Contemporary Authors®

ISSN 0275-7176

Contemporary Authors®

A Bio-Bibliographical Guide to
Current Writers in Fiction, General Nonfiction,
Poetry, Journalism, Drama, Motion Pictures,
Television, and Other Fields

volume 170

The Gale Group

DETROIT • SAN FRANCISCO • LONDON • BOSTON • WOODBRIDGE, CT

Library of Congress Catalog Card Number 62-52046
ISBN 0-7876-2675-9
ISSN 0010-7468

Printed in the United States of America

10 9 8 7 6 5 4 3 2 1

Contents

Indexing note: All *Contemporary Authors* entries are indexed in the *Contemporary Authors* cumulative index, which is published separately and distributed with even-numbered *Contemporary Authors* original volumes and odd-numbered *Contemporary Authors New Revision Series* volumes.

As always, the most recent *Contemporary Authors* cumulative index continues to be the user's guide to the location of an individual author's listing.

Preface

Contemporary Authors (*CA*) provides information on approximately 100,000 writers in a wide range of media, including:

- Current writers of fiction, nonfiction, poetry, and drama whose works have been issued by commercial publishers, risk publishers, or university presses (authors whose books have been published only by known vanity or author-subsidized firms are ordinarily not included)

- Prominent print and broadcast journalists, editors, photojournalists, syndicated cartoonists, graphic novelists, screenwriters, television scriptwriters, and other media people

- Authors who write in languages other than English, provided their works have been published in the United States or translated into English

- Literary greats of the early twentieth century whose works are popular in today's high school and college curriculums and continue to elicit critical attention

A *CA* listing entails no charge or obligation. Authors are included on the basis of the above criteria and their interest to *CA* users. Sources of potential listees include trade periodicals, publishers' catalogs, librarians, and other users.

How to Get the Most out of *CA:* Use the Index

The key to locating an author's most recent entry is the *CA* cumulative index, which is published separately and distributed with even-numbered original volumes and odd-numbered revision volumes. It provides access to *all* entries in *CA* and *Contemporary Authors New Revision Series* (*CANR*). Always consult the latest index to find an author's most recent entry.

For the convenience of users, the *CA* cumulative index also includes references to all entries in these Gale literary series: *Authors and Artists for Young Adults, Authors in the News, Bestsellers, Black Literature Criticism, Black Writers, Children's Literature Review, Concise Dictionary of American Literary Biography, Concise Dictionary of British Literary Biography, Contemporary Authors Autobiography Series, Contemporary Authors Bibliographical Series, Contemporary Literary Criticism, Dictionary of Literary Biography, Dictionary of Literary Biography Documentary Series, Dictionary of Literary Biography Yearbook, DISCovering Authors, DISCovering Authors: British, DISCovering Authors: Canadian, DISCovering Authors: Modules* (including modules for Dramatists, Most-Studied Authors, Multicultural Authors, Novelists, Poets, and Popular/Genre Authors), *Drama Criticism, Hispanic Literature Criticism, Hispanic Writers, Junior DISCovering Authors, Major Authors and Illustrators for Children and Young Adults, Major 20th-Century Writers, Native North American Literature, Poetry Criticism, Short Story Criticism, Something about the Author, Something about the Author Autobiography Series, Twentieth-Century Literary Criticism, World Literature Criticism, World Literature Criticism Supplement,* and *Yesterday's Authors of Books for Children.*

A Sample Index Entry:

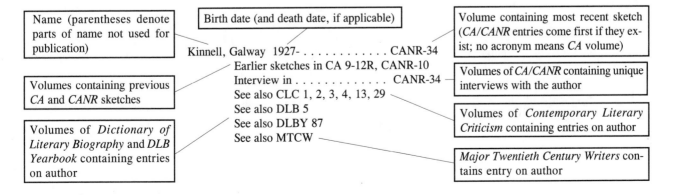

Name (parentheses denote parts of name not used for publication)	Birth date (and death date, if applicable)	Volume containing most recent sketch (*CA/CANR* entries come first if they exist; no acronym means *CA* volume)

Kinnell, Galway 1927- CANR-34
Earlier sketches in CA 9-12R, CANR-10
Interview in CANR-34
See also CLC 1, 2, 3, 4, 13, 29
See also DLB 5
See also DLBY 87
See also MTCW

Volumes containing previous *CA* and *CANR* sketches

Volumes of *Dictionary of Literary Biography* and *DLB Yearbook* containing entries on author

Volumes of *CA/CANR* containing unique interviews with the author

Volumes of *Contemporary Literary Criticism* containing entries on author

Major Twentieth Century Writers contains entry on author

How Are Entries Compiled?

The editors make every effort to secure new information directly from the authors; listees' responses to our questionnaires and query letters provide most of the information featured in *CA*. For deceased writers, or those who fail to reply to requests for data, we consult other reliable biographical sources, such as those indexed in Gale's *Biography and Genealogy Master Index,* and bibliographical sources, including *National Union Catalog, LC MARC,* and *British National Bibliography.* Further details come from published interviews, feature stories, and book reviews, as well as information supplied by the authors' publishers and agents.

An asterisk (*) at the end of a sketch indicates that the listing has been compiled from secondary sources believed to be reliable but has not been personally verified for this edition by the author sketched.

What Kinds of Information Does an Entry Provide?

Sketches in *CA* contain the following biographical and bibliographical information:

* **Entry heading:** the most complete form of author's name, plus any pseudonyms or name variations used for writing

* **Personal information:** author's date and place of birth, family data, ethnicity, educational background, political and religious affiliations, and hobbies and leisure interests

* **Addresses:** author's home, office, or agent's addresses, plus e-mail and fax numbers, as available

* **Career summary:** name of employer, position, and dates held for each career post; resume of other vocational achievements; military service

* **Membership information:** professional, civic, and other association memberships and any official posts held

* **Awards and honors:** military and civic citations, major prizes and nominations, fellowships, grants, and honorary degrees

* **Writings:** a comprehensive, chronological list of titles, publishers, dates of original publication and revised editions, and production information for plays, television scripts, and screenplays

* **Adaptations:** a list of films, plays, and other media which have been adapted from the author's work

* **Work in progress:** current or planned projects, with dates of completion and/or publication, and expected publisher, when known

* **Sidelights:** a biographical portrait of the author's development; information about the critical reception of the author's works; revealing comments, often by the author, on personal interests, aspirations, motivations, and thoughts on writing

* **Biographical and critical sources:** a list of books and periodicals in which additional information on an author's life and/or writings appears

Obituary Notices in *CA* provide date and place of birth as well as death information about authors whose full-length sketches appeared in the series before their deaths. These entries also summarize the authors' careers and writings and list other sources of biographical and death information.

Related Titles in the *CA* Series

Contemporary Authors Autobiography Series complements *CA* original and revised volumes with specially commissioned autobiographical essays by important current authors, illustrated with personal photographs they provide. Common topics include their motivations for writing, the people and experiences that shaped their careers, the rewards they derive from their work, and their impressions of the current literary scene.

Contemporary Authors Bibliographical Series surveys writings by and about important American authors since World War II. Each volume concentrates on a specific genre and features approximately ten writers; entries list works written by and about the author and contain a bibliographical essay discussing the merits and deficiencies of major critical and scholarly studies in detail.

Available in Electronic Formats

CD-ROM. Full-text bio-bibliographic entries from the entire *CA* series, covering approximately 100,000 writers, are available on CD-ROM through lease and purchase plans. The disc combines entries from the *CA, CANR,* and *Contemporary Authors Permanent Series* (*CAP*) print series to provide the most recent author listing. The *CA CD-ROM* is searchable by name, title, subject/genre, nationality/ethnicity, and personal data, as well as by using Boolean logic. The disc is updated every six months. For more information, call 1-248-699-4253.

Contemporary Authors is also available on CD-ROM from SilverPlatter Information, Inc.

Online. The *Contemporary Authors* database is made available online to libraries and their patrons through online public access catalog (OPAC) vendors. Currently, *CA* is offered through Ameritech Library Services' Vista Online (formerly Dynix).

GaleNet. *CA* is available on a subscription basis through GaleNet, an online information resource that features an easy-to-use end-user interface, the powerful search capabilities of the BRS/Search retrieval software, and ease of access through the World-Wide Web. For more information, call 1-248-699-4253.

Magnetic Tape. *CA* is available for licensing on magnetic tape in a fielded format. The database is available for internal data processing and nonpublishing purposes only. For more information, call 1-248-699-4253.

Suggestions Are Welcome

The editors welcome comments and suggestions from users on any aspects of the *CA* series. If readers would like to recommend authors for inclusion in future volumes of the series, they are cordially invited to write the Editors; or call at 1-248-699-4253; or fax at 1-248-699-8054.

CA Numbering System and Volume Update Chart

Occasionally questions arise about the *CA* numbering system and which volumes, if any, can be discarded. Despite numbers like "29-32R," "97-100" and "169," the entire *CA* print series consists of only 170 physical volumes with the publication of *CA* Volume 170. The following charts note changes in the numbering system and cover design, and indicate which volumes are essential for the most complete, up-to-date coverage.

CA First Revision
- 1-4R through 41-44R (11 books)
  Cover: Brown with black and gold trim.
  There will be no further First Revision volumes because revised entries are now being handled exclusively through the more efficient *New Revision Series* mentioned below.

CA Original Volumes
- 45-48 through 97-100 (14 books)
  Cover: Brown with black and gold trim.
- 101 through 170 (70 books)
  Cover: Blue and black with orange bands.
  The same as previous *CA* original volumes but with a new, simplified numbering system and new cover design.

CA Permanent Series
- *CAP*-1 and *CAP*-2 (2 books)
  Cover: Brown with red and gold trim.
  There will be no further *Permanent Series* volumes because revised entries are now being handled exclusively through the more efficient *New Revision Series* mentioned below.

CA New Revision Series
- *CANR*-1 through *CANR*-73 (73 books)
  Cover: Blue and black with green bands.
  Includes only sketches requiring significant changes; **sketches are taken from any previously published *CA*, *CAP*, or *CANR* volume**.

If You Have:	You May Discard:
CA First Revision Volumes 1-4R through 41-44R **and** *CA Permanent Series* Volumes 1 and 2	*CA* Original Volumes 1, 2, 3, 4 Volumes 5-6 through 41-44
CA Original Volumes 45-48 through 97-100 **and** 101 through 170	**NONE:** These volumes will not be superseded by corresponding revised volumes. Individual entries from these and all other volumes appearing in the left column of this chart may be revised and included in the various volumes of the *New Revision Series*.
CA New Revision Series Volumes *CANR*-1 through *CANR*-73	**NONE:** The *New Revision Series* does not replace any single volume of *CA*. Instead, volumes of *CANR* include entries from many previous *CA* series volumes. All *New Revision Series* volumes must be retained for full coverage.

A Sampling of Authors and Media People
Featured in This Volume

Pinckney Benedict

An award-winning short story writer, Benedict sets many of his visceral and often violent tales in the hills of West Virginia. A former student of writer Joyce Carol Oates, Benedict is also the author of the novel *Dogs of God.*

Sharon Butala

Canadian novelist Butala won acclaim for her memoir *The Perfection of the Morning: An Apprenticeship in Nature,* which tells of, among other things, the writer's life-changing move to Saskatchewan.

Anthony Daniels

A psychiatrist by trade, Daniels is also a travel writer who has issued such volumes as *Coups and Cocaine: Two Journeys in South America* and *Monrovia Mon Amour: A Visit to Liberia.*

John Dewey

A philosopher, academician, and prolific writer, Dewey is best appreciated as an education reformer. Opposing programs of rote memorization, Dewey promoted a more flexible educational approach designed around the psychology of the student.

Tananarive Due

Due, a journalist, writes horror novels distinctive for largely featuring African American characters. Her works include *My Soul to Keep* and *The Between,* which was a Bram Stoker Award finalist.

Lawrence Freedman

A political scientist described as "one of Britain's leading academic strategic theorists," Freedman is the author of *War, The Gulf Conflict, 1990-1991: Diplomacy and War in the New World Order,* and *The Revolution in Strategic Affairs.*

Marjorie Garber

Garber is a professor of English and a Shakespeare scholar who, in the 1990s, began writing on such contemporary topics as gender issues and sexuality. In 1998 she issued the volume *Symptoms of Culture*, a collection of essays.

Mary C. Henderson

Author of *Theatre in America*, winner of the 1987 George Freedley Memorial Book Award, Henderson specializes in theatrical topics. Her works include *The New Amsterdam: The Biography of a Broadway Theatre.*

Johannes V. Jensen

Remembered for the Danish novel cycle "The Long Journey," which traces the history of mankind to the discovery of North America, Jensen received the Nobel Prize for literature in 1944.

Alfred Kinsey

Kinsey's *Sexual Behavior in the Human Male,* the result of extensive and revolutionary surveys on sexual practices, provoked controversy upon its publication in 1948. The volume and its companion on female sexual behavior brought serious discourse on sexuality into the open.

Alan Macfarlane

Historian Macfarlane, who has served as a scholar at the University of Cambridge, writes primarily on premodern-era England. Among his titles are *Witchcraft in Tudor and Stuart England* and *The Savage Wars of Peace: England, Japan, and the Malthusian Trap.*

Gustav Mahler

Austrian composer Mahler is renowned for his symphonies, which feature such titles as *Titan, Resurrection,* and *Symphony of a Thousand.* Much of Mahler's correspondence has been collected in volumes like *Mahler's Unknown Letters.*

Sanjay Nigam

Born in India, Nigam is the author of *The Non-Resident Indian and Other Stories* and the novel *The Snake Charmer,* which was inspired by the tale "Charming," published in the former volume.

Theodore Roosevelt

Roosevelt—soldier, rancher, politician, avid sportsman, and twenty-sixth president of the United States—was a prolific writer on history and political science as well as the outdoors.

Kate Summerscale

A London-based journalist, Summerscale wrote a biography on Standard Oil heiress Marion Barbara "Joe" Carstairs titled *The Queen of Whale Cay: The Eccentric Story of "Joe" Carstairs, Fastest Woman on Water.*

Leslie Kanes Weisman

Weisman, a professor of architecture and author of *Discrimination by Design,* proposes that, historically, architecture was designed for men's comfort at the expense of women and children.

A

ABLEMAN, Michael 1954-

PERSONAL: Born August 18, 1954, in Wilmington, DE; son of Bernard and Helen (Kramer) Ableman; married Jeanne Marie Herman; children: Aaron. *Avocational interests:* Music, making instruments, weaving.

ADDRESSES: Home—598 North Fairview Ave., Goleta, CA 93117; fax 805-967-0116. *E-mail*—michael abl@aol.com. *Agent*—Martha Casselman, Box 342, Calistoga, CA 94515-0342.

CAREER: Fairview Gardens, Goleta, CA, founder and executive director of Center for Urban Agriculture, farm manager, 1981—. Photographer, with solo exhibitions at Oakland Museum, Santa Barbara Museum of Art, University of Kansas, Santa Barbara Museum of Natural History, Camera Work Gallery, San Francisco Art Institute, and Field Museum of Natural History. Lecturer at educational institutions in the United States and abroad, including University of Denmark; public speaker. Creator of good gardens at Santa Barbara AIDS Hospice, Midland School, and Jordan Downs (housing project), Los Angeles, CA.

AWARDS, HONORS: Governors Environmental and Economic Leadership Award, 1977, for Center for Urban Agriculture; Food Hero Award, *Eating Well,* 1995.

WRITINGS:

From the Good Earth, Abrams (New York City), 1993.

On Good Land: The Autobiography of an Urban Farm, Chronicle Books (San Francisco, CA), 1998.

Columnist, *National Gardening.* Contributor of articles and photographs to periodicals. Guest editor, *Race, Poverty, and the Environment.*

SIDELIGHTS: Michael Ableman told *CA:* "The farm at Fairview Gardens was founded in 1895. It is now surrounded by urban development, but it continues to produce some one hundred varieties of fruits and vegetables, as well as fresh eggs, cheese, and breads. Over the past decade, through tours, classes, a community-supported agriculture program, a summer concert series, and other events, the farm has become an important community/education center and national model for urban agriculture. We have successfully raised the funds to secure Fairview Gardens and preserve it under a protective conservation easement. I am currently researching energy and water conservation strategies and expanding the educational outreach of the nonprofit center."

*   *   *

ADAMS, Deborah 1956-

PERSONAL: Born January 22, 1956, in TN. *Avocational interests:* Horseback riding and competing in endurance races, volunteer work for domestic violence prevention programs.

ADDRESSES: Home—Route 4, Box 664, Waverly, TN 37185.

CAREER: Novelist. Nashville State Technical Institute, adjunct faculty member (teaches online writing courses).

MEMBER: Sisters in Crime, Appalachian Writers' Association, Kentucky State Poetry Society (officer), Green Rivers Writers' Association.

WRITINGS:

All the Great Pretenders, Ballantine (New York City), 1992.
All the Crazy Winters, Ballantine, 1992.
All the Dark Disguises, Ballantine, 1993.
All the Hungry Mothers, Ballantine, 1994.
All the Deadly Beloved, Ballantine, 1995.
All the Blood Relations, Ballantine, 1997.

SIDELIGHTS: Deborah Adams writes mystery novels set in the fictional town of Jesus Creek, Tennessee. Born in 1956, Adams is a seventh-generation member of a Tennessee family, and she has remained in that state. In an interview published on her own Internet web site devoted to mysteries, Adams was asked if she was born to write. "Well, in the way that some people are born to be botanists," she answered. "I've always loved writing and I've done all I can to improve my skills. I like to think I'm a better writer now than when I wrote my first book." In the interview, Adams said, "I don't want to sound syrupy, but I just want to write. I'd prefer to get paid for doing it, but bottom line? I don't care what you call it, I don't care what genre it fits into." Besides writing, Adams is involved in a domestic violence prevention organization, is an avid horsewoman who participates in twenty-five-mile endurance races, and teaches writing courses, via the internet, through the Nashville State Technical Institute.

Adams's Jesus Creek series employs a different protagonist for each novel. In *All the Dark Disguises* (1993), the heroine is Kay, a wiseacre waitress who was, at one time, a newspaper reporter. A Ginsu knife-wielding serial killer, called the "Night Terror," is menacing Jesus Creek, and Kay makes it her business to track him down, putting herself in peril before the novel's end. Patrick S. Jones wrote in *Kliatt* that *All the Dark Disguises* "is never dull, but sometimes Adams' cleverness gets in the way of the mystery and suspense."

The protagonist of Adams's fourth novel, *All the Hungry Mothers* (1994), is Janet Ayres, a nanny to the Leach household. The busy Sarah Elizabeth Leach, who works at a library, teaches classes at a university, and does volunteer work for a domestic violence hotline, hires Janet to care for her two-year-old. Janet befriends Mary Ann, a young mother who lives next door with a faithful husband—or so it seems. Janet learns about the horrors of domestic violence second-hand through her employer's work and first-hand through what she observes next door. *Publishers Weekly* called *All the Hungry Mothers* a "well-intentioned but ultimately unsatisfying Southern gothic."

Police Chief Robert Lee "Reb" Gussler relates a tale of murder and betrayal in *All the Deadly Beloved* (1995). Patrice and Steven Gentry arrive in Jesus Creek after doing medical work in Somalia. Steven is the head of the town's medical clinic and Patrice is the much-admired second-shift nursing supervisor at the local nursing home. Steven is unfaithful, seducing several women in the town. When Patrice turns up murdered, he has a perfect alibi—he was sleeping with another woman at the time. Unfortunately, his alibi is too good—two different women claim to have been with him when Patrice was killed. Don Sandstrom commented on Adams's series in *Armchair Detective,* noting that Adams effectively portrays life in a small town with "humor [that] is subtle and on target rather than being a series of one-liners."

Other books in the Jesus Creek series include *All the Great Pretenders* (1992), *All the Crazy Winters* (1992), and *All the Blood Relations* (1997).

BIOGRAPHICAL/CRITICAL SOURCES:

PERIODICALS

Armchair Detective, winter, 1996, p. 107.
Kliatt, July, 1993, pp. 4-5.
Publishers Weekly, April 18, 1994, p. 59.

OTHER

Deborah Adams's Internet web site, http://members.aol.com/dkadams (July 9, 1997).*

*   *   *

ADAMS, Nicholas
See MACDONALD, James D.

ADAMS, Walter 1922-1998

OBITUARY NOTICE—See index for *CA* sketch: Born August 27, 1922, in Vienna, Austria; died of pancreatic cancer, September 8, 1998, in East Lansing, MI. Economics professor and author. An expert on antitrust matters, Adams received a bachelor's degree from Brooklyn College (now Brooklyn College of the City University of New York) and master's and doctorate degrees from Yale University. After serving in Europe during World War II and fighting in the Battle of the Bulge, he returned to the United States and taught briefly at Yale before joining the staff at Michigan State University in 1947, where he stayed until his death. Always a member of the economics department, Adams served as Michigan State's president from April 1969 to January 1970. He stepped down to return to teaching, although thousands of students and numerous faculty urged him to remain president. Adams was a visiting professor at the universities of Paris and Grenoble, France, and at the Salzburg Seminar and Falkenstein Seminar. In addition, he attended to his duties at Michigan State and in 1991 was named one of the country's ten best professors by *Rolling Stone* magazine. The author or co-author of fourteen books about economics, his most recent work, *The Tobacco Wars,* was published the week before his death. His 1987 book *The Bigness Complex: Industry Labor and Government in the American Economy* was named one of the ten best business books that year by *Business Week* magazine. Other works by Adams include *The Brain Drain* and *The Test.* He contributed to *Tariffs, Quotas and Trade: Problems of the International Economy* and co-wrote *Antitrust Economics on Trial.* He wrote more than thirty journal articles and pamphlets during his career, which also included testifying before the U.S. Congress on trade issues.

OBITUARIES AND OTHER SOURCES:

PERIODICALS

Chicago Tribune, September 17,1998, sec. 3, p. 12.
New York Times, September 11, 1998, p. A25.
Washington Post, September 12, 1998, p. B6.

*   *   *

ADDISON, Paul S. 1966-

PERSONAL: Born April 15, 1966, in Edinburgh, Scotland; married, wife's name Stephanie, April 4, 1992; children: Michael, Hannah. *Education:* University of Glasgow, M.Eng., 1989, Ph.D., 1992. *Avocational interests:* Family activities.

ADDRESSES: Office—School of the Built Environment, Napier University, Edinburgh, Scotland. *E-mail*—p.addison@napier.ac.uk.

CAREER: Napier University, Edinburgh, Scotland, lecturer in fluid mechanics, 1992—.

MEMBER: International Association of Hydraulic Research, Institute of Physics, Institution of Civil Engineers (graduate member), Scottish Hydraulics Study Group, American Society of Civil Engineers (associate member).

WRITINGS:

Fractals and Chaos, IOP Publishing (Philadelphia, PA), 1997.

WORK IN PROGRESS: An introductory textbook on "wavelet transforms" and their applications in science and engineering; research on fractal-based turbulent diffusion, wavelet transforms and turbulence, wavelet transforms and non-destructive testing, fractal cracking, modeling traffic pollution in the urban environment, car-following dynamics, and open-channel flows.

SIDELIGHTS: Paul S. Addison told *CA:* "My scientific literary work is motivated by a desire to explain research-level topics in a logical and clear manner in order to facilitate greater access by the wider scientific and engineering community."

*   *   *

AGEE, Chris 1956-

PERSONAL: Born January 18, 1956, in San Francisco, CA; married Noirin McKinney (an art critic and administrator); children: Jacob. *Education:* Harvard University, B.A., 1979; Queen's University (Ireland), M.A., 1987.

ADDRESSES: Agent—The Daedalus Press, 24 the Heath, Cypress Downs, Dublin 6W, Ireland.

CAREER: Poet. Belfast Institute of Further and Higher Education, Belfast, Ireland, lecturer in literacy, 1979; Queen's University, School of Education, Ireland, lecturer, 1985-90; Open University in Northern Ireland, tutor; University of East London, Belfast branch, adult education advisor.

MEMBER: Member of the board of directors of *Poetry Ireland,* 1988—.

WRITINGS:

In the New Hampshire Woods (poetry), Daedalus Press (Dublin, Ireland), 1992.
Scar on the Stone (poetry), Dufour Editions, Inc., 1998.
The Sierra de Zacatecas, (poetry), bilingual version with Spanish translations by Raphael Vargas, Ediciones Papeles Privados (Mexico City), 1998.

SIDELIGHTS: Although he was born in the United States, Chris Agee has spent much of his life in Ireland, teaching and writing, and is now an Irish citizen. He received his education at Andover and Harvard; while at Harvard he became interested in the philosopher Roberto Unger and the poet and translator Robert Fitzgerald, who was Agee's advisor for his senior thesis on W. H. Auden.

Agee originally went to Belfast to assist a Harvard professor who was doing research on medical ethics. He established residency in Ireland, moving there permanently in 1979, when he began lecturing on literacy at various Irish institutes of higher education. He wrote his graduate thesis on Eugene Watters, an Irish poet, and received an M.A. from Queen's College in 1987.

Agee's first collection of poems, *In the New Hampshire Woods,* reflects his life in both his native and adopted homelands. The first part of the book focuses on his experience as a young man in America, exploring the landscapes of the New England coast, Block Island, and Squam Lake, New Hampshire. Reviewer Jonathan Allison wrote in *A Dictionary of Irish Literature* that Agee "might be considered a poet of the environment and wilderness, and his poems evoke the minutest details of New Hampshire's flora and fauna."

Allison remarked that Agee's poems have a "mystical undercurrent," perhaps arising from his interest in nature and Eastern religion. Allison called the book is "very literary," noting its "allusions to Auden, Eliot, Frost, and Lowell." *In the New Hampshire Woods,* concluded Allison, "is never stuffy, and the language is always charged and energetic."

BIOGRAPHICAL/CRITICAL SOURCES:

BOOKS

Hogan, Robert, editor, *Dictionary of Irish Literature,* two volumes, Greenwood Press (Westport, CT), 1996.*

* * *

ALLEN, Ronald J. 1948-

PERSONAL: Born July 14, 1948, in Chicago, IL; son of J. Matteson (an engineer) and Carolyn (Latchum) Allen; married Debra Jane Livingston (marriage ended, June, 1982); married Julie O'Donnell, September 2, 1984; children: Sarah, Adrienne, Michael, Carol. *Education:* Marshall University, B.S. (magna cum laude), 1970; University of Michigan, J.D. (magna cum laude), 1973.

ADDRESSES: Home—1812 North Hudson, Chicago, IL 60614. *Office*—School of Law, Northwestern University, 357 East Chicago Ave., Chicago, IL 60611; fax 312-503-2035. *E-mail*—rjallen@nwu.edu.

CAREER: University of Nebraska, visiting professor of law, 1973-74; State University of New York at Buffalo, assistant professor, 1974-77, associate professor of law, 1977-79; University of Iowa, Iowa City, visiting professor, 1978-79, professor of law, 1979-84; Northwestern University, School of Law, Chicago, IL, visiting professor, 1984, professor, 1984—, Stanford Clinton, Jr., Research Professor, 1990-91; John Henry Wigmore Professor of Law, 1992—, fellow of Center for the Humanities, 1994-95. University of Michigan, visiting professor, 1982; Duke University, professor, 1983; Federal Judicial Center, lecturer, 1987; University of Adelaide, university distinguished visiting scholar, 1991; Marshall University, distinguished lecturer, 1991. Supreme Court of Illinois, member of Inquiry Board, Attorney Registration and Disciplinary Commission, 1989-92, member of Hearing Board, 1992; Constitutional Rights Foundation of Chicago, member of board of directors, 1992—. Children's Memorial Hospital, member of board of directors of John Thomas Graziano Fund, 1993-98.

MEMBER: American Bar Association, American Law Institute, Nebraska State Bar Association, Iowa Bar Association, Illinois Bar Association, Yeager Society of Scholars (Marshall University; member of board of directors, 1992—), Coif, Saddle and Cycle Club (member of board of governors, 1993—; vice president, 1996-98).

AWARDS, HONORS: Grants from Nellie Ball Trust Fund, 1980-84, and Corporate Counsel Center, Northwestern University, 1985-87; named Citizen of the Year, Constitutional Rights Foundation, 1990.

WRITINGS:

Constitutional Criminal Procedure: An Examination of the Fourth, Fifth, and Sixth Amendments and Related Areas, Little, Brown (Boston, MA), 1985, teacher's manual, 1985, 2nd edition (with Kuhns), 1991, 3rd edition (with Kuhns and Stuntz), 1995.
(With Kuhns) *An Analytical Approach to Evidence: Text, Problems, and Cases,* Little, Brown, 1989, teacher's manual, 1989, 2nd edition (with Kuhns and Swift), 1997.
(With Kuhns) *Federal Rules of Evidence with Legislative History and Case Supplement,* Little, Brown, 1989, 2nd edition (with Kuhns and Swift), 1996.
(With Brander and Stulberg) *Arthritis of the Hip and Knee: The Active Person's Guide to Taking Charge,* Peachtree Publishers (Atlanta, GA), 1998.
The Nature of Juridicial Proof, Princeton University Press (Princeton, NJ), 1999.
(With Stuntz, Hoffman, Livingston, and Steiker) *Criminal Procedure,* Little, Brown, in press.

Contributor to law books. Contributor of numerous articles and reviews to law journals. Member of board of consulting editors, *Psychology, Public Policy, and Law,* 1995—; member of advisory board, *Journal of Criminal Law and Criminology,* 1995—, and *International Commentary on Evidence,* 1997—.

*   *   *

ALTOFF, Gerard T(homas) 1949-

PERSONAL: Born October 8, 1949, in Gettysburg, PA; son of Paul Edward (a bookkeeper) and Mary (an executive secretary; maiden name, Weaver) Altoff; married Cynthia Hamilton (a paramedic), April 12, 1971; children: Kristin Heather. *Ethnicity:* "Caucasian." *Education:* Attended Dixie College, St. George, UT; Federal Law Enforcement Training Center, graduated (with distinction), 1980. *Politics:* Independent. *Religion:* Independent. *Avocational interests:* Military history.

ADDRESSES: Home—50 Park Ave., P.O. Box 153, Put-in-Bay, OH 43456. *Office*—National Park Service, 93 Delaware Ave., P.O. Box 549, Put-in-Bay, OH 43456. *E-mail*—gerryaltoff@nps.gov.

CAREER: U.S. Forest Service, Ashley National Forest, Dutch John, UT, forest aide, 1972; National Park Service, Washington, DC, park technician at Zion National Park, Springdale, UT, 1972-75, district naturalist at Theodore Roosevelt National Park, Medora, ND, 1975-79, chief ranger and historian at Perry's Victory and IPM, Put-in-Bay, OH, 1979—. Speaker at schools. *Military service:* U.S. Coast Guard, gunner's mate, 1967-71; served in Vietnam.

MEMBER: Association of National Park Rangers, Council on America's Military Past, American Legion.

AWARDS, HONORS: Freeman Tilden Award, Midwest Region, National Park Service, 1996; Author's Award, Eastern National Park and Monument Association, 1996, for *Amongst My Best Men;* John Lyman Book Award, North American Society for Oceanic History, 1997, and Local History Publication Award, Bowling Green State University, 1998, both for *A Signal Victory.*

WRITINGS:

Deep Water Sailors—Shallow Water Soldiers: Manning the United States Fleet on Lake Erie, 1813, Perry Group, 1993.
Amongst My Best Men: African-Americans and the War of 1812, Perry Group, 1996.
(With David C. Skaggs) *A Signal Victory: The Lake Erie Campaign, 1812-1813,* Naval Institute Press (Annapolis, MD), 1997.

Author of the booklet "Oliver Hazard Perry and the Battle of Lake Erie." Contributor to books, including *The Great Lake Erie,* 1987; and *War on the Great Lakes,* 1991. Contributor to periodicals, including *Journal of Lake Erie Studies, Leatherneck, Northwest Ohio Quarterly,* and *Michigan Historical Quarterly.*

WORK IN PROGRESS: A revised edition of the booklet "Oliver Hazard Perry and the Battle of Lake Erie."

* * *

AMUNDSEN, Roald Engelbregt Gravning 1872-1928

PERSONAL: Born July 16, 1872, in Borge, near Oslo, Norway; missing and presumed dead June, 1928; son of Jens Amundsen (a shipowner). *Education:* Attended high school in Christiana, 1890; attended two years of medical school, c. 1891-92; attended Christiana Public Sailors' School.

CAREER: Explorer. Worked on seal-hunting boats, c. 1894-97; Antarctic expedition, first mate with the *Belgica* under Captain Adrien de Gerlache de Gomery, 1897-99; licensed as sea captain, 1900; pursued ice navigation in the Arctic circle, 1901-02; Northwest Passage expedition, leader, 1903-06; South Pole expedition, leader, 1910-12; entered shipping business, c. 1912; Northeast Passage expedition, leader, 1918-20; flies over North Pole (with Lincoln Ellsworth and Umberto Nobile), 1926. Lecturer and author.

WRITINGS:

To the Magnetic Pole and through the Northwest Passage, Geographical Journal (London), 1906.
Roald Amundsen's "The North West Passage"; Being the Record of a Voyage of Exploration of the Ship Gjoa 1903-1907, Constable (London), 1908.
Captain Amundsen's Own Narrative of His Attainment of the South Pole, New York Times Co. (New York City), 1912.
Expedition to the South Pole, Bulletin of the American Geographical Society (Washington, DC), 1913.
The South Pole: An Account of the Norwegian Antarctic Expedition in the Fram, 1910-1912, translated by A. G. Chater, J. Murray (London) and L. Keedick (New York City), 1913.
The Hop-Off: Radiograms of the Amundsen-Ellsworth Polar Flight, W. Hyans (New York City), 1925.
My Polar Flight, Hutchinson (London), 1925.
(With Lincoln Ellsworth and others) *Our Polar Flight: The Amundsen-Ellsworth Polar Flight,* Dodd, Mead (New York City), 1925.

(With Lincoln Ellsworth and others) *First Crossing of the Polar Sea,* George H. Doran (New York City), 1927, published as *The First Flight across the Polar Sea,* Hutchinson (London), 1927.
Roald Amundsen—My Life as an Explorer, Doubleday, Page (Garden City, NY), 1927.
The Amundsen Photographs, edited by Roland Huntford, Hodder & Stoughton (London), 1987.

SIDELIGHTS: Roald Engelbregt Gravning Amundsen began his career in polar exploration when he became the first man to navigate the Northwest Passage, sailing from the Atlantic Ocean to the Pacific through the straits north of the North American continent. His voyage, which is described in his book *Roald Amundsen's "The North West Passage"; Being the Record of a Voyage of Exploration of the Ship Gjoa 1903-1907,* lasted from 1903 until 1906. During this trip Amundsen made surveys of the north magnetic pole that led to the discovery that the pole's position is not stationary. Amundsen is perhaps best remembered, however, as the man who successfully raced Britain's Robert F. Scott to the South Pole. Amundsen, who was known as a resourceful and able leader, and the four other members of the Norwegian Polar Expedition reached the South Pole on December 14, 1911, more than a month in advance of the British expedition. Amundsen's other accomplishments include completing the Northeast Passage, thus becoming the first man to sail around the world within the Arctic Circle, and participating in the first dirigible flight over the North Pole.

Born into a shipping family and, some might argue, a nautical culture, Amundsen was apparently drawn to the sea from early childhood. In particular, Amundsen had, by all accounts, set his sights on polar exploration, his enthusiasm fired by the accounts of Sir John Franklin's doomed expedition to discover the Northwest Passage. However, upon leaving secondary school in Christiana (now Oslo), Amundsen acquiesced to his mother's wishes and enrolled in medical school.

Amundsen might have remained there, had he not lost both his parents in 1893. Suddenly on his own, a mediocre and unmotivated medical student, he abandoned his studies to pursue training as a sailor. He worked on board a seal-hunting vessel for the following three years, until word reached him of a Belgian polar expedition led by established explorer Adrien de Gerlache de Gomery. Amundsen managed to sign on as first mate, and their ship, the *Belgica,* set sail for the Arctic in 1897. Without suspecting it, Amundsen was on his way to his first command: the *Belgica* promptly froze into the surface ice of the Arctic Sea and remained there immobilized for over a year, effectively stranding the ship for the winter. The crew was decimated by scurvy and other diseases, and when de Gomery took to his bed, command of the ship fell to Amundsen. The men of the *Belgica* were the first to successfully winter in the Arctic, and the trials of this voyage established Amundsen as a capable captain.

For all that he had endured on the *Belgica,* Amundsen was eager to lead his own expedition to the Arctic, and spent the next few years fundraising and, having learned firsthand the importance of timing, carefully planning a schedule. Amundsen bought his own ship, a seventy-foot, forty-seven-ton sloop called the *Gjoa,* in 1901. Two years later, having rigged the ship for Arctic conditions, he set out from the city of Christiana.

Amundsen's career was a series of historical firsts. In 1903, he became the first man to navigate the Northwest Passage, which links the Atlantic and Pacific oceans just to the south of the Arctic ice cap. In the course of this three-year exploration, Amundsen discovered the "wandering" of magnetic north, which had been roving since its discovery in 1831 by James Clark Ross. He was forced to stop over on various islands along the way, and during this time, recorded his observations of the indigenous Eskimos (who taught him how to drive dog teams). Once in Alaskan waters, the *Gjoa* froze into the ice, and Amundsen made the final leg of the trip by dogsled, traveling overland to Eagle City, Alaska, to report his success by telegraph.

The volume *Roald Amundsen's "The North West Passage"; Being the Record of a Voyage of Exploration of the Ship Gjoa 1903-1907* contained the explorer's account of the expedition. A *New York Times* critic observed, "With the skill of the true artist, the Northwest Passage is there, the real hero of the story, behind all the humorous and sometimes tragic adventures with which this excellent narrator entertains his readers." A contributor to *Nature* commented, "Though the book would not lose by condensation in places, it is singularly free from the trivialities with which such volumes are often loaded. But an appendix of scientific results would have given more permanent value to these volumes." P. F. Bicknell in *Dial,* however, was more enthusiastic, stating that Amundsen's "straightforward narrative makes not only one of the best books of Arctic exploration, but one of the best

books of adventure of any sort that have ever been written." And a *Spectator* reviewer remarked, "The observations which Captain Amundsen makes on the mode of life, manners, and struggle for existence of the inhabitants near the Northwest Passage are quite the most interesting and valuable in the volume."

With the Passage behind him, Amundsen apparently felt confident enough to set his sights on the North Pole itself. His funds exhausted, and lacking a ship, Amundsen set off on a world lecture tour to raise more money. His fame was already such that not much time was needed—Norway's greatest explorer of the previous generation, Nansen, lent Amundsen his own ship, the *Fram.* Then, in April, 1909, word came that American explorer Robert Peary had reached the North Pole first. Amundsen lost no time— he set his sights instead on the Antarctic. Robert Scott, of England, had already embarked on a much-publicized second attempt to reach the South Pole, and Amundsen secretly resolved to beat him there.

Amundsen arrived at the Bay of Whales, in Antarctica, in January of 1911. From there, sixty miles closer to the Pole than Scott's base camp at Cape Evans, he set out with his dogsleds, making surprisingly good time. On December 14, 1911, Amundsen achieved the most famous of his "firsts," becoming the first man to set foot on the South Pole, beating Scott by more than one month.

Although somewhat slowed down by World War I, Amundsen was determined to return to the Arctic. He acquired his own ship, the *Maud,* christening it with a block of ice, and embarked in 1918 to attempt the Northeast Passage. This was the largest and best-equipped polar expedition up to that time, but upon arrival in Arctic waters the Maud was frozen solid into the ice and would not emerge again for two years. Eventually Amundsen was forced to retreat to Seattle to repair the *Maud.* His second attempt at the Passage, launched in 1922, met with no more success than the first, leaving the explorers stranded in the ice for three more years. However, if nothing else, this prolonged stay in the north enabled Amundsen's team to make a more extensive study of Arctic conditions than had ever been undertaken before.

Taking another tack, Amundsen began looking for backers to fund his flight over the North Pole, and found one in Lincoln Ellsworth, an American aviator. With Ellsworth along as a colleague, Amundsen set out on May 21, 1925, with two planes. Despite mechanical troubles that led to the complete failure of one of the aircraft, all the men returned safely, having come within less than a hundred miles of the North Pole. The following year, Amundsen returned with Ellsworth and an Italian pilot, Umberto Nobile, and successfully flew over the North Pole in the dirigible *Norge,* becoming in the process the first men to fly from Europe to America. These events were described in the volume *Our Polar Flight: The Amundsen-Ellsworth Polar Flight,* which Amundsen wrote with Ellsworth and others. According to H. E. Armstrong in the *New York Times,* "The narrative of the often baffled preparations to start the plane for the return flight, while rations ran low and hope seemed to be fading, is one of the strongest pieces of writing Amundsen has ever done." In the *New York World* J. O. Swift commented, "The elements of boyish enthusiasm, gentle wit, and mature judgment in whatever story Roald Amundsen . . . has to tell make his description of the flight . . . absorbing reading."

In May, 1928, Nobile's aircraft, the *Italia,* was reported down in the Arctic Sea. Amundsen volunteered his assistance in the rescue attempt, and three hours after setting forth from Tromso, Norway, the signals from his airplane stopped coming. Eventually, the rescue parties returned, and Amundsen was presumed dead.

BIOGRAPHICAL/CRITICAL SOURCES:

BOOKS

Carlsson, Karl Alex, *A Twentieth-Century Viking Voyage,* [New York City], 1934.

Davis, Paxton, *A Flag at the Pole: Three Soliloquies,* Atheneum, 1976.

Flaherty, Leo, *Roald Amundsen and the Quest for the South Pole,* Chelsea House, 1992.

Frazier, Carla, *To the South Pole,* Raintree, 1979.

Hanssen, Helmer, *Voyages of a Modern Viking,* Routledge, 1936.

Hesselberg, Theodor, *Various Papers on the Projected Cooperation with Roald Amundsen's North Polar Expedition,* I Kommission Hos Cammermeyers Boghandel, 1920.

Holt, Kare, *The Race,* Joseph, 1976.

Humble, Richard, *The Expeditions of Amundsen,* F. Watts, 1991.

Huntford, Roland, *The Last Place on Earth,* Pan Books (London) and Atheneum (New York City), 1985.

Huntford, Roland, *Scott and Amundsen,* Hodder & Stoughton, 1979, Putnam, 1980.

Keller, F. M., *North to Eighty-Eight Degrees,* [Sommerville, NJ, and New York City], 1927.

Kugelmass, J. Alvin, *Roald Amundsen: A Saga of the Polar Seas,* J. Messner, 1955.

Langley, Andrew, *The Great Polar Adventure: The Journeys of Roald Amundsen,* Chelsea Juniors, 1994.

Mason, Antony, *Peary and Amundsen: Race to the Poles,* Raintree Steck-Vaughn, 1995.

Mason, Theodore, K., *Two against the Ice, Amundsen and Ellsworth,* Dodd, Mead, 1982.

Matthews, Rupert, *The Race to the South Pole,* Bookwright Press, 1989.

Partridge, Bellamy, *Amundsen, the Splendid Norseman,* Frederick A. Stokes, 1929.

Taylor, J. Garth, *Netsilik Eskimo Material Culture. The Roald Amundsen Collection from King William Island,* Oslo Universitetsforlaget, 1974.

Turley, Charles, *Roald Amundsen, Explorer,* Methuen, 1935.

Vaeth, Joseph Gordon, *To the Ends of the Earth: The Explorations of Roald Amundsen,* Harper, 1962.

PERIODICALS

Athenaeum, July 11, 1908.

Bookman, November, 1908.

Boston Transcript, July 3, 1925.

Dial, August 16, 1908.

Nation, September 17, 1908.

Nature, September 17, 1908.

New York Times, July 4, 1908; January 10, 1926.

New York World, December 13, 1925; January 10, 1926.

Saturday Review of Literature, June 27, 1908.

Spectator, November 21, 1908.

Springfield Republican, July 24, 1925.*

* * *

ANGELL, David (F.)
(David F. Angell)

PERSONAL: Male.

ADDRESSES: Office—147 Herbert Road, Arlington, MA 02174, phone: 617-646-1587, fax: 617-646-7594. *Agent*—Waterside Productions, 2191 San Elijo Avenue, Cardiff-by-the-Sea, CA 92007-1839. *E-mail*—http:\\www.angell.com.

CAREER: Computer industry analyst, journalist, consultant, and author specializing in emerging technologies. Founder, @ngell.com (consulting and technical communications firm).

MEMBER: Computer Press Association.

WRITINGS:

ISDN for Dummies, IDG Books Worldwide (San Mateo, CA, Foster City, CA and Braintree, MA), 1995.
Windows Remote Access Toolkit Wiley Computer (New York City), 1997.
Internet Information Server 4 for Dummies, IDG Books Worldwide (San Mateo, CA, Foster City, CA and Braintree, MA), 1998.

Regular contributor to computer-industry magazines and others including *PC Magazine, PC Week, Internet World,* and *NetGuide.*

WITH BRENT HESLOP

Mastering SunOS, Sybex (San Francisco), 1990.
The First Book of Microsoft Word 5, H. W. Sams (Carmel, IN), 1990.
Mastering SunOS 5.0: SVR4, UNIX System V Release 4, Sybex, 1991.
The First Book of Microsoft Word for Windows, H. W. Sams, 1991.
The First Book of Microsoft Word 5.5, revised by Lisa Bucki, illustrated by Don Clemons, H. W. Sams, 1991.
The Windows 3.1 Font Book, Peachpit Press (Berkeley, CA), 1992.
(As David F. Angell) *Mastering Solaris 2,* Sybex, 1993.
The Instant Internet Guide: Hands-On Global Networking, Addison-Wesley (Reading, MA), 1994.
The Elements of E-Mail Style: Communicate Effectively Via Electronic Mail, Addison-Wesley, 1994.
PC World Word for Windows 6: Handbook, IDG Books Worldwide, 1994.
The Internet Business Companion: Growing Your Business in an Electronic Age, Addison-Wesley, 1995.
Mosaic for Dummies, Windows Edition, IDG Books Worldwide, 1995.
Word for Windows 95 Bible, IDG Books Worldwide, 1995.

(With Bill Mann) *Mosaic for Dummies,* IDG Books Worldwide, 1995, updated 1996.
Word 97 Bible, IDG Books Worldwide, 1997.

SIDELIGHTS: Busy and prolific computer consultant David F. Angell has authored at least eighteen books with more, presumably, to come. He is the founder as well of a thriving consulting firm known as @ngell.com which helps small businesses cope with the mysteries of the ever-changing internet and communications technology. Angell contributes regularly to a variety of computer magazines, thus sharing with the public at large his insights into such matters as how to best manipulate the latest software.

Of Angell's books, most have been co-written with Brent Heslop. Among these have been *The Internet Business Companion: Growing Your Business in an Electronic Age* (1995), which received an enthusiastic review from Michael Erbscloe via the online magazine *Internet Book Reviews.* The reviewer particularly commended the book's practical management advice. Raved Erbschloe, "There are countless books that cover the technical aspects of the Internet . . . but if you are a business person that needs guidance and real down-to-earth business planning support *The Internet Business Companion* is a great tool." Less welcome was a *Los Angeles Times Book Review* piece by Daniel Akst assessing the writing team's *The Elements of E-Mail Style: Communicate Effectively via Electronic Mail.* Mincing no words, Akst excoriated the book's writing style as well as its advice, and concluded that in fact, good e-mail writing was little different from plain old good writing. The team of Angell and Heslop, however, continued to produce numerous successful books that were useful to a large number of regular computer users and businesspeople, such as *Word 97 Bible.* On his own, Angell wrote *ISDN for Dummies,* in 1995, and most recently *Windows Remote Access Toolkit.*

BIOGRAPHICAL/CRITICAL SOURCES:

PERIODICALS

Los Angeles Times Book Review, October 30, 1994, p. 10.

OTHER

Book Stacks—Author's Pen, www.books.com, 1992.
Internet Book Reviews, www.telepath.com/telepath/reviews, 1997.

Virtual Computer Library: Book Reviews, http://wwwhost.utexas.edu/computer/ vcl/bkreviews, 1997.
@ngell.com, http://angell.com/books.html, 1997.*

* * *

ANGELL, David F.
   See ANGELL, David (F.)

* * *

ANTHONY, Joseph 1964-

PERSONAL: Born October 10, 1964, in Denver, CO; son of Ward R. (a physician) and Doris M. (an occupational therapist; maiden name, Hammes) Anthony; married Cris Arbo (an illustrator), January 1, 1991; children: Alina Fae. *Education:* Attended St. John's College, Annapolis, MD, and St. John's College, Santa Fe, NM. *Politics:* "Don't like it." *Religion:* "Life."

*ADDRESSES: Home and office—*Buckingham, VA. *Agent—*Dawn Publications, 14618 Tyler Foote Rd., Nevada City, CA 95959.

CAREER: Author and screenwriter. Also works as a carpenter. Local Interagency Network for Children, member of board of directors, 1994-96. *Military service:* U.S. Navy, 1987-91; musician.

AWARDS, HONORS: Benjamin Franklin Silver Medal, Publishers Marketing Association, 1998, for *The Dandelion Seed.*

WRITINGS:

FICTION; FOR CHILDREN

The Dandelion Seed, illustrated by Cris Arbo, Dawn Publications (Nevada City, CA), 1997.
In a Nutshell, illustrated by Chris Arbo, Dawn Publications, in press.

WORK IN PROGRESS: Reformer, "an action/adventure screenplay about technology to reform criminals"; *Up!* "a dramatic screenplay about a psychic healer with Down's syndrome"; *Earthpainting,* "an animated and live-action feature film, with Cris

Arbo"; "several children's books, all parables about the meaning of life, including *Little Blue Library* and *A, Be, and See* (an alphabet book)."

SIDELIGHTS: Joseph Anthony commented: "I began writing because my wife needed a screenwriter for her film. I read screenplays and books about screenwriting, and I wrote a script for her. Then I wrote it again. Nine years and almost as many drafts later, *Earthpainting* is almost ready for the big screen.

"My writing has grown through the process of writing my other films and my children's books. Each is a story about finding one's highest calling and expressing it because I believe that calling, that 'soul purpose,' is a divine gift. It needs our constant attention. Above all things, it is why we are here, and when we are true to that deepest part of our self, where God speaks to us, everything else falls into place. Everything. In fact, the way I see it, the only real problem in the world is that people don't follow that dream of their highest potential, their divine spark. Every other problem is a symptom of that one. I want to get this message out in a big way, and in my lifetime, film is the best medium for doing that.

"Children's parables are another great way of communicating that message. When I sign a copy of my book for somebody, I always add a reminder to 'live your dream!'"*

* * *

APPLETON, Victor
   See MACDONALD, James D.

* * *

ARANYOS, Kakay
   See MIKSZATH, Kalman

* * *

ARNOTE, Ralph 1926-1998

PERSONAL: Born November 14, 1926; died June 26, 1998.

CAREER: Novelist. Tor and Forge Books, New York City, head of ID sales, 1980-94.

WRITINGS:

MYSTERY NOVELS

Fallen Idols, Tor (New York City), 1994.
Fatal Secrets, Tor, 1994.
False Promises, Forge (New York City), 1995.
Weekenders' Club, Forge, 1995.
Evil's Fancy, Forge, 1996.
Hong Kong, China, Forge, 1996.
A Rage in Paradise, Forge, 1997.
Fast Lane, St. Martin's Press (New York City), 1998.

SIDELIGHTS: Ralph Arnote was a mystery writer and avid traveler whose works often incorporate his knowledge of Chinese culture and exotic locations. In *Fallen Idols* Arnote launched a paperback series and introduced protagonist Willy Hanson, a publishing and entertainment executive who is determined to bring to justice the Chinese narcotics and sex peddler Onyx Lu. The 1994 novel *Fatal Secrets* continues the saga of Hanson and his sexy nemesis, whose unsavory enterprises include a Los Angeles night club specializing in sex and cocaine. Penny Kaganoff, in *Publishers Weekly,* found the novel "diverting" but complained about the "unbelievable premise of a two-fisted publishing executive and Chinese characters speaking in pidgin English."

False Promises, published in 1995, offers a third installment in the series as Lu stalks Hanson to seek revenge for his previous interference in her affairs. Clarence Petersen, writing in Chicago *Tribune Books,* noted that the writing in *False Promises* succeeds through its "nonstop suspense" as well as "a fine sense of place" drawn from the author's travels. The 1996 work *Evil's Fancy* centers on a homicide investigation conducted by private investigator Coley Doctor, who had been featured earlier in the series, and Hanson, a friend of the wealthy victim. Lorrie K. Inagaki, reviewing the novel in *Armchair Detective,* noted that "colorful characters" add interest to the story and concluded that the book offers "entertainment and nonstop action, without a hint of seriousness."

Hong Kong, China, which was published in 1996, marked Arnote's hardcover debut. Set in Hong Kong on the eve of the July 1, 1997 transfer of power from Britain to China, the story weaves together the lives of such diverse characters as Lacy Locke, a Wall Street banker who travels to Hong Kong to assess

investment prospects; the Dutch entrepreneur Claude Van Hooten and his partner in a successful apparel operation, Moia Hsu—the daughter of a Mainland Chinese official; Liu Wing, a brutal Red Army general embittered by his unsuccessful bid for the love of Moia Hsu; and Brandon Poole, a wealthy representative of the now-departing British colonial power. In a negative assessment of the novel in *Kirkus Reviews,* a critic labeled the work "a trashy and rather tedious tale" and particularly faulted the "inane plotting and witless dialogue." However, Sybil Steinberg, reviewing *Hong Kong, China* in *Publishers Weekly,* characterized the novel as "a stylish if evanescent financial thriller" and noted that "colorful cameo characters . . . contribute to the action, played out against the well-evoked, exotic scenery of Hong Kong."

BIOGRAPHICAL/CRITICAL SOURCES:

PERIODICALS

Armchair Detective, spring, 1996, pp. 229-230.
Kirkus Reviews, July 15, 1996, p. 985.
Publishers Weekly, December 6, 1993, p. 70; August 19, 1996, p. 53.
Tribune Books (Chicago), January 1, 1995, p. 2.*

* * *

ARTSYBASHEV, Mikhail (Petrovich) 1878-1927

PERSONAL: Surname also transliterated as Artsuibashev, Artzibashef, Artzibasheff, Artzibashev, Artzybashef, and Artzybashev; born November 6, 1878, in Kharkov, Russia; died of tuberculosis, March 3, 1927, in Warsaw, Poland; father a landowner and retired army officer, mother a landowner; married, 1898. *Education:* Attended the Imperial Academy of fine arts, Russia.

CAREER: Novelist and playwright. Journalist and cartoonist for Russian newspapers, c. 1894; publisher of *Svoboda* (a weekly magazine), Russia, c. 1912-15, 1917-23; editor and publisher of anti-Soviet newspaper, Warsaw, Poland, c. 1923-27.

WRITINGS:

NOVELS

Sanin, 1907, translation published as *Sanine,* B. W. Huebsch (New York City), 1915.

U posledney cherty, 1912, translation published as
   Breaking Point, M. Secker (London), 1915.
Dikie, 1923, translation published as *The Savage,*
   1924.

PLAYS

Revnost, 1913, translation published as *Jealousy,*
   1923.
Vragi, 1913, translation published as *Enemies,* 1927.
Zakon dikarya, 1913, translation published as *The
   Law of the Savage,* 1923.
Voyna, 1915, translation published as *War,* 1915, and
   as *War: A Play in Four Acts,* A. A. Knopf (New
   York City), 1916.

OTHER

Smert' Lande (novella), 1904, translation published as
   Ivan Lande, 1916.
The Millionaire (short stories), B. W. Huebsch (New
   York City), 1915.
Tales of the Revolution (short stories), B. W. Huebsch,
   1917.
Zapisky pisatelya (essays), 1925.

SIDELIGHTS: Mikhail Artsybashev is chiefly remembered as the author of *Sanin* (*Sanine*), an immensely
popular novel of its time that detailed the sensual
exploits of an unapologetic egoist. Extremely rebellious and nihilistic in spirit, Artsybashev was preoccupied with sex and death and with the stultification
of the free expression of individual will by social
conventions. In all of his works, society crumbles as
its members succumb to despair and suicide; only
Sanine, through his unabashed individualism and sensuality, avoids the spiritual malaise suffered by
Artsybashev's other characters. However, in his later
works, Artsybashev even doubts the viability of his
own creed of anarchism as a response to the human
condition and ultimately concedes the utter futility of
being.

The only son of small landowners, Artsybashev was
born in the Kharkov region of southern Russia. He
was extremely unhappy in school, the brutal discipline
of which he later described in his first short story,
"Pasha Tumanov." He demonstrated an early aptitude
for painting, and his father, a retired army officer
who wanted his son to pursue a military career, reluctantly allowed him to study art. While attending art
school, Artsybashev began writing, at first experimenting primarily with poetry. In 1898 he provoked

a bitter feud with his father by marrying a woman of
a slightly lower social class, and thereafter his father
refused to support him financially. When Artsybashev
left a year later to study at the Imperial Academy of
fine arts, he earned money by drawing cartoons and
writing articles for local newspapers. During the unsuccessful Revolution of 1905, which Artsybashev
supported, he wrote several short stories that recorded
some of the bloodiest and most dramatic events of the
uprising.

In 1907 the publication of *Sanine* brought Artsybashev
immediate fame and inspired numerous imitations as
well as *Sanine* cults which many young people organized in order to give expression to their defiance of
tradition and restraint. Translated into every major
European language, the novel was widely censored
for its promotion of unrestrained sexuality and rebellion against authority. His next novel, *U posledney
cherty* (*Breaking Point*), was similarly rebellious in
tone, and after its publication in 1912 Artsybashev
was imprisoned for several months as an enemy of the
czarist government, an experience that further confirmed his nihilistic and anarchistic beliefs. At this time
Artsybashev began writing dramas as well as fiction
and soon began to publish *Svoboda,* a weekly magazine that became a vehicle for his opinions. The paper
was suppressed after the outbreak of World War I,
but was revived after the Bolshevik Revolution in 1917.

Because of his anarchistic beliefs, Artsybashev soon
became estranged from the Bolsheviks and was persecuted by them: *Svoboda* was again suppressed, he was
imprisoned several times, and his books were placed
on the "forbidden list." In 1923 Artsybashev left
Russia for Poland, where he published bitter invec-
tives against the Bolsheviks. He died of tuberculosis
in Warsaw in 1927.

Sanine, Artsybashev's most widely read work, was a
succes de scandale that glorified the defiant egoism of
its eponymous protagonist. Rejecting the authority of
society to limit his behavior, Sanine believes that only
through self-willed activity, and not socially induced
passivity, can life be lived to the fullest. *Renaissance
and Modern Studies* contributor Nicholas Luker wrote
that "Sanin embodies Artsybashev's advocacy of the
natural life free of moral and social constraints," and
that the dominance that he exerts over all of the other
characters attests to the efficacy of his world-view.
Sanine regards those who are constrained by society
as vulgar and stupid, and the numerous suicides at the
end of the novel as evidence that their social order is
crumbling.

While the novel was widely denounced as pornographic, some critics defended the artistic merit and philosophical sophistication of the work. In his *Books in General, second series,* critic J. C. Squire, writing under the pseudonym Solomon Eagle, claimed that *Sanine* is worth studying because "it discusses 'sex problems' with unusual honesty. . . . It gives a vivid picture, within certain limitations, of Russian life. . . . And it reflects the welter of thoughts and aspirations which are common to the whole contemporary Western world." Many critics have viewed Sanine as a literary descendant of German philosopher Friedrich Nietzsche's *Ubermensch* ("superman") because of his unapologetic self-assertion; however, Artsybashev disavowed this comparison and instead pointed to the influence of Max Stirner, a nineteenth-century philosopher who argued that the suppression of human will by civilization and government subverted the natural expression of life. Early commentary on *Sanine* often discussed the work in relation to contemporary politics: Gilbert Cannan wrote in his preface to the first English translation that the novel "was written in the despair which seized the Intelligentsia of Russia after the last abortive revolution" in 1905. However, Artsybashev contended that the novel was written in 1903, but because of its controversial nature was withheld from publication until 1907; thus, later critics argued that interpreting the novel as a reaction to the failed Revolution of 1905 overestimates the social purpose of the book. Sanine, although openly defiant of all authority, has no interest in revolution nor in joining with others to achieve social change; he looks upon the submission of others to authority only as a sign of their own weakness.

While *Sanine* is in part an apology for the uncompromising pursuit of pleasure, *Breaking Point* emphasizes the bankruptcy of sensuality as a way of life. Sanine is never bored by his pursuit of pleasure; Dchenev, the central character in *Breaking Point,* becomes satiated and no longer interested in self-assertion. James Huneker, who, in his book *Unicorns,* described *Breaking Point* as "the most poignant and intolerable book I ever read," called Artsybashev "a prophet of pessimism." Death and suffering pervade the novel, a fact that has led many critics to compare it to the works of Fyodor Dostoevsky. However, whereas Dostoevsky saw suffering as a vehicle for redemption, Artsybashev recognized only the universality and inescapability of suffering. He concluded that the only response to endless and meaningless suffering is suicide, reflecting a pure intellectual nihilism that is the major theme of the novel. Artsybashev's dramas, like his novels, deal explicitly with sex and relations between men and women. They focus on what the author saw as the inevitable unhappiness of marriage, an institution that inhibits the natural desires of its participants. In his plays Artsybashev continued to express the "anarchical individualism" that is the hallmark of his fiction.

Early critical reaction to Artsybashev's works concentrated on his frank treatment of sexuality and unabashed sensuality. Many critics dismissed *Sanine* as prurient; in his *Contemporary Russian Literature: 1881-1925,* D. S. Mirsky, who called the novel "the Bible of every schoolboy and schoolgirl in Russia," maintained that it "contributed to that moral deterioration of Russian society, especially of provincial schoolgirls." Other critics, however, lauded Artsybashev for his daring frankness and found literary value in his works, praising their philosophical depth and artistic candor. Later critics, accustomed to what seemed at the time sensational excesses, have recognized the value in Artsybashev's articulation of the moral, social, and intellectual turmoil of his age. Marc Slonim, in his *Modern Russian Literature: From Chekhov to the Present,* remarked that Artsybashev's works are of historical interest, because he "represented and reflected the era of reaction on the eve of World War I."

BIOGRAPHICAL/CRITICAL SOURCES:

BOOKS

Artsybashev, Mikhail, *Sanine,* introduction by Gilbert Cannan, B. W. Huebsch (New York City), 1915.

Artsybashev, Mikahail, *Sanine,* preface by Ernest Boyd, Viking Press, 1926.

Clark, Barrett H., and George Freedley, editors, *A History of Modern Drama,* Appleton-Century, 1947, pp. 370-481.

Eagle, Solomon [pseudonym of J. C. Squire], *Books in General, second series,* Alfred A. Knopf (New York City), 1920, pp. 81-85.

Huneker, James, *Unicorns,* Scribner (New York City), 1917, pp. 49-52.

Mirsky, D. S., *Contemporary Russian Literature: 1881-1925,* Alfred A. Knopf, 1926, pp. 139-141.

Olgin, Moissaye J., *A Guide to Russian Literature: 1820-1917,* Harcourt, Brace and Howe, 1920, pp. 265-269.

Slonim, Marc, *Modern Russian Literature: From Chekhov to the Present,* Oxford University Press, 1953, pp. 153-183.

Zavalishin, Vyacheslav, *Early Soviet Writers,* Praeger, 1958, pp. 61-67.

PERIODICALS

Bookman, Volume XL, number 2, 1915, pp. 135-138.
Nation, October 14, 1915, pp. 461-462; January 30, 1924, pp. 119-120.
New Republic, January 30, 1915, pp. 27-28.
New York Times Book Review, July 1, 1917, p. 249, May 25, 1924, p.9.
New Zealand Slavonic Journal, 1985, pp. 89-104.
Renaissance and Modern Studies, Vol. XXIV, 1980, pp. 58-78.
Slavonic and East European Review, January, 1966, pp. 76-87.*

*   *   *

ASHBY, Godfrey W. 1930-

PERSONAL: Born June 11, 1930, in Llandrillo-ym-Rhos, Wales; son of William (a farmer) and Vera Ashby; married, wife's name Valerie, November 30, 1957; children: Garmon, John Mark, Mary, Philip, Ruth, Charles. *Ethnicity:* "British." *Education:* King's College, London, A.K.C., 1952, B.D. (with honors), 1953, Ph.D., 1969. *Politics:* Social Democrat. *Religion:* Anglican. *Avocational interests:* Old Testament, ornithology.

ADDRESSES: Home—Box 2685, Knysna 6570, South Africa.

CAREER: Church of the Province of South Africa, began as priest, became bishop, 1957-88; priest of the Church of England, 1988-95. Affiliated with Rhodes University, 1969-75, and University of the Witwatersrand, 1986-88. *Military service:* Served in Intelligence Corps, 1949-51.

MEMBER: South African, British, and international societies devoted to the study of the Old Testament.

WRITINGS:

Saintfire, S.C.M. Press, 1988.
Go out and Meet God: Exodus, Eerdmans (Grand Rapids, MI), 1998.

WORK IN PROGRESS: Research on Lamartine's beliefs.

SIDELIGHTS: Godfrey W. Ashby told *CA:* "I have written to communicate insights, particularly those I feel have been neglected or misrepresented. Also I try to put across biblical truths to non-experts. In the area of Old Testament I have had to take what opportunities for publication came my way, since the market is limited.

"I was inspired both by my mentors of years ago and by my experiences in South Africa over a lifetime. More recently the work of Lamartine, the French poet and statesman, has interested me. I believe he was a man of faith, not a deist, and has been neglected.

"I write in longhand first, after assembling all the materials in note form and after having studied all the relevant works. Then I put the manuscript on the word processor and revise and correct."

*   *   *

ASHTON, Dianne 1949-

PERSONAL: Born June 21, 1949, in Buffalo, NY; daughter of Irving (in business) and Miriam (a bookkeeper; maiden name, Keller) Ashton; married Richard M. Drucker (a teacher), October 23, 1988. *Ethnicity:* "Jewish." *Education:* Adelphi University, B.A., 1971; studied at Kibbutz Palmach Tsuba, Israel, 1971; graduate study at University of Massachusetts at Amherst, 1975; Temple University, M.A., 1982, Ph.D. (with distinction), 1986. *Politics:* Democrat. *Religion:* Jewish. *Avocational interests:* Travel, music, art, reading.

ADDRESSES: Home—Cherry Hill, NJ. *Office*—Department of Philosophy and Religion, Bunce Hall, Rowan University, 201 Mullica Hill Rd., Glassboro, NJ 08028-1701. *E-mail*—ashton@jupiter.rowan.edu.

CAREER: University of Pennsylvania, Philadelphia, teacher of general studies, 1987; La Salle University, Philadelphia, lecturer in religion, 1986-88; Rowan University, Glassboro, NJ, professor of religion, 1987—, and director of American studies, past chairperson of Department of Philosophy and Religion. Lecturer at Gratz College and Netzky Institute, 1986-88; Rutgers University, lecturer, 1988; guest lecturer at colleges and universities, including University of Utah, 1989, Temple University, 1992, Ocean County College, Bergen County College, and University of

Maryland at College Park, all 1993, and University of Minnesota—Twin Cities, 1996.

AWARDS, HONORS: American Jewish Archives, Franklin fellowship, 1984, Rapoport fellowship, 1988, Marguerite R. Jacobs fellowship, 1998; *Rebecca Gratz* was selected as recommended reading by New Jersey Council for the Humanities, 1998.

WRITINGS:

(Contributor) Sari Thomas, editor, *Communication Theory and Interpersonal Interaction,* Ablex Publishing (Norwood, NJ), 1984.
(Editor with Ellen M. Umansky, and coauthor of introductions) *Four Centuries of Jewish Women's Spirituality: A Sourcebook,* Beacon Press (Boston, MA), 1991.
The Philadelphia Group: A Guide to Archival and Bibliographic Collections, Center for American Jewish History, Temple University (Philadelphia, PA), 1993.
(Contributor) Murray Friedman, editor, *When Philadelphia Was the Capital of Jewish America,* Associated University Presses (Philadelphia), 1993.
(Contributor) Maurie Sacks, editor, *Active Voices: Women in Jewish Culture,* University of Illinois Press (Urbana, IL), 1995.
Jewish Life in Pennsylvania, Pennsylvania Historical Association, 1998.
Rebecca Gratz: Women and Judaism in Antebellum America, Wayne State University Press (Detroit, MI), 1998.

Contributor to periodicals, including *Religious Studies Review, American Jewish History, Jewish Folklore and Ethnology Review, Liturgy,* and *Transformations.*

WORK IN PROGRESS: Research on Jewish women during the American Civil War era.

SIDELIGHTS: Dianne Ashton told *CA:* "I have loved the process of writing since childhood. I became an academic because I could always find something to write about by researching other people's lives, even if I could not come up with a story of my own.

"I am an immensely curious person, probably in both senses of that phrase. I find the conditions of human life fascinating and religion in all its permutations—belief, material artifacts, culture—probably the most

curious thing about being human. I am grateful that so many people appreciate my written work, which emerges almost completely out of my own interests. I pay fairly close attention to the work of scholars I admire in the fields of American studies, Jewish studies, and women's studies, but my research projects appeal primarily to me. I hope they will please others when they are completed. I enjoy the process.

"When I write, I sit down at the computer and just pour words onto the screen as fast as I think of them. I organize, edit, substantiate, cite, and generally improve the flow as I go along. I do countless revisions, but I like revising. I like figuring out better ways to shape a sentence, paragraph, chapter, or phrase.

"I prefer to write about topics that allow me to explore issues and subtleties in American religious life. I think scholarship is more interesting when it is exploring nuances and seeming contradictions than when it is telling a single narrative that overarches a historical era. Nonetheless, I think narrative structure is crucial in a volume. The reader has to like the book! My challenge is to construct an enjoyable, readable, credible, and intellectually challenging book out of the complexities in the material that I have researched. I find it fun."

*   *   *

ASHWORTH, Andrea 1969-

PERSONAL: Born May 16, 1969, in Manchester, England; daughter of Anthony (a painter and decorator) and Lorraine (Chatfield) Clarke. *Education:* Oxford University, B.A., M.A., D.Phil., 1996; Yale University, M.A. program, 1991.

ADDRESSES: Home—Jesus College, Oxford, OX1 3DW, England. *Agent*—Michelle Kass Associates, 36-38 Glasshouse St., London W1R 5HR, England. *E-mail*—andrea.ashworth@ell.ox.ac.uk.

CAREER: Educator. Jesus College, Oxford, junior research fellow in English literature, 1997—.

AWARDS, HONORS: Henry Fellowship, 1990; British Academy Award for Graduate Study, 1992-95; honorary D.Phil., Hertford College, Oxford, 1996; YADDO and Hawthornden writer's fellowships, 1997.

WRITINGS:

Once in a House on Fire: A Memoir, Metropolitan Books (New York City), 1998.

Once in a House on Fire has been translated into more than ten languages.

WORK IN PROGRESS: A novel.

SIDELIGHTS: In 1998, at the age of twenty-eight, writer Andrea Ashworth became one of the youngest fellows of Jesus College at Oxford University. Although the institution is generally considered a bed of privilege and wealth, Ashworth experienced neither of these while growing up. Instead, during her short lifetime, she had been more accustomed to poverty, mental and physical abuse, racial slurs and the pain associated with death. In her first published book, titled *Once in a House on Fire: A Memoir,* Ashworth recalls a childhood in which she spent more time merely trying to survive than aspiring to have any type of literary career. However, the positive critical response to *Once in a House on Fire,* as well as her collegiate achievements—she studied at Oxford and Yale—are evidence of Ashworth's ability to overcome such obstacles.

Described through Ashworth's eyes, the book is the story of her upbringing and family life in Manchester, England and Canada during the 1980s. Ashworth, the oldest of three sisters, experienced tragedy very early. "My father drowned when I was five years old," her book begins. "By the time I was six, our mother's stomach was swollen full of a third child. . . . A looming, red-faced man, quite a bit older than her, stepped into our house for tea and was introduced to Laurie (middle sister) and me as our new daddy." From this point forward, until she made her liberating "flight" to Oxford, Ashworth endured her fair share of hardship. Her new stepfather was an alcoholic prone to beating his wife and her children. She describes how her mother had to wear dark sunglasses during the dreary English winters just to hide her bruised and battered eyes.

Ashworth writes in her book that her mother, Lorraine, was finally able to rid herself of her second husband's abuse only to meet Terry ("Tez"), a small-time criminal with a good deal of money. After Tez and Lorraine were married, he was apprehended for his unlawful activities and sent to prison. When he returned, he too took to beating the family, especially

Ashworth's mother, who was so viciously attacked that she was eventually hospitalized. Ashworth's youngest sister, Sarah, began burning and wounding herself, because she said "it hurts less" than the domestic abuse.

Ashworth gives intriguing descriptions of "our mother," as she suffers through terrible bouts of depression and serious headaches, as well as a host of injuries sustained from the beatings at the hands of her husbands. Ashworth expresses the belief that her mother was so terrified of being alone that she would tolerate almost anything, including the beatings and abuse, in order to be with a man. Still, the daughters show a great deal of love for their mother.

Throughout their trials and tribulations, the family moved around constantly, sometimes being taken in by other people, and often sleeping on cots or the floor. They also moved to Canada for a brief, but ill-fated period. In addition to the abuse the girls must endure at home, they also found plenty outside of the household. Because their biological father was Maltese, the girls acquired his dark skin, a fact that caused others to call them "wogs" and "dirty Pakis."

According to critics there are moments of hope and inspiration in Ashworth's book. Their struggles force the sisters to bond, and their relationship with one another is touching. Fortunately for Andrea, she was also able to find solace elsewhere. She took a liking to literature and even wrote poetry herself. Delving into the works of such diverse authors as Shakespeare, D. H. Lawrence, Judy Blume, James Joyce, Graham Greene, and T. S. Eliot, Ashworth was able to find "sonnets and odes that make miserable things seem sublime." Somehow, despite her stepfather's attempts to stunt her intellect—she writes "In our house, homework makes you a rebel"—she was also able to excel in the classroom, particularly in the subjects of science, art, and literature. At the urging of several of her teachers, she applied for entrance to Oxford and succeeded.

Ashworth's memoir ends as she prepared to leave her mother to attend college. Both of her sisters were also in the process of transition: Laurie moved into a girls hostel and Sarah awaited a decision whether or not she would be placed in a foster home. Nina Barret, in a review for the *Plain Dealer,* wrote, "It's a haunting and disturbing ending, and one that makes it actually disappointing to read in her author's biography that

Ashworth is now trying her hand at fiction. It's not that you doubt she has the literary talent; it's just that you want to hear more about the way her new life went—the way she really lived it and the way she can surely make it sing."

After its release, *Once in a House on Fire* received a great deal of critical praise. Carol West of the *New York Times Book Review* called the book "mesmerizing and poetic," while Mary Paumier Jones, in a review for *Library Journal*, commented, "That she can have achieved the distance and art to produce such a memoir is enough to make many an older writer jealous." A contributor from *Publishers Weekly* was struck by Ashworth's memory and vivid descriptions, stating that the book "stands out for its integrity, lack of self-pity, colorful Manchester dialect and realistic dialogue." Similarly, a contributor from *Kirkus Reviews* wrote that *Once in a House on Fire* is "written in short, cinematic bursts of memory" and "its strengths [lie] in its physical detail."

Grace Fill, reviewing the book for *Booklist,* found it "written with fresh honesty." Ashworth's writing, wrote Fill, "leaves a strong desire for more." Dan Cryer, in a review for *Newsday,* also praised the book, commenting, "Though the bleak conditions of child abuse she portrays are the stuff of talk-show stereotype, the book rises above stereotype on every page." Cryer added that the book's "portrayal of a girl's discovery of intellectual pleasure, like tasting a forbidden fruit, is touching and thrilling."

BIOGRAPHICAL/CRITICAL SOURCES:

BOOKS

Ashworth, Andrea, *Once in a House on Fire: A Memoir,* Metropolitan Books (New York City), 1998.

PERIODICALS

Booklist, April 15, 1998, p. 1398.
Kirkus Reviews, April 15, 1998; May 11, 1998.
Library Journal, June 1, 1998.
Los Angeles Times, June 16, 1998.
Newsday, May 11, 1998.
Newsweek, July 27, 1998.
New Yorker, August 24 & 31, 1998.
New York Times Book Review, July 12, 1998.
Plain Dealer, May 10, 1998.

Publishers Weekly, April 13, 1998, p. 66.
Redbook, December, 1998.

OTHER

Amazon.com, http://www.amazon.com (September 11, 1998).

*   *   *

AUDEH, Azmi S.   1932-

PERSONAL: Born September 7, 1932, in Nazareth, Palestine (now Israel); naturalized U.S. citizen; son of Salim (a carpenter) and Kamilah Audeh; married Nuhiela Habiby (marriage ended); married Salwa Habiby, May 25, 1993; children: Hilda Audeh Bliss, Liela Audeh Haynes. *Ethnicity:* "Palestinian." *Education:* Israel Institute of Technology, B.Sc., 1957; University of Tennessee, M.Sc., 1962. *Politics:* Republican. *Religion:* Christian. *Avocational interests:* Wood work.

ADDRESSES: Home and office—5546 Homestead Way, Boulder, CO 80301. *E-mail*—Asaudeh@aol. com.

CAREER: 3M Co., Camarillo, CA, senior engineer, 1963-66; Ampex Corp., Culver City, CA, engineering manager, 1966-71; Burroughs Corp., Westlake Village, CA, vice-president for engineering, 1971-82; Storage Technology Corp., Louisville, CO, chief engineer, 1982-88, retired, 1988. Worked as writer and as a consultant to control-system component suppliers. Holder of patents related to the design of control systems, such as computer digital tape instrumentation and computer peripherals.

MEMBER: Institute of Electrical and Electronics Engineers.

WRITINGS:

Carpenter from Nazareth: A Palestinian Portrait, Audeh Publishers (Boulder, CO), 1998.

Contributor to engineering journals.

SIDELIGHTS: Azmi S. Audeh told *CA:* "The Palestinian-Israeli conflict is a byword for violence. Most local events capture world attention, provoking polarization, strong feelings, and raw emotions. No conflict in history has ever aroused such passions and fanaticism outside its regional boundaries, and none has been more distorted by prejudice and propaganda. For every confrontation and every act of terrorism, there is an anguished, deeply moving story.

"My book, *Carpenter from Nazareth: A Palestinian Portrait,* deals with the life of an average Arab Palestinian, born when the conflict was still in its infancy. He grew up to witness his beloved country torn by conflict and later occupied by foreigners. Destruction was the norm, followed by the loss of family and friends and the questioning of the very identity of his people."

*   *   *

AUERBACH, Michael 1949-

PERSONAL: Born August 19, 1949, in New York, NY; son of Dory (a realtor) and Hortense (a realtor; maiden name, Moses) Auerbach; married Eileen Coelus (an obstetrician), August 11, 1984; children: Sarah Adalie, Samuel Chapman. *Ethnicity:* "Jewish." *Education:* Emory University, B.S., 1970; New York Medical College, M.D., 1975. *Politics:* Democrat. *Religion:* Jewish. *Avocational interests:* Golf, piano, sports statistics.

ADDRESSES: Home—17 Jackson Manor Ct., Phoenix, MD 21131. *Office*—9000 Franklin Square Dr., Baltimore, MD 21237; fax 410-682-8093. *E-mail*—michaela@helix.org.

CAREER: Cleveland Clinic, Cleveland, OH, in internal medicine, 1978; Columbia University, New York City, in hematology and oncology, 1981; Franklin Square Hospital Center, Baltimore, MD, chief of hematology and oncology and director of Comprehensive Cancer Center, 1986—. Georgetown University, clinical professor.

MEMBER: American College of Physicians (fellow), American Society of Hematology, American Society of Clinical Oncology.

WRITINGS:

Conversations about Cancer, Williams & Wilkins (Baltimore, MD), 1997.

Contributor to medical journals.

SIDELIGHTS: Michael Auerbach told *CA:* "I write to educate the lay public, not so much on content, but on how to question physicians when dealing with cancer in their families. My writing is inspired by the incredible, if not shocking, lack of awareness that educated people have about cancer and by how poorly facts are conveyed by health care providers."

*   *   *

AVISE, John C.

PERSONAL: Male. *Education:* University of Michigan, B.S., 1970; University of Texas at Austin, M.A., 1971; University of California, Davis, Ph.D., 1975.

ADDRESSES: Office—Department of Genetics, University of Georgia, Athens, GA 30602.

CAREER: University of Georgia, Athens, assistant professor of zoology, 1975-79, associate professor, 1979-84, professor of genetics, 1984—.

MEMBER: American Association for the Advancement of Science (fellow), National Academy of Science, American Ornithological Union (fellow), Society for the Study of Evolution (president, 1994), American Academy of Arts and Sciences (fellow), American Genetic Association (president-elect, 2000).

AWARDS, HONORS: Brewster Award, American Ornithological Union, 1997; Pew fellow in marine conservation, 1998.

WRITINGS:

Molecular Markers: Natural History and Evolution, Chapman & Hall (New York City), 1994.
(Editor with J. L. Hamrick) *Conservation Genetics: Case Histories from Nature,* Chapman & Hall, 1996.
The Genetic Gods: Evolution and Belief in Human Affairs, Harvard University Press (Cambridge, MA), 1998.
Phylogeography: The History and Formation of Species, Harvard University Press, 1999.

Contributor of about two-hundred articles to scientific journals. Served as member of editorial board, *Sys-*

tematic Zoology, Paleobiology, Genetica, Genetics, Molecular Biology and Evolution, Journal of Molecular Evolution, Annual Review of Ecology and Systematics, Oxford Surveys in Evolutionary Biology, Molecular Phylogenetics and Evolution, and *Proceedings of the National Academy of Sciences.*

SIDELIGHTS: John C. Avise told *CA:* "My laboratory is interested in the study of the natural history, phylogeography, and evolution of natural populations through the use of molecular genetic markers. Laboratory methods include a variety of protein and DNA assays, with particular emphasis on restriction site and sequence analyses of mitochondrial DNA, alone or in conjunction with allozymes, microsatellites, and other nuclear gene markers. Topics studied range from micro- to macro-evolutionary, and research has been conducted on all major vertebrate groups and selected invertebrates. In most cases, the primary focus is on understanding the natural histories and evolution of organisms through application of molecules as genetic markers, but a secondary concern includes the elucidation of features of the protein and DNA molecules themselves.

"Effort in the laboratory has also been devoted to concepts and theories of population genetics and speciation. The theory and practice of evolutionary genetics are highly relevant to conservation biology, an area that provides an underlying theme to most of our research. I am also interested in evolutionary-genetic findings as applied to the human species, and that is the topic of my book *The Genetic Gods: Evolution and Belief in Human Affairs.*

*   *   *

AZOULAY, Dan 1960-

PERSONAL: Born June 17, 1960, in Toronto, Ontario, Canada; married Raya Neumann, 1984; children: Alyssa, Adam. *Education:* University of Toronto, B.A., 1983; York University, M.A., Ph.D., 1991.

ADDRESSES: Home—1005 Lemar Rd., Newmarket, Ontario, Canada L3Y 1S2. *Office*—Department of History, Atkinson College, York University, North York, Ontario, Canada M3J 1P3. *E-mail*—dazoulay@yorku.ca.

CAREER: Trent University, Peterborough, Ontario, sessional instructor, 1989—; York University, North York, Ontario, sessional instructor in history, 1995—.

WRITINGS:

Keeping the Dream Alive: The Survival of the Ontario CCF/NDP, 1950-1963, McGill-Queen's University Press (Montreal, Quebec), 1997.
(Editor) *Canadian Political Parties: Historical Readings,* Irwin (Toronto, Ontario), 1998.
(Contributor) E. A. Montigny and L. Chambers, editors, *Papers in Post-Confederation Ontario History,* University of Toronto Press (Toronto), in press.

Contributor of articles and reviews to periodicals, including *Journal of Women's History, Ontario History, Labour/Le Travail, Journal of Commonwealth and Comparative Politics,* and *Canadian Historical Review.*

WORK IN PROGRESS: Editing *Not Only the Lonely,* a collection of letters to the "personals" section of a monthly magazine from western Canada, 1905-25; *Let the Seller Beware,* a history of Canadian women in the consumer movement, 1900-50.

SIDELIGHTS: Dan Azoulay told *CA:* "I am motivated to make Canadian history more accessible to the average person, and I want to contribute to the body of knowledge in my field. I really enjoy wading through historical documents and then piecing bits of evidence together to recreate an era long past. It's a bit like traveling in time and being an investigator all at once. I am influenced by popular historians and journalists who seem to bring history to life better than professional historians do."

B

BAGRITSKY, Eduard
See DZYUBIN, Eduard Georgievich

*   *   *

BAIUL, Oksana 1977-

PERSONAL: Born November 16, 1977, in Dnepropetrovsk, Ukraine, of the former Union of Soviet Socialist Republics (USSR); immigrated to the United States, 1994; naturalized citizen; daughter of Sergei and Marina (a French teacher; deceased) Baiul.

ADDRESSES: Home—Newark, DE. *Agent*—c/o William Morris Agency, 1325 Avenue of the Americas, New York, NY 10019.

CAREER: Ice skater, 1991—. Author.

AWARDS, HONORS: Second-place award, women's figure skating European Championships, 1993; first-place award, women's World Figure Skating Championships, 1993; Gold Medal for women's figure skating, Olympic Games in Lillehammer, Norway, 1994.

WRITINGS:

(With Heather Alexander) *Oksana: My Own Story,* Random House (New York City), 1997.
Secrets of Skating, compiled by Christopher Sweet, photography by Simon Bruty, foreword by Dorothy Hamill, Universe Publishers (New York City), 1997.

SIDELIGHTS: Russian figure skater Oksana Baiul began to receive the attention of American sports fans in 1991, when she placed twelfth in the Soviet Championships. By 1993 she was receiving international attention as the second-place winner in the European Championship in Helsinki, and later that year, as winner of the World Championships in Prague. But only by winning the Gold Medal for women's figure skating at the 1994 Olympic Games at the age of sixteen did Oksana Baiul become an international household name.

Baiul overcame great odds to make it to the top of her sport; that story is told in her autobiography, *Oksana: My Own Story*. But she also paid a great price as a result of her instant notoriety and sudden riches, a story her book leaves out, but which has been followed by all those interested in skating and sports news in general.

Oksana: My Own Story traces Baiul's origins to Dnepropetrovsk, the Soviet missile-factory town in the Ukraine where she was born in 1977. Baiul was raised by her mother and maternal grandparents from the age of two, after her father Sergei deserted the family. It was her grandfather who got her started in skating by buying Oksana her first pair of skates when she was four. He foresaw a future in dance for her, and viewed the skating rink as a "training ground" for a career in the ballet. But Baiul took to the ice instantly, and there she remained under the training of Stanislav Korytek, called "one of the finest Ukrainian coaches" by Ami Walsh in *Newsmakers 1995*. Her mother Marina managed to cover the costs of Baiul's training from her salary as a French teacher. But Marina Baiul's life was cut short in 1991, at the age of thirty-six, when she died of ovarian cancer. Having already lost her grandparents, and only having glimpsed her father at her mother's funeral, Baiul was effectively orphaned by her mother's death.

Fortunately for her, Baiul's coach Korytek, who defected to Canada within a few weeks of Marina Baiul's death, begged Galina Zmievskaya, another excellent skating coach, to take Baiul as a student. Zmievskaya's protege and later son-in-law Victor Petrenko also encouraged her to coach Baiul, having sensed the young skater's potential. Within a short time Baiul was living with Zmievskaya in her small Odessa apartment, sharing her youngest daughter's bedroom.

Within two years Baiul began to win medals in major competitions, including a win at the World Championships in 1993. But the pressure of these events was hardly comparable to the upcoming Winter Olympic Games. If the pressure of the games themselves was not enough, women's figure skating was in the spotlight more than usual that year because of the intensive coverage of the Harding-Kerrigan scandal. The scandal began in January, 1994, when a man (who was later discovered to have been hired by figure skater Tonya Harding's boyfriend) attacked Nancy Kerrigan as she trained in Detroit's Cobo Arena. Although Kerrigan's knee was injured in the attack, she was able to skate at the Olympic Games, as was Harding, who had not been disqualified by her boyfriend's actions.

Baiul had her own injuries to contend with going into the final competition; she ran into another skater while training on the night before the finals and suffered a bad cut to her shin and bruises on her back. But despite the overwhelming attention being focused on women's skating, and despite her own painful injuries, Baiul skated a nearly flawless program and managed to beat the heavily favored Kerrigan by a narrow margin. In so doing, Baiul arrested the attention of one of the largest television-viewing audiences ever, and secured herself a place in the figure skating pantheon.

Baiul's book ends at this climactic point, but once having garnered the world's attention, Baiul has not lost it. Many other publications have kept the public apprized of her post-Olympic life. Baiul's fairy-tale vault to the heights of fame, and the wealth that came as a result of her decision to turn to professional skating, product endorsements, and her creation of a line of jewelry, did not guarantee her happiness or continuous success.

Within six months of her Olympic win, Baiul, her coach, and her coach's family had moved to Simsbury, Connecticut, to help establish the International Skating Center for training professional and amateur skaters. But Baiul, suffering from some chronic injuries, had begun to tire of the rigors of skating, and turned her sights on more diverting pastimes. Without parental guidance to keep her stable and focused, and with her coach unable to fill that gap, Baiul, who had gained weight and height that threw off her skating, began to lose her drive to skate. By mid-1996 she had begun to drink heavily. On January 12, 1997, after attending an ice skating event in Hartford and then drinking heavily at a nearby bar, Baiul drove her Mercedes off a two-lane highway at a speed of close to 100 miles per hour, and into roadside brush. As Richard Jerome wrote in *People Weekly,* "The January mishap was rife with metaphor: Ice princess skids out of control." She and her passenger, a skater named Ari Zakarian, were lucky to survive the accident, from which she sustained a mild concussion and cut scalp, and he a broken finger. According to Jerome, Baiul put her luck down to her mother's protection from beyond the grave, and forswore drinking after that event.

Baiul's car accident not only made her stop drinking, but brought her focus back to skating, once her injuries had healed. But the return to skating was not accompanied by a return to the oversight of her Ukrainian coach, from whom she had begun to feel a lack of faith and support. Baiul told Jerome, "I don't think they [the coach and her family, including skater Victor Petrenko] believe in me anymore." She turned instead to U.S. choreographer Sara Kawahara, with whom she worked in Los Angeles. Baiul has begun to skate professionally again, to the delight of audiences who showed their appreciation with standing ovations.

Reviews of *Oksana: My Own Story* were generally positive, although some reviewers waxed more enthusiastic than others. Writing for the *School Library Journal,* Janice C. Hayes admired the books high-quality photographs and heavy, snow-flake embossed paper, as well as its "charming and heartwarming story." Conversely, Deborah Stevenson, writing for the *Bulletin of the Center for Children's Books,* called the book "a hardcover souvenir brochure" that does not bring readers "any real closeness to the glamorous world" they are eager to read about. *Booklist* contributor Chris Sherman felt the book would appeal to preteen skating fans. While she noted that the work doesn't reveal much new information, she considered Baiul's autobiography "interesting reading."

BIOGRAPHICAL/CRITICAL SOURCES:

Newsmakers 1995, Gale (Detroit, MI), 1995.

PERIODICALS

Booklist, May 1, 1997, pp. 1489-1491.
Bulletin of the Center for Children's Books, May, 1997, pp. 312-313.
People Weekly, June 23, 1997, pp. 71-75.
School Library Journal, May, 1997, p. 142.
Time, January 26, 1998, pp. 64-67.*

*   *   *

BALD, Wambly 1902-

PERSONAL: Born 1902 in Chicago, IL. *Education:* University of Chicago, (philosophy), 1924.

ADDRESSES: Agent—Ohio University Press, Scott Quadrangle, Athens, OH 45701.

CAREER: Paris Tribune, Paris, France, journalist, columnist, and proofreader, 1929-33.

WRITINGS:

On the Left Bank, edited by Benjamin Franklin V, Ohio University Press (Athens, OH), 1987.

Contributor of fiction to the *New Review*; contributor to *Boulevardier*. Contributor of stories to anthologies, including "Flow Gently," *Readies for Bob Brown's Machine,* edited by Bob Brown, Roving Eye Press (Cagnes-sur-Mer), 1931; and "Dreary," *Americans Abroad An Anthology,* edited by Peter Neagoe, Servire (The Hague), 1932.

SIDELIGHTS: Wambly Bald is known primarily for his newspaper columns and writings that captured the essence of the Parisian Left Bank during the early twentieth century. Bald was born in Chicago but relocated to France in 1929 after graduating from the University of Chicago in 1924. Between 1929 and 1933 he wrote a column for the *Paris Tribune* (a French edition of the *Chicago Tribune*). He also worked as a proofreader for the paper, refusing frequent offers of advancement.

In a review of Bald's work in the *New Republic,* Jerrold Siegel suggested that Bald arrived in Paris on the tail end of the expatriate movement and that his writing reflects the hollow endeavor that being an expatriate had become. Prior to 1929 Americans had trekked to Paris and its Left Bank in an esoteric search for artistic, literary, and intellectual inspiration. By the time Bald arrived the movement was on the decline. Siegel called Bald's writing undeveloped, and noted that one of Bald's peers had named him "the greatest living non-writer."

Bald attempted to capture the bohemian mood in Paris by telling "tall tales" and by mixing surrealism and factual prose. He poked fun at those who took themselves too seriously and was not afraid to cover the unique and possibly untouchable egos of some of the era's more famous personalities.

According to reviewer Andrea Barnet of the *New York Times Book Review,* Bald was a "master of the one-liner and the telling anecdote." Aldous Huxley, for example, was described by Bald as someone "who had been concentrating for seventy-five years," even though he was only thirty-eight at the time.

Bald's column, titled "La Vie de Boheme," covered notable gossip and society personalities of the day, including F. Scott Fitzgerald and painter Henry C. Lee, as well as relatively unknown people. Additionally he advocated for certain literary endeavors such as the publication of *New Review,* a literary magazine that published some of Bald's own work. Benjamin Franklin V in the *Dictionary of Literary Biography* described Bald's column as having an "irrepressible spirit" and suggested that Bald's main literary gift was his "keen observation of bohemian Paris and his ability to capture its essence." Nonetheless Bald became bitter over time with the bohemian ideal that he had pursued. Toward the end of his tenure with the *Tribune* he commented that "art is a solace but no solution" and that he had grown weary of the lifestyle that he attempted to cover.

In 1934 Bald headed back to the United States after the Parisian edition of the *Tribune* merged with the *Paris Herald.* Bald's columns were later edited and published in 1987 in *On the Left Bank.* While a *Publishers Weekly* reviewer found that the material covered nothing new about the era, *New York Times Book Review* contributor Barnet called the presentation a "stylish commentary by a witty raconteur."

BIOGRAPHICAL/CRITICAL SOURCES:

BOOKS

Dictionary of Literary Biography, Volume 4, Gale
    (Detroit, MI), 1980.

PERIODICALS

New Republic, September 28, 1987, pp. 30-34.
New York Times Book Review, March 1, 1987, p. 21.
Publishers Weekly, December 5, 1986, p. 58.*

* * *

BALTAUSIS, Vincas
    See KREVE (MICKEVICIUS), Vincas

* * *

BASTIANICH, Lidia Matticchio 1947-

PERSONAL: Born February 21, 1947, in Pula, Italy;
naturalized U.S. citizen; daughter of Vittorio and
Erminia Motika-Matticchio; married Felice Bastianich;
children: Joseph, Tanya Bastianich Manual. *Ethnicity:*
"Italian." *Education:* Attended Hunter College and
Queens College, both of the City University of New
York. *Avocational interests:* Gardening, singing.

ADDRESSES: Office—Felidia Restaurant, 243 East
58th St., New York, NY 10022; fax 212-935-7687.
Agent—Jane Dystel, Jane Dystel Literary Management, 1 Union Sq. W., New York, NY 10003. *E-
mail*—lidia@lidiasitaly.com.

CAREER: Buonavia Restaurant, Forest Hills, NY,
owner, 1972-81; Felidia Restaurant, New York City,
owner, 1981—. Villa Secondo, Fresh Meadows, NY,
owner, 1979-81; Becco Restaurant, co-owner, 1992—;
Frico Bar and Restaurant, co-owner, 1995—; Lidia's
Restaurant, Kansas City, MO, co-owner, 1998—;
Lidia's Flavors of Italy, partner. Esperienze Italian
Travel, president, 1997—.

Guest on television programs, including guest chef for
Julia Child's Cooking with Master Chefs, broadcast
by Public Broadcasting Service in 1994. UNICEF,

chairperson of Roman Holidays fund-raising benefit,
1991, member of advisory board, 1994, cochairperson
of Celebration of Women charity event, 1998, and
member of New York Metropolitan Committee. Good
Samaritan Hospital (for victims of war in Bosnia),
founder, 1994. James Beard Foundation, member.

MEMBER: International Italian Guild of Professional
Restaurateurs, Distinguished Restaurants of North
America, American Academy in Rome, American
Institute of Wine and Food, Culinary Institute of
America, National Organization of Italian American
Women, Women Chefs and Restaurateurs (cofounder;
member of board of directors, 1997), Les Dames
d'Escoffier, Caterina de Medici Society, New York
State Restaurant Association.

AWARDS, HONORS: Best Pasta in America Award,
National Pasta Association, 1986; Innovation Award
and named woman of the year in restaurant category,
Women's Institute of the Center for Food and Hotel
Management, 1987; Grand Award, Restaurant Wine
List, 1988; Emmy Award nomination, Academy of
Television Arts and Sciences, 1994, for *Julia Child's
Cooking with Master Chefs;* five-star review, Passport
to New York Restaurants, 1995, for Felidia Restau-
rant; Felidia Restaurant was also listed among Top
Ten Italian Restaurants, *Wine Spectator,* 1997; Mayor
Vincent A. Cianci, Jr. Award, 1998; award from
New York Association of Cooking Teachers, 1998.

WRITINGS:

(With Jay Jacobson) *La Cucina di Lidia,* Doubleday
    (New York City), 1990.
Lidia's Italian Table, Morrow (New York City),
    1998.

Editor of the column "A Celebration of Life," *New
York Times Magazine,* 1991-98.

*WORK IN PROGRESS: Lidia's Italian Table with
Friends and Family.*

SIDELIGHTS: Lidia Matticchio Bastianich told *CA:*
"I have been a professional chef and restaurant owner
for nearly thirty years. I am a native Italian who
immigrated to the United States when I was twelve
years old. Through the years I have collected a multitude of information on the culture of Italian cuisine,
and writing is a way for me to record and maintain
my Italian heritage. I feel this need to record my life
experiences for myself and my family, and then to
share the record with the interested public.

"My work is influenced by M. F. K. Fisher, James Beard, Marcella Hazan, Julia Child, and Anna Gossetti. Dumas and Jane Davidson are also authors whose work I admire and enjoy. For me, to share a recipe is to share history and culture. Food is life and must be shared among people, not just in recipes. I continuously collect recipes, through my work, restaurants and cooking, my travels and friends, both familial and professional. I add cultural, scientific, and personal experiences in a narrative form to the list of recipes and techniques. In the narrative, my passion and sentiments for the subject flow freely."

*   *   *

BATAILLE, Christophe 1971-

PERSONAL: Born October 14, 1971, in Versailles, France; son of Alain and Edith Bataille; married Maguelone Fallot, September 14, 1996. *Ethnicity:* "French." *Religion:* Christian.

ADDRESSES: Home—19-21 Rue Dumoncel, 75014 Paris. *Office*—GRASSET, 61 Rue des Saints-Peres, 75006 Paris.

CAREER: Fiction writer. Editor at Edition GRASSET, Paris, France.

AWARDS, HONORS: Winner of the Prix du Premier Roman, for *Annam,* 1993.

WRITINGS:

Annam, Arlea (Paris), 1993, translated by Richard Howard published as *Annam,* New Directions (New York City), 1996.
Absinthe, Arlea (Paris), 1994.
Le Maitre des Hevres, Arlea (Paris), 1997.

SIDELIGHTS: Christophe Bataille's first novel, *Annam,* published when he was only twenty-one, won Bataille the prestigious French Prix du Premier Roman (First Novel Prize) in 1993, immediately establishing him as an important writer. In the United States, where it was published three years later in a translation by poet Richard Howard, it has also met with great literary acclaim.

The novel dramatizes key elements of one of France's earliest official involvements with Vietnam, more than fifty years in advance of its colonization of

Saigon. In 1787 the emperor of Vietnam, a boy of seven named Canh, travels to France to beg Louis XVI for help in the form of soldiers and missionaries. The French king denies Canh's request for aid, and before long both Canh and Louis XVI are dead: Canh from pneumonia and Louis guillotined, along with many other members of the French aristocracy, in the bloody French revolution. Although Canh's plea for help falls on deaf ears within the French court, it has been heard by a retired bishop who is inspired to spread the teachings of Christ among the Vietnamese. Two ships embark to Vietnam in 1789, loaded not only with Dominican missionaries, but with soldiers whose objective it is to aid Prince Regent Nguyen Anh, an expatriate now living in Siam, in his bid to regain leadership of his homeland.

Those missionaries who survive the voyage and the diseases of the jungle fulfill their purpose of claiming souls, while at the same time establishing parishes, constructing dikes, and teaching the French language to the natives. Back in France the revolution takes heads and reconfigures French government, law, and history to the cry of "Liberty, Equality, Fraternity!"—with little attention toward this small Vietnamese mission. France's effort to support Nguyen Anh's return to power (and their support for the missionaries) dwindles and dies. When Nguyen Anh finally comes to power through his own efforts in 1800, he decides to take revenge on the French for betraying their original alliance. He orders that all the French Dominican monks and nuns be put to death. Only one monk and one nun escape murder, protected by the remoteness of the tiny mountain enclave they inhabit with its Vietnamese villagers. Gradually, their distance from the land and church that sent them and from other Christian clergy results in the weakening of their religious vows until they become much like the villagers they had once sought to convert.

The reception of the English translation of Bataille's novel echoed the enthusiasm the book met in its original French version. *Publishers Weekly* lauded both the writer and the excellent translation. Bataille's *Annam, Publishers Weekly* enthused, is "built around short sentences [and] achieves a cumulative lyricism that poignantly captures the unfulfilled promise and tragedy of the period of colonial history it depicts. In a similarly appreciative response, Ray Olson, writing for *Booklist,* applauded the novel's "elegant" minimalism and its resultant emotional depth. And a contributor to *Kirkus Reviews* described the novel as "skillfully understated" and the translation "beautiful." A number of reviewers pointed out that Bataille published the acclaimed novel at the young age of twenty-one.

BIOGRAPHICAL/CRITICAL SOURCES:

PERIODICALS

Booklist, September 15, 1996, p. 218.
Kirkus Reviews, August 1, 1996, p. 1095.
Publishers Weekly, August 5, 1996, p. 432.

*   *   *

BEARANGER, Marie
   See MESSIER, Claire

*   *   *

BECKINGHAM, Charles Fraser   1914-1998

OBITUARY NOTICE—See index for *CA* sketch: Born February 18, 1914, in Houghton, Huntingdonshire, England; died September 30, 1998. Professor and author. Beckingham, a scholar in several areas, graduated from Queens College, Cambridge, in 1935 and received his master's degree there in 1939. He worked as a cataloguer in the department of printed books at the British Museum for ten years, then joined the British Foreign Office in 1946. He stayed at the Foreign Office until 1951, working in a secret branch, then left for a post at Manchester University as an Islamic history lecturer. While at that university he helped translate and edit *Some Records of Ethiopia, 1593-1646, Being Extracts from the History of High Ethiopia or Abassia,* and helped edit *The Prester John of the Indies: The Translation of Lord Stanley of Alderley, 1881.* In 1965 he moved to the University of London's School of Oriental and African Studies as a full professor and from 1969 to 1972 was head of the Near and Middle East Department. Other books on Prester John followed, including *The Achievement of Prester John: An Inaugural Lecture Delivered on 17 May 1966* and *Prester John, the Mongols, and the Ten Lost Tribes,* which was published in 1996.

OBITUARIES AND OTHER SOURCES:

PERIODICALS

Times (London), October 6, 1998.

BELLM, Dan   1952-

PERSONAL: Born August 19, 1952, in Springfield, IL; son of C. V. and Mary E. Bellm; married Yoel Kahn, June 16, 1991; children: Adam. *Education:* Boston College, B.A., 1973; University of Michigan, M.A., 1976.

ADDRESSES: Home—61 Ford St., San Francisco, CA 94114. *E-mail*—danbellm@aol.com.

CAREER: Writer, poet, and translator.

MEMBER: National Writers Union, Poetry Society of America, Squaw Valley Community of Writers, Media Alliance.

AWARDS, HONORS: Walt Whitman Award finalist, 1997.

WRITINGS:

Story in a Bottle (poetry), Norton Coker Press (San Francisco), 1991.
(And editor) *Family Day Care Handbook,* California Child Care Resource and Referral Network (San Francisco), 1993.
(Translator) Alberto Blanco, *Angel's Kite/Estrella de Angel,* (children's fiction), Children's Book Press (Emeryville, CA), 1994.
(With Marcy Whitebook and Patty Hnatiuk) *The Early Childhood Mentoring Curriculum: A Handbook for Mentors,* National Center for the Early Childhood Work Force (Washington, DC), 1996.
(With Mary Whitebook) *Taking on Turnover: An Action Guide for Child Care Center Teachers and Directors,* National Center for the Early Childhood Work Force (Washington, DC), 1998.
(With Molly Fisk and Forrest Hamer) *Terrain* (poetry), Hip Pocket Press (Nevada City, CA), 1998.
One Hand on the Wheel (poetry), Roadhouse Press (Berkeley), 1999.
Buried Treasure (poetry), Cleveland State University Press, 1999.

OTHER

"Child Care Resource and Referral Agencies," *ERIC Digest,* Clearinghouse on Elementary and Early Childhood Education, available at http://ericps. crc.uiuc.edu, 1991.

Contributor of articles, book reviews, and poetry to publications, including the *Nation, Mother Jones, Village Voice, San Francisco Chronicle,* and *Poetry.*

SIDELIGHTS: Dan Bellm is a writer and poet who has also contributed book reviews, articles, and poetry to national publications. He has written several volumes dealing with topics such as mentoring children, prevention of child abuse in residential care, and children's day care. Bellm also writes articles for organizations such as the Clearinghouse on Elementary and Early Childhood Education. His other works include *Story in a Bottle,* a book of poetry, and *Angel's Kite/Estrella de Angel,* a bilingual children's book, which he translated.

His publication "Child Care Resources and Referral Agencies," is included on the web site of the Children's Research Center at the University of Illinois at Urbana-Champaign. In this paper, funded by the United States Department of Education, Bellm stresses the need for planning to overcome the lack of superior services for child care programs for families with young children. He calls the current care system "at best, a patchwork quilt: a fragmented and often confusing array of public and private programs, housed in a variety of settings, and frequently subject to eligibility guidelines that vary widely."

Writing of the growth of Child Care Resource and Referral Agencies (CCR&Rs), Bellm commented that some "are housed in state or other public agencies. But most are community-based organizations that have been created by parents or child care advocates in response to local needs."

Bellm describes how CCR&Rs can improve child care by providing parents with information about child care resources, offering training to child care providers, collecting and analyzing child care data to offer better services, and encouraging partnerships between the public sector and the private sector.

BIOGRAPHICAL/CRITICAL SOURCES:

OTHER

Barnes and Noble, http://www.barnesandnoble.com (October 6, 1998).
ERIC Digest, Clearinghouse on Elementary and Early Childhood Education, http://ericps.crc.uiuc.edu (October 14, 1998).

BENDALL, Molly 1961-

PERSONAL: Born in 1961.

ADDRESSES: Office—English Department, University of Southern California, Los Angeles, CA, 90089-0354.

CAREER: Writer.

AWARDS, HONORS: George Dillon Memorial Prize, *Poetry,* 1994.

WRITINGS:

After Estrangement (poetry), Peregrine Smith (Salt Lake City), 1992.

SIDELIGHTS: According to a *Publishers Weekly* reviewer, *After Estrangement,* Molly Bendall's first book of poetry, contains lush and mysterious language, even if the larger structure of its poems is not always effective. Bendall, according to this reviewer, has a knack for "absurd juxtaposition." While Bendall often uses effective images (for example, a lip cut by a lover's fingernail), the reviewer finds it less effective when the poetry resorts to a disjointed question-and-answer format.

Bendall originally studied as a ballet dancer, and Daniel Kunitz in *Parnassus* finds that her language is similarly "nimble and dancing." But for Kunitz, the effective juxtapositions between the images in the poetry are disjointed and seem out of place. Bendall's poetry works best when she slows down to a more reflective pace, according to the reviewer, as in the poem "Pavlova," which effectively paints a picture of a dancer working through ballet drills.

In *After Estrangement,* Bendall often writes of dancers or other people in the arts. Calvin Bedient in *Poetry* calls Bendall "a rare inventor in the field of style and poetic movement" and claims that her poetry works because she perfectly pairs elegant language with personalities who think in a unique and disjointed way. According to Bedient, the technique works and the reader is assured of the deliberateness of each word, even when the poetry is unconventional. Bedient finds impressive the contrasts in Bendall's poetry, remarking that her work would be "exquisite if it did not also exude a power that is part formidable invention and part menace." Bendall's perception of the world includes "enchantment and misgiving," "estrangement and ambiguity."

BIOGRAPHICAL/CRITICAL SOURCES:

PERIODICALS

Parnassus, February, 1992, pp. 476-479.
Poetry, June, 1993, pp. 176-180.
Publishers Weekly, July 6, 1992, p. 51.*

*   *   *

BENEDICT, Pinckney 1964-

PERSONAL: Born in 1964, in southern WV; son of Cleve (a farmer and politician) Benedict; married Laurie Philpot (a writer), 1990. *Education:* Attended a private high school in Pennsylvania; Princeton University, B.A., 1986; University of Iowa (Writers' Workshop), M.F.A., 1988.

ADDRESSES: Agent—c/o Doubleday, 1540 Broadway, New York, NY 10036. *E-mail*—benedict@ hope.edu.

CAREER: Fiction writer, 1987—. Hope College, Holland, MI, associate professor (English); Pushcart Anthology Series, contributing editor. Has also taught creative writing at Ohio State University, Oberlin College, and Princeton University.

AWARDS, HONORS: Nelson Algren Short Story Award, *Chicago Tribune,* 1986, for the short story "The Sutton Pie Safe"; Steinbeck Award (Britain); shortlisted for Hammett Award for Excellence in Crime Writing; Henfield Foundations Transatlantic Review Awards; *Town Smokes, The Wrecking Yard,* and *Dogs of God* were named Notable Books by *New York Times Book Review.*

WRITINGS:

Town Smokes (stories), Ontario Review Press (New York City), 1987.
The Wrecking Yard and Other Stories (stories), Doubleday (New York City), 1992.
Dogs of God (novel), Doubleday (New York City), 1994.

Contributor of stories and nonfiction to publications, including *Ontario Review, Grazia* (Italy), *Gunzo* (Japan), and *The Oxford Book of American Short Stories.* Also author of one-act, full-length, and musical plays.

WORK IN PROGRESS: A screenplay for *Dogs of God* for Gerard de Thame Films, London.

SIDELIGHTS: Pinckney Benedict is an award-winning short story writer and novelist whose visceral and often violent tales—which have won him comparison to William Faulkner and Cormac McCarthy, among others—paint a grim picture of life in the mountainous regions of West Virginia. Benedict was born and makes his home in West Virginia, although he grew up on a dairy farm in the flatlands around Lewisburg.

Benedict told Bruce Weber of *New York Times Book Review* that many of his stories concern "neighboring counties, where it's more mountainous. And the mountains are pretty wild places," filled with "a lot of very . . . independent people" with "strong personalities." West Virginia is sometimes called a "border" state, because Northerners think of it as a Southern state and Southerners regard it as not Southern enough in its culture. "Neither region wants us," Benedict told *U.S. News & World Report* contributor Viva Hardigg. "So it does feel like we're sort of a doorway. And that's fine. Because that's the area I like to explore in my work—these places where there's no mainstream to be outside of."

Benedict studied under the famous and prolific novelist Joyce Carol Oates—herself prone to the use of lavish violence in her fiction—while at Princeton University, and Oates urged him to write about West Virginians, paying particular attention to their dialect. "It was immediately apparent to other students and to me that Pinckney stood out," Oates told Jim Naughton, a staff writer for the *Washington Post.* "He was just on another level. He has a precocious sense of what he wanted to write about and he's more mature emotionally." Upon Oates's suggestion, Benedict studied the stories of Breece D'J Pancake, a West Virginian writer whose works were published posthumously after the author committed suicide in 1979. Reading Pancake's stories further supported Benedict's decision to write about the people of West Virginia in the laconic style he shared with Pancake. At Oates's prompting he submitted a short story, "The Sutton Pie Safe," to the *Chicago Tribune*'s annual Nelson Algren Award contest and he won.

That story was included in Benedict's first collection of short stories, *Town Smokes,* published in 1987. Among the protagonists in this collection are a fifteen-year-old son who despises his father for dying in a lumbering accident and a young man who kills his sick dog with a .45 pistol. In another piece, a mother wakes her son in the middle of the night to rescue his intoxicated stepfather from an enraged moonshiner. Diane McWhorter, writing for the *New York Times Book Review,* praised *Town Smokes* as "an often heart-stopping literary performance." "The assured tone that distinguishes this debut would be remarkable for any author, but it's especially notable given the age of Pinckney Benedict," stated Richard Panek in Chicago *Tribune Books.* "At twenty-three, he has delivered a collection that is almost free of immature material. Aside from one attempt at magical realism that misses, all the stories in *Town Smokes* command respect through their impressive authority." "Symbolism this rich would bring on gout in less authentically felt stories," remarked McWhorter. "Mr. Benedict has taken big risks—particularly in using a dialect that, failing perfect pitch, would have badly got on one's nerves—and his prose achieves excellent harmony between voice and virtuosity. His lyricism never plays his flinty characters false."

Five years later, Benedict followed *Town Smokes* with *The Wrecking Yard and Other Stories.* In this collection, Benedict portrays confrontations between so-called ordinary folks and outsiders: among others, a fight between a boy and a crazed Vietnam veteran, a girl from a carnival who electrocutes her lovers, and the punishment of a rapist by a posse. Writing for Chicago *Tribune Books,* Douglas Glover maintained that "Benedict's style is laconic and deadpan. He gets comic mileage from the tension between the dry, matter-of-fact way he writes and the terrible and outlandish things he describes." Glover concluded, Benedict "is at his weakest when he strays into the present or the real. . . . He is at his best when he ignores the contemporary siren calls of sentimental realism and interpersonal sensitivity and simply lets the violence overflow, propelling the reader into a world of strange and macabre beauty." "With his second book," Nancy Willard of the *New York Times Book Review* remarked, "he has established himself as a highly original writer whose vision of the American frontier is as contemporary as it is compelling."

Benedict flexed his literary muscles further in his next offering, *Dogs of God* (1994), his first novel. On a remote mountaintop, Tannhauser, a mad, twelve-fingered drug lord—he hints that he also has a tail—grows marijuana, utilizing the labor of enslaved Mexicans. His sprawling, though decaying, mountain compound was once, at turns, a prison for women, a resort hotel, and a military installation. Tannhauser has dubbed it "El Dorado." Little does Tannhauser know that DEA agents are planning a raid and that the corrupt local sheriff is helping them as a means of covering up his own misdeeds. Into this hell on earth wanders Goody, a boxer who once killed a man in a fixed match and who must now engage in a bare-knuckle fight with one of Tannhauser's men for the amusement of visiting Mafiosi. The novel ends with a massacre in which nearly every major character dies.

Many critics lavished praise on the novel. *Los Angeles Times* reviewer Chris Goodrich coined the word "Benedictland" to describe the novel's setting, which "brims with odd characters and creatures driven by primal, irrefutable urges. These desires regularly fail to make sense to the reader, but part of this novel's magnetic attraction is a logic both alien and commonplace, a logic that doesn't so much defy analysis as render it irrelevant." Goodrich called *Dogs of God* "about as fine a first novel as one could want." Writing in the Chicago *Tribune Books,* William O'Rourke commented that Benedict "is a superior writer and his garrulous miscreants grow downright likable." Alexander Harrison wrote in the *Times Literary Supplement* that he found the novel "graphic and hard-boiled." Harrison noted a great depth in Benedict's writing, "the calm, ambiguous tone of Benedict's writing poses questions, not only about his characters but about the wider world from which they seem so cut off."

Oates offered perhaps the pithiest critique of *Dogs of God*—*U.S. News & World Report* contributor Viva Hardigg related Oates's reaction upon reading a copy of the manuscript that Benedict had sent her: "Pinckney, you're going to set the tourist industry in West Virginia back one hundred years." Pinckney wryly replied, "I may have some vested interest in keeping tourists out."

BIOGRAPHICAL/CRITICAL SOURCES:

PERIODICALS

Bloomsbury Review, May/June 1995, p. 23.
Georgian Review, winter, 1987, pp. 819-826.
Los Angeles Times Book Review, February 2, 1992, p. 6; March 27, 1994, pp. 3, 7.
New Statesman & Society, July 1, 1994, pp. 39-40.
New York Times Book Review, July 12, 1987, pp. 13-14; February 9, 1992, p. 14; February 6, 1994, p. 31.
Publishers Weekly, March 27, 1987, pp. 42-43.
Times Literary Supplement, March 6, 1992, p. 21; July 1, 1994, p. 20.

Tribune Books (Chicago), June 1, 1987, p. 3; January 26, 1992, p. 7; February 27, 1994, pp. 3, 11.
U.S. News & World Report, May 16, 1994, p. 63.
Washington Post, November 2, 1987, pp. C1, C12.*

*   *   *

BENGTSSON, Frans (Gunnar) 1894-1954

PERSONAL: Born October 4, 1894, in Roessjoeholm, Sweden; died December 19, 1954, in Stockholm, Sweden. *Education:* Lund University, baccalaureate degree, 1920, licentiate, 1930.

CAREER: Novelist, poet, and translator.

AWARDS, HONORS: Annual prize from the Swedish Academy, 1938, for *Karl den XII:s levnad.*

WRITINGS:

NOVELS

Roede Orm, sjoefarare i vaesterled (title means "Red Orm on the Western Way"), 1941, translation by Barrows Mussey published as *Red Orm,* Scribner (New York City), 1943, translation by Michael Meyer published, along with *Roede Orm, hemma i oesterled,* as *The Long Ships: A Saga of the Viking Age,* Knopf (New York City), 1954.
Roede Orm, hemma i oesterled (title means "Red Orm at Home and on the Eastern Way"), 1945, translation by Meyer published, along with *Roede Orm, sjoefarare i vaesterled,* as *The Long Ships: A Saga of the Viking Age,* Knopf (New York City), 1954.

POETRY

Taerningkast (title means "Throw of the Dice"), 1923.
Legenden om Babel (title means "The Legend of Babel"), 1925.
Dikter, 1950.

ESSAYS

Litteratoerer och militaerer (title means "Literature and Military Men"), 1929.
Silverskoedarna (title means "The Silver Shields"), 1931.

De langhariga merovingerna och andra essayer (title means "The Long-Haired Merovingians"), 1933.
Saellskap foer en eremit, 1938.
A Walk to an Ant Hill, and Other Essays, translated by Michael Roberts and Elspeth Schubert (nee Harley), Norstedt (Stockholm), 1950, also published by American-Scandinavian Foundation (New York City), 1951.
Folk som sjoeng och andra essayer, 1955.

OTHER

Karl den XII:s levnad (biography), 1935-36, translation by Naomi Walford published as *The Life of Charles XII, King of Sweden 1697-1718,* Norstedt, 1960, translation by Walford also published as *The Sword Does Not Jest: The Heroic Life of King Charles XII of Sweden,* St. Martin's Press (New York City), 1960.
Den lustgard som jag minns (memoirs), 1953.
Tankar i groengraeset (essays and lectures), 1953.
Breven till Tristan (letters), 1986.

Also translator into Swedish of the *Chanson de Roland,* John Milton's *Paradise Lost,* and Henry David Thoreau's *Walden.*

SIDELIGHTS: Frans Bengtsson is considered one of the most distinguished figures in twentieth-century Swedish literature. He is known principally for his imaginative and witty treatment of historical subjects in such works as *Karl den XII:s levnad* (*The Sword Does Not Jest: The Heroic Life of King Charles XII of Sweden*) and *Roede Orm* (*The Long Ships: A Saga of the Viking Age*). Adamantly opposed to the spirit of modernity, Bengtsson greatly admired medieval literature as well as the English tradition of contemplative and critical prose exemplified by Edward Gibbon, Charles Lamb, and William Hazlitt. In both his fiction and nonfiction, Bengtsson eschewed detailed renderings of character psychology, concentrating rather on portraying heroic figures and accurately depicting the times in which they lived.

Bengtsson was born and raised in the southern province of Skane, a region traditionally devoted to farming and shipping and imbued with the lore of seafaring that features strongly in *The Long Ships.* While studying at Lund University, Bengtsson completed a doctoral thesis on Geoffrey Chaucer and published two collections of verse, *Taerningkast* and *Legendem om Babel.* These volumes, which include evocations of heroic themes as well as revivals of medieval verse forms, prefigure the concerns of Bengtsson's major works. Bengtsson later published accomplished Swedish translations of the *Chanson de Roland,* John Milton's *Paradise Lost,* and Henry David Thoreau's *Walden.* During his lifetime his work received both scholarly recognition and popular acclaim; his epic biography of Charles XII won the Swedish Academy's annual prize in 1938, and *The Long Ships* became a bestseller. Bengtsson died in 1954. Following his death, Lawrence S. Thompson, surveying Bengtsson's life and works for *Kentucky Foreign Language Quarterly,* remarked: "Frans G. Bengtsson belongs to no school of creative writers or historians. He would have been promptly rusticated from an into which any overzealous critic might have matriculated him. He may not endure through the centuries that have laughed and wept with Villon, but for those of us who can revel in a pure display of genius, a rousing story, and a mastery of prose and poetic style, Bengtsson has a firm position in twentieth century literature."

Bengtsson's studies of historical figures focus on men of action, including Francois Villon, Oliver Cromwell, and Stonewall Jackson. In these works he sought to integrate scholarly precision and artistic gracefulness, qualities that are most evident in *The Sword Does Not Jest.* The quasi-legendary stature of the ascetic monarch Charles XII was considered by critics to be the ideal vehicle for Bengtsson's talents. The energetic and compelling narrative of the biography avoids interpretation of his psychological motivation, while nevertheless providing a rich portrayal of his life. Moreover, Bengtsson's deft and lucid handling of military matters received universal praise, prompting one critic to call the biography the greatest interpretation of military matters since Julius Caesar's *Commentaries.* In an assessment of *The Life of Charles XII, King of Sweden 1697-1718* in the *American-Scandinavian Review,* Gurli Hertzman-Ericson remarked: "What one admires in Frans G. Bengtsson is not merely his erudition, his skill in hammering out the metal of speech in sounding rhythms, and his capacity to assimilate the historical material, but rather his power to paint a vivid and harmonious portrait of an almost legendary figure who has stood closer to the heart of the Swedish people than any other. . . . And yet he does not become in Frans G. Bengtsson's picture a remote or hazy ideal; he stands out as a human being with a sense of humor and of reality and with a rare fidelity not only to ideas but also to his fellow men."

Considered by some critics to be his masterpiece, *The Long Ships* reflects Bengtsson's fascination with medieval civilization. Spanning the tenth and eleventh centuries, this novel traces the life of Orm, a Viking from Skane living in the reign of Harald Bluetooth. Orm's adventures provide an elaborate depiction of Dark Age Europe, featuring Ireland, the Black Sea kingdom of the Bulgars, and the opulent caliphate of Cordoba. Critics have noted that *The Long Ships* is suffused with satire. For example, Orm converts to both Islam and Christianity while maintaining a resolutely pagan outlook. Commenting on *The Long Ships* and *The Sword Does Not Jest* in his *A History of Swedish Literature,* Swedish critic Alrik Gustafson stated: "In both of these works [Bengtsson] shoulders his learning effortlessly, with the skill of a scholar who defies the dust of learning and recaptures those vital realities of life in the past which have too often been written about in heavy, measured, lifeless periods." In a review of the 1943 translation of *Roede Orm, sjoefarare i vaesterled,* which was published as *Red Orm, New York Times Book Review* contributor Hal Borland asserted: "*Red Orm* is a Viking story from the first line, swift-paced, true to its times, excellently done. It is escape fiction only in conveying to perfection the whole flavor of a vanished period and people." *Scandinavian Studies* contributor Walter W. Gustafson expressed similar sentiments, declaring *The Long Ships* "a book that is eminently readable from beginning to end, full of verve and gusto almost in the Chaucerian manner. . . . In general, one can say that it is a thrilling book of Viking tales to be read for sheer pleasure and also for profit as an authentic reconstruction of Viking folkways and manner of life."

BIOGRAPHICAL/CRITICAL SOURCES:

BOOKS

Bengtsson, Frans G., *The Sword Does Not Jest: The Heroic Life of King Charles XII of Sweden,* translated by Naomi Walford, with an introduction by Eric Linklater, St. Martin's Press (New York City), 1960, pp. ix-xiii.

Gustafson, Alrik, *A History of Swedish Literature,* University of Minnesota Press, 1961, pp. 438-540.

PERIODICALS

American-Scandinavian Review, December, 1937, pp. 354-355; spring, 1955, pp. 89-90; spring, 1961, p. 86.

Kentucky Foreign Language Quarterly, vol. II, no. 2, 1955, pp. 75-79.

New Statesman & Nation, March 6, 1954, p. 294.

New York Herald Tribune Book Review, September
    19, 1954, p. 5.
New York Herald Tribune Weekly Books, April 18,
    1943, p. 10.
New York Times Book Review, April 25, 1943, p. 6.
Saturday Review, December 17, 1960, p. 25.
Scandinavian Studies, May, 1955, pp. 115-117.
Times Literary Supplement, August 5, 1960, p. 491.*

*   *   *

BENNETT, Brian (Scott) 1953-

PERSONAL: Born January 3, 1953, in Sacramento,
CA; son of Richard (in real estate) and Marjorie (a
homemaker; maiden name, Miller) Bennett; married
Shelley Zellman, June 20, 1992; children: Skye Richard. *Avocational interests:* Photography, yoga, meditation, filmmaking.

ADDRESSES: Home—Studio City, CA.   *E-mail*—
bri@ix.netcom.com.

CAREER: Composer and writer. Recordings include
the album *Trance,* released in 1998.

MEMBER: National Academy of Television Arts and
Sciences.

WRITINGS:

(With wife, Shelley Zellman) *Autobiography of an
    Angel* (nonfiction), Journey into Light, 1998.

Composer of the score for the television series *The
Bradshaw Experience.*

*   *   *

BENSON, Ann

PERSONAL: Female.

ADDRESSES: Agent—c/o Delacorte Press, 1540 Broadway, NY 10036-4094.

CAREER: Writer.

WRITINGS:

*Beadweaving: New Needle Techniques and Original
    Designs,* Sterling, 1993.
*Ann Benson's Beadwear: Making Beaded Accessories
    and Adornments,* Sterling, 1994.
Beadwork Basics, Sterling, 1994.
*Two-Hour Beaded Projects: More than Two Hundred
    Designs,* Sterling, 1996.
The Plague Tales (thriller), Delacorte (New York
    City), 1997.

SIDELIGHTS: Ann Benson is the author of various
works on beading as well as a medical thriller novel.
Among her beadwork volumes is *Beadweaving: New
Needle Techniques and Original Designs,* which
Sharon Bateman, writing in *Lapidary Journal,* deemed
"wonderfully entertaining" and "a book well worth
having."

Benson made a departure from her previous publications with *The Plague Tales,* a medical thriller that
crosses the fourteenth and twenty-first centuries. The
hero of the historical portion is Alejandro Canches, a
fourteenth-century Spanish physician who has been
dispatched to England to protect King Edward's court
from the plague epidemic that is ravaging Europe.
Canches's arrival will bear tragic consequences. The
central figure of the futuristic storyline is Janie
Crowe, a former surgeon now working as a federal
archaeologist in London. Crowe is still mourning the
loss of her family during one of the gruesome epidem-
ics plaguing the region. Indeed, the illnesses are so
lethal that armed units roam the streets killing anyone
who appears to be suffering from a contagious disease.

Critics had generally favorable views of the novel.
Gene Lyons in *Entertainment Weekly* said it was "surprisingly literate, chockful of curious lore and considerable suspense"; Lesley C. Keogh in *Library Journal*
called the book "a harrowing medical novel that will
give readers both nightmares and thrills"; and a *Publishers Weekly* reviewer said that "Benson's debut is
assured and accomplished in both the past and the
present."

BIOGRAPHICAL/CRITICAL SOURCES:

PERIODICALS

Entertainment Weekly, July 25, 1997, p. 66.
Lapidary Journal, September, 1996, p. 79.
Library Journal, June 1, 1997, p. 144.
Publishers Weekly, May 19, 1997, p. 63*

BIALIK, Chaim Nachman 1873-1934

PERSONAL: First name also transliterated as Hayim and Hayyim; middle name also transliterated as Nahman and Nahhman; surname also transliterated as Byalik; born January 9, 1873, in Radi, Volhynia district, Ukraine, Russia; immigrated to Berlin, Germany, 1921; emigrated to Tel Aviv, Israel, 1924; died following surgery, July 4, 1934, in Vienna, Austria; buried in Tel Aviv, Israel; father, a Talmudic scholar and innkeeper; married, 1893. *Education:* Attended a Talmudic academy, Belorussia, 1890-91; studied Russian and German language in Odessa, 1891-93. *Religion:* Jewish.

CAREER: Writer and lecturer. Worked in the timber trade, 1893-97; teacher of Hebrew in a small town near the Prussian border, 1897-1900, in Odessa, Russia, beginning in 1900; co-editor of *Ha-Shiloach* (a Hebrew-language journal), Odessa, beginning c. 1905; founded a publishing firm, Odessa, c. 1920s.

WRITINGS:

POETRY

Poems from the Hebrew, 1924.
Selected Poems, 1926.
Far over the Sea, 1939.
Complete Poetic Works, 1948.

OTHER

Law and Legend or Halakah and Aggada (essay), 1925.
And It Came to Pass (legends and short stories), 1938.
Aftergrowth and Other Stories (autobiography and short stories), 1939.
Knight of Onions and Knight of Garlic (legend), 1939.
The Hebrew Book (essay), 1951.
Bialik Speaks (conversations), 1970.

SIDELIGHTS: Regarded as the most important Hebrew poet of the twentieth century, Chaim Nachman Bialik contributed greatly to that century' renaissance of Hebrew literature and modernization of the Hebrew language. His verses reflect the personal sufferings of his childhood as well as the sufferings of the Diaspora—the Jewish people in exile from their ancient homeland. Through works such as "The City of Slaughter" and "The Scroll of Fire," he called upon Jews to assert their national independence and to take pride in the traditions of their culture, and these con-

cerns have led to his adoption as "the national poet of Israel." According to critic Israel Efros in his introduction to *Selected Poems of Hayyim Nahman Bialik,* Bialik "stirred Jewish life to its utmost and gave modern Hebrew literature a new and vigorous impulse and a place in contemporary world literature."

Born in a village in the Volhynia district of the Ukraine, Bialik was five years old when his family moved to Zhitomir where his father, a pious Talmudic scholar, supported them by working as an innkeeper. Two years later, Bialik's father died unexpectedly, and Bialik was sent to live with his grandparents in order to ease the financial strain on his widowed mother. He was given rigorous instruction in Jewish law and tradition in his grandfather's orthodox household and, at sixteen, was enrolled in a prestigious Talmudic academy in Belorussia. He excelled equally in religious and secular studies there and, while still a student, composed his popular poem "To the Bird." In 1891 he left the academy and traveled to Odessa, the center of Eastern European Jewish culture. In Odessa Bialik was befriended by several prominent scholars, including Ahad Ha'am, a leading Zionist philosopher whose writings he greatly admired, and J. H. Ravnitzky, who later became Bialik's patron and business partner. Ha'am influenced and encouraged Bialik and effectively launched his literary career by publishing several of his verses in *Ha-Shiloach,* an influential Hebrew-language journal.

When Bialik received news that his grandfather was dying, he returned home. He married in 1893 and worked for his father-in-law in the timber trade for several years before returning to Odessa where his friends had secured a teaching position for him. At about this time, due in part to the patronage of Ha'am, Ravnitzky, and others, Bialik's poetry began to receive international renown. On a visit to Palestine in 1909, for example, he was greeted everywhere as a national spokesman and hero. In Odessa he worked as a co-editor of *Ha-Shiloach* and established a publishing firm which prospered until it was closed by the Bolsheviks. In 1921 he left the Ukraine to join other Hebrew writers in Germany and eventually settled in Palestine in 1924. He died in Vienna after undergoing surgery in 1934.

Rooted in his orthodox religious training, Bialik's early works were largely inspired by Biblical and Talmudic writings. His extensive knowledge of Judaic tradition and literature enabled him to create verses based on ancient forms and themes while thoroughly transforming the academic Hebrew language in which he wrote. Agreeing with many scholars of the era, William A. Drake wrote in his 1928 volume *Contemporary European Writers,* that Bialik had "conclusively proven the supreme flexibility of Biblical Hebrew beneath the hand of an artist." Closely linked to his use of the Hebrew language is his choice of Zionist subjects and themes. Writing for the Diaspora, Bialik exhorted his audience to recognize its duty to defend itself against antisemitism, to resist cultural assimilation, and to reclaim its ancient homeland. In "The City of Slaughter" and other poems written after the 1903 Kishinev pogroms, Bialik denounced the cowardice of acquiescent Jews who had failed to defend themselves or their property. The visionary, though sometimes chastening nature of his nationalist poetry has led some admirers to proclaim him a prophet, while most observers have noted that at the very least he should be credited with rousing and inspiring the Jews of the Diaspora. Many appreciative critics, including Drake, Efros, and Israel Goldstein, have praised Bialik's patriotic verses. Goldstein asserted in his *Toward a Solution* that Jews everywhere are indebted to Bialik "who has given [them] a tongue to speak with, a national song to cherish and a national hope by which to live."

Several observers have suggested that very personal preoccupations lie beneath the nationalistic sentiment of Bialik's verses, and they have linked the sorrow associated with his childhood to the subsequent topics and themes of his poetry. These critics see the premature loss of his father and separation from his mother as an important emotional source of Bialik's poetry. In many of his verses he examined the pain of separation or exile, and in a number of his later works he brooded on death. Bialik's childhood environment offered him an escape from unhappiness, and his love of nature inspired his mature verses as well. Efros called his nature poetry "radiant songs of nature, . . . novel in their joyousness and abandon." Other works are drawn on well-known Hebrew legends, such as "The Scroll of Fire," Bialik's allegorical epic, which is set at the time of the destruction of the first temple of Jerusalem.

Bialik's examination of universal issues and their implications in the lives of individuals has gained him international praise, and he has been enthusiastically proclaimed as the counterpart in Hebrew literature of such authors as Shakespeare and Goethe. His continuing appeal for the Jewish people has been concisely explained by *Encounter* contributor David Aberbach, who suggested that Bialik, "in life-long mourning for his childhood, . . . spoke meaningfully to a people in

perpetual mourning for its lost nationhood." Bialik's unique expression of Jewish culture has led to his stature as the greatest Hebrew poet of this century, a judgment forcefully expressed by Amos Elon in *The Israelis: Founders and Sons.* Elon declared: "None before Bialik nor after has expressed the Jewish will to live in words and rhymes of such beauty and poetic force; he is rightly known today as the national poet of Israel." Menachem Ribalow, a central figure in the Hebrew cultural movement in the United States in the first half of the twentieth century, expressed adoration for Bialik in his *The Flowering of Modern Hebrew Literature: A Volume of Literary Evaluation,* declaring that "Hayyim Nahman Bialik is without question the greatest name in modern Hebrew poetry, one of the greatest in the entire history of Jewish literature. One must go back to the prophets for a parallel to Bialik in the use of the Hebrew idiom. Since the close of the Biblical canon, no writer has ever used the Hebrew language with such perfection."

BIOGRAPHICAL/CRITICAL SOURCES:

BOOKS

Alter, Robert, *The Tradition: Modern Jewish Writing,* Dutton (New York City), 1969, pp. 226-240.

Bialik, Hayyim, *Selected Poems of Hayyim Nahman Bialik,* edited by Israel Efros, revised edition, Bloch Publishing, 1965, pp. xvii-xxxvii.

Burnshaw, Stanley, T. Carmi and Ezra Spicehandler, editors, *The Modern Hebrew Poem Itself,* Holt, Rinehart and Winston (New York City), 1965, pp. 18-34.

Drake, William A., *Contemporary European Writers,* John Day Company, 1928, pp. 279-284.

Caplan, Samuel and Harold U. Ribalow, editors, *The Great Jewish Books: And Their Influence on History,* Horizon Press, 1952, pp. 317-339.

Elon, Amos, *The Israelis: Founders and Sons,* Holt, Rinehart, and Winston (New York City), 1971.

Goldstein, Israel, *Toward a Solution,* G. P. Putnam's Sons, 1940, pp. 197-201.

Halkin, Simon, *Modern Hebrew Literature: Trends and Values,* Schocken Books, 1950, p. 26ff.

Lipsky, Louis, *A Gallery of Zionist Profiles,* Farrar, Straus and Cudahy, 1956, pp. 106-112.

Ribalow, Menachem, *The Flowering of Modern Hebrew Literature: A Volume of Literary Evaluation,* edited and translated by Judah Nadich, Twayne, 1959, pp. 25-57, 58-87.

Spiegel, Shalom, *Hebrew Reborn,* Meridian Books, 1930, pp. 293-312.

Waxman, Meyer, *A History of Jewish Literature: Volume IV, from 1880-1935,* Part One, Thomas Yoseloff, 1941, pp. 199-338.

Yudkin, Leon I., *Escape to Siege: A Survey of Israeli Literature Today,* Routledge & Kegan Paul, 1974, pp. 19-38.

PERIODICALS

Daedalus, summer, 1966, pp. 740-762.
Encounter, June, 1981, pp. 41-48.
Jewish Quarterly Review, April, 1907, pp. 445-466.
Judaism, summer, 1984, pp. 301-308.
Yiddish, fall, 1973, pp. 75-79.*

*   *   *

BIERSTEDT, Robert   1913-1998

OBITUARY NOTICE—See index for *CA* sketch: Born March 20, 1913, in Burlington, IA; died September 8, 1998, in Charlottesville, VA. Educator, sociologist, and author. Bierstedt's interest in sociology and constitutional law shaped his career and directed his focus toward issues such as the relationship between church and state and academic freedom. After completing undergraduate work in philosophy at the University of Iowa, Bierstedt continued graduate studies at the University of Columbia in philosophy and sociology; he obtained a Ph.D. in 1946.

Bierstedt served on the faculties of colleges including City Colleges in New York, New York University, and the University of Virginia. Bierstedt also served as the director of the American Civil Liberties Union (ACLU) during the 1960s and 1970s. Bierstedt authored several sociological works, including *The Social Order* (1957), *Power and Progress: Essays on Sociological Theory* (1974), and *American Sociological Theory* (1981).

OBITUARIES AND OTHER SOURCES:

BOOKS

Who's Who in America, Marquis Who's Who, 1999.

PERIODICALS

New York Times, September 17, 1998, p. B15.

BING, Stanley
See SCHWARTZ, Gil

*   *   *

BIRKLAND, Thomas A.   1961-

PERSONAL: Born September 19, 1961, in Seattle, WA; son of James R. (an engineer) and Kathleen S. (a teacher and electrical designer) Birkland. *Ethnicity:* "Caucasian (Norwegian, Swedish, etc.)." *Education:* University of Oregon, B.A. (cum laude), 1984; Rutgers University, M.A., 1985; University of Washington, Seattle, Ph.D., 1995.

ADDRESSES: Home—Albany, NY. *Office*—217 Milne Hall, Nelson A. Rockefeller College of Public Affairs and Policy, State University of New York at Albany, 135 Western Ave., Albany, NY 12222; fax 518-442-5298. *E-mail*—birkland@csc.albany.edu; http://www.albany.edu/~birkland.

CAREER: New Jersey Department of Transportation, Trenton, research analyst in Office of Policy Analysis, 1985-87; Office of the Governor, Trenton, aide in Independent Authorities Unit, 1987-88; New Jersey Department of Transportation, assistant manager of strategic planning, 1988-90; State University of New York at Albany, assistant professor of public affairs and political science and adjunct assistant professor of biological sciences, all 1995—, codirector of Biodiversity, Environment, and Conservation Program, 1995—, director of Public Policy Program, 1997-99. University of Washington, Seattle, worked as instructor.

MEMBER: American Political Science Association, Association for Public Policy Analysis and Management, Academy of Management, Earthquake Engineering Research Institute, Western Political Science Association, Midwest Political Science Association.

AWARDS, HONORS: Fellow of Earthquake Engineering Research Institute and Federal Emergency Management Agency, 1993-94; grants from New York State Office of Mental Retardation and Developmental Disabilities, 1998-99, New York State Office for the Aging, 1998-2000, and National Science Foundation, 1998-2000.

WRITINGS:

After Disaster: Agenda Setting, Public Policy, and Focusing Events, Georgetown University Press (Washington, DC), 1997.

Contributor of articles and reviews to periodicals, including *Judge's Journal, Environment, Policy Studies Journal, International Journal of Mass Emergencies and Disasters, Environmental Management, Journal of Public Policy,* and *Coastal Management.*

WORK IN PROGRESS: The Public Policy Toolkit: A Guide to Key Concepts and Terms, with Scott Barclay, for M. E. Sharpe (Armonk, NY).

SIDELIGHTS: Thomas A. Birkland told *CA:* "My writing is most often oriented toward academic audiences, so my primary motivation for writing is professional responsibility. To view academic writing as simply 'a job,' however, is to deny the artistic and expressive nature of writing. A charge leveled against academic writing is that the author's voice must not appear, or at best should be subordinate to the rather patterned recitation of research results. I disagree: the challenge in academic writing is to find the appropriate voice for the material being presented, while not writing mechanically. This voice is important, and I think it helps to engage the reader to a greater extent than would a dry recitation of facts. The actual voice should stay consistent even while the content and audience change. My work in *Environment* magazine is quite different from something that I would submit to the *Journal of Public Policy. After Disaster* is a rather different book than *The Public Policy Toolkit,* but while the form is different, I think my voice is consistent.

"The voice I seek is that of a patient teacher and an enthusiast. I want to both teach and motivate readers to understand and to be more interested and more involved in the policy making process. These desires to teach and to communicate motivate me to write on the policy process and the environment. Every article or book I write is an expression of the deep interest I have in the subject matter. I have chosen the environment as the focus of my research and writing because of my love of nature, my experiences in some of the most beautiful places on earth, and my belief that we can and should leave the earth to future generations in a condition that promotes human progress and the physical integrity of the earth.

"My academic career has been influenced by a number of academics, including my doctoral adviser, Peter May, John Kingdon, E. E. Schattschneider, Deborah Stone, Frank Baumgartner, and Bryan Jones. While I tend to write for a specialist audience, I would like to think of myself as a *writer* as well as an academic. I would like to write as clearly and directly as Ernest Hemingway. I seek to achieve the descriptive powers and passion for the natural world exemplified by John Muir and John Steinbeck. Overall I would hope my work carries on the legacy of Rachel Carson, whose *Silent Spring* awakened us all to the threat of unthinking exploitation of the earth. Her book and her writing are clear and stark, yet she also offers a message of hope: we can get out of the mess we've made. I hope my work somehow helps achieve this goal."

*   *   *

BLECHMAN, Elaine A(nn) 1943-

PERSONAL: Born September 15, 1943, in Boston, MA; married Joshua Friedman, May, 1997; children: Reva Blechman. *Ethnicity:* "Jewish." *Education:* University of California, Los Angeles, B.A. (with honors), 1966, M.A., 1968, Ph.D., 1971.

ADDRESSES: Home—220 Green Rock Dr., Boulder, CO 80302. *Office*—Department of Psychology, Campus Box 345, Muenzinger Psychology Bldg., University of Colorado at Boulder, Boulder, CO 80309-0345. *E-mail*—eblechman@cu.campuscw.net.

CAREER: Brentwood Veterans Administration Hospital, Brentwood, CA, intern in clinical psychology, 1969-71; University of Maryland at College Park, assistant professor of psychology, 1971-73; Yale University, New Haven, CT, assistant professor of psychiatry, 1973-77; Wesleyan University, Middletown, CT, research associate professor, 1977-83, research professor, 1983-84; Yeshiva University, Albert Einstein College of Medicine, Bronx, NY, professor of psychiatry, 1984-89; New York City Department of Health, New York City, senior research scientist, 1990; University of Colorado at Boulder, professor of psychology, 1990—. State University of New York Health Sciences Center, Brooklyn, professor, 1990. National Institute of Mental Health, member of Family Research Consortium, 1982-90; State of Colorado, member of Maternal Substance Abuse Commission, 1990—; Office of the Boulder County District Attorney, consultant, 1995—.

MEMBER: American Psychological Association (fellow; divisional president, 1982; member of board of scientific advisers and board of scientific affairs, both 1989-92), American Psychological Society (founding member), Association for Clinical Psychosocial Research (fellow), Association for the Advancement of Behavior Therapy, Life History Society, Society for Behavioral Medicine, Society for Clinical and Preventive Psychology (founding member), Society for Prevention Research, Society for Psychotherapy Research, Society for Research on Adolescence, Society for Research on Child and Adolescent Psychopathology, Society for Research on Psychopathology.

AWARDS, HONORS: Award for research on women, American Psychological Association, 1986; citation for outstanding textbook, American Library Association, 1989, for *Handbook of Behavioral Medicine for Women;* grants from National Institute of Mental Health, Sigma Xi, State of Connecticut, National Institutes of Health, and National Institute of Drug Abuse.

WRITINGS:

(Contributor) A. Brodsky and R. Hare-Mustin, editors, *Women and Psychotherapy,* Guilford (New York City), 1980.

(Editor and contributor) *Behavior Modification with Women,* Guilford, 1984.

(Contributor) R. F. Dangel and R. A. Polster, editors, *Behavioral Parent Training: Issues in Research and Practice,* Guilford, 1984.

Solving Child Behavior Problems: At Home and at School, Research Press (Champaign, IL), 1985.

(Contributor) C. E. Schaefer and S. Reid, editors, *Game Play: Therapeutic Uses of Childhood Games,* Wiley (New York City), 1986.

(Editor with K. D. Brownell, and contributor) *Handbook of Behavioral Medicine for Women,* Pergamon (New York City), 1988.

(Contributor) Schaefer, editor, *Handbook of Parent Training: Parents as Co-therapists for Children's Behavior Problems,* Wiley, 1989.

(Editor and contributor) *Emotions and the Family: For Better or for Worse,* Lawrence Erlbaum (Hillsdale, NJ), 1990.

(Contributor) R. D. Peters, R. J. McMahon, and V. L. Quinsey, editors, *Aggression and Violence throughout the Lifespan,* Sage Publications (Newbury Park, CA), 1992.

(Editor, with E. M. Hetherington, and contributor) *Stress, Coping, and Resiliency in Children and Families,* Lawrence Erlbaum, 1996.

(Editor with Brownell, and contributor) *Behavioral Medicine for Women: A Comprehensive Handbook,* Guilford, 1998.

(Contributor) Schaefer, editor, *Handbook of Parent Training,* Wiley, 1998.

Prosocial Family Therapy for Juvenile Offenders: A Practitioner's Guidebook, Lawrence Erlbaum, in press.

Author of the book *Schools and Families Together: Cost-Effective Interventions for High-Risk Youth,* in press. Contributor of more than fifty articles to professional journals, including *Aggressive Behavior, Applied and Preventive Psychology, Addictive Behaviors, Journal of Abnormal Child Psychology, Behavior Therapist,* and *Family Psychologist.* Member of editorial board, *Child and Family Behavior Therapy* and *Advances in Clinical Child Psychology;* past member of editorial board, *Behavioral Counseling Quarterly, Cognitive Therapy and Research, Family Studies Review Yearbook, Journal of Applied Behavior Analysis,* and *Journal of Clinical Psychology.*

*   *   *

BLEDSOE, Glen L(eonard) 1951-

PERSONAL: Born April 10, 1951, in Gary, IN; son of John William (a steel worker) and Loretta Radcliffe (a child-care provider; maiden name, Dix) Bledsoe; married Karen Elizabeth Lytle (a teacher and writer), June 28, 1992; children: Gabriel Scott, James Wesley Solonika (stepson). *Ethnicity:* "British." *Education:* Indiana University—Bloomington, B.A., 1983; attended School of the Art Institute of Chicago, 1980; Willamette University, M.A.T., 1991. *Avocational interests:* Guitar, shin-shin toitsu aikido.

ADDRESSES: Home—Salem, OR. *E-mail*—GlnBledsoe@aol.com; http://members.aol.com/SublimeArt/Studios.

CAREER: U.S. Steel Co., chemical technician, 1972-78; Rubino's Music Center, Portage, IN, luthier and seller of musical instruments, 1976-80; Keizer Elementary School, Keizer, OR, teacher, 1991—, team leader, 1995—, web page designer and webmaster of http://keizer.salkeiz.k12.or.us, 1995—. Lansing Art Gallery, Lansing, MI, interim director, 1981; also works as artist-in-residence. Willamette University, cochairperson of Education Consortium, 1996—.

MEMBER: Society of Children's Book Writers and Illustrators.

WRITINGS:

JUVENILES; WITH WIFE, KAREN BLEDSOE

Classic Ghost Stories II, Lowell House (Los Angeles, CA), 1998.
Classic Sea Stories, Lowell House, 1999.
Creepy Classics III, Lowell House, 1999.
Classic Mysteries II, Lowell House, in press.
Classic Adventure Stories, Lowell House, in press.

OTHER

Contributor of articles to the periodicals *HyperCard* and *Computing Teacher;* contributor of art to *Oregon Focus.* Contributor of illustrations to the compact disc accompanying *Real World Bryce II* by Susan Kitchens.

SIDELIGHTS: Glen L. Bledsoe told *CA:* "My wife and I have our separate writing projects, but when we work together we have a unique approach. I usually write the first few chapters to a novel, then, using a y-cord, we both plug into my Macintosh computer. From there we take turns as inspiration moves us. We leap-frog through entire chapters very quickly that way. Later we swap chapters for editing and rewriting. The result is a flowing, seamless product. We have completed five novels, as yet unpublished, and have as many more to finish."

*   *   *

BLEDSOE, Karen E(lizabeth) 1962-

PERSONAL: Born April 15, 1962, in Salem, OR; daughter of Don James (an accountant and Christmas tree farmer) and Harriet Elizabeth (a medical technologist and Christmas tree farmer; maiden name, Hiday) Lytle; married Glen Leonard Bledsoe (a teacher and writer), June 28, 1992; children: Gabriel Scott (stepson), James Wesley Solonika. *Ethnicity:* "Scots/Bohemian/English." *Education:* Willamette University, B.S., 1985, M.A.T., 1991; Oregon State University, M.S., 1988. *Avocational interests:* Gardening, shin-shin toitsu aikido.

ADDRESSES: Home—Salem, OR. *Office*—Division of Natural Science and Mathematics, Western Oregon University, Monmouth, OR 97361. *E-mail*—Kestrel B@aol.com; http://members/aol/com/SublimeArt/Studios.

CAREER: Temporary and substitute teacher at public schools in Salem, OR, 1991-95; Western Oregon University, Monmouth, instructor in biology, 1995—. Oregon Academy of Science, science education cochairperson and web page designer, 1996—; Oregon Collaborative for Excellence in the Preparation of Teachers, faculty fellow, 1997—; Oregon Public Education Network, team coach for Master WEBster web page design contest, 1998-99. U.S. Forest Service, seasonal biological technician, 1985; City of Salem, seasonal recreational leader and environmental educator, 1989-94.

MEMBER: Society of Children's Book Writers and Illustrators, National Biology Teachers Association, Oregon Science Teachers Association, Phi Delta Kappa.

WRITINGS:

JUVENILES; WITH HUSBAND, GLEN L. BLEDSOE

Classic Ghost Stories II, Lowell House (Los Angeles, CA), 1998.
Classic Sea Stories, Lowell House, 1999.
Creepy Classics III, Lowell House, 1999.
Classic Mysteries II, Lowell House, in press.
Classic Adventure Stories, Lowell House, in press.

OTHER JUVENILES

(With Candyce Norvall) *365 Nature Crafts,* Publications International, 1997.
Best Friends, Publications International, 1997.
School Memories Album, Publications International, 1998.
Millennium Album, Publications International, 1998.

SIDELIGHTS: Karen E. Bledsoe told *CA:* "Writing and teaching are natural careers for me. I've always liked telling what I know to a captive audience.

"Words have been my toys since I first taught myself to read at the age of three. I spent many hours manufacturing little books, hand-illustrated and bound with a stapler. Inventions were a favorite theme, followed closely by mysteries, code books, and adventure stories. When I wasn't writing, I was gobbling up books as fast as I could get my hands on them. Books were my best friends during my school years when we moved every year—sometimes twice a year. I was a wallflower and had difficulty making friends.

"In junior high and high school, when the family was more settled and I finally had friends again, I turned to more challenging themes in both my reading and writing: high fantasy, supernatural adventure, lengthy sagas. I churned out the usual dreary, self-pitying poetry characteristic of angst-ridden teen writers, wrote for the school yearbook, and got a fair start on a lengthy fantasy novel that I may yet finish. My best subjects were English and science, and I chose the life sciences as my college path.

"College and a disastrous marriage occupied the next eight years of my life. Though I had little energy to spare for it, I still dabbled at writing. With a sister-in-law, I completed my first novel, a cliche-ridden romantic spoof that will never see the light of print (nor was it meant to) but which taught me much about what it takes to finish a book. Earning my bachelor's degree and a master of arts in botany during this period taught me plenty about perseverance in adverse circumstances.

"Finding that teaching was more to my liking than scientific research, I enrolled in the master of arts in teaching program at Willamette University, where I earned my teaching certificate and met my current husband. The two events marked a new era in my life. In the mutually supportive environment we've nurtured in our home, we have both blossomed creatively. We always have projects going: novels in progress, web pages going up, art work, music, gardening, while the television slowly gathers dust. When we write, it is often literally together, with two keyboards plugged in series into the back of a Macintosh. Our publishing successes have been modest so far, but we intend to persevere until we can retire from teaching and earn our living as writers."

*   *   *

BLOSSFELD, Hans-Peter 1954-

PERSONAL: Born July 30, 1954, in Munich, Germany; son of Otto and Camilla (Bloechl) Blossfeld; married Erika Gutsmuethl, December 22, 1980; children: Gwendolin Josephine, Pia Nicoletta. *Education:* Free University of Berlin, Habilitation, 1987; University of Mannheim, Ph.D., 1984; University of Regensburg, M.S., 1980.

ADDRESSES: Home—Getkensweg 7, 28879 Grasberg, Germany. *Office*—Lehrstuhl fuer Allgemeine Soziologie, Fakultaet fuer Soziologie, Universitaet Bielefeld, Postfach 100131, 33501 Bielefeld, Germany; fax 49-521-106-6443. *E-mail*—hpb@post.uni-bielefeld.de.

CAREER: University of Mannheim, Mannheim, Germany, research scientist for a comparative analysis of social structure with mass data, 1980-84; Max Planck Institute for Human Development and Education, Berlin, Germany, senior research scientist, 1984-89; European University Institute, Florence, Italy, professor of political and social sciences, 1989-92, external professor, 1992-95; University of Bremen, Bremen, Germany, professor of sociology and social statistics, 1992-98. Performed civil service, 1974-75.

WRITINGS:

Bildungsexpansion und Berufschancen: Empirische Analysen zur Lage der Berufsanfaenger in der Bundesrepublik, Campus (New York City), 1985.

(With A. Hamerle and K. U. Mayer) *Ereignisanalyse: Statistische Theorie und Anwendung in den Wirtschafts-und Sozialwissenschaften,* Campus, 1986.

(Contributor) D. L. Parkes, B. Sellin, and M. Tessaring, editors, *Education/Training and Labor Market Policy,* Volume I, s'Gravenhage, 1986.

(Contributor) Wolfgang Teckenberg, editor, *Comparative Studies of Social Structure: Recent Research on France, the United States, and the Federal Republic of Germany,* M. E. Sharpe (Armonk, NY), 1987.

Kohortendifferenzierung und Karriereprozess: Eine Laengsschnittstudie ueber die Veraenderung der Bildungs-und Berufschancen im Lebenslauf, Campus, 1989.

(With Hamerle and Mayer) *Event History Analysis,* Lawrence Erlbaum (Hillsdale, NJ), 1989.

(Contributor) David Magnusson, Lars Bergmann, and other editors, *Problems and Methods in Longitudinal Research: Stability and Change,* Cambridge University Press (Cambridge, England), 1991.

(Editor with Yossi Shavit, and contributor) *Persistent Inequality: Changing Educational Attainment in Thirteen Countries,* Westview Press (Boulder, CO), 1993.

(Contributor) G. Esping-Andersen, editor, *Changing Classes: Stratification and Mobility in Post-Industrial Societies,* Sage (London), 1993.

(Editor and contributor) *The New Role of Women: Family Formation in Modern Societies,* Westview Press, 1995.

(With Goetz Rohwer) *Techniques of Event History Modeling: New Approaches to Causal Analysis,* Lawrence Erlbaum, 1995.

(Contributor) Karen O. Mason and An-Magritt Jensen, editors, *Gender and Family Change in Industrialized Countries,* Clarendon Press (Oxford, England), 1995.

(Contributor) Robert Erikson and Jan O. Jonsson, editors, *Can Education Be Equalized? The Swedish Case in Comparative Perspective,* Westview Press, 1996.

(Editor with Catherine Hakim, and contributor) *Between Equalization and Marginalization: Women's Part-Time Work in Europe and the United States of America,* Oxford University Press (Oxford, England), 1997.

(Editor with Gerald Prein, and contributor) *Rational Choice Theory and Large-Scale Data Analysis,* Westview, 1997.

(With Reinhard Stockmann) *Globalization and Changes in Vocational Training Systems in Developing and Advanced Industrialized Societies,* M. E. Sharpe, 1999.

Contributor of more than sixty articles and reviews to scholarly journals, including *American Journal of Sociology, Quality and Quantity, Sociological Methods and Research, Sociology of Education, Journal of Marriage and the Family,* and *International Journal of Sociology.* Editor, *European Sociological Review.*

WORK IN PROGRESS: Research on household dynamics and social inequality.

*   *   *

BLUM, Lenore (Carol) 1943-

PERSONAL: Born December 18, 1942, in New York, NY; married Manuel Blum (a mathematician), 1961; children: a son. *Education:* Attended Carnegie Tech (Pittsburgh); Simmons College, B.S., 1963; Massachusetts Institute of Technology, Ph.D. (mathematics), 1968; University of California at Berkeley, postdoctoral student.

ADDRESSES: Home—700 Euclid Ave., Berkeley, CA 94708-1334.

CAREER: Air Force Office of Science and Research, fellow, 1968-69; University of California, Berkeley, lecturer in mathematics, 1969-71, adjunct professor of computer science, beginning in 1989, Mathematical Sciences Research Institute, deputy director, c. 1990—; Mills College, research associate in mathematics, 1971-77, mathematics and computer science department, founder, 1973, chair, 1973-86, associate professor of mathematics, 1977—, Letts-Villard chair of mathematics and computer science, 1978—, Letts-Villard professor, 1978—; International Computer Science Institute, Theory Group, research scientist, 1988—. Math/Science Network, Expanding Your Horizons Conferences, founder, co-director, 1975-81; member of Mathematics Panel, Project 2061.

MEMBER: American Association for the Advancement of Science, American Mathematical Society (vice president, 1990-92), Association for Women in Mathematics (president, 1975-77), Association of Women in Science, Sigma Xi.

WRITINGS:

(With Stephen Smale and Mike Shub) *Complexity and Real Computation,* Springer (New York City), 1997.

Author of books and films for the Math/Science Network, including *Count Me In, The Math/Science Connection,* and *Four Women in Science;* served as editor of *International Journal of Algebra and Computation,* 1989-91; contributor of essays to journals, including *Information and Control* and *The Mathematical Intelligencer.*

SIDELIGHTS: Lenore Blum has played an integral role in increasing the participation of girls and women in mathematics. She was one of the founders of the Association for Women in Mathematics (AWM), acting as its president from 1975 to 1978. The AWM has membership totaling over 1,500 women and men. In addition to local, national and international meetings, the AWM sponsors the Emmy Noether Lecture series and has organized symposiums. The organization provides a list of women who are available to speak at high schools and colleges and also contributes to the *Dictionary of Women in the Mathematical Sciences.*

Blum was born in 1943 and as a child enjoyed math, art, and music. Finishing high school at sixteen, Blum applied to the Massachusetts Institute of Technology (MIT), but was denied admission repeatedly. After being turned down by MIT, Blum attended Carnegie Tech in Pittsburgh, Pennsylvania. She began studying architecture, then changed her major to mathematics. For her third year, Blum enrolled at Simmons, a

Boston-area college for women. However, Blum found that she did not have to put forth much effort in the math classes. She then cross-registered at MIT, graduated from Simmons, and received her Ph.D. in mathematics from MIT in 1968. Blum continued her education as a postdoctoral student and lecturer at the University of California at Berkeley.

According to a biography written by Lisa Hayes for the web site *Biographies of Women Mathematicians*, "Blum's research, from her early work in model theory, led to the formulation of her own theorems dealing with the patterns she found in trying to use new methods of logic to solve old problems in algebra." The work she did on this project became her doctoral thesis, which earned her a fellowship. Blum has also had the honor of reporting on work she did with Stephen Smale and Mike Shub in developing a theory of computation and complexity over real numbers.

Blum has written mathematical books with her husband, Manuel Blum, who is also a mathematician. They collaborated on a paper that proposed designing computers that had the ability to learn from example, much in the way young children learn. Blum has studied this project to discover why some computers learn the methods they do. Blum has been involved in other fields of research, in addition to working with her husband, which includes work in developing a new (homotopy) algorithm for linear programming.

When Blum was hired to teach algebra at Mills College, she was not happy with the program and sought a way to make the classes more interesting to the students and to the instructors. In 1973 she founded the Mills College Mathematics and Computer Science Department. Blum served as chair or co-chair of the department for thirteen years. While at Mills, Blum received the Letts-Villard Research professorship. Since 1988 she has been a research scientist in the Theory Group of the International Computer Science Institute (ICSI). In 1989 Blum was employed as an adjunct professor of Computer Science at Berkeley. During the 1980s Blum became a research mathematician full-time, giving numerous talks at international conferences.

To further girls and women's participation in mathematics, Blum founded the Math/Science Network and its Expanding Your Horizons conferences. The Network began as an after-school problem-solving program. The aim of the program is to get high school girls interested in math and logic. The confer- ence now travels nationwide. Blum served as its co-director from 1975 to 1981. Blum has written books and produced films, including *Count Me In, The Math/Science Connection,* and *Four Women in Science.*

In addition to her work with the Math/Science Network, Blum is involved in the Mills College Summer Mathematics Institute for Undergraduate Women (SMI). The SMI is a six-week intensive mathematics program. Twenty-four undergraduate women are selected from across the nation to participate. According to the Mills College SMI internet page, the program aims "to increase the number of bright undergraduate women mathematics majors that continue on into graduate programs in the mathematical sciences and obtain advanced degrees."

Blum is an active member of several mathematical societies. She is a fellow of the American Association for the Advancement of Science and the American Mathematical Society (AMS), where she served as vice president from 1990 to 1992. Blum represented the AMS at the Pan African Congress of Mathematics held in Nairobi, Kenya, in the summer of 1991. At that time she became dedicated to creating an electronic communication link between U.S. and African mathematics communities. Blum also served as a member of the Mathematics Panel of Project 2061. The project was to determine how much a typical adult must know about science and technology to be prepared for the return of Halley's Comet. In addition, Blum served as the first woman editor of the *International Journal of Algebra and Computation* from 1989 to 1991.

Blum is the deputy director at the Mathematical Sciences Research Institute (MSRI) at U.C. Berkeley. She has participated in MSRI's Fermat Fest and has been an organizer of MSRI's "Conversations" between mathematics researchers and mathematics teachers.

BIOGRAPHICAL/CRITICAL SOURCES:

BOOKS

Perl, Teri, *Women and Numbers: Lives of Women Mathematicians,* Wide World Publishing, 1993.

OTHER

Biographies of Women Mathematicians, http://www.scotlan.edu/lriddle/women/blum.html (December, 1998).

Database Systems & Logic Programming, http:// sunsite.ust.hk/dblp/db/indices/a-tree/b/Blum:Le nore.html (December, 1998).

Lenore Blum's Home Page, http://www.msri.org/ staff/bio/lblum.html (December, 1998).

Mills College Summer Mathematics Institute for Undergraduate Women [SIM web site], http://aug3. augsburg.edu/pkal/resources/ptw/mills.html (December, 1998).*

* * *

BOGACKI, Tomek

PERSONAL: Male.

ADDRESSES: Agent—c/o Farrar, Straus & Giroux Inc., 19 Union Square W., New York, NY 10003.

CAREER: Writer and illustrator of children's books.

WRITINGS:

FOR CHILDREN; AND ILLUSTRATOR

Cat and Mouse, Farrar, Straus (New York City), 1996.
Cat and Mouse in the Rain, Farrar, Straus (New York City), 1997.
I Hate You! I Like You!, Farrar, Straus (New York City), 1997.
Cat and Mouse in the Night, Farrar, Straus (New York City), 1998.
The Story of a Blue Bird, Farrar, Straus (New York City), 1998.

ILLUSTRATOR

Walter Kreye, *The Giant from the Little Island,* North-South, 1990.
Andrew Matthews, *Crackling Brat,* Holt (New York City), 1993.

SIDELIGHTS: A writer and illustrator of picture books for young children, Tomek Bogacki has earned a fair amount of critical praise for several of his works. His books, primarily directed at the preschool/kindergarten age group, often focus on differences that exist between the main characters, and how they can be overcome. For example, in *Cat and Mouse,* published in 1996, Bogacki features a young mouse and a young cat who, despite warnings from their mothers, put aside their traditional adversarial relationship to become fast friends. The lesson that Bogacki attempts to get across to children is that they can overcome inner fears to tolerate those unlike themselves, and in the process learn more about the world around them.

Bogacki broke into the picture-book genre solely as an illustrator. In 1990 he collaborated with author Walter Kreye to produce *The Giant from the Little Island,* a traditional German fairy tale about a giant whose island home is flooded, forcing him to seek a life elsewhere. In the process, the giant encounters a throng of individuals who attempt to take advantage of him because of his immense strength and size. Just as the giant is ready to proclaim the world a cruel one, he meets a little boy who has a dream of "flying to the stars." The giant decides to help him achieve this noble cause. Reviewers thought Bogacki's bright illustrations added a visual dimension to the warm tale. Ruth Smith, who reviewed the book for *School Library Journal,* commented that Bogacki's "Impressionistic watercolor paintings give a dreamlike quality" to the German fable.

In 1993 Bogacki provided illustrations for another work titled *Crackling Brat,* a book of fairy tales written by author Andrew Matthews. As in *The Giant from the Little Island,* the pictures are impressionistic, in an attempt to appeal to a younger audience. Suzanne Hawley of *School Library Journal* said Bogacki's illustrations made Matthews' characters appear "outlandish." Bogacki's experience on these two books led him to take greater control of his projects. From this point forward, he would not only be the illustrator, but also take on the writing duties in his books.

In 1996 *Cat and Mouse*—the first of a series that also includes *Cat and Mouse in the Night* and *Cat and Mouse in the Rain*—was published. The story follows the unlikely friendship between the two main characters. As the story begins, both young characters are warned by their mothers that they should stay away from each other because they are enemies. When the two encounter each other in a big field, neither is sure who the other is, because the cat has never seen a mouse and the mouse has never seen a cat. When, to both of their surprise, they figure out each others' identity, each attempts to ward off and scare the other. Ironically, the cat and mouse realize they don't have anything against one another and end up playing together for the rest of the day. When they finish playing, each of them returns home to tell their curious siblings of the experience. "How could you have fun with a cat?" one of the mice asks the little mouse. The cat fields similar questions about the mouse. In the end, all the cats and mice become playmates. Bogacki's illustrations are of a tempera style in which the animals are portrayed in a simplistic, out-of-proportion style.

Pam Gosner, reviewing *Cat and Mouse* for *School Library Journal,* called the story a "simple parable," noting that it "has charm." Gosner also applauded the story's theme of friendship between "those who look different." While a contributor for *Kirkus Reviews* believed the book was "hauntingly illustrated," the same contributor had a problem with the story's disregard of the natural predator/prey relationship between cats and mice. Using words such as "eloquent," a contributor for *Publishers Weekly* called *Cat and Mouse* a "simple, appealing book," and dubbed Bogacki's artwork "both wistful and solid."

In 1997 Bogacki released *Cat and Mouse in the Rain,* which reunites the "curious little mouse" and the "curious little cat" for a drizzly day romp. The friends again neglect to heed the advice of their mothers to stay out of the wet weather. This time their playful session includes a little frog who teaches them how to make the most of such a rainy day. Heide Piehler of *School Library Journal* lauded the book, especially its "simple straightforward text and colorful double-page tempera paintings." A year later, Bogacki published a installment in his series, titled *Cat and Mouse in the Night.*

Also in 1997 Bogacki published *I Hate You! I Like You!,* a picture book that again explores the subject of differences. The book contains two odd-looking characters, one big and the other small. In the course of the first half of the book, the smaller character declares to the other, "I hate you!," and then precedes to chide his companion about the look of his tail, eyes, fur, teeth and even his shape. The larger character, taken aback by the storm of criticism, is about to dart off, until the smaller creature has a change of opinion. "I like you!," he proclaims to the larger character. The two end up becoming friends. The layout that Bogacki uses throughout the book takes into account his pre-school audience: Each illustrated page contains only one line of text, while the pictures, with a predominance of blue, green, orange and yellow, are simple and coarse, in an appeal to younger, untrained eyes. Also, as the little character berates the other, Bogacki's illustrations actually show how the two character's attributes benefit one another. Martha Topol, review-

ing *I Hate You! I Like You!* for *School Library Journal,* called it "a powerful in-your-face statement" which she believed will "either turn off readers entirely or will excite them with its emotional truth."

The busy Bogacki published *The Story of a Blue Bird* in 1998, a picture book about the first flying experience of a little blue bird. As the story begins, the blue bird's mother tries to coax him into leaving the nest and taking flight. But, like anyone attempting something for the first time, the baby bird is frightened and refuses to go. Still, the young bird is terribly curious about what it is like to fly, so he badgers his mother with a flurry of questions about what is beyond their nest. The mother grows tired of these questions and, in an attempt to make her young one hush and go to sleep, she tells him that "nothing" is outside of the nest and beyond the trees. The little bird begins to ponder the meaning of "nothing" and one night decides to leave the nest on foot and find out exactly what nothing is. On his quest, he meets a green bird. "What are you looking for?" the green bird asks him. When the young blue bird says "nothing," the green bird tells him to follow him. The green bird takes wing and begins to fly. The blue bird, so curious about finding out what "nothing" is, forgets his fear of flying and follows the other bird. "And they flew high, and they flew low. They flew here, and they flew there," Bogacki writes of their flight. The book is another example of Bogacki's exploration of how to overcome inner fears of the unknown.

In *The Story of a Blue Bird,* Bogacki's illustrations reflect how the little blue bird sees the world, before and after his first big flight, with the colors changing accordingly. Many critics adored the book, but some were confused as to why the author/illustrator failed to resolve the question of what "nothing" means. A contributor for *Publishers Weekly* called *The Story of a Blue Bird* "visually voluptuous" and "sensually alluring." The same contributor also believed that some readers would get hung up on the question of "nothing." Comparing *The Story of a Blue Bird* to Bogacki's previous books, a *Kirkus Reviews* reviewer concluded that "this one is neat, tidy, and charmingly—but utterly—elusive."

BIOGRAPHICAL/CRITICAL SOURCES:

PERIODICALS

School Library Journal, February, 1991, p. 71; June, 1994, p. 111; September, 1996, p. 171; March, 1997, p. 148; August, 1997, p. 128.

Kirkus Reviews, June 15, 1996, p. 895; January 1, 1998, pp. 53-54.

Publishers Weekly, July 8, 1996, p. 83; January 5, 1998, p. 66.*

*   *   *

BONANNO, Joseph 1905-

PERSONAL: January 18, 1905, in Sicily, Italy; immigrated to U.S., 1924; married Fay, c. 1920s; children: Salvatore, Catherine, Joseph.

ADDRESSES: Home—Tucson, AZ. *Agent*—c/o Simon & Schuster, Simon & Schuster Building, 1230 Avenue of the Americas, New York, NY 10020.

CAREER: Mafioso, c. 1910-68, head of Bonanno crime family, 1931-68; member of Mafia Commission, 1933-68. Legal businesses included a funeral home, laundromat, and cheese company.

WRITINGS:

(With Sergio Lalli) *A Man of Honor: The Autobiography of Joseph Bonanno,* Simon & Schuster (New York City), 1983.

ADAPTATIONS: The made-for television film *Love, Honor & Obey: The Last Mafia Marriage,* 1993, portrays the marital relationship of Bonanno's son Salvatore ("Bill") Bonanno; Bonanno himself is played by Ben Gazzara.

SIDELIGHTS: When Joseph Bonanno, former boss of the Mafia family that bears his name, published his memoirs in 1983, a number of interested readers sought out the book. *A Man of Honor: The Autobiography of Joseph Bonanno* promised to offer inside knowledge on the workings of the Mafia, though in fact—according to several reviewers—it consists of little more than an attempt to portray its author in the best possible light. But one reader saw something of particular interest in *A Man of Honor.* A future Mayor of New York City, Rudolph Giuliani was a federal prosecutor in the mid-1980s, and in *A Man of Honor* he discovered information he had been seeking. "Reading that book," Ed Magnuson of *Time* reported, ". . . helped Giuliani realize that the little understood 1970 RICO [Racketeer Influenced and Corrupt Organizations] Act could be used against the

Mob." Referring to the Mafia's "board of directors," comprised of the heads of the five "families" controlling New York's underworld, Giuliani told *Time,* "Bonanno has an entire section devoted to the Commission. . . . It seemed to me that if he could write about it, we could prosecute it."

Bonanno's own words would help lead to a short sentence for the author, by then already in his eighties. On September 6, 1985, he went to jail in Tucson, Arizona—his adopted home after he "retired" from the Mob in 1968—on contempt charges arising from his refusal to answer Giuliani's questions regarding revelations in his book. According to Arnold H. Lubasch in the *New York Times,* Bonanno evaded Giuliani's questions by pleading poor health. Thus when Giuliani said, "In 1933, did you become a member of the commission of the Mafia or La Cosa Nostra?", Bonanno replied, "My doctors instructed me and recommended me not to testify because the extreme stress could be fatal." Then Giuliani held up a copy of *A Man of Honor.* "Mr. Bonanno," he said, "is this a copy of your book?" Bonanno answered, "I believe in God and I believe in my doctors."

Charged with contempt and sentenced to prison, Bonanno was moved to a prison hospital in Springfield, Missouri. He failed to win his appeals, despite the fact that his lawyer, the celebrated William Kunstler, told the judge "Everything is in the book" meaning there was no need for Bonanno himself to testify. But the author of *A Man of Honor* was nothing if not a survivor, and a decade later, in 1995, James Barron in the *New York Times* reported on Bonanno's ninetieth birthday celebration in Tucson. Bonanno, as it turned out, had been released after serving just a year, because the federal judge had lifted the contempt charge. Since then, he has lived quietly in his desert home.

Among the items Barron noted at the party was a cake in the shape of the Leaning Tower of Pisa ("The real [tower] was engineered by a Bonanno") and a party program which included a page of "Bonannoisms." These, Barron observed, were "long on sentiment but short on grammar." As an example, he quoted the following: "Friendships, connections, family ties, trust, loyalty, obedience, is the glue that holds us together." Such use of language seems a far cry from that found in the introduction to the book reputedly authored by Bonanno, lines which set the tone for the entire volume: "I wish to provide an honest portrait of myself and of my times so that you may judge for yourself what kind of man I am. . . . I've often been described as a gangster, a racketeer, a mobster. . . . I am not unmindful of my past. Who knows better than I my mistakes and my accomplishments? This book does not attempt to foist apologies or deny facts. To arrive at a balanced picture of a man, one must make a thorough examination."

Such a "thorough examination," suggested Walter Goodman in the *New York Times,* is exactly what is lacking in *A Man of Honor;* as for the writing style, which bears little resemblance to what one would expect from a Mafia don, Goodman noted that "This autobiography was written for Mr. Bonanno by Sergio Lalli, who does pretty well, given the interesting areas he must skirt, the dubious material he must impart, and the posturings he must treat with respect." Lalli, Goodman observed, owed a "stylistic debt to Mario Puzo," whose novel, *The Godfather,* he seemed to be imitating. Robert Fox of the *Times Literary Supplement* also found something a little suspect in the Mafia boss's apparently well-developed facility with language. Bonanno, Fox noted, acknowledges his poor grasp of English grammar. *A Man of Honor,* is comprised of "an atrocious mixture of styles," Fox concluded, stating further that the book is brimming with "the sentimentality of a very violent man."

Indeed, the facts of Bonanno's life offer a portrait quite different from that in his book. Born in Sicily, he first came to America with his family in 1908, when he was three years old; but the Bonannos returned to their Sicilian home town of Castellamare de Gulfo. There the young Bonanno became involved with the "Men of Honor," as Mafia members are known; and by 1924 was compelled to flee Sicily for Cuba and ultimately the United States. Three years after his arrival in New York, Bonanno became involved in the War, a battle from which emerged the Commission, led by Charlie "Lucky" Luciano.

The Commission established the five families as the controlling forces in the New York Mob; already at twenty-six, Bonanno had become the youngest don, or family chief, and now he likewise became the youngest Commission member. Among his innovations was the design of the "double coffin," which allowed mobsters to bury two bodies at once: on top, a loved one who happened to have died, and beneath a special trap door, a second body—usually of someone who died under less-than-natural circumstances—that the gangsters needed to remove from sight.

After thirty years as family head in New York, Bonanno moved to Arizona and became involved in a plot with Profaci family boss Joe Maglicco to kill off several powerful Mafia bosses, including Carlo Gambino and Sam Giancana. When the Commission learned of this plot, they demanded that both conspirators appear before them. Maglicco did, and the Commission served him a fifty thousand-dollar fine and an order to retire. He died two weeks later, reportedly from high blood pressure. For obvious reasons, Bonanno refused to appear before the Commission, but after being kidnapped and held for almost two years by his own cousin, he agreed to turn over his family's assets—valued at two billion dollars a year—to the Commission.

Bonanno retired to Haiti in the mid-1960s, but after the Commission tried to kill his son Salvatore (nicknamed "Bill"), Bonanno responded by launching the "Bananas War." He waged it ruthlessly, and was at the point of getting the Commission to back down when, after suffering a heart attack, he decided to retire. Thereafter he lived peacefully in Arizona, the very tranquility of his existence—given the nature of the men who wished him ill—proof of his former high stature within the Mob. Other than his brush with prison and his ninetieth birthday party, his chief claim to fame in retirement has been his book, which Ann Hill Punnett of the *Christian Science Monitor* recommended for its educational qualities if nothing else: "This book is not necessarily to be avoided. If learning is knowledge, then an understanding of the underworld and its power is an education in itself. Here the knowledge just happens to be imparted by a mob boss who knows whereof he speaks."

BIOGRAPHICAL/CRITICAL SOURCES:

BOOKS

Bonanno, Joseph, with Sergio Lalli, *A Man of Honor: The Autobiography of Joseph Bonanno,* Simon & Schuster, 1983.

PERIODICALS

Christian Science Monitor, September 2, 1983, p. B8.
Newsday, April 15, 1993, p. 3.
New Statesman, September 16, 1983, p. 24.
New York Times, May 23, 1983, p. C17; September 6, 1985, p. A1; October 13, 1985, p. 63; January 18, 1995, p. B1.
Time, September 29, 1986, p. 16.
Times Literary Supplement, September 23, 1983, p. 1012.

OTHER

"Joseph Bonanno," *Murder, Inc.COM,* http://www.
murderinc.com/fam/bonn.html (October 5, 1998).*

—Sketch by Judson Knight

* * *

BOON, Debbie 1960-

PERSONAL: Born April 17, 1960, in Surrey, England; daughter of John Richard (a business owner)
and Kathleen Barbara (Skid) Jenkins; married Nicholas Eric Boon (a graphic designer), 1985; children: Henry Nicholas, George Louis, Cecily Grace
Matilda. *Education:* Degree from Loughborough College of Art and Design. *Religion:* Church of England.

ADDRESSES: Home—The Old Grammar School, Melton Rd., Wymondham, Leicestershire, LE14 ZAR,
England. *Office*—The Chapel, Melton Rd., Wymondham, Leicestershire, LE14 ZAR, England.

CAREER: Roy Walker Design Associates, Nottingham,
England, illustrator-designer, 1980-83; Pencil Box
Design, Nottingham, co-founder and co-managing director, 1983-97; Aspire Design, Leicestershire, England, co-founder and co-managing director, 1997—.

WRITINGS:

SELF-ILLUSTRATED; POETRY FOR CHILDREN

My Gran, Macdonald Young (London), 1997.
Aunt Sal, Macdonald Young (London), 1998.
Gio's Pizzas, Macdonald Young (London), 1998.

WORK IN PROGRESS: Two children's books. Also
"researching ideas on children with special needs, as
very little visual material is produced to which young
children can relate."

SIDELIGHTS: By way of introduction, Debbie Boon
shared a poem about herself:

"You've heard of Michael Rosen? He's more well
known than me. / Babette Cole and Dick King Smith,
but just you wait and see . . . / for now that I've got
started, you'll hear a whole lot more of Debbie

Boon—she's coming to you, just wait for what's in
store! Her kids think she's *quite* crazy; Her mum is
oh! so proud; Her husband's seen to raise a brow
when she reads out loud!

"A writer, illustrator, and a mum of three. . . . /
Time for things creative too? That's a tough one—let
me see. . . . / I'll sit at the kitchen table and scribble
down a line; I have to pick my moment, there's pre-
cious little time! A verse may come into my head; I'll
jot it down on paper. / I could be shopping or in bed;
it's really quite a caper!

"This brainstorm lasts a couple of days with ditty
after ditty. / I try them out on all my chums who
sigh—'Oh! ain't she witty!' But finally I've got it
down; it's there in all its glory. / My book is now all
there in words, and YES! I've got a story!

"Where do my ideas come from? and how long does
it take to write these books and illustrate the stories
that I make? Well, it may start with a scribble or an
image in my head; It could have been inspired by
something someone said! A book, a place, a person,
a photo someone took; and that may spark the pictures
that spread across my book.

"With *My Gran* it was easy—a love of all things
French. / Then came our *Aunt Sally*; I wrote sitting
on a bench, whilst Sally chatted of the times she'd
nannied for my kids—and the things they'd gotten up
to would make you raise your lids! Next, of course
was Gio, inspired by a certain cook, and so *Gio's
Pizzas* grew into my very latest book.

"It's very hard to say how long it takes to do a book
because the fun of doing them outweighs the work it
took."

In her first self-illustrated picture book, *My Gran,*
Boon follows a young girl as she enthusiastically describes her one-of-a-kind grandmother. Gran is un-
mistakably and wonderfully French: "My gran's a
French gran / a laze on the bench gran . . . a choco-
late in bowls gran / an 'any more rolls?' gran."
Accompanying the "rollicking rhyme," noted *School
Librarian* critic Lucinda Jacob, are "exuberant and
assured" pictures that evoke "the scenes of southern
France." A *Kirkus Reviews* critic raved about the way
that "joy bursts forth from these pages," and declared
that the gloriously eccentric gran, who stomps grapes
to make wine and drives a big yellow truck, "is in
every way, a child's dream."

BIOGRAPHICAL/CRITICAL SOURCES:

BOOKS

Boon, Debbie, *My Gran,* Macdonald Young, 1997.

PERIODICALS

Kirkus Reviews, March 1, 1998, p. 335.
School Librarian, November, 1997, p. 184.*

* * *

BOSSELAAR, Laure-Anne 1943-

PERSONAL: Born in 1943, in Belgium; married Kurt Brown, a poet. *Education:* Warren Wilson Program for Writers, M.F.A.

ADDRESSES: Agent—c/o Milkweed Editions, 430 First Avenue N., Suite 400, Minneapolis, MN 55401.

CAREER: Worked for radio and television stations in Belgium and Luxembourg; editor of poetry anthologies; poetry translator.

WRITINGS:

The Hour between Dog and Wolf: Poems, BOA Editions (Rochester, NY), 1997.
(Editor with Kurt Brown) *Night Out: Poems about Hotels, Motels, Restaurants, and Bars,* Milkweed Editions (Emeryville, CA), 1997.

Also author of *Artemis,* a book of poems written in French, published in France, 1982.

SIDELIGHTS: Poet Laure-Anne Bosselaar, who was born in Belgium during World War II, lived in several European countries before moving to the United States, where she earned an M.F.A. from the Warren Wilson Program for Writers. Bosselaar's first book, *Artemis,* a collection of poems written in French, was published in France. Since moving to the United States, Bosselaar, who is fluent in five languages, has worked on translations of American poetry into French. She has also translated Flemish poetry into English and edited poetry anthologies. With her husband, poet Kurt Brown, she edited *Night Out: Poems about Hotels, Motels, Restaurants, and Bars,* which includes poems by such notable U.S. poets as Raymond Carver, Lawrence Ferlinghetti, Jorie Graham, Maxine

Kumin, Galway Kinnell, Charles Simic, Thom Gunn, Joy Harjo, and Derek Walcott, as well as many selections from lesser-known writers. Scott Veale, in *New York Times Book Review,* admired the collection as "a clever homage to restless souls and creatures of the night." Veale liked the book's range of moods, from the dark to the whimsical, but pointed out that many of the best selections "are odes to transient hotels, seedy bars and all-night diners."

Bosselaar's first collection of poetry in English, *The Hour between Dog and Wolf,* was published in 1997. The book contains poems that both recall her European childhood and the aftermath of war, and works that reflect on her experiences in America. Poet Charles Simic, in his foreword to the collection, praised Bosselaar's "authentic poetic voice," writing that she recognizes "the complexities and the endless contradictions" of the trials of modern life. Wyn Cooper, in *Ploughshares,* admired Bosselaar's "large" themes and her sensual descriptions that "evoke [life] in every color, smell, texture, and taste." Cooper noted that one of the book's strengths is its technical and thematic variety, from long narrative works about the poet's childhood experiences to shorter lyric poems on North American and European landscapes to poems about romantic love. Cooper found these love poems "the most moving" in this "unforgettable" collection.

BIOGRAPHICAL/CRITICAL SOURCES:

BOOKS

Bosselaar, Laure-Anne, *The Hour Between Dog and Wolf,* BOA Editions (Rochester, NY), 1997.

PERIODICALS

New York Times Book Review, July 6, 1997, p. 14.
Ploughshares, fall, 1997.*

* * *

BRADFORD, Roy Hamilton 1921-1998

OBITUARY NOTICE—See index for *CA* sketch: Born July 7, 1921, in Belfast, Ireland; died September 2, 1998. Politician, broadcaster, and novelist. Bradford's political career was at its most visible when he served on the Northern Ireland Assembly between 1973 to 1974, even though he lost his seat in an upset election. Bradford also worked as a broadcaster for the British Broadcasting Corporation (BBC) and authored several novels. Bradford grew up in Ireland and graduated from college in 1942 with a degree in German and French. After working in military intelligence in France and Germany, he moved to London in 1950 where he pursued interests in restaurants and insurance and eventually worked as a writer and a broadcaster for the BBC and Instructional Television (ITV). Bradford became visible in politics in the mid sixties when he was elected as a representative to Northern Ireland's parliament. He continued to rise in politics and served as the Minister of Commerce in the province he represented beginning in 1969. He served in the 1970s as a member of the Northern Ireland Assembly but lost his seat in 1974. Bradford was known as a liberal, friendly, and calm politician and he continued to advocate calm discussion and mediation between Northern Ireland and the Commonwealth until late in his life. Bradford authored several novels during his life, including *Excelsior* (1960) and *The Last Ditch* (1951). He published the biography *Rogue Warrior of the SAS* in 1987.

OBITUARIES AND OTHER SOURCES:

BOOKS

Who's Who, St. Martin's Press, 1998.

PERIODICALS

London Times, September 7, 1998.

* * *

BRADSHAW, Timothy 1950-

PERSONAL: Born May 20, 1950, in the United Kingdom; son of Anthony and Ruth (Fleming) Bradshaw; married Ann Kaufmann, 1972; children: Sam, Ben, Dan. *Ethnicity:* "White, mongrel Celtic." *Education:* Oxford University, law degree, 1972; University of Nottingham, Ph.D., 1984. *Avocational interests:* Cricket, music.

ADDRESSES: Home—54 St. Giles, Oxford OX1 3LU, England. *Office*—Regents Park College, Oxford University, Oxford OX1 2LB, England; fax 01-86-528-8121. *E-mail*—timothy.bradshaw@regents.ox.ac.uk.

CAREER: Curate of the Church of England, 1976-79; Trinity College, Bristol, England, lecturer, 1979-90; Oxford University, Regents Park College, Oxford, England, senior tutor, 1990—. Ecumenical representative of the Church of England with the Orthodox Church; minister of a local church.

MEMBER: Society for the Study of Theology.

WRITINGS:

Purity and Orthodoxy, Rutherford House, 1984, Edwin Mellen (Lewiston, NY), 1986.
The Olive Branch, Paternoster, 1992.
(Editor) *The Way Forward?,* Hodder & Stoughton (London), 1997.
Grace and Truth in the Secular Age, Eerdmans (Grand Rapids, MI), 1998.
Praying and Believing, Smith & Henry, 1998.

WORK IN PROGRESS: A work on church doctrine; research on theology, Barth, and the church.

SIDELIGHTS: Timothy Bradshaw told *CA:* "My writing on Christian theology is motivated by 'faith seeking understanding.' I am keen to address modern challenges to the church, to promote ecumenism, and to articulate on Anglican orthodox self-understanding. I am also interested in Jewish-Christian thought and life."

* * *

BRATT, James D. 1949-

PERSONAL: Born September 11, 1949, in Grand Rapids, MI; son of Bert (a teacher) and Anita (Ribbens) Bratt; married Tina M. Bruinsma, July 21, 1973; children: Peter A., Suzanne A., David W., Eric J. *Ethnicity:* "Dutch-American." *Education:* Calvin College, B.A., 1971; Yale University, Ph.D., 1978. *Politics:* Democrat. *Religion:* Protestant. *Avocational interests:* Cross-country skiing, hiking, baseball.

ADDRESSES: Home—2321 Everest S.E., Grand Rapids, MI 49507. *Office*—Department of History, Calvin College, 3201 Burton S.E., Grand Rapids, MI 49546; fax 616-957-8551. *E-mail*—jbratt@calvin.edu.

CAREER: University of Pittsburgh, Pittsburgh, PA, began as assistant professor, became associate professor of religious studies, 1978-87; Calvin College, Grand Rapids, MI, professor of history, 1987—. Institute for the Study of American Evangelicals, member of advisory board; Grand Rapids Area Council on the Humanities, consultant.

MEMBER: Organization of American Historians, American Society of Church History, Conference on Faith and History.

WRITINGS:

Dutch Calvinism in Modern America, Eerdmans (Grand Rapids, MI), 1984.
(Editor) *Viewpoints: Exploring the Reformed Tradition,* CRC Press (Boca Raton, FL), 1991.
(With Christopher Meehan) *Gathered at the River: Grand Rapids, Michigan, and Its People of Faith,* GRAHC (Grand Rapids), 1993.
(Editor) *Abraham Kuyper: A Centennial Anthology,* Eerdmans, 1997.

WORK IN PROGRESS: Abraham Kuyper: A Biography, publication by Eerdmans expected in 2001; research on U.S. religion before the Civil War.

SIDELIGHTS: James D. Bratt told *CA:* "I have been particularly concerned to explore the religious subculture that shaped me, to interpret it to its current denizens and to outside observers, and to achieve for all three of these audiences (insiders, outsiders, and myself) a critical appreciation of its virtues and an understanding of how its virtues are (necessarily?) entwined with its defects. I've tried the same exercise on broader communities of faith and their interaction with American society and culture, under the notion that the thing believers (of whatever creed) most need is not self-congratulation, but a sense of the perils they face in imposing their vision on others and in being imposed upon by social power. Humor, irony, and humble resolution would be the best outcomes of my work, though I cannot say that these have their way with me. The book I most wish I had written is Henry May's *The Enlightenment in America.*"

* * *

BREIVIK, Patricia Senn 1939-

PERSONAL: Born August 17, 1939, in Pittsburgh, PA; daughter of Elmer W. and Leona (Frey) Senn; married Agnar Ove Breivik, 1961 (marriage ended);

married Clyde C. Walton, July 7, 1979; children: (first marriage) Kenneth Agnar. *Ethnicity:* "Caucasian." *Education:* Attended Florida State University, 1958, Silliman University, Hunter College of the City University of New York, and University of Oslo; Brooklyn College of the City University of New York, B.A., 1968; Pratt Institute, M.L.S., 1969; Columbia University, D.L.S., 1974. *Religion:* Protestant.

ADDRESSES: Home—Detroit, MI. *Office*—University Libraries, Wayne State University, 5155 Anthony Wayne Dr., Detroit, MI 48202. *E-mail*—p.breivik @wayne.edu.

CAREER: Fund raiser for church-related activities, New York City, 1962-67; school librarian, New York City, 1969-70; Brooklyn College of the City University of New York, Brooklyn, NY, humanities reference librarian, 1970; Pratt Institute, Brooklyn, lecturer, 1971-72, assistant professor and assistant dean of Graduate School of Library and Information Science, 1972-76; Sangamon State University, Springfield, IL, dean of library services and associate professor, 1976-79; University of Colorado at Denver, director of Auraria Library and professor, 1979-90, special assistant to the president, 1984-90; Towson State University, Towson, MD, associate vice president for information resources, 1990-95; Wayne State University, Detroit, MI, dean of university libraries, 1995—. University of Wisconsin, American Council on Education fellow in academic administration, 1983-84; Columbia University, visiting professor, 1988. Western Interstate Commission for Higher Education, member of steering committee for Regional Telecommunications Cooperative Project, 1988-89, member of advisory board, 1992-93; Colorado Telecommunications Advisory Commission, chairperson, 1989; Governor's Information Technology Board, chairperson of Education Work Group, 1993-95; Accrediting Council on Education in Journalism and Mass Communications, member, 1998—. Baltimore County Police Department, member of Futurists Group, 1994-95.

MEMBER: EDUCOM, National Forum on Information Literacy (founding chairperson, 1989—), American Council on Education (chairperson of Council of Fellows, 1985-88), American Association for Higher Education (chairperson of Information Literacy Action Community, 1989-95), Fellowship of Christian Librarians and Information Specialists (president, 1986-88), Association of College and Research Libraries (president, 1995-96), American Library Association (member of council, 1986-90; chairperson of Carroll Preston Baber Research Award Jury, 1985-86), Beta Phi Mu.

AWARDS, HONORS: Service Award, Fellows Program, American Council on Education, 1990; Library Literature Award, G. K. Hall and Co. (publisher), 1990; Crystal Apple Award, American Association of School Librarians, 1992, for special contributions to school library media programs; Leadership-Baltimore County Award, 1991-92; Miriam Dudley Instruction Librarian Award, Association of College and Research Libraries, 1997.

WRITINGS:

Open Admissions and the Academic Library, American Library Association (Chicago, IL), 1977.
(Editor with E. Burr Gibson, and contributor) *Funding Alternatives for Libraries,* American Library Association, 1979.
Planning the Library Instruction Program, American Library Association, 1982.
(Editor and contributor) *Managing Programs for Learning outside the Classroom,* Jossey-Bass (San Francisco, CA), 1986.
(Editor with Robert Wedgeworth, and contributor) *Libraries and the Search for Academic Excellence,* Scarecrow Press (Metuchen, NJ), 1988.
(With E. Gordon Gee) *Information Literacy: Revolution in the Library,* Macmillan (New York City), 1989.
(Contributor) Glen E. Mensching and Teresa B. Mensching, editors, *Coping with Information Illiteracy: Bibliographic Instruction for the Information Age,* Perian Press (Ann Arbor, MI), 1989.
(With J. A. Senn) *Information Literacy: Educating Children for the Twenty-First Century,* Scholastic Inc. (New York City), 1994, 2nd edition, National Education Association (Washington, DC), 1998.
Student Learning in the Information Age, Oryx (Phoenix, AZ), 1997.

Editor of continuing education column, *Journal of Education for Librarianship,* 1974-76. Contributor of about forty articles to library journals, including *Journal of Academic Librarianship, Reference Librarian, American Libraries, Educational Record, Journal of Liberal Education,* and *Change.*

SIDELIGHTS: Patricia Senn Breivik told *CA:* "Once I began to understand the empowerment that access to relevant information can bring to people, I wanted to

be part of making those connections happen, especially for those people who face more than 'their share' of challenges. That has been the motivating factor in my career, including my writing. In particular I have worked with a growing number of broadly based national organizations to promote educational practices and other opportunities that will prepare people for lifelong learning by becoming information-literate. Representatives from these organizations keep me inspired and working as hard as I can.

"My writing process—born of necessity—is writing in short spurts. I start with a clear-cut vision for the publication and write whatever is closest to mind in available time slots, usually of twenty-to-sixty minutes duration. Then I put the pieces together. It's far from efficient, but it works within my administrative demands."

*   *   *

BREMERMANN, Hans-Joachim   1926-1996

PERSONAL: Born September 14, 1926, in Bremen, Germany; naturalized U.S. citizen; died of cancer, February 21, 1996, in Berkeley, CA; son of Bernard and Berta (Wicke) Bremermann; married Maria Isabel Lopez-Ojeda (a professor), 1954. *Education:* University of Muenster, M.A., Ph.D., 1951.

CAREER: University of Muenster, Muenster, Germany, instructor of mathematics, 1952, assistant professor, 1954-55; Stanford University, Stanford, CA, research association, 1952-53, visiting assistant professor, 1953-54; Institute for Advanced Study, staff member, 1955-57, 1958-59; University of Washington, assistant professor, 1957-58; University of California, Berkeley, associate professor of mathematics, 1959-64, associate professor of mathematics and biophysics, 1964-66, member of executive committee for biophysics and medical physics group, 1964-68, member of bioengineering group, 1972-76, professor of mathematics and biophysics, 1966-91; University of California, San Francisco, member of bioengineering group, 1991-96. Harvard University, research fellow, 1953. Co-founder, *Journal of Mathematical Biology.*

MEMBER: American Mathematics Society, Austrian Mathematics Society, American Association of Artificial Intelligence, German Mathematics Association, Biophysics Society, American Association for the Advancement of Science (fellow).

AWARDS, HONORS: Lifetime Achievement Award, Evolutionary Programming Society; also recipient of other honors and awards.

WRITINGS:

Distributions, Complex Variables, and Fourier Transforms, 1965.

Contributor to *Proceedings of the IEEE Conference on Man, Systems and Cybernetics,* IEEE (Anaheim, CA), 1971; also contributor to journals, including *Mathematics Annual, Journal of Mathematical Biology,* and *Experientia.*

SIDELIGHTS: Hans-Joachim Bremermann made his home in many American universities throughout his career. To them all he brought the benefits of his training in the famed Muenster school of thought in complex analysis, as well as his enthusiasm for new fields ripe for mathematical modeling. Although he began his work in pure mathematics, Bremermann published papers on such varied and controversial subjects as artificial intelligence, human evolution, and the AIDS crisis. He was a leader among those inventing new buzzwords for the dawn of the twenty-first century: complexity theory, fuzzy logic, neural nets. He even speculated on an eponymous "Bremermann limit" to the ultimate computational capacity of all matter in the universe—a sort of intellectual thermodynamics.

Bremermann was born to Bernard and Berta (nee Wicke) Bremermann in Bremen, Germany, on September 14, 1926. His education was apparently unremarkable, perhaps even interrupted during World War II, but that changed in the late 1940s. Once Bremermann turned twenty and began his doctoral work at the University of Muenster, he joined the circle of analysts led by Heinrich Behnke. The year 1949 was an especially active one, in which many German mathematicians and physicists returned to Germany or emigrated to other European countries. They brought with them a mix of new ideas and inventions.

By the early 1950s Bremermann had devised a general solution to what was known as the Levi problem, previously only solvable in two dimensional forms. He had also immigrated to the United States and married Maria Isabel Lopez Perez-Ojeda, a professor. Their marriage would last forty-two years, until his death.

A new set of functions introduced by Pierre Lelong and Kiyoshi Oka in the early 1940s set the foundation for Bremermann's continued investigations. He disproved a generalization of the Bochner and Martin conjecture of 1948, offering a simpler proof instead. It was later incorporated into a 1966 textbook on complex analysis that remained in use for many years. By 1959 Bremermann had attacked an even older problem of Peter Dirichlet's involving continuous functions, proving it could be solved in two classes of domains.

Bremermann and a few other ambitious colleagues were already experimenting with aspects of quantum field theory. By the 1960s, he was involved in biology and computer science as well. Graduate classes in programming and Turing machines had sparked Bremermann's interest in the new technology, but a more practical motivation came in the form of John von Neumann's computer, nicknamed MANIAC. While attempting to program the machine, Bremermann quickly saw the need for the introduction of more subtle algorithms into MANIAC's brute computational processes. He was inspired to set out an agenda for the development of artificial intelligence in a publication funded by the Office of Naval Research and distributed throughout Europe and the United States. One tactic Bremermann used was to devise and employ evolutionary or "genetic" search procedures. He saw their future in training what he called "perceptrons," and finally witnessed their implementation in automated reasoning or "neural nets" in 1989.

During the 1980s Bremermann moved from genetic algorithms in computing to computer models of evolution. Arguing against group-selection models, he supported the Red Queen hypothesis. This still-controversial vision of the human body posits a complex system as host to a churning population of rapidly mutating parasites. Biology and computer analysis continued to overlap as his "Bremermann optimizer" method came to be used in the fields of genetics, bioscience, and cybernetics.

Bremermann took memberships in a variety of scientific clubs and organizations devoted to mathematics both pure and applied. He published in just as wide a variety of publications including one he co-founded, the *Journal of Mathematical Biology.*

Aside from teaching and conducting research at Stanford University, Bremermann also held posts at the University of Washington and the Institute for

Advanced Study at Princeton, New Jersey. Bremermann also returned to the University of Muenster to teach, before settling permanently in California. He held joint professorships in mathematics and biophysics at the Berkeley campus of the University of California until his retirement in 1991. Bremermann's wife served at San Francisco State University as professor emeritus of romance language literature. She survived him upon his death from cancer on February 21, 1996 in Berkeley. The year before Bremermann's death he was feted with such honors as the Evolutionary Programming Society's lifetime achievement award, and an invitation to speak at the Dalai Lama's sixtieth birthday celebration.

BIOGRAPHICAL/CRITICAL SOURCES:

PERIODICALS

Biosystems, vol. 34, 1995, pp. 1-10.
Notices of the AMS, September, 1996.
Society for Mathematical Biology Newsletter, April, 1992.*

*   *   *

BRENNA, Duff

PERSONAL: Male.

ADDRESSES: Home—Poway, CA. *Agent*—c/o Doubleday, 1540 Broadway, New York, NY 10036. *E-mail*—dbrenna@mailhost1.csusm.edu.

CAREER: California State University in San Marcos, teacher of creative writing. Employed as a dairy farm worker.

AWARDS, HONORS: Recipient of National Endowment for the Arts grant; Novel Award, Associated Writing Programs, 1988, for *The Book of Mamie; Milwaukee Magazine* fiction award.

WRITINGS:

The Book of Mamie (novel), University of Iowa Press (Iowa City), 1989.
The Holy Book of the Beard, Nan A. Talese/Doubleday (New York City), 1996.
Too Cool, Doubleday (New York City), 1998.

SIDELIGHTS: "There is much to be admired in Duff Brenna's ambitious first novel. A work of varied textures and unusual richness, it has an energy that catches hold from the very first sentence," states Harry Middleton in the *New York Times Book Review.* The Mamie of the title is a young retarded girl on the run across rural Wisconsin from her physically and sexually abusive father. She meets up with the narrator, fifteen-year-old Christian Foggy, who bonds with her and helps in her flight across the state. With her father, John Beaver, in quick pursuit, Mamie and Christian encounter numerous adventures and misadventures as they both mature during their odyssey.

Middleton continues of *The Book of Names,* "It is a story of lost youth and life lived deeply. And it portrays a transformation that is at once comic and tragic, as the trauma of Mamie's life is peeled away, revealing a young woman of immense complexity and compassion." Middleton concludes that the novel "is a risky, graceful book. Its story is told in language that is lean and unpretentious, a language forged out of the hard landscape of the rural Middle West." A *Kirkus Reviews* critic describes the book as "an intelligent, lively picaresque coming-of-age tale about a backwoods adolescent who travels with a sort of idiot savant who has the strength and vitality of a folk-tale hero." The reviewer adds that the novel "survives some bagginess and dull spots to succeed as a sort of modern folk tale." A *Publishers Weekly* reviewer perceives similar elements, stating that "this picaresque yarn has the exuberance and broad humor of a folk tale."

Brenna's second novel, *The Holy Book of the Beard,* focuses on Jasper John, a man in his early twenties who arrives in East San Diego from Colorado in search of a new life. He obtains work as a busboy at Fat Stanley's Diner and there meets a cast of unusual characters whose lives, relationships, and escapades comprise the novel's action. A *Publishers Weekly* reviewer describes the book as "alternately sad, funny, grotesque and sexy," adding, "Vivid characters, rich dialogue and spellbinding narrative make this odd mix of tragedy, myth and ribaldry memorable and often moving." Nicholas Birns writes in the *New York Times Book Review* that *The Holy Book of the Beard* "is a showcase for the raffish, the down-and-out and the free-spirited." While acknowledging some plot flaws, Birns nevertheless finds that the book "should not be underestimated. Loaded with all the ingredients of an underground classic, engrossing and uproarious, it is nearly impossible to put down. . . . Most important, though, Mr. Brenna writes with an

honesty and vigor that make his characters and his vision matter."

Readers meet sixteen-year-old Triple E, the main character of *Too Cool,* escaping to Colorado in a stolen Oldmobile after breaking out of Goodpastures Correctional Facility. His passengers include his girlfriend Jeanne, fourteen-year-old cousin Ava, and Ava's boyfriend Tom. With the police in pursuit, Triple E stalls the car in a snowbank on an unplowed road in an attempt to avoid a roadblock. As the story continues, it shifts between his current predicament and the events that led Triple E to this moment. Richard Bernstein explains in the *New York Times,* "As Triple E struggles to find a way for him and Jeanne to survive, his memories come in new-hallucinatory form. The idea here is for the boy-man to face the explosive rage, the death wish, the primitive urgins and the craving for love that brought him face to face with death." A reviewer for *Booklist* describes Brenna's characters as "both rough-talking and deeply philosophical," and writes that their "only desire is to be free to be themselves." Bernstein concludes, "What especially characterizes *Too Cool* is not just compassion but the honed intelligence of a skilled writer who has brilliantly evoked the airtight, impenetrable inner logic of youth determined at all cost to find its own way."

BIOGRAPHICAL/CRITICAL SOURCES:

PERIODICALS

Booklist, June 1, 1998, p. 1720.
Kirkus Reviews, October 1, 1989, p. 1419; June 15, 1998, p. 826.
New York Times, July 27, 1998, p. E4.
New York Times Book Review, January 7, 1990, p. 12; March 17, 1996, p. 28.
Publishers Weekly, September 29, 1989, p. 59; January 1, 1996, p. 56.
West Coast Review of Books, March/April, 1990, p. 31.*

*   *   *

BREYMAN, Steve 1960-

PERSONAL: Born May 6, 1960, in Milwaukee, WI; son of James (an engineer) and Patricia (an office manager; maiden name, Pasch) Breyman; married Sheryl Evans (a special educator), May, 1981; children: Karl, Natasha, Vanessa. *Education:* University of California, Santa Barbara, Ph.D., 1992. *Politics:* "Green Party."

ADDRESSES: Office—Department of STS, Rensselaer Polytechnic Institute, Troy, NY 12180-3590. *E-mail*—breyms@rpi.edu.

CAREER: Marquette University, Milwaukee, WI, visiting assistant professor, 1991-93; Rensselaer Polytechnic Institute, Troy, NY, assistant professor, 1993—. Environmental Advocates, Albany, NY, member of board of directors. *Military service:* U.S. Army, 1978-80.

MEMBER: Common Cause (secretary of board of directors).

AWARDS, HONORS: Named teacher of the year, Rensselaer Alumni Association, 1998.

WRITINGS:

Movement Genesis, Westview Press (Boulder, CO), 1997.
Why Movements Matter, State University of New York Press (Albany, NY), 1999.

*   *   *

BRINKLEY, Douglas 1961(?)-

PERSONAL: Born c. 1961, in Atlanta, GA; father a health care worker; mother an English teacher. *Education:* Attended Ohio State University; Georgetown University, Ph.D., 1989. *Politics:* "Liberal Democrat."

ADDRESSES: Office—Eisenhower Center for American Studies, 923 Magazine St., New Orleans, LA 70130.

CAREER: Historian and educator. Hofstra University, Long Island, NY, associate professor of history, 1990-93; University of Louisiana, associate professor; Eisenhower Center for American Studies, University of New Orleans, director, 1994—. Contributor to National Public Radio; consultant to television documentary projects.

WRITINGS:

NONFICTION

(With Townsend Hoopes) *Driven Patriot: The Life and Times of James Forrestal,* Knopf (New York City), 1992.

Dean Acheson: The Cold War Years, 1953-1971, Yale University Press (New Haven, CT), 1992.

The Majic Bus: An American Odyssey, Harcourt (New York City), 1993.

Jimmy Carter: The Triumph and the Turmoil, Random House (New York City), 1996.

(With Hoopes) *FDR and the Creation of the United Nations,* Yale University Press, 1997.

The Unfinished Presidency: Jimmy Carter's Journey beyond the White House, Viking (New York City), 1998.

American Heritage History of the United States, Viking, 1998.

OTHER

(Contributor) Stephen Ambrose, *Rise to Globalism: American Foreign Policy since 1938,* Penguin (Baltimore, MD), 1971.

(Co-editor with Clifford Hackett) *Jean Monnet: The Path to European Unity,* St. Martin's Press (New York City), 1992.

(Co-editor with Natalie A. Naylor and John Allen Gable) *Theodore Roosevelt, Many-Sided American,* Heart of the Lakes (Interlaken, NY), 1992.

Dean Acheson and the Making of U.S. Foreign Policy, St. Martin's Press, 1993.

(Co-editor with David R. Facey-Crowther) *The Atlantic Charter,* Volume 8 of "Franklin and Eleanor Roosevelt Institute Series on Diplomatic and Economic History," St. Martin's Press, 1994.

(Author of introduction) Jimmy Carter, *Why Not the Best? The First Fifty Years,* University of Arkansas Press (Fayetteville), 1996.

(Author of introduction) Theodore Dreiser, *A Hoosier Holiday,* Indiana University Press (Bloomington), 1997.

(Editor) Hunter S. Thompson, *The Proud Highway: Saga of a Desperate Southern Gentleman 1955-1967,* Villard (New York City), 1997.

(Author of introduction) Carl Thomas Rowan, *South of Freedom,* Louisiana State University Press (Baton Rouge), 1997.

(Co-editor, with Richard T. Griffiths) *John F. Kennedy and Europe,* Eisenhower Center Studies on War and Peace, Louisiana State University Press, 1999.

Contributor to periodicals, including *New York Times, Foreign Affairs, Washington Post, New Yorker,* and *Atlantic Monthly.*

SIDELIGHTS: Douglas Brinkley is a historian who has produced many biographies and edited several collections of historical essays. He is also a history professor with a love of literature and music, and an educator who feels strongly that learning should be experiential and participatory. With interests and accomplishments ranging from authorship, history, and academia to popular culture, Brinkley claimed in a *USA Today* article that he has "an extremely high energy level, didn't need a lot of sleep, and looked forward to getting up every day and writing a book or teaching." He refuses to compartmentalize work and leisure in his life, claiming that, for him, these are one and the same.

One of Brinkley's earliest works, 1992's *Driven Patriot: The Life and Times of James Forrestal,* which he co-authored with Townsend Hoopes, details the biography of Forrestal, a workaholic who put work before pleasure and ascended from Wall Street into high government appointments, including positions in the Pentagon. One of Forrestal's notable career achievements was his organization of navy construction efforts during World War II. As Forrestal rose to higher prominence in government, he took a stronger stand against Communism and helped shape the beginnings of the Cold War. The job was not without its pressures, and Forrestal eventually suffered a mental breakdown and committed suicide. *New Republic* reviewer Jacob Heilbrunn called *Driven Patriot* the first biography to integrate its subject's work with the rest of his life. Brinkley's biography provides readers with a glimpse into Forrestal's icy demeanor, including his failed marriage, his self-imposed distance from his children, and his absorption in his work. One reviewer claims that the author shows Forrestal's downfall to be caused by his virtues, namely "determination, self-reliance, and discipline."

Brinkley's other 1992 biography, *Dean Acheson: The Cold War Years, 1953-1971,* details the life of a man who first served as secretary of state to President Harry S. Truman and later advised the Johnson, Kennedy, and Nixon administrations. Acheson helped shape foreign policy during the Cold War, particularly in its early years, and was a fierce believer that the United States' stand against the Communist threat was not to be dealt with lightly. He worked with presidents whom he originally despised—including Richard Nixon—to advise them on foreign policy.

Acheson was responsible for setting the hard-line tone against the Soviet Union during early U.S. foreign policymaking, and was not interested in compromise or negotiation. Reviewing *Dean Acheson,* several critics hailed Brinkley's work for its clarity. *Times Literary Supplement* contributor Warren Kimball concluded that Brinkley offered the reader a "fascinating, slightly off-center perspective on the Cold War world and the mentality which governed American foreign policy" for the duration of that time. On the other hand, *Commentary* reviewer Jeffrey Salmon faulted Brinkley for taking a condescending tone and implied that "he knows the world better than his subject." Brinkley also edited *Dean Acheson and the Making of U.S. Foreign Policy,* a collection of essays that includes criticism as well as praise for Acheson, and lists written works and speeches by the former statesman.

In 1993 Brinkley published *The Majic Bus, An American Odyssey.* The book recounts a unique teaching experiment which Brinkley created in 1992 and which was, by most accounts, extraordinarily successful. In order to give students a first-hand glimpse and experience of American history and culture, Brinkley organized a six-week, for-credit course that was conducted on a cross-country bus trip. Students visited historically and culturally significant sites, met important American authors, delved into a required reading list, and listened to lectures Brinkley created during the trip. Teacher and students traveled against a backdrop of American music ranging from blues to jazz to rock—all of which Brinkley claimed provided historical context to the lessons that the students were learning. According to Brinkley, the cross-country class format was a more effective learning experience than four years of university work would have been. He has continued to offer the course, focusing on civil rights, environmental issues, and other significant aspects of U.S. history. According to Brinkley, his intent is to make history and literature fun; not to "simply study America, but to grab it by the scruff of the neck." Reviewing *The Majic Bus, Voice of Youth Advocates* reviewer Janet Polacheck called Brinkley's writing "headlong and voracious" and claims that Brinkley's concept of teaching is among the most exciting she has encountered. *Kliatt* reviewer R. Bruce Schauble grasped Brinkley's infectious teaching methods, and appreciated the usual eloquence with which Brinkley relates the story of the bus trip.

In 1997, amid complaints and doubts about the effectiveness of the United Nations, Brinkley's *FDR and the Creation of the United Nations,* co-authored with Townsend Hoopes, was published. *New York Times Book Review* reviewer Rudy Abramson concluded that the book contributed a great deal of insight into the contemporary issues the United Nations faces. Brinkley and Hoopes outline the history of the organization and offer suggestions for improving its late-twentieth-century status, rather than advising that it be disbanded.

Brinkley has also written two biographies of former president Jimmy Carter, 1996's *Jimmy Carter: The Triumph and the Turmoil,* and *The Unfinished Presidency: Jimmy Carter's Journey beyond the White House,* which was published in 1998, and which focuses on Carter's post-presidential years. Several reviewers noted *The Unfinished Presidency*'s insights into Carter's personality, or what a *New York Times* reviewer called the "elusive, and sweet yet angular" aspects of Carter. Colman McCarthy of the *Washington Post Book World* called Brinkley's treatment of his subject "thoroughly readable, forcefully written, and detailed." The book details why Carter has been more successful since leaving office than he was as president. Brinkley's biography of Carter shows some of the former president's less than positive attributes as well: driving competitiveness, an occasional mean streak, and episodes of self righteousness. However, his overall treatment of Carter is positive, and Brinkley sheds a favorable light on Carter's values, energy, and pursuit of a simple lifestyle. In his review of *The Unfinished Journey, Salon* contributor Theo Spencer maintained that Brinkley's support of Carter resulted in a portrayal of a less than three dimensional person, claiming that Brinkley failed to provide the reader sufficient insight into why Carter strove to become president in the first place.

Brinkley feels strongly that the teaching of history should not be overspecialized; in fact, he maintains, it should be integrated with humanities and other liberal arts pursuits. In both his writing and his teaching, he often integrates literature into an historical context. During the Majic Bus Tour, for example, Brinkley included Graceland on the itinerary—not only because he felt that Elvis Presley was a significant part of U.S. history, but because Presley's music shaped part of that history and the frenzy of media and public attention surrounding Presley during his life and after his demise epitomizes the commercialization of America. In an article for the *Washington Post Educational Review,* Brinkley wrote in defense of so-called "Generation X students," born between 1961 and 1981, claiming that they are not nearly as apathetic and cynical as the public believes them to be. Brinkley stated that he believed all educators have an obligation to understand their students' points of view, and that history teachers should include a broader context in their lessons.

BIOGRAPHICAL/CRITICAL SOURCES:

PERIODICALS

American Historical Review, June, 1993, p. 972; December, 1993, p. 5.
American History Illustrated, November-December, 1992, p. 23.
Book Watch, May, 1993, p. 4.
Choice, March, 1993, p. 1224.
Commentary, February, 1993, p. 64.
Economic Books, winter, 1991, p. 59.
Economist, February 20, 1993, p. 92.
Foreign Affairs, May, 1991, p. 197; winter, 1991, p. 197; winter, 1992, p. 204; May, 1994, p. 159; July-August, 1995, p. 142.
Guardian Weekly, January 31, 1993, p. 20; July, 1995, p. 142.
Historian, autumn, 1993, p. 55.
History: Reviews of New Books, winter, 1994, pp. 59, 61; winter, 1995, p. 95.
Journal of American History, June, 1993, p. 335; December, 1993, p. 1156; September, 1994, p. 796.
Kliatt, September, 1994, p. 42.
London Review of Books, October 21, 1993, p. 15.
New Republic, October 5, 1992, p. 38; December 28, 1992, p. 36.
New Yorker, July 6, 1992, p. 80; November 20, 1992, p. 175.
New York Review of Books, August 13, 1992, p. 33; December 17, 1992, p. 11.
New York Times Book Review, May 3, 1992, p. 11; November 8, 1992, p. 7; February 5, 1995, p. 28; June 11, 1995, p. 58.
Publishers Weekly, February 24, 1992, p. 38; October 19, 1992, p. 66; June 13, 1994, p. 62; December 19, 1994, p. 52.
Times Literary Supplement, September 3, 1993, p. 7.
USA Today, June 24, 1998.
Utne Reader, July-August, 1993, p. 123.
Voice of Youth Advocates, October, 1993, p. 256.
Wall Street Journal, June 2, 1993, p. A12.
Washington Monthly, June, 1992, p. 54.
Washington Post Book World, December 13, 1992, p. 1.
Washington Post Education Review, April 3, 1994, p. 1.

OTHER

Booknotes Transcript, http://www.booknotes.org/transcripts/10024.htm (April, 1993).
Salon, http://www.salonmagazine.com/books/sneaks/1998/05/19sneaks.html (May 19, 1998).*

—*Sketch by Catherine Dybiec Holm*

* * *

BRITT, Brian (Michael) 1964-

PERSONAL: Born August 28, 1964, in Omaha, NE; son of Gerald and Janice (Gitter) Britt; married Jessica Meltsner, August 19, 1989; children: Lucy, Anna. *Ethnicity:* "Irish and German American." *Education:* Oberlin College, B.A.; University of Chicago, M.A. and Ph.D.

ADDRESSES: Office—207 Major Willems, Virginia Polytechnic Institute and State University, Blacksburg, VA 24061-0135. *E-mail*—bbritt@vt.edu.

CAREER: Virginia Polytechnic Institute and State University, Blacksburg, assistant professor.

WRITINGS:

Walter Benjamin and the Bible, Continuum (New York City), 1996.

Contributor of articles and reviews to periodicals, including *Nova Religio, Literature and Theology,* and *Continuum.*

WORK IN PROGRESS: Moses: The Narrative Eclipse of the Text.

* * *

BROAD, Kendal L. 1966-

PERSONAL: Born May 15, 1966, in California; daughter of G. H. and Sharon (Feierabend) Broad. *Ethnicity:* "White." *Education:* University of California, Santa Cruz, B.A., 1990; Washington State University, M.A., 1993, Ph.D., 1998.

ADDRESSES: Office—Department of Sociology, University of Florida, P.O. Box 117330, Gainesville, FL 32611. *E-mail*—kendal@soc.ufl.edu.

CAREER: University of Florida, Gainesville, assistant professor of sociology, 1998—.

MEMBER: American Sociological Association, National Women's Studies Association.

WRITINGS:

(With Valerie Jenness) *Hate Crimes: New Social Movements and the Politics of Violence,* De Gruyter (Hawthorne, NY), 1997.

*   *   *

BROOKE, Bryan (Nicholas) 1915-1998

OBITUARY NOTICE—See index for *CA* sketch: Born February 21, 1915, in Croydon, Surrey, England; died September 18, 1998. Gastroenterologist, professor, and author. Brooke received his bachelor's degree from Corpus Christi College, Cambridge, and his medical degree from the University of Birmingham. He served in the British Army's Royal Medical Corps from 1944 to 1946, attaining the rank of lieutenant colonel before accepting a post as a lecturer in surgery at the University of Aberdeen in Scotland. From there Brooke joined the faculty at the University of Birmingham in England, where he stayed until 1963. Brooke became a professor of surgery at the University of London, St. George's Hospital, later that year and remained there until his retirement. A visiting professor at several universities in the United States and Australia, Brooke was perhaps best known for a new form of bowel surgery he devised called the Brooke ileostomy. He wrote several books, including *Ulcerative Colitis and Its Surgical Treatment, You and Your Operation, Understanding Cancer,* and *Inflammatory Diseases of the Bowel.*

OBITUARIES AND OTHER SOURCES:

PERIODICALS

Times (London), October 26, 1998.

BROOKS, Geraldine

PERSONAL: Born in Sydney, Australia.

ADDRESSES: Agent—c/o Doubleday, 1540 Broadway, New York, NY 10036.

CAREER: Journalist. *Wall Street Journal,* Middle Eastern correspondent, 1988—.

AWARDS, HONORS: Hal Boyle Award, Overseas Press Club of America, 1990, for the best daily newspaper or wire service reporting from abroad.

WRITINGS:

Nine Parts of Desire: The Hidden World of Islamic Women, Anchor Books (New York City), 1995.
Foreign Correspondence: A Pen Pal's Journey from Down Under to All Over, Anchor Books/Doubleday (New York City), 1998.

SIDELIGHTS: Geraldine Brooks the author (not to be confused with Geraldine Brooks the film and stage actress) has won awards for her Mid-East correspondence for the *Wall Street Journal,* which included covering the Persian Gulf War. She channeled a unique part of that experience into her first non-fiction book, *Nine Parts of Desire: The Hidden World of Islamic Women.* When Brooks first arrived in the Middle East she felt cut off, as a female correspondent, from much of Muslim society. But she turned that liability into an advantage when she donned the *hijab* (the black veil worn by most Muslim women in the Middle East) and thereby enabled herself to penetrate the cloistered world of Muslim women.

The title of *Nine Parts of Desire* comes from an interpretation of the Koran offered by the Shiite branch: "Almighty God created sexual desires in ten parts; then he gave nine parts to women and one to men." As Laura Shapiro, writing for *Newsweek* commented, "Good enough reason to keep women under wraps." But Brooks uncovered a complex picture in her investigation of Muslim women's lives that goes beyond the Western assumption of women's oppression and isolation from public life.

Brooks interviews a wide range of Muslim women, from belly dancers to housewives, and from activists to female army recruits; her list of interviewees includes Queen Noor of Jordan and Ayatollah Khomeini's daughter. Her discoveries are fascinating and wide-ranging, if sometimes contradictory. According to

Brooks, wrote *Booklist* contributor Mary Ellen Sullivan, sexual gratification is considered "an inherent right" for Muslim women, but genital mutilation is still a common practice. It may surprise some Americans to read that women fare better in Iran than the rest of the Middle East. Brooks explains, "To Muslim women elsewhere . . . the Iranian woman riding to work on her motorbike, even with her billowing *chador* gripped firmly in her teeth, looks like a figure of envy." By wearing the *chador* herself, Brooks discovers a camaraderie among the women that she has experienced elsewhere, as when she bakes bread with Kurdish women. But when she notices a young boy sampling bits of bread that his sister sweats to make, she sees the negative side of strict sexual divisions as well: "His sister, not much older, was already part of our bread-making assembly line. Why should he learn so young that her role was to toil for his pleasure?"

Reviews of Brooks's first book were generally very positive. Sullivan called Brooks "a wonderful writer and thinker," noting that her study gives readers new insight into the lives of Muslim women. *Publishers Weekly* called the book a "powerful and enlightening report" that brings Westerners much closer to the reality of Muslim life for women. And Laura Shapiro of *Newsweek* admired the first-hand reporting that led Brooks to an "intimacy with these women [that] made it impossible either to romanticize or to demonize the tradition that ruled them."

A few years later Brooks followed up her first book with *Foreign Correspondence,* a memoir of her childhood that focuses on the importance of foreign pen pals to her sense of an independent identity and freedom from what she then considered the boring backwater of her hometown, Sydney, Australia.

The frame of the narrative is the approaching death of Brooks's father, which brings her back to Sydney from her life as a foreign correspondent for the *Wall Street Journal.* While going through family papers she finds letters from pen pals—from as far as the United States, France, and Israel—she had long ago forgotten. Rereading these letters brings her back to her youthful sense of restlessness and early belief that "real life happened in far-off lands." During her childhood and adolescence, the pen pals fulfilled her yearning for the exotic, and gave a sense of breaking away, as *Booklist*'s Donna Seaman commented, from "Australia's mid-century, Anglo-focused insularity." The experience was formative in bringing Brooks to her current position as a traveling journalist and "fire-

man" for the *Wall Street Journal* (the term identifies journalists who can report on controversial subjects and issues). Brooks's rereading inspired her to look up her old pen pals, and among other things to tell them the story of Joannie, her pen pal from the United States who spent the summer in Switzerland and Martha's Vineyard, but whose glamorous-sounding life ended early from the ravages of anorexia.

Reviews of *Foreign Correspondence* ranged from hot to cold. Seaman termed the book a "magnetic memoir," while *Publishers Weekly* deemed it "competent but unexciting." A critic for *Kirkus Reviews* offered unadulterated praise, calling it an "evocative, superbly written tale of a woman's journey to self-understanding."

BIOGRAPHICAL/CRITICAL SOURCES:

BOOKS

PERIODICALS

Booklist, September 15, 1994, p. 88; November 1, 1997, p. 436.
Kirkus Reviews, November 1, 1997, pp. 1616-1617.
Newsweek, February 13, 1995, p. 81.
New York Times Book Review, January 8, 1995, p. 14.
Publishers Weekly, November 21, 1994, p. 64; October 27, 1997, p. 57.*

* * *

BRUNDIGE, Donald G. 1940-

PERSONAL: Born October 28, 1940, in San Diego, CA; son of George Dewitt and Bernice (Jacobsen) Brundige; married Sharron Lea Davis, December 2, 1972. *Education:* University of California, Los Angeles, B.S., 1963; California State College (now University), Los Angeles, M.S., 1969. *Avocational interests:* Outdoor recreation in general, space physics, computer programming.

ADDRESSES: Home and office—122 Mirabeau Ave., San Pedro, CA 90732. *E-mail*—bnyduk@aol.com.

CAREER: Rockwell International Corp., Seal Beach, CA, member of technical staff, 1962-79; Aerospace Corp., El Segundo, CA, senior project engineer, 1979-96; writer, 1996—. Aerospace Corp., consultant, 1996—. *Military service:* U.S. Navy, 1963-65; served in Vietnam; became lieutenant. U.S. Naval Reserve, 1965-69.

MEMBER: American Institute of Aeronautics and Astronautics, Sigma Pi Sigma, Theta Xi.

WRITINGS:

WITH WIFE, SHARRON L. BRUNDIGE

Bicycle Rides: Los Angeles and Orange Counties, B-D Enterprises, 1986.
Bicycle Rides: San Fernando Valley and Ventura County, B-D Enterprises, 1987.
Bicycle Rides: Orange County, B-D Enterprises, 1988.
Bicycle Rides: Los Angeles County, B-D Enterprises, 1989.
Bicycle Rides: Inland Empire, B-D Enterprises, 1990.
Bicycle Rides: San Diego and Imperial Counties, B-D Enterprises, 1991.
Bicycle Rides: Santa Barbara and Ventura Counties, B-D Enterprises, 1992.
Mountain Biking L.A. County (Southern Section), B-D Enterprises, 1996.
Outdoor Recreation Checklists, Outdoor Recreation Equipment, 1998.

WORK IN PROGRESS: Mountain Biking L.A. County (Northern Section), with Sharron L. Brundige, for B-D Enterprises.

SIDELIGHTS: Donald G. and Sharron L. Brundige told *CA:* "When work was beginning to dominate our lives, and time together was shrinking, we revived our mutual interest in bicycle touring. After of couple of years of bicycling in the Los Angeles area, we realized that the then-available cycling tour guides were incomplete. With encouragement from friends and family, we set out to write and publish our own book, *Bicycle Rides: Los Angeles and Orange Counties.* The success of the initial book led us to publish on-road bicycling books throughout Southern California and to venture into the mountain biking world. The early books set a Southern California standard by providing thorough trip descriptions, detailed trip maps, distance and elevation profiles, and thumbnail summaries of trip highlights and levels of difficulty.

"We started thinking about *Outdoor Recreation Checklists* over eight years before it was published. In our outdoor adventures, there were several outings in which critical gear was left at home. Hiking trips

without spare shoelaces, winter climbing trips devoid of tent repair materials, and canoeing trips with a shortage of watertight storage containers are examples. On one bicycling-by-day and motel-at-night weekend outing, we even managed to leave our luggage at home! We searched the literature for an all-around outdoor guide which identified equipment needs, but the outcome was null. This led to our latest venture, which is centered around equipment checklists for about every major outdoor activity, whether on land or water. The checklists are accompanied by gear descriptions and key tradeoffs to assist buyers or renters in selecting the 'right' equipment for their adventures.

"We are thinking through the options for our next publication in the outdoor recreation arena. What we choose will depend on the excitement level of the project and the perceived needs of the outdoor person."

*   *   *

BRUNDIGE, Sharron L(ea) 1943-

PERSONAL: Born July 4, 1943, in Flint, MI; daughter of William Richard and Margaret (Berrisford) Davis; married Donald G. Brundige (a writer), December 2, 1972. *Education:* Attended Fullerton Junior College, 1964. *Avocational interests:* Outdoor recreation in general, figurines, antiques.

ADDRESSES: Home and office—122 Mirabeau Ave., San Pedro, CA 90732. *E-mail*—bnyduk@aol.com.

CAREER: Rockwell International Corp., El Segundo, CA, member of technical staff, 1965-89; writer, 1989—.

WRITINGS:

WITH HUSBAND, DONALD G. BRUNDIGE

Bicycle Rides: Los Angeles and Orange Counties, B-D Enterprises, 1986.
Bicycle Rides: San Fernando Valley and Ventura County, B-D Enterprises, 1987.
Bicycle Rides: Orange County, B-D Enterprises, 1988.
Bicycle Rides: Los Angeles County, B-D Enterprises, 1989.

Bicycle Rides: Inland Empire, B-D Enterprises, 1990.

Bicycle Rides: San Diego and Imperial Counties, B-D Enterprises, 1991.

Bicycle Rides: Santa Barbara and Ventura Counties, B-D Enterprises, 1992.

Mountain Biking L.A. County (Southern Section), B-D Enterprises, 1996.

Outdoor Recreation Checklists, Outdoor Recreation Equipment, 1998.

WORK IN PROGRESS: Mountain Biking L.A. County (Northern Section), with Donald G. Brundige, for B-D Enterprises.

SIDELIGHTS: For more about Sharron L. Brundige, see the entry on Donald G. Brundige.

*   *   *

BURK, Frank 1942-

PERSONAL: Born September 29, 1942, in Kirksville, MO; son of Glen (in U.S. Army Corps of Engineers) and Helen (a teacher) Burk; married Janet Martin, June 18, 1965; children: Eric, Angela, Michael, Brandon, Bryan. *Education:* University of Missouri—Columbia, B.A., 1963; University of California, Riverside, Ph.D., 1969. *Religion:* None. *Avocational interests:* Civic activities.

ADDRESSES: Home—2280 Oak Park Ave., Chico, CA 95928. *Office*—Department of Mathematics, California State University, Chico, CA 95929. *E-mail*—fburk@csuchico.edu.

CAREER: California State University, Chico, member of mathematics faculty.

MEMBER: Mathematical Association of America, American Mathematical Society.

WRITINGS:

Lebesgue Measure and Integration, Wiley (New York City), 1997.

WORK IN PROGRESS: Conducting research on "real analysis."

BURNS, Edward 1946-

PERSONAL: Born in 1946.

ADDRESSES: Agent—c/o Broadway Books, 1540 Broadway, New York, NY 10036.

CAREER: Public school teacher. Has also served with the Baltimore Police Dept., Baltimore, MD, as a patrol officer and as a detective.

WRITINGS:

(With David Simon) *The Corner: A Year in the Life of an Inner-City Neighborhood* (nonfiction), Broadway (New York City), 1997.

SIDELIGHTS: Edward Burns served as a police officer in the city of Baltimore, Maryland, and has also taught in the public schools. After his retirement, he teamed with David Simon, the author of *Homicide,* to research and write about daily life in a crime-ridden, drug-plagued neighborhood of west Baltimore. The result was the 1997 book, *The Corner: A Year in the Life of an Inner-City Neighborhood.*

In *The Corner* readers are confronted with the realities that face people such as DeAndre McCullough, a fifteen-year-old boy struggling to overcome the legacy of his drug-addicted parents but handicapped by an environment in which the drug trade is a way of life. As a *Publishers Weekly* review of *The Corner* explained, "the book conveys the feeling of helplessness of those who awake every morning thinking only of their 'next blast' and the arrogance of those who condemn them for it." Ellis Cose, discussing the volume in *Newsweek,* lauded the "fascinating snapshots of life on the streets" contained between its covers as well as "a vivid sense of why it is so hard for some members of the underclass to find their way into the light." However, Paula Dempsey, reviewing the book for *Library Journal,* seemed disappointed that Burns and his co-author did not advocate social policy as a way of alleviating some of the problems they chronicled.

BIOGRAPHICAL/CRITICAL SOURCES:

PERIODICALS

Economist, October 11, 1997, p. 110.
Library Journal, August, 1997 p. 113.
Newsweek, November 3, 1997, pp. 66, 68.

New York Times Book Review, November 23, 1997, p. 7.
Publishers Weekly, July 14, 1997, p. 74.*

* * *

BUTALA, Sharon (Annette) 1940-

PERSONAL: Born August 24, 1940 in Nipawin, Saskatchewan, Canada; daughter of Achille Antoine (a mechanic) and Margaret Amy Alexis (a homemaker; maiden name, Graham) Le Blanc; married (divorced); married Peter Noble Butala (a rancher), 1976; children: (first marriage) Sean Anthony Hoy. *Ethnicity:* "French Canadian/Irish/Scots." *Education:* University of Saskatchewan, B.Ed. (English), 1962, B.A. (art), 1963, post-graduate diploma (special education), 1973.

ADDRESSES: Home—Box 428, Eastend, Saskatchewan S0N 0T0, Canada. *Agent*—Westwood Creative Artists, 94 Harbord St., Toronto, Ontario M5S 1G6, Canada. *E-mail*—sharon.noble@sk.sympatico.ca.

CAREER: Educator, artist, and author. Teacher of English, then special education, in Saskatchewan, Nova Scotia, and British Columbia, 1963-83; full-time writer, 1983—.

MEMBER: Saskatchewan Writers' Guild, Writers' Union of Canada, P.E.N.

AWARDS, HONORS: Long Fiction Award, Saskatchewan Writers' Guild, 1983; Best Novel Award nomination, *Books in Canada,* 1984, for *Country of the Heart;* Major Drama Award, Saskatchewan Writers' Guild, 1985; Governor General's Award nomination, 1986, for *Queen of Headaches;* Annual Contributors Award, Canadian Fiction Magazine, 1988; 'B' Award, Canada Council, 1988; Senior Arts Grant, Saskatchewan Arts Board, 1989; Silver Award for Fiction, National Magazine Awards, 1991; Runner-up, Commonwealth Writers Award, 1991; Author's Award for Paperback Fiction, Foundation for the Advancement of Canadian Letters, 1992; Gold Saskatchewan Award, Western Magazine Awards, 1992, 1993 and 1994; Governor General's Award nomination, 1994, for *The Perfection of Morning;* Nonfiction Prize and "Spirit of Saskatchewan" Prize, Saskatchewan Book Awards, 1994; Marian Engel Award, Writers' Development Trust, 1998.

WRITINGS:

NOVELS

Country of the Heart, Fifth House Publishers (Saskatoon, Saskatchewan), 1984, HarperCollins Canada, 1999.
The Gates of the Sun, Fifth House Publishers (Saskatoon, Saskatchewan), 1986, HarperCollins Canada, 1994.
Luna, Fifth House Publishing (Saskatoon, Saskatchewan), 1988, HarperCollins Canada, 1994.
Upstream, Fifth House Publishers (Saskatoon, Saskatchewan), 1991, HarperCollins Canada, 1996.
The Fourth Archangel, HarperCollins Canada, 1992.
The Garden of Eden, HarperCollins Canada, 1998.

SHORT STORY COLLECTIONS

Queen of the Headaches, Coteau Books (Moose Jaw, Saskatchewan), 1985.
Fever, HarperCollins (New York City), 1990.

OTHER

Harvest, with photography by Todd Korol, Fifth House Publishers (Saskatoon, Saskatchewan), 1992.
The Perfection of the Morning: An Apprenticeship in Nature, HarperCollins (New York City), 1994.
Coyote's Morning Cry: Meditations and Dreams from a Life in Nature, HarperCollins (Toronto), 1995.
Perfection of the Morning: A Woman's Awakening in Nature, Hungry Mind Press (Saint Paul, MN), 1997.

Contributor to numerous Canadian literary magazines and periodicals. Also author and producer of five plays.

WORK IN PROGRESS: Wild Stone Heart: Hauntings at the Heart of Nature, a nonfiction book.

SIDELIGHTS: Saskatchewan author Sharon Butala commenced her writing career relatively late in life and through a rather roundabout way. In 1976, when she was thirty-six, she found she had fallen in love with Peter Butala and wished to marry him. The fly in the ointment was that geography separated them. She lived in Saskatoon with the teenage son of her first marriage and was pursuing a master's degree in special education and a career as an academic. Her mother, her sisters, and their families, and a close circle of female friends also lived in Saskatoon. Peter, on the other hand, owned a ranch in the most arid region of Canada—the Palliser Triangle in southwestern Saskatchewan. Despite her misgivings the rhythm of life on the ranch moved her. As Butala told Linda Leith in *Books in Canada,* during a May cattle drive at Peter's ranch, Butala "spent the entire day perched on the coral watching the men work—in the middle, she joked afterwards, of a Roy Rogers movie. But though she made light of it, she was actually 'stirred so deeply that everything in my old life—friends, job, family, politics—paled beside it.'" Surprising her friends and family, she moved to be with Peter (her son stayed in Saskatoon to finish high school).

Butala was under no delusions that she was fleeing to Eden, but nothing in her earlier life had prepared her for the hardscrabble existence on the prairie. While Butala's husband was away minding his cattle herd, reported George Woodcock, writing for *Quill & Quire,* Butala found herself alone, "thrown back starkly on herself, or rather, on herself and Nature, seen at its barest and its purest in the dry ice-scraped plateau where some of the true prairies survived. She was driven inward to examine the sources of herself, but also outward into the world of dreams and visions, which in this isolation took on a special importance, partly because they were indeed striking and clearly significant of changes of both outer and inner life."

In an article for *Canadian Geographic,* Butala related how the landscape was changing her: "The longer I stayed [on the prairie], the more I saw of [the meadows, buttes, and 'box' canyons], and the more fascinated I grew. Everywhere we went, the enormity and silence of this diffusely populated landscape opened my psyche to mysteries I'd not examined in the hurly-burly of city life. I could feel my soul expanding to admit—to encompass—this splendour." It was these circumstances that provoke Butala to write—first journals, then short stories and novels, all set in the prairie lands of Saskatchewan.

Butala considers herself primarily a writer of fiction, but her most well-received book, *The Perfection of the Morning: An Apprenticeship in Nature* (1994), is a memoir of her life-changing move to Saskatchewan, of her development as a writer, and of her burgeoning appreciation of nature. Leith praised the results in *Books in Canada,* commenting that Butala is at ease in this environment. Leith wrote that Butala's "insights are hard-won, her voice honest and true. She is a wonderful guide." John Bemrose, reviewing *The*

Perfection of the Morning for *Maclean's,* called it "one of the most perceptive and moving meditations ever written by a Canadian on that mysterious and often misunderstood presence that we call nature."

Butala is also the author of several novels. Her first, *Country of the Heart* (1984), tells the story of Lannie, an unsettled young woman who journeys back to the Saskatchewan farm of her adoptive parents. Alberto Manguel, a reviewer for *Books in Canada* found Butala's debut promising. He praised her writing as "straightforward, unadorned, [and] tight-fisted with metaphors." However, Sherie Posesorski reviewed the novel negatively in a *Quill & Quire* review, calling the book "a black-and-white photo" of the three protagonists in "an out-of-focus background, dominated by Butala's thumb print on the camera lens." Despite such criticism, *Country of the Heart* was generally well received and was nominated for the 1984 *Books in Canada* first novel award.

The Gates of the Sun (1986), a more ambitious novel, follows the life of Andrew Samson on the Saskatchewan prairie. The novel has four sections, each section detailing a different stage in Andrew's development. In the first part Andrew is an eight-year-old emigre yearning to ride horses and live a free life on the land. In part two he is a grown man who makes a living by cattle rustling. His mother's death and his incarceration for rustling causes him to reassess his life and he becomes a respected rancher and raises a family in the third part of the novel. Part four shows him as an old man wondering what has happened to the plains now being converted to farmlands and oil fields. Barbara Novak gave a mixed report of *The Gates of the Sun* in *Books in Canada:* "Butala is more successful at physical descriptions than she is at exploring the emotional core of her characters, where she tends to be somewhat heavy-handed. . . . At its best, however, *The Gates of the Sun* expresses a prairie existentialism that is profoundly moving."

Luna (1988), Butala's next novel, tells about the trials and tribulations of two sisters and their aging aunt living on the prairie. The women engage in various power struggles with the men in the novel—the worst involves the rape of one of the women's sixteen-year-old daughter—and the women offer each other emotional and spiritual solace. Cary Fagan, reviewing the work for *Books in Canada,* felt that the novel is overpowered by feminist dialectics, but praised Butala's gift for physical description: "Butala lets the reader see the grasshopper swarms, feel the cold of a cattle drive at thirty below, sympathize with the unending work and financial worry." Judith Carson was more unequivocal in her praise in a *Canadian Forum* review: "[Butala] is not an intellectual writer or elitist or wordsmith, but a storyteller, a chronicler. There is a satisfying mix of evocative description, readable dialogue, both internal and external. Butala clearly articulates what it means to be a woman in the modern world and I believe she speaks across cultures."

Upstream (1991) features Chloe, a Saskatchewan woman coping with her mixed French/English heritage. Her husband, whom she has supported through graduate school, is leaving her for another woman. She drives across country to Quebec to visit her parents and to sort out her life. A *Kirkus Reviews* critic dismissed the book as "meandering . . . and only mildly engaging" and Rita Donovan complained about the book's "unevenness" in a *Books in Canada* review: "It is a good story. But one finds oneself wishing that it could have been a slightly better novel."

The Fourth Archangel (1992), Butala's next novel, is perhaps her most unusual one. The residents of Ordeal, a small prairie town in Saskatchewan, face the impending millennium with trepidation. Many of them are having mystical experiences and visions. A local prostitute suffers from stigmata, phantom trains rush by on abandoned train lines, ghosts of Western pioneers materialize in the streets, a minister dreams of Ordeal becoming a perfect town floating in the sky— the wonders tumble forth. It is the summer of the year 2000 and the weather is sweltering. The farmers despair because their crops are not thriving, but they join forces to protect the town and their rustic ways. "All in all, it's a strange mixture of a book," wrote Eric McCormack in a review for *Books in Canada,* claiming the book provided "considerable reading pleasure." Philip Bull, writing for *Quill & Quire,* called it "a touching and vivid tale of a vanishing world."

Butala has also published two collections of short stories. Her first collection, *Queen of the Headaches* (1985), was published to mixed reviews. "Some of the stories, which are mostly about the people of the Saskatchewan farmlands, do not succeed, but others are almost perfect examples of their genre," wrote Hilda Kirkwood in a review of the collection for *Canadian Forum.* Kirkwood particularly noted "Arlene," the story of a pregnant hippie woman welcomed and then rejected by a commune. John Greenwood of *Books in Canada* complained that Butala could be "heavy-handed" at times, but noted that "the best stories are those that get away from . . . didactic plots." One of these stories, according to Greenwood, is "The Mission" which he called "a curious, gentle piece." *Queen of the Headaches* was nominated for the Governor General's Literary Award in 1986.

Butala's second book of short stories, *Fever,* came out in 1990 to favorable reviews. Joan McGrath, in a review for *Canadian Materials,* noted that "all of [the stories] have enormous power and resonance." Rachel Rafelman, reviewing the collection for *Books in Canada,* wrote that the stories' "reward is at best a brief and painful awareness that life is random and experience idiosyncratic." Ann Jansen, writing for *Quill & Quire,* saw some interesting differences between Butala's first and second story collections. In both collections, Jansen found, the stories are about "ordinary people," but in *Fever* the characters find themselves "caught in out-of-the-ordinary situations. . . . [in] ambiguous landscapes . . . though reality generally clicks firmly in again after the temporary distortions."

In 1998 Butala's sixth novel, *The Garden of Eden,* was published. Similar to her nonfiction *The Perfection of the Morning* in theme, the novel tells of Iris, a middle-aged woman married to a Saskatchewan farmer. Following her husband's death, Iris finds herself trying to deal with emotional and spiritual issues ranging from guilt at having placed her mother in a retirement home to her loveless marriage. Iris is also driven in the novel to reestablish contact with Lannie, the orphaned niece she raised who has fled to refugee work in Ethiopia with her own emotional issues. "One of the book's finest achievements is the way it weaves details from the natural world into the lives of its protagonists, so that the flight of a bird, the smell of soil, become an integral part of their thinking and feeling," wrote John Bemrose in a review for *Maclean's.* He added, "For Butala, nature is obviously the fundamental ground of human life."

Butala has also written a book of spiritual observations, *Coyote's Morning Cry: Meditations and Dreams from a Life in Nature* (1995). In it she offers twenty short essays on such topics as vulnerability, alienation, and belonging. Some critics compared it unfavorably to her earlier non-fiction work, *The Perfection of Morning.* "The book has the feel of a rushed afterthought to the runaway bestseller," wrote Anne Francis in *Quill & Quire,* "and readers deserve better from this obviously talented writer." On the other hand, Pat Barclay, writing for *Books in Canada,* called it a "slim but insightful volume."

Butala told *CA:* "We are currently negotiating with foreign publishers for the rights to publish several of my books, and I anticipate writing and publishing many more books before I reach old age. Long ago I made the decision to accept the ranching and farming subculture of southwest Saskatchewan as my literary world."

BIOGRAPHICAL/CRITICAL SOURCES:

BOOKS

McFague, Sallie, *Super, Natural Christians: How We Should Love Nature,* Fortress Press (Minneapolis, MN), 1997.

PERIODICALS

Beaver, February, 1995, p. 53.
Books in Canada, October, 1984, pp. 31-32; April, 1986, p. 24; August/September, 1986, pp. 13-14; October, 1988, pp. 8-9; March, 1991, p. 50; October, 1991, p. 38; April, 1994, pp. 26-27; December, 1994, p. 16; October, 1995, p. 40.
Canadian Book Review Annual, 1994, p. 51; 1996, p. 237.
Canadian Forum, January, 1987, p. 39; February/March, 1989, pp. 33-34; July/August, 1992, p. 28.
Canadian Geographic, November-December, 1992, p. 118; July-August, 1995, p. 44.
Canadian Literature, spring, 1993, p. 157; winter, 1995, p. 201.
Canadian Materials, March, 1991, p. 115.
Kirkus Reviews, January 15, 1997, pp. 76-77.
Maclean's, July 1, 1994, pp. 38-40; May 9, 1994, p. 48; October 26, 1998.
Montreal Gazette, September 19, 1998.
Publishers Weekly, April 14, 1997, p. 72.
Quill & Quire, July, 1984, p. 73; February, 1986, p. 39; September, 1986, pp. 81-82; December, 1990, pp. 21, 23; April, 1992, p. 23; February, 1994, p. 23; September, 1994, p. 63; September, 1995, pp. 61-62.
Toronto Star, August 27, 1998.

*   *   *

BUTLER, Daniel Allen   1957-

PERSONAL: Born January 24, 1957, in Gary, IN; son of Harold E. (an architect) and Lottie (Nabors) But-ler; married Eleanor Anne Lang (a registered nurse), March 27, 1993; children: Thomas Harold Robert (deceased). *Ethnicity:* "Scots."   *Education:* Hope College, B.A., 1979; graduate study at University of Erlangen. *Religion:* Presbyterian.

ADDRESSES: Home and office—13265 Southwest 49th Ct., Miramar, FL 33027. *E-mail*—Butler1918 @aol.com.

CAREER: Writer. 42nd Royal Highland Regiment (Black Watch) Re-enactment Group, regimental sergeant major. Active in Scottish-American community in south and central Florida. *Military service:* U.S. Army, 1980-87; became captain; received Bronze Star, Meritorious Service Medal, Army Achievement Medal, and Army Commendation Medal.

MEMBER: Royal British Legion.

WRITINGS:

"Unsinkable": The Full Story of RMS Titanic, Stackpole (Mechanicsburg, PA), 1998.

WORK IN PROGRESS: The Day the Lusitania Died, a history of the *Lusitania* disaster and the politics leading up to and surrounding it; *Waterloo: A Hundred Days of Glory,* a detailed account of the 1815 campaign that resulted in the final defeat of Napoleon Bonaparte.

SIDELIGHTS: Daniel Allen Butler told *CA:* "My primary motivation for writing is that I simply like to tell a good story. History can be far more intense and interesting than fiction could ever hope to be, provided it's presented the right way. Far too much history today is presented without drama, without passion, without the emotions that motivated the men and women living through the events described. I want to redress that balance and make my readers understand the excitement, the fear, the anger, the ambition, the cowardice, and the courage of the people who made the events that we call history—and in doing so, make those events more real and understandable to the readers. I want to bring life to what is all too often a dead past.

"There are probably a multitude of indirect influences on my writing, but few that I could describe as direct. My perspectives take years, sometimes decades, to develop and are the result of continual re-evaluation of the sources I have available on a subject. My writing style is very visual. I visualize the scene I'm writing about and then simply describe what I see. This is a process that can happen any time, anywhere. The visualization begins and the description starts to write itself. All I have to do is get it down on paper. It's difficult to describe, because it isn't the result of a conscious effort. I don't sit at my computer and write for a specified amount of time each day, or for a specific number of pages. Sometimes I'll go a week without writing anything, then suddenly I'll write for twenty-four hours without stopping. It's certainly not a system I would try to teach in school!

"The subjects I write about are subjects that have fascinated me for years. They can be battles and military campaigns, disasters, lives of individuals, or stories of entire nations. I suppose it's safest to say I'm a drama junkie—the more dramatic the story, the more likely I'll be interested in it."

*   *   *

BUTLER, Francelia McWilliams 1913-1998

OBITUARY NOTICE—See index for *CA* sketch: Born April 25, 1913, in Cleveland, OH; died September 18, 1998, in Windham, CT. Academic and writer. Butler, a social activist, graduated from Oberlin Col-

lege in 1934 but did not receive her master's degree until 1959 when she graduated from Georgetown University following her husband's death. In 1963 she received her doctorate in Renaissance literature from the University of Virginia and joined the English faculty at the University of Tennessee at Knoxville, where she stayed until 1965. Later that year she moved to the University of Connecticut and made strides to move children's literature courses out of the academic basement and into the humanities. Children's literature courses met with disdain from many professors but Butler viewed them as a serious discipline, establishing the journal *Children's Literature* and creating the children's literature division of the Modern Language Association. During this time she was named a Ford Foundation fellow at the University of North Carolina's Institute of Medieval and Renaissance Studies and also served as a Fulbright lecturer at Jagellonian University in Krakow, Poland. She wrote several books, including *The Strange Critical Fortunes of Shakespeare's Timon of Athens, Children's Literature: A Module, Sharing Literature with Children,* and *Master Works of Children's Literature of the Seventeenth Century.*

OBITUARIES AND OTHER SOURCES:

PERIODICALS

New York Times, September 25, 1998, p. B10.

C

CABRERA, Jane 1968-

PERSONAL: Born July 30, 1968, in Berkhamsted, England; daughter of Bernard and Jill Johnson; married Julian Cabrera (a writer and disc jockey), August 29, 1995. *Education:* Watford College of Art, higher national diploma (graphic design; with distinction). *Politics:* "Green." *Avocational interests:* Environmental activism, travel, nature crafts, mural painting, cooking, country walks, and socializing with friends.

ADDRESSES: Home—7 Saint Marks Mansions, Balderton Street, London WIY ITG, England. *Office*— The Drawing Room, Panther House, 38 Mount Pleasant, London WCIX 40P, England.

CAREER: Apollo Arts and Antiques (magazine), art director, 1989-91; freelance graphic designer for clients including the British Broadcasting Corporation (BBC) Children's Books, Reed Children's Books, Dorling Kindersley, HarperCollins, Tiger Print (design group), and HIT Entertainment PLC, 1991-98; illustrator, 1997—. Speaker on children's book design and illustration at schools in England.

MEMBER: Amnesty International, Greenpeace, Friends of the Earth.

WRITINGS:

SELF-ILLUSTRATED; FICTION FOR CHILDREN

Cat's Colours, Reed, 1997, published in the United States as *Cat's Colors,* Dial (New York City), 1997.
Dog's Day, Reed, 1998.

Panda Big and Panda Small, Dorling Kindersley, 1998.

ILLUSTRATOR; FICTION FOR CHILDREN

Joyce Dunbar, *Egg Day,* David & Charles, in press.

Also contributor of illustrations to travel magazine.

WORK IN PROGRESS: Alien Visits Planet Shape, Egmont, expected publication in 1999; *Rory and the Lion,* Dorling Kindersley, expected publication in 1999; *Over in the Meadow,* David & Charles, expected publication in 2000.

SIDELIGHTS: Jane Cabrera commented: "I feel I am at the beginning of my illustrating career. My true love is children's books (and children), but I hope to expand into other fields.

"I've been working as a graphic designer for ten years—mainly on a freelance basis within children's publishing—and slowly I developed my illustration work and have now left design behind to fully concentrate on illustration and children's stories. But I still design my own books and will always be interested in typography. I work in a studio in Clarkenwell, London, sharing space and ideas with six other illustrators."

Cabrera's first self-illustrated book, *Cat's Colours* (published in the United States as *Cat's Colors*), showcases her design and typography experience, as well as her sense of playfulness. A *Publishers Weekly* critic appreciated the zeal with which Cat, a "sassily rendered kitten," is "put . . . through its paces," as she tries to find her favorite color. Pawing at the reader's sense of suspense, Cat presents "all the crayon-box basics . . . in lavishly brushed, eye-popping double-page paintings," lauded *Bulletin of the Center for Children's Books* critic Elizabeth Bush. What is Cat's preferred palette choice? "Is it Red?" asks a contented Cat, "Red is the rug where I snooze by the fire." Cat teases the reader with nine colors before revealing that orange is her favorite, because it's the color of her mother. *School Library Journal* writer Melissa Hudak promised that this "sweet ending" will be a "delightful surprise for toddlers." A *Publishers Weekly* reviewer commented on the book's visual impact, noting that "the book's playfulness extends to the typography . . . which skips and tumbles on the page." The reviewer also commended Cabrera's illustrations as full of "tactile vitality and a just-ripped-from-the-easel freshness." A *Books* critic praised *Cat's Colours* as "a vibrant, joyful, and engaging piece of work."

Working at numerous freelance positions and travelling throughout the world, Cabrera is an experiential student of life. At the young age of twenty-nine, she was credited by *Books* with "breaking the mould" when it came to illustrating picture books for preschoolers. And while Cabrera commented that travel and children are chief among her interests, she admitted she has another predilection: "My main passion is the environment. I am very concerned for the future of our planet and that of the children on it. I'm involved in a lot of green groups and believe that people need to take more responsibility for their own lives and environments, and escape the clasp of mass commercialization led by big multinationals. I feel it's time to put people and nature before profits, before it's too late. My husband and I try to live a low-impact lifestyle as much as it's possible within a big city. We try to consume less and monitor what we do consume by establishing the source of the product and the impact its production and destruction (through waste disposal) have had on the environment and the country of origin (especially important in developing countries).

"We were fortunate enough to have a one-year honeymoon! We travelled on a low budget through India, Nepal, and Southeast Asia. This trip reinforced my beliefs that we live in one world and that our actions in developed countries directly affect the poverty in less-fortunate countries. It was also incredibly inspiring, and I filled many sketchbooks.

"My ambition is to produce children's environmental books. Not only would the stories be environmental, but the production would be too—from recycled/sustainable paper, to non-toxic inks, and the production workers would be treated ethically.

"My other hobbies include mural painting for toddlers' bedrooms, life drawing, long country walks, and cooking and eating. (I'm a vegetarian of fourteen years and a big fan of organic food.) I also enjoy reading; collecting children's books; making mobiles, picture frames, blinds, etc. from collected nature finds (driftwood, leaves, and even broken pottery and nineteenth-century clay pipes from the River Thames); but my main hobby is socializing with my friends!"

BIOGRAPHICAL/CRITICAL SOURCES:

BOOKS

Cabrera, Jane, *Cat's Colors,* Dial, 1997.

PERIODICALS

Books, June, 1997, p. 21.
Bulletin of the Center for Children's Books, July, 1997, pp. 388-389.
Children's Book Review, August, 1997, p. 158.
Kirkus Reviews, January 15, 1997, p. 138.
Publishers Weekly, April 21, 1997, p. 70.
School Librarian, August, 1997, p. 130.
School Library Journal, May, 1997, p. 93.*

* * *

CALBERT, Cathleen 1955-

PERSONAL: Born June 2, 1955, in Jackson, MI; daughter of Emile and Mary Helen (Weickart) Calbert; married Christopher Lewis Mayo, August 1, 1992. *Education:* University of California at Berkeley, B.A., 1977; Syracuse University, M.A., 1984; University of Houston, Ph.D., 1989. *Politics:* Liberal.

ADDRESSES: Home—563 King Road, Tiverton, RI 02878. *Office*—Rhode Island College, 600 Mt. Pleasant, Providence, RI 02908. *E-mail*—ccalbert@brainiac.com.

CAREER: Poet. Rhode Island College, Providence, RI, assistant professor, 1990-95; associate professor of English, 1995—.

MEMBER: Modern Language Association, Associated Writing Programs, Writers' Union, Poetry Society of America.

AWARDS, HONORS: Discovery Prize, *Nation,* 1990; Gordon Barber Memorial Award, Poetry Society of America, 1994; Bullis-Kizer Award, *Poetry Northwest,* 1998.

WRITINGS:

My Summer As a Bride: Poems, Riverstone (West Chester, PA), 1995.
Lessons in Space (poetry), University Press of Florida (Gainesville), 1997.
Bad Judgment: Poems, Sarabunde Books (Louisville, KY), 1999.

Has contributed poems to publications including *New Republic, Nation, Paris Review, Harvard Review, Ploughshares,* and to *The Best American Poetry, 1995.*

SIDELIGHTS: Cathleen Calbert is a creative writing professor at Rhode Island College and a working poet. Calbert's poems have appeared in various periodicals such as the *New Republic, Paris Review, Harvard Review,* and *Ploughshares.* She also has two books to her credit.

Her first collection of poems, *My Summer As a Bride,* was published in 1995. A mere two years later *Lessons in Space* was published. Literary observer Richard Howard, quoted on The University Press of Florida's online service, compared Calbert's poems to "*pomes,* indeed, delectable within the rind, but guarded, sly." In the title poem to *Lessons in Space,* Calbert explores the imagery of the 1986 space shuttle disaster: "Once again, a bad year for the / skies. / Ice on the wings. Terrorist/activities. / The shuttle shooting stars, a/white blossoming, / newscasters suddenly speaking / of the face of God." The University Press of Florida's online service reviewer described Calbert's poems as "sudden blooms in provisional, temporary spaces," noting that Calbert gives meaning to the "small details" in life.

BIOGRAPHICAL/CRITICAL SOURCES:

OTHER

Sarabande Books, www.SarabandBooks.org (January 18, 1999).

University Press of Florida, http://nersp.nerdc.ufl.edu /~upf/spring /calbert.html (September 24, 1998).

*   *   *

CANN, Kate 1954-

PERSONAL: Born June 9, 1954, in London, England; daughter of Eric (an engineer) and Irene (a homemaker; maiden name, Waller) Waller; married Jefferson Cann (a marketing director), October 21, 1978; children: Hester, John. *Education:* Kent University, B.A., 1977, M.A., 1978. *Politics:* "Left." *Religion:* "Broad." *Avocational interests:* "Running, reading, the theatre, my dog, long conversations, wine, and most of all, friends and family."

ADDRESSES: *Home*—34 Denton Rd., East Twickenham, Middlesex, TWI 2HQ, England. *Agent*—A.P. Watt, 20 John St., London, WCIN 2DR, England.

CAREER: Time-Life Books, London, England, copyeditor, 1979-83. Freelance editor; writer.

WRITINGS:

FICTION; FOR YOUNG ADULTS

Diving In, Women's Press (London), 1996.
In the Deep End, Women's Press, 1997.
Sink or Swim, Women's Press, 1998.
Footloose, Scholastic, Inc. (New York City), 1999.

NONFICTION; FOR YOUNG ADULTS

Living in the World, illustrated by Derek Matthews, F. Watts (New York City), 1997.

WORK IN PROGRESS: "I'm interested in doing books for ten- to twelve-year-old boys. I have one on the back burner I hope to finish—kind of Mad Max meets Iron John! There's very little around for these sophisticated, macho, reluctant readers."

SIDELIGHTS: Kate Cann commented: "I got the idea for my first novel, *Diving In,* when I was working as an editor of teen books. Quite a few of these books, naturally, dealt with love and sexuality, and they fell into two distinct camps. Happy relationships were trashy, fantasy romances. More literate books took a distinctly gloomy view—abuse, unwanted pregnancy, rape.

"I started to think about writing a book that treated the whole theme of young sexuality with depth, in a *positive* and realistic way. I wanted an honest, intelligent character; I wanted to stress the emotional power of a first sexual relationship.

"As I did my research I became increasingly depressed with the double standard in our society. We bombard kids with sexual images in advertising, music videos, and films, yet sex education lessons are often just basic biology lessons. Where are the discussions about feelings—where is the idea that sex can be a fulfilling, holistic experience, not a thing apart but something with implications for the whole of your life?

"I was delighted when the Women's Press agreed to publish *Diving In;* less delighted when they said I'd have to tone down some of the more explicit passages, or school and library sales would be affected. Then the book was picked up for a teen-magazine promotion, and the response from readers was so encouraging the publishers asked me to go ahead with the sequel, *In the Deep End,* which talks directly about a girl's first full sexual relationship. Again, the response to the book has been great; it is going to be reprinted, and sales of foreign rights are going well— Denmark, Italy, and Germany so far! Now that *Sink or Swim* has completed the trilogy, there is discussion about turning it into a television series, which would be wonderful."

Cann drew from personal experience, as both a mother and editor, to develop exactly the kind of book she had hoped to write. *Diving In,* her first novel, became the start of a trilogy that follows the relationship of Colette "Coll" and Art. The sexual pressure that Coll faces during the course of the relationship is not easily categorized, but according to *Books for Keeps* critic Val Randall, it is portrayed with "realism and sensitivity"—the very qualities that Cann had strived most ardently to convey. Randall's review of *In the Deep End,* the sequel to *Diving In,* is even more enthusiastic, as she again lauded the convincing, sympathetic, and knowing way that the author captures her young adult characters. "This book," enthused Randall, "contains some of the best writing about love and sex that I have ever read in a book for young people." Randall concluded that *In the Deep End* addresses teenage sexuality "in a way which is both emotionally stunning and morally unshakeable."

Commenting on her motivation for addressing the topic of sexuality within young adult fiction, Cann

continued: "Again and again studies show us that young people who have access to information and discussion about sex delay their first-time experiences, have fewer pregnancies and sexually transmitted diseases. I hope my books contribute to the beneficial results that sex education is known to have on young adults."

Cann described her 1999 novel *Footloose* as "a teen novel about a wonderful cataclysmic summer in Greece,"

BIOGRAPHICAL/CRITICAL SOURCES:

PERIODICALS

Books for Keeps, January, 1997, p. 27; March, 1998, p. 26.
School Library Journal, October, 1997, p. 131; January, 1998, p. 120.
Times Educational Supplement, November 29, 1996, p. 10.*

* * *

CAPONIGRO, Jeffrey R. 1957-

PERSONAL: Born August 13, 1957, in Kankakee, IL; son of Ralph A. (a finance consultant) and Barbara A. (an artist) Caponigro; married, wife's name Ellen C. (a homemaker), October 15, 1982; children: Nicholas, Michael. *Ethnicity:* "Caucasian." *Education:* Central Michigan University, B.A., 1979.

ADDRESSES: Office—Caponigro Public Relations, Inc., 4000 Town Center, Southfield, MI 48075; fax 248-355-5747. *E-mail*—jcap@caponigro.com.

CAREER: Casey Communications Management, Inc., Southfield, MI, president and chief executive officer, prior to 1995; Caponigro Public Relations, Inc., Southfield, president and chief executive officer, 1995—. Walsh College, member of board of trustees; Metropolitan Affairs Coalition of Detroit, member of board of directors.

MEMBER: Public Relations Society of America, National Investor Relations Institute.

AWARDS, HONORS: Silver Anvil, Public Relations Society of America, 1988.

WRITINGS:

The Crisis Counselor: The Executive's Guide to Avoiding, Managing, and Thriving on Crises That Occur in All Businesses, Barker Business Books, 1998.

Work represented in anthologies, including *Best Sports Stories—1978,* Dutton (New York City), 1978.

* * *

CAROSSA, Hans 1878-1956

PERSONAL: Born December 15, 1878, in Bad-Toelz, Bavaria; died September 12, 1956, in Rittsteig; son of Karl (a physician) and Maria (a schoolteacher; maiden name, Voggenreiter) Carossa; married Valerie Endlicher, 1907 (deceased, 1940); married Hedwig Kerber, 1943 (deceased, February 22, 1956); children: (first marriage) Hans Wilhelm, (second marriage) Eva. *Education:* Studied medicine at the Universities of Munich and Nuremberg, 1898-1903; University of Leipzig, M.D., 1903.

CAREER: Writer and physician. Practiced medicine in Munich, Nuremberg, and Passau, Bavaria, beginning 1903. *Wartime service:* Served as a German medical officer during World War I.

AWARDS, HONORS: Italian San Remo Prize for outstanding authors, 1938; awarded various literary prizes in Germany and Switzerland; received honorary doctorate from University of Cologne, 1938, and University of Munich, 1948.

WRITINGS:

POETRY

Stella mystica: Traum eines Toren, Meyer (Berlin), 1907.
Gedichte, Insel (Leipzig), 1910, enlarged edition published as *Gesammelte Gedichte,* 1948.

NOVELS

Doktor Buergers Ende: Letzte Blaetter eines Tagebuchs, Insel (Weisbaden), 1913, also published as *Die Schicksale Doktor Buergers,* 1930.

Der Arzt Gion: Eine Erzaehlung, Insel, 1931; translation by Agnes Neill Scott published as *Doctor Gion,* R. O. Ballou (New York City), 1933.
Geheimnisse des reifen Lebens: Aus den Aufzeichnungen Angermanns, Insel, 1936.

AUTOBIOGRAPHIES

Eine Kindheit, Insel, 1922, translation published as *A Childhood,* J. Cape & H. Smith (London), 1930; referred to collectively, along with *Rumaenisches Tagebuch, Das Jahr der schoenen Taeuschungen,* and *Der Tag des jungen Arztes,* as "Jugendgeschichte."
Rumaenisches Tagebuch, Insel, 1924, published as *Tagebuch im Kriege,* 1934; translation by Agnes Neill Scott published as *A Roumanian Diary,* Knopf (New York), 1930.
Verwandlungen einer Jugend, Insel, 1928, translated by Scott along with *Eine Kindheit* and included in *Boyhood and Youth,* Putnam (New York City), 1932; referred to collectively, along with *Eine Kindheit, Das Jahr der schoenen Taeuschungen,* and *Der Tag des jungen Arztes,* as "Jugendgeschichte."
Fuehrung und Geleit: Ein Lebensgedenkbuch, Insel, 1933.
Das Jahr der schoenen Taeuschungen, Insel, 1941; translation published as *Year of Sweet Illusions,* 1950; referred to collectively, along with *Eine Kindheit, Verwandlungen einer Jugend,* and *Der Tag des jungen Arztes,* as "Jugendgeschichte."
Ungleiche Welten, Insel, 1951.
Der Tag des jungen Arztes: Aus dem Schlussband einer Jugendgeschichte, Post-Presse (Offenbach), 1953, enlarged edition, 1955; referred to collectively, along with *Eine Kindheit, Verwandlungen einer Jugend,* and *Das Jahr der schoenen Taeuschungen,* as "Jugendgeschichte."

OTHER

Gesammelte Werke (novels, autobiography, and poetry), 2 volumes, 1949-50.
Geschichte einer Jugend (autobiography; contains *Eine Kindheit, Verwandlungen einer Jugend, Das Jahr der schoenen Taeuschungen,* and *Der Tag des jungen Arztes: Aus dem Schlussband einer Jugendgeschichte*), Insel (Wiesbaden), 1957.

SIDELIGHTS: Hans Carossa is best known for novels and works of autobiography that express his search for self-realization and his attempts to reconcile his conflicting ambitions as both a doctor and a writer.

These works reflect Carossa's admiration for Johann Wolfgang von Goethe, particularly Goethe's advocacy of individualism and the contemplative life. Critics have praised Carossa for his precise and lucid prose style, for his revival of Goethean thought, and for the humane and highly spiritual qualities that characterize his life and works.

Carossa was born in 1878 in Bad-Toelz, Bavaria. Both his father and grandfather were physicians, the profession which Carossa himself later chose. On his fifteenth birthday Carossa's parents presented him with a fifteen-volume edition of Goethe's works. Between 1898 and 1903 Carossa studied medicine in Munich, Nuremburg, and Leipzig, receiving his M.D. from the University of Leipzig in 1903. Carossa inherited his father's medical practice in 1906 and worked as a doctor in Bavaria for the rest of his life.

In 1907 Carossa published his first work, the poetry collection *Stella Mystica.* That year also marked the beginning of his correspondence with Austrian writer Hugo von Hofmannsthal, who became his mentor. Carossa published his second volume of poetry, *Gedichte,* in 1910 and for the remainder of his life continued to publish poetry on a regular basis. *Doktor Burgers Ende,* his first novel, was published in 1913. During World War I Carossa served as a medical officer on the eastern and western fronts, and his wartime experiences were recorded in his 1924 volume, *Rumaenisches Tagebuch,* (translated in 1930 as *A Roumanian Diary*). During the 1920s and early 1930s Carossa produced three more works of autobiography and the novel *Der Arzt Gion: Eine Erzaehlung (Doctor Gion),* published in Germany in 1931 and translated into English in 1933. The Nazi party's rise to power in Germany and its claim that nazism was a pure expression of Goethean thought prompted Carossa to write two works, a novel and a volume of autobiography, that condemned the party's policies and tenets. In the 1936 novel *Geheimnisse des reifen Lebens: Aus den Aufzeichnungen Angermanns* Carossa described an unnamed country in which young men dressed in black uniforms conduct mass arrests. Although the autobiographical 1941 volume *Das Jahr der schonen Tauschungen* concerns the German people's delusions of grandeur in 1900, critics believe that Carossa intended the work to be a thinly disguised critique of the Nazis' delusions of 1940. Carossa refused to give public sanction to the party's programs and institutions despite the Nazis' persistent demands for such support. However, he occasionally made concessions in return for the release of prisoners, such as Jewish writer Alfred

Mombert, from concentration camps. In his 1951 autobiographical work, *Ungleiche Welten,* Carossa recounted his life in nazi Germany. Carossa completed *Der Tag des jungen Arztes,* the final book in his autobiographical sequence, in 1955, one year before his death.

Carossa's novels and autobiographies focus on moral and spiritual issues. In these works the overarching theme is the importance of achieving a synthesis of one's artistic aspirations and one's responsibilities to society. The autobiographical works *Eine Kindheit (A Childhood),* published in 1922, and *Verwandlungen einer Jugend (Boyhood and Youth),* published in 1928, trace the development of Carossa's imaginative traits which eventually culminate in his desire to become an artist. Parallel to his artistic development is the growing awareness of his responsibility to society and the importance of self-sacrifice. In a review of *A Childhood* for *New York Herald Tribune Books,* William Maxwell declared: "So actual is this childhood that one must attribute to the author a power as potent as animates certain moments of childhood."

Carossa's final volume of autobiography, *Der Tag des jungen Arztes,* concerns the conflict between his life as a doctor and his life as a writer. *German Life & Letters* contributor A. V. Subiotto remarked: "Carossa has a finely-sharpened consciousness of the processes which determine the spiritual development of an individual, an awareness of childhood, youth and manhood as stages within one all-embracing unity and continuity in which the significance of each stage cannot be fully appreciated independently of its preceding and succeeding stages." In his fiction Carossa most clearly articulated this theme, particularly in *Doktor Burgers Ende,* a novel about a young doctor whose inability to reconcile his longings for a life devoted to art with the ethical demands of a medical career leads to suicide. Nevertheless Carossa's prose works convey a strong sense of optimism, a quality especially evident in the novel *Doctor Gion,* in which the protagonist succeeds in healing his patients both physically and spiritually. Dr. Gion guides his patients, whom critics contend are symbols of post-World War I Germany, to an understanding of the principles, such as composure and detachment in the face of turmoil, on which he believes life should be based.

In his novels and autobiographies Carossa focused on incidents of everyday life, avoiding the depiction of dramatic events or intense emotion. For example, *Doktor Burgers Ende* presents a first-person account of a doctor's daily routine, revealing the mental suffering of the troubled main character only indirectly. While some critics have argued that the anecdotes that comprise much of Carossa's work are occasionally superfluous to his larger themes, others find his meticulous attention to mundane incidents praiseworthy because in them, they argue, he observes significance in details that many writers overlook. In a review of *A Childhood* and *Boyhood and Youth*, *Bookman* contributor Edwin Muir asserted that out of seemingly trifling events Carossa "constructed . . . a more complete and proportioned image of the world than any other writer of his time."

BIOGRAPHICAL/CRITICAL SOURCES:

BOOKS

Hofrichter, Ruth J., *Three Poets and Reality: Study of a German, an Austrian, and a Swiss Contemporary Lyricist,* Yale University Press (New Haven, CT), 1942, pp. 9-41.

PERIODICALS

Bookman (New York), December, 1930, pp. 404-408.
German Life & Letters, April, 1951, pp. 171-175; April, 1953, pp. 192-195; October, 1957, pp. 34-40; July, 1979, pp. 327-331.
Hudson Review, summer, 1959, pp. 252-253.
Modern Language Review, April, 1965, pp. 229-232.
Modern Languages, March, 1975, pp. 17-21.
New German Studies, summer, 1979, pp. 91-104; autumn, 1979, pp. 205-206.
New York Herald Tribune Books, April 10, 1932, p. 2.
New York Times Book Review, June 4, 1933, p. 6.
Spectator, April 21, 1933, p. 575.*

* * *

CARR, Jonathan

PERSONAL: Male.

ADDRESSES: Agent—c/o Overlook Press, 149 Wooster, 2nd Floor, New York, NY 10012.

CAREER: British foreign correspondent; writer for *Economist;* West German financial correspondent for *Financial Times.*

WRITINGS:

Helmut Schmidt: Helmsman of Germany, St. Martin's Press (New York City), 1985.
Mahler, Overlook Press, 1997.

SIDELIGHTS: Jonathan Carr is known for his biographical works. In 1985 he published *Helmut Schmidt: Helmsman of Germany,* a biography of West Germany's chancellor during the 1970s and early 1980s. Carr charts the life of Schmidt, whom *New York Times Book Review* contributor Robert Gerald Livingston deemed "far and away West German's most popular political personality. Prior to assuming the chancellorship, Schmidt held ministerial posts in fields ranging from economics to armed services. The volume provides details of Schmidt's most significant political achievements, including reforms to the West German military and the formation of the European Monetary System, which was intended as an alternative to the influence of United States financial policies. Schmidt's career came undone in 1983 when his own Social Democratic Party voted in opposition of his defense policy involving the deployment of United States missiles.

Livingston, in his *New York Times Book Review* assessment, deemed *Helmut Schmidt* a "brisk biography [that] is precisely focused and eminently readable." Henrik Bering-Jensen, meanwhile, wrote in *American Spectator* that Carr's book constitutes a "eulogistic" biography and declared that it "tends to gloss over Schmidt's failure to counter the forces of German restlessness that grew steadily in the 1970s." Bering-Jensen added, however, that "because it can be said to represent the "conventional wisdom' on Schmidt, the book deserves close scrutiny."

Carr is also the author of *Mahler,* a biography of the Austrian composer and conductor who lived from 1860 to 1911. While charting Mahler's life and achievements, including controversial terms as the leader of orchestras in Vienna and New York City, Carr also addresses various legends about the great musician, including the tale that Mahler, believing that ninth symphonies were cursed, avoided writing one and composed, instead, the song-cycle *Song of the Earth.* This was followed by a composition of what would be, essentially, a tenth symphony. Carr notes the absurdity of this tale by relating that Mahler acknowledged the ensuing symphony—the one written after *Song of the Earth*—as his ninth. Interestingly, that ninth symphony would become his last completed work. *New York Times* reviewer Richard

Bernstein described Carr's *Mahler* as an "intelligent and absorbing biography."

BIOGRAPHICAL/CRITICAL SOURCES:

PERIODICALS

American Spectator, July, 1985, pp. 42-44.
New York Times, January 21, 1998, p. E9.
New York Times Book Review, July 14, 1985, p. 18.*

*   *   *

CARTER, Betty 1944-

PERSONAL: Born in 1944.

ADDRESSES: Agent—c/o American Library Association, 50 East Huron St., Chicago, IL 60611.

CAREER: Librarian and educator.

WRITINGS:

(With Richard F. Abrahamson and the Committee on the Senior High School Booklist of the National Council of Teachers of English) *Books For You: A Booklist for Senior High Students,* The National Council of Teachers of English (Urbana, IL), 1988.
(With Richard F. Abrahamson) *Nonfiction for Young Adults: From Delight to Wisdom,* Oryx Press (Phoenix, AZ), 1990.
Best Books for Young Adults: The Selections, the History, the Romance, American Library Association (Chicago), 1994.

SIDELIGHTS: Betty Carter compiled outstanding books for readers aged twelve to eighteen in *Best Books for Young Adults: The Selections, the History, the Romance,* a guide for librarians and media specialists responsible for collections and recommendations for teen readers. The first part of the book provides a history of the selection process. Carter draws upon American Library Association (ALA) archives in revealing the history of the lists beginning with *Books for Young People, 1930* to the current publication. Originally, the list consisted of adult books recommended for teen readers, but it now covers fiction and nonfiction for the range of teen readers. In the second section, past books selected are listed by author within each year from 1966 to the present. The "Best of the Best" is a list of titles selected at previous ALA preconferences and published as pamphlets. Nominations are broken down into categories, including multicultural, historical, and nonfiction. Carter found imaginative fiction or fantasy books were under-represented, considering their growing popularity with teens, and in this edition she focused on the genre.

"Most professionals who work with young adult reading will thank Betty Carter for making our job easier and for making us think about it," wrote Cathi Dunn MacRae in the *Wilson Library Bulletin.* Jennifer Comi Ellard wrote in *ARBA* that the book "affords an interesting glimpse into the development, growth, and . . . evolution of a dynamic committee, and . . . provides a premier reading list for young adults."

BIOGRAPHICAL/CRITICAL SOURCES:

PERIODICALS

Adoles, fall, 1995, p. 755.
A Lib, July, 1994, p. 664.
ARBA, 1995, p. 488.
Booklist, May 1, 1994, p. 1611; April 1, 1996, p. 1380.
Book Rpt, November, 1994, p. 33; January, 1995, p. 20.
Bulletin of the Center for Children's Books, October, 1994, p. 72.
Emerging Lib, March, 1995, p. 42.
Horn Book, May, 1995, p. 382.
JOYS, fall, 1994, p. 89.
J Read, December, 1994, p. 335.
Kliatt, September, 1994, p. 24.
New Ad, winter, 1995, p. 45.
School Library Journal, August, 1994, p. 16.
SLMQ, fall, 1994, p. 66.
Voice of Youth Advocates, February, 1995, p. 368.
Wilson Library Bulletin, October, 1994, pp. 118-19.*

*   *   *

CASCONE, A. G.
  See CASCONE, Annette

CASCONE, A. G.
  See CASCONE, Gina

          *   *   *

CASCONE, Annette 1960-
  (A. G. Cascone, a joint pseudonym)

PERSONAL: Born November 1, 1960, in Trenton, NJ; daughter of Peter P., Jr. (an attorney) and Shirley (Shelmet) Cascone.

ADDRESSES: Office—A. G. Cascone, Inc., 1100 Green St., Iselin, NJ 08830. *Agent*—Marcy Posner, William Morris Agency, 1325 Avenue of the Americas, New York, NY 10019. *E-mail*—agcascone@bookwire.com.

CAREER: Children's book writer.

WRITINGS:

FOR CHILDREN; WITH SISTER, GINA CASCONE, UNDER JOINT PSEUDONYM A. G. CASCONE

The Attack of the Aqua Apes (in "R. L. Stine's Ghosts of Fear Street" series), Minstrel, 1995.
Eye of the Fortuneteller (in "R. L. Stine's Ghosts of Fear Street" series), Minstrel, 1996.

FOR CHILDREN; WITH SISTER, GINA CASCONE, UNDER JOINT PSEUDONYM A. G. CASCONE; "DEADTIME STORIES" SERIES

Terror in Tiny Town, Troll (New York City), 1996.
Invasion of the Appleheads, Troll, 1996.
Along Came a Spider, Troll, 1996.
Ghost Knight, Troll, 1996.
Revenge of the Goblins, Troll, 1996.
Little Magic Shop of Horrors, Troll, 1997.
It Came from the Deep, Troll, 1997.
Grave Secrets, Troll, 1997.
Mirror, Mirror, Troll, 1997.
Grandpa's Monster Movies, Troll, 1997.
Nightmare on Planet X, Troll, 1997.
Welcome to the Terror-Go-Round, Troll, 1997.
The Beast of Baskerville, Troll, 1997.
Trapped in Tiny Town, Troll, 1997.
Cyber Scare, Troll, 1997.
Night of the Pet Zombies, Troll, 1997.
Faerie Tale, Troll, 1997.

FOR YOUNG ADULTS; WITH SISTER, GINA CASCONE, UNDER JOINT PSEUDONYM A. G. CASCONE

In a Crooked Little House, Troll, 1994.
If He Hollers, Avon (New York City), 1995.
There's No Place Like Home, Troll, 1997.

SCREENPLAYS; WITH SISTER, GINA CASCONE

Mirror, Mirror, Orphan Eyes Academy Entertainment, 1991.

OTHER

Work has been translated into Danish, French, and Italian. Also co-author of several songs for Island Records.

SIDELIGHTS: Annette Cascone does most of her writing with her sister Gina, under the joint pseudonym A. G. Cascone. She asked, in a Troll publicity flier, "What could be better than sitting around all day, making up stories with one of my very best friends?" However, it wasn't always so easy being friends with big sister, Gina. Thanks to Gina, Annette was convinced that her mother had purchased her "from a band of gypsies for fifty cents," and that the only career she "could ever hope to have was with Ringling Bros. and Barnum & Bailey Circus." As an adult, though, Annette is happy with her career choice and doesn't regret ceding her position as family clown to her younger sister, Elise.

Telling stories was the one thing that guaranteed a unified front among the young Cascone sisters. When they got in trouble, the girls found that their best defense against punishment was to make their parents "laugh, or make them cry, or scare the bejeebers out of them." That was the tactic the sisters used, for example, when they explained that they were hours late for dinner because they'd been abducted by aliens, and when they solemnly swore that a burglar broke into the house and was responsible for coloring in all the flowers on the brand new wallpaper. Annette and Gina refined their creative method of defense into an art form that has afforded them great success as writers. "These days, we get to tell our crazy stories to lots of other people," they say, "and it's a wonderful thing to be able to make a living doing something we love."

Written with sister Gina under the name A. G. Cascone, Annette Cascone's first book for young adults enrolls the reader in the elite, but hazardous atmosphere of Huntington Prep. In *A Crooked Little House,* a killer who mysteriously calls himself Iggy-Boy has claimed another victim—this time a teacher. The authors introduce a compelling group of characters, including students and school employees, every one of whom could be a potential victim or the suspect himself. "[T]he authors," commented a *Publishers Weekly* reviewer, "add enough clever false leads and snippets of suspense to keep the plot sprinting along." Claiming the book rises above the typical "teen-slasher" thriller, *School Library Journal* critic Rosalyn Pierini asserted that "mystery, suspense, and danger strengthened by skillful characterization, plotting, and a strong sense of place make for addictive reading."

BIOGRAPHICAL/CRITICAL SOURCES:

PERIODICALS

Children's Bookwatch, December, 1996, p. 65; February, 1997, p. 4; March, 1997, p. 3; July, 1997, p. 5.
Journal of Adolescent and Adult Literature, November, 1997, p. 211.
Kliatt, September, 1995, p. 9; May, 1996, p. 6.
Publishers Weekly, November 14, 1994, p. 70.
School Library Journal, April, 1995, p. 150.

OTHER

Troll Publishing publicity materials, c. 1998.*

* * *

CASCONE, Gina 1955-
(A. G. Cascone, a joint pseudonym)

PERSONAL: Born December 14, 1955, in Trenton, NJ; daughter of Peter P., Jr. (an attorney) and Shirley (Shelmet) Cascone.

ADDRESSES: Office—A. G. Cascone, Inc., 1100 Green St., Iselin, NJ 08830. *Agent*—Marcy Posner, William Morris Agency, 1325 Avenue of the Americas, New York, NY 10019. *E-mail*—agcascone@bookwire.com.

CAREER: Children's book writer.

WRITINGS:

FOR CHILDREN; WITH SISTER, ANNETTE CASCONE, UNDER JOINT PSEUDONYM A. G. CASCONE

The Attack of the Aqua Apes ("R. L. Stine's Ghosts of Fear Street" series), Minstrel, 1995.
Eye of the Fortuneteller ("R. L. Stine's Ghosts of Fear Street" series), Minstrel, 1996.

FOR CHILDREN; WITH SISTER, ANNETTE CASCONE, UNDER JOINT PSEUDONYM A. G. CASCONE; "DEADTIME STORIES" SERIES

Terror in Tiny Town, Troll (New York City), 1996.
Invasion of the Appleheads, Troll (New York City, 1996.
Along Came a Spider, Troll (New York City), 1996.
Ghost Knight, Troll (New York City), 1996.
Revenge of the Goblins, Troll (New York City), 1996.
Little Magic Shop of Horrors, Troll (New York City), 1997.
It Came from the Deep, Troll (New York City), 1997.
Grave Secrets, Troll (New York City), 1997.
Mirror, Mirror, Troll (New York City), 1997.
Grandpa's Monster Movies, Troll (New York City), 1997.
Nightmare on Planet X, Troll (New York City), 1997.
Welcome to the Terror-Go-Round, Troll (New York City), 1997.
The Beast of Baskerville, Troll (New York City), 1997.
Trapped in Tiny Town, Troll (New York City), 1997.
Cyber Scare, Troll (New York City), 1997.
Night of the Pet Zombies, Troll (New York City), 1997.
Faerie Tale, Troll (New York City), 1997.

FOR YOUNG ADULTS; WITH ANNETTE CASCONE UNDER JOINT PSEUDONYM A. G. CASCONE

In a Crooked Little House, Troll (New York City), 1994.
If He Hollers, Avon (New York City), 1995.
There's No Place Like Home, Troll (New York City), 1997.

OTHER

Pagan Babies and Other Catholic Memories, St. Martin's Press (New York City), 1982.

Mother's Little Helper, St. Martin's Press (New York City), 1986.

(With sister, Annette Cascone) *Mirror, Mirror* (screenplay) Orphan Eyes Academy Entertainment, 1991.

Author's work has been translated into Danish, French, and Italian.

SIDELIGHTS: Gina Cascone does most of her writing with her sister Annette, under the joint pseudonym A. G. Cascone. The sisters said in a Troll publicity flier that while writing, they often seem to "share the same brain." Sharing anything now seems amusing to Gina and her sister, who grew up as most siblings do—hating to share. Even as children, the sisters shared a love of books, but the books themselves were a different story. Gina was enrolled in "every [mail order] book club that existed" and remembers waiting on her porch in anticipation of the postman's delivery of each new adventure. When Gina occasionally missed the postman, her little sister Annette would beat her to the new book and color in it.

The Cascone sisters may have fought over reading stories, but they often conspired to make them up in order to "talk [their] way out of trouble." With a mother who "swore that she had ESP and another pair of eyes in the back of her head," and a father who was a criminal attorney, the girls knew that they could not make their case with mere facts, so they aimed to "make [their parents] laugh, or make them cry, or scare the bejeebers out of them."

The defiant sisters have grown up and, as adults, are grateful for their parents' sound advice to "do what you love, and the money will follow." "It's a wonderful thing," said Gina and Annette, "to be able to make a living doing something we love."

For more information on Gina Cascone's work, see the *CA* sketch for Annette Cascone.

BIOGRAPHICAL/CRITICAL SOURCES:

PERIODICALS

Children's Bookwatch, December, 1996, p. 65; February, 1997, p. 4; March, 1997, p. 3; July, 1997, p. 5.
Journal of Adolescent and Adult Literature, November, 1997, p. 211.

Kliatt, September, 1995, p. 9; May, 1996, p. 6.
Publishers Weekly, November 14, 1994, p. 70.
School Library Journal, April, 1995, p. 150.

OTHER

Troll Publishing publicity materials, c. 1998.*

* * *

CAUDILL, (Charles) Edward 1953-

PERSONAL: Born August 16, 1953, in Rowan County, KY. *Education:* University of Cincinnati, B.A., 1975; Ohio State University, M.A., 1977; University of North Carolina at Chapel Hill, Ph.D., 1986.

ADDRESSES: Home—11220 Sonja Dr., Knoxville, TN 37922. *Office*—330 Communications Bldg., University of Tennessee, Knoxville, TN 37996.

CAREER: Columbus Citizen-Journal, Columbus, OH, copy editor, 1977-83; University of Tennessee, Knoxville, professor of journalism, 1985—.

WRITINGS:

Darwin in the Press: The Evolution of an Idea, Lawrence Erlbaum (Hillsdale, NJ), 1989.
(Contributor) Perry Ashley, editor, *American Newspaper Publishers, 1951-1990,* Gale (Detroit, MI), 1993.
(Contributor) Donald Shaw, M. McCombs, and J. Kerr, editors, *Patterns: Reporting beyond News Events,* Longman (New York City), 1996.
Darwinian Myths: The Legends and Misuses of a Theory, University of Tennessee Press (Knoxville), 1997.
(Contributor) McCombs and Shaw, editors, *Communication and Democracy: Exploring the Intellectual Frontiers in Agenda-Setting Theory,* Erlbaum, 1997.
(Contributor) Michael Singletary and Gerald Stone, editors, *Clarifying Communication Theory,* Iowa State University Press (Ames), 1999.

Contributor to periodicals, including *Journalism Educator, Journalism Quarterly,* and *Journal of the History of Ideas.*

CAVE, Eric M. 1965-

PERSONAL: Born November 12, 1965, in Lund, Sweden; U.S. citizen; son of M. Donald (a professor) and Joan Adele (a social worker; maiden name, Winzler; present surname, Baltz) Cave; companion of Alyson A. Gill (an art historian); children: Meghan Fiona. *Ethnicity:* "Scotch-Irish." *Education:* Trinity University, San Antonio, TX, B.A., 1988; University of California, Irvine, M.A., 1990, Ph.D., 1994. *Politics:* Independent. *Avocational interests:* Motorcycles, horses, running.

ADDRESSES: Home—P.O. Box 3429, State University, AR 72467. *Office*—Department of English and Philosophy, Arkansas State University, P.O. Box 1890, State University, AR 72467; fax 870-972-2795. *E-mail*—ecave@toltec.astate.edu.

CAREER: Union College, Schenectady, NY, visiting assistant professor of humanities, 1994-95; Arkansas State University, State University, assistant professor of philosophy, 1995—.

MEMBER: American Philosophical Association, Society for the Philosophy of Sex and Love, Phi Beta Kappa.

AWARDS, HONORS: Justine Lambert Prize in Social Justice, University of California, Irvine, for paper titled "Rationality and the Sense of Justice."

WRITINGS:

Preferring Justice: Rationality, Self-Transformation, and the Sense of Justice, Westview Press (Boulder, CO), 1998.

Contributor to periodicals, including *Dialogue, Theory and Decision,* and *Philosophical Studies.*

WORK IN PROGRESS: Marital Pluralism; research on the philosophy of sex and love.

* * *

CHANG, Maria Hsia 1950-

PERSONAL: Born March 17, 1950, in Hong Kong; naturalized U.S. citizen; daughter of Pao-en (a teacher, editor, and publisher) and Huang-lu (a teacher) Chang; married A. James Gregor (a professor), December 22, 1987; children: Charles Elmo, Gabriel Raphael. *Ethnicity:* "Chinese." *Education:* University of California, Berkeley, B.A., 1973, M.A., 1975, Ph.D., 1983. *Politics:* Republican. *Religion:* Agnostic. *Avocational interests:* Arts and crafts, physical fitness, making jewelry.

ADDRESSES: Home—Reno, NV. *Office*—Department of Political Science, University of Nevada, Reno, NV 89557-0060; fax 702-784-1473. *E-mail*—mariac@scs.unr.edu.

CAREER: Washington State University, Pullman, visiting assistant professor of political science, 1980-82; University of Puget Sound, Tacoma, WA, assistant professor of political science, 1983-89; University of Nevada, Reno, professor of political science, 1989—. U.S. Office of Personnel Management, lecturer at national security seminars, 1992—; Diversity Coalition for an Immigration Moratorium, member of national advisory board, 1995-97; Carrying Capacity Network, member of board of advisers, 1997—; consultant on Chinese immigration and political asylum cases in the United States and Canada.

MEMBER: Association of Chinese Social Scientists in North America, American Association for Chinese Studies (member, board of directors).

AWARDS, HONORS: Fellow of Hoover Institution on War, Revolution, and Peace, 1984, and Chiang Ching-kuo International Foundation, 1995.

WRITINGS:

(Co-author) *The Taiwan Relations Act and the Defense of the Republic of China,* Institute of International Studies, University of California, Berkeley, 1980.
(Co-author) *Ideology and Development: Sun Yat-sen and the Economic History of Taiwan,* Institute of East Asian Studies, University of California, Berkeley, 1981.
(Co-author) *The Republic of China and U.S. Policy,* Ethics and Public Policy Center, 1983.
(Co-author) *The Iron Triangle: A U.S. Security Policy for Northeast Asia,* Hoover Institution (Stanford, CA), 1984.
The Chinese Blue Shirt Society, Institute of East Asian Studies, University of California, Berkeley, 1985.
(With Yuan-li Wu and others) *Human Rights in the People's Republic of China,* Westview Press (Boulder, CO), 1985.

(Editor with Bih-jaw Lin and others) *The Aftermath of the 1989 Tiananmen Crisis in Mainland China,* Westview Press, 1992.

The Labors of Sisyphus: The Economic Development of Communist China, Transaction Books (New Brunswick, NJ), 1998.

Contributor to periodicals, including *Journal of Strategic Studies, Communist and Post-Communist Studies, Asian Survey, Political Communication and Persuasion, Terrorism, China Quarterly,* and *Journal of Asian Studies.*

WORK IN PROGRESS: The Return of the Dragon: China's New Nationalism.

SIDELIGHTS: Maria Hsia Chang told *CA:* "What inspired and continues to motivate me to write and conduct research, corny as it may sound, is the desire to search for the truth. The original inspiration came from a philosophy of science course I took as an undergraduate student at the University of California, Berkeley. I like to think that my writing and research are contributing, however modestly, to the trove of accumulated truths and information concerning China, political science, and whatever other subject may interest me in the future.

"My writing process is laborious and rather tortuous. I need a substantial chunk of uninterrupted time to write, preferring the early morning hours. I have learned that it is alright to write less than perfectly, an ability that was made possible entirely by the blessed personal computer and its word processor. I write an initial draft, then revise continuously until a chapter is complete. Good writing is truly a craft, to which an author must be dedicated."

*   *   *

CHARLEBOIS, Lucile C. 1950-

PERSONAL: Born December 22, 1950, in Northampton, MA; daughter of John J. (in business) and Alma R. (a homemaker; maiden name, Plante) Charlebois. *Ethnicity:* "French Canadian." *Education:* College of Our Lady of the Elms, B.A. (summa cum laude), 1969; Middlebury College, M.A., 1970; attended Universidad Complutense de Madrid, 1971, and New York University, 1972-74; University of Massachusetts at Amherst, Ph.D., 1982.

ADDRESSES: Home—800 State St., No. 202, West Columbia, SC 29169-7101. *Office*—Department of Spanish, Italian, and Portuguese, 713 Welsh Humanities, University of South Carolina—Columbia, Columbia, SC 29208; fax 803-777-7828. *E-mail*—charlebois1@garnet.cla.sc.edu.

CAREER: Department of Public Welfare, Springfield, MA, social worker, 1968-69; College of Our Lady of the Elms, Chicopee, MA, instructor in Spanish, 1970-76, head of modern language department, 1975-76; Volunteers for Educational and Social Services, Austin, TX, teacher of Spanish in Uvalde, TX, 1976-77; College of Our Lady of the Elms, instructor in Spanish, 1977-78; Residencia Buendia, Cuenca, Spain, instructor in English, 1981; University of Nebraska—Lincoln, visiting assistant professor, 1982-83, assistant professor of Spanish, 1983-88; University of South Carolina at Columbia, assistant professor, 1988-94, associate professor of Spanish, 1994—, director of Spanish Tutorial Center, 1988-92. Broadcaster, programmer, and scriptwriter for the Spanish-language radio program *Encrucijada,* West Springfield, MA, 1975-76.

MEMBER: Asociacion Internacional de Hispanistas, American Council on the Teaching of Foreign Languages, Asociacion de Linguistica y Filologia de Latinoamerica, Twentieth-Century Spanish Association of America, American Association of Teachers of Spanish and Portuguese, Asociacion de Pensamiento Hispanico, Council of Editors of Learned Journals, Philological Association of the Carolinas, South Carolina Association of Teachers of Spanish and Portuguese, Delta Epsilon Sigma.

WRITINGS:

Understanding Camilo Jose Cela, University of South Carolina Press (Columbia), 1998.

Contributor to books. Contributor of articles and reviews to periodicals, including *Nueva Revista de Filologia Hispanica, Hispanic Journal, Insula,* and *Segismundo. Anales de la Literatura Espanola Contemporanea,* member of editorial advisory council, 1983—, interim editor, 1984; *Siglo XX/Twentieth Century,* editor, 1983-85, book review editor, 1986-90; member of editorial board, *Studies in Twentieth-Century Literature,* 1983-88; editor, *Textos: Works and Criticism/Creacion y Critica,* 1998—.

WORK IN PROGRESS: La Cuentistica de Camilo Jose

Cela; research on the essays, theater, and poetry of Camilo Jose Cela.

*   *   *

CHERTOW, Marian R. 1955-

PERSONAL: Born April 14, 1955, in Syracuse, NY; daughter of Bernard (a chemical engineer) and Doris (a county legislator) Chertow; married Matthew Nemerson, November, 1985; children: Elana, Joy. *Education:* Barnard College, B.A., 1978; Yale University, M.P.P.M., 1981. *Politics:* "Sensible center." *Avocational interests:* Theater, politics.

ADDRESSES: Home—New Haven, CT. *Office*—School of Forestry and Environmental Studies, Yale University, 205 Prospect St., New Haven, CT 06511; fax 203-432-5556. *E-mail*—marian.chertow@yale. edu.

CAREER: Town of Windsor, CT, assistant to assistant town manager, 1983-86; Connecticut Resources Receiving Authority (bonding authority), Hartford, president, 1986-88; U.S. Conference of Mayors, Washington, DC, senior fellow, 1988-89; Yale University, New Haven, CT, director of industrial environmental management at School of Forestry and Environmental Studies, 1991—. Tax Exempt Proceeds Fund, member of board of directors; Connecticut Council for Environmental Quality, appointed member; Technology for Connecticut, Inc., member. Shubert Theatre, member of board of directors.

MEMBER: National Urban Fellows.

AWARDS, HONORS: Regional Merit Award, U.S. Environmental Protection Agency, 1997, for a project on next-generation policy reform.

WRITINGS:

Garbage Solutions: A Public Official's Guide to Recycling and Alternative Solid Waste Management Technologies, U.S. Conference of Mayors (Washington, DC), 1989.
(Editor with Daniel Esty) *Thinking Ecologically: The Next Generation of Environmental Policy,* Yale University Press (New Haven, CT), 1997.

Member of editorial board, *BioCycle* and *Journal of Industrial Ecology.*

WORK IN PROGRESS: Accelerating Commercialization of Environmental Technology.

*   *   *

CHIRA, Susan

PERSONAL: Children: two.

ADDRESSES: Agent—c/o HarperCollins, 10 East 53rd St., New York NY 10022.

CAREER: Journalist. *New York Times,* New York City, deputy foreign editor.

WRITINGS:

A Mother's Place: Taking the Debate About Working Mothers Beyond Guilt and Shame, HarperCollins (New York City), 1998.

SIDELIGHTS: The arguments for and against mothers working outside the home were recharged with the appearance of Susan Chira's first book, *A Mother's Place.* In the book, Chira, deputy foreign editor of *The New York Times* and the mother of two children, challenges what she considers the "backlash" against working mothers that gained momentum in the 1980s and that she felt was preached by such childcare specialists as Penelope Leach and Dr. Spock. It is possible, Chira concludes, for children of working mothers to develop in healthy and happy ways, while children whose mothers feel forced by social pressures to stay home can suffer the negative effects of the mother's frustration or depression. Chira bases her arguments on current scientific research, interviews with over forty mothers and several fathers, and her own personal experience as a woman who struggled with her choice not to abandon her career when she had children of her own. "For years, I believed I had to choose between work and children," she notes, "and I allowed my fears to still my desire to become a mother." Many reviewers responded enthusiastically to Chira's message. In the *New York Times Book Review,* Carol Tavris wrote that *A Mother's Place* is a "splendid book" that is well researched and smoothly written. Tavris found Chira's last chapter, on "Reimagining Motherhood," in which the author argues for efforts to make child care more widely accessible, "brilliant." Tavris questioned the need for such a book in the first place. She made the point that "[t]he need for this book means that one of the most important messages of contemporary feminism and decades-old research in the social sciences has yet to penetrate even the skin of American culture: namely, that a mother's working does not . . . harm children." Marilyn Nissenson, in the *New York Times Book Review,* wrote that "Chira offers a solid, measured account" of how the backlash against working mothers is damaging to women and children, and concluded that "Working mothers could not ask for a better champion." Some critics, however, found fault with Chira's argument. *Kirkus Reviews* considered *A Mother's Place* "somewhat fragmented because the author never fully develops any of the many ideas she throws out." A *Publishers Weekly* contributor, however, called *A Mother's Place* "forcefully argued [and] well-documented," concluding that the book lends "an important perspective to the debate."

BIOGRAPHICAL/CRITICAL SOURCES:

BOOKS

PERIODICALS

Kirkus Reviews, May 11, 1998.
New York Times Book Review, May 3, 1998, p. 16; May 15, 1998.
Publishers Weekly, April 27, 1998, p. 54.

OTHER

Parenting and Families, available at http://www.amazon.com
ParentTime, available at http://www.pathfinder.com/ParentTime/Growing/ bustmyth.html.*

*   *   *

CHITWOOD, Michael 1958-

PERSONAL: Born April 27, 1958, in Rocky Mount, VA; son of T. W. (a mill worker) and Elaine (Franklin County, VA treasurer) Chitwood; married Jean Sink, 1980; children: two. *Education:* Attended Emory College and Henry College; University of Virginia, M.F.A. (creative writing), 1986.

ADDRESSES: Agent—c/o Down Home Press, P.O. Box 4126, Asheboro, NC 27204.

CAREER: Writer, poet, and journalist. *Independent Weekly,* Chapel Hill, NC, columnist, 1995-98; WUNC

radio, Chapel Hill, commentator, 1995—. Worked in maintenance at a fabric mill.

AWARDS, HONORS: Participant, Poets and Writers Inc. Exchange Program, 1988; North Carolina Literature fellow, 1989.

WRITINGS:

Salt Works: Poems, Ohio Review Books (Athens), 1992.
Whet: Poems, Ohio Review Books (Athens), 1995.
The Weave Room, University of Chicago Press (Chicago), 1997.
Hitting below the Bible Belt: Blood Kin, Baptist Voodoo, Grandma's Teeth, and Other Stories from the South, Down Home Press (Asheboro, NC), 1998.

Contributor of poems, essays, and stories to national publications.

SIDELIGHTS: Michael Chitwood is a freelance journalist and poet who grew up in the foothills of Virginia's Blue Ridge Mountains. His poetry reflects the lives of the people of the region, as in "Kin," when he says, "You could farm under their fingernails / and dwell in that land forever." In reviewing his collection *Whet: Poems,* a *Virginia Quarterly Review* writer noted that Chitwood's ear "is finely tuned." The reviewer said that Chitwood's poems are often dark but sometimes show "a sly sense of humor," and called him "a poet worth spending time with." A reviewer for *Poetry Daily,* felt Chitwood's poems "fuse narrative with the colloquial lyricism of the language of the people and the place."

Chitwood worked in the weave rooms of a J. P. Stevens Company textile mill in Rocky Mount, Virginia during his summer breaks from college. In 1996 he revisited the mill with his father, who had retired after three decades there. The memories called up resulted in Chitwood's collection, *The Weave Room,* a collection of poems about workers and their lives during a summer of union organizing. According to reviewers, the poems in this collection reflect the strong religious ties of the community. Peter Landstrom, editor of *Listen!,* wrote that "from the church choir to workers singing unheard songs at their looms, the singing and the song provide a constant undercurrent for the poems." Landstrom called *The Weave Room* "a powerful book. . . . part memoir part social history."

BIOGRAPHICAL/CRITICAL SOURCES:

PERIODICALS

Listen!, March, 1998.
Poetry, April, 1993, p. 32; February, 1994, p. 260; May, 1994, pp. 76-77.
Virginia Quarterly Review, spring, 1996, p. 64.

OTHER

North Carolina Arts Council, http://www.ncarts.org (September 10, 1998).
Poetry Daily, http://www.poems.com/home.htm (September 10, 1998).

* * *

CHRISTENSEN, Allan Conrad 1940-

PERSONAL: Born December 16, 1940, in New York, NY; Italian citizen; son of G. Raymond and Jane Elisabeth (Conrad) Christensen; companion of Philip Tyler Rand (a professor). *Ethnicity:* "Norwegian." *Education:* Harvard University, A.B., 1962; attended University of Oslo, 1962-63; Princeton University, Ph.D., 1968. *Politics:* "Democratici di Sinistra." *Religion:* Agnostic. *Avocational interests:* Music (especially opera).

ADDRESSES: Home—Via Monserrato 6, 00186 Rome, Italy. *Office*—John Cabot University, Via Lungara 233, 00165 Rome, Italy; fax +39-06-687-3168. *E-mail*—scituat@tin.it.

CAREER: University of California, Los Angeles, assistant professor of English, 1967-73; New School, Rome, Italy, lecturer, 1973-81; John Cabot University, Rome, professor of English, 1981—.

AWARDS, HONORS: Fulbright fellow in Norway, 1962-63.

WRITINGS:

Edward Bulwer-Lytton: The Fiction of New Regions, University of Georgia Press (Athens), 1976.
A European Version of Victorian Fiction: The Novels of Giovanni Ruffini, Rodopi Editions (Amsterdam, Netherlands), 1996.
(Co-editor) *The Challenge of Keats: Bicentenary Essays,* Rodopi Editions, in press.

Contributor to scholarly journals. Assistant editor, *Nineteenth-Century Fiction,* 1970-73.

WORK IN PROGRESS: Research on the treatment of cultural disease in novels by Manzoni, Ainsworth, Dickens, Kingsley, James, and others.

* * *

CHUNG, Lily

PERSONAL: Born in Hong Kong; naturalized U.S. citizen; daughter of Ping Kwan and Meilen (Ling) Chung; married Glen Wan, February, 1975. *Education:* Chinese University of Hong Kong, B.A., 1963; Kent State University, M.A., 1967; University of Minnesota—Twin Cities, Ph.D., 1972. *Religion:* "Multi."

ADDRESSES: Home and office—Pacifica, CA; fax 650-355-7539. *E-mail*—lwanju@aol.com.

CAREER: High school teacher in Hong Kong, 1963-65; instructor in geography at colleges in Hong Kong and Pennsylvania, 1969-75; Wells Fargo Bank, San Francisco, CA, employee, 1976-95; City College of San Francisco, San Francisco, instructor in Chinese metaphysics, 1996-97. Practitioner of *feng shui* and divination; instructor in Chinese metaphysics and talk show host for a Chinese radio station, 1996-97.

MEMBER: Society of Metaphysicians (London).

WRITINGS:

The Path to Good Fortune: The Meng, Llewellyn Worldwide, 1997.
Easy Ways to Harmony, Gold Medal Books, 1999.

Author of the book *Human Geography for Hong Kong,* 1977. Columnist, *Asian Week,* 1992—.

WORK IN PROGRESS: A book about a divination system of the *I Ching;* research on natural law.

SIDELIGHTS: Lily Chung told *CA:* "My motivation for writing began with frustration about the uncontrollable changes in our lives. Why does our luck change beyond our control while our endowment does not change? If we are so smart, why can't we succeed all the time? The answer is cyclical cosmic flows.

"This is not a new topic. The formulas on how the flows of the five elements affect human destiny have been applied and proven by the huge Chinese population for more than a thousand years. Chinese are blessed with three mysterious metaphysical documents: the lunar calendar which registers the timely cosmic flows, *I Ching* which preaches natural law, and the number plate from which *feng shui* was originated. These tools have to come out to benefit the world. Authentic Chinese metaphysicians who have mastered the subject through a lifetime of devotion don't speak English. Those who are making waves on the global stage on this subject don't read Chinese. I feel the need to bridge the gap.

"I first completed the most important task by converting the lunar calendar into English. It is a Bible for all Chinese metaphysicians, a tool with which to chart the personal flow and the grand cosmic flow in order to design the best possible environment for the individual. None of the western practitioners on Chinese *feng shui* are aware of this procedure, because the tool only recently became available.

"My research on many great political leaders in the western world, hundreds of Nobel Prize winners and Olympic gold medalists, and many others has supported these formulas. Luck plays the key! This is the subject of my book, *The Path to Good Fortune: The Meng.*

"As an advocate of natural law, I have also completed a manuscript on the most functional *I Ching* divination system. It is a vital key to learn the natural law. My second book, *Easy Ways to Harmony,* summarizes some of these findings. All of us want and try hard to be successful, but the privilege is assigned to only a few by birth. Can we do something about it? My system offers some help. We can identify our endowment and the problem spot that keeps us from fulfilling our goals. By attuning to the flows, we can turn our luck into success. My passion is to find out the truth about luck.

*   *   *

CLAPP, Nicholas 1936-

PERSONAL: Born May 1, 1936, in Providence, RI; son of Roger (a lawyer) and Helen Clapp; married Kathryn Kelly (a probation officer), March 31, 1962; children: Cristina, Jennifer. *Education:* Brown University, B.A., 1957; University of South Carolina, M.A., 1962. *Avocational interests:* Archeology, photography, desert and mountain backpacking.

ADDRESSES: Office—1551 South Robertson Blvd., Los Angeles, CA 90035.

CAREER: Documentary filmmaker and writer. Trustee, American Center of Oriental Research. *Military service:* Served in U.S. Army.

MEMBER: International Documentary Association (director).

AWARDS, HONORS: Recipient of over seventy awards for film making, including several Academy Award nominations and Emmy Awards.

WRITINGS:

The Road to Ubar: Finding the Atlantis of the Sands, Houghton Mifflin (Boston), 1998.

WORK IN PROGRESS: Sheba: With Eyes Shining as Stars.

SIDELIGHTS: While working on a project in southern Arabia for the World Wildlife Fund in the 1980s documentary filmmaker Nicholas Clapp became fascinated with the area. On his return to Los Angeles he began to research the region in hopes of developing another project he could work on there with his wife, Kay. A book shop owner recommended that Clapp read Bertram Thomas's *Arabia Felix,* which includes an account of the fabled ancient city of Ubar. Legends claim that Ubar, once a thriving trade center, descended into wickedness and was destroyed by Allah. Clapp was immediately intrigued, especially when clues from other sources, such as *The Arabian Nights,* suggested that the seemingly fictitious city had really existed. Though he was not trained as an archaeologist, Clapp set out to find Ubar—and succeeded.

Researching the city, conducting the expedition and writing the resulting book took Clapp almost twelve years. Clapp read extensively about Ubar's history and determined its probable site. He also obtained help from the National Aeronautics and Space Administration, which allowed him to use radar images from the space shuttle to search for traces of the ancient city beneath the desert sands. Landsat and SPOT—remote sensing satellites—provided images that revealed evidence of tracks through the sand. These tracks were identified as old caravan routes that converged near the Empty Quarter where Ubar was believed to be buried. With a team of experts, including British explorer Sir Ranulph Fiennes, Clapp returned to Arabia to begin excavations.

The Road to Ubar: Finding the Atlantis of the Sands, Clapp's account of his search for the site, recounts the difficulties and triumphs the team faced and its ultimate success in identifying the remains of an ancient city that once was an important link in the frankincense trade. Clapp argues that the city was probably destroyed by a distant earthquake between 300 and 500 A.D. after several centuries of prosperity. But he also points out that the growth of Christianity in the region, which diminished demand for frankincense, was instrumental in the city's decline as a mercantile center.

Clapp's book attracted much favorable attention. Critics for *Publishers Weekly, Kirkus Reviews,* and *Library Journal* gave it positive reviews, and the book reached the *Los Angeles Times* bestseller list. Bob Sipchen of the *Los Angeles Times* wrote that Clapp's "contagious enthusiasm blazes through his prose." *New York Times* critic Michiko Kakutani praised Clapp's account as "a delightfully readable, if often highly speculative, volume that's part travel journal, part Walter Mittyesque daydream and part archeological history." Kakutani pointed out, however, that the chapter in which Clapp uses myth and imagination in an attempt to re-create the life of an Ubar ruler, weakens the book and "fails to fulfill any useful function" in an otherwise "gripping real-life story."

In an online discussion with readers at Barnes and Noble's web site, Clapp explained that one of the most exciting things about finding Ubar was the chance to compare mythic accounts of the city with historical facts. "We researched the city in myth, then found what it was really like, then were able to go back and see where the myth was accurate," he noted. He found that, in many ways, the myths were truthful.

Clapp's search for Ubar was the subject of a 1996 Nova documentary program for Public Television titled *Lost City of Arabia.*

BIOGRAPHICAL/CRITICAL SOURCES:

PERIODICALS

Archaeology, July-August, 1992, p. 6.
Booklist, February 1, 1998.

Discover, January, 1993, pp. 56-58.
Kirkus Reviews, January 15, 1998.
New York Times Book Review, February 27, 1998.
Publishers Weekly, January 19, 1998, p. 364.
USA Today, May, 1998, p. 80.

OTHER

Amazon.com, http://www.amazon.com (September 10, 1998).
Barnes & Noble, http://www.barnesandnoble.com (September 2, 1998).
NASA Observatorium Education, http://www.observe. ivv.nasa.gov (September 2, 1998).
New York Times on the Web, http://www.nytimes. com/books98/02/22/daily/ubar-book-review.html (September 2, 1998).
Nova #2312: Lost City of Arabia transcript, http:// web-cr02.pbs.org/wgbh/nova/transcripts/2312lo st.html (September 10, 1998).

*   *   *

CLARK, Larry

PERSONAL: Male.

ADDRESSES: Agent—c/o Douglas & McIntyre, 1615 Venables St., Vancouver, BC, Canada V5L 2H1.

CAREER: Canadian author. *Military service:* Canadian Forces Supplementary Radio System, Inuvik, Northwest Territories, electronic spy, 1972-74.

WRITINGS:

Doomsday Minus Four, Douglas & McIntyre (Vancouver), 1981.

SIDELIGHTS: Canadian author Larry Clark's debut novel, a thriller titled *Doomsday Minus Four,* was published in 1981. Using the experience he gained while employed as a spy for the Canadian Forces Supplementary Radio System (CSFRS) during the early 1970s, Clark wrote a novel about a modern world in which personal privacy is a thing of the past. When Clark worked for the CFSRS, as well as when the book was published, the world was locked in the grips of the Cold War, which pitted the United States against the now-defunct U.S.S.R. in an ideological battle that had nuclear annihilation as a backdrop. In *Doomsday Minus Four* Clark relates the actual

activities of the U.S. National Security Agency (NSA), an agency that is able to listen in on nearly every telecommunications transmission. Clark admitted that during his work "voice intercept operators" were used to monitor Russian activities, such as radio broadcasts and radar frequencies. "We actually monitor Russian radar as it monitors their own aircraft," Clark told Larry Faustmann in an interview for *Maclean's*. "And we can make voice prints of anyone. So when a bomber takes off, we not only know it, we know who's flying it. We even monitor control-tower conversations," he said.

The book, contains detailed accounts of "burning sky" flights in which United States Hercules aircraft, loaded with electronic intelligence devices, fly high speed missions over Soviet airspace to determine Soviet response time. As a result, Soviet aircraft fly over United States and North Atlantic Treaty Organization (NATO) targets to test there response time. In Clark's opinion, between the 1960s and the early 1980s nearly one hundred United States pilots have died or been taken captive. He writes that these dangerous cat-and-mouse actions became a game for both players. For a former government employee to write about such activities during those tense times presented quite a quandary for both Canadian and United States intelligence agencies. Clark suggests that he and his book are not a threat to national security. "The Russians know what we're doing."

Of course, the novel is only a fictional story which Clark fits into the context of that intelligence/counter-intelligence environment. In the book, a Soviet plane on an intelligence mission over the heart of United States airspace is shot down and destroyed. Many in the defense department are outraged that the plane made it that far without being detected by the elaborate and expensive defense system used to detect just such an invasion. When an inquiry is set in motion, a cover-up of the incident by a conspiratorial group occurs. Internal security forces get rid of all those who have knowledge of the event. However, an inquisitive reporter suspects corruption and keeps probing. To make matter worse, tension between the two superpowers has escalated, and nuclear war becomes a serious possibility.

Clark claims that his motivation for writing *Doomsday Minus Four* was to make readers aware of the spying activities of the NSA, including their monitoring of citizen's telephone calls, as well as the intelligence flights of both countries. People should be aware of these activities, he feels, "before World War III starts because of an error." Although the Canadian Forces confirmed that Clark had been an employee, they stressed that Clark's book was merely "fiction."

Although some critics appreciated *Doomsday Minus Four*, others questioned its plausibility, and quality. Faustmann called it "a foreboding tale." Joan McGrath of *Quill & Quire* labeled it a "chilling book" that was "written in oddly impersonal, jargon-ridden prose." Douglas Hill, reviewing the book for *Books in Canada*, was, however, less impressed. The novel, wrote Hill is "all artificial and lifeless." Feeling he could not recommend the book, Hill declared the story "not at all inventive, and about as exciting as corn starch."

BIOGRAPHICAL/CRITICAL SOURCES:

PERIODICALS

Books in Canada, December, 1981, p. 30.
Maclean's, December 21, 1981, pp. 19-20.
Quill & Quire, April, 1982, p. 26.*

*   *   *

CLARKE-RICH, Elizabeth L. 1934-

PERSONAL: Born May 14, 1934, in Red Oak, VA; daughter of Fred (a farmer) and Lena (a homemaker; maiden name, Yancey) Lockett; married William J. Clarke, December 27, 1954 (divorced, 1986); married Amos K. Rich, November 20, 1998; children: (first marriage) Carol, Charles F. *Education:* Virginia State College (now University), B.A., 1950; attended Rutgers University, 1960-61; Catholic University of America, M.L.S., 1969. *Politics:* Democrat. *Religion:* Protestant. *Avocational interests:* Reading, playing the piano and organ, singing, dramatics.

ADDRESSES: Home—11611 Tyre St., Upper Marlboro, MD 20772.

CAREER: Writer. Elementary school teacher at public schools in Charlotte County, VA, 1950-52; social studies teacher and librarian at public schools in Charlotte County, 1953-55; elementary school principal in Mecklenburg County, VA, 1956-59; Prince George's County Public Schools, Prince George's County, VA, librarian, 1960-66, resource teacher,

1967-69, high school librarian, 1970-89. Worked as a university librarian in Maryland.

MEMBER: Maryland Retired Teachers Association, National Writers Association, Smithsonian Institution, MEMO, Girls' Social Club, Library of Congress (associate member, 1997).

AWARDS, HONORS: Outstanding Educator's Award, Prince George's County Public Schools, 1985; ASF Intercultural Award, 1987; World Poetry Organization, Golden Poet Award, 1992, Outstanding Achievement in Poetry Award, 1997.

WRITINGS:

We Ain't Arrived Yet (poems), Clarke Productions, 1991.
The Big Mistake, illustrated by Douglas Gillam, Jr., Scythe Publications (Nashville), 1995.
And the Winner Is. . . (sequel to *The Big Mistake*), Winston-Derek (Nashville), 1998.

WORK IN PROGRESS: Fly Me to the Moon, the story of an African-American youngster who flies to the moon on a bicycle propelled by a whirlwind.

SIDELIGHTS: Elizabeth L. Clarke-Rich commented: "I grew up on a farm in southern Virginia during the Depression years. Being an only child, I had to find my own pleasures. I developed a great love of the natural world, and for all forms of animal life. Animals became my companions and special friends.

"It was commonplace to ride horses and feed them corn. I would also carry foodstuff to the chickens and pigs. Rabbits were regular visitors, and squirrels were seen scampering around and scaling trees. Occasionally, snakes would show up near barns and storage buildings. Once in a while they would make surprise visits to our house, especially during dry seasons. My dad explained that they were looking for water. The two species that were most common in our area were black snakes and moccasins. My parents explained that the black snake was harmless, but to be aware of the poisonous moccasin.

"In addition to the animals, I'd entertain myself in the woods. I got a special kick out of creating leaf designs and riding tree limbs.

"As a youngster, I became an avid reader. I also developed an interest in writing. It probably started with keeping a diary. And then, I got into writing

poetry and short stories. My interests expanded when I became an adult, but basically I used the same genre through the years. In the future I plan to write a couple of novels.

"I view poetry primarily as a journey into the human psyche. I believe it should illuminate the feelings, emotions, and conflicts that we humans experience. In essence, it should touch the heart and soul and should induce challenge and creative thought.

"With children's books, I want to make children smile and laugh and stimulate their imaginations. Moreover, the subject matter and illustrations should motivate them to read more extensively.

"I am passionate about writing, and hope to continue to write until I'm a hundred plus."*

*   *   *

COHEN, Leah Hager

PERSONAL: Born in the United States; father's name, Oscar (a superintendent at the Lexington School for the Deaf); mother also employed at the Lexington School for the Deaf; married; children: one son. *Education:* Hampshire College, received degree in writing; Columbia University School of Journalism, received degree in writing.

ADDRESSES: Home—Boston, MA. *Agent*—c/o Avon Books, 1350 Avenue of the Americas, New York, NY 10019.

CAREER: Educator and author. Emerson College, professor, c. 1990s.

AWARDS, HONORS: Train Go Sorry: Inside a Deaf World was chosed by the American Library Association as one of the Best Books of 1994.

WRITINGS:

Train Go Sorry: Inside a Deaf World (nonfiction), Houghton Mifflin (Boston), 1994.
Glass, Paper, Beans: Revelations on the Nature and Value of Ordinary Things (nonfiction), Doubleday (New York City), 1997.
Heat Lightning (novel), Avon (New York City), 1997.

SIDELIGHTS: Leah Hager Cohen's first three books have won praise for their convincing exploration of three vastly different subjects. Her first book, 1994's *Train Go Sorry: Inside a Deaf World,* reflects Cohen's own personal background as the hearing, second-generation American granddaughter of two deaf immigrants. The book itself chronicles a coming-of-age period at the Lexington School for the Deaf in New York City, a school her grandfather attended, and at which her father, Oscar, works as superintendent and her mother is also employed. Given this personal attachment and involvement with the institution in question, Cohen is well prepared to discuss the tremendous tumult the school experienced in 1988. Tensions arose when those students involved in the deaf pride movement protested the pressure being applied to them to undergo risky cochlear implant surgery, even if that surgery offered the possibility of functional hearing. The protestors instead espoused the view that deafness is something about which to be proud. To cast these difficult issues against a more human backdrop, Cohen focuses her attention on two particular students at the school: Sofie, a Russian immigrant struggling gamely to learn both standard English and English sign language, and James, who must adjust to the major differences between the school and the ghetto in which he was raised.

Reviewers praised Cohen's tight, even look into a world that most readers will never see. A *Kirkus Review* contributor praised the book as "an intimate portrait of a tight knit subculture that, ironically, is coming of age as it shrinks in size, the result of medical advances against meningitis and other causes of deafness—a situation that Cohen terms, with typical awareness of both sides, 'bittersweet.'" A *Publishers Weekly* reviewer offered similar comments, noting: "If Cohen's narrative is disjointed, her commitment and her descriptive gifts make her book memorable." Janis Ansell, writing in *School Library Journal,* recommended the book as an important sociological tool: "A careful reading of *Train Go Sorry* provides exposure to the urban poor and our country's many immigrants (both past and present)," Ansell maintained.

In Cohen's next book, 1997's *Glass, Paper, Beans: Revelations on the Nature and Value of Ordinary Things,* she is inspired by the newspaper in her hand, the mug on her table, and the coffee steaming in that mug to investigate the personal stories that surround the origin of these diverse objects. She brings the reader to the world of Ruth, a glassworker in Ohio who might have made the glass from which Cohen

drinks. Similarly, the reader meets Basilio, who tends to the coffee trees, and Brent, a Canadian logger. Accompanying these portraits of the human faces behind the objects that we use daily are detailed explanations of the facts behind the objects—the fact that lightning strikes can produce a type of glass from sand, for example.

Critics expressed mixed opinions about both subject and approach in *Glass, Paper, Beans.* Several reviewers noted that, unlike Cohen's first book, *Glass, Paper, Beans* does not involve topics with which the author is intimately familiar. Chase Collins of the *Chicago Tribune* wrote: "research and human interest can be a tough pair to marry . . . *Glass, Paper, Beans* lacks the passionate intellect and felt experience of *Train Go Sorry.*" Ilse Heidmann of *Library Journal* echoed these comments, asserting: "Despite its unusual focus and well-constructed sentences, her book gets bogged down in a plethora of tedious details and unrelated observations." Nevertheless, other reviewers responded favorably to Cohen's attention to detail and wealth of commentary. A *Publishers Weekly* reviewer, who praised Cohen's "sparkling, nimble prose," observed that "Cohen's acumen in focusing on these specific people makes her journey and ours particularly pleasurable; she signals connections among commodities and geography and time, supply and demand, raw materials and market forces."

Heat Lightning, Cohen's first novel, was published in 1997. It tells the story of two orphaned sisters whose parents are said to have died while saving a boatload of partygoers. Narrated by Mole (derived from Martha), the younger of the two sisters, *Heat Lightning* delves deeply into the tumultuous issues of identity that surround the onset of puberty, particularly in a small town. Because facts surrounding their parents' drowning are somewhat vague, the two girls have constructed an elaborate set of fables that lionize their dead parents. During one particularly hot summer when the girls are twelve and eleven, this fable unravels disastrously, leaving Mole and her sister Tilly terribly uncertain about their beliefs and feelings. Adding to the problems are the Rouens, their new next-door neighbors. Even as Tilly is attracted to the Rouens' fourteen-year old son, she must endure his father's own attempt to seduce her. Despite these crises, Mole and Tilly ultimately find peace with their family's past.

Reviews for *Heat Lightning* were highly favorable. A *Kirkus Reviews* contributor praised "Cohen's taut, unsentimental prose . . . [which] brilliantly evokes

Mole's strange imaginary world. . . . [The book is] a radiant coming-of-age story in which every character rings true." A *Publishers Weekly* reviewer observed that Cohen's "sensuous language bursts with charged imagery, as do her descriptions of a rural hamlet whose apparent summertime languor hides simmering emotions." Joanna Burkhardt, writing in *Library Journal,* applauded *Heat Lightning,* asserting: "Beautifully written and told . . . [the] vivid description and detail make these characters come alive."

BIOGRAPHICAL/CRITICAL SOURCES:

PERIODICALS

Chicago Tribune, February 23, 1997, p. 9.
Kirkus Reviews, December 1, 1993, p. 1500; May 15, 1997, pp. 736-37.
Library Journal, January 1, 1997, p. 127; June 1, 1997, p. 144.
Publishers Weekly, December 6, 1993, p. 62; November 25, 1996, p. 60; May 5, 1997, p. 193.
School Library Journal, December, 1994, p. 145.*

*   *   *

COLISH, Marcia L.   1937-

PERSONAL: Born July 27, 1937, in Brooklyn, NY; daughter of Samuel (an orthodontist) and Daisy (a homemaker; maiden name, Kartch) Colish. *Education:* Smith College, B.A. (magna cum laude), 1958; Yale University, M.A., 1959, Ph.D., 1965.

ADDRESSES: Home—143 East College St., Apt. 310, Oberlin, OH 44074. *Office*—Department of History, Oberlin College, Oberlin, OH 44074; fax 440-775-8124. *E-mail*—marcia.colish@oberlin.edu.

CAREER: Skidmore College, Saratoga Springs, NY, instructor in history, 1962-63; Oberlin College, Oberlin, OH, instructor, 1963-65, assistant professor, 1965-69, associate professor, 1969-75, professor, 1975—, Frederick B. Artz Professor of History, 1985—, department head, 1973-74, 1978-81, and 1985-86. Case Western Reserve University, lecturer, 1966-67; Institute for Advanced Study, member of School of Historical Studies, 1986-87; Ohio State University, affiliate of Center for Medieval and Renaissance Studies, 1996—; member of advisory board for Centre for Classical, Oriental, Medieval, and Renaissance Studies at University of Groningen,

1991—, Franciscan Institute at St. Bonaventure University, 1993-96, and Netherlands Research School for Medieval Studies, 1995—. Ohio Humanities Council, member of executive board, 1978-81, vice-chairperson, 1979-81.

MEMBER: International Society for the Classical Tradition, Societe Internationale pour l'Etude de Philosophie Medievale, Medieval Academy of America (fellow; chairperson, 1986-87; member of council, 1987-90, and executive committee, 1989-92; president, 1991-92), American Historical Association, Renaissance Society of America, American Association of University Professors, Medieval Association of the Midwest (member of council, 1978-81), Midwest Medieval Conference (member of council, 1976-77; president, 1978-79), Central Renaissance Conference, Phi Beta Kappa.

AWARDS, HONORS: National Endowment for the Humanities, younger scholar fellow, 1968-69, senior fellow, 1981-82, grant, 1993; visiting scholar, American Academy in Rome, 1968-69; travel grants, American Council of Learned Societies, 1974 and 1987; fellow of Institute for Research in the Humanities, University of Wisconsin—Madison, 1974-75; visiting scholar, Harvard University and Weston School of Theology, both 1982; Guggenheim fellow, 1989-90; visiting fellow, Yale University, 1989-90; Wilbur Cross Medal, Yale Graduate School Alumni Association, 1993; fellow at Woodrow Wilson Center, 1994-95; Rockefeller Foundation resident, Villa Serbelloni, Bellagio, Italy, 1995; Haskins Medal, Medieval Academy of America, 1998, for *Peter Lombard;* grant, American Philosophical Society, 1998; D.H.L., Grinnell College, 1999.

WRITINGS:

The Mirror of Language: A Study in the Medieval Theory of Knowledge, Yale University Press (New Haven, CT), 1968, revised edition, University of Nebraska Press (Lincoln), 1983.
(Contributor) Patrick Henry, editor, *Schools of Thought in the Christian Tradition,* Fortress (Philadelphia, PA), 1984.
The Stoic Tradition from Antiquity to the Early Middle Ages, Volume I: *Stoicism in Classical Latin Literature,* Volume II: *Stoicism in Latin Christian Thought through the Sixth Century,* E. J. Brill (Leiden, the Netherlands), 1985.
(Contributor) Aldo S. Bernardo and Saul Levin, editors, *The Classics in the Middle Ages,* State University of New York Press (Binghamton), 1990.

(Contributor) Maryanne Cline Horowitz, editor, *Race, Gender, and Class: Early Modern Ideas of Humanity,* University of Rochester Press (Rochester, NY), 1992.

(Contributor) Mark D. Jordan and Kent Emery Jr., *Ad Litteram: Authoritative Texts and Their Medieval Readers,* University of Notre Dame Press (Notre Dame, IN), 1992.

Peter Lombard, two volumes, E. J. Brill, 1994.

(Contributor) John Van Engen, editor, *The Past and Future of Medieval Studies,* University of Notre Dame Press, 1994.

(Contributor) William Caferro and Duncan G. Fisher, editors, *The Unbounded Community: Papers in Christian Ecumenism in Honor of Jaroslav Pelikan,* Garland Publishing (New York City), 1996.

Medieval Foundations of the Western Intellectual Tradition, 400-1400, Yale University Press, 1997.

(Contributor) John Dunn and Ian Harris, editors, *Great Political Thinkers: Machiavelli,* Edward Elgar (Aldershot, England), 1997.

Co-editor, "Garland Medieval Casebooks," Garland Publishing, 1998—. Contributor of articles and reviews to periodicals, including *Apollo, American Journal of Jurisprudence, Journal of the American Academy of Religion, Renaissance Quarterly,* and *Church History. Journal of the History of Ideas,* contributing editor, 1985-89, member of editorial board, 1989—, member of board of directors, 1998—; member of editorial board, *Assays,* 1979-96, and *American Historical Review,* 1991-94.

*   *   *

COLLINS, Tess

PERSONAL: Born in KY. *Education:* University of Kentucky, B.A. (journalism).

ADDRESSES: Home—San Francisco, CA. *Office*—Curran Theatre, 445 Geary Blvd., San Francisco, CA 94102. *Agent*—c/o Ballantine Books, 201 East 50th St., New York, NY 10022.

CAREER: Curran Theatre, San Francisco, CA, manager. Freelance writer, c. 1997—.

AWARDS, HONORS: Oswald Award for Creative Writing.

WRITINGS:

Tossing Monte (play), produced in San Francisco, c. 1997.

The Law of Revenge (novel), Ballantine (New York City), 1997.

WORK IN PROGRESS: A sequel to *The Law of Revenge.*

SIDELIGHTS: Born in the Appalachian Mountain region of eastern Kentucky, Tess Collins moved to San Francisco, California in 1979. Since that time, she has become manager of the Curran Theatre—a facility that has hosted such spectacles as Andrew Lloyd Webber's *Phantom of the Opera.* Collins writes as well, and her first play, *Tossing Monte,* debuted in 1997 in a small theater across the street from the Curran. That same year saw the release of her first novel, a work of suspense titled *The Law of Revenge.*

The Law of Revenge introduces protagonist Alma Mae Bashears, who is, like the author, a native of Appalachia transplanted to San Francisco. An attorney, Alma has just landed a position with a prestigious Bay Area law firm when her family calls her home to represent her brother, accused of murdering a hometown big shot. She arrives, only to find that the prosecuting attorney in the case is the man who, during her adolescence, led the gang rape that has left her emotionally scarred. *The Law of Revenge* was assessed by internet magazine reviewer Ron Hogan in *Beatrice,* who reported that Alma's "efforts to clear her brother's name bring her head-to-head with the local political machine and with emotions she's suppressed for years." Harriet Klausner, commenting in the internet publication *Under the Covers,* asserted that Collins "captures the atmosphere of Appalachia and the essence of its hill people with a tenderness, vividness and accuracy that is positively brilliant."

Hogan's *Beatrice* review also included a brief interview in which Collins discussed her first novel and her writing career in general. Collins told Hogan that writing a mystery had been secondary to "wanting to write a book about the area of the country I grew up in, in Appalachia." However, recognizing the commercial aspect of fiction writing, she opted to combine her interest in regional storytelling with the conventions of the modern legal fiction genre. She also told Hogan that she plans a sequel to *The Law of Revenge,* again featuring Alma, and implied that she planned to do many books with Alma as the protagonist. Commenting on the fact that *The Law of Revenge* ends with Alma not returning to San Francisco, Collins told Hogan that "it felt as if she had to stay a little longer." However, for subsequent books, Collins noted that "[s]he's the kind of character who, after what she's been through in this story, could eventually [move] to any city and still maintain her Appalachian roots." She concluded by letting Hogan know that despite her work with the Curran Theatre, she "would definitely like to be writing fulltime."

BIOGRAPHICAL/CRITICAL SOURCES:

OTHER

Beatrice, http://www.beatrice.com/interviews/collinst (January 20, 1998).
Under the Covers, http://www.silcom.com/~manatee/collins_law.html (November 21, 1997).*

*   *   *

COOK, Timothy E. 1954-

PERSONAL: Born August 16, 1954, in Van Nuys, CA; son of Thomas E. (a personnel manager) and Audrey J. (a secretary) Cook; companion of Jack Yeager (a professor). *Ethnicity:* "European-American." *Education:* Pomona College, B.A., 1976; University of Wisconsin, Ph.D., 1982. *Politics:* "Yes." *Religion:* "No." *Avocational interests:* Classical music.

ADDRESSES: Home—Williamstown, MA. *Office*—Stetson Hall, Williams College, Williamstown, MA 01267; fax 413-597-4194. *E-mail*—timothy.cook@williams.edu.

CAREER: Williams College, Williamstown, MA, assistant professor, 1981-88, associate professor, 1988-92, professor, 1993—. Harvard University, adjunct professor at Kennedy School of Government, 1998—.

MEMBER: American Political Science Association (member of executive council and administrative committee, 1994-96).

AWARDS, HONORS: American Political Science Association, congressional fellow, 1984-85, Pool Award, 1993, and Graber Prize, 1995.

WRITINGS:

Making Laws and Making News, Brookings Institution (Washington, DC), 1989.
(With M. Just and others) *Crosstalk,* University of Chicago Press (Chicago), 1996.
Governing with the News, University of Chicago Press, 1998.

SIDELIGHTS: Timothy E. Cook told *CA:* "Politics is too changeable and time-bound for any of us who study it to imagine that we can be contributing to the knowledge of the ages. Instead, I have come to see writing books as a way of entering into dialogues with people with whom I could not possibly come into contact and, through that dialogue, making a difference in the way the world runs and is run. My writing is influenced by a desire for social justice and a strong sense that politics—in its most positive sense—can be found in unexpected places.

"Some friends of mine who are scholars and writers have to get everything down on paper before they start trimming. My process is exactly the reverse, almost a process of slow accretion in my mind as I encounter new evidence, new challenges, and new ideas over a period of months, even years. I remember reading a quotation from a composer—it was either Witold Lutoslawski or Michael Tippett—that when he listened to a piece of music by someone else, it became transformed into what it might have been in his hands. My writing draws from the same impulse."

*   *   *

COPPEE, Francois 1842-1908

PERSONAL: Born January 26, 1842, in Paris, France; died May 23, 1908, in Paris; father a civil servant. *Education:* Attended the Lycee St. Louis.

CAREER: Writer. Employed as a clerical worker, Ministry of War, France, c. 1862.

AWARDS, HONORS: Academie Francaise, elected member, 1884.

WRITINGS:

POETRY

Le reliquaire, 1867.

Les intimites, 1868.
La greve des forgerons, 1869.
Poemes modernes, 1869.
Les humbles, 1872.
Le cahier rouge, 1874.
Une idylle pendant le siege, 1874.
Olivier, 1875.
Promenades et interieurs, 1875.
L'exilee, 1876.
Contes en vers et poesies diverses, 1886.
Arriere-saison, 1887.
Les paroles sinceres, 1891.
Dans la priere et dans la lutte, 1901.
Des vers francais, 1906.

PLAYS

Le passant, 1869; translation published as *The Passer-by,* 1885, translated as *The Wanderer,* G. F. Nesbitt and Co. (New York City), 1890.
Deux douleurs, 1870.
Le luthier de Cremone, 1876; translation published as *The Violin Maker of Cremona,* De Witt (New York City), 1892.
Severo Torelli, 1883.
Les Jacobites, 1885.
Rivales, 1893; translation published as *The Rivals,* Harper (New York City), 1893.
Le tresor, 1893; translation published as *The Treasure,* 1895.
Pour la couronne, 1895; translation published as *For the Crown,* 1896.
Le pater, 1896; translation published as *Pater Noster,* Samuel French (New York City), 1915; performed in the United States as *The Prayer.*

OTHER

Vingt contes nouveaux (short stories), 1883.
Oeuvres completes de Francois Coppee (poetry, plays, short stories, and novels), 10 volumes, 1888-92.
Henriette (novel), 1889, translation published as *Henriette; or, A Corsican Mother,* Worthington Co. (New York City), 1889.
Ten Tales by Francois Coppee (short stories), Harper and Brothers, 1890.
Toute une jeunesse (novel), 1890, translation published as *The Days of My Youth,* Belford and Company (New York City), 1890, translated as *Disillusion; or, The Story of Amedee's Youth,* G. Routledge and Sons (New York City) 1890, translated as *A Romance of Youth,* Maison Mazarin (Paris, France), 1905.

Les vrais riches (short stories), 1892; translation published as *True Riches,* D. Appleton and Company (New York City), 1893, translated as *Blessed Are the Poor,* 1894.
Mon franc parler (nonfiction), 1894.
Le coupable (novel), 1897, translation published as *The Guilty Man,* G. W. Dillingham Company (New York), 1911.
La bonne souffrance (essays), 1898, translation published as *Happy Suffering,* 1900.
Tales for Christmas and Other Seasons (short stories), Little, Brown (Boston), 1900.
Oeuvres de Francois Coppee (poetry, plays, short stories, novels), 1907.

SIDELIGHTS: Francois Coppee was one of the most popular and respected literary figures in late nineteenth-century France. Although he began his career under the tutelage of the Parnassian poets, whose central tenet was the absolute rejection of all forms of literary Romanticism, he later developed distinctly Romantic tendencies in his own works and focused in particular on the courageous endurance of the poor. Coppee's popularity was the direct result of this sympathetic treatment of the economically dispossessed, and while his diverse writings were critically acclaimed for their stylistic sophistication, he was known to the vast majority of his readers simply as "the poet of the humble," an epithet coined by *French Essays and Profiles* author Stuart Henry. Henry remarked: "[Coppee's] verse was simple in effect, like his stories. It was written for plain people, and no other writer was then more widely read and beloved by the general French public."

Born in Paris, Coppee was the son of a civil servant whose meager income afforded the family only a marginal existence. The adversity of the poet's youth was further exacerbated by his poor health, and his education was frequently interrupted by severe illness. Coppee nevertheless completed his primary education and attended the Lycee St. Louis, where he developed a keen interest in poetry. After his father's death in 1862, Coppee was forced to accept a clerical position in the Ministry of War in order to provide for his mother and sister, but he continued to write poetry and to hope for a literary career.

In 1863 Coppee became acquainted with Catulle Mendes, a successful and flamboyant poet to whom he confided his literary aspirations. Although Mendes disliked the poems Coppee initially showed him, he offered the younger man some direction, believing him capable of much better work. In addition, Mendes introduced Coppee into the Parnassian circle, which included such prominent figures as Stephane Mallarme and Leconte de Lisle, the acknowledged leader of the group. Coppee's natural talent soon earned the respect of the Parnassians, and the 1867 publication of his first volume of poetry, *Le reliquaire,* brought the approval of the larger critical community. Popular success came two years later, when his verse comedy *Le passant* was performed at the *Theatre Odeon* with Sarah Bernhardt in the starring role.

The majority of Coppee's subsequent works were equally well received, and in 1884 he was accorded the highest honor available to a French author: membership in the prestigious Academic Francaise. Having secured his reputation as a poet and critic, Coppee went on to publish novels and short stories, beginning in 1889 with the novel *Henriette.* Near the end of his life Coppee underwent a religious conversion, and the works he published between 1897 and his death in 1908 reflect their author's strong Catholic faith.

Although Coppee created works in a wide variety of genres, he is best known for his popular poetry, his verse dramas, and his *contes en vers,* or verse tales. His early poems, collected in the volumes *Le reliquaire* and *Les intimites,* exemplify Parnassian ideals of rigid formalism, semantic precision, and objective response. Later, when Coppee had abandoned objective response in favor of a more emphatic approach to his subject matter, he nevertheless adhered to the primary stylistic tenets of the Parnassians. As a result, both his poetry and his prose have been applauded for their simplicity and clarity, while his images are described as precise and powerfully realistic. Coppee's sentimental characterizations of the oppressed poor and his realistic depictions of Parisian life, most notably those of the very collection *Les humbles,* have also been widely praised. In his *On Life and Letters,* Anatole France declared: "Francois Coppee is a born poet; verse is his mother-tongue. He speaks it with charming facility. But—and all poets are not thus endowed—he also writes, when he wishes, an easy, laughing, limpid prose."

Coppee's literary reputation, however, does not extend beyond the borders of France. In part because of their reliance upon the subtleties of the French language for their style, few of his works have been translated into English and many of the extant translations are considered markedly inferior to the originals. Within his own country, however, Coppee is praised for his skillful concretization of Parnassian

literary theories as well as for his championing of the poor, and he is considered by many to be a major figure in the development of French poetry. In an assessment of some of the characteristics of Coppee's poetry, *English Illustrated* contributors E. Prothero and R. E. Prothero asserted: "Coppee is a *parisien parisiennant,* a Parisian of Parisians. Paris is his native place, his home, his mistress. He studies every aspect of her life with the ardor of a lover. . . . In Paris his thoughts habitually dwell. Her streets are the stage on which are played his humble tragedies; each stone in her pavements is a friend; at every corner an association greets him; down every alley in her gardens flits some phantom of his youth; her trees sheltered alike his first loves and his first rhymes."

The reviewers continued, "Paris, as a whole, is to him a personal living being. . . . He has made every detail of her humble life his own. He does not chaunt the glories of her great streets, or palaces. But, as in *Les Humbles,* he dedicates his genius to sing of the weak and forlorn, the pariahs on whom a gay society rarely bestows even a smile, the obscure heroes and unknown heroines whom his pity detects among her newsvendors, nurses, grocers, foundlings, and motherless child-mothers. Others have sung of Parisian life, but none have treated it in Coppee's peculiar vein. . . . He is not only the poet of Paris, but the poet of her solid, unostentatious virtues."

BIOGRAPHICAL/CRITICAL SOURCES:

BOOKS

Blunt, Hugh Francis, *Great Penitents,* 1921, Books for Libraries Press, 1967.

Coppee, Francois, *A Romance of Youth,* with a preface by Jose de Heredia, 1905, Current Literature Publishing Company, 1910.

Coppee, Francois, *Ten Tales,* with an introduction by Brander Matthews, 1991, Books for Libraries Press, 1969.

France, Anatole, *On Life and Letters,* third series, translated by D. B. Stewart, John Lane/The Bodley Head Ltd., 1922.

Henry, Stuart, *French Essays and Profiles,* E. P. Dutton & Company, 1921.

Matthews, Brander, *Aspects of Fiction and Other Ventures in Criticism,* 1896, Literature House/Gregg Press, 1970.

Shaw, Bernard, *Dramatic Opinions and Essays with an Apology,* Volume 1, Brentano's, 1907.

Smith, Hugh Allison, *Main Currents of Modern French Drama,* Henry Holt and Company, 1925.

PERIODICALS

Appleton's Journal, March, 1880, pp. 231-239.
English Illustrated, vol. 8, 1890-91, pp. 655-661.
PMLA, December, 1928, pp. 1039-1054.
Review of Reviews, January, 1895, pp. 96-97.*

* * *

CORDY, Michael

PERSONAL: Male.

ADDRESSES: Home—London, England. *Agent*—c/o William Morrow & Co., Inc., 1350 Avenue of the Americas, New York, NY 10019 .

WRITINGS:

The Miracle Strain, Morrow (New York City), 1997.

SIDELIGHTS: With his debut novel, *The Miracle Strain,* Michael Cordy created what his publisher called a new genre: the "genetic thriller." The book combines elements of the classic thriller with knowledge of new developments in DNA mapping, in a novel that *Publishers Weekly* deemed "a potent cocktail of high-tech science and apocalypse." The novel, set in the near future, tells the story of ace geneticist Dr. Tom Carter, who is targeted for assassination by the Brotherhood of the Second Coming, an extremist religious sect. When the killer misses his aim and murders Carter's wife by mistake, Carter begins a quest for the truth. The scientist eventually uncovers a bizarre plot: the Brotherhood is cleansing the world of blasphemers, and it considers Carter guilty because his genetics work—the Genescope he has developed that can decode a human being's DNA from a single cell—is too much like playing God.

But the zealots soon find themselves in need of Carter's help. The scientist has begun to work on the genetic code of Jesus Christ, hoping to be able to identify elements that made Christ a healer, and then perhaps find a way to use this information to save the life of his daughter, destined to die from the same rare disease that would have killed Carter's wife if she had not first been murdered. The Brotherhood, too, is interested in Jesus's DNA—this information, it hopes, will enable the sect to confirm that the suspected new Messiah is, in fact, a genetic match for Christ.

Cordy got the idea for his plot, he explained in an interview posted on his publisher's website, after reading Michael Crichton's *Jurassic Park* while on a rainy vacation with his wife, Jenny. He began wondering what would happen if scientists could explore the genes of history's great figures. Since DNA is passed on from father to son, he asked himself, would the genes of Jesus be the genes of God? Though the idea, he admitted, seemed "preposterous," it certainly offered the "big story with a mind-blowing idea" that he dreamed of one day writing. A marketing executive with a degree in English but no idea how to write a novel and no professional training in science, he went ahead with research to determine if his premise was credible. He scoured copies of *Scientific American* and *New Scientist* for information and visited the biochemistry department at London's University College. "It was frightening how close science already is to the kind of areas I explore in *The Miracle Strain,*" he noted.

The novel's blend of religious extremism and biotechnology proved a big success. Though a *Publishers Weekly* reviewer found Cordy's writing undistinguished and sometimes even careless, praise was given to the book's clever plot twists and fast-paced action. A contributor to *Library Journal* considered *The Miracle Strain* imaginative and filled with suspense. While a critic for *Booklist* deemed the novel "unusually thrilling" and predicted it would be a bestseller. Indeed, movie rights to the book were sold to Disney for more than one million dollars before the novel even appeared in bookstores, and ten foreign publishers snapped it up as their lead title for their fall sale lists.

Cordy's combination of science and action, said a contributor to the *San Francisco Chronicle,* resulted in "an engrossing and intelligent work that reads like a cross between Michael Crichton and Umberto Eco." In fact, these two writers were among the many that Cordy read to teach himself the nuts-and-bolts of novel writing. He credited Mario Puzo's *The Godfather* as his model for conveying information through dialogue.

Cordy, who lives in London, spent two years working on *The Miracle Strain* after leaving his demanding marketing job to write full time. He emphasized in the interview that his wife, a statistician, not only supported him financially during this period but also helped analyze the book's plot and inspired him to strive for excellence. He now hopes to continue his career as a full-time novelist.

BIOGRAPHICAL/CRITICAL SOURCES:

PERIODICALS

Booklist, August, 1997, p. 1846.
Denver Post, September 28, 1997.
Library Journal, August, 1997, p. 125.
Publishers Weekly, July 21, 1997, p. 181.

OTHER

William Morrow's web page "A Conversation with Michael Cordy," http://www.williammorrow. com/wm/longauthor.html?auth_id=3797 (July 22, 1998).
San Francisco Chronicle, http://www.sfgate.com. (March 1, 1998).*

*   *   *

CORNELL, Gary

PERSONAL: Male. *Education:* Brown University, Ph.D.

ADDRESSES: Office—c/o Department of Math, University of Connecticut, 196 Auditorium Rd., Math Sciences Bldg., Room 102, Storrs, CT 06269. *E-mail*—cornell@math.uconn.edu.

CAREER: Professional computer programmer, author, and educator. University of Connecticut, professor of mathematics.

AWARDS, HONORS: Reader's Choice Award, *Visual Basic Programmer's Journal,* 1997, for *Visual Basic 4 for Windows 95 Handbook.*

WRITINGS:

(With William Abikoff) *The Basic Adam,* J. Wiley (New York City), 1984.
(With William Abikoff) *The Basic Apple IIc: A Self-Teaching Guide,* J. Wiley (New York City), 1985.
ProDOS and Beyond, J. Wiley (New York City), 1985.
(Editor, with Joseph. H. Silverman) *Arithmetic Geometry,* Springer Verlag (Heidelberg, Germany), 1986.

Basics for DOS, Windcrest (Blue Ridge Summit, PA), 1991.
QuickBASIC 4.5, Windcrest (Blue Ridge Summit, PA), 1991.
Visual Basic for Windows Inside & Out, Osborne McGraw-Hill (Berkeley, CA), 1992.
Visual Basic 3 for Windows Handbook, Osborne McGraw-Hill (Berkeley, CA), 1993.
Teach Yourself Word for Windows, Osborne McGraw-Hill (Berkeley, CA), 1994.
(With Cay S. Horstmann and Troy Strain) *Delphi Nuts & Bolts: For Experienced Programmers,* Osborne McGraw-Hill (Berkeley, CA), 1995.
(With Troy Strain) *Visual Basic 4 Nuts & Bolts: For Experienced Programmers,* Osborne McGraw-Hill (Berkeley, CA), 1995.
(With Cay S. Horstmann and Joanne Cuthbertson) *The Visual Basic 4 for Windows 95 Handbook,* Osborne McGraw-Hill (Berkeley, CA), 1995.
(With Cay S. Horstmann and Dave Jezak) *Activex: Visual Basic 5 Control Creation Edition,* Prentice Hall (Upper Saddle River, NJ), 1997.
(With Cay S. Horstmann) *Core Java 1.1: Fundamentals,* Prentice Hall (Upper Saddle River, NJ), 1997.
(With Cay S. Horstmann) *Core Java 1.1: Advanced Features,* Prentice Hall (Upper Saddle River, NJ), 1997.
(With Cay S. Horstmann and Dave Jezak) *Core Visual Basic 5,* Prentice Hall (Upper Saddle River, NJ), 1997.
(With Cay S. Horstmann and Troy Strain) *Visual Basic 5 from the Ground Up,* Osborne McGraw Hill (Berkeley, CA), 1997.
(With Cay S. Horstmann and Kamal Abdali) *Cgi Programming with Java,* Prentice Hall (Upper Saddle River, NJ), 1998.
(With Cay S. Horstmann and Kim Topley) *Core Java Foundation Classes,* Prentice Hall (Upper Saddle River, NJ), 1998.
(With Pratik Patel) *Core NT Web Server with CDROM,* Prentice Hall (Upper Saddle River, NJ), 1998.
(With Cay S. Horstmann and Janet L. Traub) *Core Visual J,* Prentice Hall (Upper Saddle River, NJ), 1998.
Learn Microsoft Visual Basic Scripting Edition Now, Microsoft Press (Redmond, CA), 1998.
(Editor, with Joseph H. Silverman and Glenn Stevens) *Modular Forms and Fermat's Last Theorem,* Springer Verlag (Heidelberg, Germany).

SIDELIGHTS: Gary Cornell is a best-selling author of computer programming books and an expert on Visual Basic (VB), Java, and Delphi. His books cover earlier versions of VB, DOS, and Apple systems. His recent Core series, written with Cay S. Horstmann and Dave Jezak, is designed for the serious programmer who wishes to write commercial-quality code and build real applications. The first book in the series, *Core Visual Basic 5,* is a major advance for developers, bringing the power of object-oriented programming and ActiveX controls to the VB development environment. It introduces VB for expert programmers familiar with other languages and includes coverage of new features and detailed comparisons with previous releases. It explains the development of ActiveX EXEs and DLLs and object-oriented VB5 programming techniques. The book covers profiling, testing and optimizing VB applications. The series continues with Core Java 1 and 2, fundamentals and advanced.

BIOGRAPHICAL/CRITICAL SOURCES:

PERIODICALS

Byte, October, 1992, p. 256.
Computer Book Review, October, 1985, p. 53; February, 1986, p. 5.
New Technical Books, January, 1988, p. 94; January, 1993, p. 5.
PC/Computing, December, 1997, p. 200.
SciTech Book News, February, 1987, p. 8; August, 1992, p. 4; September, 1996, p. 5.*

*　　　*　　　*

COYKENDALL, Ralf (W., Jr.) 1929-

PERSONAL: Born November 22, 1929, in White Plains, NY; son of Ralf (an advertising media sales representative and writer) and Lin (an artist) Coykendall; married, wife's name Patricia (deceased); children: Jill Coykendall Callaway, Dale (daughter), Liz Coykendall Rice, Lee (daughter), Ralf W. III.

ADDRESSES: Home and office—93 Fields Rd., Manchester Center, VT 05255-9526.

CAREER: Artist and writer, c. 1965—. Worked as advertising copywriter, columnist, editor, and decoy manufacturer.

MEMBER: Southern Vermont Artists, American Museum of Fly Fishing.

WRITINGS:

Coykendall's Sporting Collectibles Price Guides, Lyons & Burford, 1990, 3rd edition, Chilton (Radnor, PA), 1996.
(Editor) *The Golden Age of Fly-Fishing,* Countryman Press (Woodstock, VT), 1997.

Other books include *You and Your Retriever, Wildfowling at a Glance,* and *Modern Decoys.* Author of "Sporting Collectibles," a monthly column in *Outdoor Life,* 1999—. Contributor to magazines, including *Sports Afield, Guns and Ammo,* and *Antique Weekly.*

WORK IN PROGRESS: Editing *The Tranquillity Stories* by H. P. Shelton; editing *The Golden Age of Gunning;* a fish and game cookbook.

SIDELIGHTS: Ralf Coykendall told *CA:* "Two things in my youth shaped the 'why' and 'what' I write about today: *I Wanted to Write* by Kenneth Roberts and growing up in a family where hunting and fishing were a part of life. In my youth I devoured the historical novels of Roberts, and when I read *I Wanted to Write* I knew somehow where I was headed. One only writes well about subjects that one knows and understands, and it is no surprise that I 'headed outdoors' to find success. My first book, *You and Your Retriever,* published in the 1960s, was the direct result of owning, training, hunting, and field-trialing an exceptional retriever. The pattern was set. *Wildfowling at a Glance* and *Modern Decoys* reflected participation afield and in the decoy manufacturing business. Hunting and fishing and all that go with them were my forte and the niche for my writing career."

*　　　*　　　*

CRAWFORD, Mark 1954-

PERSONAL: Born September 5, 1954, in Chicago, IL; son of Justin C. (an engineer) and Janet Patricia (a teacher; maiden name, Doyle) Crawford; married Mary K. Zietz, 1986. *Education:* University of Western Ontario, B.Sc. (with honors), 1976; University of Toronto, M.Sc., 1981. *Avocational interests:* Sports, travel, music.

ADDRESSES: Office—5101 Violet Lane, Madison, WI 53714. *E-mail*—mandm@itis.com.

CAREER: Mining geologist, 1977-95; freelance writer, 1995—.

WRITINGS:

Toxic Waste Sites, American Bibliographical Center-Clio Press (Santa Barbara, CA), 1997.
Physical Geology, Cliff's Notes (Lincoln, NE), 1997.
Encyclopedia of the Mexican-American War, American Bibliographical Center-Clio Press, 1998.
Courage on Lesser Fields, McFarland and Co. (Jefferson, NC), 1998.
Endangered Habitats and Ecosystems, American Bibliographical Center-Clio Press, 1998.

SIDELIGHTS: Mark Crawford told *CA:* "I am drawn to just about any topic except business and finance. I choose subjects that interest me and that I may know nothing about. This is the way I learn. For me, history is incredibly important, because there is so much that can be learned and applied to the present.

"Good nonfiction *must* be thoroughly researched, but don't distill primary material until it is reduced to dry facts. Maintain the personal feel and drama by using choice quotations. This advice can be applied to almost any topic."

*   *   *

CRIMMINS, G(erald) Garfield 1940-
(Jerry Crimmins)

PERSONAL: Born February 9, 1940, in Minneapolis, MN; son of John Emmett (an architect and property assessor) and Inez (an interior designer; maiden name, Wood; present surname, Danesen) Crimmins. *Ethnicity:* "Irish American." *Politics:* None. *Religion:* "None/retired Catholic." *Avocational interests:* Gardening, travel.

ADDRESSES: Home—153 Roberts Ave., Glenside, PA 19038. *Agent*—Susan Gainsburg, Writers House, Inc., 21 West 26th St., New York, NY 10010. *E-mail*—revesguy@aol.com.

CAREER: Moore College of Art, Philadelphia, PA, professor of art, 1968-99. Artist, with solo and group exhibitions in major U.S. cities; art represented in private and institutional collections, including Phila-

delphia Museum of Art, Pratt Institute, Minneapolis Museum of Art, and Philadelphia Free Library. *Military service:* U.S. Marine Corps, 1958-64.

AWARDS, HONORS: Purchase award, Philadelphia Museum of Art, 1980; grants from National Endowment for the Arts, 1980 and 1983, Pennsylvania Council on the Arts, 1980, and Pollock-Krasner Foundation, 1991.

WRITINGS:

Anatomical Notes, ICUC Press, 1975.
Thicker Than Blood, Cold Chair Press, 1976.
The Song of the Fair Haired, ICUC Press, 1977.
A Visitor's Guide to La Republique de Reves, Synapse, 1980.
The Secret History of La Republique de Reves, Oracle Press (Baton Rouge, LA), 1984.
The Republic of Dreams, Norton (New York City), 1998.

Some writings have appeared under the name Jerry Crimmins.

WORK IN PROGRESS: A sequel to *The Republic of Dreams.*

*   *   *

CROSSETTE, Barbara

PERSONAL: Female. *Education:* Muhlenberg College, B.A.; University of Colorado, M.A.

ADDRESSES: Office—The New York Times, UN Secretarial Building, Room 453, New York, NY 10017.

CAREER: New York Times, New York City, Bangkok bureau chief, 1984-88, New Belhi bureau chief, 1988-91, Washington correspondent, 1991-93, and United Nations bureau chief, 1994—. Fulbright Professor of Journalism at Punjab University and at the Indian Institute for Mass Communications, New Delhi, 1980. Columbia University, Southern Asia Institute, research associate.

AWARDS, HONORS: George Polk Award for foreign reporting, 1991, for coverage of the assassination Rajiv Gandhi.

WRITINGS:

(Editor) *America's Wonderful Little Hotels and Inns*, Dutton (New York City), 1980.

(Editor with Wendy Lowe) *America's Wonderful Little Hotels and Inns: Eastern Region*, Congdon & Weed (New York City), 1984.

(Editor with Wendy Lowe) *America's Wonderful Little Hotels and Inns: Western Region*, Congdon & Weed (New York City), 1984.

India: Facing the Twenty-First Century, Indiana University Press (Bloomington), 1993.

So Close to Heaven: The Vanishing Buddhist Kingdoms of the Himalayas, Knopf (New York City), 1995.

The Great Hill Stations of Asia, Westview Press (Boulder, CO), 1998.

SIDELIGHTS: Barbara Crossette's three books on the Far East are informed to some extent by her years as a *New York Times* correspondent based in New Delhi, India. One is an analysis of India's present and future; two are travel books, but only in part. In the 1980s, she edited American hostelry guides. Most recently, Crossette served as U.N. bureau chief for the *Times*.

Crossette and Wendy Lowe teamed up to write several volumes comprising *America's Wonderful Little Hotels & Inns*. These volumes collect observations from tourists who have completed a questionnaire. One volume includes states to the east of the Mississippi River, eastern Canada, and Puerto Rico; the other includes states to the west of the Mississippi River and western Canada. Denise P. Donavin, a reviewer for *Booklist*, wrote "the entries tend to be extremely individualistic, differing markedly in length, tone, and detail." *Publishers Weekly* reviewer Ray Bongartz commented that many descriptions include remarks by travelers that adds "some depth to the overall effect." *Library Journal* called the 1980 edition a "fine and useful guide."

In *India: Facing the Twenty-First Century* (1993), "Crossette's rage at what she saw . . . seethes on every page," declared *New York Times* writer Thomas Thornton. What she saw, according to a *Publishers Weekly* review was "[s]taggering corruption at all levels," including caste discrimination, the burning of brides with inadequate dowries, exploited child workers, a massive uneducated and impoverished population, and on going violence. Her portrait of India examines contemporary urban life, religion, the role of women, and the country's perception of interna-

tional allies and enemies. Crossette holds politicians responsible for India's woes, specifically Indira Gandhi and Indira's son Rajiv Gandhi. Crossette believes hope for India's future lies with a more visible middle class and growing activist movements.

Reviews of *India: Facing the Twenty-First Century* were favorable. Thornton criticized Crossette for failing to discuss India's ability to build a nation despite economic and political problems. However, Thornton called her "a skilled and honest reporter" and commented that readers familiar with India "will find her reporting filled with sharp insights." *Publishers Weekly* called the book "compelling."

With *So Close to Heaven: The Vanishing Buddhist Kingdoms of the Himalayas*, Crossette journeys to Bhutan, a country where Tantric Buddhism endures, and until recently, one of the few remaining places on earth that remained unaffected by Western civilization. According to *New York Times* writer Pico Iyer, Crossette "unravels the intricacies of Buddhism with commendable clarity."

Crossette's 1998 book, *The Great Hill Stations of Asia*, examines the history of Asia's hill stations and discusses the impact of an emerging middle class on the region's economics, politics, and religion. Crossette's first encounter with a hill station occurred while teaching at a university in India near the Himalayan foothills. One night she noticed a cluster of lights which, she discovered, belonged to Kasauli, at an elevation over 6,000 feet the first of several hill stations she would visit. In 1977 Crossette toured similar sites in India, Burma, Sri Lanka, Malaysia, and Indonesia.

Hill stations in India were originally high-elevation retreats built by British colonials to escape the hot Indian low lands. Over time, they became unique little towns perched in valley nooks from 5,000 to 8,000 feet above sea level, complete with clubs, a village church, a library, medical facilities, lodgings, a race course, a golf course, botanical gardens, hiking trails, and schools. After colonialism faded away, the close to one hundred hill stations in existence suffered a period of decline, but they have again become retreats for the elite, "locals," and tourists. Their recent successes, Crossette points out, may be their undoing, as trees come down for roads and golf courses, as environmental problems mount, and as tourists press for entertainment facilities such as theme parks, discos, casinos, and restaurants. Crossette pays a good deal of attention to the history of these places but notes they are "becom[ing] more a part of Asian than of Western history." Still, they are unique. Says Crossette, they "cannot be mass-produced or even reproduced anywhere but where they are."

BIOGRAPHICAL/CRITICAL SOURCES:

PERIODICALS

Booklist, July 1984, p. 1503.
Christian Science Monitor, July 21, 1998, p. 15.
Library Journal, January 1, 1980, p. 101.
New York Times Book Review, November 21, 1993, p. 37; October 13, 1996, p. 32.
Publishers Weekly, September 2, 1983, p. 30; September 20, 1993, pp. 57-59.

OTHER

Washington Post Online, http://washingtonpost.com (September 24, 1998).*

—*Sketch by Richard Chapman*

D

DALTON, Sheila

PERSONAL: Born in Middlesex, England; daughter of Christopher William (a contract administrator) and Vola Molly (a government office manager) Dalton; married Gordon Wyatt, 1982; children: Adam Dalton-Wyatt. *Citizenship:* Canadian. *Ethnicity:* "British." *Education:* Received B.A. (English; with honors), M.L.S. *Politics:* Liberal/Socialist. *Religion:* Agnostic. *Avocational interests:* Insight meditation, herbalism, psychoanalysis, and psychology.

ADDRESSES: Agent—Carolyn Swayze. *E-mail*—sage spirit@hotmail.com.

CAREER: Freelance writer and poet, 1982—. Freelance editor and reference librarian. Previous positions include bartender and art gallery assistant.

MEMBER: Writers' Union of Canada, League of Canadian Poets, Canadian Poetry Association, CANSCATP, Canadian Alliance in Solidarity with the Native Peoples.

AWARDS, HONORS: "Our Choice" Award, Canadian Children's Book Centre, for *Trial by Fire;* Short Fiction Prize, *Cross-Canadian Writers' Quarterly,* 1984, for "Dreams of Freedom, Dreams of Need"; runner-up, Kalamalka New Writers Society Award for Booklength poetry manuscript, for *Blowing Holes through the Everyday.*

WRITINGS:

Bubblemania (picture book), illustrated by Bob Beeson, Orca Book Publishers (Victoria, British Columbia, Canada), 1992.

Blowing Holes through the Everyday (poetry) HMS Press (London, Ontario, Canada), 1993.
Tales of the Ex Fire-Eater: A Novel (novel), Aurora Editions (Winnipeg, Alberta, Canada), 1994.
Doggerel (picture book), illustrated by Kim LaFave, Doubleday (Toronto, Ontario, Canada), 1996.
Catalogue (picture book), illustrated by Kim LaFave, Doubleday (Toronto, Ontario, Canada), 1998.
Trial by Fire (young adult), Napoleon Publications (Toronto, Ontario, Canada), 1998.

WORK IN PROGRESS: A novel for adults entitled, *The Girl in the Box.*

SIDELIGHTS: Many of Canadian author and poet Sheila Dalton's published books have been aimed at a juvenile audience. She is the author of the picture books *Bubblemania, Doggerel,* and *Catalogue.* Dalton is also the author of the adult novel, *Tales of the Ex Fire-Eater,* and a poetry collection for adults titled *Blowing Holes through the Everyday.*

Dalton's *Bubblemania,* with illustrations by Bob Beeson, is a counting book, that relates the tale of David, a young boy who blows a big bubble that eventually traps his friends, relatives, and much of his town. To save his loved ones, David takes it upon himself to pop his wondrous creation. *Bubblemania* met with genial reviews. Rhea Tregebov in *Books in Canada* thought that the illustrations of the book were somewhat "hectic," but praised Dalton's work as "energetic." Tregebov also noted that the story is suitable for all age groups, from "toddlers . . . learning to count," preschoolers learning to read, and "early readers." Catherine McInerney in *Canadian Materials* hailed *Bubblemania*'s "imaginative text," while Janet McNaughton in *Quill & Quire* concluded:

"Bubblemania is not only a good counting book, but it's the best one I've seen in a while."

Blowing Holes through the Everyday, a poetry collection, discusses topics such as medical tests, being a tourist, and why some women sexually tease men. According to Bert Almon in *Canadian Book Review Annual,* Dalton includes a preface to this work in which she puts forth her theory that poetry offers the reader a connection to life's enigmas. Almon felt that the volume "assume[s] the mystery" more than it provides the reader an experience of it, but he did concede that "Dalton has talent." Whereas Mark Young in *Scene* said, "Her Poetry is as rich and varied . . . as any recent works I've read. She is capable of many poetic voices, yet is still able to imprint them with her own voice, which makes extraordinary these poems of the ordinary and the 'everyday.'"

Tales of the Ex Fire-Eater is no literary metaphor. The heroine of the book, whose real name is Antoinette but who is called Fido, actually is attempting to escape her past as a circus fire-eater. Antoinette is only fourteen but has lived with the circus all of her life, at first with her mother, then solo after her mother's disappearance. Her bisexual boyfriend, in training to be a tightrope walker, talks her into leaving with him and living in Toronto, where he abandons her for another boy. Eventually, Antoinette returns to the circus. Janet Money in *Canadian Book Review Annual* hailed the novel as "a fascinating web of characters and symbols" and predicted that it "would probably make a good film." Eva Tihanyi in *Books in Canada* praised *Tales of the Ex Fire-Eater* as well, citing "the remarkable consciousness of Antoinette herself" as superseding even the "wealth of colourful secondary characters."

In 1996 Dalton's *Doggerel* became available to child audiences. The book features illustrations of many different breeds and types of dogs done by Kim LaFave, with Dalton's light-hearted rhyming verses accompanying them. This effort, too, met with positive reviews. Steve Pitt in the *Canadian Book Review Annual* announced that the author's "rhyme and rhythm standards [are] consistently high" in *Doggerel* while remaining "delightfully silly."

Dalton told *CA:* "People sometimes ask me if I prefer writing for children or for adults. And I answer that I like both, for very different reasons. They seem to come from different parts of the psyche. Writing for diverse age groups keeps me in touch with different stages of life. Certainly, writing for children helps me create young characters in my books for adults, and vice versa."

BIOGRAPHICAL/CRITICAL SOURCES:

PERIODICALS

Books in Canada, summer, 1992, p. 36; October, 1995, p. 51.
Canadian Book Review Annual, 1994, pp. 204-205; 1995, pp. 165-166; 1996, pp. 496-497.
Canadian Materials, September, 1992, p. 207.
Quill & Quire, May, 1992, p. 32; April, 1996, p. 38.
Scene, May/June, 1994, p. 8.

* * *

DANIELS, Anthony 1949-

PERSONAL: Born October 11, 1949, in London, England. *Avocational interests:* Travel.

ADDRESSES: Home—England. *Agent*—c/o John Murray Publishers Ltd., 50 Albemarle St., London W1X 4BD, England. *E-mail*—ADan530211@aol .com.

CAREER: Psychiatrist and medical journalist.

WRITINGS:

Coups and Cocaine: Two Journeys in South America, Overlook Press (Woodstock, NY), 1986.
Fool or Physician: The Memoirs of a Sceptical Doctor, J. Murray (London), 1987.
Zanzibar to Timbuktu, J. Murray (London), 1988.
Sweet Waist of America: Journeys around Guatemala, Hutchinson (London), 1990.
Utopias Elsewhere: Journeys in a Vanishing World, Crown (New York City), 1991, published in England as *The Wilder Shores of Marx: Journeys in a Vanishing World,* Hutchinson (London), 1991.
Monrovia Mon Amour: A Visit to Liberia, J. Murray (London), 1992.

Contributor to medical journals under a pseudonym.
WORK IN PROGRESS: A social history of arsenic, with notes on antimony, strychnine, and prissic acid.

SIDELIGHTS: Though he makes his living as a psychiatrist, British author Anthony Daniels is best known for his travel writings. Most of Daniels's adventures take place not in the relatively safe and familiar capitals of the West, but in Third World locales including nations in Latin America and Africa, and even—as he recorded in *Utopias Elsewhere: Journeys in a Vanishing World* (1991), his recollections of a 1989 trip—the rapidly diminishing world of Marxist police states. In the introduction to *Utopias Elsewhere,* he wrote, "I have long been fascinated by the passing of ways of life. In 1975, shortly after I qualified as a doctor, I went for a few months to work in Rhodesia, as [the present nation of Zimbabwe] was then still called. I wanted to witness the last gasp of the colonial world before it passed into an oblivion from which it would be rescued only by vilification."

Daniels's first book, *Coups and Cocaine: Two Journeys in South America* (1986), took him to Peru, Bolivia, Ecuador, Brazil, Chile, and Paraguay, where he saw another threatened way of life. In this case, however, politics were not the defining factor; drugs were. Among the more hair-raising of his stories, as noted by reviewers both in the *Christian Science Monitor* and the *Times Literary Supplement,* was a visit to four Americans convicted of drug-smuggling and incarcerated in a Bolivian jail. John Ure of the *Times Literary Supplement* faulted Daniels for "trying the stuff [cocaine], and accepting the gift of cocaine from a casual acquaintance (admittedly he flushed it down the sink fairly promptly thereafter). He was perhaps lucky to get home safely. This is a lively traveller's tale." Gail Pool of the *Christian Science Monitor* likewise took issue with Daniels's sardonic attitude, calling him "an unpleasant guide" who "ridicule[s] and insult[s] other Westerners and non-Indian natives"; but, she conceded, the book was "an interesting mix" of "description, history, and anecdote."

Daniels's irreverent treatment of his subject matter has sometimes rankled critics, as for instance in *Utopias Elsewhere,* which was published in his native England as *The Wilder Shores of Marx.* His anti-Communism offended Paula M. Zeiselman in *Library Journal,* who called the book "patronizing and condescending. . . . an early 1950s throwback to when 'Commie pinkos' lurked behind every bush." Daniels made it clear in his book that he is no fan of totalitarianism, a fact for which he is unapologetic: "I make no claim," he writes in the introduction, "to have travelled in a neutral frame of mind. But neutrality is not a precondition of truth, which itself is not necessarily the mean between two extremes. One

does not expect neutrality of someone investigating Nazism, and would be appalled if he affected it; why, then, expect it of someone investigating a different, but longer-lasting, evil?"

In gathering material for the book, written as the peoples of Eastern Europe had begun to overthrow Communism, Daniels deliberately travelled to the more remote outposts of Marxist Leninism, some of them entirely outside the Soviet orbit: Albania and Romania in Eastern Europe, Vietnam and North Korea in East Asia, and Cuba in the Caribbean. Except for Vietnam, which had a thriving black market that promised to grow into a free market someday, Daniels saw little hope in these countries. Indeed, while Romania and Albania both experienced an end to Communism shortly after he completed his book, both nations have since encountered great difficulties in adjusting to a more democratic form of government.

Because of the restricted nature of these countries, Daniels tended to travel with tour groups of Westerners, many of whom were true believers in communism. Some members of the delegation visiting North Korea, for instance, were liberals concerned over issues such as animal rights; but the majority were "not the kind of people to wax sentimental over the fate of dumb beasts. They were hard-faced communists, who dressed tough and cut their hair short so their heads should appear as bony as possible."

Also pithy are Daniels's observations regarding the triumphs of socialism. Again, because he travelled in extremely controlled countries, he was not allowed to see much in the form of poverty or repression, but what he did see was clear enough. Ruminating, while in Albania, on the state of consumer goods in countries with command economies, he asked, "What, I wondered, is the defining characteristic of communist shoddiness? . . . What have the tubes of Bulgarian toothpaste on sale in kiosks in Tirana in common with the packets of Czechoslovak soap or East German buttons also on sale there?" After considering various qualities such as skewed labels and rusty metal cans, he concluded that "it is the printing and design of packaging that is most thoroughly characteristic . . . of communist manufacture. The paper or cardboard is always rough and absorbent, so that ink often sends little spidery strands through it; the calligraphy is crude and inelegant. The labels bear as little information as possible: *toothpaste,* they say, or *soap,* and nothing else. This is because the alternatives to *toothpaste* and *soap* are not other brands, but no toothpaste at all and no soap." On the other hand, he goes on to say, these labels are not entirely superfluous, since plums bottled in Communist countries tend to be "revoltingly indistinguishable from cherries, olives, apricots" and other similarly small and cylindrical items of fruit.

To Ross Clark of the *Times Literary Supplement, Utopias Elsewhere* was "an excellent travelogue," and Donald Lyons of the *Wall Street Journal* wrote that Daniels's "synthesizing eye is sharp." He quoted as an example Daniels's description of Cuban dictator Fidel Castro's Havana: "It . . . is an inhabited ruin; the inhabitants are like a wandering tribe that has found the deserted metropolis of a superior but dead civilisation and decided to make it home." Arnold Beichman of the *National Review* praised Daniels for "a perfectly timed, different kind of travel book exquisitely written by a practicing British psychiatrist with a sardonic style, a keen eye, and a sense that the struggle for democratic civilization is far from over."

In contrast to *Utopias Elsewhere* is Daniels' *Monrovia Mon Amour: A Visit to Liberia* (1992) in which he confronts an autocracy that has nothing to do with communism—one, indeed, that owed its continued existence partly to U.S. support. Daniels, wrote Bill Berkeley in the *Times Literary Supplement,* "paints a vivid and disquieting portrait. . . . [He] has a keen eye for the quirky detail and he writes with a wry [Evelyn] Waugh-like scepticism. His portraits of some of the protagonists in Liberia's on-going military stalemate are devastatingly accurate." Alice Joyce of *Booklist* noted the "cast of appalling characters" with whom Daniels met, including "the maniacal killer General Prince Y. Johnson." The book, she concluded, is "informative reporting on the present-day conditions of this African nation that is required, if painful, reading."

Daniels told *CA:* "I have always tried in my travel writing to tell the unvarnished truth. Contrary to what some critics have suggested, to do otherwise is true condescension. When Liberians or inhabitants of communist countries tell me they recognize the truth of what I have written, I feel gratified."

BIOGRAPHICAL/CRITICAL SOURCES:

BOOKS

Daniels, Anthony, *Fool or Physician: The Memoirs of a Sceptical Doctor,* J. Murray (London), 1987.

PERIODICALS

Booklist, January 15, 1993, p. 873.
Christian Science Monitor, March 6, 1987, p. B4.
Library Journal, July, 1991, p. 119.
National Review, October 21, 1991, p. 46.
New Statesman & Society, April 19, 1991, p. 32.
Times Literary Supplement, June 20, 1986, p. 674; March 29, 1991, p. 22; July 31, 1992, p. 9.
Wall Street Journal, May 11, 1992, p. A8.

—*Sketch by Judson Knight*

*   *   *

DAVID, Jonah M.
See JONES, David Martin

*   *   *

DAVID, Thomas 1940-

PERSONAL: Born October 28, 1940, in Budapest, Hungary; son of Josef (a surgeon and medical director) and Marianne (a painter) DaVid; married, wife's name Karin (died, 1987); married Li Qin (a surgeon), 1996; children: Nathalie, Nicole, Annamaria. *Ethnicity:* "Hungarian." *Education:* University of Veterinary Medicine of Budapest, Dr.Med.Vet. (summa cum laude), 1964; University of Veterinary Medicine of Vienna, Mag.Vet.Med. *Politics:* Liberal. *Religion:* Roman Catholic. *Avocational interests:* Offshore sailing, art, photography, aquarell painting.

ADDRESSES: Office—Oesterreichisches Zellkultur-Forschungslabor, Margaretenstrasse 2-4/III/14, A-1040 Vienna, Austria; fax 00-43-1-58-518-0513. *Agent*—Juergen Braunschweiger, Grendelstrasse 15, Lucerne, Switzerland. *E-mail*—codtea-nutritional@mail.xpoint.at.

CAREER: Oesterreichisches Zellkultur-Forschungs-labor, Vienna, Austria, president and chief scientist. Conducted research on polygonal pelvic osteotomy, 1969-86, ethnomedicine (cancer and immunodeficiency) and biotherapy against cancer, 1986—.

AWARDS, HONORS: Austrian Cross of Honor, 1994.

WRITINGS:

Griechenland (art and photography), Terra Magica, 1982.
Istria (art and photography), Terra Magica, 1983.
Crete (art and photography), Terra Magica, 1984.
Salzburg (art and photography), Bertelsmann (Munich, Germany), 1986.
Miracle Medicines of the Rainforest, Inner Traditions (Rochester, VT), 1997.

WORK IN PROGRESS: Research on cancer and immunodeficiency using tropical herbs, particularly the author's CoD tea.

*   *   *

DEAN, Eric T., Jr. 1950-

PERSONAL: Born May 31, 1950, in Chicago, IL; son of Eric T. (a college professor) and Betty (a homemaker; maiden name, Garrett) Dean. *Education:* Swarthmore College, B.A., 1972; Indiana University—Bloomington, J.D., 1978; Purdue University, M.A., 1988; Yale University, M.Phil., 1993, Ph.D., 1996. *Politics:* Democrat. *Religion:* Presbyterian.

ADDRESSES: Home—213 Willow St., New Haven, CT 06511. *Office*—Marcus Law Firm, 111 Whitney Ave., New Haven, CT 06510; fax 203-789-8705. *E-mail*—Etdean@aol.com.

CAREER: U.S. Peace Corps, Washington, DC, tuberculosis control worker in Hahm Pyong and Seoul, South Korea, 1972-75; Legal Services of Northern Indiana, attorney in Lafayette, Kokomo, and Fort Wayne, 1978-81; attorney in private practice, Crawfordsville, IN, 1981-89; Purdue University, West Lafayette, IN, instructor in history, 1989; Yale University, New Haven, CT, instructor in history, 1993 and 1995; Marcus Law Firm, New Haven, real estate attorney, 1996—.

MEMBER: American Historical Association, Connecticut Bar Association, New Haven County Bar Association.

AWARDS, HONORS: Yale University, Mellon fellow,

1992-93, John F. Enders fellow, 1994, Whiting fellow in humanities, 1995-96; Albert J. Beveridge grant, American Historical Association, 1993-94; Mark C. Stevens fellow, Bentley Historical Library, University of Michigan, 1993-94; fellow, Indiana Historical Society, 1993-94; William M. E. Rachal Award, *Virginia Magazine of History and Biography,* 1995, for the article "'We Live under a Government of Men and Morning Newspapers': Image, Expectation, and the Peninsula Campaign of 1862;" shared Best Book Award, Political Psychology Section, American Political Science Association, 1998, for *Shook over Hell.*

WRITINGS:

Shook over Hell: Post-Traumatic Stress, Vietnam, and the Civil War, Harvard University Press (Cambridge, MA), 1997.

Contributor to law and history journals, including *Civil War History, Journal of American Studies, History of Psychiatry, Southern Historian, Cincinnati Law Review,* and *Michigan Historical Review.*

WORK IN PROGRESS: Research on the impact of the media on contemporary views and conceptions of the American Civil War.

SIDELIGHTS: Eric T. Dean, Jr. told *CA:* "*Shook over Hell* investigates the complexities and myriad images of war, both for the participants as well as the civilians and commentators or historians. I was struck by how war shatters all ideas and notions of stability, order, and continuity for the soldiers who experience the chaos of combat and the death of comrades; how veterans grapple with anger and resentment in their attempt to come to terms with what they experienced; and how civilians understand so little of the raw brutality of war, and resort to various clumsy myths to attempt to understand war. I concluded that our ideas of both the Vietnam War (a 'bad war') and the Civil War (a 'good war') have become wrapped up in predictable cliches, which needed to be critically evaluated. I see *Shook over Hell* as a broad-ranging challenge to rethink our seemingly simplistic ideas of war, particularly the idea of 'good' or 'justified' wars, and the idea of the veteran as victim or hero.

"My writing is shaped by my having practiced law for something like fifteen years. As a lawyer, one is called upon to analyze complex factual situations and offer clear options to one's clients. I believe this kind of rigorous training and tutelage prepares one well to tackle and evaluate complicated and extensive bodies of historical evidence.

"As a legal services attorney, I represented clients who were involuntarily committed to mental hospitals, and I had occasion to ponder the meaning of insanity and mental health. My interest in mental health issues ties into the concept of post-traumatic stress disorder, which is so central to our conception of the Vietnam veteran (the veteran as a psychiatric victim). This concern led me to investigate the psychiatric problems and readjustments of veterans of the American Civil War, something which had never before been studied."

*   *   *

de las CASAS, Walter 1947-

PERSONAL: Born February 3, 1947, in Havana, Cuba; naturalized U.S. citizen; son of Mario and Aracelia (Vivo) de las Casas. *Ethnicity:* "Hispanic." *Education:* Iona College, B.A. (cum laude), 1970; Hunter College of the City University of New York, M.A., 1977; doctoral study at City University of New York, 1987-94. *Politics:* Liberal Democrat.

ADDRESSES: Home—323 Dahill Rd., Apt. 1A, Brooklyn, NY 11218-3848.

CAREER: Poet and educator. High school Spanish teacher in Brooklyn, NY, 1978-94; Science Skill Center High School, Brooklyn, teacher of Spanish language and literature, 1994-96.

MEMBER: American Association of Teachers of Spanish and Portuguese.

WRITINGS:

La Ninez Que Dilata (poems), Editorial Catoblepas, 1986.
Libido (poems; in Spanish), Linden Lane Press, 1989.
Tributes (poems), E. Press, 1993.

WORK IN PROGRESS: Discourse, a work in English; *Human,* a work in English; *Hojas Dispersas,* a work in Spanish.

SIDELIGHTS: Walter de las Casas told *CA:* "Poetry is the lyrical expression of my intimate, interior, psychological life and of human relationships. It is also the lyrical expression of knowledge.

"Poetry should be transparent, a clean windowpane through which living feeling shines."

*   *   *

DELRIO, Martin
See MACDONALD, James D.

*   *   *

DESAUTELS, Denise 1945-

PERSONAL: Born 1945, in Montreal, Canada.

ADDRESSES: Agent—c/o Editions de Noirot, 1835 boul des Hauteurs, St. Hippolyte, Quebec J0R 1P0, Canada.

CAREER: French-Canadian poet.

AWARDS, HONORS: Prix du Gouverneur General (Governor General's Prize) for poetry, 1993, for *Le Saut de l'ange.*

WRITINGS:

Comme miroirs en feuilles (poems), drawing by Leon Bellefleur, Editions du Noroit (Quebec), 1975.
Marie, tout s'eteignait en moi, drawings by Leon Bellefleur, Editions du Noroit (Saint-Lambert, Quebec), 1977.
La promeneuse et l'oiseau suivi de Journal de la promeneuse, Editions du Noroit (Saint-L'Ambet, Quebec), 1980.
L'ecran, precede de, Aires du tempts, with two drawings by Francine Simonin, Noroit (Quebec), 1983.
(With Anne-Marie Alonzo and Raymonde April) *Nous en reparlerons sans doute,* Editions Trois (Laval, Quebec), 1986.
Un livre de Kafka a la main, suivi de La Blessure, avec huit photographies de Jocelyne Alloucherie,

Editions du Noroit (Saint-Lambert, Quebec), 1987.

Lecons de Venise, Editions du Noroit (Saint-Lambert, Quebec), 1990.

Mais la menace est une belle extravagance suivi de Le Signe Discret, avec huit photographies d'Ariane Theze, Noroit (Saint-Lambert, Quebec), 1991.

Le Saut de l'ange: autour de quelques objets de Martha Townsend, Editions du Noroit/L'Arbre a paroles (Quebec), 1992.

(With Anne-Marie Alonzo) *Lettres a Cassandre,* afterword by Louise Dupre, Trois (Laval, Quebec), 1994.

SIDELIGHTS: The prominent Quebecois poet Denise Desautels belongs, according to *Canadian Literature* reviewer Cedric May, in the company of two of the foremost contributors to the contemporary literature of that province, Gaston Miron and Gerald Godin. May expressed this opinion in a review of volumes by all three eminent writers; the Desautels work under consideration was a set of two collections, *Mais la menace est une belle extravagance* and *Le Signe discret.* That 1991 volume manifested, from the outset, some attributes typical of Desautels' publications: it coalesced two small collections into one, and it was accompanied by visual art, in this case eight photographs by Ariane Theze.

The titles of the two collections are translated literally as "But Menace is a Beautiful Extravagance" and "The Discreet Sign." Both, according to May, showed Desautels's skill in translating the poetics of her own life and in dealing with issues of language and semiotics (the study of signs and symbols). In *Le Signe discret,* Desautels plays with the word "septembre", May noted. Images of the ninth month of the year are set before the reader, fleetingly, in the form of memories which have been removed from their everyday context. These, May asserted, show the poet's desire "to verbalise a fluid and free perception of reality." May quoted an illuminating statement Desautels made in 1985 in answer to the question, "Why write poetry?": "Pour questionner les mots et me questionner a travers eux. Hors de la norme et de l'usage quotidien, hors du piege, associer mot et mouvement." ("To question words and to question myself through them. Outside of the norm and of everyday usage, outside of the trap, to associate word and movement.") Self-discovery for Desautels went along with the questioning of language.

Desautels used the visual to help question the verbal in her prize-winning 1992 book, *Le Saut de l'ange:*

autour de quelques objets de Martha Townsend, translated literally as "The Leap of the Angel: Around Some Objects of Martha Townsend". Canadian artist Martha Townsend was the creator of three-dimensional objects, photos of six of which were included in the book. The objects were, for Desautels, "catalysts of a new dimension in the life of a narrator overcome by solitude and a sense of loss," as Sarah Lawall of the University of Massachusetts observed in *French Review.* Like the Townsend objects, the country of Ireland was also a strong, recurring symbol in the book; both these symbols had to do with separation from a childhood sense of belonging and the wish to overcome that separation. The book, Lawall believed, chronicled an emotional journey from individual pain to communal awareness—to the recognition "that visions, perspectives, and emotions are held in common, especially the vision of art. . . ." Lawall asserted that Desautels' tribute to Townsend revealed "the richness of her own personal and poetic imagination." Intrinsic to the volume were not only Desautels's own poetry, but also quotations from several Canadian and European authors important to Desautels, including Peter Handke and Marguerite Duras.

Desautels's commentary upon visual art had been even more explicit in her 1990 book, *Lecons de Venise* (Lessons from Venice) which was a collection of brief prose meditations upon the sculptures of Michel Goulet as presented at the 1988 Venice Biennial. In a review written in French for the *French Review,* Andrea Moorhead questioned whether Desautels' text had successfully decided upon a direction; much of it, Moorhead disclosed, consisted of autobiographical material concerning the writer's personal and professional preoccupations, presented "tout en essayant febrilement de comprendre les sculptures" ("in the midst of trying feverishly to understand the sculptures"). Of the three sections of the book, Moorhead found the third to contain its heart. She wrote, "C'est ici que l'expression autobiographique essaie de feconder la sculpture, de combler le vide conceptuel constamment nie par Desautels" ("It is here that the autobiographical expression tries to fecondate the sculpture, to fill the conceptual void constantly repudiated by Desautels.") Goulet's sculptures, in Moorhead's view, confronted one with a self-referential quality, an atmosphere of physical and psychological doubt which was "anti-femme": the antithesis of Desautels's feminist autobiographical approach in this "sincere et interrogateur" ("sincere and questioning") book.

BIOGRAPHICAL/CRITICAL SOURCES:

PERIODICALS

Canadian Literature, winter, 1991, pp. 228-231.
French Review, March, 1993, pp. 683-684; March, 1995, pp. 746-747.*

*   *   *

DESMOINAUX, Christel 1967-

PERSONAL: Born March 28, 1967, in Nogent-sur-Marne, France; daughter of Alain (a managing director) and Ginette (Mathieu) Desmoinaux. *Education:* Attended Met de Penninghen (art school), Paris, France, 1984-86; Ecole de Communication Visuelle, Paris, 1986-88. *Avocational interests:* Travel, cinema, languages, literature, music, theater.

ADDRESSES: Home and office—57, rue de Tolbiac, 75013 Paris, France.

CAREER: Illustrator, 1988—.

WRITINGS:

SELF-ILLUSTRATED; FOR CHILDREN

Comme Il Rougit, M. Souris! Bordas, 1989.
Julia N'En Rate Pas Une! Fleurus (Paris, France), 1991.
Panique dans L'Ascenseur, Fleurus, 1991.
A la Ferme, Nathan, 1992.
Au Zoo, Nathan, 1992.
Henri, Tete-en-L'Air, Hachette, 1992.
L'Oeuf de Madame Poule (title means "Mrs. Hen's Egg"), Hachette, 1998.

ILLUSTRATOR; FOR CHILDREN; IN ENGLISH TRANSLATION

Anael Dena, *Les Chiffres,* Nathan, 1995, translation by Janet Neis published as *Numbers,* Gareth Stevens (Milwaukee, WI), 1997.
Anael Dena, *Les Lettres,* Nathan, 1995, published as *Letters,* Gareth Stevens (Milwaukee, WI), 1997.
Anael Dena, *Les Contraires,* Nathan, 1996, published as *Opposites,* Gareth Stevens (Milwaukee, WI, 1997.

Anael Dena, *Les Couleurs,* Nathan, 1996, published as *Colors,* Gareth Stevens (Milwaukee, WI), 1997.

ILLUSTRATOR

Frederique Rotillon, *Des Vacances Inoubliables,* Nathan, 1990.
Odile Hellmann-Hurpoil, *Le Nan-nan D'Aurelien,* Tournai, 1991.
Agnes Vandewiele, *Toute une Journee,* Nathan, 1992.
Dolores Mora, *10 Histoires de Sorcieres,* Champigny-sur-Marne, 1993.
Agnes Vandewiele, *Ma Maison,* Nathan, 1993.
Dolores Mora, *Le Grillon Violoniste,* Champigny-sur-Marne, 1994.
Eve Tharlet, *Jeux de Plein Air et d'Interieur,* Champigny-sur-Marne, 1995.
Sophie Bellosguardo, *Petite Methode Pour Commencer a Nager: Des 4 Ans,* Retz, 1997.
Jack Delaroche, *J'ai Pas Peur Des Ombres!* Fleurus, 1998.

ILLUSTRATOR; WRITTEN BY CLAUDE CLEMENT

Baby-sitter de Choc, Fleurus, 1989.
Un Dejeuner Mouvemente, Fleurus, 1989.
Drole de Plombier, Fleurus, 1989.
Papa Fait un Regime, Fleurus, 1989.
Le Professeur est en colere, Fleurus, 1989.
Tonton Catastrophe, 1989.
Quel Malheur! Un Enfant Bricoleur, Fleurus, 1990.
Un Dimanche Tres Agite, Fleurus, 1991.
Genial! L'Anniversaire de Juliette, Fleurus, 1991.
Boudu, Chien Savant, Fleurus, 1994.
Docteur Mamie, Fleurus, 1994.
Juliette Gagne Sa Vie, Fleurus, 1994.
La Mob de Vincent, Fleurus, 1994.
Les Soucis de Felicie, Nathan, 1994.
Bouzou le Loup Est Amoureux, Nathan, 1995.
Bravo la Famille, Fleurus, 1995.
La Foire a Tout, Fleurus, 1995.
La Grande Kermesse, Fleurus, 1995.
Dur, Dur, le Pique-nique! Fleurus, 1996.
La Fete des Meres, Fleurus, 1996.
Poulette-Douillette: d'Apres un Conte Traditionnel, Nathan, 1996.
Ah, Quel Mariage! Fleurus, 1997.
Le Carnaval de Juliette, Fleurus, 1997.

ILLUSTRATOR; WRITTEN BY JACOB AND WILHELM GRIMM

Hansel et Gretel, Champigny-sur-Marne, 1992.

Blanche-Neige, Champigny-sur-Marne, 1994.
Le Loup et les 7 Chevreaux, Hachette, 1996.

OTHER

Illustrator of the cartoon series *Bravo la Famille,* for the television station Francez 3, 1993.

WORK IN PROGRESS: "A book for little children on Moses in a collection called 'La Bible des Tout-Petits.'"

SIDELIGHTS: Christel Desmoinaux commented: "As far as I remember, I've always enjoyed drawing. At the age of eight or nine, I used to spend hours putting the stories I imagined on paper, sitting at the little table in the living room, while my parents were watching television. Like books, drawing always provided a good way to enter a secret world of my own where all that I wanted could happen to my heroes, most of them beautiful princesses. By the age of eleven, I knew I would prefer working in an artistic profession if I had the chance, which, with the help and support of my parents, luckily occurred.

"Illustrating for children is, of course, a link with my own childhood. There are a few pictures [from my childhood reading] I remember vividly (one from *Bluebeard,* for example), and I like to think that some of my pictures will make lasting impressions on the children who are now reading my books.

"I am interested in a lot of things in addition to illustration. I enjoy traveling to other countries; I have a great interest in cinema; and I like reading—in English, if possible, to stay in practice. I share my life with an English man, which also helps! We are thinking of moving in a year or two, to discover working and living in different countries, such as Australia. Of course, I love Paris, which is, culturally speaking, a place where you always have an infinity of choices when you want to go out."*

*   *   *

DEWEY, John 1859-1952

PERSONAL: Born October 20, 1859, in Burlington, VT; died of pneumonia and complications resulting from a broken hip, June 1, 1952, in New York, NY; son of Archibald (a grocer) and Lucina (Rich) Dewey; married Harriet Alice Chipman (a philosophy student), July 28, 1886, (died, 1927); married Roberta Lowitz

Grant, December, 1946; children: (first marriage) four sons (one adopted), four daughters; (second marriage) John, Adrienne (adopted Belgian war orphans). *Education:* University of Vermont, B.A., 1879; Johns Hopkins University, Ph.D., 1884.

CAREER: Oil City High School, Oil City, PA, teacher, 1879-81; Lake View Seminary, Charlotte, VT, teacher, 1881-82; University of Michigan, Ann Arbor, Department of Philosophy, professor, 1884-87; University of Minnesota, Department of Mental and Moral Philosophy, chair, 1887; University of Michigan, Department of Philosophy, University philosophy chair, 1888-94; University of Chicago, Department of Philosophy, chair, 1894-1905; Columbia University, Department of Philosophy, chair in philosophy, 1905-30, professor emeritus in residence, 1930-52. Lecturer at numerous universities, colleges, schools, and professional meetings, and in Japan and China (1919-20), Turkey (1924), Mexico (1926), and the Soviet Union (1928); charter member of teacher's union, Teachers League of New York, 1913, vice president, 1916-19; assisted in founding of New School of Social Research, New York City, 1919; cofounder of University-in-Exile for professors fleeing Nazi Germany and fascist states, 1933.

MEMBER: Philosophical Society, Students' Christian Association, American Psychological Association (president, 1899), American Philosophical Association (president, 1905), American Association for the Advancement of Science (president, 1909), American Association of University Presidents (cofounder, first president, 1913), Hull House (Chicago; member of board of trustees), Henry Street Settlement (New York City; member of board of trustees), American Civil Liberties Union, American Committee for the Outlawry of War (cofounder, 1921), League for Industrial Democracy (charter member; vice president; president, 1939-41), People's Lobby (chairman), American Committee for Cultural Freedom (co-founder)

AWARDS, HONORS: Honorary president, National Education Association, 1932; also recipient of numerous other awards and honors.

WRITINGS:

EDUCATION

My Pedagogic Creed, E. L. Kellogg (New York City), 1897, Progressive Education Association (Washington, DC), 1929.

The School and Society; Being Three Lectures by John Dewey Supplemented by a Statement of the University Elementary School, University of Chicago Press (Chicago, IL), 1899, published as *The School and Society,* edited by Jo Ann Boydston, with a preface by Joe R. Burnett, Southern Illinois University Press (Carbondale), 1980.

The Elementary School Record, University of Chicago Press (Chicago, IL), 1900.

The Educational Situation, University of Chicago Press (Chicago, IL), 1902, Arno Press (New York City), 1969.

The Child and the Curriculum, University of Chicago Press (Chicago, IL), 1902, 1959.

The School and the Child; Being Selections from the Educational Essays of John Dewey, Blackie & Son (London), 1907.

Ethical Principles Underlying Education, University of Chicago Press (Chicago, IL), 1908.

Moral Principles in Education, Houghton Mifflin (Boston), 1909, Southern Illinois University Press (Carbondale), 1975.

Educational Essays by John Dewey, Blackie & Son (London), 1910.

Interest and Effort in Education, Houghton Mifflin (Boston), 1913, Southern Illinois University Press (Carbondale), 1975.

(With Evelyn Dewey) *Schools of To-morrow,* E. P. Dutton (New York City), 1915, published as *Schools of Tomorrow,* Dutton (New York City), 1962.

Democracy and Education: An Introduction to the Philosophy of Education, Macmillan (New York City), 1916, 1963.

Progressive Education and the Science of Education, Progressive Education Association (Washington, DC), 1928.

The Sources of a Science of Education, H. Liveright (New York City), 1929, 1970.

American Education Past and Future, University of Chicago Press (Chicago, IL), 1931.

The Way Out of Educational Confusion, Harvard University Press (Cambridge, MA), 1931, Greenwood Press (Westport, CT), 1970.

Education and the Social Order, League for Industrial Democracy (New York City), 1934.

Experience and Education, Macmillan (New York City), 1938, Collier Books (New York City), 1963.

Education Today, edited and with a foreword by Joseph Ratner, G. P. Putnam's Sons (New York City), 1940, Greenwood Press (Westport, CT), 1969.

Philosophy of Education, also published as *Problems of Men,* Philosophical Library (New York City), 1946.

The Child and the Curriculum, and The School and Society, introduction by Leonard Carmichael, University of Chicago Press (Chicago, IL), 1956, introduction by Philip W. Jackson, University of Chicago Press (Chicago, IL), 1990.

Dewey on Education, introduction and notes by Martin S. Dworkin, Columbia University Teachers College (New York City), 1959.

Dictionary of Education, Philosophical Library (New York City), 1959, edited by Ralph B. Winn, with a foreword by John Herman Randall, Jr., Greenwood Press (Westport, CT), 1972.

The Relation of Theory to Practice in Education, Association for Student Teaching (Cedar Falls, IA), 1962.

John Dewey on Education: Selected Writings, edited and with an introduction by Reginald D. Archambalt, Modern Library, 1964.

Lectures in the Philosophy of Education, 1899, Random House (New York City), 1966.

Selected Educational Writings, with an introduction and commentary by F. W. Garforth, Heinemann (London), 1966.

Philosophy and Education in Their Historic Relations, compiled by Elsie Ripley Clapp, edited and with an introduction by J. J. Chambliss, Westview Press (Bolder, CO), 1993.

Also author of National Education Association addresses, including *General Principles of Educational Articulation,* 1929, *Education and or Present Social Problems,* 1933, and *Education for a Changing Social Order,* 1934. Author of *Selected Statements about the American Federation of Teachers,* American Federation of Teachers (Chicago), c. 1950s.

PHILOSOPHY

Outlines of a Critical Theory of Ethics, Michigan Register Publishing Company (Ann Arbor, MI), 1891, Greenwood Press (New York City), 1969.

The Significance of the Problem of Knowledge, University of Chicago Press (Chicago, IL), 1897.

(Editor) *Studies In Logical Theory, With the Co-operation of Members and Fellows of the Department of Philosophy,* University of Chicago Press (Chicago, IL), 1903, AMS Press (New York City), 1980.

(With James H. Tufts) *Ethics,* Columbia University Press, 1908, H. Holt (New York City), 1938, Holt (New York City), Rinehart, & Winston, 1961.

The Influence of Darwin on Philosophy, and Other Essays in Contemporary Thought, H. Holt (New

York City), 1910, Prometheus Books (Amherst, NY), 1997.

German Philosophy and Politics, H. Holt (New York City), 1915, G. P. Putnam's Sons (New York City), 1942, Books for Libraries Press (Freeport, NY), 1970.

Essays in Experimental Logic, University of Chicago Press (Chicago, IL), 1916, Dover (New York City), 1953.

Reconstruction in Philosophy, H. Holt (New York City), 1920, enlarged edition with a new introduction by the author, Beacon Press (Boston), 1948.

The Quest for Certainty: A Study of the Relation of Knowledge and Action, Minton, Balch, 1929, Putnam (New York City), 1960.

Logical Conditions of a Scientific Treatment of Morality, University of Chicago Press (Chicago, IL), 1930.

Philosophy and Civilization, Minton, Balch, 1931, P. Smith (Glouchester, MA), 1968.

Logic, the Theory of Inquiry, H. Holt (New York City), 1938, Holt (New York City), Rinehart, 1960.

Theory of Valuation, University of Chicago Press (Chicago, IL), 1939.

(With Arthur F. Bentley) *Knowing and the Known,* Beacon Press (Boston), 1949, Greenwood Press (Westport, CT), 1975.

Theory of the Moral Life, with an introduction by Arnold Isenberg, Irvington Publishers (New York City), 1960, 1980.

PSYCHOLOGY

Psychology, Harper Brothers (New York City), 1887.

Leibniz's New Essays Concerning the Human Understanding, S. C. Griggs (Chicago), 1888, Hillary House (New York City), 1961.

Psychology and Social Practice, University of Chicago Press (Chicago, IL), 1901, published as *Philosophy, Psychology and Social Practice: Essays,* selected, edited and with a foreword by Joseph Ratner, Putnam (New York City), 1963.

Interest as Related To Will, 1903.

How We Think, D. C. Heath (Boston), 1910, published as *How We Think, A Restatement of the Relation of Reflective Thinking to The Educative Process,* D. C. Heath, 1933, Regnery (Chicago), 1971, published as *How We Think,* Prometheus Books (Buffalo, NY), 1991.

Creative Intelligence, H. Holt (New York City), 1917.

Human Nature and Conduct: An Introduction to Social Psychology, H. Holt (New York City), 1922,

published with a new introduction by John Dewey, Modern Library (New York City), 1930.

Experience and Nature, Open Court (Chicago), 1925, Dover, 1958.

Context and Thought, University of California Press (Berkeley, CA), 1931.

Types of Thinking Including a Survey of Greek Philosophy, with an introduction by Samuel Meyer, Philosophical Library (New York City), 1984.

POLITICS AND POLITICAL PHILOSOPHY

The Ethics of Democracy, Andrews & Company (Ann Arbor, MI), 1888.

The Public and Its Problems, H. Holt (New York City), 1927, Swallow Press, 1991.

The Philosophy of John Dewey, selected and edited by Joseph Ratner, H. Holt (New York City), 1928.

Individualism, Old and New, Minton, Balch & Company (New York City), 1930.

Characters And Events: Popular Essays in Social and Political Philosophy, edited by Joseph Ratner, H. Holt (New York City), 1929, Octagon Books (New York City), 1970.

A Common Faith, Yale University Press (New Haven, CT), 1934, 1991.

Liberalism and Social Action, G. P. Putnam's Sons (New York City), 1935, Capricorn Books, 1963.

Freedom and Culture, G. P. Putnam's Sons (New York City), 1939, Capricorn Books, 1963.

What Is Democracy? Its Conflicts, Ends and Means, Cooperative Books (Norman, OK), 1939.

Intelligence in the Modern World: John Dewey's Philosophy, edited and with an introduction by Joseph Ratner, Modern Library, 1939.

John Dewey on Henry George, and What Some Others Say, Robert Schalkenbach Foundation (New York City), 1927.

TRAVEL AND FOREIGN AFFAIRS

Conditions among the Poles in the United States: Confidential Report, 1918.

(With Alice Chipman Dewey) *Letters from China and Japan,* edited by Evelyn Dewey, E. P. Dutton (New York City), 1920.

China, Japan and the S.A., Republic Publishing (New York City), 1921.

Impressions of Soviet Russia and the Revolutionary World, Mexico—China—Turkey, New Republic (New York City), 1929, Columbia University Teachers College (New York City), 1964.

The Case of Leon Trotsky, Harper & Brothers (New York City), 1937.

Tragedy of a People: Racialism in Czecho-Slovakia, American Friends of Democratic Sudetens (New York City), 1946.

The John Dewey Report, Milli Egitim Bakanligi, Test Ve Arastirma Bros (Ankara, Turkey), 1960.

CONTRIBUTOR

Art And Education: A Collection of Essays by John Dewey and Others, Barnes Foundation Press (Merion, PA), 1929, 1954.

(Author of introduction) Jane Addams, *Peace and Bread in Time of War,* King's Crown Press (New York City), 1945.

The Morning Notes of Adelbert Ames, Jr., including a Correspondence with John Dewey, Rutgers University Press (New Brunswick, NJ), 1960.

John Dewey and Arthur F. Bentley: A Philosophical Correspondence, Rutgers University Press (New Brunswick, NJ), 1964.

(With Leon Trotsky and George Novack) *Their Morals and Ours: Marxist Versus Liberal Views on Morality,* Merit Publishers (New York City), 1966.

Creative Intelligence: Essays in the Pragmatic Attitude, Octagon Books (New York City), 1970.

Not Guilty: Report of the Commission of Inquiry into the Charges Made against Leon Trotsky in the Moscow Trials, Monad Press (New York City), 1972.

Science, Technology, and Society, compiled and edited by Julius A. Sigler, University Press of America (Lanham, MD), 1997.

SELECTED AND COLLECTED WORKS

The Wit and Wisdom of John Dewey, edited and with an introduction by A. H. Johnson, Greenwood Press (Westport, CT), 1949, 1969.

John Dewey: His Contribution to the American Tradition, Bobbs-Merrill (Indianapolis, IN), 1955.

On Experience, Nature, and Freedom; Representative Selections, edited and with an introduction by Richard J. Bernstein, Liberal Arts Press (New York City), 1960.

The Collected Works of John Dewey, 1882-1953, Series I: *The Early Works, 1882-1898,* edited by Jo Ann Boydston, Southern Illinois University Press (Carbondale), 1969-72, Series II: *The Middle Works, 1899-1924,* edited by Jo Ann Boydston, with an introduction by Joe R. Burnett, Southern Illinois University Press (Carbondale), 1976-1983, Series III: *The Later Works, 1925-1953,*

edited by Jo Ann Boydston, with an introduction by Sidney Hook, with a new introduction by John Dewey, edited by Joseph Ratner, Southern Illinois University Press (Carbondale), 1981-90.

John Dewey: The Essential Writings, edited by David Sidorsky, Harper & Row (New York City), 1977.

The Essential Dewey, edited by Larry A. Hickman and Thomas M. Alexander, Indiana University Press (Bloomington), 1998.

John Dewey, edited, with an introduction by Malcolm Skilbeck, Collier-Macmillan (London), 1970.

The Philosophy Of John Dewey, edited with an introduction and commentary by John J. McDermott, Putnam Sons (New York City), 1973.

Lectures on Psychological and Political Ethics, 1898, edited and with an introduction by Donald F. Koch, Hafner Press (New York City), 1976.

The Moral Writings of John Dewey, edited, with an introduction and notes by James Goinlock, Hafner Press (New York City), 1976.

The Philosophy of John Dewey, edited by Pal Arthur Schilpp and Lewis Edwin Hahn, Open Court (La Salle, IL), 1989.

Lectures on Ethics, 1900-1901, edited and with an introduction by Donald F. Koch, Southern Illinois University Press (Carbondale), 1991.

The Political Writings, edited, with introduction, by Debra Morris and Ian Shapiro, Hackett (Indianapolis, IN), 1993.

OTHER

The Open Door, United States Book Company (New York City), 1891.

Construction and Criticism, Columbia University Press (New York City), 1930.

(Editor) *New York and the Seabury Investigation: A Digest and Interpretation of the Reports by Samuel Seabury concerning the Government of New York City, Prepared by a Committee of Educators and Civic Workers under the Chairmanship Of John Dewey,* The City Affairs Committee of New York, 1933.

Art as Experience, Minton, Balch, 1934, Capricorn Books (New York City), 1959.

(Editor) *The Living Thoughts of Thomas Jefferson,* Longmans, Green (New York City), 1940.

(Editor, with Horace M. Kallen) *The Bertrand Russell Case,* Viking Press (New York City), 1941.

David Dubinsky: A Pictorial Biography, foreword by William Green, introduction by Walter P. Reuther, Inter-allied Publications (New York City), 1951.

The Lived Experience, edited with an introduction and commentary by John J. McDermott, Putnam (New York City), 1973.

Lectures in China, 1919-1920, translated from the Chinese and edited by Robert W. Clopton and Tsuin-chen O, University Press of Hawaii (Honolulu), 1973.

The Poems of John Dewey, edited, with an introduction by Jo Ann Boydston, Southern Illinois University Press (Carbondale), 1977.

Also author of *Interpretations of the Culture-Epoch Theory,* from the National Hebart Society Yearbook, 1896. Author of numerous articles, lectures, papers, and essays.

SIDELIGHTS: More than a generation after his death, John Dewey remains one of the towering figures of American intellectual life. Often considered the nation's greatest philosopher, in this capacity he was without a doubt ranked with fellow pragmatist William James, or with his mentor C. S. Peirce. Working at a time when psychology was just emerging as a discipline, Dewey's writings in philosophy often concerned the subject of "how we think" (the title of one of his books), and his name has enjoyed enormous stature within the psychological community as well as among philosophers. Likewise he was influential in the realm of politics: as a charter member of the democratic socialist League for Industrial Democracy and the American Committee for the Outlawry of War; as an active member of the American Civil Liberties Union and other organizations; and as a trustee of Jane Addams's Hull House and the Henry Street Settlement in New York City, Dewey helped to define the shape of American liberalism in the twentieth century.

However, his work and his writings in the areas of philosophy, psychology, and politics were secondary to the principal interest of Dewey's career: education. Of the scores of books and the hundreds of articles that he wrote or edited in his lifetime, a large number are concerned with this topic. In his view, education held a position at the center of all concerns, both individual and social: through education—an education built around a recognition of how the mind actually works—young people became productive members of a democracy. With the democratic system under attack in Dewey's lifetime, first from the authoritarian systems represented by the Central Powers in World War I, and later by the totalitarian menace of Nazi Germany and Soviet Russia, this concern was far from academic.

How, then, to best train students? Dewey saw the key in new advances within the pragmatic school of philosophy, and in the new field of psychology. Pragmatism, perhaps the only school of philosophy developed in America—its influence in Europe has been minimal—takes the practical approach implied by its name: instead of sticking rigidly to preconceived notions, pragmatists say, one should gain knowledge from actual facts and experiences, and adjust one's thinking with changing circumstances. At the same time, the nascent discipline of psychology offered an increased understanding of the mind's complexities, along with the promise of new keys to unlock its mysteries. Influenced by these movements, Dewey held that teachers should build their presentation of information around the child, rather than vice versa. In the 1880s, when Dewey began his writing career, this view was far from the norm: educators overwhelmingly subscribed to notions of rote learning and heavy discipline in the classroom. These ideas had prevailed in the 1800s, as they had for centuries before—the schoolroom scenes in Mark Twain's *Tom Sawyer* and countless other nineteenth-century novels offer modern readers a view of these old methods in practice—and Dewey's *The School and Society* (1899) represented a radical break with the past.

Within a few decades, however, Dewey and his followers had swept away the traditional modes, and his system—really a further development of ideas first presented by Rossea (1712-78) and Pestalozzi (1745-1827)—prevailed in the classroom. In the period following his death in 1952 there was a reaction to Dewey's methods, or as Joe R. Burnett suggested in a 1979 *Teachers College Record* article entitled "Whatever Happened to John Dewey?" a reaction to what many believed to be Dewey's methods. But by the 1990s, almost 150 years after his birth, there was a resurgence of interest in Dewey and his ideas.

Many consider it fitting that a man of such wide-ranging influence should have enjoyed an extremely long and full life: ninety-two years, two wives, a total of ten children, and more than fifty books. The son of a well-to-do grocer in Burlington, Vermont, Dewey had his early education interrupted by the Civil War, in which his father Archibald served as quartermaster for the First Vermont Cavalry. Separated from their father for three years, the Dewey family moved to Virginia after the war, and in 1867 returned to Vermont, where Archibald became the owner of a tobacco shop. Dewey returned to school in Burlington, and in 1872 entered high school. His parents were religious conservatives of the Congregationalist Church, and they brought up their son to be both a sober young man and a serious student.

At the age of fifteen in 1875, Dewey enrolled in the University of Vermont, where he studied under H. A. P. Torrey. Following gradation in 1879, he took a job as a teacher in Oil City, Pennsylvania, but this did not last long. In 1881 he moved to Vermont for another teaching position, but after he published two articles in the *Journal of Speculative Philosophy* in 1882, he was persuaded by Torrey to earn his doctorate in philosophy at Johns Hopkins University in Baltimore.

Having earned his Ph.D. in 1884, Dewey joined the faculty of the University of Michigan at Ann Arbor, during which time he continued to study the subjects that had influenced him as a student. In some regards, the German idealist philosophy of Immanuel Kant and G. W. F. Hegel seemed an odd fit with more recent developments in "scientific" psychology, but Dewey sought to bring the two together, as evidenced by the title of his undergraduate thesis, *The Psychology of Kant*. On the strength of two articles on psychology in the journal *Mind* in 1886, Dewey's reputation began to spread. That year was to prove pivotal: also in 1886—when Dewey married one of his students, Harriet Alice Chipman—he began to take an interest in education after taking part in a University-sponsored study of high schools in Michigan.

By the late 1880s Dewey was shifting away from the idealist approach of Kant and Hegel toward the pragmatism of Peirce, who had been one of his professors at Johns Hopkins. In 1894 he took a position as the chairman of the philosophy department at the University of Chicago, and became instrumental in developing that institution's school of education—one of the first such schools in the United States. Columbia University in New York City had a similar program at its teachers college, and after some disagreement with the administration at Chicago, in 1905 Dewey joined the Columbia faculty. There he wold remain until his death nearly half a century later.

Dewey's first notable work was *The School and Society,* in which he presented ideas that he would later elaborate on in *Democracy and Education* (1916), one of his most influential books. By the first decade of the twentieth century, Dewey's writings had made him well-known within the intellectual community, and his name would soon become a household word. The strength of his work lay not necessarily in his writing—many critics faulted his tendency toward wordiness and opaque phraseology—or even in the

innovative qualities of his ideas, many of which he borrowed from other thinkers. Rather, it was the strength of his conviction, coupled with the fact that Dewey was a man of his time, which made his books the influential body of work they remain.

Another "early" book—Dewey had already been publishing for twenty years by this point—which attracted attention was *Ethics* (1908), written with James H. Tufts. The volume presents an overview of moral problems, examining the historical development of ideas about morality, varieties of moral views, and the present moral climate. *Ethics* was, a critic in the *Nation* wrote, "Above the level of textbooks." *Booklist* (which at that time still went by the name *American Library Association Booklist*) called it "the best general introduction [to the subject] in English." The reviewer called its treatment of ethical questions both "modern" and "conservative," terms which well characterized Dewey's pragmatic liberalism.

With *How We Think* (1910), Dewey began to develop his ideas about the psychology of education. Despite its title, in fact, the book is more about the challenges facing the elementary school system than psychology or epistemology. Though commenting that the book is "too compact for desultory reading," a critic in *Booklist* nonetheless declared *How We Think* "the best book on the subject for both teachers and students." H. Aldington Bruce in the *New York Times Book Review* held that "No school teacher—more especially no teacher of the very young—should fail to read it carefully, and it may be studied to equal advantage by the parents." So influential were Dewey's ideas by 1933, when the book was reissued, that a critic in the *Saturday Review of Literature* treated the work as an established classic: "The book itself contributed to the reforming movement, which with all its persisting faults has made the atmosphere of schooling more wholesome, more fresh-airy than when the Dewey campaign began."

A part of Dewey's genius, like that of influential contemporaries such as Sigmund Fred or H. G. Wells, was the timeliness of his work. Hence in 1915, when America was on the verge of war with Germany, he produced *German Philosophy and Politics*. The *New York Times Book Review* treated its publication almost as a news event, presenting its review with the headline "German Spirit Due to Kant, Not Nietzsche" and the sub-heading, "Professor Dewey Traces Prussian Militarism Back to the Famous Philosopher of the Eighteenth Century and His Categorical Imperative." Dewey's point was that whereas the roots of German militarism had often been attributed to Friedrich Nietzsche's idea of the "Superman," the origins lay further back, in the seemingly innocuous doctrines of Kant. The latter presented the idea of the State as the supreme expression of a higher moral law, a notion further developed by Hegel ("the State is the march of God through history") and others. As these views sifted down to the German populace, Dewey suggested, they created a nation more willing than most to fight and die for their kaiser and their fatherland. It was perhaps fitting that *German Philosophy and Politics* was reissued in 1942, when the United States once again fond itself at war with Germany.

In 1915 Dewey published *Schools of Tomorrow,* in which he and his daughter Evelyn examined applications of new educational methods in Gary, Indiana, and elsewhere. Hence, Dewey wrote in his preface, "There has been no attempt in this book to develop a complete theory of education nor yet review any systems or discuss the views of prominent educators." Dewey would approach those topics in one of his most important works, published the next year: *Democracy and Education: An Introduction to the Philosophy of Education.* The book represented a more defined expression of ideas which Dewey had been developing for years, and within its pages he began to bring together his views on the best society alongside his concept of the best educational system. Though critics noted that such an approach was not novel—Plato had done it nearly 2,500 years before with his *Republic*—once again, Dewey's work was well-suited to his time.

In *Democracy and Education* Dewey linked the history and development of democratic institutions with that of the scientific method, as well as of industry. In each case, humankind experimented, learning from its mistakes and in the process exploring more workable ideas. "Since democracy stands in principle for free interchange, for social continuity," Dewey wrote, "it mst develop a theory of knowledge which sees in knowledge the method by which one experience is made available in giving direction and meaning to another." A reviewer in the *New Republic* praised Dewey for challenging readers to think: "It is impossible to read this book quickly, not because it is unclear but because it evokes a constant activity on the part of the reader." The review concluded, "It is a great book because it explores [its topic] more deeply and more comprehensively than any other [work] that could be named the best hope of liberal men." Another critic lauded the volume as "a notable

contribution to the philosophy of education. In the flood of modern educational literature it would be difficult to find another work in which the theory of education attains, by the depth and breadth of its thought, the dimensions of a philosophy. . . . To us it seems that the presentation is much clearer and more definite than that of the writer's philosophical papers, which have not seldom seemed baffling and evasive." The review ran in the *Nation* on May 4, 1916. Two generations later, in its September 21, 1992 issue, the same publication polled a variety of thinkers concerning the most important books on education, and William H. Schuber of the John Dewey Society presented *Democracy and Education* as a seminal work still highly relevant in the 1990s.

Following World War I, Dewey and his wife Alice travelled to China and Japan. In Tokyo he delivered the lectures published as *Reconstruction in Philosophy* (1920), which a *Booklist* reviewer called "concrete, clearly written and unusually free from abstruse reasoning and technical diction." Dewey's "interpretation of the reconstruction of ideas and ways of thought now going on in philosophy," as he put it in his preface—along with his idea that morality should not be absolute but rather geared toward the greatest good for the greatest number—won him a large audience in the Far East. As for his lectures in China, many of those were lost, but reappeared in English in 1973 by a roundabout path, translated from the Chinese back into their original language. To many, *Lectures in China, 1919-1920* presents a thinker at the height of his powers, operating in an environment pregnant with change as it entered the modern world.

Dewey's and Alice's *Letters from China and Japan* (1920), on the other hand, offered a more personal side of Dewey and his wife. "The letters included in this volume," wrote a critic in the *New York Times Book Review,* "are written under the spur of first impressions. They have not either been revised or touched up in any way. You are never expected to remember that Mr. Dewey is really a Ph.D., or that his wife reads 'deep books.' They make you see the cherry trees in bloom, the Mikado [Japan's emperor] passing with his symbols, the chrysanthemums on the panels of his carriage; the Chinese women of the middle classes at home, and the panorama of Chinese villages and streets."

Nearly a decade later, Dewey published a collection of letters from his travels in the 1920s, *Impressions of Soviet Russia and the Revolutionary World, Mexico—China—Turkey* (1929). This correspondence, much of it already published in the *New Republic,* shows a sense of the "vitality and courage and confidence of life" which Dewey fond in these societies, each of which was in the throes of modernization. Jessica Smith in the *Nation,* which generally supported the Bolshevik revolution in Russia, gave the book a favorable review, and quoted Dewey's qualified praise for the Soviet system: "The people go about as if some mighty and oppressive load had been removed, as if they were newly awakened to the consciousness of released energies." In the year of the book's publication, Josef Stalin was consolidating his grip on power, and beginning a quarter-century reign of terror; soon Dewey would become disillusioned with Communism, and through the League for Industrial Democracy and other organizations, he would seek to counteract the Communist appeal among liberals and democratic socialists.

In 1922 another of Dewey's pivotal works was published: *Human Nature and Conduct: An Introduction to Social Psychology.* In this book he more directly approached the topic implied in the title of *How We Think.* "It is the outstanding feature of Mr. Dewey's book," wrote M. T. McClure in the *Nation,* "that in neither instinct nor intelligence is to be fond the basal fact of social significance." Rather, what motivates behavior, in Dewey's view, is habit itself: "In understanding what men do and why they do as they do," McClure went on, "it is to habit that we must turn. . . . The problem of social psychology is not to explain how our socialized ways of acting are instincts writ large, but how existing institutions and customs fashion and shape the individual." Astin Hay of the *New York Times Book Review* wrote that "it would be doing Professor Dewey an injustice if we did not mention that, fine and penetrating as is his analysis of mind and character, the application of his fully ripened thought to the big questions of morality and social life is no less stimulating and enlightening."

Experience and Nature (1925), with its presentation of Dewey's metaphysics, represented the fulfillment of a promise to readers who had asked for a thorough exploration of his beliefs about ultimate questions. Joseph Ratner, longtime editor of Dewey's works, presented *The Philosophy of John Dewey* in 1928, one of the earliest of many collected and selected works which gave newcomers an overview of Dewey's philosophy. In another collection, *Characters And Events: Popular Essays in Social and Political Philosophy* (1929), Dewey gave his insights on a number of people and movements that had shaped the postwar world.

Meanwhile Dewey explored, in works such as *The Public and Its Problems* (1927) and *Individualism, Old and New* (1930) the topics of education, ethics, democracy, and knowledge that continued to concern him. In *A Common Faith* (1934), the son of devout Congregationalists sought to offer a "new" type of morality divorced from religion. Even if his concern with ethics was not new, Dewey's treatment of religious faith per se showed that his interests were continuing to expand even in the eighth decade of his life. So, too, did *Art as Experience,* also published in 1934, a treatment of aesthetics which Dewey wrote "to restore continuity between the refined and intensified forms of experience that are works of art[,] and the everyday events, doings, and sufferings that are universally recognized to constitute experience"—in other words, to make art relevant.

In 1934 Dewey still had eighteen years of life, another marriage—Alice died in 1927—and several more books ahead of him. Among the latter were *Liberalism and Social Action* (1935); *Freedom and Culture* (1939), a liberal response to attempts by conservatives to control standards in art and popular culture; and a collection of fifty years' worth of essays, *Problems of Men* (1946, sometimes called *Philosophy of Education*.) In the late 1940s, with fellow philosopher Arthur F. Bentley, Dewey wrote *Knowing and the Known* (1949), one of his last works published while he was alive. Dewey died in 1952, having experienced some tumultuous periods of human history in a lifetime that began two years before the Civil War and ended with American troops embroiled in the Korean conflict.

Dewey's death did not stop the flow of publications, including a volume of his correspondence with Bentley (1964). A work of particular interest, because of the insights it offered concerning Dewey himself, was *The Poems of John Dewey* (1977). Dating to the 1910s, while he was at Columbia—where he had hidden them away in his desk—many of these were written for his student Anzia Yezierska, with whom Dewey had a short but intense affair. The quality of the poetry itself, many critics held, was not high: "one concludes," Daniel L. Gillory wrote in *Library Journal,* "that Dewey was wise in concealing these poems." Nonetheless, the book offered, as a reviewer for *Choice* observed, "an insight into the creative mentality of a seminal American thinker."

Jo Ann Boydston received particular praise for her work as editor, which the *Choice* critic considered "a model of excellence." By that time, she had already edited several volumes in a vast series published by Southern Illinois University Press (Carbondale), *The Collected Works of John Dewey, 1882-1953,* the final portion of which—*The Later Works, 1925-1953*—saw publication in 1990. In 1993 Donald F. Koch in *Ethics* reviewed a new collection called *John Dewey: The Political Writings.* Koch noted that the book's editors, Debra Morris and Ian Shapiro, had commented on "recent interest in [Dewey's] work in an effort to find a 'third way' in response to the 'exhaustion' of liberal and socialist world views." In a world which had seen the fall of Communism, and in an America which had begun to question many liberal precepts concerning crime, welfare, and other concerns, Dewey was still relevant. But the question remained, Koch asked, whether he offered a "comprehensive, articulate political standpoint" for "working out practical responses to current social problems." Answering that question would take time, and "there is much more to be done."

BIOGRAPHICAL/CRITICAL SOURCES:

BOOKS

Alexander, Thomas M., *John Dewey's Theory of Art, Experience, and Nature: The Horizons of Feeling,* State University of New York Press (Albany), 1987.

Alibone's Critical Dictionary of English Literature: A Supplement, Gale (Detroit, MI), 1965.

American Decades, 1910-1919, Gale (Detroit, MI), 1996.

American Decades, 1920-1929, Gale (Detroit, MI), 1996.

Appell, Morey L., *John Dewey: Pattern for Adventuring,* introduction by Carl R. Rogers, Morey L. Appell Human Relations Foundation (Greenwich, CT), 1988.

Archambalt, Reginald D., editor, *Dewey on Education; Appraisals,* Random House (New York City), 1966.

Bernstein, Richard J., *John Dewey,* Washington Square Press (New York City), 1966.

Boisvert, Raymond D., *Dewey's Metaphysics,* Fordham University Press (New York City), 1988.

Boydston, Jo Ann, editor, *Guide to the Works of John Dewey,* Southern Illinois University Press (Carbondale), 1970.

Boydston, Jo Ann, editor, *John Dewey's Personal and Professional Library: A Checklist,* Southern Illinois University Press (Carbondale), 1982.

Boydston, Jo Ann and Robert L. Andersen, editors, *John Dewey: A Checklist of Translations, 1900-1967,* Southern Illinois University Press (Carbondale), 1969.

Boydston, Jo Ann and Kathleen Polos, *Checklist of Writings about John Dewey, 1887-1973,* Southern Illinois University Press (Carbondale), 1969.

Brickman, William W., editor, *John Dewey: Master Educator,* Society for the Advancement of Education (New York City), 1961.

Bullert, Gary, *The Politics of John Dewey,* Prometheus Books, 1983.

Coughlan, Neil, *Young John Dewey: An Essay in American Intellectual History,* University of Chicago Press (Chicago, IL), 1975.

A Dictionary of American Authors, fifth edition, Gale (Detroit, MI), 1969.

Damico, Alfonso J., *Individual and Community: The Social and Political Thought of John Dewey,* University Presses of Florida (Gainesville), 1978.

Dearborn, Mary V., *Love in the Promised Land: The Story of Anzia Yezierska and John Dewey,* Free Press (New York City), 1988.

Dewey, John, *Reconstruction in Philosophy,* H. Holt (New York City), 1920, enlarged edition with a new introduction by the author, Beacon Press (Boston), 1948.

Dewey, Robert E., *The Philosophy of John Dewey: A Critical Exposition of His Method, Metaphysics, and Theory of Knowledge,* Martins Nijhoff (The Hague, Netherlands), 1977.

Durant, Will, *Contemporary American Philosophers,* Haldeman-Julius (Girard, KS), 1925.

Edman, Irwin, editor, *John Dewey: His Contribution to the American Tradition,* Greenwood Press (Westport, CT), 1955.

Essays in Honor of John Dewey, on the Occasion of His Seventieth Birthday, October 20, 1929, Octagon Books (New York City), 1956.

Encyclopedia of Psychology, Gale (Detroit, MI), 1996.

Hook, Sidney, *John Dewey, An Intellectual Portrait,* John Day Co. (New York City), 1939, Prometheus Books, 1995.

Horne, Herman Harrell, *The Democratic Philosophy of Education: Companion to Dewey's Democracy And Education: Exposition And Comment,* Greenwood Press (Westport, CT), 1932, 1978.

John Dewey: Guide to Correspondence and Manuscript Collections, Dewey Center (Carbondale, IL), 1971.

Johnson, A. H., editor, *The Wit and Wisdom of John Dewey,* Greenwood Press (Westport, CT), 1949.

Levine, Barbara, editor, *Works about John Dewey, 1886-1995,* Southern Illinois University Press (Carbondale), 1996.

Levitt, Morton, *Fred and Dewey on the Nature of Man,* Greenwood Press (Westport, CT), 1960.

Meyer, Samuel, editor, *Dewey and Russell—An Exchange,* Philosophical Library, 1985.

Moore, Edward C., *American Pragmatism: Peirce, James, and Dewey,* Greenwood Press (Westport, CT), 1961.

Mossenberger, Sidney, editor, *Dewey and His Critics: Essays from the Journal of Philosophy,* Journal of Philosophy (New York City), 1977.

The Philosopher of the Common Man: Essays in Honor of John Dewey to Celebrate His Eightieth Birthday, Greenwood Press (Westport, CT), 1940, 1968.

Reference Guide to American Literature, third edition, St. James Press (Detroit, MI), 1994.

Rockefeller, Steven C., *John Dewey: Religious Faith and Democratic Humanism,* Columbia University Press, 1991.

Rosen, Norma, *John and Anzia: An American Romance,* Syracuse University Press (Syracuse, NY), 1997.

Ryan, Alan, *John Dewey and the High Tide of American Liberalism,* W. W. Norton (New York City), 1995.

Thinkers of the Twentieth Century, second edition, St. James Press (Detroit, MI), 1987.

The Twentieth-Century Biographical Dictionary of Notable Americans, Gale (Detroit, MI), 1968.

Williams, Bruce, compiler, *John Dewey, Recollections,* University Press of America, 1982.

PERIODICALS

American Historical Review, July, 1965, pp. 1137-1138.

American Library Association Booklist, February, 1909, p. 39; June, 1910, p. 372; October, 1915, pp. 6, 9; November, 1915, p. 97; June, 1916, p. 404; December, 1916, p. 102; July, 1917, p. 423.

Booklist, July, 1920, p. 341; December, 1920, p. 92; July, 1925, p. 356; November, 1928, p. 52; October, 1929, p. 8; April, 1929, p. 280; January, 1931, p. 188; November, 1931, p. 90; July, 1933, p. 349; May, 1934, p. 272; October, 1934, p. 50; October, 1935, p. 32; November 15, 1938, p. 91; December 1, 1939, p. 126; November 1, 1940, p. 83; June 1, 1946, p. 311; September 1, 1955, p. 4; October 1, 1966, p. 141; May 15, 1969, p. 1026; February 1, 1974, p. 558; February 1, 1978, p. 890.

Choice, May, 1965, p. 180; November, 1965, pp. 588-589; July, 1966, p. 436; September, 1966, p.

555; September, 1969, p. 827; September, 1973, p. 999; May, 1974, p. 452; October, 1976, p. 995; March, 1977, p. 77; April, 1977, p. 216; April, 1978, p. 226; July, 1980, p. 709; January, 1982, p. 638; July, 1984, p. 1620; November, 1991, p. 462; March, 1994, p. 1079.

Continuing Education, winter 1989, p. 117.

Education Journal, March, 1982, p. 83.

Ethics, January, 1978, pp. 186-187; April, 1985, p. 776; July, 1992, pp. 851-853; April, 1995, p. 686.

Harvard Educational Review, February, 1983, p. 103.

Library Journal, September 15, 1940, p. 761; May 15, 1946, p. 755; July, 1955, p. 1591; June 1, 1966, p. 2832; May 1, 1969, p. 1880; January 15, 1974, p. 134; March 15, 1974, p. 760; January 15, 1978, p. 172; May 15, 1984, p. 984.

Nation, November 5, 1908, 438; May 5, 1910, p. 464; July 29, 1915, p. 152; May 4, 1916, p. 480; July 24, 1920, pp. 103-104; December 8, 1920, pp. 658-660; July 5, 1922, pp. 20-21; October 31, 1928, pp. 457-458; June 19, 1929, p. 744; October 22, 1930, pp. 446-447; June 20, 1934, pp. 710-711; September 26, 1934, pp. 358-359; September 11, 1935, pp. 303-304; December 2, 1939, pp. 621-622; June 6, 1942, p. 664; December 10, 1955, p. 518; September 21, 1992, p. 302.

New Republic, June 26, 1915, pp. 210-211; July 1, 1916, p. 231; September 2, 1916, p. 118; May 24, 1922, p. 379; March 25, 1925, p. 129; August 24, 1927, p. 22; November 4, 1931, pp. 330-331; April 25, 1934, pp. 315-316; December 6, 1939, p. 206; May 17, 1939, pp. 51-52; December 23, 1940, p. 877.

New Statesman, February 16, 1929, p. 612.

New Yorker, October 22, 1938, p. 99; October 29, 1949, p. 115.

New York Herald Tribune Books, August 5, 1928, p. 1; October 20, 1929, p. 3.

New York Review of Books, April 22, 1965, p. 16.

New York Times Book Review, November 5, 1910, p. 617; July 18, 1915, p. 257; August 15, 1915, p. 291; April 15, 1917, pp. 141-142; May 30, 1920, p. 285; October 8, 1922, pp. 5, 26; October 23, 1927, p. 15; July 14, 1929, p. 5; April 21, 1929, p. 12; October 20, 1929, pp. 5, 36; December 21, 1930, p. 2; May 31, 1931, p. 28; September 30, 1934, p. 10; September 1, 1935, p. 9; November 20, 1938, p. 16; June 9, 1946, p. 7.

Publishers Weekly, January 8, 1973, p. 61.

Review of Metaphysics, June, 1979, p. 745.

Saturday Review of Literature, October 15, 1927, p. 198; October 26, 1929, pp. 309-310; December

21, 1929, p. 585; July 1, 1933, p. 682; October 22, 1949, p. 15.
Scientific American, September, 1965, p. 270.
Social Studies, September/October, 1977, pp. 220-221.
Teachers College Record, winter 1979, p. 209.
Times Literary Supplement, January 11, 1917, p. 20; February 16, 1967, p. 123.*

—Sketch by Judson Knight

* * *

DI, Zhu Xiao 1958-

PERSONAL: Name is pronounced "Jew Shau Dee;" born June 17, 1958, in Nanking, China; immigrated to the United States, 1987. *Ethnicity:* "Asian." *Education:* Nanjing Teachers' University, B.A., 1982; University of Massachusetts at Boston, M.A., 1989; Massachusetts Institute of Technology, M.C.P., 1991.

ADDRESSES: Home—357 Commercial St., No. 619, Boston, MA 02109; fax 617-496-9957. *E-mail*—zhu_xiao_di@ksg.harvard.edu.

CAREER: Jiangsu Education College, Nanjing, China, assistant professor of English, supervisor of field education, liaison officer, and interpreter, 1982-87; Harvard University, Cambridge, MA, research assistant at Fairbank Center for East Asian Research, 1987-89; Cognetics, Inc., research assistant, 1989-90; Management Strategies, Inc., assistant to the president, 1991-92; University of Massachusetts at Boston, assistant study director at Center for Survey Research, 1992-93, senior assistant director, 1993-97; Harvard University, research associate at Joint Center for Housing Studies, 1997—. Consultant to Arthur Andersen and Co.

WRITINGS:

(With JinMin Chen) *English-Speaking Nations* (textbook), Jiangsu Education Press (Nanjing, China), 1984.
Thirty Years in a Red House: A Memoir of Childhood and Youth in Communist China, foreword by Ross Terrill, University of Massachusetts Press (Amherst, MA), 1998.

Contributor to Chinese management journals and other periodicals, including *Preventive Medicine* and *Public Opinion Quarterly.*

SIDELIGHTS: Zhu Xiao Di told *CA:* "I started writing in China in the early 1980s, including freelance travel stories and essays, and I translated fiction and essays from English into Chinese. I came to America in 1987 for graduate studies, but I ended up as a permanent resident in the United States and am currently in the process of becoming an American citizen. The published version of *Thirty Years in a Red House* is the eighth draft, completed in four years while I had a full-time research job to support my family. The idea for my title came from *Twenty Years in the Hull House* by Jane Adams and the best Chinese classic novel *Dreams in a Red Chamber.* Just as the latter makes real the history of Chinese society in past centuries, I was hoping that my book will do the same for twentieth-century Chinese history. Also, my reflection on the life of my father, who is a central figure in my book, mirrors Jane Adams's reflection on individual and institutional humanitarian efforts to help other human beings."

* * *

DICK, David 1930-

PERSONAL: Born February 18, 1930, in Cincinnati, OH; son of Samuel Stephens (a surgeon) and Lucile Barnes (a homemaker; maiden name, Crouch; later surname, Rogers) Dick; married Rose Ann Casale (divorced, 1978); married Eulalie Anne Cumbo, March 17, 1978; children: Samuel S. II, Deborah Ann Dick Farr, Catherine Neal Dick O'Shields, Nell Britton Dick Blankenship, Ravy Bradford. *Ethnicity:* "English/Dutch." *Education:* University of Kentucky, B.A., 1956, M.A., 1964. *Religion:* Episcopalian.

ADDRESSES: Home and office—Plum Lick Publishing, Inc., P.O. Box 68, North Middletown, KY 40357-0068; fax 606-383-4366. *E-mail*—ddick@ uky. campus.mci.net.

CAREER: WHAS-Radio and Television, Louisville, KY, journalist, 1959-66; CBS, Inc., correspondent in Washington, DC, Atlanta, GA, Caracas, Venezuela, and Dallas, TX, 1966-85; *Bourbon Times,* Paris, KY, publisher, 1988-91; Plum Lick Publishing, Inc., North Middletown, KY, president, 1992—. University of Kentucky, professor, 1985-96. Kentucky Humanities

Council, member, 1994—. *Military service:* U.S. Navy, 1951-55; became petty officer second class.

MEMBER: Professors Emeriti (club of University of Kentucky).

AWARDS, HONORS: Emmy Award, Academy of Television Arts and Sciences, 1972; inducted into Kentucky Journalism Hall of Fame, 1987; D.Hum., Cumberland College, 1996.

WRITINGS:

The View from Plum Lick (nonfiction), Plum Lick Publishing (North Middletown, KY), 1992.
Follow the Storm (nonfiction), Plum Lick Publishing, 1993.
Peace at the Center (nonfiction), Plum Lick Publishing, 1994.
A Conversation with Peter P. Pence (fiction), Plum Lick Publishing, 1995.
The Quiet Kentuckians (nonfiction), Plum Lick Publishing, 1996.
The Scourges of Heaven (historical novel), University Press of Kentucky (Lexington, KY), 1998.
Home Sweet Kentucky (sequel to *The Quiet Kentuckians*), Plum Lick Publishing, in press.

WORK IN PROGRESS: Sylva's Gift, a sequel to *The Scourges of Heaven,* completion expected in 2000.

SIDELIGHTS: David Dick told *CA:* "My primary motivation for writing is to achieve a greater sensitivity for the humanities. Those who particularly influence my work are Theodore Dreiser, Ernest Hemingway, Stephen Crane, Charles Dickens, Robert Penn Warren, Wendell Berry, and Wallace Stegner, and, of course, Mark Twain.

"My writing process places, as Stegner has suggested it should, discovery before construction. I arise in the early morning and write during most of the morning hours. I continue in all seasons until the project is completed.

"My first five books were inspired by a passion for the good earth and many of those good people who live on it and for it and by it. My sixth book, *The Scourges of Heaven,* was inspired by the life of my great-grandmother, who lived from 1830 to 1865. She probably lost her first husband and son to cholera. I have been interested in primitive theology, which teaches that God punishes his children for sin by sending them scourges."

DICK, Ron 1931-

PERSONAL: Born October 18, 1931, in Newcastle-upon-Tyne, England; son of Arthur John Craig (an electrical engineer) and Lilian (Provost) Dick; married Pauline Lomax, October 15, 1955; children: Gary Charles, Peta Noelle Dick Enoch. *Ethnicity:* "Caucasian." *Education:* Attended Royal Air Force College, 1950-52, Royal Air Force Staff College, 1966, Joint Services Staff College, 1969, and Royal College of Defence Studies, 1972-74.

ADDRESSES: Home—3011 Jenny Lane, Woodbridge, VA 22192; fax 703-492-8934. *E-mail*—rafron@ aol.com.

CAREER: Royal Air Force, career officer, 1950-88, retiring as air marshal; National Air and Space Museum, Washington, DC, Smithsonian international fellow, 1988-91; Air University, Maxwell Air Force Base, AL, visiting lecturer on the history of air power, 1991-94; writer and public speaker, 1994—. Military assignments included aerobatic pilot, pilot of historic aircraft, flying instructor, exchange flight commander, flight commander on a nuclear strike squadron, and Vulcan squadron commander in Cyprus; air attache at British embassy in Washington, DC, 1980-83; head of British Defence Staffs in the United States, 1984-88.

MEMBER: International Association of Eagles, Royal Aeronautical Society (fellow).

AWARDS, HONORS: Clarkson Trophy and Wright Jubilee Trophy, both 1955-56, both for aerobatic flying; Companion, Order of the Bath, 1988.

WRITINGS:

(Contributor) *The Means of Victory: RAF Bomber Command,* Charterhouse Publications (London), 1992.
(Contributor) *Classic RAF Battles,* Arms & Armour Press (London), 1995.
Lancaster: RAF Heavy Bomber, with photographs by Dan Patterson, Howell Press (Charlottesville, VA), 1996.
Messerschmitt Bf109: Luftwaffe Fighter, with photographs by Patterson, Howell Press, 1997.
Spitfire: RAF Fighter, with photographs by Patter-son, Howell Press, 1997.
American Eagles: A History of the United States Air Force, with photographs by Patterson, Howell Press, 1997.

Reach and Power: The Heritage of the United States Air Force in Pictures and Artifacts, U.S. Government Printing Office (Washington, DC), 1997.

Contributor to other books, including *Oxford Companion to American Military History,* Oxford University Press (New York City). Contributor to magazines, including *Flight Journal, Air and Space Smithsonian,* and *Air Power History.*

WORK IN PROGRESS: *The Aviation Century: A History of Human Flight and How It Has Changed the World,* with photographs by Patterson, publication by Boston Mills Press (Erin, Ontario) expected in 2000; *Hurricane: Hawker's Hero,* with photographs by Patterson.

SIDELIGHTS: Ron Dick told *CA:* "As a schoolboy in London, I spent many hours looking skyward, watching the great aerial combats of the Battle of Britain. That experience inspired me to become a pilot in the Royal Air Force, a career which captured me for thirty-eight years. Although I retired from the service in 1988, my enthusiasm for flying remained undiminished, and I found an outlet in telling others about aviation, either by lecturing or by writing.

"The compulsion to write about aviation has its roots in the fact that, as the twenty-first century approaches, most people have come to take aircraft and flying very much for granted. Most of the wonder and excitement of the early days has gone, as generations have grown up with aircraft as an everyday phenomenon. Few people pursue the thought that aviation changed the world more than any other development in the twentieth century—technologically, militarily, politically, economically, and sociologically. Not a single human being anywhere on earth is untouched by the effects of aviation. It is a story well worth the telling—full of adventure, drama, courage, disaster, success, inspiration, enterprise, unlooked for curses, and unexpected blessings. What more could an author ask?"

*　　*　　*

DOCKREY, Karen 1955-

PERSONAL: Born May 28, 1955, in Bloomington, IL; married, husband's name Bill; children: two. *Educa-*

tion: Southern Baptist Theological Seminary (Louisville, KY), M.Div.

ADDRESSES: *Office*—8CPH, 3558 South Jefferson Ave., St. Louis, MO 63118. *E-mail*—kdockrey@mindspring.com.

CAREER: Youth minister, 1980—; writer, 1984—.

AWARDS, HONORS: Named to Youth Sunday School Writers Hall of Fame, 1991; named Outstanding Tennessee Teacher, 1991.

WRITINGS:

Getting to Know God, Broadman & Holman (Nashville, TN), 1984, study guide, 1986.
Friends: Finding and Keeping Them, Broadman & Holman, 1985.
Dating: Making Your Own Choices, Broadman & Holman, 1987.
What's Your Problem?, Chariot Victor Publishing (Colorado Springs, CO), 1987.
Family Survival Guide (leader's and student's versions), Chariot Victor, 1988.
Living until Jesus Comes, Scripture Press (Wheaton, IL), 1989.
When Everyone's Looking at You, Chariot Victor, 1989.
Junior High Retreats and Lock-Ins, Group Books (Loveland, CO), 1990.
(With John Hall) *Holiday Specials and Boredom Busters,* David C. Cook (Elgin, IL), 1990.
Youth Workers and Parents: Sharing Resources for Equipping Youth, Scripture Press, 1990.
Why Does Everybody Hate Me?, Zondervan (Grand Rapids, MI), 1991.
The Youth Worker's Guide to Creative Bible Study, Victor (Wheaton, IL), 1991.
Does Anybody Understand? Devotions for Teens on Family Survival, Chariot Family (Elgin, IL), 1992.
What's a Kid like Me Doing in a Family like This?: Leader's Book, Chariot Victor, 1992.
From Frustration to Freedom, Chariot Victor Publishing, 1992.
It's Not Fair!: Through Grief to Healing, Woman's Missionary Union (Birmingham, AL), 1992.
(With Johnnie Godwin and Phyllis Godwin) *Holman Student Bible Dictionary,* Broadman & Holman, 1993.
Will I Ever Feel Good Again?: When You're Overwhelmed by Grief and Loss, Fleming H. Revell (Grand Rapids), 1993.
Are You There, God?, with leader's guide, Victor, 1993.

When a Hug Won't Fix the Hurt, Victor, 1993.

I Thought You Were My Friend!, with leader's guide, Victor, 1994.

(With Beth Matthews and Andrew Adams) *I Only See My Dad on Weekends: Kids Tell Their Stories about Divorce and Blended Families,* Chariot Victor, 1994.

(With others) *Ready for Life,* Victor, 1994.

Tuned-Up Parenting: Eight Studies to Invite Harmony in Your Home, Chariot Victor, 1994.

(With Emily Dockrey) *You'll Never Believe What They Told Me: Trusting God through Cancer and Other Serious Illness,* Chariot Victor, 1994.

Alone but Not Lonely, Woman's Missionary Union, 1994.

Curing the Self Hate Virus, Woman's Missionary Union, 1994.

Growing a Family Where People Really Like Each Other, Bethany House (Minneapolis, MN), 1996.

Fun Friend-Making Activities for Adult Groups, Vital Ministry, 1997.

Am I in Love? Twelve Youth Studies on Guy/Girl Relationships, Concordia (St. Louis, MO), 1997.

YouthCare: Giving Real Help That Makes a Real Difference, Woman's Missionary Union, 1997.

Facing Down the Tough Stuff, Chariot Victor, 1998.

Contributor to books, including *Parenting: Questions Women Ask, True Love Waits, The Busy Woman's Guide to Balancing Your Life,* and *Growing Close.* Contributor to periodicals, including *Christian Parenting Today, Living with Teenagers, Today's Christian Woman, Decision, ParentLife,* and *Youthworker Journal.*

SIDELIGHTS: Karen Dockrey commented: "Youth are wonderful. When we let them talk, draw, and otherwise learn for themselves, they fall in love with the Bible and its Author. My books are meant to show you how to guide youth in this way."

BIOGRAPHICAL/CRITICAL SOURCES:

PERIODICALS

School Library Journal, February, 1994, p. 133.
Voice of Youth Advocates, April, 1992, p. 54.*

*   *   *

DONATI, Sara
   See LIPPI, Rosina

DOSSEY, Larry 1940-

PERSONAL: Born in 1940. *Education:* University of Texas at Austin, B.A.; Southwestern Medical School, Dallas, TX, M.D., 1967.

ADDRESSES: Home—Santa Fe, NM. *Agent*—c/o Harper & Row, 10 East 53rd St., New York, NY 10022.

CAREER: Medical doctor and author of books on spirituality and medicine. Dallas Diagnostic Association, physician (Internal Medicine); Medical City Dallas Hospital, chief of staff; Isthmus Institute of Dallas, president; National Institutes of Health, Office of Alternative Medicine, Panel on Mind/Body Interventions, co-chair; *Alternative Therapies,* executive editor. *Military service:* Battalion surgeon in Vietnam.

AWARDS, HONORS: Delivered the annual Mahatma Gandhi Lecture, New Delhi, India, 1988; chosen by *Utne Reader* as one of the Visionaries of 1996.

WRITINGS:

Space, Time, and Medicine, Shambhala (Boston), 1982.

Beyond Illness: Discovering the Experience of Health, Shambhala, 1984.

Recovering the Soul: A Scientific and Spiritual Search, Bantam (New York City), 1989.

Meaning and Medicine: Lessons from a Doctor's Tales of Breakthrough and Healing, Bantam (New York City) 1991.

Healing Words: The Power of Prayer and the Practice of Medicine, Harper-Collins (San Francisco), 1993. *Prayer Is Good Medicine: How to Reap the Healing Benefits of Prayer,* Harper (New York City), 1996.

Be Careful What You Pray for . . . You Just Might Get It: What We Can Do about the Unintentional Effects of Our Thoughts, Prayers, and Wishes, Harper (New York City), 1997.

Contributor of articles to periodicals.

SIDELIGHTS: Reared in a fundamentalist farming community near Waco, Texas, Larry Dossey believed he had a calling to the ministry. In his teen years he played piano at his church and toured with a revival preacher. College turned him around, though, and he became an agnostic. He only turned his attention back to religion—this time Eastern varieties such as Taoism and Buddhism—while attending medical school. Dossey confessed to Peter Steinfels in a *New York Times* interview that a chronic condition was partly responsible for his investigations. "I was afflicted—or blessed—with severe migraines from the sixth grade on," he said. "I almost dropped out of medical school out of fear I might harm a patient." Steinfels filled in the rest of the story: "Seeking relief [Dossey] began studying biofeedback and other mind-body therapies and ended up convinced that neither medicine nor modern physics substantiated the familiar view of a strictly material universe. Eventually he became a regular practitioner of meditation, even while keeping his distance from the kind of straightforward prayer he had known in his youth." Dossey's spiritual quest would later become grist for the many books he would write about spirituality and healing. He went on to a distinguished medical career after graduating. When he returned from Vietnam, where he served as a battalion surgeon during the war, he finished his residency at Veterans Administration Hospital and Parkland Hospital in Dallas, Texas and began exploring connections between science and religion. In particular Dossey searched out medical studies demonstrating the power of prayer to heal sick patients. In the 1980s Dossey began writing a series of popular books about his findings. He also lectures widely on the topic and in 1988 he was chosen to deliver the annual Mahatma Gandhi lecture in New Delhi, India, the only physician ever to receive this honor. Dossey currently co-chairs the Panel on Mind/Body Interventions at the Office of Alternative Medicine of the National Institutes of Health.

Dossey's 1993 book, *Healing Words: The Power of Prayer and the Practice of Medicine,* made it to the *New York Times* best-seller list, and sold close to 150,000 copies in the first three years after its release. Dossey cites double-blind studies in the book that, he claims, show that prayer is effective even for patients who do not know that someone is praying for them. He even claims that there are studies that support the effectiveness of prayer in affecting the behavior of white blood cells, yeast colonies, and germinating seeds. Writing for the *Christian Science Monitor,* Richard A. Nenneman gave this assessment of how the author feels on the issue of prayer: "Dossey thinks there are as many approaches to prayer as there are personality types. But he seems to favor the kind of praying in which the individual tries to learn God's will, to draw closer to whatever he defines as this power outside himself—rather than a prayer of giving the Almighty specific instructions." *Kirkus Reviews* praised the book for "rais[ing] new

questions . . . about an old but little-studied phenomenon."

Dossey has written several other books that explore similar themes. *Space, Time, and Medicine* (1982) examines the role the human mind plays in combating illness. *Publishers Weekly* calls it "a lively book that sparkles with ideas." Bruce Hepburn, reviewing the book for *New Statesman,* warns readers to prepare "against this audacious onslaught by the disturbing ideas of an author who, if short on proof, is as strong as they come on stimulating speculation." *Library Journal* refers to it as a "quietly revolutionary book." *Beyond Illness: Discovering the Experience of Health* (1984) is a collection of essays that discusses polarities such as health and illness, life and death, and doctor and patient. Dossey's next book, *Recovering the Soul: A Scientific and Spiritual Search* (1989) studies human consciousness and the probable existence of a Universal Mind. His 1991 book, *Meaning and Medicine: Lessons from a Doctor's Tales of Breakthrough and Healing,* looks at how a person's mindset can affect the outcome of an illness.

Dossey's follow-up to *Healing Words,* the 1996 book, *Prayer Is Good Medicine: How to Reap the Healing Benefits of Prayer,* tries to build a bridge between scientific critics on one side and religious critics on the other. As he had done in his previous book, Dossey cites the latest studies on the healing power of prayer. He lays out his arguments in the first two parts of the book—"The Evidence" and "The Controversy"—and he concludes that both medicine and prayer have a place in the healing regimen. The book's other two sections, "What Is Prayer?" and "How to Pray," act together as a how-to manual for praying.

Prayer Is Good Medicine answers the questions of those who doubt the power of prayer, noted Dr. Cindy L. A. Jones in the *Bloomsbury Review.* "It helps to pave the way for spiritual healing, not only among religious traditions, but between science and religions. Dossey reminds us that the life of prayer is not necessarily an easy one, but by learning the lessons of simplicity and tolerance we can hope to find peace." Ray Olson, writing for *Booklist,* found *Prayer Is Good Medicine* to be a "comforting, sometimes eye-opening little book," but takes the author to task because he "repeats some points too often for so short a book."

Dossey looks at the flip side of the prayer phenomenon in his 1997 book, *Be Careful What You Pray for*

. . . You Just Might Get It: What We Can Do about the Unintentional Effects of Our Thoughts, Prayers, and Wishes. Studying prayer practices in a variety of cultures, Dossey muses that prayer may not always be benevolent, that it can even be harmful if the person doing the praying has an evil intention. He even includes advice on how to protect oneself from evil prayer.

In a review of the book for *National Catholic Reporter,* Clarence Thomson wrote, "You can search far and wide among New Age spiritual writings and find little or nothing on sin, repentance or evil—themes embedded in the liturgy and spirituality of the Christian tradition. Dossey takes evil seriously." Thomson further praised the author: "Dossey is a good scientist, a thoroughly holistic doctor and even a good writer. . . . He faces the problem of evil, embedded everywhere in ambiguity and malice. And as he does, he inadvertently makes a great case for the need for spiritual direction." *Publishers Weekly* lauded the book as well, calling it an "intelligent and passionate work" that will help convince "readers . . . that their personal interventions into the divine order are effective."

BIOGRAPHICAL/CRITICAL SOURCES:

PERIODICALS

Bloomsbury Review, November/December 1996, p. 13.
Booklist, October 15, 1991, p. 391; June 1, 1996, p. 1638.
Christian Science Monitor, February 11, 1994, p. 19.
Kirkus Reviews, September 1, 1993, p. 1113.
Library Journal, May 15, 1982, p. 1002; October 1, 1984, 1853; September 1, 1991, p. 254; November 1, 1991, p. 124.
National Catholic Reporter, December 12, 1997, p. 17.
New Statesman, September 10, 1982, p. 23.
New York Times, December 1993.
Publishers Weekly, April 2, 1982, p. 77; September 21, 1984, p. 80; October 11, 1991, p. 56; June 10, 1996, p. 92; September 29, 1997, p. 82.

OTHER SOURCES

Biography of Larry Dossey, M.D., http://www.annonline.com/interviews /961024/biography. html (July 21, 1998).
Biography of Larry Dossey, M.D., http://www.mysticfire.com/NIDossey.html (July 21, 1998).*

DRAPER, Sharon M(ills)

PERSONAL: Born in Cleveland, OH; daughter of Victor (a hotel manager) and Catherine (a gardener) Mills; married Larry E. Draper (an educator); children: Wendy, Damon, Crystal, Cory. *Education:* Pepperdine University, B.A.; Miami University (Oxford, OH), M.A.

ADDRESSES: Office—2650 Highland Ave., Cincinnati, OH 45219. *E-mail*—TTYGER@aol.com.

CAREER: Junior- and senior-high school teacher, 1972—. Public speaker, poet, and author.

MEMBER: International Reading Association, American Federation of Teachers, National Board for Professional Teaching Standards (member of board of directors, 1995—), National Council of Teachers of English, Ohio Council of Teachers of English Language Arts, Conference on English Leadership, Delta Kappa Gamma, Phi Delta Kappa, Women's City Club.

AWARDS, HONORS: First prize, *Ebony Magazine* Literary Contest, 1991, for short story, "One Small Torch"; Coretta Scott King Genesis Award for an outstanding new book, American Library Association (ALA), 1995, for *Tears of a Tiger;* Best Book for Young Adults, ALA, Best Books, Children's Book Council and Bank Street College, Books for the Teen Age, New York Public Library, and Notable Trade Book in the Field of Social Studies, National Council for the Social Studies, 1995, for *Tears of a Tiger,* and 1998, for *Forged by Fire;* Outstanding High School English Language Arts Educator, Ohio Council of Teachers of English Language Arts, 1995; Midwest regional winner of the NCNW Excellence in Teaching Award, 1996; Governor's Educational Leadership Award from the Governor of Ohio, 1996; National Teacher of the Year, 1997; Coretta Scott King Genesis Award, ALA, 1998, for *Forged by Fire.*

WRITINGS:

FOR CHILDREN

Ziggy and the Black Dinosaurs, Just Us Books (East Orange, NJ), 1994.
Ziggy and the Black Dinosaurs: Lost in the Tunnel of Time, Just Us Books, (East Orange, NJ), 1996.
Ziggy and the Black Dinosaurs: Shadows of Caesar's Creek, Just Us Books (East Orange, NJ), 1997.

FOR YOUNG ADULTS

Tears of a Tiger, Simon & Schuster (New York City), 1994.

Forged by Fire, Simon & Schuster (New York City), 1997.

Romiette and Julio, Simon & Schuster (New York City), 1999.

Jazzimagination, Scholastic, Inc., 1999.

OTHER

Also author of *Let the Circle Be Unbroken* (children's poetry), and *Buttered Bones* (poetry for adults). Contributor of poems and short stories to literary magazines, and of an award-winning essay, "The Touch of a Teacher," to *What Governors Need to Know about Education,* Center for Policy Research of the National Governor's Association.

SIDELIGHTS: Sharon M. Draper is a teacher and writer with a philosophy that guides her in how she teaches and what she writes. That philosophy is evident in her remarks to *Something About the Author* (*SATA*) about being honored as the 1997 National Teacher of the Year: "It is a wonderful honor, but also an awesome responsibility—to be the spokesperson and advocate for education in America. I was ready for this challenge, however, because I had been preparing for this work my entire life." Reading, teaching, and writing are all connected for Draper, who wanted to be a teacher since childhood. In an interview with Jon Saari, Draper said, "I was an avid reader. I read every single book in the elementary school library, all of them. I did not plan to be a writer until much, much later. I tell kids all the time that in order to be a good writer it is necessary first to be a good reader. You need some information in your head. Reading is input. Writing is output. You can't write without input.

"Reading should not be a painful experience," Draper commented in the *AAYA* interview. Her experience teaching public school since 1972 has given her some definite ideas on the reading habits of teens. "I know what kids like—what they will read, and what they won't. Although I have nothing against Charles Dickens, many teenagers would rather gag than read him. Dickens wrote for his contemporaries—young people of a hundred and fifty years ago. American students might need to know about the world of London in the 1860s, but they would much rather read about their own world first. Not only will they read

about recognizable experiences with pleasure, but they will also be encouraged to write as well."

Draper advises other teachers to read aloud the first chapter of *Tears of a Tiger* (her first young adult novel) to students and then put the book down. "The kids break their necks getting the book. They fight over who gets to read it next. If you can capture their attention very early in a book, then you'll be successful." From her own teaching experiences, Draper knows the obstacles teachers face in getting students to read. "I want them to enjoy what they are reading. I want them to learn from it, but I don't want them to know they are learning something in the process. The best learning is painless. If I get too didactic, teenagers will turn it off if they think I am preaching at them. I try not to do that."

Draper has firm ideas on how to cultivate an idea in fiction. "The idea grows as the characters develop, and it is a kind of combined effort with characters, idea, and theme. And that drives what the plot is going to be." A book evolves for Draper and is not a predetermined plan she sticks to. "It's not as if I have a preconceived notion, 'I am going to teach students about this particular goal and make a book about it.' Instead it's the other way around: The characters and plot drive the theme." According to Draper, research has an essential place in the writing process. "If a writer wants reality and accuracy, research, even into seemingly insignificant things, is very important," she told Saari. "For example, in the third Ziggy book, which is called *Shadows of Caesar's Creek,* the kids go on a field trip to a placed called Caesar's Creek State Park, and there they meet up with Shawnee Indians that live in Ohio. In order to make it real and true I had to do the research. I spent time with the Shawnee Indians in Ohio. I spent several days at the park so that my writing had validity."

Given her commitment to teaching, Draper often must squeeze time out of her busy day by writing early in the morning or late at night after family members are in bed. Those odd times, though, provide the necessary ingredient for her creative work, which is "absolute silence, absolutely no interruptions for long periods of time. It's basically impossible, but that's what I need," she said to Saari.

In 1994 Draper began her "Ziggy" series, writing for a young audience about African American history and folklore. Ziggy and his friends call themselves the Black Dinosaurs, and they have a number of adventures that appeal to the younger reader. In the first book, *Ziggy and the Black Dinosaurs,* Draper sets an entertaining tone that drew a positive response from readers and critics. In the second book, *Lost in the Tunnel of Time,* Ziggy and friends, on a field trip to the Ohio River, learn about the Underground Railroad and the tunnels the slaves used to escape the South. In the third volume, *Shadows of Caesar's Creek,* Draper makes connections between African Americans and Native Americans.

In the fall of 1994 Draper published the young adult novel *Tears of a Tiger,* a story about Andy Jackson, an African American youth who struggles to make sense of the death of his best friend, Robert, in an automobile accident in which Andy was the driver. Andy must live with his friend's last words: "Oh God, please don't let me die like this! Andy!" The two teenagers had been drinking beer with their friends Tyrone and B. J. in celebration of a victory by their high school basketball team. Tyrone and B. J. are able to move past the awful pain caused by the accident: Tyrone finds support from his girlfriend Rhonda, B. J. through religion. Andy, however, is racked with guilt, grief, and pain that does not subside with time.

According to critics, *Tears of a Tiger* shows the difficulties in healing a damaged teenager. Andy's coach is understanding, as is his girlfriend, Keisha, despite Andy's frequent childish displays of bad behavior which work to mask his anguish. Neither, however, are available in the hour of his greatest need—the night he kills himself with a shotgun. Draper also places in her narrative characters who represent institutional attitudes confronting the young black male. In one episode, two teachers discuss how Andy's grief cannot be all that serious since he is black. Andy also internalizes some ideas about himself that prevent him from realizing his full capabilities; for example, he thinks he cannot be successful academically because he is a basketball player. Merri Monks, writing in *Booklist,* observed that "Andy's perceptions of the racism directed toward young black males—by teachers, guidance counselors, and clerks in shopping malls—will be recognized by African American YAs."

"*Tears of a Tiger* is written for high school students—on their level, in their style, about their world," Draper told *SATA.* "The main characters are African American males, but it's written for all teenagers. The characters are just ordinary kids trying to get through high school. The book does not deal with drugs or gangs or sex. It does, however, deal with

parents, girlfriends, and homework. It also discusses the problems of drinking and driving, racism and teen suicide."

Critics of *Tears of a Tiger* found that Draper effectively uses dialog to advance the story. Kathy Fritts, writing in the *School Library Journal,* pointed out that "the characters' voices are strong, vivid, and ring true. This moving novel will leave a deep impression." Furthermore, Draper's use of news stories, journal entries, homework assignments, and letters give the novel an immediacy that adds to its power. Although some critics faulted Draper for a tendency to be preachy, most commented similarly to Monks, who remarked that the work's "characters and their experiences will captivate teen readers." In *Publishers Weekly,* a reviewer concluded that "the combination of raw energy and intense emotions should stimulate readers." Dorothy M. Broderick, critiquing the work in *Voice of Youth Advocates,* wrote: "Suffice to say, not only is Draper an author to watch for, but that this is as compelling a novel as any published in the last two decades." Roger Sutton, writing in the *Bulletin of the Center for Children's Books,* stated that "rather than a tidy summary of suicide symptoms and 'ways to help,' readers instead get a grave portrait of unceasing despair and a larger picture of how young African-American men like Andy get lost in a system that will not trust or reach out to them." *Tears of a Tiger* has received several national honors, including the Coretta Scott King Genesis Award.

Forged by Fire, the 1997 sequel to *Tears of a Tiger,* has a similar socially relevant nexus for its plot. Child sexual abuse and drug addiction replace suicide and racism, yet both books reach a tragic finality. Draper wrote *Forged by Fire*'s first chapter as a short story, "One Small Touch," published in *Ebony.* The novel went on to win Draper her second Coretta Scott King Award.

Gerald Nickelby, the hero of this story, is a minor character in *Tears of a Tiger*—a friend of Robert. (The car accident and Robert's death are retold here). Gerald, at age three, is burned in a fire when left alone by his mother, Monique. After his hospital stay, Gerald is not returned to his mother. Instead he lives with his Aunt Queen, a loving and supportive woman. Six years later, Monique reenters Gerald's life after Aunt Queen dies. Monique has married Jordan Sparks, the father of Angel, Gerald's new half-sister. Gerald learns that Sparks has sexually abused Angel and through the testimony of the children,

Sparks is sent to prison. When Sparks returns six years later (Gerald is now fifteen), Monique, who indulges too much in drugs, lets him return to family life where he once again attempts to sexually harm Angel.

Tom S. Hurlburt, reviewing *Forged by Fire* in *School Library Journal*, assessed the book's impact this way: "There's no all's-well ending, but readers will have hope for Gerald and Angel, who have survived a number of gut-wrenching ordeals by relying on their constant love and caring for one another." Candace Smith, writing in *Booklist*, concluded that "Draper faces some big issues (abuse, death, drugs) and provides concrete options and a positive African American role model in Gerald."

Draper commented: "I feel very blessed that I have had so much success in such a short time. I hope that my books can continue to make a difference in the lives of young people."

BIOGRAPHICAL/CRITICAL SOURCES:

BOOKS

Something about the Author, Volume 98, Gale, 1998.

PERIODICALS

American Visions, December-January, 1995, p. 39.
Booklist, November 1, 1994, p. 492; April 1, 1995, p. 1416; March 15, 1996, p. 1278; February 15, 1997, pp. 1016-1017.
Bulletin of the Center for Children's Books, January, 1995, p. 164; June, 1997, p. 355.
Children's Book Review Service, February, 1997, p. 82.
Children's Bookwatch, February, 1995, p. 3.
Ebony, December, 1990, pp. 18C-19C.
Emergent Librarian, September, 1996, p. 24.
English Journal, January, 1996, p. 87.
Horn Book Guide, spring, 1995, p. 88.
Jet, May 12, 1997, p. 25.
Kirkus Reviews, December 1, 1996, p. 1735.
Publishers Weekly, October 31, 1994, p. 64; January 15, 1996, p. 463; March 25, 1996, p. 85; December 16, 1996, p. 61.
School Library Journal, February, 1995, p. 112; March, 1995, p. 202; August, 1996, p. 142; March, 1997, p. 184.

Social Education, April, 1995, p. 215.
Voice of Youth Advocates, February, 1995, p. 338; June, 1997, p. 108.

OTHER

Children's Literature Web Guide, http://www.acs.ucalgary.ca/~dkbrown/ala98.html (June 5, 1998).
Cincinnati Public Schools, http://www.cpsboe.k12.oh.us/general/recognition_walnuthills.html (June 5, 1998).
Ohio Department of Education, http://school improvement.ode.ohio.gov/TOY/draper.html (June 5, 1998).
Simon Says Kids, http://www.simonsays.com/kid zone/teach/celebration/draper.html (June 5, 1998).
Skillsbank, http://www.skillsbank.com/pages/rc teache.html (June 5, 1998).

Interview with Jon Saari, The Gale Group, December 15, 1998.*

*   *   *

DRURY, Allen (Stuart) 1918-1998

OBITUARY NOTICE—See index for *CA* sketch: Born September 2, 1918, in Houston, TX; died of cardiac arrest, September 2, 1998, in San Francisco, CA. Journalist and novelist. Drury was best known for his insider's knowledge of Washington, D.C., and infused his novels with characters who made readers wonder if they were based on real politicians. He learned about the nation's capital while covering the Senate for the *New York Times.* Drury graduated from Stanford University in 1939 and worked at several newspapers, including *The Tulare Bee, Bakersfield Californian, Washington Evening Star,* and the wire service United Press International before joining the staff at the *Times.*

While Drury covered the Senate by day he spent his free time working on his first novel, *Advise and Consent,* which deals with political intrigue and sexual scandal relating to the appointment of the secretary of state. When the book was published in 1959 it became an instant hit with critics and readers alike and won the Pulitzer Prize for literature in 1960. In 1962 the book was made into a film starring Henry Fonda, Walter Pidgeon, Charles Laughton, and Franchot Tone, but by then Drury had already left the *Times* to serve as a political correspondent for *Reader's Digest.* He continued writing novels, including six sequels to *Advise and Consent.* Other titles include *A Shade of Difference, Capable of Honor, Preserve and Protect, Toward What Bright Glory?* and *Decision.* In addition he wrote five nonfiction books dealing with topics that included politics and travel. He completed his last novel, *Public Men,* two weeks before his death.

OBITUARIES AND OTHER SOURCES:

PERIODICALS

Chicago Tribune, September 4, 1998, sec. 2, p.10.
CNN Interactive (electronic), September 3, 1998.
Los Angeles Times, September 3, 1998, p. A24.
New York Times, September 3, 1998, p. C20; September 3, 1998.

*   *   *

DUE, Tananarive 1966-

PERSONAL: Name is pronounced *tah-nah-nah-REEVE doo;* born in 1966; daughter of Patricia (a civil rights activist; maiden name, Stephens) Due. *Education:* Northwestern University, B.S., University of Leeds (England), M.A.

ADDRESSES: Home—Miami, FL. *Office*—c/o Harper Collins Publishers, 10 East 53rd St., New York, NY 10022.

CAREER: Journalist and novelist. Columnist for the *Miami Herald;* former intern at the *New York Times* and *Wall Street Journal.* Has performed with the Rockbottom Remainders, a rock band that includes authors Stephen King, Dave Barry, and Amy Tan, as keyboardist/vocalist/dancer.

AWARDS, HONORS: Finalist, Bram Stoker Award for Outstanding Achievement in a First Novel, Horror Writers Association, 1995, for *The Between.*

WRITINGS:

The Between (novel), HarperCollins (New York City), 1995.
My Soul to Keep (novel), HarperCollins (New York City), 1997.

Contributor to *Naked Came the Manatee,* Putnam, a comic thriller written by thirteen southern writers, each contributing a chapter.

WORK IN PROGRESS: Researching a nonfiction book on the civil rights movement in Florida, to be co-authored by her mother, Patricia Stephens Due.

SIDELIGHTS: Tananarive Due is a journalist based in Miami whose two novels are nearly unique in the genre of mystery/horror in featuring African American characters. *The Between,* Due's first novel, is "a skillful blend of horror and the supernatural," according to a reviewer for *Publishers Weekly.* The story centers on a forty-year-old social worker in Miami's inner city who is plagued by nightmares that seem to indicate either his insanity or his status as a person "in between" life and death. As a child, Hilton James barely escaped death by drowning in the same accident that killed his grandmother; now, as the husband of the only African American woman judge in Miami, he seems to be receiving messages through his subconscious that indicate his survival all those years ago was a mistake that must be rectified. Due's portrait of Hilton's crumbling personality is "sympathetic and credible," according to a *Publishers Weekly* critic, who nevertheless felt that the rest of the cast fails to achieve the same verisimilitude. M. J. Simmons, who reviewed *The Between* for *Library Journal,* noted that rather than a tale of supernatural horror, Due's first novel, which was nominated for the Bram Stoker Award by the Horror Writers Association, is "a chilling and sympathetic portrait of a man whose madness needs explanation in the psychic realm." Although Simmons found Due's ending a disappointment, Lillian Lewis, who reviewed the book for *Booklist,* praised Due's "intriguing and suspenseful plot," concluding that "Due may very well develop a loyal following with her first novel."

Due followed *The Between* with *My Soul to Keep,* another tale of supernatural horror, in which a reporter discovers that her otherwise-perfect husband is actually a five hundred-year-old member of an Ethiopian band of immortals willing to kill to keep its members existence a secret. Due increases the tension as David reveals his secret to Jessica, endangering himself and the family he has come to love when the brotherhood sends another member of the band to make sure their secret does not get out. *Booklist* critic Lewis found Due's second novel "more compelling than her first" and compared *My Soul to Keep* with Octavia Butler's *Kindred* for its grounding in "African and African-American heritage and culture."

Critics lauded Due's realistic details and strong sense of family life, which provide a convincing foundation for a somewhat melodramatic plot. *My Soul to Keep* is "a novel populated with vivid, emotional characters that is also a chilling journey to another world," concluded a reviewer for *Publishers Weekly.*

BIOGRAPHICAL/CRITICAL SOURCES:

PERIODICALS

Booklist, May 15, 1995, p. 1631; July 19, 1997.
Houston Chronicle, August 13, 1997.
Kirkus Reviews, May 15, 1997, p. 738.
Library Journal, June 1, 1995, p. 158.
Publishers Weekly, April 24, 1995, p. 60; June 2, 1997, p. 55.
Washington Post Book World, November 23, 1997.*

* * *

DUNNETT, Alistair M(acTavish) 1908-1998
(Sir Alistair MacTavish Dunnett)

OBITUARY NOTICE—See index for *CA* sketch: Born December 26, 1908, in Kilmacolm, Renfrewshire, Scotland; died September 2, 1998. Oil executive, journalist, editor, playwright, and author. Dunnett's rich and varied contributions during his life included revamping a sagging Scottish newspaper, contributing to the oil industry in Scotland, and authoring a number of plays and other works. Dunnett grew up in a strict Glasgow household, and while the desire to write was sparked early on in his life, he initially took a job in banking. Later he decided that finance was not the field for him and he launched a boy's magazine with a friend. His journalism career continued to build and by the late 1930s he had served on the staff of several newspapers. During World War II Dunnett served as press officer for the Scottish Secretary of State. After the war Dunnett worked in editorial capacities for the *Daily Mirror* and *The Scotsman.* Dunnett gave the latter publication a new look, added exciting writers, and gave the paper a nationalist identity. Dunnett served on the board of Thomson Scottish Petroleum beginning in 1972. He was knighted in 1995 for his many contributions to society during his life. Dunnett authored two plays including *The Original John Mackay* (1956) and *Fit to Print* (1962). He also wrote *Quest by Canoe* (1956; with James Adam) and the autobiography *Among Friends* (1984).

OBITUARIES AND OTHER SOURCES:

BOOKS

Who's Who, St. Martin's Press, 1998.

PERIODICALS

London Times, September 4, 1998.

* * *

DUNNETT, Sir Alistair MacTavish
See DUNNETT, Alistair M(acTavish)

* * *

DURAN, Jane 1947-

PERSONAL: Born January 1, 1947; U.S. citizen; married Richard Duran (a professor of education). *Ethnicity:* "White." *Education:* University of California, Berkeley, B.A. (with honors), 1968; University of California, Berkeley, Ph.D. (psychology), 1977; Rutgers University, Ph.D., 1982.

ADDRESSES: Agent—c/o Pennsylvania State University Press, 820 North University Dr., University Support Bldg. 1, University Park, PA 16802.

CAREER: Rutgers University, New Brunswick, NJ, coadjutant, 1981; Trenton State College, Trenton, NJ, visiting assistant professor, 1982-83; Hamilton College, Clinton, NY, visiting assistant professor, 1983-84; University of California, Santa Barbara, fellow in education, 1984-85; affiliated scholar in philosophy, 1985-87; Mount St. Mary's College, Los Angeles, CA, assistant professor, 1987-88; University of California, Santa Barbara, research associate and lecturer in philosophy, 1988-98, member of Sociology Network Theory Seminar, 1990-97, and Science, Culture, Technology, and Society Discussion Group, 1995-98. California Polytechnic State University, San Luis Obispo, lecturer, 1985 and 1986; Johns Hopkins University, associate of Center for Research on Students Placed at Risk, 1995-98; guest lecturer at colleges and universities, including University of Pittsburgh, 1987.

MEMBER: American Philosophical Association, American Society for Aesthetics, Society for Women in Philosophy, Society for Philosophy and Psychology, Philosophy of Science Association, Society for the Study of Women Philosophers (member of executive board), American Association of University Professors, American Association of University Women.

AWARDS, HONORS: Fellow, Johns Hopkins University, 1977; grant from National Center for Research on Cultural Diversity and Second Language Learning, 1991-95.

WRITINGS:

(Contributor) Patrick Grim, editor, *Philosophy of Science and the Occult,* State University of New York Press (Albany, NY), 1982.
(Contributor) Mary Vetterling-Braggin, editor, *"Femininity," "Masculinity," and "Androgyny": A Modern Philosophical Discussion,* Littlefield, Adams (Totowa, NJ), 1982.
Epistemics, University Press of America (Lanham, MD), 1989.
Toward a Feminist Epistemology, Rowman & Littlefield (Totowa), 1991.
Knowledge in Context, Rowman & Littlefield, 1994.
Philosophies of Science/Feminist Theories, Westview (Boulder, CO), 1997.
(Contributor) Lynn Hankinson Nelson, editor, *Feminist Interpretations of Quine,* Pennsylvania State University Press (University Park, PA), 1998.

Contributor of more than forty articles to philosophy journals, including *Critica, Philosophy of Science and the Occult, International Journal for Philosophy of Religion, Social Epistemology, Monist,* and *British Journal for the Philosophy of Science.* Coeditor, *Philosophica,* 1990, and *Journal of Aesthetics and Comparative Literature,* 1993; member of editorial board, *Metaphilosophy.*

*   *   *

DUTTON, Geoffrey (Piers Henry)   1922-1998

OBITUARY NOTICE—See index for *CA* sketch: Born August 2, 1922, in Anlaby, Kapunda, Australia; died September 17, 1998. Educator, editor, and author. Dutton was well known for publishing prolifically, encouraging the growth of the arts in his native Australia, and promoting a nationalistic independence for

the country. Dutton was born in Australia into a family wealthy from land and sheep farming. He followed his Australian college education with a stint at Oxford in England, but found the austerity of England in the late 1940s difficult to get used to. During the war Dutton served as a RAAF instructor and spent a little over a month in military jail for a disciplinary offense. He traveled extensively in Europe and spent more time in England, but eventually returned to Australia to teach literature at Adelaide University. After 1962 he wrote on a full-time basis. He was also responsible for establishing two premier Australian literary magazines, and for creating dialog and a sense of identity in the Australian art community. Dutton believed that Australia needed to stop thinking of itself as a monarchy, and became active in the Australian Republican movement in 1990—a movement which encouraged independence for Australia. Dutton's writing included literary criticism, biography, novels, travel writing, art appreciation, and poetry. His work *The Australian Aborigine Portrayed in Art* won the 1978 Weickhardt Prize. He also published an autobiography, *Warts and All* (1994).

OBITUARIES AND OTHER SOURCES:

PERIODICALS

Times (London), October 12, 1998.

*   *   *

DYSON, Esther 1951-

PERSONAL: Born July 14, 1951, in Zurich, Switzerland; daughter of Freeman (a physicist) and Esther (a mathematician; maiden name, Huber) Dyson. *Education:* Harvard University, B.A. (economics), 1972. *Avocational interests:* Swimming.

ADDRESSES: Office—EDventure Holdings, 375 Park Avenue, New York, NY 10152-0002.

CAREER: Computer newsletter publisher, journalist, and venture capitalist. *Forbes* magazine, reporter, 1974-77, columnist, 1987—; New Court Securities, securities analyst, 1977-79; Oppenheimer & Co., president, 1980-82; Rosen Electronics Newsletter; *Release 1.0,* editor and publisher, 1982—; EDventure Holdings, owner and president, 1982—; *Computer Industry Daily,* editor and publisher, 1985; Mayfield

Software Partners, limited partner; *Guardian Magazine,* London, columnist; *Content Magazine,* columnist; National Public Radio, commentator. Member, President's Export Council, Subcommittee on Encryption; National Information Infrastructure Advisory Council, Information Privacy and Intellectual Property Subcommittee, co-chair, 1994-1996. Sits on the boards and committees of several organizations and foundations including the Institute for East/West Studies, Perot Systems Corporation, Global Business Network, Institute for Research on Learning, and the Eurasia Foundation.

MEMBER: Women's Forum, Association of Data Processing Service Organizations, Software Publications Association.

AWARDS, HONORS: Von Neumann Medal (Hungary), 1996.

WRITINGS:

Release 2.0: A Design for Living in the Digital Age, Broadway Books (New York City), 1997.

Contributor of articles to professional journals and periodicals including *Harvard Business Review, Forbes,* and *Wired.*

SIDELIGHTS: Esther Dyson, a computer visionary whose newsletter *Release 1.0* is one of the most influential in the industry, has led an adventurous life. Dyson's father is the renowned British astrophysicist Freeman Dyson; a math prodigy, he also writes on a variety of subjects and his interests range from subatomic physics to space travel and peace issues. Her mother, the Swiss mathematician Verena Huber-Dyson, received her Ph.D. from the same institution as Albert Einstein.

Dyson was born in Zurich, Switzerland, in 1951, but she and her brother George were raised in the university town of Princeton, New Jersey. It was a heady time. In a *New York Times* interview Dyson told Claudia Dreifus, "Two of our neighbors were Nobel Prize winners. A third developed color television. As children, my brother, George, and I played on the derelict remains of one of the first computers, which was on the grounds of the Institute for Advanced Studies, where my father worked. Mrs. Hans Berthe [wife of a key architect of the A-bomb] was my godmother. Edward Teller [father of the H-bomb] came to the house often."

Dyson's parents divorced when she was five. She recalled, in the same *New York Times* interview, her father's claim that she said, "Oh, who needs a mother when the milk is gone." Her mother moved to Berkeley, California, taught math at the university there, and plunged herself into a bohemian lifestyle. She numbered among her friends fellow mathematician and famous protest song writer Tom Lehrer. Dyson spent time on both coasts while growing up, continuing to develop a fascination with computers.

Essentially stateless, Dyson had to have special passports made up for her on her family's frequent trips abroad. She caught the nomadic bug. At the age of twelve she planned and executed an extended trip to England on her own. Applying herself to academics, she matriculated at Harvard at the age of sixteen, majoring in economics. By her own admission Dyson was not a good student at Harvard, preferring instead to devote her energies to the *Harvard Crimson,* the campus newspaper.

After graduating in 1974 Dyson went to work for *Forbes* magazine. An early indicator of her perceptive flare was an article she wrote for the magazine after she had spent her savings and her vacation time in Japan. She predicted that Japan would threaten the U.S. computer industry, and she correctly discerned that the threat would be in hardware, not software. After her three-year stint at Forbes, Dyson worked as a securities analyst on Wall Street. After that she scaled back, working for the *Rosen Electronics Newsletter.* When its founder, Ben Rosen, divested the newsletter due to a conflict of interest with his venture capital activities, he sold it to Dyson. She rechristened it *Release 1.0* and, except for a short hiatus when she signed on to edit a doomed daily electronic newspaper that focused on the computer industry, Dyson has published *Release 1.0* continuously since 1982.

Unlike most computer industry newsletters that cover short-term trends and breaking news, *Release 1.0* takes the long view. According to the EDventure Internet web page (EDventure is the holding company for the newsletter), "*Release 1.0* pioneered coverage and analysis of client/server technology (1986), object-oriented programming (1987), group-ware (1986), document management (1988), and the commercial potential of the Internet (1991)." Many subscribers to her newsletter are the CEOs, venture capitalists, and stock pickers whom the computer industry revolves around. Those ideas that engage Dyson "will matter in the industry," noted Paulina Borsook in a

Wired magazine article. Dyson "has a kind of distant early warning system that . . . the most influential people in the computer industry (a.k.a., her subscribers) look to when they design new products, create new markets, and try to change the world. For them, Esther is a one-woman think tank," Borsook commented. Even more influential than her newsletter is Dyson's annual PC Forum, open only to subscribers. The forum is more famous for the networking and deal-making that go on in the hallways than for its speakers or presentations. "What I try to do is find worthy ideas and people and get attention for them," Dyson told Dreifus of the *New York Times.* "I meet a lot of people, read a lot of stuff and try to promote new ideas."

A typical month finds Dyson traveling to far-flung areas of the world attending conferences and researching newsletter topics. Due to an interest in Eastern Europe's emerging computer market, Dyson started a new newsletter named *Rel-EAST.* It, too, has a corresponding forum, the annual East-West High Tech Forum. Her efforts have earned her kudos from that quarter of the globe. Hungary awarded her the Von Neumann Medal in 1996 for "distinction in the dissemination of computer information" and the Russian *Who's Who in the Computer Market* included Dyson at number 23 in the list of the most influential people in Russia's computer industry. Dyson also holds a variety of posts on corporate boards and for non-profit organizations. Chief among these—at least measured in what visibility it gives her—is her chairing of the Electronic Frontiers Foundation, an organization devoted to preserving civil liberties in the digital realm.

In 1997 Dyson put forth some of her newest predictions in book form in *Release 2.0: A Design for Living in the Digital Age.* Many predictions have to do with the Internet and with the culture that it is spawning—how it will change education, commerce, intellectual property rights, and even social relations. Talking about her book to Donna Seamann of *Booklist,* Dyson said, "I see [the Internet] as an environment for human beings, not as an alien or separate place. . . . By writing the book, I hope to encourage—this sounds really corny—more good people to get on the net and not be scared." A contributor to *Publishers Weekly* noted that "Dyson doesn't present many surprises here for those familiar with her thought, but nearly everything she says is worth hearing." Derek Bickerton, reviewing *Release 2.0* for the *New York Times,* praised Dyson's work: "one of her goals is to demystify the Net and

thus disarm those who would demonize it. . . . A system that lets people communicate globally, instantly and often free of charge, must seem to many the way witchcraft seemed in the Middle Ages; anything that helps dispel such attitudes must be salutary." Bickerton, however, criticized what he saw as a "narrowness of vision" on Dyson's part in her predictions that the whole world will be "wired" in the near future. Bickerton pointed out in the *New York Times* inequities between the very poor and the electronic elite that will only widen as technology marches forward.

BIOGRAPHICAL/CRITICAL SOURCES:

BOOKS

Current Biography Yearbook 1997, Gale, (Detroit, MI), 1997.

PERIODICALS

Booklist, December 1, 1997, p. 601.
Library Journal, November 1, 1997, p. 108.
Publishers Weekly, September 29, 1997, pp. 78-79.
New York Times, July 7, 1996.
New York Times Book Review, November 30, 1997, p. 6.

OTHER

EDventure Holdings, Esther Dyson biography, http://www.edventure.com /bios/esther.html (July 21, 1998).
Release 1.0, http://www.edventure.com/release1/release1.html (July 21, 1998).
Wired, "Release" by Pauline Borsook, http://www.wired.com/wired/1.5 /features/dyson.html (July 21, 1998).*

*   *   *

**DZYUBIN, Eduard Georgievich   1895-1934
(Eduard Bagritsky, a pseudonym)**

PERSONAL: Born November 4, 1895, in Odessa, Ukraine; died of chronic asthma, February 16, 1934, in Kuntsevo, U.S.S.R. (now Ukraine); son of a shopkeeper; married. *Education:* Educated in Odessa. *Politics:* Communist.

CAREER: Poet, translator, and essayist, c. 1918-34. Worked briefly for the Odessa Police Department; staff writer for satirical magazines *Pero v spinu* (title means, "A Pen in the Back") and *Tablochko* (title means, "Apple"). *Military service:* Served in the Russian Army during World War I; served in the Soviet Army during the Communist Revolution.

WRITINGS:

AS EDUARD BAGRITSKY; POETRY, EXCEPT AS NOTED

Duma pro Opanasa (title means "Lay of Opanas"), 1925.
Yugozapad (title means "Southwest"; includes "Pigeons," "The Watermelon," and "The Cigarette Box"), 1928.
Pobediteli (title means "The Victors"), 1932.
Poslednyaya noch (title means "The Last Night"), 1932.
Sobranie sochinenii (poetry and prose), two volumes (second volume unpublished), 1938.
Dnevniki, Pisma, Stikhi (diary, letters, and poetry), 1964.
Stikhotvoreniya i poemy, 1964.

Also the author of *Fevral* (title means "February").

SIDELIGHTS: Eduard Georgievich Dzyubin, who wrote under the name of Eduard Bagritsky, is regarded by many as one of the important poets from the early years of the Soviet Union. He was born in Odessa, Ukraine, in 1895, the son of a Jewish shopkeeper. Though many of the poems he penned painted his youth as a time of deprivation, his family maintained an average standard of living. He was, however, sickly as a child. Bagritsky attended school in Odessa, and determined upon a literary career early on, though he was employed for brief stints with the Odessa police and both the Russian and Soviet Armies during and following World War I. He also served as a staff writer on two satirical magazines, *Pero v spinu* and *Tablochko*. After his nation was transformed into the communist Soviet Union, Bagritsky joined the Constructivists writing group. Though his poetry was greatly praised by Soviet critics, and often explored "revolutionary" themes, his work was never considered completely true to communist ideology, having throughout it a great deal of influence from the earlier Romantic school. Some of Bagritsky's best-known works include *Duma pro Opanasa, Yugozapad,* and the unfinished *Fevral*, on which he was working on when he died of chronic asthma in 1934. Despite the fact that Bagritsky's widow served in a Soviet prison for nearly twenty years, she was able to assist in the publication of two posthumous collections of the poet's writings; not only poetry, but essays and correspondence.

Duma pro Opanasa, which became available to Soviet readers in 1925, is Russian for "The Lay of Opanas." According to Alexander Kaun in his 1943 book *Soviet Poets and Poetry,* "the very name of the elegy, *Duma,* suggests Bagritsky's affinity with the celebrated Taras Shevchenko (1814-1861), author of numerous *dumy* (the name applied to Ukrainian folk epics and songs); the text reveals further signs of this kinship." Kaun went on to explain that in *Duma pro Opanasa,* "Opanas is an Ukrainian peasant, unwittingly swept by the waves of revolution and civil wars." The main forces in the Communist Revolution were three—the Reds, who wanted to implement a communist government; the Whites, who were loyal to the Czarist cause; and the Greens, who favored a ruralist anarchy. Opanas falls in with the Greens, and after a raid in which Opanas' group surprises and captures a Red unit, Opanas is assigned to execute the communist leader, a Jew named Kogan. Opanas is troubled by the thought of shooting an unarmed man, and offers Kogan an opportunity to escape. Kogan refuses, and meets his execution with courage. Later, when Opanas himself is captured by the Reds, Kogan's inspiring example causes him to confess to executing the Red leader, and to meet his own execution with bravery.

Kaun gave high praise to *Duma pro Opanasa,* hailing the lengthy poem's "power and colorfulness" and went on to declare that "Bagritsky combines a gift for describing dramatic scenes, battles, surging crowds, executions, with the typical Ukrainian badinage that one finds in Gogol or Shevchenko." Kaun further noted that the poet "tempers the pathos of fratricidal war and pitiless carnage by the contrasting tone of everydayness, by bits of homely colloquialism and banter, of folk song and folk wisdom." Renato Poggioli, in 1960's *The Poets of Russia, 1890-1930,* was less enthusiastic about *Duma pro Opanasa,* opining that with it, Bagritsky had "reduced poetry to a picturesque fancy, episodic and anecdotal, superficial and fragmentary, in brief, almost to a parody of itself." Reporting in 1971's *Russian Literature under Lenin and Stalin, 1917-1953* that *Duma pro Opanasa* "for a long time was regarded by Soviet critics as one of the masterpieces of Soviet poetry," Gleb Struve also asserted that "its free and quick-changing meter recalls Ukrainian folk songs," and that "there are in it some beautiful evocations of the Ukrainian landscape."

Bagritsky's 1928 collection *Yugozapad* ("Southwest") includes individual poems such as "Pigeons," "The Watermelon," and "The Cigarette Box." Struve, again in *Russian Literature under Lenin and Stalin,* cited these three poems in particular as "deserv[ing] a place in any anthology of modern Russian poetry." In "The Cigarette Box," the poem's narrator has stayed up chain-smoking late into the night, and is tormented by nightmares of pre-revolutionary Russian poets. As Boris Thomson explained in his 1978 volume *Lot's Wife and the Venus of Milo: Conflicting Attitudes to the Cultural Heritage in Modern Russia,* "as the nightmare continues, Bagritsky is forced to undergo the flogging which they underwent and to experience all the horrors of the Tsarist past. As dawn comes," Thomson continued, "the figures of the nightmare reveal themselves to have been only the trees and currant-bushes of his garden." Following this realization, the poet advises his son to destroy the trees and bushes in order to promote new growth—symbolically also advising him to abandon the poetic techniques of the past. Thomson labeled "The Cigarette Box" a "startling" poem, and took from it the conclusion that "where almost all other Soviet writers would proudly place themselves in the Decembrist tradition, Bagritsky sees only the horror and the demoralization; Russian history is a long nightmare that must be obliterated if a new and healthier race is ever to inherit the world."

Bagritsky's last major work, the unfinished *Fevral* or "February," is based upon an incident from his own life, but is greatly changed. In *Lot's Wife and the Venus of Milo,* Thomson quoted the poet as explaining: "All this actually happened to me, just as I describe it. Yes, the schoolgirl and the search. I hardly added anything at all, but what was essential for the idea. First," Bagritsky revealed, "the bandits we were looking for, turned out not to be in the house. Second," the poet continued, "when I saw this schoolgirl, with whom I had once been in love, and who had now become an officers' prostitute, well, in the poem I send everyone out, and jump on the bed on top of her. It was, so to say, a break with the past, a settling of accounts with it. In actual fact," Bagritsky pointed out, "I was completely bewildered and couldn't get out of the room fast enough." Thomson believed that the poetic description of the rape itself, by contrast, shows that the narrator "is concerned simply to possess and humiliate; all the gestures are violent and brutal." Later, according to Thomson, the narrative shows remorse on the part of the rapist and "the tone changes dramatically: from action to introspection, from self-assertion to self-justification, from aggression almost to apology." Thomson applauded *Fevral* as Bagritsky's "extraordinary bid to settle accounts once and for all with the past." He reported that it had been the poet's intent to "insert some 'lyrical interludes' into the work," before he died. Thomson went on to express: "It is hard to believe that these would have enriched the poem any further; if anything they would have diluted it. As it stands it is already a self-contained and unified work of art."

BIOGRAPHICAL/CRITICAL SOURCES:

BOOKS

Kaun, Alexander, *Soviet Poets and Poetry,* University of California Press, 1943.

Poggioli, Renato, *The Poets of Russia, 1890-1930,* Harvard University Press, 1960.

Struve, Gleb, *Russian Literature under Lenin and Stalin, 1917-1953,* University of Oklahoma Press, 1971.

Thomson, Boris, *Lot's Wife and the Venus of Milo: Conflicting Attitudes to the Cultural Heritage in Modern Russia,* Cambridge University Press, 1978.*

—*Sketch by Elizabeth Wenning*

E

EDWARDS, P. D. 1931-

PERSONAL: Born March 2, 1931, in Melbourne, Australia; son of Harry Salter (in business) and Marjorie Wood (Willis) Edwards; married Ann Jean Mitchell, June 30, 1962; children: Alan David, Paul Richard Keith, John Peter, Gwendolen Marjorie. *Ethnicity:* "Caucasian." *Education:* Attended University of Queensland, 1949-52, and Birkbeck College, London, 1958-60. *Politics:* Socialist. *Religion:* None.

ADDRESSES: Home—125 Kenmore Rd., Kenmore, Queensland 4069, Australia. *Office*—Department of English, University of Queensland, St. Lucia, Brisbane, Queensland 4072, Australia; fax 61-73-365-2799. *E-mail*—p.edwards@uq.net.au.

CAREER: University of Queensland, Brisbane, Australia, lecturer in English, 1954-58 and 1961; University of Sydney, Sydney, Australia, began as lecturer, became senior lecturer in English, 1962-68; University of Queensland, professor of English, 1969-96, pro-vice-chancellor for humanities, 1985-90.

WRITINGS:

Anthony Trollope, Routledge & Kegan Paul (London), 1968.
Anthony Trollope: His Art and Scope, St. Martin's Press (New York City), 1978.
Anthony Trollope's Son in Australia, University of Queensland Press (Brisbane, Australia), 1982.
Idyllic Realism from Mary Russell Mitford to Hardy, St. Martin's Press, 1988.
Dickens's "Young Men," Ashgate Publishing (Brookfield, VT), 1997.

ELLIS, Edward Robb 1911-1998

OBITUARY NOTICE—See index for *CA* sketch: Born February 22, 1911, in Kewanee, IL; died September 7, 1998, in New York, NY. Historian, diarist, and author. Ellis is best known for the lengthy and detailed diary of his life which he started as a young boy in Kewanee, IL. When Ellis was sixteen years old and bored in his small Midwestern town, he dared some friends to see who could keep a diary going for the longest time. While his diary starts with the title "Hog Capital of the World," referring to his home town, Ellis's diary tracked his life and career as a newspaper journalist through several cities, including his arrival in New York City. According to his diary, he knew immediately that he loved the city and realized that he should have been born there. Ellis wrote daily and was interested in the stories of many people. He compiled a history of New York City titled *The Epic of New York City* (1966) which one writer called the best of its kind. He also compiled histories of the Depression and of World War I. In 1995, Ellis published a small portion of his diary (which encompassed seventy volumes) titled *A Diary of the Century: Tales from America's Greatest Diarist.*

OBITUARIES AND OTHER SOURCES:

BOOKS

Who's Who in Entertainment, 1998-99.

PERIODICALS

New York Times, September 9, 1998, p. B12.
Washington Post, September 12, 1998, p. B7.

EMERSON, Ken 1948-

PERSONAL: Born October 29, 1948, in Huntington, WV; son of Robert K. (an attorney) and Roberta Esther (a museum director; maiden name, Shinn) Emerson; married Ellen Ketchum O'Meara (a teacher), June 27, 1981; children: Maude. *Education:* Attended Groton School, Harvard University, and Yale University.

ADDRESSES: Home—42 Harrison Ave., Montclair, NJ 07042. *Office*—The Century Foundation, 41 East 70th St., New York, NY 10021. *Agent*—Gloria Loomis, Watkins Loomis Agency, 133 East 35th St., Suite 1, New York, NY 10016. *E-mail*—Emersonrk@aol.com.

CAREER: Boston Phoenix, Boston, MA, writer and editor, 1968-77; *New York Times Magazine,* New York City, editor; *Newsday,* New York City, "New York Viewpoints" editor, 1990-95.

AWARDS, HONORS: Anschutz Distinguished Fellowship in American Studies, Princeton University, 1998-99.

WRITINGS:

NONFICTION

Doo-dah!: Stephen Foster and the Rise of American Popular Culture, Simon & Schuster (New York City), 1997.

Contributor to periodicals, including *Nation, New Republic,* and *Sports Illustrated.*

WORK IN PROGRESS: A history of the Brill Building.

SIDELIGHTS: Journalist Ken Emerson delves into the life of one of the most influential songwriters in American history in his 1997 book *Doo-dah!: Stephen Foster and the Rise of American Popular Culture.* Foster wrote about two hundred songs, including "Oh! Susannah," "Old Folks at Home" (also known as "Swanee River"), "Camptown Races," "My Old Kentucky Home," "Jeanie with the Light Brown Hair," "Beautiful Dreamer," and "Old Black Joe." As Emerson reveals, Foster also wrote songs for minstrel shows that featured white performers in blackface and skits about slavery. Emerson also recounts that Foster often sold the rights to his songs for very little money, and died an alcoholic, in poverty, at the age of thirty-seven. Yet Foster's songs

remain popular, and Emerson describes their influence on the development of an American music that incorporates qualities of both European and African-American music.

Commentators noted Emerson's thorough research when reviewing *Doo-Dah!.* A *Publishers Weekly* contributor called Emerson's studies "exhaustive" and observed that his findings have "been meticulously worked into a vivid portrait of nineteenth-century America." Writing in *Library Journal,* Michael Colby noted that *Doo-Dah!* "goes a long way towards dispelling the myths that have surrounded the composer." However, David Thigpen, writing in Chicago *Tribune Books,* maintained that the exhaustive approach has a downside, noting that "to dig deeply into Foster's life is to scrape away much of the magic of his magnificent songs." According to Thigpen, Foster's pro-slavery sympathies should be understood within the climate of his times: "Even as we are made aware of the many skeletons rattling around in Foster's closets, Emerson places him in a historical context that makes his life and art compelling."

BIOGRAPHICAL/CRITICAL SOURCES:

PERIODICALS

Atlantic, June, 1997, p. 122.
Kirkus Reviews, March 15, 1997, p. 433.
Library Journal, May 1, 1997, p. 105.
Los Angeles Times Book Review, May 4, 1997, p. 4.
New York Times Book Review, June 22, 1997, p. 5.
Publishers Weekly, March 31, 1997, pp. 53-54.
Tribune Books (Chicago), May 4, 1997, p. 5.
Village Voice, June 17, 1997, pp. 55-56.
Washington Post Book World, May 11, 1997, p. 3.

*   *   *

ESPAILLAT, Rhina P. 1932-

PERSONAL: Born January 20, 1932, in Santo Domingo, Dominican Republic; naturalized U.S. citizen; daughter of Homero and Dulce Maria (Batista) Espaillat; married Alfred Moskowitz, June 28, 1952; children: Philip Elias, Warren Paul; foster-children: Gaston W. Dubois. *Ethnicity:* "Hispanic." *Education:* Hunter College, B.A., 1953; Queens College, M.S.E., 1964. *Avocational interests:* Drawing, gardening, needlework.

ADDRESSES: Home and office—12 Charron Drive, Newburyport, MA 01950. *E-mail*—espmosk@Juno.com.

CAREER: Teacher and poet. New York City public schools, teacher, 1953-54; Jamaica High School, NY, teacher, 1965-80; New York City Board of Education, consultant, 1984-89.

MEMBER: Academy of American Poets, Women Poets of New York, Poets & Writers, Fresh Meadows Poets, Poetry Society of America, Powow River Poets, New England Poetry Club, Newburyport Art Association.

AWARDS, HONORS: Gustav Davidson Memorial Award, Poetry Society of America, 1986 and 1989; Croton Review Annual Award, 1987; T. S. Eliot Prize, 1998, for *Where Horizons Go; Sparrow* Sonnet Award, 1997; Howard Nemerov Sonnet Award, 1998; also recipient of awards from *Orbis, Lyric, Amelia,* and World Order of Narrative and Formalist Poets.

WRITINGS:

Lapsing to Grace: Poems and Drawings, Bennett & Kitchel (East Lansing, MI), 1992.
Where Horizons Go, Thomas Jefferson University Press (Kirksville, MO), 1998.

Contributor of poetry to anthologies and textbooks, including *Looking for Home: Women Writing about Exile,* Milkweed Editions, 1990; *In Other Words: Literature by Latinas of the United States,* Arte Publico Press, 1994; *A Formal Feeling Comes: Poems in Form by Contemporary Women,* Story Line Press, 1994; *Patchwork of Dreams: Voices from the Heart of the New America,* The Spirit That Moves Us Press, 1996; *Anthology of Magazine Verse & Yearbook of American Poetry,* Monitor Book Co., 1997; and *The Muse Strikes Back: A Poetic Response by Women to Men,* Story Line Press, 1997.

Contributor of poetry to numerous publications, including *American Scholar, Commonwealth, Ekphrasis, Formalist, Hellas, Ladies' Home Journal, Lyric, Manhattan Poetry Review, New York Times, Orbis, Piedmont Literary Review, Pivot, Plains Poetry Journal, Poet Lore, Poetry,* and *Voices International.*

ADAPTATIONS: Various poems have been set to music and used as part of visual art works.

WORK IN PROGRESS: Seeking publication for four completed manuscripts; contributing twenty poems to the collection *Landscapes with Women: Four American Poets,* for Singular Speech Press.

SIDELIGHTS: Rhina P. Espaillat told *CA:* "I began writing at the age of six, in Spanish, inspired by my paternal grandmother, who loved—and wrote—poetry, but never published any. At seven, as the daughter of political exiles in the U.S., I learned English and by eight had begun to write in my second and now dominant language, but have retained fluency in Spanish and publish poems in both languages.

"Early and enduring influences on my English-language poetry include the Elizabethans, the Metaphysical poets of the seventeenth century, Emily Dickinson, Thomas Hardy, A. E. Houseman, Charlotte Mew, and such twentieth-century poets as Robert Frost, W. B. Yeats, W. H. Auden, Edna St. Vincent Millay, Sara Teasdale, Elinor Wylie, and Stanley Kunitz.

"While there are many individual poems in free or experimental forms that I love, the poems that I return to with the greatest satisfaction tend to be formal, metrical, and consciously musical. I've never believed that strict form hampers communication, but feel, in fact, that formal constraints serve to stimulate the imagination, liberate it from the commonplace, and heighten the expressivity of language by subjecting it to tension that charges and enriches it. I am heartened and delighted to note that formal verse has begun to come back into favor as one of the legitimate choices available to the poet.

"When I advise young poets, as I do often as a teacher and workshop leader, my advice is always the same: read a great deal, roam the centuries in your reading, be aware of how language is used in what you read, write for the ear as well as the mind and heard, and revise your work as if it were not yours."

*　　*　　*

ESTES, Daniel J(ohn)

PERSONAL: Married Carol Ann Towle, June 20, 1975; children: Jonathan, Christiana, Joel. *Education:* Cedarville College, B.A., 1974; Dallas Theological Seminary, Th.M., 1978; Cambridge University, Ph.D., 1988.

ADDRESSES: Home—6619 McVey Blvd., West Worthington, OH 43235. *Office*—Cedarville College, Box 601, Cedarville, OH 45314. *E-mail*—estesd@cedarville.edu.

CAREER: Dallas Theological Seminary, Dallas, TX, instructor at Lay Institute, 1977; assistant pastor of a Baptist church, Columbus, OH, 1978-84; Cedarville College, Cedarville, OH, assistant professor, 1984-90, associate professor, 1990-95, professor of Bible, 1995—, assistant academic vice president, 1993—, director of Honors Program, 1995—. Clintonville Baptist Church, assistant pastor, 1989-93.

MEMBER: Society of Biblical Literature, Evangelical Theological Society.

AWARDS, HONORS: Amy Writing Award, 1991; Sears Roebuck Award for teaching excellence and campus leadership, 1991.

WRITINGS:

(Contributor) Michael Baumann and David Hall, editors, *God and Caesar,* Christian Publications (Camp Hill, PA), 1994.
Hear, My Son: Wisdom and Pedagogy in Proverbs 1-9, Eerdmans (Grand Rapids, MI), 1997.

Contributor to periodicals, including *Bibliotheca Sacra, Catholic Biblical Quarterly,* and *Vetus Testamentum.*

WORK IN PROGRESS: Song of Songs, an Old Testament commentary, for Marshall Pickering (London, England), completion expected in 2000; *Handbook on the Poetical Books,* Baker Book (Grand Rapids), 2003.

*   *   *

ESTY, Daniel C. 1959-

PERSONAL: Born June 6, 1959, in MA; son of John (an educator) and Katherine (a management consultant) Esty; married Elizabeth Henderson (a lawyer), October 20, 1984; children: Darah, Thomas, Jonathan. *Education:* Harvard University, B.A., 1981; attended Oxford University, 1981-83; Yale University, J.D., 1986. *Religion:* Congregationalist. *Avocational interests:* Ice hockey.

ADDRESSES: Home—Cheshire, CT. *Office*—Center for Environmental Law and Policy, Yale University, P.O. Box 208215, New Haven, CT 06520-8215; fax 203-432-3817. *E-mail*—daniel.esty@yale.edu.

CAREER: Arnold & Porter, Washington, DC, attorney, 1986-89; U.S. Environmental Protection Agency, Washington, DC, special assistant to the administrator, 1989-90, deputy chief of staff, 1990-91, deputy assistant administrator for policy, 1991-93; Institute for International Economics, Washington, DC, senior fellow, 1993-94; Yale University, New Haven, CT, professor of law and director of Center for Environmental Law and Policy, 1994—, associate dean of School of Forestry and Environmental Studies, 1998—. American Farmland Trust, member; U.S. Trade Representative-Public Advisory Committee, member. Planning and Zoning Commission, Cheshire, CT, member, 1995-99.

MEMBER: American Bar Association, Council on Foreign Relations.

AWARDS, HONORS: Rhodes scholar in England, 1981-83; U.S. Environmental Protection Agency, Fitzhugh Award, 1992, and New England regional merit award, 1997; named among the "world's one hundred most influential environmental leaders" by *Earth Times,* 1998.

WRITINGS:

Greening the GATT, Institute for International Economics (Washington, DC), 1994.
(Editor with Marian R. Chertow) *Thinking Ecologically: The Next Generation of Environmental Policy,* Yale University Press (New Haven, CT), 1997.
Sustaining the Asia Pacific Miracle, Institute for International Economics, 1997.

WORK IN PROGRESS: Research on international environmental protection, trade and the environment, and global environmental governance.

*   *   *

EVANS, David C(hristian) 1940-

PERSONAL: Born January 9, 1940, in Bakersfield, CA; son of Edwin Ben (a high school and junior college administrator) and Dorothy Louise (a registered nurse) Evans; married Carolyn Kay Hemmerling, December 18, 1965; children: Andrew David, Peter Christian, Daniel Edwin. *Ethnicity:* "Caucasian." *Education:* Stanford University, B.A., 1961, M.A., 1969, Ph.D., 1978; Princeton University, graduate study, 1961-62. *Avocational interests:* Snorri Sturluson, Coen brothers films.

ADDRESSES: Home—Richmond, VA. *Office*—Department of History, University of Richmond, Richmond, VA 23173; fax 804-289-8313. *E-mail*—devans @richmond.edu.

CAREER: Stanford University, Stanford, CA, lecturer in history, 1973; University of Richmond, Richmond, VA, instructor, 1973-78, assistant professor, 1978-84, associate professor, 1984-91, professor of history, 1991—, associate dean of School of Arts and Sciences, 1995—. Saga University, exchange professor, 1994. *Military service:* U.S. Navy, 1963-66; became lieutenant junior grade.

MEMBER: American Historical Association, Association for Asian Studies, Phi Beta Kappa.

WRITINGS:

(Editor) *The Japanese Navy in World War II: In the Words of Former Japanese Naval Officers,* Naval Institute Press (Annapolis, MD), 1986.

(With Mark R. Peattie) *Kaigun: The Strategy, Tactics, and Technology of the Imperial Japanese Navy,* Naval Institute Press, 1997.

(With Peattie) *Sunburst: The Rise of Japanese Naval Aviation,* Naval Institute Press, in press.

F

FAGAN, Louis J. 1971-

PERSONAL: Born May 29, 1971. *Education:* Attended Fulton-Montgomery Community College, 1992; State University of New York College at Oneonta, B.A. (magna cum laude), 1995; State University of New York College at New Paltz, M.A., 1997.

ADDRESSES: Home—Johnstown, NY.

CAREER: Listener, editorial assistant, 1995-96; State University of New York at Cobleskill, adjunct instructor in English, 1997—. Gives readings of his stories, including appearances at Oneonta Out Loud, 1996, and *Reader's Theater,* Colonial Little Theater, 1998.

WRITINGS:

New Boots (novel), A-Peak Publishing, 1999.

Contributor to *Listener.*

WORK IN PROGRESS: Angelo, a novel.

SIDELIGHTS: Louis J. Fagan told *CA:* "In 1991 the film *Dances with Wolves*—with its complex characters, humanistic themes, artistic direction—inspired me to no end. Yet, at the age of twenty, I had no idea how or what to do with that feeling. Some years later, I enrolled in a fiction workshop with published author Charlotte Zoe Walker. There I connected inspiration with passion and found it was writing that I needed. I write for both selfish and selfless reasons. I write to acquire that feeling of need ful-filled. I write to fuel a flame in another soul, as *Dances with Wolves* did to me.

"I think my work, stylistically, has a modernized Henry James feel to it. Melville, Hawthorne, Whitman, Thoreau, Emerson, Wharton, and Woolf can all be found in my work stylistically and theoretically, as well. Furthermore, inspired by the medieval works I have encountered, I even try to incorporate alliteration. I think growing up on *Dances with Wolves, Dead Poets Society, Swing Kids,* and the like has allowed me to combine the modern, quick, and visual aspects of film with the literary aspect to produce a modern/classical fiction.

"I keep a pad under my bed and a pen on my nightstand, so I can jot down ideas or phrases even if I'm about to fall asleep. I have a complete story roughly started in my head and on a few sheets of paper when I sit down at the computer. I write a book in about three months, four or five hours a night. During those three months, I live and breathe that book. It is always on the threshold of my thought, so, when I sit to write, I play some inspiring piece of music, light incense, and let the words pour out.

"*New Boots* started as one sentence: 'Connie lifted the corner of the clear thin sheet and pulled it from the page.' I was strictly working with the sound and poetics of the sentence when I wrote it. It lay under my bed for six months until I was filled with a burst of energy, having completed my graduate work, taken my competency examination, and finished my first semester of teaching. I took this natural high and channeled it into writing. I combined my love of nature and my love for a good story and birthed my first novel."

FAGGEN, Robert

PERSONAL: Male.

ADDRESSES: Office—Athenaeum 214, Claremont McKenna College, Claremont, CA 91711. *E-mail*—r_faggen@benson.mckenna.edu.

CAREER: Claremont McKenna College, Claremont, CA, currently associate professor of literature; Claremont Graduate School, currently adjunct associate professor.

WRITINGS:

Robert Frost and the Challenge of Darwin, University of Michigan Press (Ann Arbor), 1997.
(Editor) *Striving towards Being: The Letters of Thomas Merton and Czeslaw Milosz,* Farrar, Straus (New York City), 1997.
(Editor and author of introduction) Edwin Arlington Robinson, *Selected Poems,* Penguin Books (New York City), 1997.
(Editor) Robert Frost, *Early Poems,* Penguin Twentieth-Century Classics (New York City), 1998.

Contributing editor to the *Paris Review.*

WORK IN PROGRESS: "An interview with the late poet Denise Levertov is forthcoming in the *Paris Review.* I am also editing the Cambridge Companion to Robert Frost."

SIDELIGHTS: A professor of literature at Claremont McKenna College, Robert Faggen has edited collections of poetry by Robert Frost and Edwin Arlington Robinson and has edited a book of correspondence between Czeslaw Milosz and Thomas Merton. Faggen has also written a study on the influence of Darwinian theory in the work of Frost.

Early Poems, which contains the poems from Robert Frost's first three books as well as selections from poems Frost wrote in the early 1920s, was published as part of Penguin's "Twentieth-Century Classics" series. Faggen edited the collection, contributing an introduction and notes that clarified Frost's relationship to traditional poetic themes and forms. Faggen also showed that the poet's interest in science and philosophy was evident in these early works. Faggen expanded on this theme in *Robert Frost and the Challenge of Darwin,* which the publisher describes as "the first book-length assessment of the influence of scientific thought on the work of Robert Frost." The study, for which Faggen had access to the poet's unpublished notebooks, establishes the importance of science in American culture from the transcendentalist movement of the mid-1800s to the pragmatism of the early-1900s. Through close readings of Frost's poems, Faggen shows that the poet's attitudes toward nature and his interest in matters relating to human equality, race, gender, and religion, were influenced by his reading of Darwinian theory.

Faggen attained critical recognition with *Striving towards Being: The Letters of Thomas Merton and Czeslaw Milosz,* his edition of the collected correspondence between Polish poet and Nobel laureate Czeslaw Milosz and Thomas Merton, an American Trappist monk and poet who wrote prolifically on spiritual and social themes. Merton had become interested in Milosz's work after reading a translation of *The Captive Mind* (1952), a collection of essays that Milosz had written while living in exile in Paris (Milosz immigrated to the United States in 1960). The book, which was not well regarded in France, sharply criticized Polish intellectuals for accepting the dehumanizing effects of communism and found a fairly receptive audience when it was published in translation in America in 1953. Faggen explains that Merton was attracted to Milosz's view that a "third way," a system that rejected both communism and consumer capitalism, could be found as a solution to the problem of social organization. In 1958 the monk wrote to Milosz, expressing admiration for the book. Milosz, who was familiar with Merton's poetry, answered and the two began a correspondence that lasted through the years of the Cold War, Vatican II, and Vietnam. The letters form, in Faggen's words, "a mutually edifying dialogue, a concerto grosso, between two powerful voices seeking to maintain faith in some of the most turbulent years of the late 20th century."

Striving towards Being received several respectful reviews. Steve Schroeder of *Booklist* called it a "rare opportunity to share an intimate conversation," and *Publishers Weekly* deemed it "one of those books that touches your soul" and especially appreciated the way in which the writers' letters showed each man's spiritual struggle. Phoebe Pettingell, in the *New Leader,* also admired the insights gained about each writer through their collected letters. "We can appreciate the fact that in these letters," she wrote, "each man crawled out of his shell and exposed aspects of his thinking and personality seldom fully on display in the public works." Martha Bayles, in the *Wilson Quarterly,* observed that Faggen elucidated some important points in *Striving towards Being* about the correspondents' relationship. Faggen wrote that Merton "recognized that [*The Captive Mind*] was not simply a condemnation of Communism but an attempt to understand the lure of Marxism in the wake of the erosion of the religious imagination"—a nuanced understanding that Milosz appreciated. Faggen further pointed out that Milosz, a practicing Catholic, saw in Merton a figure who could serve as a "spiritual father."

In 1997 Faggen drew on his expertise in matters relating to Milosz in an interview with the poet for *Books and Culture Magazine*. In that piece, Milosz expounded on his early life in Poland, his work in the resistance during World War II, his complex views on religion, and his correspondence with Merton. He also answered Faggen's questions on the development of individual poems and on new works.

Faggen has also edited the *Selected Poems* of Edwin Arlington Robinson. His introduction to the volume explores Robinson's place within the modern tradition and his influence on poets such as Eliot, Pound, Frost, and Berryman.

BIOGRAPHICAL/CRITICAL SOURCES:

BOOKS

Faggen, Robert, editor, *Striving towards Being: The Letters of Thomas Merton and Czeslaw Milosz*, Farrar, Straus (New York City), 1997.

PERIODICALS

Booklist, February 1, 1997, p. 909.
Books & Culture Magazine, September/October, 1997, p. 14.
Library Journal, December, 1996, p. 100.
New Leader, March 24, 1997, pp. 13-15.
Publishers Weekly, December 2, 1996, p. 51.
Wilson Quarterly, summer, 1998.

OTHER

Amazon.com, http://www.amazon.com/exec/obidos/ts/bo...id=907961641/sr=1-1/002-3306978-3033069 (October 9, 1998).
Barnes and Noble, http://www.barnesandnoble.com/...OL1RNBLQS2A6UAG&isbn=0472107828 (October 6, 1998).
Claremont McKenna College faculty, http://faculty.mckenna.edu/CMC_Faculty/Fac_Profile.ASP?Fac=24 (October 5, 1998).

University of Michigan Press, http://www.press.umich.edu/titles/10782.html (October 5, 1998).

*   *   *

FAIRCHILD, B(ertram) H. (Jr.) 1942-

PERSONAL: Born October 17, 1942, in Houston, TX; son of Bertram (a machinist) and Locie (Swearingen) Fairchild; married Patricia Lea Gillespie (a Math teacher), October 12, 1968; children: Paul, Sarah. *Education:* University of Kansas, B.A., 1964, M.A., 1968; University of Tulsa, Ph.D., 1975. *Religion:* Episcopal. *Avocational interests:* Running, music, Kansas basketball.

ADDRESSES: Home—706 West 11th St., Claremont, CA 91711. *Office*—California State University, 5500 University Parkway, San Bernardino, CA 92407. *E-mail*—Bhfairchil@aol.com; fairchld@mail.csusb.edu.

CAREER: Poet, 1977—. C & W Machine Works, Liberal, Kansas, until 1966; Hercules, Inc., Lawrence, Kansas, 1966-67; Kearney State College, Kearney, Nebraska, instructor, 1968-70; University of Tulsa, teaching fellow, 1970-73; Southwest Texas State University, assistant professor, 1973-76; Texas Woman's University, associate professor, 1976-83; California State University, San Bernardino, professor, 1983—.

MEMBER: Association of Literary Scholars and Critics.

AWARDS, HONORS: National Endowment for the Arts Fellowship in Poetry, 1988-89; National Book Award finalist, 1998; Capricorn Book Award, 1996; Beatrice Hawley Award, 1997; Seaton Poetry Award, 1997.

WRITINGS:

Such Holy Song: Music as Idea, Form, and Image in the Poetry of William Blake (literary criticism), Kent State University Press (Kent, OH), 1980.
Arrival of the Future (poetry), illustrated by Ross Zirkle, Swallow's Tale Press, 1985, Livingston Publishing, 1985.
The Art of the Lathe: Poems, Alice James Books (Farmington, ME), 1998.

Also author of the essay "Local Knowledge," *Princeton Quarterly Review of Literature,* 1991. Contributor of poetry and articles to periodicals, including *Poetry, Southern Review, Hudson Review, TriQuarterly, Sewanee Review, Salmagundi, Threepenny Review, Prairie Schooner, Georgia Review, Thoth, Essays in Literature, Blake Studies, St. Louis Literary Supplement: A Review of Literature, Politics, and the Arts, Journal of Popular Film, Literature/Film Quarterly, Studies in American Humor,* and *Statements on Language and Rhetoric.*

WORK IN PROGRESS: Rave On, a book of poems.

SIDELIGHTS: Author and poet B. H. Fairchild's first published book was a critical study of another poet. *Such Holy Song: Music as Idea, Form, and Image in the Poetry of William Blake,* which saw print in 1980, looked at the influence of music on the work of the famed late eighteenth-century poet who pioneered Romanticism and created such masterpieces as *Songs of Innocence and of Experience* and *The Four Zoas.* In fact, it is primarily these two sets of poems by Blake that Fairchild uses to assert his premise that music is supremely important to Blake's poetic creations.

As Brian Wilke pointed out in the *Rocky Mountain Review, Such Holy Song* itself "has a kind of simple ABA sonata form." The critic explained that chapter one provides a framework for the rest of the book. The next three chapters explore "the theoretical and mythic meaning of music for Blake," "melos" in the *Songs of Innocence and of Experience,* and the "sound effects, . . . musico-dramatic form, and . . . musical imagery" in *The Four Zoas.* The last chapter sums up the book. Fairchild also asserts that melody, in Blake's creative realm, is likened "to the visual . . . and the poetic line, . . . representing the right, healthy form of imagination. . . ." In addition, the author includes information about Blake's living conditions, which included a home near "pleasure gardens" where music was frequently performed.

Critical response to *Such Holy Song* was generally positive. Wilke noted that the chapter dealing with *The Four Zoas* is "the best part of the book." Wilke particularly appreciated the explanation "of the poem's sound effects, which Fairchild brings excitingly alive." *Choice* felt that Fairchild explored his subject matter and proved his points "clearly and effectively," and declared the volume to be "the first direct attempt to render as accurately as possible the musicality" of Blake's poetry.

Fairchild has also published volumes of his own poetry, notably 1985's *Arrival of the Future,* with illustrations by Ross Zirkle; and 1998's *The Art of the Lathe: Poems.* The poet has also contributed to poetry magazines. A 1984 issue of *Poetry,* for instance, features Fairchild's "Flight," which includes an introductory note about how some sufferers from epilepsy describe feeling as if they have gone out of their bodies during an attack, and have the illusion that "another presence is entering one's own person"; they themselves are also unsure of their own return into their bodies. Fairchild's poem goes on to describe an epileptic narrator's feelings of shame after having an attack of the disease in front of his wife and son: "Yesterday my wife held me here / as I thrashed and moaned, her hand / in my foaming mouth, and my son / saw what he was warned he might." The narrator then turns to a description of what he experienced during the attack.

BIOGRAPHICAL/CRITICAL SOURCES:

PERIODICALS

Choice, January, 1981, p. 658.
Poetry, October, 1984, pp. 29-30.
Rocky Mountain Review, vol. 35, no. 2, 1981, pp. 165-166.

*   *   *

FAISSLER, Margareta (A.) 1902-1990

OBITUARY NOTICE—See index for *CA* sketch: Born January 24, 1902, in Sycamore, IL; died November 11, 1990, in Baltimore, MD. History teacher. Faissler attended Wellesley College, where she earned a bachelor's degree in 1924 and a master's in 1925. She obtained her Ph.D. from the University of Chicago in 1936, majoring in European diplomatic history. She began her career as a history teacher at Miss Holley's School in Dallas, TX, in 1924, moving to Holland Hall, in Tulsa, OK, in 1926, and finally to Roland Park Country School in Baltimore in 1931, retiring as head of the History Department there in 1967. After her retirement she taught for a short time at Goucher College. She was a member of the American Historical Association (where she served as a member of the committee on teaching), National Council for Social Studies, and Teachers Association of Independent Schools of the Baltimore Area. Her first publication, *European Diplomacy in the Balkan Peninsula, 1913-*

1914, was published in 1938. Her last two books included *Modern Times* (with Carlton J. H. Hayes), a high school text that went through three editions in 1965, 1970, and 1983; and *Mainstreams of Civilization: Teacher's Manual,* published by Macmillan in 1966. She also contributed essays to *Slavonic Yearbook* and other professional history publications.

OBITUARIES AND OTHER SOURCES:

PERIODICALS

Baltimore Sun, November 27, 1990, p. 4B.

—*Obituary by Robert Reginald*

* * *

FARRER-HALLS, Gill   1958-

PERSONAL: Born February 7, 1958, in Weybridge, England; daughter of James Anthony (an engineer) and Mary Clare (a physiotherapist; maiden name, Briscoe) Farrer-Halls; companion of Robert Beer (an artist and writer). *Ethnicity:* "Caucasian." *Education:* Bulmershe College, B.A. (with honors), 1984. *Religion:* Buddhist. *Avocational interests:* Music, nature.

ADDRESSES: Home—29a Miranda Rd., London N19 3RA, England; fax 01-71-263-6357. *Agent*—Liz Puttick, 46 Brookfield Mansions, Highgate West Hill, London N6 6AT, England.

CAREER: Meridian Trust, administrator of Buddhist Film and Video Archive and videotape producer, 1991-98. Also works as aromatherapy teacher.

WRITINGS:

The World of the Dalai Lama, Quest Books (Wheaton, IL), 1998.
Handbook of Buddhist Wisdom, Godsfield Press, 1999.

WORK IN PROGRESS: Research on the sacred use of essential oils.

SIDELIGHTS: Gill Farrer-Halls told *CA:* "For me, writing is a process of discovery and my main creative expression. The desire to take information de-

rived from my own understanding and experience and make it clear and accessible to others is another consideration.

"As I work mainly in the field of Buddhism, I am influenced by Buddhist teachers both alive and dead. These include individuals from Buddhist countries like the Dalai Lama from Tibet, and contemporary western Buddhists like Stephen Batchelor, who is British. I am also inspired by the ideals and philosophy of Buddhism, primarily the central idea that all beings desire to find happiness and avoid suffering.

"When I am writing a book, I work with ideas most of the time. It is a part of my life. I attempt the discipline of writing each day, though as I am a freelancer and have other work, this is not always possible, I write directly into a word processor and edit as part of the process. Each piece of writing is edited while it is being written, the day after that, and one other time in relation to the surrounding pieces. I drink a lot of tea and go for a walk in the park after a few hours work. This allows thoughts to arise spontaneously, and I can muse over them before returning to work.

"My own life has vastly improved through my encounter with Buddhism, and the desire that others may improve their lives through such an encounter is a major inspiration. Buddhism proscribes proselytism and encourages people to have a strong interest before leaping into it. I feel that books on Buddhism can provide sufficient information for people to decide for themselves whether they wish to pursue this spiritual path, without trying to convert one's readers.

"The simplicity and beauty of the essence of the Buddhist view of the world is inspiring and a challenge to my own understanding. I deepen my learning and understanding through writing, and this helps prevent complacency and pride."

* * *

FERGUSON, Charles Albert   1921-1998

OBITUARY NOTICE—See index for *CA* sketch: Born July 6, 1921, in Philadelphia, PA; died of a heart attack and strokes, September 2, 1998, in Menlo Park, CA. Linguist, educator, and author. Ferguson pursued a career in linguistics and founded the Center for Allied Linguistics in Washington, D.C. He was also responsible for creating an Arabic language school for U.S. State Department employees posted in Beirut, Lebanon. Ferguson received his Ph.D. in linguistics from the University of Pennsylvania in 1945. For the majority of his career he taught linguistics in colleges including Harvard University and Stanford University. Ferguson worked for the State Department between 1946 and 1955, serving in a linguistic capacity both in the U.S. and overseas. He wrote and edited a number of linguistically oriented works including *Agreement in Natural Language: Approaches, Theories, Descriptions* (editor, with Michael Barlow; 1988), *Phonological Development: Models, Research, Implications* (editor, with Lise Menn and Carol Stoel-Gammon; 1992), and *Language in the USA* (1981).

OBITUARIES AND OTHER SOURCES:

BOOKS

Who's Who in America, Marquis Who's Who, 1995.

PERIODICALS

Washington Post, September 20, 1998, p. B6.

* * *

FERRELL, Carolyn

PERSONAL: Female. *Education:* Attended City University of New York.

ADDRESSES: Agent—c/o Houghton Mifflin Company, 222 Berkeley St., Boston, MA 02116.

CAREER: Writer.

AWARDS, HONORS: Fulbright Scholar; Los Angeles Times Art Seidenbaum Award for First Fiction, 1998, for *Don't Erase Me.*

WRITINGS:

Don't Erase Me, Houghton Mifflin (Boston), 1997.

SIDELIGHTS: Short story writer Carolyn Ferrell earned critical respect with her first collection, *Don't Erase Me,* which received the Art Seidenbaum Award for First Fiction from the *Los Angeles Times.* Many of the eight stories in the book were inspired by Ferrell's first-hand experience of inner-city life; she

worked as director of a South Bronx family literacy program for a period of time, and renders this world of single-parent families, teen pregnancy, gang presence, and AIDS in her fiction.

Ferrell's stories, found a *Kirkus Reviews* critic, "mingle a welcome touch of poetry with rough urban realism." Other reviewers, too, admired the author's poetic prose and her ability to capture authentic speech patterns. *New York Times Book Review* contributor Katherine Whittemore noted that Ferrell's language "is intimate in the way you used to hope a good book could be, until you were disappointed once too often by shock tactics masquerading as literature." A *Washington Post* critic commended Ferrell's "rich realism" and "gift for the authentic spoken voice. . ." Among the works in this debut collection, reviewers singled out "Proper Library," which focuses on gay teenager Lorrie, and "Tiger-Frame Glasses," which tells of a girl who creates elaborate fantasies in response to the cruelty of her peers, as exceptional. Also admired was the title story, in which a young mother begins a diary that progresses backwards from the moment she learns that her stepfather infected her with HIV.

"More than simple authenticity," concluded the *Kirkus Reviews* contributor, "Ferrell offers a complex vision of ghetto life . . .: work satisfying as art, and disturbing as sociology."

BIOGRAPHICAL/CRITICAL SOURCES:

PERIODICALS

Booklist, May 1, 1997, p. 1479.
Kirkus Reviews, April 15, 1997, p. 574.
New York Times Book Review, September 14, 1997.
Publishers Weekly, April 21, 1997, p. 59.
Washington Post Book World, September 14, 1997.*

* * *

FLAMINI, Roland

PERSONAL: Male.

ADDRESSES: Agent—c/o World Trade Press, 1505 Fifth Ave., San Rafael, CA 94901.

CAREER: Time magazine, New York City, correspondent; freelance writer, c. 1975—.

WRITINGS:

NONFICTION

Scarlett, Rhett, and a Cast of Thousands: The Filming of Gone with the Wind, Macmillan (New York City), 1975.

Pope, Premier, President: The Cold War Summit That Never Was, Macmillan (New York City), 1980.

Ava: A Biography, Coward, McCann (New York City), 1983.

Ten Years at Number 10: Images of a Decade in Office, Aurum Press (London), 1989.

Sovereign: Elizabeth II and the Windsor Dynasty, Delacorte (New York City), 1991.

Thalberg: The Last Tycoon and the World of M-G-M, Crown (New York City), 1994.

Passport Germany: Your Pocket Guide to German Business, Customs, and Etiquette, World Trade Press (San Raphael, CA), 1997.

Contributor of articles to periodicals, including *Time, Town & Country, Architectural Digest, People, Los Angeles Magazine,* and *Connoisseur.*

SIDELIGHTS: Roland Flamini has made a career as a correspondent for *Time,* but in addition to writing pieces for other periodicals such as *People* and *Architectural Digest,* he has also penned several books. Beginning with 1975's *Scarlett, Rhett, and a Cast of Thousands: The Filming of Gone with the Wind,* Flamini's full-length book titles include *Pope, Premier, President: The Cold War Summit That Never Was, Sovereign: Elizabeth II and the Windsor Dynasty,* and *Thalberg: The Last Tycoon and the World of M-G-M.*

Scarlett, Rhett, and a Cast of Thousands is an "evocation of an era when the national pulse seemed to beat in time with Hollywood's," according to Dorothy Rabinowitz in *Saturday Review.* In this volume, Flamini tells the story of how Margaret Mitchell's best-selling novel was translated to the screen by David O. Selznick. Before it was announced that Selznick would look for a relative unknown to fill the role of Scarlett O'Hara, people lobbied on behalf of their favorite actresses. Tallulah Bankhead, for instance, had a unanimous resolution passed on her behalf by the Alabama Public Service Commission. After the announcement seeking an unknown was made, however, Selznick was besieged by aspiring Scarletts, including one who had herself delivered to his home as a birthday gift. Flamini provides plenty of details about what happened after Vivien Leigh was

chosen, including tidbits about leading man Clark Gable. He does, according to Jean V. Naggar in the *New York Times Book Review,* "a splendid job of amassing all the details and organizing them into a readable, entertaining book." The critic went on to assess *Scarlett, Rhett, and a Cast of Thousands* as "not only informative" but "fun." Similarly, Rabinowitz concluded the volume was "first-rate and serious entertainment."

Flamini's next book, *Pope, Premier, President,* was published in 1980. The project came about because the author had been assigned by *Time* magazine to cover news from the Vatican. In doing his research, Flamini decided to tell more fully the story of the Vatican's gradual warming towards Communist nations. As his volume's subtitle implies, the author's starting point is the offer on behalf of Pope John XXIII to mediate Cold War-era peace talks between U.S. President John F. Kennedy and Soviet Premier Nikita Khrushchev. The offer was refused, but Flamini goes on to discuss the papal encyclical, *Pacem in Terris,* issued by John XXIII that, as Genevieve Stuttaford of *Publishers Weekly* explained, "modified the church's hard line." When Pope John was succeeded by Pope Paul VI, this softening continued, in Flamini's estimation, in spite of the fact that Paul VI was considered to be a much more conservative Pope than John XXIII had been. Stuttaford judged that *Pope, Premier, President* "provides some revealing insights on church politics," while *Time* hailed the work as "a valuable history" lacking "the sanctimonious, overripe prose" of many books about the Vatican.

Flamini returned to the subject of film and film stars with his 1983 work, *Ava: A Biography.* Chronicling the life of actress Ava Gardner, the volume devotes a large portion of text to Gardner's brief marriage to singer Frank Sinatra. *Ava* did not meet with the critical approval that has greeted most of Flamini's other books. In a review for the *Washington Post Book World,* Christopher Schemering compared it unfavorably with Charles Higham's biography of the same actress and noted that "Flamini presents Gardner as a rootless, often violent spitfire with a voracious sexual appetite." Irwin R. Blacker, in a review for the *Los Angeles Times Book Review* dismissed *Ava* as "primarily froth."

Sovereign, Flamini's 1991 volume, focuses on Queen Elizabeth II but also provides information about other members of the British royal family. Of the Queen, Flamini's readers find out that she purposely sets her face in a frown for public appearances to prevent herself from breaking out in giggles. He also reveals that she can do a devastating impression of former U.S. First Lady Nancy Reagan. When the two women met during a royal visit to the Reagan ranch in California in 1983, Mrs. Reagan kept apologizing for the freakishly bad stormy weather, while Elizabeth II is quoted by the author as saying: "Don't be silly. It's an adventure." Flamini also discusses Elizabeth II's husband, Prince Philip, and the Prince's opinion of the couple's eldest son, Charles, Prince of Wales. Noted Florence King in the *New York Times Book Review:* "Without laboring the point . . . Flamini causes us to speculate whether this overly sensitive People's Prince is too idealistic and well meaning for his and Britain's good." *Sovereign* also contains anecdotes about the Queen Mother that display her sense of humor. King compared the book favorably with other tomes about the royal family, calling *Sovereign* "far and away the best of the lot." A *Kirkus* reviewer approved of the chronicle as well, describing it as "an informed and credible if still discreet portrait" and "a good read, with a lot of inside detail."

Former Metro-Goldwyn-Mayer executive Irving Thalberg is the subject of Flamini's 1994 effort, *Thalberg: The Last Tycoon and the World of M-G-M.* Thalberg was considered so important to the film industry of the 1920s and 1930s that the Academy Awards have a special Oscar named after him given to actors, directors, and other film people who have displayed integrity and high artistic standards during the course of their careers. Born with a heart defect that caused doctors to predict he'd be dead by the age of thirty, Thalberg only beat their estimates by seven years. Still, as Flamini attests, he accomplished a great deal in his chosen profession during his short lifetime. Flamini discusses Thalberg's professional accomplishments, such as the discovery of actress Joan Crawford and the production of classic films such as *Anna Christie, Mutiny on the Bounty,* and *A Night at the Opera*—and his one grand incident of short-sightedness in turning down the film rights to *Gone with the Wind.* The author also reveals more personal items about Thalberg, such as the fact that he lived with his mother even after his marriage to actress Norma Shearer. Of Thalberg and Shearer, Flamini also claims: "One of their private jokes was to dine together by candlelight wearing each other's clothes: Thalberg in an Adrian creation complete with make-up, Norma wearing one of his suits."

While praising other books on Thalberg's life, Sheridan Morley in the London *Times* conceded that

"Flamini has done a perfectly competent job with a difficult subject." L. S. Klepp, discussing the biography in *Entertainment Weekly,* praised it as a "brisk tour behind the myth" that "reveals an intelligent, iron-willed, but not exactly colorful man."

Flamini has also penned books about former British Prime Minister Margaret Thatcher, and a business travelers' guide to Germany.

BIOGRAPHICAL/CRITICAL SOURCES:

PERIODICALS

Entertainment Weekly, March 25, 1994, pp. 48-49.
Kirkus Reviews, March 1, 1991, pp. 297-298.
Los Angeles Times Book Review, February 27, 1983, p. 4.
New York Times Book Review, March 7, 1976, p. 23; June 9, 1991, pp. 40, 42.
Publishers Weekly, August 29, 1980, p. 359.
Saturday Review, January 10, 1976, p. 57.
Time, January 19, 1981 pp. 83-84.
Times (London), August 14, 1994, sec. 7, p. 5.
Times Literary Supplement, June 14, 1991, p. 6.
Washington Post Book World, April 24, 1983, pp. 10-11.*

* * *

**FRANK, A. Scott
See FRANK, (A.) Scott**

* * *

FRANK, Gerold 1907-1998

OBITUARY NOTICE—See index for *CA* sketch: Born August 2, 1907, in Cleveland, OH; died September 17, 1998, in Philadelphia, PA. Journalist and writer. Frank's career began after he graduated from Ohio State University in 1929 and received his master's degree from Case Western Reserve University in 1933. He got a job as a staff writer at the *Cleveland News,* where he stayed until 1937 when he took a post with the *Journal-American,* based in New York. He also served as a war correspondent with the Overseas

News Agency in the Middle East. His interest in Judaism led him to contribute to *Behind the Silken Curtain,* which detailed the efforts of the Anglo-American Committee of Inquiry on Palestine, which played a large part in the founding of Israel. He later donated a film he had made about life in a Polish shtetl to the Yivo Institute for Jewish Research. Although he was a successful mystery writer and received two Edgar awards for his novels *The Deed* and *The Boston Strangler,* Frank was best known for his work as the ghostwriter of numerous books about celebrities, mostly women. His first of that sort was *I'll Cry Tomorrow,* on which he collaborated with Mike Connolly and singer Lillian Roth to produce a story about Roth's life. He later worked with gossip columnist Sheilah Graham on the story of her romance with F. Scott Fitzgerald, *Beloved Infidel.* Both books were made into successful films. Frank also collaborated with Zsa Zsa Gabor and Diana Barrymore on books about their life experiences. He frequently worked on books without credit but was the sole author of *An American Death: The True Story of the Assassination of Dr. Martin Luther King, Jr., and the Greatest Manhunt of Our Time* and *Judy,* a biography of Judy Garland.

OBITUARIES AND OTHER SOURCES:

BOOKS

Who's Who in America, Marquis, 1995.

PERIODICALS

Chicago Tribune, September 24, 1998, sec. 1 p.9.
New York Times, September 19, 1998, p. A13.
Washington Post, September 21, 1998, p. B6.

* * *

FRANK, Larry 1926-

PERSONAL: Born May 6, 1926, in Los Angeles, CA; son of Laurence P., Sr. (a stockbroker) and Julliette (Guggenheim) Frank; married Alyce Kahn; children: Ross, Melissa, Chad. *Education:* Attended University of California, Los Angeles, 1944-45, and University of California, Berkeley, 1946-49. *Politics:* Democrat. *Avocational interests:* Collecting North American Indian art, New Mexico Spanish colonial art, books, folk art, toys, and religious art.

ADDRESSES: Home—P.O. Box 290, Arroyo Hondo, NM 87513; fax 505-776-8539.

CAREER: President of a company that buys and sells North American Indian art and New Mexico Spanish colonial art, Arroyo Hondo, NM, c. 1963—. *Military service:* U.S. Navy; served during World War II.

WRITINGS:

Historic Pottery of the Pueblo Indians, New York Graphic Society (Boston, MA), 1974.
Indian Silver Jewelry of the Southwest, New York Graphic Society, 1978.
New Kingdom of the Saints, Red Crane Books (Santa Fe, NM), 1994.
Train Stops (stories), Sunstone Press (Santa Fe), 1998.

WORK IN PROGRESS: A novel.

* * *

FRANK, (A.) Scott 1960(?)-
(A. Scott Frank)

PERSONAL: Born c. 1960. *Education:* University of California at Santa Barbara, received degree, 1982.

ADDRESSES: Agent—c/o Beth Swofford, Creative Artists Agency, 9830 Wilshire Blvd., Beverly Hills, CA 90212.

CAREER: Screenwriter.

MEMBER: Writers Guild of America.

WRITINGS:

SCREENPLAYS

(As A. Scott Frank) *Plain Clothes,* Paramount, 1988.
Dead Again, Paramount, 1991.
Little Man Tate, Orion, 1991.
Get Shorty, Metro-Goldwyn-Mayer, 1995.
Heaven's Prisoners, New Line Cinema/Savoy Pictures, 1996.

Also author of the television screenplays *Fallen Angels* (with others) and *Birdland* (with Walter F. Parkes).

SIDELIGHTS: Scott Frank has written a variety of movie and television screenplays. The movie *Dead Again* featured a Frank screenplay that tells the story of a deceased couple who are reincarnated again under different circumstances. Kenneth Branagh and Emma Thompson star, first as a married couple (she has been murdered; he is about to be executed for her murder), then as a private detective (Branagh) trying to uncover the identity of a woman with amnesia. Reviewer David Ansen of *Newsweek* warned readers to lower their expectations slightly when viewing the film (and Branagh's role) and claimed that it was tough to "shake the feeling that you were watching a talented cast playing an elaborate game of Let's Pretend." However, Ansen credited the movie with being "cotton candy, but . . . well spun." Stanley Kaufmann of the *New Republic* expressed disapointment with an effort that "aims so low."

Little Man Tate, a movie starring and directed by Jodie Foster, appeared in 1991. The story concerns a working-class, street smart, but uneducated woman with a seven-year-old prodigy son. Foster struggles with how to provide stimulation for her son and is faced with competition from a rich psychologist who feels the boy should be attending a school for gifted children. While a *Rolling Stone* reviewer gave Foster accolades for her efforts and called the film "passionately involving" and Foster "sharply intuitive" in her directing and acting, the reviewer compared Frank's screenplay to a "soap opera."

In 1993 Frank, with other writers, adapted six short stories for television in a six-installment program called *Fallen Angels*. The program featured actors such as Tom Cruise and Laura Dern and pays tribute to the 1940s stories that it is based on. According to reviewer John Leonard in *New York,* the program is shot artfully to give it a vintage feel but, as was the case with the stories of that time, "it sounds like *faux* Hamlet . . . and is hard on women." Leonard rated it "at least as interesting as the overrated B-movies" from which it is taken.

Frank also worked with Walter F. Parkes to write the screenplay for *Birdland,* a television show that featured a psychiatric staff and patients in a hospital with the title name. Reviewer Tony Scott of *Variety* concluded that the screenwriters did not succeed in creating compelling story possibilities, given the setting and the characters.

Frank's screenplay *Get Shorty* takes a look at the social workings of movie making and shows the entire process of the creation of Hollywood cinema. The story, based on an Elmore Leonard novel, stars John Travolta as a former assistant loan shark who ends up in the Hollywood movie business. Reviewer Stuart Klawans in the *Nation* claimed that the "cynical bite" of the original story is lost in its translation to cinema, however, the reviewer appreciated the "light entertainments" of the movie, even though it is presented in "cartoonlike . . . style."

The movie *Heaven's Prisoners* features a plane crash and a cop who is drawn into the underworld of Louisiana, but according to Greg Evans of *Variety,* the film has the slow pace of bayou backwaters rather than the high-pressure pace that drove the movie *The Big Easy* (also a crime story based in Louisiana). Evans noted the "film's provocative, moody touch" (such as a grippingly real presentation of the aftermath of a plane crash) but claimed that these "don't add up to much." Evans concluded that "despite a dark grainy look, [the] film never achieves . . . Gothic gloom."

BIOGRAPHICAL/CRITICAL SOURCES:

BOOKS

Contemporary Theatre, Film, and Television, Volume 11, Gale (Detroit, MI), 1994.

PERIODICALS

Cosmopolitan, September, 1991, p. 62; October, 1991, p. 54.
Nation, December 4, 1995, pp. 724-725.
New Republic, September 16 and 23, 1991, p. 30; November 13, 1995, p. 32.
Newsweek, September 9, 1991, p. 67.
New York, August 2, 1993, p. 52.
Rolling Stone, October 31, 1991, pp. 97-99.
Variety, January 3-9, 1994, p. 57; May 20, 1996, p. 30.*

*   *   *

FREEDMAN, Lawrence (David) 1948-

PERSONAL: Born December 7, 1948, in Tynemouth, England; son of Julius (a Lieutenant Commander) and Myra (a homemaker; maiden name, Robinson) Freedman; married Judith Anne Hill (an academic lawyer),

September 1, 1974; children: Samuel, Ruth. *Ethnicity:* "Human." *Education:* Manchester University, England, B.A., 1970; York University, B. Phil., 1971; Oxford University, D. Phil., 1975. *Religion:* Jewish. *Avocational interests:* Tennis, political caricature.

ADDRESSES: Office—Department of War Studies, Kings College, The Strand, London, WC2R 2LS, England. *E-mail*—LFREED0712@aol.com.

CAREER: Political sciences educator. York University, teaching assistant, 1971-72; Nuffield College, Oxford, research fellow, 1974-75; International Institute for Strategic Studies, London, research associate, 1975-76; Royal Institute for International Affairs, London, research fellow, 1976-78, head of policy studies, 1978-82; Department of War Studies, Kings College, London, and professor, 1982—, department head, 1992-97, chair of Board of War Studies, 1997—; Center for Defence Studies, London, honorary director, 1990—.

MEMBER: Center for Defence Studies (former chair), Committee on International Peace and Security, Social Science Research Council, International Institute for Strategic Studies (council member, 1984-92), Royal Institute for International Affairs.

WRITINGS:

U.S. Intelligence and the Soviet Strategic Threat, Macmillan (Basingstoke, England), 1977, Westview Press (Boulder, CO), 1977, Princeton University Press (Princeton, NJ), 1986.

The Price of Peace: Living with the Nuclear Dilemma, Royal Institute of International Affairs (London), 1978, Holt (New York City), 1986.

The West and the Modernization of China, Royal Institute of International Affairs (London), 1979.

Britain and Nuclear Weapons, Humanities Press, (Atlantic Highlands, NJ), 1981.

The Evolution of Nuclear Strategy, St. Martin's Press (New York City), 1981, reprinted, 1989.

(Editor) *The Troubled Alliance: Atlantic Relations in the 1980s,* St. Martin's Press (New York City), 1983.

Atlas of Global Strategy, Facts on File (New York City), 1985.

Arms Control: Management or Reform?, Routledge & Kegan Paul (London), 1986.

Terrorism and International Order, Routledge & Kegan Paul (London), 1986.

Strategic Defence in the Nuclear Age, International Institute for Strategic Studies (London), 1987.

Britain and the Falklands War, Blackwell (New York City), 1988.

(With Martin Navias and Nicholas Wheeler) *Independence in Concert: the British Rationale for Possessing Strategic Nuclear Weapons,* University of Maryland (College Park, MD), 1989.

The South Atlantic Crisis of 1982: Implications for Nuclear Crisis Management, RAND (Santa Monica, CA), 1989.

(Editor, with Philip Bobbitt and Gregory F. Treverton) *U.S. Nuclear Strategy: A Reader,* New York University Press, (New York City), 1989.

(With Virginia Gamba-Stonehouse) *Signals of War: The Falklands Conflict of 1982,* Faber and Faber (Boston, MA), 1990, Princeton University Press (Princeton, NJ), 1991.

(Editor) *Europe Transformed: Documents on the End of the Cold War,* St. Martin's Press (New York City), 1990.

(Editor) *Military Power in Europe: Essays in Memory of Jonathan Alford,* St. Martin's Press (New York City), 1990.

(Editor, with John Saunders) *Population Change and European Security,* Macmillan (New York City), 1991.

(Editor, with Michael Clarke) *Britain in the World,* Cambridge University Press (New York City), 1991.

(Editor, with Paul Hayes and Robert O'Neill) *War, Strategy and International Politics: Essays in Honour of Sir Michael Howard,* Oxford University Press (Oxford, England), 1992.

(With Efriam Karsh) *The Gulf Conflict, 1990-1991: Diplomacy and War in the New World,* Princeton University Press, (Princeton, NJ), 1993.

Military Intervention in European Conflicts,(Political Quarterly Special Issue), Blackwell (London), 1994.

(Editor) *War,* Oxford University Press (New York City), 1994.

(Editor) *Strategic Coercion: Concepts and Cases,* Oxford University Press (New York City), 1998.

The Revolution in Strategic Affairs, Oxford University Press (New York City), 1998.

The Politics of British Defence, 1979-1998, Macmillan (New York City), 1999.

WORK IN PROGRESS: "Kennedy's Wars: Laos, Berlin, Cuba and Vietnam"; an official history of the Falklands Campaign; an introduction to contemporary strategy.

SIDELIGHTS: Lawrence Freedman, a political scientist heading up the department of war studies at

King's College in London, has been called "one of Britain's leading academic strategic theorists," according to *Choice* reviewer F. S. Pearson. His many works include well-received discussions of global and nuclear strategy, nuclear arms, case studies of two recent wars, and collections of writings intended for lay readers, students, and specialists.

Freeman's first six books focus on cold war weaponry and strategic issues, but they all transcend the era. In *U.S. Intelligence and the Soviet Strategic Threat* (1977), a case study of inter-continental ballistic missile postures between the two superpowers, Freedman offers a "general overview of intelligence work," commented a *Choice* reviewer. Freedman understands that for intelligence to be truly useful one must "[get] inside his potential adversary's mind," observed the a critic for the *Economist*.

The Price of Peace: Living with the Nuclear Dilemma (1978) examines, through a series of essays and lectures, the nuclear arms debate, including topics such as arms control, disarmament, the anti-nuclear movement, and the advantages and disadvantages of nuclear and conventional defense. Pearson found the study "more relevant to European than North American audiences" in a review for *Choice*. A *Publishers Weekly* reviewer noted Freedman's doubts about President Reagan's "Strategic Defense Initiative," or "Star Wars" program. In Freedman's opinion, the Star Wars program is "imbued with a contrived sense of scientific adventure." The *Publishers Weekly* critic faulted Freedman for too much debate and too few recommendations.

Britain and Nuclear Weapons (1981) chronicles the development of nuclear weapons in Great Britain during the second half of the twentieth century and into the future. Freedman also discusses the reasons for Great Britain's acquisition of nuclear weapons. Patrick W. Murphy, a critic for *Perspective*, declared *Britain and Nuclear Weapons* to be "lucid, clear, and to the point."

In *The Evolution of Nuclear Strategy* (1981) Freedman examines the evolution of nuclear strategy, and post-1945 attempts by the nuclear powers to establish feasible nuclear arms policies. A *Choice* reviewer called the book "excellent," and observed that "the entire range of the nuclear debate is described in language of clarity and precision." According to *Choice* reviewer Bradley Hooper, "Freedman denies that an effective policy . . . has been formulated anywhere."

To this day, noted Hooper, the horror of the potential devastation of nuclear weapons has guided nuclear arms strategies.

Freedman's *Atlas of Global Strategy* (1985) was called an "excellent encyclopedia of strategy and conflict" by A. C. Tuttle of *Choice*. In this book Freedman explores the history of politics and the military, concentrating on the superpowers, especially the United States and the Soviet Union. He also discusses terrorism, warfare since 1945, nuclear proliferation, Poland's solidarity movement, and the revolution in Iran. Photographs and more than one hundred maps round out this reference work. Dennis Felbel, a reviewer for *Library Journal*, noted that the maps contribute "geographical perspective" to the study.

In *Strategic Defence in the Nuclear Age* (1987), a short publication in the Adelphi Papers series published by the International Institute for Strategic Studies, Freedman looks at defense and policy issues and the outcome for NATO and the Strategic Defensive Initiative.

After the Cold War ended Professor Freedman turned his attention to conflicts in the Falklands and the Persian Gulf. Two books dealing with the Falklands conflict are *Britain and the Falklands War* (1988) and *Signals of War: The Falklands Conflict of 1982* (1990). In *Britain and the Falklands War*, according to *Choice* reviewer J. A. Weeks, Freedman provides "an excellent examination" of the military, political and social issues involved in the war. Anthony Farrar-Hockley in the *Times Literary Supplement* called the book "illuminating" and "perceptive." *Signals of War*, written by Freedman and Virginia Gamba-Stonehouse (an Argentine civilian specialist in strategic issues) provide a study of the war and explore the diplomatic attempts to restore peace without war. According to *Times Literary Supplement* reviewer Eduardo Crawley, the authors argue that the war was, in part, a product of the influence of outdated geopolitical thinking by the Argentine military, and also a result of inevitability. If Prime Minister Margaret Thatcher had not acted, her government would have fallen, observed Crawley.

The Gulf Conflict, 1990-1991: Diplomacy and War in the New World Order (1993) written by Freedman and Efriam Karsh, takes an evenhanded look at the Gulf War. It was deemed "one of the most comprehensive and analytical books" of the Gulf War by *Library Journal*'s Nadia Entessar. According to the authors, Saddam Hussein's primary goal was to "establish hegemony over Kuwait, insuring its complete financial, political, and strategic subservience to his wishes," rather than annexation of Kuwait. Despite the probable truth of the alleged remarks made by Prince Bandar bin Sultan, the Saudi Arabian Ambassador to Washington, that "he who eats Kuwait for breakfast is likely to ask for something else for lunch," Hussein did not strike at the Saudis before the allied coalition was in place. Further, the authors speculate that Hussein did not use chemical weapons because he wanted "to keep the allied war aims limited to Kuwait" rather than targeting Iraq (and himself). They also note Hussein's miscalculation that Arab nations would never join the West in resistance to his moves. "Saddam deceived them all," and "the local fury at this deception" helped create a "coherent international response," claim the authors. According to H. D. S. Greenway in the *New York Times Book Review,* "Mr. Freedman and Mr. Karsh conclude that the gulf war may reinforce Washington's 'basic predilection to stay clear of civil wars, rely on air superiority and fight land wars with the maximum mobility'. . . . it is unlikely," wrote Greenway, "that there will be a better balanced or more comprehensive chronicle" of the Gulf war.

War, Freedman's 1994 book, discusses the history of war since the early nineteenth century, and examines the principles of war, including its causes, strategies, and sociological and ethical concerns with firsthand accounts by individuals who have participated in warfare. Geoffrey Best, writing in the *Times Literary Supplement,* observed that *War* "seems original in its attempted comprehensiveness." Writing in *Foreign Affairs,* Eliot A. Cohen observed that Freedman "has transcended the genre brilliantly" with "a marvelous variety of authors" who have been arranged "with splendid effect."

Freedman argues in his 1998 book, *The Revolution in Strategic Affairs,* that America's use of advanced information technology and guided weapons has transformed military operations. The book discusses the tactics and weapons that powerful governments may use against weaker governments.

Freedman told *CA:* "My basic approach has always been to explore alternative lines of argument and consider the policy options as they face governments. That is, what I prefer to explain what policy debates are (or were) about rather than act simply as an advocate."

BIOGRAPHICAL/CRITICAL SOURCES:

PERIODICALS

Air Power History, spring, 1995, pp. 54-55.

Albion, spring, 1994, p. 197.

American Academy of Political and Social Science Annals, November, 1978, p. 170.

American Political Science Review, June, 1979, p. 681; March, 1980, p. 148; June, 1983, p. 528; March, 1992, p. 285.

American Reference Books Annual, vol. 17, 1986, p. 249.

Americas: A Quarterly Review of Inter-American Cultural Study, July, 1992, p. 110.

Armed Forces & Society, winter, 1994, p. 319.

Booklist, November 1, 1982, p. 341; January 15, 1986, p. 712; April 1, 1986, p. 1126; September 1, 1986, p. 9; January 1, 1993, p. 787.

British Book News, January, 1981, p. 28; June, 1984, p. 342; July, 1985, p. 390; December, 1985, p. 722; November, 1987, p. 751.

Bulletin of the Atomic Scientists, June-July, 1981, pp. 45-46; December, 1983, pp. 42-43; January-February, 1987, p. 56.

Choice, December, 1978, p. 1437; May, 1982, p. 1321; March, 1986, p. 1137; July/August, 1987, p. 1752; June, 1988, p. 1522; May, 1989, p. 1574; February, 1991, p. 912; November, 1991, p. 401; December, 1991, p. 651.

Christian Century, July 15, 1987, pp. 634-635.

Christian Science Monitor, January 15, 1982, p. B6.

Commonweal, May 7, 1993, pp. 25-26.

Contemporary Sociology, September, 1992, p. 694.

Economist, January 14, 1978, pp. 106-108; February 28, 1981, p. 92; December 5, 1981, p. 111.

English Historical Review, April, 1993, p. 425.

Ethics, January, 1996, p. 495.

Foreign Affairs, spring, 1981, p. 948; fall, 1989, p. 200; September-October, 1983, p. 154; June, 1984, p. 1257; no. 2, 1993, p. 181; no. 4, 1993, p. 154; July-August 1994, p. 167.

Foreign Policy, spring, 1998, pp. 48-63.

Guardian Weekly, June 12, 1983, p. 18; May 13, 1990, p. 26; January 31, 1993, p. 28.

Harper's Magazine, February, 1983, p. 66.

Historian, spring, 1994, p. 587.

History Today, June, 1993, p. 58; August, 1995, p. 57.

Journal of American History, June, 1996, pp. 298-299.

Journal of Military History, January, 1994, pp. 141, 176; January, 1995, p. 187.

Kirkus Reviews, October 1, 1982, p. 1133; August 15, 1986, p. 1263.

Library Journal, November 15, 1982, p. 2180; February 15, 1986, p. 173; January 1993, p. 146.

London Review of Books, November 5, 1992, p. 7.

New Republic, June 19, 1995, pp. 43-45.

New Statesman & Society, April 27, 1990, p. 40.

New York Review of Books, March 17, 1983, p. 3.

New York Times Book Review, January 25, 1987, p. 33; January 24, 1993, p. 2; June 6, 1993, p. 40; December 5, 1993, p. 68; July 23, 1995, p. 20.

Perspective, January/February, 1982, p. 24.

Perspectives on Political Science, summer, 1992, p. 170; winter, 1995, p. 61.

Political Science Quarterly, fall, 1982, p. 518; fall, 1993, p. 547.

Presidential Studies Quarterly, spring, 1994, p. 396.

Publishers Weekly, November 5, 1982, p. 67; August 29, 1986, pp. 383-384.

Reference & Research Book News, February, 1990, p. 40; October, 1992, p. 13.

Reference Book Review, no. 1, 1986, p. 3.

Review of Politics, April, 1983, p. 282.

Third World Resources, January, 1993, p. 22.

Times Educational Supplement, November 28, 1980, p. 23; June 12, 1987, p. 32; June 15, 1990, p. B7; May 24, 1991, p. 23; March 25, 1994, p. 10.

Times Literary Supplement, April 16, 1982, p. 427; June 6, 1986, p. 614; October 31, 1986, p. 1214; September 16, 1988, p. 1022; May 11-17, 1990, p. 492; January 29, 1993, p. 22; April 30, 1993, p. 26; February 3, 1995, p. 25.

Virginia Quarterly Review, summer, 1993, p. 97.

Wall Street Journal, January 21, 1983, p. 22; February 4, 1987, p. 28.

Washington Post Book World, May 1, 1983, p. 1.

Wilson Quarterly, autumn, 1987, p. 151.

OTHER

Oxford University Press, http://www.oup-usa.org (October 6, 1998).

*   *   *

FREESE, Gene Scott 1969-

PERSONAL: Born March 19, 1969, in Bryan, OH; son of Marty J. and Barbara (Ely) Freese. *Ethnicity:* "Caucasian." *Education:* Purdue University, B.A., 1991. *Avocational interests:* Martial arts, motorcycles, horses, marathons.

ADDRESSES: Home—4115 East Indian School, No. 222, Phoenix, AZ 85018.

CAREER: Scottsdale Healthcare, Scottsdale, AZ, electrocardiogram technician, 1995—. Certified fitness trainer.

WRITINGS:

Hollywood Stunt Performers, McFarland & Co. (Jefferson, NC), 1998.

WORK IN PROGRESS: Luck of the Damned, a novel; *Hollywood Man: The Life and Films of William Smith; Video Villains: Bad Guys on Screen,* completion expected in 2000.

SIDELIGHTS: Gene Scott Freese told *CA:* "Through motion picture and athletic endeavors I have encountered a number of entertaining stories and interesting personalities. It is my intention to transfer this knowledge into print for the enjoyment of a wider audience."

*   *   *

FREGA, Donnalee 1956-

PERSONAL: Born December 27, 1956, in Kenmore, NY; daughter of Donald (a machinist) and Georgetta (an art teacher; maiden name, Herl) Wells; married Alvin Frega (a sculptor), August 12, 1980; children: Carl, Kurt, Emma Lee. *Education:* State University of New York College at Fredonia, B.A. (summa cum laude), 1978, M.A. (summa cum laude), 1982; Duke University, Ph.D., 1989.

ADDRESSES: Home—North Carolina. *E-mail*—fregad @wilmington.net.

CAREER: University of North Carolina at Wilmington, assistant professor of English, 1990-96; Duke University, Durham, NC, visiting scholar in English, 1997-99.

WRITINGS:

Speaking in Hunger: Gender, Discourse, and Consumption in Richardson's "Clarissa," University of South Carolina Press (Columbia, SC), 1998.

Walking the Wire: Telling a Circus Family's Story, St. Martin's Press (New York City), in press.

Contributor to periodicals, including *Southern Literary Journal, Pennsylvania English, Southern Quarterly, Studies in the Literary Imagination, Coastal Chronicles,* and *Works and Days: Essays in the Socio-Historical Dimensions of Literature and the Arts.*

WORK IN PROGRESS: Letters to Ian, a novel; creative nonfiction in the areas of women's studies and biography.

SIDELIGHTS: Donnalee Frega told *CA:* "I was pregnant with my third child when I was denied tenure at the University of North Carolina at Wilmington 'for lack of sufficient publications in print.' I immediately accepted an appointment as a visiting scholar in the English department at Duke University and have since divided my time between parenting and writing.

"My first book, *Speaking in Hunger: Gender, Discourse, and Consumption in Richardson's "Clarissa,"* was published in 1998. Using Samuel Richardson's novel *Clarissa* as a focal point, I draw on historical and literary scholarship, psychology and clinical studies, feminist theory, religious studies, and hagiography to examine the broad range of socio-cultural factors which have defined 'abnormal' eating practices from the eighteenth century through the present. I argue that when what is today called 'anorexia' is viewed as an interpersonal language—a dangerous strategy employed by both sexes against unrealistic expectations of perfection, rather than as a private repudiation of life 'suffered' primarily by women, much of its mystery is dispelled.

"My next book is a work of creative nonfiction, *Walking the Wire: Telling a Circus Family's Story,* which follows four generations of performing women from the Brumbach family (the famous circus family immortalized in Elia Kazan's movie *Man on a Tightrope*). The book chronicles the funny and turbulent friendship that develops when a trained feminist scholar and academic critical theorist confronts a family of gypsy (Romani) circus artists, whose tools for living are magic, fantasy, and illusion.

"I am currently at work on a novel, tentatively titled *Letters to Ian,* about a mother who copes with her young son's death by appropriating the child's voice to maintain a correspondence with his British pen pal."

FRITH, Katherine Toland 1946-

PERSONAL: Born June 11, 1946, in New York; daughter of John M. and Marjorie (Canavan) Toland; married Michael Frith, August 10, 1973; children: Giles, John Sebastian. *Ethnicity:* "Caucasian." *Education:* Chestnut Hill College, B.S., 1967; University of Massachusetts at Amherst, M.Ed., 1983, Ed.D., 1985. *Politics:* Liberal. *Religion:* "I believe all religions are great." *Avocational interests:* Travel.

ADDRESSES: Home—711 Sunset Rd., State College, PA 16803. *Office*—125 Carnegie Bldg., College of Communications, Pennsylvania State University, University Park, PA 16801; fax 814-867-1106. *E-mail*—Katherine@frith.com.

CAREER: Iowa State University, Ames, teacher of journalism for five years; Pennsylvania State University, University Park, faculty member, c. 1988—, currently associate professor of advertising, past chairperson of advertising program. Fulbright professor in Malaysia, 1986-87, and Indonesia, 1993; Nanyang Technological University, visiting senior fellow, 1996-98; Asian Mass Communication and Information Center, Singapore, member.

Worked as an advertising copywriter in New York City, for such firms as J. Walter Thompson, N. W. Ayer, and Grey Advertising.

MEMBER: International Association of Mass Communications Researchers, American Academy of Advertising, Association for Education in Journalism and Mass Communications.

WRITINGS:

(Editor) *Advertising in Asia: Communication, Culture, and Consumption,* Iowa State University Press (Ames, IA), 1996.
(Editor) *Undressing the Ad: Reading Culture in Advertising,* Peter Lang Publishing (New York City), 1998.

Contributor to periodicals, including *Journalism Quarterly, Current Issues and Research in Advertising, Media Asia,* and *Journalism Educator.*

WORK IN PROGRESS: A book on advertising and global culture.

FUGUET, Alberto

PERSONAL: Born in Chile. *Education:* Attended University of Chile and University of Iowa.

ADDRESSES: Home—Santiago, Chile. *E-mail*—afug uet@mcl.cl.

CAREER: Writer and freelance journalist.

WRITINGS:

(With others) *Premios Literarios: Concurso Alonso de Ercilla,* Pehuen (Santiago, Chile), 1989.

La Azarosa y Sobreexpuesta Vida de Enrique Alekan, El Mercurio (Santiago, Chile), 1990.

Sobredosis: Cuentos, Editorial Planeta Chilena (Santiago, Chile), 1990.

Mala Onda, Planeta (Buenos Aires, Argentina), 1991, translation by Kristina Cordero published as *Bad Vibes,* St. Martin's Press (New York City), 1997.

(With others) *Santiago, Pena Capital: Narraciones,* Documentas (Santiago, Chile) 1991.

(Editor, with Sergio Gomez) *Cuentos con Walkman,* Planeta, Biblioteca del Sur (Santiago, Chile), 1993.

Por Favor, Rebobinar, Planeta (Santiago, Chile), 1994.

SIDELIGHTS: Alberto Fuguet grew up in Encino, California, then moved to Chile, where he learned Spanish. Jose Donoso, Chile's premier writer, invited Fuguet to attend a workshop at his home and became a mentor to the young writer. Donoso had taught creative writing at the University of Iowa during the 1960s and encouraged Fuguet to apply to their International Writers Program. Fuguet entered in 1994, eager to publish in English, having already published three books in Spanish. He was hopeful since "I was Latino, and everything Latino was 'hot.'. . . There seemed to be a Spanish-Language wave that I wanted to ride on my South American board," said Fuguet in a *Salon* interview.

His first story, submitted to the *Iowa Review,* was rejected as being a something that could have taken place in America. Fuguet said, "Add some folklore and a dash of tropical heat and come back later. That was the message I heard." As Fuguet examined the work of Hispanic writers, he found that they fit a formula. Stories centered on migrant farm workers, political refugees, or barrio violence, plots far removed from the urban life of the young Chilean writer.

His luck changed when *Mala Onda* was accepted for publication by a New York publishing house. Fuguet said in a *Salon* (internet) interview that his editor "was fed up with Garcia Marquez wannabes and is a true believer in cultural realism, a sort of NAFTA-like writing that he felt I exemplified. . . . Unlike the ethereal world of Garcia Marquez's imaginary Macondo, my own world is something much closer to what I call 'McOndo'—a world of McDonald's, Macintoshes, and condos." Fuguet said he and other young apolitical writers watch cable television, movies, and are net-connected, "far away from the jalapeno-scented, siesta-happy atmosphere that permeates too much of the South American literary landscape." Fuguet feels that present-day writers who model their novels after the writers of the 1960s (like Garcia Marquez, Carlos Fuentes, and Mario Vargas Llosa) "have transformed fiction writing into the fairy-tale business, cranking out shamelessly folkloric novels that cater to the imaginations of politically correct readers—readers who, at present, aren't even aware of Latino cultural realism."

Many of the influences on Fuguet come from pop culture, especially movies. He was at one point a film critic. His favorite American authors include Hemingway, Fitzgerald, Charles Bukowski, Richard Price, Ethan Canin, and Michael Chabon. He uses the internet for research and worked with the translator of *Mala Onda* (published as *Bad Vibes*) via e-mail. The book has been described as a South American *Catcher in the Rye,* and the first edition published in Spanish in 1991 triggered increased sales for *Catcher.* Fuguet's protagonist is seventeen-year-old Matias Vicunas, living a bored life within Santiago's middle class in the 1980s. Matias demonstrates his antisocial rebellion through the use of sex, drugs, and rock and roll. He has one sympathetic teacher, a left-wing anti-Semite, ironic because Matias's practicing-Catholic mother has a secret—her ancestors were Jewish. Matias's father is a swinger, and the two share coke and hookers. Matias seeks innocence like Holden Caulfield, with whom he identifies. A critic for *Kirkus Reviews* said that Fuguet's feel for Chile in the 1980s, like America in the 1950s, is reinforced by a "time-warping soundtrack, . . . slangy translation, . . . [and] cool pop references. . . . Here is what the new economic prosperity engenders culturally, he implies, and thank goodness we have such a clever novelist to guide us."

Fuguet commented in *Salon,* "I feel very comfortable at my desk in Santiago, writing about the world around me. A world that comes to me through television, radio, the Internet, and movies, which I send back through my fiction. My Latin American fiction."

BIOGRAPHICAL/CRITICAL SOURCES:

PERIODICALS

Booklist, November 15, 1994, p. 583.
Kirkus Reviews, January 15, 1997.
Library Journal, March 1, 1997, p. 102.
Publishers Weekly, February 24, 1997, p. 62.

OTHER

Salon, http://www.salonmagazine.com/june97/magi cal970611.html (June 11, 1997).*

* * *

FULTZ, Jay 1936-

PERSONAL: Full name James R. Fultz, Jr.; born January 21, 1936, in Parsons, KS; son of James R. (a truck farmer and in furniture sales) and Dorothy (a schoolteacher and librarian; maiden name, Santelle) Fultz. *Ethnicity:* "Caucasian." *Education:* Kansas State College of Pittsburg (now Pittsburg State University), B.A., 1963, M.A., 1965; University of Nebraska—Lincoln, Ph.D., 1978. *Politics:* Democrat. *Religion:* Protestant. *Avocational interests:* Nutrition and disease prevention, reading, movies, "hamlet hunting," walking, unsolved mysteries, collecting Dick Tracy comic strips from the 1930s and 1940s.

ADDRESSES: Home—1024 South 28th St., Parsons, KS 67357.

CAREER: Northwest Missouri State College (now University), Maryville, teacher of English composition and literature, 1965-66; Eastern College (now University of Baltimore), Baltimore, MD, teacher of English composition and literature, 1966-67; South Dakota State University, Brookings, instructor in English, 1967-70; University of Nebraska—Lincoln, instructor in English, 1975-82; University of Nebraska Press, Lincoln, editorial associate, 1984-87, editor of Bison Books, 1987-98; freelance editor and writer, 1998—. Guest on television programs, including a biography of Donna Reed broadcast by Arts and Entertainment in 1998 and the series *Intimate Por-*

trait, broadcast by Lifetime in 1999. *Military service:* U.S. Army, Public Information Branch, 1958-61.

MEMBER: Friends of the Parsons Public Library.

AWARDS, HONORS: Maude Hammond Fling fellow at Library of Congress, University of Nebraska, 1974.

WRITINGS:

In Search of Donna Reed, University of Iowa Press (Iowa City, IA), 1998.

Contributor to periodicals, including *Journal of Scholarly Publishing, Literature/Film Quarterly, Western Humanities Review,* and *Midwest Quarterly.*

WORK IN PROGRESS: Will Linton of Angerica, a political satire; "profiles of half-forgotten Hollywood stars."

SIDELIGHTS: Jay Fultz told *CA:* "If I have a prose style, I hope it's been formed on Oscar Wilde, Scott Fitzgerald, James Agee, and Raymond Chandler. I more or less consciously imitated all of them because they wrote with unusual clarity and grace, with poetic precision, in a complex but natural (even vernacular) rhythm. Early on, I soaked up Fitzgerald's work. My doctoral dissertation was on James Agee's film scripts and from exhaustive acquaintance I fell into the master's style: triplicate adjectives, cascading clauses, unexpected visual metaphors at the turn of a comma. I was *thinking* like him, or so I thought. Journalists are in disrepute during Monicagate, and rightfully so, but some of the sharpest, tightest writing still comes from them. I learned far more about syntax from H. L. Mencken, Walter Lippmann, Scotty Reston, and Stewart Alsop than I ever did from any composition class.

"I chose to write about Donna Reed because she was a star who struck me sometime in adolescence and kept on shining for me in maturity. She had a place in my psyche long before I ever wrote about her, and that made the writing trickier, more fraught with pitfalls. So far everything I've written has developed special interests from different parts of my past. This gives a satisfying sense, personal beyond words, of recurrence and continuity; but I'd probably have to chuck the sense if I wrote to support a large family.

"*In Search of Donna Reed* is not, I think, a typical celebrity biography. Taking great care with the research and writing, I tried to transcend a genre that is not much respected because it is expected to be trivial and gossipy. There's wasn't much dirt on Donna Reed, who had been ignored by biographers. She was, I discovered, a rich subject: a cultural icon, yet unhyped; a strong and brilliant woman who was far more interesting than her television persona, Donna Stone. To capture her substance, I had to proceed from a respect for her and gradually come to an understanding. During my research I became more interested in the person than the celebrity. I tried to show how her civilized and principled life matters in this more cynical time.

"Nowadays, any show-biz biographer who is sympathetic toward his or her subject is accused to writing hagiography. I think this charge is unfair. Popular biography is evidently *supposed* to be a debunking, and indeed much of it shows little or no liking of the subject, an attitude that is hardly conducive to judicious or thoughtful treatment.

"*In Search of Donna Reed* was harder to write than my doctoral dissertation. There wasn't much external excitement in Donna Reed's life, so the challenge was to make it interesting without falsifying. How well I succeeded isn't for me to judge, but members of her family have praised my portrait as the only real one of her that they've read."

G

GARBER, Marjorie

PERSONAL: Married (divorced).

ADDRESSES: Office—English Department, Harvard University, Cambridge, MA 02138.

CAREER: Harvard University, Cambridge, MA, professor of English, 1981—, and director of the Center for Literary and Cultural Studies. Also taught at Yale University, New Haven, CT.

WRITINGS:

Dream in Shakespeare: From Metaphor to Metamorphosis, Yale University Press (New Haven, CT), 1974.

Coming of Age in Shakespeare, Methuen (New York City), 1981.

Shakespeare's Ghost Writers: Literature as Uncanny Causality, Methuen (New York City), 1987.

Vested Interests: Cross-Dressing and Cultural Anxiety, Routledge (New York City), 1992.

Vice Versa: Bisexuality and the Eroticism of Everyday Life, Simon & Schuster (New York City), 1995.

Dog Love, Simon & Schuster (New York City), 1996.

Symptoms of Culture, Routledge (New York City), 1998.

EDITOR

Cannibals, Witches, and Divorce: Estranging the Renaissance, Johns Hopkins University Press, 1987.

(With Jann Matlock and Rebecca L. Walkowitz) *Media Spectacles,* Routledge (New York City), 1993.

(With Rebecca L. Walkowitz) *Secret Agents, The Rosenberg Case, McCarthyism, and 'Fifties America,* Routledge (New York City), 1995.

(With Paul B. Franklin and Rebecca L. Walkowitz) *Field Work: Sites in Literary and Cultural Studies,* Routledge (New York City), 1996.

WORK IN PROGRESS: (With Rebecca L. Walkowitz) *One Nation under God? Religion and Contemporary American Culture,* for Routledge, expected in 1999; (with Nancy J. Vickers) *Medusa,* an anthology, for Routledge, expected in 1999; (with Beatrice Hanssen and Walkowitz) *The Turn to Ethics,* expected in 2000.

SIDELIGHTS: Marjorie Garber established herself as a Shakespeare scholar during the 1970s and 80s, while teaching at Yale and since 1981 at Harvard. She later turned her analytical skills to broader contemporary issues of gender, sexuality, and cultural representation. As the author and editor of numerous books, Garber has addressed both academic and general audiences on a range of topics. Her work belongs to the postmodernist and New Historicist schools of analysis and draws upon the theories of Sigmund Freud, Michel Foucault, and others.

Garber was credited with breaking new ground in literary study when she wrote *Dream in Shakespeare: From Metaphor to Metamorphosis* (1974), a cataloging and analysis of the increasingly complex use of dream in Shakespeare's plays. Dorothy Sternlicht commented in *Library Journal* that this was "the first critical work to deal extensively and adequately" with the subject of dream in Shakespeare, and considered the book to be "intelligent" and "insightful." A reviewer for *Choice* concurred that nowhere else was the topic considered so carefully, and noted that although there were "echoes of dissertationese at times," it was still "an illuminating and vigorous reading."

In her book *Coming of Age in Shakespeare* (1981) Garber again regards the full corpus of plays in a discussion of the playwright's treatment of rites of passage, from childhood through death. Cyrus Hoy, writing for *Sewanee Review,* considered Garber to be acting "in the manner of a cultural anthropologist cum literary critic" and commended her for making "some very shrewd inductions about the varieties of human experience that mark the stages along life's way in Shakespeare's theater." A *Choice* reviewer found that Garber's use of psychological and anthropological theory created "a wondrous potpourri and source for student essays in many areas," although sometimes Garber discusses material that "would be obvious to most scholars." Rosamond Putzel commented in *Library Journal* that Garber's character "analyses and comparisons . . . are intriguing and original."

In response to the more-than a century-old controversy that not all of Shakespeare's plays should be attributed to a single author, Garber turned to the plays themselves for insight on the issue of authorship. Beginning with an essay titled "Shakespeare's Ghost Writers" (1985), she applied postmodern literary theory—namely that of New Historicism and theorist Michel Foucault—to the subject. Arthur F. Kinney of the *Philological Quarterly* considered this strategy to be "a dazzling move." Subsequently, Garber produced a book that expanded on the title and subject of the paper: *Shakespeare's Ghost Writers: Literature as Uncanny Causality* (1987). In *Shakespeare Quarterly,* Margreta de Grazia found that "[the book] employs an intriguing tactic for removing Shakespeare from the empowered center: it makes him ubiquitous." She also explained, "the controversy . . . over Shakespeare's authorship is seen to emanate from how the plays themselves problematize the concept of origin, especially in relation to authorship and paternity." De Grazia concluded that Garber had succeeded in giving new life to an often tired subject, saying, this "is a brave new book, for in justifying another book on Shakespeare, it has attempted nothing less than to make literature newly consequential."

Taking with her many of the same analytical and theoretical tools used in her Shakespearean studies, Garber leapt from topics rooted in the English Renaissance to those of contemporary America. She pro-

duced the book *Vested Interests: Cross-Dressing and Cultural Anxiety* in 1992, offering an encyclopedic examination of the then-blossoming issue of cross-dressing and the attendant subjects of gender and sexuality. Key ideas that Garber introduced include the status of the cross-dresser as a third identity separate from that of man or woman, and the significance of cross-dressing as more than a means to cross social boundaries. Writing for the *Nation,* David Kaufman noted that the book "is bound to become the new, comprehensive bible on the subject [of cross-dressing]" and found that the author "has uncovered a surprising abundance of data and examples of cross-dressing from the worlds of history, literature, biology, anthropology, film, music, psychoanalytic theory, and popular and mass culture." Julie Wheelwright, in a review for *New Statesman,* perceived that "the confusion and even discomfort provoked by this separation of sex from gender has provided literary critic Marjorie Garber with fertile terrain." Wheelwright concluded, "[the book] does . . . offer a provocative and highly readable analysis of a contemporary obsession, even for those without a rigorous grounding in Freudian theory." *New Republic* reviewer Anne Hollander found the book to be "filled with startling lore and vivid anecdotes" but concluded that "this study seems to be based on its own kind of blindness. . . . In all her formulations about transvestism, Western culture seems deprived of its richly uneven and messy continuity." Hollander criticized the author for not considering the larger framework of the history of clothing over the ages, reaching back to a time when women's and men's fashions were not so dissimilar.

Garber's next book, *Vice Versa: Bisexuality and the Eroticism of Everyday Life* (1995), expanded on her work on gender and identity. Using illustrations from the lives of many famous writers, actors, musicians, and artists, *Vice Versa* takes an anecdotal as well as analytical look at bisexuality in western culture. Garber's major contention is that sexuality can be properly seen as a continuum from heterosexual to homosexual, and from monosexual to bisexual. Together with *Vested Interests, Vice Versa* presents a new history of sexuality. Larissa MacFarquhar, a reviewer for *Nation,* felt Garber was "at her finest doing close readings of the byzantine entanglements bisexuality gets you into," but concluded, "it's difficult to imagine who this book is for. She evidently set out to be accessible and entertaining to the average highbrow and break new theoretical ground at the same time, but she hasn't succeeded." Conversely, *Booklist* commentator Patricia Monaghan commented that the author's approach is more appealing than those of Camille Paglia, Norman Mailer, and Michel Foucault. In "brilliant conceptual moves . . . [she] appl[ies] the ideas of narratology to sexual life . . . we do not have a sexual identity, but a sexual story," remarked Monaghan. A *Publishers Weekly* critic called the book an "erudite, provocative study of bisexuality."

The subject of Garber's next book, *Dog Love* (1996) might seem a departure. A critic for *Kirkus Reviews* considered it to be a "wry, literate study of dogs in human culture" in which "Garber smartly charts the contested ground that separates human from canine." A *Publishers Weekly* reviewer noted that Garber "trains her formidable interpretive gifts" on the topic of dogs and while the discussion is not particularly new, it "unfolds . . . with such agility and imagination as to compel attention." *New York Times Book Review* critic Andrew Sullivan was less taken with Garber's stories of famous dogs and dogs in literature. He commented, "The significance she ascribes to dogs, the profundity she sees in human relations with dogs, the depth and passion she brings to the subject—all these are, I'm afraid, beyond me."

Symptoms of Culture (1998), a collection of Garber's new and previously published essays, served to synthesize the full range of her previous work. The essays juxtapose the minute with the macroscopic to uncover the meanings behind American cultural obsessions. Linda Nochlin, writing in *Bookforum*, commented: "In her ability to move from High Culture to pop culture, from media representations of the Scopes Trial to the implications of the second-best bed from the Renaissance to the White House, Garber at times recalls the early Roland Barthes . . . The point is to make the reader see what she didn't see before, become a warier consumer of cultural artifacts and establishment verities, yet to do it without solemn preaching or professorial one-upsmanship, to do it with grace and humor." *Globe and Mail* contributor Mark Kingwell explained: "Culture, she says is like a rebus, the sort of visual puzzle, composed of punning images and plays on words, that decodes only through imagination and lateral thinking. The puzzlement, and the pleasure, lie less in the message that is hidden than in the manner of its hiding."

Garber's editorial work includes *Cannibals, Witches, and Divorce: Estranging the Renaissance* (1987), a collection of essays from the English Institute dating from 1984 and 1985. In general, these essays utilize a postmodern approach to reading the works of Spenser, Shakespeare, and Milton, considered the most important figures from the English Renaissance. Garber also served as a co-editor for *Media Spectacles* (1993), a grouping of essays on the issues and events which became "media circuses" during the early 1990s, that Matthew P. McAllister, writing for *Film Quarterly,* deemed to be "short on explicit theory but long on insightful analysis." Garber has edited two other books: *Secret Agents, The Rosenberg Case, McCarthyism, and 'Fifties America* (1995), and *Field Work: Sites in Literary and Cultural Studies* (1996).

BIOGRAPHICAL/CRITICAL SOURCES:

PERIODICALS

Afterimage, December, 1992, p. 16.
American Theatre, July, 1992, p. 44.
Belles Lettres, fall, 1992, p. 46.
Booklist, December 15, 1991, p. 733; May 15, 1995, p. 1617; January 1, 1996, p. 732.
British Book News, April, 1982, p. 255.
Canadian Literature, autumn, 1992, p. 140.
Choice, July/August, 1974, p. 758; April, 1982, p. 1068.
Chronical of Higher Education, January 22, 1992, p. A7.
Clio, winter, 1983, p. 204.
Colonial Literature, spring, 1983, p. 199; June, 1994, p. 185.
Contemporary Sociology, March, 1994, p. 209.
Dog Fancy, January, 1997, p. 39.
Drama Review, winter, 1994, p. 197.
Film Quarterly, fall, 1994, pp. 61-62.
Hungry Mind Review, fall, 1995, p. 9.
Journal of American History, December, 1996, pp. 1078-1079.
Journal of English and Germanic Philology, April, 1975, p. 235; July, 1984, p. 235.
Journal of Homosexuality, no. 4, 1994, p. 185.
Journal of Popular Culture, spring, 1993, p. 211.
Kirkus Reviews, September 15, 1991, p. 1197; April 1, 1995, p. 441; September 1, 1996, p. 1293.
Lambda Book Report, March, 1992, p. 48; May, 1992, p. 14; March, 1993, p. 42; March, 1994, p. 46; September, 1995, p. 19.
Library Journal, April 15, 1974, p. 1135; January 1, 1982, p. 95; November 1, 1991, p. 120; May 15, 1995, p. 85.
London Review of Books, November 5, 1992, p. 25; February 8, 1996, p. 15.
Los Angeles Times Book Review, July 30, 1995, p. 2.
Modern Language Review, January, 1977, p. 149.

Modern Philology, February, 1977, p. 149; August, 1984, p. 95.

Ms., September, 1995, p. 80.

Multicultural Review, July, 1992, p. 74.

Nation, February 24, 1992, pp. 239-242; July 17, 1995, pp. 102-104.

New Republic, August 31, 1992, pp. 34-41.

New Scientist, May 17, 1997, p. 44.

New Statesman, May 8, 1992, p. 35; January 19, 1996, p. 39.

New Yorker, July 17, 1995, p. 79.

New York Times Book Review, December 15, 1991, p. 11; May 31, 1992, p. 29; January 31, 1993, p. 32; July 9, 1995, p. 6; November 17, 1996, pp. 11-12.

Observer, May 3, 1992, p. 55; April 18, 1993, p. 62; January 21, 1996, p. 14; June 1, 1997, p. 18.

Partisan Review, no. 1, 1993, p. 161.

Philological Quarterly, fall, 1989, pp. 433, 459.

Publishers Weekly, October 18, 1991, p. 48; April 24, 1995, p. 54; September 23, 1996, p. 68; April 13, 1998, pp. 66-67.

Renaissance Quarterly, spring, 1983, p. 140.

Review of English Studies, November, 1975, p. 472.

San Francisco Review of Books, no. 4, 1991, p. 28; September, 1995, p. 30.

Sewanee Review, April, 1984, pp. 256-270.

Shakespeare Quarterly, winter, 1987, pp. 527-531; fall, 1989, pp. 345-348; fall, 1993, p. 363.

Sight and Sound, August, 1992, p. 42.

Spectator, February 3, 1996, p. 38.

Times Literary Supplement, January 29, 1982, p. 100; August 26, 1988, p. 934; May 28, 1993, p. 10; June 14, 1996, p. 10; June 20, 1997, p. 6.

Tribune Books (Chicago), February 9, 1997, p. 1.

Tulsa Studies in Women's Literature, spring, 1996, p. 175.

Victorian Studies, winter, 1993, p. 207.

Virginia Quarterly Review, summer, 1974, p. R76; autumn, 1987, p. 120.

Voice Literary Supplement, June, 1992, p. 23; June, 1995, p. 4.

Washington Post Book World, June 18, 1995, p. 5.

Women's Review of Books, January, 1992, p. 11; November, 1995, p. 7.

Yale Review, April, 1992, pp. 197-206.

*   *   *

GATTI, Anne 1952-

PERSONAL: Born May 28, 1952; daughter of William (a lawyer) and Verette Finlay; married Will Gatti (a writer and teacher), 1973; children: Thomas, Georgia. *Education:* St. Anne's College, Oxford University, degree in English, 1973. *Religion:* Roman Catholic. *Avocational interests:* Walking, fishing, gardening, theatre.

ADDRESSES: Home and office—17 Boltons Ln., Pyrford, Woking Surrey, England. *E-mail*—Gatti @dircon.co.uk.

CAREER: Collins Harvill, London, editorial assistant, 1976-78; Reader's Digest, London, researcher, 1978-80; Eaglemoss Publications, London, editor, 1980-81; freelance writer and editor, 1984—.

WRITINGS:

FICTION; FOR YOUNG ADULTS

(Editor) Edna O'Brien, *Tales for the Telling: Irish Folk and Fairy Stories,* illustrated by Michael Foreman, Antheneum (New York City), 1986.

(Editor) Kiri Te Kanawa, *Land of the Long White Cloud: Maori Myths,* illustrated by Michael Foreman, Arcade, 1989.

(Reteller) *Aesop's Fables,* illustrated by Safaya Salter, Harcourt (San Diego), 1992.

(Reteller) *Tales from the African Plains,* illustrated by Gregory Alexander, Dutton (New York City), 1995.

(Reteller) *The Magic Flute,* illustrated by Peter Malone, Chronicle Books (San Francisco), 1997.

NONFICTION; FOR YOUNG ADULTS

Isabella Bird Bishop (biography), Hamilton, 1988.

OTHER

Stepping Out (youth information handbook), Wolf-hound, 1985.

SIDELIGHTS: Anne Gatti commented: "I greatly enjoy the challenge of presenting traditional or established tales in an accessible way for the children of the twentieth century, while retaining the original spirit of the tale. I have been fortunate to work as editor to Edna O'Brien on a collection of Irish traditional tales, and to Dame Kiri Te Kanawa on her personal collection of Maori tales. I hope to follow my African tales with another selection, possibly from Persia."

Gatti specializes in splendor, retelling stories in books that bring the original wonder and magic of the tales to new generations of children. Most recently, Gatti gave what a *Publishers Weekly* reviewer called "the royal treatment" to Mozart's opera *The Magic Flute*. The story follows the classic opera: Prince Tamino battles evil with his comic bird-friend Papageno in order to save Pamina, his true love. "There's plenty of bewitching material here," according to a *Publishers Weekly* reviewer, while a *Kirkus Reviews* critic commented that "Gatti keeps tempo . . . with pleasingly swift scene changes and quick character portraits." Included with the book, is an audio CD with excerpts that correspond to the picture spreads. A *Publishers Weekly* reviewer asserted that *The Magic Flute* can be well appreciated as a "stand-alone" or an "integrated . . . audio experience."

Another of Gatti's books is her version of *Aesop's Fables*. The author selected fifty-eight of the original fables and, according to reviewer Denise Anton in *School Library Journal*, gave them "a fresh and totally inviting look" with a linguistic style that is "sparse but evocative." A *Kirkus Review* critic praised the author's economical retelling for keeping with "strict classical tradition," while a *Books for Keeps* reviewer commended the "extremely well-handled" retelling of the stories. Calling Gatti's version of Aesop's Fables "luxurious," *School Librarian* contributor Val Booler suggested that this "attractive book . . . would make a nice gift."

BIOGRAPHICAL/CRITICAL SOURCES:

PERIODICALS

Booklist, May 1, 1995, pp. 1569-1570.
Books for Keeps, May, 1992, p. 29.
Kirkus Reviews, October 15, 1992, p. 1305; November 15, 1997, p. 1706.
Publishers Weekly, November 23, 1992, p. 63; February 6, 1995, p. 84; November 24, 1997, p. 74.
School Librarian, November, 1992, p. 138.
School Library Journal, October, 1992, p. 101; June, 1995, p. 119.*

*   *   *

GEIRINGER, Hilda 1893-1973
(Hilda Pollaczek-Geiringer)

PERSONAL: Born September 28, 1893, in Vienna, Austria; naturalized U.S. citizen, 1945; died of influenzal pneumonia, March 22, 1973, in Santa Barbara, CA; daughter of Ludwig (a textile manufacturer) and Martha (Wertheimer) Geiringer; married Felix Pollaczek (a mathematician), 1921 (divorced, 1925); married Richard von Mises (a professor of aerodynamics and applied mathematics), November 5, 1943 (died, 1953); children: (first marriage) Magda Tisza. *Education:* University of Vienna, Ph.D., 1917. *Religion:* Jewish.

CAREER: Mathematician. *Fortschritte der Mathematik,* editor, 1919-20; University of Berlin, Institute of Applied Mathematics, Berlin, Germany, first assistant under Richard von Mises, 1921-27, lecturer, 1927-33, professor emeritus, 1965—73 Institute of Mechanics, Belgium, research associate, 1933; Istanbul University, Istanbul, Turkey, professor of mathematics, 1934-39; Bryn Mawr College, Bryn Mawr, PA, lecturer, 1939-44; Wheaton College, Norton, MA, professor and chair of mathematics department, 1944-59. Brown University, instructor in program for advanced instruction and research in mechanics, summer, 1942; Harvard University, research fellow in mathematics, beginning 1954.

MEMBER: American Academy of Arts and Sciences (fellow), Sigma Xi.

AWARDS, HONORS: Honorary degree, Wheaton College, 1960; honored with a special presentation by the University of Vienna on the fiftieth anniversary of her graduation from that institution, 1967.

WRITINGS:

(As Hilda Pollaczek-Geiringer) *Fondements mathematiques de la theorie des corps plastiques isotropes* (title means "Mathematical Foundations of the Theory of Isotropic Plastic Bodies"), Memorial des Sciences Mathematiques/Gauthier Villars (Paris), 1937.
Geometrical Foundations of Mechanics, [Providence, RI], 1942.
(Compiler and editor) Richard von Mises, *Probability, Statistics, and Truth,* revised edition, 1957.
(With G. S. S. Ludwig and Richard von Mises) *Mathematical Theory of Compressible Fluid Flow,* 1958.
(Contributor and compiler) Richard von Mises, *Mathematical Theory of Probability and Statistics,* revised edition, 1964.

Contributor to journals, including *Encyclopedia of Physics*.

SIDELIGHTS: Hilda Geiringer was an applied mathematician who made important contributions to the theory of plasticity of materials. She formulated the Geiringer equations for plane plastic deformations in 1930. She also pursued research in probability, statistics, genetics, and numerical methods. A refugee from Europe during World War II, Geiringer was among the European mathematicians who brought an emphasis on applied mathematics to the United States, where pure mathematics predominated. In the summer of 1942 she participated in the development of an applied mathematics program at Brown University, presenting a series of lectures on the geometric foundations of the mechanics of a rigid body. After the death of her second husband, mathematician Richard von Mises, in 1953, Geiringer worked on the publication of new editions of his works as well as her own research.

Geiringer was born in Vienna, on September 28, 1893. She was the daughter of Ludwig, a textile manufacturer, and Martha Wertheimer Geiringer. She showed a talent and interest in mathematics at an early age. Her parents supported her studies in mathematics at the University of Vienna, where she received a Ph.D. in 1917 for her thesis on double trigonometric series. In 1919 and 1920 Geiringer assisted the editor of *Fortschritte der Mathematik* ("Advances in Mathematics").

During the following year Geiringer moved to Germany to work at the Institute of Applied Mathematics in Berlin, under Richard von Mises, a founder of mathematical aerodynamics and contributor to probability theory. This was the beginning of Geiringer's productive career in applied mathematics. She began to publish papers on probability and on the mathematical characterization of plasticity, the bending of material after deformation. In 1927 Geiringer became a lecturer at the University of Berlin.

Geiringer, who was Jewish, was removed from the University in 1933; she moved to Belgium and then to Turkey. From 1934 to 1939 she was professor of mathematics at the Istanbul University. There, she learned Turkish for her lectures. When war broke out in 1939 Geiringer fled to the United States, where she taught at Bryn Mawr from 1939 to 1944. During this period, Geiringer published papers on

probability as well as notes for her lectures at Brown.

Geiringer married Felix Pollaczek in 1921. They had one daughter, Magda, born in 1922, but they divorced in 1925. Geiringer took Magda with her to Istanbul and then to the United States. In 1943 Geiringer married von Mises, who had also come to the United States via Turkey. He became a lecturer and then professor of aerodynamics and applied mathematics at Harvard. Geiringer became a U.S. citizen in 1945.

From Bryn Mawr, Geiringer went to Wheaton College in Norton, Massachusetts, where she became chairman of the Mathematics Department. In the late 1940s, Geiringer wrote several papers on statistics applied to Mendelian genetics and two papers on numerical methods. In the early '50s she took up plasticity again in a more general form. After the death of von Mises, Geiringer worked at Harvard under a grant from the Office of Naval Research to complete his work.

In 1957 Geiringer published a new edition of his book *Probability, Statistics, and Truth*. Her work with G. S. S. Ludwig and von Mises, *Mathematical Theory of Compressible Fluid Flow*, appeared in 1958. The new edition of von Mises's *Mathematical Theory of Probability and Statistics*, with Geiringer's supplementary material, was published in 1964. Geiringer wrote papers and lectured on probability during this period and wrote an article titled "The Mathematical Theory of the Inelastic Continuum" with A. F. Freudenthal for the *Encyclopedia of Physics*.

Geiringer retired from Wheaton in 1959, but continued her research work at Harvard. Wheaton gave her an honorary degree in 1960. Geiringer was made Professor Emeritus by the University of Berlin in 1956, and was honored by the University of Vienna on the fiftieth anniversary of her graduation. On March 22, 1973, during a visit with her younger brother, Karl, a noted musicologist, in Santa Barbara, Geiringer died of influenzal pneumonia.

BIOGRAPHICAL/CRITICAL SOURCES:

PERIODICALS

American Journal of Physics, 1943, pp. 67-73.
American Mathematical Monthly, October, 1980, pp. 607-621.

Boston Sunday Globe, March 25, 1973.
New York Times, July 19, 1953, p. 25; March 24, 1973, p. 36.
Wheaton Newsletter, September, 1959.*

*   *   *

GEORGE-BROWN, George Alfred 1914-1985
(Lord George-Brown)

PERSONAL: Original surname, Brown; surname changed to George-Brown by deed poll, 1970; born September 2, 1914, in London, England; died of complications following surgery to correct internal hemorrhaging, June 2, 1985, in Truro, England; son of George Brown (a truck driver); married Sophie Levene, 1937 (marriage ended, 1982); children: two daughters. *Religion:* Anglican.

CAREER: Politician and author. Created life peer, Baron George-Brown of Jevington, Sussex, 1970. Worked as clerk, in fur sales, and as a union organizer. Member of Parliament (Labour), Belper Division of Derbyshire, 1945-70. Parliamentary Private Secretary to Minister of Labour and National Service, 1945-47, and Chancellor of the Exchequer, 1947; Joint Parliamentary Secretary, Ministry of Agriculture and Fisheries, 1947-51; Minister of Works, 1951; First Secretary of State and Secretary of State for Economic Affairs, 1964-66; Secretary of State for Foreign Affairs and Deputy Prime Minister, 1966-68. Deputy Leader, Labour Party, 1960-70; contender for Labour Party leader, 1963; president, Social Democratic Alliance, 1981-85. Helped draft United Nations Security Council Resolution 242 (on Middle East); participated in British effort to mediate Vietnam War. Productivity counsellor, Courtaulds Ltd. (textile firm), 1968-73; deputy chair, G. C. Turner Group Ltd., 1977-85, and J. Compton, Sons & Webb (holding company) Ltd., 1980-85; director, Diebold Computer Leasing, 1973-85, British Northrop Ltd., 1978, GT Japan Investment Trust Ltd., 1980-85, and Commercial Credit Services Ltd. Founder, Air Compton (holding company), 1982.

MEMBER: Council for International Contact Trust (chair, 1974-85).

AWARDS, HONORS: Order of Cedar of Lebanon, 1971; Biancamano Prize (Italy), 1972; named Freeman, City of London, 1978.

WRITINGS:

In My Way: The Political Memoirs of Lord George-Brown, St. Martin's Press (New York City), 1971.

(Editor and author of introduction) *The Voice of History: Great Speeches of the English Language,* Sidgwick & Jackson (London), 1979, Stein & Day (New York City), 1980.

(Contributor with Hugh Todd-Naylor Gaitskell) *Britain and the Common Market: Texts of Speeches Made at the 1962 Labour Party Conference by Hugh Gaitskell and George Brown, together with the Policy Statement Accepted by the Conference* (speech), Labour Party (London), 1962.

ADAPTATIONS: In My Way was translated into French as *Memoires de choc,* with introduction by Maurice Schumann, Fayard (Paris), 1973.

SIDELIGHTS: "I've come from the wrong side of the sticks, darling," George Alfred George-Brown told *Washington Post* interviewer Sally Quinn in 1972, "and I bought my toll ticket to get across the bridge." George-Brown, who almost became leader of the Labour Party, and thus prime minister of Great Britain, in 1963, was born into the family of a poor London truck driver in 1914. He apprenticed in the fur industry, was a sales clerk for a time, and worked as a teamster and union organizer. He entered electoral politics in 1945 when he was chosen for a seat in Parliament on the Labour ticket; he remained in that house for twenty-five years, during which time he frequently served in the Labour "shadow cabinet" when Conservative governments were in power.

From 1963 to 1968, during the Harold Wilson administration, he was variously a deputy prime minister and a cabinet minister for economic and foreign affairs. In the latter role, he achieved importance on the international scene for his instrumental role in the adoption of United Nations Security Council Resolution 242, which called on the Arab states to recognize Israel's right to exist and called on Israel to withdraw to its pre-Six-Day-War borders. The resolution, never implemented, has remained a key text in later Middle East peace efforts. Brown also attempted to mediate the Vietnam War as part of a British team.

In 1968 he resigned as Foreign Secretary, declaring that Wilson had not consulted him during a gold crisis. Interviewer Quinn, however, makes plain that George-Brown's resignations were frequent occurrences at Ten Downing Street—a special file was kept there for them, according to the Quinn—and that, like previous resignations, this one had not been intended to be accepted. Wilson accepted it, in part, because of Brown's increasingly controversial nature as an outspoken, hard-drinking, sometimes painfully blunt personage. Brown was known for his intellectual brilliance, his "memorable foghorn voice," as it was termed by *Washington Post* writers Richard Pearson and J. Y. Smith, and his ability to communicate with people across the socioeconomic spectrum. He was also known for the alcohol consumption—sometimes amounting to six drinks before lunch, according to a *Chicago Tribune* obituary—that resulted in his two drunk-driving convictions. He was known for brash familiarity in his communications with members of royalty, and for sharply confronting foreign diplomats and office-holders, including Soviet leader Nikita Khruschev during his 1956 visit to London.

Two years after his 1968 resignation from the cabinet, George-Brown lost his House of Commons seat in a nationwide conservative sweep. In order to remain in political life, he applied for a seat in the House of Lords and chose the name Lord (or Baron) George-Brown. According to a *New York Times* obituary, he told an interviewer in 1970, "It's ridiculous to give me that stupid title. I'm not a lord and I wish I could drop the damn thing."

During the 1970s George-Brown became disillusioned with Labour, the party he had joined as a young man; he resigned in 1976, citing as his reason the lack of democracy in Britain's labor unions. He said at that time, "This is the saddest night of my life. . . . After 45 years I've left for the same bloody reasons I joined." Leaving Labour headquarters, he slipped and fell into the gutter, prompting jeers and unflattering newspaper headlines. He then entered business as director or officer of various corporations, most visibly the textile firm of Courtaulds.

His book, *In My Way: The Political Memoirs of Lord George-Brown*, was published in Britain in 1971 to a wave of publicity and in direct competition with the autobiography of Harold Wilson, which was published during the same season. At a pre-publication party, he joked to representatives of the press and industry that the experience of reading proofs over Christmas had depressed him and that the book was "absolutely bloody lousy." He opined, however, that it ought to sell well, a prediction that was borne out. In 1979 he edited a book of speeches, titled *The Voice of History: Great Speeches of the English Language*. In 1982 he

left his wife Sophie after forty-five years of marriage, and died of surgical complications after an episode of severe internal bleeding in 1985. Responding to George-Brown's death, Labour spokesperson Denis Healy said, as quoted in the *New York Times:* "[George-Brown] lacked a degree of self-discipline that would have taken him straight to the top. At his best George was a markedly successful parliamentarian. His off moments saddened his colleagues and Conservative opponents alike." Similar sentiments had been expressed by George-Brown himself, as quoted by Pearson and Smith in the *Washington Post:* "I'm no saint. And there were hard drinkers in my family. Of course, I've sometimes woken up next morning and thought, 'Damn!' Of course, I've sometimes wished I'd kept my mouth shut at dinner." Pearson and Smith, commenting on Brown's personality, declared: "He was rough, blunt, and emotional. Even his detractors, who were numerous, admired his honesty."

BIOGRAPHICAL/CRITICAL SOURCES:

PERIODICALS

Bookseller, January 2, 1971.
Chicago Tribune, June 5, 1985.
New York Times, June 4, 1985.
Washington Post, February 9, 1972; June 4, 1985.*

*   *   *

GEORGE-BROWN, Lord
   See GEORGE-BROWN, George Alfred

*   *   *

GIARD, Robert 1939-

PERSONAL: Born July 22, 1939, in Hartford, CT; son of Robert (a maintenance worker) and Antoinette (a housekeeper; maiden name, Peculis) Giard; companion of Jonathan G. Silin (an educator and author). *Education:* Yale University, B.A., 1961; Boston University, M.A., 1965. *Avocational interests:* Reading, film.

ADDRESSES: Home and office—43 Meeting House Lane, Box 1011, Amagansett, NY 11930.

CAREER: Photographer, 1971—.

AWARDS, HONORS: Lambda Literary Award, best visual arts/photography book, Lambda Literary Foundation, 1997, for *Particular Voices.*

WRITINGS:

Particular Voices: Portraits of Gay and Lesbian Writers, MIT Press (Cambridge, MA), 1997.

WORK IN PROGRESS: Portraits of gay and lesbian writers, early activists, and gay places.

SIDELIGHTS: Robert Giard told *CA:* "I am gay. I am a photographer, and I am a reader whose academic training was in English, American, and comparative literature. I began the photographic archive, *Particular Voices,* in 1985, and I continue to work on it. My intention is to preserve gay and lesbian history. I am an archivist, a preservationist."

*   *   *

GILLETTE, J(an) Lynett 1946-

PERSONAL: Born October 27, 1946, in St. Louis, MO; daughter of Louis J. (a United States Air Force pilot) and Zella Elizabeth (a homemaker; maiden name, Bodenhamer) Anderson; married David D. Gillette (a paleontologist), April 2, 1971 (marriage ended, 1993); children: Jennifer Rene. *Education:* Southern Methodist University, B.A. (journalism), 1969, graduate study (anthropology) 1969-71; Boise State University, B.S. (geology), 1981. *Avocational interests:* Hiking.

ADDRESSES: Agent—c/o Publicity Director, Dial, 375 Hudson St., New York, NY 10014.

CAREER: Department of Physical Anthropology, National Museum of History, Smithsonian Institution, Washington, DC, technician/research assistant, 1972-74; oil exploration geologist for small independent oil and gas companies, Dallas, TX, 1981-83; Ruth Hall Museum of Paleontology, curator of paleontology, Abiquiu, NM, 1986-97. Southwest Paleontology Foundation, president, 1987-92; served on National Ghost Ranch Foundation Board, 1987-91.

MEMBER: National Center for Science Education, Geological Society of America, Society of Vertebrate Paleontology, Society of Children's Book Writers and Illustrators.

WRITINGS:

Dinosaur Diary: My Triassic Homeland, illustrated by Catherine Larkin, Petrified Forest Museum Association, 1988.
The Search for Seismosaurus: The World's Longest Dinosaur, illustrated by Mark Hallett, Dial (New York City), 1994.
Dinosaur Ghosts: The Mystery of Coelophysis, illustrated by Douglas Henderson, Dial (New York City), 1997.

WORK IN PROGRESS: Early Humans of Ice Age Days, "an archaeology/paleontology book"; "a biography of a fossil collector who lived in Victorian England."

SIDELIGHTS: J. Lynett Gillette commented: "Sometime during the last year of my undergraduate studies I realized that I wasn't ready to make use of my journalism major. I wanted to write but felt I didn't have enough in-depth knowledge of any particular subject. I went on to follow interests in archaeology, geology, paleontology, and museums. Now, after twenty-five years, I am returning to writing, this time with a deep appreciation for and love of the process of discovery in the sciences. I write for young people, hoping that some of their wonderful energy and creativity can be put to use in the future—solving all the puzzles that remain."

As an undergraduate, Gillette studied journalism, but her interests in archaeology, geology, and paleontology led her into the life of a scientist. Gillette gained work experience at the Smithsonian Institution's National Museum of Natural History, studied graduate-level anthropology, and earned a second bachelor's degree—this time in geology. Eventually, she became curator of a paleontology museum at Ghost Ranch, the dig site featured in her book, *Dinosaur Ghosts: The Mystery of Coelophysis.*

Approximately 225,000,000 years ago Coelophysis, a small canine-sized dinosaur, scampered over the area that is now New Mexico. In 1947 paleontologists found hundreds of Coelophysis skeletons packed, well preserved, in New Mexico's red mud. In her book *Dinosaur Ghosts: The Mystery of Coelophysis,* Gillette poses possible answers to the question of how so many dinosaurs came to be buried together. *Horn*

Book reviewer Margaret A. Bush noted that Gillette creates "an intriguing setting" from which she systematically conducts an exploration of the mystery. Using the scientific method, Gillette introduces the reader to several hypotheses, including poisoned water and volcanic eruption; she then supports or refutes each hypothesis with photos and explanations of the existing physical evidence. *Booklist* contributor Lauren Peterson called Gillette's dig for answers a "fascinating" one that will "help young scientists gain insight into the process of formulating and testing hypotheses." Concluding her book with an explanation of the most current hypothesis, Gillette adds that scientists modify their ideas to fit new evidence—encouragement that critic Bush proclaimed "an open call to future scientists." A *Kirkus Reviews* critic thought *Dinosaur Ghosts* "an involving book about a topic of guaranteed interest to children."

Also with an alluring topic, Gillette's first book, *The Search for Seismosaurus: The World's Longest Dinosaur,* examines dinosaurs that are on the opposite end of the size spectrum. Remains of a Seismosaurus estimated to have been one hundred fifty feet long have been excavated from the sandstone of New Mexico. Beckoned by what *Booklist* reviewer Denia Hester called "fascinating but sometimes very technical" text, photographs of the dig site, and paintings of dinosaurs, readers—young and old—are invited to join the dig. The format of *The Search for Seismosaurus* "appears to be designed for grade 3-4 readers," noted *Appraisal* reviewer and librarian Kathleen A. Dummer, but the text is "at an 8th grade reading level. . . . Much of the information may be beyond the intended audience." Donald L. Wolberg, a specialist who reviewed the book for *Appraisal,* however, saw merit in the scientific work that made it intriguing to readers of all ages, commenting that it is "also worth a look by adults interested in paleontology and dinosaurs." An un-romanticized, nitty-gritty look at paleontology, this window overlooking a dinosaur dig, is "worthwhile," wrote Wolberg, "especially for a young enthusiastic reader with an interest in dinosaurs, fossils, or science."

BIOGRAPHICAL/CRITICAL SOURCES:

PERIODICALS

Appraisal, spring-summer, 1994, pp. 11-12.
Booklist, March 15, 1994, p. 1346; April 1, 1997, p. 1328.
Bulletin of the Center for Children's Books, March, 1993, pp. 221-222; July-August, 1997, p. 394.

Horn Book, July-August, 1997, p. 475.
Kirkus Reviews, January 15, 1997, p. 142.
School Library Journal, March, 1994, p. 228.*

*   *   *

GLADKOV, Fyodor (Vasilyevich) 1883-1958

PERSONAL: Born June 21, 1883, in Chernavka, Russia; died December 20, 1958, in Moscow, U.S.S.R. (now Russia). *Education:* Attended the Normal School, Tiflis, Russia. *Politics:* Communist.

CAREER: Writer. Worked as a teacher, 1902-17.

WRITINGS:

NOVELS

Izgoi (title means "The Outcasts"), published in the journal *Zavety,* 1912.
Ognennyi kon' (title means "The Fiery Steed"), 1923.
Tsement, 1925, English translation published as *Cement,* 1929, Raduga Publishers, 1985.
Staraya sekretnaya, 1927.
Novaya zemlya, 1931.
Energiya (title means "Energy"), 1932-38.
Tragediya Lyubashi, 1935.
Povest' o detstve (title means "A Tale of Childhood"), 1949.
Vol'nitsa (title means "A Free Gang"), 1950.
Likhaya godina (title means "A Woeful Year"), 1954.
Myatezhnaya yunost' (unfinished), 1958, English translation published as *Restless Youth,* 1959.

OTHER

Malen'kaya trilogiya (short stories), 1936.
Opalyonnaya dusha (short stories), 1943.
Klyatva (short stories), 1944.
Sobranie sochineniya (novels, short stories, plays, and essays), 8 volumes, 1958-59.

SIDELIGHTS: Fyodor Gladkov is best known for his proletarian novel *Tsement* (*Cement*), in which he documented the changes that occurred in Russia following the revolution of 1917. As a member of the Communist party, Gladkov strongly supported the postrevolutionary regime, and in *Cement* he enthusiastically endorsed governmental plans for reorganizing Russian society. However, despite the generally affirmative tone of the novel, Gladkov did not refrain from exposing what Gleb Struve called, in his *Soviet Russian Literature,* "the seamy side of this new life."

Gladkov was born in the village of Chernavka to a peasant family only one generation removed from serfdom. Although his parents were too poor to send him to school, a family friend taught him to read and write; soon after, he began reading the classics of Russian literature, including the works of Leo Tolstoy, Fyodor Dostoevski, and Mikhail Lermontov. At the age of seventeen Gladkov began to write for local newspapers and to work as a tutor, earning enough money to attend the Normal School in Tiflis, where he quickly became involved in the burgeoning revolutionary movement. Gladkov's subsequent activities during the abortive revolution of 1905 resulted in his exile to Siberia.

Returning to Russia after three years in exile, Gladkov settled in the Black Sea port of Novorossiysk, and it was there that he wrote his first novel, *Izgoi.* Upon completion of the manuscript, he sent it to Vladimir Korolenko, who was then editor of the liberal journal *Russkoe Bogatstvo.* Korolenko rejected the manuscript but encouraged Gladkov to submit the work to the smaller journal *Zavety,* where it was published in 1912. Gladkov continued to write and teach until the outbreak of the revolution in 1917, whereupon he abandoned both to resume his revolutionary activities.

After participating in the revolution and the ensuing civil war, Gladkov devoted himself exclusively to literature, hoping to aid in the creation of a new national literature for his newly transformed country. However, *Ognennyi kon',* his first postwar novel, fell far short of his expectations, and it was only with the publication of *Cement* in 1925 that he succeeded in producing a novel that celebrated the life of the proletariat in a manner favored by the government. The book was immediately popular with readers and critics, while its pro-communist sentiments earned the approval of the government and thus allowed him freedom to continue writing and publishing in the Soviet Union. Gladkov subsequently produced a number of other works, but he was never able to duplicate the success of *Cement,* and at his death in 1958 he was still known primarily as the author of that novel.

In *Cement* Gladkov sought to describe in a realistic and inspiring manner the emergence of a new socialist society from the turmoil of war and revolution, focusing in particular on the collectivization of Russian industry and the transformation of traditional values. Although he was thoroughly optimistic about the eventual success of the former, he foresaw major difficulties in altering centuries-old Russian social institutions. These attitudes are reflected in *Cement,* where the characters' efforts to rebuild and restart a cement factory as a collective endeavor are significantly more successful than their efforts to collectivize their interpersonal relationships. Nevertheless, the primary message of the novel remains, as Marc Slonim described it in his *Soviet Russian Literature: Writers and Problems 1917-1977,* "the victory of confidence over skepticism, of effort over indolence, of labor over inactivity."

Observers note that the major reason for the initial popularity of *Cement* in Russia was the relevance of the plot; Russian citizens, struggling to rebuild their own cities and factories, were indeed inspired by the triumph of Gladkov's workers. Critics, however, have been divided on the question of its merits. Many of Gladkov's socialist contemporaries found his prose style no different from that of nineteenth-century romantic fiction, while non-socialists found his overt didacticism unpalatable. The majority of critics today find Gladkov's characters unconvincing and his prose style stilted, but they concede that the work as a whole is powerful in its effect and acknowledge its influence on the development of Soviet socialist literature. Vyacheslav Zavalishin, in his *Early Soviet Writers,* declared: "Gladkov is not a very important writer, but he has brought home with force—if only by virtue of dogged repetition—the important theme in postrevolutionary Russian letters of the dissolution of the individual personality in the storm of the revolution and the subsequent attempt of those carried to power—the organizers who had retained the storm's dynamic energy—to impose their will, to suppress and obliterate the individuality of the executors, who had lost their energy and strength of will."

BIOGRAPHICAL/CRITICAL SOURCES:

BOOKS

Brown, Edward J., *Russian Literature since the Revolution,* revised edition, 1969, Harvard University Press, 1982.

Gladkov, Fyodor, *Cement,* translated by Liv Tadge and with a foreword by Berta Brainina, 1981, reprinted, Raduga Publishers, 1985.

Maguire, Robert A., *Red Virgin Soil: Soviet Literature in the 1920s,* Princeton University Press, 1968.

Slonim, Marc, *Soviet Russian Literature: Writers and Problems 1917-1977,* second revised edition, Oxford University Press, 1977.

Struve, Gleb, *Russian Literature under Lenin and Stalin,* University of Oklahoma Press, 1971.

Struve, Gleb, *Soviet Russian Literature,* Routledge & Kegan Paul, 1935.

Zavalishin, Vyacheslav, *Early Soviet Writers,* Praeger, 1958.

PERIODICALS

American Slavic and East European Review XIII, 1954, pp. 72-88.
Germano-Slavica, fall, 1979, pp. 85-103.
Modern Language Journal, autumn, 1983, pp. 303-304.
Nation, December 4, 1929, pp. 695-696.
Nation and Athenaeum, February 2, 1929, pp. 620, 622.
New Republic, May 15, 1929, pp. 367-368.
New Statesman, February 9, 1929, pp. 576-578.
New York Herald Tribune Books, July 14, 1929, p. 2.*

* * *

GLYMAN, Caroline A. 1967-

PERSONAL: Born November 28, 1967, in Lake Forest, IL. *Education:* University of Illinois at Urbana-Champaign, B.A., 1989; graduate work in advertising at Northwestern University, 1989. *Avocational interests:* Holistic health, ayurveda, aromatherapy, dance, horseback riding, astrology, crystology, numerology, feng shui, kundalini yoga.

ADDRESSES: Home—1765 Shore Acres Dr., Lake Bluff, IL 60044. *Office*—Forest House Publishing Co., Inc., P.O. Box 738, Lake Forest, IL 60045-0738.

CAREER: Forest House Publishing Co., Inc., Lake Forest, IL, writer, 1990-93, executive assistant, 1997—. Massage practitioner.

MEMBER: Associated Bodywork and Massage Professionals.

WRITINGS:

Learning Your ABC's of Nutrition, illustrated by Dee Biser, Forest House (Lake Forest, IL), 1992.
What's above the Sky? A Book about the Planets, illustrated by Biser, Forest House, 1992.
The Birthday Present, illustrated by Biser, Forest House, 1993.

SIDELIGHTS: Caroline A. Glyman commented: "I write to share important lessons that I have learned from my life experiences. I like to enlighten people and hope that the awareness they gain from my work will help them improve themselves and their lives. I write about subjects that stir my emotions—topics that make me feel the most joy or the most pain. I always try to make my art entertaining, inspiring, and uplifting."*

* * *

GODSHALK, C. S.

PERSONAL: Female; married; has children.

ADDRESSES: Home—Boston, MA. *Agent*—Henry Holt & Co., 115 West 18th St., 6th Floor, New York, NY 10011.

CAREER: Writer and freelance journalist. Formerly owned an import/export business in Southeast Asia; worked in a children's cancer hospital, and with inmates of a penitentiary.

WRITINGS:

Kalimantaan, Holt (New York City), 1998.

Contributor of short stories to anthologies, including *Best American Short Stories,* edited by Mark Helprin, Houghton (Boston), 1988; *Best American Short Stories,* edited by Richard Ford, Houghton (Boston), 1990; and *An Iowa Review Reader,* edited by David Hamilton, University of Iowa Press, 1996.

WORK IN PROGRESS: A contemporary novel set in New England.

SIDELIGHTS: C. S. Godshalk began writing *Kalimantaan* (Malay for the island of Borneo) in the 1970s while living in Singapore. Godshalk moved fourteen times in ten years with her husband and small children as she added to the story. The book began with her discovery of letters, diaries, and journals of people who lived in the setting of her nineteenth-century novel.

The book is loosely based on the life of Sir James Brooke (1803-68), whose history was also fictionalized by Joseph Conrad in *Lord Jim*. Brooke was the actual ruler of Sarawak, the raj of Godshalk's *Kalimantaan*. In the novel, Gideon Barr, an officer of the East India Company, returns to his birthplace on the coast of Borneo in the Malaysian archipelago and becomes a rajah, trading in spices and opium in a land inhabited by aboriginal headhunters, Dyak pirates, and Chinese traders. Kai Maristed wrote in the *Boston Globe* that the first one hundred pages, which details the building of Barr's empire, "dwells on landscapes and fauna, Malaysian alliances and the logic of headhunting cultures. . . . Barr is guest or host of such an array of colonial 'characters' that for all their eccentricities these buccaneers and Dutchmen, churchmen and chieftains become difficult to distinguish one from another. The text itself is jungle-like—bristling with unattributed pronouns and unglossed native vocabulary." David W. Henderson wrote in *Library Journal* that *Kalimantaan* "is not easy reading. . . . but to the willing, it will prove rewarding."

As the value of Barr's dynasty becomes apparent to the British government, settlers are sent to populate Sarawak—medical professionals, salesmen, clergy, entertainers, wives, and teachers. The newcomers include criminals and adventurers drawn to the faraway outpost. Barr travels to England, with the intention of marrying his widowed cousin, but decides at a face-to-face meeting that she is too old. He chooses instead the cousin's eighteen-year-old daughter Amelie, or Melie, less than half his age. Through Melie, a *Publishers Weekly* reviewer noted, Godshalk's "steady narrative strength" is revealed, and the reader is "able to absorb the rich, sodden beauty of the archipelago," the astonishing variety of characters, "and the humanity in the 'phenomenon' of Barr himself." Melie adjusts "to her husband . . . in a gradual process of familiarization and tragedy that draws the reader in," wrote Frank Caso in *Booklist*. Her adaptation to the primitive life is compounded by illness and homesickness. It is said that Barr keeps a "black queen" in a love nest nearby. Melie's first two pregnancies are stillbirths. Her first living child, a daughter, dies at age four of cholera. Melie conceives

again, the twin boys die, as does a native boy she has taken in.

Annette Kobak wrote in the *New York Times Book Review* that Barr built his raj despite "insurmountable difficulties: entrenched and murderous piracy . . . monsoons . . . cholera. . . . The warring Dyak tribes [who] take heads not just as trophies but to gain the life force. . . . [and] the British have their own 'head tax,' meant to encourage adventurers to kill pirates." All of this brought about the slaughter of which Barr was accused. The citizens of Sarawak counter the terrors of life in the raj by busily constructing churches, expansive lawns, classifying plant life, and by devising a new system of weights and measures. Barr writes letters to his mother, who died in Borneo when he was six, to fill the void of her loss. Kobak believed the plot is indicative of "the whole enterprise of empire as a venture of displaced love, as well as of willful blindness." Kobak called Godshalk a "born storyteller" and noted that her understanding of the story as "a human, not just a colonial, predicament amplifies the narrative from a highly accomplished novel of the contradictions of empire to a brilliantly subtle panorama of life forces played out in the face of death." *Boston Phoenix* reviewer Scott Stossel concluded that *Kalimantaan* is "ambitious, beautifully written, with a richly woven tapestry of themes and ideas, it may also be the best historical novel of the past ten years."

In an online interview at *Barnesandnoble.com*, Godshalk stated that "I think what lies at the heart of my writing . . . is an enduring fascination with people who are trying to live normal lives in brutal places. And this certainly is true of my short fiction, which is very much unlike *Kalimantaan*. It's contemporary, and it for the most part takes place in this country. And in part, my short fiction has this in common with the novel. Certainly the people I discovered in this history—especially in the letters and personal diaries that I came upon—were people like you and me, who were living and loving and raising families in a savage environment. This sets what it means to be human in high profile, and it provides rich ground for fiction."

BIOGRAPHICAL/CRITICAL SOURCES:

PERIODICALS

Booklist, March 15, 1998, p. 1202.
Boston Globe, April 19, 1998, p. N3.
Library Journal, March 15, 1998, p. 92.
New York Times Book Review, April 26, 1998, p. 8.

Publishers Weekly, January 29, 1996, p. 95; January 12, 1998, p. 42.

OTHER

Barnes & Noble, http://www.barnesandnoble.com (1998).
Boston Phoenix, http://www.phx.com/archive/books (1998).*

* * *

GOLDMAN, E(leanor) M(aureen) 1943-

PERSONAL: Born November 14, 1943, in Oakland, CA; daughter of Errett George Bryan (a telephone company worker) and Rachel Leader (a bookkeeper); married Donald Lauren Exter (divorced, 1982); children: Alice Liddell Exter, Simeon Exter III, Anna Jessamyn Exter, Max Frederick Exter. *Education:* San Francisco State College, B.A. (English), 1968.

ADDRESSES: Home—RR4, S18A, C20, Gibsons, British Columbia V0N 1V0, Canada. *Agent*—Laura Blake, Curtis Brown Ltd., 10 Astor Place, New York, NY 10003. *E-mail*—inkslinger@sunshine.net.

CAREER: Writer. Worked as a litigation secretary in San Francisco during the 1960s, and in British Columbia from 1981-92.

AWARDS, HONORS: Best Books for Young Adults, American Library Association (ALA), 1996, for *Getting Lincoln's Goat;* Quick Picks, ALA, 1996, for *The Night Room.*

WRITINGS:

FOR MIDDLE GRADE READERS

Money to Burn, Viking (New York City), 1994.
Shrinking Pains, Viking, 1996.

FOR YOUNG ADULT READERS

The Night Room, Viking, 1995.
Getting Lincoln's Goat: An Elliot Armbruster Mystery, Delacorte (New York City), 1995.

ADAPTATIONS: The Night Room has been optioned by Jane Startz Productions, Inc.

SIDELIGHTS: E. M. Goldman commented: "Like most writers, I have always written except for long spaces when I've been cranky about not writing. My small measure of success arrived after anyone with sense would have given up. This may be preferable to being published posthumously.

"Mostly, when I write, I seize on an idea that intrigues me and explore the Great What-if. The characters appear in response to the basic idea. That is, the basic idea leads to plans for scenes and a goal—a maze for my mice. The characters react to their experiences and to each other because of who they are, and each may change because of these experiences and associations. Each had better interest me because I have to spend months with them.

"I always know where a book will end, but the journey is full of surprises. Sometimes I sit at my desk laughing at something I have written. Sometimes I weep when bad things happen to the characters. Sanity is not part of the job description for a novelist. On the other hand, I only have to commute down the hall, and the wardrobe can't be beat.

"While it is a compliment when someone says that s/he devoured the book at a single gulp, my internal response is sometimes, 'If I spent three months writing it, then *you* should sit there for three months reading it.' (Real reply: 'Really! What a compliment! Thank you so much.')

"I wish that I could claim to be well disciplined, but I wander away entirely too easily. Or the computer Scrabble game often appears when I intend to write. I'll intend to play one game, then go for two out of three and three out of five.

"Like many other writers, when I am honest-to-gosh involved in creating, I always play music—any kind, as long as I enjoy it and the music doesn't demand attention in its own right. Music helps to put me into a space where my thoughts are completely in my work, and the music is only heard in a minimal way. Editing requires silence. And a sharp pencil. And a back-up on disk.

"Advice to aspiring writers: It may be easier and less painful to hit yourself over the head with a hammer. You obtain faster results that way, too. And attention. But, if you must write, then you must. I advise taking literature classes and avoiding writing courses. Books on writing are fine, and I particularly recommend those by Dwight Swain and Lawrence Block.

"Also important: Learn a trade. Consider it background, not to mention a source of income. Live life as a participant, not as an observer.

"Take care of your teeth. Go clean your room."

Goldman's books for middle and young adult readers feature adolescent protagonists who learn lessons on the way to becoming responsible adults. Sometimes these lessons are learned the hard way. In *Money to Burn* buddies Matt and Lewis face the prospect of a boring summer until they happen across a suitcase containing $400,000. The boys decide to enlist the aid of Dermot, a local eccentric, to help them spend the money without arousing their parents' suspicions. Keeping the money turns out to be more trouble than it is worth, however, when friends of the dead drug dealer to whom the suitcase belonged come looking for the loot, and the trio are caught in the middle. Of *Money to Burn, School Library Journal* contributor Bruce Anne Shook said, "This is a rollicking adventure, full of suspense, action, and humor." Sarah Ellis, a *Quill & Quire* contributor, enthused, "The writing is crisp, the plot rolls right along, and the whole book provides one ingenious answer to the perennially fascinating question, 'What would you do if you had a fortune?'"

Goldman's next book, *The Night Room,* aimed at young adult readers, has a darker theme than *Money to Burn.* Seven high school juniors are chosen to participate in a virtual reality program in which they are transported to their ten-year class reunion. Based on questionnaires the students had filled out, their fantasy futures are revealed to them, bringing happiness, heartbreak, and many surprises. A measure of suspense is added when a disgruntled computer hacker places a virus in the program and one of the participants, Sandy, is remembered at the virtual reunion as the girl that died in her junior year. The remaining students band together to find out what is wrong with the program before Sandy "attends" the reunion. According to *School Library Journal* contributor Lyle Blake Smythers, the characters, which are built on stereotypes such as the jock and the genius, "become real individuals as the book progresses." "The mix of players is well-differentiated through effective dialogue and the suspense judiciously leavened with an authentic measure of high school camaraderie, competition, and romance," stated Roger Sutton in the *Bulletin of the Center for Children's Books.* A *Kirkus Reviews* contributor asserted that, "this novel will reach deep inside readers' own hopes and dreams."

Still in a mysterious vein but with a large dose of humor, *Getting Lincoln's Goat* is Goldman's next title for middle-grade readers. The star of this comic mystery is budding teen detective Elliot Armbruster. Fifteen-year-old Elliot dreams about the glamorous life of a private eye and decides to dive into the profession when the school's mascot, Lincoln the goat, disappears. He enlists the help of his friends Bruno and Francine, and a real-life private eye. A *Kirkus Reviews* contributor called *Getting Lincoln's Goat,* "a hoot," and Chris Sherman in *Booklist* said, "readers will enjoy the mayhem, goofy mystery, and interplay between the very likeable characters." In addition to a lively story, Phyllis Simon, a reviewer in *Quill & Quire,* noted that Goldman's book "takes a cheeky look at some of the hackneyed phrases and attitudes found in pulpy detective fiction." Carrol McCarthy, a *School Library Journal* contributor, pointed out that *Getting Lincoln's Goat* "is more about finding oneself than finding a goat."

BIOGRAPHICAL/CRITICAL SOURCES:

PERIODICALS

Booklist, March 1, 1994, p. 1252; January 1, 1995, p. 816; April 15, 1995, p. 1493.
Bulletin of the Center for Children's Books, July-August, 1994, pp. 356-357; February, 1995, pp. 197-198.
Canadian Children's Literature, no. 81, 1996, pp. 69-73.
Kirkus Reviews, April 15, 1994, p. 556; February 15, 1995, p. 224; October 1, 1996, p. 1466.
Publishers Weekly, December 12, 1994, p. 62; April 24, 1995, p. 72.
Quill & Quire, May, 1994, p. 33; June, 1995, p. 58.
School Library Journal, April, 1994, pp. 127-128; March, 1995, p. 225; May, 1995, pp. 120-121; September, 1996, p. 202.*

*   *   *

GONZALEZ, Victor Hugo 1953-

PERSONAL: Born November 19, 1953, in Mexico; son of Pedro and Sara (Franco) Gonzalez. *Ethnicity:* "Mexican." *Education:* Rio Hondo Community College, A.A., 1976; Whittier College, B.A., 1979; California State University, graduate study, 1984. *Religion:* Roman Catholic.

ADDRESSES: Home—9622 Rex Rd., Pico Rivera, CA 90660.

CAREER: Instituto Tecnologico Superior, Mexico, professor of English and French, summer, 1985; Kendall Industries, Mexico, documentation translator, 1986; Century 21 (real estate company), Whittier, CA, salesperson, 1986-88.

WRITINGS:

Boundless Journal: The Stranger (novel), 1stBooks Library (Bloomington, IN), 1998.

WORK IN PROGRESS: Surreal Adventures and *Conde.*

SIDELIGHTS: Victor Hugo Gonzalez told *CA:* "Since the 1980s many music recording companies have produced songs about an unknown man, known only as 'the stranger.' In my novel, Alberto dreams about writing a book of his own adventures. Soon he forgets about his dream. For years later, he causes an involuntary disturbance at the Playboy Club in Los Angeles, where he acquires a nickname, 'the stranger.' Gossip about him reaches beyond the club's walls. Rock songs about a mysterious stranger begin to be heard on the radio. Alberto thinks about the book he wanted to write and decides to take his own challenge. He has to lead a double life, with a double identity, and he develops an alter ego. The stranger takes control of Alberto and makes a name in rock music. After fourteen years of songs about the stranger, Alberto annuls the stranger to write his book."

*   *   *

GORUP, Radmilla J(ovanovic)

PERSONAL: Born in Yugoslavia; naturalized U.S. citizen; daughter of Matija and Milka (Trojancevic) Jovanovic; married Ivan Gorup (a chemical engineer), June 15, 1963; children: John Matthew, Alexander Mark. *Ethnicity:* "Serbian." *Education:* University of Belgrade, B.A., 1959; St. John's University, Jamaica, NY, M.A., 1973; Columbia University, M.A., 1977, M.Phil., 1979, Ph.D., 1986. *Religion:* Serbian Orthodox. *Avocational interests:* Linguistics, sociolinguistics, art, travel.

ADDRESSES: Home—7 Somerset Dr. N., Great Neck, NY 11020. *Office*—Department of Slavic Languages,

718 Hamilton Hall, Columbia University, New York, NY 10025; fax 516-482-5728. *E-mail*—rjg26 @columbia.edu.

CAREER: Columbia University, New York City, instructor in Slavic languages, 1980-86, lecturer, 1994, currently adjunct associate professor of Slavic languages, University of California, Berkeley, lecturer in Slavic languages, 1986-93.

MEMBER: North American Society for Serbian Studies (member, board of directors, 1990-92; president, 1996-98), Linguistic Society of America, Modern Language Association of America, American Association of Teachers of Slavic and East European Languages, American Association for the Advancement of Slavic Studies, Columbia School Linguistic Society (member, board of directors, 1997—).

WRITINGS:

The Prince of Fire, University of Pittsburgh Press (Pittsburgh, PA), 1998.

Contributor of articles, reviews, and translations to periodicals, including *World Literature Today, Serbian Studies,* and *Slavic and East European Journal.* Guest editor, *Review of Contemporary Fiction,* summer, 1998.

WORK IN PROGRESS: Research on children in literature and on "Serbo-Croatian Deixis."

*   *   *

GOVIER, Trudy 1944-

PERSONAL: Born August 3, 1944, in Edmonton, Alberta, Canada; daughter of George and Doris (Kemp) Govier; married Anton Colijn, 1974; children: Caroline, Peter, Douglas. *Ethnicity:* "Canadian." *Education:* University of Alberta, B.A. (history), 1965; University of Waterloo, Ph.D. (philosophy), 1971. *Politics:* "Left of center." *Religion:* Agnostic. *Avocational interests:* Swimming, singing, cyling, piano.

ADDRESSES: Home and office—3207 Canmore Rd. N.W., Calgary, Alberta T2M 4J8, Canada. *Agent*— c/o McGill-Queen's University Press, 3430 McTavish St., Montreal, Quebec H3A 1X9, Canada. *E-mail*— govier@home.com.

CAREER: Writer and philosopher. Trent University, Peterborough, Ontario, former philosophy professor.

MEMBER: Canadian Philosophical Association, Project Ploughshares Calgary, Western Affairs Committee, Association for Informal Logic and Critical Thinking, Concerned Philosophers for Peace.

AWARDS, HONORS: Gold Medal in Arts, University of Alberta, 1965; doctoral scholarship, Canada Council, 1968-71; research grants, Social Sciences and Humanities Research Council of Canada, 1983-85 and 1989-94.

WRITINGS:

A Practical Study of Argument, Wadsworth (Belmont, CA), 1985.
Problems in Argument Analysis and Evaluation, De Gruyter, 1987.
(Editor) *Selected Issues in Logic and Communication,* Wadsworth (Belmont, CA), 1988.
God, the Devil, and the Perfect Pizza: Ten Philosophical Questions, Broadview Press, 1989.
Social Trust and Human Communities, McGill-Queen's University Press (Montreal), 1997.

Contributor to periodicals, including *Hypatia.*

WORK IN PROGRESS: A book on issues of revenge, forgiveness and acknowledgement with special interest in reconciliation politics.

SIDELIGHTS: Trudy Govier is the author of several philosophical studies. Her most successful book, *A Practical Study of Argument,* has been read by audiences in many countries and has been reissued four times since its 1987 publication.

Among Govier's other publications is *Selected Issues in Logic and Communication,* for which she served as editor. The book contains sixteen essays on subjects ranging from misapprehension of political commentary to critical discrimination in the age of media saturation. Dianne Romain, writing in *Canadian Philosophical Reviews,* affirmed that the "collection's strength lies in the high quality and diversity of the essays." She added that the volume's essays "offer a host of ways to critique mass media and other communication and provide good reading for an upper division critical thinking or communications studies course."

Govier followed *Selected Issues in Logic and Communication* with *God, the Devil, and the Perfect Pizza: Ten Philosophical Questions,* which is structured as a series of philosophical debates and brief fictional accounts. Among the issues addressed in this volume are electronic consciousness, the nature of numbers, conscience, the irrational aspects of rationality, and even likely survival strategies in contemporary times. Alan R. Drengson wrote in *Canadian Philosophical Reviews* that Govier "manages to catch authentically the way in which philosophical problems can arise for us in the normal course of life." He asserted, "Her book has the virtue of helping us to recover part of this larger, richer context, and for that reason alone it serves a valuable end." Drengson concluded his review by affirming that Govier's book is "a pleasure to read" and declaring that he was "impressed by Govier's ability to weave the major issues . . . into coherent dialogues and stories."

Govier told *CA:* "Though I remain interested in argument and critical thinking, my main concern over the past several years has been with topics in social philosophy. I spent a number of years studying issues of trust and distrust. I'm now fascinated with issues of reconciliation, especially with the attitudes of revenge and forgiveness which are so important to them. I'm thinking about how the ethical issues shade into politics."

BIOGRAPHICAL/CRITICAL SOURCES:

PERIODICALS

Argumentation and Advocacy, winter, 1994, pp. 182-184.
Canadian Philosophical Reviews, December, 1989, pp. 480-483; July, 1990, pp. 268-270.
Dialogue, April, 1991, pp. 640-645.
Journalism Quarterly, winter, 1988, p. 1042.
Quill & Quire, February, 1990, p. 25.

*   *   *

GREENE, Stanley A. 1929-

PERSONAL: Born April 27, 1929, in Rochester, NY; married Katherine Marine, November 1, 1959; children: Susan. *Education:* University of Arizona, B.S., 1952; University of Pennsylvania, M.B.A., 1954.

ADDRESSES: Home—829 Winter Rd., Rydal, PA 19046.

CAREER: Lawyers Co-operative Publishing Co., Rochester, NY, product manager, 1961-68; Auerbach Publishers, Philadelphia, PA, marketing manager for computer reference publications, 1968-73; *Legal Intelligencer,* Philadelphia, general manager, 1975-80; Warman Publishing Co. (publisher of antique price guides), Philadelphia, owner and president, 1980-89.

AWARDS, HONORS: Award for outstanding reference book, Reference Librarians Association, 1995.

WRITINGS:

(Editor with Richard Pohanish) *Hazardous Materials Handbook,* Van Nostrand (New York City), 1996.
(Editor with Pohanish) *Rapid Guide to Chemical Incompatibilities,* Van Nostrand, 1997.
(Editor with Pohanish) *Hazardous Substances Resource Guide,* 2nd edition, Gale (Detroit, MI), 1997.
(Editor with Pohanish) *Electronic and Computer Industry Guide to Chemical Safety and Environmental Compliance,* Wiley (New York City), 1998.
(Editor with Pohanish) *Hazardous Chemical Safety Guide for the Machining and Metalworking Industries,* McGraw (New York City), 1999.

* * *

GRIFFITH, William E(dgar) 1920-1998

OBITUARY NOTICE—See index for *CA* sketch: Born February 19, 1920, in Remsen, NY; died of a stroke, September 29, 1998, in Cambridge, MA. Educator and author. Although Griffith spent a large part of his career teaching political science at Massachusetts Institute of Technology, he was also recognized as an expert on communism and the Cold War and he once served as an advisor to President Jimmy Carter's national security advisor. Griffith received an M.A. and Ph.D. from Harvard University. He served in the United States Army during World War II and continued his involvement in military affairs by administering de-Nazification efforts in Bavaria after the war for the U.S. army. Griffith became an expert on cold war issues and served as an advisor to Radio Free Europe during the 1950s at the height of tense Soviet/U.S. relations. Between 1959 and 1990 Griffith taught political science at MIT and administered related academic research projects. Griffith edited several works that addressed political science and Soviet relations, including *The Soviet Empire: Expansion and Detente*

(1976), *The European Left* (1979), and *Europe: The Opening Curtain* (1989).

OBITUARIES AND OTHER SOURCES:

BOOKS

Who's Who in America, 1990-1991, Marquis Who's Who, 1991.

PERIODICALS

Washington Post, October 7, 1998, p. B6.

* * *

GROBSTEIN, Clifford 1916-1998

OBITUARY NOTICE—See index for *CA* sketch: Born July 20, 1916, in New York, NY; died of pneumonia, September 6, 1998, in La Jolla, CA. Scientist, educator, and author. Grobstein was known for his contributions to cancer research and his writings which focused on the ethics of scientific research. He also contributed to the field of developmental biology. Grobstein earned degrees in biology and zoology and graduated with a Ph.D. from the University of California at Los Angeles. After working for the National Cancer Institute for ten years, Grobstein taught biology at Stanford and eventually headed that department. In 1965 he began teaching at the University of California in San Diego, where he served as a professor and administrator for the remainder of his career. Grobstein was noted by his peers as being able to acknowledge and analyze the human implications of biological research. For example, he suggested in his writings that cloning would take a prevalent role in society for creating new life. Grobstein authored several publications addressing scientific research, including *A Double Image of the Double Helix* (1979), *From Chance to Purpose* (1981), and *Science and the Unborn* (1988).

OBITUARIES AND OTHER SOURCES:

BOOKS

Who's Who in America, Marquis Who's Who, 1994.

PERIODICALS

New York Times, September 13, 1998, p. A63.

GROSS, Jonathan David 1962-

PERSONAL: Born November 26, 1962, in New York; son of Theodore L. Gross (a university president); married Jacqueline Russell, March, 1993; children: Sheri Nicole. *Ethnicity:* "Jewish." *Education:* Haverford College, B.A., 1985; Columbia University, M.A., 1986, Ph.D., 1992. *Politics:* Democrat.

ADDRESSES: Home—3812 North Whipple, Chicago, IL 60618. *Office*—Department of English, DePaul University, 802 West Belden Ave., Chicago, IL 60614-3214; 773-267-8502. *E-mail*—jgross@wppost.depaul.edu.

CAREER: DePaul University, Chicago, IL, assistant professor, 1992-98, associate professor of English, 1998—. University of Santa Clara, guest lecturer, 1995.

AWARDS, HONORS: Grant from National Endowment for the Humanities, 1992; grant for England, DePaul University, 1993; Mayer Fund fellow, Huntington Library, 1994; Gladys Krieble Delmas travel grant, American Council of Learned Societies, 1994.

WRITINGS:

(Editor and author of introduction) *Byron's "Corbeau Blanc": The Life and Letters of Elizabeth Milbanke, Lady Melbourne (1751-1818),* Rice University Press (Houston, TX), 1997.
(Contributor) *Mapping Male Sexualities,* Fairleigh Dickinson University Press (Madison, NJ), in press.

Contributor of articles and reviews to scholarly journals, including *European Romantic Review, European Legacy, Studies in English Literature,* and *Philological Quarterly.* Bibliographer, *Keats-Shelley Journal,* 1997-98.

WORK IN PROGRESS: Byron: The Erotic Liberal, for St. Martin's Press (New York City).

*   *   *

GUERIF, Francois 1944-

PERSONAL: Born November 16, 1944, in La Limouzimere, France; son of Jean and Jeanne (Baudry) Guerif; married, 1970; children: two sons.

ADDRESSES: Home—12 Boulevard Saint Martin, 7510 Paris, France. *Office*—106 Boulevard Saint Germain, 75006 Paris, France.

CAREER: Editions Fayard, former editor; Editions Fleuve Noire, former editor; Editions PAC, editor; Editions Rivages, Paris, former editorial director. Editor of journal *Polar.*

AWARDS, HONORS: Ellery Queen award, 1997.

WRITINGS:

Paul Newman, Editions PAC, 1975.
Robert Redford, Editions PAC, 1976.
Marlon Brando, Editions PAC, 1976.
(With Pascal Merigeau) *John Wayne: le Dernier Giant,* Editions du Grand Bouchet (Paris), 1979.
Le Film Noir Americain, Editions H. Veyrier (Bordeaux), 1979.
Le Cinema Policier Francais, Editions H. Veyrier (Bordeaux), 1981.
(With Raymond Boyer) *Brigitte Bardot: And God Created Woman,* photographs by Sam Levin, translated by Anne Collier, Delilah Communications (New York City), 1983.
Clint Eastwood, Editions H. Veyrier (Bordeaux), 1983, St Martin's Press (New York City), 1986.
Vincente Minnelli, Edilig (Paris), 1984.
Paul Newman, Editions H. Veyrier (Bordeaux), 1987.
Francois Truffaut, Edilig, 1988.
Steve McQueen, Editions J'ai Lu (Paris), 1988.
Sans Espoir de Retour: Samuel Fuller, Editions H. Veyrier (Bordeaux), 1989.
Le film Policier, Editions J'ai Lu (Paris), 1989.
James M. Cain: Biographie, Nouvelles Editions Seguier, 1992.
Conversations with Claude Chabrol, Deuvel, 1999.

WORK IN PROGRESS: Writers of the Twentieth Century: James Ellroy, a television movie.

SIDELIGHTS: Francois Guerif, editorial director of Paris's Editions Rivages mystery collection, and editor of the review *Polar,* has been instrumental in promoting American crime writers in France. Starting in 1978 with a small collection called "Red Label," Guerif introduced French readers to Fredric Brown's novel *We All Killed Grandma,* Robert Bloch's *Firebug,* James Cain's *The Magician's Wife,* and David Goodis's *The Wounded and the Slain.* After the company went out of business, Guerif took a position with Fayard, where he published three more novels by

Goodis and two by Jim Thompson. His next move was to Fleuve Noir, and then to Rivages. His association with Rivages has been a happy one; expanding on their demonstrated commitment to foreign literature, he helped develop their Rivages/Thriller collection with titles from Robin Cook, and James Ellroy. Ellroy remains his most successful writer to date.

In an online interview with Brad Spurgeon Guerif explained that he likes to promote American writers who are not well known to French readers—either those who have never been published in France, or those whose work had gone out of print there. He credits Ellroy as the "motor of the collection," describing to Spurgeon the risk he took in publishing the author's *Blood on the Moon* in 1987. "I found he had a way of talking about violence that was very different," Guerif remembered. "I thought this was someone completely modern." Success was not instantaneous, though; the book did nothing until Guerif's friend, writer Jean-Patrick Manchette, gave it a rave review in the daily *Liberation*. That review launched the book, and along with it Guerif's collection. In addition to Ellroy, Guerif admires American writers Charles Willeford, Jim Thompson, and David Goodis. Guerif has stated that he believes he reinvigorated the career of the latter after publishing all of Goodis's out-of-print novels, which were then made into films.

Guerif has also written several books on film, particularly film noir. Only two of his titles have been published in the United States, however: 1983's *Brigitte Bardot: And God Created Woman,* written with Raymond Boyer, and *Clint Eastwood* (1986). His books on American film giants include works on Vincente Minnelli, Paul Newman, and John Wayne, and a biography of thriller writer James M. Cain, whose books were made into film noir classics. In addition, Guerif has written books on American film noir and the French police film.

French Review's Allen Thiher admired Guerif's study of Truffaut (*Francois Truffaut,* 1988), noting that the book "sets forth a coherent network of concerns that could serve as a springboard to new readings" and finding the filmography that concludes the book thorough and helpful. Christopher Schemering in *Library Journal,* however, wrote that Guerif's book on Eastwood suffered from "an unbalanced critical viewpoint" that ignored valid criticism of Eastwood's use of screen violence, as well as discussion of his alleged misogyny.

A critic of French mystery writing as well, Guerif edits *Polar,* a review he started in 1979. Each issue focuses on a theme or a writer, and contains interviews, short stories, and a complete bibliography. In 1997, the Mystery Writers of America awarded Guerif the Ellery Queen award.

BIOGRAPHICAL/CRITICAL SOURCES:

PERIODICALS

French Review, February 1990, p. 568.
Library Journal, May 1, 1986, p. 129.

OTHER

Spurgeon, Brad, "Interview with Francois Guerif," http://www.mygale.org/00/polarweb/spurgeon/guerif.htm (28 Jan. 1998).

* * *

GUGGENBUHL, Allan 1952-

PERSONAL: Born March 24, 1952, in Zurich, Switzerland; son of Adolf (a psychiatrist) and Anne (a sculptress; maiden name, Craij) Guggenbuhl; married, wife's name Beatrice (a social worker), August 7, 1981; children: Valenz, Alexandre, Raphael. *Education:* University of Zurich, M.A., 1982, Ph.D., 1997; C. G. Jung Institut, Diploma, 1994. *Religion:* Protestant.

ADDRESSES: Home—Mittelstrasse 21, 8008 Zurich, Switzerland. *Office*—Unter Zaunel, 8001 Zurich, Switzerland; fax +41-1-383-6959. *E-mail*—algugg@swissonline.ch. *Agent*—Monika Menne, Raudramerstrasse 31, 8102 Obeiengstringen, Switzerland.

CAREER: Deputy director of outpatient clinic for group psychotherapy of children and adolescents; lecturer in psychology at a teacher-training college in Zurich, Switzerland.

WRITINGS:

Men, Power, and Myths, Continuum (New York City), 1997.
The Incredible Fascination of Violence, Spring, Woodstock, 1996.

GUIVER, Patricia

PERSONAL: Born in England.

ADDRESSES: Agent—c/o Putnam Berkley Publishing Group, 200 Madison Avenue, New York, NY 10016.

CAREER: Novelist. Society for the Prevention of Cruelty to Animals (SPCA), Orange County Chapter, head.

WRITINGS:

MYSTERY NOVELS; "DELILAH DOOLITTLE PET DETECTIVE SERIES"

Delilah Doolittle and the Purloined Pooch, Berkley (New York City), 1997.
Delilah Doolittle and the Motley Mutts, Berkley (New York City), 1998.
Delilah Doolittle and the Careless Coyote, Berkley (New York City), 1998.

SIDELIGHTS: Patricia Guiver is the creator of a series of mysteries featuring pet detective Delilah Doolittle, a sleuthing British widow who lives in Surf City, California. Doolittle's specialty is animals and particularly finding missing pets. Her companion is a Doberman pinscher named Watson, with a nose for investigation. In their first adventure, *Delilah Doolittle and the Purloined Pooch,* the duo is on the trail of a missing German Shepherd, Herbert Fitzherbert. When they find a human corpse in the dog's doghouse, the investigation takes a much different turn. A commentator for *Publishers Weekly* noted the debut of the pet detective series, calling the *Purloined Pooch* "mildly amusing" for its details on pet ownership and the services that deal with pets.

In *Delilah Doolittle and the Motley Mutts,* Doolittle again finds a corpse instead of a hound, this time that of a parks and recreation worker with whom she wanted to discuss the illegal trapping going on in the wetlands of Surf City. After another murder takes places, Doolittle begins to wonder if the trapping and missing dog are linked. Gloria Miller, in the *Literary Times,* called the Motley Mutts "a delightful, well-crafted whodunit that reads fast and will hold your interest and keep you on your toes." She concluded, "You don't have to love animals to enjoy this book by Patricia Guiver! The supporting cast of motley mutts are adorable!"

Guiver is also the author of *Delilah Doolittle and the Careless Coyote.* In this book Delilah is searching for the beloved Abyssinian cat belonging to Mavis Bryde. Mavis believes her neighbor, who she suspects of practicing witchcraft, is behind the cat's disappearance. When Delilah tries to meet with the neighbor, however, she finds that she has been murdered. Harriet Klausner, in a review for *Under the Covers,* commented that the book would be "especially enjoyed by Anglophiles and animal lovers."

BIOGRAPHICAL/CRITICAL SOURCES:

PERIODICALS

Publishers Weekly, August 18, 1997, pp. 89-90.

OTHER

In Orange County, http://www.inorangecounty.com/orangemedia/sites/books/pg-writers_harvest.asp (1998).
Literary Times, http://www.tlt.com/revs/revs_con.htm (March 28, 1988).
Mystery Reader Reviews, http://www.themystery reader.com/guiver-delilah.html (February 8, 1998).
Under the Covers, http://www.silcom.com/~manatee/guiver_delilah.html (August 29, 1998).*

H-I

HACKETT, Bob
See HACKETT, Robert A(nthony)

*   *   *

HACKETT, Robert A(nthony) 1952-
(Bob Hackett)

PERSONAL: Born May 27, 1952, in London, England; son of Ambrose M. and Joyce E. C. (Underwood) Hackett; married Angelika Kahrkling (a translator), 1980; children: Karina, Melanie. *Ethnicity:* "Anglo." *Education:* Simon Fraser University, B.A. (with honors), 1973; Queen's University, Kingston, Ontario, M.A., 1976, Ph.D., 1983. *Politics:* "Unabashedly progressive, neo-modernist." *Religion:* "Fundamentally agnostic." *Avocational interests:* Travel, desert, and shoreline solitude.

ADDRESSES: Home—Burnaby, British Columbia, Canada. *Office*—School of Communication, Simon Fraser University, Burnaby, British Columbia, Canada V5A 1S6; fax 604-291-4024. *E-mail*—hackett@sfu.ca.

CAREER: Simon Fraser University, Burnaby, British Columbia, assistant professor, 1984-92, associate professor of communications, 1992—. NewsWatch Canada, codirector; Canadian Centre for Policy Alternatives, research associate.

MEMBER: Society for Socialist Studies.

WRITINGS:

Pie in the Sky: A History of the Ontario Waffle, Canadian Dimension, 1980.
News and Dissent, Ablex Publishing (Norwood, NJ), 1991.
Sustaining Democracy? Journalism and the Politics of Objectivity, Garamond Press (Toronto, Ontario), 1998.

Some writings appear under the name Bob Hackett. Member of editorial board, *Journalism Studies.*

WORK IN PROGRESS: The Missing News: Filters and Blind Spots in Canada's Press; research on media democratization as a social movement.

*   *   *

HAKIM, Catherine 1948-

PERSONAL: Born May 30, 1948; citizenship, British. *Education:* University of Sussex, B.A. (with honors), 1969; University of Essex, Ph.D., 1974.

ADDRESSES: Office—Department of Sociology, London School of Economics and Political Science, University of London, Houghton St., London WC2A 2AE, England; fax 01-71-955-7405. *E-mail*—c.hakim@lse.ac.uk.

CAREER: Conducted field research in Caracas, Venezuela, 1969-72; Tavistock Institute, London, England, research officer, 1972-74; British Office of Population Censuses and Surveys (now Office of

National Statistics), London, senior research officer, 1974-78; British Department of Employment, London, principal research officer, 1978-89; University of Essex, Colchester, England, professor of sociology and director of ESRC Data Archive, 1989-90; University of London, London School of Economics and Political Science, London, began as Morris Ginsberg fellow, became senior research fellow in sociology, 1993—.

MEMBER: Royal Statistical Society (fellow), British Sociological Association, Social Policy Association.

WRITINGS:

(Contributor) M. Bulmer, editor, *Censuses, Surveys, and Privacy,* Macmillan (London, England), 1979.

(With W. R. Hawes) *Labour Force Statistics,* Open University Press (Milton Keynes, England), 1982.

Secondary Analysis in Social Research: A Guide to Data Sources and Methods with Examples, Allen & Unwin (London), 1982.

(Contributor) Bulmer, editor, *Essays on the History of British Sociological Research,* Cambridge University Press (Cambridge, England), 1985.

Research Design: Strategies and Choices in the Design of Social Research, Allen & Unwin, 1987.

(Contributor) E. McLaughlin, editor, *Understanding Unemployment: New Perspectives on Active Labour Market Policies,* Routledge (London), 1992.

Key Issues in Women's Work: Female Heterogeneity and the Polarisation of Women's Employment, Athlone Press (London), 1996.

(Editor with H.-P. Blossfeld, and contributor) *Between Equalization and Marginalization: Women Working Part-Time in Europe and the USA,* Oxford University Press (Oxford, England), 1997.

Social Change and Innovation in the Labour Market: Evidence from the Census SARs on Occupational Segregation and Labour Mobility, Part-Time Work and Student Jobs, Homework and Self-Employment, Oxford University Press, 1998.

(Contributor) G. Dench, editor, *Rewriting the Sexual Contract,* Transaction Publishers (New Brunswick, NJ), in press.

Contributor of about forty articles to professional journals, including *European Societies, British Journal of Sociology, European Sociological Review, Work, Employment, and Society, Journal of Historical Sociology,* and *International Journal of Comparative Labour Law and Industrial Relations.*

WORK IN PROGRESS: Revising *Research Design: Strategies and Choices in the Design of Social Research,* publication by Routledge expected in 2000; *Preference Theory: Predicting Work-Lifestyles in the Twenty-First Century.*

*   *   *

HALL, Timothy L. 1955-

PERSONAL: Born October 28, 1955, in Tyler, TX; son of Norris (a tax assessor) and Betty (a homemaker; maiden name, Lewis; present surname, Pettit) Hall; married Lee Nicholson, November 20, 1977; children: Benjamin, Amy. *Education:* University of Houston, B.A. (summa cum laude), 1978; Rice University, graduate study, 1978-80; University of Texas, J.D. (with honors), 1983. *Politics:* Republican. *Religion:* Christian. *Avocational interests:* Woodworking.

ADDRESSES: Home—311 Phillip Rd., Oxford, MS 38655. *Office*—Law Center, University of Mississippi, University, MS 38677; fax 601-232-7731. *E-mail*—lwhall@olemiss.edu.

CAREER: U.S. Court of Appeals for the Fifth Circuit, judicial clerk, 1983-84; Hughes & Luce, Austin, TX, litigation associate, 1984-89; University of Mississippi, University, assistant professor, 1989-93, associate professor, 1993—, Mitchell, McNutt, Threadgill, Smith & Sams Lecturer in Law, 1997-98. University of Texas, visiting professor, 1994. Member of State Bar of Texas, U.S. Court of Appeals for the Fifth Circuit, and U.S. District Court for the Western District of Texas.

MEMBER: Association of American Law Schools (member of executive committee, section on law and Religion, 1994, 1995, 1996), Coif.

WRITINGS:

(Editor and contributor) *Ready Reference: American Justice,* Salem Press (Englewood Cliffs, NJ), 1996.

(With Michael L. Harrington) *The University of Mississippi: In Principle and Practice,* Simon &

Schuster (New York City), 3rd edition, 1997, 4th edition, 1998.
(Editor and contributor) *Ready Reference: Censorship,* three volumes, Salem Press, 1997.
(Editor and contributor) *Civil Rights Encyclopedia,* three volumes, M. E. Sharpe (Armonk, NY), 1997.
(Editor and contributor) *Ready Reference: Women's Issues,* three volumes, Salem Press, 1997.
(Editor and contributor) *Ready Reference: Family Life,* three volumes, Salem Press, 1998.
Separating Church and State: Roger Williams in America, University of Illinois Press (Champaign, IL), 1998.
Entering the University, Simon & Schuster, in press.

Contributor to law journals.

*   *   *

HAMBLY, Barbara 1951-

PERSONAL: Born August 28, 1951, in San Diego, CA. *Education:* University of California at Riverside, M.A. (medieval history); also studied at University of Bordeaux, France.

ADDRESSES: Agent—c/o Del Rey Books, 201 East 50th St., New York, NY 10022.

CAREER: Freelance writer. Has worked as a research assistant, high school teacher, and karate instructor.

MEMBER: Science Fiction Writers of America (president).

WRITINGS:

"DARWATH" SERIES

The Time of the Dark, Del Rey (New York City), 1982.
The Walls of Air, Del Rey, 1983.
The Armies of Daylight, Del Rey, 1983.
Mothers of Winter, Del Rey, 1996.
Icefalcon's Quest, Del Rey, 1998.

"SUN WOLF" SERIES

The Ladies of Mandrigyn, Del Rey, 1984.
The Witches of Wenshar, Del Rey, 1987.

The Unschooled Wizard, (includes *The Ladies of the Mandrigyn* and *The Witches of Wenshar*), Doubleday (New York City), 1987.
The Dark Hand of Magic, Del Rey, 1990.

"SUN-CROSS" SERIES

The Rainbow Abyss, Del Rey, 1991.
Magicians of the Night, Del Rey, 1992.
Sun-Cross (includes the novels *The Rainbow Abyss* and *Magicians of the Night*), Guild America, 1992.

"THE WINDROSE CHRONICLES" SERIES

The Silent Tower, Del Rey, 1986.
The Silicon Mage, Del Rey, 1988.
Darkmage (includes *The Silent Tower* and *The Silicon Mage*) Doubleday, 1988.
Dog Wizard, Del Rey, 1993.

"STAR TREK" SERIES

Ishmael: A Star Trek Novel, Pocket (New York City) 1985.
Ghost Walker, Pocket, 1991.
Crossroad, Pocket, 1994.

OTHER NOVELS

The Quirinal Hill Affair, St. Martin's Press (New York City), 1983, published as *Search the Seven Hills,* Ballantine, 1987.
Dragonsbane, Del Rey, 1986.
Seven Hills, Ballantine, 1987.
Search the Seven Hills, Del Rey, 1987.
Those Who Hunt the Night, Del Rey, 1988, published in England as *Immortal Blood,* Unwin (London), 1988.
Beauty and the Beast (novelization of television script), Avon (New York City), 1989.
Song of Orpheus (novelization of television script), Avon, 1990.
Stranger at the Wedding, Del Rey, 1994, published in England as *Sorcerer's Ward,* HarperCollins (London), 1994.
Bride of the Rat God, Del Rey, 1994.
Travelling with the Dead, Del Rey, 1995.
Star Wars: Children of the Jedi, Del Rey, 1995.
A Free Man of Color, Bantam, 1997.
Star Wars: Planet of Twilight, Del Rey, 1997.
Fever Season, Bantam, 1998.

OTHER

(Editor) *Women of the Night,* Warner Aspect, 1994.
(Editor) *Sisters of the Night,* 1995.

Contributor of short fiction to anthologies and other publications, including *Xanadu 2,* edited by Jane Yolen and Martin H. Greenberg, 1994; *South from Midnight,* Southern Fried Press, 1994; *Sandman: Book of Dreams,* 1996; and *War of Worlds: Global Dispatches,* 1996. Also author of scripts for animated cartoons.

WORK IN PROGRESS: Dragonshadow, for Del Rey, expected 1999.

SIDELIGHTS: Barbara Hambly's life experiences are as varied as her fiction. The ex-model, clerk, high school teacher, black belt karate instructor, and technical writer enjoys dancing, painting, studying historical and fantasy costuming, and carpentry—and she occasionally uses these varied activities as fodder for her writing. While Hambly's novels are primarily sword-and-sorcery fantasies, she also writes in a variety of other genres—everything from vampire stories to science fiction; recently she has enjoyed success with historical mysteries such as the popular *Free Man of Color* and *Fever Season,* and she has created novelizations based on the characters in television shows like *Beauty and the Beast* and *Star Trek.*

Hambly, who has served as president of the Science Fiction Writers of America, has said that she feels the urge to write is something that's inherent. "I think a person is a writer if they HAVE to write," she said during a July 1997 online chat session with Barnes and Noble. "This is not an easy way to make a living. I think I would be doing this even if I were not making money at it. I think people who are true writers write because they have to. They can't NOT do it. They have stories in them to tell, and they have to tell them." Hambly is considered a gifted storyteller who has garnered a wide readership, and critics have praised her work. "Hambly's writing is witty and fast-paced," wrote Elizabeth Hand of the *Washington Post Book World.* David Langford, in the *St. James Guide to Fantasy Writers,* remarked that Hambly "has a special talent for reclaiming and reworking familiar themes of fantasy, making them over into a seamless gestalt which is very much her own."

Hambly was born in the Naval Hospital of San Diego, California, on August 28, 1951. She grew up in southern California, attended the University of California, Riverside, and studied for a time at the University of Bordeaux in southern France. As a girl, she was an avid reader. She fell in love with fantasy fiction after reading L. Frank Baum's classic turn-of-the-century children's tale *The Wizard of Oz;* she decided to become a writer. Hambly took a step in this direction when in 1975 she earned a master's degree in medieval history. This gave her both the research skills and the knowledge base to craft historical novels.

Hambly took her first step toward a writing career in 1978 when she penned a fantasy novel for her own enjoyment. She sold the book to a publisher on its first submission, despite the fact she did not yet have an agent. "I always wanted to be a writer but everyone kept telling me it was impossible to break into the field or make money," Hambly said in an interview with Elisabeth Sherwin in the *Davis Enterprise.* "I've proven them wrong on both counts."

However, it wasn't until 1982 that her writing career took off with publication of *The Time of the Dark,* the first book in the "Darwath Trilogy." The story centers on a race of creatures known as the "Dark Ones" who are eyeless, can fly, and have a taste for human flesh. Two citizens of Los Angeles, graduate student Gil Patterson and auto mechanic Rudy Solis, are drawn into the alternate world to do battle with the Dark Ones in their attack on a parallel earth. Reviewer Michael W. McClintock of *Science Fiction and Fantasy Book Review* found fault with the book, but wrote that Hambly "draws Gil and Rudy effectively, and the plot shows at least the possibility of interesting development." Susan L. Nickerson in *Library Journal* described *The Time of the Dark* as "heart stopping," and noted that Hambly had written an "unusually effective" fantasy work.

The second book, *The Walls of Air,* published a year later, continues the adventure of Gil and Rudy, who have been taken to the Dark Ones' parallel world. There Rudy becomes a wizard and Gil is transformed into an elite guard. Reviews for this novel were mixed. Nickerson however, praised Hambly's plot for its "brisk action" and a feeling of impending menace which "keeps the reader deeply involved." The third book in the saga, *The Armies of Daylight,* gave devotees an answer to the riddle of the Dark. Roland Green of *Booklist* wrote that Hambly's work features "intelligent characterization, sound storytelling, and creative use of magic." Thirteen years after *The Armies of Daylight,* Hambly resurrected Rudy and Gil in 1996 for the novel *Mother of Winter*. Here the characters must save the earth from a glacial freeze. "The story is involving, and the narrative intelligent," according to a *Publishers Weekly* reviewer.

Aside from the "Darwath" novels, the prolific Hambly has written more than two dozen other books. Among them is *Ishmael: A Star Trek Novel,* published in 1985. In Hambly's tale, one of a popular series of books based on the characters created by the late Gene Roddenberry, Spock travels back in time to visit the Earth in 1867 in an effort to thwart a Klingon plan to change human history. Roland Green of *Booklist* praised Hambly's effort, recommending it "not only for Star Trek collections but as a good novel in its own right." *Ishmael* grabs the reader's attention throughout "with humor, action and personal interplay," according to Roberta Rogow of *Voice of Youth Advocates*. Hambly added two other books to the "Star Trek" series: *Ghost Walker* in 1991 and *Crossroad* in 1994.

Hambly delved into the adventures of Princess Leia and Luke Skywalker in *Children of the Jedi* and *Planet of Twilight,* part of a series of books based on George Lucas' popular *Star Wars* films. Critics were enthusiastic. "In her hands, the heroes of the New Republic take on a maturity and credibility that enhance their already engaging personalities," reviewer Jackie Cassada of *Library Journal* wrote of *Children of the Jedi.* Hambly's contribution rated "among the best in the series," a *Booklist* reviewer declared. The story takes Leia, Luke, Han Solo and Chewbacca on a journey to find the missing children of the Jedi. In *Planet of Twilight,* published in 1997, two factions battle for power on a planet called Nam Chorios. "Hambly is superior to most of the other SW authors at vivid word building [and] humor," wrote Roland Green of *Booklist.*

Perhaps Hambly's most successful original creation is the "Sun Wolf" series, which chronicles the adventures of what Langford described as "the unbrutal mercenary Sun Wolf and his hard-bitten lady second-in-command Starhawk." *The Ladies of Mandrigyn,* the first book in the series, is a gory adventure about Sun Wolf's battle with the wizard Altiokis. It also deals with his realization of the aging process, the emergence of his own innate wizard potential, and the realization that he loves Starhawk, his longtime loyal follower. The work should "please most fantasy readers," *Library Journal* reviewer Janet Cameron predicted. Subsequent books in the "Sun Wolf" series are *The Witches of Wenshar* and *The Dark Hand of*

Magic. Hambly gave further proof of her versatility when she wrote *Dragonsbane,* a dragon fantasy novel. The book relates the adventures of a character named Prince Gareth as he deals with a demonic parent, love, rioting subjects, and a black dragon. "High school readers of both sexes will applaud with equal fervor," wrote Frank Perry of *Voice of Youth Advocates.*

In 1988 Hambly went off in another direction when she crafted a vampire story. Hambly's inventive effort had an odd twist: the vampires are the victims. *Those Who Hunt the Night* deals with a mysterious being who slashes open the coffins of vampires in London and lets in lethal sunlight that allows the stalker to kill the victims as it drinks their blood. A frightened vampire enlists the help of an ex-spy to find the culprit. Susan M. Schuller, writing in *Voice of Youth Advocates,* stated that Hambly "delves into vampire lore with gusto, detailing the lust for blood and the killing urge among the undead."

While Hambly has said that she enjoyed writing her vampire book, she was so busy with other projects that a decade passed before she returned to the genre. *Traveling with the Dead* follows the adventures of James Asher, a former British espionage agent, and his wife Lydia who battle to prevent an alliance between human governments and the living dead. A *Library Journal* critic believed that *Traveling with the Dead* "captures both the subtle ambiance of turn-of-the-century political intrigue and the even more baroque pathways of the human and the inhuman heart." A reviewer in *Publishers Weekly* remarked that Hambly's "vivid portraits" of the vampires "allow them to emerge as memorable personalities distinct from the viewpoints they represent."

Hambly has also ventured into the field of mystery writing. Her first novel in that genre was *A Free Man of Color,* published in 1997. Set in nineteenth-century New Orleans, the book follows the exploits of Benjamin January, a free Creole with dark brown skin. January, a trained surgeon, returns to Louisiana after living in Paris and promptly becomes a murder suspect. Hambly explained in her Barnes and Noble online interview that she did extensive research at the Historic New Orleans Collection in preparation for writing of the book. "I did not think so much about writing in the voice of a black man, as writing in the voice of a historical character from another time and place," she said in an online chat. Hambly's attention to detail paid off handsomely. Marilyn Stasio of the *New York Times Book Review* praised *A Free Man of*

Color as a "stunning first mystery;" Dick Adler of the Chicago *Tribune Books* described it as being "magically rich and poignant." Assessing the author's work, a *Kirkus Reviews* contributor observed that Hambly has a talent for "goldstained description."

In *Fever Season,* the sequel to *A Free Man of Color,* January works at New Orlean's Charity Hospital while city is in the grip of a cholera epidemic. January also realizes that free men of color are disappearing, and his investigations into the matter lead to a horrifying conclusion. According to a *Publishers Weekly* critic, *Fever Season* is "Complex in plotting, rich in atmosphere, and written in powerful, lucid prose." A *Booklist* reviewer called the work "rich, intense, and eye-opening."

Although she juggles a seemingly unbelievable schedule, Hambly prides herself on the professionalism and thoroughness with which she practices her art. Her books go through first, second, and third drafts. Hambly begins her stories by writing a hard copy on a computer, printing it out and then going over it with a pen and rewriting, sometimes large portions, by hand. The technique has served her well. Hambly explained during the Barnes and Noble online chat that if ever she suffers from writer's block—an inability to follow through on her story—she retraces what she has written. She believes that hold-ups in her writing are likely her subconscious telling her that something is not right.

Hambly continues to maintain a hectic pace. She is working on a sequel to *Dragonsbane,* is in the process of writing *Graveyard Dust,* the third book in the Benjamin January mystery series, and she has a new fantasy novel called *Fading of the Light* in the works. Hambly, who divides her time between Los Angeles and New Orleans, shares her two homes with her author-husband, George Alec Effinger, and the couple's two Pekinese cats. Hambly has said that her greatest writing gift is always having a story to tell. As she explained in her Barnes and Noble online interview, "If everyone has one superpower, mine is—thank God and knock on wood—that so far, I seem to have a cast-iron Muse; I seem to be able to work under just about any condition."

BIOGRAPHICAL/CRITICAL SOURCES:

BOOKS

St. James Guide to Fantasy Writers, Gale (Detroit), 1995.

PERIODICALS

Booklist, September 1, 1983, p. 31; July, 1985, p. 1519; April 1, 1995, p. 1355; February 1, 1997, p. 907; May 15, 1998.
Davis Enterprise (CA), October 29, 1995.
Kirkus Reviews, August 1, 1996, p. 1107; May 15, 1997, p. 741; November 15, 1997, p. 1678.
Library Journal, May 15, 1982, p. 1014; March 15, 1983, p. 603; March 15, 1985, p. 599; March 15, 1995, p. 101; August, 1995, p. 122; September 15, 1996, p. 101; June 1, 1997, p. 148.
New Statesman, November 28, 1986, p. 35.
New York Times Book Review, August 2, 1998, p. 24.
Publishers Weekly, March 13, 1995, p. 63; September 4, 1995; September 16, 1996, p. 74; May 5, 1997, p. 197; April 27, 1998, p. 48.
Science Fiction and Fantasy Book Review, September, 1982, pp. 30-31.
Tribune Books (Chicago), July 6, 1997, p. 2.
Voice of Youth Advocates, February, 1986, pp. 393-394; August/October, 1986, p. 162; April, 1989, p. 42; October, 1995, p. 232; August, 1998, p. 210.
Washington Post Book World, January 29, 1989, p. 6.

OTHER

Barnes and Noble Online Chat, http://www.barnes andnoble.com/comm...y_1.asp?userid=5U6D0X F5G8&pcount=0 (January 27, 1999).*

* * *

HARRIS, Lynn 1969-

PERSONAL: Born February 3, 1969, in Boston, MA. *Education:* Yale University, received degree, 1990. *Avocational interests:* Playing ice hockey.

ADDRESSES: Home—New York, NY. *Office*—Just Friends Productions, P.O. Box 150214, Brooklyn, NY 11215. *E-mail*—bg@breakupgirl.com.

CAREER: Comedy performer and writer. Performer in New York City at comedy clubs, including Gotham Comedy Club. Member of women's hockey team, the Brooklyn Blades. Guest on television shows, including *Crook and Chase, Entertainment Extra, Today,* and *USA Live.*

WRITINGS:

(With Larry Berger) *Tray Gourmet: Be Your Own Chef in the College Cafeteria,* illustrations by Chris Kalb, Lake Isle Press, 1992.

(With J. D. Heiman) *MTV's "Singled Out" Guide to Dating,* MTV Books, 1996, Pocket (New York), 1996.

He Loved Me, He Loves Me Not: A Guide to Fudge, Fury, Free Time, and Life beyond the Breakup, illustrations by Chris Kalb, Avon (New York), 1996.

Contributor of articles to periodicals, including *Glamour, Ladies' Home Journal, New York Daily News, Smarty Pants,* and *Time Out New York.*

SIDELIGHTS: Lynn Harris is a comic performer and writer who is known for her humorous observations about male-female relationships. Her writings include two volumes published in 1996: *MTV's "Singled Out" Guide to Dating,* on which she collaborated with J. D. Heiman, and *He Loved Me, He Loves Me Not: A Guide to Fudge, Fury, Free Time, and Life Beyond the Breakup,* a humorous self-help book for women trying to survive the end of a relationship.

BIOGRAPHICAL/CRITICAL SOURCES:

PERIODICALS

Entertainment Weekly, August 2, 1996.*

*   *   *

HARRIS, Ruth Roy 1927-

PERSONAL: Born July 14, 1927, in San Jose, CA; daughter of David Golden (a chiropractor) and Rosa (a teacher; maiden name, Lebrecht) Roy; married Isadore Harris (a physicist), October 9, 1960; children: Jonathan Golden, Geoffrey Roy. *Education:* University of California, Berkeley, A.B. (with honors), 1949; George Washington University, M.A., 1953, Ph.D., 1975. *Avocational interests:* Music, gardening, swimming.

ADDRESSES: Home—Silver Spring, MD.

CAREER: Redding Record-Searchlight, women's editor and reporter, 1949-50; U.S. House of Represen-

tatives, Washington, DC, staff assistant, 1950-51; U.S. Food and Drug Administration, Washington, DC, librarian, 1951-52; Central Intelligence Agency, Washington, DC, intelligence officer, 1953-63; George Washington University, Washington, DC, archivist at university library, 1974-75; contract historian, 1978-79; C & W Associates (historical consultants), research historian, 1980-81; History Associates, Inc., senior historian, 1981-94, director of research, 1992-94; historical consultant, 1994—. Montgomery County Library Board, Montgomery County, MD, member of board of trustees, 1977-85; American Association of University Women, volunteer state historian for Maryland Division, 1985-88; Long Branch Library, chairperson of advisory committee, 1994-95; Concert Society at Maryland, volunteer historian and archivist, 1995—.

MEMBER: Society for History in the Federal Government (chairperson of Archival Concerns Committee, 1984-85), Washington History of Medicine Society, Phi Beta Kappa.

AWARDS, HONORS: Grant from Eleanor Roosevelt Institute, 1974-75; Distinguished Technical Communication Award, Society for Technical Communication, 1990, for *American Contributions to the New Age of Dental Research.*

WRITINGS:

American Contributions to the New Age of Dental Research, National Library of Medicine, 1988.

Dental Science in a New Age: A History of the National Institute of Dental Research, Iowa State University Press (Ames, IA), 1992.

Contributor to books, including *Argonne National Laboratory, 1946-96,* University of Illinois Press (Champaign, IL). Contributor to periodicals, including *Pacific Historical Review, Public Historian,* and *Isis.*

WORK IN PROGRESS: The Changing Face of Dental Science: The National Institute of Dental and Craniofacial Research in the 1980s and 1990s.

SIDELIGHTS: Ruth Roy Harris told *CA:* "I like to write, to hunt for information, to piece together the findings to make a story. As for science—it is important to convey the meaning of scientific research, especially basic, in such a way that the average reader can understand the significance of a particular work."

BIOGRAPHICAL/CRITICAL SOURCES:

PERIODICALS

Journal of Dental Hygiene, March-April, 1993, p. 114.

*   *   *

HASLER, Julie 1963-

PERSONAL: Born May 26, 1963, in Hertford, England; daughter of Wilfred John and Doris Ruby (Woolcott) Croft. *Ethnicity:* "White." *Education:* Attended secondary school. *Politics:* Conservative. *Religion:* Atheist. *Avocational interests:* Nursing and finding homes for stray and abused cats, animal rights and anti-vivisection activities.

ADDRESSES: Home and office—561 Howlands, Welwyn Garden City, Hertfordshire AL7 4HT, England.

CAREER: Review (newspaper), St. Albans, England, pasteup artist, 1978-80; freelance designer, writer, model, and film "extra," 1985—. Welwyn Hatfield Line, bus driver, 1986-87. Lecturer on cross-stitch and needlepoint topics; guest on television and radio programs. Fundraiser for local women's refuge and cats' protection league.

MEMBER: Creative Industries Association, Creative Crafts Association.

WRITINGS:

Cats and Kittens Charted Designs, Dover (New York City), 1986.
Kate Greenaway Alphabet Charted Designs, Dover, 1986.
Peter Rabbit Iron-On Transfer Patterns, Dover, 1987.
Wild Flowers in Cross Stitch, Blandford, 1988.
Dogs and Puppies in Cross Stitch, Blandford, 1988.
Kate Greenaway Cross Stitch Designs, David & Charles (Newton Abbot, England), 1989.
Kate Greenaway Iron-On Transfer Patterns, Dover, 1990.
The Little Tale of Benjamin Bunny, Dover, 1990.
The Little Tale of Tom Kitten, Dover, 1991.
Needlepoint Designs, Blandford, 1991.
Egyptian Charted Designs, Dover, 1992.

Cats and Kittens in Cross Stitch, Cassell, 1992.
Decorative Charted Designs for Children's Clothing and Accessories, Dover, 1993.
Wild Animals in Cross Stitch, Cassell, 1993.
The Crafty Cat Workbasket, David & Charles, 1993.
(With Valerie Janitch) *Five Hundred Cross Stitch Charted Designs,* David & Charles, 1993.
Cuddly Cats and Kittens in Cross Stitch, Merehurst, 1993.
Silhouettes in Cross Stitch, David Porteous, 1993.
Cats: A Cross Stitch Alphabet, David Porteous, 1993.
Teddy Bears in Cross Stitch, Merehurst, 1994.
Christmas in Cross Stitch, Merehurst, 1994.
Julie Hasler's Cross Stitch Designs, Batsford, 1994.
Nursery Cross Stitch, David Porteous, 1995.
Clowns in Cross Stitch, Merehurst, 1996.
Cross Stitch Gifts for Special Occasions, Cassell, 1996.
(With Janitch) *Five Hundred Flower and Animal Charted Designs,* David & Charles, 1996.
Julie Hasler's Cross Stitch Projects, David & Charles, 1996.
Julie Hasler's Fantasy Cross Stitch, Zodiac Signs, Mythical Beasts, and Mystical Characters, David & Charles, 1997.
(With Janitch) *Five Hundred Alphabets in Cross Stitch,* David & Charles, 1998.
Needlepoint Cats, David & Charles, 1998.
Native American Cross Stitch, David & Charles, 1999.

Contributor to needlecraft books, including *The Complete Book of Cross Stitch,* by J. Alford, A. Beezley, and others, Merehurst. Contributor to periodicals, including *Your Cat, Cat World, Popular Crafts, Needlecraft, Beautiful Stitches, Cross Stitcher,* and *Classic Stitches.*

WORK IN PROGRESS: Needlepoint Dogs, for David & Charles; research on dog breeds and history.

SIDELIGHTS: Julie Hasler told *CA:* "I was first introduced to cross-stitch while recovering in hospital from a serious motorcycle accident at the age of sixteen. At eighteen I had my first design published in a monthly craft magazine, and at twenty-one I wrote my first book on the subject."

BIOGRAPHICAL/CRITICAL SOURCES:

PERIODICALS

Baltimore Sun, November 22, 1993.
Cross Stitch, Christmas, 1997.

HAYES, Ellen (Amanda) 1851-1930

PERSONAL: Born September 23, 1851, in Granville, OH; died in 1930; daughter of Charles Coleman (a tanner) and Ruth Rebecca (Wolcott) Hayes. *Education:* Oberlin College, A.B., 1878; studied at McCormick Observatory, University of Virginia, 1887-88.

CAREER: Adrian College, Adrian, MI, principal of women's department, 1878; Wellesley College, Wellesley, MA, teacher of mathematics, 1879-83, associate professor, 1883-88, professor and chair of department of mathematics, 1888-97, professor of applied mathematics and chair of department of applied mathematics, 1897-1904, professor of astronomy, 1904-16.

MEMBER: American Association for the Advancement of Science (fellow), History of Science Society (founding member).

WRITINGS:

Lessons on Higher Algebra, Press of F. I. Brown (Boston), 1891, revised edition 1894.

Elementary Trigonometry, J. S. Cushing (Boston, MA), 1896.

Algebra for High Schools and Colleges, J. S. Cushing (Norwood, MA), 1897.

Calculus with Applications: An Introduction to the Mathematical Treatment of Science, Allyn & Bacon (Boston, MA), 1900.

Letters to a College Girl, G. H. Ellis (Boston, MA), 1909.

Two Comrades, E. L. Grimes (Boston, MA), 1912.

Wild Turkeys and Tallow Candles, The Four Seas Company (Boston, MA), 1920.

How Do You Know? A Handbook of Evidence and Inference, Nation Press Printing Co. (New York City), 1923.

The Sycamore Trail, The Relay, 1929.

Editor, *Relay* (newspaper), c. 1923-30. Contributor of articles to journals and periodicals, including *Science.*

SIDELIGHTS: Ellen Hayes was born on September 23, 1851. Her maternal grandparents, originally from Granville, Massachusetts, founded the small town of Granville, Ohio, in 1805 and it was in their home that Hayes was born. Hayes' grandparents, as well as her parents, would set the stage for her love of learning, career, and political interests.

Hayes' father, Charles Coleman Hayes, made his living as a tanner after serving as an officer in the Civil War. Her mother, Ruth Rebecca (Wolcott), taught all six of her children to read, gave them a smattering of astronomy, and instructed them in botany, supplying them with the names plants in Latin. Both generations, parents and grandparents, believed in education without regard to gender. Hayes' mother had been trained as a teacher and graduated from the Granville Female Academy, a school that enjoyed the support of, and accepted as a trustee, Hayes' grandfather, Horace Wolcott. Although Hayes' father was uneducated, he too encouraged the education of his children.

Hayes left the home instruction supplied by her mother when she was seven and went to the Centerville school. That school had only one room for all levels of instruction and kept no grades. At age sixteen Hayes was herself a teacher at a country school, saving the money she earned to attend college. After entering Oberlin College in 1872 as a preparatory student, Hayes began her college career as a freshman in 1875. Her endeavors mainly centered on the fields of mathematics and science, but she also became well versed in English literature, Greek, Latin, and history. Her mother's introduction to astronomy must have left a lasting impression because Hayes spent time at the Leander McCormick Observatory at the University of Virginia from 1887 to 1888, where she studied the Minor Planet 267, confirming its definite orbit, and producing other important papers on Comet *a* and planetary conic curves.

After graduating from Oberlin with a bachelor of arts degree, Hayes spent a year as the principal of the women's department at Adrian College in Michigan. In 1879 she became a teacher of mathematics at Wellesley College. By 1888 she was a full professor and had assumed the role of chair of the department. In 1897 a department of applied mathematics was created at Wellesley and Hayes took the helm. Her responsibilities included giving instruction in seven levels of applied mathematics.

Although Hayes spent thirty-seven years at Wellesley, the association was often far from congenial because of Hayes' view on education and politics. She was never silent or restrained about either subject. Hayes was adamant about females taking mathematics and science courses and highly critical of the school for allowing students to choose electives that would make it possible for them to evade these studies. Reforms concerning working conditions, politics, and the education of women was something Hayes worked toward all her life. Her views on and support of the union movement and workers rights caused her to receive threats and to be arrested. She closely studied the Russian Revolution of 1917 as it unfolded, writing and speaking openly about the situation. Although Hayes never affiliated herself with the Communist party and disagreed with many of its doctrines, her association with socialist causes did much to brand her a radical and incite serious criticism from Wellesley College. Upon her retirement from Wellesley, Hayes was denied the honorary position of Professor Emeritus usually bestowed on teachers for lengthy and faithful service.

At the age of seventy-two Hayes began her own newspaper. The *Relay* was published monthly and was devoted to giving publicity to facts and movements that Hayes believed were not accurately presented in the mainstream press. Her description of the publication was that "the *Relay* plans to camp in a hut by the side of the road and to keep a lamp or two burning—in the hope of being a friend to wayfarers and especially to the limping Under Dog." Other books written after her retirement include *The Sycamore Trail,* a novel set during the Civil War, and *How Do You Know?,* a book which asks readers to question the origin of their beliefs and superstitions, and study the nature of evidence. Most of Hayes' work was self-published.

Upon her death in 1930, Hayes' brain was donated to the Wilder Brain Collection at Cornell University. The epitaph assigned to her by her friends was her favorite quotation: "It is better to travel hopefully, than to arrive."

BIOGRAPHICAL/CRITICAL SOURCES:

BOOKS

Brown, Louise, *Ellen Hayes: Trail-Blazer,* [West Park, NY], 1932.
Moskol, Ann, *Women of Mathematics: A Biobibliographic Sourcebook,* edited by Louise S. Grinstein and Paul J. Campbell, Greenwood Press (Westport, CT), 1987, pp. 62-66.

PERIODICALS

Scrapbook of the History Department of Mathematics (Wellesley College Archives), 1944, pp. 41-46.
Wellesley Magazine, February, 1931, pp. 151-152.

OTHER

Biographies of Women Mathematicians, http://www.scotlan.edu/lriddle/women/chronol.htm (December, 1998).*

*   *   *

HAYNSWORTH, Leslie   1966-

PERSONAL: Born July 23, 1966, in Greenville, SC; daughter of Harry J. IV (a professor of law) and Patricia (a homemaker; maiden name, Foster) Haynsworth. *Ethnicity:* "White." *Education:* Duke University, A.B., 1988; University of South Carolina, M.A., 1990; University of Virginia, Ph.D., 1999.

ADDRESSES: Home—1401 Woodrow St., Columbia, SC 29205; fax 803-799-2447. *Agent*—David Hendin, DH Literary, Inc., P.O. Box 990, Nyack, NY 10960. *E-mail*—Inhworth@aol.com.

CAREER: University of Virginia, Charlottesville, instructor, 1992-95; Chernoff/Silver and Associates (advertising agency), Columbia, SC, copywriter, 1997-98; Columbia College, Columbia, adjunct assistant professor, 1999.

MEMBER: Modern Language Association of America.

WRITINGS:

(With David Toomey) *Amelia Earhart's Daughter,* Morrow (New York City), 1998.

*   *   *

HENDERSON, Mary C.   1928-

PERSONAL: Born July 16, 1928, in Newark, NJ; daughter of Thomas (in business) and Divina (a homemaker; maiden name, Gionatasio) Malanga; married Robert M. Henderson, February 14, 1953 (divorced, 1983); children: James M., Douglas A., Stuart A. *Education:* Rutgers University, B.A. (with honors); University of Pittsburgh, M.A.; New York University, Ph.D.; also attended Columbia University and

Graduate Center of the City University of New York. *Politics:* "Independent/liberal." *Religion:* None. *Avocational interests:* Sculpture, travel, gardening.

ADDRESSES: Home and office—1 Polly's Lane, Congers, NY 10920-1107; fax 914-268-5767. *Agent*—Fifi Oscard Agency, 24 West 40th St., New York, NY 10018. *E-mail*—ADEM1134@aol.com.

CAREER: Freelance writer. Adelphi University, Garden City, NY, adjunct lecturer in theater and costumer, 1955-60; American University, Washington, DC, lecturer in theater and costumer, 1960-64; William Paterson College of New Jersey, Wayne, assistant professor of speech and theater, 1966-72; Montclair State College, Upper Montclair, NJ, assistant professor of speech and theater, 1973-74; Museum of the City of New York, New York City, assistant curator of theater collection, 1975-77, associate curator, 1977-78, curator, 1978-85; University of Bridgeport, Bridgeport, CT, adjunct faculty member in theater department, 1986-87; Archives for the Performing Arts, San Francisco, CA, executive director, 1987-88; White Barn Theatre Museum, Westport, CT, curator, 1992—.

Pace University, adjunct professor, 1976-77; New York University, adjunct professor, 1976-87; Columbia University, extension lecturer in colonial theater history, 1977; British and American Academy, special lecturer, 1979; Hunter College of the City University of New York, adjunct associate professor, 1983-84, 1987; lecturer at colleges and universities, including Denison University, 1974, Ohio State University, 1977, Institute for Architecture and Urban Studies, 1977, and C. W. Post College of Long Island University, 1985; New York University, member of alumni council, 1991-92.

New York Public Library for the Performing Arts, archivist of Jo Mielziner Collection, 1989-93, and George Becks Theatre Prompbook Collection, 1992-96; British Broadcasting Corp., guest historian, 1993; leader of walking tours for Pace University, Queens College of the City University of New York, Cooper-Hewitt Museum, and Smithsonian Institution; lecturer at museums; exhibition curator; consultant to television producers for programs such as *Sixty Minutes* and *The Best of Families.* City of New York, member of mayor's theater advisory council, 1982-83; York Players, honorary board member, 1982-87; Artsangle, member of advisory board, 1984-88; Theater Hall of Fame, member of executive board, 1992-94; Lucille Lortel Foundation, member of board of directors.

MEMBER: American Society for Theatre Research (member of executive committee, 1986-89), League of Professional Theatre Women (member of board of directors, 1985-89), Theatre Communications Group, Authors Guild, Theatre Library Association, Douglass Society of Distinguished Alumnae, Phi Beta Kappa.

AWARDS, HONORS: Grant from State of New Jersey, 1970; Guggenheim fellow, 1983; George Freedley Memorial Book Award, 1987, for *Theater in America;* National Endowment for the Humanities, travel grant, 1990, fellowship, 1991; grant from Graham Foundation, 1994; Award for Excellence in Theatre Education, Broadway Theatre Institute, 1995.

WRITINGS:

The City and the Theatre, James White (Clifton, NJ), 1973.
Theater in America, Abrams (New York City), 1986, revised edition, 1996.
Broadway Ballyhoo, Abrams, 1989.
(Contributor) Adele Heller and Lois Rudnick, editors, *1915: The Cultural Moment,* Rutgers University Press (New Brunswick, NJ), 1991.
(Contributor) *The Cambridge Guide to the American Theatre,* Cambridge University Press, 1993.
The New Amsterdam: The Biography of a Broadway Theatre, Hyperion (New York City), 1997.
(Contributor) *The Cambridge History of the American Theatre,* Cambridge University Press, 1998.

Author of exhibition catalogs. Contributor of articles and reviews to periodicals, including *Playbill, Architectural Digest, Broadside, New York Times,* and *Variety.* Editor, *Performing Arts Resources,* 1975-80.

WORK IN PROGRESS: Revising *The City and the Theatre; Jo Mielziner and the Theatre of His Time; Miracle on Forty-Second Street: The Ford Center for the Performing Arts;* research on American theater in the 1920s.

SIDELIGHTS: Mary C. Henderson told *CA:* "Fulltime writing is one of several careers I've had in my life. It probably was always there in my quill of potential future endeavors, but I suppose that if I hadn't been forced into earning a living after being 'evacuated' from my last nine-to-five (and then some) job, I would have used it as an adjunct to some other principal livelihood.

"When I started writing in a serious way, I was a college teacher, living in a time of the fiercest publish-or-perish era in American higher education. If my first book, *The City and the Theatre,* established my credentials as a writer, it came out *after* I had left academia—or rather, when teaching itself became an adjunct to another livelihood. My tenure as the curator of the Theatre Collection of the Museum of the City of New York provided many opportunities for writing, since I was responsible for grinding out essays for the exhibition catalogs. Besides, I was writing about my greatest passion, the theater.

"My magnum opus, *Theater in America,* was published in 1986, within a year after I had left my job at the museum. Since then, I have been a freelance writer, completing five books, of which two have been published and the others are awaiting publication at some future date. I have also written a number of articles for periodicals and newspapers and contributed to several anthologies of essays centered on American theater.

"Unfortunately, as interest in live theater in general is declining, so is the market for books and essays on the subject outside of academic walls. They are now a hard sell. If it were not for the support from foundations and special commissions, it is doubtful that I would have survived as a freelance writer working in such a narrow field. In the next few years, I intend to spread my wings a bit and try dramatic writing. We'll see.

"As a nonfiction writer and essayist, I found my god and guide in E. B. White. *Elements of Style* has become laminated to my psyche: I no longer need to consult it. What I learned from White (and a few others) was to concentrate on the rhythm and movement of language, to seek strong and descriptive verbs, to use adjectives and adverbs sparingly, and to think straight before putting a word down on paper.

"Because of what I write about, the writing is always prefaced by many weeks, months, even years of research before I boot up my computer. After I have digested most of what I have discovered on the subject, I spend a good deal of time thinking of what I want to say and how I want to say it. When I have found my starting point and the internal logic of the subject, I begin writing. Each spurt of creation is followed by painstaking self-editing and polishing until I am sure that it is ready for the editors. Then come the agonizing hours of cutting and fixing to please the editors. Finally, the process ends.

"To me, writing appears to be an ageless occupation. I will keep at it until the end of my days—or until I can no longer find anyone to publish my words."

* * *

HENKE, Shirl

PERSONAL: Married, husband's name Jim (a retired English professor); children: a son. *Education:* Received bachelor's and master's degrees (history). *Avocational interests:* Reading, travel, cooking, working in her greenhouse.

ADDRESSES: Office—P.O. Box 72, Adrian, MI 49221. *Agent*—c/o St. Martin's Press, 175 Fifth Ave., New York, NY 10010. *E-mail*—shenke@c4systm.com.

CAREER: Romance novelist. Former teacher at the university level.

AWARDS, HONORS: Romantic Times award nominee, for *Bride of Fortune* and *McCrory's Lady;* Career Achievement nominee for Sensual Historical Romance, *Romantic Times,* 1996-97.

WRITINGS:

ROMANCE NOVELS

Golden Lady, 1986.
Love Unwilling, Warner (New York City), 1987.
Capture the Sun, 1988.
Summer Has No Name, 1991.
Bouquet, NAL-Dutton (New York City), 1994.
A Fire in the Blood, Dorchester (New York City), 1994.
Love a Rebel, Love a Rogue, Dorchester (New York City), 1994.
Broken Vows, Dorchester (New York City), 1995.
McCrory's Lady, Dorchester (New York City), 1995.
Bride of Fortune, St. Martin's Press (New York City), 1996.
The Endless Sky, St. Martin's Press (New York City), 1998.
Sundancer, St. Martin's Press (New York City), 1999.

ROMANCE NOVELS; "GONE TO TEXAS TRILOGY"

Cactus Flower, Warner (New York City), 1988.

Moon Flower, Warner (New York City), 1989.
Night Flower, Warner (New York City), 1990.

ROMANCE NOVELS; "DISCOVERY DUET"

Paradise and More, Dorchester (New York City), 1991.
Return to Paradise, Dorchester (New York City), 1992.

ROMANCE NOVELS; "NIGHT WIND" SERIES

Night Wind's Women, Leisure (New York City), 1991.
White Apache's Woman, Dorchester (New York City), 1993.
Deep as the Rivers, St. Martin's Press (New York City), 1997.

ROMANCE NOVELS; "ROCKY MOUNTAIN" SERIES

Terms of Love, Dorchester (New York City), 1992.
Terms of Surrender, Dorchester (New York City), 1993.

OTHER

Contributor to anthologies, including "Love for Sail," *A Dream Come True,* 1992; "Billy Jo and the Valentine Crow," *Old-Fashion Valentine,* 1993; "Falling in Love," *Secrets of the Heart,* 1994; and *The Topaz Man Presents: A Dream Come True/Five Love Stories,* Topaz, 1994.

SIDELIGHTS: Shirl Henke is the author of numerous historical romance novels, many of which are set in the American west. Her novel *Bride of Fortune* is a Mexican variant of Mark Twain's *The Prince and the Pauper,* in which the American-born illegitimate son of a Mexican landowner meets his wealthy, legitimate brother while they are fighting during the Mexican revolution of the 1860s, and the two change places. A *Publishers Weekly* reviewer noted a couple of "credibility gaps," but stated that they are "offset . . . by passionate love scenes, engaging characters and a well-researched, fast-paced plot."

Henke placed the setting of another of her books farther north. *The Endless Sky,* which features Chase Remington—a half-breed who is torn between his love for a white woman and his Native American roots—exposes the reader to many aspects of life on the frontier. A *Publishers Weekly* reviewer complimented Henke on "the intensity of her writing" and her "thor-

ough research." Among the most interesting passage in *The Endless Sky,* according to the critic, is the account of the battle at Little Bighorn, told from a Native American point of view.

In the novel *Deep as the Rivers,* Henke introduces the character of Colonel Samuel Shelby, who travels into the western wilderness on a secret mission for President James Madison on the eve of the War of 1812. The plot involves a complicated contest of wills between Shelby and the beautiful but headstrong Olivia St. Etienne, whom he has "won" in a gambling contest.

BIOGRAPHICAL/CRITICAL SOURCES:

PERIODICALS

Publishers Weekly, March 25, 1996, p.81; January 13, 1997, p.72; December 1, 1997, p.51.

OTHER

Dorchester Publishing, http://westernbookclub.com (February 8, 1999).
My Unicorn—Shirl Henke Bibliography, http://www.myunicorn.com/bibl6/bibl0632.html (February 8, 1999).
Romance Communications, http://www.romcom.com (February 8, 1999).
Romance Reader, http://www.theromancereader.com (February 8, 1999).
Romantic Times, http://www.romantictimes.com (February 8, 1999).
Under the Covers, http://www.silcom/com/~manatee/henke_endless.html (February 8, 1999).*

*   *   *

HERRICK, Steven 1958-

PERSONAL: Born December 31, 1958, in Brisbane, Australia; son of William (a factory worker) and May (a homemaker; maiden name Clulow) Herrick; married Catherine Gorman (a bank officer); children: Jack Gorman, Joe Gorman. *Education:* University of Queensland, B.A., 1982. *Avocational interests:* "Playing soccer and coaching my sons' soccer team."

ADDRESSES: Office—P.O. Box 116, Hazelbrook, New South Wales 2780, Australia. *Agent*—Glen Leitch

Management, 103 Oxford St., Darlinghurst, New South Wales 2010, Australia.

CAREER: Poet, 1988—.

MEMBER: Poets Union.

AWARDS, HONORS: Shortlisted for Australian Children's Book of the Year for Older Readers, Children's Book Council, 1997, for *Love, Ghosts & Nose Hair.*

WRITINGS:

POETRY; FOR CHILDREN

My Life, My Love, My Lasagne, illustrated by Annmarie Scott, University of Queensland Press, 1997.
Poetry to the Rescue, illustrated by Catherine Gorman, University of Queensland Press, 1998.

PICTURE BOOKS

The Place Where the Planes Take Off, illustrated by Annmarie Scott, University of Queensland Press, 1995.

POETRY; FOR YOUNG ADULTS

Caboolture, Five Islands, 1990.
Water Bombs: A Book of Poems for Teenagers, Jam Roll, 1992; University of Queensland Press, 1995.

NOVELS IN VERSE; FOR YOUNG ADULTS

Love, Ghosts, & Nose Hair, University of Queensland Press, 1996.
A Place like This, University of Queensland Press, 1998.

POETRY; FOR ADULTS

The Esoteric Herrick: Poems & Things, illustrated by Roger Norris, Red Hill, 1982.
The Sound of Chopping, Five Islands, 1994.

WORK IN PROGRESS: The Spangled Drongo, "a verse-novel for children," expected publication in 1999; "an untitled verse-novel for young adults," expected publication in 1999.

SIDELIGHTS: Steven Herrick commented: "I'm a poet. Why? Simple, because I love poetry. I love the power of poetry and the potential of poetry. I've always believed that poetry can talk to an audience or reader in the most concise, direct, and thought-provoking way.

"For the past ten years I've been doing more than two hundred performances per year in schools, clubs, festivals, pubs, and universities throughout the world. I've read to people ages five to eighty-five and have been pleased to see their excited reactions to the spoken word.

"I have a touch of the evangelist in me when it comes to poetry—I want the public to recognize poetry as an enjoyable, entertaining medium. That's why I not only write poetry, but I also read it in front of an audience. I believe writers need to see (and hear) how an audience reacts to their writing. Performing my poetry allows me that luxury.

"And why do I write verse-novels like *Love, Ghosts & Nose Hair* and *A Place like This*? Because everyone kept saying that young adults don't like poetry. And yet I kept performing my work in high schools and enjoying the experience. And the students appeared to enjoy listening and reacting, which led me to the verse-novel format.

"I wanted to write a poetry book that told a story. I wanted a reader to pick it up, start reading, and not be able to say, 'It's just poetry; it doesn't say anything.' So I write verse-novels about teenagers—about the relationships they have with each other and the world. Because I like the immediacy of poetry, I write all the poems in the first person.

"Poetry allows me into the personality of each character—his or her thoughts, emotions, insecurities, and ambitions. The verse-novel form lets me tell the story from a number of perspectives, and, hopefully, with an economy of words. In short, it allows each character to tell the story in his or her own language, from his or her own angle."

One of Herrick's verse-novels, *Love, Ghosts, & Nose Hair,* possesses exactly the writing format that Herrick prefers. A series of first-person poems, the novel looks at how a family copes with the death of a loved one. Each voice examines the loss from its own perspective, like one of several cameras set to catch the same action from its own unique angle.

The predominant perspective belongs to Jack—a sixteen-year-old writer who is preoccupied with sex, sports, and nose hair; but the reader also gets glimpses of Jack as seen from his sister's and father's perspectives. *Magpies* critic Anne Hanzl commented that *Love, Ghosts & Nose Hair*—a "sad, funny, moving, and thoughtful" book . . . will ensure that [Herrick's] audience of young adult and other readers continues to grow."

Herrick continued, reflecting on his hopes for his readers: "One of the great joys I feel in visiting so many schools is talking to children and young adults. I listen to what they say and how they say it. I hope my books reflect some of what I've heard over the years. I hope they get more people of all ages reading poetry and believing that poetry, as a medium, can tell a story as well as prose."

Herrick has shared his enthusiasm for poetry with audiences in Australia, Canada, the United Kingdom, the United States, and Singapore. He is also a frequent guest on live radio shows and has appeared on various Australian television programs. Herrick's writing and performance styles are similar, reported *Sydney Morning Herald* critic Shelli-Anne Couch, in that they are "extraordinarily simple on the surface but spliced with subtle bites and small twists." The straightforward quality common to Herrick's spoken and written word, was also noted by Felicity Norman in *Magpies,* where she wrote that Herrick's writings possess the "directness and immediate impact" required of performance poetry.

With *Water Bombs: A Book of Poems for Teenagers,* Herrick uses his frank style to mark the milestones of two lives in stand-alone poems that collectively reveal the cyclical nature of life. The reader glimpses verbal snapshots of Joe and Debbie's lives—from their own childhood dreams to their hopes for their children. In "almost everyday speech," observed Norman, *Water Bombs* "speaks easily to its audience and will be very popular."

BIOGRAPHICAL/CRITICAL SOURCES:

PERIODICALS

Australian Book Review, June, 1994, p. 53; September, 1998, p. 44.
Magpies, September, 1992, p. 24; July, 1996, p. 33.
Sydney Morning Herald, April 26, 1994, p. 23.*

HILL, David 1942-

PERSONAL: Born June 24, 1942, in Napier, New Zealand; married Elizabeth Smith; children: Peter, Helen. *Education:* Victoria University of Wellington, New Zealand, M.A. (with honors), 1964. *Avocational interests:* Reading, tramping, travelling, "cheering for the All Blacks" (the New Zealand national rugby team).

ADDRESSES: Home—21 Timandra Street, New Plymouth, New Zealand. *E-mail*—dhill@taranaki.ac.nz.

CAREER: High school teacher in New Zealand and England, 1968-82; writer, 1983—. *Military service:* New Zealand Army, 1965-68.

AWARDS, HONORS: AIM Children's Book Merit Award, Booksellers New Zealand, 1993, for *See Ya, Simon,* and 1996, for *Take It Easy;* Special Needs Award, *Times Educational Supplement,* 1995, for *See Ya, Simon;* New Zealand Post Children's Book Merit Award, Booksellers New Zealand, 1997, for *Cold Comfort;* Esther Glen Medal, New Zealand Library Association, 1997, and New Zealand Post Children's Book Merit Award, Booksellers New Zealand, 1998, both for *Fat, Four-Eyed and Useless.*

WRITINGS:

NOVELS; FOR YOUNG ADULTS

See Ya, Simon, Mallinson Rendel (Wellington, New Zealand), 1992, Viking (London, England), 1993, Dutton (New York City), 1994.
Curtain Up, Heinemann (Auckland, New Zealand), 1995.
Kick Back, Ashton Scholastic (Auckland, New Zealand), 1995.
Take It Easy, Mallinson Rendel, 1995, Dutton, 1997.
The Winning Touch, Ashton Scholastic, 1995.
Cold Comfort, Mallinson Rendel, 1996.
Seconds Best, Ashton Scholastic, 1996.
Treasure Deep, Mallinson Rendel, 1997.
Fat, Four-Eyed and Useless, Scholastic New Zealand, 1997.
Comes Naturally, Mallinson Rendel, 1998.
Give It Hoops, Scholastic New Zealand, 1998.
Boots 'n' All, Scholastic New Zealand, 1999.

DRAMA; FOR YOUNG ADULTS

Get in the Act: Three One-Act Plays, Heinemann, 1985.

Ours but to Do: A Two-Act Play for Teenagers, Longman (Auckland, New Zealand), 1986.

A Time to Laugh: A Play for Teenagers, Longman, 1990.

Takes Two, Heinemann, 1995.

Be All Right, New House, 1998.

TEXTBOOKS

On Poetry: Twelve Studies of Work by New Zealand Poets, Heinemann, 1984.

Response to the Short Story, Longman, 1985.

(With Sarah Davey) *Just Write,* Longman, 1989.

English, 2nd edition, Longman, 1992.

Gossip Writing, Wairarapa Education Resource Centre (Masterton, New Zealand), 1993.

(With Christine Ryan) *You Know Something: Research Using the Encyclopedia,* illustrated by Alison Green, Curriculum Concepts (New Plymouth, New Zealand), 1994.

(With Christine Ryan) *Right Number: Research Using the Telephone Book,* illustrated by Eugene Kreisler and Alison Green, Curriculum Concepts, 1994.

(With Christine Ryan) *Having a Word: Research Using the Thesaurus,* illustrated by Brendon Watts, Curriculum Concepts, 1994.

Life on Other Planets, illustrated by Peter Lole, Rainbow Reading Programme (Nelson, New Zealand), 1997.

FOR ADULTS

(With Elizabeth Smither) *The Seventies Connection,* McIndoe (Dunedin, New Zealand), 1980.

Moaville Magic, illustrated by Eric Heath, Hodder & Stoughton (Auckland, New Zealand), 1985.

(With Elizabeth Smither) *Taranaki,* photographs by Jane Dove, Hodder & Stoughton, 1987.

The Boy, illustrated by Chris Slane, Benton Ross (Auckland, New Zealand), 1988.

More From Moaville, Hodder & Stoughton, 1988.

The Year in Moaville, Inprint (Lower Hutt, New Zealand), 1991.

SOUND RECORDINGS

A Bit of a Blow: The Inglewood Tornado: Interviews, Learning Media (Wellington, New Zealand), 1991.

Dairy Farmer: An Interview with a Dairy Farmer, Learning Media, 1992.

Contributor to sound recordings *Grampa's Place: Molestation,* Replay Radio, 1984; *Science Project* (contains "Nightrunner"), Learning Media, 1992; *Some Light on the Problem,* Learning Media, 1992; *Tough Talk,* Learning Media, 1994; *Papaka and Koura* (recorded in Maori), Te Pou Taki Korero (Te Whanganui a Tara, New Zealand), 1995; *Once Bitten,* Learning Media, 1996; *Danger Dog,* Learning Media, 1997; *Double Act* (contains "Moving On"), Learning Media, 1998.

OTHER

Introducing Maurice Gee, Longman, 1981.

(With Christina Calveley) *The New Zealand Family Quiz Book,* Penguin (Auckland, New Zealand), 1982.

(With June Melser) *New Zealand Disasters,* illustrated by John Cole, adapted from *New Zealand Disasters* by Eugene Grayland, Longman, 1983.

The Games of Nanny Miro (picture book for children with parallel text in English and Maori), translated by Irene Curnow, illustrated by June Grant, Moana (Tauranga, New Zealand), 1990.

Having a Word (storybook adaptation of *Having a Word: Research Using the Thesaurus*), illustrated by Brendon Watts, Pinnacle (New Plymouth, New Zealand), 1996.

You Know Something, (storybook adaptation of *You Know Something: Research Using the Encyclopedia*), illustrated by Alison Green, Pinnacle, 1996.

Work represented in several drama anthologies, including "Been There" and "Nice to Know You," *On Stage Book 3: Four Plays for Secondary Schools,* Longman, 1989; "Branches," *Generations: Plays for Young People,* Longman, 1993; "A Day at a Time," *White Lies,* New House (Auckland, New Zealand), 1994. Contributor to periodicals in New Zealand (including *School Journal, Allsorts,* and *Landfall*), Australia, the United Kingdom, and the United States. Work has been published in Australia, Japan, Denmark, Germany, and Holland.

ADAPTATIONS: See Ya, Simon was recorded by Radio New Zealand, 1994, told by Peter Hambleton. *Take It Easy* was recorded by Radio New Zealand, 1996, told by Eryn Wilson.

SIDELIGHTS: An internationally recognized author of juvenile and adult fiction, as well as textbooks, New Zealand native David Hill is perhaps most highly praised for *See Ya, Simon,* his novel for young adults. *See Ya, Simon* chronicles a year in the life of a teenage boy named Simon. Sadly, the year is Simon's last, as he is dying of muscular dystrophy. The story is narrated by Nathan, Simon's compassionate best friend, who accepts Simon's situation and tries to make his last year a memorable one. The two boys have the typical teenage adventures with classmates, teachers, and girls, all the while coping with the realization that Simon will never see adulthood. Although Simon is disabled by his disease, Hill portrays him as well-adjusted, popular, and fun-loving. Several critics have been impressed with the way in which Hill refrains from over-dramatizing the tragedy of Simon's death at such a young age. *School Library Journal* contributor Renee Steinberg observed that "the author avoids a maudlin tone, thus adding to the book's power." A reviewer for *Publishers Weekly* called *See Ya, Simon* "a noble counterpart to weepy melodramas about dying teens." The critic also praised Hill's depiction of Simon and Nathan's relationship, calling the novel "a glowing and memorable tribute to a stalwart, life-affirming friendship." Deborah Stevenson in *Bulletin of the Center for Children's Books* claimed that the book has "enough boyish life and charm to appeal to a far wider audience than would a sentimental dying-by-inches drama." Hill himself noted his tendency to downplay tragedy, commenting: "I like using dialogue, corny jokes, ordinary domestic events. . . . I hate the depression when it won't fit."

Another of Hill's novels for young adults portrays a teenager's attempts at dealing with death. In *Take It Easy,* the main character, Rob, has just lost his mother and as a result is having trouble communicating with his father. In the hope of escaping his problems, Rob goes with five other teenagers on a camping expedition through the New Zealand bush country. The trip turns into a disaster when the group's guide dies and the kids must fend for themselves, dealing with bad weather and injuries as they try to make it back home. Critics lauded Hill's use of realism in this novel. A *Kirkus Reviews* contributor observed that "every brush with danger . . . is so vivid that . . . readers will feel as wrung out as if they've actually been along for the ride." Tracy Taylor noted in a *School Library Journal* review that "The emotions of these young people are realistically developed." In a *Booklist* review, Chris Sherman called *Take It Easy* "a fast-paced story with credible teen characters."

Hill turned to more light-hearted themes with two sports novels, *Seconds Best* and *Give It Hoops. Seconds Best* follows the story of a group of high-school cricket players who start off as the underdogs, but, with the help of an enthusiastic teacher, make their

way to the regional championships. In a *Magpies* review, Kevin Steinberger declared that in this book, "young cricketers—boys and girls—will quickly find themselves and familiar experiences and dilemmas." In *Give It Hoops,* the high school senior basketball team in a small rural community has barely enough players and a coach with a bad attitude. The team's adventures make for what a *Reading Time* reviewer called "a rattling good basketball story: brutal, honest, well-researched, well paced and well written."

Hill commented: "I'm a very timetabled writer. I try to work very regular hours—8:30 a.m. to 3:30 p.m., five days a week, plus an hour each evening. I make huge numbers of notes before I start, because I like to have details worked out in advance. In spite of this, I always change my mind as I write—writing is a process of discovery.

"I like writing about fears and embarrassments; I reckon that these are common ground which we all recognise, and I believe that writing anything which gives you that 'I know that' response is likely to be effective.

"I like writing for kids and teenagers because they're such a truthful audience. They recognise padding and boring bits very quickly, and they keep you on your toes."

BIOGRAPHICAL/CRITICAL SOURCES:

PERIODICALS

Booklist, September 1, 1997, pp. 105-106.
Bulletin of the Center for Children's Books, September, 1994, pp. 13-14; June, 1997, p. 360.
Junior Bookshelf, August, 1993, p. 153.
Kirkus Reviews, May 15, 1997, p. 801.
Magpies, March, 1997, pp. 33-34.
Publishers Weekly, June 6, 1994, p. 66.
Reading Time, May, 1998, p. 33.
School Librarian, November, 1993, p. 153; July, 1994, p. 116; June 1997, p. 118.*

*   *   *

HOLBROOK, Teri

PERSONAL: Born in Atlanta, GA; married Bill Holbrook (syndicated cartoonist); children: two. *Edu-*

cation: College of William and Mary, graduated with degree in linguistics and anthropology. *Avocational interests:* Pottery.

ADDRESSES: Home—Atlanta, GA. *Agent*—c/o Bantam Books, 1540 Broadway, New York, NY 10036-4094. *E-mail*—BTHolbrook@compuserve.com.

CAREER: Mystery novelist. Former journalist. Has spoken or made appearances at the University of Georgia, Emory University, Cluefest, Malice Domestic, Bouchercon, Sleuthfest, Southeastern Booksellers Association, and the Houston SinC conference. Community liaison for C.O.P.S., a crime prevention program.

MEMBER: Sisters in Crime, Women's National Book Association, Mystery Writers of America.

AWARDS, HONORS: Georgia Press Association Award for Best Feature Writing; (with others) Penney-Missouri Award runner-up; Agatha Award nomination, Anthony Award nomination, Macavity Award nomination, and Georgia Author of the Year Award nomination, all 1996, all for *A Far and Deadly Cry;* Edgar Award nomination for Best Paperback Original, Anthony Award nomination for Best Paperback Original, Agatha Award nomination for Best Novel, and Macavity Award nomination for Best Novel, all 1997, all for *The Grass Widow.*

WRITINGS:

A Far and Deadly Cry, Bantam (New York City), 1995.
The Grass Widow, Bantam (New York City), 1996.

Contributor of the short story "Both Feet" to the anthology *Murder They Wrote II,* edited by Beth Foxwell. Contributor and editor, with Toni P. Kelner, D. R. Meredith, Marlys Millhiser, Deborah Adams, Elizabeth Daniels Squire, Charlaine Harris, to "The Femmes Fatales," a bi-annual newsletter.

WORK IN PROGRESS: Sad Water, a novel set in West Yorkshire, England, for Bantam Books, expected in 1999.

SIDELIGHTS: Teri Holbrook's *A Far and Deadly Cry,* is her first novel in a mystery series featuring Gale Grayson, an Atlanta native living in England. Grayson's husband, an accused terrorist, commits suicide, leaving her pregnant with their daughter. Three years later, when the babysitter is killed, the Scotland Yard inspector who had been investigating Grayson's husband investigates the babysitter's death. Grayson probes the facts behind the murder as she becomes suspect in connection with the crime. Marvin Lachman wrote for *Armchair Detective,* that Holbrook handled well the "prickly relationship" which develops between Grayson and Inspector Halford "showing the shifting uncertainties of human interaction. . . . Holbrook is also good at dialogue and displays a knack for presenting highly dramatic confrontations."

Holbrook's second novel in the series, *The Grass Widow,* takes place in Statlers Cross, Georgia. Gale Grayson, returned to her birthplace, is writing a book on southern women. She gets caught up in the legend of Linnie Cane, who, in 1925, hung herself from the pecan tree in her yard. When Linnie's minister grandson is murdered, Grayson delves into the family secrets that have haunted the town since Linnie's death. Shirley Gibson Coleman, in *Library Journal,* called the book "well-written and fast-moving." A reviewer for *Publishers Weekly* commented positively on Holbrook's "stellar telling."

BIOGRAPHICAL/CRITICAL SOURCES:

BOOKS

Heising, Willetta L., *Detecting Women 2,* Purple Moon Press (Dearborn, MI), 1996.

PERIODICALS

Armchair Detective, spring, 1996, p. 174.
Library Journal, November 15, 1996, p. 88.
Publishers Weekly, November 4, 1996, p. 70.

OTHER

The Femmes Fatales, http://members.aol.com/femmesweb (February 5, 1999).
Mystery Author Teri Holbrook, http://members.aol.com/altsinc/tholbrook (February 5, 1999).
Writers Write, http://www.writerswrite.com/journal/dec97/yeatts.htm (February 5, 1999).*

*   *   *

HOLMES, Donald J. 1924-
(Don Joseph)

PERSONAL: Born June 9, 1924, in Columbus, OH; son of George Wilbur (in business) and Katharine (a homemaker; maiden name, Conard) Holmes; married Paula Schatzman (an architect); children: Robb, Todd. *Ethnicity:* "Anglo." *Education:* Ohio State University, B.A. and M.D.; University of Michigan, M.Sc. *Politics:* Independent. *Religion:* Independent. *Avocational interests:* Reading, writing.

ADDRESSES: Home and office—Tucson, AZ. *E-mail*—paulaaia@aol.com.

CAREER: Board-certified neuropsychiatrist, 1947—; physician, 1952—. University of Michigan, Ann Arbor, member of medical school faculty, 1955-69; visiting professor; lecturer in the United States and abroad. *Military service:* U.S. Merchant Marine and U.S. Marine Corps Reserve, 1943-46.

WRITINGS:

The Adolescent in Psychotherapy, Little, Brown (Boston, MA), 1964.
Psychotherapy, Little, Brown, 1972.
(Under pseudonym Don Joseph) *Skinnerball!* (novel), Vantage (New York City), 1978.
Illuminati Conspiracy: The Sapiens System (novel), New Falcon Press, 1985.

WORK IN PROGRESS: Angels in the Wings, a nonfiction work; *An Unholy Trinity,* a murder mystery, for 1stBooks Library (Bloomington, IN); *Double Feature in Paradise,* a play; *Storm Port,* a novel.

SIDELIGHTS: Donald J. Holmes told *CA:* "I'm a physician specializing in the practice of psychiatry, with more than forty years of experience. In the past I've done a lot of lecturing, with better than sixty visiting professorships and invitational lectures here and abroad. I have written most of my life and am still writing, with hope for further successes ever burning. Closest to my heart is the nonfiction work, *Angels in the Wings,* which I can't reasonably publish until the copyright of an earlier book of similar content reverts to me."

*   *   *

HOOK, Geoffrey R(aynor) 1928-
(Jeff Hook)

PERSONAL: Born December 27, 1928, in Hobart, Tasmania, Australia; son of Marryat Raynor (a picture framer) and Violet Beatrice (a teacher; maiden name, McSherry) Hook; married Pauline Beryl Lowe (a teacher), May 6, 1961; children: David, Brendan, Martin, Warwick, Sarah. *Education:* Hobart Technical College, Diploma of Commercial Art, 1953. *Religion:* Roman Catholic. *Avocational interests:* Cycling.

ADDRESSES: Home and office—2 Montana St., Glen Iris, Victoria 3146, Australia.

CAREER: Davies Brothers Ltd., Hobart, Australia, press artist, 1951-64; *Herald and Weekly Times,* Melbourne, Australia, editorial cartoonist, 1964-93, editorial cartoonist for *Sunday Herald-Sun,* 1993—. Work represented in international cartoon collections, corporate collections in Australia, and in the collection of political cartoons at the National Museum of Australia, Canberra. Royal Victorian Institute for the Blind, life member of board of governors, 1991—; City of Boroondara, member of planning committee for cultural facilities, 1993-94, and environmental strategy planning committee, 1994-95. Xavier College Foundation, member, 1973-85.

MEMBER: Australian Guild of Realist Artists, Illustrators Association of Australia, Australian Black and White Artists' Club, Melbourne Press Club (life member; past president).

AWARDS, HONORS: Award for humorous illustration, Australian Black & White Club Bulletin, 1981; International Cartoon Festival, award for best political cartoon, 1987, and Press Award, best political cartoon, 1991; nominated for Children's Book of the Year, Children's Book Council of Australia, 1998, for *Jamie the Jumbo Jet;* named to master list, Young Australian Best Book Awards, for *The Superoo of Mungalongaloo.*

WRITINGS:

AUTHOR AND ILLUSTRATOR, UNDER NAME JEFF HOOK

Jamie the Jumbo Jet, Wren (Melbourne, Australia) 1971.
Hook Book: Cartoons by Jeff of the Sun, Herald and Weekly Times (Melbourne), 1978.
The Hook Book, No. 2, Herald and Weekly Times, 1979.
The Penguin Hook, Penguin Australia, 1984.
The Laugh's on Us: Cricket's Finest Tell Their Funniest, Swan Publishing (Byron Bay, Australia), 1989.
Ashes: Battles and Bellylaughs, Swan, 1990.

More Laughs on Us, Swan, 1991.
Just for Kicks, Swan, 1992.
Look Who's Laughing Now, Swan, 1995.

AUTHOR AND ILLUSTRATOR, UNDER NAME GEOFFREY HOOK

(With David Rankine), *Kangapossum and Crocoroo,* Heinemann (Milsons Point, NSW, Australia), 1969.

Other self-illustrated books include *Boom, Bust, and Polka Dots,* 1992.

ILLUSTRATOR, UNDER NAME JEFF HOOK

Harvey E. Ward, *Down Under without Blunder: Guide to the English Spoken in Australia, with a Random Sample of Australian Words and Phrases, and Translations of Some Australian Pronunciations,* Tuttle (Rutland, VT), 1967.
Stan Marks, *Animal Olympics,* Wren, 1972.
Osmar White, *The Superoo of Mungalongaloo,* Wren, 1973.
Don Burnard, *Towards a Life of Loving: Preparing for Marriage,* Hill of Content, (Melbourne), 1975.
Keith Dunstan, *It's All Up Hill,* Pegasus Books (Melbourne), 1979.
Burnard, *Towards a Life of Loving: Pre-Marriage Education,* Hill of Content, 1980.
Lou Richards and Tom Prior, *The Footballer Who Laughed,* Hutchinson of Australia, 1981.
O. White, *The Further Adventures of Dr. A. A. A. McGurk, M.D.,* Puffin Australia, 1981.
John Clifford White and William K. Halliwell, *Dole Bludger's Handbook,* Sun, 1983.
O. White, *McGurk and the Lost Atoll,* Puffin Australia, 1983.
Joan Weaver and Feyne Weaver, *Everyman's Guide to—Down Under,* Rigby (New York City), 1984.
Lorraine Wilson, *Sydney Swans,* Nelson (Melbourne), 1984.
Wilson, *Melbourne,* Nelson, 1984.
Wilson, *Richmond,* Nelson, 1984.
Wilson, *Carlton,* Nelson, 1984.
Desmond Zwar, *Golf: The Dictionary,* Sun, 1984.
Richards, *The Footballer Who Laughed Again,* Hutchinson, 1986.
Doug Walters, *One for the Road,* Swan, 1988.
Maureen Stewart, *Tall Tales from the Speewah: Australian Stories That Are Bigger and Better,* Puffin Australia, 1988.

Jane Fraser, *Plainly Jane: Best Bits from "The Australian" Weekly Column,* Sun, 1988.
June Factor, compiler, *Ladies and Jellyspoons: Favourite Riddles and Jokes of Australian Children,* Puffin Australia, 1989.
Alan Veitch, *Horses Don't Bet on People,* Random House Australia, 1991.
Rod Marsh, *Two for the Road,* Swan, 1992.
Ken Piesse, *Just for Kicks, Two,* Swan, 1994.
Brendan Hook, *Harry the Honkerzoid,* Penguin Australia, 1997.
B. Hook, *Planet of the Honkerzoids,* Puffin Australia, 1998.

WRITTEN BY KEITH DUNSTAN; PUBLISHED BY SUN BOOKS

Footy: An Aussie Rules Dictionary, 1983.
A Cricket Dictionary, 1983.
Tennis: A Dictionary, 1984.
Racing: The Horse-Racing Dictionary, 1985.
Health and Fitness: The Dictionary, 1985.
Wine: The Wine Dictionary, 1985.
Hook, Line, and Sinker: The Dictionary, 1986.
Bowls: The Lawn Bowls Dictionary, 1986.
Skiing: The Skiing Dictionary, 1987.

SIDELIGHTS: Geoffrey R. Hook commented: "I was born in Tasmania. As a cadet press artist on the *Hobart Mercury,* I completed a course in graphic art at the Hobart Technical College. I started my career as a press artist and part-time cartoonist on the *Hobart Mercury,* moved to Melbourne and started at the *Sun News Pictorial* (later to become the *Herald-Sun*), in 1964.

"I was very fond of adapting my career as a cartoonist to amuse my five children. The illustration of *Kangapossum and Crocoroo* was my first involvement. I was also making up bedtime stories, often told in the dark. It was following a visit to Boeing's huge plant at Everett, Washington, that *Jamie the Jumbo Jet* came into my mind. The children enjoyed the story so much that I decided to illustrate it, and it was first published in 1971.

"When writing and illustrating, I hope to entertain children and provide them with a love and enjoyment of reading. In my drawing, I aim for accuracy and humor. *Jamie the Jumbo Jet* is an example of my working method—I first drew the illustrations. Next came the adaptation of my oral narrative into the written form—rather like captions on a cartoon. When illustrating other people's work I confer with the author, the publisher, and the designer of the book, and illustrate key situations accordingly. I have to feel in tune with the stories I illustrate. Music is always part of my working environment.

"I have traveled widely in the course of my work, including visits to the United Kingdom, Europe, the United States, Vietnam (during that war), and China. I am fond of cycling for relaxation. I rode across the Rockies in the United States during the celebration of the United States bicentennial. I rode from Melbourne to Sydney in 1988, as part of our own bicentennial celebrations, and took part in the Eleventh Anniversary Great Victorian Bikeride in 1994."*

*   *   *

HOOK, Jeff
   See HOOK, Geoffrey R(aynor)

*   *   *

HOWARD, Linda 1950-
   (Linda S. Howington)

PERSONAL: Born August 3, 1950, in Gadsden, AL; married Gary F. Howington.

ADDRESSES: Home—116 Louise Avenue, Gadsden, AL 35903. *Agent*—Robin Rue, Anita Diamant Agency, 310 Madison Ave, New York, NY 10017.

CAREER: Bowman Transportation, Gadsden, AL, secretary, 1969-86. Romance novelist, beginning c. early 1980s.

WRITINGS:

All That Glitters, Silhouette (New York City), 1982.
An Independent Wife, Silhouette, 1982.
Against the Rules, Silhouette, 1983.
Come Lie with Me, Silhouette, 1984.
Tears of the Renegade, Silhouette, 1985.
Sarah's Child, Silhouette, 1985.
The Cutting Edge, Silhouette, 1985.
Midnight Rainbow, Silhouette, 1986.
MacKenzie's Mountain, Silhouette, 1989.
A Lady of the West, Pocket Books (New York City), 1990.

Duncan's Bride, Silhouette, 1991.
Angel Creek, Pocket Books, 1991.
The Touch of Fire, Pocket Books, 1992.
MacKenzie's Mission, Silhouette, 1992.
Heart of Fire, Pocket Books, 1993.
Dream Man, Pocket Books, 1995.
After the Night, Pocket Books, 1995.
Shades of Twilight, Pocket Books, 1996.
Son of the Morning, Pocket Books, 1997.
Kill and Tell, Pocket Books, 1997.

"SARAH'S CHILD" SERIES

Almost Forever, Silhouette, 1986.
Bluebird Winter, Silhouette, 1987.

"MIDNIGHT RAINBOW" SERIES

Diamond Bay, Silhouette, 1987.
Heartbreaker, Silhouette, 1987.
White Lies, Silhouette, 1988.

SIDELIGHTS: Since 1982 Linda Howard has been publishing romance novels regularly, sometimes as many as three in one year. Her works have included stand-alone novels set in the current day, novels in a series, and romance novels that cross into the historical and the science fiction genres.

Howard is known for being able to develop interesting and believable characters, from heroes and heroines to the minor characters who share in the story. According to Barbara E. Kemp, a writer for *Twentieth-Century Romance and Historical Writers,* Howard's heroes and heroines, while fulfilling the expectations of her genre, do not "degenerate into romance stereotypes."

An overview of her novels and some of their reviews give a sense of the breadth of Howard's work as well as its reception. Her debut novel, *All That Glitters,* is set in the cut-throat boardrooms and file cabinet-lined halls of the business world, as are the "Sarah's Child" series including *Almost Forever,* and *The Cutting Edge.* In *All That Glitters,* the hero, Nikolas Constantinos, is powerfully drawn to Jessica Stanton, the woman whom he makes his mistress; at the same time he despises what he mistakes as her gold-digger marriage to a wealthy older man. This leads him to manipulate her into giving up her stockholdings to him, and to hate himself for loving her.

This pattern of a hero who cannot help loving a woman whose fatal flaws are actually only the result of false information or misunderstandings repeats itself in a number of Howard's books. "Their attempts," wrote Kemp of Howard's heroes, "to manipulate and even dominate their women lead to deep rifts in their relationships that are difficult to heal." This creates the tension in many of Howard's novels. In the "Sarah's Child" series also set in the world of high finance, Rome Matthews weds Sarah, but does not want to share her with any offspring. After she becomes pregnant he threatens to have nothing to do with the child. In *Almost Forever* (the second novel in the "Sarah's Child" series), Rome's second-in-command, Max Conroy, beguiles Claire Westbrook in order to take over the business she has been so indispensable to. And in *The Cutting Edge,* Brett Rutland, who cannot stay away from Tessa Conway, also cannot help but emotionally brutalize her because he has reason to think she has stolen company funds.

In the "Midnight Rainbow" series of books, including *Diamond Bay, Heartbreaker,* and *White Lies,* the venue shifts to the dark world of government undercover agents, where the need for constant cover-ups and subterfuges makes male-female misunderstandings all the more unavoidable. The main action in "Midnight Rainbow" is set in Central America, where the hero, Grant Sullivan, has been called out of retirement to find and save the heroine, Jane Greer, from rebel forces. In *Diamond Bay* Kell Sabin, Grant Sullivan's supervisor, takes central stage; this time the heroine, Rachel Jones, does the saving when she aids and then tends Sabin's wounds after a violent exchange with the enemy, thus putting herself in grave danger. *White Lies* lives up to its title by involving its hero, Jay Granger, in a "deadly charade to trap a dangerous criminal," commented Kemp. "These men, living in the shadows, find it difficult to admit their need of anyone, which makes their developing relationships even more tenuous," wrote Kemp.

As the 1980s rolled toward the 1990s, Howard's venue began to shift toward the nineteenth-century wild West. One of her early ventures in this arena is *A Lady of the West.* The story follows Victoria Waverly, an aristocratic daughter of the Old South who must marry a roughhousing New Mexican cattle rancher, Frank McLain, in order to help her family restore its credit and good name after the ravages of the Civil War. Victoria has much to resent in the manners and character of her new husband; little does she know that others hold grudges against him as well. The Sarratt boys, sons of the former owner of McLain's ranch, have returned twenty years after McLain murdered their father to take their revenge.

But McLain's recent marriage to Victoria poses problems for the Sarratts: McLain's death will result in her inheritance. The fact that Jake Sarratt has fallen in love (and most decidedly in lust) with Victoria complicates matters even further—either she must be convinced to marry him or he must end her life as well. A *Publishers Weekly* reviewer enjoyed the sweeping momentum of the plot, especially when the "mostly likable protagonists are caught up in intrigue and sheer survival." But the reviewer felt that the book's romantic element interrupted its momentum with "ordinary lovers' spats."

Angel Creek followed not long behind *Lady of the West;* it tells the story of Dee Swann, a Colorado homesteader who doesn't welcome suitors or ranchers who want to water their cattle at her creek, one of the few dependable water supplies in the area. Her attitude about suitors begins to change however, when Lucas Cochran, who inherits the neighboring farm, enters her life. Dee soon finds herself hobbled by an accident and must turn to Lucas for aid. Their proximity lends heat to their attraction for each other, "[b]ut as the relationship blossoms, the land withers in a dry spell" that increases the attraction of the local ranchers for Angel Creek. A *Publishers Weekly* reviewer found Howard's characters "engaging," but the novel "otherwise routine."

Howard's next novel moved further west, to the 1870s Arizona Territory. In *The Touch of Fire,* Howard's heroine, Annie Parker, practices medicine in Silver Mesa, where she is the only doctor for many miles around. But before long she is forced onto the trail, having been kidnapped by outlaw Rafe McCay, whose gunshot wound she has been brought along to treat as he hurries to avoid bounty hunters. Although bad times have hardened Rafe, prolonged proximity to Annie begins to gentle his cold heart, as is evidenced by his willingness to face death along with Annie as she tarries in an Apache village trying to save lives after an epidemic outbreak. "Minimal tension" as a result of encounters with bounty hunters "leads to the maximal tension of myriad graphic sexual encounters," wrote the *Publishers Weekly* reviewer, who was moved by the segment in the Apache Village but not otherwise overly impressed with the novel.

According to Kemp, *Heart of Fire* signaled a new direction for Howard's work. This novel relates the story of Jillian Sherwood, an archeologist who is determined to save her archeologist father's reputation and her own by finding a lost city of Amazonian women her father believed existed in the deep South

American jungle. Armed with her father's map and her own iron will, Jillian is accompanied by Rick, her half-brother, Steven Kates, a financial backer looking for valuables to rob, and Ben Lewis, their jungle guide. At first, wrote Kemp, the character of Lewis appears "to be . . . [a] typical lonewolf [hero]." However, Kemp noted, important differences, including the bantering tone that Ben and Jillian engage in, add humor to the novel without detracting from its romantic or adventurous elements. Jillian is not a typical Howard heroine either: instead of 'patiently wait[ing] for Ben to accept her love,' "[s]he is in charge and in control." A *Publishers Weekly* critic panned *Heart of Fire,* taking issue with the "charmed lives" the characters seemed to lead, facing the most dangerous and life-threatening situations without losing a night's sleep, let alone a life. As a result, wrote the critic for *Publishers Weekly,* the book lacks real suspense.

Howard took yet another direction in her novel *Dream Man,* a tale of murder and psychic events. Here she teams hard-boiled Orlando police detective Dane Hollister with a young woman who volunteers information about a serial killer after having dreamed the murders from the killer's viewpoint and seen the grisly details through his eyes. Hollister is instantly suspicious of her crackpot claims, and Marlie Keen, the psychic "witness," regrets ever having volunteered her assistance after her psychic abilities are met with mockery and doubt. The characters, however, cannot deny their attraction to each other. Dane Hollister is the ideal foil, as well as partner to Marlie. Marlie convinces Dane to give her approach a chance, and after she confirms several key facts of the murders he begins to believe in her gift. A *Publishers Weekly* reviewer was also convinced, declaring that Howard has researched "the procedure used to develop a serial killer's profile and brings this process cinematically alive." The critic called *Dream Man* "Howard's best work yet." A contributor to *Library Journal* concurred, noting "this sensual, suspenseful . . . story succeeds in blending a number of romance genres."

Howard's *After the Night* is a sexy Southern romance, full of gothic hints of murder, revenge, and class tension. The families at war are the "dirt-poor" Devlins and the powerful, old-money Rouillards of Louisiana. The heroine, Faith Devlin, has returned to the Southern town from which her family was forcefully evicted after Gray Rouillard discovered what looked like the elopement of Faith's mother Renee and Gray's father Guy. With no resources, the four-

teen-year-old Faith was forced to try to heal her dying baby brother on her own, and her failure has made revenge upon Gray and the Rouillards a sweet dream for her. Her desires are conflicted, however, because her youthful passion for Gray has not been diminished by the years of anger and distance. *Publishers Weekly* found the protagonists of this steamy Southern tale unsympathetic, but noted that "provocative secondary characters and borderline erotica" compensate for this, "creating a sexy speed read."

Shades of Twilight (1997) offers another Southern gothic, this time set in Alabama with its focus on intrigue within a wealthy family. The heroine, Roanna Davenport, is an orphan whose shy and unpolished nature has aggravated her relatives' cool feelings toward her. Her only champion is her cousin, Webb Tallant. She develops an enormous crush on him, but her dreams of love are shattered when he marries another cousin, Jessie. Jessie is killed shortly after the wedding, and Webb leaves the estate. Ten years later he returns at the request of his dying great-aunt Lucinda. Tensions run high as a result of Lucinda's idea to make Webb her heir, and over the unsolved murder of Jessie for which many hold Webb responsible. The romance between Webb and Roanna kindles quickly into flame, but not everyone is so well disposed toward him. In fact, he is being stalked by someone bent on murdering him. *Library Journal* called *Shades of Twilight* "Southern Gothic at its steamiest." Roanna and Webb need "a good shaking," deemed *Publishers Weekly,* "as they misinterpret each other's actions to excess." The review acknowledged Howard's ability to keep the flame high under the romance and the plot tense and exciting.

Published at nearly the same time as the genre-conforming *Shades of Twilight, Son of the Morning* takes a real genre-bending turn. The story involves a translator of ancient scripts, Grace St. John, whose husband and brother are killed by the Foundation, a no-good organization bent on stealing ancient treasures that only Grace can help them find. The story takes a real leap when Grace discovers a way to transport herself back to the fourteenth century and into the arms of Niall of Scotland, of whom she has been having passionate dreams that now can be realized. Niall, as a member of the Knights Templar and as a Guardian of the Treasure, is linked directly to the holy objects the Foundation wants to attain. *Publishers Weekly* gave the book a mixed review, faulting "a heroine whose actions defy credibility" and a slow-paced plot, but appreciating its "fascinating premise . . . gripping passages and steamy sex."

Quill and Quire enjoyed the "cross-over into historical fantasy."

In early 1998 Howard published *Kill and Tell*. Set mainly in New Orleans, this present-day romance places nurse Karen Whitlaw in the center of a deadly intrigue that hinges on a package sent to her by a father she barely knows, and which she puts away unopened. When her father is murdered a few months later, Karen is called to New Orleans by detective Marc Chastain, who awakens long-forgotten desires in her. But she is also identified by her father's murderers, who will stop at nothing to obtain the contents of that mysterious package. A reviewer for *Publishers Weekly* put Howard at the top of her game with this thriller-romance. Comparing this work to past novels, the review applauded Howard's writing talent and, in this novel, her deft handling of the plot line and minor characters.

BIOGRAPHICAL/CRITICAL SOURCES:

BOOKS

Twentieth-Century Romance and Historical Writers, third edition, St. James Press (Detroit), 1994.

PERIODICALS

Library Journal, May 15, 1995, p. 60; February 15, 1997, p. 184.
Publishers Weekly, August 10, 1990, p. 437; October 4, 1991, p. 84; August 24, 1992, p. 76; June 21, 1993, p. 102; May 1, 1995, p. 51; October 16, 1995, p. 54; May 27, 1996, p. 76; February 10, 1997, p. 81; December 15, 1997, p. 54.
Quill and Quire, May, 1997, p. 17.*

* * *

HOWINGTON, Linda S.
See HOWARD, Linda

* * *

HUBBARD, Bill
See HUBBARD, William M.

HUBBARD, William M. 1954-
    (Bill Hubbard)

PERSONAL: Born August 16, 1954, in Albuquerque, NM; son of Jim and Lorraine Hubbard; married, wife's name Debbie J. (a property manager), 1985. *Ethnicity:* "Anglo." *Education:* McMurry College, B.A., 1976; Oral Roberts University, graduate study, 1976-79. *Politics:* Republican. *Religion:* Christian. *Avocational interests:* Marathon running, mountain biking, cross-country skiing.

ADDRESSES: Home and office—P.O. Box 593, Red River, NM 87558; fax 505-754-6679. *E-mail*—rr4 marsh@yahoo.com. *Agent*—Wanda Evans, 4601 50th St., Suite 100, Lubbock, TX 79412.

CAREER: Lubbock Police Department, Lubbock, TX, homicide sergeant, 1979-95; Red River Marshal's Office, Red River, NM, deputy marshal, 1995—. New Mexico Office of the Medical Investigator, deputy medical investigator, 1996—. Texas Commission on Law Enforcement, certified master peace officer, 1995; New Mexico Department of Public Safety, certified executive peace officer, 1998. Women's Protective Services, Lubbock, vice president, 1984-88.

MEMBER: Police Management Association, Sigma Tau Delta.

AWARDS, HONORS: Named officer of the year, Lubbock Optimist Club, 1985; Law Enforcement Officer Courage and Integrity Award, MacArthur Justice Center, Washington, DC, 1994.

WRITINGS:

(Under name Bill Hubbard) *Substantial Evidence* (nonfiction), New Horizon Press (Far Hills, NJ), 1998.

WORK IN PROGRESS: The Race Card, a true story of a racially motivated hate crime; *Texas Lawman,* an autobiography.

SIDELIGHTS: William M. Hubbard told *CA:* "I realize that a cop with an English degree is a dangerous combination. Bearing that in mind, I try to find true crime stories which have some historical significance, as well as some universal appeal. In writing *Substantial Evidence,* I felt that both of these conditions had been met, plus it was a painfully true story that had happened to me. When I sat down and began writing, my greatest motivation was that I believed the people in Texas had a right to know the *whole* story about what had happened in their midst. It had been covered on a daily basis by a wide variety of newspapers, but there were still gaps as opposing sides sought to put their own spin on the story in the media.

"In learning to write and (more importantly) having a love for writing, I am still largely influenced by my writing professor in college, Dr. Joyce Armstrong Carroll, who now directs the New Jersey Writing Project in Texas. She not only teaches, but also imparts passion to her students. I truly am fortunate to have studied with her.

"I also try to read a lot of other writers who are successful in this genre, and I still enjoy most everything written by Joseph Wambaugh. The fact that he was a real cop before he became a successful writer leads me to believe that I have a bit of identity with him. However, only a few of Wambaugh's books have been nonfiction, which is the area where I am concentrating at present.

"In order to write true crime, an immense amount of compilation and research must take place before the writing begins. I find that I can poke along for months compiling and organizing my sources without feeling much pressure. When the writing actually begins, however, I turn into a total maniac, shutting out the whole world for weeks as I do nothing but get an initial draft down on paper. Once that is done, I am able to back off and be in a less obsessive mode for the editing and rewriting that make the manuscript ready to find a publisher.

"Little did I know when I headed into a law enforcement career over twenty years ago that I was building a stockpile of material for what would later become my writings. Once I have been able to write the most compelling of these stories, I hope to use the leftover incidents, characters, and situations to try my hand at police fiction."

*   *   *

HUFFMAN, Jennifer Lee 1950-

PERSONAL: Born December 26, 1950, in Mount Pleasant, MI; daughter of John Robert (a professor) and Jane Pearl (Martin) Lee; married Damon R. Huffman, December 15, 1974 (marriage ended January 16, 1996); children: Jeremy, Trevor, Damon II. *Ethnicity:* "White." *Education:* Attended University of Grenoble, 1971; Albion College, B.A., 1973; attended Institut de Francais, Villefrance-sur-Mer, France, 1975; Michigan State University, M.A. (summa cum laude), 1982. *Politics:* Republican. *Religion:* Christian Scientist. *Avocational interests:* Water sports, skiing, horseback riding, reading historical novels, working as a soccer referee.

ADDRESSES: Home—Petoskey, MI. *Office*—Torch Lake Publishing, P.O. Box R, Petoskey, MI 49770; fax 616-348-0756. *E-mail*—torchlake@racc2000.com.

CAREER: High school French teacher, Albion, MI, 1973-75; City of Lansing, MI, clerk and receptionist for mayor's office, 1975-76; manager of an apartment complex in Lansing, 1976-78; GMI Engineering and Management Institute, Flint, MI, assistant director of financial aid, 1983-85; Rehabitat Systems of Michigan (adult foster care homes), director of administration and finance, 1986-96; Jennifer Lee Huffman Family Limited Partnership, general partner, 1989—. Torch Lake Publishing, owner. Bas de Laine Investment Club, president.

WRITINGS:

(Coauthor) *What Fits You?* (career planning manual), University of Michigan—Flint, 1980.
Money and Marriage: Choices, Rights, and Responsibilities, Torch Lake, 1999.

Contributor to *Christian Science Sentinel.*

WORK IN PROGRESS: Money and Remarriage and *Money and Children.*

SIDELIGHTS: Jennifer Lee Huffman told *CA:* "At New Trier High School, one of my English teachers would tell the student that 'the only way to know if you have learned something well is to be able to explain it to someone else.' My motivation for writing is to clarify the truths that I experience, which in turn may help others through some of life's challenges.

"I began writing articles for a religious magazine twenty years ago and coauthored a career planning book for the University of Michigan—Flint in 1980. My writing came to a halt for about fifteen years while I became involved in the business world. My husband and I bought rental properties, restaurants, and four adult foster care homes, and I was the financial administrator for all of them. This was in addition to being a full-time mother to three boys.

"Even during these busy years, I would write out different financial scenarios for families and try to figure out ways to simplify the money process for couples. The money choices and values of hundreds of families were intriguing to me during my work as assistant director of financial aid at a college.

"To clarify my ideas, I began writing *Money and Marriage* seven years ago when we moved to northern Michigan. When my marriage of twenty-one years ended, it became important for me to write about the use of money in marriage as a tool to growth, rather than a method for control, domination, or codependence. Before the book was finished, I began teaching adult education classes based on my manuscript. I found many people who were not able to communicate their money choices, ideas, goals, and values to the ones they loved the most. Many couples do not know how to cultivate financial self-sufficiency (rather than codependency) in intimate relationships. Money use, values, and choices are usually the last things discussed by couples.

"The purpose of my book is to help couples find practical solutions to the forty or more financial stages of long-term marriages, and to help them set up a useful financial system for their families, all in a safe and satisfying environment. Financial values and choices are explored in the many worksheets, which are meant to be shared with the spouse or prospective spouse."

*   *   *

HUGGINS, James Byron 1959-

PERSONAL: Born August 14, 1959; married, wife's name Karen; children: two. *Education:* Troy State University, B.A. (journalism), 1981.

ADDRESSES: Home—Decatur, AL. *Agent*—c/o Simon & Schuster, 1230 Avenue of the Americas, New York, NY 10020.

CAREER: Hartselle Enquirer, writer, c. 1981-85; worked for the Christian Underground of Eastern

Europe helping to smuggle information in and out of Iron Curtain countries, first in TX, 1985-87, then Romania, beginning 1987; later returned to U.S. and wrote for a small newspaper; joined Huntsville Police Department, Huntsville, AL, as a uniform patrolman; became full-time writer.

AWARDS, HONORS: Decorated as Field Training Officer, Huntsville Police Department.

WRITINGS:

NOVELS

A Wolf Story, Harvest House Publishers (Eugene, OR), 1993.
The Reckoning, Harvest House (Eugene, OR), 1994.
Leviathan, Thomas Nelson (Nashville, TN), 1995.
Cain, Simon & Schuster (New York City), 1997.

SIDELIGHTS: In his first four novels, James Byron Huggins made leaps from a small Christian press in Oregon to a well-known evangelical publisher in Nashville to a broad-based industry giant in New York City. His first three novels were bestsellers in the Christian market; the fourth was a crossover venture. The first, the 1993 novel *A Wolf Story,* was deemed "chilling," by *Booklist*'s religious fiction specialist John Mort, who made the assessment in a review of a later Huggins novel, *Cain.*

The Reckoning, published in 1994, is a tale about an attempt to stop a group of Satanists from obtaining an ancient parchment that gives how-to instructions for installing the Antichrist into power. Its hero, a converted assassin named Gage, must kill again in order to stop the evil forces; thus, he learns that God is someone who demands bloodshed. *Booklist*'s Mort predicted correctly that the novel was a good choice for this genre's bestseller list. He felt that Gage was "as adept at shedding blood as any character in a Don Pendleton novel" and "more fully realized" than such characters. Moreover, Mort found the evil antagonists in this novel genuinely frightening.

Huggins' 1995 thriller *Leviathan* was referred to by some critics as being in the Michael Crichton or Robin Cook vein, with Christian theology added. The menace referred to in the title is a genetically engineered monster, a Komodo dragon raised to the status of a high-tech weapon. The hero, electrician Jackson Connor, who works on the research project that created the monster, learns of this threat to society and battles it with the help of a scholar-priest named Thor Magnusson. Again assessing the novel for *Booklist*, Mort was impressed by Huggins's technical knowledge but sensed an inevitable resemblance to tales of Godzilla. A *Publishers Weekly* reviewer commented that Huggins's writing was weighed down by "preaching and melodrama" but added that "once the action gets up to steam, he takes readers on a merry, entertaining ride." In *Library Journal*, Henry Corrigan observed that "in Connor we finally have a character whose goodness is fully drawn and credible."

Huggins again found success with his 1997 crossover novel *Cain*, the movie rights to which were bought by action movie star Bruce Willis. The title character, created by Maggie, a CIA scientist, represents the embodiment of murder. Cain drinks blood to keep up his strength, and his chosen source as the novel unfolds is Maggie's six-year-old daughter, Amy. Retired commando Colonel James Solomon comes out of retirement to fight Cain; a series of violent events leads to what a *Publishers Weekly* reviewer called "a gruesome climax in an English seaside castle during a spectacular thunderstorm." The *Publishers Weekly* reviewer noted a preponderance of technical jargon and theological speeches in the book version, but aside from these, called it a "breakneck action thriller." The *Publishers Weekly* reviewer also praised the fast action and said that *Cain* "becomes more entertaining as its events become increasingly incredible." In *Booklist*, Mort, noting that crossover publication had given Huggins "a freer hand," wrote, "Huggins turns in a suspenseful performance, no question."

BIOGRAPHICAL/CRITICAL SOURCES:

PERIODICALS

Booklist, January 15, 1995, p. 897; September 1, 1995, p. 17; June 1, 1997, p. 1619-20.
Library Journal, September 1, 1995, p. 158; August, 1997, p. 129.
Publishers Weekly, September 25, 1995, p. 48; June 9, 1997, p. 39.

OTHER

Interview with James Byron Huggins, http://www.annonline.com/interviews/970822/biography.html (February 5, 1999).*

HUTCHINS, Nigel 1945-

PERSONAL: June 4, 1945, in Tynemouth, England; Canadian citizen. *Avocational interests:* Antiques, sailing, diving.

ADDRESSES: Office—c/o Limestone Productions, Box 216, Streetsville, Ontario L5M 2B8, Canada.

CAREER: Film and television designer and decorator; writer. NABET 700, union member.

MEMBER: Freedom in the Clothworkers Company of the City of London.

AWARDS, HONORS: Ontario Arts Council grant, 1967-68, 1971, 1982; "Insect Play" design selected for World Pavilion "Man and His World", Montreal, 1969; Heritage Ottawa Award, 1975, for overall contribution to the field of preservation; Heritage Canada Award of Honour, 1976, for contribution to the heritage of Canada; Ontario Renews Award honorable mention, 1982; LACAC Award, city of Brockville, 1987.

WRITINGS:

Restoring Old Houses, Van Nostrand Reinhold (Toronto and New York City), 1980, Grammercy Publishing Company (New York City), 1985.
Restoring Houses of Brick and Stone, Fleet, 1982, Van Nostrand Reinhold (Toronto and New York City), 1983.

WORK IN PROGRESS: A home dictionary.

SIDELIGHTS: Several reviewers described Nigel Hutchins's first book, *Restoring Old Houses,* as appealing and attractive because of its many photos, drawings, and diagrams. With contents ranging from historical information to practical guidelines, it covers topics such as building a stone wall and doing decorative stenciling. Although acknowledging Hutchins's vast experience and knowledge of the field (he is a Canadian building contractor and consultant on preservation), Sally Bird in *Quill & Quire* pronounced the book's appendix "helpful" and its bibliography "excellent." The author's viewpoint that "technology and modern lifestyles can harmonize" with historical preservation permeates this work and distinguishes *Restoring Old Houses* from others on the topic, according to Douglas Birdsall in *Library Journal*. William Heine stated in the *London Free Press* that the volume is an "excellent work."

Also visually rich in its inclusion of photos and sketches of subjects ranging from tools to finished buildings, Hutchins' next work, *Restoring Houses of Brick and Stone,* chronicles the history of masonry from ancient times to the present. The book covers topics such as stone cutting, brick making, house inspection, the causes of masonry damage, halting and repairing decay, installing new foundations, and refurbishing interior and exterior finishes. *Restoring Houses of Brick and Stone* uses historic homes in Ontario as examples and includes a bibliography and glossary. In *Quill & Quire,* James Bugslag assessed Hutchins's second effort as not detailed enough for beginners and said that it dealt more with "routine building maintenance and repair rather than [with] historic preservation or restoration." However, Birdsall, in *Library Journal,* believed *Restoring Houses of Brick and Stone*'s useful advice is balanced by Hutchins's concern for good taste and the preservation of historical buildings. This reviewer lauded it as "a worthy companion to the author's first book." A reviewer deemed the work "unique and useful" in *Booklist.*

Hutchins told *CA:* "Living with the past, today, is the essence of good architectural preservation. Although designated historic neighborhoods are important, the challenge is to marry historic structures with contemporary lifestyles and commerce."

BIOGRAPHICAL/CRITICAL SOURCES:

PERIODICALS

Antiques Journal, April, 1981, p. 53.
Booklist, July, 1983, p. 1376.
Century Home, March-April, 1983.
Colonial Homes, May-June, 1981.
Historic Preservation, November/December, 1983.
Library Journal, April 1, 1981, p. 806; June 15, 1983, p. 1269.
London Free Press, February 28, 1981.
Old-House Journal, July/August, 1991.
Quill & Quire, February, 1981, p. 48; April, 1983, p. 32.

*   *   *

HUTCHINSON, Bill 1947-

PERSONAL: Born March 10, 1947, in Philadelphia, PA; son of Herman R. (a business executive) and Ethel (a homemaker; maiden name, Williamson) Hutchinson; married Lori Webber (a consultant), July 17, 1976; children: Katharine, Tucker. *Ethnicity:* "Caucasian." *Education:* Pomona College, B.A., 1969; Claremont Graduate School, M.Ed., 1971; San Francisco Theological Seminary, M.Div., 1990. *Avocational interests:* Travel, hiking, skiing.

ADDRESSES: Home and office—20735 Fifth St. E., Sonoma, CA 95476; fax 707-939-1417. *E-mail*—hutchpc@aol.com.

CAREER: Minister of United Church of Christ; United Way of the Bay Area, San Francisco, CA, associate campaign director, 1974-81; Marin Interfaith Task Force on Central America, Mill Valley, CA, director, 1985-95; Hew Hope Church, Sonoma, CA, founding minister, 1990-94; Hutchinson Personnel Consulting, Sonoma, co-owner, 1996—.

Christians for Peace in El Salvador, president of board of directors, 1999-2000; United Way of Sonoma, Mendocino, and Lake Counties, member of board of directors, 1996-2002.

AWARDS, HONORS: Received award from University Press of Colorado, 1999, for *When the Dogs Ate Candles.*

WRITINGS:

When the Dogs Ate Candles: A Time in El Salvador, University Press of Colorado (Niwot, CO), 1998.

WORK IN PROGRESS: A screenplay, *Mirtala.*

SIDELIGHTS: Bill Hutchinson told *CA:* "During the latter half of the 1980s and early half of the 1990s, I was the director of the Marin Interfaith Task Force on Central America. In that role I administered an accompaniment project on behalf of threatened human rights workers in El Salvador, traveled there many times, and met people whose work and courage inspired my book *When the Dogs Ate Candles: A Time in El Salvador.* Subsequently I developed the story of Mirtala Lopez, as recounted in the book, into a screenplay.

"Earlier in my life I wrote several manuscripts—a novel and a young adult novel—which were never published. I am still hoping."

HYMAN, Timothy 1946-

PERSONAL: Born April 17, 1946, in Hove, Sussex, England; son of Alan (a screenwriter and author) and Noreen (Gypson) Hyman; married Judith Ravenscroft (a fiction writer), March 22, 1982. *Education:* Slade School of Fine Art, University of London, Diploma, 1967. *Politics:* "Left/anarchist." *Avocational interests:* The novels of John Cowper Powys, Italian cinema.

ADDRESSES: Home—62 Myddelton Sq., London EC1R 1XX, England.

CAREER: Artist (painter) and freelance lecturer.

AWARDS, HONORS: Leverhulme Award, 1993; Wingate Award, 1997.

WRITINGS:

Bonnard, Thames & Hudson (London, England), 1998.
Bhupen Khakhar, Mapin (India), 1998.

Contributor of more than a hundred articles to magazines and newspapers, including *London, Artscribe, Modern Painters,* and *Times Literary Supplement.*

WORK IN PROGRESS: Sienese Painting, for Thames & Hudson, completion expected in 2000; *Stanley Spencer,* Tate Galley, 2001.

SIDELIGHTS: Timothy Hyman told *CA:* "For the past twenty years I've been in the awkward category of a 'painter who writes.' Most of my energies have been devoted to painting (which remains my chief source of income). I began to write as a crusader—in defense of artists unregarded or misunderstood—and that remains my central motivation. Of course I am also writing about the artists from whom I have learned the most and to whom I feel closest, and that quest for self-understanding determines my critical viewpoint.

"The focus of my book on Bonnard is a subjective pictorial space—a new space for the self—which obviously links to my own practice as a painter. It is partly my interest in the representation of the city of London that now fuels my research on Ambroyio Lorenzetti and Sienese painting. For me, the writing and the painting are integral and interdependent, even if the gear changes are sometimes troublesome."

IANNUZZI, "Joe Dogs"
See IANNUZZI, Joseph

*   *   *

IANNUZZI, Joseph 1931-
("Joe Dogs" Iannuzzi)

PERSONAL: Born in 1931, in Port Chester, NY; son of Joe and Molly Iannuzzi; married (divorced); children: five. *Politics:* Democrat. *Religion:* Catholic. *Avocational interests:* Sports.

ADDRESSES: Agent—Sterling Lord Literistic, 65 Bleecker St., New York, NY 10012.

CAREER: Chef in Cleveland, OH; Mafia associate, Gambino Family, c. 1950-81; Federal Witness Protection Program member, 1981—. *Military service:* U.S. Army, 1948-50, awarded Silver Star and Purple Heart with a cluster.

WRITINGS:

Joe Dogs: The Life and Crimes of a Mobster, Simon & Schuster (New York City), 1993.
The Mafia Cookbook, edited by Bob Drury and Carolyn Beauchamp, Simon & Schuster (New York City), 1993.

WORK IN PROGRESS: A book about life in the Federal Witness Protection Program; *Cooking on the Lam,* a second book combining recipes with tales of Mob life.

SIDELIGHTS: In December of 1985, Gambino Family crime boss Paul Castellano was gunned down outside a favorite eatery, Manhattan's Sparks Steak House. To those who follow underworld events—or at least, those who follow these events inasmuch as they are known to the public at large—this murder led to the rise of the infamous crime boss John Gotti. Less well-known, however, is the role played by Joseph "Joe Dogs" Iannuzzi, a former Mafia associate turned federal witness, in assisting federal agents' attempts to convict Castellano for racketeering. Though his own men ended Castellano's life, the testimony of Iannuzzi and others helped to usher in the beginning of the end for the "Five Families" of New York crime.

Despite the fact that his first book, *Joe Dogs: The Life and Crimes of a Mobster* (1993), was an autobiography, relatively little is known about Iannuzzi's life. And given the fact that he has resided in the Federal Witness Protection Program ever since informing on former mentor Tommy Agro and others in 1981, it is not likely that more facts will emerge unless Iannuzzi—living under an assumed identity—discloses them. It is known that Iannuzzi was fourteen years old when he was first arrested, and that his stepfather kicked him out a year later. He learned how to cook from his mother, and served in the United States Army, where he developed his cooking skills while on K.P. duty. Afterward he went to work as a chef in a Cleveland, Ohio, restaurant, and worked in various restaurants for several years, then migrated to Florida, where he became involved with the Mafia.

Iannuzzi never became a "made man," that is, a formal member of Cosa Nostra, but his criminal credentials are without doubt. Albert Mobilio, reviewing a number of Mob-related books in *Harper's,* used Iannuzzi as an example when contrasting real mobsters with the glorified versions that appear in films such as *The Godfather:* "The all too real 'Joe Dogs' hardly fascinates, but he does know how to win friends and influence people." Mobilio then quoted a pithy excerpt from *Joe Dogs:* "If you don't do what I tell you, I'll kill your father. I won't kill you, but I'll maim you. And you will have to live with the fact that you got your father killed. We will even let your mother live, but let her know the reason her husband got killed." After recounting the details of a beating delivered under Iannuzzi's direction, Mobilio observed: "No grandiose threat or Taoist hoodoo here; this beating is strictly business."

"Business" for Iannuzzi, who gained his nickname as a result of his penchant for betting on dog races, consisted of fixing horse races, narcotics trafficking, loan-sharking, and of course beating up people who failed to pay back their loans, along with the exorbitant interest rates charged by the Mob. In 1981 he himself became the object of a beating when he ran afoul of Agro: "I had a terrible accident," he recalled, "I kept walking into this baseball bat [along] with this iron pipe. Some of my pals were trying to see if my head was harder than those two instruments. It was, barely." After that, he became a federal witness, and played a role in more than ten Mafia trials. "I put away twenty of the top Mafia in New York and Florida," he recalled, "although most of them wound up doing it to themselves—including Tommy Agro and a chief of police."

According to Manuel Perez-Rivas in *Newsday,* twelve years after splitting with Cosa Nostra, Iannuzzi says he was inspired to write his autobiography by a 1991 biography of Castellano, *Boss of Bosses.* Referring to *Boss of Bosses* authors Joseph O'Brien and Andris Kurins, two federal agents, he said, "I figured if those guys could write a book like that, then maybe so could I." The resulting volume, in the words of a *Booklist* reviewer, is "colorful, to say the least." The reviewer warned that the book was "not for the squeamish": in addition to its graphic descriptions of violence, it is riddled with profanity and racial slurs. "Iannuzzi seems to take it all—including the threats and beatings—in stride," concluded the reviewer, "laughing and poking fun at the world's most dangerous criminals and their foibles." A *Library Journal* reviewer called his writing style "brutally frank," as well as "glib and fast-paced." Publisher Simon & Schuster capitalized on these characteristics, promising in their promotional material that the autobiography was "written by an insider whose style is as authentic, brutal, and hard-edged as the world he inhabited."

While he was with the Mob, Iannuzzi assured his place among his comrades with his culinary skills, and later he said, "I don't know which I liked better, being a crook or a cook." On the heels of his earlier success with *Joe Dogs*—he reportedly netted a quarter-million dollars in a two-book deal—he published *The Mafia Cookbook.* But it is far more than a cookbook: "Each recipe," noted Manuel Perez-Rivas, "comes with a detailed list of where and when Joe Dogs prepared the meal, and which mobsters (or in some cases, FBI agents) were present, with their crime families and ranks duly noted."

The Mafia Cookbook contains some thirty-five recipes for delicacies such as Veal Marsala and Caponata, Iannuzzi's specialties, as well as Shrimp Scampi Gambino-style and Baked Chicken a la Joe Dogs. It is also seasoned with plenty of underworld wisdom, such as the following: "If any guy wants to join your crew and tells you he's just out of the joint, take him to dinner. If he orders anything but steak or lobster, he's lying and probably a Fed." He also includes anecdotes that illustrate aspects of his former associates, as for instance the comment made by Colombo Family boss Thomas DiBella after Iannuzzi served a Mandarin Pork Roast: "Joey, I want you to know how much I enjoyed that meal. I know it was some kind of southern dish, because Little Dom tells me you're from the south. So where exactly in South Brooklyn you from?" Iannuzzi also makes asides such as the following, when recounting a Shrimp Scampi meal he made for Nick "Jiggs" Forlano: "Now I know you're gonna say, whoa, half a pound of butter and sour cream? But remember, these guys ain't exactly concerned about their cholesterol count. So when serving guests with more normal appetites, just keep the sauce on the side."

Iannuzzi's editors on *The Mafia Cookbook* deleted the profanities because, he said, "They didn't think the housewives, you know, would want to read all that stuff." Nonetheless, he is handy with gallows humor, introducing a Bouillabaisse recipe with the words, "A nice fish stew for someone who some day may sleep with the fishes." Likewise "Revenge, like my Cicoria Insalata (Dandelion Salad) is best eaten cold." But aside from all the gallows humor and the anecdotes, what about the recipes themselves? Maya Sinha in *Mother Jones* called them "world-class," and Marion Kane in the *Toronto Star* praised the book as "a wonderfully witty little tome packed with [Iannuzzi's] and his cohorts' favorite (and, I must add, excellent) recipes."

In a review of Iannuzzi's cookbook and another by a former Mafioso, Selwyn Raab of the *New York Times* examined the importance of food to Mob culture. Not only was Castellano gunned down outside a restaurant, he observed, but the FBI wiretap that helped to bring down his operation was placed in the favorite gathering-spot of his Staten Island mansion: the kitchen. "These volumes," Raab observed, "demonstrate the central role that gluttony plays in mob life. . . . There is a practical side, too. A portly frame is more intimidating than a pencil-line figure when collecting loan-shark debts and carrying out other nefarious assignments." Viva Hardigg of *U.S. News & World Report* posed the question: "Weren't any of their deeds distasteful enough to incur loss of appetite? 'No way,' [Iannuzzi] says. 'Fuggeddaboudit.'"

Iannuzzi told *CA:* "I'm just learning how to use a computer. I used to write long-hand and friends would help me with typing. Now I'm learning how to type and work on a computer, and it's fascinating, but it was a lot easier just to steal them—*that* I know how to do."

BIOGRAPHICAL/CRITICAL SOURCES:

BOOKS

Iannuzzi, Joseph, *Joe Dogs: The Life and Crimes of a Mobster,* Simon & Schuster, 1993.

PERIODICALS

Booklist, July, 1993, p. 1927.
Harper's, October, 1997, pp. 68-77.
Library Journal, May 15, 1993, p. 84.
Mother Jones, May, 1995, p. 78.
Newsday, July 19, 1993, p. 15; August 30, 1993, p. 1.
New York Times, July 14, 1993, p. C1.
Toronto Star, August 25, 1993, p. E1.
U.S. News & World Report, September 20, 1993, p. 14.

—*Sketch by Judson Knight*

*   *   *

IROH, Eddie

PERSONAL: Born in Nigeria.

ADDRESSES: Home—London, England. *Agent*—c/o Heinemann Educational Publishing, Halley Court, Jordan Hill, Oxford OX2 8EJ, England.

CAREER: Novelist. *The Guardian,* Lagos, Nigeria, cofounder and former managing editor; radio and television broadcaster and writer and producer for ENTV (Nigerian television network); USAfrica Median Networks, executive editor of international projects and columnist for *USAfricaonline; Black Business Journal,* columnist.

AWARDS, HONORS: Recipient of fiction awards.

WRITINGS:

NOVELS; "NIGERIAN CIVIL WAR" TRILOGY

Forty-Eight Guns for the General, Heinemann (London, England), 1976.
Toads of War, Heinemann (London, England), 1979.
The Siren in the Night, Heinemann (London, England), 1982.

OTHER NOVELS

Without a Silver Spoon, Spectrum Books (Ibadan, Nigeria), 1981.

SIDELIGHTS: Nigerian novelist Eddie Iroh is known for his trilogy of novels about his country's civil war of 1967-1970, a war begun when Biafra attempted to secede and ended when the Biafran rebellion collapsed amid starvation and violence. The first novel of the three, *Forty-Eight Guns for the General* (1976), focuses on white mercenaries who are hired by the Biafran side, and in particular, a colonel named Rudolph. These mercenaries delay fighting in order to increase their revenues; when fighting does come, they lose men and materials and thus prestige. They attempt to mutiny against their employers, but the attempt is quashed with the help of Rudolph's Biafran second-in-command.

Reviewing Iroh's fictional account of these events in *World Literature Today,* Ossie Onuora Enekwe of Columbia University expressed admiration for a pervasive sense of "irony and paradox" that was "skillfully heightened by punning and repetition." However, Enekwe also commented on the book's "melodrama and sensationalism" and stereotyped characters. The novel, the reviewer concluded, was a work of journalistic fiction, "superb" as a thriller rather than a work of literary art. Nigerian novelist Chikwnye Okonjo Ogunyemi, in a scholarly assessment of Nigerian war novels in *Comparative Literature Studies,* called *Forty-Eight Guns for the General* "brutally funny in the style of *Catch-22*" and called attention to Iroh's preference for short, action-packed scenes, "racy" dialogue, and straightforwardly narrated episodes of sex and drinking.

The second novel in the trilogy, *Toads of War,* appeared in 1979; it was called "a *roman a these*" in Ogunyemi's article, the thesis being that the promise of Biafra had deteriorated into a reality of war propaganda and social-class tension. The first-person narrator is a Biafran soldier who has lost an arm; much of the novel is devoted, however, to a good-hearted prostitute. According to David Dorsey in *World Literature Today,* "The novel is essentially a simple suspense story, but its many features of daring originality and earnest didacticism merit serious attention." Its structure, consisting of forty-four brief, titled chapters, among which are sections in the third person, quotations from poetry (including footnotes), and a six-page summary of a play the characters see, was for Dorsey "at once ambitious and naive." These devices, as well as the device of foreshadowing, made for increased suspense, in Dorsey's view. That critic found *Toads of War* well-blended in different forms and intents, artistically liberating, craftsmanlike, and successful in depending on "its sardonic but sympathetic moral vision."

The trilogy concludes with *The Siren in the Night* (1982), which Dorsey, again in *World Literature To-*

day, called "less ambitious" than its two predecessors, "but a greater artistic success." The novel's protagonist and antagonist, respectively, are two colonels who never meet: Ben Udaja, who becomes disenchanted with the rebels and successfully moves his allegiance to the federal army; and villainous security chief Mike Kolawole, whose mistress has been killed in an operation led by Udaja. Kolawole hatches a complicated scheme to assassinate Udaja, which is only foiled at the novel's end. For Dorsey, this was "a plot of elaborate intrigue with laudably spare violence." He remarked favorably on the "mordant humor" of Iroh's social commentary. The reviewer commented that he was most impressed by the characterizations, particular of Kolawole and his expatriate daughter. Kolawole, Dorsey attested, was "believable, sometimes even admirable." All in all, Dorsey wrote, *Siren in the Night,* "shorn of most idiosyncrasies which marred the other two novels," was both "an engaging example of popular fiction" and "a conscious tribute to the spirit of reconciliation." For *Library Journal* reviewer Peter Sabor, *The Siren in the Night* served as a "tense, chilling" reading experience.

BIOGRAPHICAL/CRITICAL SOURCES:

PERIODICALS

Comparative Literature Studies, summer, 1983, pp. 203-216.
Library Journal, November 15, 1982, p. 2190.
World Literature Today, winter, 1978, p. 166; winter, 1980, p. 161; autumn, 1983, p. 679.

OTHER

Black Business Journal Online, http://www.bbjonline.com (February 5, 1999).
USAfricaonline, http://www.usafricaonline.com (February 5, 1999).*

* * *

IRWIN, Ann(abelle Bowen) 1915-1998
(Hadley Irwin, a joint pseudonym)

OBITUARY NOTICE—See index for *CA* sketch: Born October 8, 1915, in Peterson, IA; died of complications from hepatitis C, September 13, 1998, in Des

Moines, IA. Educator and author. Irwin was known for her young adult novels that dealt with troubling teenage issues such as suicide, incest, and racism. Irwin took her ideas for these books from the many teenagers she came to know during years of high school teaching. Irwin grew up in and attended school in Iowa, where she majored in music. She taught high school for the next thirty years, teaching both music and English. In her fifties she returned to school and earned a master's degree which qualified her to teach at the college level. In the late 1960s Irwin and another college professor, Lee Hadley, teamed up and co-authored several young adult novels that were published under the pseudonym Hadley Irwin. The books were popular with young readers both in the U.S. and overseas, and several were made into television movies or television specials. Works that Irwin co-authored under the pseudonym Hadley Irwin included: *The Original Freddie Ackerman* (1992), *Jim Dandy* (1994), and *Sarah with an H* (1995).

OBITUARIES AND OTHER SOURCES:

PERIODICALS

New York Times, September 20, 1998, p. 51.
Washington Post, September 18, 1998, p. B6.

*   *   *

IRWIN, Hadley
   See IRWIN, Ann(abelle Bowen)

J

JACKSON, Richard D(ean) W(ells) 1967-

PERSONAL: Born February 9, 1967, in Livingstone, Zambia; citizen of New Zealand; son of David George (a minister) and Kathryn Marjory (a minister; maiden name, Goffin) Wells; married Michelle Denise Angela Jackson (a music teacher), December 5, 1993. *Ethnicity:* "European." *Education:* University of Canterbury, B.A., 1989, M.A. (with first class honors), 1992, Ph.D., 1998. *Politics:* "Liberal—democratic, green, pacifist." *Religion:* Christian. *Avocational interests:* Fly fishing, guitar, basketball, movies.

ADDRESSES: Home—28B Howard St., MacAndrew Bay, Dunedin, New Zealand. *Office*—Department of Political Studies, University of Otago, Box 56, Dunedin, New Zealand; fax 03-479-7174. *E-mail*—richard.jackson@stonebow.otago.ac.nz.

CAREER: University of Otago, Dunedin, New Zealand, teaching fellow, 1996—, chairperson of Foreign Policy School, 1997-98.

MEMBER: Institute of International Affairs (president of Dunedin branch, 1998), APSA, AFSAAP.

AWARDS, HONORS: Scholar, Peace and Disarmament Education Trust, 1994-96.

WRITINGS:

(With Jacob Bercovitch) *International Conflict: A Chronological Encyclopedia of Conflicts and Their Management, 1945-1995,* Congressional Quarterly (Washington, DC), 1997.

Contributor to *Peace and Change.*

WORK IN PROGRESS: African Conflict Management in the Post-Cold War Era; Negotiation versus Mediation in International Conflict; research on collapsed states.

* * *

JAMES, Caryn

PERSONAL: Born in Providence, RI.

ADDRESSES: Office—*New York Times,* 229 West 43rd St., New York, NY 10036. *Agent*—Gloria Loomis, Watkins Loomis Agency, 113 East 135th St., Suite 1, New York, NY 10016.

CAREER: New York Times, New York City, chief television critic. Has also worked as a *New York Times* film critic and cultural reporter, and as an editor for the *New York Times Book Review.*

WRITINGS:

Glorie, Zoland Books (Cambridge, MA), 1998.

Contributor to periodicals, including *New York Times, TV Guide,* and *Vogue.*

SIDELIGHTS: Caryn James, chief television critic for the *New York Times,* published her first novel in

1998. Set in an unnamed New England town, *Glorie* is the story of Gloria Carcieri, an octagenerian whose beloved husband of fifty years, Jack, has been dead for seven years. Glorie now lives alone in the house she shared with Jack, across the street from her vigilant daughter, Louisa, and Louisa's husband Patrick, a bland accountant whom Louisa refers to as "Ivory Soap." Glorie has never warmed to Patrick, or even to her own granddaughter, Blanche, whom she finds pretentious, yet Glorie finds herself sleeping at their house every night.

At the heart of the novel is Glorie's struggle to retain the home she shared with Jack. Several of Patrick's aunts live in a high-rise nursing home in town, and Patrick, along with Louisa, thinks that a similar arrangement would be best for Glorie. Glorie resists their efforts as best she can, going so far as to steal the deed to her house from Patrick's home office files, and later giving the new owner of the house the "Evil Eye." Glorie is a complex woman, by turns defiant and despairing. Her advanced age brings her new worries, such as whether she is going senile. After checking for symptoms of senility, Glorie comforts herself by noting that she is "still sane enough to look for them."

As the novel progresses, Glorie dyes her hair to its original red and fantasizes about scolding the young doctor who seems to ignore Glorie's presence as he tells Louisa that Glorie is "fine for a woman her age." While Glorie wrestles with age and the loss of her home, she is consumed by the spirit of her departed husband. She talks with Jack, who calms her fears. As James wrote in the novel, "She would not think time had ended for him. There was a version of her husband that could follow her anywhere."

James, flaunting her day-job expertise, used contemporary television as a source for Glorie's reality and her fantasy life. Critics generally agreed that James successfully made the transition from columnist to novelist. Hilma Wolitzer of the *New York Times* called *Glorie* "an especially stirring and charming novel." Richard Burgin, also in the *New York Times,* said that James takes risks and writes "convincingly" about a "flawed but mostly sympathetic heroine" and "a number of other elderly characters." According to a review in *Publishers Weekly,* James feels that Glorie's story "is a testament to the courage and will of many women of an earlier era who were raised to be wives and mothers unprepared for lives without their husbands."

BIOGRAPHICAL/CRITICAL SOURCES:

BOOKS

James, Caryn, *Glorie,* Zoland Books (Cambridge, MA), 1998.

PERIODICALS

American Spectator, September, 1993, pp. 70-71.
Library Journal, April 15, 1998, pp. 112-113.
New York Times, May 14, 1998; May 17, 1998.
Publishers Weekly, January 12, 1998, pp. 32-38.

OTHER

Barnes & Noble, http://www.barnesandnoble.com (September 24, 1998).

*   *   *

JENNINGS, Paul 1943-

PERSONAL: Born April 30, 1943, in Heston, England; immigrated to Australia, 1949; son of an engineer and a homemaker; married, c. late 1970s (divorced, c. 1984); married Claire (a consultant and lecturer in language and literacy), c. mid-1980s; children: Gemma, Bronson, Sally, Andrew, Lind, Tracy. *Education:* Frankston Teachers College, 1963; Lincoln Institute, 1972. *Avocational interests:* Playing the button accordion, classic English cars.

ADDRESSES: Home—Belgrave, Victoria, Australia. *Office*—P.O. Box 189, Belgrave, Victoria 3160, Australia.

CAREER: Writer, speech pathologist, and special education teacher, 1963-68; Ministry of Education, Australia, speech pathologist, 1972-75; Burwood State College, lecturer in special education, 1976-78; Language and Literature, Warrnambool Institute of Adult Education, senior lecturer, 1979-88; full-time writer, 1989—.

AWARDS, HONORS: Young Australian Best Book awards, 1987, for *Unreal! Eight Surprising Stories,* 1988, for *Unbelievable! More Surprising Stories,* 1989, for *The Cabbage Patch Fib* and *Uncanny! Even More Surprising Stories,* 1990, for *The Paw Thing,* 1991, for *Round the Twist,* 1992, for *Quirky Tales! More Oddball Stories* and *Unmentionable! More*

Amazing Stories, 1993, for *Unbearable! More Bizarre Stories,* 1994, for *Spooner or Later* and *Undone! More Mad Endings,* and 1995, for *Duck for Cover* and *The Gizmo;* Ashton Scholastic award (with Ted Greenwood and Terry Denton), 1993, for *Spooner or Later;* Australian Environment Award, 1994, for *The Fishermen and the Theefyspray* (illustrated by Jane Tanner). Jennings has also been a repeat winner of a number of other Australian child-selected awards, including Canberra's Own Outstanding List (COOL) Award, West Australian Young Readers' Book Award, Kids Own Australian Literature Award (KOALA), Kids Reading Oz Choice (KROC) Award, Books I Like Best Yearly (BILBY) Award, and South Australian CROW Award. For his body of work, Jennings has received the Gold Puffin Award, the Angus & Robertson Bookworld Award, and has been honored as an Appointed Member, General Division, of the Order of Australia.

WRITINGS:

JUVENILE

Unreal! Eight Surprising Stories, Penguin, 1985, Viking (New York City), 1991.
Unbelievable! More Surprising Stories, Penguin, 1986, Viking (New York City), 1995.
Quirky Tails! More Oddball Stories, Penguin, 1987, Puffin (New York City), 1990, Puffin Books, 1995.
The Cabbage Patch Fib, illustrated by Craig Smith, Penguin, 1988.
Uncanny! Even More Surprising Stories, Penguin, 1988, Viking (New York City), 1991.
The Paw Thing, illustrated by Keith McEwan, Penguin, 1989.
Round the Twist, Penguin, 1990.
Unbearable! More Bizarre Stories, Penguin, 1990, Viking Penguin 1995, 1998.
The Naked Ghost, Burp! and Blue Jam, Longman Cheshire (Australia), 1991.
Unmentionable! More Amazing Stories, Penguin, 1991, Viking (New York City), 1993.
Round the Twist 1, Puffin (New York City), 1993.
Undone! More Mad Endings, Penguin, 1993, Viking (New York City), 1995.
The Gizmo, illustrated by Keith McEwan, Penguin, 1994.
The Gizmo Again, illustrated by Keith McEwan, Penguin, 1995.
Uncovered! Weird, Weird Stories, Penguin, 1995, Viking (New York City), 1996.
Come Back Gizmo, 1996.

Thirteen! Unpredictable Tales from Paul Jennings, Viking (New York City), 1996.
Sink the Gizmo, illustrated by Keith McEwan, Puffin (New York City), 1997.
Wicked, Penguin, 1998.
Singenpoo Strikes Again, Puffin (New York City), 1998.
(Contributor) *Listen Ear and Other Stories to Shock You Silly,* Puffin (New York City), 1998.

PICTURE BOOKS

Teacher Eater, illustrated by Jeannette Rowe, William Heinemann, 1991.
Grandad's Gifts, illustrated by Peter Gouldthorpe, Rigby Heinemann, 1991, Viking (New York City), 1993.
(With Ted Greenwood and Terry Denton) *Spooner or Later,* Viking (New York City), 1992.
The Fisherman and the Theefyspray, illustrated by Jane Tanner, Penguin, 1994.
(With Ted Greenwood and Terry Denton) *Duck for Cover,* Penguin, 1994.

ADAPTATIONS: Round the Twist was adapted as a television series by the Australian Children's Television Foundation, 1990.

WORK IN PROGRESS: A movie script based on the author's four *Gizmo* novellas.

SIDELIGHTS: Paul Jennings is not yet the household name in North America that he is in his native Australia. However, the growing positive attention of reviewers and readers on this side of the globe indicates that his work will soon be well known to North American readers. His imaginative, off-beat tales for pre-teen readers, which have been likened to the best-selling "Goosebumps" stories of R. L. Stine, are phenomenally popular in Australia. In fact, Jennings receives so much fan mail from young readers—about five thousand letters per year—that he employs two secretaries to help him keep up with replies. Writing in a 1995 article for *Australian Way* magazine, freelance journalist Terry Lane described Jennings as "a one-man industry," and, indeed, he is nothing if not prolific. Jennings has written a succession of critically acclaimed bestsellers since 1989, the year that he quit his job as a special education teacher to become a full-time writer. Total sales of his books now exceed three million copies, and Jennings has won a host of awards, including the Order of Australia for his service to children's literature.

Although Jennings's stories might raise eyebrows among parents, critics have praised his efforts for getting kids to sit down and *read* in the first place. Echoing that comment, Jennings once commented in *Something about the Author,* "Some adults think I should write about the sorts of things that they think kids *should* read. I only want to write the sorts of things that I think kids *want* to read. Books are fantastic. That's what I want my readers to think."

Jennings lives in Australia, but he was actually born in the English town of Heston, near London, on April 30, 1943. Six years later, with the country still mired in the economic aftermath of World War II, Jennings's parents packed up their son Paul and younger sister Ruth, and immigrated to Australia. There they settled in the city of Melbourne, where Jennings's father found work as an engineer. "I had a good childhood," Jennings writes in an autobiographical sketch that appears on his internet homepage. "I can remember all the good parts . . . very clearly. I can also remember all the fears and feelings of childhood that aren't so good. Feeling very small and powerless. The guilt and the embarrassment. The monster that I was quite sure lurked in the shadows. These are the things that I write about in my stories and which make some children ask, 'How do you know what it feels like to be me?' It's because I haven't forgotten those feelings."

Jennings told interviewer Fay Gardiner of *Scan* magazine that his father was a man who "had very high expectations; he was a very ambitious man." On the prompting of the elder Jennings, who decided that his son should receive vocational training, Jennings quit high school in his senior year to enroll at Frankston Teachers College. "In those days, you didn't need matriculation because there was a shortage of teachers," he explained to Gardiner. After receiving his certificate, Jennings taught for the next five years in the primary school system. His work there with young people who suffered from learning disorders got him interested in this specialized area of education. Jennings returned to college to study speech pathology—the science of speech disorders. He earned an undergraduate degree from Lincoln Institute in 1972, and then spent three years working for the Ministry of Education. In 1976 he became a lecturer in Special Education at Burwood State College, near Sydney.

In 1979 Jennings moved on to become a senior lecturer in Language and Literature at Warrnambool Institute of Adult Education in Warrnambool, a re-gional city in the state of Victoria. It was during the latter part of this ten-year period that Jennings's first marriage crumbled, and he was left on his own to raise the couple's four young children. As an outlet for some of the raw emotions he was feeling, Jennings joined a creative writing class and began writing stories for young people. He recalled in an interview with Mary Jo Fresch of the Australian magazine *Dragon Lode* that he was "very interested in families with single parents to legitimize them as proper families." He was also frustrated by what he felt was a lack of good stories for young readers.

Jennings told Fresch that in his work he had observed that many of the books available in libraries for what he calls "reluctant readers" were either poorly written or "talked down" to children. Worst of all, they were dull. In an article in *Magpies,* Jennings defined a "reluctant reader" as being "a child for whom adults have not been able to find a good enough book." Jennings decided he would write such books for readers in the eight- to twelve-year-old age group. In preparation for doing so, he began to systematically study the structure, language, and plots of childrens' stories. This helped him devise a series of informal guidelines to avoid the common mistakes other authors made. The Jennings recipe for readability called for stories for young readers to be clearly and concisely written; to have predictable language patterns, short sentences, and chapters; and to include no more than two or three main characters. But above all, Jennings decided, a successful story needs a plot that is imaginative, humorous, and unpredictable. "Magic is a must," he explained in his *Magpies* article. "You can't write for children unless you can remember what it is like to be a child."

Jennings had written four brief books related to his teaching work, but he had dreamed of writing fiction for many years. In an autobiographical sketch posted on his British publisher's internet page, he recalled, "One of my early attempts to get published was sending a story in to the *Women's Weekly* [magazine] when I was sixteen. They rejected the story and I was so upset by this that I didn't write again until I was thirty-nine." Encouraged by his experiences in the writing course that he was taking, Jennings submitted one of his stories to the Australian office of Penguin Publishers. As a result, he was offered an advance of four hundred dollars Australian to write some more. Jennings later told a reporter for the local newspaper, the *Warrnambool Standard,* that it took him about a year to write the seven more stories needed for the book; his efforts paid off handsomely.

Unreal! Eight Surprising Stories was an instant bestseller. Most books for young readers available in Australian bookshops were imports written by British or American authors, and so reviewers and readers alike loved that one of their own had written a book with an Australian perspective, vernacular, and settings. But even better was the realization that the stories, full of humor, plot twists, and deliciously unexpected endings, were good enough to appeal to readers anywhere. That assessment was confirmed when *Unreal!* was subsequently reprinted in Great Britain and North America—after some of the Australianisms had been amended for the overseas markets. (This would become standard practice for all of Jennings's books.) A critic in *Publishers Weekly* praised this debut collection for being "light, fast-paced entertainment sure to satisfy appetites for the grotesque." Jeanne Marie Clancy of *School Library Journal* wrote, "Both the vocabulary and the terse, journalistic style coupled with a frequent first-person point-of-view make (*Unreal!*) a natural for reluctant readers and story-tellers."

Surprised and delighted by the success of *Unreal!*, Jennings promptly went to work on a new book, *Unbelievable! More Surprising Stories.* Once again, the reception was favorable. "Stories like these can sometimes be just crazy enough to keep a child's interest going where other books fail," commented a reviewer in Jennings's hometown newspaper, the *Melbourne Herald.* "They are also shorter and less demanding than novels, which makes them an interesting alternative for reluctant or bored readers."

Having now hit his literary stride, Jennings began writing feverishly. He produced a succession of best-selling books—sometimes two per year—through the late 1980s and into the 1990s. The Jennings formula clearly works, for kids love his stories. His books often deal with bizarre topics; for example, there are stories about such things as a haunted outhouse, fly-killing cow "dung custard," a dead man's tattoos which come to life, and a boy's embarrassment at having to wear pink underpants with fairies on them. Predictably, some adults regard such dark humor as distasteful; reviewing the 1987 short story collection *Unbelievable,* Bill Boyle of the British publication *Books for Keeps* dismissed Jennings's fiction as "definitely an acquired taste." Jennings responded to such comments by defending his work to all who would listen. "Some people feel that bleak humor is an inappropriate form to use with children. I don't agree," he explained in a 1988 speech he gave at a conference of Australian educators (a transcript of which was

subsequently published in *Magpies*). "As George Bernard Shaw said, 'Life does not cease to be funny when someone dies anymore than it ceases to be serious when someone laughs.'"

With the emergence of Jennings as an important new Australian writer, people began paying more attention to what he was saying and how he was saying it. Some thoughtful reviewers pointed out that there are recurring themes in Jennings's fiction. Embarrassment is one; the vagaries of father-son relationships and the uncertainties of childhood are a couple of the others. Jennings does not deny that he tries to deal in his writing with what he feels are universal themes for young readers. "I guess basically what I do is observe very closely the world children live in now and I put the feelings I had as a child on top of it," he told Fay Gardiner.

A great many readers around the world apparently agreed with Karen Jameyson of *Horn Book* when she hailed Jennings as a "short story magician." Jennings continued to win fans with each new book. He wrote a succession of short story collections that proved popular with readers, including *Quirky Tales: More Oddball Stories* (1987), *Uncanny! Even More Surprising Stories* (1988), *Unbearable! More Bizarre Stories* (1990), *Unmentionable! More Amazing Stories* (1991), and *Undone! More Mad Endings* (1993), and *Thirteen! Unpredictable Tales from Paul Jennings* (1996). Critics have also continued to praise Jennings's books, which have won him a shelf full of literary awards, including Young Australian Best Book Awards each year from 1987 to 1995.

Despite his phenomenal success, Jennings has refused to rest on his laurels and has tried his hand at longer fiction. He wrote two books about a clever cat: *Paws* and a sequel called *Singenpoo Strikes Again.* Jennings also created a four-part series that began with a 1994 novella called *The Gizmo,* which recounts the strange adventures of a boy who on a dare steals a mysterious electronic gizmo from a market stall. The unlucky thief discovers that the device sticks to anyone who touches it and that it exchanges the unlucky person's clothes for those of any passersby. Ann Darnton of *School Library Journal* praised *The Gizmo* as "an amusing and well-written book," while George Hunt of *Books for Keeps* described it as "a lurid and slightly risque story [that] . . . might well appeal to older readers who are more at home with comic books." Jennings related the further adventures of the Gizmo in three other books: *The Gizmo Again, Come Back Gizmo,* and *Sink the Gizmo.*

Jennings moved in another new direction when he collaborated with fellow children's author Morris Gleitzman to write a six-part "serial story" called *Wicked.* According to reviewer Elaine McQuade of *School Librarian, Wicked* "is a wild, fantastic, roller-coaster of an adventure, full of 'slobberers' and evil rates and other gross creatures. But underlying the gripping story is a sensitive examination of the death of a parent, of the effects of divorce, and of the difficulties of living within a step family."

In recent years Jennings has also worked successfully with various illustrators to create picture storybooks. Sometimes the themes have been serious; that was the case when Jennings wrote the text for *The Fisherman and the Theefyspray,* an impassioned book about animal conservation and endangered species that won an Australian Environment Award. At times, Jennings's themes have been light-hearted, as was the case in *The Cabbage Patch Fib,* a hilarious lesson in the "facts-of-life." And at other times, Jennings's themes have been educational as well as fun, as was the case in *Spooner or Later,* a game book where silly illustrations are accompanied by "spoonerisms"—wordplay in which the beginnings of the words in a phrase are reversed, so "read the book" becomes the nonsensical "bead the rook." Jennings delights in this kind of humor, but he notes it also has a more serious purpose. Picture books are a publishing genre which he feels have been neglected as a potential tool to grab reluctant young readers. "Picture books are capable of giving enormous pleasure," Jennings explained in an essay for *Magpies.* "It is only the stigma of being seen with them that confines picture books to the lower grades."

Given the popularity and the strong visual component of Jennings's storytelling, some felt it inevitable that film producers would come knocking on his door. In 1990 he was enlisted to begin writing scripts based on his stories for a weekly Australian television series called *Round the Twist.* Then, in an unabashed marketing ploy, Jennings joined forces with illustrators Glenn Lumsden and David de Vries to start recycling the scripts into a series of comic books. Reviewing their first effort, *Round the Twist 1,* Kevin Steinberger of *Magpies* noted that while the publication had "great visual appeal," it—and others pending in the series—would be "less imaginative reads than the original short stories which have already proved their appeal convincingly."

Regardless of what television critics or book reviewers have said, the *Round the Twist* television series was a hit. In response, Jennings has now written television scripts for more than two dozen of his short stories, and he has decided to try his hand at writing for the movies. According to information that Jennings posted on his web site in the fall of 1998, he was hard at work on a script for a feature film. "This is all highly secret but I can tell you that [it] is based on my four Gizmo books," he teased.

BIOGRAPHICAL/CRITICAL SOURCES:

BOOKS

Children's Literature Review, Volume 40, Gale, 1996.
Something About the Author, Volume 88, Gale, 1996.

PERIODICALS

Australian Way, December, 1995.
Booklist, October 15, 1988, p. 423; March 15, 1990, pp. 1467, 1471; August, 1991, p 2147; March 15, 1993, p. 1314; January 1, 1995, p. 816.
Books for Keeps, July, 1986, p. 17; September, 1987; July, 1989, p. 10; July, 1991, p. 12; September, 1993, p. 13; November, 1995, p. 12; September, 1996, p. 16.
Bulletin of the Center for Children's Books, September, 1991, p. 43.
Carousel, winter, 1996, p. 23.
Children's Book Review Service, December, 1991, p. 47.
Dragon Lode, November, 1994.
Five Owls, May/June, 1996, p. 104.
Horn Book, July/August, 1992, pp. 497-500.
Junior Bookshelf, April, 1996, p. 78.
Kirkus Reviews, October 15, 1991, p. 1344; January 1, 1993, p. 62.
Magpies, September, 1988, pp. 9-12; March, 1990, pp. 5-9; September, 1990; September, 1993, p. 39; November, 1993, pp. 33-34; July, 1998.
Melbourne Herald, October 30, 1986.
New Advocate, fall, 1996, pp. 327-328.
Publishers Weekly, October 11, 1991, pp. 63-64; December 11, 1995, p. 71; August 31, 1998, p. 21.
Puffin Post, spring, 1996.
Reading Time, vol. 42, no. 2, p. 17.
Scan, May, 1991.
School Librarian, December, 1991, p. 117; summer, 1998.

School Library Journal, January, 1992, p. 113; November, 1993, p. 156; January, 1995, p. 108; November, 1995, p. 152.

Tribune Books (Chicago), February 12, 1995, p. 6.

Voice of Youth Advocates, October, 1995, p. 234.

Warrnambool Standard, November 16, 1985.

OTHER

Paul Jennings' Homepage, http://people.enternet.com/ ~jennings/educ/wrtt.htm (December, 1998).

Puffin homepage, http:/www.puffin.co.uk/living/ aut_25.htm (December, 1998).*

* * *

JENSEN, Johannes V(ilhelm) 1873-1950
(Ivar Lykke, a pseudonym)

PERSONAL: Born January 20, 1873, in Farso, Denmark; died November 25, 1950, in Copenhagen, Denmark; son of Hans and Marie Kirstine Jensen; married Else Marie Ulrik, 1904; children: three sons. *Education:* Studied medicine at the University of Copenhagen, 1893-96. *Religion:* Freethinker, from Lutheran background.

CAREER: Writer. Worked as a reporter for *Politiken* (Danish newspaper), beginning 1896.

AWARDS, HONORS: Nobel Prize for literature, 1944.

WRITINGS:

NOVELS

Danskere (title means "Danes"), 1896.

Einar Elkoer, 1898.

Kongens Fald, 1901, translation published as *The Fall of the King,* 1933.

Hjulet (title means "The Wheel"), Gyldendal (Copenhagen), 1905.

Broeen (part of the novel cycle "Den lange Rejse," or "The Long Journey"), 1909, translated by Arthur Chater and published with *Det tabte Land* as *Fire and Ice,* Gyldendal (London), 1922.

Skibet (part of the novel cycle "Den lange Rejse," or "The Long Journey"), 1912, translated by Arthur Chater and published with *Broeen, Norne-*

Goest, Det tabte Land, Christofer Columbus, and *Cimbrernes Tog* in the *The Long Journey,* Gyldendal (London), 1922-24.

Norne-Goest (part of the novel cycle "Den lange Rejse," or "The Long Journey"), 1919 translated by Arthur Chater and published with *Broeen, Skibet, Det tabte Land, Christofer Columbus,* and *Cimbrernes Tog* in *The Long Journey,* Gyldendal (London), 1922-24.

Det tabte Land (part of the novel cycle "Den lange Rejse," or "The Long Journey"), 1919, translated by Arthur Chater and published with *Broeen, Skibet, Norne-Goest, Christofer Columbus,* and *Cimbrernes Tog* in *The Long Journey,* Gyldendal (London), 1922-24.

Christofer Columbus (part of the novel cycle "Den lange Rejse," or "The Long Journey," 1921, translated by Arthur Chater as *Christopher Columbus,* Knopf (New York City), 1924, also published with *Broeen, Skibet, Norne-Goest,* and *Cimbrernes Tog* in *The Long Journey,* Gyldendal (London), 1922-24.

Cimbrenes Tog (part of the novel cycle "Den lange Rejse," or "The Long Journey"), 1922, translated by Arthur Chater as *The Cimbrians* and published with *Broeen, Skibet, Norne-Goest,* and *Christofer Columbus* in *The Long Journey,* Gyldendal (London), 1922-24.

The Long Journey (includes *Broeen, Skibet, Norne-Goest, Christofer Columbus,* and *Cimbrenes Tog*), three volumes, translated by Arthur Chater, Gyldendal (London), 1922-24.

Dr. Renaults Fristelser, 1935.

Also wrote serial novels under the pseudonym Ivar Lykke, c. 1893-96.

SHORT STORY COLLECTIONS

Himmerlandsfolk (title means "Himmerland People"), Gyldendal (Copenhagen), 1898.

Nye Himmerlandshistorier, Gyldendal (Copenhagen), 1904.

Himmerlandshistorier: Tredie Samling, Gyldendal (Copenhagen), 1910.

Olivia Marianne, 1915.

Kornmarken, 1932.

POETRY

Digte (title means "Poems"), 1906.

Digte: Tredie Udgave, 1921.

Aarstiderne, 1923.

Verdens Lys, 1926.

Den jydske Bloest, 1931.
Paaskebadet, 1937.

TRAVEL ESSAYS

Den gotiske Renaissance (title means "The Gothic Renaissance"), 1901.
Madame d'Ora, Gyldendal (Copenhagen), 1904.
Skovene, 1904.
Introduktion til vor Tidsalder, 1915.

ESSAYS

Den ny Verden, 1907.
Nordisk Aand, 1911.
Aestetik og Udvikling, 1923.
Evolution og Moral, 1925.
Dyrenes Forvandling, 1927.
Aandens Stadier, 1928.

FABLES; ADAPTER

Nye Myter, 1908.
Myter: Ny Samling, 1910.
Myter: Fjerde Samling, 1912.
Mollen, 1944.

OTHER

Intermezzo (short stories and travel essays), 1899.
Myter og Jagter (fables and short stories), 1907.
Rudyard Kipling (biography), 1912.
The Waving Rye (essays and short stories), 1958.

Contributor of poetry and prose to Danish journals.

SIDELIGHTS: Johannes V. Jensen was one of the foremost Danish writers during the first half of the twentieth century and the winner of the Nobel Prize for literature in 1944. His best-known work, the novel cycle "Den lange Rejse" ("The Long Journey"), traces the history of humanity from the emergence of the species to the discovery of America and reflects his interest in biological science and the evolutionary theories of Charles Darwin. Jensen wrote in a variety of genres, including poetry, drama, and short story, and the best of these works are noted for their sensitive characterizations and adept presentations of the natural landscape, as well as for expressing Jensen's wide-ranging travel experiences and his enthusiastic promotion of the technological advancements of modern civilization. *Seven Arts* contributor Paul Rosenfeld declared: "The strength and freshness of [Jensen's] genius, the deep richness and nervousness of his style, the boldness and originality of his ideas, place him among the dominant literary figures of the hour. . . . It was Whitman who first announced the coming of a race of men for whom no past existed, whose dreams were drawn to no sunken ages, who were whole-heartedly alive and whole-heartedly a part of their own time. Such a one is Jensen. And so it is given him to reveal to his day its grand proportions."

Born in Farso, in north Jutland, Jensen was educated at home until the age of eleven when he entered the Viborg Cathedral School. He began medical studies at the University of Copenhagen in 1893 and supported himself during his studies by writing a number of serial novels for a popular magazine under the pseudonym Ivar Lykke. A competent but restless student, Jensen began a succession of travels to the United States, France, and Spain in 1896 as a reporter for the Danish newspaper *Politiken*. He subsequently withdrew from the university, intending instead to pursue a career as a journalist. In the mid-1890s he published the novels *Danskere* (title means "The Danes") and *Einar Elkoer*, as well as the short story collection *Himmerlandsfolk* (title means "Himmerland People"), which is considered his most important work from this period. Maintaining a professional association with *Politiken* throughout his life, Jensen continued a series of international travels, visiting the Far East, Africa, and the United States, a country which he counted among his favorite travel destinations. Greatly inspired by the vitality of American life at the turn of the century, Jensen celebrated American inventiveness and vigor in the companion novels *Madame d'Ora* and *Hjulet* (title means "The Wheel"), which are set in Chicago and New York. With the publication of *Kongens Fold* (*The Fall of the King*) in 1901, Jensen turned from journalistic travel essays and novels with contemporary settings to historical works centered on evolutionary theory. His subsequent novels comprising *The Long Journey* amplify his views on the development of civilization. A popular lecturer and well-known cultural figure within Denmark, Jensen received little international attention before the English edition of *The Long Journey* was published in the early 1920s. He was later awarded the Nobel Prize in recognition of his numerous contributions to national and world literature. For the remainder of his life he continued to travel extensively and contributed essays, short stories, and poems to Danish journals. Jensen died in 1950.

Jensen's early novels *Danskere* and *Einar Elkoer*, which reflect a youthful aestheticism and fin de siecle disillusion, are representative of the introspective literature prominent in Denmark at the close of the nineteenth century. Later renouncing these works, Jensen stated, "I myself do not have copies of them, and I would read them again only with reluctance." The first work to bring him acclaim, *Himmerlands-folk,* and subsequent volumes of stories set in the Himmerland, are largely based on Jensen's recollections of the region surrounding his childhood home in Farso. These works are praised for their skillful delineation of landscape and local cultural traditions as well as for the combination of irony and sensitivity that distinguishes Jensen's character portraits. In an article in *Books Abroad,* Jens Nyholm asserted: "Jensen, through his individualistic style, has given a new tone to the Danish language. Through him, it has gained in power and expressiveness. Nature description has become nature revelation; the vigor of manhood, and the sweetness, the mellowness of womanhood, have been embodied in words as never before."

Jensen's fondness for the Himmerland region greatly influenced his outlook on the evolution of human civilization, which formed the chief focus of many of his mature works. Beginning with *Den gotiske Renaissance* (title means "The Gothic Renaissance"), a collection of newspaper articles written in Spain and France, Jensen praised the achievements and spirit of the "Gothic," or Anglo-Saxon, people, a race he believed had developed from the prehistoric inhabitants of Scandinavia, and he sought to revitalize the spirit of innovation in the descendants of this race by emphasizing the technological accomplishments of modern industrial nations. *The Long Journey,* an epic work presenting his view of civilization from its beginnings in Scandinavia to Christopher Columbus's discovery of America, depicts the struggle against nature as the impetus for human cultural progress and intellectual development. While the cycle combines elements from the Bible, ancient mythology, and the Icelandic sagas, it also evidences Jensen's knowledge of geography and anthropology, as well as the evolutionary theories of Charles Darwin. Applying Darwin's theory of natural selection to intellectual history, Jensen celebrated in *The Long Journey* the originators of such significant developments in human history as the discovery of fire, the invention of tools and modes of transportation, the emergence of art and architectural styles, and the undertaking of important human migrations. Considered Jensen's greatest achievement. *The Long Journey* has been described as a scientific counterpart to the Old Testament, and it remains the work for which he is principally known outside Denmark.

Jensen's prolific output also included writings in such various genres as drama, poetry, short story, essay, and what he termed "myth," or a brief work focusing on a moment of historical significance and combining literary characteristics of the short story, fable, and essay. His concept of myth—"short flashes of the essence of things that illumine man and time"—has been compared to James Joyce's idea of epiphany, and Jensen's mythological stories are considered innovative and significant literary achievements. Also a respected poet, Jensen published his works regularly in Danish periodicals, and a number of his lyrical poems on patriotic subjects became well known in Denmark during his lifetime when they were set to music. The themes of Jensen's poems reflect those of his prose writings and include the celebration of nature, the advancement of time, and the achievements of human progress. Greatly influenced by the American poet Walt Whitman, Jensen wrote predominantly in free verse, and his works have been praised as powerfully expressive, yet he is not widely known as a poet outside Denmark, a situation that commentators suggest is due to the difficulty of translating his works for a wider audience. Within Denmark, however, he remains a highly esteemed contributor to Danish culture and national identity. *American-Scandinavian Review* contributor Aage Marcus commented: "Jensen has more than any other Danish writer become the interpreter of his race and his nation. He has once for all given conscious expression to the mentality of the Nordic race, and has enabled his people to find themselves by obtaining a foothold in that Denmark which, unaffected by political changes, goes back to the dawn of time."

BIOGRAPHICAL/CRITICAL SOURCES:

BOOKS

Jensen, Johannes V., *The Long Journey,* translated by A. G. Chater, with a preface by Francis Hackett, Alfred A. Knopf (New York), 1945, pp. xi-xvii.

Rosenfeld, Paul, *Men Seen: Twenty-Four Modern Authors,* Dial Press (New York City), 1925, pp. 313-322.

Rossel, Sven H., *Johannes V. Jensen,* Twayne Publishers, 1984.

PERIODICALS

American Norvegica, vol. III, 1971, pp. 272-293.

American-Scandinavian Review, June-July, 1932, pp. 339-347; winter, 1943, pp. 343-346.

Books Abroad, April, 1945, pp. 131-135.

Literary Digest International Book Review, April, 1923, pp. 18-19, 61.

New Republic, May 7, 1945, pp. 648-649.

New Statesman and Nation, April 29, 1933, p. 535.

New Yorker, April 28, 1945, pp. 78, 81.

New York Times Book Review, February 25, 1923, pp. 3, 24; April 30, 1933, p. 6; April 15, 1945, pp. 4, 28.

Orbis Literarum, vol. 23, 1968, pp. 225-232.

Scandinavian Studies, winter, 1989, pp. 55-67.

Scandinavica, May, 1962, pp. 114-123; May, 1985, pp. 17-34.

Seven Arts, January, 1917, pp. 281-286.*

Sewanee Review, July, 1925, pp. 331-334.*

*   *   *

JOHANSEN, Iris

PERSONAL: Female; children: two.

ADDRESSES: Home—Atlanta, GA. *Agent*—c/o Bantam Books, 1540 Broadway, New York, NY 10036.

CAREER: Romance and romantic suspense novelist. Previously worked for a major airline.

WRITINGS:

NOVELS

"SHAMROCK" SERIES

York the Renegade, Bantam Books (New York City), 1986.

"DELANEYS OF KILLAROO" SERIES

Matilda the Adventuress, Bantam Books (New York City), 1997.

Wild Silver, Bantam Books (New York City), 1988.

Satin Ice, Bantam Books (New York City), 1988.

Also author of the novella "Christmas Past," published in *The Delaney Christmas Carol,* with novellas by Kay Hooper and Fayrene Preston, Doubleday (New York City), 1992.

"WILD DANCER" TRILOGY

The Wind Dancer, Bantam Books (New York City), 1991.

Storm Winds, Bantam Books (New York City), 1991.

Reap the Wind, Bantam Books (New York City), 1991.

OTHER NOVELS

Stormy Vows, Bantam Books (New York City), 1983.

Tempest at Sea, Bantam Books (New York City), 1983.

The Reluctant Lark, Bantam Books (New York City), 1983.

The Bronzed Hawk, Bantam Books (New York City), 1983.

The Lady and the Unicorn, Bantam Books (New York City), 1984.

The Golden Valkyrie, Bantam Books (New York City), 1984.

The Trustworthy Redhead, Bantam Books (New York City), 1984.

Return to Santa Flores, Bantam Books (New York City), 1984.

No Red Roses, Bantam Books (New York City), 1984.

Capture the Rainbow, Bantam Books (New York City), 1984.

Touch the Horizon, Bantam Books (New York City), 1984.

The Forever Dream, Bantam Books (New York City), 1985.

White Satin, Bantam Books (New York City), 1985.

Blue Velvet, Bantam Books (New York City), 1985.

A Summer Smile, Bantam Books (New York City), 1985.

And the Desert Blooms, Bantam Books (New York City), 1986.

Always, Bantam Books (New York City), 1986.

Everlasting, Bantam Books (New York City), 1986.

'Til the End of Time, Bantam Books (New York City), 1987.

Last Bridge Home, Bantam Books (New York City), 1987.

Across the River of Yesterday, Bantam Books (New York City), 1987.

The Spellbinder, Bantam Books (New York City), 1987.

Magnificent Folly, Bantam paperback (New York City), 1987, Doubleday Loveswept hardcover (New York City), 1989.

One Touch of Topaz, Bantam Books (New York City), 1988.

Star Light, Star Bright, Bantam Books (New York City), 1988.

This Fierce Splendor, Bantam Books (New York City), 1988.

Man from Half Moon Bay, Bantam Books (New York City), 1988.

Blue Skies and Shining Promises, Bantam Books (New York City), 1988.

Strong, Hot Winds, Bantam Books (New York City), 1988.

Notorious, Doubleday Loveswept hardcover, 1990.

Wicked Jake Darcy, Bantam Books (New York City), 1990.

Tender Savage, Bantam Books (New York City), 1991.

The Golden Barbarian, Doubleday Loveswept (New York City), 1990, Bantam, 1992.

The Tiger Prince, Bantam Books (New York City), 1993.

Star Spangled Bride, Bantam Books (New York City), 1993.

The Magnificent Rogue, Bantam Books (New York City), 1993.

The Beloved Scoundrel, Bantam Books (New York City), 1994.

Midnight Warrior, Bantam Books (New York City), 1994.

Dark Rider, Bantam Books (New York City), 1995.

Lion's Bride, Bantam Books (New York City), 1995.

The Ugly Duckling, Bantam Books (New York City), 1996.

Long After Midnight, Bantam Books (New York City), 1996.

The Face of Deception, Bantam Books (New York City), 1998.

And Then You Die, Bantam Books (New York City), 1998.

SIDELIGHTS: Popular romance and romantic suspense novelist Iris Johansen is a prolific writer, having published seven novels in 1984, eight novels in 1988, and more than one novel in most other years since 1983. Quantity of output, however, has not stopped her from being an innovator, in the view of Barbara E. Kemp in *Twentieth-Century Romance and Historical Writers.* "She has stretched the boundaries of the standard formulas in the category romance field and has written some of the best historical romance novels," declared Kemp. Johansen writes category romances set in several historical eras and has become known for the conviction with which she describes bygone places and people. Her characterizations are considered among the more complex in the genre. As for sex, Kemp pointed out that the presence of one or more long seduction scenes is a hallmark of Johansen's work, and that, although the seduction often contains "an element of punishment," it is always made clear that the heroine is not in real physi-

cal danger. Commented Kemp, "The uncertainty of remaining safely on the edge of possible pain adds sexual tension to the stories."

Several of Johansen's novels have belonged to Bantam/Doubleday's Loveswept line of romances, beginning with *Stormy Vows,* Johansen's first novel, published in 1983. However, her historical novels have taken her—and her readers—into far corners of the earth. In particular, Johansen has made two imaginary countries, the Middle Eastern kingdom of Sedikhan and the Balkan state of Tamrovia, her own. Characters recur from book to book, and the two nations are linked by marriage; thus, Johansen's loyal readers can follow the fortunes of favorite characters such as recovering drug addict David Bradford (who originally appeared *The Trustworthy Redhead*), who finds love and contentment in *Touch the Horizon* with a woman, Billie Callahan, herself a star of *Capture the Rainbow.*

Johansen's novels are sometimes included in established series which feature novels written by several authors. For example, in the "Shamrock" Trilogy, a series about the Delaney brothers of Ireland, Johansen wrote *York the Renegade* while the two other novels were written by Kay Hooper and Fayrene Preston. The "Delaneys of Killaroo" series is a spinoff of the Shamrock tales, focusing on three sisters in the Australian branch of the Delaney family. Although not officially part of the Delaney series, the novel *This Fierce Splendor* deals with a male character who is a Delaney. The trio of authors contributing to the trilogy also wrote a Christmas book, *The Delaney Christmas Carol,* in which each writer contributed a novella.

As an individual Johansen wrote the novels comprising the "Wind Dancer" Trilogy of 1991, the first two volumes of which received considerable acclaim from romance reviewers. The novels, spanning much of European history, deal with the Andreas family's quest for a legendary golden statue called the Wind Dancer. The first novel, *The Wind Dancer,* is set in sixteenth-century Italy, and the second, *Storm Winds,* in France during the Reign of Terror near the end of the eighteenth century. *The Wind Dancer,* which had a first printing of 700,000 copies, is "a lively and imaginative blend of romance and adventure," according to *Publishers Weekly;* that magazine's reviewer also applauded the character of Lorenzo Vasaro, the hero's friend, who is "an unlikely but likable character . . .[,] a worldly-wise and intriguing blend of ruthlessness and charm."

Peggy Kaganoff, another *Publishers Weekly* reviewer, called *Storm Winds* "a diverting romance" with "plot twists worthy of a mystery novel." However, Kaganoff felt that the concluding segment of the trilogy, *Reap the Wind,* suffered under the weight of the author's apparent aspiration to make it a contemporary spy novel involving the CIA and the KGB. Kemp, while expressing opinions similar to those of *Publishers Weekly* regarding the relative merits of the three volumes in the trilogy, pointed out that "a disappointing novel by Johansen is still far better than the work of many other authors."

Johansen went on to produce other well-received romance novels in the 1990s. Of *The Magnificent Rogue,* published in 1993, a *Booklist* commented, "Passion and suspense abound in [this]. . . robust romance. . . . Spellbinding romantic fiction from a master of the genre." *Library Journal's* Bettie Alston Spivey called the 1994 novel *The Beloved Scoundrel,* a romance of the Napoleonic era, "absorbing" and thought readers would find it a page-turner by an author who "has outdone herself here." The same year Johansen produced *Midnight Warrior,* a tale of England and Wales set in 1066. Kristin Ramsdell of *Library Journal* commented on the book and wrote: "Believable,thoughtfully constructed characters, complex plotting, and lively dialog characterize this sensual historical."

Johansen achieved a personal milestone in 1996 with the publication of *The Ugly Duckling.* It was her most prestigious publication to date, although not the "hardcover debut" that a *Kirkus Reviews* critic termed it (at least two of her previous novels had been placed between hardcovers, but in the Loveswept line rather than as solo creations). In *The Ugly Duckling,* commented the *Kirkus Reviews* critic, "megaseller Johansen abandons the lush historical romances that have made her reputation and stakes out the proven market of Nora Roberts and Sidney Sheldon." The heroine, Nell, is the plain wife of a rich man who, along with their daughter, is murdered before her eyes; Nell herself is thrown off a cliff and survives but is disfigured. Hero Nicholas, pursuing the drug dealers who killed Nell's family, takes her under his wing and sees that she receives state-of-the-art plastic surgery that turns her into a beauty. He also teaches her martial arts. Nell and Nicholas set out to destroy the villains and do so with the help of what the *Kirkus Reviews* critic called "inventive surprises." A *Publishers Weekly* reviewer called *The Ugly Duckling* "spectacular" and elaborated: "The romance here is suspenseful, and the suspense is romantic; for fans of

each, this is a keeper." *Booklist's* Brad Hooper announced that, in *The Ugly Duckling,* "the romantic suspense genre is done a good turn."

Having achieved this new level of success, Johansen went on to create another successful thriller with her next book, *Long After Midnight,* a tale of scientific breakthroughs and corrupt corporations. The heroine, Kate, is a high-level working mother doing important research for top scientist Noah Smith and trying to give her nine-year-old son a good life at the same time. When Noah's lab blows up and attempts are made on Kate's life, Kate and Noah go into hiding to escape from the psychopathic hit man who is stalking them. Kate has two love interests, Noah and his solder-of-fortune friend Seth. Noting that the plot premise contains some familiar, conventional elements, a *Publishers Weekly* critic added that "Johansen knows how to take the formula and run with it," appealing to readers with her believable characters, effective dialogue, and interesting plotting. The review also noted that a plot strand involving the heroine's father, an Alzheimer's patient, gives "the deft but somewhat protracted finish a moving, unexpected touch."

BIOGRAPHICAL/CRITICAL SOURCES:

BOOKS

Vasudevan, Aruna, editor, *Twentieth-Century Romance and Historical Writers,* third edition, St. James Press (London), 1994, pp. 353-354.

PERIODICALS

Booklist, September 1, 1993, p. 34; March 1, 1996, p. 1076.
Kirkus Reviews, February 15, 1996, p. 249.
Library Journal, December, 1993, pp. 174-175; May 15, 1994, p. 66.
Publishers Weekly, January 4, 1991, p. 68; April 26, 1991, p. 55; September 13, 1991, pp. 73-74; November 30, 1992, p. 49; July 26, 1993, p. 63; January 3, 1994, p. 78; July 4, 1994, p. 57; March 13, 1995, p. 65; December 4, 1995, p. 58; February 26, 1996, p. 84; May 18, 1996, p. 25; December 30, 1996, p. 54; November 10, 1997, p. 54; August 17, 1998, p. 45.

OTHER

Bantam, Dell, Doubleday Online (website), http://www.bdd.com (January 29, 1999).

Books@Random, http://www.randomhouse.com (January 29, 1999).*

* * *

JOHNSON, Bettye
   See ROGERS, Bettye

* * *

JOHNSON, Cait 1952-

PERSONAL: Born September 23, 1952, in Andover, MA; daughter of Robert John (an inventor) and Patricia Marie (a craftsperson; maiden name, Lewis) Johnson; married William David Peters, 1974 (divorced, 1980); companion of Stuart Hannan (a special effects designer and musician); children: (first marriage) Reid Johnson. *Ethnicity:* "Anglo." *Education:* St. Mary's College of Maryland, B.A. (cum laude), 1974; Ohio State University, M.F.A., 1979. *Politics:* Liberal Democrat. *Religion:* "Earth-centered spirituality." *Avocational interests:* Singing and performance, fabric arts, sculpting goddess figurines "from anything handy," walking in the woods.

ADDRESSES: Home—R.R.1, Box 382, Clinton Corners, NY 12514; fax 914-266-4007. *E-mail*—caitjohnson@hotmail.com.

CAREER: Teacher, workshop, and ritual facilitator at healing and spiritual centers, 1981—.

AWARDS, HONORS: First prize, Maryland State Poetry Contest, 1970.

WRITINGS:

Tarot for Every Day: Ideas and Activities for Bringing Tarot Wisdom into Your Daily Life, Shawangunk Press, 1994.
(With Maura D. Shaw) *Tarot Games: Forty-Five Playful Ways to Explore Tarot Cards Together; a New Vision for the Circle of Community,* HarperSanFrancisco (San Francisco, CA), 1994.
(With Shaw) *Celebrating the Great Mother: A Handbook of Earth-Honoring Activities for Parents and Children,* Inner Traditions (New York City), 1995.

Cooking like a Goddess: Bringing Seasonal Magic into the Kitchen, Inner Traditions, 1997.

Author (with Elizabeth Cunningham) of the book *Naked Masks,* 1998.

WORK IN PROGRESS: Sow at the Fair, a book of poems with illustrations by Ann duBois; *River of Birds,* a novel; *Bone Time,* poems; "Dark Blessing," a performance piece for narrator and six characters; a divination deck for women, with art by Melissa Harris.

SIDELIGHTS: Cait Johnson told *CA:* "My nonfiction has been fueled by involvement with the women's spirituality movement and the compulsion to share what I know about connecting—with the seasons, with the natural world, and with our own inner wisdom. Now, after two books on the Tarot, one on earth-centered activities for parents and children, and one that is as much a recipe for playful, sacred, and connected living as it is a seasonal vegetarian cookbook, my focus is changing. I've carried on a clandestine affair with poetry, fiction, and performance nearly all my life. Now the same spirit of creative play that infuses my nonfiction is urging me to bring those elements more fully into my life and work."

* * *

JONES, David Martin 1951-
   (Jonah M. David)

PERSONAL: Born August 21, 1951, in Cardiff, Wales; son of John Cynan (a clerk) and Betty (a nurse; maiden name, Hutchings) Jones. *Ethnicity:* "Welsh." *Education:* University of Reading, B.A. (with honors), 1971; McMaster University, M.A., 1973; University of Toronto, doctoral study, 1975-76; London School of Economics and Political Science, London, Ph.D., 1984. *Politics:* Liberal. *Religion:* Atheist.

ADDRESSES: Office—Department of Government, University of Tasmania, G.P.O. Box 252-22, Hobart, Tasmania 7001, Australia. *E-mail*—d.m.jones@utas.edu.au.

CAREER: Teacher at secondary schools in Brent borough, London, England, 1975-77; Brent Educational Workshop, London, coordinator of truancy project,

1981-88; history teacher and department head at a girls' school in Bushey, England, 1988-90; National University of Singapore, Singapore, lecturer in political science, 1990-95; University of Tasmania, Hobart, Australia, senior lecturer in political theory, 1995—. University of London, teacher at London School of Economics and Political Science, 1984-90, researcher at Centre for Urban Education, King's College, 1987-90, and visiting fellow in war studies; North East London Polytechnic, teacher fellow, 1986-87.

WRITINGS:

(Contributor) Stephen Ball, editor, *Michel Foucault and Education: Disciplines and Knowledge,* Routledge (New York City), 1990, 2nd edition, 1992.
(With D. A. Bell, D. Brown, and K. Jayasuriya) *Towards Illiberal Democracy in Pacific Asia,* St. Martin's Press (New York City), 1995.
(Contributor) Chan Kwok Bun, editor, *Crossing Borders: Transmigration in the Asia Pacific,* Prentice-Hall (Toronto, Ontario), 1995.
(Contributor) P. Mclaren and J. Giarelli, editors, *Critical Theory and Educational Research,* State University of New York Press (Albany, NY), 1995.
Political Development in Pacific Asia, Polity Press (Oxford, England), 1997.
(Contributor) D. Goldblatt and R. Maidment, editors, *Pacific Studies,* Open University (Milton Keynes, England), 1998.
Conscience and Allegiance: The Political Significance of Oaths and Engagements, University of Rochester Press (Rochester, NY), 1999.
The Image of East Asia in Western Social and Political Thought, St. Martin's Press, in press.

Contributor of articles and reviews to professional journals, popular magazines, and newspapers, including *National Review* (under pseudonym Jonah M. David), *World Today, Humboldt Journal of Social Relations, Comparative Politics, Contemporary Security Policy, Constitutional Political Economy, National Interest,* and *Pacific Review.* Book review editor, *Asian Journal of Political Science,* 1992-95.

SIDELIGHTS: David Martin Jones told *CA:* "I have always found writing both therapeutic and satisfying, something that, as Paul Bowles observed, 'keeps the evil on the outside.' The difficulty with writing is its obsessive nature; it is also difficult to find an audience, or more precisely a publisher or editor, who believes that what I write might reach an audience.

"What motivates me to write on issues of contemporary politics is generally an experience that I have had which seems to conflict with a prevailing academic or ideological (currently the two are disturbingly interchangeable) orthodoxy. In terms of the anxiety of influence, I was fortunate to have attended the London School of Economics government department when the skeptical legacy of Michael Oakeshott, Elie Kedourie, and Ernest Gellner prevailed. It was through this influence that I gradually realized that jargon was often an excuse for thought and that it was the duty of a writer to try and express ideas in an interesting manner. To think clearly is also to write clearly.

"With regard to the subjects I have chosen, they are all ultimately concerned with the languages of self-understanding and self-disclosure. Whether writing on seventeenth-century understandings of conscience and obligation, or twentieth-century Asian reinvention of traditional values, I am interested in the ways in which culture and contingent historical experience shape political destiny. In this context, I am currently interested in the manner in which a contemporary politics of identity selectively deploys the historical record."

*   *   *

JOSEPH, Don
See HOLMES, Donald

*   *   *

JUNKER, Patricia 1952-

PERSONAL: Born August 16, 1952, in Ohio. *Education:* University of Toledo, B.A. (magna cum laude), 1974; University of Michigan, M.A., 1980.

ADDRESSES: Office—M. H. de Young Memorial Museum, Fine Arts Museums of San Francisco, Golden Gate Park, San Francisco, CA 94118. *E-mail*—pjunker@famsf.org.

CAREER: Toledo Museum of Art, Toledo, OH, fellow, 1976-77; Smith College, Northampton, MA, intern at art museum, 1978-80, curatorial assistant, 1980-82; University of Rochester, Rochester, NY, curator of American art and chief curator at Memorial

Art Gallery, 1982-90; University of Wisconsin—
Madison, curator of collections at Elvehjem Museum
of Art, 1990-92; Fine Arts Museums of San Francisco, San Francisco, CA, assistant curator of American paintings, 1992-94, acting head of American
art department, 1994-96, associate curator of American art, 1996—. John Steuart Curry Foundation,
member of board of directors, 1992-96; American
Decorative Arts Forum, member of board of directors, 1998—.

MEMBER: Midwest Art History Association (member
of board of directors, 1992), Upper Midwest Conservation Association (member of board of directors, 1992).

AWARDS, HONORS: National Endowment for the
Arts, fellowship, 1976-77, internship, 1978-80;
scholar of Association of Art Museum Directors at
Attingham Summer School, England, 1982; Henry
Allen Moe Prize, New York State Historical Association, 1991, for *Winslow Homer in the 1890s;* grant
from Henry Luce Foundation.

WRITINGS:

*Promoted to Glory: The Apotheosis of George
Washington,* Museum of Art, Smith College
(Northampton, MA), 1980.
*The Course of Empire: The Erie Canal and the New
York Landscape, 1825-1875,* University of Wash-
ington Press (Seattle, WA), 1984.
Winslow Homer in the 1890s: Prout's Neck Observed,
Hudson Hills (New York City), 1990.
(Contributor) *Facing Eden: One Hundred Years of
Landscape Art in the San Francisco Bay Area,
1895-1995,* University of California Press (Ber-
keley, CA), 1995.
John Steuart Curry: Inventing the Middle West,
Hudson Hills, 1998.

Coauthor of *The Rockefeller Collection of American
Art at the Fine Arts Museums of San Francisco,*
Abrams (New York City). Author of exhibition cata-
logs. Contributor to periodicals, including *Triptych,
Magazine Antiques,* and *Porticus.*

K

KAPLAN, Robert S. 1940-

PERSONAL: Born May 2, 1940, in NY. *Education:* Massachusetts Institute of Technology, B.S. and M.S.; Cornell University, Ph.D.

ADDRESSES: Office—Harvard Business School, Boston, MA 02163.

CAREER: Carnegie-Mellon University, Pittsburgh, PA, member of industrial administration faculty, c. 1968-84, dean of Graduate School of Industrial Administration, 1977-83; Harvard University, Business School, Boston, faculty member, 1984—, became Marvin Bower Professor of Leadership Development. Technion-Israel Institute of Technology, member of academic committee of board of trustees; Balanced Scorecard Collaborative, director.

AWARDS, HONORS: Outstanding Educator Award, American Accounting Association, 1988; CIMA Award, Chartered Institute of Management Accountants, 1994; honorary doctorate, University of Stuttgart, 1994.

WRITINGS:

(With H. Thomas Johnson) *Relevance Lost: The Rise and Fall of Management Accounting,* Harvard Business School Press, 1991.
(Editor) *Measures for Manufacturing Excellence,* Harvard Business School Press, 1992.
(With David Norton) *The Balanced Scorecard: Translating Strategy into Action,* Harvard Business School Press (Boston), 1996.
(With Robin Cooper) *Cost and Effect: Using Integrated Cost Systems to Drive Profitability and Performance,* Harvard Business School Press, 1998.

Co-author of five other books, including *Implementing Activity-based Cost Management: Moving from Analysis to Action.* Author of the four-part videotape series, "Measuring Corporate Performance," produced by HBS Management Productions, 1994. Contributor to business and management journals.

* * *

KARINTHY, Frigyes 1887-1938

PERSONAL: Born in 1887, in Budapest, Hungary; died of a brain hemorrhage in August, 1938. *Education:* Attended University of Budapest; attended medical school.

CAREER: Writer and translator.

WRITINGS:

Naszutazas a fold kozeppontja fele (novel), 1902.
Igy irtok ti: parodiak (parodies), two volumes, 1912.
Holnap reggel (drama), 1916.
Tanar ur kerem! (short stories), 1916, translation by Istvan Farkas published as *Please Sir!,* Corvina (Budapest), 1968.
Utazas faremidoba (novel), 1917.
Capillaria: regency (novel), 1921; translation by Paul Tabori published as *Voyage to Faremido. Capillaria,* Living Books, 1966.

The Drama: A Farce-Satire in One Act (drama),
    translated by Edmond Pauker, Longmans, Green
    (New York City), 1922.
Ki kerdezett? (essays), 1926.
Nem mondhatom el senkinek: versek (poetry), Szepiro-
    dalmi Konyvkiado (Budapest), 1930.
Meg mindig igy irtok ti (parodies), 1934.
Utazas a koponyam korul (memoir), 1938; translation
    by Vernon Duckworth Barker published as *A
    Journey 'Round My Skull,* 1938.
Grave and Gay: Selections from His Work, selected
    by Istvan Kerekgyarto, with an afterword by
    Karoly Szalay, Corvina, 1973.

Also author of *Three Plays: The Singing Lesson; The
Long War; The Magic Chair,* published in the journal
Performing Arts, 1982; translator of Jonathan Swift's
Gulliver's Travels into Hungarian.

SIDELIGHTS: Hungarian author Frigyes Karinthy
was noted for his numerous satirical and parodic essays and short stories. Critics praise his best works
for their insight into the grotesqueries and inanities
of individuals living out what Karinthy perceived to
be the tragedy of modern life. After the beginning
of the World War I, Karinthy produced fewer satirical works and began writing pieces that directly
protested social and political injustice. His last book,
1938's *Utozas a koponyam korul* (*A Journey 'Round
My Skull*), a memoir describing his affliction with
a brain tumor from diagnosis through surgery, is
considered a unique autobiographical accomplishment.

Paul Tabori, in his introduction to *Voyage to
Faremido. Capillaria,* his translation of Karinthy's
1921 novel, *Capillaria,* remarked: "As a parodist
[Karinthy] was without peer. . . . I know a good
many other writers who have dabbled in this particular literary form—yet I have not hesitation in saying
that none of them could touch Karinthy. He had a
wonderful ability of grasping the essential quality,
the basic nature of any writer, Hungarian or foreign. His parodies could be wild and mad exercises
of the imagination running amuck . . . ; but in most
cases they were of high literary quality in themselves. Whether it was Ibsen or Conan Doyle,
Dickens or Zola, the Hungarian Endre Ady or
Ferenc Molnar whom he picked for his victim, the
persiflage and satire were pinpointed brilliantly,
showing up the faults or exaggerations of the most
eminent authors. He was like a master taxidermist;
his stuffed animals were so life-like that they almost
moved."

Karinthy was born in Budapest in 1887. He published
his first novel, *Naszutazas a fold kozeppontja fele,* in
1902 and began publishing regularly in 1906. He
entered the University of Budapest to study mathematics and natural science, then attended medical school
for a time. Because the rigorous discipline of his
course of study prevented him from pursuing his wide
range of intellectual interests, Karinthy left the university and became a journalist. He soon gained acclaim as a brilliant member of Budapest's cafe society
and as a writer of skillful parodies of well-known
European authors; his first collection of these works,
Igy irtok ti, appeared in 1912.

After the outbreak of World War I, he openly criticized the devastating effects of the war; he also translated Jonathan Swift's *Gulliver's Travels* into Hungarian during this period. His two sequels to Gulliver's
journal, *Utazas faremidoba* and *Capillaria,* were published in 1917 and 1921 respectively. Karinthy frequently wrote for cabarets, theaters, and a number of
influential Hungarian periodicals until he began experiencing the psychic disturbances which accompany a
brain tumor; early in 1938, he submitted to an operation to remove the tumor. Although the surgery was
successful, Karinthy died of a brain hemorrhage in
August, 1938.

Karinthy's best works use humor as a vehicle for
sociopolitical and philosophical commentary. While
much of his writing is entertaining, Joseph Remenyi
observed in *Poet Lore:* "Karinthy, as a humorist, was
somewhat of a literary wizard. . . . His joviality was
speculative; but he was sufficiently the artist who felt
the pathetic unmeaningness of many things and hap-
penings, and was hurt by them, but, in a creative
sense, was also intrigued with their place in human
destiny. His jesting articulateness, his vivacious com-
municativeness jeopardized his reputation as a 'serious' writer; his 'slang', the argot of 'literary' cafes,
detracted from his reputation as a genuine literary
artist—a reputation, however, to which he was entitled. In a world of political and social masqueraders
it was easy to mistake his nimbly expressed, but not
light work for sheer virtuosity. He had the solitariness
of a clown, with no sneering contempt for his fellow-
man whom he amused, but possessing a mastery of
facts, understanding and adroitness of expression that
made him superior to his surroundings. There was
cosmic conviviality in Karinthy, the source of which
was his sense of universality."

Such works as *Capillaria* and *A Journey 'Round My
Skull* exemplify Karinthy's ability to make serious

subject matter amusing. *Capillaria* recounts relationships and conflicts between men and women in the form of a traveller's journal, allowing Karinthy to comment on the disparate conceptions that men and women hold of each other. *A Journey 'Round My Skull* is Karinthy's account of his brain disease, beginning with his first suspicions of the disorder and culminating in his precise description of the operation, which was performed using only a local anesthetic. The memoir presents a detailed picture of his physical and mental state through the course of his brain disease, during which Karinthy scrutinized the slow disconnection of the link between intellect and body and attempted to understand the nature of that link. In *A Journey 'Round My Skull,* Karinthy applied to his own experience the intense powers of observation that are displayed in his social commentary. While some critics maintain that Hungary's social and political upheaval prevented Karinthy from consistently producing the quality of work of which he was capable, he is nevertheless credited with producing works notable for their wit and insight.

BIOGRAPHICAL/CRITICAL SOURCES:

BOOKS

Karinthy, Frigyes, *Grave and Gay: Selections from His Work,* edited by Istvan Kerekgyarto, with an afterword by Karoly Szalay, Corvina Press (Budapest), 1973.
Karinthy, Frigyes, *Voyage to Faremido. Capillaria,* translated and with an introduction by Paul Tabori, Living Books, 1966.

PERIODICALS

New Statesman, February 4, 1939, pp. 180, 182.
Poet Lore, spring, 1946, pp. 69-79.
Times Literary Supplement, February 18, 1939, p. 101.*

*   *   *

KATZ, Avner 1939-

PERSONAL: Born March 11, 1939, in Kibbutz Ramat-Rachel, Israel; son of Moshe (a member of Kibbutz Ramat-Rachel) and Hanna (a member of Kibbutz Ramat-Rachel; maiden name, Mazusky) Katz; mar-

ried Ayeleth Hershler (a translator), September 10, 1964; children: Efrat, Erella Katz-Aran, Aya. *Education:* Graduate of Bezalel Academy of Art, 1960; Central School of Arts & Crafts (post-graduate studies), 1964-66. *Religion:* Jewish.

ADDRESSES: Home and office—12 She'erit Israel St., Ramat-Hasharon 47201, Israel.

CAREER: Artist and writer/illustrator of books for children and adults. Bezalel Academy of Art, Jerusalem, Israel, Avni Institute for Painting, Tel Aviv, Israel, and Ha'mifrasha for Painting, Tel Aviv, Israel, instructor, 1976-80; University of Haifa, Israel, instructor, 1978—, head of creative arts department, 1988-91, associate professor, 1993—. *Military service:* Army service, 1959-62.

Solo exhibitions include "Tempera on Paper," Dugit Gallery, Tel Aviv, Israel, 1972; "Works on Paper," Artist House, Jerusalem, Israel, 1974; "Works on Paper," July M. Gallery, Tel Aviv, 1975; "Ceramic Sculptures," July M. Gallery, 1982; "Illustration-painting," Herzliya Museum of Art, Israel, 1987; "Oil Painting," July M. Gallery, 1990; "Lino Cuts," Ramat-Gan Museum of Art, Israel, 1990; "Lino Cuts," Art Gallery, Detroit, MI, 1991; "Illustrations 1970-1991," South Wing, Israel Museum, Jerusalem, 1991; "Paintings," July M. Gallery, 1992; "Paintings," Noga Gallery, Herzliya, 1993; "Papers," Herzliya Museum of Art, 1993; "Illustrations," Every Picture Tells a Story Gallery, Los Angeles, CA, 1994; "Air Mail," July M. Gallery, 1995; "Illustrations," Yad Lebanim Gallery, Ramat-Hasharon, Israel, 1995; "Works on Paper," Art Gallery, Haifa University, Israel, 1996; "Illustrations: Animals," Yad Lebanim Gallery, 1997; "Illustrations," Seminar Oranim Library, Tiveon, Israel, 1997; "Love Poems: paintings inspired by Nathan Alterman's love poems," Bialick House, Tel Aviv, 1998; "Sculptures," July M. Gallery, 1998; "Love Poems: paintings inspired by Nathan Alterman's love poems," Art Gallery, Kibbutz Mahanayim, 1998; "Illustrations," Widener Library, Harvard University, Cambridge, MA, 1999.

Group exhibitions include "The Bienalle for Etching," Harro, England, 1971; "Five Artists Paint," Yodfat Gallery, Tel Aviv, 1974; "Artist House," Jerusalem, 1974; "Autumn," Gordon Gallery, Tel Aviv, 1975; "Paintings," Gordon Gallery, 1976; Israel Museum, 1979; "Illustrations," Ruth Young Wing, Israel Museum, 1980; "Illustrations," Beit Ariela Library, Tel Aviv, 1981; "Paintings," Bugrashov Gallery, Tel

Aviv, 1986; "Paintings," Haifa Museum of Art, 1987; "Posters," Ramat-Gan Museum of Art, 1987; "Illustrations," Ruth Young Wing, Israel Museum, 1987; "Paintings," Rega Gallery, Tel Aviv, 1988; "Art & Architecture," Israel Museum, 1989; "Paintings" (traveling exhibition), Omanut La'am, Israel, 1990; "Illustrations: Israeli Artist Exhibit," Albatros Gallery, Prague, Czechoslovakia, 1991; "Paintings: Pa'atei Ma'cerav" (traveling exhibition), Omanut La'am, 1992; "Paintings: Soldiers in Art," Habima Theatre, Tel Aviv, 1993; "Bialik '93: Illustrations," Beit Ariela Library, 1993; "Illustrations," Beit Shturman, Kibbutz Ein Harod, Israel, 1994; Illustrations, Ma'alot Culture Center, Israel, 1994; and "Illustrations," Tel-Hai Museum, Israel, 1994.

Group exhibitions also include "Paintings," Beit Yad Lebanim, Ramat-Hasharon, 1995; "Masks, International Exhibition for Children in Need," 1995; "Paintings: Art Gallery Presents Art Teachers," Haifa University, 1995; "Bienalle of Illustration," Slovakia, 1995; "Paintings," Lenochach Ha'acher, Yetsirat Gallery, Haifa, 1995; "Paintings," Efter's Arts Center Gallery, Ma'alot, Israel, 1995; "Paintings: Mangal," Askola Design Gallery, Tel Aviv, 1996; "Paintings," Yad Lebanin Gallery, 1996; "Illustrations," Ruth Young Wing, Israel Museum, 1996; "Paintings: Figura," July M. Gallery, 1996; "Illustrations," Ort Bravda Gallery, Karmiel, Israel, 1997; "Paintings: Sharing Jerusalem," El Wasity Gallery, East Jerusalem, 1997; "Painting," Yad Lebanim Museum, Petach Tikva, Israel, 1998; "Illustrations: Adama," Ruth Young Wing, Israel Museum, 1998.

AWARDS, HONORS: International Prize for Children's Literature, International Board of Books for Youth, Prague, Czechoslovakia, 1980; Ben Itzhak Prize for Children's Illustrations, Israel Museum, Jerusalem, 1980, 1984, 1988, 1996, and 1998; Nahum Gutman Prize for Illustrations, 1985; Josef Lada Award for Children's Illustrations, Prague, Czechoslovakia, 1991; Discount Bank and Israel Museum Prize for the Israeli Artist, 1996.

WRITINGS:

SELECTED TITLES FOR CHILDREN; AND ILLUSTRATOR; IN ENGLISH TRANSLATION

Mishehu Motse Keter, Keter Publishing, 1979, translated as *The King Who Was Not,* Prion, 1989.
Ahava Rishona, Keter Publishing, 1989, translated as *My First Love,* Prion, 1989.

Veaz Hatzab Bana lo Bai't, Keter Publishing (Jerusalem, Israel), 1979, translated as *Tortoise Solves a Problem,* HarperCollins, 1993.
Hakayas Hakatan, Am Oved Publishers (Tel Aviv, Israel), 1979, translated as *The Little Pickpocket,* Simon & Schuster, 1996.

SELECTED TITLES FOR CHILDREN; AND ILLUSTRATOR; IN HEBREW

Chamor Af (title means "The Flying Donkey"), Am Oved, 1979.
Mishehu Motse Perach (title means "Tommy and the Flower"), Keter, 1979.
Mishehu Motse Keter (title means "Tommy and the Crown"), Keter, 1979.
Shabtai Vehatsipor (title means "Shabtai and the Bird"), Israel Museum (Jerusalem), 1985.
Hutz Miprat Ze Oh Aher, Hacol Emet (title means "Apart From a Few Details, Everything is True"), Shva Publishing (Tel Aviv), 1986.

OTHER

Illustrator of more than one hundred and forty titles in Hebrew. Author and illustrator of twelve humorous horoscope books. Contributor of short stories and poems to anthologies.

WORK IN PROGRESS: Illustrations for several books in a series of Greek mythology for children for Zabam Publishers; illustrations and an adaptation of *Gulliver's Travels,* by Jonathan Swift.

SIDELIGHTS: Avner Katz commented: "As an artist (illustrator, author, and painter) I am inspired and motivated by my childhood and personal experience and biography. I was born in Kibbutz Ramat-Rachel near Jerusalem, Israel. When I was nine years old, the [Israeli] War of Independence broke out, the kibbutz was bombed and all the families, including ours, evacuated to air raid shelters in Jerusalem. Afterwards, we transferred from place to place for three whole years. When my family came back to Ramat-Rachel, the place was in ruins and had to be rebuilt in a new spot.

"This break from home and landscape at such a young age, the wandering as a refugee, and the return to the ruins, is a traumatic experience that I have carried with me all these years. I became a nostalgic child (and then a nostalgic grownup), longing and yearning for the home I once had. I still carry these feelings in me. As an author for children, I express in my stories a longing for a utopian world and a search for a safe home, as exemplified in such books as *Tortoise Solves a Problem, The Little Pickpocket,* and many others. I write and illustrate my stories humorously and lightly although the experience that motivates me is so deep. As an illustrator for other authors, I get very much involved with the text and I create a dialogue between myself and the text while bringing into it my own images and personal interpretation.

"As a painter, I deal with very personal and autobiographical subjects and materials. One of the subjects I consider most vital is peace. I live in a country which is divided between two nations, Jews and Arabs. I strongly wish that the peace process will succeed, that there will be no more wars, and no one will ever have to leave his home and land and become a refugee. Every person and every child deserves to live safely in his home and homeland."

Katz explores the want of a home in his tale *Tortoise Solves a Problem,* a story that explains how tortoises came to have their shells. Back in the days when all the animals had a home except the tortoise, three wise tortoises send a young upstart to learn all about architecture and building with the hope that he would design a suitable abode. After several fantastic ideas that fall flat, the tortoise elders tell the youngster that they will no longer go to look at these houses, he must bring the tortoise home to them. From there, an idea is born which leads to success. A critic for *Kirkus Reviews* asserted that, "Though the outcome is foreseeable, the means of getting there are not only entertaining, but an amusing analog to some well-known human behavior." Critics also admired the artwork, including *Booklist* reviewer Janice Del Negro who noted that the inside illustration, "with its white backgrounds, low horizon lines, and dead-on perspectives, has immediacy and vigor." Donnarae MacCann and Olga Richard in a review in *Wilson Library Bulletin* admired Katz's graceful drawings of the tortoises, noting, "One can easily believe that Katz has sketched them from life in a tortoise modeling school."

Katz continued his success with *The Little Pickpocket.* When his mother's pouch proves too noisy, a young kangaroo named Joey sets out to find a better pocket. After he ventures over the countryside, testing the pockets of little boys and hobos, artists and musicians, Joey decides there is no place like home and returns to the warmth of his mother's pouch. The story has "a wry sense of humor that young readers and listeners would enjoy," stated Kathy Mitchell in

School Library Journal. Writing in *Five Owls,* critic Mary Lou Burket enthused, "While the story follows a straight, conventional course, the pictures are airy, strange, and magically benign."

BIOGRAPHICAL/CRITICAL SOURCES:

PERIODICALS

Booklist, January 15, 1993, p. 921.
Five Owls, May-June, 1996, p. 108.
Kirkus Reviews, January 1, 1993, p. 63.
Publishers Weekly, April 1, 1996, p. 76.
School Library Journal, September, 1993, pp. 208-209; July, 1996, p. 66.
Wilson Library Bulletin, October, 1993, pp. 118-119.*

*   *   *

KATZ, Molly

PERSONAL: Female.

ADDRESSES: Agent—c/o Ballantine Books, 201 East 50th St., New York, NY 10022.

CAREER: Mystery novelist and former stand-up comedian.

WRITINGS:

Nobody Believes Me, Ballantine (New York City), 1994.

SIDELIGHTS: Molly Katz's first novel, *Nobody Believes Me,* tells the story of a woman who falls in love with the wrong man. The heroine of the story is Lynn Marchette, a Boston talk show host whose show may be headed for national syndication. Through her hard work, Lynn manages to overcome her impoverished East Tennessee childhood but not her low self-esteem. While in Los Angeles on a business trip, she falls for Greg Alter, who is by all appearances the "perfect man." Although charmed by Greg's attentions, Lynn begins to feel acutely uncomfortable when Greg pressures her into uncharacteristic behaviors such as getting a tattoo and engaging in sex in public places. When Lynn abruptly ends the relationship, she is surprised to find that her friends are not supportive;

they are convinced her low self-esteem is once again leading her to reject a suitable partner and the success she deserves. To make matters worse, Greg will not take no for an answer. Finally, Lynn seeks advice from one of her talk show guests, Detective Mike Delano, who agrees to help Lynn prove that it is Greg who is stalking her.

Katz's novel received mixed reviews. A *Publishers Weekly* reviewer found the plot to be "formulaic" and unconvincing, but praised Katz's main characters as "well-wrought" and "skillfully depicted . . . caught in a downward spiral of doubt, insecurity, self-hatred and shame." *Library Journal* reviewer Rebecca House Stankowski found that Katz's novel "bristles with suspense." A *Kirkus Reviews* contributor noted that the tension in the novel arises not so much from Greg's stalking as from the lack of supportive relationships in Lynn's life and the potential cost to her career. The reviewer concluded the review declaring that "Katz does an extraordinary job of disguising pivotal clues in seemingly frivolous details, fashioning a pulp story into an absorbing thriller."

BIOGRAPHICAL/CRITICAL SOURCES:

PERIODICALS

Kirkus Reviews, April 1, 1994 , p. 423.
Library Journal, May 15, 1994, p. 100.
Los Angeles Times Book Review, July 3, 1994, p. 6.
Publishers Weekly, May 2, 1994, p. 285.*

* * *

KAUFMAN, Kenn 1956(?)-

PERSONAL: Born c. 1956, in IN.

ADDRESSES: Agent—c/o Houghton Mifflin Co., 222 Berkeley St., Boston, MA 02116.

CAREER: Birder, artist, author, tour leader. Former associate editor, *American Birds*.

AWARDS, HONORS: Set record for most North American bird species sighted in a year; Ludlow Griscom Distinguished Birder Award, American Birding Association, 1992.

WRITINGS:

(With Les Line and Kimball L. Garrett) *The Audubon Society Book of Water Birds*, Abrams (New York City), 1987.
(Also illustrator) *A Field Guide to Advanced Birding: Birding Challenges and How to Approach Them*, Houghton (Boston), 1990.
(Illustrator) Kaufman, Lynn Hassler, *Deserts*, Houghton, 1993.
Lives of North American Birds, Houghton, 1996.
(Author of introduction and bird notes) Porter, Eliot, *Vanishing Songbirds: The Sixth Order: Wood Warblers and Other Passerine Birds*, Little Brown (Boston), 1996.
Kingbird Highway: The Story of a Natural Obsession That Got a Little out of Hand, Houghton, 1997.

SIDELIGHTS: Since he was a child, Kenn Kaufman had been fascinated by birds. Determined to set a record for observing birds, he took his first solo birding trip at the age of sixteen, hitchhiking across the country to observe bird species. In 1973 when Kaufman turned nineteen, he set out again to see how many birds he could spot in one year, posting a record of 671 species. *Kingbird Highway: The Story of a Natural Obsession That Got a Little out of Hand* is Kaufman's own story of his unique 69,000-mile trip, during which he survived on very little money (less than one thousand dollars during the entire year), took odd jobs for cash, and occasionally ate cat food when the money ran low. The book provides a close look at the unique culture and passion of other birders Kaufman meets along the way, as well as glimpses into the details of hitchhiking and living on the road.

Other adventures Kaufman encountered include being hit on by male drivers, totaling a bus in Alaska, and evading a rancher with a gun in Oklahoma. According to Frank Graham Jr. of *Audubon*, Kaufman's single-minded drive is typical of expert and passionate birders. "I don't know how a normal person thinks of birds or looks at them," said Kaufman in *Audubon*, "By the age of six, I had narrowed my interest down to birds and I've never been interested in anything else."

One of Kaufman's earliest books about birds, *The Audubon Society Book of Water Birds*, earned him praise from a *Time* reviewer for the "easy, intelligent prose" which helped readers get beyond the pictures and gave a glimpse into the lives of particular birds. *A Field Guide to Advanced Birding* gives detailed identification information for the thirty-five birds that are most difficult to recognize. Kaufman instructs the reader on how to watch for the more subtle characteristics of birding—behavior, molting and plumage, for example—in identifying these birds. Henry T. Armistead of *American Reference Book Annual* recommended the book, particularly for its field guides, and praised the "well-written text" as well as the "useful line drawings" by Kaufman. Another book by Kaufman, *Lives of North American Birds,* was praised by reviewers for its detailed information on bird behavior, written in language for the layperson.

BIOGRAPHICAL/CRITICAL SOURCES:

PERIODICALS

American Reference Books Annual, vol. 22, 1991, pp. 632-633.
Audubon, January, 1988, p. 14-.
Birder's World, December, 1997, pp. 94-95.
Booklist, May 15, 1997, p. 1549.
Kirkus Reviews, May 1, 1997, p. 697.
Library Journal, January, 1997, p. 88; May 15, 1997, p. 97.
Natural History, July, 1997, p. 12.
New York, June 10, 1985, pp. 56-65.
Publishers Weekly, May 12, 1997, p. 71.
SciTech Book News, spring, 1990, p. 13.
Time, December 21, 1997, p. 66.
Utne Reader, January, 1997, p. 96.

OTHER

Amazon.com, http://www.amazon.com (January 29, 1999).
Kenn Kaufman Interview, http://www.birdwatching. com/tips/kkaufman.html (January 29, 1999).
Peterson Online, http://www.petersononline.com/ birds/kingbird (January 29, 1999).*

*   *   *

KEEGAN, Marcia 1943-

PERSONAL: Born in 1943. *Education:* University of New Mexico, B.S.; attended New York Photographers School.

ADDRESSES: Home—823 Don Diego, Santa Fe, NM 87501.

CAREER: Albuquerque Tribune, Albuquerque, NM, journalist and photographer, 1963-64; *Albuquerque Journal,* Albuquerque, editor of "Home Living" Sunday supplement, 1964-68; freelance photographer, 1969-88; Clear Light Publishers, Santa Fe, NM, cofounder, 1988, president and book designer, 1988—. Lecturer and workshop presenter at educational institutions, including New York University, New School for Social Research, Long Island University, and St. John's University, Jamaica, NY. Photographs of Native American and Tibetan cultures have been exhibited internationally in group and solo shows; work represented in permanent collections at major U.S. museums, including Library of Congress, Metropolitan Museum of Art, Lincoln Center Museum of Performing Arts, Princeton University Gallery, and Albuquerque Museum.

MEMBER: International PEN, International Women's Writers Guild, American Society of Magazine Photographers, Society of Woman Geographers, Association on American Indian Affairs, Native American Indian Women's Association, Authors Guild, Southwest Writers Association, University Women.

AWARDS, HONORS: Grant from Creative Artists Program, New York City, 1972.

WRITINGS:

AUTHOR AND PHOTOGRAPHER

Taos Pueblo and Its Sacred Blue Lake, Messner (New York City), 1972.
Mother Earth, Father Sky, Grossman/Viking, 1974.
Southwest Indian Cookbook, Morgan & Morgan (Dobbs Ferry, NY), 1977.
We Can Still Hear Them Clapping, Avon (New York City), 1975.
Oklahoma, Abbeville Press (New York City), 1979.
The Dalai Lama's Historic Visit to North America, Clear Light (Santa Fe, NM), 1981.
New Mexico, Oxford University Press, 1984.
Enduring Culture, Clear Light, 1991.
Pueblo Boy, Dutton (New York City), 1991.
Ancient Wisdom, Living Tradition, Clear Light, 1998.
Pueblo People: Ancient Traditions, Modern Lives, Clear Light, 1998.

OTHER

(Photographer) *Only the Moon and Me,* Lippincott (Philadelphia, PA), 1968.

(Photographer) *Moonsong Lullaby,* Morrow (New York City), 1981.

(Photographer) *Ocean of Wisdom,* Clear Light, 1989.

Contributor to books. Contributor to magazines, including *National Geographic, Natural History, Smithsonian, Forbes, Esquire, Woman's Day,* and *Newsweek.*

* * *

KEERY, James 1958-

PERSONAL: Born February 10, 1958, in Coleraine, Northern Ireland; son of Robert (a nuclear engineer) and Rosemary (a teacher; maiden name, Turner) Keery; married Julie Mary Addis (a dental hygienist), September 6, 1986; children: Jennifer, Jack. *Education:* Churchill College, Cambridge, B.A. (with honors), 1979; University of Durham, Postgraduate Certificate of Education, 1980. *Politics:* "New Labour!" *Religion:* "Confirmed Methodist; agnostic." *Avocational interests:* Postwar British poetry.

ADDRESSES: Home—22 Chiltern Rd., Culcheth, Warrington, Cheshire WA3 4LL, England. *Office*—Fred Longworth High School, Tyldesley, Wigan, England.

CAREER: High school English teacher, Wigan, England, 1980-86; Fred Longworth High School, Wigan, teacher, 1986-95, head of English department, 1995—. Warrington District Council for the Protection of Rural England, chairperson, 1990-97. Gives readings from his works.

WRITINGS:

That Stranger, the Blues (poems), Carcanet Press (Manchester, England), 1996.

(Contributor) S. Sakurai, editor, *The View from Kyoto: Essays on Twentieth-Century Poetry,* Reinsen (Japan), 1998.

(Editor) *Collected Poems of Burns Singer,* Carcanet Press, in press.

Work represented in anthologies, including *New Poetries,* Carcanet Press, 1994. Contributor of poems, articles, and reviews to periodicals, including *PN Review, New Welsh Review, Poetica, Rialto,* and *Honest Ulsterman.*

WORK IN PROGRESS: A biography of Burns Singer.

SIDELIGHTS: James Keery told *CA:* "It is funny, perhaps even unusual, but I've never been able to shake off the feeling that I've written my last poem. Often I find I *have,* for months at a time, and perhaps it's natural that a poem should be accompanied by a sense that a spring has run dry. I suppose it's because I tend to write from a present that's already past.

"I can't speak about intention in what is (for me) an unconscious activity, but I find that, when I write, my attention is exclusively to the sound, the rhythm, not so much of the words as of the originating impulse. I'd better draw a distinction between what I mean by this and the lyric epiphany, for the kind of impulse I mean is as likely to give rise to discursive prolixity as to anything more succinct and imagistic. My first collection, *That Stranger, the Blues,* is made up of both—though most of the prolix dialogic pieces are actually snippets from a series of 'sinless confessional epics' that still come under the heading of work in progress. But each of my poems has its originating impulse, in which it is in some sense implicit. I arrive at it by endless retyping of a line, or perhaps two, at a time until I can hear it in what I read."

* * *

KERFERD, G(eorge) B(riscoe) 1915-1998

OBITUARY NOTICE—See index for *CA* sketch: Born January 20, 1915, in Melbourne, Australia; died August 9, 1998. Educator, scholar, and author. Kerferd believed that an understanding of the classics—particularly Greek classics—was crucial to an understanding of human nature and society in general. Kerferd's love of Greek philosophy shaped his career. He earned his first degree in Latin and Greek in Australia, where he grew up. Kerferd then traveled to England and served as a lecturer at Durham University. Between 1942 and 1946 Kerferd returned to Australia to lecture at Sydney University; he also met and married his wife during that time. He later returned to England and continued to serve in a number of academic positions. Kerferd veered away from the status quo in his teaching and strove to challenge his students with new and stimulating methods. He also advocated for university libraries to increase their acquisitions. He was known among his peers as a tireless worker and a person who enjoyed a friendly and challenging argument. His writings covered classical studies and included: *The Sophistic Movement* (1981), *The Sophists and Their Legacy* (1983) and *Italian Translation* (1988).

OBITUARIES AND OTHER SOURCES:

BOOKS

International Authors and Writers Who's Who, 1993-1994, International Biographical Center, 1994.

PERIODICALS

Times (London), August 21, 1998.

*   *   *

KILPATRICK, Alan Edwin

PERSONAL: Ethnicity: "American Indian (Cherokee)." *Education:* Northeastern State University, B.A., 1970; Loyola Marymount University, M.A. (film and television production), 1974; University of California, Los Angeles, M.A. (archaeology), 1985, Ph.D., 1989.

ADDRESSES: Home—5292 Stone Ct., San Diego, CA 92115. *E-mail*—akilpatr@mail.sdsu.edu.

CAREER: University of California, Santa Cruz, lecturer at Oakes College, 1989-91; University of Minnesota—Twin Cities, Minneapolis, assistant professor of American Indian studies, 1991-93, McKnight Land Grant Professor, 1993; San Diego State University, San Diego, CA, professor of American Indian studies, 1993—, department head, 1997. University of California, Los Angeles, extension lecturer in archaeology, 1989-90; speaker at colleges and universities, including Hamline University, New York University, and Adams State College, all 1992, Carleton College, Northfield, MN, 1993, Dartmouth College, 1995, University of Maine, 1996, and University of Kansas, 1997; public speaker. Museum of Man, Balboa Park, CA, member of board of directors, 1994—; San Diego Commission for Arts and Culture, member, 1996—.

AWARDS, HONORS: American Scandinavian fellow in Sweden, 1986; Fulbright fellow in Sweden, 1988; McKnight international travel grant, University of Minnesota, 1992; Archibald Hanna visiting fellowship, Yale University, 1993; grant from National

Endowment for the Humanities, 1995; visiting scholar, American Museum of Natural History, 1996; Southwest Center for Environmental Research and Policy Planning grant, U.S. Environmental Protection Agency, 1997 and 1998.

WRITINGS:

The Night Has a Naked Soul: Witchcraft and Sorcery among the Western Cherokee, Syracuse University Press (Syracuse, NY), 1997.
(Contributor) Douglas R. Parks, editor, *American Indian Contributions to Anthropology,* University of Oklahoma Press (Norman), 1998.

Scriptwriter for *Paths to Progress,* an educational film produced by United Indian Development Association, 1976, and for episodes of the television series *Knowledge,* broadcast by NBC-TV, 1975-76. Contributor of articles and reviews to periodicals, including *American Indian Culture and Research Journal, American Indian Quarterly,* and *Wicaza Sa Review.*

WORK IN PROGRESS: Madness, Possession, and Witchcraft: A Review of Native American Mental Health, 1880-1960; On the Trail of the Moon Goddess: The Tlazoteotl-Ixcuina Cult.

*   *   *

KINSEY, Alfred (Charles) 1894-1956

PERSONAL: Born June 23, 1894, in Hoboken, NJ; died of an embolism, August 25, 1956, in Bloomington, IN; son of Alfred Seguine (an educator) and Sarah Ann (Charles) Kinsey; married Clara Brachen McMillen, 1921; children: Donald (deceased), Bruce, Anne, Joan. *Education:* Attended Stevens Institute; Bowdoin College, B.S. (biology; magna cum laude), 1916; Harvard University, Sc.D.

CAREER: Indiana University, professor of zoology, 1920-56.

WRITINGS:

Introduction to Biology, Lippincott (Philadelphia), 1926.
Field and Laboratory Manual in Biology (companion text to *Introduction to Biology*), Lippincott, 1927.

The Gall Wasp Genus Cynips: A Study in the Origin of the Species, Indiana University Studies (Bloomington), 1930.

The Origin of Higher Categories of Cynips, Indiana University Publications, 1936.

Methods in Biology, Lippincott, c. 1937.

(With Merritt Lyndon Fernald) *Edible Wild Plants of Eastern North America,* Idlewild Press (Cornwall-Hudson, NY), 1943, revised by Reed Collins, Harper (New York City), 1958.

(With W. B. Pomeroy and C. E. Martin) *Sexual Behavior in the Human Male,* W. B. Saunders, 1948.

(With W. B. Pomeroy and C. E. Martin) *Sexual Behavior in the Human Female,* W. B. Saunders, 1953.

SIDELIGHTS: Arguably the most influential sex researcher in modern America, zoologist Alfred Kinsey was the first to study human sexual behavior using modern scientific methods. His *Sexual Behavior in the Human Male* (1948) and *Sexual Behavior in the Human Female* (1953) were the results of extensive research in which thousands of subjects were interviewed in detail; the studies reported on sexual activities in clear and unprejudiced language and included findings on such matters as masturbation and homosexual behavior—subjects that until then were not openly discussed. Though the books aroused intense controversy, especially from extreme conservatives, they were also hailed as the first morally neutral studies on sexual behavior. The Kinsey studies found a wide readership and stimulated open discussion of sexual matters, establishing a benchmark by which subsequent research in sexual behavior was measured.

Born in 1894 in Hoboken, New Jersey, Kinsey was the oldest of three children in a family of evangelical Methodists. His upbringing was extremely strict. His father, Alfred Seguine Kinsey, a faculty member at the Stevens Institute of Technology, was an authoritarian parent who forbade popular music, dancing, tobacco, and drink in his household and who refused to allow his teenage children to date. Kinsey was often sickly as a child, suffering from rickets, rheumatic fever, and typhoid fever. He hated Hoboken, where he spent his first ten years, and was happier when the family moved to the more suburban South Orange, New Jersey. He enjoyed nature hikes in the surrounding hills and marshes and began collecting botanical specimens. He joined the Boy Scouts in 1910, became an Eagle Scout, and in high school became a scout leader. Encouraged in his zoological

interests by his high school biology teacher, Natalie Roeth, Kinsey wrote a paper in high school titled "What Do Birds Do When It Rains?" This piece was distinguished by its precise empirical observations of animal behavior—qualities that were characteristic of all of Kinsey's professional work.

Although Kinsey wished to pursue a career in biology, he bowed to his father's pressure and attended the Stevens Institute, where he studied mechanical engineering. After two years, however, he persuaded his father to allow him to transfer to Bowdoin College in Brunswick, Maine. There he studied biology, earning his B.S. magna cum laude in 1916 and giving the commencement address at graduation. In 1916 Kinsey received a scholarship to attend Harvard University's Bussey Institution, where he began graduate work in entomology under William Morton Wheeler, the leading authority on the social behavior of insects. At Harvard, Kinsey developed a special interest in the gall wasp, an ant-sized insect with an extremely short life-span—often less than a few hours. After completing his Sc.D. at Harvard, Kinsey received a Sheldon Traveling Fellowship which enabled him to spend a year touring the southwestern United States to further his study of gall wasps. In 1920, he joined the zoology faculty at Indiana University in Bloomington, where he spent his entire teaching career.

In 1921 Kinsey married Clara Brachen McMillen of Fort Wayne, Indiana, a top chemistry student at Indiana University. The marriage produced four children: Donald, who died at age three of diabetes, Bruce, Anne, and Joan. Though Clara gave up her own career to raise the children and to assist her husband in his research, the Kinseys' friends considered the marriage to have been a happy one in which Clara was an equal partner. She was able to share in her husband's intellectual enthusiasms and actively supported his research throughout his career.

In his early years at Indiana University Kinsey continued with his study of the gall wasp and worked on an innovative high school text, *An Introduction to Biology,* published in 1926. The book was remarkable for its friendly tone, its urging that students observe nature for themselves, and its strong position on evolution, which had caught the country's attention in 1925 with the Scopes trial in Tennessee. The text became a significant success and went into several later editions, providing Kinsey with some financial independence. After completing a companion text for *An Introduction to Biology,* Kinsey concentrated on the gall wasp, spending eighteen years on this subject.

During this period he travelled throughout the United States, Mexico, and Guatemala, collecting hundreds of thousands of specimens. His research culminated in the publication of *The Gall Wasp Cynips: A Study in the Origin of the Species* in 1930, followed in 1936 by *The Origin of Higher Categories of Cynips.* These works were distinguished by their reliance on large scientific samples, clear writing, and enthusiasm for the subject—characteristics that would also be evident in Kinsey's later studies on human sexual behavior. The gall wasp texts strengthened Kinsey's reputation as the leading authority on the subject and an innovative genetics theorist.

Shortly after the publication of his second book on the gall wasp, Kinsey began teaching a noncredit course in marriage for Indiana University seniors. This course had been requested by students the previous spring. When Kinsey began research for the course, he wrote in his "Historical Introduction" to his study on men, he was "struck with the inadequacy of the samples on which such studies were being based, and the apparent unawareness of the investigators that generalizations were not warranted on the bases of such small samples." He determined to embark on his own more rigorous and extensive research.

With the support of the university, Kinsey began. He wanted to compile the biggest possible sample of people and spent years recording sexual histories from individuals. Realizing that it was essential to establish trust with his subjects so that they would feel free to answer questions honestly and without embarrassment, he avoided the use of written questionnaires and relied on a complex code by which to notate answers. Kinsey also developed especially sensitive interviewing skills, learning to read body language and avoid euphemistic or confusing terminology. Through these techniques, he amassed huge amounts of data.

By the early 1940s Kinsey had gathered over 1,700 case histories—enough data to apply for grants. He received a grant of twenty-three thousand dollars from the National Research Council's Committee for Research in Problems of Sex (funded by the Rockefeller Foundation) in 1941. With this help, Kinsey was able to hire additional staff, including W. B. Pomeroy (listed as co-author of the two Kinsey reports), who conducted thousands of additional interviews. Other grants followed, enabling Kinsey to establish the Institute for Sex Research at Indiana University in 1947. By the following year Kinsey and his colleagues were ready to release their findings.

Sexual Behavior in the Human Male was published by a respected medical publisher, W. B. Saunders, in 1948. The 804-page book, which sold 185,000 copies in its first year, made the *New York Times* bestseller list. It reported Kinsey's results in plain, direct, nonjudgmental language. Among its findings: that extramarital and premarital sexual activity was more prevalent than generally assumed; that virtually all males masturbate; that masturbation does not cause mental illness; and that more than one in three men reported engaging in at least one homosexual encounter. The book's underlying message, says Kinsey's biographer James H. Jones in an article in the *New Yorker,* was tolerance; he "bombarded his readers with the theme of sexual diversity," according to Jones, and "took pains to show that many forms of sexual behavior labelled criminal or rare were actually quite common."

Though the Kinsey report enjoyed overwhelmingly positive response from the mainstream press and early polls suggested that many American readers accepted Kinsey's conclusions, intense criticism was leveled at the book, especially from conservative and religious organizations. These attacks focused on Kinsey's subject matter rather than methodology. Within the scientific community, however, the book elicited mixed reactions. Anthropologist Margaret Mead, for example, objected that Kinsey's reliance on the orgasm as the basic unit of measurement removed "sexual behavior [from] its interpersonal context." Critic Lionel Trilling echoed Mead's concerns. Most insulting to Kinsey was the attack from British anthropologist Geoffrey Gorer, who sharply criticized Kinsey's samplings. Gorer insisted that quality research had to come from random samples; Kinsey used "grab" samples—he questioned only subjects who wished to participate without trying to get a fair representation of an entire group. Kinsey passionately defended his techniques, arguing that he had never claimed to present a perfect sample and insisting that his work had revealed the truth about sexual behavior.

Despite some concern that funding for his Institute might be suspended due to the controversy generated by his first report on sexual behavior, Kinsey continued his sex research with his team, publishing *Sexual Behavior in the Human Female* in 1953. Like the first study, this book caused a sensation, reporting on controversial findings such as high rates of sex outside marriage, low rates of frigidity, the rapidness of erotic response, and evidence for clitoral orgasm. The book sold 250,000 copies in the U.S. alone, put

Kinsey's photo on the cover of *Time,* and drew the vehemence of the religious right. It also prompted the Rockefeller Foundation, which had suffered intense pressure from conservative board members, finally to withdraw funding for the Kinsey Institute. In addition, Kinsey was labelled a subversive and accused by Congress of aiding Communism by undermining traditional American morals.

Discouraged, Kinsey doggedly continued his work and searched for new sources of financial support. He began work on a large-scale study of sex-offenders, but his health had been affected by the stress. He began relying on sleeping pills and other medications. After a lecture trip to England and Europe in 1955 Kinsey developed heart trouble requiring several hospitalizations. In the spring of 1956, after a research trip to Chicago, he was admitted to the Bloomington Hospital with pneumonia which exacerbated his heart condition. He died at age sixty-two on August 25. The immediate cause of death was an embolism resulting from a bruise he had suffered while gardening.

Kinsey had lived the life of a model scientist and established his reputation as the preeminent authority on sexual behavior in America. But in 1997 James H. Jones issued a biography that introduced startling new information about Kinsey. Kinsey was, Jones asserts, a homosexual, masochist, and exhibitionist who craved extreme forms of sexual arousal—aspects of his identity he carefully guarded from the public. This proclivity made Kinsey especially attracted to subjects who shared this orientation, skewing his samples and resulting in a misrepresentation of male behavior. The statistic that thirty-seven percent of men had reported engaging in at least one homosexual act, for example, seems inordinately high; a 1994 survey from the University of Chicago's "National Health and Social Life Survey," cited by Jones in his *New Yorker* article, reports the number of gay or bisexual men in the United States as only 2.8 percent.

Jones concludes that "[Kinsey's] methodology and his sampling technique virtually guaranteed that he would find what he was looking for." Also extremely troubling was evidence that suggested Kinsey was inclined to condone sexual activity between adults and children. Jones cites evidence from Glenway Westcott, a man who'd been one of Kinsey's subjects, indicating that Kinsey had told him he'd once condemned adult-child sexual relationships but later came to believe that few children who reported being molested appeared to have been psychologically harmed by the behavior. Westcott felt that Kinsey's implication was

that any harm was caused by society's condemnation, not by the act itself.

Jones's biography reveals that the impetus for Kinsey's research was probably linked to his own secret sexual desires. In his *New Yorker* article, Jones portrays Kinsey as a "strong-willed patriarch who created around himself a kind of utopian community in which sexual experimentation was encouraged." But Jones also points out that Kinsey was "a covert crusader who was determined to use science to free American society from what he saw as the crippling legacy of Victorian repression."

Despite the controversies surrounding Kinsey's statistics, his studies profoundly changed American attitudes toward sexual behavior. In the years following the publication of his research, many laws relating to sexual matters were liberalized and sex education for children was promoted. The institute he founded at Indiana University, renamed the Kinsey Institute for Research in Sex, Gender, and Reproduction in 1984, continues its research and publications.

BIOGRAPHICAL/CRITICAL SOURCES:

BOOKS

Jones James H., *Alfred C. Kinsey: A Public/Private Life,* Norton (New York City), 1997.
McGuire, William and Leslie Wheeler, *American Social Leaders,* ABC-Clio (Santa Barbara, CA), 1993.
Notable Twentieth-Century Scientists, Gale (Detroit), 1995.

PERIODICALS

American Journal of Public Health, April, 1948.
Booklist, March 1, 1948; November 1, 1953.
Bookmark, January, 1944.
Canadian Forum, May, 1948; January, 1954.
Chicago Sun, January 27, 1948.
Chicago Sunday Tribune, September 13, 1953, p. 3.
Commonweal, April 23, 1948.
Harvard Law Review, January, 1954.
Kirkus Reviews, December 15, 1947.
Library Journal, February 1, 1948.
Manchester Guardian, December 4, 1953, p. 4.
Nation, May 1, 1948, pp. 471-472; October 10, 1953.
New Republic, February 9, 1948; November 9, 1953.
New Yorker, January 3, 1948; September 19, 1953; August 25, 1997, pp. 99-113.

New York Herald Tribune, February 1, 1948; September 13, 1953.

New York Times, January 4, 1948, p. 4; September 13, 1953, p. 3.

San Francisco Chronicle, January 18, 1948, p. 25; September 13, 1953.

Saturday Review of Literature, March 13, 1948; September 26, 1953.

School and Society, August 28, 1948.

Social Forces, March, 1948.

Social Studies, October, 1948.

Weekly Book Review, October 24, 1943.

Yale Review, spring, 1948.*

—*Sketch by Elizabeth Shostak*

* * *

KISSINGER, Rosemary K.
  See UPDYKE, Rosemary K.

* * *

KLEIN, Christian Felix   1849-1925

PERSONAL: Born November 25, 1849, in Dusseldorf, Germany; died January 22, 1925; son of an official in the Dusseldorf finance department; married Anne Hegel; children: one son, three daughters. *Education:* University of Bonn, Ph.D., 1868.

CAREER: University of of Goettingen, lecturer, until 1871, chair of mathematics, beginning 1886, founder of mathematical center; University of Erlangen, professor of mathematics, 1871-75; Technische Hochschule, Munich, professor of mathematics, 1875-80; University of Leipzig, professor, 1880-86. *Wartime service:* Worked as a medical orderly during the Franco-Prussian War.

AWARDS, HONORS: Copley Medal, Royal Society, 1912; recipient of numerous other awards and honors.

WRITINGS:

Famous Problems of Elementary Geometry and Other Monographs, 1894, reprinted, Chelsea, 1956.
The Evanston Colloquium, 1911.

Gesammelte Mathematlsche Abhandlungen, 1921-23.
Development of Mathematics in the Nineteenth Century, 1926-27, reprinted, Mathematical Science Press, 1979.
Elementary Mathematics from an Advanced Standpoint, translated by E. R. Hedrick and C. A. Noble, 1939.

Editor, *Mathematische Annalen* (mathematical journal), beginning in 1872.

SIDELIGHTS: Christian Felix Klein is arguably one of the most influential mathematicians of the nineteenth century. He is best known for building the mathematical community at the University of Goettingen which became a model for research facilities in mathematics world wide.

Klein was born on November 25, 1849 in Dusseldorf, the son of an official in the local finance department. Klein graduated from Gymnasium (the German equivalent of an academic high school) in Dusseldorf and began studying at the University of Bonn in 1865. At Bonn he fell under the influence of Julius Plucker, one of the best-known geometers of the century. Plucker had moved the center of his interest to physics, and it had been in physics that Klein originally wanted to work, but Plucker returned to his original interest in geometry and took Klein with him. After Plucker's death in 1867 Klein became responsible for finishing a manuscript of Plucker's which gave him an early introduction to the scholarly community and, in particular, to Alfred Clebsch, another prominent geometer of the time.

After receiving his doctorate in 1868 Klein spent a year traveling between Goettingen, Berlin, and Paris. Of the three, he enjoyed Goettingen immensely, did not like Berlin, and had to leave Paris ahead of schedule because of the outbreak of the Franco-Prussian War. Some of his travels were spent with the young Norwegian mathematician Marius Sophus Lie, whose ideas on geometry and analysis were much in common with Klein's.

Klein's patriotism led him to enlist as a medical orderly during the Franco-Prussian war, but before the year was over he had returned to Dusseldorf, suffering from typhoid fever. The next year Klein qualified as a lecturer at Goettingen, but the following year he accepted a chair at the University of Erlangen. The complexities of academic promotion within the German university system at the time frequently required moving about from one university to another, merely for the sake of promotion within the original university.

It was the custom for a new professor to deliver an inaugural address at a German university, and in 1872 Klein followed suit at Erlangen. At the time, it was difficult to speak of one geometry, as recent developments had led to a collection of geometries whose relation to one another was unclear. There was the familiar Euclidean geometry, based on the ordinary axioms including the parallel postulate (which stipulated that there was exactly one parallel to a line through a point not on that line). There were at least two non-Euclidean geometries, one denying the existence of any parallels through a point not on a line, the other allowing the existence of an infinite number of parallels. Finally, projective geometry, which had been known since the seventeenth century, had been given a more quantitative turn in the work of Arthur Cayley, among others.

As outlined by Klein, geometry is the study of the properties of figures preserved under the transformations in a certain group. Which group of transformations one started with determined the geometry in which one was working. For example, if the transformations were limited to rigid motions, then one had Euclidean geometry. If projections were allowed, then one had projective geometry. If an even wider class were included, then one could end up with topology. This view (called the Erlangen program) has infused the spirit, not just of geometry, but of mathematics as a whole ever since.

In 1872 Klein took over editing *Mathematische Annalen* after the death of Clebsch. Under his editorship this became the leading mathematical journal in the world and it was to remain so until World War II. By 1875 Klein had left Erlangen for the Technische Hochschule in Munich and in 1880 went to the University of Leipzig. In 1884 he was invited to take the place of James Joseph Sylvester at Johns Hopkins University in Baltimore, but he declined. He did make several visits to the United States subsequently, where both his personal influence and those of his students were strong. Finally, in 1886 Klein achieved the goal of a chair at Goettingen.

Two factors in particular led Klein to successfully create a mathematical center at Goettingen. One was personal, as he was married to Anne Hegel, a descendant of German philosopher Georg Wilhelm Friedrich Hegel. Her striking beauty may have been a draw even for those who were not yet convinced of the mathematical attractions of her husband. In the course of their married life the Kleins had one son and three daughters.

The other factor was not so pleasant. One of the subjects on which Klein had been working while at Leipzig were automorphic functions, transformations of the complex plane into itself that satisfied certain conditions. Unfortunately for Klein, the year 1884 turned into a competition with the younger French mathematician Henri Poincare seeking fundamental results. Although Klein's work during this period was of a high quality, he felt that he had not lived up to expectations and suffered a nervous breakdown.

Thereafter Klein immersed himself in creating a major mathematical center at Goettingen. The mathematical discussions did not stop with the classroom walls, but continued at the Kleins' home or on walks into the woods around Goettingen. One feature of the institute was a room filled with geometrical models to help with visualization. The presence of such a room was a reminder of Klein's antipathy to the abstract style of analysis favored by Karl Weierstrass at Berlin. Klein wanted his mathematics to have intuitive content, which explains why he was anathema to Weierstrass. Klein attracted many of the leading German mathematicians to Goettingen, the most outstanding being David Hilbert. Goettingen's creative atmosphere also encouraged the presence of women and foreign visitors in the lecture hall.

At the time of Klein's retirement shortly before the outbreak of World War I, he could take pride in having brought together a mathematical research community the likes of which the world had never seen. In 1912 he received the Copley Medal of the Royal Society, one of many honors. His last years were saddened by the death of his son on the battlefield during the war, and he died on January 22, 1925.

Within ten years of his death the Nazi government had undertaken the dismantling of the research community in Goettingen. When the Institute for Advanced Studies was founded at Princeton in the 1930s, it modeled itself after Goettingen, thus allowing Klein's dream of a mathematical community to live on.

BIOGRAPHICAL/CRITICAL SOURCES:

BOOKS

Yaglom, I. H., *Felix Klein and Sophus Lie,* translated by Sergei Sossinsky, Birkhauser (Boston), 1988.*

KNECHT, Heidi 1961-

PERSONAL: Born April 13, 1961, in Newark, NJ; daughter of Eli G. (an engineer) and Phyllis (a home-maker; maiden name, Steiner) Katz; married Mitchell Knecht (a telecommunications professional), July 23, 1983; children: Julie Nicole, Hilary Leah. *Education:* Tufts University, B.A., 1982; New York University, M.A., 1986, M.Phil., 1987, Ph.D., 1991.

ADDRESSES: Office—Thinking Strings, P.O. Box 334, Short Hills, NJ 07078. *E-mail*—hknecht@ thinkingstrings.com.

CAREER: University of Miami, Coral Gables, FL, adjunct assistant professor, 1991-96; New York University, New York City, visiting scholar, 1996—. Thinking Strings, associate, 1998—.

MEMBER: Society for American Archaeology.

WRITINGS:

(Contributor) Jean Hudson, editor, *From Bones to Behavior,* Center for Archaeological Investigations, Southern Illinois University at Carbondale, 1993.
(Editor with Anne Pike-Tay and Randall White, and contributor) *Before Lascaux: The Complex Record of the Early Upper Paleolithic,* CRC Press (Boca Raton, FL), 1993.
(Editor and contributor) *Projectile Technology,* Plenum (New York City), 1998.

Contributor to scholarly journals, including *Scientific American.*

*   *   *

KNIPPENBERG, Joseph M. 1957-

PERSONAL: Born May 9, 1957, in San Francisco, CA; son of Josephus Jacobus Maria and Ingeborg Katherina (Buttenhauser) Knippenberg; married Charlotte Lee Boggus, December 19, 1992; children: William Robert Joseph, Charlotte Taylor Katharina. *Ethnicity:* "Dutch/Austrian." *Education:* James Madison College, Michigan State University, B.A., 1977; University of Toronto, M.A., 1978, Ph.D., 1986. *Politics:* Moderate conservative. *Religion:* Presbyterian.

ADDRESSES: Home—1763 Remington Rd., Atlanta, GA 30341-1439. *Office*—Department of Political Science, Oglethorpe University, 4484 Peachtree Rd., Atlanta, GA 30319-2797. *E-mail*—jknippenbeg@fac staff.oglethorpe.edu.

CAREER: Oglethorpe University, Atlanta, GA, assistant professor, 1985-92, associate professor of political science, 1992—; Boston College, visiting scholar, 1988-89; Emory University, Atlanta, GA, visiting associate professor of political science, 1994.

MEMBER: American Political Science Association, Southern Political Science Association, Midwestern Political Science Association, National Association of Scholars, Georgia Association of Scholars (trustee 1994—, president 1994-98).

AWARDS, HONORS: Faculty Appreciation Award, Omicron Delta Kappa, Oglethorpe University, 1991; Service award, Alpha Phi Omega, Oglethorpe University, 1995; Donald C. Agnew Distinguished Service award, Oglethorpe Students Association, 1995; Award for Teaching Excellence and Leadership, Vulcan Materials Co., 1996; fellow, John M. Olin Foundation, 1988-89; Salvatori Fellow in Academic Leadership, Heritage Foundation, 1992-94; Research grantee, Earhart Foundation, 1991; Pew Summer Seminar, Calvin College, 1998.

WRITINGS:

(Editor, with Peter Augustine Lawler) *Poets, Princes, and Private Citizens: Literary Alternatives to Modern Politics,* Rowman & Littlefield (Lanham, MD), 1996.

Also contributor to periodicals.

WORK IN PROGRESS: A monograph on reason, faith, and liberalism in the German Enlightenment.

SIDELIGHTS: Though his specialty is political theory, Joseph M. Knippenberg chose literature as the focus of his first book, a scholarly anthology he edited with Peter Augustine Lawler. Seeking to show that "poets, playwrights, and novelists are still teachers," Knippenberg and Lawler collected articles from a range of political science specialists in a volume that explores the relationships between literature and politics. The fourteen articles in *Poets, Princes, and Private Citizens: Literary Alternatives to Postmodern Politics* examine philosophical, moral, and political issues in works by such writers as Homer, Miguel de

Cervantes, Angl Machiavelli, Aristophanes, William Shakespeare, Charles Dickens, Herman Melville, Albert Camus, Jane Austen, Flannery O'Connor, Walker Percy, and Paul Scott. Rather than employing the analytical devices of literary criticism, the contributors consider social and political thought in poetry, drama, and fiction. According to G. L. Jones in *Choice,* this approach succeeds in "stimulating interest in a more traditional approach to the study of literature." Jones, who found the editors' selection of material "provocative," recommended the volume highly for academic audiences.

An associate professor of politics at Oglethorpe University in Atlanta, Georgia, where he has received numerous awards for teaching, Knippenberg also contributes articles to scholarly publications. He has been a visiting scholar at Boston College and a visiting associate professor at Emory University. He has served since 1994 as trustee and president of the Georgia Association of Scholars, an affiliate of the National Association of Scholars. He is also a regular member of the American Political Science Association, and the Southern Political Science Association.

Knippenberg told *CA:* "For me, teaching, research, and writing are intimately connected. The questions I address in my writing are the same ones I pose to my students. At present I'm most interested in the 'theological-political problem'—that is, how individuals understand the relationship between divine authority and political authority. In liberal societies such as ours, we 'resolve' the question by privatizing it. But moral claims often and inevitably have a public dimension that we ignore at our peril."

BIOGRAPHICAL/CRITICAL SOURCES:

PERIODICALS

Books in Canada, March, 1998, pp. 31-32.
Choice, April, 1997, p. 1417.

* * *

KNOWLES, Elizabeth 1947-

PERSONAL: Born March 19, 1947, in Petersfield, Hampshire, England; daughter of Arthur Heygate (a doctor) and Sheila (a homemaker; maiden name, Dudgeon) Knowles. *Education:* University of Exeter, B.A. (with honors), 1970. *Religion:* Anglican.

ADDRESSES: Home—41 Newland, Witney, Oxfordshire OX8 6JN, England. *Office*—Oxford University Press, Great Clarendon St., Oxford OX2 6DP, England; fax 01-86-526-7810. *E-mail*—eknowles@oup.co.uk.

CAREER: Oxford University Press, Oxford, England, staff member, then senior editor of English dictionary, 1983-93, managing editor of Oxford quotation dictionaries, 1993—.

WRITINGS:

The Oxford Dictionary of New Words, Oxford University Press (Oxford, England), 1997.
The Oxford Dictionary of Phrase, Saying, and Quotation, Oxford University Press, 1997.
The Oxford Dictionary of Twentieth Century Quotations, Oxford University Press, 1998.

WORK IN PROGRESS: The Oxford Dictionary of Quotations, 5th edition, for Oxford University Press.

* * *

KOLLER, Jackie French 1948-

PERSONAL: Born March 8, 1948, in Derby, CT; daughter of Ernest James (an electrical engineer) and Margaret (a homemaker; maiden name, Hayes) French; married George J. Koller (a president of a hospital) July 11, 1970; children: Kerri, Ryan, Devin. *Education:* University of Connecticut, B.A., 1970.

ADDRESSES: Home—Westfield, MA. *Agent*—c/o Atheneum, Simon & Schuster Inc., 1230 Avenue of the Americas, New York, NY 10020.

CAREER: Author.

MEMBER: Society of Children's Book Writers and Illustrators (former regional advisor).

AWARDS, HONORS: Recipient of numerous awards, including American Library Association Best Books for Young Adults, American Library Association Notables, International Reading Association Teacher's Choice, International Reading Association Young Adult's Choice, American Bookseller's Association Pick of the Lists, New York Public Library Reluctant Reader Recommended List, Bulletin for the Center for Children's Books Blue Ribbon, Bank Street College Annual Book Award, Honor Book and Junior Library Guild.

WRITINGS:

FOR CHILDREN

Impy for Always, Little, Brown (Boston), 1989.
The Dragonling, Little, Brown, 1990.
Mole and Shrew, Atheneum (New York City), 1991.
Fish Fry Tonight!, Crown (New York City), 1992.
Mole and Shrew Step Out, Atheneum, 1992.
The Dragonling, Archway Minstrel, 1996.
A Dragon in the Family, Archway Minstrel, 1996.
No Such Thing, Boyds Mills Press, 1997.
Dragon Quest, Archway Minstrel, 1997.
Mole and Shrew, All Year Through, Random House, 1997.
Dragons of Krad, Archway Minstrel, 1997.
Dragon Trouble, Archway Minstrel, 1997.
Dragons and Kings, Archway Minstrel, 1998.

FOR YOUNG ADULTS

Nothing to Fear, Harcourt (New York City), 1991.
If I Had One Wish. . . , Little, Brown, 1991.
The Last Voyage of the Misty Day, Atheneum, 1992.
The Primrose Way, Harcourt, 1992.
A Place to Call Home, Atheneum, 1995.
The Falcon, Atheneum, 1998.

OTHER

Also contributor of the long poem *What If?,* to *Cobblestone;* "Home Early," published in *Spider,* 1994; and "'Oink!' Said the Cat," published in *Ladybug,* 1996.

WORK IN PROGRESS: The Promise, for Knopf, 1999; *One Monkey Too Many,* for Harcourt, 1999; *Bouncing on the Bed,* for Orchard, 1999; *Nickommoh! A Thanksgiving Celebration,* 1999; a short story, "Brother, Can You Spare a Dream?," to appear in *Time Capsule Anthology,* edited by Don Gallo, for Bantam, 2000.

SIDELIGHTS: Jackie French Koller has spent her life immersed in stories, listening as her mother read to her when she was a baby; conjuring up make-believe adventures to entertain herself; and developing a lifetime habit of avid reading. As a young mother, Koller found herself steeped in books again, this time for her infant daughter, Kerri. Like giving birth over and over again, the stories that Koller had inside her be-

gan emerging. "At first I wrote them for Kerri and the two little brothers who followed her, but gradually I began to share them with others, and people began to encourage me to try publication," Koller said in an interview with Diane Andreassi. After her youngest child was out of diapers Koller began attending writers' conferences where she learned her trade. Six years and hundreds of rejection slips later she began her journey as a professional writer. Koller sold *Impy for Always,* a chapter book, and just a couple of weeks later sold a novel, *Nothing to Fear.* Her writing has been praised by reviewers like Esther Sinofsky of *Voice of Youth Advocates,* who applauded Koller's second historical fiction novel, *The Primrose Way.* Sinofsky felt the book would be good for teachers of history, women's studies, and multiculturalism. "Recommend this book to young adults who enjoy good historical fiction," the critic remarked.

Koller's life and at least two books were inspired by her parents, who met at the end of World War II, married soon after, and moved to Connecticut. Koller's mother, Margaret, was one of nine children who grew up in poverty in New York City during the Great Depression. Margaret's father was an abusive alcoholic who rarely worked, and her mother supported their family by working as the janitor of their building. Margaret's family was often hungry and poorly clothed, so as a sophomore in high school Koller's mother dropped out of school to work full-time so she could help support her brothers and sisters. Koller's mother's childhood struggles inspired *Nothing to Fear.* Koller's father's life was equally difficult and was the backdrop for her short story "Brother, Can You Spare a Dream?" Koller's paternal grandfather was also an alcoholic. Koller's father, Ernest, was a teen when his father went to jail for killing a woman in a hit-and-run accident. Meanwhile Koller's grandmother took up with a hobo.

After Koller's grandfather was released from jail, her grandparents went through a number of separations and reconciliations until they finally divorced. Determined to make a better life for himself, Ernest graduated from high school and put himself through engineering school by working four jobs. World War II began and Koller's father joined the Navy as an officer. He met Margaret and they were married. "Needless to say, my parents didn't have the best role models in the marriage or parenting department, and they hit many snags along the way, but they tried hard to give us children the best life they possibly could, and my memories of early childhood are good ones," Koller said in the interview with Andreassi.

As a youngster, Koller developed the ability to entertain and amuse herself. "I didn't have any imaginary friends per se, but I developed a vivid imagination and was forever pretending," she told Andreassi. "I would dream up great adventures for my siblings and friends to act out, and I, of course, was always the star, the hero, or, one might say, the main character, for as I look back now I can see that those early games of pretend were my first attempts at creating stories." A tomboy who was quite bossy around children her age, Koller described herself as "the one who came up with the ideas for what we should do and how we should do it." Koller was very quiet, however, around adults because she was raised with the philosophy that children should be seen and not heard: "I was a great listener, though, and loved to creep to the top of the stairs and eavesdrop when my parents were having guests or parties."

As soon as Koller could read to herself, it became a constant pastime. She loved to curl up in a cozy corner or in the crook of a tree and read for hours. Her favorites, books that her mother gave her and had been her best loved novels, were *Black Beauty, Heidi, Little Women* and fairy tales. "I could never get enough fairy tales," Koller explained in the interview with Andreassi. As a youngster, school work came easily to her, and she was a straight A student. As she grew bored and disenchanted with the work, her grades dropped; however, she rarely got less than a B. "These days I would have been put in accelerated classes and challenged, and I would probably have had a much better school experience, but in the post war years there were thirty-five kids in a class and little time or money for special programs," Koller explained to Andreassi.

As an adolescent Koller was tall, bright, and tomboyish; this did not put her on the "most popular list" in school. By the time she entered sixth grade, she had sprouted to five foot eight inches tall, which made her the tallest student in the class. "To make matters worse, I got 103 on my first science test and word spread that not only was I a giant, I was a brain, too—the kiss of death for a girl back then," Koller told Andreassi. She had a hard time making friends and finally connected with other misfits who were also struggling. In high school, Koller remembers, she was often the last to be chosen by team captains, sat out dance after dance at school events, and never was asked for a date. Adding to that turmoil, her parents were having troubles and home was not a refuge. She took solace in books and nature. Living near woods, beautiful ponds, and streams, Koller

went hiking alone after school and found herself daydreaming at length, making up stories in which she was beautiful, popular, glamorous, famous, mysterious—whatever she felt like that day. She would return home, dive into a book, and lose herself in the story and characters, leaving all the pain of the real world behind.

During this time, Koller never dreamed of being a writer. "I didn't think it was something an ordinary person could do, and no one ever told me otherwise," Koller told Andreassi. While she always wrote well, no teacher ever encouraged her to pursue it as a career. In fact, it was her art work that drew the most attention and initially she thought she might be an animator. She considered art school, until her father convinced her it was a risky business. Instead, Koller enrolled at the University of Connecticut and studied interior design, but the subject never really excited her. Her social life, however, took off. She was no longer the tallest woman in class, and she finally fit in because being smart was admired in college. "I had friends and dates and was courted by the most prestigious sororities on campus, and had to pinch myself sometimes to see if I was still really me underneath," Koller told Andreassi.

Koller met George J. Koller her junior year, and they were married in 1970. Her husband went on to graduate school, and she supported them by working in the insurance industry. With the birth of her first child, Kerri, also came the beginning of her new career as a writer. As Koller read to her infant child, her own imagination became rekindled and her daydreams became reality in print. At first she wrote her stories solely for Kerri (and later Kerri's two younger brothers), and gradually Koller began to share them with others who encouraged her to get them published.

Koller's first young adult work, *Nothing to Fear,* is about an Irish immigrant family living in poverty in New York City during the Depression. The only family income is what Danny can make shining shoes and what his mother earns doing laundry. His father leaves town to seek work and Danny becomes the man of the house. Pregnant and weary, his mother loses her laundry work and Danny begins begging for food. The family finally finds relief, ironically, by helping a sick and hungry stranger who appears at their doorstep. Rosemary Moran of *Voice of Youth Advocates* described the story as "in turn depressing and enriching." Ann Welton of *School Library Journal* stated that the work had a strong "plot line and numerous interesting supporting characters will hold readers' attention." Zena Sutherland, in a review for *Bulletin of the Center for Children's Books,* commented less favorably, finding the book "believable but banal." She felt the novel doesn't offer "fresh twists" to already published fiction about the Depression. However, a critic in *Kirkus Reviews* remarked that *Nothing to Fear* is an "involving account of the Great Depression . . . conjuring an entire era from the heartaches and troubles of one struggling family."

In 1992 came *The Last Voyage of the Misty Day,* which Koller described as being inspired by her father's lifelong love of the sea and fascination with boats of all kinds. The story concerns Denny, who moves with her mother from New York City to the coast of Maine after her father's death. Struggling with a new climate and isolation, Denny meets her odd neighbor, Mr. Jones, who works endlessly repairing the wrecked boat that he has made his home. She ultimately learns that people aren't always what they seem. Susan Knorr of *School Library Journal* described the work on the boat as "nicely integrated" into the plot, but she also felt that Denny's "overblown emotional shifts, along with occasional trite dialogue" may put readers off. Zena Sutherland in *Bulletin of the Center for Children's Books,* however, found the book's conclusion rewarding, commenting that it "moves to a dramatic ending."

By this time Koller had begun to hone her own writing style and was building a tunnel to the publishing world. Another 1992 novel, *The Primrose Way* is about a sixteen-year-old girl, Rebekah Hall, who comes to live with her Puritan father in seventeenth-century Massachusetts. Pretending that she is converting the local Native Americans, Rebekah befriends Qunnequawese, the chief's niece. This awakens a cultural understanding between the two. Rebekah's interest in the Native American way of life makes her question the Puritan salvation. Her problems worsen as she falls in love with the tribe's holy man, Mishannock. According to Koller, getting inside the psyche of her characters meant learning the history of the time and cultural mores. "I try to find as much original source material as possible—diaries, journals, letters—and then I also read extensively, including ethno-historical studies on the people and times," Koller told Andreassi. While some reviewers found flaws in the novel, as with Ilene Cooper in *Booklist* who wrote, "Koller has a few awkward moments at first," most gave the work high praise. Sinofsky wrote in *Voice of Youth Advocates* that Koller has written a "beautiful story" of Rebekah searching for her identity, with "carefully researched" scenes de-

picting early Massachusetts. A contributor in *Kirkus Reviews* proclaimed that Koller creates a vivid landscape that "successfully de-romanticizes the early settlers' struggles and avoids the absolutes (us-good, them bad)." Barbara Chatton in *School Library Journal* was equally impressed, remarking: "Koller's carefully researched book incorporates authentic language in a readable text."

Koller did extensive research about the foster care system, even interviewing a social worker, before she introduced her readers to Anna O'Dell in *A Place to Call Home.* In the book fifteen-year-old Anna returns home from school one day and finds her infant brother, Casey, screaming. Anna instantly knows that her alcoholic mother has left them for good. This time, however, her mother is found drowned in a lake, having committed suicide. Anna is determined to keep her five-year-old sister, Mandy, and Casey together with her. Anna, who is biracial, shows her intelligence, strength, and determination to fight for "the greater good for her family," according to Hazel Moore in a review for *Voice of Youth Advocates.* Carolyn Noah of *School Library Journal* called this novel an "eloquent depiction of impoverishment and courage." She went on to say that the novel is "fast paced" and "compelling," with "satisfying social values." Merri Monks of *Booklist* stated that *A Place to Call Home* is a "finely written novel that shows the tragic" outcome of sexual abuse and family rejection. In fact, these issues are Koller's main concern with society today. "We pay a lot of lip service to the importance of family values and education, but very little ever changes," Koller told Andreassi. "Children should be our number one national priority—their health, their well being, their education. Children's caregivers should be among the most highly respected and highly paid professions we have."

In *The Falcon,* published in 1998, Koller uses a journal format to bring out a secret about Luke, the work's protagonist. Luke's self-destructive behavior lands him in a psychiatric hospital, and he must heal a deep emotional scar on his way to recovery. "Luke's strong voice comes through quite believably throughout," according to Roger Leslie in *Booklist.* Paula Rohrlick of *Kliatt* called the novel an "involving and often suspenseful tale."

Koller, whose hobbies include making ginger bread houses, lives and writes at home, on ten acres on a mountaintop in Western Massachusetts with her husband, her youngest son, and two Labrador retrievers. She writes at least seven hours a day, four times a week. "I talk to myself a lot," Koller told Andreassi. "That's the only way I can describe it. I get an idea for a story and I decide on the main character and then I walk around having conversations with that character until I know him or her well enough to start putting his/her story down on paper." Koller said that she always keeps her audience in mind while she is writing and that she often stops and asks herself if the story is going to hold the interest of a reader, and whether or not it is a subject to which a young reader can relate. "Sometimes I start out thinking I'm writing a picture book and then realize that it's getting too involved and sophisticated, so I'll start over with an older audience in mind and write the story as a chapter book or novel," Koller told Andreassi. "I hope young readers will see themselves or others that they know in my books and that my books will encourage a love of reading."

BIOGRAPHICAL/CRITICAL SOURCES:

PERIODICALS

Booklist, October 15, 1992, p. 418; October 15, 1995, p. 396; April 15, 1998, p. 1436.
Bulletin of the Center for Children's Books, March, 1991, p. 168; April, 1992, p. 211; January, 1993.
Horn Book Guide, December, 1995.
Kirkus Reviews, March 1, 1991; September 15, 1992, p. 1189.
Kliatt, July, 1998.
School Library Journal, May, 1991, p. 93; June, 1992, p. 116; September, 1992, p. 278; October, 1995, p. 155.
Voice of Youth Advocates, October, 1991, p. 228; June, 1992; December, 1992, p. 280; February, 1996, p. 373.

OTHER

Interview with Diane Andreassi, The Gale Group, fall, 1998.*

* * *

KONING, (Angela) Christina 1954-

PERSONAL: Born April 8, 1954, in Kuala Belait, Borneo; daughter of Geert Julius (an engineer) and Angela Vivienne (a teacher; maiden name, Thompson) Koning; married Eamonn Stephen Vincent, May 16, 1981 (divorced, 1994); children: Anna Cordelia,

James Connor. *Ethnicity:* "White." *Education:* Girton College, Cambridge, M.A. (with honors), 1975; attended Newcastle College of Art, 1975-76; doctoral study at University of Edinburgh. *Politics:* "Not strongly committed, but left of center." *Religion:* Agnostic. *Avocational interests:* Art, music, travel, gardening.

ADDRESSES: Home and office—London, England. *Agent*—Derek Johns, A. P. Watt Ltd., 20 John St., London WC1N 2DR, England. *E-mail*—ckoning@ interbase.co.uk.

CAREER: Writer. Tate Gallery, worked in Publications Department, 1978; Transworld Publishers Ltd., member of export sales staff, 1978-81. Lecturer at educational institutions, including University of Greenwich, 1993-94, Universidad Catolica Andres Bello and Universidad Simon Bolivar, both in Venezuela, 1994, and Birkbeck College, London. Appeared on British television programs, including *Espresso,* Channel 5, and *Woman's Hour,* British Broadcasting Corp.

WRITINGS:

A Mild Suicide (novel), Lime Tree, 1992.
The Good Reading Guide to Children's Books, Bloomsbury, 1997.
Undiscovered Country (novel), Penguin (London), 1998.

Work represented in anthologies, including *A Treasury for Mothers,* Michael O'Mara, 1998. Columnist for *Guardian,* 1987-89. Contributor of articles, stories, and reviews to magazines and newspapers, including *She, Times* (London), *Observer, Roman Holiday, London for Kids,* and *You.* Books editor, *Cosmopolitan* and *M.*

WORK IN PROGRESS: Chinese White, a novel; research on travel in the Far East.

SIDELIGHTS: Christina Koning told *CA:* "I have written stories and poems for as long as I can remember, but I started writing seriously when I was a student at Cambridge and Edinburgh universities. Apart from a couple of short stories, I didn't attempt to get anything published until much later, when I was already working as a freelance journalist.

"My first novel, *A Mild Suicide,* which is set in Edinburgh in 1977, was written over three years, during which I was bringing up two young children and living in somewhat straitened circumstances.

Looking back, I think that I chose to write about what was (for me) a rather wild and hedonistic time—the late 1970s—because it was an escape from the difficulties under which I was then living. The novel deals with love, sex, and art—subjects to which I have returned in subsequent works. If there was one author who influenced the work more than another it was Wyndham Lewis, the subject of my unfinished doctoral thesis, from whose own first novel *Tarr* I derived the title.

"My second novel, *Undiscovered Country,* was published after a hiatus during which I wrote another novel (as yet unpublished) and a collection of short stories. The novel, which is set in Venezuela in 1953, was inspired to some extent by the lives of my late parents, who met in South America in the early 1950s while both were working for the Shell petroleum company. While researching the book, including a visit to Venezuela where I had spent my early childhood, I became fascinated by the expatriate lifestyle, with its curious mixture of privilege and footlessness. The postcolonial theme is one which continues to absorb me; I'm also very interested in the work of other writers (Rushdie, Kureishi, Ishiguro, Mo) who are exploring similar ideas from a different perspective.

"I am currently working on another novel, *Chinese White,* which is set partly in Sussex, England in 1968, and partly in Shanghai in 1911. The book deals with aspects of colonialism, art, love, and other preoccupations."

BIOGRAPHICAL/CRITICAL SOURCES:

PERIODICALS

Guardian, February 26, 1998.
Independent, February 23, 1998.
Observer, January 18, 1998.
Scotsman, January 24, 1998.
Spectator, February 7, 1998.
Sunday Telegraph, February 15, 1998.
Times (London), January 24, 1998.
Times Literary Supplement, February 13, 1998.

*   *   *

KOST, Bruce 1950-

PERSONAL: Born August 1, 1950, in Louisville, KY; son of Ray (an electrician and business owner) and Marie (a postal worker; maiden name, Borman) Kost; married, wife's name Deborah, June 10, 1972 (divorced August 20, 1975); children: Sandy Kost Youngblood, Shane, Lee Kost Tufley. *Ethnicity:* "Caucasian—German and Irish." *Education:* Attended Ventura Junior College, 1973-75, and Pasadena City College, 1975-76. *Politics:* Independent. *Religion:* Christian. *Avocational interests:* Hang gliding, cliff climbing, scuba diving, snow skiing, tennis.

ADDRESSES: Home—P.O. Box 70184, New Orleans, LA 70172-0184. *Office*—Business Office, Tidewater Marine, Inc., Amelia, LA.

CAREER: Tidewater Marine, Inc. (offshore service provider), Amelia, LA, able-bodied seaman, 1991—. *Military service:* U.S. Navy, Seabees, 1969-71; served in Vietnam; received Bronze Star, Vietnam Campaign Medal with device, Vietnam Service Medal with insignia, and Combat Action Ribbon.

WRITINGS:

Reclusive Authority (science fiction), American Literary Press (Baltimore, MD), 1998.

WORK IN PROGRESS: The Youngblood Project; Fountain of Longevity; Captain Terragon, the Early Days, completion expected in 2000; research on the social behavior and psychology of ants.

SIDELIGHTS: Bruce Kost told *CA:* "I was motivated to write because I had a story that I wanted to tell. I also wanted to explore the possibility that I may have any writing talent. My way of ascertaining that was to do it.

"Because of the psychic development classes I was taking when I began, Marion Zimmer Bradley was required reading, and her work inspired a portion of my own. *Reclusive Authority* begins on the psychic note, and I draw from my own experiences and apply them to several of the characters in the book. Not all of my writings will follow a psychic theme, but the volumes in the *Reclusive Authority* series will. I also plan to develop stories about Wren Dover, the psychic's home planet.

"I started writing a short story, 'Hastur's Dream,' for Marion Zimmer Bradley's 'Darkover' series. Thirty-thousand words into the story, I learned that she had discontinued accepting manuscripts for the series. That prompted me to write my first novel. In writing the short story, I completed the end first, and then I wrote five different scenes before settling on the beginning chapters. In the novel, I wrote from the beginning to the end. Even though I had an outline, the story deviated from it, as it seemed to evolve on its own.

"I've led a nomadic life for thirty years. I've wandered across the United States coast to coast, north to south, and I've wandered around the world, visiting Egypt, Spain, Italy, Bahrain, Portugal, Gibraltar, Guam, Diego Garcia, and, of course, Vietnam. I've also been to Puerto Rico, Ecuador, Panama, and through the Canal Zone and Mexico. I wander and work. I've drawn on all of my experiences in writing *Reclusive Authority* and the following novels. If I become an established writer, the wanderings will not stop. Since I was in Vietnam in the late sixties, I have an urge to wander."

*　　*　　*

KRAMER, Edna E.
See LASSAR, Edna Ernestine Kramer

*　　*　　*

KRAMER, Edna Ernestine
See LASSAR, Edna Ernestine Kramer

*　　*　　*

KREVE (MICKEVICIUS), Vincas 1882-1954
(Vincas Baltausis, a pseudonym)

PERSONAL: Born October 19, 1882, in Subartonys, Lithuania; immigrated to the United States, 1947; died July 7, 1954, in Marple Township, PA. *Education:* Studied philology at the University of Kiev, 1904-05; University of Lvov, Ph.D., 1908.

CAREER: Writer, educator, and critic. Teacher of Russian language and literature at secondary schools, Ukraine, c. 1908-20; University of Kaunas, Lithuania, professor of Slavic literatures, 1920-40, dean of the Faculty of Humanities, 1925-37; Prime Minister of Lithuanian foreign affairs, 1940-44; University of Pennsylvania, professor of Slavic literatures, 1947-53.

WRITINGS:

SHORT STORY COLLECTIONS

Dainavos salies senu zmoniu padavimai, 1912.
Sutemose, 1921.
Rytu pasakos, 1930.
Miglose, 1944.
The Herdsman and the Linden Tree, Maryland Books (New York), 1964.

PLAYS

Sarunas, Dainavos kunigaikstis, 1911.
Zentas, 1921.
Mindaugo mirtis, 1935.
Skirgaila, 1935.
Dangaus ir zemes sunus, 1949.

OTHER

Vinco Kreves rastai (short stories and plays), 10 vols., 1921-30.
Raganius (novel), 1938.
(As Vincas Baltausis) *Pagunda* (novel), 1950, translation published as *The Temptation,* 1950.

SIDELIGHTS: Vincas Kreve is considered Lithuania's greatest modern writer. Portraying heroic figures from medieval legends as well as the common people of his own day, Kreve dedicated his fiction to expressing the independent spirit of the Lithuanian people. During the late nineteenth and early twentieth centuries, Lithuanian literature was devoted to creating a revival of national consciousness in order to counteract the longstanding cultural influence of Poland and political domination by Russia. When a forty-year ban on all publications in the Lithuanian language was repealed by the Russians in 1904, the desire to establish a national culture motivated Lithuanian writers to focus on the past greatness of their country. Influenced by authors who celebrated the development of Lithuania as a powerful European empire during the Middle Ages, Kreve based his earliest works on heroic legends, medieval history, and folklore, while his subsequent works included depictions of Lithuanian peasant life and the political plight of modern Lithuanians.

Born in the village of Subartonys, Kreve grew up hearing the folksongs and folktales of southeastern

Lithuania. His early education was conducted at a seminary in Vilinius, and at the age of twenty-two he entered the University of Kiev to study philology. He went on to graduate work in the same field at the University of Lvov in the Soviet Ukraine. Concerning his experiences as a student, Kreve later wrote: "When, while studying at the university, I had occasion to meet students of a different national background who boasted about their glorious past history, I was seized by a desire to show the others that our history is greater than theirs." After his graduation in 1908, Kreve taught Russian language and literature at secondary schools in the Ukraine. He also began writing adaptations of folktales which he included in his first collection of stories, 1912's *Dainavos salies senu zmoniu padavimai*. On returning to Lithuania in 1920, Kreve became professor of Slavic literatures at the University of Kaunas. Over the next two decades, he played a major role in the cultural affairs of his country by founding and editing several journals. In 1940, when Soviet control was reinstated after twenty years of Lithuanian autonomy, Kreve entered Lithuanian political life by becoming Prime Minister of Lithuania's foreign affairs. In the satirical 1950 novel *Pagunda* (translated as *The Temptation*), he related in fictional form some of his frustrating experiences in dealing with the totalitarian Soviet regime. Regarding this work, Charles Angoff declared in his introduction to Raphael Sealey's 1965 translation of *Pagunda:* "It is surely one of the best portraits of what it means to be a Communist functionary and a Communist intellectual that has yet appeared in print." In 1944 Kreve resigned from his office and left Lithuania. He spent the next three years living in exile in Austria before ultimately immigrating to the United States, where he accepted a professorship at the University of Pennsylvania. From 1947 until his death in 1954 Kreve devoted himself to teaching and writing.

Throughout his career Kreve utilized Lithuanian legend and folklore in developing his central subject: the independent spirit of the Lithuanian people. In his earliest works Kreve depicted figures from Lithuanian legends, such as medieval princes and knights, in order "to re-create that Lithuania of old which with one hand fought off the onslaught of Western Europe while with the other it conquered the large part of that country which is now Russia." Kreve described the heroic figures in his work as "giants" who represented the "spirit and soul of old Lithuania." One of Kreve's most successful illustrations of this spirit is the 1911 drama *Sarunas, Dainavos kunigaikstis,* in which the legendary prince Sarunas leads his country into battle in an attempt to unite the tribes of Lithuania. Although he is defeated, the struggle to consolidate Lithuania's tribes is continued after his death. In another dramatic work, 1935's *Skirgaila*, Kreve again delineated the struggle for independence and political unity in Lithuania, a struggle now carried on by the wrathful prince Skirgaila who led Lithuania into battle against invading Teutons. Critics have seen in Kreve's emphasis on the turmoil medieval Lithuania experienced in the struggle for political unification and independence an analogy to the situation of modern Lithuania.

The spirit of the Lithuanian people is further defined in Kreve's stories of peasant life. These works focus primarily on the peasants living in Kreve's native region of Dzukija at the turn of the century, emphasizing their essential goodness and primitive faith in the life-giving powers of nature. Together with his renditions of Lithuanian legends, Kreve's peasant stories made him one of his country's most representative and beloved authors. Praising Kreve's part in the renewal of a Lithuanian national consciousness, Alfred Senn wrote in his essay in the 1956 volume *World Literatures:* "Kreve has indeed created a new spiritual world for the Lithuanians. He has given Lithuanian culture a new physiognomy. No other Lithuanian in the entire course of Lithuanian history can boast a similar success."

BIOGRAPHICAL/CRITICAL SOURCES:

BOOKS

Kreve, Vincas, *The Herdsman and the Linden Tree,* translated by Albinas Baranauskas, Pranas Pranckus, and Raphael Sealey and with and introduction by Charles Angoff, Manyland Books, 1964.
Kreve, Vincas, *The Temptation,* translated by Raphael Sealey and with an introduction by Charles Angoff, Manyland Books, 1965.
Remenyi, Joseph, and others, *World Literatures,* University of Pittsburgh Press, 1956.
Schirokauer, Arno, and Wolfgang Paulsen, editors, *Corona: Studies in Celebration of the Eightieth Birthday of Samuel Singer,* Duke University Press, 1941.

PERIODICALS

Books Abroad, summer, 1964, pp. 265-267.
Studi Baltici, Vol. 1, 1952, pp. 11-23.*

KUROSAWA, Akira 1910-1998

OBITUARY NOTICE—See index for *CA* sketch: Born March 23, 1910, in Tokyo Japan; died of a stroke, September 6, 1998, in Tokyo, Japan. Director, screenwriter, and author. Kurosawa was revered for his films that combined traditional Japanese folklore with Western film technology like Panavision and Dolby sound. Kurosawa is credited with bringing Japanese films to the world's attention and at the time of his death was considered among the best directors of all time. Born in Tokyo to a large family, Kurosawa originally wanted to be a painter and studied at the Tokyo Academy of Fine Arts. Not finding success as a painter, he answered an ad for Tokyo's P.C.L. Studios, which was searching for six men to become apprentice assistant directors. Kurosawa was accepted into the program after an interview with Kajiro Yamamoto, Japan's renowned director, and presenting an essay he had written saying that films could always be better than they had been. Yamamoto insisted Kurosawa learn all aspects of filming, including screenwriting, and after seven years, in 1943, he was allowed to direct his first film, *Sanshiro Sugata* ("Judo Saga"). The film was successful and Kurosawa began work on his next picture, 1944's *The Most Beautiful.* It was while working on that film that Kurosawa met his future wife, Yoko Yaguchi, who then retired from acting to be Kurosawa's companion until her death in 1985.

One of Kurosawa's best-known films, and the first to win international acclaim, was 1950's *Rashomon,* which won the 1951 Oscar for best foreign film and the best picture award at the Venice International Film Festival. The film, about an attack on a nobleman and his wife in a forest in medieval Japan, tells the story from the viewpoints of the attacker, the woman, the murdered nobleman and a woodcutter who was in the forest. Each viewpoint is depicted plausibly, making truth the theme of the film in that each person believes him or herself to be telling the truth. The 1950s and 1960s were prolific times for Kurosawa, who made about fifteen films during that period. His works frequently were based on the writing of William Shakespeare, Feodor Dostoevski, and the American author Ed McBain, and he cited directors John Ford and John Huston as role models. In 1952 his film *Ikiru* ("To Live!") was released. Considered to be one of Kurosawa's best films, it tells the story of a Japanese bureaucrat who learns to appreciate life shortly before he dies of cancer. Another acclaimed film, *Seven Samurai,* soon followed. *Samurai* tells the story of seven out-of-work samurai warriors who are hired by a group of peasants to defend their village from bandits. The samurai want to live by the warrior ideology which, incidentally, Kurosawa had satirized in his 1945 film *They Who Step on the Tiger's Tail.* *Seven Samurai* was remade by United Artists as a western and released in America as *The Magnificent Seven.* Kurosawa received his second Silver Lion Award from the Venice Film Festival for *Samurai.*

The films Kurosawa made during the late 1960s were assailed by critics and led him to slash his wrists in a 1971 suicide attempt. His critical failures and bad behavior on movie sets, where he often threw tantrums, resulted in difficulty finding financial backing for his subsequent films. He turned to outsiders for funding and finally returned to films in 1976 with *Dersu Uzula,* which was financed by Russians and filmed in Siberia. The picture resulted in Kurosawa's second Academy Award, as well as Italy's Donatello Prize and the Moscow Film Festival First Prize.

In 1985 Kurosawa's film *Ran* startled viewers with its Japanese retelling of King Lear and its realistic battle scenes. It was a critical and commercial success and returned Kurosawa to the forefront of filmmaking. He was nominated for a best director Oscar for *Ran* and also received a special trophy for achievement at the Cannes Film Festival. In 1989 Kurosawa received his third Academy Award, an honorary Oscar for lifetime achievement. His most recent films include *Akira Kurosawa's Dreams* and *Rhapsody in August,* which starred Richard Gere. In addition to his numerous films and screenplays, Kurosawa also wrote the book *Something like an Autobiography* in 1982.

OBITUARIES AND OTHER SOURCES:

PERIODICALS

Los Angeles Times, September 6, 1998; September 7, 1998.
New York Times, September 7, 1998, p. Al.
Times (London), September 7, 1998.
USA Today, September 7, 1998.
Washington Post, September 7, 1998, p. D6.

*   *   *

KUZMIN, Mikhail (Alexeyevich) 1872-1936

PERSONAL: Born October 6, 1872, in Yaroslavl, Russia; died of pneumonia, March 1, 1936, in

Leningrad (now St. Petersburg), USSR (now Russia); companion of Vsevolod Knyazev (a poet; committed suicide, 1913); companion of Yury Yurkun. *Education:* Attended St. Petersburg University; studied music under Nikolay Rimsky-Korsakov at the St. Petersburg Conservatory, 1891-94.

CAREER: Poet, playwright, and novelist.

WRITINGS:

PLAYS

Istorya rytsaria d'Alessio, 1905.
O Alexee, cheloveke Bozhem, 1907.
Venetsianskie bezumtsy, 1912; translation published as *Venetian Madcaps,* 1973.

POETRY

Seti (title means "Nets"), [Russia], 1908.
The Chimes of Love (poetry set to music), [Russia], 1910.
Osennie ozera (title means "Autumn Lakes"), [Russia], 1912.
Glinyanie golubki (title means "Clay Doves"), [Russia], 1914.
Dvum (title means "Pathfinder"), [USSR], 1918.
Zanaveshennye kartinki (title means "For the Two"), [USSR], 1920.
Alexandryskie pesni, [USSR], 1921; translation published as *Alexandrian Songs,* 1980.
Ekho, [USSR], 1921; translation published as *Echo,* 1921.
Nezdeshnie vechera (title means "Otherworldly Evenings"), [USSR], 1921.
Paraboly (title means "Parabola"), [USSR], 1923.
Forel razbyvaet lyod, 1929; translation published as *The Trout Breaks the Ice,* 1980.

NOVELS

Krilya, 1906; translation by Neil Granoien and Michael Green published as *Wings: Prose and Poetry,* Ardis (Ann Arbor, MI), 1972.
Plavayushchie puteshestvuyushchie, 1914.

OTHER

O prekrasnoy yastnosti (essay), 1910.
Sobranie sochineny (poetry, plays, novels, short stories, and essays), 9 volumes, 1914-18.
Sobranie stikhov (title means "Collected Poetry"), 3 volumes, edited by John E. Malmstad and Vladimir

Markov, Wilhelm Fink Verlag (Munich), 1977-78.
Selected Prose and Poetry (poetry, short stories, and plays), edited and translated by Michael Green, Ardis, 1972.
Prose, 8 volumes, edited and with an introduction by Vladimir Markov, Berkeley Slavic Specialties (Berkeley, CA), 1984-88.

SIDELIGHTS: A controversial figure of early twentieth-century Russian literature, Mikhail Kuzmin wrote esoteric and allusive poems, plays, and novels that are remembered as much for their frank treatment of homosexuality as for their literary merit. Writing in a period when Russian Symbolism was the dominant literary movement, Kuzmin rejected what he perceived as its false metaphysical pretensions, advocating instead an aesthetic based on concrete experience. In his *Nikolai Gumilev on Russian Poetry,* Nikolai Gumilev declared: "Mikhail Kuzmin holds one of the first places among contemporary Russian poets. Only a few are blessed with such an amazing harmony of the whole, combined with free diversity of details. As a spokesman, however, for the views and feelings of a whole circle of people united by a common culture and by rights ascended to the crest of life, he is a poet of this earth, and finally, his fully developed technique never overshadows the image, but only inspires it."

Born into a family of the minor nobility in the city of Yaroslavl, Kuzmin was educated at St. Petersburg University and initially planned a career as a composer. He began to study under Nikolay Rimsky-Korsakov at the St. Petersburg Conservatory, but discontinued his musical education in 1894, completing only three years of a seven-year course. The following year, he traveled to Egypt with his mother, and he settled in Alexandria after she returned to Russia; his years in the city were to inspire his most acclaimed collection of poetry, 1921's *Alexandryskie pesni* (translated in 1980 as *Alexandrian Songs*). In 1897 he visited Italy, later basing much of his 1906 novel *Krilya* (translated in 1972 as *Wings: Prose and Poetry*) on his experiences there. Returning to St. Petersburg, Kuzmin again turned to composing music. *Istorya rytsaria d'Alessio* was originally intended as the text for a musical piece he had written, but it became his first professional literary work when it was published as a drama in 1905. A year later, the literary journal *Vesy* published *Wings.* The novel's subject, a young artist's homosexual encounters in Italy, caused a scandal in St. Petersburg literary circles, and the controversy over Kuzmin intensified with the 1908 publication of *Seti,* a collection of poetry that contained explicitly erotic scenes. Between 1910 and 1917 Kuzmin wrote numerous dramas, becoming a prominent figure in St. Petersburg's theater community. After the Bolshevik Revolution in October of 1917, Kuzmin's opportunities for publishing original work were limited, so he turned to writing reviews and translating the works of William Shakespeare and other writers. After 1929, the year in which his noted poem cycle *Forel razbyvaet lyod* (translated in 1980 as *The Trout Breaks the Ice*) appeared, government regulations dictated that Soviet literature fulfill a primarily didactic function, and Kuzmin's works were proscribed for their aestheticism as well as their controversial subject matter. In his *Literature and Revolution,* Leon Trotsky deemed them "completely and entirely superfluous to a modern post-October man." Kuzmin died of pneumonia in 1936.

In his works Kuzmin often depicted love and sex in a way that challenged conventional morality, insisting that the pursuit of human affection is the individual's most solemn obligation. This theme is realized in a variety of historical and geographical settings, ranging from the ancient Rome of *Alexandrian Songs* to the eighteenth-century Venice of his 1912 play, *Venetsianskie bezumtsy* (translated in 1973 as *Venetian Madcaps*). While his concern for an idealized past is a trait that he shares with the Russian Symbolists, critics note that in his poetry he spurned their usage of complex and personal metaphors to express primarily metaphysical concepts. Kuzmin's ecstatic celebration in *Alexandrian Songs* of "Chablis on ice, a toasted bun," is often cited as an example of his intention to mine spirituality from everyday experience. This sentiment has led critics to stereotype Kuzmin as a poet of trivial pleasures, but such later works as *The Trout Breaks the Ice* contain expressionistic and surreal imagery that indicates the versatility of his imagination. In this cycle of poems, considerably more complex than *Alexandrian Songs,* the trout is a symbol for love, which is active and unpredictable, while the ice represents the enemies of love—repression and death.

In his dramas, Kuzmin subscribed to the aesthetic beliefs of director Vsevelod Meyerhold, who rejected the theatrical realism then popular in Russia in favor of stylized and experimental productions and who brought his vision of a new Russian theater to Kuzmin when they collaborated on various productions. Kuzmin's dramas featured elaborate costumes and scenery and incorporated his own songs and poems, and these aspects of production were considered as important as

the acting and writing. Alexandr Blok's successful drama *The Fairground Booth* of 1906 exerted a strong influence on Kuzmin, and in works such as *Venetian Madcaps* he exhibits an ironic humor that critics have compared to Blok's. Kuzmin used fiction as the forum for presenting and elaborating his theories of human relationships. Like *Wings,* his 1914 novel *Plavayushchie puteshestvuyushchie* depicts complicated entanglements and both heterosexual and homosexual partnerships, examined in detail during late-night arguments in bohemian cafes. In his novels' frequent philosophical dialogues, characters also discuss art, religion, and literature in a manner that has been described as "dilettantish," but has also been praised for its socially progressive vision. *Russian Literature Triquarterly* contributor Neil Granoien remarked: "Diaghileff once described an esthete as one who is incorrigible in his insistence upon forgetting life and in his refusal to face it. Perhaps this rather imperious view suited the imposing person of the critic and entrepreneur for whom success in life was success itself. But the picture of the artist and the esthete as superior beings disdainful of the world would not have suited Kuzmin. He preferred to think of himself and the artist as joyous celebrants in the miraculous ritual of life, and *Wings* is a part of the liturgy."

The Soviet publication of Kuzmin's collected writings and the English translations of many of his works sparked a renewal of critical interest in the 1970s. Recent commentators have unearthed complexities in Kuzmin's themes and techniques, celebrating the diversity of his achievements and recognizing his influence on such important Russian poets as Velimir Khlebnikov and Anna Akhmatova, who once called Kuzmin "my wonderful teacher." Such critical efforts, in the words of *Slavic Review* contributor Simon Karlinsky, "should help restore Kuzmin to his rightful place among the foremost Russian poets of this century."

BIOGRAPHICAL/CRITICAL SOURCES:

BOOKS

Gibian, George, and H. W. Tjalsma, editors, *Russian Modernism: Culture and the Avant-Garde, 1900-1930,* Cornell University Press, 1976.

Gumilev, Nikolai, *Nikolai Gumilev on Russian Poetry,* edited and translated by David Lapeza, Ardis, 1977.

Kuzmin, Mikhail, *Selected Prose and Poetry,* edited and with an introduction by Michael Green, Ardis, 1980.

Kuzmin, Mikhail, *Wings: Prose and Poetry,* edited and translated by Neil Granoien and Michael Green, with a preface by Vladimir Markov, Ardis, 1972.

Mirsky, Prince D. S., *Contemporary Russian Literature: 1881-1925,* Knopf, 1926.

Poggioli, Renato, *The Poets of Russia: 1890-1930,* Harvard University Press, 1960.

Slonim, Marc, *Modern Russian Literature: From Chekhov to the Present,* Oxford University Press, 1953.

Trotsky, Leon, *Literature and Revolution,* translated by Rose Strunsky, International Publishers (New York), 1925.

PERIODICALS

Russian Literature Triquarterly, vol. 7, 1973, pp. 243-266; Vol. 11, 1975, pp. 393-405.

Russian Review, July, 1963, pp. 289-300.

Slavic Review, March, 1975, pp. 44-64; September, 1979, pp. 92-96.

South Atlantic Bulletin, January, 1976, pp. 22-31.*

L

laFAVOR, Carole S.

PERSONAL: Born in Minnesota; daughter of Doris laFavor (present surname, Harrod); children: Theresa. *Ethnicity:* "Native American/Ojibwa." *Education:* St. Mary's (now St. Catharine's) College, Minneapolis, MN, A.A. and R.N. *Politics:* "Politics of justice for the poor and people of color." *Religion:* "Traditional Native spirituality." *Avocational interests:* "Anything having to do with the outdoors, nature, and other living things."

ADDRESSES: Home and office—3932 Oakland Ave. S., Minneapolis, MN 55407. *E-mail*—cslaf@aol.com.

CAREER: Minnesota American Indian AIDS Task Force, Minneapolis, MN, nurse consultant, 1996—, and past member of board of directors. Positively Native (national organization by and for Native American Indian, Alaskan, and Hawaiian natives with HIV/AIDS), member of board of directors and past administrator; member of President Bill Clinton's Council on HIV/AIDS; past member of board of directors, National Minority AIDS Council, National Native American AIDS Prevention Center, National Association of People with AIDS, and Aliveness Project. Public speaker at schools and colleges, clinics, medical and nursing conferences, and tribal councils; guest on television and radio programs; subject of videotapes, including *Her Giveaway: A Spiritual Journey with AIDS* and *An Interruption in the Journey: Living with HIV.*

AWARDS, HONORS: Service Award, McKnight Foundation, 1988; annual award, National Minority AIDS Council, 1988; Coalition Builder Award, Urban Coalition, 1991; Indian Health Service Award, 1992; Courage Award, U.S. Department of Human Ser-

vices, 1994; Distinguished Service Award, National Native American AIDS Prevention Center, 1998.

WRITINGS:

Along the Journey River (Ojibwa mystery novel), Firebrand Books (Ithaca, NY), 1996.
Evil Dead Center (Ojibwa mystery novel), Firebrand Books, 1997.

Contributor to periodicals. Editor, *Positively Native,* a newsletter, 1993-97.

SIDELIGHTS: Carole laFavor told *CA:* "My interest in writing about Native America grew as I read more and more non-native authors' works on native culture and traditions. As native people began writing, a truer picture of ourselves began to emerge. To that end, I participated in the Loft's Inroads Writers Program in Minneapolis, led by local Ojibwa author Jim Northrup.

"Both of my books, *Along the Journey River* and *Evil Dead Center,* include composites of native folks I have met in my travels around the United States, my family, and others in my personal life. I write about Ojibwa life and traditions out of respect and gratitude to all the courageous native people, past and present, who continue to fight for native culture."

*   *   *

LAGATREE, Kirsten M. 1948-

PERSONAL: Born November 6, 1948, in New York, NY; daughter of Robert Edmund and Marion

(McCormick) Lagatree; married John Barth (an internet journalist), September 27, 1990. *Education:* University of Chicago, M.A.

ADDRESSES: Home—Falls Church, VA. *Agent*—Nancy Yost, Lowenstein Associates, 121 West 27th St., New York, NY 10001. *E-mail*—klagatree@aol. com.

CAREER: Los Angeles Times, Los Angeles, CA, columnist. Worked as reporter, news director, managing editor, producer, and broadcast journalist for public radio programs, 1981-93.

WRITINGS:

Feng-Shui: Arranging Your Home to Change Your Life, Villard Books (New York City), 1996.
(With Alice Bredin) *The Home Office Solution,* Wiley (New York City), 1998.
Feng-Shui at Work, Villard Books, 1998.

WORK IN PROGRESS: Checklists for Life, for Random House (New York City), completion expected in 2000.

* * *

LAMMERS, Stephen E. 1938-

PERSONAL: Born October 22, 1938, in Davenport, IA; son of Edward J. and Helen G. Lammers; married, wife's name Noel K., June 18, 1960; children: Amy Lammers McCumber, Benjamin J. *Education:* Marquette University, A.B., M.A., 1962; Brown University, Ph.D., 1971. *Religion:* Roman Catholic.

ADDRESSES: Home—620 Weygadt Dr., Easton, PA 18042. *Office*—Department of Religion, Lafayette College, Easton, PA 18042; fax 610-330-5585. *E-mail*—lammerss@lafayette.edu.

CAREER: Lafayette College, Easton, PA, professor of religion, 1969—.

MEMBER: Society of Christian Ethics, American Academy of Religion.

AWARDS, HONORS: Grants from National Endowment for the Humanities, 1981-82, and Pennsylvania Humanities Council, 1983.

WRITINGS:

On Moral Medicine, Eerdmans (Grand Rapids, MI), 1998.

WORK IN PROGRESS: A Recasting of the Christian Just War Tradition (tentative title), completion expected in 2000.

* * *

LANDAU, Edmund Georg Hermann 1877-1938

PERSONAL: Born February 14, 1877, in Berlin, Germany; died February 19, 1938, in Berlin, Germany; buried in the Berlin-Weissensee Jewish cemetery; son of Leopold (a gynecologist) and Johanna (Jacoby) Landau; married Marianne Ehrlich, 1905; children: two daughters, two sons. *Education:* Berlin University, Ph.D., 1899, also received advanced degree in mathematics, 1901. *Religion:* Jewish.

CAREER: Berlin University, Berlin, Germany, teacher of mathematics, became professor of mathematics, 1901-09; University of Goettingen, Goettingen, Germany, professor, 1909-34. Lecturer of mathematics at other universities, including Cambridge and Brussels.

AWARDS, HONORS: Honorary doctorate, University of Oslo, c. 1929.

WRITINGS:

Neuer beweis der gleichung, [Berlin], 1899.
Handbuch der Lehre von der Verteilung der Primzahlen, 2 volumes, B. G. Teubner (Berlin and Leipzig), 1909, with an appendix by Paul T. Bateman, Chelsea (New York City), 1974.
Vorlesungen uber zahlentheorie, 3 volumes, S. Hirzel (Leipzig), 1927, Chelsea (New York City), 1946-47, translation by Jacob E. Goodman, with exercises by Paul T. Bateman and Eugene E. Kohlbecker, published as *Elementary Number Theory,* Chelsea (New York City), 1958.
Darstellung und begrundung einiger neuerer ergebnisse der funktionentheorie, J. Springer (Berlin), 1929.
Grundlagen der analysis (Das rechnen mit ganzen, rationalen, irrationalen, komplexen zahlen), Akademische verlagsgesellschaft (Berlin), 1930, Chelsea (New York City), 1946, translation by F.

Steinhardt published as *Foundations of Analysis: The Arithmetic of Whole, Rational, Irrational, and Complex Numbers,* Chelsea (New York City), 1951.

Einfuhrung in die differentialrechnung und integral-rechnung, P. Noordhoff, 1934, translation by Melvin Hausner and Martin Davis published as *Differential and Integral Calculus,* Chelsea (New York City), 1951.

Uber einige neuere fortschritte der additiven zahlen-theorie, Cambridge University Press (Cambridge, England), 1937.

Collected Works, edited by L. Mirsky and others, Thales Verlag (Essen), 1985.

Also author or contributor to other books. Author of articles and papers contributed to periodicals.

SIDELIGHTS: Edmund Georg Hermann Landau profoundly influenced the development of number theory. His primary research focused on analytic number theory, especially the distribution of prime numbers and prime ideals. An extremely productive author of at least 250 publications, Landau's writings had a distinct style. His prose was carefully crafted, highlighted by lucid, comprehensive argumentation and a thorough explanation of the background knowledge required to understand it, with Landau's writing style becoming more succinct over the course of his career. He was forced to retire from teaching at the behest of Nazi anti-Semitic policies.

Born in Berlin on February 14, 1877, Landau was the son of Leopold, a gynecologist, and Johanna (Jacoby) Landau. Johanna Landau came from a wealthy family with whom the Landaus lived in an affluent section of Berlin. Although Leopold Landau was an assimilated Jew and a German patriot, in 1872 he helped found a Judaism academy in Berlin. Landau himself studied in Berlin at the Franzoische Gymnasium (French Lycee), graduating two years early at age sixteen. He promptly began studying at Berlin University. Landau had published twice before receiving his Ph.D; both pieces explored chess-related mathematical problems.

Under the tutelage of Georg Frobenius, Landau was awarded his doctorate at Berlin University in 1899 at the age of twenty-two. His dissertation dealt with what became his life's work: number theory. Landau began teaching at Berlin in 1901, when he earned the advanced degree which allowed him to teach mathematics. He proved to be a popular lecturer at the university because of his personal excitement over the carefully prepared material he presented to his students.

Landau's first major accomplishment as a mathematician came in 1903 when he simplified and improved upon the proof for the prime number theorem conjectured by Carl Gauss in 1796 and demonstrated independently by Jacques Hadamard and C. J. de la Vallee-Poussin in 1896. In Landau's proof the theorem's application extended to algebraic number fields, specifically to the distribution of ideal primes within them.

Landau married Marianne Ehrlich (daughter of Paul Ehrlich, a friend of Landau's father, who won the 1908 Nobel prize in medicine or physiology) in 1905 at Frankfurt-am-Main, and fathered two daughters and two sons (one of whom died before age five). He served as a professor of mathematics at Berlin until 1909.

Landau published his first major work in 1909, the two-volume *Handbuch der Lehre von der Vertiolung der Prizahalen.* The volumes were the first orderly discussion of analytic number theory, and were used for many years in universities as a research and teaching tool. Landau's texts are still considered important documents in the history of mathematics.

In the same year Landau became a full professor at the University of Goettingen. Although the faculty at Berlin tried twice to keep Landau on staff, the government wanted to make Goettingen a center of German mathematical learning. They succeeded in their objective, and Landau stayed there until 1934. In 1913 Landau even declined an offer from a university in Heidelberg for a chair position in favor of his place at Goettingen. Although he was still a charismatic, inspiring teacher, by the 1920s he was criticized for his rigid, almost perfectionistic lecture style. A demanding lecturer, he insisted that one of his assistants sit through his presentations so any errors could be immediately corrected.

Landau continued his father's support of Jewish institutions. In 1925 he gave a lecture on mathematics in Hebrew at the Hebrew University in Jerusalem, an institution Landau heartily embraced. His activities there continued when he took a sabbatical from Goettingen and taught a few mathematics classes between 1927 and 1928. Landau even contemplated staying in Jerusalem at one point.

Landau published another important treatise in 1927, the three volumes comprising *Vorlesungeuber Zahlentheorie* ("Elementary Number Theory"). In these texts Landau brought together the various branches of number theory in one comprehensive text. He thoroughly explored each branch from its origins to the then-current state of research. Two years later, the widely respected Landau received a honorary doctorate of philosophy from the University of Oslo in Norway. The next year Landau published another landmark book, titled *Grundlagen der Analysis* ("Foundations of Analysis"). Beginning with Giuseppe Peano's axioms for natural numbers, this volume presented arithmetic in four forms of numbers: whole, rational, irrational, and complex.

The Nazi Party and their policies of discrimination against Jews led to a premature end to Landau's academic career. In late 1933 he was forced to cease teaching at Goettingen, although he was one of the last Jewish professors to be purged from that institution. While technically not subject to the 1933 non-Aryan clause attached to Nazi civil servant laws, all Jewish mathematical professors were forced to leave Goettingen. Landau stayed on through the summer and fall terms of 1933, but he could only teach classes through assistants. Landau would sit in the back of every class, ready to teach at any moment if his ban was raised.

On November 2, 1933, Landau attempted to resume teaching his class. The students, alerted to this perceived impropriety in advance, boycotted his lecture. SS Guards were stationed at the entrance in case a student did not want to boycott; only one got in. When it was clear he would not be allowed to lecture, Landau returned to his office. The boycotting students explained by letter that they no longer wanted to be taught by a Jew or be indoctrinated in his mode of thought.

In 1934 Landau was given his retirement leave, and he and his family moved back to Berlin. Although he never taught in Germany again, he did lecture out of the country at universities such as Cambridge in 1935 and Brussels in 1937. Landau died in Berlin of natural causes on February 19, 1938, and was buried in the Berlin-Weissensee Jewish cemetery.

BIOGRAPHICAL/CRITICAL SOURCES:

PERIODICALS

Mathematical Intelligencer, fall, 1991, pp. 12-18; spring, 1995, pp. 12-14.*

LANGLEY, Charles P(itman), III 1949-

PERSONAL: Born April 6, 1949, in New Bern, NC; son of Charles P., Jr. and Eva (Connor) Langley; married Anne Smevog Langley (an educational consultant), October 26, 1985; children: Catherine, Anna. *Education:* University of North Carolina, Chapel Hill, A.B., 1971, M.D., 1975. *Religion:* Presbyterian. *Avocational interests:* Music, literature, foreign language.

ADDRESSES: Home—82 Fairview Farms, Shelby, NC, 28150. *Office*—808 Schenck St., Shelby, NC, 28150.

CAREER: Shelby Medical Associates, physician (internal medicine), 1979—, president. Elder at the Shelby Presbyterian Church.

MEMBER: American Medical Association, American Society of Internal Medicine, Phi Beta Kappa.

WRITINGS:

Catherine and Geku: The Adventure Begins, Research Triangle, 1996.
Catherine, Anna, and Geku Go to the Beach, Research Triangle, 1997.

WORK IN PROGRESS: North, East, South, West: Catherine, Anna, and Geku Take a Trip—an organized approach to expanding French vocabulary.

SIDELIGHTS: Dr. Charles P. Langley practices medicine in Shelby, North Carolina, where he lives with his wife, Anne, and two daughters, Catherine and Anna.

In the hopes of stimulating his children's imaginations and teaching them values, Langley began telling them adventure stories with themes of trust and friendship. These stories grew to become the author's first two published works, *Catherine and Geku: The Adventure Begins* and *Catherine, Anna, and Geku Go to the Beach.*

According to Langley, Geku, a fantastic giant bird featured in both books, "on one level . . . represents the inner spirit and imagination of the child. On another level, he represents the ideal in a parent figure: A companion who teaches, inspires, stimulates, builds confidence, and provides security."*

LASSAR, Edna Ernestine Kramer 1902-1984
(Edna E. Kramer, Edna Ernestine Kramer)

PERSONAL: Born May 11, 1902, in New York, NY; died of pneumonia, July 9, 1984, in New York, NY; daughter of Joseph (in men's clothing sales) and Sabine (Elowitch) Kramer; married Benedict Taxier Lassar (a high school French teacher, guidance counselor, and clinical psychologist), July 2, 1935. *Education:* Hunter College, B.A. (mathematics; summa cum laude), 1922; Columbia University, M.A. (mathematics), 1925, Ph.D. (mathematics, with a minor in physics), 1930. *Avocational interests:* Travel.

CAREER: DeWitt Clinton High School, Bronx, NY, mathematics teacher, 1922-23; Wadleigh High School, Manhattan, NY, mathematics teacher, 1923-29; New Jersey State Teachers College, Montclair, NJ, instructor of mathematics, 1929-32, assistant professor, 1932-34; Thomas Jefferson High School, Brooklyn, NY, teacher in mathematics, 1934-48; Columbia University, Division of War Research, statistical consultant, c. 1941-48; New York Polytechnic Institute, instructor, 1948-65.

MEMBER: American Mathematical Society, Mathematical Association of America, Societe Mathematique de France, Association for Women in Mathematics, American Association for the Advancement of Science, History of Science Society, New York Academy of Sciences.

AWARDS, HONORS: Elected to Hunter College Hall of Fame, 1972.

WRITINGS:

(As Edna Ernestine Kramer) *Polygenic Functions of the Dual Variable w and the Laguerre Group,* Lutcke & Wulff, 1930.

(As Edna Ernestine Kramer) *A First Course in Educational Statistics,* John Wiley and Sons (New York City), 1935.

(As Edna Ernestine Kramer) *Mathematics Takes Wings: An Aviation Supplement to Secondary Mathematics,* Barrie & Edwin (New York City), 1942.

(As Edna E. Kramer) *The Main Stream of Mathematics,* Oxford University Press (New York City), 1951.

(As Edna Ernestine Kramer; with Oscar F. Schaaf and others) *Experiences in Mathematical Discovery,* National Council of Teachers of Mathematics (Washington, DC), 1966.

(As Edna E. Kramer) *The Nature and Growth of Modern Mathematics,* Hawthorn Books (New York City), 1970.

Contributor to periodicals, including *American Journal of Mathematics, Scripta Mathematica, Newsletter of the Southeast Asian Mathematics Society,* and *Mathematics Teacher.* Contributor of chapters to *Dictionary of Scientific Biography,* edited by Charles Coulston Gillispie, Scribners (New York City), 1972-77.

SIDELIGHTS: Edna Ernestine Kramer Lassar was a mathematics professor who made her mark by writing books about math concepts for general readers. *The Nature and Growth of Modern Mathematics,* first published in 1970 under the name Edna E. Kramer, was her crowning achievement. In a review in *Science,* Donald J. Dessart concluded that the volume "richly deserves a place on any mathematical bookshelf."

Lassar was born on May 11, 1902, in New York City. She was the eldest child of Joseph Kramer and Sabine Elowitch Kramer, Jewish immigrants from Rima-Sombad, Austro-Hungary (now Czechoslovakia). Lassar's father worked mainly as a salesman of men's clothing. However, both of her parents showed a strong intellectual bent; Joseph was interested in political science, and Sabine enjoyed opera. Education was highly valued in their home. Lassar was named for an uncle, Edward Elowitch, who had died at age nineteen shortly before her birth. This uncle had been a gifted math student, and Lassar later explained that she was motivated as a child to excel in the subject partly in his honor.

In 1922 Lassar received a B.A. degree in mathematics from Hunter College in New York City. After graduation she began teaching high school math, first at DeWitt Clinton High School in the Bronx, and then at Wadleigh High School in Manhattan. At the same time, Lassar attended graduate school at Columbia University, where she received a Ph.D. degree in 1930. She was only the third woman to earn a doctorate in pure mathematics from that institution. Her advisor at Columbia was Edward Kasner, who had published papers on polygenic functions of one complex variable. For her dissertation, Lassar developed an analogous theory of polygenic functions of the dual variable.

Lassar had originally hoped to obtain employment as a mathematical researcher, but such positions were scarce during the Depression of the 1930s. She gravitated instead toward teaching. In 1929 Lassar became the first female instructor of mathematics at the New Jersey State Teachers College in Montclair. Five years later she returned to the New York City public school system, taking a job at Thomas Jefferson High School in Brooklyn, thereby doubling her salary. Her first book, *A First Course in Educational Statistics,* appeared in 1935. It was followed by another educational volume, *Mathematics Takes Wings: An Aviation Supplement to Secondary Mathematics,* in 1942.

On July 2, 1935, Lassar married Benedict Taxier Lassar, a high school French teacher and guidance counselor who later became a clinical psychologist. The couple shared a passion for travel, which they indulged in with trips across the United States, Canada, and the Near and Far East. Lassar's husband was supportive of her career, helping with library research and manuscript typing. Two of her books were dedicated to him.

During World War II Lassar had found an opportunity to apply her academic knowledge of statistics to practical use. While still teaching high school, she also worked part-time at Columbia University as a statistical consultant to the school's Division of War Research. Her work there included probabilistic analyses of the war in Japan. In 1948 Lassar became an instructor at the New York Polytechnic Institute. She remained at the institute until her retirement in 1965.

Lassar collected real-life examples, historical tidbits, and enrichment activities to enliven her math lessons. By 1951 her collection had grown into a book, *The Main Stream of Mathematics.* This work explores mathematical history and concepts from ancient times to the early twentieth century. The theme was later expanded in *The Nature and Growth of Modern Mathematics,* a comprehensive thirty-chapter work that emphasizes twentieth-century math through the 1960s. This book was widely praised for its lively style and clear explanations. It was chosen as a Science Book of the Month Club offering, and a *Kirkus Reviews* contributor lauded Lassar for "the remarkable lucidity of her expression and her attack."

Lassar suffered from Parkinson's disease for the last decade of her life. She died of pneumonia on July 9, 1984, at her home in New York City. One of Lassar's special interests had been the historical achievements of women in mathematics. Her unique blend of talent in both math and language assured her own place in the history of the field.

BIOGRAPHICAL/CRITICAL SOURCES:

BOOKS

Halmos, Paul R., *I Want to Be a Mathematician: An Automathography,* Springer-Verlag (New York City), 1985.
Lipsey, Sally Irene, *Women of Mathematics: A Bio-bibliographic Sourcebook,* edited by Louise S. Grinstein and Paul J. Campbell, Greenwood Press (New York City), 1987, pp. 114-120.

PERIODICALS

Kirkus Reviews, January 15, 1970, p. 91.
Mathematical Reviews, nol 42, 1971, p. 2911.
New York Times, July 25, 1984, p. D23.
Publishers Weekly, July 27, 1984, p. 78.
Science, October 23, 1970, p. 432.

OTHER

Biographies of Women Mathematicians: http://www. scottlan.edu/lriddle/women/chronol.htm (December, 1998).*

* * *

LATZER, Barry 1945-

PERSONAL: Born in 1945, in Bronx, NY; married, wife's name Sandra A. (a school librarian); children: Miriam. *Education:* Brooklyn College of the City University of New York, B.A., 1966; University of Massachusetts at Amherst, Ph.D., 1977; Fordham University, J.D., 1985.

ADDRESSES: Home—183 Oakdene Ave., Teaneck, NJ 07666. *Office*—Department of Government, John Jay College of Criminal Justice of the City University of New York, 445 West 59th St., New York, NY 10019; fax 212-237-8742. *E-mail*—proflatzer@aol. com.

CAREER: John Jay College of Criminal Justice of the City University of New York, New York City, professor of law, 1978—. Graduate Center of the City University of New York, professor, 1978—; lecturer at colleges and universities, including Fordham University, 1984, and Universita degli Studi di Trento, 1996. Member of State Bars of New York and New Jersey; Kings County District Attorney's Office, New

York City, assistant district attorney in Appeals Bureau, Criminal Court Bureau, and Early Case Assessment Bureau, 1985-86; Supreme Court of the State of New York, member of Indigent Defendants' Appeals Panel, Appellate Division, 1987—. Guest on television and radio programs.

MEMBER: National Association of Scholars, City University of New York Association of Scholars (member of executive committee).

WRITINGS:

(Contributor) B. Price and P. J. Baunach, editors, *Criminal Justice Research: New Models and Findings,* Sage Publications (Beverly Hills, CA), 1980.
State Constitutions and Criminal Justice, Greenwood Press (Westport, CT), 1991.
State Constitutional Criminal Law, Clark, Boardman, Callaghan (Rochester, NY), 1995, annual supplements, 1996-98.
(Contributor) G. Alan Tarr, editor, *Constitutional Politics in the States,* Greenwood Press, 1996.
Death Penalty Cases: Leading U.S. Supreme Court Cases on Capital Punishment, Butterworth-Heinemann (Woburn, MA), 1998.
(Contributor) Andrew Karmen, editor, *Crime and Justice in New York City,* McGraw (New York City), 1998.

Contributor of articles and reviews to law journals. Contributing editor, *Criminal Law Bulletin,* 1991—.

*   *   *

LAVENSON, James H.   1919-1998
   (Jim Lavenson)

OBITUARY NOTICE—See index for *CA* sketch: Born June 8, 1919, in Philadelphia, PA; died of a stroke, September 19, 1998, in Rockport, ME. Lavenson was well known in the marketing industry for his charismatic, humorous public speaking style. He also brought sales ideas that were ahead of their time to customer service transactions in the hotel industry. Lavenson graduated from college and served in World War II as a captain. After the war he joined his father's advertising agency and in the 1960s he worked as an executive for the Hotel Corporation of America. In the 1970s Levenson was noticed when he succeeded in improving the failing Plaza Hotel in

New York City. Levenson restored architectural integrity to the hotel dining room, which attracted customers and increased revenues. In one of his speeches which became a classic in the hotel industry, Levenson described how he instilled the idea in Plaza Hotel management that every employee see their job as actively selling to the customer. His publications mainly addressed marketing and included: *Selling Made Simple, Think Strawberries,* and *How to Earn an MBWA Degree.* He also authored the novel *Sensuous Animal.*

OBITUARIES AND OTHER SOURCES:

BOOKS

Who's Who in America, Marquis Who's Who, 1999.

PERIODICALS

New York Times, September 26, 1998, p. A13.

*   *   *

LAVENSON, Jim
   See LAVENSON, James H.

*   *   *

LEMAY, Laura

PERSONAL: Born in Boston, MA. *Education:* Carnegie Mellon University, graduated, 1989.

ADDRESSES: *Agent*—c/o Macmillan Computer Publishing, 201 West 103rd St., Indianapolis, IN 46290. *E-mail*—lemay@lne.com; ladmin@lne.com.

CAREER: Writer on topics related to Java and HTML. Former technical writer for Sun Microsystems and Kaleida.

WRITINGS:

Teach Yourself Web Publishing with HTML in a Week, Sams Publishing (Indianapolis, IN), 1995, revised edition published as *Teach Yourself Web Publishing with HTML 3.0 in a Week,* Sams.net (Indianapolis, IN), 1996, third edition published as *Teach Yourself Web Publishing with HTML 3.2 in a Week,* Sams.net (Indianapolis, IN), 1996, fourth edition with revisions by Arman Danesh published as *Teach Yourself Web Publishing with HTML 4 in a Week,* Sams.net (Indianapolis, IN), 1997.

Teach Yourself More Web Publishing with HTML in a Week, Sams.net (Indianapolis, IN), 1995.

Teach Yourself Web Publishing with HTML in 14 Days, Premier Edition, Sams.net (Indianapolis, IN), 1995.

(With Charles L. Perkins) *Teach Yourself Java in 21 Days,* Sams.net (Indianapolis, IN), 1996, second edition, 1997, third edition, 1998.

Teach Yourself Java in 21 Days, Software Edition, Howard Sams Publishing (Indianapolis, IN), 1996.

Teach Yourself Web Publishing with HTML 3.2 in 14 Days, Professional Reference Edition, Sams.net (Indianapolis, IN), 1996, second edition with revisions by Arman Danesh published as *Teach Yourself Web Publishing with HTML 4 in 14 days,* Howard Sams Publishing (Indianapolis, IN), 1997.

(With Michael G. Moncur) *Laura Lemay's Web Workshop: JavaScript,* Sams.net (Indianapolis, IN), 1996.

(With Brian K. Murphy and Edmund T. Smith) *Creating Commercial Web Pages,* Sams.net (Indianapolis, IN), 1996.

(With Ned Snell) *Laura Lemay's Web Workshop: Netscape Navigator Gold 3,* Sams.net (Indianapolis, IN), 1996.

(With Denise Tyler) *Laura Lemay's Web Workshop: Microsoft FrontPage,* Sams.net (Indianapolis, IN), 1996.

(With Ted Foley) *Laura Lemay's Web Workshop: Shockwave and Multimedia,* Sams.net (Indianapolis, IN), 1996.

(With Justin Couch and Kelly Murdock) *Laura Lemay's Web Workshop: 3D Graphics and VRML 2.0,* Sams.net (Indianapolis, IN), 1996.

(With Charles L. Perkins and Roger Cadenhead) *Teach Yourself SunSoft Java Workshop in 21 Days,* Sams.net (Indianapolis, IN), 1996.

(With Daniel I. Joshi and Charles L. Perkins) *Teach Yourself Java in Cafe in 21 Days,* Sams.net (Indianapolis, IN), 1996.

Teach Yourself Web Publishing with HTML 3.0 in a Week, Software Edition, Sams.net (Indianapolis, IN), 1996.

(With Charles L. Perkins and Michael Morrison) *Teach Yourself Java in 21 Days, Professional Reference Edition,* Sams.net (Indianapolis, IN), 1996, second edition, 1997.

Teach Yourself Java for Mac, Hayden Books (Indianapolis, IN), 1996.

(With Charles L. Perkins and Timothy Webster) *Teach Yourself Java for Macintosh in 21 Days,* Hayden Books, 1996.

(With others) *Laura Lemay's Java 1.1 Interactive Course,* Waite Group Press (Corte Madera, CA), 1997.

(With Molly E. Holzschlag) *Laura Lemay's Guide to Sizzling Web Site Design,* Sams.net (Indianapolis, IN), 1997.

(With Patrick Winters and Charles Perkins) *Teach Yourself Visual J++ in 21 Days,* second edition, Sams.net (Indianapolis, IN), 1997.

Official Marimba Guide to Castanet, Sams.net (Indianapolis, IN), 1997.

(With Ned Snell) *Laura Lemay's Web Workshop: Netscape Navigator Gold 3, Deluxe Edition,* Sams.net (Indianapolis, IN), 1997.

Teach Yourself Java 1.2 in 21 Days, Macmillan Computer Publishing (Indianapolis, IN), 1998.

Teach Yourself Perl in 21 Days, Macmillan Computer Publishing (Indianapolis, IN), 1998.

BIOGRAPHICAL/CRITICAL SOURCES:

PERIODICALS

Booklist, September 15, 1996, p. 193.
Library Journal, March 1, 1996, p. 101; June 1, 1997, p. 140.
New Scientist, January 18, 1997, p. 41.
PC Magazine, June 25, 1996, p. 69.
Quill and Quire, May, 1996, pp. 20-21.
Technical Communication, February, 1996, p. 93.
Technology and Learning, May, 1997, p. 39.
Whole Earth Review, summer, 1995, p. 86.

OTHER

Laura Lemay's Home Page, http://www.lne.com/lemay/ (January 26, 1999).
Laura's Web Zone, http://www.lne.com/Web/ (January 26, 1999).*

* * *

LEPLIN, Jarrett 1944-

PERSONAL: Born November 20, 1944, in San Francisco, CA; son of Emanuel (a musician) and Anita (a teacher) Leplin. *Education:* Amherst College, B.A.,

1966; University of Chicago, M.A., 1967, Ph.D., 1972. *Religion:* "Opposed." *Avocational interests:* "Tennis, haute cuisine."

ADDRESSES: Home—5623 Brisbane Dr., Chapel Hill, NC 27514. *Office*—Department of Philosophy, Box 26170, University of North Carolina at Greensboro, Greensboro, NC 27402; fax 336-334-4720. *E-mail*—j_leplin@uncg.edu.

CAREER: University of North Carolina at Greensboro, professor of philosophy.

MEMBER: Philosophy of Science Association.

WRITINGS:

A Novel Defense of Scientific Realism, Oxford University Press (Oxford, England), 1997.

Editor of five books. Contributor of about fifty articles to philosophy journals.

*   *   *

LEPORE, Jill 1966-

PERSONAL: Born August 27, 1966, in Worcester, MA; married Timothy Leek. *Education:* Tufts University, B.A., 1987; University of Michigan, M.A., 1990; Yale University, M.Phil, 1993, Ph.D., 1995.

ADDRESSES: Office—History Department, Boston University, 226 Bay State Rd., Boston, MA 02215. *E-mail*—jlepore@bu.edu.

CAREER: Yale University, acting instructor in American studies, 1993-95; University of California at San Diego, San Diego, assistant professor of history, 1995-96; Boston University, Boston, MA, assistant professor of history, 1996—.

MEMBER: American Antiquarian Society, American Historical Association, American Studies Association, Organization of American Historians, Massachusetts Historical Society (member, steering committee, 1997—).

AWARDS, HONORS: Fellow, Whitney Humanities Center, Yale University, 1994-95; fellow, Charles

Warren Center, Harvard University, 1996-97; named "Young Americanist," Harvard University, 1998; research grant, American Philosophical Society, 1998.

WRITINGS:

The Name of War: King Philip's War and the Origins of American Identity, Knopf (New York City), 1998.
The Age of Encounters: A History in Documents, Oxford University Press (New York), in press.

Contributor of the chapters "Literacy and Reading in Puritan New England" in *Perspectives on Book History: Artifacts and Commentary,* 1999, "'Till I Have No Country': The Problem of Indian Speech in Early America" in *The Young Americanists,* 1999; also contributor of articles and reviews to the *Journal of American History, American Historical Review,* and *American Quarterly,* among others.

WORK IN PROGRESS: Native Tongues: Webster, Sequoyah, Gallaudet, and the Language of Nations (expected 2000); researching Noah Webster.

SIDELIGHTS: Boston University academic Jill Lepore won solid praise for her first book, *The Name of War: King Philip's War and the Origins of American Identity,* published by Knopf in 1998. Deemed the most murderous of conflicts ever to have spilled blood on American soil, the 1675 war began, as Lepore explains, with a rumor and a suspicious murder of a prominent Algonquian preacher near Plymouth Colony. Yet fear and distrust on both sides were the underlying root of the hostilities: New England's indigenous peoples and the European newcomers had engineered a shaky coexistence and even began to assume some of the other's customs, as her book details. The massacre, however, eradicated any hope of Native American hegemony or independence.

In *The Name of War,* Lepore chronicles the year-and-a-half conflict which began when Wampanoag leader Metacom, also known as King Philip, launched an attack on Plymouth Colony. An alliance of Algonquian tribes decimated over half the English settlements in New England, and colonial militia groups pursued them in turn across much of modern-day Connecticut and Rhode Island, slaughtering women and children along the way; torture and mercilessness occurred on both sides. Lepore portrays prominent figures of the era, including Puritan theologian Cotton Mather, the Harvard-educated convert John Sassamon, and Mary

Rowlandson, who wrote a captivity chronicle that became the first North American bestseller.

King Philip's War concluded with the quartering and beheading of its namesake, his skull enshrined on a pole in Plymouth Colony. The victorious colonists then shipped many of the surviving Algonquian off as slaves, a violation of the tenet at the time that held slavery acceptable only when the captives were "heathens." The New England economy was devastated by the war and took three decades to prosper again; Lepore, who begins *The Name of War* with the observation that "war is a contest of injuries and of interpretation," devotes equal space to the postwar ramifications. What has been termed America's "first civil war" curiously faded from significance in the annals of American history by the early nineteenth century, and the author offers insight into how such obliterations become possible and even obligatory to the victor. She also interviewed present-day descendants of Wampanoag and writes of the land claims that were still pending in the late twentieth century as a result of King Philip's War.

Reviewers cited Lepore's use of first-person accounts from the diaries of English settlers and the subsequent retelling of the war in plays, poems, and fiction, as especially noteworthy features of her debut. A *Publishers Weekly* reviewer found *The Name of War* "engrossing," while a *Booklist* critic called it "a powerful book that doesn't shy away from depicting the sheer horror of what must be termed a race war." *New York Times Book Review* critic Edward Countryman declared that Lepore's "contribution to a developing literature on historical American identity lies with her elucidation of how people attached meanings to the war's gruesome events." *Boston Globe* reviewer Barry O'Connell called Lepore's debut "a model of what multicultural history can be," a work that in tone "escapes all the parochialisms that afflict so many historians. . . . Her achievement in this book puts her in the company of our best contemporary prose stylists. It takes only a few sentences to be caught up." O'Connell concluded that a reader of the book will cast aside "the unexamined belief that Indians disappeared or became extinct or were, before the war, ever simply minor and marginal presences in the region."

BIOGRAPHICAL/CRITICAL SOURCES:

PERIODICALS

Booklist, January 1, 1998.
Boston Globe, March 1, 1998, p. F1.
Library Journal, March 1, 1998, p. 104.
New York Times Book Review, February 15, 1998.
Publishers Weekly, December 15, 1997, p. 39.

* * *

LIATSOS, Sandra Olson 1942-

PERSONAL: Born March 22, 1942, in Lynn, MA; daughter of John Thura Olson and Florence Barbara Colantuno; married Charles Emmanuel Liatsos, May 14, 1967. *Education:* Salem State College, B.S.; California State University at Northridge, M.A.; University of California, Los Angeles, Ed.D. *Avocational interests:* Reading, participating in a book discussion group, painting landscapes, singing in the Santa Ynez Valley Chorale, going to movies, playing golf, hiking in the woods, and enjoying nature.

ADDRESSES: Home and office—1210 Deer Trail Lane, Solvang, CA 93463. *Agent*—Marian Reiner, 20 Cedar St., New Rochelle, NY 10801.

CAREER: North Reading, MA, elementary school teacher, 1962-73; author, 1973—.

MEMBER: Society of Children's Book Writers and Illustrators.

WRITINGS:

FOR CHILDREN

Bicycle Riding, and Other Poems, illustrated by Karen Dugan, Boyds Mills (Honesdale, PA), 1997.
Poems to Count On: Thirty Terrific Poems and Activities to Help Teach Math Concepts, Scholastic, 1995.

OTHER

Contributor of poetry to textbooks, anthologies, and children's magazines including *Cricket, Ranger Rick, Jack and Jill,* and *Sports Illustrated for Kids.* Also author of *Reading Comprehension: A Springboard to Creative Thinking,* a paperback reading game book for classroom use.

SIDELIGHTS: A former teacher, Sandra Olson Liatsos has created useful learning tools in poetic form. She has also written a collection of poetry that captures the exuberance of childhood—in thoughts, feelings, and actions. In the twenty-two poems collected in *Bicycle Riding, and Other Poems,* Liatsos calls upon her own childhood fantasies and family experiences.

Liatsos commented on why she enjoys her work: "I write for children because I love to do it. It gives me a feeling of joy and buoyancy. It brings me back to my own childhood, its feelings of surprise and awe and pure pleasure. To share my poems with today's children gives me a strong reason for being in the world."

BIOGRAPHICAL/CRITICAL SOURCES:

PERIODICALS

Hopscotch, June-July, 1994, p. 23.
Kirkus Reviews, May 15, 1997, p. 803.
School Library Journal, May, 1997, p. 121.*

* * *

LIEBERMAN, Susan (Abel) 1942-

PERSONAL: Born August 11, 1942, in Pittsburgh, PA; married Michael W. Lieberman (a physician), November, 1968; children: Jonathan, Seth.

ADDRESSES: Home—1506 Driscoll St., Houston, TX 77019. *E-mail*—susan@lieberman.net.

CAREER: Super Summers, Inc., Houston, TX, executive director, 1993—. Rice University, director of Leadership Rice, 1998—.

WRITINGS:

New Traditions: Redefining Celebrations for Today's Family, Farrar, Straus (New York City), 1991.
(With Nathalie A. Bartle) *Venus in Blue Jeans: Encouraging Candid Talk between Mothers and Daughters on Sex,* Houghton (Boston, MA), 1998
The Real High School Handbook, Houghton (Boston, MA), 1997.

Also author of *The KIDFUN Activity Book,* Harper Collins (New York City).

LIEBMAN, Roy 1936-

PERSONAL: Born August 4, 1936, in Brooklyn, NY; son of Harry (a carpenter) and Belle (a homemaker) Liebman; divorced; children: Janine, Marissa Liebman Tragesser. *Ethnicity:* "Caucasian." *Education:* Brooklyn College (now of the City University of New York), B.A., 1958; Pratt Institute, M.L.S., 1961; California State University, Los Angeles, M.A., 1978.

ADDRESSES: Home—5900 El Canon Ave., Woodland Hills, CA 91367. *Office*—California State University, 5151 State University Dr., Los Angeles, CA 90032; fax 323-343-6500. *E-mail*—rliebma@calstatela.edu.

CAREER: California State University, Los Angeles, librarian, 1969—. International Performing Arts Index, member of advisory board.

MEMBER: California Library Association.

WRITINGS:

Silent Film Performers, McFarland & Co. (Jefferson, NC), 1996.
From Silents to Sound, McFarland & Co., 1998.

Contributor to reference books, including *The Encyclopedia of Propaganda, The Sixties in America,* and *Magill Legal Guide.* Contributor of more than a hundred articles and reviews to professional journals and other magazines, including *Silent Film Monthly.*

WORK IN PROGRESS: The Wampas Baby Stars, publication by McFarland and Co. expected in 2000; *The Vitaphone Films: A Catalogue,* 2002.

SIDELIGHTS: Roy Liebman told *CA:* "I continue to relish the moment when a respected film historian told me that I was now a film historian, too. Was it akin to being anointed? I had 'officially' metamorphosed from mere film buff-dom to being a recognized writer, a fate for which I had always hoped I was destined.

"My first taste of the possibilities came when I won a one-act play contest as a senior at Brooklyn College. Its perhaps too-weighty theme concerned a Joe McCarthyesque politician who smears his opponent. Its one-night run cried to me: validation! I had something to say that someone else wanted to hear.

"Although I later published several articles in professional journals related to my work as a university librarian, along with more than a hundred book reviews, they were hardly the stuff of great creativity. In the early eighties my long-dormant 'talent' for writing one-act plays was revived. The Los Angeles School District commissioned me to write a series of playlets for children, built around themes of stereotyping. The seven that resulted were performed in elementary schools and were included in a teachers' manual issued by the school district. It was book-like, not quite an actual book yet, but getting closer.

"Finally I found my niche. Long a fan of silent movies, I was curious about the mostly now-obscure actors and actresses in those faded and scratchy flickers. A few stars of that monumental era were remembered, but so many hundreds more had been forgotten. Film preservation was just coming into its own, and newly preserved films were becoming more widely viewed. A new picture-going generation was discovering them in universities, revival theaters, and on cable television. It seemed natural that this generation would, like me, want to know more about those long-dead or barely alive performers. Where could people do either formal or informal research about them? The result was my first book, *Silent Film Performers,* a reference book that provides fans and researchers with hundreds of published and archival resources for three-hundred-fifty silent stars and lesser lights, some of them really obscure.

"A work on where to find information on silent film personalities seemed to lead naturally into providing biographical information and commentary on these performers. Because I am interested in both the silent cinema and early talking pictures, I next wrote to about five-hundred actors and actresses who made the transition from the silents to the talkies. Even more obscure players were included in *From Silents to Sound.*

"Many of the actresses I had researched had been Wampas Baby Stars in the twenties and early thirties. That discovery provoked me to write the first book about these women. Many of the performers about whom I had written also had appeared in sound shorts produced by Vitaphone Corporation. These were among the earliest talking shorts ever made. This will lead to the publication of a catalogue of Vitaphone films, probably the first catalogue ever published about any company's film shorts.

"Success, however minor, breeds recognition. I also do such varied writing as articles for the magazine *Silent Film Monthly,* entries for major reference works, book reviews for a CD-ROM service, and even press packets for a local musical theater group."

* * *

LIN, Chia-Chiao 1916-

PERSONAL: Born July 7, 1916, in Fukien, China; became U.S. citizen; son of Kai and Y. T. Lin; married Shou-Ling Liang, 1946; children: one daughter. *Education:* National Tsing Hua University, B.Sc., 1937; University of Toronto, M.A. (applied mathematics), 1941; California Institute of Technology, Ph.D. (aeronautics), 1944.

ADDRESSES: Office—Department of Mathematics, Massachusetts Institute of Technology, Cambridge, MA 02139.

CAREER: National Tsing Hua University, China, assistant, 1937-39; California Institute of Technology, Pasadena, began as assistant engineer, became research engineer, 1943-45; Brown University, Providence, RI, began as assistant professor, became associate professor of applied mathematics, 1945-47; Massachusetts Institute of Technology, Cambridge, began as assistant professor, became professor, 1947-87, professor emeritus, 1987—.

MEMBER: National Academy of Science, American Astronomers Society, Society of Industrial and Applied Mathematics (president, 1972-74), American Mathematics Society, American Academy of Arts and Sciences (fellow), American Philosophical Society, American Physics Society, Institute for Aerospace Science (fellow).

AWARDS, HONORS: John Von Neumann lecturer, Society of Industrial and Applied Mathematicians—American Mathematical Society, 1967; Otto Laporte Memorial lecturer, American Physics Society, 1973; received honorary L.L.D. from Chinese University—Hong Kong, 1973; Timoshenko Medal, American Society of Mechanical Engineers, 1975; Award for Applied Mathematics and Numerical Analysis, National Academy of Science, 1977; Fluid Dynamics Prize, American Physics Society and U. S. Office of Naval Research, 1979; DSD Prize, 1979.

WRITINGS:

On the Motion of Vortices in Two Dimensions, University of Toronto Press (Toronto), 1943.

The Theory of Hydrodynamic Stability, 1955, Cambridge University Press (Cambridge, England), 1966.

(With L. A. Segel) *Mathematics Applied to Deterministic Problems in the Natural Sciences,* with material on elasticity by G. H. Handelman, Macmillan (New York City), 1974.

Selected Papers of C. C. Lin, 2 volumes, edited by David J. Benney, Frank H. Shu, and Chi Yuan, World Scientific (Teaneck, NJ), 1987.

(With G. Bertin) *Spiral Structure in Galaxies: A Density Wave Theory,* MIT Press (Cambridge, MA), 1996.

Contributor to periodicals and journals, including *Handbuch der Physik-Encyclopedia of Physics, Astrophysical Journal,* and *Proceedings of the National Academy of Sciences.*

SIDELIGHTS: Born in Fukien, China, on July 7, 1916, to Kai and Y. T. Lin, Chia-Chiao Lin pursued his undergraduate studies at the National Tsing Hua University in China, receiving a B.Sc. in 1937. He was awarded a master's degree in applied mathematics from the University of Toronto in 1941 and a Ph.D. in aeronautics from the California Institute of Technology in 1944. A former student of Theodore von Karman whose varied background includes mathematics, aeronautics, and fluid mechanics, Lin's work has contributed to multiple disciplines within the scientific community, as well as to government and industry. His importance lies in his use of mathematical modeling to create new formal tools for theoretical investigation in a number of sciences, including meteorology, oceanography, astrophysics, chemical engineering, and planetary sciences. He is also the author of several book, including *Spiral Stucture in Galaxies: A Density Wave Theory, The Theory of Hydrodynamic Stability,* and *Mathematics Applied to Deterministic Problems in the Natural Sciences.*

Following early work on fluid mechanics, Lin turned to concentrate on the hydrodynamics of superfluid helium and, later, on astrophysics. It was his work in this latter field that led to his development of the density wave theory of the spiral structure of galaxies, which provided an answer to one of the most long-standing puzzles in astronomy. This theory attempts to explain the formation of galaxies, their shapes (elliptical, normal spiral, barred spiral, etc.), and their luminosity.

Scientists had long recognized that the shapes of galaxies appeared to have a certain regularity—a regularity that could be governed by wave phenomena. The density wave theory was developed to explain these patterns and to analyze their dynamical implications; such implications include star formation, which the theory explains as being triggered by galactic shocks induced by a low-amplitude density wave pattern. The density wave theory also classifies spiral galaxies by associating specific shapes with particular wave patterns, or "modes"; according to Lin, normal spiral modes and barred spiral modes correspond to normal spiral galaxies and transition barred galaxies and some barred spiral galaxies. Lin's theory has since been confirmed by a wealth of observational data and has provided a model for applying theoretical mathematics and physics—often in conjunction with computer science—to other disciplines.

Lin has been instrumental in the exchange of information between scientists in the United States and China and has organized trips by Chinese scientists to the United States. He has served as an advisor to the Chinese government on issues involving education and as an educational consultant for applied mathematics groups. He is a member of the National Academy of Science's Committee on Support of Research in the Mathematical Sciences; he served as the president of the Society for Industrial and Applied Mathematics and the chairman of the Committee on Applied Mathematics of the American Mathematical Society.

After a two-year stint as assistant and later associate professor of applied mathematics at Brown University, Lin took a position at Massachusetts Institute of Technology as professor of applied mathematics in 1947; he later became a professor emeritus. He has also worked at Jet Propulsion Laboratories, and has served as a consultant to a number of industries. Lin married Shou-Ling Liang in 1946; they have one daughter.*

*   *   *

LINKIN, Harriet Kramer 1956-

PERSONAL: Born February 25, 1956, in New York, NY; daughter of Abram (a builder) and Thea (a homemaker; maiden name, Karp) Kramer; married Larry Linkin (a programmer and analyst), August 1,

1982. *Ethnicity:* "White Jewish." *Education:* Queens College of the City University of New York, B.A. (summa cum laude), 1979; University of Michigan, M.A., 1982, Ph.D., 1985.

ADDRESSES: Home—2242 Sunrise Point Rd., Las Cruces, NM 88011. *Office*—Department of English, New Mexico State University, Las Cruces, NM 88003; fax 505-646-7725. *E-mail*—hlinkin@nmsu. edu.

CAREER: University of Michigan, Ann Arbor, lecturer in English, 1985-86; New Mexico State University, Las Cruces, assistant professor, 1986-93, associate professor of English, 1993—, director of graduate studies in English, 1998-2001. Western Michigan University, visiting professor, 1991-92.

WRITINGS:

(Editor with Stephen C. Behrendt, and contributor) *Approaches to Teaching British Women Poets of the Romantic Period,* Modern Language Association of America (New York City), 1997.
(Contributor) Jackie DiSalvo, G. A. Rosso, and Christopher Z. Hobson, editors, *Blake, Politics, and History,* Garland Publishing (New York City), 1998.
(Editor with Behrendt, and contributor) *Romanticism and Women Poets: Opening the Doors of Reception,* University Press of Kentucky (Lexington, KY), 1999.

Contributor of articles and reviews to periodicals, including *European Romantic Review, Studies in Romanticism, Nineteenth-Century Contexts, Legacy: Journal of American Women Writers,* and *Journal of Narrative Technique.* Member of editorial board, *Pedagogy: Critical Approaches to Literature, Language, and Composition,* 1997—; member of editorial advisory board, *British Women Romantic Poets, 1789-1832,* 1998—.

WORK IN PROGRESS: The Legend of Mary Tighe: Psyche, Romanticism, and Reception.

*   *   *

LIPPI, Rosina 1956-
    (Rosina Lippi-Green; Sara Donati, a pseudonym)

PERSONAL: Born in 1956, in Chicago, IL; daughter of Arturo (a cook) and Mary Ennis (a waitress) Lippi;

married William Green (a mathematician), July 16, 1988; children: Elizabeth Green. *Ethnicity:* "Italian/ northern European." *Education:* University of Illinois, B.A (linguistics; with highest distinction), 1982; Princeton University, M.A./Ph.D. (linguistics), 1987. *Politics:* Liberal. *Avocational interests:* Linguistics, critical language studies.

ADDRESSES: Office—Western Washington University, Department of English, 341 Humanities Building, Bellingham, WA 98226-9055. *Agent*—Jill Grinberg, Scovil Chichak Galen Literary Agency Inc., 381 Park Ave. S., Suite 1020, New York, NY 10016. *E-mail*—rlg@cc.wwu.edu.

CAREER: Professor, writer, and lecturer. Western Washington University, Bellingham, WA, 98226-9055, associate professor. Formerly taught at University of Michigan, Ann Arbor.

MEMBER: Linguistics Society of America, American Academy of Arts and Letters, A.W.P.

WRITINGS:

NOVELS

Homestead, Delphinium Books (Harrison, NY), 1998.
(Under pseudonym Sara Donati) *Into the Wilderness,* Bantam Books, 1998.

ACADEMIC; AS ROSINA LIPPI-GREEN

Language Ideology and Language Change in Early Modern German: A Sociolinguistic Study of the Consonantal System of Nuremburg, John Benjamins, 1994.
English with an Accent: Language, Ideology, and Discrimination in the United States, Routledge (London), 1997.

Contributor of short fiction and academic articles to periodicals.

WORK IN PROGRESS: (As Sara Donati) *Down to the Sea,* a novel, for Bantam Books.

SIDELIGHTS: Rosina Lippi holds degrees in linguistics and has written and lectured widely on language-related subjects. Lippi began writing short stories as a child and has had several published in periodicals. She spent four years in the Bregenz Forest area of the Austrian Alps, the setting of her first novel, *Homestead.* The book contains twelve linked vignettes, covering a period extending from 1909 to 1977 in the fictional village of Rosenau, with its population of 363, and surrounding homesteads. Included are clan charts and a glossary explaining the language and customs of the region.

Homestead chronicles the cycles of farming and life and focuses on three generations of women whose names provide titles for the book's chapters. It opens with the arrival of a postcard in the isolated town's post office, addressed to Anna Fink. Because of naming customs, the postcard signed "Your Anton" could be intended for any one of seven women. The letter's effect on Anna of Bengat homestead begins the interwoven tales.

The women experience the effects of World War I as their men fail to return, leaving the women feeling vulnerable and unprotected. The stories revolve around family, community, and love, reflecting the cares and longings of most women. Angelika, of the Bent Elbow homestead, "measures her own worth by the quality of the cheese she makes for her husband," commented a *Booklist* reviewer. One story, called "moving and poignant" by a reviewer for *Publishers Weekly,* tells of an Italian deserter who offers comfort to spinster Johanna, who has never known love. Each link to the outside world has a profound effect on the villagers, but by the book's end, they have become integrated into "the continuing cycles of birth, marriage, death and the changing seasons," according to the *Publishers Weekly* reviewer, who concluded that it is the "cumulative effect" of the individual stories that pulls the reader into a period and place "at once strange and universal."

Lippi told *CA:* "My primary interest is historical fiction told from a woman's perspective. *Homestead* is my effort to look at the repercussions of the world wars on women who lead quiet lives in a remote place, but who have vivid internal lives, wants and sorrows and needs that any other woman will identify with. *Into the Wilderness* is another such attempt, in a different approach to the frontier mythology based around Daniel Boone and the idea of wilderness. Here I wanted to retell some of those stories from the perspective of the women as well."

BIOGRAPHICAL/CRITICAL SOURCES:

PERIODICALS

Booklist, February 15, 1998.
People Weekly, August 31, 1998, p. 40.
Publishers Weekly, January 26, 1998, p. 71; June 22, 1998, p. 85.

OTHER

Amazon.com, http://www.amazon.com (September 2, 1998).
Rosina Lippi-Green web site, http://wally.english.wwu.edu/rlg (September 2, 1998).

*   *   *

LIPPI-GREEN, Rosina
   See LIPPI, Rosina

*   *   *

LYKKE, Ivar
   See JENSEN, Johannes V(ilhlem)

M

MACDONALD, James D. 1954-
(Robyn Tallis, Nicholas Adams, Victor Appleton, Martin Delrio, joint pseudonyms)

PERSONAL: Born 1954, in White Plains, NY; son of a chemical engineer and an artist; married Debra A. Doyle (a writer and teacher); children: four. *Education:* University of Rochester, received degree (medieval studies). *Avocational interests:* Science fiction, cats, computers.

ADDRESSES: Home—Colebrook, NH. *Agent*—c/o Avon Books, 1230 Avenue of the Americas, New York, NY 10019. *E-mail*—doylemacdonald@sff.net.

CAREER: Journalist and science fiction author. *Military service:* United States Navy, served fifteen-year tour of duty as both an emlisted man and an officer.

AWARDS, HONORS: Mythopoetic Fantasy Award for children's literature, 1992, for *Knight's Wyrd*; named to New York Public Library Books for the Teen Age list, 1993, for *Knight's Wyrd*; Best Young Adult Science Fiction Award, *Science Fiction Chronicle*, 1997, for *Groogleman*.

WRITINGS:

NOVELS; "CIRCLE OF MAGIC" SERIES; WITH WIFE, DEBRA A. DOYLE

School of Wizardry, Troll Books (Mahway, OH), 1990.
Tournament and Tower, Troll Books (Mahway, OH), 1990.
City by the Sea, Troll Books (Mahway, OH), 1990.
The Prince's Players, Troll Books (Mahway, OH), 1990.

The Prisoners of Bell Castle, Troll Books (Mahway, OH), 1990.
The High King's Daughter, Troll Books (Mahway, OH), 1990.

NOVELS; "MAGEWORLDS" SERIES; WITH WIFE, DEBRA A. DOYLE

The Price of the Stars, Tor (New York City), 1992.
Starpilot's Grave, Tor (New York City), 1993.
By Honor Betray'd, Tor (New York City), 1994.
The Gathering Flame, Tor (New York City), 1995.
The Long Hunt, Tor (New York City), 1996.

NOVELS; "BAD BLOOD" SERIES; WITH WIFE, DEBRA A. DOYLE

Bad Blood, Berkley (New York City), 1993.
Hunter's Moon, Berkley (New York City), 1994.
Judgment Night, Berkley (New York City), 1995.

OTHER NOVELS; WITH WIFE, DEBRA A. DOYLE

Timecrime, Inc. (Robert Silverberg's "Time Tours" no. 3), Harper (New York City), 1991.
Night of the Living Rat (Daniel Pinkwater's "Melvinge of the Megaverse" no. 2), Ace (New York City), 1992.
Knight's Wyrd, Harcourt (New York City), 1992.
Groogleman, Harcourt (New York City), 1996.

OTHER NOVELS UNDER JOINT PSEUDONYM ROBYN TALLIS; WITH WIFE, DEBRA A. DOYLE

Night of Ghosts and Lightning ("Planet Builders" no. 2), Ivy, 1989.

Zero-Sum Games ("Planet Builders" no. 5), Ivy, 1989.

OTHER NOVELS UNDER JOINT PSEUDONYM NICHOLAS ADAMS; WITH WIFE, DEBRA A. DOYLE

Pep Rally ("Horror High" no. 7), Harper (New York City), 1991.

OTHER NOVELS UNDER JOINT PSEUDONYM VICTOR APPLETON; WITH WIFE, DEBRA A. DOYLE

Monster Machine ("Tom Swift" no. 5), Pocket Books (New York City), 1991.
Aquatech Warriors ("Tom Swift" no. 6), Pocket Books (New York City), 1991.

OTHER NOVELS UNDER JOINT PSEUDONYM MARTIN DELRIO

Mortal Kombat (movie novelization; adult and young adult versions), Tor (New York City), 1995.
Spider-Man Super-Thriller: Midnight Justice, Byron Preiss Multimedia/Pocket Books (New York City), 1996.
Spider-Man Super-Thriller: Global War, Byron Preiss Multimedia/Pocket Books (New York City), 1996.
Prince Valiant (movie novelization), Avon (New York City), 1997.

OTHER

Contributor, with Doyle, of short stories to anthologies, including "Bad Blood" in *Werewolves,* edited by Jane Yolen and Martin Greenberg, Harper Junior Books, 1988; "Nobody Has to Know" in *Vampires,* edited by Jane Yolen and Martin Greenberg, Harper Collins, 1991; "The Last Real New Yorker in the World" in *Newer York,* edited by Lawrence Watt-Evans, Roc, 1991; "Now and In the Hour of Our Death" in *Alternate Kenndys,* edited by Mike Resnick and Martin Greenberg, Tor, 1992; "Uncle Joshua and the Grooglemen" in *Bruce Coville's Book of Monsters,* edited by Bruce Coville, Scholastic, Inc., 1993; "Why They Call It That" in *Swashbuckling Editor Stories,* edited by John Betancourt, Wildside Press, 1993; "The Queen's Mirror" in *A Wizard's Dozen,* edited by Michael Stearns, Harcourt, 1995; "Crossover" in *A Wayfarer's Dozen,* edited by Michael Stearns, Harcourt, 1995; "Witch Garden" in *Witch Fantastic,* edited by Mike Resnick and Martin Greenberg, DAW, 1995; "Holly and Ivy" in *Camelot,*

edited by Jane Yolen, Philomel, 1995; "Please to See the King" in *The Book of Kings,* edited by Richard Gilliam and Martin Greenberg, Roc, 1995; "Stealing God" in *Tales of the Knights Templar,* edited by Katherine Kurtz, Warner, 1995; "Ecdysis" in *Otherwere,* edited by Laura Ann Gilman and Keith R. A. DeCandido, Berkley/Ace, 1996; "Up the Airy Mountain" in *A Nightmare's Dozen,* edited by Michael Stearns, Harcourt, 1996; and "Jenny Nettles" in *Bruce Coville's Book of Spine Tinglers,* edited by Bruce Coville, Scholastic, Inc., 1996.

Contributor of short stories to anthologies, including (with Alan Rodgers) "Rosemary—Scrambled Eggs on a Blue Plate" and "Souvenirs" in *Alternate Kennedys,* edited by Mike Resnick and Martin Greenberg, Tor, 1992; and "A True Story" in *Bruce Coville's Book of Ghosts,* edited by Bruce Coville, Scholastic, Inc., 1994.

WORK IN PROGRESS: City of the Dreadful Night, Erassi: The Professor Story's ("Mageworlds" series no. 6), and *The Stars Asunder,* all for Tor Books.

SIDELIGHTS: In close collaboration with his wife, Debra A. Doyle, James D. Macdonald writes science fiction and fantasy for children, young adults, and adults. In an interview with Amazon.com, Macdonald related that he writes the first drafts of the stories and novels and that his wife works on the revisions. Macdonald said, "I have final say on the plot and characters, she has final say on the words and descriptions." He commented that the books of J. R. R. Tolkien have had an impact on his writing and said that he also enjoys reading the work of Robert Heinlein and Alexandre Dumas. Together, Macdonald and Doyle have written over twenty novels and innumerable short stories, primarily fantasy and science fiction for young adults.

Doyle and MacDonald's first series, "Circle of Magic" (1990), intended for an elementary and junior high school audience, consists of six novels chronicling the story of Randal and his adventures in fulfilling his destiny to become a wizard. *School of Wizardry* introduces twelve-year-old Randal, who is determined to become a wizard after a wayfaring wizard visits his home. Initially delighted to be admitted as an apprentice into the famous Schola Sorceriae (School of Wizardry), he soon realizes that he must conquer many enemies before becoming a master wizard, among them Lord Fess, who plans to destroy the school and gain supreme power through his evil spells.

Tournament and Tower, the second installment in the "Circle of Magic" series, opens with Randal being granted permission to graduate from the School of Wizardry with the provision that he refrain from using his magic until Balpesh, the master wizard, exonerates him for breaking his pledge not to use a weapon. In the meantime, Randal becomes a squire to his cousin Walter. In a tournament, Walter sustains serious injuries, but Randal, lacking his magical powers, cannot rescue Walter. Balpesh, who can rescue him, is himself in great peril. It is up to Randal to free the wizard, who can then save Walter and restore to Randal his magical powers.

In *City By the Sea,* Randal, now a fifteen-year-old journeyman wizard, embarks on one of his most hazardous undertakings when he accepts a statue from a dying stranger and promises to fulfill the man' deathbed wish that the statue be brought to Dagon, a soldier of fortune. Randal soon learns that the statue has magical powers of its own, and that Dagon is not the only person seeking the statue.

The series continues with *The Prince' Players,* which places Randal and his friend Lys on their way to visit Prince Vespian's palace. Here, Randal learns tricks of illusion from the court's master wizard, Petrucio. he thinks his new talent is to be used in royal stage productions; instead, he discovers that Petrucio has more diabolical plans for his new skills. A dangerous adversary seeks to conquer Prince Vespian's kingdom drawing Randal and Lys into political intrigue.

In *The Prisoners of Bell Castle,* Randal confronts Lord Fess, his old enemy, when he and his friends agree to guard a boatload of gold needed as wages for Baron Ector's armies, who have put Fess's ancestral home, Bell Castle, under siege. When the gold disappears, Randal is implicated in the theft and must triumph over Lord Fess in order to prove his innocence and recover the gold. The final novel in the *Circle of Magic* series, *The High King's Daughter* follows Randal, Walter and Lys as they journey into Elfland to rescue Diamante, the High King's daughter, and restore her to her rightful throne. In order to do so, they must enter a magical realm and confront Lord Hugo de la Corre, who has proclaimed himself High King in Diamante's absence.

Doyle and Macdonald's fantasy novel, *Knight's Wyrd,* won the Mythopoetic Fantasy Award for Children's Literature in 1992 and was placed on the acclaimed new York Public Library Books for the Teen Age list in 1993. *Knight's Wyrd,* combines a realistic story of knighthood with the fantasy elements of magic, dragons and wizards. Just as young Will Odosson is about to be knighted, the castle wizard predicts his wyrd (fate): Will is not destined to inherit his father's title and lands and will soon meet death. Although the wizard's prophecy comes to pass, it does not occur in the manner Will expects. A young man of strong character, Will becomes a knight despite his wyrd and leaves home seeking adventure. In the course of the novel, Will rescues Isobel, his betrothed, is doublecrossed by his Duke, and becomes entangled in high magic. Indeed, he does meet death, but it is in the form of Lord Death, who observes Randal slay the ogre who cannot be killed. A *Kirkus Reviews* critic praised *Knight's Wyrd's* "strong sense of time, place, and code of honor." A *Horn Book* reviewer called it "a lively story," and a *School Library Journal* critic recommended it as "suspenseful," with a lively tempo.

In their next series, the spine-tingling "Bad Blood" series, Macdonald and Doyle explore the kind of horror stories told around campfires after dark. *Bad Blood,* which takes its name from the series, begins with hair-raising tales shared around a campfire in the woods. But Valerie Sherwood and her friends never expected any of the stories to come true. After all, Jay's strange tale of moonlight and werewolves was just make believe. That night, however, they hear the beast prowling around the camp and they remember Jay's words: "By morning, you'll all be dead."

In *Hunter's Moon,* the sequel to *Bad Blood,* Valerie, now a werewolf, uses her power to protect her community from a group of vampires while trying to live a "normal" suburban life. But soon she suspects that werewolves are powerless against vampires and she must find a way to save her loved ones. In *Judgment Night,* the final installment, Valerie is haunted by her own nightmares and by the Wendigo, an ancient force that calls to her from the mountains and thrives on her fear.

The popular "Mageworlds" series, begun in 1992, focuses on the centuries-long conflict between the human Republic and the mysterious Mageworlds. In *The Price of the Stars,* the first in the series, Beka Rosselin-Metadi is tired of consistently hearing about her parents herois roles in the human galaxy's history. When her mother is murdered on the Senate floor, however, she finds new pride in her heritage and vows to bring the assassin to justice. Her father offers her *Warhammer,* his cherished ship, for her use in capturing the murderer. As the plot develops, Beka plans her own demise so that she can, with a different identity, conquer the dangerous enemies of the galaxy.

In *Starpilot's Grave,* Beka continues the search for the man who arranged her mother's assassination, but soon it is revealed that the Magelords have breached the Republic's stronghold. Beka, in searching for her mother's killer, infiltrates the Magezone and learns that the Republic is far more vulnerable than she ever imagined. The Magelords have triumphed over the Republic in the third of the series, *By Honor Betrayed.* Confronted with betrayal and surrounded by enemies, Beka strives to reclaim what she can from the wreckage of the Republic.

The Gathering Flame, fourth in the "Mageworlds" series, describes Beka's parents' contributions to the Republic's struggle against the Magelords. The novel chronicles attempts by the Magelords to ravage the galaxy, planet by planet. However, the Magelords must take on three individuals to succeed in their plans: Perada Rosselin, Domina of Entibor, Jos Metadi (a notorious privateer who prefers to battle Mage ships one-on-one), and Errec Ransome, who is acquainted with the customs of the Magelords but has confidences he will not reveal. When the Magelords attack Entibor, the three must work together.

In *The Long Hunt,* set in the era following the Second Magewar, Entibor faces attack by the Magelords. Meanwhile, on the planet Khesat, a crisis unfolds and all depends on Jens Metadi-Jessan D'Rosselin, unwilling heir to the throne. Warring factions and criminal guilds know that control of the heir means control of Khesat and the galaxy. But young Jens, eager for adventure, sets off with his cousin Faral to see the galaxy. However, in their travels they encounter more action than anticipated. Writing in *Locus,* Carolyn Cushman called the "Mageworlds" series "a space opera with unusual depth, and some wonderful characters I'm eager to see in further adventures."

A critic for *Science Fiction Chronicle* declared *Groogleman* "the best young adult science fiction" of 1996. In this fantasy novel, the plot centers around thirteen-year-old Dan Henchard, a student healer who must save his teacher Leezie, a natural healer, from her abductor. Dan, believing the kidnapper is the Groogleman, travels to the Dead Lands in search for Leezie, knowing that failure means certain death for him. Along the way he receives help from a hunter named Joshua and in the process learns much about himself. Selections from "historical documents" intro-

duce each chapter and provide clues to the secret purpose of the Grooglemen. A reviewer for *Realm of Fantasy* magazine wrote that *Groogleman* is "filled with adventure and action—a must read," and a *Science Fiction Chronicle* writer praised it as "an old fashioned post collapse adventure."

In an interview with *Amazon.com,* Macdonald explained that he attempts to write every day but said that "can be an hour or it can be ten hours, depending on how things are going." Reflecting that he served fifteen years in the U.S. Navy as both an enlisted man and an officer before becoming a full-time writer, he advised would-be writers to "go out and have a life to write about, then write and keep writing."

BIOGRAPHICAL/CRITICAL SOURCES:

PERIODICALS

Bulletin of the Center for Children's Books, December, 1996, p. 132.
Horn Book, January-February, 1993, pp. 89-90; March-April, 1996, p. 202.
Kirkus Reviews, October 1, 1992.
Locus, August, 1995.
Realms of Fantasy, April, 1997.
School Library Journal, December, 1996, pp. 120-121.
Science Fiction Chronicle, April/May, 1997.

OTHER

Amazon.com, http://www.amazon.com (December 11, 1998).
Doyle and Macdonald—About Our Books, http://www.sff.net/people/doylemacdonald (December 11, 1998).*

*   *   *

MACFARLANE, Alan (Donald James) 1941-

PERSONAL: Born December 20, 1941, in Assam, India; son of Donald Kennedy and Iris (Stirling) Macfarlane; married Gillian Ions, c. 1966 (divorced); married Sarah Harrison, 1981. *Education:* Attended Sedbergh School; Worcester College, Oxford, M.A., D.Phil.; London School of Economics, M.Phil.; School of Oriental and African Studies, Ph.D. *Avocational interests:* Walking, gardening, music, second-hand book hunting.

ADDRESSES: Home—25 Lode Rd., Lode, Cambridge CB5 9ER, England. *Office*—King's College, Cambridge CB2 1ST, England.

CAREER: University of Cambridge, Cambridge, England, senior research fellow in history at King's College, 1971-74, lecturer, 1975-81, reader in social anthropology, 1981-91. Has lectured at other academic institutions, including Liverpool University, London School of Economics, and University of Lancaster.

AWARDS, HONORS: Rivers Memorial Medal, 1984; William J. Goode Award, American Sociological Association, 1987.

WRITINGS:

NONFICTION

Witchcraft in Tudor and Stuart England: A Regional and Comparative Study, Harper (New York City), 1970.
The Family Life of Ralph Josselin, A Seventeenth-Century Clergyman: An Essay in Historical Anthropology, Cambridge University Press (Cambridge), 1970, Norton (New York City), 1977.
(Editor) *The Diary of Ralph Josselin, 1616-1683,* Oxford University Press (London), 1976.
Resources and Population: A Study of the Gurungs of Nepal, Cambridge University Press (New York City), 1976.
(With Sarah Harrison and Charles Jardine) *Reconstructing Historical Communities,* Cambridge University Press (New York City), 1977.
The Origins of English Individualism: The Family, Property, and Social Transition, Blackwell (Oxford), 1978, Cambridge University Press (New York City), 1979.
(With Harrison) *The Justice and the Mare's Ale: Law and Disorder in Seventeenth-Century England,* Cambridge University Press (New York City), 1981.
A Guide to English Historical Records, Cambridge University Press (New York City), 1983.
Marriage and Love in England: Modes of Reproduction, 1300-1840, Blackwell (New York City), 1986.
The Culture of Capitalism (essays), Blackwell (New York City), 1987.
(With Indrabahadur Gurung) *Gurungs of Nepal: A Guide to the Gurungs,* Ratna Pustak Bhandar (Kathmandu, Nepal), 1990.

The Savage Wars of Peace: England, Japan, and the Malthusian Trap, Blackwell (Cambridge, MA), 1997.

SIDELIGHTS: British academician and author Alan Macfarlane has published several works in the field of historical anthropology. Though he has also written about the Gurung people of Nepal, he has focused primarily on English people living in pre-modern centuries. Macfarlane is perhaps best known for his 1978 volume, *The Origins of English Individualism: The Family, Property, and Social Transition.* In this and other books he has asserted the controversial argument that England never really had the pre-industrial peasant society posited by nineteenth-century communist theorist Karl Marx and used by Marxist philosophers ever since as part of their theoretical justifications. Some of Macfarlane's other titles include *Resources and Population: A Study of the Gurungs of Nepal, Witchcraft in Tudor and Stuart England: A Regional and Comparative Study, Marriage and Love in England: Modes of Reproduction, 1300-1840,* and *The Culture of Capitalism.*

One of Macfarlane's first books was 1970's *Witchcraft in Tudor and Stuart England.* In it, he examines many of the accusations of witchcraft made in England during the sixteenth and seventeenth centuries in which those found guilty were often burned to death at the stake. Macfarlane focuses particularly on the English county of Essex, and takes into account the records of assizes and trials available to scholars. As Lee Ash pointed out in *Library Journal,* the author places far more emphasis on the economic and social circumstances surrounding each case than he does on the religious issues involved. Similarly, an *Economist* reviewer observed that Macfarlane "reject[s] general explanations which relate witchcraft to the battle between religions or the survival of a pagan cult." Ash went on to declare *Witchcraft in Tudor and Stuart England* to be "probably one of the most significant modern contributions" to the subject.

In the same year that *Witchcraft in Tudor and Stuart England* saw print, Macfarlane's *The Family Life of Ralph Josselin, A Seventeenth-Century Clergyman: An Essay in Historical Anthropology* became available to interested readers. The author gathered the basic material for this work from Josselin's existing diary, which he later edited as a more inclusive version than that first printed. Josselin was a Puritan clergyman who kept a diary from 1616 to 1683—including the time when the long line of British monarchs was interrupted by the Puritan-supported protectorate of

Oliver Cromwell—but according to one of the reviewers of the volume, Macfarlane does not make clear to which specific Puritan sect the minister belonged. He is more concerned with analyzing Josselin's references to his various and many family members. Critics have had mixed response to Macfarlane's study of Josselin. Austin Woolrych in the *English Historical Review* maintained that the author "would surely have reached more generally valid conclusions if he had extended his detailed analysis to the life records of other Puritan clergymen such as Oliver Heywood, Henry Newcome, Thomas Jolly and Adam Martindale." A *Times Literary Supplement* commentator, however, gave high praise to *The Family Life of Ralph Josselin,* calling it "a crisply written and penetrating study of a man's mind, circumstances and environment," and predicting that historians would decree that "Macfarlane has . . . added something very worthwhile indeed to our knowledge and understanding."

Macfarlane, according to Alan Ryan in *Listener,* "sets out the central features of a peasant society such as did exist in Eastern Europe, and such as historians have supposed to exist in England" in *The Origins of English Individualism.* Ryan went on to explain: "The central features concern the way families relate to the land; property is family property and heads of households cannot alienate it except to avert disaster; there is, thus, no land market. Labour," the reviewer continued, "is provided from within the family; family members automatically have a right to subsistence from family land and a duty to work it; in consequence, the age of marriage is low, because the pool of labour has to be kept up by the family unit of cultivation." Macfarlane then reveals to the reader that English society as it has existed since the middle ages has contained practices in opposition to the peasant model. Such practices include property owners being able to choose who to bestow their property upon; the frequent sale of land; commoners working for wages; and an average marriage age much higher than that of true peasant societies.

Spectator contributor Colin Welch, reviewing Macfarlane's *The Origins of English Individualism,* reported that "his thesis provoked roars of dissent from academic bigwigs who . . . took a quite opposite and then conventional view. Some were very rude." *The Origins of English Individualism* did draw praise from some critics, however, including Ryan, who hailed it as "an altogether admirable piece of work." *Choice* judged it to be "a very important work implying new directions and interpretations for English,

economic, and social history." "Most history collections will need it," affirmed Richard C. Hoffman in *Library Journal.*

Macfarlane further explored the way English marriage customs helped prepare the country for the Industrial Revolution in his 1986 effort, *Marriage and Love in England: Modes of Reproduction, 1300-1840.* According to Macfarlane, the English during the years of the book's subtitle engaged in marital and familial practices that greatly differed from those of the Marxist peasant model. In the latter model, parents usually choose spouses for their children, often formalizing the marriage before the bride and groom reached adulthood. By contrast, in England people generally chose their own marriage partners—frequently for love, though parents, of course, often tried to influence the choice. Also, marriage was generally put off until the man could be confident of an income that would support a wife and children, and until the woman could bring a large portion of money into the marriage from her dowry. *Marriage and Love in England* met with much approbation from critics. "Much of what Macfarlane says about marriage is already well-known," asserted R. A. Houlbrooke in the *English Historical Review.* "His originality lies in the bold and incisive way in which he demonstrates the connections between different parts of the pattern, illuminates it by means of challenging comparisons, and sets it in the larger context of social history." Ferdinand Mount lauded *Marriage and Love in England* in his *Spectator* appraisal as "a spirited and authoritative work."

The Culture of Capitalism, which appeared in 1987, is a collection of Macfarlane's essays providing an expanded explanation of his assertion that capitalism gained a head start in England and, to a lesser degree, in other Western European nations. In the words of Jack A. Goldstone in *Journal of Economic History,* "Macfarlane's book is devoted to showing that in a variety of ways—in their attitudes toward property, kin, evil, nature, and love—English peasants, as far back as we can trace the evidence, show 'modern' attitudes, with a high degree of rationality, flexibility, and individualism." Goldstone added that *The Culture of Capitalism* "raise[s] important hypotheses." *Spectator* contributor Colin Welch declared Macfarlane's analysis in this volume to be "calm . . . fruitful . . . original and penetrating."

Macfarlane has published other books since *The Culture of Capitalism,* including 1997's *The Savage Wars of Peace: England, Japan, and the Malthusian Trap.*

BIOGRAPHICAL/CRITICAL SOURCES:

PERIODICALS

Choice, June, 1979, pp. 598-599.
Economist, January 23, 1971, p. 51.
English Historical Review, April, 1971, pp. 412-413;
　April, 1987, pp. 419-422.
Journal of Economic History, December, 1991, pp.
　1001-1003.
Library Journal, March 1, 1971, p. 843.
Listener, December 14, 1978, p. 790.
Spectator, February 15, 1986, pp. 21-22; September
　5, 1987, pp. 28-29.
Times Literary Supplement, August 7, 1970, p. 870.*

—*Sketch by Elizabeth Wenning*

*　　*　　*

MACINTYRE, Sheila Scott 1910-1960
(Sheila Scott)

PERSONAL: Born April 23, 1910, in Edinburgh, Scotland; died of cancer, March 21, 1960, in Cincinnati, OH; daughter of James Alexander (a rector at Trinity Academy) and Helen Myers (Meldrum) Scott; married Archibald James Macintyre, December 27, 1940; children: Alister William, Douglas Scott, Susan Elizabeth. *Education:* Attended Edinburgh Ladies' College (now Mary Erskine School), 1926-28; University of Edinburgh, M.A. (mathematics; with first class honors), 1932; Girton College, Cambridge, B.A. (with first class honors), 1934; University of Aberdeen, Ph.D., 1949. *Religion:* Presbyterian.

CAREER: St. Leonard's School for Girls, Saint Andrews, Scotland, mathematics teacher, 1935-39; James Allen's School for Girls, London, England, mathematics teacher, 1940; Stowe School, Buckinghamshire, England, mathematics teacher, 1940-41; University of Aberdeen, Aberdeen, Scotland, assistant lecturer, 1941-49, became lecturer, 1949-59; University of Cincinnati, OH, visiting associate professor of mathematics, 1959-60.

MEMBER: Royal Society of Edinburgh (fellow), Edinburgh Mathematical Society, Mathematical Association (Great Britain).

AWARDS, HONORS: Newton Bursary (faculty award), Spence Bursary, and the Bruce of Grangehill Math-

ematical Scholarship, all from the University of Edinburgh.

WRITINGS:

(As Sheila Scott; with Edith Witte) *German-English Mathematical Vocabulary,* [Edinburgh], 1955, Interscience (New York City), 1956, second edition published as *Mathematical Vocabulary (German-English),* Interscience, 1966.

Contributor to journals, including *Proceedings of the Cambridge Philosophical Society, Journal of the London Mathematical Society,* and *Proceedings of the Royal Society of Edinburgh.*

SIDELIGHTS: Although Sheila Scott Macintyre's career was ended prematurely by cancer, she successfully juggled professional and family responsibilities while continuing to publish in her field. Her success in academics reflected the growing tolerance in Western society toward women entering higher education and specializing in previously male-dominated subjects. Macintyre's relationship with her husband, Archibald James Macintyre, was professional as well as personal, a successful role model for working couples of today. They worked on joint papers, served the British war effort together, and taught at the same universities, moving as a family from one post to the next. Along with Edith Witte, Macintyre produced the *German-English Mathematical Vocabulary,* a bilingual mathematics dictionary.

Helen Myers Meldrum and James Alexander Scott, both natives of Scotland, had their only child on April 23, 1910. Macintyre was first sent to school at Trinity Academy in Edinburgh, where her father would serve as rector from 1925 to 1942. In 1926 she entered what was then known as Edinburgh Ladies' College, and in two years she became a "dux," or valedictorian, in mathematics and in her studies overall. This attracted the attention of the faculty of the University of Edinburgh, who granted Macintyre two bursaries. She was also awarded the Bruce of Grangehill Mathematical Scholarship.

Macintyre's M.A. was granted in 1932 with first class honors in mathematics and natural philosophy, and Edinburgh's faculty encouraged her to enter Cambridge University to pursue another B.A. of higher esteem. By the early 1930s women were allowed to be "wranglers," or top-rung math students, at Girton, the women's college of Cambridge. In two years

Macintyre placed as a wrangler. This qualified her for a year-long research project, supervised by Mary Lucy Cartwright, who specialized in integral functions. The year bore fruit with Macintyre's first publication at the age of twenty-five.

Another year of research followed, which Macintyre did not find as equally satisfying. She spent the next five years teaching at girl's schools in Scotland, among them St. Leonard's, in the town of St. Andrews, and James Allen's School for Girls.

Archibald James Macintyre had earned a Ph.D. at Cambridge, but he did not meet his future wife until 1933, when they were introduced by a fellow academic in Scotland. After a lengthy courtship, they married on December 27, 1940. By this time, World War II took precedence for all citizens of Great Britain. The Macintyres worked in the same department at Aberdeen and taught courses sanctioned by the War Office and the Air Ministry. Macintyre took a year off between 1943 and 1944 for the birth of her first child, Alister William, before resuming her duties. She was retained for a permanent post as assistant lecturer at that time and simultaneously launched a thesis project. Her second son, Douglas Scott, was delivered almost the same day as her doctorate on the Whittaker constant. Unfortunately, this child succumbed to enteritis just before his third birthday.

A year later the Macintyres' daughter, Susan Elizabeth, was born. Over the next five years Macintyre raised their two children, continued to teach, and published a handful of papers on various problems related to the theory of functions of a complex variable. At least one commentator noted her ability to find "new and original problems" as well as her knack for refining older techniques and existing proofs. Macintyre also joined up with a member of the German department to produce a bilingual dictionary of mathematical terms, published in 1955.

The year 1958 seemed to mark a new phase of the Macintyres' careers. Long active in the Edinburgh Mathematical Society, Macintyre was elected a full Fellow of the Royal Society of Edinburgh. She published her last paper on Abel's series. Macintyre and her family, with her father, joined Archibald at the University of Cincinnati. The couple served as visiting research professors there for a few years, where she was particularly successful and popular with her students. Macintyre died at age fifty on March 21, 1960.

BIOGRAPHICAL/CRITICAL SOURCES:

BOOKS

Fasanelli, Florence D., *Women of Mathematics,* edited by Louise S. Grinstein and Paul J. Campbell, Greenwood Press (Westport, CT), 1987.

PERIODICALS

Bulletin of the London Mathematical Society, no. 1, 1969, pp. 368-381.
Edinburgh Mathematical Notes, vol. 43, 1960, p. 19.
Journal of the London Mathematical Society, vol. 36, 1961, pp. 254-256.
Yearbook of the Royal Society of Edinburgh, 1961, pp. 21-23.*

*   *   *

MACOMBER, Debbie

PERSONAL: Born in the U.S.; married, husband's name, Wayne; children: four.

ADDRESSES: Home—Port Orchard, WA. *Agent*—c/o Harper, 10 East 53rd St., New York, NY 10022.

CAREER: Freelance writer, beginning c. 1970s.

WRITINGS:

ROMANCE NOVELS

Morning Comes Softly, Harper (New York City), 1993.
A Season of Angels, Harper, 1993.
One Night, Harper, 1994.
The Trouble with Angels, Harper, 1994.
Someday Soon, Harper, 1995.
Touched by Angels, Harper, 1995.
Sooner or Later, Harper, 1996.
Mrs. Miracle, Harper, 1996.
This Matter of Marriage, Mira (Don Mills, Ontario, Canada), 1997.
Three Brides, No Groom, Silhouette (New York City), 1997.

Montana, Mira, 1998.
Can This Be Christmas?, Mira, 1998.

ROMANCE NOVELS; SILHOUETTE "SPECIAL EDITIONS"

Starlight, 1985, reprinted, Mira, 1995.
Reflections of Yesterday, 1986, reprinted, Mira, 1995.
White Lace and Promises, 1986.
All Things Considered, 1987.
Navy Wife (for the "Navy" series), 1988.
The Playboy and the Widow, 1988, reprinted, Mira, 1996.
For All My Tomorrows, 1989, reprinted, Mira, 1996.
Navy Blues (for the "Navy" series), 1989.
The Sheriff Takes a Wife (for the "Manning Sisters" series), 1990.
The Cowboy's Lady (for the "Manning Sisters" series), 1990.
Fallen Angel, 1990, reprinted, Mira, 1996.
The Courtship of Carol Sommars, 1990.
Navy Brat (for the "Navy" series), 1991.
Navy Woman (for the "Navy" series), 1991.
Navy Baby (for the "Navy" series), 1991.
Marriage of Inconvenience (for the "Those Manning Men" series), 1992.
Denim and Diamonds, 1992, reprinted, Mira, 1997.
Stand-in Wife (for the "Those Manning Men" series), 1992.
Bride on the Loose (for the "Those Manning Men" series), 1992.
Borrowed Dreams, 1993.
Hasty Wedding, 1993.
Groom Wanted (for the "From This Day Forward" series), 1993.
Bride Wanted (for the "From This Day Forward" series), 1993.
Marriage Wanted (for the "From This Day Forward" series), 1993.
Baby Blessed, 1994.
Same Time, Next Year, 1996.
Just Married, c. 1995.

ROMANCE NOVELS; SILHOUETTE "INSPIRATIONS"

A Girl Like Janet, 1984.
Thanksgiving Prayer, 1984.
Heartsong, 1984.
Undercover Dreamer, 1984.
The Gift of Christmas, 1984.
Love Thy Neighbor, 1985.

ROMANCE NOVELS; PUBLISHED BY SILHOUETTE

The Trouble With Caasi, 1985.

Christmas Masquerade, 1985.
That Wintry Feeling, 1985.
Promise Me Forever, 1985, reprinted, Mira, 1995.
Adam's Image, 1985.
A Friend or Two, 1985.
Yesterday's Hero, 1986.
Yesterday Once More, 1986, reprinted, 1996.
Laughter in the Rain, 1986.
Jury of His Peers, 1986.
Friends—And Then Some, 1986.
Shadow Chasing, 1986, reprinted, Mira, 1997.
Sugar and Spice, 1987.
No Competition, 1987.
Love'n Marriage, 1987.
Mail-Order Bride, 1988.
Cindy and the Prince (for the "Legendary Lovers" series), 1988.
Some Kind of Wonderful (for the "Legendary Lovers" series), 1988.
Almost Paradise (for the "Legendary Lovers" series), 1988.
Any Sunday, 1988.
Almost No Angel, 1989.
The Way to a Man's Heart, 1989.
The Bachelor Prince, 1994.
Wanted: Perfect Partner (for the "Yours Truly" series), 1995.

ROMANCE NOVELS; PUBLISHED BY HARLEQUIN

The Matchmakers, 1986.
Love by Degree, 1987.
Yours and Mine, 1989.
A Little Bit Country, 1990.
Country Bride, 1990.
Rainy Day Kisses, 1990.
First Comes Marriage, 1991.
Father's Day, 1991.
Here Comes Trouble, 1991.
The Forgetful Bride, 1991.
My Hero, 1992.
The Man You'll Marry, 1992.
Valerie (for the "Orchard Valley Trilogy"), 1992.
Stephanie (for the "Orchard Valley Trilogy"), 1992.
Norah (for the "Orchard Valley Trilogy"), 1993.
Lone Star Lovin', 1993.
Ready for Romance, 1993.
Ready for Marriage, 1994.
Marriage Risk (for the "Midnight Sons" series), 1995.
Daddy's Little Helper (for the "Midnight Sons" series), 1997.
Ending in Marriage (for the "Midnight Sons" series), 1997.

Brides for Brothers (for the "Midnight Sons" series), 1997.

Because of the Baby (for the "Midnight Sons" series), 1997.

Falling for Him (for the "Midnight Sons" series), 1997.

ROMANCE NOVELS; HARLEQUIN "HEART OF TEXAS" SERIES

Lonesome Cowboy, 1998.
Texas Two-Step, 1998.
Caroline's Child, 1998.
Dr. Texas, 1998.
Nell's Cowboy, 1998.
Lone Star Baby, 1998.

CONTRIBUTOR

Christmas Treasures '86, Silhouette, 1986.
Valentine Anthology, Harlequin, 1991.
Christmas Treasures '91, Silhouette, 1991.
To Have and to Hold, Harlequin, 1992.
Christmas Treasures '92, Silhouette, 1992.
To Mother with Love, Silhouette, 1993.
Men in Uniform, Harlequin, 1994.
Purrfect Love, Harper, 1994.
Three Mothers and a Cradle, Silhouette, 1995.
A Spring Bouquet, Zebra (New York), 1996.
Home for Christmas, Harlequin, 1996.
Christmas Kisses, Silhouette, 1996.
That Summer Place, Mira, 1998.

SIDELIGHTS: Best-selling romance novelist Debbie Macomber began her writing career in the 1970s. Since then, she has penned and published over one hundred books. Macomber has written for several major publishers of romantic fiction, such as Harper, Harlequin, Silhouette, and Mira. Among her popular titles are *Heartsong, A Season of Angels, Someday Soon,* and *Montana.* The author has also contributed to many romantic anthologies, including *To Have and to Hold, Purrfect Love, A Spring Bouquet,* and *Christmas Kisses.*

With 1984's *Heartsong,* Macomber had the honor of penning the first book in Silhouette's "Inspiration" series—a collection aimed at Christian readers. The heroine of *Heartsong* is Skye Garvin, who teaches kindergarten, does hospital volunteer work, and is a member of her church choir. At the hospital she meets Jordan Kiley, who is recovering from a car accident. Though their relationship is not without its challenges, the pair eventually work out their differences. According to a *Publishers Weekly* reviewer,

"Macomber does a neat job" of combining "the themes of love and religion," and declared that readers attracted to these themes "will undoubtedly enjoy" *Heartsong.*

Though aimed at a more mainstream audience, Macomber's novels featuring angels as protagonists include *A Season of Angels,* which was published in 1993. It features the heavenly trio of Shirley, Goodness, and Mercy, assigned to aid in the lives of three human beings—Leah, a neonatal nurse unable to have her own baby; Monica, a minister's daughter whose prudery interferes with her ability to find true love; and Timmy, a young boy who has petitioned God for a father.

A critic for *Publishers Weekly* gave *A Season of Angels* a somewhat mixed review, making comparisons with the film *It's a Wonderful Life* and noting that "[a]lthough the angels are amusing, the humans whose lives they mean to set right lack character."

Someday Soon became available for fans of Macomber's work in 1995. This novel features a widow named Linette Collins, whose gentle ways endear her to a formerly confirmed bachelor named Cain Maclellan. Unfortunately, Cain has an extremely dangerous career attempting to rescue hostages from international terrorists. Linette has already lost one great love in her life, and fights against loving another man she could very easily lose to death.

Though a *Publishers Weekly* critic questioned the ultimate compatibility of Linette and Cain, the reviewer conceded that Macomber's "portrayal of a relationship that develops slowly and steadily" in spite of numerous stumbling blocks "can be convincing." Kristin Ramsdell in the *Library Journal* favored *Someday Soon* as well, affirming that "the emotionally involving characters make the story work."

This Matter of Marriage, one of Macomber's 1997 efforts, tells the tale of Hallie McCarthy, who is much better at attaining career goals than at finding true love. The reader follows her on dates with what a *Publishers Weekly* commentator termed "two-dimensional dorks," waiting for her to realize what she could have with her divorced neighbor and confidante, Steve Marris. The *Publishers Weekly* reviewer maintained that the novel "goes limp" after Hallie makes this discovery, but assured readers that Macomber addresses women's affairs "with gentle humor and charm."

In the same year as *This Matter of Marriage,* Macomber's *Three Brides, No Groom* also saw print. This novel centers on a college sorority reunion. Three women who were close friends and all on the verge of marriage as they were graduating from college meet and tell the stories of their individual breakups, for it is revealed that none of them married to the men to whom they were engaged while in school. The reviewer for *Publishers Weekly* faulted "characters [that] are fundamentally archetypes," but noted that the conclusion is "still satisfying." A *Library Journal* reviewer concluded that *Three Brides, No Groom* "exudes . . . warmth and gentle humor."

One of Macomber's efforts for 1998, *Montana,* has enjoyed great popular success, showing up on bestseller lists from *USA Today. Montana*'s heroine is Molly Cogan, a woman with two children who is divorced from their criminal father. She is invited by her grandfather to move to his ranch in Montana, and she thinks it will be a suitable environment for her children. She commits herself completely to the idea when Sam Dakota, an employee of her grandfather's, informs her that the old man is dying. Once Molly arrives, she is attracted to Sam, despite his having a mysterious reputation among their neighbors. When her grandfather tries to push Molly into marriage with Sam, however, she discovers that she has questions that must be answered before she can commit to marriage with Sam.

Macomber has had a prolific output during the late 1990s. Among her projects is the "Heart of Texas" series for which she is has contracted with Harlequin. These novels are all set in the fictional town of Promise, in the Texas hill country. As the author herself describes on her web page, Promise is "a ranching community . . . a place with a mysterious past. A place that still keeps secrets. But Promise has a heart of goodness, and the people there—most of them, anyway!—know what really matters in life. Love, family, community."

BIOGRAPHICAL/CRITICAL SOURCES:

PERIODICALS

Library Journal, May 15, 1995, p. 60; August, 1997, p. 68.
Publishers Weekly, January 13, 1984, p. 66; November 15, 1993, p. 75; April 10, 1995, p. 59; March 10, 1997, p. 64; August 25, 1997, p. 69.

OTHER

Debbie Macomber web site, http://www.nettrends. com/ debbiemacomber/.*

—Sketch by Elizabeth Wenning

* * *

MAGONA, Sindiwe 1943-

PERSONAL: Born August 27, 1943, in Tsolo, South Africa; daughter of Sigongo Penrose and Lilian Lili (Mabandla) Magona; children: Thembeka (daughter), Thokozile (daughter), Sandile (son). *Ethnicity:* "Xhosa (African)." *Education:* St. Matthew's Training School, Higher Primary Teachers Certificate, 1961; University of London, General Certificate of Education; University of South Africa, B.A.; Columbia University, M.S., 1983.

ADDRESSES: Home—3030 Johnson Ave., Bronx, NY 10463. *Office*—United Nations, 1 United Nations Plaza, Suite S-805M, New York, NY 10017; fax 212-963-1658. *Agent*—Aaron M. Priest Literary Agency, Inc., 122 East 42nd St., Suite 3902, New York, NY 10168. *E-mail*—magona-gobado@un.org.

CAREER: Domestic worker, 1963-67; primary schoolteacher, Cape Town, South Africa, 1967-80; high school teacher of Xhosa language, Cape Town, 1977-81; United Nations, New York City, press officer, 1984—.

MEMBER: International Women's Writing Guild, PEN America, United Nations Society of Writers, Bhala Writers Association.

AWARDS, HONORS: Honorary doctorate from Hartwick College; named among Xhosa heroes of South Africa.

WRITINGS:

To My Children's Children, Interlink Publishing (Brooklyn, NY), 1994.
Living, Loving, and Lying Awake at Night (fiction), Interlink Publishing (Brooklyn, NY), 1994.
Forced to Grow, Interlink Publishing (Brooklyn, NY), 1998.
Mother to Mother (fiction), David Philip, 1998.

Also author of *Push-Push and Other Stories.*

WORK IN PROGRESS: Penrose and Lilian, a memoir of the author's parents; *The Last School Year,* a novel.

SIDELIGHTS: Sindiwe Magona told *CA:* "I come to writing with no great training except my life and the lives of the people of whom I am a part. For so long, others have written about us; I write to change that, instead of moaning about it. We are people of an oral tradition; however, times have changed and our stories must be told in the mode of the time. I write so that African children in my country can see someone like them doing this miraculous thing that for so long has not belonged to us. I write to add to the rising voice of my people, dispersed throughout the world. We need to leave footprints, to show we have lived. And so, I write.

"Although I have read the classics, my inspiration comes from reading works by women, especially African women or writers who are of African descent. The first book by a black woman writer that I ever held in my hand was *I Know Why the Caged Bird Sings* by Maya Angelou. This writer remains my all-time favorite. I regard her as my writing ancestor. I also take delight in Tony Morrison, Ellen Kuzwayo, and Miriam Tlali.

"I write best when I feel very strongly about a subject. At this time, it is South Africa—particularly the lives of African people there—lives that were squandered, wasted, stunted, brutalized, and sacrificed to the ideology of apartheid. We may be in the era of the new South Africa, but the lives being lived out in that country are still very much rooted in the old order. The legacy of that iniquitous system will still play havoc with the lives of many. That is not to say I am pessimistic about my country's future or the future of my people. No; indeed, the opposite is true. To have survived apartheid is no small feat. It is the song of these unsung heroines and heroes I'd like to write about: the millions whose greatness went unnoticed, disguised in acts labeled ordinary or traditional.

"This is linked to my reasons for writing. I want to inspire young black women to make what I call the transition, so that more of us will write our stories instead of telling them. Writing for the African woman is but a transition: old wine in new bottles. She has been telling stories for ages. I myself am in the process of making the transition from telling to writing."

MAHLER, Gustav 1860-1911

PERSONAL: Born July 7, 1860, in Kaliste, Bohemia, Austria (now part of the Czech Republic); died May 18, 1911; son of Bernhard (a distiller) and Marie (Hermann) Mahler; married Alma Schindler, 1902; children: two daughters. *Education:* Studied at the Vienna Conservatory, 1875-78. *Religion:* Jewish, converted to Catholicism as an adult.

CAREER: Conductor and composer. Conducted in small theaters in Austria, 1880-83; Court Theater of Kassel, musical director, 1883; Municipal Theater of Leipzig, second conductor, 1886-88; Budapest Opera House, musical director, 1888—; Hamburg Opera House, first conductor, 1891-97; Imperial Opera, Vienna, 1897-1907, deputy director and artistic director general for life; New York Philharmonic Orchestra, New York City, guest conductor; Metropolitan Opera, New York City, guest conductor.

WRITINGS:

COLLECTED LETTERS

Gustav Mahler: Memories and Letters, edited by Alma Mahler, translation by Basil Creighton, edited by Donald Mitchell, University of Washington Press (Seattle, WA), 1975.
Selected Letters of Gustav Mahler, translation by Eithne Wilkins, Ernst Kaiser, and Bill Hopkins, Faber (London, England), 1979.
Gustav Mahler, Selected Letters, edited by Knud Marten, Farrar-Strauss-Giroux (New York City), 1979.
Gustav Mahler, Richard Strauss: Correspondence, 1888-1911, edited by Herta Blaukopf, translation by Edmund Jephcott, University of Chicago Press (Chicago, IL), 1984.
Mahler's Unknown Letters, edited by Herta Blaukopf, translation by Richard Stokes, Northeastern University Press (Boston, MA), 1987.
Symphony No. 2 in C Minor ("Resurrection") Facsimile, edited by Gilbert Kaplan, Kaplan Foundation (New York City), 1987.
Adagietto: Facsimile, Documentation, Recording, edited by Gilbert Kaplan, Kaplan Foundation (New York City), 1992.

CANTATAS

"Das Klagende Lied," 1878-80.

SONGS

"Three Songs for Tenor and Pianoforte," 1880.
"Five Songs for Voice and Pianoforte," 1880-83.
"Nine Songs for Voice and Pianoforte," 1887-90.
"Four Songs for Voice and Pianoforte," 1888-91.
"Songs of a Wayfarer," 1884.
"The Youth's Magic Horn," 1892-99.
"Songs on the Death of Children," 1901-04.
"Five Songs," 1901-02.

SONG-SYMPHONY

The Song of the Earth, 1911.

SYMPHONIES

Symphony No. 1 in D Major (Titan), 1889.
Symphony No. 2 in C Minor (Resurrection), 1895.
Symphony No. 3 in D Minor, 1902.
Symphony No. 4 in G Major, 1901.
Symphony No. 5 in C Sharp Minor, 1904.
Symphony No. 6 (Tragic), 1906.
Symphony No. 7 in E Minor, 1909.
Symphony No. 8 (Symphony of a Thousand), 1909.
Symphony No. 9 in D Major, 1910.
Symphony No. 10 in F Sharp Minor (Adagio), 1911.

Many of Mahler's scores have been reproduced and published.

SIDELIGHTS: Gustav Mahler was an Austrian conductor and composer of the Romantic period. He completed nine symphonies but died before finishing his tenth. It is believed that very early symphonies may have been destroyed during the bombing of Dresden during World War II. His earlier works reflect his love of nature, and later compositions have themes based in philosophy and religion. Mahler conducted the New York Philharmonic Orchestra and at the Metropolitan Opera during four trips to the United States toward the end of his life.

Mahler was born of Jewish parents in Bohemia, part of the Austro-Hungarian empire, and spent most of his childhood in Iglau (Jihlava), Moravia, where his father operated a brandy distillery. The family was poor, and half of the family's fourteen children died in infancy. Mahler studied piano as a child under Iglau conductor Franz Viktorin and later under Johannes Bosch. Mahler taught other children before making his own debut as a pianist at age ten. He studied formally at the Vienna Conservatory, writing songs and chamber music, and graduated with honors.

Out of financial necessity, he conducted in small theaters during the season from fall through spring and composed most of his own works during summers, concentrating only on the symphony and the lieder. His experimentation with chamber music was confined to his days as a student; and, although he felt opera to be the greatest art form, he never composed an opera. He was influenced by Bruckner, Bach, Beethoven, and Wagner and himself influenced young composers of the time.

Mahler began his career conducting in small theaters in Austria, and in 1883 he became musical director of the Court Theater of Kassel. He worked for a short time in Prague, then conducted at the Municipal Theater of Leipzig. In 1888 he was appointed musical director of the Budapest Opera House where he came to the attention of Johannes Brahms. Because of a dispute, he left to become first conductor of the Hamburg Opera in 1891 and stayed for six years. In 1897 he became artistic director of the Imperial Opera in Vienna.

Mahler married Alma Schindler in 1902. The couple had two daughters, but the eldest died of diphtheria in 1907. During the same year Mahler was diagnosed with heart disease. During his years with the Vienna Opera Mahler raised the standards of performance of the instrumentalists and performers, so much so that it outraged many of his associates. By 1907 his relationship with the Vienna Opera was so strained and his health and loss of his daughter weighed so heavily upon him that he left the Opera and accepted an invitation to conduct in the United States. He was very well received and took a position as conductor of the New York Philharmonic Society. He traveled back and forth to Austria over the next several years, performing in the United States and composing during summers. His health deteriorated as he suffered increasing angina attacks. His final symphony, *Symphony No. 10 in F Sharp Minor,* was drafted but never completed. He last stood at the podium in New York City on February 21, 1911. Mahler returned to Austria and died in a sanatorium on May 18, 1911.

There are no records of writings by Mahler, other than personal letters, many of which are presented in a number of collections. He wrote letters daily, and these provide insight into his feelings about his life, work, and his views. *Gustav Mahler, Selected Letters,* edited by Knud Marten, contains over four hundred letters spanning his life as a young man in 1877 until the final year of his life in 1911. The book contains an introduction and notes to guide the reader in understanding the circumstances and people to whom the letters were written. Included are Mahler's letters to and from his family, including Alma's mother and stepfather. Friends with whom Mahler corresponded included archeologist Friedrich Lohr, attorney Emil Freund, and Arnold Berliner, who had helped Mahler master English. Mahler wrote to many in the music and art worlds, including Bruno Walter, who became a close friend and who interpreted Mahler's music following his death. "The book, however, is not only an example of meticulous scholarship, but a living document of the composer's personality," wrote Paul A. Pisk in the *American Music Teacher*. "The romanticism of his youth, his passionate emotions, the various, often tragic phases of his career as creative artist and conductor, become apparent."

Mahler and Richard Strauss were friends and rivals, who shared the practical aspects of their art through correspondence. *Gustav Mahler, Richard Strauss: Correspondence, 1888-1911* by Herta Blaukopf, with translation by Edmund Jephcott, contains ninety letters written by Mahler and Strauss, an important conductor of his works. Alma's view of the relationship between the two men was that it had been hostile, but Robert W. Richart wrote in *Library Journal* that the collection offers a different viewpoint of their relationship. Richart said they "championed each other's works." "The letters are lively and entertaining reading," wrote C. Isaac in *Choice*. Blaukopf's collection *Mahler's Unknown Letters,* translated by Richard Stokes, also includes telegrams and postcards to seventeen friends, family members, colleagues, and critics. Short essays provide overviews of the relationships between Mahler and the recipients. K. Pendle wrote in *Choice* of the "striking" difference in tone used by Mahler in his communications with his associates as compared to that found in letters to his sister Justine, and to friends. "Mahler's letters are always fluent and direct, charged with energy, usually dashed off at great speed in odd moments between rehearsals," wrote David Matthews in the *Times Educational Supplement*. Donald Mitchell wrote in the *Times Literary Supplement* that the letters to Hermann Behn, Mahler's close friend, "are among the most valuable in the book. . . . We encounter, for instance, the flustered composer who has absent-mindedly left behind him in Hamburg what he desperately needs on holiday at Steinbach." Said Mahler, "Just imagine, I've left the sketches for the 1st movement of my third in my desk. I'm in utter despair. I beg you to go immediately to Hamburg. I enclose the two keys to

my desk. Look in one of the compartments on the right side and you'll find a bundle of papers wrapped in manuscript paper marked: "Drafts" or "Sketches" or something similar. Please do this without delay and send it to me by express! I can do nothing before I have this!. . . . Wire me as soon as you receive this letter, to tell me if I can count on you!" Of course, Mahler could count on his dear friend, who found the sketches.

Mahler biographer Henry-Louis de la Grange attended a 1990 symposium titled "Mahler in America 1907-1911." Sue Taylor wrote in the *St. Louis Post-Dispatch* that de la Grange began by "eloquently discrediting Alma and others who viewed Mahler as a depressed, morose neurotic. . . . De la Grange contended that Mahler did not arrive in America a physical and mental wreck. Instead, it was Mahler's physical and emotional strengths . . . that allowed him to replace despair with creativity." During this period, Mahler wrote his *Symphony No. 9 in D Major*. His work with the New York Philharmonic was supported by Andrew Carnegie and Joseph Pulitzer through a half million dollar contribution. Leonard Slatkin conducted the St. Louis Symphony in a performance of Mahler's *Symphony No. 3 in D Minor* during the two-day event and participated as a speaker.

The symposium was organized by Gilbert Kaplan, a financier whose passion for Mahler's *Symphony No. 2 in C Minor (Resurrection)* caused him to learn to conduct the piece. Kaplan purchased the score of this favorite symphony in 1984 and published a facsimile edition, which includes an essay by Kaplan and the contents of Mahler's letters referencing the work. David Matthews wrote in the *Times Literary Supplement* that "the facsimile reproduction is of superb quality, faithfully duplicating the various colours and textures of Mahler's pens and pencils. . . . Even before he finished the last page of the score . . . Mahler had probably begun to revise it. . . . It is fascinating to compare the manuscript with the final published score, as there are differences on every page."

Kaplan also published *Adagietto: Facsimile, Documentation, Recording*. Matthews said "it comprises two finely reproduced facsimile full scores of the Adagietto from the Fifth Symphony, Mahler's autograph fair copy and Alma Mahler's copy which was used as a basis for the published score." Alma often wrote out the scores of entire symphonies for her husband. The Adagietto was written as a love song to Alma, but there is no documentation available as to whether Mahler began work on the piece before or after he had met her. Kaplan notes similarities between the Adagietto's opening phrase and the first movement of Mahler's *Symphony No. 6 (Tragic),* also a tribute to Alma. Matthews said Kaplan could have mentioned his *Symphony No. 10 in F Sharp Minor (Adagio),* "where the long passage of string music near the end of the finale . . . represents Mahler's reaffirmation of his love for Alma after the trauma of his discovery of her infidelity." Also included are seventeen letters written by Mahler to Alma, a monograph edited by Kaplan, and a compact disc of the Adagietto played by the London Symphony Orchestra conducted by Kaplan. Stephen E. Hefling wrote in *Notes* that "Kaplan argues compellingly that most conductors today considerably distort the music with tempos far slower than Mahler intended: eleven-and-a-half- to fourteen-minute renditions are currently commonplace, whereas the composer and his chosen interpreters averaged seven to nine minutes. Kaplan's own lucid and polished reading of the movement with the London Symphony Orchestra . . . clocks just under eight minutes." Hefling pointed out that sixteen of the letters to Alma were included in her *Gustav Mahler: Memories and Letters,* but that the additional letter included by Kaplan "is the chillingly frank one in which Mahler asks his fiancee whether she can give up her music 'in order to possess and also be mine instead.'" This letter was included in Henry-Louis de La Grange's *Mahler* (1973). Hefling concluded that the volume "draws upon excellent scholarly sources to make readily accessible the documents of an extraordinary moment in the work of a composer whose life and creativity were closely intertwined."

Jonathan Carr's is the most recent biography of Mahler. Reviewer Noel Malcolm, writing in the *Telegraph,* noted the varying accounts of Mahler's character. "Dominant among these has been the version given by his highly-strung and at times well-nigh nymphomaniac wife, Alma. Her account, depicting him as a doom-laden neurotic, had some influence on the popular view of the composer. . . . But serious biographers of Mahler learnt long ago to treat her outpourings with great caution." Malcolm said Carr "does not hesitate to present the Jewish composer's 'conversion' to Catholicism as a straightforward ploy to secure his appointment to the most coveted job of all, the directorship of the court Opera in Vienna." Malcolm said "every generation needs its own updated account; and this generation should be grateful for one written with such a combination of no-nonsense clarity and real enthusiasm."

BIOGRAPHICAL/CRITICAL SOURCES:

BOOKS

Adorno, Theodor Wiesengrund, *Mahler: A Musical Physiognomy,* Faber and Faber (London, England), 1992, reprinted, translation by Edmund Jephcott, University of Chicago Press (Chicago, IL), 1996.

Blaukopf, Kurt, *Mahler: A Documentary Study,* Allen Lane, 1973, reprinted, translation by P. R. J. Ford, Oxford University Press (Oxford, England), 1976.

Blaukopf, Kurt, *Gustav Mahler,* Proscenium Press, 1985.

Bruno, Walter, *Gustav Mahler: Theme and Variations,* translation by James Galston, Quartet, 1990.

Burnett, James, *The Music of Gustav Mahler,* Fairleigh Dickinson University Press (Cranbury, NJ), 1985.

Carr, Jonathan, *Mahler: A Biography,* Overlook Press (New York City), 1997.

Cooke, Deryck, *Gustav Mahler: An Introduction to His Music,* Faber (London, England), 1980, reprinted, Cambridge University Press (New York City), 1988.

Delmar, Norman, *Mahler: Symphony 6, A Study,* Da Capo Press (New York City), 1982.

Esselstrom, Michael J., *A Conductor's Guide to Symphonies I, II, and III of Gustav Mahler (Studies in the History and Interpretation of Music,* Volume 60, Edwin Mellen Press (Lewiston, NY), 1998.

Floros, Constantin, *Gustav Mahler: The Symphonies,* Amadeus Press (Portland, OR), 1993, 1997.

Franklin, Peter, *Mahler: Symphony No. 3,* Cambridge University Press (New York City), 1991.

Franklin, Peter, *The Life of Mahler (Musical Lives),* Cambridge University Press (New York City), 1997.

Fulop, Peter, editor, *Mahler Discography,* E. P. Dutton, 1995.

Gartenberg, Egon, *Mahler: The Man and His Music,* Schirmer Books, 1978.

Greene, David B., *Mahler, Consciousness and Temporality,* Gordon and Breach Science Pub., 1984.

Haylock, Julian, *Gustav Mahler: An Essential Guide to His Life and Works,* Trafalgar Square, 1997.

Hefling, Stephen E., editor, *Mahler Studies,* Cambridge University Press (New York City), 1997.

Holbrook, David, *Gustav Mahler and the Courage to Be,* Da Capo Press (New York City), 1981.

Hopkins, Robert G., *Closure and Mahler's Music: The Role of Secondary Parameters (Studies in the*

Criticism and Theory of Music), University of Pennsylvania Press (Philadelphia, PA), 1990.

Kaplan, Gilbert, editor, *The Mahler Album,* Harry N. Abrams (New York City), 1995.

Kennedy, Michael, *The Master Musicians—Mahler,* J. M. Dent and Sons, 1974, 1990.

La Grange, Henry-Louis, *Gustav Mahler:* Volume 1, Doubleday (New York City), 1973.

La Grange, Henry-Louis, *Gustav Mahler: Vienna: The Years of Challenge (1897-1904),* Volume 2, Oxford University Press (Oxford, England), reprinted, Clarendon Press (New York City), 1995.

Lebrecht, Norman, *Mahler Remembered,* Faber (London, England), 1987.

Mitchell, Donald, *Gustav Mahler: Songs and Symphonies of Life and Death,* Volume 3, University of California Press (Berkeley, CA), 1985.

Mitchell, Donald, *Gustav Mahler: The Early Years,* Volume 1, University of California Press (Berkeley, CA), 1995.

Raynor, Henry, *Mahler,* Macmillan (London, England), 1975.

Reilly, Edward R., *Gustav Mahler and Guido Adler: Records of a Friendship,* Cambridge University Press (New York City), 1982.

Roman, Zoltan, *Gustav Mahler's American Years, 1907-1911: A Documentary History,* Pendragon Press (Stuyvesant, NY), 1989.

Russell, *Light in Battle with Darkness Mahler's Kindertotenlieder,* Peter Lang (New York City), 1991.

Samuels, Robert, *Mahler's Sixth Symphony: A Study in Musical Semiotics, (Cambridge Studies in Music Theory and Analysis),* 6, Cambridge University Press (New York City), 1995.

Seckerson, Edward, *Mahler (The Illustrated Lives of the Great Composers),* Omnibus (New York City), 1996.

Smoley, Lewis M., *The Symphonies of Gustav Mahler: A Critical Discography,* Greenwood Publishing Group (Westport, CT), 1986.

Smoley, Lewis M., *Gustav Mahler's Symphonies: Critical Commentary on Recordings Since 1986 (Discographies, No. 66),* Greenwood Publishing Group (Westport, CT), 1996.

Walter, Bruno, *Gustav Mahler,* Da Capo Press (New York City), 1978.

PERIODICALS

American Music Teacher, April, 1981, p. 49.
American Scholar, fall, 1997, p. 513.
Audio, September, 1990, p. 33.
Atlantic, November, 1982, p. 111.

Choice, June, 1985, p. 1506; July, 1988, p. 1704.
Commentary, May, 1986, p. 57.
Guardian Weekly, January 20, 1985, p. 22.
Horizon, June, 1986, p. 43.
Library Journal, January, 1985, p. 81.
Musical Quarterly, spring, 1985, p. 200; spring, 1990, p. 175; spring, 1993, p. 47; summer, 1996, p. 276.
Nation, February 7, 1987, p. 158.
National Review, February 22, 1985, p. 44.
New York Times Book Review, February 3, 1985, p. 23.
Notes, December, 1985, p. 293; June, 1989, p. 832; September, 1991, p. 274; June, 1994, p. 1566.
Opera News, December 7, 1985, p. 24; September, 1995, p. 71.
Publishers Weekly, December 14, 1984, p. 46.
Stereo Review, May, 1981, p. 40.
Telegraph, September 14, 1997.
Times Educational Supplement, April 24, 1987, p. 24.
Times Literary Supplement, December 7, 1984, p. 1401; June 19, 1987, p. 657; July 17, 1987, p. 772; November 13, 1992, p. 12.*

—Sketch by Sheila Velazquez

* * *

MALVASI, Mark G. 1957-

PERSONAL: Born November 23, 1957, in Niles, OH; son of Joseph Anthony and Ira Gene (Bowser) Malvasi; married Catherine E. Kelly (marriage ended July 25, 1992); married Meg Greene (a writer), October 6, 1995. *Ethnicity:* "Italian-American." *Education:* Hiram College, B.A., 1980; University of Chicago, M.A., 1982; University of Rochester, Ph.D., 1991. *Politics:* Independent. *Religion:* Roman Catholic. *Avocational interests:* Reading, gardening, music (composition and performance), cooking, raising dogs, ice hockey.

ADDRESSES: Home—13803 Sterlings Bridge Rd., Midlothian, VA 23112. *Office*—Department of History, Randolph-Macon College, P.O. Box 5005, Ashland, VA 23005-5505. *E-mail*—malvasi@aol.com.

CAREER: University of Puget Sound, Tacoma, WA, assistant professor of American history, 1989-90; University of South Carolina at Columbia, fellow of National Historical Publications and Records Commission, "John C. Calhoun Papers," 1990-91; University of Alabama, Tuscaloosa, assistant professor of American history, 1991-92; Randolph-Macon College, Ashland, VA, associate professor of American history, 1992—.

MEMBER: American Historical Association, Historical Society (vice president of Chesapeake branch, 1998), St. George Tucker Society, Phi Beta Kappa.

WRITINGS:

The Unregenerate South: The Agrarian Thought of John Crowe Ransom, Allen Tate, and Donald Davidson, Louisiana State University Press (Baton Rouge, LA), 1997.

(Contributor) Robert Pacquette and Louis Ferliger, editors, *Slavery and Southern History,* University of North Carolina Press (Chapel Hill, NC), 1999.

(Contributor) Clyde N. Wilson, editor, *Lost Causes Regained: The Work of M. E. Bradford,* University of Missouri Press (Columbia, MO), 1999.

Contributor to periodicals, including *Modern Age, Southern Partisan, Chronicles: Magazine of American Culture,* and *Journal of the Early Republic.*

WORK IN PROGRESS: Merigan, a novel of Italian-American life, completion expected in 2000; *The Last Patriots: Tradition and Tragedy in Southern Conservative Thought,* an analysis of the southern conservative critique of modernity and the accomplishments and limitations of the southern conservative intellectual tradition.

SIDELIGHTS: Mark G. Malvasi told *CA:* "I write to satisfy what cannot be satisfied, to quench the unquenchable: my curiosity. I desire to know and to understand all sorts of things, even the most apparently trivial. Writing about them enables me to do so. I have come to believe that I do not really know or understand anything until I have studied it enough to write about it. Writing also reveals to me on almost a daily basis my vast and growing ignorance of most of the world. To me, writing is a deeply and inherently humbling activity.

"I do not like to explore too thoroughly the influences on my thinking and writing, not because I claim originality of mind, but because the number and variety of writers who have influenced me are legion. In general, though, two sorts of writers have shaped my work: those who have taught me how to organize material and those who have enabled me to see the world through new eyes or, more precisely, to see the world more clearly through my own eyes.

"I have learned more about the structure and organization of writing from poets, essayists, and novelists than from historians. William Shakespeare, Michel de Montaigne, Samuel Johnson, Jonathan Swift, Mark Twain, Marcel Proust, Owen Barfield, and C. S. Lewis have exercised important influences on me in this regard. One work of history that deserves mention here is Shelby Foote's masterpiece *The Civil War: A Narrative.* In my view, Foote's work, in its sophisticated organization and refined art, is from beginning to end an example of the historian's craft at its finest.

"It is harder to identify those writers whose work has helped to form the core of my ideas and my world view. Glancing at the bookshelf in my study, I can make an argument to include virtually every book I see. The writer who has exercised the most enduring influence on the formation of my mind, however, is Alexis de Tocqueville. His understanding of the contours, promise, and dangers of the world in which we now live remains unsurpassed. I have yet to encounter a mind that was at once as honest and as meticulous as his. He taught me that writing is as much a moral as an aesthetic undertaking. As a writer, Tocqueville represents an ideal to which I can only hope to aspire.

"Writing is a craft. My process of writing really begins with reading, for it is through reading the works of others that I learn how to organize ideas and manage words. I approach the craft with the logic and discipline of a businessman. I research slowly and painstakingly; I write quickly; I edit carefully and extensively. I take pleasure in the process of writing. The real pleasure, though, is not in the process itself, but in the sense of accomplishment and satisfaction of having written something well.

"I write about southern history and literature principally because I enjoy reading and studying these topics. Upon my first exposure to the literature of the South, I discovered that most southern writers believed in the sinful nature of man as the one unalterable reality of human life. I shared their conviction and, as a consequence, not being southern myself, grew curious about the history of the society and the region that had shaped the outlook and the work of these men and women. The elegiac tone of much southern writing also appealed to my sensibilities and captured my imagination.

"In addition, I write about matters southern because they are presently out of fashion. It seems to me an integral responsibility of writers to explore ideas that others have abandoned, discarded, dismissed, or rejected, if only to learn whether they may retain even a germ of wisdom about the human condition. At last I write about the South not primarily to do justice to southern literature and history, neither of which requires my defense, but to uncover and state the truth or, more modestly, to eliminate as much untruth about them as it is within my power and ability to do.

"I am now attempting to write fiction because of my convictions about the evolution of history and historical consciousness; that is, the mental and emotional climate that describes how certain men and women, living in a particular time and place, were inclined to feel, think, and believe. In my present work I am more and more wrestling with two different conceptions of history: the scholarly and the existential. In following this line of inquiry I have been guided and inspired by the insights of Johan Huizinga, Eric Hobsbawm, and especially John Lukacs. For all of us there is a kind of shadow region between history and memory, between the *recorded* past found in documents and books and subject to relatively dispassionate investigation and analysis and the *remembered* past that forms the background to one's own life. This shadow region, this no-man's land of time, is by far the hardest part of history for historians, or for anyone else, to comprehend. In my work, then, I am trying to reproduce the world around me by drawing on the world within me."

*　　*　　*

MARK, Samuel EuGene 1953-

PERSONAL: Born January 28, 1953, in Henry County, IN; son of Norman E. and Mary A. (Todd) Mark. *Ethnicity:* "White." *Education:* Ball State University, B.A. (history), B.S. (anthropology and geology), 1980; studied Arabic at U.S. Army Defense Language Institute, 1983-84; Texas A&M University, M.A., 1993, Ph.D., 1999.

ADDRESSES: Office—1401, FM 2818 No. 302, College Station, TX 77840.

CAREER: Archaeologist. Molasses Reef Project, conservation technician, 1987-88; Texas A&M University, College Station, librarian in Nautical Archae-

ology Program, 1993-97, Mr. and Mrs. Ray H. Siegfried II fellow, 1997-98. Work as archaeologist includes ship recording, artifact photography, and illustration. *Military service:* U.S. Army, Military Intelligence, 1983-87; served in the Middle East; became sergeant.

WRITINGS:

From Egypt to Mesopotamia: A Study of Predynastic Trade Routes, Texas A&M University Press (College Station, TX), 1997.

Contributor of articles and reviews to periodicals, including *American Journal of Archaeology, International Journal of Nautical Archaeology,* and *Isis.*

SIDELIGHTS: Samuel EuGene Mark told *CA:* "I write because an archaeologist who does not publish is little more than a treasure hunter.

"Before writing, I try to read extensively. Since my interests are historical or archaeological in nature, I try to read extensively on the periods that precede and succeed my period of interest. This allows me to get a better feel for trends. My first concern is to outline the general pattern suggested by the evidence. Once a pattern is defined, I return to the original source and try to disprove the pattern I see. I then try to find someone who disagrees with this point of view to see if he or she can find any flaws in the pattern. I have learned that research and criticism should not be taken personally. Even if people are vindictive in their comments, the writer should still try to find merit in what they say, because it strengthens the work in the long run.

"I enjoy the subjects about which I write. My advice is: never write on anything you do not like. It will become work."

*　　*　　*

MARSHALL, Adre 1942-

PERSONAL: Born June 18, 1942, in Uitenhage, South Africa; daughter of Louis Botha (a medical practitioner) and Elizabeth (a teacher; maiden name, Brinton) Bok; married Rodney Marshall (a medical practitioner), November 25, 1967; children: Delia, Helene, Andrew. *Ethnicity:* "Caucasian South African." *Education:* University of Stellenbosch, B.A., 1962, B.A.

(with honors), 1963, M.A., 1985; University of Paris, degree, 1964; University of Cape Town, Ph.D., 1993. *Politics:* "Floating between a variety of unsatisfactory parties." *Avocational interests:* Classical music, theater, hiking, bird watching.

ADDRESSES: Home—3 Glenthorne Lane, Rondebosch, Cape Town, South Africa.

CAREER: University of Stellenbosch, Stellenbosch, South Africa, lecturer in English, 1965-67; University of Port Elizabeth, Port Elizabeth, South Africa, lecturer in French, 1968 and 1970, lecturer in English, between 1983-86; University of Cape Town, Cape Town, South Africa, lecturer in English, 1988-95.

WRITINGS:

The Turn of the Mind: Constituting Consciousness in Henry James, Fairleigh Dickinson University Press (Madison, NJ), 1998.

Contributor to *English Studies in Africa.*

WORK IN PROGRESS: Poetry.

SIDELIGHTS: Adre Marshall told *CA:* "My book *The Turn of the Mind: Constituting Consciousness in Henry James* represents the culmination of a lifelong interest in the fiction of James. This interest was first aroused when, as a teenager, I picked up a tattered copy of *The Beast in the Jungle* in a second-hand book shop. Later, university studies further stimulated my enthusiasm for James's fiction, and I based both my master's and doctoral dissertations on the study of James's work. Apart from academic writing, I have always enjoyed dabbling in genres such as poetry and the short story. As it is extremely difficult to find a publisher for poetry in South Africa, it is unlikely that my poems will ever merit a mention!"

*   *   *

MARSHALL, Bridget M(ary) 1974-

PERSONAL: Born March 28, 1974, in Harrisburg, PA; daughter of William (a salesman) and Margaret Marshall. *Education:* Lehigh University, B.A. (summa cum laude), 1996; University of Massachusetts at Amherst, graduate study, 1997—.

ADDRESSES: Home—736 North West St., Carlisle, PA 17013. *Office*—Writing Program, Bartlett Hall, University of Massachusetts at Amherst, Amherst, MA 01003. *E-mail*—bmarshal@english.umass.edu.

CAREER: Payment Technologies, Inc., Carlisle, PA, technical and business writer, 1994-97; Lehigh University Writing Center, Bethlehem, PA, writing tutor, 1995-96; University of Massachusetts at Amherst, teaching associate, 1997—. Performer with the Kerouac Players, 1994-96; violinist in Lehigh University Orchestra, 1992-94.

MEMBER: Phi Beta Kappa, Sigma Tau Delta, Omicron Delta Kappa, Phi Eta Sigma.

AWARDS, HONORS: Animal Crackers was named an "outstanding selection" by Parent Council, 1997.

WRITINGS:

Animal Crackers: A Tender Book about Death and Funerals and Love, illustrated by Ron Boldt, Centering Corp., 1998.

Composer of *Josephine the Mouse Singer,* performed in 1993. Author of the column "Dear Phoebe Valentine" in *Red Moon Martini* (Bethlehem, PA), 1995. Contributor to newspapers and periodicals, including *Red Moon Martini, Amaranth Journal of Creative Arts* and *Lehigh Review.*

WORK IN PROGRESS: Research on the following topics: animation, Hemingway, and the new music culture.*

*   *   *

MASO, Carole

PERSONAL: Born in New Jersey; father a musician, mother a nurse; companion of Helen Lange. *Education:* Vassar College, B.A., 1977.

ADDRESSES: Office—Brown University, Box 1852, Providence, RI 02912. *Agent*—Georges Borchardt Inc., 136 East 57th St., New York, NY 10022. *E-mail*—Carole_Maso@brown.edu.

CAREER: Writer. Illinois State University, Normal, IL, writer-in-residence, 1991-92; George Washington University, Washington, DC, writer-in-residence,

1992-93; Columbia University, New York City, associate professor, 1993; Brown University, Providence, RI, professor and director of creative writing, 1995—. Has worked as a waitress, an artist's model, and a fencing instructor.

AWARDS, HONORS: CAPS, grant for fiction, 1983; W. K. Rose, fellowship in the creative arts, 1985; New York Foundation for the Arts, grant, 1987; National Endowment for the Arts, literature grant, 1988; Lannan Literary fellowship for fiction, 1993.

WRITINGS:

Ghost Dance, Perennial Library (New York), 1987, reprinted, Ecco Press (Hopewell, NJ), 1995.
The Art Lover: A Novel, North Point Press (San Francisco), 1990, reprinted, Ecco Press, 1995.
Ava: A Novel, Dalkey Archive Press (Normal, IL), 1993.
The American Woman in the Chinese Hat, Dalkey Archive, 1994, reprinted, Plume (New York), 1995.
Aureole, Ecco, 1996.
Defiance: A Novel, Dutton (New York), 1998.

Contributor to *Tasting Life Twice: Literary Lesbian Fiction by New American Writers,* edited by E. J. Levy, Avon Books, 1995.

WORK IN PROGRESS: Novel, *The Bay of Angels.*

SIDELIGHTS: Carole Maso is a professor of English and author whose first book, *Ghost Dance,* is the story of a family's disintegration and an exploration of loss. "Carole writes beautifully, with a depth of imagination and fine descriptive power—but plot, continuity, and climax generally conceded to a novel are most difficult to pull from the thick cloudy contest of ephemeral memories," proclaimed Alicia Dulac in *Best Sellers.* A *Publishers Weekly* reviewer opined: "Comparable more to musical than to literary forms, this first novel resembles a tone poem."

The novel is not organized into chapters but rather into five parts that are further divided. "*Ghost Dance*'s unconventional structure is not a pretentious, arty overlay," claimed Leslie Lawrence in *Sojourner.* "The structure is born of necessity; the story could be told no other way. This is not a novel about character development or about how one event leads to another. It is a novel that succeeds in conveying the enormity and fertility of one woman's mind." *Library Journal* reviewer Jeanne Buckley called Maso's prose "repeti-

tious and dreamlike, and her poetic images are sharp and evocative." *Kirkus Reviews* said that Vanessa tells the story "in an emotion-charged and montage-like narrative that roams freely from deep in the past right up to the present."

The narrator of *Ghost Dance* is Vanessa Turin, daughter of the distinguished, beautiful, and mad poet Christine Wing. Vanessa's father is a quiet man, devoted to his wife. Fletcher, Vanessa's brother, is an activist, and her grandfather travels west to learn from the Native Americans. "The children observe marriages of opposites, parents and grandparents," explained E. M. Broner in the *Women's Review of Books.* "Their father is silent, their mother's life and living are words. Their Italian grandmother is practical; her husband is a visionary, a moralist. . . . The children are the heirs of these symbiotic traits. Vanessa, the eldest, inherits her mother's physical form, and, like the mother, writes. Fletcher, the brother, a year younger, speaks out for the silent things that have no speech themselves, flora, fauna, the environment." As the novel progresses, Vanessa loses her mother to an automobile accident and her father when he departs on an unannounced pilgrimage. Fletcher journeys to remote places and sends Vanessa postcards with muddled messages.

Ron Burnett remarked in the *Christian Science Monitor* that *Ghost Dance* is not so much a story as it is "a mode of recall by a narrator who really isn't telling a story at all but trying to build a rationale for her own existence." Vanessa becomes addicted to cocaine and then heroin. She has an affair with her mother's female lover of over two decades. The sections of the book are connected by imagery. "Snow, for example, is at once cocaine, the asbestos in a worker's lungs, and the setting for the massacre of Native Americans at Wounded Knee," observed Meredith Sue Willis in the *New York Times Book Review.* Cyra McFadden, in her assessment for the *Los Angeles Times Book Review,* characterized the language of the novel as "dense" and "lyrical" and contended that Maso "takes enormous risks, juggling level upon level of metaphor. . . . The book's strengths are greater than its flaws, however, and the flaws are honorable, born of ambition and abundant talent. I can't remember a more striking depiction of madness, or the labyrinth of family ties." *Booklist* reviewer Joanne Wilkinson called *Ghost Dance* "[a] stunning debut."

Maso's second novel, *The Art Lover,* is dedicated to Gary Falk, a friend of hers who died of AIDS. Linda L. Rome, writing in *Library Journal,* said that the "nontraditional novel presents an experimental face to the reader." The main character, Caroline, is a poet and writer who returns to New York from an artists' colony to settle the estate of her father, an art historian who had told her that art is everything. She accepts his belief but feels that her mother's suicide may have been linked to her father's philosophy. As Caroline's childhood friend is dying of AIDS, "Caroline begins to feel that retreating into art may in fact be nothing but an exquisite form of betrayal," explained William Ferguson in the *New York Times Book Review*. At one point, Caroline is replaced by Maso's persona, describing her work on the novel as her own friend is dying. Photographs of art, reviews, start charts, poems, and newspaper clippings are scattered throughout the story, "often as ironic counterpoint," said Ferguson. He maintained that although the book contains many "imaginative levels," *The Art Lover* "is fully coherent, moving and elegiac, a genuine consolation."

"[*The Art Lover*] is more a deconstructionist art gallery of the author's sensibility than a conventional novel," wrote Carol Muske Dukes in the *Los Angeles Times Book Review*. "These 'pieces' form a puzzle, an album of memories, though the style is in no way retrospective; it is as contemporary and self-conscious as a style can get in our post-structuralist age." Dukes characterized the images as "sensual, obsessed—with long passages of intoxicating beauty. . . . Maso has found an innovative way to see, like a laser, into the human heart." A *Publishers Weekly* reviewer asserted that Maso "brings to life a 'bombardment of images and sounds,' fashioning a pattern of astonishing complexity and beauty."

A critic for *Publishers Weekly* compared Maso's third novel to James Joyce's *Ulysses* in that the protagonist Ava Klein recalls her past on the last day of her life as she dies from a rare cancer of the blood. The reviewer contended that *Ava* "presents heartbreakingly familiar emotions in an utterly original form." L. Winters opined in *Choice* that *Ava* is "mysterious and richly allusive. . . . Maso contributes new insights into women's inner life."

In the novel, Ava is a thirty-nine-year-old professor of literature at Hunter College who reflects upon her marriages to an Italian film director, a French pilot, and a Latin American. Her current partner is a Czech writer. Wendy Smith observed in the *New York Times Book Review* that references to Ava's literary mentors (such as Nabokov and Neruda) "signal that this novel's goals are modernist: to stimulate new kinds of

thinking through new kinds of writing, to refract reality through the prism of an individual consciousness rather than mimicking it with an omniscient, third-person narration." Smith noted Ava's memories of New York as it had been and said that "her memories of vanished amenities are not just sentimental expressions of the typical complaint . . . but mirror Ava's sense of her own vital forces ebbing away. . . . Although Ava's memories come to her on the eve of death, they all celebrate life." "Maso has written another spellbinder in this current novel," declared Cherry W. Li in *Library Journal*.

The title of Maso's fourth novel, *The American Woman in the Chinese Hat,* refers to the central character, Catherine, a young American writer traveling on a grant whose female lover decides not to join her on the French Riviera. Rejected, Catherine writes and cries in cafes and engages in sexual adventures with a variety of men, including a seventeen-year-old artist's model. "This book may shock the genteel reader, but others will be enthralled," observed Jim Dwyer in *Library Journal*. "Language is the shape of her pain and her desire: she continually inscribes her life . . . , reinventing herself in the pages of her notebook," contended a *Publishers Weekly* reviewer. A critic for *Kirkus Reviews* who assessed *The American Woman in the Chinese Hat* as "[a]ll voice and no story" remarked: "You . . . wait fruitlessly for its beautiful brushstrokes and wispy episodes to come together and grab the back of your neck." Tom Sleigh in the *New York Times Book Review* maintained that "Ms. Maso seems to identify passionately with her narrator's plight, but as the novel cycles through pickups and love affairs, devolving eventually into Catherine's madness, the relationship between the wily Ms. Maso and her first-person narrator grows steadily more complex . . . forcing us to assess and reassess not only our attitudes toward Catherine but Ms. Maso's own attitude toward her narrator." Sleigh noted Maso's "sophisticated use of verbal collage" and movement "from internal monologue to fragmentary perception" and praised her "rigorous associative logic"; she added that "there is nothing slack or frenzied about Ms. Maso's writing: despite the overheated plot and setting, the depiction of Catherine's suffering is provocatively cool."

A *Publishers Weekly* reviewer called Maso's fifth book, *Aureole*, "a lesbian erotic fantasia so drunk with language games, impressionistic imagery and self-referential play as to be almost plotless." The book is composed of poetry and vignettes in mainly French settings, often on the beach, and sometimes involving food. Barbara Hoffert declared in *Library Journal* that Maso has entered "rarefied territory" in this "extended prose poem . . . with only a hint of character and plot to guide the reader." A critic for *Kirkus Reviews* expanded on this critical assessment, commenting: "Although the poetic sequences contain striking passages and vivid images, they can't convey a story in any recognizable sense, running the high risk of rapidly coming to seem pointless."

"For Maso, *Defiance* is definitely a new thing," asserted Matthew Debord in *Publishers Weekly;* he concluded that Maso's sixth novel "employs a recognizable structure and manages to live up to its billing as a thriller by suspensefully manipulating a reader's expectations until its brutal, macabre conclusion." *Defiance*'s protagonist, Bernadette O'Brien, is a former Harvard physics professor awaiting execution on death row in a Georgia prison for the murder of two of her male students. Bernadette keeps a journal which Elizabeth Bukowski described in the *Wall Street Journal* as "a dizzying swirl of memories and mathematics, black humor and hallucinatory voices." Bukowski called *Defiance* "a sharp exploration of new extremes of cynicism and darkness." Bernadette had been a child prodigy in a working-class Irish family; she had been mistreated and had witnessed her father's abuse of her mother and his infidelities. She does not see herself as a victim and rejects the social workers and feminists who urge her to plead mental illness to win a stay of execution. Faye A. Chadwell in *Library Journal* considered Maso's "unsympathetic, explicit" treatment of her central character's dark side "the novel's greatest strength."

BIOGRAPHICAL/CRITICAL SOURCES:

BOOKS

Contemporary Literary Criticism, Volume 44, Gale (Detroit), 1987, pp. 57-61.

PERIODICALS

American Book Review, August, 1994, p. 4.
Belles Lettres, winter, 1991, p. 56; summer, 1993, p. 2; summer, 1994, p. 76.
Best Sellers, September, 1986, p. 204.
Bloomsbury Review, November, 1990, p. 33.
Booklist, May 1, 1986, p. 1283; May 1, 1993, p. 1570.
Boston Review, August, 1990, p. 29.
Choice, September, 1993, p. 121.

Christian Science Monitor, July 18, 1986, p. 22.
Harper's Bazaar, August, 1987, p. 108.
Kirkus Reviews, April 15, 1986, p. 572; March 15, 1990, p. 370; March 1, 1994, pp. 237-38; August 15, 1996, p. 1179.
Lamda Book Report, May, 1994, p. 42; September, 1994, p. 17.
Library Journal, July, 1986, p. 110; May 15, 1990, p. 95; April 1, 1993, p. 132; October 1, 1993, p. 152; February 1, 1994, p. 113; November 1, 1996, p. 108; April 1, 1998, p. 124.
Los Angeles Times Book Review, July 27, 1986, p. 3; July 1, 1990, p. 2; May 16, 1993, p 6; July 31, 1994, p. 6; November 24, 1996, p. 1.
New Pages, fall, 1986, p. 18.
New Yorker, September 15, 1986, p. 120.
New York Times Book Review, July 20, 1986, p. 18; June 24, 1990, p. I20; December 12, 1993, p. 23; May 15, 1994, p. 31; August 6, 1995, p. 32; October 8, 1995, p. 40.
Parnassus, January, 1995, p. 146.
Publishers Weekly, April, 25, 1986, p. 66; March 23, 1990, p. 64; March 15, 1993, p. 67; March 28, 1994, p. 83-4; April 10, 1995, p. 60; September 30, 1996, p. 63; April 27, 1998, p. 38-9.
San Francisco Review of Books, September, 1996, p. 48.
Sojourner, December, 1986, pp. 38-39.
Tribune Books (Chicago), August 8, 1993, p. 6.
Virginia Quarterly Review, winter, 1987, p. 21.
Voice Literary Supplement, May, 1993, p. 33.
Wall Street Journal, April 24, 1998, p. W4.
Women's Review of Books, September, 1986, p. 13; January, 1991, p. 16.*

*   *   *

MATERA, Lia 1952-

PERSONAL: Born in 1952, in Canada; children: a son. *Ethnicity:* Italian American. *Education:* Hastings College of Law, graduated 1981.

ADDRESSES: Home—Santa Cruz, CA. *Agent*—c/o Simon & Schuster, 1230 Avenue of the Americas, New York, NY 10020.

CAREER: Writer of murder mysteries. *Hastings Constitutional Law Quarterly,* editor-in-chief, until c. 1981; Stanford Law School, teaching fellow, c. early 1980s.

AWARDS, HONORS: Anthony and Macavity Award nominations, 1990, for *The Good Fight;* Edgar Award nomination, 1991, for *Prior Convictions;* Edgar Award and Anthony Award nominations, 1991, for *A Radical Departure;* Anthony Award and Macavity Award nominations, 1991, for *Where Lawyers Fear to Tread;* Shamus Award for Best Short Story, 1996, for "Dead Drunk".

WRITINGS:

MYSTERY NOVELS; "WILLA JANSSON" SERIES

Where Lawyers Fear to Tread, Bantam (New York City), 1987, Ballantine (New York City), 1991.
A Radical Departure, Bantam (New York City), 1988, Ballantine (New York City), 1991.
Hidden Agenda, Bantam (New York City), 1987, Ballantine (New York City), 1992.
Prior Convictions, Simon & Schuster (New York City), 1991, Ballantine (New York City), 1991.
Last Chants, Simon & Schuster (New York City), 1996, Ballantine (New York City), 1997.
Star Witness, Simon & Schuster (New York City), 1997.
Havana Twist, Simon & Schuster (New York City), 1998.

MYSTERY NOVELS; "LAURA DIPALMA" SERIES

The Smart Money, Bantam (New York City), 1988, Ballantine (New York City), 1991.
The Good Fight, Simon & Schuster (New York City), 1990, Ballantine (New York City), 1990.
A Hard Bargain, Simon & Schuster (New York City), 1992, Ballantine (New York City), 1992.
Face Value, Simon & Schuster (New York City), 1994, Pocket Books (New York City), 1994.
Designer Crimes, Simon & Schuster (New York City), 1995, Pocket Books (New York City), 1996.

Also author of short stories contributed to anthologies, including "Counsel for the Defense," *Sisters in Crime,* Berkley Books, 1989; "Destroying Angel," *Sisters in Crime 2,* Berkley Books, 1990; "Easy Go," *Deadly Allies,* Bantam, 1992; "The River Mouth," *Mysterious West,* Harper, 1994; "Do Not Resuscitate," *Crimes of the Heart,* Berkley Books, 1995; "Performance Crime," *Women on the Case,* Delacorte, 1996; and "Dead Drunk," *Guilty as Charged,* Pocket Books, 1996.

Matera's novels have been published in Germany, Denmark, Norway, Japan, and Finland.

SIDELIGHTS: Lia Matera is a novelist who writes within the murder mystery genre, often specializing in mysteries that carry on the sociopolitical debates of the 1960s. *Where Lawyers Fear to Tread,* the first in a series featuring protagonist Willa Jannson, is set in the cloistered community of Malhousie Law School in San Francisco. Willa is a law student and a member of the school's law review. When law review editors and a professor die mysterious deaths, Willa endeavors to find the killer. One of the obstacles that Willa must work against is her distrust of the police, a sentiment instilled in Willa by her politically liberal parents. In the course of her investigation, Willa finds that she herself may be in danger. While a reviewer for *Booklist* felt that Matera's protagonist spent "too much time accusing practically every character of being the killer," the critic also praised the "smooth wit and interplay" of the characters. Kathleen Maio, who reviewed the book for *Wilson Library Bulletin,* called it "an exceptional debut."

Matera continued her series with the novels *A Radical Departure* and *Hidden Agenda. Hidden Agenda* begins with Willa, who attended a legal aid-oriented law school, working at a low-paying job. Willa's boss suddenly dies after ingesting hemlock, and subsequently Willa is mysteriously offered a high-paying job at a prestigious law firm. Forsaking her Marxist parents, Willa accepts the job but is terribly distressed when her new boss is fatally poisoned during a corporate retreat. Though a reviewer for *Publishers Weekly* felt that the novel "is angry, and devoid of humor or emotions other than hate," a *Booklist* critic praised the novel as "offbeat and very funny."

Prior Convictions finds Willa resigning from her lucrative job as a corporate lawyer in Los Angeles and moving back to San Francisco. To the delight of her hippie parents, a job as clerk for politically liberal federal court judge Michael J. Shanna awaits Willa in San Francisco. An elaborate string of events is set in motion when a friend, acting on behalf of Rita Delacourt, a 1960s political activist, asks Willa to her estranged husband and himself a lawyer, to find out what he plans to do if Rita were to seek a divorce. Willa complies, but that the phone call causes Judge Shanna to excuse himself from a securities fraud case that Phil is working on. Thus begins the spinning of a tangled web that catches Willa when Rita, who has turned state's evidence against her fellow revolutionaries and placed her husband Tom Rugieri in prison, is found dead. A critic for *Kirkus Reviews,* though noting some problems with the novel, wrote, "Matera's wit, grace with language, irreverence toward the legal system, and wry dissection of being a child of children of the Sixties make this a standout . . . work." A *Publishers Weekly* reviewer declared, "Matera once again demonstrates that she is one of today's best mystery writers."

Last Chants, Matera's 1996 effort, catches up with lawyer Jansson as she is en route to work when she encounters mythology professor and old family friend Arthur Kenna, who is brandishing a gun on the street. Arthur later explains to Willa that his assistant, Billy Seawuit, has been killed, and that someone is trying to frame him for the murder. Willa must track down the real killer to clear Arthur, but to do so she must learn about shamanism, a religion that was practiced by Billy. In a starred review for *Booklist,* Stuart Miller wrote, "Effectively blending the seemingly incongruous elements of high-tech computing and ancient mythology, Matera has produced a first-rate mystery, exhibiting her usual hallmarks of excellent plotting, solid characterizations, and brisk pacing." Marilyn Stasio, commenting in the *New York Times Book Review,* declared, "It's a treat to watch the normally level-headed Willa crawling around in the woods searching for naked gods." "Matera's skills make an accomplished, compelling mystery of material that could have been a lightweight, New Age yarn," wrote a *Publishers Weekly* reviewer.

Matera continued the Willa Jansson series with *Star Witness* (1997) and *Havanna Twist* (1998). In *Star Witness* Willa is talked into defending a man who is charged with vehicular homicide. While under hypnosis the defendant says that he is innocent of the crime as he was not in fact in his car at the time of the crime but the victim of a UFO abduction. Harriet Klausner, in a review for *Under the Covers,* wrote that "Matera constructs her usual brilliant who-done-it while subtly weaving a lot of known UFO lore into the story line."

Matera began a second series of mystery novels in 1988 with *The Smart Money* and *The Good Fight,* which feature wealthy attorney Laura DiPalma as an amateur sleuth. The third novel in the series, *A Hard Bargain* finds Laura retired from her law career and living in northern California with Hal, her cousin and lover. Laura and Hal are visited by Laura's former law partner, Sandy Arkelett, who is seeking help in connection with a suicide. The chronically depressed Karen Clausen McGuinn has killed herself, but her husband Ted has left a loaded gun with her each day, and Sandy smells a rat. Ted, an African-American paramedic, is disliked by his in-laws, and he seems to

be the likely suspect. Matera probes the personalities of the characters as she drives the story toward a grim ending in a novel that was praised by critics.

The trials and tribulations of Laura DiPalma are continued by Matera in *Face Value.* Laura has returned to the practice of law and moved back to San Francisco to start her own practice. Her first client, Margaret Lenin, wants to sue her spiritual guru, Brother Mike Hover, because tapes made by Brother Mike at Lenin's sex-therapy sessions have been popping up in adult video stores. Lenin eventually drops the case, and Laura takes on another client: Brother Mike himself, who is being sued by Arabella de Janeiro, an exotic dancer who has romantic ties to Margaret. The mystery deepens when Laura responds to a late-night phone call from Margaret and finds six dead strippers at Arabella's workplace, The Back Door. A *Kirkus Reviews* critic commented, "Matera's look at the dehumanizing power of sexual manipulation . . . is so unblinking that you'll look right past the story's coincidences in your hurry to get to the hair-raising finale."

Designer Crimes pits Laura DiPalma against Connie Gold, a district attorney and Laura's archenemy. The book opens with a flash-forward prologue describing Laura's arrest, and then the first chapter reverts back in time to a meeting between Laura and another lawyer, Jocelyn Kinsley. Laura is seeking to enlist Jocelyn to file a slander suit against a former employer when Kinsley is mowed down by a masked man. Before Kinsley dies, she utters the words "designer crimes," and Laura must discover the meaning behind the words to save her own skin. Pat Dowell of the *Washington Post Book World* called *Designer Crimes* a "sizzling" novel "clenched in a no-holds-barred struggle of murderous dimensions."

BIOGRAPHICAL/CRITICAL SOURCES:

PERIODICALS

Armchair Detective, summer, 1991, p. 357; winter, 1992, p. 39.

Booklist, August, 1997, p. 1721; November 15, 1988, p. 543; January 1, 1990, p. 894; March 15, 1991, p. 1457; April 15, 1992, p. 1507; February 15, 1994, p. 1064; June 1, 1995, pp. 1735, 1741; April 15, 1996, p. 1423; April 15, 1997, p. 1410; April 15, 1998.

Chicago Tribune, June 15, 1997.

Dallas Morning News, May 29, 1998.

Entertainment Weekly, June 21, 1996, p. 59.

Houston Chronicle, June 7, 1998.

Kirkus Reviews, November 15, 1989, p. 1637; January 15, 1991, p. 79; March 15, 1992, p. 358; December 1, 1993, p. 1491; April 15, 1995, p. 512; May 1, 1996, p. 645.

Library Journal, January, 1995, p. 176; April 1, 1995, p. 129; April 1, 1996, p. 148; June 1, 1996, p. 157.

New York Times Book Review, January 21, 1990, p. 35; March 24, 1991, p. 37; June 9, 1991, p. 22; May 24, 1992, p. 25; February 20, 1994, p. 18; June 18, 1995, p. 31; June 23, 1996, p. 28; June 29, 1997; May 17, 1998.

Pittsburgh Post-Gazette, May 31, 1998.

Publishers Weekly, July 3, 1987, p. 58; October 28, 1988, p. 74; November 17, 1989, p. 44; February 1, 1991, p. 68; April 19, 1991, p. 64; March 30, 1992, p. 92; April 6, 1992, p. 59; December 20, 1993, p. 53-54; April 10, 1995, p. 56; April 15, 1996, p. 53; April 14, 1997, p. 59; April 6, 1998.

Rapport, no. 2, 1994, p. 21.

San Francisco Chronicle, July 7, 1997; April 30, 1998.

San Francisco Examiner, July 1, 1997.

San Hose Mercury News, June 15, 1997.

St. Petersburg Times, June 14, 1998.

Tribune Books (Chicago), May 3, 1992, p. 6; February 6, 1994, p. 6; June 4, 1995, p. 6.

Wall Street Journal, April 10, 1991, p. A20.

Washington Post Book World, April 21, 1991, p. 10; June 18, 1995, p. 11; June 22, 1997.

Wilson Library Bulletin, October, 1987, p. 101; February, 1989, p. 88-89.

Women's Review of Books, July, 1991, p. 32.

OTHER

Feminist Mystery Corner, http://www.feminist.org/arts/mys_revstar.html (February 5, 1998).

Lia Matera's Web Site, http://www.scruz.net/~lmatera/LiaMatera.html (February 5, 1999).

Under the Covers, http://www.silcom.com/~manatee/matera_star.html (May 8, 1997).*

*   *   *

MATSON, Cathy

PERSONAL: Female. *Education:* Roosevelt University, B.A. (with highest honors), 1977; Columbia University, M.A., 1979, M.Phil., 1981, Ph.D. (with distinction), 1985.

ADDRESSES: Office—Department of History, University of Delaware, Newark, DE 19716.

CAREER: United Automotive, Aerospace, and Agricultural Implement Workers of America, Chicago, IL, instructor in Spanish, 1974-77; Cambridge University, Cambridge, England, tutor in U.S. history, 1981; Columbia University, New York City, instructor in history, 1982; State University of New York, Center for Labor Studies, adjunct teacher of history and labor studies, 1982-84; University of Tennessee, Knoxville, assistant professor of history, 1985-90; University of Delaware, Newark, associate professor of history, 1990—. Lecturer at colleges and universities, including Trinity College, Hartford, CT, 1985, Johns Hopkins University, 1994, and University of Pennsylvania, 1998; public speaker.

WRITINGS:

(Contributor) Conrad Wright and William Pencak, editors, *New York and the Rise of American Capitalism,* University Press of Virginia (Charlottesville, VA), 1988.

(With Peter Onuf) *A Union of Interests: Politics and Economy in the Revolutionary Era,* University Press of Kansas (Lawrence, KS), 1990.

(Contributor) Stephen L. Schechter and Richard B. Bernstein, editors, *New York and the Union: Contributions to the American Constitutional Experience,* New York State Library (Albany, NY), 1990.

(Contributor) Pencak and Paul A. Gilje, editors, *New York in the Age of the Constitution,* University Press of Virginia, 1992.

Merchants and Empire: Trading in Colonial New York, Johns Hopkins University Press (Baltimore, MD), 1997.

(Contributor) Gilje, editor, *Wages of Independence: Capitalism in the Early American Republic,* Madison House (Madison, WI), 1997.

Contributor of articles and reviews to academic journals, including *American Quarterly, William and Mary Quarterly,* and *Journal of the Early Republic.*

*   *   *

McCORMICK, Charles H(oward) 1932-

PERSONAL: Born June 2, 1932, in Akron, OH; son of Durward (a brake operator) and Mary Virginia

(McCormick) McMillin; adopted son of C. E. (a pharmacist) and Ruth (Loew) McCormick; married Margie Lee Kepler (a librarian), November 4, 1962. *Education:* Kent State University, B.A. (cum laude), 1959; Yale University, M.A., 1960; American University, Ph.D., 1971. *Politics:* Independent. *Religion:* Atheist. *Avocational interests:* Working as a museum volunteer, building model ships, photography, computers, classical music.

ADDRESSES: Home—9906 Walker House Rd., No. 6, Gaithersburg, MD 20886-0518. *E-mail*—chmc cor.grd.hist@aya.yale.edu.

CAREER: National Aeronautic and Space Administration, Houston, TX, contract assistant and specialist, 1961-63; U.S. National Park Service, Washington, DC, historian, 1964-68; Fairmont State College, Fairmont, WV, began as assistant professor, became professor of history, 1970-95. *Military service:* U.S. Air Force, 1952-55.

MEMBER: American Historical Association, Organization of American Historians, Phi Alpha Theta, Pi Gamma Mu.

AWARDS, HONORS: Woodrow Wilson fellow, 1960.

WRITINGS:

Leisler's Rebellion, 1689-1691, Garland Publishing (New York City), 1989.
This Nest of Vipers: McCarthyism and Higher Education in the Mundel Affair, 1951-1952, University of Illinois Press (Champaign, IL), 1989.
Seeing Reds: Federal Surveillance of Radicals in the Pittsburgh Mill District, 1917-1921, University of Pittsburgh Press (Pittsburgh, PA), 1998.

Contributor of articles and reviews to history journals, including *West Virginia History.*

WORK IN PROGRESS: Research on "the less visible aspects of anti-left zealotry in America between the world wars."

*   *   *

McMASTER, H. R. 1962-

PERSONAL: Born July 24, 1962, in Philadelphia, PA; son of Herbert and Marie McMaster; married, July 27, 1985; children: Katharine, Colleen, Caragh. *Ethnicity:* "Caucasian." *Education:* United States Military Academy, B.S., 1984; University of North Carolina, Ph.D., 1996. *Religion:* Roman Catholic.

ADDRESSES: Home—4025 Hidden Springs Court, Fort Irwin, CA 92310. *Agent*—c/o HarperCollins, 1000 Keystone Industrial Park, Scranton, PA 18512. *E-mail*—hrmcm@aol.com.

CAREER: U.S. Army, 1984—, served in the Gulf War, attained rank of lieutenat colonel. Has taught history at West Point Military Academy.

AWARDS, HONORS: Gil Robb Wilson Arts and Letters Award; Best History Book Award, New York Military Affairs Symposium.

WRITINGS:

Dereliction of Duty: Lyndon Johnson, Robert McNamara, the Joint Chiefs of Staff, and the Lies that Led to Vietnam, HarperCollins (New York City), 1997.

WORK IN PROGRESS: A Greater Power: Eagle Troop, 2nd U.S. Calvary in Desert Storm.

SIDELIGHTS: Lieutenant colonel H. R. McMaster has had a distinctive career in the U.S. Army, serving in the Gulf War during the early 1990s. He has also taught history at West Point Military Academy. His first book, *Dereliction of Duty: Lyndon Johnson, Robert McNamara, the Joint Chiefs of Staff, and the Lies that Led to Vietnam,* saw print in 1997.

As the subtitle explains, *Dereliction of Duty* analyzes the causes of the United States' failure to win the Vietnam War. McMaster asserts in his book that the war effort was doomed from the start because U.S. President Lyndon B. Johnson, who served during most of the war era, was more concerned with implementing the domestic policy known as the War on Poverty than with properly conducting a foreign conflict. According to McMaster, rather than asking his Joint Chiefs for accurate military advice, Johnson instead persuaded them to confirm decisions he had already made and rewarded them by settling power struggles within their respective branches of the military.

Also receiving criticism in *Dereliction of Duty* are then-Secretary of State Dean Rusk and advisors William and McGeorge Bundy. McMaster also claims, in the words of Arnold R. Isaacs in the *Washington Post Book World*, that President Johnson "and his aides blundered ahead step by step, hoping that each new action would convince the Vietnamese Communists to give up and thus make the next step unnecessary." *Dereliction of Duty* is supplemented by illustrations.

Critics responded positively to McMaster's book. Though Isaacs expressed some difficulties with laying so much of the blame upon President Johnson because of "the complete absence of evidence that the Joint Chiefs had any useful advice on how to win the war in Vietnam, even if anyone had been listening," he hastened to add that this "should not detract from the value of McMaster's research." A *Kirkus Reviews* critic noted that McMaster's arguments are similar to those put forth by David Halberstam in his 1972 book, *The Best and the Brightest,* but cited the availability of more recently released official transcripts in allowing McMaster to give "more attention to" the part played by the Joint Chiefs of Staff. The *Kirkus Reviews* critic finished by calling McMaster's effort "a relentless, stinging indictment of the usual Johnson administration Vietnam War suspects." A *Publishers Weekly* reviewer also applauded McMaster's work, hailing *Dereliction of Duty* as a "seminal analysis" that "demonstrates in particular that an officer's moral courage is as important as his willingness to face physical risk." Isaacs went on to praise the volume as "well written and full of enlightening new details," concluding that it "adds significantly to the historical record of a great national failure—a failure that clearly occurred on both sides of the Potomac [i.e., White House and Pentagon] and that was all the more tragic because, as is now mercilessly clear, it was so unnecessary."

BIOGRAPHICAL/CRITICAL SOURCES:

PERIODICALS

America, January 17, 1998, pp. 22-24.
Booklist, April 15, 1997, p. 1363.
Foreign Affairs, July, 1997, p. 153.
Insight on the News, June 9, 1997, pp. 14-15.
Kirkus Reviews, April 1, 1997, p. 529.
Los Angeles Times Book Review, May 11, 1997, p. 6.
Marine Corp Gazette, August, 1997, p. 73.
New York Times Book Review, July 20, 1997, p. 31.
Parameters, autumn, 1997, pp. 162-166.
Publishers Weekly, April 21, 1997, p. 56.
Washington Post Book World, May 25, 1997, p. 4.
Wilson Quarterly, summer, 1997, p. 100.

McNEIL, Linda L. 1946-

PERSONAL: Born June 9, 1946, in Fort Collins, CO; daughter of James H. (a federal government administrator) and Virginia L. (a state employee; maiden name, Simmons) Bright; married LeRoy C. McNeil, 1975 (divorced, c. 1982). *Education:* University of Colorado at Boulder, B.S., 1969. *Avocational interests:* Scuba diving, hiking, biking, travel, reading.

ADDRESSES: Home—Golden, CO. *Office*—P.O. Box 280234, Lakewood, CO 80228. *E-mail*—linmcneil@aol.com.

CAREER: Porter Memorial Hospital, Denver, CO, staff physical therapist, 1969-71; legal secretary, bookkeeper, and real estate salesperson, 1971-72; Westland Manor Nursing Home, Lakewood, CO, staff physical therapist, 1972-74; Rehab Therapy, Inc., Arvada, CO, owner and president, 1974-87; InSpeech, Inc., Arvada, CO, manager, 1987-89; Choices and Changes Unlimited, Golden, CO, speaker, trainer, and writer, 1989—. Western Home Health, owner and president, 1981-85; Best Home Health Care, owner and president, 1981-85.

MEMBER: National Speakers Association, National Association of Female Executives, Colorado Speakers Association.

WRITINGS:

Seven Keys to Changing Any Attitude or Circumstance in Your Life, privately printed, 1997.
Seven Keys to Changing Your Life, Health, and Wealth, privately printed, 1998.

Contributor to periodicals, including *Physical Therapy Products* and *Advance for Directors in Rehabilitation.* Past member of editorial board, *Physical Therapy Today.*

SIDELIGHTS: Linda L. McNeil told *CA:* "My primary motivation for writing is my desire to help one million people do their own choices and changes with the same life-transforming results I have. My life is a miracle, and I wish to share hope and inspiration. I have done so as a professional speaker for more than ten years.

"What motivates my work is my experience as professional speaker and my personal life changes, which include losing one-third of my body weight and keeping it off for eighteen years, overcoming alcoholism, dangerously high blood pressure, two unhappy marriages, and near-bankruptcy. I listen to others who share the same problems and those who have changed for real, for good.

"My writing process is simple and straightforward. The first time I just sat down at the computer and created the acronym 'CHANGES.' The major principles came to me in about ninety minutes. Then I added my own life experiences and those of others I knew who had overcome much. The book was completed in about three months. The second book was a result and outgrowth of the first, based on feedback and workshops. It was also clear that a workbook portion was needed, and I did not want to create and sell an empty 'journal.' So the second book encourages the reader to be inspired, motivated, then answer a number of questions at the end of each of the seven keys.

"What inspired me to write was a number of course and seminar participants who asked me when I was going to write a book and go beyond the limited scope of physical therapy. These are individuals whose opinions I value very much, and who know I live my life fully in the joyful 'present moment' experience.

"Change fascinates me because there is so much happening so fast. We can all be overwhelmed by lightning-fast techno-changes, business down-up-right-sizing, et cetera. Many people know that their problem is about attitudes, especially when they have personal habits which they know must be changed (by choice), but they don't know how to choose to change. I have tried to give them very basic, simple (not easy, however) tools to use to deal with change."

*   *   *

MEADE, Glenn

PERSONAL: Born in Ireland.

ADDRESSES: Agent—c/o St. Martin's Press, 175 Fifth Ave., New York, NY 10010.

CAREER: Novelist.

WRITINGS:

NOVELS

Snow Wolf, St. Martin's Press (New York City), 1996.
Brandenburg, St. Martin's Press (New York City), 1997.

Also the author of novels published in Ireland.

SIDELIGHTS: Glenn Meade had novels published in his native Ireland before his 1996 espionage thriller, *Snow Wolf,* became available to American audiences. His next book in the same genre was *Brandenburg,* which saw print the following year. *Snow Wolf* and *Brandenburg* have been compared by critics with books from such masters of espionage fiction as Robert Ludlum and Frederick Forsyth.

Snow Wolf is based on the fictional speculation that Soviet dictator Josef Stalin might have been assassinated by a spy rather than dying from a cerebral hemorrhage in 1953. The novel has a present-day framework, in which a journalist from the *Washington Post* named William Massey tries to find out the truth behind his father Jake's death in Moscow over forty years before. The young Massey eventually finds Anna Khorev, a survivor of the spy operation Snow Wolf, which Jake was involved with when he died.

Khorev then narrates the main story, set in 1953. She relates that she herself had escaped from a Soviet gulag when she was recruited by the CIA to guide the senior Massey and Alex Slanski to a place where they might make the attempt on Stalin. Many actual historical figures are featured in Khorev's tale, including U.S. Presidents Harry S. Truman and Dwight D. Eisenhower; another important (though fictional) character in the novel is KGB agent Yuri Lukin, who attempts to foil the assassination plot.

Critics gave predominantly favorable responses to *Snow Wolf.* Though Gilbert Taylor in *Booklist* felt that "credulity and suspense have worn thin" by the novel's end, Michele Leber in the *Library Journal* pronounced the book "great summer reading." A *Publishers Weekly* critic affirmed that although "the Cold War may be on ice, . . . Meade shows that it can still freeze readers' attention and chill their blood."

Brandenburg takes as its premise the survival of an illegitimate son of Nazi leader Adolf Hitler. This son, named Karl Schmeltz, is the nucleus of a group of neo-Nazis who first hide out in South America, then plot to take over Germany. Opposing them is a British army officer named Joseph Volkmann, who has found out about their plot through a journalist named Erica Kranz, whose cousin was murdered after accidentally overhearing one of the neo-Nazi group's meetings. Volkmann must also enlist the help of Wolfgang Lusch, described by a *Kirkus Reviews* critic as "a patriotic terrorist," to try to wrest a nuclear missile from where the group has placed it in an abandoned monastery.

Brandenburg received positive remarks from reviewers as well. Though a *Publishers Weekly* reviewer mentioned some pacing problems, the critic also declared that the author "spins out this involving yarn with skill and clarity." In addition, the critic cited "a final confrontation worth its outstanding premise." Taylor, in another *Booklist* piece, labeled *Brandenburg* "fast, sly, and slick" and went on to assert that "this thriller delivers the goods—tension, action, plot twists—until the smoke clears on the last page." A *Kirkus Reviews* critic summed up the novel as "another literate and suspenseful thriller from an estimable storyteller who proves that beginners luck had nothing to do with his impressive debut."

BIOGRAPHICAL/CRITICAL SOURCES:

PERIODICALS

Booklist, June 1, 1996, pp. 1679-1680, 1686; May 1, 1997, p. 1482.
Kirkus Reviews, April 1, 1996, p. 477; April 1, 1997, p. 492.
Kliatt, November, 1996, p. 45.
Library Journal, May 1, 1996, p. 132; October 1, 1996, p. 47; November, 1996, p. 106.
Publishers Weekly, April 8, 1996, p. 53; March 31, 1997, p. 72; April 28, 1997, p. 47.
Washington Post Book World, August 4, 1996, p. 8.*

*   *   *

MERRILL, Helen Abbot 1864-1949

PERSONAL: Born March 30, 1864, in Orange, NJ; died May 1, 1949, in Wellesley, MA; daughter of George Dodge (in business and an inventor) and

Emily Abbot Merrill. *Education:* Wellesley College, B.A., 1886; attended University of Chicago, 1896-97; attended University of Goettingen, 1901-03; Yale University, Ph.D., 1903.

CAREER: Classical School for Girls, New York City, instructor in Latin, history, and mathematics, 1886-89; Dutch Reformed Church, New Brunswick, NJ, teacher, 1889-91; Walnut Lane School, Philadelphia, PA, teacher of Latin and mathematics, 1891-93; Wellesley College, Wellesley, MA, instructor of mathematics, 1893-1901, associate professor, 1902-15, professor, 1915-32, chair of mathematics department, 1916-32, named Lewis Atterbury Stimson professor, named professor emerita, 1932.

MEMBER: Mathematical Association of America (board of trustees, 1917-19, vice president, 1920), American Association for the Advancement of Science, American Association of University Women, American Mathematical Society, National Historical Society (member of executive committee), Deutsche Mathematiker Vereinigung, New York Wellesley Club (first president), Phi Beta Kappa, Sigma Xi.

WRITINGS:

(With Clara E. Smith) *Selected Topics in College Algebra,* Norwood Press (Norwood, MA), 1914.
(With Smith) *A First Course in Higher Algebra,* Macmillan (New York City), 1917.
Mathematical Excursions: Side Trips along Paths Not Generally Traveled in Elementary Courses in Mathematics, Norwood Press (Norwood, MA), 1933.

Contributor to journals and periodicals, including *Transactions of the American Mathematical Society* and *Mathematics Teacher.* Served as editor of Mathematical Society of America's newsletter.

SIDELIGHTS: Helen Abbot Merrill took up mathematics as a vocation and avocation at a time when women were rarely visible in the field. She was most active as an instructor, co-writing textbooks as well as publishing articles on pedagogy. Merrill also wrote a "mathematical amusement" book, a populist work for young readers titled *Mathematical Excursions.* Even in her spare time she was devoted to broader aspects of her profession, joining many mathematical, academic, and scientific organizations, and serving as vice president of both the Mathemati-

the

cal Association of America and the American Mathematical Society.

Merrill was born March 30, 1864, in Orange, New Jersey, near Thomas Edison's facilities at Llewellyn Park. Her family traced its ancestry back to 1633, when Nathaniel Merrill settled in Massachusetts. Her father, George Dodge Merrill, had many business concerns and was also an inventor. Her siblings included a sister, Emily, and two brothers, Robert and William, who both grew up to become Presbyterian ministers.

Merrill began high school in 1876 at Newburyport, and entered Wellesley College six years later in one of the first graduating classes in the history of the college. Originally her major was classical languages, an interest she would keep up throughout her life. However, as a freshman she committed to mathematics. At that time Wellesley was still considered something of an experiment, but Merrill responded to the close-knit atmosphere and wrote a history of her graduating class as a commemorative booklet.

Merrill graduated with a B.A. after four years and began her career as a teacher. Working at the Classical School for Girls in New York, Merrill was allotted courses in Latin and history as well as mathematics. She was assigned to a variety of students, including "mill girls" from New Brunswick, New Jersey, and immigrant children in the Germantown section of Philadelphia.

In 1893 Merrill was asked to return to Wellesley, this time as an instructor, in exchange for a stipend and housing. Helen Shafer, who had hired Merrill, allowed her time off intermittently for graduate studies at the universities of Chicago, Goettingen, and eventually Yale. Merrill earned a Ph.D. from Yale in 1903 and her thesis on "Sturmian" differential equations was published the same year. Merrill moved up from instructor to associate professor status at Wellesley. The college benefitted directly from Merrill's excursions, as she introduced courses in functions and descriptive geometry for her undergraduate students based on her graduate work.

Merrill dedicated herself to providing a "flowery path" for her young charges to follow into the normally thorny subject of mathematics. She did not lower her standards for undergraduates; in fact, the courses Merrill taught were often in subjects generally offered only at the graduate level. However, she

was quick to offer tailored assistance to any young woman she considered a diamond in the rough.

After being promoted to full professor in 1916, Merrill was appointed head of the mathematics department the next year. She was particularly active as associate editor of the Mathematical Association of America's (MAA) monthly newsletter, member of the executive council, and later vice president in 1920. With fellow MAA member Clara E. Smith, who would also serve as vice president of the group, Merrill authored two textbooks. Merrill remained at Wellesley until her retirement, when she was named a Lewis Atterbury Stimson professor.

Merrill was also an amateur historian, fulfilling archival duties at Wellesley. She was elected as an executive committee member of the National Historical Society. Her interest in music and language led her to become a student again, taking summer courses at the University of California at Berkeley. She also traveled across Europe and the Americas. Merrill retired as professor emerita in 1932, and died at her home in Wellesley on May 1, 1949.

BIOGRAPHICAL/CRITICAL SOURCES:

BOOKS

A Century of Mathematics in America, Volume 2, edited by Peter Duren, American Mathematical Society (Providence, RI), 1989.
National Cyclopedia of American Biography, Volume 42, reprint, University Microfilms (Ann Arbor, MI), 1967-71.
Women of Mathematics, edited by Louise S. Grinstein and Paul J. Campbell, Greenwood Press (Westport, CT), 1987.
Women in the Scientific Search: An American Bio-bibliography, 1724-1979, The Scarecrow Press (Metuchen, NJ), 1985.

PERIODICALS

New York Times, May 3, 1949, p. 25.
Yale University Obituary Record, July 1, 1949, p. 142.

OTHER

Biographies of Women Mathematicians, http://www.scottlan.edu/lriddle/women/chronol.htm (December, 1998).*

MESIBOV, Gary B. 1945-

PERSONAL: Born June 28, 1945, in Rockville Centre, NY; son of Harold and Rhoda (Meister) Mesibov; married, wife's name Laurie (an attorney and professor), August 13, 1967; children: Brian, Todd. *Education:* Attended Rutgers University, 1963-64; Stanford University, A.B., 1967; University of Michigan, M.A., 1968; Brandeis University, Ph.D., 1974. *Religion:* Society of Friends (Quakers). *Avocational interests:* Running.

ADDRESSES: Home—710A Greenwood Rd., Chapel Hill, NC 27514-5923. *Office*—Division TEACCH, CB 7180, Medical School Wing E, University of North Carolina at Chapel Hill, Chapel Hill, NC 27599-7180; fax 919-966-4127. *E-mail*—Gary_mesibov@unc.edu.

CAREER: University of Guam, Mangilao, began as instructor, became assistant professor of psychology, 1968-71, department head, 1969-71; University of North Carolina at Chapel Hill, postdoctoral fellow in clinical child psychology, 1974-75, psychologist in Division for Disorders of Development and Learning, 1975-79, assistant professor, 1975-81, associate professor, 1981-87, professor of psychology, 1987—, coordinator of adolescent and adult services for Division TEACCH, 1979-82, associate director of the division, 1983-87, codirector, 1988-92, director, 1992—. Lecturer at colleges and universities. State of North Carolina, head of Advisory Committee to Assess Community-Based Residential Needs of Autistic People, 1979-80; D. T. Watson Educational Services Professional Advisory Board, member, 1995—. Residential Services, Inc. (administrators of group homes), head of programming committee, 1975-77, president, 1980-81, head of adult homes committee, 1983—; Murdoch Center, member of human rights committee, 1980-81; Orange Enterprises, Inc. (administrators of sheltered workshops), member, 1982-87.

MEMBER: American Psychological Association (fellow), Society of Clinical Psychology, Society of Pediatric Psychology (member of executive committee, 1979-84; president, 1982), Society of Clinical Child Psychology, Society of Mental Retardation, Society of Child and Youth Services, American Association on Mental Deficiency, Association for Children and Adults with Learning Disabilities, National Society for Children and Adults with Autism (co-chairperson of professional advisory board, 1991-92), Southeastern Psychological Association, North Carolina Psychological Association, North Carolina Society for Children and Adults with Autism (member of executive board, 1979—).

AWARDS, HONORS: Certificate of Appreciation, Orange County Association for Retarded Citizens, 1982; Distinguished Professional Contribution Award, Society for Pediatric Psychology, 1989; Mesibov Award, Residential Services, Inc., 1990; Belgium's Opleidingscentrum International Award, 1994; Mary G. Clarke Award, North Carolina Psychological Association, 1994; MAPP Award, More Able Autistic People (international organization), 1995; Distinguished Professional Contributions Award, American Psychological Association, 1997; grants from North Carolina Developmental Disabilities Council, North Carolina Division of Vocational Rehabilitation Services, National Institute of Mental Health, North Carolina Department of Human Resources, U.S. Department of Education, National Society for Children and Adults with Autism, and U.S. Department of Housing and Urban Development.

WRITINGS:

(With L. W. Adams and L. G. Klinger) *Autism: Understanding the Disorder,* Plenum (New York City), 1998.

Contributor to scholarly books. Contributor of about sixty articles and reviews to professional journals. *Journal of Pediatric Psychology,* associate editor, 1976-82, member of editorial board, 1982—; *Journal of Autism and Developmental Disorders,* associate editor, 1983—, acting editor, 1988-89; member of editorial board, *Journal of Clinical Child Psychology,* 1986—, and *Journal of Cognitive Rehabilitation,* 1989—.

EDITOR WITH E. SCHOPLER, AND CONTRIBUTOR

Autism in Adolescents and Adults, Plenum, 1983.
The Effects of Autism on the Family, Plenum, 1984.
Communication Problems in Autism, Plenum, 1985.
Social Behavior in Autism, Plenum, 1986.
Neurobiological Issues in Autism, Plenum, 1987.
Diagnosis and Assessment in Autism, Plenum, 1988.
High-Functioning Individuals with Autism, Plenum, 1992.
Behavioral Issues in Autism, Plenum, 1994.
Learning and Cognition in Autism, Plenum, 1995.
Asperger Syndrome or High Functioning Autism?, Plenum, 1998.

MESSIER, Claire 1956-
(Marie Bearanger)

PERSONAL: Born February 7, 1956, in Marquette, MI; daughter of Donald Eugene and Patricia Charlotte (Johnson) Messier; divorced. *Education:* Milwaukee Stratton Business College, B.B.M. *Avocational interests:* Scuba diving and snorkeling.

ADDRESSES: Home—1128 South 74th St., West Allis, WI 53214. *Office*—1555 North Rivercenter Dr., Suite 201, Milwaukee, WI 53212. *E-mail*—claire@gspub.com.

CAREER: Gareth Stevens, Inc., Milwaukee, WI, marketing associate, 1987—. Horizon Travel, travel consultant, 1988—.

WRITINGS:

AS MARIE BEARANGER; "COLORS OF THE SEA" SERIES; WRITTEN WITH ERIC ETHAN; PHOTOS BY W. GREGORY BROWN

Coral Reef Builders, Gareth Stephens (Milwaukee), 1997.
Coral Reef Feeders, Gareth Stephens (Milwaukee), 1997.
Coral Reef Hunters, Gareth Stephens (Milwaukee), 1997.
Coral Reef Partners, Gareth Stephens (Milwaukee), 1997.
Coral Reef Survival, Gareth Stephens (Milwaukee), 1997.

WORK IN PROGRESS: An autobiographical novel.

SIDELIGHTS: Claire Messier commented: "I chose to coauthor [the *Colors of the Sea*] children's series for a number of reasons. First, I am an avid scuba diver and snorkeler and love the water. We had an opportunity to take an adult 'coffee book' and rework it into five volumes for children. It was a fun project for me, and I was not paid any royalty or fee.

"I have no other plans for a children's book or series in my immediate future. However, I have been working on an autobiographical novel for a number of years and hope to have it completed soon.

"I chose the pseudonym Marie Bearanger because my border collie's name is Bearanger and my middle name is Marie."*

MIKSZATH, Kalman 1847-1910
(Kakay Aranyos, Scarron, pseudonyms)

PERSONAL: Born January 1, 1847, in Szklabonya, Hungary; died May 28, 1910, in Budapest, Hungary; married Ilona Mauks, 1873 (divorced, c. 1874; remarried, c. 1882). *Education:* Attended the University of Budapest, studied law.

CAREER: Writer. Nograd County, Hungary, worked as a jurist for the chief administrative officer, c. late 1860s; worked as a journalist and apprentice lawyer, c. early 1870s.

WRITINGS:

NOVELS

Nemzetes uraimek: Macsik, a nagyerejue, 1884, originally published in serial form under the title *Macsik, a nagyerejue,* 1882 and 1883.
Szent Peter esernyoeje, published in the journal *Uj Idoek,* 1895, English translation by B. W. Worswick, with an introduction by R. Nisbet Bain, published as *St. Peter's Umbrella,* Harper (New York City), 1900.
Beszterce ostroma: Egy kueloenc ember toertenete, 1896, English translation by Dick Sturgess published as *The Siege of Beszterce,* Corvina (Budapest, Hungary), 1982.
Prakovszky, a siket kovacs, 1897; English translation published as *Prakovszky, the Deaf Blacksmith,* 1962.
Uj Zrinyiasz: Tarsadalmi es politikai szatirikus rajz, 1898.
Kueloenoes hazassag, 2 volumes, 1901; English translation published as *A Strange Marriage,* Corvina, 1964.
A szelistyei asszonyok, 1901.
Akli Miklos cs. kir. udv. mulattato, 1903.
A ven gazember, 1906.
Jokai Mor elete es kora, 2 volumes, 1907.
A Noszty fiu esete Toth Marival, 3 volumes, 1908.
Ket Valasztas Magyarorszagon, 1910.
A fekete varos, 3 volumes, 1911.

SHORT STORY COLLECTIONS

Elbeszelesek, 2 volumes, 1874.
A tot atyafiak, 1881.
A jo palocok, 1882, English translation published as *The Good People of Palocz,* with an introduction by Clifton Bingham, Dean (London), 1893.

OTHER

Also wrote under the pseudonyms Kakay Aranyos and Scarron; contributor of articles and editorials to a daily newspaper in Szged, Hungary, c. 1878.

SIDELIGHTS: Kalman Mikszath was a prominent Hungarian short story writer, novelist, and political commentator during the late nineteenth and early twentieth centuries. Described by critics as "the Hungarian Mark Twain," he is best known for lighthearted, anecdotal narratives satirizing the social and political institutions of his day. Mikszath's works earned him wide popular and critical acclaim during his lifetime and posthumous recognition as the most important Hungarian fiction writer of the period. In his *Kalman Mikszath,* Steven C. Scheer declared: "Mikszath's place in the world of literature is more important than either the immediate influences upon him or his own immediate influence upon his followers. In his work there is a strange mixture of eighteenth-century self-consciousness and an early twentieth-century modernity. . . . His vision of life combined with his particular embodiment of that vision is still awaiting a potential influence in a hopefully more open and more tolerant future. His works are there, and they speak a language of their own, and that language happens to be one of the major languages in the world of literature."

Mikszath was born in 1847 in the village of Szklabonya in Nograd County, near the Czechoslovakian border of Hungary. Although his family was of modest means—his father worked as an innkeeper and, occasionally, as a butcher—it counted among its ancestors members of the Lutheran landed gentry. According to biographers, Mikszath was a sickly child whose father hired local storytellers to entertain him whenever he was confined to bed; in this way, he gained an extensive knowledge of regional folklore. After completing his secondary education at schools in Rimaszombat and Selmecbanya, Mikszath studied law at the University of Budapest. While still at the university, he published his first essays, and began to seriously consider becoming a writer. Mikszath left the university without taking his examinations; thereafter he worked for two years as a jurist for the chief administrative officer of Nograd County, then as a journalist and apprentice lawyer, while writing fiction in his spare time. In 1873 he married Ilona Mauks, the daughter of his former employer, despite her father's objection that Mikszath would not be able to support a wife on a writer's income. Mikszath indeed earned very little at this time, and his first book of short stories, whose publication he financed himself in 1874, proved a failure. A year later his wife became ill and returned to her father's home to convalesce; Mikszath, unwilling to earn his living by means other than writing, yet wishing to spare his wife further hardship, persuaded her to divorce him.

Beginning in 1878 Mikszath began to gain recognition for his articles and editorials written for a daily paper in Szged. Returning to Budapest, he worked first as an assistant editor of *Orszag-Vilag,* then as editor and staff writer with *Pesti-Hirlap,* and soon developed a following for his witty, satirical writings about Parliamentary activities and other political matters. While exposing what he considered to be examples of corruption and injustice, Mikszath always tempered his indictments with humor and an apparent willingness to forgive the transgressions described. Gradually, he became one of the most popular and respected political commentators in Hungary. During this time Mikszath, who had formerly sympathized with the progressive Independence Party, switched his allegiance to the more conservative Liberal Party, becoming good friends with its leader, Kalman Tisza. His success as a journalist was paralleled by equal good fortune in his literary endeavors. Two collections of his short stories, *A tot atyafiak* and *A jo palocok,* published in 1881 and 1882, were warmly received by both critics and the public. Confident in his newfound fame and financial solvency, he began to court his former wife, eventually persuading her to marry him again.

Throughout the remainder of his career Mikszath wrote prolifically, with continued success. He was appointed to several prestigious literary societies and received many other honors, including acceptance into the Hungarian Academy. His work as a journalist brought him considerable political power as well as popular acclaim, and in 1892 he was elected Parliamentary representative of Fogaras, an area in southeastern Transylvania. He continued to serve as a member of Parliament, and to write, for the rest of his life. In 1908, the government changed the name of his birthplace to Mikszathfalva in his honor, and presented him with a gift of an estate that had belonged to his ancestors. He died in 1910, several days after festivities were held to celebrate his fortieth year as a professional writer.

Commentators have divided Mikszath's career as a fiction writer into three periods: a romantic period, characterized by idyllic representations of childhood, romantic love, and fabulistic evocations of peasant life; an ironic period, characterized by cynical yet good-humored portrayals of humanity's baser instincts; ad a realistic period, characterized by increasingly pessimistic depictions of social and political life. The works of Mikszath's first period include numerous children's stories; highly praised for their affectionate portrayals of children, many of these have become classics of Hungarian children's literature. The short stories and novels of Mikszath's second, ironic, period are much like his political writings, describing the failings he found in his society yet never offering outright condemnation or advocating reform. The theme of greed, recurrent in his fiction, is exemplified in the story "A gavallerok," about the inhabitants of a small town whose odd predilection for acting out elaborate charades designed to gratify their desire to be rich baffles an out-of-town observer. Mikszath also explored the shortcomings he found in society through the theme of the conflict between the ideal and reality. For example, in "Gallamb a kalitkaban," which consists of two variations on a single story line, Mikszath portrayed two cultivated gentlemen proving their friendship for one another through a series of noble, self-sacrificing gestures and two politicians engaged in ruthless attempts to do each other in.

Many of Mikszath's other novels and short stories of this period contrast the delusions of misconceptions of his characters with the truth, which is ironically evident both to readers and to the story's narrator. The protagonist of one early novel, the 1896 volume *Beszterce ostroma* (*The Siege of Beszterce*), is an eccentric nobleman who, oblivious to the realities of modem Hungary, insists on behaving like a feudal lord. A comic treatment of a similar theme is 1898's *Uj Zrinyiaz,* about a sixteenth-century warrior hero who, resurrected in the present day, creates havoc by applying battlefield methods to his new career as a bank manager. Mikszath's best-known novel, 1895's *Szent Peter esernyoeje* (translated in 1900 as *St. Peter's Umbrella*), concerns an old umbrella mistakenly regarded as evidence of a miracle by the inhabitants of a village. While Mikszath emphasized the comic absurdity of the situations he depicted, he also usually chose to elicit the reader's sympathy for his hapless protagonists.

The fiction of Mikszath's final period increasingly reflected his distress at the unsavory dealings he witnessed in politics, the problems brought about by the inequities of the class system, and the deteriorating state of the nation, both domestically and in its international position. In his last works, he evokes situations of inhumanity, suffering, and amorality. The hero of his 1901 novel *Kueloenoes hazassag* (translated in 1964 as *A Strange Marriage*) is forced to marry the pregnant mistress of a local priest, and must spend the rest of his life struggling to escape the match in order to be reunited with the woman he truly loves. In his 1908 work, *A Noszty fiu esete Toth Marival,* an unscrupulous nobleman schemes to replenish his family fortune by seducing an heiress. Commentators regard the last novel Mikszath completed before his death, 1911's *A fekete varos,* as his bleakest in outlook. It concerns a pair of young lovers whose happiness is destroyed by a senseless and violent political feud.

During his lifetime, Mikszath's fiction was overshadowed by that of his popular contemporary Mor Jokai; today, however, his works are the subject of increasing interest both within Hungary and elsewhere. As *American Slavic and East European Review* contributor Joseph Remenyi remarked: "In comparison with the common run of Hungarian novelists and storywriters, Mikszath is exceptional indeed, and it is fair to say that his literary importance transcends the political and cultural boundaries of his native land."

BIOGRAPHICAL/CRITICAL SOURCES:

BOOKS

Mikszath, Kalman, *St. Peter's Umbrella,* translated by B. W. Worswick, with an introduction by R. B. C., Folio Society, 1966, pp. 7-9.
Scheer, Steven C., *Kalman Mikszath,* Twayne, 1977, pp. 140-149.

PERIODICALS

American Book Collector, September, 1965, p. 6.
American Slavic and East European Review, vol. VIII, no. 3, 1949, pp. 214-225.
Dial, September 1, 1901, p. 139.
Nation, November 22, 1900, pp. 409-410.
Times Literary Supplement, December 7, 1962, p. 949; January 21, 1965, p. 52.*

* * *

MILLER, James M. 1933-

PERSONAL: Born August 7, 1933, in Lancaster, PA; son of James M. and Ruth H. (Ober) Miller; married

Elva Jean Lehman, December 26, 1955; children: Gregory J., Robert Alan. *Ethnicity:* "Caucasian." *Education:* Elizabethtown College, B.S., 1955. *Politics:* Independent. *Religion:* United Methodist. *Avocational interests:* Jogging, gardening, sports, music.

ADDRESSES: Home—8 Oxford Lane, Madison, NJ 07940. *Office*—c/o Department of Chemistry, Drew University, Madison, NJ 07940; fax 973-408-3572. *E-mail*—jmiller@drew.edu.

CAREER: Drew University, Madison, NJ, began as assistant professor, became professor and professor emeritus, 1959—. Jemcor Ltd., vice president; consultant to Johnson & Johnson, Inc. and Gow-Mac Instrument Co.

MEMBER: American Chemical Society, American Association for the Advancement of Science, American Association for Clinical Chemistry.

AWARDS, HONORS: American Chemical Society, North Jersey Teacher Affiliates Award, 1983, and E. Emmett Reid Award, 1992; Petix Supporter of Science Award, New Jersey Association of Science Teachers, 1984.

WRITINGS:

Separation Methods in Chemical Analysis, Wiley (New York City), 1975.
Chromatography: Concepts and Contrasts, Wiley, 1988.
(With McNair) *Basic Gas Chromatography,* Wiley, 1998.
(Editor and contributor) *Chemical Analysis in a GMP Environment,* Wiley, in press.

WORK IN PROGRESS: Research on chiral separations by capillary electrophoresis.

SIDELIGHTS: James M. Miller told *CA:* "I have felt that, as a teacher in a small college, I could help further science by recording the advancement in my field in readable books."

*   *   *

MIRUKA, Okumba

PERSONAL: Male.

ADDRESSES: Office—c/o East African Educational Publishers, Brick Court, Mpaka Road, Woodvale Grove, P.O. Box 45314, Nairobi, Kenya.

WRITINGS:

(With Leteipa Ole Sunkuli) *A Dictionary of Oral Literature,* Heinemann Kenya (Nairobi, Kenya), 1990.
Encounter with Oral Literature, East African Educational Publishers (Nairobi, Kenya), 1994.

(Contributor) *Delusions-Essays on Social Construction of Gender,* edited by Wanjiku Mukabi Kabira, Masheti Masinjila, and Wanjiku Mbugua, African Women's Development and Communication Network (FEMNET) (Nairobi, Kenya), 1994.

SIDELIGHTS: Okumba Miruka researched and wrote on the subject of African oral literature, focusing on Kenya. His contributions in the area of gender politics on behalf of the African Woman's Development and Communication Network (FEMNET) in Nairobi, Kenya have been in training, workshops, and as contributor to a collection of essays.

A Dictionary of Oral Literature is a compilation of selected vocabulary terms used to discuss oral literature, and includes songs, proverbs, folktales, and other texts from many areas of Africa. The work also contains an appendix that includes discussions of topics such as "Image," "Narrative Formulae," and "Audience in Orature." Also included is a bibliography and a list of entries.

Joseph L. Mbele, reviewing *A Dictionary of Oral Literature* in *Research in African Literatures,* found, to some extent, that the definitions included were satisfactory but he faulted the omission of some important terms such as "motif" and "tale type." According to Mbele, "These omissions reflect, in part, current East African scholarship on oral literature and also the basic problem . . . which terms to include and which to exclude." Mbele also felt that many of the definitions were incomplete. In spite of this, Mbele, who calls the book "useful" because it offers a foundation for examining the definitions, commented: "This book is also an interesting anthology of texts that should engage the attention of students of African oral tradition."

Encounter with Oral Literature contains chapters on riddle, proverb, oral poetry, and narrative and raises questions about the structure, audience, and reason for each genre in understanding traditional oral literature as it exists in Kenya. B. Harlow writes in *Choice* that "readers can apply the interpretations more broadly . . . especially useful for introductory purposes."

Delusions-Essays on Social Construction of Gender was produced by FEMNET, an organization that works with government and media to "mainstream gender at the policy levels." FEMNET studies the adaptation of western models, taking into account the differences between them and African culture, rituals, and traditions. Wanjiku Mukabi Kabira, project coordinator for FEMNET, says the book "contributes to the effort to dismantle these structures and to expose the social mythology that encourages male dominance and women's oppression."

Miruka's contribution to the book is titled "Gender and Politics," wherein he explores the role of women in political life. Miruka states that women's rights, were once broader in scope, "in ancient Egypt, Britain, and Japan, . . . queens and empresses ruled their empires." He points out that women had property, herds, and control of money, but the system was somehow overturned and new values introduced whereby women were "devalued and subjugated." Miruka cites the low percentages of women in government worldwide and said "By 1991, there were only seven women heads of state." According to a report of a UN-sponsored group meeting on the role of women in public life, "Women 2000" (Vienna, 1991), women are more likely to "organize a web culture of affiliation" while men are more hierarchical in their approach to public life. Miruka stresses the success of groups and initiatives influenced by women's positive qualities, especially in voluntary, community, neighborhood, and grassroots environmental groups. Miruka comments that studies show that women who do enter politics do not use their positions to expressly represent women's interests and actually tend to think and act in ways similar to their male colleagues. Miruka refers to Professor Ali Mazrui's article in the *Daily Nation* in which Mazrui asserts that "the true impact of women on decisions concerning war and peace can only be discovered when the power system as a whole has acquired true sexual balance."

BIOGRAPHICAL/CRITICAL SOURCES:

PERIODICALS

Choice, January, 1996, p. 786.

Daily Nation, June 9, 1992.
Research in African Literatures, vol. 24, no. 2, summer, 1993.*

* * *

MITCHELL, John C. 1955-

PERSONAL: Born December 20, 1955, in Palo Alto, CA; son of John W. (a professor) and Carol C. Mitchell; married Diane Frank (a dancer), June 30, 1986; children: Laura, John. *Education:* Stanford University, B.S., 1978; Massachusetts Institute of Technology, M.S., 1982, Ph.D., 1984.

ADDRESSES: Office—Department of Computer Science, Stanford University, Stanford, CA 94305-9045; fax 650-725-4671. *E-mail*—mitchell@cs.stanford.edu; www.stanford.edu/~jcm.

CAREER: American Telephone and Telegraph, Bell Laboratories, member of technical staff, 1984-88; Stanford University, Stanford, CA, professor of computer science, 1988—.

WRITINGS:

Theoretical Aspects of Object-Oriented Programming, MIT Press (Cambridge, MA), 1994.
Foundations for Programming Languages, MIT Press, 1996.

* * *

MIYAMOTO, Yuriko (Chujo) 1899-1951

PERSONAL: Born February 13, 1899, in Koishikawa, Tokyo, Japan; died January 21, 1951; daughter of Chujo Seiichiro (an architect) and Yoshie (Nishimura); married Araki Shigeki (a linguist and academic researcher), August, 1919 (divorced, 1924); married Miyamoto Kenjii (a literary critic), February, 1932. *Education:* Attended Ochanomizu Women's High School, 1910-16; attended Nihon Women's University, 1916; attended Columbia University, 1918-19. *Politics:* Communist.

CAREER: Novelist and short story writer.

MEMBER: All-Japan Proletarian Artists' Association, Shin Nihon Bungakukai (New Japanese Literature Association), Fujin Minshu Kurabu (Women's Democratic Club).

AWARDS, HONORS: Mainichi Publishing Culture Award, 1947.

WRITINGS:

Mazushiki hitobito no mure (novel), Genbunsha (Tokyo), 1917.

Hitotsu no mebae (short stories), Shinchosha (Tokyo), 1918.

Nobuko (novel), Kaizosha (Tokyo), 1928, partially translated as *Nobuko* in the journal *Bulletin of Concerned Asian Scholars,* 1975.

Chujo Yuriko shu/Uno Chiyo shu, Heibonsha (Tokyo), 1930.

Atarashiki Shiberia yokogiru, Naigaisha (Tokyo), 1931.

Chujo Yuriko shu (collection), Kaizosha (Tokyo), 1931.

Chibusa, Chikuson Shobo (Tokyo), 1937.

Asu e no seishin, Jitsugyo no Nihonsha (Tokyo), 1940.

Asa no kaze, Kawade Shobo (Tokyo), 1940.

Sangatsu no daiyon nichiyo, Kinseido (Tokyo), 1940.

Bungaku no shinro, Kozan Shoin (Tokyo), 1941.

Watakushitachi no seikatsu, Kyoryoku Shuppansha (Tokyo), 1941.

Watakushitachi no kengetsu, Jitsugyo no Nihonsha (Tokyo), 1946.

Shinjitsu ni ikita joseitachi, Soseisha (Tokyo), 1946, also puvlished as *Shinjitsu ni ikita josei,* Shin Nihon Shuppansha (Tokyo), 1989.

Fuchiso (novel), Bungei Shunjusha (Tokyo), 1947, partially translated as *The Weathervane Plant* in *Journal of the Association of Teachers of Japanese,* 1984.

Banshu heiya (novel), Kawade Shobo, 1947, partially translated as *The Banshu Plain* in *Ukiyo: Stories of the Floating World of Post-War Japan,* 1954.

Utagoe yo okore (literary criticism), Kaihosha (Tokyo), 1947.

Atarashii fujin to seikatsu, Nihon Minshu Shugi Bunka Renmei (Tokyo), 1947.

Kofuku ni tsuite, Onkeisha (Tokyo), 1947.

Sakka to sakuhin, Sanne Shoten (Tokyo), 1947.

Fujin to bungaku (literary criticism), Jitsugyo no Nihonsha, 1947.

Dohyo (novel), three volumes, Chikuma Shobo (Tokyo), 1947-50.

Onna kutsu no ato, Takashimaya Shuppanbu (Tokyo), 1948.

Futatsu no niwa (novel), Chuo Koronsha (Tokyo), 1948.

Josei no rekishi, Fujin Minshu Shinbun Shuppanbu (Tokyo), 1948.

Shiroi kaya, Shinkyo Geijutsusha (Tokyo), 1948.

Bungei hyoronshu, Kindai Shisosha (Tokyo), 1949.

Fujin no tame ni (essays), 1949.

Watashitachi mo untaeru, 1949.

Heiwa no mamori, Shin Nihon Bungakukai (Tokyo), 1949.

Mosukuwa no inshoki (travel), Tokyo Minpo Shuppansha (Tokyo), 1949.

Miyamoto Yuriko bunko (collection), eight volumes, 1949-51.

Juninen no tegami (letters), Chikuma Shobo (Tokyo), 1950.

Nihon no seishun, Shinjusha (Tokyo), 1951.

Heiwa o warera ni, Iwasaki Shobo (Tokyo), 1951.

Wakai josei no tame ni, 1951.

Miyamoto Yuriko, 1951.

Miyamoto Yuriko zenshu (collection), fifteen volumes, 1951-53, thirty volumes, Shin Nihon Shuppansha, 1979-86.

Miyamoto Yuriko shu (collection), edited by Yoshida Akira, Chikuma Shobo, 1954.

Miyamoto Yuriko hyoron senshu (collection), four volumes, 1964-65.

Nobuko jidai no nikki, 1920-23 (diary), 1976.

SIDELIGHTS: Yuriko Miyamoto is considered one of the most important Japanese novelists of the post-World War II period. She is best known for her autobiographical novels in which she integrated accounts of her personal development with descriptions of Japanese history, politics, and society. In these works Miyamoto also conveyed her strong feminist perspective and socialist political convictions. In an essay in the *Journal of the Association of Teachers of Japanese,* Brett de Bary stated: "As the saga of the evolution of a Japanese feminist, the life story narrated in Miyamoto's oeuvre is of compelling historical interest. It is for the clarity with which the elements of that struggle are revealed, and in those moments when we cannot fail to be moved by the intensity of her protagonist's quest, that Miyamoto's work achieves its enduring literary power."

Miyamoto was born into a wealthy and prominent family in 1899. When she was eighteen, she issued her first work, *Mazushiki hitobito no mure,* a novel that features an introspective and idealistic young protagonist who wants to improve conditions for the peasants on her grandfather's estate. The following year, Miyamoto traveled to New York with her father. There she attended classes at Columbia University and met and married a Japanese graduate student. Miyamoto and her husband were divorced in 1924 after they returned to Japan, and critics suggest that her unsuccessful first marriage helped shape her awareness of the social limitations imposed on women. During the mid-1920s, Miyamoto formed an important friendship with Yuasho Yoshiko, a scholar of Russian literature, and for three years the two women lived in Moscow, where Miyamoto became convinced that socialism would solve many problems and improve the status of women in her own country. Returning to Japan in 1930, she became involved in the proleterian literature movement and served as editor of a women's journal. In 1931 she joined the Communist party, and in 1932 she married Miyamoto Kenji, a prominent figure in the party. Over the next twelve years, Miyamoto was intermittently imprisoned for her political activities. She continued to write during this period, and a number of her works were banned. When World War II ended, Miyamoto and her husband were reunited, and afterward she enjoyed the most prolific phase of her career. However, Miyamoto's health had been damaged by her years of imprisonment and by the frenetic pace of writing and political activity she maintained after the war. She died in 1951.

Miyamoto's autobiographical novels are often discussed as part of the tradition of the I-novel, a Japanese novelistic form in which the author focuses on his or her personal development and experiences, often without using fictional devices. In *Nobuko,* for example, Miyamoto described her life in New York City, while *Dohyo* relates the process by which the author came to accept Marxist doctrine. Miyamoto's novels differ from the I-novel, however, in her integration of the protagonist's experiences with social issues and historical events, especially the status of women, class inequality, and the suffering of the Japanese people during World War II. In *Fuchiso,* a novelist and her husband re-establish their relationship and adjust to normal life after years of separation while the husband was imprisoned during the war. *Banshu Heiya* focuses on both the main character's relationship with her husband's family and the destruction Japan experienced as a result of the war. Miyamoto has been praised for her insightful portrayal of human relationships, particularly that of the husband and wife in *Fuchiso,* and for her evocative

descriptions of the devastation and misery following the Japanese surrender. Miyamoto's blending of individual experiences and history in her works has been recognized as an important contribution to Japanese literature. As Noriko Mizuta Lippit has written in her Reality and Fiction in Modern Japanese Literature, Miyamoto "created a new form of autobiography, one in which the protagonist emerges as an historic figure of the age, experiencing fully its limitations and possibilities."

BIOGRAPHICAL/CRITICAL SOURCES:

BOOKS

Lippit, Noriko Mizuta, *Reality and Fiction in Modern Japanese Literature,* M. E. Sharpe, 1980, pp. 146-162.
Keene, Donald, *Dawn to the West, Japanese Literature of the Modern Era: Fiction,* Volume 1, Holt, Rinehart & Winston, 1984, pp. 1113-1166.

PERIODICALS

Journal of the Association of Teachers of Japanese, April, 1984-85, pp. 7-33.
Literature East and West, March, 1974, pp. 90-102.

*　　*　　*

MOHIN, Ann 1946-

PERSONAL: Born January 31, 1946, in Baltimore, MD; daughter of Edward J. and Josephine (Gross) Purcell; married William Mohin, July 7, 1978. *Education:* University of Maryland, B.A., 1976; postgraduate work at College Park, MD, 1978.

ADDRESSES: Home and office—338 Pike Rd., McDonough, NY 13801. *Agent*—c/o Bridge Works Publishing Co., Box 1798, Bridge Lane, Bridgehampton, NY 11932. *E-mail*—anchor@clarityconnect.com.

CAREER: Writer of essays, fiction, and poetry; sheepfarmer; formerly a freelance editor in Washington, DC, 1968-79.

MEMBER: National League of American Pen Women, Authors' Guild, Women's National Book Association, National Writers Union, International Women's Writing Guild.

AWARDS, HONORS: America's Best Novel Competition finalist, Writers' Foundation, 1995, 1997; Special Opportunity Grant, New York State Foundation of the Arts, 1996, 1998; Great New Writers Selection, Barnes and Noble, 1998, for *The Farm She Was: A Novel.*

WRITINGS:

The Farm She Was: A Novel, Bridge Works Publishing (Bridgehampton, NY), 1998.

Contributor of short stories, poems, and travel essays to periodicals.

ADAPTATIONS: The Farm She Was: A Novel has been optioned for film.

WORK IN PROGRESS: The second novel of a rural trilogy.

SIDELIGHTS: Novelist Ann Mohin lives with her husband in an 1845 post-and-beam house in the small town of McDonough, New York. Situated on a two hundred-acre farm, they are caretakers of their land and livestock, including sheep, cows, horses, and chickens. In an online interview with Nicola Davies, Mohin revealed that she writes in a twenty-seven-foot RV she has named Phil "because it sounds so obnoxious to say, 'I'm going to the office.'" Mohin's first novel, *The Farm She Was,* is set in rural upstate New York, and she pointed out "most of what I learned about farming, maintaining the land, and animal husbandry is contained in this book. In that sense it is autobiographical, but in no other."

The Farm She Was is the story of the life of Irene Leahy, a ninety-year-old woman holding onto her farm and way of life as she ages and faces death. The book of memories and reflections described in her journals begins with her childhood. As a girl, Irene had a very special relationship with her father, who died when she was seventeen, leaving her to take his place and care for the family's sheep farm. Her narration unfolds to reveal life on a small family farm and the nostalgia for a simpler, but not easier, time.

The novel details the physical and mental efforts of animal caregiving and the joys of country life. Irene's day-to-day chores provide a view of the specifics of sheep husbandry necessary to sustain a healthy and productive flock, as well as other skills critical to the survival of the small farmer.

Absorbed with the needs of her farm, Irene grows older alone, never marrying or having children. Her only romantic relationship is with a local veterinarian, whom she loses in World War II. Irene says her family "has been lambs and piglets, calves, goats and foals. . . . The vegetable garden was my passion and a generation of fruit and nut trees still thrive on the land I tilled. The milk and maple syrup, the flowers and golden honey, for a taste of these things I traded colorless time." Irene cherishes the farm and the possessions of her father and is determined to hold onto everything she has worked for. Real estate agents offer to buy her land, but Irene cannot bear to see the farm developed and subdivided. A social services worker and a local minister try to convince her to sell and live in a nursing home. Irene resists, determined to finish her life on the farm, with her old dog, Joe. "I scratch his salt and pepper muzzle. . . . he licks my misshapen hands."

Booklist reviewer Grace Fill commented of Mohin that "there is an aching poignancy in her writing about the physical process of aging." Karen Propp stated in the *Women's Review of Books* that *The Farm She Was* "is full of many lovely, lyrical moments." Propp concluded that the character of Irene and "Mohin's careful attention to life on the farm," resulted in "an interesting, quiet novel." Kimberly G. Allen noted in *Library Journal* that Mohin's writing reflects "sensitivity and gentle humor." A film version of *The Farm She Was* was planned soon after the publication of the book.

BIOGRAPHICAL/CRITICAL SOURCES:

PERIODICALS

Booklist, March 15, 1998, p. 1202.
Library Journal, March 1, 1998, p. 128.
Women's Review of Books, July, 1998, pp. 26-27.

OTHER

One Woman's Writing Retreat, http://www.prairie den.com/front...visiting_authors/mohin_bio. html, September 10, 1998.

*   *   *

MOLONEY, Susie

PERSONAL: Born Susie Schledwitz; daughter of Don

(owner of a trucking firm) Schledwitz; married Mick Moloney (a contractor); children: Josh, Michael. *Education:* Attended the University of Winnipeg and Red River Community College.

ADDRESSES: Home—Little Current, Manitoulin Island, Northern Ontario, Canada.

CAREER: Writer, newspaper columnist. Worked odd jobs, including waitressing and magazine editing.

WRITINGS:

Bastion Falls, Key Porter Books (Toronto), 1995, reprinted, Delacorte (New York City), 1997.
A Dry Spell: A Novel, Delacorte (New York City), 1997.

Author of syndicated column "Funny Girl" for Ontario newspapers.

SIDELIGHTS: Susie Moloney is a horror writer and columnist whose column "Funny Girl" runs in four Northern Ontario newspapers. Moloney's mother died of cancer when she was eleven, and she became estranged from her father during her teen years. She said in an interview in *Maclean's* magazine, "As a kid, I used to watch TV programs and then rewrite the plots into story form." She was fascinated by *Tales from the Crypt* comic books and later as an adult became an *X-Files* fan. Moloney was a single mother at age nineteen and wrote while her young son slept. Her first novel about wolves was never published. She wrote a vampire novella but said she realized that "Anne Rice had done blood lust better."

Moloney moved to Manitoulin Island at the northern end of Lake Huron when her husband Mick was offered a job there and then began to write her first published novel, *Bastion Falls*. The story is set in a northern Ontario town where the residents are hit by an unexpected and very strange snow storm which becomes so intense that the residents, who are used to bad weather, cannot get home and take shelter in a mall. The storm has an evil element known only by a teenaged psychic. Jennifer Williams wrote in *Quill & Quire* that, "like the slowly gathering storm, the pace of the novel gradually quickens," but Williams felt that although the snowfall creates suspense, "certain aimless, drifting passages should have been cleared to make a shorter path for the reader."

Moloney's second novel, *A Dry Spell,* was sold on the basis of a prologue, three chapters, and an outline.

David Keymer wrote in *Library Journal* that Moloney "tries to generate interest, but she builds too little tension much too slowly." The prologue introduces Tom Keatley, a rainmaker who travels to drought-stricken towns. "The myth of the rainmaker—the rootless wanderer with the power to make both women and farmlands blossom under his touch—is given a Stephen King-like twist," wrote a *Publishers Weekly* reviewer. Tom is contacted by Karen Grange, a banker who is forced to foreclose on family farms in Goodlands, North Dakota, as they fail from four years' lack of rain. Diane Turbide wrote in *Maclean's* that Moloney "writes sensitively" about Karen's shopping addiction, a storyline based on a woman Moloney had actually met, "a bona fide shopaholic" who "ended up in jail after she had embezzled to finance her extravagant purchases."

Tom pits his power against that of the spirit of a woman who was raped decades ago and who has cast the "dry spell" on the town. The spirit causes disasters and takes over the wills of the town's young women as it moves to destroy the town and everyone in it. Turbide also compared Moloney's "part romance and part horror thriller" to Stephen King novels "with its primal struggle between good and evil, its psychic elements mingling with the mundane, and its detailed exploration of small-town life." Film rights to *A Dry Spell* were purchased by Paramount and Cruise-Wagner Productions.

BIOGRAPHICAL/CRITICAL SOURCES:

BOOKS

Wilson, Joyce M., editor, *Canadian Book Review Annual,* University of Toronto Press, 1996, p. 171.

PERIODICALS

Booklist, August, 1997, p. 1848.
Books in Canada, December, 1995, p. 36.
Entertainment Weekly, September 12, 1997, p. 133.
Kirkus Reviews, July 15, 1997, p. 1055.
Library Journal, August, 1997, p. 133.
Maclean's, September 1, 1997, pp. 74-75.
People Weekly, September 22, 1997, p. 34.
Publishers Weekly, May 13, 1996, p. 30; July 21, 1997, p. 180.
Quill & Quire, October, 1995, pp. 27-28; July, 1997, p. 22; August, 1997, p. 30.
New York Times Book Review, January 18, 1998, p. 17.*

MOORE, Greg 1946-

PERSONAL: Born December 25, 1946, in Shelbyville, IN; son of Robert E. (a director of buildings and grounds for a school district) and Bette (a stenographer; maiden name, Harding) Moore; married Carol J. Sternke (a teacher), August 9, 1969; children: Amanda, Carrie, Robert. *Ethnicity:* "Caucasian." *Education:* Purdue University, B.S., 1970; University of Tennessee at Chattanooga, M.B.A., 1975. *Religion:* Lutheran. *Avocational interests:* Walking, reading.

ADDRESSES: Home—48 Tenby Chase Dr., Newark, DE 19711. *Office*—Integrated Technology Research, 913 Market St., P.O. Box 1790, Wilmington, DE 19899-1790; fax 302-234-2990. *E-mail*—moorege@aol.com.

CAREER: Integrated Technology Research, Wilmington, DE, director, 1997—.

MEMBER: Association of Corporate Travel Executives, Travel and Tourism Research Association.

WRITINGS:

Travel Services Contracting Agreements, ITR Publishing (Wilmington, DE), 1997.
Seduced by a Mile (novel), ITR Publishing, 1998.

WORK IN PROGRESS: Frequent flyer impact research; research on corporation/airline negotiating strategies.

SIDELIGHTS: Greg Moore told *CA:* "My writing is driven most often by the desire to bring applied research to the business travel industry. Most corporate travel managers and chief financial officers are unfamiliar with research being conducted that could improve their performance. I review the body of research on a given topic and publish work directed at corporate managers."

* * *

MOORE, Philip N(icholas) 1957-

PERSONAL: Born November 29, 1957, in Atlanta, GA; son of Nicholas George (a realtor and business owner) and Addy Marie (Todd) Moore. *Ethnicity:* "White/Greek." *Education:* Attended Georgia State University. *Politics:* "Republican/Conservative." *Religion:* Baptist. *Avocational interests:* Reading, research, travel to the Middle East, learning Hebrew and Greek, Bible study and interpretation.

ADDRESSES: Home—2995 Slaton Dr. N.W., Atlanta, GA 30305.

CAREER: Realtor.

AWARDS, HONORS: D.D., Immanuel Baptist Theological Seminary, 1998.

WRITINGS:

The End of History: Messiah Conspiracy, Ramshead Press International (Atlanta, GA), 1996.
Nightmare of the Apocalypse, Ramshead Press International, 1997.
Eternal Security for True Believers, Ramshead Press International, 1997.
A Liberal Interpretation of the Prophecy of Israel: Disproved, Ramshead Press International, 1997.
What If Hitler Won the War?, Ramshead Press International, 1998.
The End of Earth as We Know It, Ramshead Press International, 1999.

WORK IN PROGRESS: Israel and the Apocalypse Prophecies of Newton, for Ramshead Press International, completion expected in 2000; research on Newton, end-time prophecy, current events, and Jewish messianism.

* * *

MORDELL, Louis (Joel) 1888-1972

PERSONAL: Born June 28, 1888, in Philadelphia, PA; became British subject, 1929; died March 12, 1972, in Cambridge, England; son of Phineas (a Hebrew scholar) and Annie Feller Mordell; married Mabel Elizabeth Cambridge, 1916; children: a daughter, a son. *Education:* St. John's College, Cambridge University, B.A., 1910. *Avocational interests:* Travel.

CAREER: Cambridge University, researcher, 1910-13, Sadleirian Professor of pure mathematics, 1945-53; Birkbeck College, London, member of faculty, 1913-20; Manchester College of Technology, lecturer, 1920-22; University of Manchester, member of faculty, 1922-23, Fielden professor of pure mathematics and head of mathematics department, 1923-45.

AWARDS, HONORS: Received Smith's Prize; Sylvester Medal, Royal Society of London, 1949; Larmor Medal and Berwick Prize, both from the London Mathematical Society.

WRITINGS:

Three Lectures on Fermat's Last Theorem, Cambridge University Press (Cambridge, England), 1921.
A Chapter in the Theory of Numbers, 1947: An Inaugural Lecture, Cambridge University Press (Cambridge, England), 1947.
Reflections of a Mathematician, Canadian Mathematical Congress, McGill University (Montreal), 1959.
A Norm Ideal Bound for a Class of Biquadratic Fields, Trondheim, 1969.
Diophantine Equations, Academic Press (New York City), 1969.

Contributor to journals, including *Proceedings of the London Mathematical Society,* and *American Mathematical Monthly.*

SIDELIGHTS: Louis Mordell, who is best known for his work in pure mathematics and the development of the finite basis theorem, became fascinated with mathematics at an early age. Born in Philadelphia, Pennsylvania on January 28, 1888, to Hebrew scholar Phineas Mordell and Annie Feller Mordell, both Jewish immigrants from Lithuania, Mordell was introduced to complex mathematical concepts through used books he purchased at a bookstore. He already had a solid grasp of mathematics when he entered Central High School in Philadelphia at the age of fourteen, and he completed that school's four-year mathematics course in two years.

In 1907 Mordell placed first on Cambridge University's scholarship examination and accepted a scholarship to St. John's College at the British school. His interest in Cambridge dated back to his self-taught days, when the used books he studied presented numerous examples from Cambridge scholarship and tripos papers. Two years later, he took the first part of the mathematical tripos and placed third, behind P. J. Daniell and E. H. Neville. Following this success, he pursued research in the theory of numbers. There was little interest in this area of study in England at that time, and Mordell was largely self-taught. His focus was the integral solutions of the Diophantine equation

$y2 = x3 + k$, which dates back to the 1600s and the mathematician Pierre de Fermat. Mordell, however, greatly expanded the work in this area, determining the solubility for many new values of k, among other things. His work earned him a Smith's Prize but this high honor did not immediately lead to a college fellowship.

Mordell continued his research and acted as a tutor, and in 1913 joined the faculty of Birkbeck College in London. In 1916 he married Mabel Elizabeth Cambridge, with whom he later had a daughter and a son. Mordell remained at Birkbeck College until 1920, and much of his work there focused on modular forms, which resulted in two important advances. His first discovery involved the *tau* function—the set of coefficients of a specific modular form—which had previously been introduced by Srinivasa Ramanujan. Mordell proved Ramanujan's theory that the tau function has the property of multiplicativity. The theory was studied, proven, and popularized by Erich Hecke in 1937. The second discovery involved the representation of integers as the sum of a fixed number of squares of integers. Mordell's work in this area was also furthered by Hecke.

Mordell accepted a lecturer position at Manchester College of Technology in 1920, and remained there for two years. It was during this period that Mordell developed the finite basis theorem, based on earlier work by Jules Henri Poincare. It is this work for which Mordell is best known, and it was later furthered by Andre Weil. In his theorem, Mordell determined that there exist a finite number of rational points on any curve of genus greater than unity. "Mordell's conjecture," as this determination was commonly called, was proven by Gerd Faltings in 1983.

In 1922 Mordell transferred to the University of Manchester, and in 1923 was named Fielden professor of pure mathematics and head of the mathematics department at that school. In 1924, while still a citizen of the United States, he was named to the Royal Society. Mordell became a British subject in 1929.

Mordell remained at Manchester until 1945 and the school became known as a leading center for mathematics during his tenure. Mordell himself explored the theory of numbers and made significant advances in the area of the geometry of numbers while at Manchester. His work during this period was political as well as scientific, as he devoted much time to assisting European refugees. Mordell even secured temporary and permanent positions at the university for some of the immigrants.

Mordell left Manchester in 1945 to succeed Godfrey Harold Hardy as Sadleirian professor of pure mathematics at Cambridge. At this time he also became a fellow of St. John's College at Cambridge. Mordell advanced Cambridge's reputation as a highly reputable research school before his retirement in 1953. He continued to work with other mathematicians, especially beginners, but also used the time to travel. Cambridge continued to be his home, however, and he died there after a brief illness in 1972.

BIOGRAPHICAL/CRITICAL SOURCES:

BOOKS

Biographical Memoirs of Fellows of the Royal Society, Volume 19, 1973, pp. 493-520.

PERIODICALS

Acta Arithmetica, vol. 9, 1964, pp. 1-22.*

* * *

MORGAN, Bernice B.

PERSONAL: Born in St. John's, Newfoundland, Canada.

ADDRESSES: Agent—c/o Breakwater Books, Box 2188, 100 Water St., St. Johns, Newfoundland NF A1C 6E6, Canada.

CAREER: Writer. Member of editorial board of Killick Press; served on several community-based committees, including the St. John's Library Board and The Newfoundland Writers' Guild.

AWARDS, HONORS: Runner-up for Canadian Library Association's Young Adult Book Award, 1993, for *Random Passage;* Canadian Authors Association Prize for Fiction, for *Waiting for Time.*

WRITINGS:

The Very Thought of Thee: Adventures of an Arctic Missionary, Zondervan (Grand Rapids, MI), 1952.

(Selected and edited with Helen Porter and Geraldine Rubia) *From This Place: A Selection of Writing by Women of Newfoundland and Labrador,* Jesperson Press (St. John's, Newfoundland), 1978.

Random Passage, Breakwater, 1992.
Waiting for Time, Breakwater, 1995.

SIDELIGHTS: Bernice Morgan is the editor, along with Helen Porter and Geraldine Rubia, of *From This Place: A Selection of Writing by Women of Newfoundland and Labrador,* an anthology of literature from women writers of eastern Canada. In addition, Morgan is the author of the young adult novels *Random Passage* and *Waiting for Time.*

Random Passage, set during the early nineteenth century, concerns seventeen-year-old Lavina Andrews, who flees from England with her extended family when her father gets in trouble with the law. A detailed account of a family's survival in a brutal climate and geographical area, *Random Passage* was a runner-up for the 1993 Canadian Library Association's Young Adult Book Award. Douglas Hill pointed out in *Books in Canada* that Morgan successfully conveys the hardships and privations endured by Canadian pioneers—"the novel is . . . thick with chronology and accurate"—but questioned whether it spoke beyond the conventions of plot and dialogue. A contributor to *Emergency Librarian,* however, praised *Random Passage* as a "beautifully written story. . . . This is a complex and engrossing look at family loyalties."

Waiting for Time, also set in Newfoundland, spans a period from the early nineteenth century to the mid-twentieth century and focuses on a female character from each era. The two women, who settle in roughly the same geographical location, are distantly related. The novel touches on such existential topics as the meaning and significance of "place" and the influence of the past on the present-day. Robert C. Ruttan, writing in *Books in Canada,* stated that *Waiting for Time* is a "compelling story" and "a difficult book to put down."

BIOGRAPHICAL/CRITICAL SOURCES:

PERIODICALS

Atlantic Books Today, spring, 1995, p. 16.
Books in Canada, summer, 1992, p. 62; March, 1995, p. 42.

Canadian Book Review Annual, 1995, p. 181.
Emergency Librarian, September, 1993, pp. 62-63.*

* * *

MORGAN, Lorrie (Loretta Lynn) 1959-

PERSONAL: Born June 27, 1959, in Nashville, TN; daughter of George Morgan (a country music singer); married Ron Gaddis (marriage ended); married Keith Whitley (a musician; died, 1989); married Jon Randall (a musician); children: Morgan, Jesse.

*ADDRESSES: Home—*Hendersonville, TN. *Office—* Lorrie Morgan Entertainment, 1709 19th Ace St., Nashville, TN 37212-3701.

CAREER: Vocalist. Signed to RCA Records, Nashville, 1989—. Recordings include *Leave the Light On,* 1989; *Something in Red,* 1991; *Watch Me,* 1992; and *War Paint,* 1994. Actor in television films, including *Proudheart,* 1993, and *The Enemy Within,* ABC, 1995.

WRITINGS:

(With George Vecsey) *Forever Yours, Faithfully,* Ballantine (New York City), 1997.

SIDELIGHTS: Forever Yours, Faithfully offers an autobiographical account of the highs and lows in the life of popular country singer Lorrie Morgan. Now a respected musician in her own right, Morgan's early career benefited from her status as the daughter of George Morgan, a famous country musician at Nashville's Grand Ole Opry. Her pedigree in the musical world was no help in Morgan's private life, however, as she writes about her past failed marriages, most notably her relationship with gifted musician Keith Whitley, who drank himself to death in 1989.

Written with the help of George Vecsey, Morgan's book offers titillating details on numerous celebrities, starting with the philandering Whitley and also including Kenny Rogers, Troy Aikman, and Tennessee senator and actor Fred Thompson, each of whom Morgan dated. An *Entertainment Weekly* review describes the book as "heavily padded," and criticizes Morgan's lack of soul searching on the failings of her marriages. Still, fans of the country singer will likely appreciate the chance to learn so many personal details about the star.

BIOGRAPHICAL/CRITICAL SOURCES:

BOOKS

Carlin, Richard, editor, *Big Book of Country Music,* Penguin (New York City), 1993.

PERIODICALS

Entertainment Weekly, November, 1997.*

* * *

MORRIS, Sylvia Jukes

PERSONAL: Born in England; immigrated to the United States; married to Edmund Morris (a writer).

*ADDRESSES: Home—*New York, NY and Washington, DC. *Agent—*c/o Random House, 201 East 50th St., New York, NY 10022.

CAREER: Writer.

WRITINGS:

Edith Kermit Roosevelt: Portrait of a First Lady, Coward, McCann & Geoghegan (New York City), 1980.
Rage for Fame: The Ascent of Clare Boothe Luce, Random House (New York City), 1997.

SIDELIGHTS: Rage for Fame: The Ascent of Clare Boothe Luce by Sylvia Jukes Morris is the controversial chronicle of the life of Luce from birth to midlife. The biography is the result of years of access to Luce, her diaries, and papers. The title is taken from a quote by English satirist John Wolcot, a phrase which thirteen-year-old Luce chose to use under her photo in her eighth grade Catholic high school yearbook.

Grace Lichtenstein, who reviewed *Rage for Fame* in the *Washington Post,* said of Luce, "Spunky, beautiful, athletic, shrewd yet shallow, fascinating to men and women alike, she was hot stuff, all right; and this book, which ends in 1943 with her election to Congress, spills over with juicy details."

Luce was born in 1903 to a teenaged mother and musician/salesman father twenty-five years her mother's senior. According to Morris, although the relationship lasted nearly a decade, Luce's parents never married and her mother, who occasionally worked as a call girl, lusted after money and the good life. She eventually left Luce's father, engaged in a relationship with a millionaire benefactor, then married a Connecticut doctor. Luce rose from a poor and unstable childhood to marry, at age twenty, millionaire George Tuttle Brokaw. The marriage produced one daughter, Ann, and ended in divorce after six years, with Luce receiving a substantial settlement. She worked for a short time at *Vogue,* then moved on to *Vanity Fair* and a relationship with its editor, Donald Freeman. In a *New York Times* review, Michiko Kakutani wrote that "once her position at the magazine was secure, Clare began to pull away from Freeman and focus her attentions on the married financier Bernard Baruch." After Freeman's death, as the result of an automobile accident, Luce assumed his position.

Kakutani observed, "As *Rage for Fame* progresses, the stories—many of them pure soap opera—rapidly pile up. We hear about Clare Brokaw's whirlwind romance with Henry Luce, who the second time he glimpsed her announced that he was leaving his children and wife of eleven years. We hear about her flirtations with Randolph Churchill, Buckminster Fuller, Joseph P. Kennedy, and his son John." In a *USA Today* review, Deirdre Donahue describes how Henry Luce, media giant and founder of *Time, Life,* and, *Fortune* magazines, "fell like an axed log for the beauteous Clare. It was the French 'coup de foudre' (a stroke of lightning), Luce told her." Henry Luce left his wife and two sons for Clare and a marriage that would last until his death in 1967.

As a wartime journalist, Clare Booth Luce covered Europe, Africa, and China. Lichtenstein wrote in the *Washington Post,* "Morris presents Luce as a 'facile' journalist, more interested in the surface of things than in underlying developments, too lazy to do the necessary leg work, even, at times, 'less than truthful.'" Lichtenstein described Luce's volatile relationship with columnist Dorothy Thompson and Luce's decision that "she, not Thompson, was to be the leading Republican female pundit." Marsha Vande Berg, in a review for *Bookpage,* wrote that Luce "was a woman who turned her relationships with men, her striking good looks, a quick intelligence and unflinching ambition, to her own advantage."

Michelle Easton, president of the *Clare Boothe Luce Policy Institute,* wrote for *crisismagazine.com* that the book "manages to make a brilliant, fascinating woman seem merely common. . . . While Luce was born three years after the turn of the century and died in 1987, she became the quintessential modern conservative woman . . . 'The Woman of the Century.'" *USA Today* reviewer Donahue observed that *Rage for Fame* has "many splendid qualities" and a "reasoned tone." Donahue wrote that Morris "admires Luce's gifts and is able to discuss her personal life—active sex life included—in a manner that doesn't make you feel trapped in the dirty laundry bin. But she does not veer from Luce's considerable character flaws." Donahue summarized, "Morris reveals Luce the human being, neither demonizing nor canonizing her."

BIOGRAPHICAL/CRITICAL SOURCES:

PERIODICALS

Booklist, July 1, 1980, p. 1587.
Choice, October, 1980, p. 313.
Horn Book, October, 1980, p. 553.
Newsweek, June 23, 1980.
New York Times, May 30, 1997.
Publishers Weekly, May 19, 1997, p. 60.
Times Literary Supplement, February 27, 1998, p. 12.
USA Today, September 11, 1997.
Virginia Quarterly Review, winter, 1991, p. 34.
Washington Post, June 8, 1997.

OTHER

Bookpage, http://www.bookpage.com, July, 1997.
Crisis, http://www.crisismagazine.com, September, 1997.*

*   *   *

MUCHMORE, Jo Ann 1937-

PERSONAL: Born February 4, 1937, in Memphis, TN; daughter of Leslie (a cattleman and rancher) and Marion (Spaulding) McBride; married Gareth B. Muchmore (divorced, 1977; deceased, 1983); children: Leslie McBride Muchmore (deceased, 1978). *Education:* Stephens College, A.A., 1955; Oklahoma State University, B.S., 1957; M.A., 1968. *Politics:* Democrat. *Religion:* Episcopalian. *Avocational interests:* Reading, playing Scrabble, traveling.

ADDRESSES: Home—Ponca City, OK. *Agent*—c/o Holiday House Inc., 425 Madison Ave., New York, NY 10017.

CAREER: Adobe Theatre, Corrales, NM, artistic director, 1970-77; Temple Civic Theatre, Temple, TX, managing director, 1977-79, 1983-91; *Dick Cavett Show,* Public Broadcasting Service (PBS), production assistant, 1979-82; Poncan Theatre, Ponca City, OK, executive director, 1991-97. Guest director and actress at various theaters in the southwest United States, 1965—; active in Ponca City Chamber of Commerce.

MEMBER: Oklahoma Arts Institute (board member), Ponca City Library (board member), Poncan Theatre Development Fund (advisor).

AWARDS, HONORS: Governor's Arts in Education Award, State of Oklahoma, December, 1994.

WRITINGS:

A Forever Thing, My Dears (essays), American Printing, 1991.
Johnny Rides Again, Holiday House, 1995.

SIDELIGHTS: Jo Ann Muchmore commented: "As a theater director and manager, my primary career has always involved a great deal of day-to-day writing: publicity releases, actor biographies, theater programs, dramaturgical essays. The book *A Forever Thing, My Dears* is a compilation of those essays brought out in Temple, Texas, and sold to benefit that theater's endowment fund. Since a director and an actress are story tellers, I'd always wanted to write fiction. The inspiration to actually do so finally came when I realized I had something that I felt was impor-

tant to say, and that the people to say it to were children. *Johnny Rides Again,* within the framework of a story with many humorous lights, attempts to give children a road map to life's continuation after loss."

Muchmore, an energetic and active woman, has managed not only to continue life following personal losses, but to challenge life to new experiences. At an age when many people retire, Muchmore produced her first novel, *Johnny Rides Again,* which a *Publishers Weekly* critic lauded as a "promising debut." The critic admired the author's depiction of the protagonist, Rose Marlin, calling her a "plucky yet vulnerable" ten-year-old. Mourning her mother's death from cancer, Rose is further devastated when the family's beloved dog, Johnny, dies only months later. To make matters worse, Rose's father and brothers buy a puppy, naming him "New Johnny"; then her father begins dating a local schoolteacher. The disloyalty is just too much for Rose. Over the course of the book, Rose and her family adjust to life's changes, while "a lively Texan tone," observed by *Bulletin of the Center for Children's Books* critic Deborah Stevenson, "keeps things fresh." Stevenson also appreciated the smart and plentiful humor in *Johnny Rides Again,* concluding that its protagonist, Rose, "is tough and honest without being cliched; kids will enjoy her company."

BIOGRAPHICAL/CRITICAL SOURCES:

PERIODICALS

Bulletin of the Center for Children's Books, June, 1995, p. 354.
Publishers Weekly, April 17, 1995, p. 60.
School Library Journal, April, 1995, pp. 134-136.*

N-O

NEELY, Barbara

PERSONAL: Female.

ADDRESSES: Home—Jamaica Plain, MA. *Agent*—c/o St. Martin's Press, 175 Fifth Avenue, New York, NY 10010.

CAREER: Mystery novelist and short story writer.

AWARDS, HONORS: Agatha Award, Anthony Award, and Macavity Award, all for best first mystery novel, all 1993, all for *Blanche on the Lam.*

WRITINGS:

NOVELS

Blanche on the Lam, St. Martin's Press (New York City), 1992.
Blanche among the Talented Tenth, St. Martin's Press (New York City), 1994.

Also author of short stories in various anthologies.

SIDELIGHTS: Barbara Neely began her writing career as the author of short stories. With her first novel, the 1992 mystery *Blanche on the Lam,* Neely "entertainingly corrected," as Charles Champlin put it in the *Los Angeles Times Book Review,* the absence of female African American writers and characters in that genre. As the novel opens Neely's heroine, Blanche White, is a domestic working in North Carolina. Her name means "White White," but her personality is anything but that: Blanche is feisty, independent, strong-willed, and proudly uninfatuated with her white employers.

Blanche is jailed for writing $42.50 in bad checks, a misfortune she fell into because four of her employers left town without paying her. She manages to escape and ends up working for the Carters, a "Faulknerian cast of oddballs," according to *Kirkus Reviews,* who may be involved in some arcane plots against one another in quest of an inheritance. Aunt Emmeline, the rich recluse whose inheritance is sought, may be an alcoholic; Cousin Mumsfield, a mildly retarded young man, may be more clever than he seems; and Miz Grace and Everett, Blanche's employers, are affluent neurotics. This family constitutes, Champlin suggests, "[a] Eugene O'Neill plot seen from the pantry door," for Blanche, given the society in which she must operate, can only observe them rather than openly investigate, a limitation which, in Champlin's admiring view, Neely overcomes with "special ingenuity."

After the local sheriff is murdered, Blanche stirs things up enough for suspicion to be thrown not only upon her, but also upon an innocent African American gardener. Forced to solve the crime in order to avoid being accused of it, Blanche successfully takes charge in what *Publishers Weekly* called a "deftly written debut" novel. *Publishers Weekly* appreciated *Blanche on the Lam,* too, for paying "heartfelt tribute to the community and culture of a working-class African American woman." A contributor to *Kirkus Reviews* approved of the "prickly view of class-clashes, race relations, and family foibles" but described the author's "folk-talk" style as somewhat "forced" in this "quirky" novel. For Champlin, a major attraction of the book was Blanche's hard-nosed social commentary. Champlin was not alone in looking forward to Neely's follow-up novel, and *Blanche on the Lam* received three major awards as best first mystery novel of 1993.

The hoped-for sequel, and presumably the second in a projected longer series, was *Blanche among the Talented Tenth.* The scene has shifted from North Carolina to Boston, without a reduction in the racism of the surrounding community, but with an added spotlight on a different form of class snobbery, that of light-skinned middle-class blacks toward their darker-skinned, less affluent brothers and sisters. Blanche, a working-class, dark-skinned woman whose obvious talents make the phrase "talented tenth" sound ironic, pays a summer visit to a niece and nephew on Amber Cove, a Maine resort frequented by middle-class African Americans.

Having ensconced herself in the local community against the grain of some of its members, Blanche learns that the local gossip, Faith Brown, has been electrocuted in her bathtub, and that an MIT professor named Hank has apparently drowned himself in the ocean, after leaving a note confessing to Faith's murder. That seems cut-and-dried, but Blanche suspects that something more is involved, and as she probes into local history and current relationships, she finds ample material for suspense and scandal.

This second novel was seen by at least two reviewers as less gripping, in its mystery plot, than *Blanche on the Lam; Kirkus Reviews* felt that the whodunit element was less effective than Neely's "acerbic portrait of class infighting at its most corrosive." *Publishers Weekly* wrote, "Blanche continues to appeal in her so-what-if-I've-got-an-attitude way, but while . . . *Blanche on the Lam* was a mystery with a bit of message, this one is a message with a bit of mystery." Blanche herself, however, and the varied environments into which she might conceivably be set, remained so captivating that thousands of readers eagerly anticipated a third installment.

BIOGRAPHICAL/CRITICAL SOURCES:

BOOKS

Heising, Willetta L., *Detecting Women 2,* Purple Moon Press (Dearborn, MI), 1996.

PERIODICALS

Kirkus Reviews, December 15, 1991, pp. 1560-1561; July 1, 1994, p. 889.
Los Angeles Times Book Review, March 8, 1992, p. 8.
Publishers Weekly, January 20, 1992, p. 50; July 18, 1994, p. 238.

NELSON, Michael 1929-

PERSONAL: Born April 30, 1929, in Bromley, England; son of Thomas Alfred (a carpenter) and Dorothy Pretoria (Bevan) Nelson; married, wife's name Helga Johanna, March 26, 1960; children: Patrick, Paul, Shivaun. *Education:* Magdalen College, Oxford, M.A., 1953.

ADDRESSES: Home—21 Lansdowne Rd., London W11 3AG, England.

CAREER: Reuters News Agency, London, England, general manager, 1952-89.

MEMBER: Garrick Club.

WRITINGS:

War of the Black Heavens: The Battles of Western Broadcasting in the Cold War, Syracuse University Press (Syracuse, NY), 1997.

WORK IN PROGRESS: Queen Victoria on the Riviera, completion expected in 2000.

*   *   *

NERSESSIAN, V(rej) N. 1948-

PERSONAL: Born December 25, 1948, in Tehran, Iran; citizenship, British; son of David and Sandukht Nersessian; married, wife's name Leyla (a librarian), 1979; children: Tiran, Zhirayr. *Ethnicity:* "Armenian." *Education:* Attended Armenian College, Calcutta, India, and Seminary of Holy Etchmiadzin, Armenia; King's College, London, B.D. (with honors) and Ph.D.

ADDRESSES: Home—32 Beechwood Ave., South Harrow, Middlesex HA2 8BY, England. *Office*—British Library, 96 Euston Rd., London NW1 2DB, England; fax 01-71-412-7858. *E-mail*—Vred.Nersessian@mail.bl.uk.

CAREER: Ordained Armenian Orthodox priest; British Library, London, England, curator in charge of Christian Middle East collections, 1976—.

MEMBER: Royal Asiatic Society, Society of Armenian Studies.

WRITINGS:

The Tondrakian Movement, Kahn & Averill (London), 1987.

Armenia, Clio Press (Oxford, England), 1993.

(Editor) *Armenian Church Historical Studies,* Temple Press, 1993.

A Bibliography of Articles on Armenian Studies in Western Journals, 1869-1995, Curzon Press (London), 1997.

(Editor) *Komitas: Armenian Sacred and Folk Music,* Curzon Press, 1998.

Editor of the collection *Essays on Armenian Music,* 1987. Contributor to books, including *Grove's Dictionary of Music and Musicians, An Encyclopedia of the History of the Written and Printed Word, Encyclopedia of European Languages, Everyman Companion to East European Literature,* and *The Oxford Guide to Literature in English Translation,* Oxford University Press.

*   *   *

NIGAM, Sanjay (Kumar) 1959-

PERSONAL: Born in 1959, in India. *Ethnicity:* "Asian Indian."

ADDRESSES: Agent—c/o William Morrow and Co., 1350 Avenue of the Americas, New York, NY 10019.

CAREER: Fiction writer and medical doctor. Harvard Medical School, Boston, associate professor of medicine.

WRITINGS:

The Non-Resident Indian and Other Stories, Penguin (New Delhi, India), 1996.

The Snake Charmer, Morrow (New York City), 1998.

Writer of academic works and contributor of short stories to periodicals, including *Kenyon Review, Story, Natural History,* and *Grand Street.*

WORK IN PROGRESS: A long novel.

SIDELIGHTS: Sanjay Nigam is a medical doctor, teacher, and author. In his first book, a collection of fiction titled *The Non-Resident Indian and Other Stories,* Nigam tells the tale of Trishanku, a mortal who

desires immortality. "Trishanku pays for his brief stay with the gods by spending eternity 'stuck' between heaven and earth watching souls transmigrate from one life to the next," wrote Robbi Clipper Sethi in an online review for *IndiaStar.* "Trishanku is Nigam's metaphor for the non-resident Indian, 'stuck' in a variety of North American locales." The non-resident Indians are found across the United States in Nigam's stories, including such locations as New York, New Mexico, New Jersey, and Texas, and two of his characters are influenced by the work of the transcendentalist Henry David Thoreau. "When Nigam's narration settles into the consciousness of his strongest characters, the stories develop beautifully," wrote Sethi. "In 'The Window' a chemist's dissatisfaction with his well-paying career in the pharmaceutical industry is believably and touchingly represented."

One of the stories in *Non-Resident Indian and Other Stories* evolved into Nigam's first novel. The original story, titled "Charming," was the only story of the collection set entirely in India. In an online interview with WordsWorth Books, Nigam said the short story expanded into *The Snake Charmer* over a period of ten years, during most of which he was writing it "in my head." Arthur J. Pais, writing in *India Today,* called the novel "a luminous fable about ego, vanity and attempts at redemption." A *Publishers Weekly* reviewer called it a tale "about the fleeting nature of fame and fortune and about a life 'ruined by a single moment of stupidity.'"

Nigam's main character, Sonalal, is a New Delhi snake charmer, "unsentimentally portrayed in his never-ending quest to fulfill his sexual, financial, and artistic needs," wrote Frank Caso in *Booklist.* "His trouble, already suggested by his wife's acerbic wit and the distance of his two sons, escalates when he hits a false note," wrote Sethi in a review for *IndiaStar.* "Raju, his cobra of fifteen years, old and tired from nine hours of one of the best days in Sonalal's career, bites the hand that feeds him." Furious, Sonalal commits an act that will haunt him, biting his snake in half, then weeping with "guilt for having murdered one he loved more than his own sons," according to Shobori Ganguli in a review for *Pioneer.* A group of foreign journalists witnesses the killing, giving Sonalal instant fame. The money he receives from the reporters and tour guides enables him to live in a style far more luxurious than Sonalal could have ever hoped.

Despite his newfound fame and fortune, Sonalal becomes impotent in his despair at the loss of his snake and turns to magicians, doctors, and sex therapists for redemption. Eventually, his temporary fortune dwindles and he returns to his native village to catch and train a new snake. "Nigam's best writing is in dialogues . . . where the characters reveal themselves and their situations convincingly and dramatically," said Sethi, adding that "the novel weakens some when summary becomes necessary to show the passage of time before Sonalal captures a new cobra and takes up his art again. The novel's suspense, however, never flags." Sethi called Nigam a "unique new voice in Indian-American fiction." *New York Times* reviewer Richard Bernstein called *The Snake Charmer* "an engaging, light-as-a-feather tale of a comically stubborn struggle." "An exceptional novel," commented Guy Amirthanayagam in *Washington Post Book World*. A reviewer for *Kirkus Reviews* called *The Snake Charmer* "a small gem of a story that entertains, moves and, naturally, charms."

Nigam told *CA*: "I guess I was attempting to write a modern day fable of sorts, about the quest for lasting meaning in life and redemption, and how difficult it is to find either."

BIOGRAPHICAL/CRITICAL SOURCES:

PERIODICALS

Booklist, April 15, 1998, p. 1429.
Detour, June/July, 1998, p. 56.
India Today, July 27, 1998.
Kirkus Reviews, April 15, 1998.
Library Journal, April 15, 1998, p. 114.
New York Times, July 6, 1998.
Pioneer, November 28, 1998.
Publishers Weekly, April 6, 1998, p. 56.
Redbook, June, 1998.
Washington Post Book World, May 31, 1998.

OTHER

IndiaStar, http://www.indiastar.com (September 10, 1998).
WordsWorth Books, http://www.wordsworth.com (September 10, 1998).

* * *

NKALA, Nathan 1941-
(Odunke, a joint pseudonym)

PERSONAL: Born October 25, 1941, in Umuawulu, Awka L.G., Nigeria; son of Okonkwo (a farmer and

palmwine tapper) and Ndita Udunkwo (a homemaker; maiden name Uzonso Nwobu) Nkala; married Fanny Ebele Ezenwaji (an educator), August 25, 1975; children: Chike, Doris, Kenechi, Obidi. *Education:* University of Ibadan, B.A. (with honors), 1965; University of Nigeria, M.A., 1982. *Religion:* Christian. *Avocational interests:* Reading and writing, scrabble, lawn tennis.

ADDRESSES: Home—P.O. Box 1093, Enugu, Nigeria. *Agent*—c/o Fouth Dimension Publishing Co. Ltd., House 16, Fifth Ave., City Layout, PMB 01164, Enugu, Nigeria.

CAREER: Civil service of Eastern Nigeria, began in administrative class, 1965, became Director General/Administrative Secretary, beginning 1992; freelance writer, c. 1988—.

MEMBER: Nigerian Institute of Management (MNIM), Institute of Personnel Management of Nigeria (AIPM), ODUNKE Community of Artists (executive member).

AWARDS, HONORS: Short story prize, Radio Netherlands, 1971; Macmillan Nigeria Prize, 1981.

WRITINGS:

(With others) *The Insider, Stories of War and Peace from Nigeria,* Nwamife (Enugu, Nigeria), 1971.
(With others, under the joint pseudonym Odunke) *OJADILE* (play), OUP, 1977.
Mezie, the Ogbanje Boy (novel), Macmillan (Nigeria), 1981.
Bridal Kidnap, Leadway Books (Onitsha, Nigeria), 1988.
(With others, under the joint pseudonym Odunke) *ONUKWUBE* (play), UPL, 1988.
Drums and the Voice of Death (novel), Fourth Dimension Publications (Enugu, Nigeria), 1996.
(With Patricia Davison) *Lobedu* (nonfiction), Heritage Library of African Peoples, 1997.

Also contributor of chapters to books, including "Towards an Inspired Policy for the Management of Urban Development in Anambra State," *The Nigeria Manager: Challenges, Development and Effectiveness,* Longman UK, 1982; "Inter-Cadre Career Paths and Over-Establishment," *Management Study of Anambra State Civil Service,* UNN, 1982; "Traditional Channels of Communication and Rural Development Policy Implementation: The Neglected Symbiotic Relationship," *Mass Communication and National Development,* edited by Ikechukwu Nwosu, Frontier Publishers, 1990; and "The Role of Top Management in Government-owned Companies," *Managing Government-owned Companies,* edited by Pita Ejiofor, Fourth Dimension.

WORK IN PROGRESS: Before the Bar-Beach Show, a novel, for Fourth Dimension (Enugu, Nigeria); (with others, under joint pseudonym Odunke) *Di-Ji-Muta Ofeke,* a play, for UPL; *Biographical Notes on African Writers,* a nonfiction book; research on oral literature among the Igbo people, the "human anchorage" to modern African literature.

SIDELIGHTS: Nathan Nkala is a Nigerian writer who has authored several books. His book *Drums and the Voice of Death* is a novel about the Nigerian Civil War and is divided into four main sections and a prologue. The novel's prologue introduces readers to protagonist Kanayo, who is facing a death sentence for committing "robbery with violence." As the novel progresses, Kanayo flashes back to his participation in the Nigerian Civil War. The first two sections deal with events before that conflict, as the Igbo people of eastern Nigeria get ready to declare themselves as the nation of Biafra. The third section describes the war itself, ending in the defeat of the Igbo people. The fourth portrays the war's aftermath, in which Kanayo and his fellows deal with their ensuing feelings of powerlessness by planning a robbery.

In addition to Kanayo, *Drums and the Voice of Death* is peopled with characters such as Ichere Aku, an evil lawyer who, as Chimalum Nwankwo put it in his review of the novel for *World Literature Today,* "repeatedly and amazingly manages to pull away from a deserved death." Another character, Colonel Onyeanatugwu, is based upon a real-life colonel in the Biafran Army. Nwankwo cited "the novel's admixture of elegant prose with lyric poetry" and went on to conclude that *Drums and the Voice of Death* "will find a good place in the treasury of works from the Nigerian civil war."

BIOGRAPHICAL/CRITICAL SOURCES:

BOOKS

Nkala, Nathan, *Drums and the Voice of Death,* Fourth Dimension, 1996.

PERIODICALS

Okike, October, 1996, p. 121.
World Literature Today, spring, 1997, p. 441.

NOLAN, Han 1956-

PERSONAL: Born August 25, 1956, in Birmingham, AL; married September 12, 1981. *Education:* University of North Carolina at Greensboro, B.S., 1979; Ohio State University, master's degree (dance), 1981. *Avocational interests:* Reading, hiking, running, swimming, "I love to move and be outside."

ADDRESSES: Office—c/o Harcourt Brace & Company, 525 B St., Suite 1900, San Diego, CA 92101-4495.

CAREER: Writer. Teacher of dance, 1981-84.

MEMBER: Society of Children's Book Writers and Illustrators, PEN.

AWARDS, HONORS: People's Choice Award and National Book Award nominee, both 1996, both for *Send Me down a Miracle;* New York Public Library Best Books for the Teen Age list, 1994, for *If I Should Die before I Wake,* 1996, for *Send Me Down a Miracle,* and 1997, for *Dancing on the Edge;* American Library Association Best Books citation and National Book Award, both 1997, both for *Dancing on the Edge.*

WRITINGS:

If I Should Die before I Wake, Harcourt, 1994.
Send Me down a Miracle, Harcourt, 1996.
Dancing on the Edge, Harcourt, 1997.

WORK IN PROGRESS: A Face in Every Window, a young adult novel, for Harcourt.

SIDELIGHTS: The 1997 winner of the National Book Award for her young adult novel, *Dancing on the Edge,* Han Nolan speaks directly to teenage readers in a voice at once empathic and down-home humorous. The author of three published novels, Nolan has already captured a wide and loyal readership with her themes of tolerance and understanding, and with her youthful protagonists who discover—in the course of her books—who they are and what they want. "Thoughtful is how I would describe my books," Nolan told J. Sydney Jones in an interview. "I put a lot of thought into my novels and I hope they are also thought-provoking, but I guess that is for someone else besides me to judge."

From the beginning of her career she Nolan out to write novels for younger readers. "I really love the

YA readership, teens. I like how their minds work. They're just coming into their own; it's an exciting, new, and scary time for them. They are learning how the world works. It's feverish and passionate. Also, I liked my own teen years. It's a time for us to wake up. We're no longer blind children led by our parents." Nolan hopes her books provide a chance for teens "to enter a private world and stop and think about their lives," as she told Jones. "They need this chance to go somewhere private and think about things that they might not be able to talk about with their friends."

Nolan's books have dealt with neo-Nazis, religious zealotry, and the lies a family promulgates to supposedly protect its children. Her characters—Hilary, Charity, Miracle—are young women on the cusp, emerging into an uncertain adulthood from shaky adolescence. They are young women who must learn to stand up for themselves—to throw off the influences of adults and peers and find their own center in a turbulent universe. In *If I Should Die before I Wake,* Hilary becomes a time-traveler to learn a lesson of tolerance, literally trading places with the Jews who she professes to hate. Her own experience of the dark night of the Holocaust changes her profoundly and allows her to become her own person. Likewise, Charity in *Send Me down a Miracle* learns—in a less dramatic manner perhaps—to stand up for herself and thus be able to deal with her domineering father. And Miracle, the protagonist of *Dancing on the Edge,* must pass through the private hell of psychosis before she puts to rest the secrets that have riven her family.

Born in the South, Nolan was raised in the North, specifically the northeast urban sectors around New York City. As a result, she has something of a dual citizenship to regional America: roots in the Southern sensibility of languorous tales after dinner, and feet firmly planted in the go-ahead urban ethic. The next to youngest of five children, Nolan and the rest of her family "moved around a lot," as she told Jones, "something that teaches you how to make new friends quickly." Friends and neighborhoods changed, but a constant in the family was a love of books and the arts. "We were big time readers in my family. I remember my father used to bring three books home every night for my mother, and she would finish them by the next morning."

Like the rest of her family, Nolan loved books and reading from an early age. "As a young child, the book that really influenced me to become a writer was *Harriet the Spy.* After reading that, I of course wanted to be a spy not a writer, but I did begin keeping journals of my observations like Harriet. It's the journal-keeping that was so influential, that helped turn me into a writer. I still keep journals." Later favorite authors were Charles Dickens and John Steinbeck. "I also loved to write stories, and began putting them down on paper as soon as I learned how to write."

School was another matter, however. "Elementary school was very difficult for me," Nolan related in the interview with Jones. "I was a hyperactive kid as a result of food allergies that I've only recently discovered. So it was hard for me to pay attention." Junior high was a more positive experience, and when she was thirteen, Nolan began dancing, an activity that enabled her to focus: "As a result, I'd say I had very happy teen years." Added to this life in New York were summers Nolan and her family spent in the South, in Dothan, Alabama, where many of her relations lived on one street. There she got into touch with another part of her heritage, listening to a favorite aunt stretch out the evening with her long tales. "My Southern relatives loved to sit and listen to these stories. Everything is a story, a blend of wit, humor, and intelligence. They had the ability to laugh at everything, including themselves. There was seriousness in these long tales, and tragedy, too. But they were always leavened with humor. When I was a child I would sit and listen for hours."

Upon graduation from high school, Nolan decided to go south for college. "I chose the University of North Carolina at Greensboro because of the dance major they offered. The program turned out to be incredibly well-rounded, requiring courses in the sciences, physical education, and education, and in addition there were all the English courses I naturally gravitated to. So I had a full education." Graduating in 1979, she went on to a master's program in dance at Ohio State where she met her future husband, who was working on his doctorate in classics. In 1981 she graduated, married, and began teaching dance. When the couple decided on adopting children several years later, Nolan also opted for a career change.

"I wanted to be home with my kids," she noted in her interview with Jones, "so I thought about work I could do at home. I always loved to write and took some creative writing classes, but it was not something you could actually do for a living. I fancied being able to write and living on Cape Cod, but those were fantasies, not reality. I just always figured I would do something more practical." Then discussing it with her husband one afternoon, he helped make the decision for her. "Suddenly he just took off, saying he'd be back in a bit. When he finally came back he had one of these writers' market guides for me, and that just started me writing."

Thus began Nolan's writing career. She studied not only markets, but every book on writing technique that she could get her hands on. She wrote stories and sent some out with no success. Then she tackled lengthier projects, writing a mystery that won some attention with a publisher but was not purchased. Nonetheless, there was encouragement in the fact that an editor had taken interest in her work. She joined or formed writers' groups where she happened to be living—in Pennsylvania and Connecticut. All the while there were children to raise in addition to learning how to become a writer. She began another mystery, but one of the characters was stubbornly going off on her own, dreaming about the Holocaust.

"This kept coming into the story and getting bigger and bigger," Nolan recalled. In addition to Nolan's subconscious at work, there were also contemporary events impinging. "Here I was in Connecticut, and I discovered that there was a KKK [Ku Klux Klan] group in town. Hate crimes were being reported, and I was appalled by this whole neo-Nazi fascination. As a young teenager I came across Viktor Frankl's *Man's Search for Meaning* in my parents' book-shelves, and reading that I remember how shocked I was to read about the Holocaust. First, that this should have been allowed to happen, and second, that I had not known about it before—that it was not being taught to us as students. There was a kind of horror I internalized then that finally found a way to come out in my writing. A sense of horror that was re-charged by events around me."

Nolan recast the character from her mystery into Hilary Burke, a young neo-Nazi who is lying in a coma in a Jewish hospital, for her 1994 novel, *If I Should Die before I Wake*. Hilary has history: her father died years before, his death caused (so Hilary believes) by a Jew, and her Bible-thumping mother temporarily abandoned her. She has found a home with a group of neo-Nazis; her boyfriend is the leader of the group. Hilary now lies in a hospital as a result of a motorcycle accident. In her coma, she sees an-other patient, an elderly Jewish woman named Chana in her room. Chana is a Holocaust survivor, but to Hilary she is sarcastically labeled "Grandmaw." Sud-denly Hilary spins back in time, trading places with

Chana, becoming herself the persecuted young girl in Poland. She experiences firsthand the horrors of the Holocaust: her father is shot; she lives in the ghetto for a time; she escapes with her grandmother from the ghetto only to be captured, tortured, and sent to Auschwitz-Birkenau. Hilary constantly drifts back to herself in the hospital. Meanwhile, her mother, a born-again Christian, and her boyfriend visit. By the end, "Hilary has come back from her own near-death experience as well as Chana's to be a more under-standing, tolerant person," Susan Levine wrote in *Voice of Youth Advocates*.

"I wanted to say to neo-Nazis 'How would you like this to happen to you?'," Nolan told Jones. "I wanted to put them into the same situations the Jews suffered. The writing of the book was very difficult. Working on the historical parts, I felt that I was actually there. I was afraid to write the book. I didn't think that I had enough talent to tackle the subject. And I'm not Jewish. But it was a story I had to tell. I was so compelled, and I wanted to write the book not so much for Jewish readers—they know their history—but for non-Jewish teenagers. To let them know, to make sure that we can't let this happen again. Just can't. I knew I was going to take some flack for the book and I did."

The first review Nolan read—or actually had read to her by her husband over the phone while attending a writer's conference—questioned the taste of the book. This was shattering enough for Nolan to later warn off a would-be purchaser of her first novel at the conference. "I told this person, 'Oh no, you don't want to read that. It got a bad review.' What did I know? I was just starting." Most reviewers, however, responded positively to this first effort. Levine went on in her *Voice of Youth Advocates* review to note that the novel is a history and ethics lesson enveloped in a riveting plot. Levine concluded that Nolan had written "an interesting and moving story." Roger Sutton, writing in the *Bulletin of the Center for Children's Books*, commented that Nolan is forthright in dealing with her material, "and her graphic de-scriptions of camp life have a morbid interest that teeters on exploitation but comes down on the side of the truth." *Booklist*'s Mary Harris Veeder stated that Nolan's "first novel has great strengths and weak-nesses." Among the latter, Veeder felt, were the time travel episodes and certain contemporary character-izations. "Chana's story, however, is brilliantly ren-dered," Veeder noted, and "carries memorable emo-tional impact." A contributor in *Kirkus Reviews* re-marked that "Nolan's first novel is ambitious indeed," and concluded that "the book as a whole is deeply felt and often compelling."

Nolan was already one hundred pages into her next novel by the time of publication of *If I Should Die Before I Wake*. "My next book was lighter," Nolan told Jones in her interview. "It was a fun book to write, because I used material from my own summers in the South. I needed something lighter after writing about the Holocaust. We were still living in Connecticut, and I was now taking my own children down to Dothan for the summers. It brought back all those old memories for me." Soon these memories were added to by the fact that Nolan and her family moved to the South, to Birmingham, Alabama.

Nolan began to find her own writing method also. Starting with a character or situation or location rather than a plot outline, she writes long enough to get to know her characters and where they want to take things. This can take up to sixty pages of manuscript, much of which gets tossed with revisions and tightening of story. "My characters are made up as I go along," Nolan explained to Jones. "They're all parts of me, composites. It's sort of like Michelangelo's theory of sculpture. The figure is already there under the stone; it's the artist's job to release it by chipping away. The first sixty pages are me chipping away at the stone."

"And there's a vagueness to the whole process. You have something you want to say in the first place. That's why you sit down to write. But it's elusive, and I tend to write around what the thing is I really want to say. Sometimes it's difficult for me to confront it, to come face to face with what it is I truly want to say. It's like I'm looking through a tiny pinhole at first, and sometimes this broadens to a window, but mostly it's a very narrow view I'm allowed through my characters and story. Much of the time I am writing in the dark. I'm seeing it all in my mind."

With *Send Me down a Miracle*, Nolan follows the fortunes of fourteen-year-old Charity Pittman as she battles for a sense of self in her hometown of Casper—a locale inspired by the Dothan of Nolan's childhood. Charity feels trapped at home with her younger sister Grace and preacher father now that her mother has left them. The father's stern interpretation of Christianity has chased away Charity's mother, but soon Charity is attracted to the cosmopolitan Adrienne Dabney, returned from New York to her family home where she sets about trying a deprivation experiment. For three weeks Adrienne locks herself away in her

inherited home, without visitors, light, or food. Emerging from the experiment, she says that Jesus has visited her, sitting in the chair in her living room. This proclamation splits the small town asunder: Charity and many others believe in the chair and its miraculous powers; Charity's father calls it all blasphemy, warning that Adrienne is evil incarnate. Caught between the prickly father whom she loves and Adrienne, who has taken her on as a friend and fellow artist, Charity must finally learn to make up her own mind. When her father comes to destroy the chair, Charity is there to stand up to him finally.

"The dichotomy of professing one's faith and actually living it is interestingly portrayed throughout this novel," commented Jana R. Fine in a *School Library Journal* review of *Send Me down a Miracle*. Fine also noted that readers were brought into the "heart of a young girl" who learns to meld her religious background with compassion and forgiveness. A critic in *Kirkus Reviews* called *Send Me down a Miracle* a "busy, hilarious, tragic story," and concluded that "readers will be dizzied by the multiple subplots and roller-coaster highs and lows" in this story of a small town. A *Horn Book Guide* contributor noted that this "offbeat coming-of-age novel is peopled with a host of peculiar, yet intriguing, characters," and *Booklist* contributor Ilene Cooper remarked that Nolan's "plot is intricate, sharp, and invigorating." *Send Me down a Miracle* was nominated for the National Book Award in 1996.

Nolan's next book, *Dancing in the Edge,* three years in the writing, was inspired by her own adopted children. "I wanted to somehow deal with the theme of adoption, the difficulty such children have in finding their own identity not knowing their birth parents. This search for identity is so vital to all of us, and some children without families have to borrow an identity to be able to find their own. I once knew a person who'd been adopted. This person used to go to the drawer where her birth certificate was kept just to make sure she really existed. So in part this novel is for those kids in search of an identity, and also it's a novel about secrets, about the damage secrets can do in a family. Children can read adults; they know when we're lying. The truth may be hard, but it's better than lies. The truth can cure."

Miracle McCloy, the young protagonist of *Dancing on the Edge,* is so named because she was delivered after her mother was killed in an accident. Her spiritualist grandmother Gigi calls it "the greatest miracle to ever come down the pike," but Miracle is not convinced. She feels a misfit, hardly special at all. She is ten at the beginning of the novel, living in Alabama with her father, Dane, a one-time child prodigy who now sits around in his bathrobe in the basement all day, and with Dane's mother, Gigi, who spends her time with matters of the occult. Dane suddenly disappears one day, and Gigi tells Miracle that her father has "melted." Gigi and Miracle then go to live with Opal, Gigi's ex-husband. Here Miracle finds some stability in the form of her gruff grandfather who buys her a bicycle and starts her in dancing lessons. Dance proves to be a momentary salvation for Miracle, something that actually makes her feel as special as everyone is always saying she is. But when she starts imitating her grandmother's occult fancies, casting spells and making love potions for her classmates, troubles arise. Accused of being a phony by another student, Miracle sets herself on fire.

Fourteen at the time of this attempted suicide, Miracle is put into a mental hospital and it is here that her Aunt Casey and a kindly doctor help her to come to terms with the secrets in her life. This second part of the novel details Miracle's therapy and recovery as she slowly uncovers the truths that have eluded her all these years. She discovers that her mother, a ballerina, was committing suicide when struck by a speeding ambulance and that she has been abandoned by her father. "Nolan skillfully discloses" the nature of her cast of offbeat characters, a *Kirkus Reviews* critic noted, calling the novel "intense" and "exceptionally well-written." Miriam Lang Budin, writing in *School Library Journal,* dubbed *Dancing on the Edge* an "extraordinary novel," and concluded that "Nolan does a masterful job of drawing readers into the girl's mind and making them care deeply about her chances for the future." *Dancing on the Edge* was nominated for a National Book Award, the first time an author has been nominated for that prestigious award two years in a row. Her novel also won the National Book Award, commended by the panel of judges as "a tale of chilling reality."

Nolan was already deep into her next novel by the time of the awards ceremony, but found taking time out from her writing and going to New York to be "great, pure fun," as she told Jones in her interview. Awards are one form of feedback for Nolan, who does not pay much attention to reviews any longer. Another form of response to her work comes in letters from fans. These letters, interestingly enough, come not just from young readers. "Adults seem to enjoy reading my books, as well as teens," Nolan told Jones. "I try to write on many different levels and

add layers of understanding to my novels. So it is heartening to know that the books speak across the generations. But in the end I think sometimes adults underestimate teenagers. If the letters I receive from young readers is any indication, we need to write to them, not write down to them. They are out there and they are hungry for good literature. Don't underestimate them."

BIOGRAPHICAL/CRITICAL SOURCES:

BOOKS

Nolan, Han, *Dancing on the Edge,* Harcourt, 1997.

PERIODICALS

ALAN Review, winter, 1998.
Booklist, April 1, 1994, p. 1436; March 15, 1996, p. 1263.
Bulletin of the Center for Children's Books, April, 1994, pp. 267-268; July, 1996, p. 382; December, 1997, pp. 135-136.
Horn Book Guide, fall, 1994, p. 322; fall, 1996, p. 304.
Kirkus Reviews, March 1, 1994, p. 308; March 15, 1996, p. 451; August 1, 1997, p. 1227.
Kliatt, July, 1996, p. 15.
Publishers Weekly, January 31, 1994, p. 90; August 18, 1997, p. 94; November 24, 1997, p. 14.
School Library Journal, April, 1994, pp. 152-153; April, 1996, p. 157; September, 1997, p. 223; January, 1998, p. 22.
Voice of Youth Advocates, June, 1994, p. 88; June, 1996, p. 99; June, 1997, p. 86.

OTHER

Interview with J. Sydney Jones, The Gale Group, conducted October 13, 1998.*

*　　*　　*

OHRT, Wallace 1919-

PERSONAL: Born June 29, 1919, in Moose Jaw, Saskatchewan, Canada; U.S. citizen; son of Norman F. (a welder) and Sigfrid (a homemaker; maiden name, Eidsness) Ohrt; married Betty Jo Martin, April 29, 1955; children: Laurie Ohrt Semke, Stephen F. *Ethnicity:* "Caucasian." *Education:* Attended University of Oregon, 1937-38, Victoria College, Victoria,

British Columbia, 1946, and University of Washington, Seattle, 1947-48. *Politics:* Independent. *Religion:* Presbyterian. *Avocational interests:* Gardening, reading, studying history.

ADDRESSES: Home—1105 Southwest 166th St., Seattle, WA 98166.

CAREER: Boeing Aircraft Co., Seattle, WA, parts fabricator, 1941-42; Boeing Co., Seattle, worked as personnel representative, staff assistant, job evaluator, procedures writer, contracts manager, staff writer, and in graphics, 1950-74; freelance technical writer and consultant, 1975-91. Teacher of English as a second language, 1994-96. *Military service:* U.S. Army Air Forces, armorer gunner; served during World War II; served in Pacific theater; became sergeant.

MEMBER: Burien Historical Society.

AWARDS, HONORS: Second place award, best nonfiction book, Pacific Northwest Writers Conference, 1977.

WRITINGS:

The Rogue I Remember (memoir), Mountaineers Books (Seattle, WA), 1979.
The Accidental Missionaries, Inter-Varsity Press (Downers Grove, IL), 1990.
Defiant Peacemaker: Nicholas Trist in the Mexican War, Texas A&M University Press (College Station), 1997.

WORK IN PROGRESS: Editing *Immigrant Girl* (tentative title), the memoirs of the author's mother, Sigfrid Ohrt; *The Wit and Wisdom of Thomas Jefferson* (tentative title), a collection of quotations.

SIDELIGHTS: Wallace Ohrt told *CA:* "Several months after World War II, I was sent home from the Pacific theater on a hospital ship. As we slogged our way from Manila to San Francisco—a thirty-day voyage on the old *Dogwood*—I got acquainted with paperback novels, cheerfully passed out by a charming Red Cross lady. What joy! The deceptively easy style of Nordhoff and Hall, Kenneth Roberts, and Samuel Hopkins Adams made me think this was something I could do. I pursued that illusion through two more years of college and one year as a starving freelancer, then settled for the greater security of corporate life. The urge returned in midlife, and I took early retirement to settle the question: could I actually become a

writer? Twenty-five years later, as I approach my eightieth birthday, with three nonfiction books published, I still count myself an apprentice.

"My original motivation for writing was, as I have indicated, to discover whether I *could* write professionally. With that question at least partially resolved, I am now motivated by a desire to discover forgotten or neglected heroes, present and past, and to bring them to the public's attention so they can receive the honor they deserve.

"I count all good writing as instructive: novels, biographies, history, short stories, articles, essays, even newspaper sports reports. Writers I particularly admire and seek to emulate include novelists Willa Cather, Conrad Richter, and A. B. Guthrie; biographer Marquis James; historian Samuel Eliot; and essayist E. B. White. I read everything I can get my hands on, including biographies by the score about everyone from Dr. Samuel Johnson to Wild Bill Hickok.

"My writing routine is not particularly novel. I seldom get started before 9:30 and work until about three o'clock, leaving enough daylight for a little gardening in season or a two-mile walk in decent weather. I write only five days a week, having become attached to the leisurely weekend during twenty-five years of corporate life. I become totally absorbed into the world I am writing about, almost to the point of losing touch with my real surroundings. Insomnia becomes chronic, but I hardly begrudge the lost sleep because it is usually compensated in increased creativity.

"A love of history has inspired me to write about historic subjects. My only complaint with history is that there is too much of it! As to the two projects in which I am now engaged, they were inspired by opposite motives, one noble, the other crass. My mother spent seven years in her eighties writing her memoirs, concluding with the statement that this was her legacy to her descendants, including those yet unborn. It is a rich legacy, needing only polishing and organizing in a somewhat more book-like form. She died at age ninety-four in 1985, and I have inherited her notes, which she called her 'stories.' I have committed myself to the necessary editing task and will probably self-publish the result. My other project is to be an anthology of pungent Jefferson quotations in a short book. The justification for this project is that it seems timely in view of the current interest in Jefferson because of recent disclosures about his hitherto mysterious sex life."

OLEINIK, Olga Arsenievna 1925-

PERSONAL: Born July 2, 1925, in Matusov, Kiev, Ukraine; daughter of Arseniy Ivanovich and Anna (Petrovna) Oleinik; married, husband's name, Chudov; children: Dmitri. *Education:* Moscow University, degree, 1947, Ph.D., 1954.

ADDRESSES: Home—Moscow University, K app 133, 117234 Moscow, Russia. *Office*—Moscow University, Department of Mathematics, 119899 Moscow, Russia.

CAREER: Moscow University, professor of mathematics, 1955—, head chair of differential equations, 1972—. Visiting scholar at universities in the United States, including the University of South Carolina.

MEMBER: Russian Academy of Sciences, Royal Society of Edinburgh (honorary), American Mathematical Society, International Society for the Interaction of Mathematics and Mechanics.

AWARDS, HONORS: Honorary doctorate, Rome University 1981; medal, College de France; "first degree" medal, Charles University, Prague; has also received various prizes from Russian institutions.

WRITINGS:

Mathematical Problems in Elasticity and Homogenization, 1992.
Homogenization of Differential Operators and Integral Functionals, 1994.
Some Asymptotic Problems of the Theory of Partial Differential Equations, 1995.

Author of books on mathematical topics published in Russian.

Has contributed more than three hundred papers to professional journals.

SIDELIGHTS: Olga Oleinik is a prolific writer and educator with eight books and nearly sixty graduate students to her credit. She teaches mainly in Russia at Moscow University, but she also travels to colloquia in America, and has held classes as a visiting scholar at such institutions as the University of South Carolina. Oleinik has also contributed more than three hundred papers to a variety of professional journals and is a member of the Russian Academy of Sciences.

She has made important findings in the area of algebraic geometry in projective space. Her books include *Mathematical Problems in Elasticity and Homogenization, Homogenization of Differential Operators and Integral Functions,* and *Some Asymptomatic Problems of the Theory of Partial Differential Equations.*

Olga Arsenievna Oleinik was born in Kiev, Ukraine on July 2, 1925. Her parents, Arseniy Ivanovich and Anna Petrovna, lived in an area known as Matusov. Olga's early years spanned times of great upheaval and difficulty in the then Soviet Union, especially World War II. She did, however, earn a degree from Moscow in 1947. She received her doctorate in 1954 and shortly thereafter began the professorship in mathematics at Moscow University that she would continue to hold throughout her career.

In 1972 Oleinik was promoted to the head chair of differential equations in her department. Her specialty is partial differential equations. Although her classes can carry such intimidating titles as "Asymptotic Properties of Solutions of Nonlinear Parabolic and Elliptic Equations and Systems," she is generous with her ideas and more than willing to give her students the right start, according to one former student. Igor Oleinik remembered how much time his "PDE" professor was willing to give to her students despite her busy schedule. Because they were fellow Ukrainians, and Oleinik is as common a name there as Smith is in America, Igor had to put up with a little teasing from fellow class members who joked that he was really Olga Oleinik's grandson.

Oleinik's studies in mathematics cover broad areas of applied mathematics and physics, such as the interactivity of liquids or gases in porous substances, the thermodynamics of bodies in different phases, as well as problems in elasticity and homogenization.

Oleinik is married and has one son, Dmitri. She holds an honorary doctorate from Rome University, granted in 1981, and is also an honorary member of the Royal Society of Edinburgh. She is a member of various societies throughout Europe. Her awards include the medal of the College de France and a "first degree" medal from Prague's Charles University, as well as various prizes from Russian institutions.

BIOGRAPHICAL/CRITICAL SOURCES:

OTHER

The Emmy Noether Lectures of the American Associa-

tion for Women in Mathematics: Profiles of Women in
Mathematics, http://www.math.neu.edu/awm/noether
brochure/Oleinik96.htm (December, 1999).*

P

PAGE, Karen 1962-

PERSONAL: Born May 8, 1962, in MI; daughter of George and Joan Page; married Andrew Dornenburg (a writer), August 25, 1990. *Education:* Northwestern University, B.A., 1983; Harvard University, M.B.A., 1989. *Avocational interests:* The "enneagram."

ADDRESSES: Office—527 Third Ave., Suite 130, New York, NY 10016. *E-mail*—KarenAPage@aol. com. *Agent*—Doe Coover, Winchester, MA.

CAREER: Lehman Brothers, New York City, investment banker, 1983-85; magazine publisher and manager, New York City, 1985-87; Braxton Associates, Boston, MA, strategy consultant, 1989-92; *Country Music,* Westport, CT, executive vice-president, 1992-94; Karen Page and Associates, New York City, president, 1994—. Harvard Business School Network of Women Alumnae, chairperson, 1992—.

MEMBER: Council of One Hundred (Northwestern University; member of executive committee, 1994—).

AWARDS, HONORS: James Beard Book Award, 1996; diploma of honor, Salon International du Livre Gourmand, 1998.

WRITINGS:

(With husband, Andrew Dornenburg) *Becoming a Chef,* Van Nostrand (New York City), 1995.
(With Dornenburg) *Culinary Artistry,* Van Nostrand, 1996.
(With Dornenburg) *Dining Out,* Wiley (New York City), 1998.

WORK IN PROGRESS: Secrets of the Harvard Superstars: What We've Learned since Harvard Business School, for Random House (New York City), completion expected in 2000; *Chef's Night Out,* Wiley, 2000; *Think Global, Cook Local,* Wiley, 2001.

* * *

PARSONS, (Quentin) Neil 1944-

PERSONAL: Born June 2, 1944, in Fulmer Chase, Burnham, Buckinghamshire, England; son of Roy (an Anglican minister) and Clare (a schoolteacher; maiden name, Waterston) Parsons; married Judy Ann Seidman (an artist), 1974 (divorced, 1988); children: Ann Neo, Jane Semane. *Ethnicity:* "South-East English (plus additives)." *Education:* Attended Moeng College, Palapye, Botswana, 1962-63; Northwestern Polytechnic, London, England, B.A., 1966; University of Edinburgh, diploma in African studies, 1967, Ph.D., 1973. *Politics:* "Democratic socialist." *Religion:* "Anglican (occasional conformist)."

ADDRESSES: Office—Department of History, University of Botswana, Private Bag UB 00703, Gaborone, Botswana; fax +267-355-2279. *E-mail*—nparsons@ noka.ub.bw.

CAREER: University of Zambia, Lusaka, lecturer in history, 1971-75; University of Swaziland, Manzini, lecturer in history, 1975-79; Oxford University, Oxford, England, research associate, 1979-80; University of Botswana, Gaborone, senior research fellow, 1980-82; National Museum and Art Gallery, Gaborone, research associate, 1983-88; Institute of Commonwealth Studies, London, England, research associate, 1988-92; University of Cape Town, Cape Town, South Africa, visiting research fellow, 1993, temporary lecturer, 1994; Botswana Society, Gaborone, research associate, 1995-96; University of Botswana, associate professor of history, 1996—. *Military service:* Royal Navy, 1958-61.

MEMBER: Botswana Society, South African Historical Society, Royal African Society (England), Society of Authors (England), African Studies Association (United States).

AWARDS, HONORS: Grant from Ford Foundation, 1983-85.

WRITINGS:

(Editor with Robin Palmer) *The Roots of Rural Poverty in Central and Southern Africa* (monograph), University of California Press (Berkeley, CA), 1977.

A New History of Southern Africa, Macmillan (London), 1982, Holmes & Meier (New York City), 1983, 2nd edition, Macmillan, 1983, Holmes & Meier, 1993.

Focus on History, three volumes, College Press (Harare, Zimbabwe), 1985-91.

Social Studies Atlas for Botswana, Botswana Society (Gaborone, Botswana), 1988.

(Editor with Michael Crowder) *Monarch of All I Survey: Bechuanaland Diaries, 1929-37 by Sir Charles Rey,* Lilian Barber (New York City), 1988.

(With Willie Henderson and Thomas Tlou) *Seretse Khama, 1921-1980,* Botswana Society, 1995.

King Khama, Emperor Joe, and the Great White Queen: Victorian Britain through African Eyes, University of Chicago Press (Chicago, IL), 1998.

Coeditor, *African Social Research,* 1972-75, and *Journal of Southern African Studies,* 1989-92; editor, *Pula: Journal of African Studies,* 1997—.

WORK IN PROGRESS: A biography of Franz Taaibosch (died in 1940), a South African-born entertainer who danced as "Clicko, the wild dancing bushman" in London, Paris, and Cuba, and performed with the Ringling Brothers Barnum and Bailey Circus Side Show in the United States; research on the history of Botswana.

SIDELIGHTS: Neil Parsons told *CA:* "I had a fairly normal, happy childhood as the youngest child of a Royal Air Force chaplain, moving between England and Egypt and Germany. After the brief agony of early adolescence, life came alive with a passion for student theater, writing, and directing, and even acting and lighting. Then, aged eighteen, I found myself 'alone' in a remote African school, enthused with the cause of African liberation and feeling slightly sick in the stomach at my first sight of a white person after six or eight weeks. Back at college in England, I reverted to student theater and journalism, but abandoned the attempt to produce a sub-Polanski horror film for graduate work in the burgeoning new academic field of African studies. A few years in Scotland got me back to Africa, to Zambia, and to an American marriage before stints in Swaziland, Oxford, Botswana, and—once liberation had almost come—South Africa. Here I am now, back in Botswana where my African adventure began, wiser but sadder, with two wonderful daughters beginning to make their ways in their own careers in any one or more of three continents.

"It was Professor George 'Sam' Shepperson, wise old Africanist and African-Americanist at Edinburgh, who taught me that the exposure of what probably happened in the past can be more exciting than the creation of any fiction—and that the biographies of flesh-and-blood individuals can tell us more about the rhythms of everyday life than abstract social histories. But it has taken years to come back to this. My earliest historical publications were attempts to apply 'underdevelopment' theory. I was also driven by the mission to explain and the need to popularize the insights of the 'new' history of Africa, especially in Africa and for school children, and later for general readers elsewhere. This has led me increasingly to research biographical studies, high and low, which break open some new vision of human nature and of the past, for me and hopefully for my readers. I have lived vicariously through the lives of an energetic British colonial official who tried but failed, an ordinary intelligent man who became an extraordinary African president, three African chiefs who visited Britain and turned the political establishment inside out, and a 'bushman' plucked from farm service in South Africa to dance in London and Paris—and to die in upstate New York. While not neglecting the importance of theory and debate in historical studies, I look forward to many more such explorations of the human spirit, bringing together the insights of my own background with insights from as many other sources as possible, to recreate the lives of people from the past like holograms in the center of a circle of reflecting mirrors."

PASCOLI, Giovanni 1855-1912

PERSONAL: Born December 31, 1855, in San Mauro, Romagna, Italy; died February 18, 1912, in Bologna, Italy. *Education:* University of Bologna, graduated, 1882.

CAREER: Writer. Worked as a teacher, c. 1882; University of Bologna, Bologna, Italy, chair of Italian literature, 1904-12.

AWARDS, HONORS: Hoefft medal for Latin poetry, from the Royal Academy of Amsterdam, c. 1891, for "Veianius"; also awarded eleven other Hoefft medals.

WRITINGS:

POETRY

Myricae, 1891.
Poemetti, 1897; divided and published in two parts as *Primi poemetti,* 1904, and *Nuovi poemetti,* 1909.
Canti di Castelvecchio, 1903.
Odi e inni, 1906.
Poemi conviviali, 1911.
Poemi italici, 1911.
Poemi del Risorgimento, 1913.
Carmina, 1914.
Poems of Giovanni Pascoli, Yale University Press (New Haven, CT), 1923.
Poems of Giovanni Pascoli, H. Vinal (New York City), 1927.
Selected Poems of Giovanni Pascoli, 1935.
Convivial Poems: Text and Translation, with an introduction and critical notes by Egidio Lunardi and Robert Nugent, Lake Erie College Press (Painesville, OH), 1979.
Selected Poems, edited and with an introduction by P. R. Horne, Manchester University Press, 1983.

CRITICISM

Minerva oscura, 1898.
Sotto il velame, 1900.
La mirabile visione, 1902.

OTHER

Tradzioni e ridzioni (translations), 1913.
Nell'Anno Mille e schemi di altri drammi (plays), 1924.

SIDELIGHTS: Giovanni Pascoli is regarded as the progenitor of modernism in Italian poetry. His early works in particular are noted for innovations that represent a departure from traditional subjects and forms. His later poetry focuses on issues associated with the Risorgimento, a nineteenth-century movement that worked toward, and eventually achieved, political unity in Italy.

The fourth of ten children, Pascoli was born in the rural village of San Mauro, Romagna. When Pascoli was twelve his father was murdered; that same year, Pascoli's mother died of heart failure and a sister died of typhus, leaving his older brother, Giacomo, as head of the family. Pascoli attended the University of Bologna but terminated his studies to take care of his younger siblings after Giacomo's death from typhus in 1875. During this time he became involved in radical politics. Biographers have surmised that Pascoli's antigovernment activities were triggered by his anger over his father's murder and the fact that, although the identity of his father's killer was widely known, the police refused to pursue the case. In 1879, after he was arrested at a political demonstration and imprisoned for over three months, Pascoli moderated his political views and began to advocate the goals of the Risorgimento. He returned to the University of Bologna and developed his interest in poetry.

Giosue Carducci, a prominent poet and teacher at the university, greatly influenced Pascoli's artistic and intellectual development. After Pascoli graduated in 1882, he held a series of teaching positions and began to publish his work in various journals. *Myricae,* his first volume of poetry, was issued in 1891. Shortly thereafter, Pascoli received the Hoefft medal for Latin poetry from the Royal Academy of Amsterdam for the poem "Veianius." Pascoli continued to write in Latin as well as Italian and was awarded the Hoefft medal twelve more times during his career. In addition to poetry, Pascoli published three volumes of criticism on the work of Dante. Pascoli's reputation as a poet facilitated his appointment to Carducci's position as chair of Italian literature at the University of Bologna when the elder poet retired in 1904. Pascoli held this post until one month before his death in 1912.

Myricae exemplifies Pascoli's modernist departure from the themes and forms of traditional Italian poetry. Rejecting the lofty subject matter, distanced perspective, and ordered verse structure of earlier Italian poets, Pascoli wrote about everyday subjects using simple, often colloquial language, impassioned descriptions, and fragmented forms. The major topics in *Myricae* are nature, peasant life, and the mystery of death. Pascoli explained the theories behind *Myricae* in "Il fanciullino," a poetic manifesto published in 1897 that stressed the notion that all poetry should be written from the viewpoint of a *fanciullino,* or young child. The poetic traits for which Pascoli was most widely recognized—fresh descriptions of nature, a sense of awe regarding the universe, and a focus on the cycle of life—stem from this theory. In an essay in the *Kentucky Foreign Language Quarterly,* Michael Ukas remarked that Pascoli "has shown, perhaps better than anyone else, the relationship that exists between all the things in this universe. Plants and animals are linked to inanimate nature, and man is related to them all. This idea, bordering on the pantheistic, is not new with Pascoli, of course. His originality lies in the fact that each thing described by him becomes a conscious being in its own right. As a result, there exists a state of active communication between all of nature's creatures. The more we realize this fact, the better will be our understanding of the universe and of ourselves. Only understanding of the world and all its creatures can lead to the poetical harmony of *fratellanza umana,* so dear to Pascoli's heart."

With his third collection, 1903's *Canti di Castelvecchio,* Pascoli departed somewhat from the tenets outlined in "Il fanciullino." Unlike Pascoli's earlier work, the poems in this volume contain autobiographical elements, most notably relating to his father's murder, and exhibit a more complex verse structure. Later volumes such as 1906's *Odi e inni* and 1913's *Poemi del Risorgimento,* with their overtly political tone, mark a significant change in Pascoli's thematic focus and have received less praise than his earlier verse. *Poet Lore* contributor Gertrude E. T. Slaughter declared: "Pascoli is . . . a man of learning. . . . As a literary scholar the mantle of Carducci seems to have fallen upon him. He has the same zeal for the enlightenment of his countrymen, the same stern faith in sanity and right reason, the same industry of scholarship. . . . And yet it was not Carducci's odes that made Pascoli a poet. He would claim attention, apart from schools and movements, for the quality of his lyrics. Our interest in him is enhanced by the fact that he embodies, more than any other living poet, the spirit which Carducci has striven to awaken. But it is because he is so genuine a poet, more than for any other reason, that he is able to carry on the work which Carducci has held out to the youth of Italy."

Criticism on Pascoli's poetry can be divided into pre- and post-1950s schools of thought. While initial re-

views expressed dismay at the poet's departure from traditional form, Pascoli found supporters in such illustrious contemporaries as Carducci and Gabriele D'Annunzio. Perhaps his most ardent critic was Benedetto Croce, who condemned Pascoli as an anticlassicist. It was not until the 1950s, when Gianfranco Contini published an in-depth analysis of Pascoli's poetic style, that Pascoli's poetry was fully recognized for its powerful language and innovative form. In her introduction to the 1983 edition of Pascoli's *Selected Poems,* which she edited, P. R. Horne commented: "In conclusion, the reader should be reminded that this rapid survey of Pascoli's innovations was undertaken with the specific and limited aim of illustrating the features of his work which were important for the subsequent development of Italian poetry. The approach is not intended to imply that technical brilliance is synonymous with poetic excellence. In fact, some of Pascoli's worst failures were occasioned precisely by technical expertise carried to excess in ways that have been adequately discussed by Croce and other critics. . . . D'Annunzio found nothing to criticize in Pascoli's onomatopoeic effects, in his use of bird-names, or in most of the mannerisms which so exasperated Croce. Could it be that Pascoli is essentially a poet's poet?"

BIOGRAPHICAL/CRITICAL SOURCES:

BOOKS

Barzun, Jacques, and George Stade, editors, *European Writers: The Romantic Century, Charles Baudelaire to the Well-Made Play,* Volume 7, Charles Scribner's Sons, 1985, pp. 1825-1854.

Burnshaw, Stanley, editor, *The Poem Itself,* Holt, Rinehart and Winston, 1960, pp. 288-289.

Galassi, Jonathan, editor, *The Second Life of Art: Selected Essays of Eugenio Montale,* Ecco Press, 1982, pp. 82-87.

Pascoli, Giovanni, *Selected Poems,* edited and with an introduction by P. R. Horne, Manchester University Press, 1983, pp. 35-39.

Phelps, Ruth Shepard, *Italian Silhouettes,* Alfred A. Knopf, 1924, pp. 33-54.

Wilkins, Ernest Hatch, *A History of Italian Literature,* Harvard University Press, 1954, pp. 460-469.

PERIODICALS

Italian Books and Periodicals, January-December, 1985, pp. 5-8.

Kentucky Foreign Language Quarterly, vol. XIII, no. 1, 1966, pp. 51-59.

Modern Language Forum, September & December, 1951, pp. 118-125.

Modern Language Review, October, 1985, pp. 833-844; January, 1989, pp. 51-65; July, 1990, pp. 595-608.

Poet Lore, winter, 1907, pp. 501-518.*

* * *

PAUL, Tessa 1944-

PERSONAL: Born October 14, 1944, in Southern Rhodesia (now Zimbabwe); daughter of Dewzil and Barbara (a nurse) Paul. *Education:* Attended Michaelis School of Art, Cape Town, South Africa.

ADDRESSES: Home—164 Shirland Rd., London W9 2BT, England.

CAREER: Writer, editor, and illustrator. *Rand Daily Mail,* Johannesburg, South Africa, worked as researcher; worked in London, England, as picture researcher for reference books and magazines.

WRITINGS:

NONFICTION

New Flowers, Cassell (London, England), 1990.

Art of Louis Comfort Tiffany, Apple Press (London), 1987.

Tiles for a Beautiful Home, Barron's (New York City), 1990.

(With Matthew Lloyd and Janet Blackmore) *Glass for a Beautiful Home,* Barron's (New York City), 1990.

New Flowers: Growing the New Garden Varieties, Abrams (New York City), 1990.

Christmas Long Ago: Christmas Past with Changing Pictures, Putnam (New York City), 1992.

Tiffany, Random House (New York City), 1992.

(With Nigel Chadwick) *The Gardener's Handbook: The Essential Guide for Success with Plants,* Holt (New York City), 1993.

Israel ("Fiesta!" series), F. Watts (New York City), 1997.

Russia ("Fiesta!" series), F. Watts (New York City), 1997.

Turkey ("Fiesta!" series), F. Watts (New York City), 1998.

Contributor of one volume to Grolier's "Library of the Oceans" series.

"ANIMAL TRACKERS" SERIES

In Fields and Meadows, Crabtree Publishing (New York City), 1997.

By Lakes and Rivers, Crabtree Publishing (New York City), 1997.

In Woods and Forests, Crabtree Publishing (New York City), 1997.

By the Seashore, Crabtree Publishing (New York City), 1997.

At the Poles, Crabtree Publishing (New York City), 1998.

Down Under, Crabtree Publishing (New York City), 1998.

In the Jungle, Crabtree Publishing (New York City), 1998.

On Safari, Crabtree Publishing (New York City), 1998.

BIOGRAPHICAL/CRITICAL SOURCES:

PERIODICALS

School Library Journal, October, 1997, p. 122.*

* * *

PELTON, Robert S(tuart) 1921-

PERSONAL: Born May 29, 1921, in Evanston, IL; son of Guy M. (a professor and financial analyst) and Nelle (a social activist; maiden name, Russell) Pelton. *Ethnicity:* "English/Irish." *Education:* University of Notre Dame, A.B. (cum laude), 1945; St. Thomas University, Rome, Italy, S.T.L., S.T.D., 1952; postdoctoral study in Spain, 1963. *Politics:* Democrat. *Avocational interests:* Swimming, tennis.

ADDRESSES: Home—Corby Hall, Notre Dame, IN 46556. *Office*—215 Hesburgh Center, University of Notre Dame, Notre Dame, IN 46556.

CAREER: Ordained Roman Catholic priest of the Congregation of the Holy Cross (CSC), 1949; University of Notre Dame, Notre Dame, IN, professor of theology, 1953-63, also department head and chairperson of Committee on the Theological Institute for Local Superiors, 1959-62; St. George's College, Santiago, Chile, religious superior and rector, 1964-

67; Catholic University of Chile, professor of theology, 1966-71; University of Notre Dame, professor of theology, 1975—, director of Notre Dame Institute for Clergy Education, director of Institute for Pastoral and Social Ministry, 1986-91, fellow, Kellogg Institute for International Studies, 1992—.

Archdiocese of Santiago, Episcopal vicar for religious institutes, 1968-71; Organization for Continuing Education of Roman Catholic Clergy, religious representative to national board of directors, 1971; Commission for Continuing Education for Holy Cross Fathers of Indiana Province, staff director, 1975; Fort Wayne-South Bend Diocesan Priests' Senate, president, 1982-83; U.S. Catholic Conference, coordinator of national research project on churches of the Americas from the perspective of the United States, 1995-96; International Consultation on Small Christian Communities, coordinator, 1996. Stanford University, visiting fellow in Latin American studies, 1991-92.

AWARDS, HONORS: Cultural scholar, government of Spain, 1963.

WRITINGS:

The Popular Church: Myth or Reality, Institute for Pastoral and Social Ministry, University of Notre Dame (Notre Dame, IN), 1984.
From Power to Communion, University of Notre Dame Press (Notre Dame, IN), 1994.
Small Christian Communities: Imagining Future Church, University of Notre Dame Press, 1997.

Contributor to magazines and newspapers, including *Notre Dame, Today's Catholic, Human Development, Emmanuel, Pastoral Life,* and *Review for Religious.* Editor, *International Papers in Pastoral Ministry,* 1991—.

WORK IN PROGRESS: The Future of Our Past, covering sixty years of the University of Notre Dame.

SIDELIGHTS: Robert S. Pelton told *CA:* "Because of a long life and experience in many cultures, I wish to share insights which show that our society and churches are constantly being challenged to change. I find this to be exhilarating, and it leads me to look into the future for even more changes and challenges. I have learned to listen carefully to people, and to walk with them as we move into even deeper sharing. I am not afraid of challenges and changes, and I am optimistic about the future."

PETTIGREW, Judith Hoyt 1943-
(Judy Pettigrew)

PERSONAL: Born March 13, 1943, in Cincinnati, OH; daughter of Charles William (an anesthesiologist) and Hazel (a homemaker; maiden name, Hoffeld) Hoyt; married John Edward Pettigrew, Jr., September 17, 1966 (marriage ended June 7, 1976); children: John Christopher, Deborah Ann. *Ethnicity:* "German." *Education:* Ohio Wesleyan University, B.A., 1965. *Politics:* Republican. *Religion:* Methodist. *Avocational interests:*Performing arts (singing, acting).

*ADDRESSES: Home and office—*Wow! Unlimited, Inc., 4850 Marieview Ct., Cincinnati, OH 45236-2012; fax 513-984-0635. *E-mail—*judypettigrew@ fuse.net. *Agent—*Barbara Rohrer, Legacies in Print, P.O. Box 30342, Cincinnati, OH 45230.

CAREER: Procter & Gamble, Cincinnati, OH, field researcher in market research, 1965-66; JP's Distinctive Marketing, Cincinnati, freelance marketing writer, 1968-76; United Air Specialist, Cincinnati, manager of product marketing, 1976-80; Union Central Life, Cincinnati, manager of marketing communications, 1980-82; Creative Consortium, Inc. (brokerage firm for marketing professionals), Cincinnati, founder and president, 1982—. Wow! Unlimited, Inc. (creator of programs and products for women), founder and chief executive officer, 1998—; Consortium for NonProfit Marketing, executive director, 1994-98.

MEMBER: Association of Women in Communications, National Association of Women Business Owners, Women Entrepreneurs, Inc., American Business Women's Association.

AWARDS, HONORS: Named communicator of the year, Women in Communications, 1995.

WRITINGS:

UNDER NAME JUDY PETTIGREW

Cincinnati Women: Jewels in the Crown, Creative Consortium Books (Cincinnati, OH), 1988.
Sure I Can Rollerskate on Jell-O!, Creative Consortium Books, 1989.
Been There. Done That. Bought the T-Shirt!, Creative Consortium Books, 1995.
From Hot Flashes to Power Surges, Creative Consortium Books, 1996.

If I Should Die before I Wake. . ., Creative Consortium Books, 1998.

WORK IN PROGRESS: A Full-Growed Woman.

SIDELIGHTS: Judith Hoyt Pettigrew told *CA:* "I write because it is cheaper than going to a therapist! My writings all reflect my life experiences. The stories, anecdotes, and vignettes are drawn from journal entries (which may be the bleak, dark side of the event). My writings look to the other side—the humorous, positive one. The greatest joy I receive from my writings is to have readers tell me that they see themselves in what I write and that it brings a smile or causes them to laugh. We all need to laugh more. I guess you would say I am on a crusade to release endorphins!"

*　*　*

PETTIGREW, Judy
   See PETTIGREW, Judith Hoyt

*　*　*

PFENNINGER, Leslie J. 1955-

PERSONAL: Surname is pronounced *Fen*-ing-er; born April 30, 1955, in Lancaster, PA; daughter of Albert Ross and Margaret D. Pfenninger. *Education:* Elizabethtown College, B.A., 1976.

ADDRESSES: Home and office—Washington, DC. *E-mail*—lesliejp@erols.com.

CAREER: U.S. Government Printing Office, Washington, DC, management consultant, 1977-84; U.S. Army, Harrisburg, PA, management consultant in manpower management, 1984-88; U.S. Commerce Department, Silver Spring, MD, management consultant, 1988-92; Internal Revenue Service, Washington, DC, management consultant, 1992—. Freelance artist and photographer.

WRITINGS:

(Contributor) *A&M Records: The First Twenty-Five Years,* A&M Records, 1988.
(Contributor) *Official Price Guide to Records,* 10th edition, House of Collectibles, 1993.

(Contributor) *Collectible CD Price Guide,* 2nd edition, Collector Books, 1997.
From Brass to Gold, Popular Culture Ink, 1999.
(Contributor) *Official Price Guide to CD's,* House of Collectibles, in press.

WORK IN PROGRESS: Publish 1-2-3 for Writers; Publish 1-2-3 for Photographers; Publish 1-2-3 for Artists, Designers, and Illustrators; two nonfiction and two fiction books.

*　*　*

PLANT, Sadie 1964-

PERSONAL: Born in 1964. *Education:* Received Ph.D.

ADDRESSES: Home—England. *Office*—c/o University of Warwick, Coventry CV4 7AL, England. *Agent*—c/o Doubleday, 1540 Broadway, New York, NY 10036. *E-mail*—S.J.Plant@warwick.ac.uk.

CAREER: Cultural studies scholar. University of Birmingham, Birmingham, England, lecturer in cultural studies; University of Warwick, Coventry, England, director of Cybernetic Culture Research Unit.

WRITINGS:

The Most Radical Gesture: The Situationist International in a Postmodern Age, Routledge (London), 1992.

Also author of *Zeros + Ones: Digital Women + the New Technoculture.*

Contributor to periodicals.

SIDELIGHTS: Sadie Plant is known for her studies in culture, particularly pertaining to cyberculture, machine intelligence, drugs, cybernetics, and cyberfeminism. Plant has written both books and articles on such subjects, including *The Most Radical Gesture: The Situationist International in a Postmodern Age* and *Zeros + Ones: Digital Women + the New Technoculture.*

In *The Most Radical Gesture* Plant focuses her attention on the deep influence of the French vanguard group, the Situationist International, and its leader Guy Debord, and on the worker and student revolutions that erupted in France and across Europe in the May of 1968. The group, founded in 1957, critiqued the ways in which post-World War II capitalism and its attendant consumerism were robbing human life of any authentic meaning. They felt that all aspects of life, from work to leisure, from romance to childrearing, were being robbed of individual significance and, through the intensive mediation of the marketplace and the media, reformulated into consumer experiences. As Plant explains, Situationism was informed by Marxism, but it extended the idea that the worker is alienated from his or her own labor by capitalism to the notion that each of us is alienated from our very self by the intervention of market forces and processes. One saying of the Angry Brigade, a group greatly influenced by Debord and the Situationists, sums up the critique: "He not busy being born is busy buying."

The publication of Guy Debord's *Society of the Spectacle* in 1967 provided not only key ideas, but what some consider a manifesto to the students and workers discontented with circumstances in France. By "society of the spectacle," according to Elizabeth Young of *New Statesman and Society,* Debord meant that as a result of the intertwining of capitalistic and media forces, we each become "spectators, totally passive consumers" of our own experiences.

According to critics, Plant places the ideas of the Situationist movement into a current-day perspective, and offers those ideas as a place from which to critique postmodern thought. Jean Baudrillard and Jean-Francois Lyotard, two of the best-known theorists of postmodernism, were strongly influenced by Debord and Situationist ideas. But, according to Plant, they drained the revolutionary potential out of Situationism by developing the postmodern notion that, rather than being alienated from authentic experience, we need to acknowledge that there is no such thing—that language itself mediates all experience and all meaning and separates us from anything outside of it, anything "real." From this perspective, since no revolutionary act can free us from language itself, then revolution has no real power to bring us into connection with authenticity, or to forge a truly different way of being in the world.

Plant finds fault with the revision of Situationist thinking for postmodernism: "The world of uncertainty and superficiality described and celebrated by the Post-Modernists is precisely that which the Situationists first subjected to passionate criticism." The Situationists, according to Greil Marcus in the

London Review of Books, are "the last utopians, haunting our every compromise." Marcus admired the clarity of Plant's writing, but missed the sense of the human beings behind the ideas in Plant's book project. Young, on the other hand, valued the perspective on Situationism brought by Plant's book, stating that "Sadie Plant's rigorous account finally gives it credit for its enormous contribution to postwar theory and revolutionary politics."

With *Zeros + Ones: Digital Women + the New Technoculture,* Plant once again produced a book examining intellectual history and culture. This time, instead of investigating a specific intellectual movement, examines the larger topic of the interconnections between women and computers. Plant traces women's traditional roles and activities throughout history to make the dual argument that women are themselves natural computers and that women are uniquely suited to use and understand computers: "singing, chanting, telling stories, dancing, . . . spinsters, weavers, and needleworkers were literally networkers as well . . . the textures of woven cloth functioned as means of communication and information storage long before anything was written down."

Plant also features the lives of women who contributed most directly to the development of the computer, including Lady Ada Lovelace, poet Lord Byron's daughter who, according to Lindsy Van Gelder in the *Nation* is "the mathematician known as the world's first software programmer (even though her software was too advanced for the hardware of the time)." Lovelace's brilliance was recognized, but the unevenness of her temperament was put down to the rigors of mathematics, a discipline that during Lovelace's time was thought to be too demanding for a woman. Part of Plant's point in writing the book is to argue that "neural nets have less to do with the rigors of orthodox logic than the intuitive leaps and cross-connections once pathologized [as] hysteria." In other words, the feminine attributes that have been condemned as unstable or weak are precisely those best suited to the broad-spectrum logic of computers.

Critiques of Plant's *Zeros + Ones* were mixed. Hilary Burton in the *Library Journal* wondered whether Plant "is just too far ahead of her time." She was put off by the broadness of the study's range, ultimately finding it confusing and ineffective. A *Publishers Weekly* critic was more enthusiastic, declaring that "the circular, crafted logic of this often brilliant work is a challenge, although readers who embrace it will be well rewarded."

The book received a lengthy review from Lindsy Van Gelder in the *Nation*. Van Gelder identified with what she called the "girl geek" underpinnings of the book, and appreciated its insistence that, rather than being naturally alienated from computer technology, women are uniquely suited to it. Van Gelder admitted that readers may be bothered by Plant's premise "that female equals fluid, connected and multitasking. Others may be put off by a certain juxtapositional glibness." Despite some reservations, Van Gelder overlooked such misgivings because "fortunately, one *does* go "Ahhh!" often enough to make *Zeros + Ones* an intriguing read."

BIOGRAPHICAL/CRITICAL SOURCES:

BOOKS

Plant, Sadie, *Zeros + Ones: Digital Women + the New Technoculture*, Doubleday (New York City), 1997.

PERIODICALS

Library Journal, October 1, 1997, p. 110.
London Review of Books, March 25, 1993, pp. 12-13.
Nation, November 3, 1997, pp. 52-53.
New Statesman and Society, vol. 5, no. 201, p. 41; January 9, 1998, pp. 44-45.
Publishers Weekly, September 8, 1997, pp. 67-68.

OTHER

geekgirl, http://www.geekgirl.com.au/geekgirl/001 stick/sadie/sadie.html (February 8, 1999).
Salon, http://www.salonmagazine.com/sept97/21st/ tech970911.html (February 8, 1999).
Zero News Datapool, http://www.t0.or.at/sadie/inter vw.htm (February 8, 1999).*

* * *

PLATT, Peter G(odfrey) 1961-

PERSONAL: Born September 7, 1961, in New Haven, CT; son of Peter Godfrey, Sr. and Gertrude (Bland) Platt; married Luisa Costanzo, August 8, 1986 (died November 22, 1987); married Nancy Hopwood Fee, June 27, 1998. *Education:* Yale University, B.A. (cum laude), 1983; Middlebury College, M.A., 1987; Oxford University, D.Phil., 1993.

ADDRESSES: Home—301 West 108th St., No. 11-C, New York, NY 10025. *Office*—Department of English, 421 Barnard Hall, Barnard College, 606 West 120th St., New York, NY 10027.

CAREER: English teacher at a school in Englewood, NJ, 1983-87; Villiers Park Program, Middleton Stoney, England, tutor, 1990; high school English teacher in San Francisco, CA, 1992-94; Barnard College, New York City, assistant professor of English, 1994—. University of Edinburgh, fellow of Institute for Advanced Studies in the Humanities, 1998.

MEMBER: Shakespeare Association of America, Renaissance Society of America, Renaissance English Text Society, Sixteenth Century Conference, Malone Society, Modern Language Association of America, Elizabethan Club (Yale University).

AWARDS, HONORS: Overseas student award, Lincoln College, Oxford, 1988-89; British Government grant, 1988-91.

WRITINGS:

Reason Diminished: Shakespeare and the Marvelous, University of Nebraska Press (Lincoln, NE), 1997.
(Editor and author of introduction) *Wonders, Marvels, and Monsters in Early Modern Culture*, University of Delaware Press (East Brunswick, NJ), 1999.
(Contributor) David Scott Kastan, editor, *A Companion to Shakespeare*, Basil Blackwell, 1999.

Contributor of articles and reviews to periodicals, including *Sidney Newsletter and Journal*, *Review of English Studies*, and *Sixteenth Century Journal*.

* * *

**PLIEKSANS, Janis 1865-1929
(Janis Rainis, a pseudonym)**

PERSONAL: Born September 11, 1865, in Rubene County, Latvia; died September 12, 1929, in Majori (near Riga), Latvia. *Education:* University of St. Petersburg, law degree, c. 1890.

CAREER: Writer and translator.

WRITINGS:

POETRY

Talas noskanas zila vakara, 1903.
Vetras seja, 1905.
Klusa gramata, 1909, also published as *Veja nestas lapas*, 1910.
Tie, kas neaizmirst, 1911.
Gals un sakums, 1912.
Sveika, briva Latvija!, 1919.

PLAYS

Uguns un nakts, 1907, English translation by R. R. Millers published as *Fire and Night: Latvia's Most Famous Play 1981, by Her Greatest Poet, Janis Rainis*, Echo Publishers West (West Menlo Park, CA), 1981.
Indulis un Arija, 1911.
Put, vejini!, 1913.
Jazeps un vina brali, 1919, English translation by Grace Rhys published as *The Sons of Jacob*, J. M. Dent (London), 1924, translation by Rhys also published as *Joseph and His Brothers*, Ziemelblazma (Vasteras, Sweden), 1965.
Speleju, dancoju, 1919.
Mila stipraka par navi, 1927.
Rigas, ragana, 1928.

TRANSLATIONS

Johann Wolfgang von Goethe, *Faust*, 1896.

Translated poetry and plays from twenty-two languages into Latvian.

OTHER

Raksti (poetry and plays), 17 volumes, 1952-65.

Editor of *Dienas lapa* (political newspaper), beginning in 1891.

SIDELIGHTS: Important both as a political activist and as a writer, Janis Plieksans—known by his pseudonym, Janis Rainis—was the most prominent figure in Latvian literature during the first three decades of the twentieth century. His poetry and dramas were strongly nationalistic, combining Latvian folklore and history with advocacy of Latvian independence from Russian and German domination. As a translator of works from twenty-two languages into Latvian, Rainis is credited with elevating Latvian literature by intro-

ducing to his compatriots the more mature literatures of Europe. Rainis is one of the few Latvian authors to earn an international reputation; in an essay translated by Karl W. Maurer in *MOSAIC: A Journal for the Comparative Study of Literature and Ideas,* Latvian writer Zenta Maurina declared: "If the poet is the voice and the central core of a nation, the interpreter of the soul of his people, . . . Janis Rainis must be such a one. As a living synthesis of West and East his mind embraced wide horizons. Though he was at home in seven languages and translated into Latvian poetry from twenty-two languages, he wrote his own plays and poems in Latvian only. German and Russian schools, imprisonment and exile could not silence the springs of his native Latvian."

The son of an estate overseer, Rainis was born in 1865. After completing his primary and secondary education in Latvia, he attended the University of St. Petersburg, graduating with a degree in law. He began his literary career in 1891 as editor of the influential political newspaper *Dienas lapa,* in which he promoted social reform and Latvian independence from Russian rule. A member of the liberal political movement New Current, Rainis was arrested in 1897 for his political activities and was exiled for six years, first to Pskov, then to Slobodsk. While in exile he wrote poetry and completed a translation of Johann Wolfgang von Goethe's *Faust.* His first published poetry collections—1903's *Talas noskanas zila vakara* and 1905's *Vetras seja*—gained him a critical reputation as Latvia's preeminent lyric poet and won him a large popular following for their passionate protests against oppression. After the 1905 Revolution, Rainis was forced to flee Latvia to avoid political persecution. He spent the next fourteen years in Switzerland, where he wrote his most important works. In 1918 Latvia was proclaimed an independent state, and Rainis returned to his homeland. For the rest of his life he continued to write while holding prominent positions in the Social Democratic Party and national government, including those of member of parliament and minister of education. Rainis also helped found the Riga Art Theater in 1920, and he served as director of the Latvian National Theater from 1921 to 1925. He died in 1929.

Rainis's work was primarily didactic in intent. As he wrote: "A great work must be done: to bring light to our brothers, to lead the nation toward a brighter, happier future. . . . The highest goal [is] development of the nation." Throughout his career, Rainis wrote poetry celebrating his homeland and advocating political action. While his 1903 volume *Talas noskanas zila*

vakara and his 1905 volume *Vetras seja* were written to inspire the struggle for national liberation, *Tie, kas neaizmirst* (published in 1911) commemorated the participants in the failed 1905 revolution and the 1919 volume *Sveika, briva Latvija!* hailed the attainment of Latvian independence. In other collections, such as 1912's *Gals un sakums*, Rainis treated personal and philosophical themes, including loneliness, the bitterness of exile, the place of the individual in society, the relationship of humanity to nature, and human destiny.

In addition to poetry Rainis was the author of fifteen dramas, most of which are written in blank verse. Many are based on episodes from Latvian history, such as 1928's *Rigas, ragana,* which describes the attack on the city of Riga by Peter the Great in 1710. Others draw on subjects from Latvian folklore, including the highly regarded 1907 play *Uguns un nakts* (*Fire and Night*). Recounting a battle between the legendary Latvian hero Bear-slayer and the evil Black Knight, *Fire and Night,* in the words of Emma S. Richards, calls for "spiritual regeneration by means of the eternal struggle between the primordial forces of good and evil." Rainis's 1919 work, *Jazeps un vina brali* (*The Sons of Jacob*), is generally considered his best play. Based on the biblical story of Joseph and his brothers, *The Sons of Jacob* is especially praised for its psychological insight and intensity of feeling. Grace Rhys, who translated the play into English in 1924, asserted in her introduction to *The Sons of Jacob* that "Rainis has poured all the passion of the persecuted exile into his study of Joseph. But he is a dramatist *par excellence,* which means he can enter into the soul of every one of his characters, animating them towards their actions, from within. Each of the brothers is separately studied, as anyone who troubles to read the book of Genesis will find out."

Rolfs Ekmanis, in his *Latvian Literature under the Soviets: 1940-1975,* remarked that "although Rainis often advanced theses, he knew how to distinguish between aesthetic and moral values," and most critics concur that Rainis's works successfully combine social advocacy with poetic artistry. Stressing humanistic ideals, his writings have also been praised for transcending their basis in Latvian culture to appeal to universal human emotions. Ekmanis commented: "[Janis Rainis was] the focal point of Latvian literary and intellectual history during the first three decades of this century. . . . His place still today is unquestionable as the greatest Latvian poet of this century—Latvians of all ranks would say their greatest writer,

deserving to be compared with the greatest names in world literature, is Rainis. . . . Rainis substantially enriched Latvian literature and brought it up to the level of that of West European literature. Brilliant and strongly individualistic, he is the best example in modern Latvian letters of the organic relationship between talent shaped by tradition and talent creating tradition."

BIOGRAPHICAL/CRITICAL SOURCES:

BOOKS

Andersons, Edgars, editor, *Cross Road Country: Latvia,* Latvju Gramata, 1953, pp. 253-268.
Andrups, Janis, and Vitauts Kalve, *Latvian Literature,* translated by Ruth Speirs, M. Goppers, 1954, pp. 113-126.
Ekmanis, Rolfs, *Latvian Literature under the Soviets: 1940-1975,* Nordland, 1978, pp. 38-78.
Ivask, Ivar, editor, *First Conference on Baltic Studies,* Association for the Advancement of Baltic Studies (Tacoma, Wash.), 1969, pp. 81-82.
Rainis, Janis, *Lauztas Priedes,* with an afterword by Jeronims Stulpans, Izdevznieciba Liesma (Riga, Latvia), 1965, pp. 116-118.
Rainis, Janis, *The Sons of Jacob,* translated and with an introduction by Grace Rhys, J. M. Dent (London), 1924, pp. v-xiii.
Rubulis, Aleksis, *Baltic Literature,* University of Notre Dame Press, 1970, pp. 115-159.
Ziedonis, Arvids, Jr., *The Religious Philosophy of Janis Rainis: Latvian Poet,* Latvju Gramata, 1969.

PERIODICALS

Journal of Baltic Studies, summer, 1974, pp. 126-135; summer/fall, 1975, pp. 141-152.
MOSAIC: A Journal for the Comparative Study of Literature and Ideas, Special Issue: The Literature of Small Countries, April, 1968, pp. 70-82.
Soviet Literature, no. 10, 1975, pp. 161-163.*

* * *

POINCARE, (Jules) Henri 1854-1912

PERSONAL: Born April 29, 1854, in Nancy, France; died of complications following prostate surgery, July

17, 1912; son of Leon (a physician and professor of medicine) Poincare; married Jeanne Louise Marie Poulain D'Andecy; children: one son, three daughters. *Education:* Attended Ecole Polytechnique; Ecole des Mines, Ph.D., 1879.

CAREER: University of Caen, Caen, France, member of faculty, 1879-81; University of Paris, Paris, France, lecturer in mathematical analysis, 1881-86, professor, 1886-1912.

MEMBER: Royal Society of London (elected foreign member, 1894), French Institut (elected to literary section, 1908), French Academie des Sciences (elected, 1887).

AWARDS, HONORS: Received numerous honors for scientific achievements.

WRITINGS:

Lecons sur la theorie mathamatique de la lumiere, G. Carre (Paris), 1889.

Electricite et Optique, G. Carre (Paris), 1890, revised edition published as *Electricite et Optique. La lumiere et les theories electrodynamiques,* G. Carre/C. Naud (Paris), 1901.

Les methodes nouvelles de la mecanique celeste, Gauthier-Villars (Paris), 1892-99.

Lecons sur la Theorie de l'elasticite, G. Carre (Paris), 1892.

Theorie mathematique de la lumiere, G. Carre (Paris), 1892.

Thermodynamique, G. Carre (Paris), 1892.

Theorie des tourbillons, G. Carre (Paris), 1893.

Les oscillations electriques, G. Carre (Paris), 1894.

Capillarite, G. Carre (Paris), 1895.

Calcul des probabilities, G. Carre (Paris), 1896.

Les rayons cathodiques et la theorie de Jaumann, G. Carre/C. Naud (Paris), 1896.

Cinematique et mecanismes; potentiel et mecanique des fluides, G. Carre/C. Naud (Paris), 1899.

Theorie du potentiel Newtonien, G. Carre/C. Naud (Paris), 1899.

La theorie de Maxwell et les oscillations hertziennes, C. Naud (Paris), 1899.

Figures d'equilibre d'une masse fluide, C. Naud (Paris), 1902.

Lecons de mecanique celeste professes a la Sorbonne, Gauthier-Villars (Paris), 1905-10.

The Principles of Mathematical Physics, translated by George Bruce Halsted, [Chicago], 1905.

La science et l'hypothese, c. 1905, translation by William John Greenstreet published as *Science and Hypothesis,* with a preface by J. Larmor, Walter Scott Publishing (London), 1905.

Le valeur de la science, E. Flammarion (Paris), c. 1907, translation by Geroge Bruce Halsted published as *The Value of Science,* Science Press (New York City), 1907.

Science et methode, E. Flammarion (Paris), 1908, translation by Francis Maitland published as *Science and Method,* with a preface by Bertrand Russell, T. Nelson (London/New York City), 1914.

Lecons sur les hypotheses cosmogoniques professes a la Sorbonne, A. Hermann (Paris), 1911.

Dernieres pensees, E. Flammarion (Paris), 1913.

The Foundations of Science; Science and Hypothesis, The Value of Science, Science and Method, translated by George Bruce Halsted, with an introduction by Josiah Royce, Science Press (New York City), 1913.

The Connection between the Ether and Matter, [Washington, DC], 1913.

La mecanique nouvelle; conference memoire et not sur la theorie de la reletivite, Gauthier-Villars (Paris), 1924.

Contributor of articles and papers to periodicals.

SIDELIGHTS: Jules Henri Poincare has been described as the last great universalist—"the last man," E. T. Bell wrote in *Men of Mathematics,* "to take practically all mathematics, pure and applied, as his province." He made contributions to number theory, theory of functions, differential equations, topology, and the foundations of mathematics. In addition, Poincare was very much interested in astronomy, and some of his best known research is his work on the three-body problem, which concerns the way planets act on each other in space. He worked in the area of mathematical physics and anticipated some fundamental ideas in the theory of relativity. He also participated in the debate about the nature of mathematical thought, and he wrote popular books on the general principles of his field, including *La science et l'hypothese* and *Le valeur de science.*

Poincare was born in Nancy, France, on April 29, 1854. The Poincare family had made Nancy their home for many generations, and the family members included a number of illustrious scholars. His father was Leon Poincare, a physician and professor of medicine at the University of Nancy. Poincare's cousin Raymond Poincare was later to serve as prime minister of France and as president of the republic during World War I. Poincare was a frail child with poor coordination; his larynx was temporarily paralyzed when he was five as a result of a bout of diphtheria. He was also very bright as a child, not necessarily an advantage in dealing with one's peers. All in all he was, according to James Newman in the *World of Mathematics,* "a suitable victim of the brutalities of children his own age."

Poincare received his early education at home from his mother and then entered the lycee in Nancy. There he began to demonstrate his remarkable mathematical talent and earned a first prize in a national student competition. In 1873 he was admitted to the Ecole Polytechnique, although he scored a zero on the drawing section of the entrance examination. His work was so clearly superior in every other respect that examiners were willing to forgive his perennial inability to produce legible diagrams. He continued to impress his teachers at the Ecole and is reputed to have passed all his math courses without reading the textbooks or taking notes in his classes.

After completing his work at the Ecole, Poincare went on to the Ecole des Mines with the intention of becoming an engineer. He continued his theoretical work in mathematics, however, and three years later submitted a doctoral thesis. He was awarded his doctorate in 1879 and was then appointed to the faculty at the University of Caen. Two years later he was offered a post as lecturer in mathematical analysis at the University of Paris, and in 1886 was promoted to full professor, a post he would hold until his death in 1912.

One of Poincare's earliest works dealt with a set of functions to which he gave the name Fuchsian functions, in honor of the German mathematician Lazarus Fuchs. The functions are more commonly known today as automorphic functions, or functions involving sets that correspond to themselves. In this work Poincare demonstrated that the phenomenon of periodicity, or recurrence, is only a special case of a more general property; in this property, a particular function is restored when its variable is replaced by a number of transformations of itself. As a result of this work in automorphic functions, Poincare was elected to the French Academie des Sciences in 1887 at the age of thirty-two.

For all his natural brilliance and formal training, Poincare was apparently ignorant of much of the literature on mathematics. One consequence of this fact was that each new subject Poincare heard about drove his interests in yet another new direction. When he

learned about the work of Georg Bernhard Riemann and Karl Weierstrass on Abelian functions, for example, he threw himself into that work and stayed with the subject until his death.

Two other fields of mathematics to which Poincare contributed were topology and probability. With topology, or the geometry of functions, he was working with a subject which had only been treated in bare outlines, and from this he constructed the foundations of modern algebraic topology. In the case of probability, Poincare not only contributed to the mathematical development of the subject, but he also wrote popular essays about probability that were widely read by the general public. Indeed, he was elected to membership in the literary section of the French Institut in 1908 for the literary quality of these essays.

In the field of celestial mechanics, Poincare was especially concerned with two problems, the shape of rotating bodies (such as stars) and the three-body problem. In the first of these, Poincare was able to show that a rotating fluid goes through a series of stages, first taking a spheroidal and then an ellipsoidal shape, before assuming a pear-like form that eventually develops a bulge in it and finally breaks apart into two pieces. The three-body problem involves an analysis of the way in which three bodies, such as three planets, act on each other. The problem is very difficult, but Poincare made some useful inroads into its solution and also developed methods for the later resolution of the problem. In 1889 his work on this problem won a competition sponsored by King Oscar II of Sweden.

The work Poincare did in celestial mechanics was part of his interest in the application of mathematics to physical phenomena; his title at the University of Paris was actually professor of mathematical physics. Of the roughly five hundred papers Poincare wrote, about seventy dealt with topics such as light, electricity, capillarity, thermodynamics, heat, elasticity, and telegraphy. He also made contributions to the development of relativity theory. As early as 1899 he suggested that absolute motion did not exist. A year later he also proposed the concept that nothing could travel faster than the speed of light. These two propositions are, of course, important parts of Albert Einstein's theory of special relativity, first announced in 1905.

As he grew older Poincare devoted more attention to fundamental questions about the nature of mathematics. He wrote a number of papers criticizing the logical and rational philosophies of Bertrand Russell,

David Hilbert, and Giuseppe Peano, and to some extent his work presaged some of the intuitionist arguments of L. E. J. Brouwer. As E. T. Bell wrote: "Poincare was a vigorous opponent of the theory that all mathematics can be rewritten in terms of the most elementary notions of classical logic; something more than logic, he believed, makes mathematics what it is."

Poincare died on July 17, 1912, of complications arising from prostate surgery. He was fifty-eight years old. During his lifetime he had received many of the honors then available to a scientist, including election to the Royal Society as a foreign member in 1894. Poincare was married to Jeanne Louise Marie Poulain D'Andecy, with whom he had four children, one son and three daughters.

BIOGRAPHICAL/CRITICAL SOURCES:

BOOKS

Bell, E. T., *Men of Mathematics,* Simon and Schuster (New York City), 1937, pp. 526-554.

Jones, Bessie Zaban, editor, *The Golden Age of Science,* Simon and Schuster (New York City), 1966, pp. 615-637.

Newman, James R., *The World of Mathematics,* Volume 2, Simon and Schuster (New York City), 1956, pp. 1374-1379.*

*   *   *

POLKINGHORNE, John Charlton 1930-

PERSONAL: Born October 16, 1930, in Weston-Super-Mare, England; son of George Baulkwell and Dorothy Evelyn (Charlton) Polkinghorne; married Ruth Isobel Martin (a statistician), 1955; children: Peter, Michael, Isobel Polkinghorne Morland. *Education:* Trinity College, Cambridge, M.A., 1956, Ph.D., 1955, Sc.D., 1974. *Religion:* Church of England. *Avocational interests:* Gardening.

ADDRESSES: Home—74 Hurst Park Ave., Cambridge CB4 2AF, England.

CAREER: Theoretical physicist and Anglican priest. California Institute of Technology, Commonwealth Fund Fellow, 1955-56; University of Edinburgh, Scotland, lecturer in mathematical physics, 1956-58; Cambridge University, Cambridge, England, lecturer in applied mathematics, 1958-65, reader in theoretical physics, 1965-68, professor of mathematical physics, 1968-79; Trinity College, Cambridge, England, fellow, 1954-86, dean and chaplain, 1986-89; Queen's College, Cambridge, England, president, beginning 1989. Ordained deacon of the Church of England, 1981; St. Andrew's, Chesterton, England, curate, 1981-82; St. Michael's, Bedminster, England, curate, 1982-84; ordained priest of the Church of England, 1982; vicar in Kent, England, 1984-86.

MEMBER: Royal Society (fellow).

AWARDS, HONORS: Knight Commander of the Order of the British Empire (K.B.E.); honorary D.D., University of Kent, 1994.

WRITINGS:

(With R. J. Eden, P. V. Landsholt, and D. I. Olive) *The Analytic S-Matrix,* Cambridge University Press (Cambridge, England), 1966.

The Particle Play: An Account of the Ultimate Constituents of Matter, W. H. Freeman (New York City), 1979.

Models of High Energy Physics, Cambridge University Press (Cambridge, England), 1980.

The Way the World Is: The Christian Perspective of a Scientist, Triangle (London), 1983.

The Quantum World, Longman (Harlow, England), 1984.

Science and Christian Belief: Theological Reflections Bottom-up Thinkers, SPCK (London), 1984.

One World: The Interaction of Science and Theology, SPCK (London), 1986.

Science and Creation, SPCK (London), 1988.

Science and Providence: God's Interaction with the World, SPCK (London), 1989.

Rochester Roundabout: The Story of High Energy Physics, W. H. Freeman (San Francisco, CA), 1989.

Reason and Reality: The Relationship between Science and Theology, Trinity International (Valley Forge, PA), 1992.

The Faith of a Physicist: Reflections of a Bottom-up Thinker, Princeton University Press (Princeton, NJ), 1994.

Quarks, Chaos and Christianity: Questions to Science and Religion, Triangle (London), 1994.

Serious Talk: Science and Religion in Dialogue, Trinity International, 1995.

Beyond Science: The Wider Human Context, Cambridge University Press (Cambridge, England), 1996.

Scientists as Theologians, SPCK (London), 1996.

Beyond Science, Cambridge University Press (Cambridge, England), 1996.

Belief in God in an Age of Science, Yale University Press (New Haven, CT), 1998.

Science and Theology: An Introduction, SPCK (London), 1998.

Polkinghorne's books have been translated into numerous languages.

SIDELIGHTS: In 1979 John Charlton Polkinghorne surprised his peers by announcing he intended to begin studying to become a clergyman for the Church of England. Many are called to "the cloth," but Polkinghorne was different from most, for he was leaving behind a successful career as a theoretical physicist that spanned nearly three decades. He claimed at the time that theoretical physics was a young man's profession. His career had been spent almost entirely at Cambridge University—he had received his undergraduate and graduate degrees there and was a professor of mathematical physics there from 1968 to 1979.

Polkinghorne did not abandon science, however, and found a way to integrate theoretical physics into his religious life by writing a number of critically acclaimed books for general readers that attempt a rapprochement between science and religion, particularly Christianity. He also practiced his new career as clergyman and academic administrator at his old haunts—he was named president of Queen's College, Cambridge University, in 1989. Polkinghorne is the only Fellow of the Royal Society (England's most prestigious science fraternity) who is also an Anglican priest.

Polkinghorne's published works include *Serious Talk: Science and Religion in Dialogue, Beyond Science: The Wider Human Context, Quarks, Chaos and Christianity: Questions to Science and Religion,* and *Belief in God in an Age of Science*—all published between 1995 and 1998. In *Serious Talk* Polkinghorne lays out a series of arguments about why scientists and theologians should engage in a dialogue. Polkinghorne expresses the belief that theology offers a "reasonable response" to the larger questions that science raises. Charles L. Currie, S.J., of St. Joseph's University, praised *Serious Talk* in *Theological Studies:* "This book is Polkinghorne at his best—. . . earnestly trying

. . . to demonstrate the possibility of a fruitful consonance between science and theology in the quest for understanding."

The topics discussed in *Beyond Science* range from evolution to the end of the universe. Polkinghorne believes, for instance, that far from flying in the face of God, the theory of evolution provides evidence of an underlying design wrought by a Supreme Being. Bryce Christensen, reviewing *Beyond Science* for *Choice,* noted Polkinghorne's belief that "science opens a genuine understanding of the harmonies of the universe." While taking exception to some of Polkinghorne's arguments, David Mermin, a physicist at Cornell University, wrote in *Nature* that "Polkinghorne's literate sense of wonder at the magical richness of things shines out on almost every page, whether or not one agrees that it implies a creator."

Belief in God in the Age of Science covers some of the same ground as *Beyond Science.* Based on the Terry lectures which Polkinghorne delivered at Yale University, the book further develops his theology of nature and posits a divine purpose behind our human destiny. He also points to the wave/particle dual nature of light as an apt metaphor for Christ's dual divinity and humanity. Christensen, who also reviewed *Belief in God in the Age of Science* for *Choice,* commented that atheists should "exercise new caution" in citing scientific proofs, because "Polkinghorne articulates a faith strengthened, not threatened, by the latest scientific research."

Polkinghorne extends the duality metaphor in *Quarks, Chaos and Christianity,* rationalizing that the dual nature of light is also a good analogy for the existence of good and evil in the world. "Applied to theological language, this is analogy that could begin to limp all too soon," Edward T. Oakes pointed out in *Commonweal,* "but I think Polkinghorne is fundamentally right: like early particle physicists, believers really don't understand how God can be good and yet there be evil in the universe—it's just that it proves impossible to give up either experience."

Since 1983 Polkinghorne had honed his themes in several books, all of which received favorable reviews. Donald MacKay of *Nature* praised Polkinghorne's "clean and straight thinking" in *The Way the World Is: The Christian Perspective of a Scientist,* published in 1983. Robert John Russell, also writing in *Nature,* positively assessed Polkinghorne's 1986 follow-up work, *One World: The Interaction of*

Science and Theology. Russell noted, "Writing with precision and elegance, Polkinghorne captures the majesty and mystery of our current view of nature." Polkinghorne's 1988 work, *Science and Creation,* fleshes out his opposition to a "God of the gaps" theology which looks at the Supreme Being who created the universe but then does not participate in the ongoing life of the universe. Keith Ward, writing for *Religious Studies,* called *Science and Creation* "a book at the frontiers of philosophy, theology, and physics, which combines a passionate concern for truth with a firm commitment of faith." *Science and Providence: God's Interaction with the World,* appearing in 1989, picks up threads developed in *Science and Creation,* namely that creation is a continual act. David Gosling, a critic for the *Ecumenical Review,* valued Polkinghorne's achievement: "Having established a scientifically credible basis for God's way of interacting with the world, John Polkinghorne has little difficulty with conventional areas of Christian theology."

In his 1994 work *The Faith of a Physicist: Reflections of a Bottom-up Thinker,* Polkinghorne adopts a novel approach to his subject: each chapter matches a phrase from the Nicene Creed to one of his scientific concerns. He calls himself a "bottom-up" thinker, one who starts with tangible physical evidence to build his theological conclusions. Thus he uses science to shed light on the nature of humanity, God, and creation; on the life, death, and resurrection of Jesus; and on Trinitarian theology. Chet Raymo of *Commonweal* thought that "on the whole, Polkinghorne steers a marvelously adept course between the Scylla of top-down theology and the Charybdis of naive scientism" in *The Faith of a Physicist.* Tony Bridge of *Contemporary Review* called it an "impressive and important book," and Patrick H. Samway of *America* commented that "Polkinghorne shows that 'faith seeking understanding' is not reserved to the realm of theology alone."

Polkinghorne has also written several books of straight science. *The Particle Play: An Account of the Ultimate Constituents of Matter,* published in 1979, is a book for laymen on recent developments in subatomic physics. A *Choice* reviewer noted that the book contains "a tremendous amount of material . . . covered in a remarkably compact fashion." *Models of High Energy Physics,* published in 1980, covers much of the same ground as *The Particle Plays,* but for a more technical audience. Polkinghorne's 1984 book *The Quantum World* falls between the other two works—more sophisticated in discourse than *The Particle Play,* but not as technically challenging as *Models of High Energy Physics.* Reviewing *The Quantum World* for *Nature,* Abraham Pais praised the book for not being a blend of "the material and the mystic." Pais wrote, "This book is short and lucid. It demands thinking but no knowledge of higher mathematics. Its language is simple."

Rochester Roundabout: The Story of High Energy Physics, Polkinghorne's 1989 work, chronicles the 1947-1977 Rochester Conferences—gatherings, sometimes annual, sometimes semi-annual, of high energy physicists. Robert G. Colodny, writing for *Science Books and Films,* referred to *Rochester Roundabout* as "an insider's book for experts." Robert W. Seidel held a similar view. Reviewing the book for *Isis,* Seidel said, "*Rochester Roundabout* is not the book from which to obtain one's first introduction to the intellectual history of high energy physics from 1950 to 1980. But for those who have a minimal acquaintance with the field the book will be useful."

Polkinghorne told *CA:* "I am a passionate believer in the unity of knowledge. In my life and in my writing I have sought to take the insights of science and the insights of religion with equal seriousness. Together this 'binocular vision' gives me a deeper understanding of reality than I would gain from either on its own."

BIOGRAPHICAL/CRITICAL SOURCES:

PERIODICALS

AB Bookman's Weekly, October 10, 1994, p. 1402.
America, March 19, 1994, p. 22.
Booklist, June 1, 1994, p. 1732; September 1, 1996, p. 48; February 15, 1998, p. 951.
British Book News, September, 1980, p. 544; April, 1986, p. 210.
Choice, September, 1980, p. 128; January, 1981, p. 694; September, 1984, p. 145; March, 1997, p. 1179.
Christian Century, December 16, 1987, p. 1155; March 18, 1982, p. 313.
Commonweal, March 10, 1989, p. 149; May 20, 1994, pp. 31-32; August 16, 1996, pp. 23-24.
Contemporary Review, June, 1994, pp. 327-328.
Dalhousie Review, spring, 1987, p. 160.
Ecumenical Review, January, 1990, pp. 76-77.
Hungry Mind Review, winter, 1995, p. 12.
Isis, June, 1992, pp. 359-361.
Library Journal, February 1, 1998, pp. 89-90.

National Review, March 22, 1985, pp. 53-54; June 27, 1994, pp. 54-57; April 6, 1998, pp. 55-59.

Nature, May 26, 1983, p. 353; April 26, 1984, p. 783; June 26, 1986, p. 825; May 4, 1989, pp. 23-24; October 31, 1996, p. 772.

New Age Journal, May, 1990, p. 80.

New Scientist, February 9, 1991, pp. 60-61.

New Technical Books, November, 1990, p. 1690.

Publishers Weekly, January 26, 1998, p. 84.

Religious Studies, December, 1989, pp. 537-538.

Religious Studies Review, October, 1989, p. 344; October, 1991, p. 335.

School Books and Films, January, 1991, p. 7.

Science Books and Films, January/February, 1991, p. 7.

SciTech Book News, October, 1990, p. 11.

Skeptic, 1995, p. 101.

Theological Studies, December, 1984, p. 793; June, 1996, pp. 383-384.

Theology Today, January, 1994, p. 613; April, 1996, pp. 140-141.

Times Educational Supplement, March 7, 1986, p. 23.

Wall Street Journal, October 10, 1994, p. A10.

Washington Post Book World, August 14, 1994, p. 13.

Zygon, March, 1987, p. 113; December, 1990, p. 504.

*   *   *

POLLACZEK-GEIRINGER, Hilda
See GEIRINGER, Hilda

*   *   *

PONTOPPIDAN, Henrik 1857-1943

PERSONAL: Born July 24, 1857, in Frederica, Jutland, Denmark; died August 21, 1943, in Charlottenlund, Denmark; son of Dines and M. Marie Kirstina Oxenboll Pontoppidan; married Mette Marie Hansen, December, 1881 (divorced, 1892); married Antoinette Cecilia Kofoed, April 9, 1892. *Education:* Attended Copenhagen Polytechnical Institute, 1873-77. *Religion:* Freethinker, from Lutheran background.

CAREER: Writer. Grundtvigian Folk High School, Denmark, teacher of natural science, 1879-82.

AWARDS, HONORS: Nobel Prize in literature, 1917.

WRITINGS:

NOVELS

Scandige menighed, 1883.

Ung elskov, 1885, revised edition, 1906.

Mimoser, 1886, English translation published as *The Apothecary's Daughter,* 1890.

Isbjornen, 1887.

Muld (part of the novel cycle "Det forjaettede land"), 1891, revised edition, 1898, English translation published as *Emanuel; or, Children of the Soil,* 1896.

Det forjaettede land (part of the novel cycle "Det forjaettede land"), Philipsen (Copenhagen), 1892, revised edition, 1898, English translation by Ms. Edgar Lucas published as *The Promised Land,* J. M. Dent (London), 1896.

Den gamle Adam, 1894.

Nattevagt, 1894.

Dommens dag (part of the novel cycle "Det forjaettede land"), 1895, revised edition, 1898.

Lykke-Per (title means "Lucky Peter"), 8 volumes, Det Nordiske Forlag (Copenhagen), 1894-1904, revised editions, 1905, 1908.

Det ideale hjem, 1900.

Lille rodhaette, 1900.

Den kongelige gaest, 1908, English translation published as *The Royal Guest,* in *The Royal Guest and Other Classical Danish Narrative,* 1977.

Torben og jytte (part of the novel cycle "De dodes rige"; title means "Kingdom of the Dead") 1912, revised edition, 1917.

Storeholt (part of the novel cycle "De dodes rige"; title means "Kingdom of the Dead") 1913, revised edition, 1917.

Toldere og syndere (part of the novel cycle "De dodes rige"; title means "Kingdom of the Dead") 1914, revised edition, 1917.

Enslevs dod (part of the novel cycle "De dodes rige"; title means "Kingdom of the Dead"), 1915, revised edition, 1917.

Favsingholm (part of the novel cycle "De dodes rige"; title means "Kingdom of the Dead"), 1916; revised edition, 1917.

Mands himmerig (title means "Man's Heaven"), Hyldendal, Norkiske Forlag (Copenhagen), 1927.

SHORT STORY COLLECTIONS

Staekkede vinger (title means "Clipped Wings"), Andr. Schous Forlag (Copenhagen), 1881.

Landsbybilleder, 1883.

Fra hytterne, 1887.
Skyer (title means "Clouds"), Gyldendalske Boghandel Forlag (Copenhagen), 1890.
Fortaellinger, 1899.

Contributor of short stories to anthologies, including *Anthology of Danish Literature,* 1971; contributor of short stories to periodicals, including *American-Scandinavian Review.*

OTHER

Asgaardsrejen (play), 1902.
Undervejs til mig selv (memoirs), 1943.

SIDELIGHTS: Considered the foremost Danish novelist of the late nineteenth century, Henrik Pontoppidan examined the cultural effects of changing class structures, sexual mores, and values during a period of transition in Danish society. Often described as a Naturalist, Pontoppidan was one of the first Danish novelists to depict the suffering of the peasantry seriously and with compassion, criticizing the idealistic and ineffectual attempts of the upper class to implement educational and political reforms. Throughout his fiction Pontoppidan satirized utopianism, whether it appeared as a neo-Rousseauistic celebration of rural life or as simple-minded liberalism, and he continually depicted the disillusion resulting from social ideals. This theme is developed most elaborately in the three cycles of novels upon which Pontoppidan's reputation is based: *Det forjaettede land (The Promised Land), Lykke-Per,* and *De dodes rige.* Although not widely read outside Denmark today, Pontoppidan's work was so esteemed during his lifetime that he received the Nobel Prize in literature for 1917.

Pontoppidan was born in Fredericia, Denmark, into a prominent Lutheran family which for generations had produced theologians and scholars. Both his father and grandfather had been Lutheran clergymen, and Pontoppidan was expected to continue the family tradition. When he was six Pontoppidan moved with his family to Randers, where he attended a Latin school and excelled in mathematics. It was his facility with this subject, together with a distaste for the restrictive lifestyle of a Lutheran cleric, that led him to apply to Copenhagen's Polytechnical Institute in 1873. Biographers note that Pontoppidan's rejection of religious life and decision to study engineering resemble the choices of the main character in his eight-volume novel cycle *Lykke-Per.* While at school, Pontoppidan

began to read such authors as Soren Kierkegaard, Fyodor Dostoevsky, and Friedrich Nietzsche, and in 1876 he began writing dramas. Realizing he preferred literature to engineering, he withdrew from school in 1877 in order to pursue a literary career. To support himself, he taught natural science at a Grundtvigian folk school, a rural high school which was part of a nationalistic and religious movement inspired by N. F. S. Grundtvig, who propagated an idealized image of both the natural life of the peasant and the potential of popular education to unify rural and urban Denmark. In sympathy with agrarian life and the suffering of the poor, Pontoppidan wrote stories portraying the peasantry as victims of social and economic forces. Representative of his work of this period is the story "Et endligt," which relates the lack of compassion displayed by several town leaders for a dying man whose family is destitute, therein presenting an indictment of the upper class for its callous response to the impoverishment of Denmark's rural population. In 1881 Pontoppidan published his first collection of short stories, *Staekkede vinger.* With the royalties advanced him, he quit teaching and married a woman of the peasant class. The marriage ended in divorce eleven years later, and biographers speculate that Pontoppidan's personal failure to live out the Grundtvigian ideal in his own life by becoming a farmer and marrying a peasant woman led him to condemn such attempts in his fiction, which is often concerned with the subject of misalliance.

Called a "literature of social consciousness," the fiction Pontoppidan produced during the 1880s treats concerns that became central to his work. The novel *Isbjornen,* for example, examines the social and political malaise of the rural population of Denmark, while *Mimoser (The Apothecary's Daughter)* traces the dissolution of two marriages as a result of the change in sexual morals occurring the Denmark in the 1880s. Pontoppidan also continued to describe the injustices experienced by the poor in short stories, including those collected in *Skyer* and *Fra hytterne. Modern Language Review* contributor W. Glyn Jones explained: "Throughout his life Pontoppidan viewed the Denmark he knew with a profound sense of tragedy; he saw it as a land of decadence and self-seeking, a mere caricature of the land that had once ruled the Baltic and whose influence had been felt far beyond, and it is in the light of this that his writings must be judged."

Upon divorcing his first wife in 1892, Pontoppidan married a woman from his own social class. With his new wife he moved to Copenhagen, where he became part of a group of freethinking artists and intellectuals that had formed around the literary critic Georg Brandes, whose critical principles were founded on a rejection of religion as a source of ethical guidance and a concomitant faith in reason and science as a guide to moral decisions. By 1912, however, Pontoppidan had become disillusioned with the social and political effects of liberal attitudes and policies he believed were typified by Brandes. In his 1943 memoir, *Undervejs til mig selv,* he wrote: "Is it not on the whole one of our most unfortunate delusions that we in our conscience—that attic full of all kinds of old, hidden superstitions and long superseded prejudices—that we in the spectral voice from that sepulchre possess a divine guide through life's labyrinth, a guide in whom we can put greater trust than in the supreme human good: our reason?" Pontoppidan continued to publish throughout his long life; he died in Copenhagen at the age of eighty-six.

Analyzing the effects of social changes on late-nineteenth-century Danish society, Pontoppidan's work was concerned with hypocrisies, abuses, and unrealistic attitudes he found in the major social movements of his age. His first extensive treatment of the effects of social reformists, *The Promised Land,* portrays the Grundtvigians, who endeavored to end poverty and illiteracy through an educational system meant to bring together cultured urbanites and the rural populace.

Pontoppidan regarded the efforts of the Grundtvigians as unnatural, naive, and overly ambitious. He believed that because the Grundtvigians refused to acknowledge the limitations imposed on a person by heredity, they naively assumed they could effect dramatic social changes by means of superficial social reforms. Representing what Pontoppidan considered the naive Grundtvigian response to the plight of the poor, the main character of the novel cycle neglects his duties as a husband and as the pastor of a village church in order to devote himself to the political cause of the peasants, but his unrealistic attitude toward the poor only leads to his personal ruin. Unlike Pontoppidan's earlier portrayals, his depiction of the lower classes in this novel cycle has been described as unsympathetic. Whereas in "Et endligt" his attack had focused on the self-absorbed wealthy Danes as the source of the problems of the poor in Denmark, the emphasis by now has shifted to include the peasants as a class of self-seekers. In *The Promised Land* the rural populace is depicted as a cunning faction of society which makes great demands on the aid supplied by the church, abusing what it views as hypo-

critical charity that is dispensed solely to gain additional votes for the parish. This change in Pontoppidan's additional votes for the parish. This change in Pontoppidan's attitude toward the peasantry is considered indicative of the development in his work from examining the effects of social ills to focusing on the underlying causes he believed originated in the character of the Danish people.

In his next major novel cycle, *Lykke-Per,* a talented young engineering student displays attitudes and opinions that reflect those current in Copenhagen during the 1880s. Specifically, Per adopts the prevailing assumption of intellectuals living in the capital that Denmark was a backward country requiring intense technological development in order to compete with the great industrialized nations of the West. Per makes the simplistic supposition that Denmark's problems will be solved with the construction of an immense and overly complex canal system of his design. Eventually he is forced to realize, however, that the project is not economically feasible, and his misjudgment is meant to represent the ill-conceived ambitions of Danish society as a whole. In *Lykke-Per* Pontoppidan wrote: "It is as if some hidden disease consumed the strength of the nation, sucked out the marrow of its best youth, and exposed the country as booty to the lust of foreign conquest."

Disillusion with facile solutions to social problems also pervades Pontoppidan's last novel cycle, *De dodes rige,* an analysis of the aftermath of the successful democratic movement in Denmark between 1900 and 1910, when an emerging liberalism had minimized the importance of traditional values such as marriage and family life without providing an adequate substitute. Pontoppidan expressed his antipathy for such trends, particularly the libertinism advocated by Brandes, who wrote that increased intellectual productivity is dependent upon "the most uninhibited freedom within the realm of Eros." Abandoning a sustained focus on any single character, *De dodes rige* presents a comprehensive view of the many popular movements originating in Denmark at the turn of the century. In an essay on *De does rige* in *Scandinavian Studies,* Kenneth H. Ober remarked: "The application of the extended myth of the divided self to Pontoppidan's delineation of his characters adds a new interest and a new dimension to the characterizations themselves and removes the atmosphere of incompleteness which seems otherwise to surround them. In addition to contributing a new depth to the novel and increasing interest in the fates of the characters, this interpretation adds an almost mythic quality to what critics have too readily labelled as a social novel. Like *Det forjaettede land* and *Lykke-Per, De dodes rige* has a philosophical substance that transcends a mere picture of the times." In studies of his works, Pontoppidan has been repeatedly praised for his ability to portray the effects this rapid social transformation had on individuals living at the time. As H. G. Topsoe-Jensen wrote in his *Scandinavian Literature from Brandes to Our Day:* "No other of the newer Danish authors has been able to present such a complete picture of his time, its intellectual movements, and its human types."

BIOGRAPHICAL/CRITICAL SOURCES:

BOOKS

Bach, Giovanni, *The History of the Scandinavian Literatures,* Kennikat Press (Port Washington, N.Y.), 1966, pp. 161-220.
Bayerschmidt, Carl F., and Erik Friis, editors, *Scandinavian Studies,* University of Washington Press, 1965, pp. 227-235.
Marble, Annie Russell, *The Nobel Prize Winners in Literature,* Appleton & Co. (New York City), 1925, pp. 197-201.
Mitchell, P. M., and Kenneth H. Ober, editors, *The Royal Guest, and Other Classical Danish Narrative,* University of Chicago Press, 1977.
Robertson, J. G., *Essays and Addresses on Literature,* reprinted, Books for Libraries Press, distributed by Arno Press, 1968, pp. 245-254.
Rossel, Sven H., *A History of Scandinavian Literature, 1870-1980,* University of Minneapolis Press, 1982, pp. 40-44.
Topsoe-Jensen, H. G., *Scandinavian Literature from Brandes to Our Day,* translated by Isaac Anderson, Norton (New York City), 1929, pp. 65-84.

PERIODICALS

American-Scandinavian Review, January, 1933, pp. 7-12; March, 1934, pp. 59-63; September, 1943, pp. 231-239.
Athenaeum, February 13, 1897, p. 210.
Dial, August 16, 1896, p. 92.
Modern Language Review, July, 1957, pp. 376-383.
Nation, September 3, 1896, p. 181.
Scandinavian Studies, August, 1957, pp. 170-183; November, 1958, pp. 191-197; February, 1965, pp. 77-90; autumn, 1978, pp. 396-402; summer, 1979, pp. 273-284.*

POULAKOS, Takis 1952-

PERSONAL: Born March 18, 1952, in Greece; U.S. citizen. *Ethnicity:* "Greek." *Education:* Miami University, Oxford, OH, Ph.D., 1987.

CAREER: University of Pittsburgh, Pittsburgh, PA, assistant professor, 1988-90; University of Iowa, Iowa City, faculty member, head of rhetoric department, 1998—.

WRITINGS:

(Editor) *Rethinking the History of Rhetoric,* Westview Press (Boulder, CO), 1993.
Speaking for the Polis: Isocrates' Rhetorical Education, University of South Carolina Press (Columbia, SC), 1997.
Classical Rhetorical Theory, Houghton (Boston, MA), 1999.

Contributor to scholarly journals.

SIDELIGHTS: Takis Poulakos told *CA:* "I have a sensitivity about language use and its political orientation."

* * *

POWELL, Kevin 1966-

PERSONAL: Born April 24, 1966, in Jersey City, NJ; son of Shirley Mae Powell. *Education:* Rutgers University, State University of New Jersey (1984-88).

ADDRESSES: Agent—c/o One World/Ballantine, 201 East 50th St., New York, NY 10022.

CAREER: New York University, New York City, instructor of English, 1990-92; *Real World,* MTV, cast member, 1992; *Vibe* staff writer, 1993—.

WRITINGS:

(Editor) *In the Tradition: An Anthology of Young Black Writers,* Harlem Writers Press (New York City), 1993.
Recognize: Poems, Harlem River Press (New York City), 1995.

Keepin' It Real: Post-MTV Reflections on Race, Sex, and Politics, One World/Ballantine (New York City), 1997.

SIDELIGHTS: In his 1997 book of essays, *Keepin' It Real: Post-MTV Reflections on Race, Sex, and Politics,* Kevin Powell offered this thumbnail sketch of himself in *Keepin' It Real:* "Over the course of the last decade I've been a flag-waving patriot, a Christian, an atheist, a Muslim, a student leader, a homeless person, a pauper, a lover, a social worker, a poet, a misogynist, an English instructor, an MTV star, a full-time journalist, an egomaniac, a manic-depressive, a bully, a punk, an optimist, a pessimist, and most of all, someone who is always trying to find and tell the truth as I see it." Powell, raised in an impoverished, single-parent home in Jersey City, explores his childhood in some of the essays—notably in "Letter to My Cousin Anthony," which concerns how he bonded with his cousin over the experience of poverty, and in "A Letter Written to You," in which he describes the incident and aftermath of a police beating he received at age fifteen. Other essays analyze the hip-hop culture Powell often covers for *Rolling Stone, Vibe,* and the *New York Times.*

Reviewing *Keepin' It Real* for the *Washington Post Book World,* Ahmed Wright noted, "With only a slight dip in the middle, *Keepin' It Real* successfully tags the sentiments and shortcomings of a *nuevo* post-teen culture." Wright also wrote that Powell's "observations comprise four blunt letters in which he tells it like it is without airs or ego." The "keepin' it real" of the book's title is a double pun. "Keepin' it real" is a catch-phrase for Generation X-ers seeking authenticity in their lives. It also refers to *The Real World,* an MTV show in which a handful of disparate Generation X-ers were thrown together as roommates for a year while a television crew filmed their lives. Powell appeared in the first season of that show.

BIOGRAPHICAL/CRITICAL SOURCES:

BOOKS

Keepin' It Real: Post-MTV Reflections on Race, Sex, and Politics, One World/Ballantine (New York City), 1997.

PERIODICALS

Booklist, September 1, 1997, p. 40.
Washington Post Book World, August 24, 1997, p. 11.*

POWELL, Robert 1942-

PERSONAL: Born August 27, 1942, in Sheffield, England; son of Henry (a steelworker) and Violet Mary (a homemaker; maiden name, Norton) Powell; married Judith Rudd, 1962 (divorced, 1972); married Maggie Milburn, 1975 (divorced, 1982); married Shantheni Chornalingam, May 12, 1990; children: Victoria Peirson, Mark, Claire Milburn, Hugh Milburn, Zara Shakira. *Ethnicity:* "Caucasian." *Education:* University of Durham, Diploma in Architecture, 1966; Open University, B.A., 1979; National University of Singapore, M.Arch., 1990. *Politics:* None. *Religion:* None. *Avocational interests:* Watercolor painting, theater, films, reading.

ADDRESSES: Home—Block 1, Pandan Valley, No. 04-103, Singapore 597625. *Office*—School of Architecture, National University of Singapore, Singapore 116290; fax 65-463-9474. *E-mail*—rpacon@mbox3.singnet.com.sg.

CAREER: Richard Turley Associates, Newcastle upon Tyne, England, assistant architect, 1963-64; Ainsworth Spark Associates (architects), Newcastle upon Tyne, began as architect, became partner, 1966-83; National University of Singapore, Singapore, senior lecturer, 1984-90, associate professor of architecture, 1990-97, adjunct associate professor, 1998-99. RPA Consultants, partner, planner, and urban designer, 1984—; Akimedia Ltd., managing director, 1997—. Singapore Ministry of National Development, planning appeals inspector, 1988-97. Morowali Nature Reserve, Sulawesi, creator of management plan, 1979-80; Operation Raleigh, Singapore, selection coordinator, 1984-90; participated in Jostedal Glacier Expedition in Norway, 1971, and Zaire River Expedition, 1974-75; People's Association Youth Movement, member of adventure activities coordinating committee, 1995-96. *Military service:* Royal Air Force, Parachute Regiment, 1966-72; became captain.

MEMBER: Royal Geographical Society (England; fellow), Royal Town Planning Institute (England), Royal Institute of British Architects, Singapore Institute of Planners, Singapore Heritage Society, Singapore Cricket Club, Changi Sailing Club.

AWARDS, HONORS: World Ironman Triathlon champion, 1985; World Short-Course Triathlon champion, 1987; nonfiction award, Book Society of Singapore, 1994.

WRITINGS:

(Editor) *Architecture and Identity,* Butterworth (London), 1986.

(Editor) *Regionalism in Architecture,* Butterworth, 1987.

Innovative Architecture of Singapore, Select Books (Singapore), 1989.

Ken Yeang: Rethinking the Environmental Filter, Landmark Books (Singapore), 1989.

(Editor) *The Architecture of Housing,* [Geneva, Switzerland], 1990.

(Editor) *Regionalism: Forging an Identity,* National University of Singapore (Singapore), 1991.

The Asian House: Contemporary Houses of Southeast Asia, Select Books, 1992.

(Editor) *Renovation Guide for Homes,* Stamford Publishing (Singapore), 1992.

(Contributor) Briffet and Sim, editors, *Environmental Issues in Development and Conservation,* SNP Publishers (Singapore), 1993.

Living Legacy: Singapore's Architectural Heritage Renewed, Singapore Heritage Society (Singapore), 1994.

(Contributor) Lee and Tham, editors, *Design for Eco-Architecture,* National University of Singapore, 1994.

The Tropical Asian House, Periplus Editions (Berkeley, CA), 1996.

Line Edge and Shade: The Search for a Design Language in Tropical Asia, Page One Publishing (Singapore), 1997.

(Contributor) Shaw and Jones, editors, *Contested Urban Heritage: Voices from the Periphery,* Ashgate (England), 1997.

The Urban Asian House: Living in the Tropical City, Thames & Hudson (London, England), 1998.

Rethinking the Skyscraper: The Complete Works of Ken Yeang, Thames & Hudson, 1999.

Contributor to architecture journals, including *World Architecture, Architectural Review,* and *Journal of Southeast Asian Architecture.* Member of editorial committee, *Singapore Institute of Architects Journal,* 1986-96; editor, *Singapore Architect,* 1997-98.

WORK IN PROGRESS: Singapore: The Architecture of a Global City, with Tan Hock Beng, publication by Akimedia (Singapore) expected in 2000; *The Asian City: History and Theory of Urbanization in Asia.*

SIDELIGHTS: Robert Powell told *CA:* "I only began to write seriously when I relocated from Europe to Asia in 1984. I am fascinated by the cultural changes and the speed of change reflected in houses and lifestyle, in urbanization and changing morphologies in Asia."

*   *   *

PRESTON, Caroline

PERSONAL: Married Christopher Tilghman (a novelist); children: three sons.

ADDRESSES: Agent—c/o Scribners, 1230 Avenue of the Americas, New York, NY. 10020

CAREER: Archivist and novelist. Archivist at Harvard University Houghton Library, Cambridge, MA, and Peabody Essex Institute, Salem, MA.

WRITINGS:

Jackie by Josie, Scribners (New York City), 1997.

SIDELIGHTS: When Caroline Preston first decided to write a novel she was thirty-nine years old, with three sons. Her husband, novelist Christopher Tilghman, encouraged her, but she found most of her support, editing help, and progress in her writers' group. She began writing a multigenerational novel set in the Midwest, where she grew up, but was diverted by journalist Edward Klein, who asked her to do some research for him at the Kennedy Library. He was writing a biography of Jackie and John F. Kennedy, and Preston's research background as an achivist at Harvard University's Houghton Library and the Peabody Essex Institute in Salem made her perfect for the job.

The research gave Preston the idea for *Jackie by Josie,* a comic novel about Josie, a graduate student whose dissertation on an obscure nineteenth-century poet is going nowhere. Her marriage to Peter, a fellow graduate student whose writings on popular culture are a raging success, is becoming strained and stale. Fortunately, she is distracted from her difficulties when she is hired to research Jackie Kennedy for a "kiss-and-tell" biography. Gradually, Josie delves into the lives of Jackie and John. Josie, described as "an edgy, lovable heroine" by Judith Viorst in the *New York Times Book Review,* begins seeing similarities between Jackie's life and her own: her lonely childhood, her parents' bitter divorce, her undependable father, and a husband who is dangerously good-looking. The book weaves Josie's own concerns about her husband's potential affair and her mother's alcoholism with her discoveries about Jackie's similarly difficult life. By the end of the book, however, both Jackie and Josie triumph, winning back their husbands, moving on in their careers, and raising healthy kids.

A *Publishers Weekly* reviewer praised the book's humor and warm family story, but remarked that "unfortunately, the various plot lines end up so neatly resolved that one longs for the untidy—but far more interesting—magic of Jackie's real-life odyssey." Sylvia Brownrigg of the *Times Literary Supplement* disagreed, praising Preston's "intelligent comedy of marriage" and noting that "the real subject of *Jackie by Josie* is marriage and infidelity. . . . Eventually [Josie] learns something from her subject about how to handle a charming philandering husband." And Kate Tuttle remarked in the *Boston Book Review* that "Her light, sure touch allows her to range over territory both funny and sad . . .[while] sharply painting the cultural landscape."

BIOGRAPHICAL/CRITICAL SOURCES:

PERIODICALS

Entertainment Weekly, February 7, 1997, p. 64.
New York Times Book Review, February 23, 1997, p.10; June 1, 1997, p. 35.
People Weekly, April 7, 1997, p. 36.
Publishers Weekly, November 25, 1996, p. 56.
Times Literary Supplement, April 18, 1997, p. 19.
Tribune Books (Chicago), February 16, 1997, p. 6.
Vogue, March, 1997, p. 328.*

* * *

PRINCE, Hugh 1927-

PERSONAL: Born September 16, 1927, in Wanstead, Essex, England; son of Louis (an art teacher) and Jessie (Counsell) Prince; married Sheila Wood (a medical doctor), 1955; children: Simon, Matthew. *Ethnicity:* "British." *Education:* University of London, B.A. (with first class honors), 1951, M.A. (with distinction), 1953, Ph.D., 1976.

ADDRESSES: Office—Department of Geography, Uni-

versity College, University of London, 26 Bedford Way, London WC1H 0AP, England.

CAREER: University of London, London, England, faculty member, 1951-65, reader in geography, 1965-92, emeritus reader and honorary research fellow, 1992—. University of Minnesota—Twin Cities, visiting professor, 1966, 1968, and 1990; Clark University, visiting professor, 1971; University of Wuerzburg, fellow, 1978. Landscape Research Group, member of board of directors, 1985—.

MEMBER: Royal Geographical Society, Institute of British Geographers, Association of American Geographers.

AWARDS, HONORS: Fellow of Deutscher Akademischer Austauschdienst (German Academic Exchange Service), 1978.

WRITINGS:

(With J. T. Coppock) *Greater London,* Faber (London), 1964.
Parks in England, Pinhorns, 1967.
(With R. J. P. Kain) *The Tithe Surveys of England and Wales,* Cambridge University Press (Cambridge, England), 1985.
Wetlands of the American Midwest, University of Chicago Press (Chicago, IL), 1997.

Honorary editor, *Area,* 1969-70; editor, *Journal of Historical Geography,* 1981-86.

WORK IN PROGRESS: Tithe Surveys for Local History, with Kain; research on parks in England.

* * *

PRUDHOMME, Rene Francois Armand 1839-1907 (Sully Prudhomme, a pseudonym)

PERSONAL: Born March 16, 1839, in Paris, France; died September 6, 1907, in Chatenay, France; son of M. Sully and Clotilde Caillat Sully Prudhomme. *Education:* Lycee Bonaparte, B.S., 1856.

CAREER: Poet. Worked as a clerk, Paris, France, 1859-60; also worked as a law apprentice.

AWARDS, HONORS: Elected to the French Academy, 1881; Nobel Prize in literature (first recipient), 1901.

WRITINGS:

POETRY; ALL UNDER PSEUDONYM SULLY PRUDHOMME

Stances et poemes, 1865.
Les epreuves, 1866.
Les solitudes: poesies, A. Lemerre (Paris), 1869.
Les destins, 1872.
La France, 1874.
Les vaines tendresses, 1875.
Le zenith (poem), published in journal *Revue des deux mondes*, 1876.
La justice (poem), 1878.
Poesie, 1865-88, A. Lemerre, 1883-88.
Le prisme, poesies diverses, A. Lemerre (Paris), 1886.
Le bonheur (poem), 1888.
Epaves, A. Lemerre, 1908.

OTHER; ALL UNDER PSEUDONYM SULLY PRUDHOMME

Oeuvres de Sully Prudhomme (poetry and prose), 8 volumes, A. Lemerre, 1883-1908.
Que sais-je? (philosophy), 1896.
Testament poetique (essays), 1901.
La vraie religion selon Pascal (essays), 1905.
Journal intime: lettres-pensee (diary), A. Lemerre, 1922.

Contributor of poetry to periodicals, including *La parnasse contemporain*.

SIDELIGHTS: One of the most highly respected French poets of the late nineteenth century, Rene Francois Armand Prudhomme was the first recipient of the Nobel Prize in literature. Writing extensively as Sully Prudhomme, he earned particular esteem for the compassion and idealism of his work, as well as for the clarity and simplicity of his poetic style. In his early verse Sully Prudhomme combined the formal precision of the Parnassians with an emotional force reminiscent of the Romantics, while in his later writings he became a philosopher-poet, composing epic verses on scientific and metaphysical themes. A critic for the *Spectator* observed that Sully Prudhomme "leads us through all the mazes of intelligence to the foot of the Christian Cross, while refusing the Christian creed. His life illustrates his doctrines by its labour, its kindness, its purity of aim and nobleness of emotion. His fine achievement is the sincere reflection of himself, and his advanced post in the vanguard of modern thought should win for him, not only the honour due to a fine poet, but the admiration of all

men of good-will, and perhaps most of those who, like the *pelerin de l'ideal* ['pilgrim of the absolute'], have been scared from the old paths by the clashing machinery of dogma."

Sully Prudhomme was born into a middle-class Parisian family in 1839. Ill health, the early death of his father, and the somber home atmosphere resulting from his mother's grief are factors often cited by biographers to explain the air of melancholy that characterized both his personality and his writings. After graduating from the Lycee Bonaparte, where he excelled in both classics and science, Sully Prudhomme intended to study mathematics in preparation for a career as a scholar and teacher. However, he was forced to curtail his studies due to a chronic eye inflammation and went to work as a clerk in a foundry, and later as an apprentice in a law office, hoping eventually to take a degree in law. During this period he wrote his first poems, which were well received among his circle of literary acquaintances and soon began to be accepted by literary journals.

After several of his poems were published in the influential journal *Le parnasse contemporain*, Sully Prudhomme became identified with the Parnassians, a group of poets who cultivated objectivity and precision in traditional verse forms as a reaction against the stylistic and emotional excesses of Romanticism. His first poetry collection, *Stances et poemes*, was published in 1865 to popular and critical acclaim, winning him such distinguished admirers as the critic Charles Augustin Sainte-Beuve. Encouraged by this reception of his work, Sully Prudhomme resolved to discontinue his legal training in order to pursue a literary career; an independent income provided by his family enabled him to devote his time to writing.

During the 1870s Sully Prudhomme's depressive nature was exacerbated by several events: his traumatic experience as a member of the Garde Mobile during the Franco-Prussian War, the onset of a chronic paralytic illness, and a series of deaths among his relatives. For the remainder of his career he avoided the social and political activities of the Parisian literary world; however, this did not prevent his becoming one of the most well-known and respected writers of the era, hailed by some commentators as a successor to Victor Hugo. He was elected to the French Academy in 1881, and in 1901 was presented with the first Nobel laureateship for literature. The Swedish Academy announced that it bestowed the honor upon Sully

Prudhomme "as an acknowledgment of his excellent merit as an author, and especially of the high idealism, artistic perfection, as well as the usual combination of qualities of the heart and genius to which his work bears witness." As his paralysis worsened in the final years of his life, Sully Prudhomme lived as a recluse, devoting himself to literature and philosophy until his death in 1907.

Throughout his career Sully Prudhomme employed the highly structured, traditional verse forms identified with the Parnassian movement. His early works, however, diverged from those of the Parnassians by focusing on human emotion and deeply personal subjects, especially romantic love. His poem "La vase brise" from *Stances et poemes,* with its metaphor of a broken flower vase as the embodiment of a shattered love affair, became a favorite among fanciers of sentimental poetry, to the bemusement of admirers of his more serious work. A number of his early verses, such as the group of poems titled "Jeunes filles," express the author's sorrow over a broken engagement. The themes of loneliness and sadness recur throughout the collections that followed *Stances et poemes,* such as 1866's *Les epreuves,* 1869's *Les solitudes,* and *Les vaines tendresses,* published in 1875; at the same time, these works also express uplifting, altruistic sentiments, many of them relating to science and the wonders of the natural world.

While rejecting Christian theology, Sully Prudhomme maintained a strong belief in a positive humanistic philosophy that celebrated human aspiration towards goodness, wisdom, and spiritual understanding. In his *Studies in Literature: 1789-1877,* Edward Dowden remarked that Prudhomme "is for ever returning to an aspiration after truth, after beauty, after simplicity of life, and yet he has never wandered far from these; and part of his moral perplexity arises from suggestions and checks to which a person of harder or narrower personality would have been insensible. There is in him something of feminine susceptibility and sensitiveness; and that a man should possess a portion of a woman's tenderness is not wholly ill."

According to commentators, Sully Prudhomme's illness and other personal tragedies moved him to turn away from confessional poetry to works that deal with profound universal themes. This change is reflected in poems such as the 1872 verse *Les destins,* a meditation on the struggle between good and evil occasioned by a disastrous fire in a Spanish church, and *Le zenith,* an 1876 apotheosis of the quest for truth in the

form of an elegy for a group of scientists killed in a ballooning accident. Influenced by the classical Roman poet and philosopher Lucretius, whose *De rerum natura* explains the scientific theories of Epicurus in verse, Sully Prudhomme also sought to use poetry to enlighten readers about recent scientific discoveries. He hoped to fuse the aesthetic and analytical functions of the human intellect in his poetry and establish an empirical foundation for the study of philosophy so that humanity's understanding of its spiritual condition could develop in the same progressive fashion as its comprehension of the physical world.

The most noted products of Sully Prudhomme's middle period are two epic poems, 1878's *La justice* and 1888's *Le bonheur,* which implement this idealistic fusion of philosophy, poetry, and science. *La justice* is a series of dialogues between a protagonist identified as the Seeker, an intellectual who despairs of finding justice in nature or society, and a Voice which assures him that justice can be found within every human soul. *Le bonheur,* which, in his *On Life and Letters,* noted French author Anatole France called "at once one of the most audacious and agreeable of philosophic poems," follows the adventures of Faustus and Stella, two lovers who pass through death and the afterlife in pursuit of knowledge and happiness. While many commentators have admired Sully Prudhomme's accomplished mingling of lyricism and philosophical insight in these poems, others have found fault with their didactic tone. In the final years of his life, Sully Prudhomme devoted himself to literary theory and philosophy. In such works as 1901's *Testament poetique,* he set forth his theories of poetics, including his explanations of prosodic form in terms of the laws of physics. *Que sais-je?* is an 1896 philosophical work expounding his ideas about the natural sciences and metaphysics. His last work, *La vraie religion selon Pascal,* which was published in 1905, concerns spiritual values in life and literature.

Sully Prudhomme made his greatest impact in his own lifetime, when his works and ideas had relevance to prevailing literary tastes and ideological fashions. Critics admired the tenderness and sincerity of his early lyric verses and the beauty and nobility of the ideas expressed in his later, more ambitious poems. Although little commentary on Sully Prudhomme has appeared in English since the 1920s, he remains a noted Figure in French literary history. In his *Punch and Judy and Other Essays,* Maurice Baring declared: "Both on account of the charm of his pure and perfect phrasing and by the consummate art and the dignity which informed all his work, Sully-Prudhomme deserved the rank which he held amongst the foremost French poets of the nineteenth century."

BIOGRAPHICAL/CRITICAL SOURCES:

BOOKS

Baring, Maurice, *Punch and Judy and Other Essays,* Doubleday, Page (New York City), 1924, pp. 216-219.

Dargan, E. Preston, and others, *Studies in Honor of A. Marshall Elliott,* Volume 1, The Johns Hopkins Press, 1911, pp. 195-208.

Dowden, Edward, *Studies in Literature: 1789-1877,* fifth edition, Kegan Paul, Trench, 1889, pp. 392-427.

France, Anatole, *On Life and Letters,* first series, translated by A. W. Evans, Dodd, Mead (London), 1911, pp. 134-145.

France, Anatole, *On Life and Letters,* second series, translated by A. W. Evans, John Lane, The Bodley Head, 1914, pp. 34-43.

Grierson, Francis, *Parisian Portraits,* John Lane, The Bodley Head, 1913, pp. 66-80.

Lalou, Rene, *Contemporary French Literature,* translated by William Aspenwall, Alfred A. Knopf, 1924, pp. 17-27.

Marble, Annie Russell, *The Nobel Prize Winners in Literature,* Appleton, 1925, pp. 21-41.

May, James Lewis, *Anatole France: The Man and His Work,* Kennikat Press (Port Washington, N.Y.), 1924, pp. 75.

Thieme, Hugo Paul, *The Technique of the French Alexandrine: A Study of the Works of Leconte de Lisle, Jose Maria de Heredia, Francois Coppee, Sully Prudhomme, and Paul Verlaine,* Inland Press, 1897, p. 68.

Warner, Charles Dudley, editor, *Library of the World's Best Literatue,* Volume XXIV, J. A. Hill (New York City), 1896, pp. 14209-14211.

PERIODICALS

French Review, December, 1971, pp. 29-37.
Spectator, July 2, 1892, pp. 16-17.*

*   *   *

PRUDHOMME, Sully
  See PRUDHOMME, Rene Francois Armand

PURDY, Jeannine M. 1959-

PERSONAL: Born December 15, 1959, in Perth, Australia; daughter of Milton Frank (an accountant) and Rosemarie Claude (a homemaker; maiden name, Gardette) Purdy. *Ethnicity:* "European Australian." *Education:* University of Western Australia, B.A., 1980, B.Jurisprudence (with first class honors), 1987, LL.B., 1988; La Trobe University, LL.D., 1995.

ADDRESSES: Home—North Beach, Australia. *E-mail*—jpurdy@ozemail.com.au.

CAREER: High Court of Australia, Canberra, associate, 1989; Royal Commission into Aboriginal Deaths in Custody, Perth, Australia, investigator in Perth and Roebounre, 1990; National Native Title Tribunal, Perth, case manager, 1995-96; Southern Cross University, Lismore, Australia, lecturer in law, 1997; Aboriginal Legal Rights Movement, Adelaide, Australia, case manager in Native Title Unit, 1998; Law Reform Commission, Perth, writer. Women's Legal Service, volunteer, 1986, and member of management committee; Fitzroy Community and Youth Center, volunteer, 1994.

WRITINGS:

(Contributor) G. Bird, G. Martin, and J. Nielsen, editors, *Majah: Indigenous Peoples and the Law,* Federation Press (Sydney, Australia), 1996.

Common Law and Colonised Peoples: Studies in Trinidad and Western Australia, Ashgate Publishing (Aldershot, England), 1997.

(Contributor) P. Fitzpatrick and E. Darian-Smith, editors, *The Laws of the Postcolonial,* University of Michigan Press (Ann Arbor, MI), in press.

Contributor to periodicals, including *Australian Feminist Law Journal, Law, Text, Culture, Journal of Legal and Social Studies, Australian Journal of Law and Society,* and *Caribbean Quarterly.*

WORK IN PROGRESS: Research on the law and practice of native title in Australia.

SIDELIGHTS: Jeannine M. Purdy told *CA:* "My primary motivation for writing has been to describe and explain something of the divergence between the promise and the practice of law. Most recently, I have been concerned by the treatment of indigenous Australians and other colonized peoples under imposed Western legal systems. In particular, I am interested in the economic, social, and historical framework which limits non-colonized peoples' recognition of the nature of ourselves and our legal systems in colonial contexts."

*   *   *

PYBUS, Cassandra

PERSONAL: Born in Australia. *Education:* Sydney University, Ph.D.

*ADDRESSES: Home—*Lower Snug, Tasmania. *Office—*c/o University of Queensland Press, P.O. Box 42, St. Lucia, Queensland 4067, Australia.

CAREER: Writer. *Island* magazine, editor, 1989-94; La Trobe University, visiting fellow in humanities.

AWARDS, HONORS: Named University of Tasmania honorary fellow; Collin Roderick Award for best Australian book, 1993, for *Gross Moral Turpitude: The Orr Case Reconsidered;* Literary Fund of Australia writers' fellowship.

WRITINGS:

Community of Thieves, Heinemann Australia (Port Melbourne, Victoria), 1991.
Gross Moral Turpitude: The Orr Case Reconsidered, Heinemann Australia (Port Melbourne, Victoria), 1993, revised as *Seduction and Consent: A Case of Gross Moral Turpitude,* Mandarin (Port Melbourne, Victoria), 1994.
(Editor) *Columbus' Blindness, and Other Essays,* University of Queensland Press (St. Lucia), 1994.
White Rajah: A Dynastic Intrigue, University of Queensland Press (St. Lucia), 1996.
Till Apples Grow on an Orange Tree (autobiography) University of Queensland Press (St Lucia), 1998.

Editor, *Australian Humanities Review* website; coordinator, *Aurora Australis* website.

SIDELIGHTS: Cassandra Pybus is a writer and historian whose first book, *Community of Thieves,* is the account of George Augustus Robinson's incarceration of Tasmanian Aborigines on Flinders Island. Pybus is a fifth-generation Tasmanian, whose ancestor Richard Pybus was a neighbor of Robinson. The last survivors of Flinders Island were eventually returned to Oyster Cove on mainland Tasmania.

When Pybus talked to a relative there about her project of documenting events, she was told, 'First we steal the blackfellas' land, then we deny them an identity, and now you want to steal their story for your own intellectual purposes.' Pybus felt there was some truth in this. Peter Read wrote in *Australian Book Review* that "Not all White Tasmanians share Pybus's sensibilities." There is an account of Robinson saying that thirty Aborigines were murdered by shepherds and thrown from the cliffs of Cape Grim. Even in the present, Pybus and others who show interest in the story have been accused of being "busybodies" and causing trouble for the Van Diemen's Land Company, in existence then and now. Read noted that visitors to Flinders Island "must tread with some delicacy when making enquiries about the Aboriginal legacy. The same may be said about other places which share a specific and separate Aboriginal and White history." Read did not "fully accept" Pybus's account of Robinson, "described by Henry Reynolds in the Foreword as 'neither the noble conciliator nor the evil "black" Robinson of recent report.' Maintaining that although "we did not steal the land, we are the inheritors of that theft," Read felt that until a "genuine peace treaty" is signed with the Aborigines, "a personalized historical understanding such as Pybus demonstrates will surely be one of the most fruitful."

In *Gross Moral Turpitude: The Orr Case Revisited* Pybus documents the first sexual harassment case in Australia. In the mid-1950s Professor Sydney Sparks Orr, chairman of the philosophy department of the University of Tasmania, was accused of seduction by student Suzanne Kemp. Orr offered to turn in his resignation, but the University chose instead to investigate, found him guilty, and dismissed him. Orr took the case to the Supreme Court on contractual grounds but added his denial of the allegations, causing him to lose the case. Professor Orr's loss in a higher court bankrupted him. Supporters saw Orr's case as a threat to academic tenure and a warning of women's growing power base. The professor's chair remained vacant for a decade. Meanwhile, he spoke at campuses, hinting at new evidence and contriving fantasies that further damaged Kemp's reputation. Academic friends began to avoid him and he was never able to secure another faculty position.

Helen Garner wrote in the *Times Literary Supplement* that Kemp, who would not be interviewed for Pybus's book, "is perceived by Pybus as a distant, rather dignified figure. Not so Orr, who is presented here in grainy close-up—a portrait of a third-rate British academic. . . . This erratic, self-obsessed man, falsified his CV, introduced into his lectures on Plato a spurious psychosexual angle, and deceived his students." Pybus holds that the seduction of a student by a professor is an abuse of power, but seduction implies a passive woman being pursued by an aggressive man. She does not condemn all sex between students and teachers, "neither will she allow for the crucial distinction between consensual sex and reprehensible, punishable harassment," wrote Garner. "The only way that she can avoid making this distinction is by over-emphasizing the power differential in the tutorial." Garner called the book "meticulously researched and written with verve."

BIOGRAPHICAL/CRITICAL SOURCES:

PERIODICALS

Australian Book Review, September, 1991, p. 6; February, 1993, p. 18; December, 1994, p. 41; October, 1996, p. 14.
Times Literary Supplement, August 20, 1993, p. 10.*

R

RAADSCHELDERS, Jos C. N. 1955-

PERSONAL: Born December 14, 1955, in Uithoorn, Netherlands; son of J. C. (a carpenter and private driver) and C. P. M. (a homemaker; maiden name, van Boheewen) Raadschelders; married Julie Bivin, July 14, 1990; children: Kitty, John. *Ethnicity:* "Caucasian." *Education:* Teachers College, Delft, Netherlands, B.A., 1979; University of Leiden, M.A., 1982, Ph.D., 1990. *Religion:* Roman Catholic.

ADDRESSES: Home—2912 Devonshire Dr., Norman, OK 73071. *Office*—Department of Political Science, 318 Dale Hall Tower, University of Oklahoma, Norman, OK 73019-2001; fax 405-325-0718. *E-mail*—raadschelders@ou.edu and www.ou.edu/cas/psc.

CAREER: University of Leiden, Leiden, Netherlands, assistant professor, 1983-92, associate professor of public administration, 1992-98; University of Oklahoma, Norman, associate professor of public administration, 1998—.

MEMBER: American Society of Public Administration.

AWARDS, HONORS: Outstanding academic book citation, *Choice,* 1998, for *Handbook of Administrative History.*

WRITINGS:

Handbook of Administrative History, Transaction Books (New Brunswick, NJ), 1998.

UNTRANSLATED WORKS

Plaatselijke Bestuurlijke Ontwikkelingen: Een Historisch-Bestuurskundig Onderzoek in Vier Noord-Hollandse Gemeenten (title means "Local Government Administrative Development, 1600-1980: An Administrative History of Four North Holland Municipalities"), VNG Publishers ('s-Gravenhage, the Netherlands), 1990.

(With Theo A. J. Toonen and Frank Hendriks) *Meso-Bestuur in Europees Perspectief: De (Randstad) Provincies uit de Pas?* (title means "Meso-Government in European Perspective: The 'Randstad' Provinces out of Touch?"), University of Leiden (Leiden, the Netherlands), 1992.

Lokale Bestuursgeschiedenis (title means "Local Government History"), Walburg Press (Zutphen, the Netherlands), 1992.

De Vierde Macht: Ambtenaren in Nederland (title means "The Fourth Power: The Civil Service in the Netherlands"), Stichting Burgerschapskunde/ Nederlands Centrum voor Politieke Vorming (Leiden), 1992.

(Editor with Toonen) *Waterschappen in Nederland: Een Bestuurskundige Verkenning van de Institutionale Ontwikkeling* (title means "Waterboards in the Netherlands: An Administrative Science Exploration of the Institutional Development"), Verloren (Hilversum, the Netherlands), 1993.

Tussen Markt en Overheid: Een Bestuursgeschiedenis van de Centrale Vereniging voor Ambulante Handel, 1921-1996 (title means "Between Market and Government: An Administrative History of the National Union for Itinerant Trade"), NUJ (Apeldoorn, the Netherlands), 1996.

(Editor with Frits M. van der Meer) *L'Entourage*

Administratif du Pouvoir Executif, Ets. Bruylant (Brussels, Belgium), 1998.

Contributor of more than a hundred articles and reviews to journals.

WORK IN PROGRESS: A book on government; a book on authority; a book on political-administrative relations; research on ethics.

SIDELIGHTS: Jos C. N. Raadschelders told *CA:* "I write to satisfy curiosity, teach students, and hopefully help citizens to understand the nature of contemporary government. I am influenced by a desire to combine insights from history, political science, public administration, and political theory to achieve a more complete understanding of the phenomenon of government.

"Ideas come to me in a flash, usually at night. I make quick notes then, upon which I elaborate and do research for as long as it takes. By the time I actually start to write, I have organized all the material into chapters and sections. The actual writing has varied from six weeks to six months, the total process (including preparation and publication) from nine months to seven years.

"I am inspired by whatever I come across and find interesting, curious, appealing. I also feel a need to fill gaps in my knowledge. History is a major source of inspiration, as are current events and colleagues who seek my collaboration."

*   *   *

RABINYAN, Dorit 1972-

PERSONAL: Born in 1972, in Kefar-Saba, Israel; daughter of Zion and Yaffa Rabinyan. *Education:* Graduated from high school. *Religion:* Jewish. *Avocational interests:* Music, cinema.

ADDRESSES: Home—5 Hagilbua St., Tel Aviv, 65223, Israel. *Office*—Am Oved Publishers Ltd., 22 Mazeh St., Tel Aviv 61003; P.O. Box 470, Tel Aviv 61003. *Agent*—The Israeli Institute of Israli Literature.

CAREER: Am-Oved Publishers, Tel Aviv, Israel, staff member. *Military service:* Israeli Army, journalist for two years.

AWARDS, HONORS: Izhac Vinner Award for literature, 1994; best drama of the year award, Film Academy Awards, 1997; *Simtat ha-shekediyot be-'Omerig'an* named one of best fifty novels written in the Jubilee, 1997.

WRITINGS:

Simtat ha-shekediyot be-'Omerig'an (novel), [Israel], 1996, translation by Yael Lotan published as *Persian Brides,* Brazilier (New York City), 1998. *Shuli's Fiance* (teleplay), 1997.

Simtat ha-shekediyot be-'Omerig'an has been published in Greece, Germany, Great Britain, Italy, Spain, and the Netherlands.

ADAPTATIONS: Persian Brides adapted to audio format by Sefarim Medabrim Co. (Tel Aviv), 1997.

WORK IN PROGRESS: Our Weddings, a novel for Am Oved, expected in 1999.

SIDELIGHTS: Israeli author Dorit Rabinyan saw her first novel published when she was twenty-two years old. Two years later her book was translated from its original Hebrew and published in the United States under the title *Persian Brides.*

Set in the Jewish quarter of a turn-of-the-century Persian village called Omerijan, *Persian Brides* paints a moving portrait of the Ratoryan family. In the temperamental Ratoryan family marriage and childbirth—the birth of a son is preferable—are of paramount importance. News of a girl's first menstruation, for example, warrants a public announcement from the rooftop and by carrier pigeon, and mothers are in the habit of inspecting their girls' private parts to see if they are still virgins. Flora, a fifteen-year-old member of the Ratoryan family, is quite pregnant. This condition seems attractive to Nazie, Flora's eleven-year-old orphaned cousin who lives with the Ratoryan's. Flora is married to a no-good cloth merchant, but this doesn't deter Nazie, who is quite taken with Flora's brother Moussa. When Flora's husband abandons her, Flora sings herself hoarse at night and Nazie, waiting for her own marriage to Moussa, consoles her.

The action in *Persian Brides* takes place over the course of two days. In this concentrated period of time, Rabinyan lends to *Persian Brides* "the feel of a nightlong wedding feast," according to *New York*

Times reviewer Michael Lowenthal. Lowenthal described the novel as "lush, lyrical, and disturbing," adding that "Rabinyan grounds her themes of sexual politics in scenes mingling exotic beauty and gritty horror. . . . She writes with the wise and leisurely assurance of a town bard." A *Booklist* reviewer called Rabinyan's novel an "earthly and sensual fairy tale" while a *Publishers Weekly* critic commented that the novel "tells one poignant, bewitching story after another, seducing us with vivid language and tales of deception, devotion, and magic." The *Publishers Weekly* critic concluded, "Rabinyan's brisk, fetching prose expertly summons a long-vanished land and renders it dazzling and delicious."

Rabinyan told *CA:* "I am happy that Israeli literature, as with my novel, is welcomed so warmly by American readers."

BIOGRAPHICAL/CRITICAL SOURCES:

PERIODICALS

Booklist, February 1, 1998.
Library Journal, January, 1998, p. 144.
New York Times, March 15, 1998.
Publishers Weekly, January 12, 1998, p. 45.

*   *   *

RADZIENDA, Tom 1963-

PERSONAL: Born April 30, 1963, in Chicago, IL; son of Frank and Nancy Radzienda. *Education:* College of Dupage, A.A., 1986; Elmhurst College, B.A., 1991; University of Sussex, M.A., 1992. *Politics:* "Political ex-patriate." *Religion:* "Existentialist." *Avocational interests:* "Photography, world travel, tennis, squash, humanism."

ADDRESSES: Home—19/262 Sukhumvit Soi 13, Bangkok 10110, Thailand. *Office*—Faculty of Humanities, Srinakharinwirot University, Sukhumvit 23, Bangkok 10110, Thailand. *E-mail*—tom@psm.swu.ac.th.

CAREER: General Binding Corp., Chicago, IL, technical coordinator, 1981-91; Srinakharinwirot University, Bangkok, Thailand, lecturer in poetry and culture, 1994—. Worked in the United States as a volunteer literacy teacher.

WRITINGS:

No More Pretty Pictures (poems), Pentameter Press, 1998.

Contributor of poems to British and American poetry magazines, including *Lynx Eye, Rustic Rub,* and *Purple Patch,* and Thai newspapers.

WORK IN PROGRESS: Lost in the Ruins of Bangkok; research on poetry as a second language.

SIDELIGHTS: Tom Radzienda told *CA:* "Why do I write? Because there's something wrong with our world. Can we return to the simple pleasures of life? The colors of a flower? Listening to the wind? Poetry will bring us to the mountains through imagination, and closer to genuine self.

"Do we even sense that modern urban life is a prison? Or are we so accustomed to it that we consider it normal? Poetry will awaken our consciousness to a purer, non-technological, unadvertised reality.

"I hope to give insight into the deep source of sorrow and pain in our society and discover a cure, rather than merely offer a distraction from the mundane demands of incorporated life. In the corporate mind, art is merely entertainment to distract us and turn us into mindless consumers. Yet art has a much deeper responsibility to awaken, incite, and inspire. Freed from the demands of making profit, art can liberate us from the dulling effects of culture, bureaucracy, and our own servile compliance with the status quo.

"No more pretty pictures. The greater beauty is in our own freedom to imagine."

*   *   *

RAINIS, Janis
See PLIEKSANS, Janis

*   *   *

RAMPTON, Sheldon M. 1957-

PERSONAL: Born August 4, 1957, in Long Beach, CA; son of Roger Harrison (a musician) and Renee (a schoolteacher; maiden name, Marchant) Rampton.

Ethnicity: "English/French/Danish." *Education:* Princeton University, B.A. *Politics:* "Left populist." *Avocational interests:* Tennis, movies, chess.

ADDRESSES: Home and office—509 Oak St., No. 4, Madison, WI 53704. *E-mail*—sheldon@execpc.com.

CAREER: Valley Times, Las Vegas, NV, reporter, 1985; *Daily Register,* Portage, WI, reporter, 1984-86; Quick Quality Press, Madison, WI, graphic artist, 1987-97; Wisconsin Coordinating Council on Nicaragua, Madison, outreach coordinator, 1993—.

WRITINGS:

Friends in Deed, Wisconsin Coordinating Council on Nicaragua (Madison), 1988.
Toxic Sludge Is Good for You, Common Courage Press (Monroe, ME), 1995.
Mad Cow U.S.A., Common Courage Press, 1997.
Trust Us, We're Experts, Putnam (New York City), 1997.

WORK IN PROGRESS: Research on the public relations industry, politics, "environmentalism," and corrupt practices.

SIDELIGHTS: Sheldon M. Rampton told *CA:* "I have always been an avid reader, and I aspired to be some kind of writer, beginning when I was still in grade school. As a child I read mysteries and science fiction, with Jules Verne, Arthur Conan Doyle, and Isaac Asimov among my favorites. In college, my interests gravitated to history, philosophy, and politics as I became something of a campus activist with a particular interest in feminism and the Central American liberation movement, an interest which began when I attended a poetry reading by the Nicaraguan poet Ernesto Cardenal.

"In college I also had the opportunity to take classes in writing from Joyce Carol Oates, John McPhee, and Steven Koch. I met E. L. Doctorow, who taught at Princeton for one semester. Although I was not one of his students, I was a huge fan of his books—in particular *Ragtime* and *The Book of Daniel.* He graciously allowed me to interview him about his writing and even bought me lunch one day, for which I am grateful. (I was poor then, and hungry.)

"One thing that I found similar about Cardenal and Doctorow is the way they incorporate details from historical and political fact into their work. Cardenal refers to his poetic method as 'constructivism.' His

poems are montages of factual information and popular themes juxtaposed in striking and thought-provoking ways. Doctorow also uses historical themes, to the point that he himself can no longer remember which of the details in his novels are factual and which are fiction. John McPhee was also a strong influence, teaching me that the techniques and attention to style which I associate with 'fictionary' writing could also be applied to what he called the 'literature of fact.'

"My primary motivation for writing today is a desire to critique the corrupting influence that money and corporate power exert upon democratic systems and values. I believe that citizen activism is necessary to counter those influences. I write, therefore, in the honorable tradition of the journalist-muckraker, whose mission is to 'comfort the afflicted and afflict the comfortable.'

"My writing process involves periods of excessive research and malingering, separated by islands of frantic activity as I race to meet deadlines. I find that I have a hard time *starting* a writing project, but once the project is underway, I enjoy the work. I like to have a writing partner against whom I can bounce ideas and to whom I can turn for help when my own intelligence and enthusiasm are exhausted. John Stauber, my current coauthor, has been a great source of inspiration."

*   *   *

REICH, Christopher 1961-

PERSONAL: Born November 12, 1961, in Tokyo, Japan; son of Willie Wolfgang and Mildred (Raible) Reich; married Susanne Wohlwend, July, 1994; children: Noelle. *Education:* Georgetown University, B.S.F.S; University of Texas at Austin, M.B.A.

ADDRESSES: Home—Austin, TX. *Agent*—Richard Pine, Arthur Pine Associates Inc., 250 West 57th St., New York, NY 10107.

CAREER: Novelist. Union Bank of Switzerland, Geneva and Zurich, portfolio manager, then Mergers and Acquisitions staff member, until 1991; Giorgio Beverley Hills Timepieces, Neuchatel, Switzerland, chief executive officer, 1992-95; writer, 1995—.

WRITINGS:

Numbered Account, Delacorte (New York City), 1998.

WORK IN PROGRESS: A novel about an American attorney chasing a former Nazi Waffen-S.S. officer in post-World War II Germany.

SIDELIGHTS: Christopher Reich, who was born in Tokyo, Japan and raised in Los Angeles, worked in banking before he committed himself to a writing career. Working for Union Bank of Switzerland, Reich started as a portfolio manager in Zurich and worked his way up the ladder to the bank's department of mergers and acquisitions in Geneva before leaving the business in 1991.

Reich's experience in high-level, sophisticated banking provided him with the background for his debut novel, *Numbered Account.* In this thriller Nick Neumann, a twenty-eight-year-old ex-Marine, leaves his beautiful fiance and a budding career at Morgan Stanley on Wall Street in favor of a job at the United Swiss Bank in Zurich, Switzerland. The job gives Nick a chance to solve the mysterious murder of his father, Alexander Neumann. The murder of Nick's father occurred seventeen years before in Los Angeles, while Alexander was working for the United Swiss Bank.

Tracking down his father's killer proves complicated for Nick. Things begin to unravel when the managers of a large, numbered bank account in the name of one "the Pasha" begin to leave the company: one experiences a nervous breakdown, one defects to a rival company, and another suffers an untimely death. Eventually the U.S. Drug Enforcement Agency visits Nick to discuss the account, and Nick finds himself sucked into a swirl of Middle East terrorism, nuclear weapons, and narcotics trafficking.

Reich uses the secretive, cut-throat world of Swiss banking to create what *Denver Post* reviewer Howard M. Kaplan called "a taut, interesting story." According to Kaplan, *Numbered Account* is "presented tautly, intricately and intensely with intelligence, chilling detail, suspense and intrigue."

BIOGRAPHICAL/CRITICAL SOURCES:

PERIODICALS

Booklist, December 1, 1997, p. 587.
Denver Post, March 8, 1998.

Entertainment Weekly, January 23, 1998, p. 58.
Forbes, January 26, 1998, p. 119.
Library Journal, December, 1997, p. 155.
People Weekly, February 16, 1998, p. 35.
Publishers Weekly, April 21, 1997, p. 23; November 10, 1997, p. 53.
Wall Street Journal, January 29, 1998, p. A16.

OTHER

Amazon.com, http://www.amazon.com (July 16, 1998).

*   *   *

RICHARD-ALLERDYCE, Diane 1958-

PERSONAL: Born October 10, 1958, in Albuquerque, NM; daughter of Victor C. (an entrepreneur) and Joyce A. (a registered nurse and hospice executive) Richard; married James W. Allerdyce, 1983 (divorced, 1989); married John R. Pickering (a professor of history), August 13, 1994; children: (first marriage) Avery J. (stepson), James V., Julia C. *Ethnicity:* "Caucasian." *Education:* Florida Atlantic University, B.A., 1982, M.A., 1983; University of Florida, Ph.D., 1988. *Politics:* Democrat. *Religion:* Unitarian-Universalist. *Avocational interests:* Music (classical, classic rock, jazz, blues).

ADDRESSES: Home—4195 Northwest Seventh Ct., Delray Beach, FL 33445. *Office*—Department of English, Lynn University, Boca Raton, FL; fax 561-237-7216. *E-mail*—DRAmoon@aol.com.

CAREER: Lynn University, Boca Raton, FL, instructor, 1985-88, assistant professor, 1988-93, associate professor, 1993-98, professor of English, 1998—, department head, 1994—, coordinator of Honors Program, 1993—, community awareness coordinator, 1992—. Palm Beach Community College, South Campus, adjunct faculty member, summers, 1985-90; Florida Atlantic University, adjunct faculty member at Central Campus, 1988-89, and Broward Center, 1992, 1993, and 1994; guest lecturer at Kent State University and Florida Atlantic University, 1988. Promise for Youth, Boca Raton, FL, member of community service task force, 1998-99.

MEMBER: Modern Language Association of America, Phi Beta Kappa.

WRITINGS:

(Contributor) Vera J. Camden, editor, *Compromise Formations: Current Directions in Psychoanalytic Criticism,* Kent State University Press (Kent, OH), 1989.

(Contributor) Paul Herron, editor, *Anais Nin: A Book of Mirrors,* Sky Blue Press (Huntington Woods, MI), 1996.

Anais Nin and the Remaking of Self: Gender, Modernism, and Narrative Identity, Northern Illinois University Press (De Kalb), 1998.

Work represented in anthologies, including *Poetic Medicine,* edited by John Fox, Putnam (New York City), 1997. Contributor of articles and reviews to periodicals, including *D. H. Lawrence Review, Anais: An International Journal,* and *Feminist Issues.*

WORK IN PROGRESS: Thick Rubber Heart, poems, completion expected in 2000; *Water like Blown Glass,* stories.

SIDELIGHTS: Diane Richard-Allerdyce told *CA:* "I write to draw a connection between my consciousness and that of the universe, and with those others who are, like me, participating in the inspiring, ongoing conversations that are constantly taking place in print. I write to make meaning and to share it, to hold myself together at the seams, to make sense of chaos, to become more aware of myself and more honest. I write to celebrate life and affirm its worth.

"Having grown up in rural Ohio in a working, middle-class family influences my work. Having lived in South Florida since 1979, I am struck by how much the changing environment here—the natural and burgeoning urban landscapes—influences me to observe the effects of humans on nature and nature on humans. Having taught at a private university for fourteen years, I am influenced by my students, who have taught me patience and humility and appreciation for difference, and my colleagues, who have shown me how to preserve friendship while resolving conflicts. Presently, my husband and children have influenced me to be fully present.

"Several professor/critics have influenced me greatly, especially Ellie Ragland, who directed my dissertation, and Daniel R. Schwarz, who directed a summer seminar I attended in 1993. Writers who I think have most influenced my creative nonfiction are Anais Nin and Alice Walker. I hope my work shows my deep admiration as well for Faulkner, Hemingway, and

Morrison. I like to think my poetry is influenced by Frost most of all.

"My writing process is sporadically steady. I write *something* nearly every day, even if it is simply a journal entry. I write poetry fairly regularly, often allowing the lines to form as I walk in the park or drive to work and later giving them shape on paper. Because I teach many classes, run a department, and help to run an honors program at Lynn University, and also participate in many activities with my children, I find it difficult to carve out blocks of time to write, especially when the task is literary criticism. When engaged with my book, *Anais Nin and the Remaking of Self,* I would indeed block out everything including my family for many hours at a time, but it was a nerve-wracking process—one in which I would be happily absorbed at the center, but whose edges were jagged and anxious. I often envy those whose lives are enough—who don't feel the need to write, as I and so many others do—but as I am cursed and blessed with this need, I honor it.

"The influences I have already mentioned led me to write about women's issues, the environment, and the process by which modernist and contemporary writers have remade themselves in the image of something they can believe in. In an essay called 'A Literary Soulmate: Some Reflections on Nin's Influence' I explained at length why I have spent nearly a decade and a half writing about Anais Nin and her work."

*   *   *

RINGER, Fritz 1934-
(Fritz K.Ringer, Klaus F. Ringer)

PERSONAL: Born September 25, 1934, in Ludwigshafen, Germany; immigrated to the United States, 1949, naturalized citizen, 1956; son of Friedrich K. (a chemical engineer) and Ernestine (Loringer) Ringer; married Mary Master (a painter), September 14, 1957; children: Monica M. Ringer Mazerai, Max K. *Ethnicity:* "German." *Education:* Amherst College, B.A., 1956; Harvard University, Ph.D., 1961. *Politics:* Democrat. *Religion:* None. *Avocational interests:* Hiking, sailing, golf, skiing.

ADDRESSES: Home—1228 South Negley Ave., Pittsburgh, PA 15217. *Office*—Department of History,

University of Pittsburgh, Pittsburgh, PA 15217; fax 412-422-0610. *E-mail*—fririt@pitt.edu.

CAREER: Harvard University, Cambridge, MA, instructor, 1960-62, assistant professor of history, 1962-66; Indiana University—Bloomington, associate professor of history, 1966-70; Boston University, Boston, MA, professor of history, 1970-84; University of Pittsburgh, Pittsburgh, PA, Mellon Professor of History, 1984—, also fellow of Center for Philosophy of Science and member of Cultural Studies Program. Center for the Study of Higher Education, Berkeley, CA, visiting fellow, 1976-77; lecturer at colleges and universities in the United States and abroad, including Princeton University, University of California, Berkeley and San Diego, University of Notre Dame, Ecole des Hautes Etudes en Sciences Sociales, University of Frankfurt, University of Marburg, University of Utrecht, University of Goeteborg, University of Oslo, and University of Madrid. American Academy of Education, member, 1995-97.

MEMBER: American Association of University Professors (member of national executive committee, 1981-83; president and chief negotiator for Boston University chapter, 1974-75, 1978-79, 1981-82).

AWARDS, HONORS: Fellow of National Endowment for the Humanities, 1969-70, 1976-77; joint fellow of National Science Foundation and Netherlands Institute for Advanced Study, 1985-86; visiting scholar, Forschungsschwerpunkt fuer Wissenschaftsgeschichte und Wissenschaftstheorie, Berlin, Germany, 1993; fellow at National Humanities Center, 1993-94; Guggenheim fellow, 1994.

WRITINGS:

The German Inflation of 1923, Oxford University Press, 1969.
The Decline of the German Mandarins, Harvard University Press (Cambridge, MA), 1969, with new introduction, University Press of New England (Hanover, NH), 1990.
Education and Society in Modern Europe, Indiana University Press (Bloomington), 1979.
(Editor with Detlef Mueller and Brian Simon, and contributor) *The Rise of the Modern Educational System,* Cambridge University Press (London), 1987.
(Contributor) W. J. Nijhof, editor, *Values in Higher Education: Bildungsideale in Historical and Con-* *temporary Perspective,* Department of Education, University of Twente/Enschede (the Netherlands), 1990.
(Contributor) Ernan McMullin, editor, *The Social Dimensions of Science,* [Notre Dame, IN], 1992.
Fields of Knowledge: French Academic Culture in Comparative Perspective, 1890-1920, Cambridge University Press, 1992.
Max Weber's Methodology: The Unification of the Cultural and Social Sciences, Harvard University Press, 1997.

Contributor to academic journals in the United States and Germany, including *Theory and Society* and *History and Theory.* Member of editorial board, *History of Education Quarterly,* 1975-81, *Journal of Modern History,* 1979-83, *Central European History,* 1979-86, and *History of Education,* 1990-98. Some writings appear under the names Fritz K. Ringer or Klaus F. Ringer.

WORK IN PROGRESS: Toward a Social History of Knowledge, for Berghahn Books; *Max Weber: A New Intellectual Biography,* Harvard University Press.

SIDELIGHTS: Fritz Ringer told *CA:* "I was a youngster in national socialist Germany. As a historian, I have been trying to come to terms with aspects of my heritage, particularly with the role and ideology of intellectuals (and especially academics) in Germany and elsewhere. I have been a critical activist in American academe as well, and am currently trying to publish a short autobiographical memoir about this, titled *Trouble in Academe,* which deals mainly with the struggle against President Silber at Boston University. I also have a strong interest in the history and philosophy of the cultural and social sciences in Germany and elsewhere. Finally, I am a committed disciple of the great German social scientist Max Weber."

*   *   *

RINGER, Fritz K.
See RINGER, Fritz

*   *   *

RINGER, Klaus F.
See Ringer, Fritz

RODRIGUEZ, Clara E.

PERSONAL: Married; children: two. *Education:* City College of the City University of New York, B.A.; Cornell University, M.A.; Washington University, St. Louis, MO, Ph.D.

ADDRESSES: Home—2160 Bolton St., No. 3-B, Bronx, NY 10462. *Office*—Division of Social Sciences, College at Lincoln Center, Fordham University, 113 West 60th St., New York, NY 10023.

CAREER: Centro Colombo-Americano, Cali, Colombia, instructor in English as a second language, 1965; New York Urban Coalition, New York City, staff associate in housing, 1969; Washington University, St. Louis, MO, instructor, 1970-71; Graduate Center of the City University of New York, New York City, research associate at Centro de Estudios Puertorriquenos, 1973; Herbert H. Lehman College of the City University of New York, Bronx, NY, head of department of Puerto Rican studies and associate of sociology department, 1974-76; Fordham University, Bronx, dean of general studies and project director for Pre-Health Professions Program, 1976-81; Fordham University, College at Lincoln Center, New York City, professor of social sciences, 1981—, member of university executive board, 1981, member of executive committee of Latin American and Latino Studies Institute, 1997—, founder of Angelo Rodriguez Memorial Trust Fund, 1990. Massachusetts Institute of Technology, visiting scholar in urban studies and planning, 1987-88; Yale University, visiting fellow in American studies, 1992; Russell Sage Foundation, visiting scholar, 1993-94; Smithsonian Institution, senior fellow at National Museum of American History, 1998.

Columbia University, guest lecturer, 1992, visiting professor, 1999; Rollins College, Alfred J. Hanna Distinguished Lecturer, 1993; guest lecturer at numerous colleges and universities, including Queens College of the City University of New York and John Jay College of Criminal Justice of the City University of New York, 1991, Harvard University, 1991 and 1992, Swarthmore College, Haverford College, and Bryn Mawr College, all 1993, and Universidad de Talca, Simmons College, University of Massachusetts at Boston, University of Groningen, University of Tuebingen, and Wesleyan University, all 1998. Cornell University, founding member of Puerto Rican Research Exchange, School of Industrial Labor Relations, 1984—. Coordinator of an illiteracy program in

Cali, 1965-66. Grass Roots Organization, founding member and member of board of directors of Youth Program and Summer Day Care Center, 1973-77; Tremont Towers Tenants Association, organizer and president, 1973-80; Aspira of America, member of educational advisory board, 1975-79; Puerto Rican Migration Consortium, founding member and member of board of directors, 1977-80; Center for Latino Family Policy, member of advisory council of Committee for Hispanic Children and Families, 1993—; Five Borough Institute, member of advisers, 1998—; New York State Economic Policy Research Council, member of coordinating committee; consultant to National Council of La Raza, Children's Television Workshop, Prescriptives Cosmetic Co., and National Puerto Rican Coalition. Bronx Museum of the Arts, member of board of trustees, 1977-80.

MEMBER: American Sociological Association (member of council, section on racial and ethnic minorities, 1988-91), American Anthropological Association, American Association for the Advancement of Science, American Public Health Association, Association for Public Policy and Management, Latin American Studies Association, Population Association of America, Sociologists for Women in Society, Union for Radical Political Economics, Eastern Sociological Society.

AWARDS, HONORS: Grants from National Institutes of Health, 1978-81, and Calder Foundation, 1979; Rockefeller fellow, 1988-89; grants from Ford Foundation, 1987, Social Science Research Council and American Sociological Association, 1988; Star Award, New York Women's Agenda, 1992; Leadership in Educational Excellence Award, National Society of Hispanic M.B.A.s, 1995; Distinguished Prize in Social Sciences, Instituto de Puerto Rico, New York City, 1997.

WRITINGS:

The Ethnic Queue in the United States: The Case of Puerto Ricans, R & E Research Associates (San Francisco), 1974.

(Editor with Virginia Sanchez Korrol and Oscar Alers) *The Puerto Rican Struggle: Essays on Survival in the United States,* Puerto Rican Migration Consortium, 1979.

(Contributor) George Mims, editor, *The Minority Administrator in Higher Education: Progress, Experiences, and Perspectives,* Schenkman (New York City), 1981.

Puerto Ricans: Born in the USA, Unwin & Hyman (Boston, MA), 1989.

(Editor with Edwin Melendez and Janice Barry-Figueroa, and contributor) *Hispanics in the Labor Force: Issues and Policies,* Plenum (New York City), 1991.

(Contributor) Ronald Takaki, editor, *From Different Shores,* Oxford University Press (New York City), 1994.

(Contributor) Roberto Santiago, editor, *Boricuas: Influential Puerto Rican Writings—An Anthology,* Ballantine (New York City), 1995.

(Editor with Korrol) *Historical Perspectives on Puerto Rican Survival in the United States,* Markus Wiener (Princeton, NJ), 1996.

(Contributor) G. Haslip-Viera and S. Baver, editors, *Latinos in New York: Communities in Transition,* University of Notre Dame Press (Notre Dame, IN), 1996.

Latin Looks: Latina and Latino Images in the Media, Westview Press (Boulder, CO), 1997.

(Contributor) Mary Romero, Pierette Hondagneu-Sotelo, and Vilma Ortiz, editors, *The Latino Experience in the United States,* Routledge (New York City), 1997.

Contributor of articles and reviews to academic journals and newspapers, including *Social Science Quarterly, American Quarterly, Women's Studies Quarterly, Ethnicity, Urban Review,* and *Ethnic and Racial Studies.* Co-editor of special issue, *Hispanic Journal of Behavioral Sciences,* 1992; founding member of editorial board, *Latino Studies Journal;* advisory editor, *Gender and Society.*

SIDELIGHTS: Clara E. Rodriguez told *CA:* "I write because I feel there are stories to be told and views to be expressed that are not present when I read what I read. I write so that those who are 'missing' can connect with my work and create the bridges that others will follow and cross many times in many different directions.

"I am influenced by my experiences in life. These include my experiences of others' experiences, whether they are personal and direct or mediated through art, media, writing, or 'history telling.' Sometimes I feel strongly and begin to write. This is often when I write my best.

"At other times, I think and then write. Still other times, I write because this is what is needed. Usually, though, I feel strongly about what I write regardless of how I got there."

RODRIGUEZ, Junius P. 1957-

PERSONAL: Born June 26, 1957, in Thibodaux, LA; son of Junius P., Sr. (a mechanic) and Mildred (a homemaker; maiden name, Degruise) Rodriguez; married Kathy J. Whitson (a college professor), November 25, 1994. *Ethnicity:* "White." *Education:* Nicholls State University, B.A., 1979; Louisiana State University, M.A., 1987; Auburn University, Ph.D., 1992. *Politics:* Democrat. *Religion:* Roman Catholic. *Avocational interests:* Travel, community service.

ADDRESSES: Home—707 South Vennum St., Eureka, IL 61530. *Office*—Eureka College, 300 College Ave., Eureka, IL 61530; fax 309-467-6386. *E-mail*—jrodrig@eureka.edu.

CAREER: High school teacher in Mathews, LA, 1979-88; Eureka College, Eureka, IL, associate professor, 1992—. Member of parish council, Lafourche Parish, LA, 1980-84.

MEMBER: Southern Historical Association, Louisiana Historical Association.

AWARDS, HONORS: Helen Cleaver Distinguished Teaching Award, 1997.

WRITINGS:

(General editor) *The Historical Encyclopedia of World Slavery,* two volumes, American Bibliographical Center-Clio Press (Santa Barbara, CA), 1997.

The Chronology of World Slavery, American Bibliographical Center-Clio Press, 1999.

WORK IN PROGRESS: An essay collection on abolitionists and higher education; research on slave revolts.

*   *   *

ROGERS, Bettye 1934-
(Bettye Johnson)

PERSONAL: Born November 4, 1934, in Smith County, TN; daughter of L. Earl and Mary (an elementary schoolteacher; maiden name, Highers) Underwood; children: Ralph Johnson, Mary Madden. *Education:* Tennessee Polytechnic University (now Tennessee Technological University), B.S. (with honors), 1958;

University of Tennessee, M.S., 1960, Ed.D., 1962. *Avocational interests:* Travel, animals, archaeology, art, Native American cultures.

ADDRESSES: Home—16 East Canyon View Dr., Ransom Canyon, TX 79366.

CAREER: East Texas State University, Commerce, associate professor, 1963-69; Texas Tech University, Lubbock, associate professor, 1970-88. South Plains Teacher Education Center, director and executive secretary, 1974-87; Texas Cooperative Teacher Center Network, president, treasurer, and executive secretary, 1980-86.

MEMBER: Phi Delta Kappa, Phi Kappa Phi, Kappa Delta Pi.

AWARDS, HONORS: Kyle Killough Award, Texas Cooperative Teacher Center Network, 1985.

WRITINGS:

Prairie Dog Town ("Smithsonian Wild Heritage Collection" series), illustrated by Deborah Howland, Soundprints (Norwalk, CT), 1993.
Paul Wylie from Cowboy to Cowboy Artist, photographs by Paul Wylie and others, privately printed, 1998.

Contributor to magazines. Author of educational materials and magazine articles, under name Bettye Johnson.

SIDELIGHTS: Bettye Rogers commented: "During my career in higher education, I wrote approximately forty articles for various state publications and for journals such as *Phi Delta Kappa* and *Journal of Teacher Education.* I was also the co-author of a small textbook on audio-visual techniques for the classroom. In conjunction with my various professional memberships and activities, I wrote, designed, and edited numerous newsletters, programs, and brochures.

"When, primarily for family reasons, I took early retirement, I wanted to write for children. The Institute of Children's Literature offered correspondence courses. I completed two. Many of my articles, for both young persons and general audiences, have been published. I particularly enjoy creating informational puzzles and word games.

My grandchildren, Allison and Valerie, have traveled far and wide with me. We enjoyed a too-short tour of Europe during Christmas of 1991, and a long-dreamed-of trip to New Zealand and Australia in 1994. We have been to all fifty of the United States, from British Columbia to Nova Scotia in Canada, and from Mexico City to Cancun in Mexico. We always seek out sites of ancient civilizations, such as Stonehenge, Chichen Itza, and the like. In addition, Valerie and I traveled to Peru in 1995, Egypt and Kenya in 1996, and Antarctica in 1998. I have also visited China, Russia, the Bahamas, Puerto Rico, and Japan.

"At home, we enjoy the local wildlife. Each evening we put out food for the raccoons, skunks, and gray foxes who live in our small community, which is built around a canyon and a lake. Sometimes a gray squirrel graces our trees, but unfortunately, population expansion is driving the wildlife to more remote regions.

"My family has built a modest, but good, art collection over the years. We have a combination of bronzes, terra cotta, and paintings in various media. Therefore my project on cowboy artist Paul Wylie was a natural. It was my first attempt at 'ground floor' biography. It involved considerable searching through public documents, as well as extensive interviews with the subject."

BIOGRAPHICAL/CRITICAL SOURCES:

PERIODICALS

School Library Journal, April, 1994, p. 90; May, 1994, p. 103.*

*   *   *

ROOSEVELT, Theodore 1858-1919

PERSONAL: Born October 27, 1858, in New York, NY; died of a coronary embolism, January 6, 1919; son of Theodore (a merchant and banker) and Martha (Bulloch) Roosevelt; married Alice Hathaway Lee (died, 1884); married Edith Kermit Carow; children: Alice, Theodore, Kermit, Ethel, Archibald, Quentin. *Education:* Harvard University, A.B., 1880. *Politics:* Republican, Progressive. *Religion:* Dutch Reformed Church.

CAREER: New York State legislature, member, 1882-84; Republican National Convention, delegate, 1884; candidate for mayor of New York City, 1886; U.S. civil service commissioner, 1889-95; New York Police Board, president, 1895-97; Assistant Secretary of the Navy, 1897-98; co-organizer of First U.S. Cavalry (Rough Riders), 1898; governor of New York, 1899-1900; vice president of the United States, 1901; president of the United States, 1901-09; special U.S. ambassador at the funeral of King Edward VII; Progressive Party candidate for president of the United States, 1912. Rancher and cattleman. American Museum of Natural History, honorary fellow, 1917.

MEMBER: American Historical Association, Phi Beta Kappa.

AWARDS, HONORS: Nobel Peace Prize, 1906; David Livingstone Centenary Gold Medal, American Geographical Society, c. 1915.

WRITINGS:

(With H. D. Minot) *The Summer Birds of the Adirondacks in Franklin County, N.Y.,* privately printed (Salem, MA), 1877.

Notes on Some of the Birds of Oyster Bay, Long Island, privately printed (New York City), 1879.

The Naval War of 1812; or, The History of the United States Navy during the Last War with Great Britain, Putnam's (New York City), 1882, published as *The Naval Operations of the War between Great Britain and the United States,* Low (London), 1910.

Hunting Trips of a Ranchman, Putnam's (New York City), 1886, published with *The Wilderness Hunter,* 1996.

Thomas Hart Benton, Houghton Mifflin (Boston), 1886.

Essays on Practical Politics, Putnam's (New York City), 1888.

Gouverneur Morris, Houghton Mifflin (Boston), 1888.

Ranch Life and the Hunting-Trail, Century (New York City), 1888.

The Winning of the West; An Account of the Exploration and Settlement of Our Country from the Alleghanies to the Pacific, four volumes, Putnam's (New York City), 1889-96.

New York, Longmans, Green (New York City), 1891.

The Wilderness Hunter: An Account of the Big Game of the United States and Its Chase with Horse, Putnam's (New York City), 1893.

(With Henry Cabot Lodge) *Hero Tales from American History,* Century (New York City), 1895.

American Ideals, and Other Essays, Social and Political, Putnam's (New York City), 1897.

The Rough Riders, Scribner (New York City), 1899.

Oliver Cromwell, Scribner (New York City), 1900.

The Strenuous Life: Essays and Addresses, Century (New York City), 1900.

California Addresses, California Promotion Committee (San Francisco, CA), 1903.

Outdoor Pastimes of an American Hunter, Scribner (New York City), 1903, enlarged edition, 1908.

Addresses and Presidential Messages of Theodore Roosevelt, 1902-1904, Putnam's (New York City), 1904.

Good Hunting, Harper (New York City), 1907.

Addresses and Papers, edited by Willis Fletcher Johnson, Sun Dial (New York City), 1908.

African Game Trails, An Account of the African Wanderings of an American Hunter-Naturalist, Scribner (New York City), 1910.

The Roosevelt Policy; Speeches, Letters and State Papers, Relating to Corporate Wealth and Closely Allied Topics, of Theodore Roosevelt, two volumes, Current Literature (New York City), 1908, expanded and edited by William Griffith, three volumes, 1919.

Outlook Editorials, Outlook (New York City), 1909.

African and European Addresses, Putnam's (New York City), 1910.

American Problems, Outlook (New York City), 1910.

The New Nationalism, Outlook (New York City), 1910.

Realizable Ideals (The Earl Lectures), Whittaker & Ray-Wiggin (San Francisco, CA), 1912.

Theodore Roosevelt: An Autobiography, Macmillan (New York City), 1913.

Progressive Principles: Selections from Addresses Made during the Presidential Campaign of 1912, edited by Elmer H. Youngman, Progressive National Service (New York City), 1913.

History as Literature, and Other Essays, Scribner (New York City), 1914.

(With Edmund Heller) *Life-Histories of African Game Animals,* two volumes, Scribner (New York City), 1914.

Through the Brazilian Wilderness, Scribner (New York City), 1914.

America and the World War, Scribner (New York City), 1915.

A Book-Lover's Holidays in the Open, Scribner (New York City), 1916.

Fear God and Take Your Own Part, Doran (New York City), 1916.

Americanism and Preparedness. Speeches, July to November, 1916, Mail & Express Job Print (New York City), 1916.

The Foes of Our Own Household, Doran (New York City), 1917.

National Strength and International Duty, Princeton University Press (Princeton, NJ), 1917.

The Great Adventure: Present-Day Studies in American Nationalism, Scribner (New York City), 1918.

Average Americans, Putnam's (New York City), 1919.

Newer Roosevelt Messages: Speeches, Letters and Magazine Articles Dealing with the War, before and after, and Other Vital Topics, edited by William Griffith, Current Literature (New York City), 1919.

Roosevelt in the Kansas City Star: War-time Editorials by Theodore Roosevelt, Houghton Mifflin (Boston), 1921.

Campaigns and Controversies, Scribner (New York City), 1926.

(With son, Kermit Roosevelt) *East of the Sun and West of the Moon,* Scribner (New York City), 1926.

Literary Essays, Scribner (New York City), 1926.

Social Justice and Popular Rule: Essays, Addresses, and Public Statements Relating to the Progressive Movement, Scribner (New York City), 1926.

Theodore Roosevelt's Diaries of Boyhood and Youth, Scribner (New York City), 1928.

Colonial Policies of the United States, Doubleday, Doran (Garden City, NY), 1937.

Theodore Roosevelt: Wilderness Writings, edited by Paul Schullery, Peregrine Smith Books (Salt Lake City, UT), 1986.

The Hunting and Exploring Adventures of Theodore Roosevelt, edited by Donald Day, Dial, 1995.

American Bears: Selections from the Writings of Theodore Roosevelt, edited by Paul Schullery, Colorado Associated University Press, 1983.

Theodore Roosevelt: An American Mind: A Selection from His Writings, edited by Mario R. Dinunzio, St. Martin's Press (New York City), 1995.

The Essential Theodore Roosevelt, edited by John Gabriel Hunt, Library of Freedom, 1998.

The Bully Pulpit: A Teddy Roosevelt Book of Quotations, edited by H. Paul Jeffers, 1998.

LETTERS

The Letters of Theodore Roosevelt and Brander Matthews, edited by Lawrence J. Oliver, University of Tennessee Press (Knoxville), 1995.

Theodore Roosevelt's Letters to His Children, 1919, *A Bully Father: Theodore Roosevelt's Letters to His*

Children, edited by Joan Paterson Kerr, Random House (New York City), 1995.

COLLECTIONS

The Works of Theodore Roosevelt, twenty volumes, National Edition, Scribner (New York City), 1926.

OTHER

Contributor to periodicals. Contributing editor to *Outlook,* 1909-14.

SIDELIGHTS: Theodore Roosevelt became the twenty-sixth president of the United States on September 14, 1901, following the assassination of President William McKinley, for whom Roosevelt was serving as vice president. Roosevelt, fondly known as "Teddy" by Americans and remembered for leading the charge up San Juan Hill during the Spanish American War, remained president following the 1904 election and served until 1909, gaining a reputation for his use of executive action and promotion of legislation to protect labor and consumers against big business abuses, his sponsorship of efforts to conserve and reclaim wildlife and natural resources through legislation and the creation of national preserves, and his foreign policies characterized by imperialism and military strength. Roosevelt was also a prolific author who issued two natural science books before he turned twenty-two and two years later produced a classic on naval warfare. In his mid-twenties, he moved west to the Dakotas, where he wrote two books on his experiences as a rancher and hunter, and then completed a biography of a U.S. Senator. Over the next twelve years, Roosevelt's literary output included two more biographies, two books of political essays, and six histories, including his four-volume magnum opus on westward expansion. His volume about his adventures in Cuba during the Spanish American War, *The Rough Riders,* was his seventeenth published work.

Before Roosevelt led his Rough Riders up Cuba's San Juan Hill, his career in politics and public service included two years in the New York state assembly, an unsuccessful run for mayor of New York City, four years as U.S. Civil Service commissioner in Washington, D.C., two years as Police Commissioner in New York City, and a year as assistant secretary of the Navy. He resigned this post, formed his volunteer cavalry unit, and sailed for Cuba in 1898. After he mustered out of the service (as Colonel Roosevelt), he was elected Governor of New York, and in 1900, was elected vice president in William McKinley's second term. Ten months later, after President McKinley was killed by an anarchist, Roosevelt was sworn in as twenty-sixth President of the United States. He was forty-two years old.

Roosevelt was an intensely energetic man, widely known for the hearty exuberance with which he went at everything. His energy was called "volcanic" by Arthur Schlesinger Jr., in the *Partisan Review.* "He was . . . voracious in his interests; except for Jefferson, no American president has ever known so much, read so widely, or dogmatized so freely in so fantastic a variety of fields."

As a child, young Roosevelt was afflicted with asthma and poor eyesight and suffered frequent bouts of illness. When he was ten years old, according to David H. Burton in *The Learned Presidency,* his father told him, "You have the mind but you have not the body, and without the body the mind can not go as far as it should." Accordingly, stated Schlesinger, Roosevelt "remade" himself, learning to ride and run and box and be tough; he wanted "to do good" and "feared being a sissy," so he redesigned his personality and made his whole life "a triumph of the will." And speaking to the issue of energy, he became an advocate and exemplar of what he later called in one of his books "the strenuous life."

Roosevelt was born October 27, 1858, the second of four children. The family was well off. Roosevelt's father, Theodore, was more a philanthropist than a businessman, according to Burton in *The Learned Presidency,* but much of the family's wealth came from his active involvement as a merchant and banker. Young Roosevelt was taught at home by private tutors, and his lifelong habit of reading widely and voraciously began early. He became quite knowledgeable about natural history, especially birds, animals, and flowers, and he consumed books on American history and adventure tales by the likes of James Fenimore Cooper and Longfellow. By the age of fifteen, he had visited England, Europe, North Africa, and the Middle East, and had lived for six months in Dresden, Germany, where he learned the language. For three years, Roosevelt was tutored fairly rigorously in preparation for Harvard, where he performed very well. He excelled in political economy and zoology; he graduated with an "honorable mention" in natural science, a membership in Phi Beta Kappa, and ranked twenty-first in a class of 177.

The future historian had only the slightest exposure to history at Harvard (there were no upper division courses at the time), and there were no science courses of the "outdoor" type (as opposed to purely laboratory courses) which would enable Roosevelt to pursue his desire to become a "naturalist" (in modern terminology, a wildlife biologist). However, he had already written one book about birds in upstate New York and another about birds in Oyster Bay, the family home on Long Island.

Despite the lack of "formal" academic training as an historian, before he graduated Roosevelt had already begun writing a history of the naval war of 1812 between Great Britain and the United States. Roosevelt knew the subject had been neglected, and he was also drawn to it by his nationalism and attraction to military life. He married in October, 1880, and continued his research while on his honeymoon, in England. By the time the publisher received the manuscript a year later, Roosevelt had just been elected as a state legislator, and was about to begin his term in office. *The Naval War of 1812; or, The History of the United States Navy during the Last War with Great Britain* "provoked no sensation," according to Raymond C. Miller in *Medieval and Historiographical Essays in Honor of James Westfall Thompson,* and Roosevelt himself once remarked that it was "dry as a dictionary." Nevertheless, the book went through three editions in its first year, and was placed on the reading list at the Naval War college in Newport and aboard every ship in the fleet. Roosevelt's treatment of both sides was so evenhanded that the British publisher of *A History of the Royal Navy* asked Roosevelt to write the chapter on the War of 1812 for the next edition; abridged and purged of much of its American bias, it became volume six of that *History* (1901). In 1897 Roosevelt revised the work considerably, and it has been reprinted numerous times.

Beyond the technical details about ships, guns, and crews, and even beyond the naval battles themselves, Roosevelt sought to expose the evils of governmental fragmentation and military unpreparedness. He blamed Jefferson and Madison for letting the fleet dwindle to only a few good ships, and called Jefferson "perhaps the most incapable executive that ever filled the presidential chair." Later, he favorably reviewed the strategic and geopolitical writings of Alfred Thayer Mahan, and as assistant secretary of the navy and later as president, he pushed "tirelessly" for a bigger, stronger, modernized navy. As critic John Milton Cooper stated in 1986, "The statesman was applying the lessons learned by the historian."

Roosevelt was a life-long omnivorous reader who valued history because it could teach him about the present; his own works favored individuals and their accomplishments over institutions or movements. He demonstrated this in his biographies of *Thomas Hart Benton* (1886), *Gouverneur Morris* (1888), and *Oliver Cromwell* (1900). Roosevelt wrote all three rather quickly and under less-than-ideal circumstances. He wrote *Benton* in three months on his Dakota ranch, far from libraries and manuscript collections; he was also busy with ranching and hunting. He wrote *Morris* in Oyster Bay without benefit of access to his subject's private papers, and *Cromwell* was largely dictated to stenographers when Roosevelt was governor of New York.

Roosevelt's *Benton* mostly covered the Missourian's thirty years in the U.S. Senate, but its focus on Benton as a western expansionist and as a nationalist served as warmup for Roosevelt's own history of the west, according to J. W. Cooke in the *Dictionary of Literary Biography*. Reviews were generally favorable and led the publisher to ask Roosevelt for a volume on Gouverneur Morris, a Constitutional Convention delegate and later U.S. Senator from Pennsylvania. While Roosevelt was not sympathetic to Morris's elitism, he again displayed his passionate interest in individuals as historical actors and in social history as well; historian John Gable noted that his biography "remained the standard work for many decades." *Oliver Cromwell* is more of a character study than a formal biography, and it was yet another example of Roosevelt's tendency to use the past as a way of explaining the present. Critic Arthur Hamilton Lee called the book "a fine, imaginative study of Cromwell's qualifications for the governorship of New York." Cooke in the *Dictionary of Literary Biography* commented that *Oliver Cromwell* was "one of the least" of Roosevelt's historical monographs, while John Milton Cooper called it his "finest single work." For Cooke, the problem is that while Roosevelt "was at his best" when he wrote about the English Civil War and the Puritan mind, "Cromwell remains shadowy and remote." On the other hand, Cooper valued the work for its "comparative perspective on revolutionary movement in the modern world" and for its reflections on the balance between thought and action in Cromwell's use of power.

History was theory for Roosevelt, but as his four-volume *The Winning of the West* shows, it was also biography. His plan was to demonstrate that the greatness of the American nation resulted from expansion into and conquest of the west by the people them-

selves, rather than by actions of government. Published serially between 1889 and 1896, *The Winning of the West* focuses on the years between 1763, when the French and Indian War ended, and 1807, with Zebulon Pike's trek west to Colorado, but its sweep is much broader. Movement toward the west is set against the backdrop of three centuries of transatlantic migration by Europeans, and that in turn rests on Roosevelt's use of mythology and ancient literature to discuss migrations of Western peoples going back over a thousand years. "During the last three centuries," Roosevelt wrote, "the spread of the English-speaking peoples over the world's vast spaces has been not only the most striking feature in the world's history, but also the event of all others most far-reaching in its effects and its importance."

Writing in 1938, Miller in *Medieval and Historiographical Essays in Honor of James Westfall Thompson* called the work "a pioneer task." Fifty years later, Burton noted in *The Learned Presidency* that Roosevelt broke new ground "very much on his own initiative," and called *The Winning of the West* "a lasting contribution to the historical literature of the frontier." Historian Frederick Jackson Turner, Roosevelt's contemporary and later friend, criticized Roosevelt's work on a number of points but praised him for exercising the skills of a "practiced historian." Turner (as quoted by Burton) also called *The Winning of the West* a "real service" because Roosevelt had "rescued a whole movement of American development from the hands of unskilled annalists."

Roosevelt did extensive research in primary materials, consulting sources in Tennessee, Kentucky, and New York, and gathering material from friends and contacts in California and Canada. He displayed knowledge of a wide range of subjects, from agriculture to weapons technology, and showed sharp appreciation of what the frontier experience meant to those who went there. As Marcus Klein pointed out in a 1994 essay, Roosevelt tended to confirm history by referring to his own frontier experience: "He knew the *type* of frontiersman, so he said, and the type did not change." The first two volumes of *The Winning of the West* feature soldiers, scouts, mountain men, traders, settlers, all types Roosevelt felt he knew, and it was their stories, their adventures, that interested him. Once the national government was established under the new constitution, the Federalists in power were too preoccupied to be of much help in westward expansion, and after them came the "spineless" Jefferson. According to Miller, "the absence of any real idea of the role of the West . . . reduces the first two volumes [of *The Winning of the West*] to a series of microscopic biographies."

For the third and fourth volumes, Roosevelt had access to more sources which, according to Miller, made the work more coherent. But he "only transformed his drama [of heroes] to a larger stage." The fourth volume begins with a long discussion of the "racial characteristics" suitable for empire building: "If the race is weak, if it is lacking in the physical and moral traits which go to the makeup of a conquering people, it cannot succeed. . . . The task must be given the race just at the time when it is ready for the undertaking." The backwoodsman fighting Indians for possession of the continent "should be both strong and good; but, above all things, [conquest] demanded that they should be strong." For Roosevelt, the winning of the west was a conflict between the forces of good and the forces of evil, a conflict between civilization and savagery, and as such, it was "in its essence just and righteous." It was perfectly proper, in Miller's words, "for bible-reading backwoodsmen to take Indian scalps."

Ultimately, for Roosevelt, the winning of the west (and everything else) was a matter of character. Native Americans were fickle, for example, while the white man was unwaveringly steadfast, and the pressures of the frontier simply intensified these differences, observed Merril E. Lewis in *The American West: An Appraisal* of Roosevelt's work. Character, "the foundation-stone of national life" for Roosevelt, was neither mysterious nor complex. "By character I mean the sum of qualities essential to moral efficiency. Among them are resolution, courage, energy, self-control, fearlessness in taking the initiative and in assuming responsibility, and a just regard for the rights of others." Though Roosevelt thought that character (rather than institutions or environmental factors like "the frontier") would likely make the future better than the past, according to Miller he could not imagine *complex* characters for example, people who had several sets of often conflicting values and he lost interest in the West when its history shifted from the backwoodsman, frontier type to those who chose to settle down.

Roosevelt's interest in the West (and its character-building qualities) was rooted in his own experience, which he reflected in personal narratives. In 1883, he invested a sizeable portion of his inheritance in a cattle ranch in the Dakotas, and he moved there in 1884 to seek solace after his mother and his wife

Alice died (on the same day, within hours of each other). Wearing his buckskin shirt and sporting a pearl-handled revolver, he immersed himself in various roles running his ranch and his cowboy crews, hunting big game, observing the flora and fauna as a naturalist, playing deputy sheriff, reading, and writing. In addition to the biography of Benton, Roosevelt wrote the first two volumes of his natural history trilogy, *Hunting Trips of a Ranchman* (1885) and *Ranch Life and the Hunting Trail* (1888); the third volume, *The Wilderness Hunter*, followed in 1893.

Hunting Trips of a Ranchman includes accounts of stalking buffalo, white-tail and black-tail deer, grizzlies, grouse, water fowl, antelope, and mountain sheep. He described these creatures as a naturalist, found many to be "most delicious eating," and was delighted that much of the Bad Lands were still untouched. But he knew his West was transitory, doomed as a frontier. "The free, open-air life of the ranchman," Roosevelt said, "the pleasantest and healthiest life in America, is from its very nature ephemeral. The broad and boundless prairies have already been bounded and will soon be made narrow." The game and Indians had been driven out by white hunters and trappers; they in turn had been displaced by cattle ranchers and cowboys, who would be soon be replaced by new settlers. In part, he believed natural selection was at work. Roosevelt the imperialist had no regrets about the near-extinction of the plains buffalo, since it opened the West to settlers, but Roosevelt the naturalist paused to note that the differences between the plains buffalo and the newly-evolved wood or mountain buffalo are due to an accelerated adaptation to a different environment. He also notes that the wars against Indians (who had no more ownership of the plains than did white hunters, he argued) were rational and just: he said that it "does no good to be merciful to the few at the cost of the many."

In *Ranch Life and the Hunting-Trail*, Roosevelt describes cowboys, range and ranch-house life, weather, and relations between ranchers and Native Americans, then turns again to hunting trips. Here, as in *Hunting Trips of a Ranchman*, the West is a testing ground and the cowboy is prominent: "the struggle for existence is very keen in the far West, and it is no place for men who lack the ruder, coarser virtues and physical qualities." However they might be "the personnel of a lost cause," as Marcus Klein wrote in *Easterns, Westerns, and Private Eyes: American Matters*, "cowboys were a race apart," and for Roosevelt they became an enduring symbol of personal as well as national recuperation. (They later made up a goodly portion of the Rough Riders.) Hunters, too, were manly paragons, and Roosevelt equated hunterly virtues courage, honor, tenacity, a willingness to accept risks and pain without complaint with civic virtues. He deplored wanton slaughter, advocated killing only for food, and inadvertently created an entire industry of "teddy bears" after news spread of how he spared the life of a bear cub.

In *The Wilderness Hunter* (1893), Roosevelt said that hunting and killing were only part of the whole: the chase alone "cultivates that vigorous manliness for the lack of which, in a nation, as in an individual, the possession of no other qualities can possibly atone." Critic Daniel Aaron in *Raritan* suggested that Roosevelt's later conservation measures ("in the opinion of many his most lasting contribution") were all about "giving unborn generations a taste of the character-building frontier experience that had toughened and tempered him." Conservation, Aaron continued, "was tantamount to social regeneration, a hedge against creeping decadence."

Roosevelt wrote little while president, though he was characteristically active and energetic. Among other things, he was the first president to ride in an automobile (1902), go underwater in a submarine (1905), or fly in an airplane (1910). He changed the official name of "The Executive Mansion" to "The White House" and with his wife Edith raised six children there. He "liberated" Panama from Columbia (1903) and started the Panama Canal, won the Nobel Peace Prize (1906) for his role in the peace treaty ending the Russo-Japanese War, and waved the flag spectacularly by sending the Great White Fleet (of battleships) around the world (1906-09).

Immediately after leaving the presidency at age fifty-two, Roosevelt went to Africa on a safari, armed with a book contract from Scribner, a large entourage including several field naturalists and taxidermists, and a substantial library of books his sister had trimmed to pocket-size and bound in pigskin to protect them from jungle rot (the "pigskin library"). In addition to stalking rhinos and elephants and many other creatures, Roosevelt the hunter and Roosevelt the naturalist wrote his almost five hundred-page *African Game Trails* (1910) as he trekked along. According to Burton, during one six-week stretch, sitting by camp fires, fatigued and in frequently adverse weather, Roosevelt managed to write forty-five thousand words. Burton pointed out that Roosevelt's contributions to scientific knowledge, "while not great, were

valiantly done," but the literary Roosevelt "passed with high marks."

In 1913, accompanied by son Kermit, Roosevelt traveled to the interior of Brazil on a scientific expedition. Conditions were much more severe than on the African trip; an infection and high fever on the part of the trip involving an exploration of the River of Doubt almost cost him his life. Nevertheless, he persevered as a writer, turning out daily notes while wearing a head net and heavy gloves as protection against insect stings. According to Burton, the resulting book, *Through the Brazilian Wilderness* (1914), was "a first rate account . . . in which Roosevelt's modesty, courage, vulnerability, and physical stamina were all visible." Further, the expedition produced important geographic, geological, and zoological information, and almost two thousand specimens of birds and mammals were collected for the American Museum of Natural Science. The Brazilian government renamed the River of Doubt "Rio Teodora" in Roosevelt's honor, and he was awarded the David Livingstone Centenary gold medal by the American Geographical Society.

The African and Brazilian books were only two of Roosevelt's post-presidential books, but they were the best and most important. His numerous others books were compilations mostly of newspaper editorials and magazine articles on various political topics of the day, book reviews and essays covering many subjects, and speeches. His Progressive "Bull Moose" third-party try for the presidency in 1912 failed. He died in his sleep of a coronary embolism on January 6, 1919; his strenuous life ended when he was just sixty years old.

Later that year, Henry A. Beers wrote in *Four Americans: Roosevelt, Hawthorne, Emerson, Whitman,* that when Roosevelt died, "it was though a wind had fallen, a light had gone out, a military band had stopped playing." It was "a general lowering in the vitality of the nation." His public standing had already diminished, however and H. L. Mencken's 1920 acerbic essay on Roosevelt set the tone for a generation's worth of negative appraisals. Mencken said that while Roosevelt was "a remarkably penetrating diagnostician, well-read, unprejudiced and with a touch of genuine scientific passion", he was also "blatant, crude, overly confidential [sic], devious, tyrannical, vainglorious, sometimes quite childish." After the Second World War, however, more favorable assessments began to appear in monographs and biographies, especially after eight volumes of

Roosevelt's letters appeared (he wrote over 150,000 letters). Writing in 1990, Aaron thought that most historians would agree that Roosevelt was the first modern president of the United States and that many would see him as the first to deal confidently with foreign heads of state and the first to ensure America's future role in global politics. He was, Aaron stated, "one of our most spectacular and entertaining presidents . . . and . . . not easy to plumb."

BIOGRAPHICAL/CRITICAL SOURCES:

BOOKS

American Orators of the Twentieth Century: Critical Studies and Sources, edited by Bernard K. Duffy and Halford R. Ryan, Greenwood Press (Westport, CT), 1987.

The American West: An Appraisal, edited by Robert G. Ferris, Museum of New Mexico Press, 1963.

Beers, Henry A., *Four Americans: Roosevelt, Hawthorne, Emerson, Whitman,* Yale University Press, 1919.

Blum, John Morton, *The Republican Roosevelt,* Harvard University Press, 1965.

Burton, David H., *The Learned Presidency,* Fairleigh Dickinson University Press, 1988.

Burton, David H., *Theodore Roosevelt,* Twayne, 1972.

Cutright, Paul Russell, *Theodore Roosevelt: The Making of a Conservationist,* University of Illinois Press, 1985.

Dictionary of Literary Biography, Gale (Detroit), Volume 47: *American Historians, 1866-1912,* 1986, Volume 186: *Nineteenth-Century American Western Writers,* 1997.

Friedenberg, Robert V., *Theodore Roosevelt and the Rhetoric of Militant Decency,* Greenwood Press, 1990.

Gatewood, Willard B., *Theodore Roosevelt and the Art of Controversy: Episodes of the White House Years,* Louisiana State University Press, 1970.

Gibson, William M., *Theodore Roosevelt: Among the Humorists, W. D. Howells, Mark Twain, and Mr. Dooley,* University of Tennessee Press, 1980.

Gould, Lewis L., *The Presidency of Theodore Roosevelt,* University Press of Kansas, 1991.

Harbaugh, William Henry, *The Life and Times of Theodore Roosevelt,* Collier Books, 1967.

Klein, Marcus, *Easterns, Westerns, and Private Eyes: American Matters, 1870-1900,* University of Wisconsin Press, 1994.

Medieval and Historiographical Essays in Honor of James Westfall Thompson, edited by James Lea

Cate and Eugene N. Anderson, Kennikat Press, 1966.

Mencken, H. L., *Prejudices: Second Series,* Knopf, 1920.

Mowry, George E., *The Era of Theodore Roosevelt, 1900-1912,* Harper, 1958.

Putnam, Carleton, *Theodore Roosevelt,* Volume 1: *The Formative Years, 1858-1886,* Scribner, 1958.

Roosevelt, Theodore, *Ranch Life and the Hunting-trail,* Century (New York City), 1888.

Roosevelt, Theodore, *The Wilderness Hunter: An Account of the Big Game of the United States and Its Chase with Horse,* Putnam's (New York City), 1893.

Roosevelt, Theodore, *The Winning of the West; An Account of the Exploration and Settlement of Our Country from the Alleghanies to the Pacific,* four volumes, Putnam's (New York City), 1889-96.

The Tocsin of Revolt and Other Essays, edited by Brander Matthews, Scribner, 1919.

Twentieth-Century Literary Criticism, Volume 69, Gale (Detroit), 1997.

PERIODICALS

American Spectator, December, 1995, pp. 72-73.

Book Buyer, vol. xviii, no. 1, 1899, pp. 5-10.

Bookman, February, 1927, pp. 726-729.

Bulletin of the New York Public Library, January/December, 1965, pp. 49-57.

Choice, July/August, 1983, p. 1618; April, 1996, p. 1380; July/August, 1996, p. 1860.

Columbia University Forum, summer, 1963, pp. 10-16.

History: Review of New Books, May/June, 1986, p. 140.

Kirkus Reviews, September 15, 1985, p. 1025.

Jack London Newsletter, May-August, 1981, pp. 80-82.

Library Journal, March 1, 1994, p. 95.

Los Angeles Times Book Review, August 3, 1997, p. 8.

Mid-America: An Historical Review, July, 1974, pp. 139-159.

New England Quarterly, December, 1943, pp. 615-626.

Nineteenth-Century Literature, June, 1997, p. 134.

Papers of the Bibliographical Society of America, vol. 39, no. 1, 1945, pp. 20-50.

Partisan Review, July/August, 1951, pp. 466-471.

Personalist, summer, 1968, pp. 331-350.

Philosophy and Rhetoric, vol. 1, no. 1, 1968, pp. 228-254.

Publishers Weekly, December 3, 1982; March 7, 1994, p. 60; August 21, 1995, p. 55.

Raritan, vol. 9, no. 3, 1990, pp. 109-126.

Smithsonian, November, 1983, pp. 86-95.

Style, winter, 1979, pp. 1-4.

Virginia Quarterly Review, vol. 62, no. 1, 1986, pp. 21-37.

Washington Post Book World, May 22, 1983, p. 16; May 8, 1994, p. 13; May 15, 1986; p. 13; November 1, 1987, p. 15.

Western American Literature, spring, 1987, p. 86.*

*   *   *

ROZBICKI, Michal J. 1946-

PERSONAL: Surname is pronounced Rose-*beet*-ski; born June 24, 1946, in Gdynia, Poland; naturalized U.S. citizen; son of Stanislaus (an economist) and Sabina (a homemaker) Rozbicki; married, wife's name Jody A. (a teacher), January 4, 1992. *Education:* Maria Curie Sklodowska University, Ph.D., 1975; University of Warsaw, Ph.D., 1984. *Politics:* Independent. *Religion:* Roman Catholic. *Avocational interests:* Music, painting.

ADDRESSES: Home—16427 Hollister Crossing Dr., Wildwood, MO 63011. *Office*—Department of History, St. Louis University, 3800 Lindell Blvd., Box 56907, St. Louis, MO 63156-0907; fax 314-977-5603. *E-mail*—rozbicmj@slu.edu.

CAREER: University of Warsaw, Warsaw, Poland, assistant professor, 1976-84, associate professor of history, 1984-90, head of American Studies Center, 1987-90; Indiana University—Bloomington, visiting associate professor of history and associate director of Polish Studies Center, both 1990-92; St. Louis University, St. Louis, MO, assistant professor, 1992-97, associate professor of history, 1997—.

MEMBER: Organization of American Historians, American Association of University Professors.

AWARDS, HONORS: Fellow of American Council of Learned Societies, 1979-80, Free University of Berlin, 1982 and 1989, Oxford University, 1984, and Rockefeller Foundation, 1990.

WRITINGS:

The Transformation of English Cultural Ethos in Colonial America: Maryland, 1634-1720, University Press of America (Lanham, MD), 1988.

Narodziny Narodu: Historia Stanow Zjednoczonych Ameryki do 1860 Roku (title means "Birth of a Nation: United States History to 1860"), Interim Press (Warsaw, Poland), 1991.

The Complete Colonial Gentleman: Cultural Legitimacy in Plantation America, University Press of Virginia (Charlottesville, VA), 1998.

Chief editor of the Polish journal, *American Studies,* 1981-95.

WORK IN PROGRESS: Research on liberty and identity among American and European ruling elites in the eighteenth century.

*   *   *

RUGG, Linda (Haverty) 1957-

PERSONAL: Born November 17, 1957, in Merced, CA; daughter of L. Dale (a small business owner) and Anna P. (a switch operator; maiden name, Barbour) Haverty; married Brian E. Rugg (a writer), May 27, 1991; children: Henry Haverty. *Ethnicity:* "European-American." *Education:* Barnard College, B.A. (cum laude), 1980; Harvard University, M.A., 1982, Ph.D., 1989. *Religion:* Roman Catholic. *Avocational interests:* Travel, birding, painting, looking at photographs.

ADDRESSES: Home—Columbus, OH. *Office*—Department of Germanic Languages and Literatures, 330 Cunz Hall, Ohio State University, 1841 Millikin Rd., Columbus, OH 43210-1229. *E-mail*—rugg.5@osu.edu.

CAREER: Ohio State University, Columbus, associate professor of German and Swedish, 1989—.

Brigham Young University, visiting professor, 1993-94; University of California, Berkeley, visiting professor, 1998.

MEMBER: Modern Language Association of America, Society for the Advancement of Scandinavian Studies.

AWARDS, HONORS: Aldo-Jeanne Scaglione Prize, best book in comparative studies, Modern Language Association of America, 1998.

WRITINGS:

Picturing Ourselves: Photography and Autobiography,
University of Chicago Press (Chicago), 1997.
(Translator from Swedish) Richard Swartz, *Room
Service: Reports from Eastern Europe* (travel),
New Press (New York City), 1998.
(Translator from German) Hans Magnus Enzens-
berger, *Zig-Zag* (cultural essays), New Press,
1998.

*WORK IN PROGRESS: Writing on the Body: Scars as
Metaphor in Literature and Film;* research on the
body in literature, metaphor, the cultural history of
Prague, ecology and literature in Scandinavia and the
United States, and Mark Twain.

SIDELIGHTS: Linda Rugg told *CA:* "I am a com-
paratist and enjoy working on broad topics that
address ideas as they appear in various cultures: the
human relationship to the environment, the meaning
of photographs in self-visualization, the relationship between literature and the 'real' world, the
history and power of writing, the construction of
racial and ethnic identity in literature, et cetera. As
an adjunct to my writing, I practice translation and
find it rewarding to bring Swedish and German texts
into English."

S

SAMAR, Vincent J(oseph) 1953-

PERSONAL: Born February 12, 1953, in Syracuse, NY; son of George E. and Harriett H. Samar. *Education:* Syracuse University, A.B. (cum laude), 1975, M.P.A. and J.D., both 1978; University of Chicago, Ph.D., 1986. *Politics:* Liberal Democrat. *Religion:* Roman Catholic.

ADDRESSES: Home—738 West Briar Pl., No. 100, Chicago, IL 60657-4533. *Office*—Department of Philosophy, Loyola University of Chicago, 928 Water Tower Campus, 820 North Michigan Ave., Chicago, IL 60611-2196; fax 312-915-8553. *E-mail*—vsamar@luc.edu.

CAREER: City of Syracuse, NY, law clerk to corporation counsel, 1977; U.S. District Court for the Northern District of New York, special summer clerk, 1980; law clerk in Chicago, IL, 1980-84; Foss, Schuman, Drake & Barnard, Chicago, law clerk, 1983-85; Coffield, Ungaretti, Harris & Slavin, Chicago, law clerk, 1985-86; Burke, Griffin, Chomicz & Wienkie, Chicago, law clerk, 1986; private practice of law (general practice and civil rights litigation), Chicago, 1986—.

Roosevelt University, lecturer, 1982-84; St. Xavier College, lecturer, 1982-84; Loyola University of Chicago, lecturer, 1984-90, visiting assistant professor, 1989-90, adjunct professor of philosophy, 1990—; Illinois Institute of Technology, adjunct professor of law, 1990—.

MEMBER: American Philosophical Association, American Civil Liberties Union (member of board of directors of Illinois chapter, 1995-97).

WRITINGS:

The Right to Privacy: Gays, Lesbians, and the Constitution, Temple University Press (Philadelphia, PA), 1991.
(Contributor) Timothy F. Murphy, editor, *Gay Ethics: Controversies in Outing, Civil Rights, and Sexual Science,* Haworth Press (New York City), 1994.
(Contributor) D. Cohen and Michael Davis, editors, *AIDS: Crisis in Professional Ethics,* Temple University Press, 1994.
Justifying Judgment: Practicing Law and Philosophy, University Press of Kansas (Lawrence), 1998.

Contributor of articles and reviews to periodicals, including *Journal of Homosexuality.*

WORK IN PROGRESS: Absolute Truth and the Internal Point of View; Is the Right to Die Dead?

BIOGRAPHICAL/CRITICAL SOURCES:

PERIODICALS

Lambda Book Report, July, 1992, p. 47.
Law and Politics Book Review, May, 1998, pp. 247-249.
National Law Journal, August 3, 1998, p. A26.

*   *   *

SAVIR, Uri

PERSONAL: Born in Israel; son of a diplomat.

ADDRESSES: Agent—c/o Random House, 201 East 50th St., New York NY 10022.

CAREER: Israeli Embassy, New York City, consul general, 1988-92, Israeli Foreign Ministry, Director-General, 1993-96; Peres Center for Peace, Tel Aviv, Israel, head.

WRITINGS:

1,100 Days That Changed the Middle East, Random House (New York City), 1998.

SIDELIGHTS: Uri Savir was director-general of Israel's Foreign Ministry when he was asked to represent his country in secret negotiations between Israel and the Palestine Liberation Organization (PLO). Negotiations began in 1992, resulting in the Oslo peace accord of 1993, with final settlement to occur in 1999. Savir's *1,100 Days That Changed the Middle East* documents the talks, most of which occurred in Oslo, Norway, but also in Geneva, Rome, Tunis, and Cairo. A *Publishers Weekly* reviewer said the negotiations that led to the "historic handshake" between Israeli Prime Minister Yitzhak Rabin and PLO chief Yasser Arafat "were far more productive than the official talks in Washington."

Savir's PLO counterpart was Ahmed Qurei, known as Abu Ala, who the Norwegian mediators jokingly told Savir was "your enemy number one." A *Booklist* reviewer wrote that the two men "often conveyed sharply conflicting views and instructions from their superiors, yet not only learned how to work together but developed a deep respect, even fondness, for each other." The Israelis were seeking security and an end to terrorism. The Palestinians were seeking an identity and respectful treatment by the Israelis. Serge Schmemann wrote in the *New York Times* that Rabin "was willing to cede half the West Bank in three stages while the final settlement was negotiated. But Mr. Rabin feared that letting the Palestinians know this would touch off a crisis, because it was far less than the Palestinians wanted." Arafat reached an agreement with Israel without knowing Rabin's original intentions.

Shimon Peres, a primary figure in the original talks, succeeded Rabin following Rabin's assassination by religious nationalist Yigal Amir. Peres supported the creation of a Palestinian state by the May 1999 deadline because, as he was quoted in Schmemann's article, "otherwise, we will have a binational state or a binational tragedy." In a review of Savir's book in the *New York Times Book Review,* Schmemann called Peres "a man who appears throughout the book several legions ahead of his fellow Israelis in his vision of what can be."

1,100 Days That Changed the Middle East, called "a brilliant book written by brilliant man," by Peres, covers the period to 1996, when Benjamin Netanyahu, in defeating Peres, was elected prime minister of Israel. It was at this point that Savir resigned from his post as director-general. The book was published in 1998, as Israel and the PLO were deadlocked in hammering out the details of possession of the West Bank. Mediators from the United States met with Netanyahu. They included Dennis Ross, special Middle East envoy, and Martin Indyk, assistant secretary of state and former ambassador to Israel. United States Secretary of State Madeline Albright met with Israeli and Palestinian leaders in London.

Schmemann noted in the *New York Times Book Review* that "given the uncertain future of the Oslo agreements today, politicians, reporters and historians are certain to sift through Savir's detailed account to buttress their continuing arguments." Schmemann wrote that, in spite of Savir's suspicions of the right-wing Netanyahu, Savir "is not a polemicist for a political cause" and "is never blind to the limitations and failings of the Palestinians." Schmemann felt that Savir was aware of the failures of the process, including "the failure of the Labor Government to spread the real message of the Oslo accords among the Israelis." Schmemann concluded that in addition to the historical peace process outlined in Savir's account, "there is another process here, a far deeper and human one. . . . Rabin, Peres and Arafat . . . gradually rose above their deep resentments and hatreds, above the profound habits of suspicion and mutual demonization, to achieve if not always friendship, then at least a recognition of a partnership in a common predicament."

BIOGRAPHICAL/CRITICAL SOURCES:

PERIODICALS

Booklist, May 15, 1998.
Kirkus Reviews, May 11, 1998.
New York Times, April 27, 1998, p. A8.
New York Times Book Review, June 7, 1998.
Publishers Weekly, April 13, 1998, p. 65.

OTHER

Amazon.com, www.amazon.com/exec/obid.../06794
2296X/002-6356449-1595632, August 27, 1998.*

*   *   *

SCARRON
See MIKSZATH, Kalman

*   *   *

SCHAEFER, George (Louis) 1920-1997

PERSONAL: Born December 16, 1920, in Wallingford,
CT; died September 10, 1997, in Los Angeles, CA;
son of Louis (in sales) and Elsie (Otterbein)
Schaefer; married Mildred Trares (an actress),
February 5, 1954. *Education:* Lafayette College,
B.A. (English), 1941; graduate work at the Yale
University School of Drama, 1942. *Avocational in-
terests:* Contract bridge, travel, theater, and film
going.

CAREER: Director and producer. Central Pacific
Base Command, U.S. Army Special Services, Honolulu, HI, director of over fifty productions, 1942-45;
City Center Theatre, New York City, executive producer and artistic director, 1949-52; Compass Productions Inc., president, 1959-86; Schaefer/Karpf Productions, founder with Merrill H. Karpf, 1982; National Council of the Arts, 1983-88; Department of
theatre, film, and television, University of California,
Los Angeles, associate dean, 1986-91, emeritus professor, 1991-97. *Military service:* U.S. Army, Special
Services, sergeant, 1942-45.

Director, for the stage, except where indicated: *Leave
It to Smith,* Pastime Players, produced in Oak Park,
IL, 1937; *Hamlet* (also known as *G.I. Hamlet*), Co-
lumbus Circle Theatre, produced in New York City,
1945, City Center Theatre, produced in New York
City, 1946; (and producer with Maurice Evans) *The
Teahouse of the August Moon,* Her Majesty's Theatre,
produced in London, 1954, producer, with Maurice
Evans, Martin Beck Theatre, produced in New York
City, 1953; (with Maurice Evans) *Man and Super-
man,* Alvin Theatre, produced in New York City,

1947, (and producer) City Center Theatre, 1949; *The
Linden Tree,* Music Box Theatre, produced in New
York City, 1948; (and producer) *She Stoops to Conquer,* City Center Theatre, 1949; (and producer) *The
Corn Is Green,* City Center Theatre, 1950; (and producer) *The Heiress,* City Center Theatre, 1950; (and
producer) *The Devil's Disciple,* City Center Theatre,
1950; (and producer) *Captain Brassbound's Conversion,* City Center Theatre, 1950; (and producer) *The
Royal Family, Richard II,* City Center Theatre, 1951;
(and producer) *The Taming of the Shrew,* City Center
Theatre, 1951; (and producer) *Dream Girl,* City Center Theatre, 1951; (and producer) *Idiot's Delight,*
City Center Theatre, 1951; (and producer) *The Wild
Duck,* City Center Theatre, 1951; (and producer)
Anna Christie, City Center Theatre, 1952; (and producer) *Come of Age,* City Center Theatre, 1952; (and
producer) *The Male Animal,* City Center Theatre,
1952; (and producer) *Tovarich,* City Center Theatre,
1952; (and producer) *First Lady,* City Center Theatre,
1952.

Also *Kiss Me Kate,* City Center Theatre, 1955; *The
Southwest Corner,* Holiday Theatre, produced in New
York City, 1955; *The Apple Cart,* Plymouth Theatre,
produced in New York City, 1956; *The Body Beauti-
ful,* Broadway Theatre, produced in New York City,
1958; (and producer) *Write Me a Murder,* Belasco
Theatre, produced in New York City, 1961, then
Lyric Theatre, produced in London, 1962; (pro-
ducer), *To Broadway with Love,* Texas Pavilion, New
York World's Fair, produced in Flushing, NY, 1964;
The Great Indoors, Eugene O'Neill Theatre, produced
in New York City, 1966; *The Last of Mrs. Lincoln,*
Kennedy Center for the Performing Arts, Opera
House, produced in Washington, DC, then American
National Theatre and Academy Theatre, produced in
New York City, both 1972; *On Golden Pond,* Center
Theatre Group, Ahmanson Theatre, produced in Los
Angeles, 1980; *Mixed Couples,* Brooks Atkinson Theatre, produced in New York City, 1980; *Another Part
of the Forest,* Center Theatre Group, Ahmanson Theatre, 1981; *Lyndon,* Wilmington Playhouse, produced
in Wilmington, DE, 1984; and *Leave It to Jane,* produced in Los Angeles, 1987. Also director of productions at the State Fair Music Hall, Dallas, TX, 1952-
56, and 1958.

Director, Major Tours including: *Hamlet,* produced in
U.S. cities, 1946-47; *Darling, Darling, Darling,* pro-
duced in U.S. cities, 1947; (with Maurice Evans)
Man and Superman, produced in U.S. cities, 1948-49;
The Teahouse of the August Moon, produced in U.S.
cities, 1954; *The Apple Cart,* produced in U.S. cities,

1957; *Zenda,* produced in U.S. cities, 1963; *The Student Prince,* produced in U.S. cities, 1973; *Ah! Wilderness,* produced in U.S. cities, 1975; and *Lyndon,* produced in U.S. cities, 1984.

Director of films, including: *Macbeth,* Prominent, 1963; *Pendulum,* Columbia, 1969; *Generation,* AVCO-Embassy, 1969; *Doctors' Wives,* Columbia, 1971; *Once upon a Scoundrel,* Carlyle, 1973; (and producer) *An Enemy of the People,* Warner Bros., 1978.

Appeared on the television special *The Television Makers,* PBS, 1987. Director of *Hallmark Hall of Fame* teleplays aired on NBC: "Hamlet," 1953; "Richard II," 1954; "Macbeth," 1954; "Alice in Wonderland," 1955; "Dream Girl," 1955; "The Devil's Disciple," 1955; "Taming of the Shrew," 1956; "The Good Fairy," 1956; "The Corn Is Green," 1956; and "Truman at Potsdam," 1976. Director and producer of *Hallmark Hall of Fame* teleplays aired on NBC: "Man and Superman," 1956; "The Little Foxes," 1956; "The Cradle Song," 1956; "Born Yesterday," 1956; "The Lark," 1957; "The Green Pastures," 1957; "On Borrowed Time," 1957; "Twelfth Night," 1957; "There Shall Be No Night," 1957; "The Yeomen of the Guard," 1957; "Dial 'M' for Murder," 1958; "Little Moon of Alban," 1958; "Kiss Me Kate," 1958; "Johnny Belinda," 1958; "Hans Brinker, or The Silver Skates," 1958; "A Doll's House," 1959; "Berkeley Square," 1959; "Ah! Wilderness," 1959; "Winterset," 1959; "Captain Brassbound's Conversion," 1960; "Macbeth," 1960; "The Tempest," 1960; "Shangri-La," 1960; "Golden Child," 1960; "Give Us Barabbas!," 1961; "The Joke and the Valley," 1961; "Time Remembered," 1961; "Victoria Regina," 1961; "Arsenic and Old Lace," 1962; "The Invincible Mr. Disraeli," 1962; "Cyrano de Bergerac," 1962; "Pygmalion," NBC, 1963; "The Patriots," 1963; "A Cry of Angels," 1963; "Abe Lincoln in Illinois," 1964; "The Fantasticks," 1964; "Little Moon of Alban," 1964; "The Magnificent Yankee," 1965; "Inherit the Wind," 1965; "The Holy Terror," 1965; "Eagle in a Cage," 1965; "Blithe Spirit," 1966; "Barefoot in Athens," 1966; "Lamp at Midnight," 1966; "Anastasia," 1967; "Soldier in Love," 1967; "Saint Joan," 1967; "The Admirable Crichton," 1968; "My Father and My Mother," 1968; "Elizabeth the Queen," 1968; "The File on Devlin," 1969; and "Gideon," 1971; also producer, "Hamlet," *Hallmark Hall of Fame,* NBC, 1970.

Executive producer and director of television series *Love Story,* NBC, 1973-74; director of television pilot

Land of Hope, CBS, 1976; director, "Hour of the Bath," *Alcoa Theatre,* NBC, 1962; and "The Hands of Donofrio," *Alcoa Premiere,* ABC, 1962.

Director of television movies: (and producer) *A War of Children,* CBS, 1972; *F. Scott Fitzgerald and The Last of the Belles,* ABC, 1974; (and producer) *In This House of Brede,* CBS, 1975; *Amelia Earhart,* NBC, 1976; (and producer) *The Girl Called Hatter Fox,* CBS, 1977; *First You Cry,* CBS, 1978; (and producer) *Who'll Save Our Children?,* CBS, 1978; with Renee Valente (and producer) *Blind Ambition,* CBS, 1979; *Mayflower: The Pilgrims' Adventure,* CBS, 1979; (and producer) *People vs. Jean Harris,* NBC, 1981; (and producer, with Aida Young) *The Bunker,* CBS, 1981; (and producer) *A Piano for Mrs. Cimino,* CBS, 1982; (and producer) *Right of Way,* HBO, 1983; (and producer, with Frank Prendergast and Charles Haid) *Children in the Crossfire,* NBC, 1984; (and producer) *Stone Pillow,* CBS, 1985; (and producer) *Mrs. Delafield Wants to Marry,* CBS, 1986; (and co-producer) *Laura Lansing Slept Here,* NBC, 1988; (and producer) *The Man Upstairs,* CBS, 1992.

Director of television specials: *One Touch of Venus,* NBC, 1955; *Harvey,* CBS, 1958; (and producer) *Gift of the Magi,* CBS, 1958; *Meet Me in St. Louis,* CBS, 1959; (and producer) *Hallmark Hall of Fame Christmas Festival,* NBC, 1959; (and producer) *The Teahouse of the August Moon,* NBC, 1962; "Do Not Go Gentle into That Good Night," *CBS Playhouse,* CBS, 1967; *U.S.A.,* PBS, 1971; (and producer) *Sandburg's Lincoln* (a series of six specials), NBC, 1974-76; (and producer) *Our Town,* NBC, 1977; *The Second Barry Manilow Special,* ABC, 1978; *Barry Manilow—One Voice,* ABC, 1980; (and producer) *Answers,* NBC, 1982; *The Deadly Game,* HBO, 1982; (and producer) *The Best Christmas Pageant Ever,* ABC, 1983; (and producer) *The Booth,* PBS, 1985; *Let Me Hear You Whisper,* 1990; "Jimmy Stewart: Hometown Hero," *Biography,* Arts and Entertainment, 1993.

MEMBER: Directors Guild of America (national board of directors, 1960-75, vice president, 1961-79, president, 1979-81), Academy of Motion Picture Arts and Sciences, Academy of Television Arts and Sciences, Caucus for Producers, Writers, and Directors, American National Theatre and Academy—West (board of directors), Variety Clubs International, Players Club, Phi Beta Kappa.

AWARDS, HONORS: Antoinette Perry Award (with Maurice Evans) for best producer of a play, 1954, for

The Teahouse of the August Moon; Look (magazine) Award, and *Radio-Television Daily* Award, both 1957, both for "The Green Pastures," *Hallmark Hall of Fame; Radio-Television Daily* Award, director of the year, 1957; Sylvania Award for outstanding dramatic series, and Peabody Award for outstanding television entertainment, both 1958, both for *Hallmark Hall of Fame; Radio-Television Daily* Award, 1959, for "Johnny Belinda," *Hallmark Hall of Fame;* Sylvania Award, Peabody Award, and Emmy Awards for best special dramatic program and best direction of a single dramatic program, all 1959, all for "Little Moon of Alban," *Hallmark Hall of Fame;* Outstanding Achievement Award, Directors Guild of America, 1960, and *TV Guide* Award for best single dramatic program on television, *Radio-Television Daily* Award for dramatic show of the year, and Emmy Awards for program of the year, outstanding program achievement in the field of drama, and outstanding directorial achievement in drama, all 1961, all for "Macbeth," *Hallmark Hall of Fame; Radio-Television Daily* Award, director of the year, 1961; both *Saturday Review* Special Commendation for Notable Production, and Emmy Award for program of the year, both 1962, for "Victoria Regina," *Hallmark Hall of Fame; Radio-Television Daily* All-American Award for producer of the year and director of the year, 1963; Honorary doctorate of literature, Lafayette College, 1963; Outstanding Achievement Award, Directors Guild of America, best television director, 1963, for "Pygmalion," *Hallmark Hall of Fame; Radio-Television Daily* Award for director of the year, 1964; Dineen Award, National Catholic Theatre Conference, 1964.

Also Emmy Award for outstanding program achievement in entertainment, 1965, for "The Magnificent Yankee," *Hallmark Hall of Fame; Radio-Television Daily* Award for director of the year, 1965; Emmy Award for outstanding dramatic program, 1968, for "Elizabeth the Queen," *Hallmark Hall of Fame;* Outstanding Achievement Award, Directors Guild of America, best television director, 1967, for "Do Not Go Gentle into That Good Night," *CBS Playhouse;* Outstanding Achievement Award, Directors Guild of America, best television director, 1968, for "My Father and My Mother," *Hallmark Hall of Fame;* Emmy Award for outstanding single program—drama or comedy, 1973, for *A War of Children;* Honorary degree, Coker College, L.H.D., 1973; Member of the Year Award, Caucus for Producers, Writers, and Directors, 1983; Emmy Award nomination, 1983, for *The Best Christmas Pageant Ever;* received more than thirty Emmy Award nominations and seventeen Direc-

tors Guild of America Award nominations; first person to win four Directors Guild America Awards.

WRITINGS:

(With James Prideaux, Israel Horovitz, and Rose Leiman Goldemberg) *The Booth,* (television special), PBS, 1985.
From Live to Tape to Film: Sixty Years of Inconspicuous Directing (autobiography), Directors Guild of America (Hollywood, CA), 1996.

SIDELIGHTS: In his many decades in theatre, television, and film, George Schaefer directed some of the twentieth century's most accomplished actors in dramatizations of some of the most celebrated literary works of all time. "From his long-ago training at the Yale School of the Drama, he was a true man of the theatre, a master of his craft, the ideal director," according to Delbert Mann in a tribute given at Schaefer's funeral in 1997 and included on *DGA Magazine*'s internet site. In the 1940s and 1950s, Schaefer directed productions of such worthy theatrical pieces as George Bernard Shaw's *Man and Superman,* and Shakespeare's *The Taming of the Shrew* and *Hamlet.* He also directed several Shakespearean plays for NBC's *Hallmark Hall of Fame* programs of the 1950s and 1960s, along with Lillian Hellman's *The Little Foxes,* Henrik Ibsen's *A Doll's House,* Shaw's *Pygmalion* and *Saint Joan,* and dozens more. According to Ted Elrick in a trubute also included on *DGA Magazine*'s internet site, Bette Davis considered Schaefer "the finest director in television," and Trevor Howard averred: "I'd play Mickey Mouse for him. I trust him. He is one of the few directors for whom I would work script unseen."

Schaefer is fondly remembered by his peers in the film industry as a tireless supporter of the Directors Guild of America (DGA), serving on several committees and as president from 1979 to 1981. Elrick quoted Schaefer's response to the question of why he had devoted so much of his energy to support of the DGA: "Partly out of a feeling of obligation that if your fellow members want you to serve, you should. And in gratitude for the opportunity to meet other directors. Except at the Guild, we rarely see each other and without the Guild I would not have been friends with such giants as King Vidor, George Stevens, Frank Capra, Fred Zinnemann, Bob Wise and so many others. In return for everything that one gives, one receives great rewards by serving the Guild." In addition to his fine attributes as a director, Schaefer "was in every way a complete gentleman," opined Mann, continuing: "He was thoughtful of others. He was generous. He was loving. He was giving, and forgiving. He was literate. He was knowledgeable." In 1996, Schaefer issued his autobiography, *From Live to Tape to Film: Sixty Years of Inconspicuous Directing.*

BIOGRAPHICAL/CRITICAL SOURCES:

PERIODICALS

Entertainment Weekly, September 26, 1997, p. 14.
Los Angeles Times, September 12, 1997, p. A20.
New York Times, September 12, 1997, p. B8.*

OTHER

DGA, http://www.dga.org/magazine/v22-4/george_schaefer.htm

*   *   *

SCHOLNICK, Ellin Kofsky 1936-

PERSONAL: Born July 10, 1936, in Brooklyn, NY; daughter of Irving (a furrier) and Celia (an interior decorator; maiden name, Greenberg) Kofsky; married Myron I. Scholnick (a historian), March 21, 1965; children: Matthew H. *Ethnicity:* "White." *Education:* Vassar College, A.B. (cum laude), 1958; University of Rochester, Ph.D., 1963. *Religion:* Jewish.

ADDRESSES: Home—Columbia, MD. *Office*—Office of Academic Affairs, 1119 Main Administration Bldg., University of Maryland at College Park, College Park, MD 20742; fax 301-405-7139. *E-mail*—es8@umail.umd.edu.

CAREER: University of Maryland at College Park, professor of psychology, 1973—, associate provost for faculty affairs, 1998—.

MEMBER: American Psychological Association (fellow), American Psychological Society, Society for Research in Child Development, Phi Beta Kappa, Sigma Xi.

WRITINGS:

(Editor) *New Trends in Conceptual Representation,* Erlbaum (Mahwah, NJ), 1983.

(Editor with S. Friedman and R. Coe King) *Blueprints for Thinking,* Cambridge University Press (New York City), 1987.
(Editor with Friedman) *The Developmental Psychology of Planning,* Erlbaum, 1997.
(Editor with K. Nelson, P. Miller, and S. Gelman) *Conceptual Development: Piaget's Legacy,* Erlbaum, 1999.

Series editor for Jean Piaget Society.

WORK IN PROGRESS: Editing *Feminist Perspectives on Development,* with P. Miller, for Routledge.

*   *   *

SCHWARTZ, Gil
(Stanley Bing)

PERSONAL: Male.

ADDRESSES: Agent—c/o Crown Publishing, 201 E. 50th St., New York, NY 10022.

CAREER: Columbia Broadcast System (CBS)Senior vice president in charge of communications.

WRITINGS:

Biz Words: Power Talk for Fun and Profit, Pocket Books (New York City), 1989.
Crazy Bosses: Spotting Them, Serving Them, Surviving Them, Morrow (New York City), 1992.
Lloyd—What Happened: A Novel of Business, Crown (New York City), 1998.

Columnist for *Fortune,* and author of "Executive Summary" column for *Esquire* magazine, both under pseudonym Stanley Bing.

SIDELIGHTS: Under the pseudonym Stanley Bing, television executive Gil Schwartz satirizes the American place of business as a regular columnist for *Esquire* and *Fortune* magazines, and in book-length works. In his first book, *Biz Words: Power Talk for Fun and Profit,* Bing offers a sly handbook to business terminology that is "really an ethics guide in disguise," according to Joan Warner in *Business Week.* Noting the inclusion of entries under such commonplace terms as "conversation," "drinks," and "briefcase," O. Gene Norman, a reviewer for *Ameri-*

can Reference Books Annual, drily concluded that "this book should be read for its wit and irreverent style rather than for a brief definition." Similarly, Bing's second book, *Crazy Bosses: Spotting Them, Serving Them, Surviving Them,* is ostensibly a reference work that defines the various types of bosses and offers humorous analyses of appropriate behavior for underlings. A reviewer for *Publishers Weekly* found the first half of this book "a thoughtful, provocative examination of corporate culture," but was caught off guard by the irreverence of the second half of the book, in which, for example, Bing advises readers to be insincere and "suck up" to certain types of bosses. Though Todd Yaeger, a contributor to *Library Journal,* agreed that Bing's striving for humorous effects can make it difficult to follow the organization of his book, he did note that the author concludes each chapter "with concrete strategies to cope with each type of crazy boss."

With *Lloyd—What Happened: A Novel of Business,* Bing branches out into fiction while retaining his satiric focus on the world of business. In this work, a typical mid-level business executive on the rise becomes less and less human as he becomes more and more successful implementing the company's layoff plans in order to prepare for a big merger. A critic for *Kirkus Reviews* called this "a tour de farce that both reviles and celebrates the pretentious, treacherous, and luxurious world of corporate middle management." Though more episodic than plot-driven, *Lloyd* was praised for its dead-on depictions of such business pitfalls as endless meetings that accomplish nothing and booze-soaked business trips; critics especially liked the inclusion of charts and graphs with titles such as "The Battle for Lloyd's Soul," and "Percent of Lloyd's Bosses Displaying Insane Behavior." "This is by far the funniest material in the book," averred Joe Queenan in the *New York Times Book Review.* Though Queenan noted that the young Kurt Vonnegut used such "sleight-of-hand tricks" as charts and graphs in a work of fiction long before Bing and that business executives were a little too easy to satirize, Harry C. Edwards on *Amazon.com* concluded that "Bing's humor captures many of the follies of business life that most readers will recognize and appreciate."

In an internet interview with Edwards, Bing described his protagonist, Lloyd, as "very much like you or me. A person who tries to be good most of the time, except when he doesn't really want to. Likes to have a drink. Likes to have friends where he works. Doesn't want it to be in a cold, unappealing environ-

ment where it's just all about 'business,' whatever 'business' is. I don't think any of us really know what that is."

BIOGRAPHICAL/CRITICAL SOURCES:

PERIODICALS

American Reference Books Annual, 1991, p. 62.
Booklist, March 15, 1998.
Business Week, May 29, 1989, p. 16.
Kirkus Reviews, February 15, 1998; May 11, 1998.
Library Journal, January, 1992, p. 148.
Newsweek, April 27, 1992, p. 61.
New York Times Book Review, May 3, 1998, p. 12.
Publishers Weekly, November 29, 1991, p. 40.

OTHER

Amazon.com, "A Conversation with Stanley Bing," http://www.amazon.com/exec/obid...g-interview/ 002-1017671-5518227 (July 28, 1998); review of *Lloyd—What Happened...*http://www.amazon.co m/exec/obid...8262/sr=1-1/002-1017671-55182 27 (July 28, 1998).*

*　　　*　　　*

SCOTT, Sheila
　See MACINTYRE, Sheila Scott

*　　　*　　　*

SCULLY, Pamela (Frederika) 1962-

PERSONAL: Born June 2, 1962, in Pretoria, South Africa; U.S. citizen; daughter of Laurence Vincent (an artist) and Christine Florence (a piano teacher; maiden name, Frost) Scully; married Clifton Charles Crais (a professor), October 16, 1987; children: Benjamin Laurence, Christine Eleanor. *Ethnicity:* "White." *Education:* University of Cape Town, B.A. (with honors), 1985, M.A. (with distinction), 1987; University of Michigan, Ph.D., 1993. *Politics:* Democrat. *Avocational interests:* Writing songs, stories for children.

ADDRESSES: Home—Granville, OH. *Office*—Department of History, Seitz House, Kenyon College,

Gambier, OH 43022; fax 740-427-5762. *E-mail—*
scully@kenyon.edu.

CAREER: Kenyon College, Gambier, OH, visiting
instructor, 1992-93, assistant professor of history,
1993—. University of Cape Town, lecturer, 1986—
92; Georgia State University, lecturer, 1991; Stanford
University, visiting scholar at Center for African
Studies, 1994-95; University of Cincinnati, Taft Memorial Fund Lecturer, 1995; Case Western Reserve
University, lecturer, 1997. New Directions (domestic
abuse shelter), volunteer, 1987-89. African National
Congress, member of United Women's Congress,
1988-89.

MEMBER: American Historical Association, African
Studies Association (member Women's Caucus).

AWARDS, HONORS: Ford Foundation fellow, 1991-
92; fellow, National Endowment for the Humanities,
1995-96.

WRITINGS:

(Contributor) Jonathan Crush and Charles Ambler,
    editors, *Liquor and Labor in Southern Africa,*
    Ohio University Press (Athens), 1992.
(Contributor) Nigel Worden and Clifton C. Crais,
    editors, *Breaking the Chains: Slavery and Its
    Legacy in Nineteenth—Century South Africa,* Uni-
    versity of the Witwatersrand Press (Johannes-
    burg, South Africa), 1992.
*Liberating the Family? Gender and British Slave
    Emancipation in the Rural Western Cape, South
    Africa, 1823-1853,* Heinemann (Portsmouth, NH),
    1997.
(Contributor) Dorothy Hodgson and Sheryl McCurdy,
    editors, *Wicked Women and the Reconfiguration
    of Gender in Africa,* Heinemann, in press.
(Contributor) Philippa Levine, Laura Mayhall, and
    Ian Fletcher, editors, *The Elusive Sisterhood of
    Woman: Women's Suffrage, Nation, and Race in
    the British Empire, 1890s-1930s,* Routledge, in
    press.

Contributor of articles and reviews to periodicals,
including *Journal of African History, Canadian Journal of African Studies,* and *American Historical Review.*

*WORK IN PROGRESS: Women, Race, and State in
Twentieth—Century South Africa,* completion ex-
pected in 2001; a pamphlet, "Race and Ethnicity in
Women's History."

*   *   *

SELTZER, David   1940(?)-

PERSONAL: Born in 1940 (some sources say 1920),
in Highland Park, IL; married Eugenia Zickermar (a
flutist); children: four (two adopted). *Education:* Attended Northwestern University School for Film and
Television.

ADDRESSES: Agent—Creative Artists Agency, 1888
Century Park E., Suite 1400, Los Angeles, CA
90067.

CAREER: Screenwriter, director, producer, and novelist. Worked with Jacques Cousteau on film documentaries; worked on staff, *I've Got a Secret* (television show); director, *My Trip to New York* (short
film).

AWARDS, HONORS: Emmy Award nomination for
achievement in news documentary programming—
program and individual, for *Adventures at the Jade
Sea;* Emmy Award nomination for achievement in
cultural documentary programming—program, 1970,
for *The Journey of Robert F. Kennedy;* Humanitas
Prize, ninety-minute category, Human Family Educational and Cultural Institute, 1977, for *Green Eyes.*

WRITINGS:

SCREENPLAYS

The Hellstrom Chronicle (documentary), Cinema 5,
    1971.
(With David Shaw) *King, Queen, Knave* (based on
    Vladimir Nabokov's novel of the same title),
    Avco Embassy, 1972.
One Is a Lonely Number (also known as *Two Is a
    Happy Number;* based on Rebecca Morris's short
    story "The Good Humor Man"), Metro-Goldwyn-
    Mayer, 1972.
The Other Side of the Mountain, Universal, 1975.
The Omen (also known as *Birthmark*), Twentieth
    Century-Fox, 1976.
Prophecy, Paramount, 1979.
Six Weeks (based on the novel by Fred Mustard
    Stewart), Universal, 1982.
Table for Five, Warner Bros., 1983.
(And director) *Lucas,* Twentieth Century-Fox, 1986.
(And director) *Punchline,* Columbia, 1988.
(With Louis Venosta and Eric Lerner) *Bird on a
    Wire,* Universal, 1990.
(And director) *Shining Through,* Twentieth Century-
    Fox, 1992.

The Eighteenth Angel, 1997.
My Giant, 1998.

TELEPLAYS

(And producer) *Adventures at the Jade Sea* (documentary), CBS, c. 1970.
Larry (adapted from Robert McQueen's book *Larry: Case History of a Mistake*), CBS, 1974.
(With David Sontag) *My Father's House,* ABC, 1975.
(And producer, with John Erman) *Green Eyes,* ABC, 1977.
(With Thom Thomas) *Private Sessions,* NBC, 1985.

OTHER

The Omen (novelization of his screenplay), New American Library, 1976.
Prophecy (novelization of his screenplay), Ballantine, 1979.

Contributor to periodicals, including *Premiere.*

SIDELIGHTS: David Seltzer's output as a screenwriter, director, and producer of both television and cinematic films has been prolific. Though many of his more critically acclaimed films, such as 1972's *One is a Lonely Number* and *Lucas,* released in 1986, did not achieve commercial success, Seltzer's popular films, including his 1976 effort, *The Omen,* and 1983's *Table for Five,* paved the way for a solid career in Hollywood.

Seltzer was born in Highland Park, Illinois, and graduated from the School for Film and Television at Northwestern University. He began his career in New York City on the staff of the popular television show *I've Got a Secret.* During this time, he directed his first short film, *My Trip to New York.* Seltzer moved to Los Angeles in 1966, where he began working as a writer for David Wolper's documentaries; later, he worked as director and producer for Wolper as well. Seltzer produced and directed National Geographic specials and *The Underworld World of Jacques Cousteau* for television.

In the 1970s Seltzer began to try his hand with screenplays for television and feature films. His first documentary, 1971's *The Hellstrom Chronicle,* was followed by a collaboration with David Shaw on a 1972 adaptation of Vladimir Nabokov's novel *King, Queen, Knave.* Seltzer's *One Is a Lonely Number,* which deals with the aftermath of divorce, did not

find a large audience but attracted critical attention as a worthwhile film ahead of its time. In 1976 Seltzer found his first major commercial success with *The Omen.* This horror film, built on the popularity of the 1973 film *The Exorcist,* was a box-office sensation, eventually spawning two sequels. *The Omen*'s plot involves the birth of the Antichrist, a baby inadvertently adopted by the American ambassador to England (portrayed by Gregory Peck) and his wife (portrayed by Lee Remick). Though some reviewers questioned the film's premise and the discretion of its creators in their choice of images and ideas represented in the film, they admitted its effectiveness as a horror genre piece; the United States Catholic Conference denounced it as "one of the most distasteful [films] ever to be released by a major studio." According to the *Motion Picture Guide* Seltzer told interviewers that he wrote the script for financial reasons. "I did it strictly for the money," he said. "I was flat broke." His novelization of the screenplay, published the same year as the movie was released, was a bestseller.

With the success of *The Omen,* Seltzer's reputation was established. He worked with Jon Erman on the screenplay for the highly praised 1977 television movie *Green Eyes,* but his next big screen project was 1979's *Prophecy,* which was viewed by many critics as a huge disappointment, given Seltzer's demonstrated abilities. Set in rural Maine, *Prophecy* injects environmental awareness into what is essentially a 1950s-era monster movie. Critics panned the film. Vincent Canby of The *New York Times* called it "epically trivial" and complained that its monsters "are as characterless as wind-up toys." Nevertheless, the film was commercially successful, and the novelization Seltzer wrote from the screenplay was a bestseller.

Seltzer's 1982 film, *Six Weeks,* failed to bring him widespread critical or public acclaim. Starring Dudley Moore and Mary Tyler Moore as adults trying to indulge the fantasy of a dying girl, the film was characterized in the *Motion Picture Guide* as a "sentimentally cloying [and] inadvertently funny" adolescent version of the exceedingly melodramatic 1970 film *Love Story. Table for Five,* Seltzer's film about a divorced father (played by Jon Voight) trying to reach out to his estranged children, was assessed by some critics as similarly melodramatic in tone, but other critics argued that the film succeeded in also being genuine and affecting. Seltzer based the story, which touches on adoption in part on his own experience as a divorced father who had adopted two Vietnamese orphans. Critic Gene Siskel, writing in the *Chicago*

Tribune, praised the "beautifully written script by David Seltzer," and declared: "the image of the American family, so often battered by the movies, is paid tribute by the actors and the writer of *Table for Five,* which turns out to be a surprisingly emotional experience." *Los Angeles Times* critic Kevin Thomas, who characterized Seltzer's *The Other Side of the Mountain* and *Six Weeks* sappy and exploitive, offered a positive review of *Table for Five* as well, primarily because in his opinion the lead character was drawn with sensitivity. Thomas remarked: "To be sure, [*Table for Five*] is not free from devisings and insensitivities, but its central character is so well drawn and so well played by Jon Voight that the film is finally deeply affecting." *Washington Post* critic Gary Arnold, however, dismissed the film as a "lavishly weepy disgrace" and a "revolting plunge into bathos," and the *New York Times*'s Janet Maslin called *Table for Five* superficial and contrived, declaring that Seltzer "packed the screenplay with platitudes," but admitting that the film "is not as hokey as it could have been."

With *Lucas,* a 1986 film that treats adolescent love, Seltzer received more definitive and consistent praise than he had with his previous works. Roger Ebert, who named the film one of the year's best, enthused, in his *Chicago Sun-Times* review: "This is a movie that is as pure and true to the adolescent experience as Truffaut's *The 400 Blows*" and noted that screenwriter Seltzer "has used an enormous amount of sensitivity. . . . He has put values into this movie." In an interview with Charles Champlin of the *Los Angeles Times,* Seltzer, who also debuted as a director with this film, emphasized that he wanted the movie to be genuine, to counter exhausted stereotypes. "I'd gotten sick of what kids were having to dine out on at the movies," he said, noting that the standard Hollywood view of teens was that they are "cynical, gullible, decadent and have a very short attention span." According to many commentators and members of the movie-going public as well, in *Lucas,* Seltzer effectively dispelled this superficial notion of teenagers, presenting characters who are complex and real.

Punchline a 1988 film about the world of stand-up comedy, was a departure for Seltzer and received a mixed reaction from critics. The movie starred Tom Hanks as a troubled medical school drop out-turned-veteran comic and Sally Field as a housewife trying to break into the business. *Los Angeles Times* contributor Sheila Benson was enthusiastic in her praise of the film, commenting: "Bold, sneaky, brilliant *Punchline*

. . . works its change-ups unmercifully. I can't remember laughing this much with tears still streaming down my face, or beginning to weep while my sides still ached from laughing." Other critics, however, considered *Punchline* formulaic, obvious, and filled with cliches. *Chicago Tribune* contributor Dave Kehr opined: "Despite a strong cast, an exceptional performance by Tom Hanks and several strong moments, *Punchline* never makes the transition from concept to movie. . . . [I]t's a film that must strain mightily to cast its promising but vague subject—stand-up comedy—into dramatic terms, and dips more than once into soapy contrivance." Seltzer defended the movie in an article for *Premiere* magazine. He had been warned that audiences would not relate to a character as "dark" as the Hanks protagonist, but Seltzer was attracted to the drama beneath the surface of comics' lives. "I took a leap," he explained, "creating a character whose outward behavior was rude and insulting." Such characters, Seltzer points out, are increasingly rare in contemporary films—which made it all the more important to him that he go ahead with the film, despite the possibility of negative reviews.

Seltzer's *Bird on a Wire,* a 1990 action-romance that starred Mel Gibson and Goldie Hawn, was not well received by critics, but 1992's *Shining Through,* a Nazi-era thriller that starred Michael Douglas and Melanie Griffith, garnered mixed assessments. Seltzer based the latter script on Susan Isaacs's bestselling novel in which a woman who discovers that her boss is an American spy insists on helping him gather secrets from the Nazis.

Seltzer's more recent screenplays include 1997's *The Eighteenth Angel* and the 1998 film *My Giant.* Since the mid-1980s, he has increasingly worked at directing and producing films as well as writing screenplays.

BIOGRAPHICAL/CRITICAL SOURCES:

BOOKS

Motion Picture Guide, 1927-1983, Cinebooks (Chicago, IL), 1985—89.

PERIODICALS

Chicago Sun-Times, March 28, 1986.
Chicago Tribune, February 23, 1983; April 2, 1986; September 30, 1988; May 18, 1990.

Los Angeles Times, February 17, 1983; May 1, 1986; September 30, 1988; May 18, 1990.

New York Times, June 20, 1972; June 25, 1976; June 15, 1979; July 24, 1979, p. 19; February 18, 1983; March 28, 1986; September 24, 1989; May 18, 1990.

New York Times Book Review, September 11, 1977, p. 3.

Premiere, October, 1988.

Washington Post, March 12, 1983; October 7, 1988.

Washington Post Book World, August 22, 1976.

OTHER

Movie Guide Database: David Seltzer, http://www. tvguide.com/movies/katz/5867.sml.*

* * *

SHAW, Scott 1958-

PERSONAL: Born September 23, 1958, in Los Angeles, CA. *Education:* Earned B.A., M.A., and Ph.D.

ADDRESSES: Home—Redondo Beach, CA. *E-mail*—DoctorShaw@aol.com.

CAREER: Writer.

WRITINGS:

Hapkido: The Korean Art of Self Defense, Tuttle (Rutland, VT), 1997.

The Ki Process: Korean Secrets for Cultivating Dynamic Energy, Samuel Weiser (York Beach, ME), 1997.

The Warrior Is Silent: Martial Arts and the Spiritual Path, Inner Traditions (Rochester, VT), 1998.

Samurai Zen, Samuel Weiser, 1999.

Zen O'Clock, Samuel Weiser, 1999.

Also created the four-volume videotape series *Hapkido,* for CFW Enterprises and Unique Publications. Contributor of more than fifty articles to magazines, including *Taekwondo Times, Inside Karate, Black Belt, Secrets of the Masters, Martial Arts Legends, Kung Fu Illustrated,* and *Kick.*

SIDELIGHTS: Scott Shaw told *CA:* "Writing is a spiritual process where the writer channels energy which he or she has encountered onto the empty page.

Writing is not about thought, nor is it about personal creativity. It is a process of divine interaction and is performed for the betterment of humanity and the world as a whole."

* * *

SHAW, Terrence 1934-

PERSONAL: Born May 27, 1934, in Morrisville, VT; son of Robert (an automobile mechanic) and Maxine (a seamstress; maiden name, Rooney) Shaw; married Gloria Purcell (a ward clerk), April 1, 1959; children: Michael Scott, Kimberly Hazel Shaw Panton, Sean. *Ethnicity:* "Caucasian." *Education:* University of Central Florida, B.A., 1972. *Politics:* Independent. *Religion:* Atheist. *Avocational interests:* Daily running and racing (including marathon), weight-lifting, reading, gardening, carpentry, travel.

ADDRESSES: Home—Ridgeville, SC. *Office*—Blackponds Publishing, P.O. Box 50190, Summerville, SC 29485.

CAREER: Isham Wholesale Produce, Hollyhill, FL, truck driver, 1963-66; Central Florida Distributing, Daytona Beach, sales representative, 1966-70; schoolteacher in Canton, NY, 1972-79; Department of Defense Dependent Schools, Alexandria, VA, teacher in the United States and Germany, 1979-95. Also worked as construction laborer, milk delivery person, cook, butcher, produce store manager, and factory worker. City of Canton, NY, director of after-school crafts, 1973-75, director of outdoor education, 1975-78. *Military service:* U.S. Air Force, 1952-56; became airman first class.

AWARDS, HONORS: Sustained Superior Performance Awards, Department of Defense Dependent Schools, 1982 and 1984, both for assignments in Germany.

WRITINGS:

The Waiter (fantasy), EOTU, 1986.

A Quiet Settlement (drama), Something beyond the Limit, 1988.

Home (mystery novel), Blackponds Publishing (Summerville, SC), 1999.

WORK IN PROGRESS: Swans Don't Sing, science fiction; *Death before Honor,* "an anti-military novel."

SIDELIGHTS: Terrence Shaw told *CA:* "When I retired from teaching in 1995 and we came home after sixteen years out of the country, I plunged into writing like a starving man dives into a Big Mac. I wrote for sixteen to eighteen hours a day, bathed in the sheer joy of creativity. Now I have changed. No longer caught up in the heat of creative freedom, I let my inbred New England Protestant work ethic have its way. Today I write eight hours a day, treating it like a job, and then spend the rest of my waking hours doing the crossword puzzle, mowing the grass or caring for the flowers, reading, running, and going to the gym. It's amazing how easily anyone (I suppose) can fill a day.

"As a teacher for twenty-odd years, I was consistently immersed in objective writing: essays, compositions, research papers, and exploratory themes. The only escapes I had from the boredom of these impersonal topics was in sponsoring the school newspaper, or locking my bedroom door at home and creating my own world on paper.

"Creative writing is God-like in the power it confers. I can make my characters do anything I want—well, almost anything. Sometimes I get so caught up in the story that the protagonist gets into a situation and must do something he or she wouldn't do. Then I either have to change the story line or go back and transform the character into another person. I don't want to do this. Instead I rewrite the story. But it's all fun.

"Every time I get an idea, and the thought develops in a logical manner, and the progress is successful, I am elated. The feeling is the same one that I get when I put myself in Mark McGwire's shoes when he knocks one out of the park.

"I haven't sold much of my work, and I know there are those who count sales as a measure of success— I know I do. However, I am enjoying myself. My goal is to write a bestseller in the next five years. Has anyone heard that before?

"Reading was something I once did only when there was nothing else to do. When I was a kid, I only read on rainy days or when a book report was due. Then I discovered Steinbeck. I don't know if I just happened to be at the perfect level of maturity when I read *Of Mice and Men,* or if he was the first good writer to whom I had been exposed. Whatever the reason, I read everything he had written up to then.

I soon was hooked on Thomas Wolfe, Kipling, and then Ayn Rand. After that I couldn't read fast enough. Today my favorite authors are Vonnegut, John Irving, Conroy, and, lately, James Lee Burke. I think the writers I have mentioned, more than any others, have influenced my writing and thinking.

"I write about my experiences, the things people tell me, and what I imagine could happen. Everything I have written and everything I will ever write is inspired by my sensual contact with life."

* * *

SHEAFFER, Mike 1950-

PERSONAL: Born October 12, 1950, in Harrisburg, PA; son of Jason P. and Vivian Sheaffer; married Anne Fontaine (a speaker and author), May 18, 1988; children: Jack, Travis, Hannah. *Ethnicity:* "Caucasian." *Education:* Texas Tech University, B.B.A., 1975. *Politics:* "Conservative Moderate." *Religion:* Christian. *Avocational interests:* Tennis, golf, organizational development, karate (first-degree black belt).

ADDRESSES: Office—c/o F.O.C.U.S. Publishing Co., 2121 Valley View Lane, Dallas, TX 75234; fax 972-406-3060. *Agent*—Jack Shaw, Marketplace Christian Network, 17340 Campbell Rd., Suite 206, Dallas, TX 75252. *E-mail*—msheaf@dallas.net.

CAREER: Hi-Line, Inc., Dallas, TX, distribution assistant, 1975-76, sales representative in Phoenix, AZ, 1976-78, sales manager, 1978-79, purchasing manager, 1980-82, national sales manager, 1983-86, president and director, 1987—. America's Crisis Pregnancy Helpline, founder and chairperson.

MEMBER: Chief Executive Officers Club, Bent Tree Bible Fellowship.

WRITINGS:

(With wife, Annie Sheaffer) *The Ultimate Gift,* F.O.C.U.S. Publishing (Dallas, TX), 1998.

WORK IN PROGRESS: Single Parent of the Year, a sequel to *The Ultimate Gift,* completion expected in 2000.

SIDELIGHTS: Mike Sheaffer told *CA:* "One weekend my wife, Annie, and I flew to Pensacola, Florida, to visit a birth mother and birth father for the purpose of adopting their baby. It had been an uphill struggle trying to build a family of our own. Just two weeks before our visit, I was shocked to hear that two murders of abortion providers had occurred outside an abortion clinic in Pensacola. The story made the national spotlight. The futility of it all—the abortions, the murders, the pro-life and pro-choice struggle—weighed heavily upon my heart. The murdering of people who were performing abortions was not the answer, any more than four-thousand abortions per day in our country was the answer.

"After concluding our day-long interview with the birth parents and their family members, Annie and I were finally catching a glimpse of hope for adopting a child. The two years prior had been filled with failed alternatives and no hope for what we had always dreamed of having—the white-picket-fence life of growing a family. I couldn't help but think that, if only there were fewer abortions, there would be more babies available for adoption. The two murders outside the abortion clinic confirmed that a middle-ground solution must be found to unlock the pro-life versus pro-choice gridlock. My mind began searching for ideas. Little did I know that, over the next two years, I would find an answer.

"My wife and I wrote *The Ultimate Gift* after having adopted two beautiful children and founding America's Crisis Pregnancy Helpline. Our book was written as a personal testimony of encouragement for anyone touched by an unplanned pregnancy, infertility, or adoption."

*   *   *

SHERMER, Michael 1954-

PERSONAL: Born September 8, 1954, in Glendale, CA; son of Richard and Lois Shermer; married Kim Ziel, July 7, 1990. *Education:* Pepperdine University, B.A., 1976; California State University, Fullerton, M.A., 1978; Claremont Graduate School, Ph.D., 1991. *Politics:* Libertarian *Religion:* Secular humanist. *Avocational interests:* "Cycling, skiing, basketball, reading, reading, and reading."

ADDRESSES: Office—P.O. Box 338, Altadena, CA 91001. *Agent*— Brockman, Inc., 5 East 59th St.,

New York, NY 10022. *E-mail*—skepticmag@aol.com.

CAREER: Glendale College, Glendale, CA, psychology instructor, 1980-86, assistant professor, 1986-91; *Skeptic* magazine, founder and publisher, 1991—; *Science Talk* radio program KPCC 89.3 FM, host, 1998—. Adjunct professor at Occidental College, 1989—, and California State University, Los Angeles, 1991-93. Skeptic Society, director, 1991—.

AWARDS, HONORS: Alumni of the Year, California State University, Fullerton, 1997.

WRITINGS:

Sport Cycling: A Guide to Training, Racing, and Endurance, Contemporary Books (Chicago), 1985.

Cycling: Endurance and Speed, Contemporary Books (Chicago), 1987.

Teach Your Child Science: Making Science Fun for the Both of You, Lowell House (Los Angeles), 1989.

(With George Yates) *Meet the Challenge of Arthritis: A Motivational Program to Help You Live a Better Life,* Lowell House (Los Angeles), 1990.

(With Arthur Benjamin) *Teach Your Child Math: Making Math Fun for the Both of You,* Lowell House (Los Angeles), 1991.

(With Arthur Benjamin) *Mathemagics: How to Look like a Genius without Really Trying,* Lowell House (Los Angeles), 1993.

Race across America, WRS Publishing (Waco, TX), 1993.

(Editor with Benno Maidhof-Christig and Lee Traynor) *Argumente und Kritik: Skeptisches Jahrbuch. Rassiismus, die Leugnung des Holocaust, AIDS ohne HIV und andere fragwuerdige Behauptungen,* IBDK Verlag (Berlin), 1997.

(Editor with Benno Maidhof-Christig and Lee Traynor) *Endzeittaumel: Propheten, Prognosen, Propaganda,* IBDK Verlag (Berlin), 1998.

Why People Believe Weird Things: Pseudoscience, Superstition, and Other Confusions of Our Time, W. H. Freeman (New York City), 1997.

O Ye of Little Faith: The Search for God in the Age of Science, W. H. Freeman (New York City), 1999.

Contributor to periodicals, including *Los Angeles Times, Complexity, Nonlinear Science,* and *Skeptic.*

WORK IN PROGRESS: Denying History: Who Says

the Holocaust Never Happened and Why Do They Say It?, University of California Press (Berkeley), 2000.

SIDELIGHTS: Michael Shermer is known for his books about the inner workings of the mind. Whether in sports training, coaching kids in math and science, or teaching science and critical thinking, critics have observed that Shermer's how-to advice allows readers to understand better how to motivate and understand themselves and others.

Sport Cycling: A Guide to Training, Racing, and Endurance details a series of long-distance road races—three trips from Seattle to San Diego and the Great American Bike Race across America, which was broadcast on ABC's *Wide World of Sports.* Along with the information about the physical training, Shermer includes "his positive point of view on hypnosis, chiropractors, mental imaging, and massage," according to *Library Journal* reviewer Thomas K. Fry.

Teach Your Child Science is a how-to guide for parents who want to cultivate their children's curiosity. Shermer contends that children lose much of their innate curiosity due to "school and social pressure," according to a reviewer in *Astronomy* magazine. By working together with their children on special science projects, parents can prevent their potential geniuses from becoming workaday drones. The book "provides good advice and sensible projects," where parents and children can both have fun, according to the *Astronomy* critic.

In *Why People Believe Weird Things: Pseudoscience, Superstition, and Other Confusions of Our Time,* Shermer analyzes the underlying reasons that humans sometimes "entertain the most fantastic notions," as *Boston Globe* reviewer Diane White put it. The root cause, according to Shermer, is a basic desire to feel good; and strange phenomena can provide comfort to some. "From psychic telephone hot lines to theories or racial supremacy," observed White, Shermer runs the gamut of topics. She concluded that the book "deserves a wide audience, perhaps among readers who think they're too smart to believe weird things."

BIOGRAPHICAL/CRITICAL SOURCES:

PERIODICALS

Astronomy, January, 1991, pp. 96-97.
Bicycling, June, 1982, p. 58; May, 1985, p. 56.

Boston Globe, April 24, 1997.
Library Journal, July, 1985, p. 89; November 1, 1993, p. 140.

* * *

SHERRY, (Michael) Norman 1935-

PERSONAL: Born July 6, 1935, in Newcastle upon Tyne, England; son of Michael and Sarah (Taylor) Sherry; married Dulcie Sylvia Brunt, June, 1960. *Education:* University of Durham, B.A., 1958; University of Singapore, Ph.D., 1964. *Avocational interests:* Reading, jogging.

ADDRESSES: Office—Department of English, 715 Stadium Dr., Trinity University, San Antonio, TX 78212; fax 210-736-7698.

CAREER: University of Singapore, Singapore, lecturer, 1961-66; University of Liverpool, Liverpool, England, began as lecturer, became senior lecturer, 1966-70; University of Lancaster, Bailrigg, England, professor of English, 1970-83, department head, 1980-83; Trinity University, San Antonio, TX, Mitchell Distinguished Professor of Literature, 1983—. University of Texas at Austin, exchange professor, 1977-78; University of Sierra Leone, visiting professor, 1980; Georgetown University, Royden B. Davis Distinguished Professor of Interdisciplinary Studies, 1992; Boston College, Lowell Lecturer, 1992; Oxford University, guest lecturer at Balliol College, 1992; gives public lectures in England and the United States. University of London, honorary research fellow, 1973; National Humanities Center in North Carolina, fellow, 1982-83; Oxford University, visiting research fellow at Merton College, 1996. Guest on media programs, including *Conrad and His Critics,* BBC-Radio 3, 1981; consultant for film *The Other Graham Greene,* British Broadcasting Corp., 1989.

MEMBER: Royal Society of Literature (fellow), Conrad Society of Great Britain (president, 1972-74), Savile Club.

AWARDS, HONORS: Book of the Year Award, *Observer,* 1971, for *Conrad's Western World;* British Council grant and Leverhulme grant, both 1977; Guggenheim fellow, 1989-90; Edgar Allan Poe Award and Book of the Year Award, *Encyclopaedia*

Britannica, both 1990, both for *The Life of Graham Greene,* Volume I, which was also selected as a notable book of 1990 by *New York Times* and biography of the decade by *Sunday Express;* citation as "one of the best eleven books of 1995," *New York Times Book Review,* for *The Life of Graham Greene,* Volume II.

WRITINGS:

Conrad's Eastern World, Cambridge University Press (London), 1966.

Jane Austen, Evans Brothers (London), 1966, Arco (New York City), 1969.

(Editor and author of notes, with Thomas Moser) Joseph Conrad, *Lord Jim,* Norton (New York City), 1968.

Charlotte and Emily Bronte, Evans Brothers, 1969, Arco, 1970.

Conrad's Western World, Cambridge University Press, 1971.

Conrad and His World, Thames & Hudson (London), 1972, Scribner (New York City), 1977, published as *Conrad,* Thames & Hudson (New York City), 1988.

(Editor and author of introduction and notes) Conrad, *An Outpost of Progress and Heart of Darkness,* J. M. Dent (London), 1973.

(Editor) *Conrad: The Critical Heritage,* Routledge & Kegan Paul (Boston), 1973.

(Contributor) Ian P. Watt, editor, *Conrad: "The Secret Agent;" A Casebook,* Macmillan (London), 1973.

(Editor and author of introduction and notes) Conrad, *Nostromo: A Tale of the Seaboard,* J. M. Dent, 1974.

(Editor and author of introduction and notes) Conrad, *The Secret Agent: A Simple Tale,* J. M. Dent, 1974.

(Contributor) Robert Ellrodt, editor, *Essays and Studies, 1975,* J. Murray (London), 1974.

(Editor and author of introduction and notes) Conrad, *The Nigger of the "Narcissus," Typhoon, Falk, and Other Stories,* J. M. Dent, 1975.

(Editor) *Conrad: A Commemoration; Papers from the 1974 International Conference on Conrad,* Barnes & Noble (New York City), 1976.

(Contributor) Philip Edwards, Vincent Newey, and Ann Thompson, editors, *KM80: A Birthday Album for Kenneth Muir,* Liverpool University Press (Liverpool, England), 1987.

Graham Greene: "The End of the Affair," British Council (London), 1989.

The Life of Graham Greene, Viking (New York City),

Volume I: *1904-1939,* 1989, Volume II: *1939-1955,* 1994, Volume III: *1956-1991,* in press.

(Editor and author of notes, with C. B. Cox) Conrad, *Youth—A Narrative; Heart of Darkness; The End of the Tether,* J. M. Dent, 1990.

(Contributor) Harry A. Wilmer, editors, *Creativity: Paradoxes and Reflections,* foreword by Linus Pauling, Chiron (Wilmette, IL), 1991.

(Author of introduction) George Gardner Herrick, *Winter Rules,* International Scholars Publications (San Francisco), 1997.

The Exquisite Time (poems), Viking (New York City), 1999.

General editor, "Variorum Edition of the Works of Joseph Conrad," Cambridge University Press, 1991—. Monthly reviewer, *Daily Telegraph,* 1974-78. Contributor of articles and reviews to academic journals and newspapers, including *Literary Review, Folio, Elle, Philological Quarterly,* and *Modern Language Review.* Editor, *Conradiana,* 1970-72.

WORK IN PROGRESS: Revising and expanding *Charlotte and Emily Bronte,* publication by Macmillan expected in 2000; revising and expanding *Jane Austen,* Macmillan, 2000; *Seeking "The Heart of Darkness,"* a documentary television film, for the Discovery Channel.

*   *   *

SIGURJONSSON, Johann   1880-1919

PERSONAL: Born June 19, 1880, in Laxamyri, Iceland; died of tuberculosis, August 30, 1919, in Copenhagen, Denmark. *Education:* Attended University of Copenhagen, 1899-c.1902.

CAREER: Playwright and poet.

WRITINGS:

PLAYS; IN DANISH, EXCEPT WHERE INDICATED

Dr. Rung, 1905.

Bondinn a Hrauni, published in Icelandic 1908, published in Danish as *Gaarden Hraun,* 1912, English translation published as *The Hraun Farm,* in *Modern Icelandic Plays,* American-Scandinavian Foundation (New York City), 1916.

Bjoerg-Ejvind og hans hustru, 1911, published in Icelandic as *Fjalla-Eyvindur,* 1912, English translation published as *Eyvind of the Hills,* in *Modern Icelandic Plays,* The American-Scandinavian Foundation (New York City), 1916.

Onsket, 1915, published in Icelandic as *Galdra-Loftur,* 1915, English translation published as *Loftur,* 1939, also published as *Loft's Wish* in journal *Poet Lore,* 1940, published as *The Wish* in *Fire and Ice: Three Icelandic Plays by Johann Sigurjonsson, David Stefansson, and Agnar Thordarson,* edited and with an introduction by Einar Haugen, University of Wisconsin Press (Madison), 1967.

Logneren, 1917, published in Icelandic as *Lygarinn,* 1939.

OTHER

Smaadigte (poetry; in Danish), 1920.

Rit (dramas, poetry, essays, and letters; in Icelandic), 2 volumes, 1941-42.

ADAPTATIONS: Eyvind of the Hills was adapted for film by Swedish director Victor Sjostrom.

SIDELIGHTS: Johann Sigurjonsson is recognized as one of the leading figures of modern Icelandic drama and a significant contributor to the early twentieth-century renaissance in Icelandic literature. In his 1911 play *Eyvind of the Hills* and in other works, he drew subjects and characters from national folk literature to present neoromantic dramas endowed with modern psychological and philosophical insights.

Born into a wealthy family in Laxamyri in northern Iceland, Sigurjonsson was educated in Reykjavik before moving to Copenhagen in 1899 to attend university. There he became increasingly interested in literature, especially in drama, which was flourishing in Denmark at the time. An honor student in veterinary medicine, Sigurjonsson soon abandoned his studies to pursue a career as a dramatist, composing his earliest works in Danish in order to reach a wider audience than his native language would afford. Recalling his early struggle for recognition, Sigurjonsson later wrote: "To begin with, I had to write in a language not my own. And then, what knowledge I had of human nature was limited to a most incomplete knowledge of myself and of a few college chums of my own age." His initial success was made possible when Norwegian dramatist Bjornstjerne Bjornson recommended his work to a prominent publisher in Copenhagen, who issued Sigurjonsson's first drama, *Dr. Rung,* in 1905. While *Dr. Rung* and his next

work, 1908's *The Hraun Farm,* received only moderate praise, critics recognize in them the developing dramatic and lyric skill that characterizes such later works as *Eyvind of the Hills* and 1915's *The Wish.* He subsequently wrote alternate Danish and Icelandic versions of each of his works, often substantially altering the plotline or ending in the second version. He produced several dramas ranging from tragedy to romantic idylls before his death from tuberculosis in 1919.

Sigurjonsson's dramas are often based on the romantic legends of Icelandic folklore, using traditional characters and motifs to examine modern themes. *Eyvind of the Hills,* for example, is patterned after the story of a legendary eighteenth-century outlaw and his wife. In Sigurjonsson's drama, the pair are pursued into exile in a mountainous region of Iceland where their love is tested by physical and psychological hardships, including isolation from society and starvation. Translated into numerous languages, produced in several countries, and filmed by Swedish director Victor Sjostrom, *Eyvind of the Hills* is Sigurjonsson's best known work. A critic for the *Nation* asserted: "To be sure, *Eyvind of the Hills* is an unusually stirring tragedy. The author is one of a group of young Icelandic writers who bear witness to the existence of a well-defined intellectual and literary renaissance in the birthplace of the most characteristic Old Norse writing. In the work of this coterie some of the sternness and majesty of that remote mediaeval literature persists. This is true especially of *Eyvind of the Hills.*"

In *The Wish,* based on a tale collected by Jon Arnason in *Icelandic Folktales and Fairystories,* Sigurjonsson updated the tale of a young man who employs magic in an attempt to murder his pregnant lover. Recognized as an outstanding lyric drama and his most accomplished work, *The Wish* also exemplifies the underlying theme of all Sigurjonsson's writings. As Einar Haugen explained in his introduction to *Fire and Ice: Three Icelandic Plays by Johann Sigurjonsson, David Stefansson, and Agnar Thordarson,* Sigurjonsson's dramas present "the ambitious man's challenge to the laws of the universe, a basically Nietzschean and Dostoievskian theme. Each of his heroes is endowed with a will to exceed his grasp, and this becomes his tragic downfall."

Although several English translations of Sigurjonsson's plays are available, his international reputation is generally limited to scholars of Scandinavian literature. His importance within his own national literature, however, remains great: he was instrumental in the growth of professional drama in Iceland and an inspiration to generations of writers who followed.

BIOGRAPHICAL/CRITICAL SOURCES:

BOOKS

Chandler, Frank W., *Modern Continental Playwrights,* Harper & Brothers (New York), 1931.
Einarsson, Stefan, *History of Icelandic Prose Writers: 1800-1940,* Cornell University Press, 1948.
Haugen, Einar, editor and author of introduction, *Fire and Ice: Three Icelandic Plays by Johann Sigurjonsson, David Stefansson, and Agnar Madison,* University of Wisconsin Press (Madison), 1967.

PERIODICALS

American-Scandinavian Review, November/December, 1916, pp. 346-354; June, 1924, pp. 346-351.
Nation, June 7, 1917, pp. 682-683.
Poet Lore, summer, 1940, pp. 147-149.
Spectator, February 10, 1917, p. 176.*

*   *   *

SILVERMAN, Joseph H. 1955-

PERSONAL: Born March 27, 1955, in New York, NY; son of Harry and Shirley Silverman; married Susan Greenhaus (an actuary), June 13, 1977; children: Deborah, Daniel, Jonathan. *Education:* Brown University, Sc.B., 1977; Harvard University, M.A., 1979, Ph.D., 1982. *Avocational interests:* Bridge, amateur theater.

ADDRESSES: Home—Needham, MA. *Office*—Department of Mathematics, Brown University, Box 1917, 151 Thayer St., Providence, RI 02912.

CAREER: Massachusetts Institute of Technology, Cambridge, Moore Instructor, 1983-85, postdoctoral fellow, 1984-86; Boston University, Boston, MA, associate professor of mathematics, 1968-91; Brown University, Providence, RI, associate professor, 1988-91, professor of mathematics, 1991—. University of Paris VII, visiting professor, 1992 and 1995. NTRU Cryptosystems, Inc., vice president, 1998—. Town of Needham, MA, member of board of direc-

tors of Extended Day Program, 1995-98, president, 1997-98, member of Town Meeting, 1992-94.

MEMBER: American Mathematical Society, Mathematical Association of America, American Contract Bridge League.

AWARDS, HONORS: National Science Foundation, fellowship, 1984-86, and grants, 1986—; fellow of Sloan Foundation, 1987-91; Lester Ford Award, Mathematical Association of America, 1994, for article "Taxicabs and Sums of Two Cubes;" Steele Prize for Mathematical Exposition, American Mathematical Society, 1998, for *The Arithmetic of Elliptic Curves* and *Advanced Topics in the Arithmetic of Elliptic Curves;* Guggenheim fellow, 1998-99.

WRITINGS:

The Arithmetic of Elliptic Curves, Springer-Verlag (New York City), 1986.
(Editor with G. Cornell) *Arithmetic Geometry,* Springer-Verlag, 1986.
(With J. Tate) *Rational Points on Elliptic Curves,* Springer-Verlag, 1992.
Advanced Topics in the Arithmetic of Elliptic Curves, Springer-Verlag, 1994.
(Editor with Cornell and G. Stevens) *Modular Forms and Fermat's Last Theorem,* Springer-Verlag, 1997.
A Friendly Introduction to Number Theory, Prentice-Hall (Englewood Cliffs, NJ), 1997.

Contributor of articles and reviews to mathematics journals. Editor, *Compositio Mathematica,* 1992—.

WORK IN PROGRESS: Diophantine Geometry: An Introduction, with Marc Hindry.

SIDELIGHTS: Joseph H. Silverman told *CA:* "I write textbooks because I love to teach mathematics. By writing I can reach a much larger audience. The books that I write are the books that I would have liked to read when I was a student."

*   *   *

SIMMONS, Charles A(lexander) 1933-

PERSONAL: Born July 25, 1933, in Savannah, GA; son of Charles A., Sr. (a journalist) and Lille Mae

Simmons; married, wife's name, Johnnie Mae (marriage ended); married Alice L. Strong, July 30, 1995; children: Jason. *Ethnicity:* "Black." *Education:* Central State University (now University of Central Oklahoma), B.A., 1980, M.A., 1981; Oklahoma State University, Ph.D., 1995. *Avocational interests:* Bowling.

ADDRESSES: Home—3304 North Maxwell Dr., Oklahoma City, OK 73121. *Office*—University of Central Oklahoma, 100 North University, Edmond, OK 73034. *E-mail*—cambox@ie.netcom.com.

CAREER: U.S. Air Force, career officer, 1949-77, manager of base telephone and radio communications systems, 1951-74, chief of squadron-level Communications-Electronics Division, 1974-75, manager of cryptographic system training program, 1975-77, and served in Thailand and Japan, retiring as sergeant; University of Central Oklahoma, Edmond, assistant professor of journalism, 1981—. Freelance photographer, with work exhibited at African American Art Exhibit, Oklahoma City, OK; conducts community workshops and school projects related to photography; judge of photography competitions. Worked as reporter for *Beach Beacon,* Savannah, GA; also worked for *Savannah Tribune* and *Savannah Herald.*

MEMBER: National Association of Black Journalists, National Set Club, Retired Enlisted Association, Air Force Sergeants Association, Ntu Art Association.

AWARDS, HONORS: Military—Meritorious Service Medal; Commendation Medal with two oak leaf clusters; Good Conduct Medal with five oak leaf clusters.

WRITINGS:

The African American Press, with Special Reference to Four Newspapers, 1827-1965, McFarland & Co. (Jefferson, NC), 1997.
African American Press Newspaper Listing, McFarland & Co., 1999.

Contributor of articles and photographs to magazines and newspapers, including *Ebony Tribune.*

SIDELIGHTS: Charles A. Simmons told *CA:* "My primary motivation for writing is twofold. First, my father was a newspaper man. Although he was not noted for his writing, the idea of writing was something I picked up just by proximity. Second, while writing, I did quite a bit of reading. One thing I found fairly absent in the history of this country is the account of major events told from a minority perspective.

"My writing process is based on simplicity. The style might change when I am writing about a modern occurrence, but it will be somewhat formal when I am dealing with historical events. More than anything else, I try to avoid the style of 'the normal' or the common ways of expression. Of course, that practice does not always get past the editors or publishers.

"If a writer is looking for a subject on which few have ventured to write, black history is a good one. I isolated black newspapers, because I've had some association with them since I was a child. It is the absence of published data in this field that keeps me researching in this area."

*   *   *

SIMONELLI, Jeanne M(arie) 1947-

PERSONAL: Born May 8, 1947, in Brooklyn, NY; daughter of Anthony (a lawyer) and Marie (a teacher; maiden name, DiMeglio) Simonelli; children: Elanor Rimassa, Rachel. *Education:* University of Oklahoma, B.A., M.A., M.P.H., Ph.D. *Politics:* "Activist." *Religion:* "Recovering Catholic; currently Episcopal." *Avocational interests:* Hiking, skiing, dogs, cats.

ADDRESSES: Home—216 Cemetery Hill Rd., Oneonta, NY 13820. *Office*—Department of Anthropology, State University of New York College at Oneonta, Oneonta, NY 138320; fax 607-436-2653. *E-mail*—simonejm@oneonta.edu.

CAREER: State University of New York College at Oneonta, professor of anthropology, 1985—. Gives readings from her works in poetry and short fiction.

MEMBER: American Anthropological Association, Society for Applied Anthropology, Society for Humanistic Anthropology.

AWARDS, HONORS: Grants from National Endowment for the Humanities, 1993, and New York State Council for the Arts, 1994; fellow of St. George's College, Jerusalem, Israel, 1997; grant from Kellogg Foundation, 1997, and from Hartwick-Chiapas Program and United University Professions, both 1998.

WRITINGS:

(Contributor) C. E. Hill, editor, *Training Manual in Medical Anthropology,* American Anthropological Association (Washington, DC), 1985.

Two Boys, a Girl, and Enough! Reproductive and Economic Decisionmaking on the Mexican Periphery, Westview Press (Boulder, CO), 1986.

Too Wet to Plow: The Family Farm in Transition, photographs by C. D. Winters, New Amsterdam Press (New York City), 1990.

(Contributor) Penn Handwerker, editor, *The Politics of Birth,* Westview Press, 1990.

(Contributor) B. Grindal and F. Salamone, editors, *Bridges to Humanity: Anthropological Friendships in the Field,* Waveland (Prospect Heights, IL), 1995.

Crossing between Worlds: The Navajos of Canyon de Chelly, School of American Research Press (Santa Fe, NM), 1997.

Contributor of articles and poems to journals, including *Voices of America, Quarterly Journal of Anthropology and Humanism, Practicing Anthropology, Man in the Northeast, Winds of Change, Social Science and Medicine, Human Organization,* and *Journal of Anthropology.*

WORK IN PROGRESS: *The Not-So-Great-New-Mexico Novel;* research on economic and religious empowerment in Chiapas, Mexico.

SIDELIGHTS: Jeanne M. Simonelli told *CA:* "How can I not write? I write to tell other people's stories, because storytelling is the oldest profession. As an anthropologist I try to tell the stories that come from other cultures, in a way that is readable by anyone. (If we have something to say, we need to say it clearly!) Sometimes a whole tale is best said in a poem, sometimes accompanied by photographs. Other times, it takes a novel, the kind you find in airport book stores. I can reach more people with these forms than I can with academic monographs, and it's much more fun to write a poem, a story, a biography."

* * *

SIMS, Anastatia 1953-

PERSONAL: Given name is pronounced A-na-*stash*-ia; born August 14, 1953, in Mobile, AL; daughter of James M., Sr. (a civil servant and contractor) and

Mamie M. Sims. *Ethnicity:* "Caucasian." *Education:* University of Texas at Austin, B.A., 1974; University of North Carolina at Chapel Hill, M.A., 1976, Ph.D., 1985. *Politics:* Democrat. *Religion:* Methodist. *Avocational interests:* Tap dancing, crossword puzzles, murder mysteries.

ADDRESSES: *Office*—Department of History, Georgia Southern University, P.O. Box 8054, Statesboro, GA 30460-8054. *E-mail*—asims@GaSou.edu.

CAREER: Indiana University at South Bend, adjunct lecturer, 1981; North Carolina State University, Raleigh, visiting instructor, 1982-84; Virginia Polytechnic Institute and State University, Blacksburg, visiting instructor, 1984-85, visiting assistant professor, 1986-87; Georgia Southern University, Statesboro, assistant professor, 1987-93, associate professor of history, 1993—. Vanderbilt University, visiting assistant professor, 1989; Duke-University of North Carolina Center for Research on Women, Rockefeller humanist-in-residence, 1990-91.

MEMBER: Society for Historians of the Gilded Age and Progressive Era, American Association of University Professors (vice president of Georgia Southern chapter, 1996-97), American Studies Association, American Association of University Women (president of Statesboro branch), Southern Association for Women Historians (life member), Southern Historical Association, Georgia Historical Society.

AWARDS, HONORS: Moore Memorial Award, Tennessee Historical Society, 1991, for the article "'Powers That Pray and Powers That Prey': Tennessee and the Fight for Woman Suffrage;" Archie K. Davis fellow, North Caroliniana Society, 1991; grants from Georgia Southern Foundation, 1992 and 1997.

WRITINGS:

(Contributor) Louis L. Queen, Rosemary Skinner Keller, and Hilah F. Thomas, editors, *Women in New Worlds: Historical Perspectives on the Wesleyan Tradition,* Volume II, Abingdon (Nashville, TN), 1982.

(Contributor) Marjorie Spruill Wheeler, editor, *Votes for Women! The Woman Suffrage Movement in Tennessee, the South, and the Nation,* University of Tennessee Press (Knoxville), 1995.

The Power of Femininity in the New South: Women and Politics in North Carolina, 1880-1930, University of South Carolina Press (Columbia), 1997.

Contributor to periodicals, including *Tennessee Historical Quarterly, North Carolina Historical Review, Tennessee Conservationist,* and *History Teacher.*

WORK IN PROGRESS: Editing *Dealing with the Powers That Be: Negotiating the Boundaries of Southern Womanhood,* with Janet Coryell, Thomas Appleton, and Sandra Treadway, for University of Missouri Press (Columbia MO); "Anne Firor Scott," to be included in *Whistlin' Dixie: Essays on the South's Most Notable Historians,* edited by Glenn Feldman, University of Alabama Press (Tuscaloosa); research for a biography of Juliette Gordon Low, founder of the Girls Scouts.

*   *   *

SLOBODKIN, Florence Gersh   1905-1994

OBITUARY NOTICE—See index for *CA* sketch: Born January 19, 1905, in New York, NY; died April 29, 1994, in Miami, FL. Children's writer and school secretary. Slobodkin studied at Hunter College and the College of the City of New York. She worked as a secretary for the New York City school system from 1926 to 1964. With her husband, well-known children's writer and illustrator Louis Slobodkin, she began writing books for the juvenile market. The first of these publications, *Too Many Mittens,* was published by Vanguard Press in 1958, and was followed by *The Cowboy Twins* (1960), *Io Sono, I Am* (1962), *Mr. Papadilly and Willy* (1964), and *Sarah Somebody* (with Louis Slobodkin, Vanguard, 1969). Most were illustrated by her husband. Slobodkin also worked closely with her husband in helping him edit his own children's books.

OBITUARIES AND OTHER SOURCES:

PERIODICALS

New York Times, May 6, 1994, p. B4.
Newsday, May 2, 1994, p. A27.

—*Obituary by Robert Reginald*

*   *   *

SPEEL, Erika

PERSONAL: British citizen.

ADDRESSES: Home—60 Deanecroft Rd., Eastcote, Pinner, Middlesex HA5 1SP, England.

CAREER: Freelance researcher, cataloger, lecturer, and writer on enameling history and related subjects, 1977—.

WRITINGS:

(Contributor) *Creative Crafts,* Elsevier-Phaidon, 1977.
Popular Enamelling, Batsford, 1984.
Dictionary of Enamelling, Ashgate Publishing (Brookfield, VT), 1998.

Contributor of more than a hundred articles to periodicals, including *Antique Dealer and Collectors' Guide* and *Glass on Metal.* Contributing editor, journal of the British Guild of Enamellers.

WORK IN PROGRESS: Research on enamel painting from the fifteenth through the twentieth centuries.

SIDELIGHTS: Erika Speel told *CA:* "I write as an outcome of my long-term personal and professional interest and involvement in enamel work. My work has included the examination and researching of objects in numerous private and public collections in the United Kingdom. Subjects of specific interest have covered Limoges-school paintings of the sixteenth century and their subsequent revival; miniature painting on enamel, especially portraiture; the individualistic work of the studio enamelers under the influence of the Arts and Crafts Movement, notably Alexander Fisher and Hubert von Herkomer; Oriental cloisonne; and the enamel work of famous makers such as Rene Lalique and Faberge and some of their contemporaries. I have also included modern aspects of traditional and innovative art work in enamels, and also objects such as heraldic enamels, enamelled coins, badges, and buttons.

"My *forte* is that I have learned the use and applications of the enamelers' materials, giving insight into how objects were made. I have been extremely fortunate to have, over many years, the opportunity to examine in detail a considerable number of representative pieces in great public and private collections. Equally important, I have been able to discuss many aspects of my findings with a variety of experts in enameling and in the technology as well as the collecting side of this important and diverse decorative art.

"Prior to the nineteenth century, only rare publications were brought out in respect of the enamelers' artistic and technological output of more than ten centuries, and some information remained in manuscripts or in volumes which are difficult to access. From the late nineteenth century, source books on processes, materials, and historical surveys were published by French, English, and other experts, with emphasis on particular periods or styles of work. I became interested in relating all the diverse branches of enameling. In this way I began reading the early histories and source books soon after I first started to learn enameling, as a teenager in the 1950s at the Central School of Art and Craft in London. My teachers were very experienced trade enamelers who had served long apprenticeships in the 1920s and 1930s. They taught directly about the nature of the materials and some of the early processes. In addition to the practical and strict basic instructions, they shared their knowledge of traditional workshop lore, terminology, and expertise. This was the background to my later preoccupation with enameling history in all its facets. I was fascinated for many years with medieval enamels, but, one by one, as I researched particular groups of work from different periods and centers, I was drawn into the intricacies and historical perspectives of each branch of enameling.

"All I heard, saw, and read over some four decades provided the background to my own writing. These sources were the templates and set the criteria on which to base my own contribution to a continuing record. The producers of the materials and the designers, artists, and craftsmen who made the work have mirrored many changes in the major arts and progression of technologies that are fundamental to our culture. It is a privilege to be able to add in some small measure to the record of the long-lived, significant, and diverse history of enameling in all its decorative and pictorial forms."

*   *   *

SPERLING, L(es) H. 1932-

PERSONAL: Born February 19, 1932, in Yonkers, NY; son of Irving (a painting contractor) and Rose (a homemaker; maiden name, Aries) Sperling; married Caroline Bonnie, August 9, 1957; children: Reisa, Sheri Sperling Sweigard. *Education:* University of Florida, B.S., 1954; Duke University, M.S., 1957,

Ph.D., 1959. *Religion:* Jewish. *Avocational interests:* Making wine at home.

ADDRESSES: Home—1134 West Market St., Bethlehem, PA 18018. *Office*—Lehigh University, 5 East Packer Ave., Bethlehem, PA 18015-3194; fax 610-758-4244. *E-mail*—lhs0@lehigh.edu.

CAREER: Buckeye Cellulose Corp., Memphis, TN, research chemist, 1958-65; Princeton University, Princeton, NJ, fellow, 1965-67; Lehigh University, Bethlehem, PA, professor of chemical engineering, 1967—. Consultant in biomedical sciences.

MEMBER: American Chemical Society, American Institute of Chemical Engineers, American Wine Society Educational Foundation (vice president), Sigma Xi.

WRITINGS:

Polymer Blends and Composites, Plenum (New York City), 1976.
Interpenetrating Polymer Networks, Plenum, 1981.
Introduction to Physical Polymer Science, Second edition, Wiley (New York City), 1992.
A Home Winemaker's Guide to Making Wine from Fruits, American Wine Society, 1993.
Polymeric Multicomponent Materials, Wiley, 1997.

Author of nine other books.

WORK IN PROGRESS: Introduction to Physical Polymer Science, Third edition, publication by Wiley expected in 2000; research on polymer chain diffusion, the molecular basis of fracture, and interpenetrating polymer networks.

SIDELIGHTS: L. H. Sperling told *CA:* "My primary motivation for book writing is self-education. While I must be an expert in some areas of the intended book, it has never been that I feel expert in all such areas. This requires a systematic approach to a study of the topic at hand, writing down the important items learned. This self-education process takes ninety percent of the time, the actual writing ten percent of the time.

"Of course, the book must be in a new area, and the information must be of general value to the field, either as teaching material or as a monograph. Who wants to write a book that isn't needed?

"I wrote one book based on my hobby, amateur winemaking. Since there was no manual available for the informed amateur about fruit winemaking, the American Wine Society put me up to it. Now, that was a fun enterprise! For starters, I interviewed fifteen recent national prize winners of the American Wine Society in the fruit wine category. (I was the sixteenth.)"

BIOGRAPHICAL/CRITICAL SOURCES:

PERIODICALS

Lehigh Week, December 8, 1998.

* * *

STARK, Marisa Kantor 1973-

PERSONAL: Born February 20, 1973, in New Jersey; daughter of Irwin (a professor) and Barbara (a teacher) Kantor; married Adam Stark (an investment banker), June 28, 1998. *Education:* Princeton University, A.B. (summa cum laude), 1995; Boston University, M.A., 1998. *Religion:* Jewish. *Avocational interests:* Shetland sheep dogs, hiking, working with the elderly.

ADDRESSES: Home—2373 Broadway, Apt. 1433, New York, NY 10024. *Agent*—Diana Finch, Ellen Levine Literary Agency, Inc., 15 East 26th St., Suite 1801, New York, NY 10010-1505. *E-mail*—marisa. stark@gte.net.

CAREER: Asbury Park Press, Asbury Park, NJ, staff writer, summers, 1992-94; Princeton Arts Council, Princeton, NJ, coordinator and teacher of writing seminars to elementary and high school students, 1995; *New Yorker,* New York City, writing assistant, 1995-96; Bruriah High School, teacher of English, speech, and communication, 1996-97; freelance writer, 1997—.

AWARDS, HONORS: Henfield Foundation *Transatlantic Review* Award, 1995.

WRITINGS:

Bring Us the Old People, Coffee House Press (Minneapolis, MN), 1998.
Ruth and Naomi (play), Unadilla Theatre, produced in East Calais, VT, 1998.

Contributor of poems, articles, and reviews to magazines and newspapers, including *Circumference, Louisiana Literature, Northeast Corridor, New York Times, Birmingham Poetry Review, Pen,* and *Hudson Valley Echoes: National Journal of Prose and Poetry.*

* * *

STEARNS, Martha Genung 1886-1972

*OBITUARY NOTICE—*See index for *CA* sketch: Born March 18, 1886, in Amherst, MA; died April, 1972, in Exeter, NH. Writer. Stearns was privately educated at home and abroad. She edited her first book, *The Transplanting,* in 1928. This was followed by *Homespun and Blue: A Study of American Crewel Embroidery* (1940), *Needle in Hand* (1950), and *Herbs and Herb Cookery through the Years* (1965). She also served as editor of the *Herb Society of America Newsletter,* and contributed numerous articles on art, handicrafts, and cooking to popular magazines. She was a member of the Herb Society of America, Colonial Dames of America, New Hampshire League of Arts and Crafts, and the Boston Society of Arts and Crafts. Her husband, the late Foster Stearns, was a well-known U.S. congressman from New Hampshire who later served as a diplomat abroad.

—Obituary by Robert Reginald

* * *

STEPHENS, Rockwell R(ittenhouse) 1900-1982

*OBITUARY NOTICE—*See index for *CA* sketch: Born February 16, 1900, in Portland, OR; died October, 1982, in South Woodstock, VT. Sportsman and sports writer. Stephens attended the University of Chicago from 1919 to 1920. He began his career as a sportswriter and an auto and travel editor for the *Chicago Daily News* from 1921 to 1926. He was a writer for Roche Advertising Company in Chicago from 1926 to 1929. He served as executive secretary for the Traffic Research-Study Foundation at Harvard University from 1929 to 1932, and as president of Ski Sport Inc. in Boston from 1933 to 1943. Stephens then went on to become the assistant manager of Research Construction Company in Cambridge, Massachusetts, from 1943 to 1945. He taught at Putney School in

Putnam, Vermont, in 1952, and at Woodstock Country School, Woodstock, Vermont, from 1953 to 1962. His first book, *The Art of Skiing* (with Charles N. Proctor), was published in 1933, and was followed by *Skiing* (with Proctor, 1936), *One Man's Forest* (with Stephen Greene; 1974), and *Axes and Chainsaws: Use and Maintenance* (Garden Way, 1977, revised edition, Storey Communications, 1988). He also contributed many essays to *Vermont Life*. He was a member of the American Tree Farm System, American Forest Institute, White Mountain Ski Runners, and many other groups.

—Obituary by Robert Reginald

* * *

STOKER, R. Bryan 1962-

PERSONAL: Born March 8, 1962, in Hickory, NC; son of Roy D. (a district engineer) and Nancy D. (a bank officer) Stoker; married, wife's name Sharyn D. (a programmer), December 14, 1985; children: Melissa L., Michelle B. *Ethnicity:* "White Caucasian." *Education:* North Carolina State University, B.S.E.E., 1984; Johns Hopkins University, M.S.E.E., 1987; California Coast University, M.B.A. and Ph.D., B.A., 1997. *Politics:* Republican. *Avocational interests:* Investing, travel, martial arts, computers, fishing.

ADDRESSES: Home—Eldersburg, MD. *Office*—Lifestyle Publishing, P.O. Box 355, Sykesville, MD 21784. *E-mail*—rstoker@erols.com.

CAREER: U.S. Department of Defense, Fort Meade, MD, division technical director, 1984—. Lifestyle Publishing, president, 1993—.

MEMBER: Theta Tau.

AWARDS, HONORS: Named master member of technical track, U.S. Department of Defense, 1998; ribbons from Toastmasters International.

WRITINGS:

Financial Freedom: A Wealth Manual for the Middle Class, Lifestyle Publishing (Sykesville, MD), 1994.

Growth and Income: How to Build a Mutual Fund Money Machine, Lifestyle Publishing, 1999.

WORK IN PROGRESS: Financial Engineering, a correspondence course; research on financial software tailored to the book *Growth and Income.*

SIDELIGHTS: R. Bryan Stoker told *CA:* "I have been fascinated with personal finances and investing since I started working at age fourteen. The concept of making my money work harder than I do seemed like the only logical thing to do. Since then I have successfully invested in stocks, real estate, mutual funds, stock options, and commodity options. Although bonds do not really appeal to me, I have even owned a few of them. I have also created a handful of businesses, the first of which was a freelance housepainting business back in high school. Of course, the most recent is my publishing company, Lifestyle Publishing. In all cases, I have always had a full-time job, either as a student or an electronics engineer, at the same time.

"So, my primary motivation for writing about personal finance, investment, and retirement stems from my incessant desire to constantly research and create new ways to invest and to convey these new concepts to my readers. Eventually, I hope to create seminars on investment and personal financial planning as well. One special goal I would like to accomplish is to create a personal finance and investment course for graduating high school and/or college students, since this seems to be one of the biggest holes in the American education system.

"My first book, *Financial Freedom: A Wealth Manual for the Middle Class,* was inspired by a realization one night, about one o'clock in the morning, that most books present generic concepts for how to invest in one thing or another, or they discuss how you can become better with a 'more positive attitude' or whatever. However, none of the books I had read pulled everything together into more or less a life-plan. I attempted to do this in *Financial Freedom* by presenting some simple, 'can't fail' steps that anyone can take to get out from under the burden of the myths created by the financial and insurance industries. Once you have obtained your freedom, the book tells you how to boost your wealth tremendously and reduce your taxes at the same time.

"My second book for the consumer, *Growth and Income: How to Build a Mutual Fund Money Machine,* emerged from more than two years of research I conducted to obtain a master's degree and a doctorate in business administration. For my long dissertation, I examined a fairly unknown investment technique called 'dollar value averaging' and compared its performance to two other automatic-investment techniques: dollar cost averaging and asset allocation. This technique is very intriguing, because it truly does buy low and sell high, unlike dollar cost averaging. For my doctoral research, I determined when and in which type of markets value averaging outperformed or underperformed dollar cost averaging and asset allocation. I also investigated the impacts of several real world constraints, including income taxes, capital gains taxes, minimum investment requirements, volatility, long-term market trends, minimum number of exchanges, and more.

"The results were sometimes unexpected, and I incorporated them into a simple step-by-step plan that anyone can use almost without thinking. An exciting bonus I never expected, I created a new hybrid technique that really supercharges the performance of your investments. Once again, I tried to incorporate the rest of a life-plan by including sections on maximizing your retirement wealth and making it last longer than you do. *Growth and Income* even includes software, special reports, and another book at no extra cost."

* * *

STORY, Jonathan 1940-

PERSONAL: Born August 12, 1940, in Chepstow, England; son of Henry Harle and Nest (maiden name, Osbourne; present surname, Williams) Story; married, wife's name Heidi, September 28, 1966; children: Henry, Christina, Nicholas, Alexander. *Education:* Attended Trinity College, Dublin, 1959-63, and Johns Hopkins University, 1969-73. *Politics:* "Liberal, conservative." *Religion:* Anglican. *Avocational interests:* Reading, music.

ADDRESSES: Home—21 Rue St. Honore, Fontainebleau, France. *Office*—INSEAD, Boulevard de Constance, Fontainebleau, France. *Agent*—Learning Partnership, London, England. *E-mail*—jonathan.story @insead.fr.

CAREER: INSEAD, Fontainebleau, France, professor, 1974-99.

MEMBER: Political Studies Association, Institut Francais de Relations Internationales.

WRITINGS:

The New Europe, Basil Blackwell, 1993.
Political Economy of Financial Integration in Europe, Manchester University Press (Manchester, England), 1997, MIT Press (Cambridge, MA), 1998.
Frontiers of Fortune, Pitman, 1999.

WORK IN PROGRESS: Contributions for books on corporate governance; research for the book *The Atlantic Century.*

SIDELIGHTS: Jonathan Story told *CA:* "Writing on complex matters of public policy is a pedagogical device to clear one's own ideas and then present them to one's readers. At least that's the way I have been writing until my recent book, *Frontiers of Fortune.* In that book my motivation was to engage better with 'fear-eaters'—the legion of highly trained people who do not, or will not, understand that the way the authorities operate is conditioned by historical or cultural favors. Major influences on me are Edmund Burke and Charles de Gaulle, among others. Depending on whether I write as a historian or as a discussant of ideas, I write according to the dictates of complex events. I have been inspired to write by the dramas of this century."

* * *

STRONG, Albertine

PERSONAL: Born in Minnesota.

ADDRESSES: Agent—c/o Harmony Books, 201 East 50th St., New York, NY 10022.

CAREER: Novelist. Has held jobs as a cosmetologist and rodeo clown. Active in drumming circle, Tonganokie, KS.

WRITINGS:

Deluge, Harmony Books (New York City), 1997.

SIDELIGHTS: A former cosmetologist and rodeo clown, novelist Albertine Strong spent much of her childhood on the White Earth and Red Lake Indian reservations, both located in remote areas of Minnesota. Being a Chippewa woman, Strong learned a great deal about the folklore and legends of her people while growing up on the two reservations. Certainly this fact, as well as the kinship she has with her family, was instrumental in writing her debut novel, *Deluge*. The book is the soul-searching tale of three generations of one mixed-blood family whose members are continuously dealing with the problems of identity. The story is narrated by A'jawac' (Aja) Sharret, whose grandfather was a Chippewa and grandmother a Swedish immigrant.

Spanning the years between 1909 and 1993, *Deluge* is an attempt by Strong to show the omnipotent importance of the familial bond, as well as the value in understanding one's ancestry. Although such topics are universal, it is no coincidence that Strong writes about them, considering how many Indian reservations in the United States are filled with despondent and aimless individuals who are still trying to come to grips with the historically altered status and present situations of their people. Within the story of Aja's family, Strong weaves in Chippewa folklore, which has played a large part in the course that the family has taken. The sly Chippewa god Wenebojo, who appears during deluges to play his mischievous trickery, is a constant character in the tale.

As *Deluge* opens, Aja's grandfather, Peke, falls victim to Wenebojo when he is thrown off of a bridge from a moving train in a torrential rain storm. He would have been left for dead if it were not for Isabel, the Swedish girl who becomes his wife. The story then moves to the character of Nina, Peke and Isabel's daughter. Nina, who feels she is better than what the reservation can offer, runs away to the city of St. Paul where she falls for a handsome Chippewa pilot named Roy. However, just as they begin their lives together, Roy is sent off to the Japanese front during World War II and then again to Korea. When he leaves for Korea, Nina decides she can do nothing but go back to the reservation of her youth, and she takes the couple's daughter Aja with her. Aja also grows to hate her background and is embarrassed by life on the reservation. For her, escape means going off to college and getting as far away from the place as possible. Yet, when she gets to Dartmouth, she finds the Ivy League setting and elitist peers detestable. After a failed marriage and giving birth to a child, Aja comes back home where she uses her education to open a school for the Chippewa children of the reservation. Upon the death of her grandmother, Aja finally faces up to her heritage. She goes through

old photographs and begins to appreciate the stories of Peke. Maturity has taught her that she can take pride in her multicultural ancestry.

Although a debut novel, *Deluge* attracted a good amount of notice from critics. A *Kirkus Reviews* contributor was impressed with Strong's storytelling ability. Despite calling the book a "standard intergenerational saga," the contributor wrote that Strong's "graceful prose and affection for Chippewa lore make for a lively, involving tale." Rebecca A. Stuhr of *Library Journal* called *Deluge* an "engrossing and moving novel." Praising it as a "lyrical first novel," a contributor for *Publishers Weekly* was reminded of the writing of Louise Erdrich, another Chippewa writer. The same critic lauded Strong for "seamlessly combining scenes of beauty, violence, grimness and humor."

BIOGRAPHICAL/CRITICAL SOURCES:

PERIODICALS

Kirkus Reviews, July 1, 1997, pp. 980-981.
Library Journal, July 1997, p. 128.
New York Times Book Review, November 16, 1997, p. 64.
Publishers Weekly, July 7, 1997, p. 48.*

*   *   *

SULLIVAN, Otha Richard 1941-

PERSONAL: Born December 28, 1941, in Hattiesburg, MS; son of Benjamin Franklin (in business) and Iola Estella (a homemaker; maiden name, Booth) Sullivan. *Education:* University of Kansas, B.S., 1965; Wayne State University, M.S., 1969, Ed.D., 1973.

ADDRESSES: Home—14187 Archdale Rd., Detroit, MI 48227. *Office*—Detroit Public Schools, 10025 Third St., Detroit, MI 48203. *Agent*—Clausen, Mays & Tahan, 249 West 34th St., New York, NY 10001.

CAREER: Classroom teacher at public schools in Detroit, MI, 1965-69; high school counselor, Highland Park, MI, 1969-70; University of Detroit, Detroit, administrator, 1970-73; director of special education for public schools, Highland Park, 1970-73; Howard University, Washington, DC, associate professor, 1977-79; ombudsman for public schools, Washington, DC, 1979-83; District of Columbia Department of Corrections, Washington, administrator, 1983-87; Highland Park Community College, Highland Park, executive vice president, 1990-91; Alcorn State University, Lorman, MS, associate professor, 1987-90; Detroit Public Schools, counselor, 1990—.

MEMBER: Council for Exceptional Children, Urban League, National Association for the Advancement of Colored People, Kappa Alpha Psi.

AWARDS, HONORS: Booker T. Washington Educator's Achievement Award, 1998.

WRITINGS:

African American Inventors and Discoverers, Wiley (New York City), 1997.

Contributor to magazines and newspapers, including *Freedomways Journal, Black Collegian, Dollars and Sense, Journal of the International Association of Pupil Personnel Workers, Natchez Democrat,* and *About Time Journal.*

WORK IN PROGRESS: A book on affirmations; a book chronicling the life of a young man growing up in Mississippi, completion expected in 2000.

SIDELIGHTS: Otha Richard Sullivan told *CA:* "My primary motivation for writing is to inform. As a teacher, I recognize that students are more involved in the educational process when they can look at individuals and their struggles and identify how these people were able to overcome adversities. Students are able to develop skills to overcome formidable challenges, and this helps them to approach and overcome other obstacles. Starting out as a teacher of social science, I immediately realized that many youths do not know their history. This lack of knowledge often leads to difficulties and wasted time before the young people come to an epiphany about how they will plan and direct their lives.

"My work is greatly influenced by my heroes, my mother and father, who taught me that education is the key that opens doors to opportunities. As a student in elementary school, I was influenced by my teachers, who introduced me to the brilliance and achievements of black Americans who were systematically missing from the pages of history, the textbooks we used, and the audiovisual materials. My favorite

teacher, Mrs. M. W. Chambers, infused black history in her classes on a daily basis, and this served to motivate students to greater achievement. Consequently, I developed a mission to write books and articles on the achievements of black Americans.

"The seeds for *African American Inventors* were sown at a middle school in Detroit, where I taught science. One day I asked students to name two black inventors. Most of them were stumped, unable to name two. I realized then that I had a responsibility to teach them about the myriad contributions of black Americans. At the same time, I began to unearth research completed some years ago at the Howard University library. I made a vow that, at the end of the year, students would identify, discuss, share, and apply the ingredients of success of many black Americans."

*   *   *

SULMASY, Daniel P. 1956-

PERSONAL: Born January 28, 1956, in New York; son of Warren J. and Margaret T. (a homemaker; maiden name, Quirke) Sulmasy. *Education:* Cornell University, A.B., 1978, M.D., 1982; Georgetown University, Ph.D., 1995. *Politics:* Independent. *Avocational interests:* Hiking, poetry, herb gardening.

ADDRESSES: Home—135 West 31st St., New York, NY 10001. *Office*—Saint Vincents Hospital and Medical Center, 153 West 11th St., New York, NY 10011; fax 212-604-8284. *E-mail*—daniel_sulmasy@nymc. edu.

CAREER: Took vows of a Franciscan friar of the Roman Catholic Church, 1990; Saint Vincents Hospital and Medical Center, New York City, attending physician, Sisters of Charity Chair in Ethics, 1998—. New York Medical College, Valhalla, director of Bioethics Institute and professor of medicine, 1998—.

MEMBER: American College of Physicians, Phi Beta Kappa, Alpha Omega Alpha.

WRITINGS:

The Healer's Calling: A Spirituality for Physicians and Other Health Care Professionals, Paulist Press (Mahwah, NJ), 1997.

WORK IN PROGRESS: Co-editor of *Methods in Bioethics,* for Georgetown University Press (Washington, DC), completion expected in 2000.

*   *   *

SUMMERSCALE, Kate 1965-

PERSONAL: Born in 1965. *Education:* Attended Oxford University and Stanford University.

ADDRESSES: Home—London, England. *Office*—c/o Viking Press, 375 Huron St., New York, NY 10014.

CAREER: Journalist and author. *Independent,* London, staff writer; *Daily Telegraph,* London, obituaries writer, became obituaries editor, 1995-96, then features writer.

WRITINGS:

The Queen of Whale Cay: The Eccentric Story of "Joe" Carstairs, Fastest Woman on Water, Viking (New York City), 1998.

SIDELIGHTS: Kate Summerscale's first book, *The Queen of Whale Cay: The Eccentric Story of "Joe" Carstairs, Fastest Woman on Water,* had its genesis in a letter she received one day in 1993 when she was an obituary writer for the *Daily Telegraph,* one of Britain's leading newspapers. The letter was written by the goddaughter of Marion Barbara "Joe" Carstairs, who had recently died at the age of 93, and the woman had enclosed some newspaper clippings about Carstairs' unusual life. Summerscale set about researching the story further and found it irresistible; from there grew the 1998 biography, *The Queen of Whale Cay.*

The words "colorful" and "iconoclastic" best describe Carstairs's life: born in 1900, she was heiress to the Standard Oil fortune and was probably unduly influenced by a mother who led a rather dissolute life. Carstairs drove an ambulance in France during World War I and was heralded in the press as the archetype of the new, modern young woman; she married only to obtain her inheritance, then immediately abandoned her husband. During the 1920s she bought motorboats, began racing them herself, and set several women's speed records over the decade. She also lived exuberantly, wore men's clothes, smoked cheroots, and sported tattoos. As Summerscale's book recounts, in Carstairs' milieu her sexuality was anything but an issue, but public opinion turned with the close of the 1920s and took an abruptly conservative shift. To escape censure, Carstairs used her considerable wealth to purchase her own island, Whale Cay, in 1934. She became de facto ruler of five hundred Bahamians, who called her "The Boss."

It was not unusual for Summerscale to chronicle the lives of the extraordinary or the eccentric; the Stanford-educated journalist was skilled at writing obituaries of both the famous and infamous for the *Telegraph*—which, like other British newspapers, does not shy away from recapping lives that were not completely exemplary. Her investigation into Carstairs's life took her from Switzerland to the Bahamas to interview those who knew her, and *The Queen of Whale Cay* is a recitation of the long list of Carstairs's adventures. The heiress had an equally interesting group of friend, including the Duke and Duchess of Windsor and actresses Tallulah Bankhead, Greta Garbo, and Marlene Dietrich. Summerscale also devotes space to Carstairs's attachment to a foot-high leather-faced Steiff doll given to her in the 1920s as a gift. She had matching suits made for "Lord Tod Wadley," as she named the doll, and created an entire persona for him that was a curious reversal of her own adventures.

A review on the online magazine *Salon* by Charles Taylor reflected that Summerscale "hasn't chosen an especially lovable subject" for a biography, and noted that she "seems constantly on the verge of affection for Carstairs without ever quite getting there, and that's hardly her fault. . . . [The book] never achieves the sparkle or the naughtiness of the era that gave rise to Joe Carstairs." Yet the *Boston Phoenix*'s Nicholas Patterson praised Summerscale, countering that the biographer indeed "develops an intelligent and intriguing picture of an iconoclastic woman and the world she created." A *Kirkus Reviews* critique termed the work "stylistically restrained and well paced . . . [an] unforgettable tale of one woman's raw hunger for immortality."

BIOGRAPHICAL/CRITICAL SOURCES:

PERIODICALS

Boston Phoenix, June 8, 1998.
Kirkus Reviews, May 11, 1998.

OTHER

Salon, http://www.salonmagazine.com/exec/obid. . ./
0670880183/002-6752410-135430, (June 9, 1998).*

*   *   *

SWOPE, Sam

PERSONAL: Male.

ADDRESSES: Agent—c/o Farrar, Straus & Giroux, 19
Union Square West, New York, NY 10003.

CAREER: Writer of children's books.

WRITINGS:

The Araboolies of Liberty Street, Potter (New York
City), 1989.
(Editor with Donald Letcher Goddard) *Saving Wild-
life: A Century of Conservation,* Abrams (New
York City), 1995.
(With Katya Arnold) *Katya's Book of Mushrooms,*
Holt (New York City), 1997.
The Krazees, Farrar, Straus (New York City), 1997.

Contributor of reviews to periodicals, including *Parenting, New York Times Book Review, Entertainment
Weekly,* and *Good Housekeeping.*

SIDELIGHTS: Sam Swope is a writer and reviewer of
children's books. In his *The Araboolies of Liberty
Street,* General Pinch and his wife maintain order and
quiet on Liberty Street, and the General threatens to
call in the army on anyone who deviates from the
norm. The Araboolies move in, a big family whose
members do not speak English and can change their
skin color at will. They paint their house in bright
zigzags, camp out in their yard, and draw the
neighborhood children into their games and colorful
lifestyle. When the General orders the army to remove the "different" house, a young girl named Joy
enlists the other children to decorate all the houses
except the General's with bright paint and balloons,
resulting in the General's being the house that is different—and dragged away. Shirley Wilton wrote in
School Library Journal that "Swope's message may
well be that diversity and individuality are good, but
what comes through in the story is the sense that
modern neighborhoods, no matter how ordinary, exist

under the threat of military enforcement." A reviewer
for *Publishers Weekly* felt the satire about fascism "is
wordy and repetitive. . . . But the messages of freedom, individualism and tolerance are strong."
"Thought-provoking at any age," was the conclusion
of Deborah Abbott after reviewing *The Araboolies of
Liberty Street* for *Booklist.*

Katya's Book of Mushrooms was co-authored with
Katya Arnold, who grew up in Russia where mush-
rooming is popular. "Perhaps this explains the convivial tone, unusual in a science book," surmised
Diana Lutz in *Horn Book.* The book is written for the
younger reader, and is intended, according to Arnold,
as an introduction that "will help families discover the
special excitement of hunting and naming mushrooms." The book uses folks names together with
scientific names and illustrations ranging from paintings and cartoons to artwork resembling woodcuts. A
Publishers Weekly reviewer called *Katya's Book of
Mushrooms* "Fungal fervor at its most contagious."

A reviewer for *Kirkus Reviews* felt that Swope's 1997
book, *The Krazees,* "borrows more than the plot from
Dr. Seuss. . . . But, heavy with nonsense words, the
derivative text makes a properly silly read-aloud."
"Children of all ages will recognize the Krazees,
nutty creatures that infest a too-quiet house and attack
only on rainy days," wrote a *Publishers Weekly* reviewer, who called the book "a gleeful fantasy for
wet-weather shut-ins." The Krazees are checkered,
striped, and polka-dotted creatures who appear to a
girl named Iggie. They do their mischief in her cup-
boards, television, and refrigerator, disappearing
when the sun reappears. *School Library Journal* reviewer Heide Piehler also compared Swope's style to
that of Dr. Seuss but concluded that it was not "as
smooth or successful." Nonetheless, Piehler did feel
that "the nonsensical rhyming text, filled with alliteration and word play, is sure to elicit giggles."

BIOGRAPHICAL/CRITICAL SOURCES:

PERIODICALS

Booklist, November 1, 1989, p. 560; February 15,
1991, p. 1214; April 1, 1997, p. 1326; June 1,
1997, p. 1675; November 15, 1997, p. 567.
Horn Book, July, 1989, p. 60; May-June, 1997, p.
336.
Kirkus Reviews, August 15, 1997, p. 1313.
New York Times Book Review, November 12, 1989,
p. 38.

Publishers Weekly, August 11, 1989, p. 457; April 17, 1995, p. 49; March 3, 1997, p. 75; June 23, 1997, p. 90.

School Library Journal, December, 1989, p. 90; April, 1997, p. 143; December, 1997, p. 101.*

* * *

SZEGO, Gabor 1895-1985

PERSONAL: Born January 20, 1895, in Kunhegyes, Austro-Hungary (now Hungary); naturalized U.S. citizen, 1940; died in 1985; son of Adolf and Hermina (Neuman) Szego; married Erzebet Anna Nemenyi (a chemist), c. 1920 (died, 1968); married Iren Vajda, 1972 (died, 1982); children: (first marriage) Peter, Veronica. *Education:* Attended Pazmany Peter University (now Eotvos Lorand University), 1912-15; University of Vienna, Ph.D., c. 1919. *Religion:* Jewish.

CAREER: Technical University of Budapest, Hungary, assistant, 1919-21; University of Berlin, Germany, associate professor of mathematics, 1921-26; University of Konigsberg, professor, 1926-34; Washington University, St. Louis, MO, professor, 1934-38; Stanford University, Palo Alto, CA, head of department of mathematics, 1938-53, professor of mathematics, 1938-60, became professor emeritus, 1960. *Military service:* Served in Austro-Hungarian calvary during World War I, 1915-19.

AWARDS, HONORS: First place, Eotvos Competition, Pazmany Peter University, 1912; prize for paper on polynomial approximations of continuous functions, Pazmany Peter University, 1913; Julius Konig Prize, 1924; posthumously honored by the dedication of a statue in Kunhegyes, Hungary, 1995.

WRITINGS:

(With George Polya) *Aufgaben und Lehrsatze aus der Analysis,* two volumes, 1925, translated by Dorothee Aeppli and C. E. Billingheimer as *Problems and Theorems in Analysis,* Springer (New York City), 1972-76.

Orthogonal Polynomials, American Mathematical Society (New York City), 1939.

(With George Polya) *Isoperimetric Inequalities in Mathematical Physics,* Princeton University Press (Princeton, NJ), 1951.

(With Ulf Grenander) *Toeplitz Forms and Their Applications,* University of California Press (Berkeley), 1958, Chelsea (New York City), 1984.

(With Ja. L. Geronimus) *Two Papers on Special Functions,* American Mathematical Society (Providence, RI), 1977.

Gabor Szego: Collected Papers, three volumes, edited by Richard Askey, Birkhauser (Boston, MA), 1982.

Contributor of papers and articles to journals.

SIDELIGHTS: Gabor Szego was a product of the German-Hungarian mathematical school. Something of a child prodigy, by age twenty, he had published a seminal paper in an internationally recognized mathematical journal. By the age of thirty he had published some thirty noteworthy papers and had co-authored, with fellow Hungarian George Polya, a famous mathematical problem book, *Problems and Theorems in Analysis.* Szego's most important theoretical work was in orthogonal polynomials and Toeplitz matrices, and he was, according to Richard Askey and Paul Nevai writing in the *Mathematical Intelligencer,* "one of the most prominent classical analysts of the twentieth century." Forced to immigrate to the United States to avoid Nazi persecution, Szego helped build the mathematics department at Stanford University, where he taught from 1938 until his retirement.

Szego was born on January 20, 1895, in Kunhegyes, then part of Austro-Hungary, to Adolf Szego and Hermina Neuman. Szego completed elementary school in the town of Szolnok, some sixty miles southeast of Budapest, and in 1912 enrolled in the Pazmany Peter University in the capital, now known as Eotvos Lorand University. It was in that same year that he won his first mathematic prize, the coveted Eotvos Competition. As Askey and Nevai noted in their article, it was fortunate for Szego that he won such a prize at the outset of his studies, for as a Jew, he might not otherwise have secured a university post. He followed this impressive beginning with a further prize the next year, this time for a paper on polynomial approximations of continuous functions.

Szego's first publication in a notable journal came in 1913 when he published the solution of a problem given by George Polya in *Archiv der Mathematik und Physik.* His first research paper, on the limit of the determinant of a Toeplitz matrix formed from a positive function, was published in 1915 and again inspired by a conjecture by Polya. As Askey and Nevai stated, "Szego spent another forty-five years working on sharpening, extending, and finding applications of the results published in this article." It was during this time also that Szego became a tutor to another mathematical prodigy, John von Neumann.

With the onset of World War I, however, this life of research came to a temporary halt. Szego joined the cavalry, though he was a self-admitted poor horseman. He remained in the army from 1915 to 1919, even after the collapse of the Austro-Hungarian Empire. He was able, while posted in Vienna, to finish his doctorate, and after the war he married Erzebet Anna Nemenyi, herself the holder of a Ph.D. in chemistry. The couple had two children, Peter and Veronica. But the effects of the war did not end with the Armistice.

The early 1920s were a turbulent time in much of Central Europe, and Hungary was no exception. Szego worked for a time as an assistant at the Technical University of Budapest, but by 1921 he and his family were forced to move to Germany in search of a more secure living. In Berlin Szego secured a post with the university for his work on orthogonal polynomial series, and became friends and worked with Issai Schur and Richard von Mises, among others. He continued his research and won the Julius Konig Prize in 1924, yet remained only an associate professor without tenure at the University of Berlin.

Together with his old acquaintance Polya, Szego collaborated on "the best-written and most useful problem book in the history of mathematics," according to Askey and Nevai. In 1925 the two published *Aufgaben und Lehrsatze aus der Analysis,* a two-volume work later translated into English as *Problems and Theorems in Analysis.* Students are introduced to mathematical research via a series of problems in analysis, number theory, combinatorics, and geometry, such that the solution to a group of problems prepares the reader for independent research in that area. Publication of this book rightly placed Szego as not only a noted researcher, but also as an educator with innovative ideas.

The following year Szego was invited to assume the position of full professor at the University of Konisgsberg, succeeding Knopp. He remained at Konisgsberg for eight years, but increasingly the situation for Jews in Germany was becoming untenable.

It slowly became apparent to Szego and his wife that they would need to move once again, and this time not simply to a neighboring country.

In 1934 Szego secured, through the intercession of friends, a teaching position at Washington University in St. Louis. The money to pay for his salary was raised by a Rockefeller grant, and by grants from local Jewish merchants as well as the Emergency Committee in Aid of Displaced Scholars. Szego remained in St. Louis until 1938, during which time he advised five Ph.D. students and worked on his seminal book, *Orthogonal Polynomials,* published in 1939. This book has become a standard reference work for both pure and applied mathematicians. Orthogonal polynomials are polynomials that first appeared in connection with numerical analysis and approximation theory. It was Szego's accomplishment to reduce many of these problems to the asymptotic behavior of certain Toeplitz determinants, which come into consideration as a variable reaches a limit, most usually infinity. Applications of Szego's theory have proved of significance in the fields of numerical methods, differential equations, prediction theory, systems theory, and statistical physics. Also, Szego's work on Toeplitz matrices led to the concept of the Szego reproducing kernel and the Szego limit theorem.

In 1938 Szego accepted an offer to lead the department of mathematics at Stanford University, in Palo Alto, California. He remained at the helm until 1953 and during those fifteen years succeeded in building the department to one of the most renowned in the world, bringing people such as Polya, Loewner, Bergman, and Schiffer to the school, and helping to train an entire generation of new mathematicians. It was while he was at Stanford also, in 1940, that Szego became a naturalized American citizen.

Szego retired from Stanford in 1960 as Professor Emeritus. His wife died in 1968, and Szego remarried in 1972 to Iren Vajda in Budapest. Ten years later, his second wife also died. In 1985, after several years of declining health, Szego passed away, leaving behind a body of work of some one hundred and forty articles and six books authored or coauthored, as well as a generation of trained mathematicians to carry on his research in orthogonal polynomials, a field which he pioneered. In 1995, the centenary of his birth, Szego was posthumously honored by the dedication of a statue in his hometown of Kunhegyes, replications of which were also installed at Washington University and at Stanford.

BIOGRAPHICAL/CRITICAL SOURCES:

BOOKS

Askey, Richard, editor, *Gabor Szego: Collected Papers,* Volume 1, Birkhauser (Boston), 1982.

PERIODICALS

Mathematical Intelligencer, vol. 18, no. 3, 1996, pp. 10-22.*

T-U

TALLIS, Robyn
See MACDONALD, James D.

*   *   *

TAYLOR, Robert Lewis 1910-1998

OBITUARY NOTICE—See index for *CA* sketch: Born September 24, 1912, in Carbondale, IL; died September 20, 1998, in Southbury, CT. Journalist, biographer, and novelist. Taylor graduated from the University of Illinois in 1933 and headed into journalism, working on the staffs of *American Boy*, the *St. Louis Post Dispatch* and then the *New Yorker*.

His first novel, *Adrift in a Boneyard*, was published in 1947 and was followed by a collection of profiles he had written called *Doctor, Lawyer, Merchant, Chief* in 1948. His biography *W. C. Fields: His Follies and Fortunes*, was published in 1949 to rave reviews and he followed it with other biographies and novels until his biggest success, *The Travels of Jaimie McPheeters*, was published in 1958. *McPheeters* told the story of a Kentucky father and son traveling to California during the gold rush years. It won that year's Pulitzer Prize for fiction and was made into a television series in 1960. Taylor continued writing a variety of books including a biography of Carry Nation that was published in 1966 and novels such as 1980's *Niagara*. His book *A Journey to Matecumbe*, which detailed the fight against the Ku Klux Klan endured by a boy and his uncle, was filmed as *The Treasure of Matecumbe* in 1976.

OBITUARIES AND OTHER SOURCES:

PERIODICALS

Los Angeles Times, October 6, 1998, p. A23.
Washington Post, October 5, 1998, p. B6.

*   *   *

TESTA, Judith (Anne) 1943-

PERSONAL: Born February 2, 1943, in New York; daughter of Emanuel E. (a musician) and Helene D. (a secretary) Testa. *Education:* Skidmore College, B.A., 1965; University of Chicago, M.A., 1967, Ph.D., 1983. *Politics:* Liberal Democrat. *Avocational interests:* Travel.

ADDRESSES: Home—411 Gayle Ave., De Kalb, IL 60115. *Office*—School of Art, Northern Illinois University, De Kalb, IL 60115; fax 815-753-7701.

CAREER: Northern Illinois University, De Kalb, professor of art, 1969—.

MEMBER: Historians of Netherlandish Art.

AWARDS, HONORS: Presidential Teaching Professorship.

WRITINGS:

The Beatty Rosarium: A Manuscript with Miniatures by Simon Bening, Davaco (Doornspijk, the Netherlands), 1986.

401

Rome Is Love Spelled Backward: Enjoying Art and Architecture in the Eternal City, Northern Illinois University Press (De Kalb, IL), 1998.

WORK IN PROGRESS: The Sunset of the Illuminated Book: The Art of Simon Bening.

* * *

THOMAS, Claudia E.   1956-

PERSONAL: Born in 1956, in San Diego, CA; married twice (marriages ended); children: two.

ADDRESSES: Home—929 10th Ave., Helena, MT 59601. *E-mail*—Siochain7@aol.com.

CAREER: Writer. Also worked as volunteer firefighter, emergency medical technician, and emergency dispatcher.

WRITINGS:

Irish Hearts: Caress across the Ocean (novel), Blaze Books (Helena, MT), 1998.

Contributor to newspapers.

SIDELIGHTS: Claudia E. Thomas told *CA:* "The second of three children of a less-than-happy marriage, I arrived on this earth, a Navy brat, via San Diego in 1956. Moving just two short years later to the Jersey side of the Hudson River across from New York City, I became a partial product of the sixties and seventies. Family, the experience of being the middle child, growing up in super-suburbia during this particular time span, the loving influence of an outstanding stepfather (entering when I was ten), traveling, marriage, and motherhood helped mold me into the person I am today.

"Of both the sad and happy experiences this life has dealt me, I have learned. I would change no part of it, for it has all served to shape the spirit within—a spirit I have grown to be comfortable with and am consistently trying to perfect, knowing full well the futility of that quest, which only lends to the magic of it all.

"My writing reflects all that I am, wish to be, and the fantasies that circle my imagination, and, I believe, the imaginations of women around the world. My primary goals and inspirations are to continue to grow and share with others, in addition to sharing and learning from others, so that we may all be a collective part of this tapestry called life.

"I moved to the Big Sky country of Montana over twenty years ago and have spent countless hours traveling the United States and Europe. Two beautiful grown children and two unsuccessful marriages later, I once again have found the freedom to travel to new heights, new adventures, and the quest for true love—an item I continue to have faith in finding. I have recently expanded my writings to include womanhood as a whole. Thus I was motivated to enter the world of love stories, which allow the imaginative and romantic spirit within to blossom and be shared."

* * *

THONE, Ruth Raymond   1931-

PERSONAL: Born November 11, 1931, in Scottsbluff, NE; married Charles Thone (an attorney, former governor, and legislator), August 16, 1953; children: Anna Thone-Salmeron, Marie J., Amy Kathryn. *Ethnicity:* "Anglo." *Education:* Attended University of Nebraska. *Politics:* "Progressive, radical." *Religion:* "Secular humanist, pagan, member of Quaker Meeting." *Avocational interests:* Reading, walking, swimming, movies, social justice, travel, friends.

ADDRESSES: Home—3045 Woodsdale Blvd., Lincoln, NE 68502.

CAREER: Writer. Nebraska Public Radio, commentator; Nebraska Humanities Committee, scholar and speaker. Leader of classes in women's issues and writing. Cofounder of Gathering Place, Gathering Place Soup Kitchen, Friends of Loren Eiseley, and Alternatives to the Military; active in Palestine Solidarity Committee, Nebraskans for Peace, Nebraskans against the Death Penalty, Center for Rural Affairs, and organizations dedicated to civil rights, alcohol and drug abuse recovery, and peace.

WRITINGS:

Women and Aging: Celebrating Ourselves, Haworth Press (New York City), 1992.
Being Home (essays), 1993.

Fat: A Fate Worse than Death? Women, Weight, and Appearance, Harrington Park Press (Binghamton, NY), 1997.

Columnist, *Lincoln Star, Friendly Woman, Sun, Nebraska Life, Grassroots Nebraska,* and *Nebraskaland.* Contributor to magazines and newspapers.

SIDELIGHTS: Ruth Raymond Thone told *CA:* "The primary motivation for my writing is to stay sane and grounded. However, all my life I have had lots to say. I have expressed my thoughts in newspaper columns, interviews and, in recent years, nonfiction, first-person essays—books and commentaries on the radio. Particular subjects of interest are women's issues, progressive politics, daily life, solitude, personal responsibility, and aging. My work is informed by my interior life, reflected in outer events and activities. In these days of old age, memory plays a major part in the way I view the world.

"The process by which I write is random, although less so than I think. In my splendid, over-full, second-story office in our house, I manage often to turn on the computer and write down what goes on continually in my head. Often I find chapters lining up for a book. I would get more writing done if I weren't obsessed with getting errands finished.

"Currently I am working on what has become chapters, on death and dying, and another manuscript about motherhood, an irreverent, sorrowful, funny look at the ill-prepared parenting of three now-grown daughters."

*   *   *

TOMLINSON, Theresa 1946-

PERSONAL: Born August 14, 1946, in Crawley, Sussex, England; daughter of Alan (a vicar) and Joan (a teacher) Johnston; married Alan Tomlinson (an architect), 1967; children: Rosie, Joe, Sam. *Education:* Attended St. Hilda's School, Whitby; attended Hull College of Education. *Politics:* Socialist. *Religion:* Agnostic.

ADDRESSES: Home—65 Hastings Rd., Sheffield, South Yorkshire S7 2GT, England. *Agent*—Caroline Walsh, David Higham Associates, 5-8 Lower John Street, Golden Square, London W1R 4HA, England.

CAREER: Author, 1987—.

MEMBER: National Association of Writers in Education, Society of Authors.

AWARDS, HONORS: Carnegie Medal Shortlist, British Library Association, 1991, for *Riding the Waves,* and 1998, for *Meet Me by the Steelmen.*

WRITINGS:

The Flither Pickers, Littlewood Press, 1987.
The Water Cat, Julia MacRae Books (London), 1988.
Summer Witches, Julia MacRae Books, 1989, Macmillan (New York City), 1989.
Riding the Waves, Julia MacRae Books, 1990, Macmillan, 1993.
The Rope Carrier, Julia MacRae Books, 1991.
The Forestwife, Julia MacRae Books, 1993, Orchard Books (New York City), 1995.
The Herring Girls, Julia MacRae Books, 1994.
The Cellar Lad, Julia MacRae Books, 1995.
Haunted House Blues, Walker Books, 1996.
Dancing through the Shadows, Julia MacRae Books, 1997, DK Ink, 1997.
Meet Me by the Steelmen, Walker Books, 1997.
Little Stowaway, Julia MacRae Books, 1997.
Child of the May, Julia MacRae Books, 1998, Orchard Books, 1998.
Ironstone Valley, A & C Black (London), 1998.

WORK IN PROGRESS: The Path of the She-Wolf, third book in "Forestwife" trilogy.

SIDELIGHTS: "I love writing about people who had a hard life, but worked together and found ways to survive," British author Theresa Tomlinson commented. "Resilience is what I admire most in human beings. I think that it is important to find exciting ways of passing a sense of history onto our children. A knowledge of the resilience of ordinary people who have lived before us can inspire modern children, and help them with their own struggles and decisions." Reviewing *The Cellar Lad,* one of Tomlinson's novels for young readers, Marcus Crouch of *Junior Bookshelf* noted that "Theresa Tomlinson has made the fictional interpretation of the English industrial revolution her own." Tomlin-son's novels, many of which are set in her native Yorkshire, are regional only in location, while their themes cross borders and continents. Daily courage in the face of hardship is a major Tomlinson motif, yet her books, as many reviewers have noted, are not heavily polemical.

They are character-driven and involve the reader in both historical and contemporary situations, generally featuring strong female protagonists. From the angst of a frustrated surfer to the exploits of Maid Marian in the forests of Sherwood, Tomlinson's novels engage young readers on several levels and generally end with an upbeat message delivered not with a sledgehammer but with a smile.

Tomlinson was raised in North Yorkshire and as a child had a strong desire to be a ballet dancer. She had no inclination to become a writer, but her parents read to her and encouraged a love of books in the young girl. "I started making little picture books for my own children when they were small," Tomlinson commented. "As the children got older, the stories got longer and I found that I enjoyed it very much." Tomlinson started her literary career writing stories inspired by the local history of North Yorkshire. "My grandparents used to tell me about the fisherwomen who arrived on the train early in the morning and stories about storms, shipwrecks, and daring lifeboat rescues."

Writing what she knew, Tomlinson first published a novel of the hard life of the wives of Yorkshire fishermen at the turn of the twentieth century. These women endured all sorts of weather to gather shellfish bait, or flithers, for their husbands. *The Flither Pickers* tells the story of the daughter of one such family, Lisa, who has the opportunity to break away from this harsh life by pursuing an education. But Lisa is torn between loyalty to her family and her desire to become a writer. Like all Tomlinson's books, this one was thoroughly researched; it also uses period photographs by Frank Meadow Sutcliffe to illustrate the text. In a *Junior Bookshelf* review, Crouch noted that Tomlinson "has written a most distinguished novel which is also a convincing piece of historical reconstruction," and also observed that the narration, rendered by Lisa, had "a rough eloquence . . . which strikes exactly the right note." Writing in *Books for Keeps,* David Bennett commented that the community of women in the novel "is realised vividly and compassionately," while in a different *Books for Keeps* review of the novel's paperback edition, Bennett concluded that the "juxtaposition of story and pictures makes up one of the best produced and affecting paperbacks I've come across in the twelve years I've been reviewing fiction for young people."

Tomlinson's next book also employed the setting of Yorkshire, but this time a bit later in history. Set in 1953, *The Water Cat* takes place in a steel-working town and involves a brother and sister who take in a stray cat. This animal turns out to be anything but a garden variety cat; in fact it is a shape-changer, a merman whose access to the sea has been cut off by the steel plant. The children vow to help the merman get back to his rightful home in the ocean. In a *Growing Point* review, Margery Fisher noted that in "plain prose which is circumstantial enough to deny disbelief the author describes the practical contrivances by which Jane and Tom manage to carry the merman/cat past the metal barrier, helped by seagulls and pigeons which put up a diversion."

Further books dealing with social and economic history include *The Rope Carrier, The Herring Girls,* and *The Cellar Lad.* The forgotten craft of rope-making is examined in the first of these, set in a village of such workers who live in the underground cottages vicinity of Sheffield, England. Minnie Dakin is born in this cave and chances are that she will die in it as well, just as generations of rope workers have before her. But when her sister Netty marries and soon thereafter falls ill, Minnie is called from the cave to help. Soon, however, she wonders if life is much better amid the growing metal industries of Sheffield. "This is social and industrial history with a human face," observed Crouch of *Junior Bookshelf,* "and very convincing it is . . . a most absorbing and attractive book, of great educational value but likely to be read with interest for its moving story and its vividly realized characters." Praising the descriptive passages, well-developed characters, and quickly-paced plot, Geoff Dubber commented in *School Librarian* that *The Rope Carrier* "is another excellent read from the pen of Theresa Tomlinson. . . . Clearly and carefully written, based loosely on real people, interspersed with some excellent contemporary lithographs of the area, this story will have wide appeal."

In *The Herring Girls,* Tomlinson once again used photographs by Sutcliffe to illustrate the lives of young nineteenth-century women who cleaned fish during the herring season. Thirteen-year-old Dory is among them, forced into the trade in order to save her family from the poor house. George Hunt, reviewing the novel in *Books for Keeps,* compared Dory's narration to "a good, honest, unadorned voice reminiscent of Laura Ingalls Wilder," while a contributor to *Junior Bookshelf* noted that the "writer presents a world that has gone forever, vividly recreating the economic hardships which then faced the poor." More social history was served up in *The Cellar Lad,* a novel dealing with attempts at getting the right to vote for all men and unionization for workers in the steel industry in Sheffield. Young Ben Sterndale and his family are caught up in these fights in a story "full of detail and very convincing," according to Linda Saunders in *School Librarian.* In a *Junior Bookshelf* review, Marcus Crouch observed that with all the difficulties facing the characters in this novel, it "would have been easy to lay on the suffering with a trowel, but here is a writer who sees her subject whole."

Tomlinson has also written books with contemporary settings and themes, dealing with issues ranging from intergenerational relationships to fighting cancer. In *Summer Witches,* she takes on the misconceptions concerning powerful women. Two young friends, Sarah and Susanna, decide to clean out an old World War II air-raid shelter uncovered in Sarah's back yard and use it as a clubhouse. In doing so, they discover evidence of earlier inhabitants of the shelter, two older women who live nearby—Lily and Rose. They have thought of Lily as something of a witch, for she is unable to speak and has wisdom of healing plants. Eventually the two young girls come to learn that Lily, far from being a witch, has a sad secret involving the shelter and a tragic incident from fifty years ago. "Gradually," a reviewer for *Junior Bookshelf* commented, "the two girls come to realise that many so-called witches of the past were really 'wise' women who knew much about the use of herbs and nature's secrets, and were seldom evil." A contributor to *Kirkus Reviews* noted that Tomlinson, with "admirable skill, . . . weaves her serious theme into an appealing, accessible story with likable, well-individualized characters and a neatly satisfying conclusion." *Horn Book* reviewer Martha V. Parravano concluded that "middle-grade girls will be hooked immediately by the private hideaway with a sense of mystery surrounding it, and the story that unfolds lives up to its enticing premise."

Steven Engelfried, writing in *School Library Journal,* described Tomlinson's *Riding the Waves* as a "strong novel about the surprising relationship that evolves between a boy and an elderly woman." Set in a small English coastal town, the novel deals with the dreams of Matt, who desperately wants to be part of a group of surfers. Such membership is elusive until Matt is forced to visit an old family friend, Florrie, for a class project. A bond is slowly formed between the two when Matt, an adoptee, learns that Florrie was long ago forced to give up her out-of-wedlock child. When Matt accompanies Florrie to the beach one day, their relationship is cemented: expecting to be embar-

rassed by the old woman, Matt is instead introduced to the surfer group who have a soft spot in their hearts for Florrie from the days when she ran a chip shop. Deborah Abbott noted in *Booklist* that this "startlingly refreshing story about an inter-generational friendship" was "well-paced" and had "an upbeat and satisfying ending." Applauding Tomlinson's well-crafted characters, Sheila Allen, writing in *School Librarian,* observed that "There are so many aspects to this book to absorb and encourage the reader. . . . Surfing, history, adoption, care of and respect for the elderly, are all woven into this very readable tale."

Tomlinson's own struggle with breast cancer inspired her novel *Dancing through the Shadows.* "When faced with a long period of treatment," Tomlinson commented, "I felt that it would be beneficial to try to keep writing, so I decided to use what was happening to me as the theme for a novel. I wrote as though I was the young daughter of a woman going through the experience. Once I'd decided to do this, I found that I felt much better. When I went to the hospital, suddenly I was a researcher, rather than a patient. It was very therapeutic. The story is quite upbeat and also suggests ways of giving help." In the novel, Ellen's mother has breast cancer, and Ellen, along with the rest of the family, is trying to be supportive. Soon Ellen begins to find some solace at an abandoned spring which her teacher discovers near the school, one that was probably once sacred and had healing powers. Restoring the natural spring to a semblance of its former pristine condition parallels the chemotherapy Ellen's mother is receiving, until both are finally restored to health. "Gracefully avoiding didacticism, Tomlinson . . . makes regular reference to the many sources of healing," noted a writer for *Kirkus Reviews.* "Readers will be borne along by the lively pace and the first-person, dialogue-heavy style." A contributor to *Publishers Weekly* observed that themes of "courage, survival and rebirth are explored in this story of a teenager coping with her mother's illness," concluding that "Tomlinson addresses painful truths about the progression of cancer and at the same time celebrates the resilience of body and spirit."

Personal experience also inspired a trilogy focusing on Marian of Sherwood Forest. Tomlinson recalled: "As a child I loved Robin Hood stories, but felt a little frustrated that Marian, the only woman that a girl could identify with, was usually locked up in a castle and needing to be rescued. I wanted to imagine Marian rushing through the forest like the men, having adventures and doing the rescuing herself." To satisfy this need for an exciting story, Tomlinson wrote *The Forestwife,* telling the story of Mary de Holt, who runs away from an arranged marriage at age fifteen. Taking to the forest with her nurse, Agnes, the pair try to find the local wise woman, the Forestwife, whom some think of as a witch. But the woman has died, and Agnes takes her role, renaming her young charge Marian, and taking her on as assistant.

Adventures there are in plenty, involving people on the run and a group of defrocked, renegade nuns. Agnes's son, Robert, is a local outlaw whom Marian initially dislikes, but soon grows to love as he becomes Robin Hood. Yet when Agnes dies, Marian's plans for marrying Robin come to an end, for she must now become the new Forestwife, enlisting the many women of the forest into a band to fight injustice. Reviewing the novel in the *Bulletin of the Center for Children's Books,* Deborah Stevenson called it "an atmospheric read about a durable heroine." In a starred review, *Booklist*'s Ilene Cooper called *The Forestwife* a "rich, vibrant tale with an afterword that describes how various legends are braided into the story." Tomlinson has followed up this initial Marian tale with two others, *Child of the May* and *The Path of the She-Wolf.*

Whether writing of the medieval forest, the plight of workers in the industrializing nineteenth century, or about contemporary teenagers facing their own modern challenges, Tomlinson fuels her stories with the theme of resiliency. In her dozen-plus novels for young readers, she reveals not only history but the ordinary men and women who created it.

BIOGRAPHICAL/CRITICAL SOURCES:

PERIODICALS

Booklist, May 1, 1993, p. 1593; March 1, 1995, p. 1241; November 1, 1997, p. 463.
Books for Keeps, May, 1992, pp. 20-21; September, 1992, p. 11; July, 1993, p. 32; May, 1996, p. 13.
Bulletin of the Center for Children's Books, May, 1991, p. 229; March, 1995, pp. 252-253.
Growing Point, June, 1989, p. 5089; January, 1991, p. 5450; January, 1992, pp. 5641-5642.
Horn Book, May-June, 1991, p. 332.
Junior Bookshelf, August, 1989, p. 181; December, 1990, p. 302; June, 1991, p. 123; December, 1991, p. 269; June, 1995, pp. 110-111; June, 1996, p. 126; October, 1996, p. 195.
Kirkus Reviews, April 15, 1991, p. 540; September 15, 1997, p. 1464; October 1, 1998, p. 1465.

Publishers Weekly, May 10, 1993, p. 72; February 13, 1995, p. 79; November 3, 1997, p. 86.
School Librarian, February, 1991, p. 33; February, 1992, p. 33; August, 1995, p. 119.
School Library Journal, May, 1993, p. 110; March, 1995, p. 225; November, 1997, p. 124; November, 1998, p. 131.
Times Educational Supplement, November 11, 1988, p. 52; December 7, 1990, p. 30; November 8, 1991, p. 38; August 11, 1995, p. 17.
Voice of Youth Advocates, June, 1995, p. 100.*

* * *

TSIPENYUK, Yuri M. 1938-

PERSONAL: Born December 4, 1938, in Kiev, U.S.S.R. (now Ukraine); son of Mikhail and Rosaliya (Turovskaya) Tsipenyuk; married Evgeniya Pronevich, August 16, 1960; children: Dmitri. *Ethnicity:* "Jewish." *Education:* Attended Moscow Institute of Physics and Technology, 1962. *Politics:* None. *Religion:* None. *Avocational interests:* Tennis, chess.

ADDRESSES: Home—Ulitza Udaltsova 4 kv. 79, 117415 Moscow, Russia. *Office*—P. L. Kapitza Institute for Physical Problems, Russian Academy of Science, Kosygina 2, 117334 Moscow, Russia; fax 095-938-2030. *E-mail*—tsip@kapitza.ras.ru.

CAREER: Russian Academy of Science, P. L. Kapitza Institute for Physical Problems, Moscow, lead scientific researcher in physics, 1962—. Moscow Institute of Physics and Technology, professor, became Soros Professor, 1997.

WRITINGS:

Principles and Methods of Nuclear Physics, Energoatomizdat, 1993.
The Physical Background of Superconductivity, MPTI Publishing, 1996.
Nuclear Methods in Science and Technology, IOP Publishing (Philadelphia, PA), 1997.
The Microtron: Development and Applications, Gordon & Breach (New York City), 1999.

Contributor of more than a hundred articles to scientific journals.

SIDELIGHTS: Yuri M. Tsipenyuk told *CA:* "The

main motivation for writing a book is the desire to present to the scientific community accumulated knowledge in my professional branch of physics. An understanding that such a book will be of interest for others is a consequence of discussions with my colleagues and friends. My writing process involves a many-sided analysis."

*   *   *

TUCKER, Anthony 1924-1998

OBITUARY NOTICE—See index for *CA* sketch: Born June 1, 1924, in Urmston, England; died September 15, 1998. Journalist. Tucker studied aeronautical engineering in Belfast at Queen's University before joining the Royal Air Force in 1942. He was a fighter pilot until 1947 but studied fine art after leaving the service. He got a job writing about the arts at the *Manchester Guardian* in 1953 and stayed there in a variety of positions until he retired. He founded the paper's features department, drew weather maps, and covered the science beat. At the time of his death he still was writing obituaries for the paper. In addition to contributing articles to magazines, Tucker wrote three books: *Climate for Living, The Toxic Metals* and, with J. A. Lauwerys and Keith Reid, *Man Nature and Ecology.*

OBITUARIES AND OTHER SOURCES:

PERIODICALS

Times (London), September 28, 1998.

*   *   *

TUCKER, John C. 1934-

PERSONAL: Born in 1934.

ADDRESSES: Office—c/o Norton, 500 Fifth Ave., New York, NY 10110.

CAREER: Attorney and writer.

WRITINGS:

May God Have Mercy: A True Story of Crime and Punishment, Norton (New York City), 1997.

SIDELIGHTS: John C. Tucker worked as a criminal lawyer before writing his first book, *May God Have Mercy: A True Story of Crime and Punishment*. Published in 1997, it told the tale of the rape and murder in Virginia of nineteen-year-old Wanda Fay Thompson, and the conviction and punishment of her brother-in-law, Ronald Keith Coleman. Coleman had a prior conviction for rape, and this made him the primary suspect of the investigation. After his arrest, he was represented legally by two public defenders who had never previously tried murder cases. As Tucker tells his readers, there were several discrepancies in the prosecution's case against Coleman—including the fact that the victim's stab wounds were four inches deep when the defendant only had a three-inch knife, and that Thompson's door showed pry marks when she would have admitted Coleman into her home voluntarily due to their relationship by marriage.

Tucker also tells of the work by many attorneys to appeal Coleman's conviction before he could be put to death in Virginia's electric chair. They did not succeed, and Coleman was electrocuted on May 20, 1992. Reviewers of *May God Have Mercy* were predominantly positive. The book, affirmed *Publishers Weekly,* "is distinguishe[d] . . . [by] his sensitive rendering of the quality of the effort on Coleman's behalf and of the dignity" of the accused as he met his end. Christine A. Moesch hailed the book in *Library Journal* as "a gripping account of what may well have been a travesty of justice." "Tucker's sterling account" of the circumstances "humanizes the death penalty issue," concluded Ellen Beauregard in *Book-list.*

BIOGRAPHICAL/CRITICAL SOURCES:

PERIODICALS

Booklist, September 15, 1997, p. 186.
Library Journal, September 15, 1997, p. 90.
Publishers Weekly, August 11, 1997, p. 398.*

*   *   *

TUNNELL, Michael O('Grady) 1950-

PERSONAL: Born June 14, 1950, in Nocona, TX; son of Billie Bob Tunnell and Mauzi Chupp; legally adopted by Grady and Trudy Chupp (maternal grandparents); married Glenna Maurine Henry (a librarian); children: Heather Anne Wall, Holly Lyne Argyle, Nikki Leigh, Quincy Michael. *Education:* University of Utah, B.A., 1973; Utah State University, M.Ed., 1978; Brigham Young University, Ed.D., 1986. *Politics:* Democrat. *Religion:* Church of Jesus Christ of Latter-day Saints (Mormon). *Avocational interests:* Reading, photography.

ADDRESSES: Office—210-A McKay Building, Brigham Young University, Provo, UT 84602. *E-mail*—mike _tunnell@byu.edu.

CAREER: Uintah School District, Vernal, UT, sixth-grade teacher, 1973-75; Wasatch School District, Heber City, UT, teacher and library/media specialist, 1976-85; Arkansas State University, Jonesboro, assistant professor of elementary education, 1985-87; Northern Illinois University, DeKalb, IL, assistant professor of language arts and children's literature, 1987-92; Brigham Young University, Provo, UT, associate and full professor of children's literature, 1992—. Children's book writer, 1993—.

MEMBER: International Reading Association, American Library Association (member of Newbery Award Committee, 1990), National Council of Teachers of English (board member and treasurer, Children's Literature Assembly, 1992-94; on board of directors, NCTE, and chair, Poetry Award Committee, 1995-97), Society of Children's Book Writers and Illustrators.

AWARDS, HONORS: American Booksellers Pick of the Lists, and Association of Mormon Letters Award in Children's Literature, both 1993, both for *Chinook!;* Association of Mormon Letters Award in Children's Literature, 1993, for *The Joke's on George;* American Booksellers Pick of the Lists, and Association of Mormon Letters Award in Children's Literature, both 1993, both for *Beauty and the Beastly Children;* Parents' Choice Award, and Cooperative Children's Book Center Choices, both 1996, Notable Children's Trade Book in the Field of Social Studies, Children's Book Council and the National Council for the Social Studies (CBC/NCSS), New York Public Library's Books for the Teen Age list, Distinguished Title, Public Library Association, Notable Books for a Global Society, International Reading Association (IRA), Notable Books in the Language Arts, National Council of Teachers of English (NCTE), and Nonfiction Honor List, *Voice of Youth Advocates,* all 1997, Carter G. Woodson Honor Book Award, NCSS, Utah Children's Informational Book Award Master List, 1997-98, and Maine Student Book Award Master List, 1997-98, all for *The Children of Topaz;* Best Books list, *Crayola Kids Magazine* and *Child Maga-*

zine, and Parents' Choice Award, all 1997, Notable Children's Trade Book in the Field of Social Studies (Selector's Choice), CBC/NCSS, Notable Children's Book, American Library Association (ALA), Notable Books in the Language Arts, NCTE, Teachers' Choices, IRA, and *Storytelling World* Honor Award, all 1998, and Utah Children's Picture Book Award Master List, 1997-98, all for *Mailing May.*

WRITINGS:

FOR CHILDREN

Chinook!, illustrated by Barry Boot, Tambourine, 1993.
The Joke's on George, illustrated by Kathy Osborn, Tambourine, 1993.
Beauty and the Beastly Children, illustrated by John Emil Cymerman, Tambourine, 1993.
(With George W. Chilcoat) *The Children of Topaz: The Story of a Japanese-American Internment Camp Based on a Classroom Diary,* Holiday House, 1996.
Mailing May, illustrated by Ted Rand, Greenwillow, 1997.
School Spirits, Holiday House, 1997.

OTHER

The Prydain Companion: A Reference Guide to Lloyd Alexander's Prydain Chronicles, Greenwood Press, 1989.
(With James S. Jacobs) *Lloyd Alexander: A Bio-Bibliography,* Greenwood Press, 1991.
(Editor with Richard Ammon) *The Story of Ourselves: Teaching History through Children's Literature,* Heinemann, 1993.
(With Jacobs) *Children's Literature, Briefly,* Merrill/Prentice Hall, 1996.

Tunnell has also written articles and short stories for children's magazines, including *Cricket* and *Spider,* and has contributed chapters and articles for numerous professional books and journals, including *Reading Teacher, Language Arts, Horn Book, Children's Literature in Education, School Library Journal, Reading Improvement, Book Links, Social Education, New Advocate* and *Journal of Educational Research.* He has also reviewed books for several publications, including *Booklist.*

WORK IN PROGRESS: Halloween Pie, illustrated by Kevin O'Malley, a picture book for Lothrop, Lee & Shepard; *If the Shoe Fits,* a picture book for Lothrop,

Lee & Shepard; a historical novel for young readers set in Nazi Germany for Holiday House; preliminary research for a historical novel set in the Mormon city of Nauvoo, Illinois, in the 1840s; second edition of *Children's Literature, Briefly,* for Prentice Hall; a professional book about children's literature (with James Jacobs and Daniel Darigan) for Prentice Hall.

SIDELIGHTS: Michael O. Tunnell is the author of several picture books, including the award-winning *Mailing May,* and of nonfiction works and novels for middle-grade readers. A professor of children's literature at Brigham Young University, Tunnell thoroughly knows the terrain of which he writes. Yet when he came to creating his own stories and novels, it was as if he were in uncharted territory. "I discovered critiquing someone else's work is an entirely different process than creating your own stories," Tunnell commented. "Perhaps I was simply too close to my own work, which made applying what I thought I knew about quality literature difficult. In any case, I had a lot to learn (and the learning has just begun!) about the creative process. I guess writers are born perhaps more than they are made. (I feel the same way about teachers.) So, part of the challenge has been to find and cultivate any spark of literary creativity with which I might have been blessed."

Born in Texas, Tunnell was raised in Canada by his grandparents. His love affair with books started at a young age. "My grandmother . . . would read to me every day," Tunnell commented. "Fairy tales, comic books, and wonderful picture books like *Caps for Sale* and *Mike Mulligan and His Steam Shovel.* I soon discovered that books were the world's best teachers and entertainers. I grew up wanting to spend my life working with books." At university he was studying for a career in law when he rediscovered this early commitment. Working part-time for an automobile dealer in Salt Lake City, Utah, he was sent to deliver a car to a customer at a nearby elementary school. "The second I walked through the school doors, I was flooded with the strangest feelings. I remembered my favorite books and my magical childhood years. The next day I changed my major to education. Since then, I've completed several degrees, all relating to reading, children's literature, and teaching." A classroom teacher and media specialist for several years, Tunnell eventually wound up teaching children' literature at the university level.

Tunnell's love of books and language encouraged him to try writing short stories as a child, and in his twenties he wrote his first novel, one that was re-

jected by more than twenty publishers. "For a number of years, instead of creating stories I channeled my writing efforts into professional educational books and journal articles," Tunnell remarked. "All the while, my desire to write books for young readers stayed strong. In the early 1990s, I found my way back to writing stories. My first effort was the manuscript for the picture book *Chinook!,* which was accepted on my third submission attempt." For this book, Tunnell harkened back to some of his own childhood memories of growing up in Alberta, Canada, and the warm, dry wind—the chinook—that blows off the eastern slopes of the Rockies. The result is a book of original tales narrated by old-timer Andrew Delaney McFadden to two ice-skating children. While out ice-fishing, McFadden pulls the children into his boat that sits on top of the ice, warning them about the possible dangers of being stranded far from shore should the weather suddenly change because of a chinook. He relates the story of one such chinook which swept down in 1888 and quickly melted the ice, explaining why he prefers to sit in a boat while ice fishing on a frozen lake. Other tales follow as McFadden gives these newly arrived siblings a taste for Western weather: tomato seeds sprouting in February; apple blossoms and fruit in winter. A cautionary tale, *Chinook!* was dubbed a "fine picture-book debut with some nicely understated tall tales" by a *Kirkus Reviews* contributor. "Few tall tales focus so intently on weather," Deborah Abbott concluded in her *Booklist* review, "and this one, with its flamboyant shift from winter to summer, radiates a gentle warmth."

The Joke's on George, Tunnell's second picture book, again employs historical situations in an amusing manner. Taken from the eighteenth-century journals of Rembrandt Peale, the book deals with an incident involving Peale's father, painter and museum keeper Charles Willson Peale, and George Washington. Visiting Peale's Philadelphia museum, the president—renowned for his courtesy to all—is fooled by one of Peale's trompe l'oeil paintings. He politely bows to two children on a staircase, but oddly they make no reaction, no response. Only when the children in question turn out to be paintings on a wall does President Washington realize that he has been fooled. Deborah Stevenson, writing in *Bulletin of the Center for Children's Books,* called *The Joke's on George* "an entertaining tale that shows Washington in a different light," and also commented that the book could lead to "some entertaining artistic discussions." A critic in *Kirkus Reviews* described the book as "a delightful vignette" and a "handsome, entertaining glimpse of times past."

Tunnell turned a traditional fairy tale on its head with his what-if rendition of Beauty and the Beast. In his *Beauty and the Beastly Children,* Tunnell imagines what might have happened after Beauty married the Beast. Beast, a.k.a. Auguste, regresses to ale drinking and darts while Beauty gives birth to rather horrid beast-like triplets. Auguste finally accepts his parental responsibilities, however, and helps to bring the unruly children around. When he does, the witch lifts the spell on the children, and finally there is a "happily ever after" ending. Tunnell related his tale in "colloquial, sassy prose," according to Susan Hepler in *School Library Journal.*

Returning to history for inspiration, Tunnell told the actual story of a girl sent by parcel post to visit her grandmother in 1914. "I especially like to write about 'little people' in history rather than the famous ones," Tunnell commented. "May Pierstorff in my picture book *Mailing May,* for instance. Parcel post was a brand new item in 1914, and May's financially strapped parents saw the new postal regulations as a way to afford sending their five-year-old daughter to visit her grandmother—for fifty-three cents they mailed her! (Her mother's cousin was the mail clerk in the railway postal car.) This may seem an insignificant bit of Americana to many people, but to me it is the marvelous story of ordinary people using creative means to solve a difficult problem. That's the stuff of history!" With a mailing label and fifty-three cents worth of stamps stuck to her coat—she is luckily under the fifty-pound parcel post limit—May sets off one morning for her visit. Her cousin Leonard is in charge of the mail, so he accompanies her on the train. Seventy-five miles later, having passed through the mountainous terrain of Idaho, she arrives safely at her grandmother's.

An American Library Association Notable Children's Book, *Mailing May* also earned high critical praise. Carolyn Phelan noted in *Booklist:* "Told in the first person from May's point of view, the story has a folksy quality and a ring of truth that will hold children's interest beyond the central anecdote." Applauding the "childlike understated quality" of the story, Betsy Groban observed in the *New York Times Book Review* that *Mailing May* "is a heartwarming period piece based on a true incident, lovingly told, beautifully illustrated and extremely well produced in an oversized format." Pat Mathews concluded in the *Bulletin of the Center for Children's Books* that "May tells the story of her bygone journey with homespun perfection, so stamp this one 'First Class' and make a special delivery to a storytime in your area."

Highly interested in historical accuracy when compiling *Mailing May,* Tunnell not only rode on the rail line which May followed, and but also found and interviewed May's son—May herself died in 1987. Additionally, he used a two-page account of the trip written by May's Cousin Leonard, the postal clerk in charge of May on her trip in February, 1914. However, for Tunnell's nonfiction book on Japanese-American internment during World War II, *The Children of Topaz,* the research was much more extensive. There was library work and also the tracking down of primary sources. "I was privileged to run into the story of Lillian 'Anne' Yamauchi Hori and her third grade class, who were interned during World War II in the Japanese-American relocation camp at Topaz, Utah. These children and their young teacher appear in no history textbooks, yet they are the ones who experienced firsthand the fallout of decisions made by well-known personalities such as Franklin Delano Roosevelt. Their illustrated class diary, an integral part of *The Children of Topaz,* helps us see and feel the effects of war hysteria and prejudice on a personal level." Tunnell and his coauthor, George Chilcoat, located the widower of the teacher as well as several of the men who, as boys, had been interned in the camp and interviewed them for the book. Female students were harder to track down because of name changes with marriage. After publication of the book however, several of the other former students contacted Tunnell and in 1996 a reunion of the class was held in Berkeley, California. "Fifteen of the twenty-three Japanese-American students, now in their sixties, attended," Tunnell related. "It was one of the most moving experiences of my life."

About a third of the class diary was used in *The Children of Topaz;* each entry is further annotated by "well-researched commentaries explaining the children's allusions, expanding upon the diary text, and placing events in socio-historical perspective," according to reviewer John Philbrook in *School Library Journal.* "Here readers are exposed to nine-year-olds writing as it happened," Philbrook concluded. *Booklist*'s Hazel Rochman noted that "the primary sources have a stark authority; it's the very ordinariness of the children's concerns that grabs you as they talk about baseball, school, becoming Scouts and Brownies." A critic in *Kirkus Reviews* commented that "Tunnell and Chilcoat provide a valuable, incisive, comprehensive text," while Elizabeth Bush concluded in a review for the *Bulletin of the Center for Children's Books* that "the ingenuous testimony left by Yamauchi's third-graders may make the Topaz story accessible to an audience slightly younger" than those for whom other such internment books have been written.

Tunnell's first novel for young readers, *School Spirits,* likewise deals with history. Set in a small town in 1958, the book is a ghost story; its writing thus combined two of Tunnell's favorite themes. "I'd say history and fantasy, not as odd a combination as some might think, are my two favorite genres when it comes to writing," Tunnell remarked. "Both history and fantasy have the ability to reveal the ageless qualities of being human. In fairytales, for instance, universal truths about the hearts and souls of people are presented in 'primary colors,' the complexities stripped away to show the basic motivations for human behaviors. In historical literature, readers are allowed to experience those same motivations throughout the millenia. History has the power to connect us to the entire human family."

Though a child of the 1950s, Tunnell once again heavily researched the period. "What music was popular? What was playing at the movies? What were the current world events? I used the town where I grew up in Alberta, Canada, as the model for Waskasoo City in the book, so I read pictorial histories of the place in order to refresh my memory. At one point, I even had to learn some particulars about locks and keys, circa 1900. Eventually I had to find a locksmith, who explained at some length what I needed to know. And I had my characters eating Oreo cookies, but I couldn't remember eating them in the fifties. Just to be sure I contacted Nabisco. Oreos hit the scene in 1912!" But Tunnell is also careful not to overburden his readers with too much history. "Authors must repress the urge to tell all the historical facts that their research has revealed. To weave historical facts deftly into the narrative is a true artform; otherwise, the story is overpowered and becomes textbook-like. That knowledge helped me when I wrote *School Spirits.*... I knew to deal carefully with all the facts about the wonderful fifties I wanted to share with my readers—still I found the job difficult, even exasperating."

School Spirits tells the story of Patrick, whose father has just become principal of Craven Hill School, a castle-like building and scene to the twentieth-century gothic tale Tunnell weaves. Though reluctant to move, Patrick quickly becomes involved in the new town, becoming friends with Nairen, the girl next door, and encountering the ghost of Barney Dawe, whose disappearance in 1920 has gone unexplained.

Patrick and Nairen soon take up the investigation, which involves researching in the town library and time-traveling down a tube-like school fire escape. Molly S. Kinney observed in *School Library Journal* that "this fast-paced story" has "solid writing and doesn't rely on buckets of blood or hacked bodies to entice readers." Writing in *Booklist,* Susan Dove Lempke noted that the "very large type makes this novel a good choice for children who are outgrowing Goosebumps books, and the 1958 setting is a change of pace from contemporary horror tales."

While still writing picture books, Tunnell has begun concentrating on longer works. "I enjoy trying my hand at the various genres and formats of literature. The economy required by the picture book format makes that sort of writing a challenge. Naturally, nonfiction books demand careful attention to factual detail, but the biggest challenge is writing nonfiction with flair. . . . The novel, however, I find the most challenging. Writing novels requires sustained imaginative output unlike picture or informational books. Creating and developing believable characters who are doing things worth reading about for one hundred pages or more is difficult yet extremely fulfilling business."

BIOGRAPHICAL/CRITICAL SOURCES:

PERIODICALS

Booklist, August 15, 1993, p. 1524; October 1, 1993, p. 349; December 15, 1993; July, 1996, p. 1818; August, 1997, p. 1908; February 15, 1998, p. 1012.
Bulletin of the Center for Children's Books, October, 1993, p. 60; September, 1996, pp. 34-35; October, 1997, p. 69.
Horn Book, July-August, 1993, p. 451; September-October, 1997, p. 564.
Kirkus Reviews, February 15, 1993, p. 235; July 1, 1993, p. 867; December 15, 1995, p. 1777; June 15, 1997, p. 958.
New York Times Book Review, March 15, 1998, p. 24.
Publishers Weekly, March 15, 1993, p. 87; July 12, 1993, p. 80; June 9, 1997, p. 45; December 8, 1997, p. 72.
School Library Journal, June, 1993, pp. 91-92; January, 1994, p. 100; August, 1996, pp. 161-162; March, 1998, p. 224.
Voice of Youth Advocates, December, 1996, p. 292; August, 1997, p. 167.

UPDYKE, Rosemary K. 1924-
(Rosemary K. Kissinger)

PERSONAL: Born April 12, 1924, in Corsicana, TX; daughter of C. C. and Polly Anna Durbin; married Herbert David Johnston (deceased); married Henry Kissinger (deceased); married Delbert N. Updyke; children: (first marriage) John Michael, Peggie Johnston Cassidy. *Education:* Attended Tyler Commercial College, Tyler, TX. *Politics:* "American." *Religion:* Catholic.

ADDRESSES: Home—183 Grand St., East Stroudsburg, PA 18301.

CAREER: Writer. American Nickeloid Co., Long Island, New York, senior secretary, 1943-63.

WRITINGS:

(As Rosemary K. Kissinger) *Quanah Parker: Comanche Chief,* Pelican (Gretna, LA), 1991.
Jim Thorpe, the Legend Remembered, Pelican (Gretna, LA), 1997.

Short story "The Cabbage Cure" published in *Teen* magazine.

WORK IN PROGRESS: A psychological mystery novel; a family history.

SIDELIGHTS: Rosemary K. Updyke commented: "I was born in Corsicana, Texas, in 1924. My mother died when I was five years old, and I was adopted by her nurse in Tyler, Texas. I attended school there through high school and continued to Tyler Commercial College, where I studied secretarial skills. World War II began, and I became a secretary to the admissions officer and then the registrar at local Camp Fannin Hospital. I married staff sergeant Herbert D. Johnston. After the war we moved to his hometown on Long Island, New York. We bought a home but eventually moved back to Tyler, where I had been raised. My son was born in New York, my daughter in Tyler. Ten years after my husband's death, I married Henry Kissinger. He died five years later, and I married Delbert Updyke. We now live in East Stroudsburg, Pennsylvania."

BIOGRAPHICAL/CRITICAL SOURCES:

PERIODICALS

Booklist, May 15, 1991, p. 1792.
Horn Book Guide, fall, 1991, p. 276; fall, 1997, p. 372.
Voice of Youth Advocates, October, 1991, p. 227.*

V

VAILL, Amanda

PERSONAL: Female.

ADDRESSES: Agent—c/o Houghton Mifflin, 222 Berkeley St., Boston, MA 02116-3764. *E-mail*—ahvail@aol.com.

CAREER: Writer and critic. Former executive editor at Viking Penguin.

WRITINGS:

Everybody Was So Young: Gerald and Sara Murphy, A Lost Generation Love Story, Houghton (Boston), 1998.

Contributor to various publications, including *Gentleman's Quarterly* and *Esquire.*

SIDELIGHTS: Amanda Vaill's *Everybody Was So Young: Gerald and Sara Murphy, A Lost Generation Love Story* was termed "fascinating and moving" and "biography at its best" by Wilda Williams in *Library Journal.* Brooke Allen wrote in the *New York Times Book Review* that Gerald and Sara Murphy were "the beautiful couple of the 1920's, and they left their mark on many works of art about the period." F. Scott Fitzgerald fashioned Dick and Nicole Diver in his *Tender Is the Night* after the Murphys. The couple also inspired works by others, including Ernest Hemingway, Philip Barry, Archibald MacLeish, John Dos Passos, and Pablo Picasso.

Young Gerald and Sara met in East Hampton, New York during the early years of the twentieth century. Gerald's father was the owner of the Mark Cross Company, known then and now for its fine leather products. Sara's father was an industrialist and both families were very wealthy. Gerald had never met his father's expectations and Sara functioned within a restrictive social world, "living life as one of the matched pieces of her mother's luggage," wrote Vaill. They became engaged in 1915, when Gerald was twenty-seven and Sara thirty-two. Her family was against the marriage. "Considering their cold and withholding families and what Sara called 'the heavy hand of chaperonage' that had always weighed firmly upon them, it is no surprise that the young Murphys looked upon their marriage not as a tie but as the beginning of glorious freedom," wrote Allen. "The Murphys cherished a Tolstoyan ideal of husband and wife working and living side by side. But this way of life was hard to bring to fruition within their parents' sphere of influence." Gerald served in the Army during World War I and studied landscape architecture at Harvard. In 1921 the Murphys took their three small children to France. Their Cote d'Azur home drew many of the artists, writers, and musicians who filled Paris at the time, and they became particularly close to Scott and Zelda Fitzgerald. The Murphys were older than the Fitzgeralds, and wealthier; and Gerald offered moral and financial support to Scott, even though "Murphy himself was all too often the butt of Fitzgerald's drunken venom," noted Allen. "He and Sara were among the few to show up at Fitzgerald's funeral. . . . Fitzgerald, however, proved himself an unreliable friend, fostering, as did Hemingway, the image of Gerald Murphy as a spoiled dilettante."

Inspired by the art of Paris, Gerald began painting in a style described by many as a kind of pop art. Gerald put aside his painting in 1929 when their youngest son, Patrick was diagnosed with tuberculosis. He and

Sara spent much of their time at the Swiss sanitarium where their son was being treated. While Patrick attempted a recovery, their older son, Baoth, developed meningitis, a complication of measles, and died in 1935. A year later, Patrick died. It appeared that the Murphys "never fully recovered from this loss," according to Christopher Lehmann-Haupt in the *New York Times Book Review*. "True, they went on creating beautiful worlds, inventing new fashions, being generous to their many friends. They both lived long lives, and Gerald gained recognition as a significant painter. . . . Eventually their surviving child, Honoria, gave them grandsons to replace at least in part what they had lost. But after the 1930's, the magic seems to have gone out of their lives."

The Murphys returned to New York. Gerald took over the Mark Cross Company, which was on the brink of failure, and turned it around, living the life he had attempted to escape. Sara became involved in volunteer work with children. Gerald died of cancer in 1964, and Sara eleven years later of pneumonia. *Booklist* reviewer Donna Seaman felt the book "restores dignity, meaning . . . luster to our impressions" of the Murphys "who have for too long been reduced to mere glitter."

BIOGRAPHICAL/CRITICAL SOURCES:

PERIODICALS

Booklist, April 15, 1998, p. 1409.
Library Journal, March 15, 1998, pp. 78-79.
New York Times Book Review, May 24, 1998; June 1, 1998.
Publishers Weekly, March 16, 1998, p. 41.*

*   *   *

VALLEE-POUSSIN, Charles Jean Gustave Nicolas de la 1866-1962

PERSONAL: Born August 14, 1866, in Louvain, Belgium; died March 2, 1962, in Louvain, Belgium; son of a professor of geology and mineralogy; married, 1900. *Education:* Jesuit College at Mons, diplome d'ingenieur, c. 1890.

CAREER: University of Louvain, assistant to Louis-Philippe Gilbert, 1891-92, professor and chair of mathematics, 1892-1962.

MEMBER: International Mathematical Union, French Academie Royales des Sciences, London Mathematical Society, Belgian Royal Academy, Legion of Honor.

AWARDS, HONORS: Prize for essay on differential equations, 1892; awarded title of baron by King of Belgium, 1928.

WRITINGS:

Cours d'analyse infinitesimale, 2 volumes, 1903-06.
Integrales de Lebesgue fonctions d'ensemble, classes de baire, 1916.
Lecons sur l'approximation des fonctions d'une variable reelle, 1919.
Lecons de mecanique analytique, 1924.
Les nouvelles methodes de la theorie du potentiel et le probleme generalise de Dirichlet: Actualites scientifiques et industrielles, 1937.
Le potentiel logarithmique, balayage et representation conforme, 1949.

Also author of papers and articles relating to mathematics.

SIDELIGHTS: Charles Jean Gustave Nicolas de la Vallee-Poussin was responsible for proving the prime number theorem. A prime number is a number that can be divided by only one and itself without producing a remainder, and Vallee-Poussin—like many others—set out to prove the relationship between prime numbers. In an article for *MAA Online,* Ivars Peterson asserted: "In effect, [the prime number theorem] states that the average gap between two consecutive primes near the number x is close to the natural logarithm of x. Thus, when x is close to 100, the natural logarithm of x is approximately 4.6, which means that in this range, roughly every fifth number should be a prime." Vallee-Poussin was additionally known for his writings about the zeta function, Lebesgue and Stieltjes integrals, conformal representation, algebraic and trigonometric polynomial approximation, trigonometric series, analytic and quasi-analytic functions, and complex variables. His writings and research, which were—and are—considered clear, stylish, and precise, were highly respected by his peers in academia and other well-placed individuals in Western society.

Despite the historical confusion posed by Vallee-Poussin's name (it is often rendered as Charles-Jean-Gustave-Nicolas, Charles-Jean Gustave Nicolas,

Charles-Joseph, Vallee Poussin, etc.), the facts surrounding his origins are well known. Vallee-Poussin was born on August 14, 1866, in Louvain, Belgium. A distant relative of the French painter Nicolas Poussin, Vallee-Poussin's father was, like himself, an esteemed teacher at the University of Louvain. (The elder Vallee-Poussin, however, specialized in geology and mineralogy.) Vallee-Poussin's family was well-off, and as a child, he found encouragement and inspiration in fellow mathematician Louis-Philippe Gilbert (some sources identify him as Louis Claude Gilbert), with whom he would eventually work.

Vallee-Poussin enrolled at the Jesuit College at Mons in southwestern Belgium, where it is said he originally intended to pursue a career in the clergy. He ultimately, however, obtained a *diplome d'ingenieur* and began to pursue a career in mathematics. In 1891, like his father and Gilbert, he became employed at the University of Louvain, where he initially worked as Gilbert's assistant. Gilbert's death the following year created an academic opening to which Vallee-Poussin was appointed in 1893, thereby earning him the title of professor of mathematics.

Although Vallee-Poussin had begun gaining recognition as early as 1892 when he won a prize for an essay on differential equations, he earned his first widespread fame four years later. In 1896, Vallee-Poussin capitalized on the ideas set forth by earlier mathematicians, notably Johann Friedrich Karl Gauss, Adrien Marie Legendre, Leonhard Euler, Peter Gustav Lejeune Dirichlet, Pafnuty Lvovich Chebyshev, and Georg Friedrich Bernhard Riemann, and proved what is now known as the prime number theorem. Vallee-Poussin shares this honor with Jacques Hadamard, who revealed his finding in the same year. Historians note, however, that Vallee-Poussin's and Hadamard's achievements were performed independently and that although both mathematicians used the Riemann zeta function in their work, they came to their conclusions in different ways.

Vallee-Poussin revealed much of his groundbreaking work in a series of celebrated books and papers. His two-volume *Cours d'analyse infinitesimale* went through several printings, and the work was consistently edited between printings to offer updated information. Initially the book was directed toward both mathematicians and students, and Vallee-Poussin used different fonts and sizes of types to differentiate between the audiences to whom a particular passage was directed. In the 1910s Vallee-Poussin was preparing the third edition of this work, but this was destroyed

by German forces, who invaded Louvain during World War I. Vallee-Poussin subsequently dedicated his 1916 *Integrales de Lebesgue fonctions d'ensemble, classes de baire* to the Lebesgue interval to compensate for the material destroyed by the Germans. Vallee-Poussin continued to publish well into his eighties, and, like *Cours d'analyse infinitesimale,* many of his writings went through various reprintings and revisions. Almost all of Vallee-Poussin's writing have been praised for their originality and the clarity of his writing style.

Vallee-Poussin, who married a Belgian woman whom he met while vacationing in Norway in the late 1890s, died on March 2, 1962, in the city of his birth. During his lifetime, he was accorded many honors. In addition to the celebrations commemorating his thirty-fifth and fiftieth anniversaries as chair of mathematics at the University of Louvain, he was elected to various prestigious institutions including the French Academie Royales des Sciences, the International Mathematical Union, the London Mathematical Society, the Belgian Royal Academy, and the Legion of Honor. In 1928 the king of Belgium also awarded him the title of baron in recognition of his years of academic tenure and his professional achievements.

BIOGRAPHICAL/CRITICAL SOURCES:

BOOKS

Burkhill, J. C., "Charles-Jean-Gustave-Nicolas de la Vallee-Poussin," in *Dictionary of Scientific Biography,* volume XIII, edited by Charles Coulston Gillispie, Charles Scribner's Sons (New York City), 1976, pp. 561-562.

Young, Laurence, *Mathematicians and Their Times: History of Mathematics and Mathematics of History,* North-Holland Publishing Company (Amsterdam), 1981, p. 306.

PERIODICALS

American Mathematical Monthly, November, 1996, pp. 729-741.

Journal of the London Mathematical Society, vol. 39, 1964, pp. 165-175.

OTHER

MAA Online, http://www.maa.org (December 23, 1996).*

VAN PATTEN, Dick 1928-

PERSONAL: Born Richard Vincent Van Patten, December 9, 1928, in Kew Gardens, NY; son of Richard (an interior decorator) and Josephine (in advertising; maiden name, Acerno) Van Patten; married Patricia Poole (a dancer), April 25, 1954; children: Nels, Jimmy, Vincent. *Education:* Attended public schools in Richmond Hills, NY. *Religion:* Catholic. *Avocational interests:* Tennis, swimming, horseback riding.

ADDRESSES: Agent—c/o Artists Agency, 10000 Santa Monica Blvd., Ste. 305, Los Angeles, CA 90067.

CAREER: Actor on stage, screen, and television, 1935—. Appeared in stage productions, including *Tapestry in Gray,* Shubert, NY, 1935; *Home Sweet Home,* Greenwich Guild Theatre, CT, 1936; *The Eternal Road,* Manhattan Opera House, 1937; *Goodbye Again,* Pine Brook Country Club, Nichols, CT, 1937; *On Borrowed Time,* Longacre, NY, 1938; *Run Sheep, Run,* Windsor, NY, 1938; *The American Way,* Center, NY, 1939; *The Woman Brown,* Wharf Theatre, Provincetown, MA, and Biltmore, New York City, 1939; *Ah! Wilderness,* Wharf Theatre, 1939, and Maplewood Theatre, NJ, 1940; *Our Girls,* Starlight Theatre, Pawling, NY, 1940; *Something about a Soldier,* Bucks County Playhouse, New Hope, PA, 1940; *Carriage Trade,* Stamford Playhouse, CT, 1940; *The Lady Who Came to Stay,* Maxine Elliott's, New York City, 1941; *The Land Is Bright,* Music Box, New York City, 1941; *Watch on the Rhine,* Majestic, Boston, MA, 1942; *Evening Rise,* Woodstock Playhouse, NY, 1942; *The Skin of Our Teeth,* Plymouth, NY, 1942; *The Snark Was a Boojum,* 48th Street Theatre, New York City, 1943; *Kiss and Tell,* Biltmore, New York City, 1943; *Decision,* Belasco, NY, 1944; *Too Hot for Maneuvers,* Broadhurst, NY, 1945; *The Wind Is Ninety,* Booth, NY, 1945; *O Mistress Mine,* Empire, NY, 1946. *Cry of the Peacock,* Locust, Philadelphia, PA, 1950; *Mister Roberts,* Alvin, NY, 1948, and Quarterdeck Theatre, Atlantic City, NJ, 1951; *Here's Mama,* Ogunquit Playhouse, ME, and Cape Playhouse, Dennis, MA, 1952; *The Male Animal,* Music Box, New York City, 1952; *The Tender Trap,* Pocono Playhouse, PA, 1955; *Oh Men! Oh Women!,* Pocono Play House, PA, 1955; *Death of a Salesman,* Long Beach Playhouse, New York City, 1955; *King of Hearts,* 1956; *Have I Got a Girl for You,* Music Box, New York City, 1963; *Don't Drink the Water,* Coconut Grove Playhouse, FL, 1968; *But Seriously. . . ,* Henry Miller's, New York City, 1969; and *Next Adaptation,* Greenwich Mews, NY, 1969. Toured in the United States and Canada in stage plays, including *Will Success Spoil Rock Hunter?,* 1957; *Golden Fleecing,* 1960; and *Strictly Dishonorable,* 1964-65.

Appeared in films, including *Reg'lar Fellers,* 1941; *Psychomania,* 1964; *Charly,* 1968; *Making It,* 1971; *Joe Kid,* 1972; *Dirty Little Billy,* 1972; *Snowball Express,* 1972; *Westworld,* 1973; *Soylent Green,* 1973; *Superdad,* 1974; *Freaky Friday,* 1976; *High Anxiety,* 1977; *Spaceballs,* 1986; *The New Adventures of Pippi Longstocking,* 1988; and *Robin Hood: Men in Tights,* 1993.

Appeared in radio plays and series, including *Young Widder Brown,* 1941; *One Foot in Heaven; Miss Hatty; Duffy's Tavern; Henry Aldrich; David Harum; Right to Happiness; Reg'lar Fellers; The March of Time; Kiss and Tell; Wednesday's Child; O Mistress Mine; Theatre; State Fair; Father of the Bride; Elmer the Great; The Major and the Minor;* and *Good Housekeeping.*

Appeared on television films and series, including *Story Hour,* 1936; *Mama,* 1949-58; *Final Ingredient,* 1959; *Dupont Show of the Month,* 1960; *Young Dr. Malone,* 1963; *The Kraft Television Theatre; Nurses; The Verdict Is Yours; Mike Hammer; Silent Service; Rawhide; Men in White; A Memory of Two Mondays,* 1971; *Partners,* 1971-72; *Hec Ramsey,* 1972; *The Crooked Hearts,* 1972; *The New Dick Van Dyke Show;* 1973-74; *When Things Were Rotten,* 1975; *Arnie; Grandpa Max,* 1975; *Ladies of the Corridor,* 1975; *The Love Boat,* 1976; *Eight Is Enough,* 1977-81 (and subsequent reunion specials); *With This Ring,* 1978; *Diary of Hitchhiker,* 1979; *Going to the Chapel,* 1988; *Jake Spanner, Private Eye,* 1989; and *WIOU,* 1990.

Appeared in videotapes, including *Couples Do It Debbie's Way,* 1988; *Single Parenting,* 1989; *Radon Free,* 1989; *Dirty Tennis,* 1989; and *Blended Families: Yours, Mine, Ours,* 1991.

MEMBER: Screen Actors Guild, Actors Equity Association.

AWARDS, HONORS: Donaldson Award, 1941, for *The Lady Who Came to Stay.*

WRITINGS:

(With Peter Berk) *Launching Your Child in Show Biz: A Complete Step-by-Step Guide,* General Publishing Group (Los Angeles, CA), 1997.

SIDELIGHTS: Actor Dick Van Patten began his show business career when he was seven years old, making his stage debut in *Tapestry in Gray* in 1935. The following year, at least a decade before most people had even heard of the medium, he was a cast member of the children's television show *Story Hour.* As Van Patten grew up, he worked continuously on both stage and in radio programs; one of his well-known roles was as Mark Brown in the *Young Widder Brown* radio series. He returned to television in 1949, playing Nels on *Mama* for nine years. Van Patten appeared in films as well. One of the few child actors to see success as an adult, he eventually became famous for his patriarchal role on the family television drama *Eight Is Enough.* His latter-day film appearances have included comedies directed by Mel Brooks—such as *High Anxiety,* which spoofed famed horror film director Alfred Hitchcock's *Vertigo; Spaceballs,* which parodied director George Lucas's *Star Wars* trilogy; and *Robin Hood: Men in Tights,* which took many of its laughs by poking fun at the popular Kevin Costner version of *Robin Hood.* Van Patten remained busy on television as well, returning for two *Eight Is Enough* reunion specials and appearing in shows such as *Going to the Chapel* and *Jake Spanner: Private Eye.* In even later projects, Van Patten has narrated nonfiction videos—on subjects ranging from detecting radon in the home to helping mesh families from the partners' previous marriages. He also made a humorous video with his son James, titled *Dirty Tennis.*

In *Single Parenting,* a video Van Patten narrated in 1989, he discusses many of the issues confronting single parents, including the negative myths about them that pervade American culture. The tape focuses mainly on the single-parent situation stemming from divorce, and offers tips on how divorced parents can limit the stress that divorce causes their children. Also included is a segment on single parenting after the death of a spouse, which discusses the stages of grief. Judy Gray gave the video high marks in *School Library Journal,* asserting that it "provides a great deal of information and should provoke thought and discussion." Van Patten also narrated 1991's *Blended Families: Yours, Mine, Ours.* This video provides viewers with a number of skits presenting various problems which may crop up when two people who already have children from previous marriages marry each other. Although Margaret B. Miller in the *School Library Journal* found *Blended Families* to be "very talky," she praised the handling of the kinds of issues that can confront blended families. Irene Wood in *Booklist,* however, found the video to be somewhat "hurried," but applauded the inclusion of "well structured and comprehensible" information.

More lighthearted was Van Patten's role in 1989's *Dirty Tennis.* This tape offers viewers tricks for winning at tennis, including wearing bizarre and visually distracting tennis clothing, and making your opponent think you are too drunk to play the match. Tom Cunneff in *People* magazine pronounced it "a must for the tennis player who'll stop at nothing to win, or to get a laugh."

BIOGRAPHICAL/CRITICAL SOURCES:

BOOKS

Contemporary Theatre, Film, and Television, Volume 1, Gale (Detroit, MI), 1984.

PERIODICALS

Booklist, March 1, 1992, p. 1293.
People Weekly, June 12, 1989, p. 20.
School Library Journal, September, 1989, p. 192; July, 1992, p. 43.*

* * *

VAN STEENHOUSE, Andrea 1943-

PERSONAL: Born February 4, 1943, in Los Angeles, CA; daughter of James (a printer) and Margaret Elliott; married Patrick Kowaleski (an attorney); children: James, John, Michael. *Education:* San Jose State University, B.A.; Central Michigan University, M.A.; Michigan State University, Ph.D. *Politics:* Independent. *Religion:* Presbyterian.

ADDRESSES: Home—Denver, CO. *Office*—222 Milwaukee, Suite 403, Denver, CO 80206; fax 303-377-1496. *E-mail*—anerus2@aol.com.

CAREER: Central Michigan University, Mount Pleasant, teacher of guidance and counselor education, 1969-71; Michigan State University, East Lansing, teacher of psychiatry, 1974-79, teacher in International Education Program in Okinawa, Japan, 1978; Stress Management, Inc., Denver, CO, president, 1979—. Stress Management, Inc., Okemos, MI, president, 1977-79. KNUS-Radio, host of *The Andrea Van Steenhouse Show,* 1982; KOA-Radio, host of *The Andrea Van Steenhouse Show,* 1983-94; KCNC-TV, host of the weekly public affairs program *Dimension 4,* 1987-88, commentator on *Answers from Andrea,* 1989-90; KUSA-TV, human behavior commentator, 1990. Colorado State Board of Psychologist Examiners, member of board of directors. Aurora Humana Hospital, chairperson and member of board of directors; member of board of directors of Adoption Option, Aurora Community Mental Health, Aurora Chamber of Commerce, and Medical Development International; honorary member of board of directors, Comitis Crisis Center and Grief Education Institute.

MEMBER: Zonta Club of Aurora (founding member; president).

AWARDS, HONORS: Womanschool Network Award, achievement by women in media, 1985; E. Ellis Graham Award, excellence in psychology, Colorado Psychological Association, 1996.

WRITINGS:

Life Lines: A Personal Journal, privately printed, 1987.
A Woman's Guide to a Simpler Life, Crown (New York City), 1996.
Empty Nest . . . Full Heart: The Journal from Home to College, Simpler Life Press, 1998.

Author of "Innervision," a column in *Aurora Sentinel,* 1985-86, "Andrea Van Steenhouse: Questions and Answers," a column in *Denver Parent,* 1988-93, and "One Slice at a Time," a column in *Rocky Mountain News,* 1989-91. Board member, *Colorado Woman.*

WORK IN PROGRESS: Clotheslines; What's Next?; Simpler Gourmet Cookbook; research on alternatives to traditional hormone replacement therapy.

SIDELIGHTS: Andrea Van Steenhouse told *CA:* "As a psychologist in private practice and a radio talk show host for many years, I began to see patterns in the emerging issues. There were a lot of people out there who were asking about the same issues over and over. I was talking with them one-on-one in my office or with very short sound bites on the air. Neither of these methods was very efficient. More importantly, it also hit me that as a wife and mother, those same issues were ones I had to deal with myself.

"I've always liked to write. To me, words are fun, instructive, and heartwarming. Writing books seemed the natural alternative to all that talking, far more time-efficient. Each of my books was written as a

reflection of events in my life and the lives of those close to me, but with the intention of stimulating readers to create their own solutions to the issue at hand. When I hear from a reader who says, 'You described my situation perfectly. How did you know?' I feel I've succeeded. Written words have done their deed.

"This success story didn't happen overnight, and certainly not without the strong and caring direction of my mentor brother, Bob Elliott, a seasoned corporate leader. He understands where I want to go and has good ideas of how to get there.

"When people ask me how I go about writing a book, my answer is that I have to have a valid idea first. That's the hardest part, for sure. In my book *Empty Nest . . . Full Heart: The Journey from Home to College,* it was the overwhelming task of sending my son John off to college that prompted the start of the book. I was seeing my own panicky look reflected in the eyes of hundreds of other parents with whom I came in contact during that too long-too short year. Developing the whole book concept takes the most concentrated energy, because each of the sub-ideas has to be fully validated as genuine and useful before I can include it. After that task, the writing is easy. I have often said to my colleagues, 'I feel this book is writing itself!'"

*   *   *

VAN TILBURG, Hans (Konrad) 1961-

PERSONAL: Born October 12, 1961, in NJ; son of Richard and Munua Van Tilburg; married Maria Da Silva, 1991; children: Sabina Fe. *Ethnicity:* "Chinese American." *Education:* University of California, Berkeley, B.A., 1985; attended NAUI College, 1987, and San Francisco State University, 1988; East Carolina University, M.A., 1994; doctoral study at University of Hawaii at Manoa. *Avocational interests:* Sailing, scuba diving.

ADDRESSES: Home—2111-A Chamberlain St., Honolulu, HI 96822. *Office*—Marine Option Program, 229 Marine Science Bldg., University of Hawaii at Manoa, 1000 Pope Rd., Honolulu, HI 96822. *E-mail*—74653.721@compuserve.com and mop@hawaii.edu.

CAREER: University of California, Berkeley, instructor in scientific diving techniques, 1985-87; worked as commercial inshore and offshore diver in Louisiana and California, 1987; sport diving instructor in California and North Carolina, 1987-92; State Historical Society of Wisconsin, diving safety supervisor and crew chief, 1993; teacher of summer field courses in maritime archaeology techniques, 1995-98. East Carolina University, diving safety supervisor, crew chief, and instructor, 1991-93; Society for Historic Preservation and Investigation, Chuuk, Micronesia, consultant; participated as investigator, dive master, crew chief, and diving safety officer for field expeditions, including Apostle Islands Shipwreck Survey, 1990, U.S.S. *Maple Leaf* Project, 1992-93, *Niagara* Project, 1993, Bermuda underwater survey, 1993, Claflin Point Project, 1995, *Ko'a* underwater reef survey, 1996, Kona Coast nautical archaeology survey, 1997, Midway Atoll initial sites survey, 1998, and landing/shipwreck inventory on Oahu, 1998. Worked as sailor aboard the sloops *Brunhilde, Mermaid,* and *Westwind,* prior to 1992; certified scuba diver, c. 1971—. Worked as a carpenter in California, 1985-91.

MEMBER: North American Society for Oceanic History, Association for Asian Studies, Society for Historical Archaeology.

WRITINGS:

(Coeditor) *Maritime Archaeology: A Reader of Substantive and Theoretical Contributions,* Plenum (New York City), 1998.
(Contributor) *International Handbook of Underwater Archaeology,* Plenum, 1999.

Contributor of articles and reviews to periodicals, including *International Journal of Nautical Archaeology, Foghorn Journal, Mains'l Haul: Journal of Maritime History, Explorations in Southeast Asian Studies,* and *American Neptune.*

WORK IN PROGRESS: Historical research on plantation landings and shipwrecks in Hawaii; research on Chinese sailors of the Pacific diaspora.

*   *   *

VASOLI, Robert H. 1925-

PERSONAL: Born July 24, 1925; married Mary Jeanne Weber; children: Anthony, Vincent, Maria,

and Theresa. *Education:* La Salle College, B.A. (magna cum laude), 1952; University of Notre Dame, M.A. (sociology), 1953; Ph.D. (sociology), 1964.

ADDRESSES: Home—1141 Blaine Ave., South Bend, IN 46616. *Office*—Department of Sociology, University of Notre Dame, South Bend, IN 46556.

CAREER: Educator and author. University of Notre Dame, teaching assistant, 1953-58, instructor, 1958-60, assistant professor, 1963-68, associate professor, 1968-91, associate professor-emeritus, 1991—; Le Moyne College, instructor, 1961-63; Valparaiso University, visiting professor, 1972; Indiana University, visiting professor, 1974-76. *Military service:* U.S. Navy, 1943-46.

MEMBER: Fellowship of Catholic Scholars.

WRITINGS:

(With John R. Maiolo) *The Labeling Perspective: A Bibliography of Research,* Council of Planning Librarians (Monticello, IL), 1975.
What God Has Joined Together: The Annulment Crisis in American Catholicism, Oxford University Press (New York City), 1998.

Contributor to books, including *Probation and Parole: Selected Readings,* edited by Robert M. Carter and Leslie T. Wilkins, John Wiley & Sons (New York City), 1970; and *The Sociology of American Poverty,* edited by H. Paul Chalfont and Joan Huber, Schenkman (Cambridge, MA), 1974.

Contributor to periodicals and reviews, including *American Catholic Sociological Review, New York Law Journal, Crime and Delinquency, Notre Dame Journal of Law, Ethic, & Public Policy, Wall Street Journal,* and *South Bend Tribune.*

WORK IN PROGRESS: Preliminary research on sanctions in the U.S. Church, and keeping *What God Has Joined Together* current.

SIDELIGHTS: Robert H. Vasoli is a retired professor of sociology who taught at the University of Notre Dame. In 1975 Vasoli, along with John R. Maiolo, published a bibliography of deviant behavior and labeling theories. Also a lay Catholic, Vasoli spent time before and after his retirement working on a book on marriage annulments that was published in 1998 as

What God Has Joined Together: The Annulment Crisis in American Catholicism.

In *What God Has Joined Together* Vasoli analyzes the Catholic Church's U.S.-based marriage tribunals and their approaches to marriage annulments. A marriage annulment is an official recognition from a Catholic Church tribunal that the marriage under consideration was invalid, and with a corresponding increase in the nation's divorce rate, a tremendous increase in marriage annulments occurred in the United States in the late twentieth century. In his book, Vasoli endeavors to chart, explain, and, through the powers of persuasion, perhaps slow or reverse the trend.

Up until 1968, the U.S. diocesan tribunal system had granted fewer than five hundred annulments annually. One decade later, some diocesan tribunals in the United States were issuing more annulments in a single year than all the tribunals in the United States had granted annually up to that point.

Reasons for annulments can vary, but approximately two-thirds of those granted in the United States are given on the grounds of "defective matrimonial consent." Vasoli concentrates on these cases to explore how judges use their own "psychological insights" and questionable jurisprudence to justify annulments that would have been denied by tribunals before the implementation of Vatican II in 1968.

Vasoli told *CA:* "Researching and writing *What God Has Joined Together* was a radical though not complete change from toiling in the fields of criminology and criminal justice. All three specialties deal with law. Two consequences of the book's publication may be worth noting. First, it enabled me to surpass Warhol's fifteen-minute fame quota—national TV appearance, reviews in mainstream publications, and a flood of mail from parties to annulments. Second, the book shows that an old dog can learn new tricks."

"*What God Has Joined Together* is the first book-length critique of the U.S. marriage tribunal system. At the very least, it demonstrates that the U.S. Catholic Church and the Vatican are poles apart on the issue of annulment."

BIOGRAPHICAL/CRITICAL SOURCES:

PERIODICALS

Library Journal, February 15, 1998, p. 148.
Time, May 12, 1997.

OTHER

Barnes & Noble, http://www.barnesandnoble.com (1998).

*   *   *

VAUGHAN, David   1924-

PERSONAL: Born May 17, 1924, in London, England; son of Albert George (a company executive) and Rose (a homemaker; maiden name, Martin) Vaughan. *Ethnicity:* "White." *Education:* Attended Wadham College, Oxford, 1942-43. *Politics:* Democrat. *Avocational interests:* Singing.

ADDRESSES: Home—New York, NY. *Office*—Cunningham Dance Foundation, 55 Bethune St., New York, NY 10014; fax 212-633-2453. *Agent*—Robert Cornfeld, 145 West 79th St., New York, NY 10024. *E-mail*—loosestrife@earthlink.net.

CAREER: Cunningham Dance Foundation, New York City, archivist, 1959—, and secretary of board of directors. Worked as an actor, singer, and dancer. John Cage Trust, member of board of trustees. *Military service:* British Army, 1944-47; became staff sergeant.

MEMBER: Dance Critics Association, Society of Dance History Scholars.

AWARDS, HONORS: De La Torre Bueno Prize, 1977, for the *Frederick Ashton and His Ballets.*

WRITINGS:

Frederick Ashton and His Ballets, Knopf (New York City), 1977, revised edition, Dance Books, 1999.
Merce Cunningham: Fifty Years, Aperture (New York City), 1997.

*   *   *

VAZIRANI, Reetika

PERSONAL: Born in India. *Education:* Attended the University of Virginia, Harvard University, and Boston University; postgraduate work in publishing and English language poetry conducted in India, China, Thailand, and Japan.

ADDRESSES: Office—P.O. Box 60 Sweet Briar College, Sweet Briar, VA 24595-1807; fax: 804-381-6173. *E-mail*—rvazirani@sbc.edu.

CAREER: Instructor, University of Virginia, 1996-97; advisory and contributing editor, Shenandoah, 1997—; Margaret Banister Writer-in-Residence, Sweet Briar College, 1998—. Also worked as personal secretary to Derek Walcott and as assistant to Rita Dove. Visiting assistant professor, University of Oregon, 1997.

MEMBER: Poetry Society of America.

AWARDS, HONORS: Discovery award, *Nation,* 1994; Barnard New Women Poets Prize, 1995, for *White Elephants;* Virginia Faulkner Award for Literary Excellence, 1997; selected to participate in *Poets and Writers* 1998 Writers Exchange program.

WRITINGS:

White Elephants (poetry), Beacon Press (Boston), 1996.

Contributor of poetry to publications, including *Nation, Kenyan Review, Callaloo, Prairie Schooner, International Quarterly, Paris Review,* and *American Voice.*

WORK IN PROGRESS: "*Inventing Maya Biswas, My Mother,* poems; *It's Me I'm Not Home,* poems; a novel."

SIDELIGHTS: Born in India, Reetika Vazirani is the Margaret Banister Writer-in-Residence at Sweet Briar College in Virginia. Vazirani's first book of poetry, *White Elephants,* "feels like a finely calibrated emotional instrument," according to a reviewer in the *Virginia Quarterly Review.* Vazirani uses Hindi words and phrasing in writing of the experience of the Indian immigrant in the United States and draws upon images of friends and family in creating her poetry. The first section of the book features the voice of Mrs. Biswas in poems titled "Mrs. Biswas Gives Advice to a Granddaughter," Mrs. Biswas Goes through a Photo Album," and others. The reviewer noted that "Letter to a Husband" "recalls and rivals" poems found in Ezra Pound's *Cathay.*

"The Rajdhani Express" is the title of the second part of *White Elephants.* The final section is titled "White Elephants," and consists of forty-two "sonnetlike pieces," explained Barbara Hoffert, writing in *Library Journal.* Hoffert felt that Vazirani "treats the immigration as an extended voyage" and said the poems "never fall into the trap of seeming exotic."

BIOGRAPHICAL/CRITICAL SOURCES:

PERIODICALS

Library Journal, June 1, 1996, p. 114.
Virginia Quarterly Review, autumn, 1996, p. 135.

*   *   *

VERBOVEN, Agnes 1951-

PERSONAL: Born August 8, 1951, in Paal, Belgium; daughter of Louis (a teacher) and Margareta (a teacher; maiden name, Reynders) Verboven; married Philippe Werck (a publisher), June 23, 1978; children: Sigrid, Kristien. *Education:* Limburgs Universitair Centrum (Diepenbeek, Belgium), Licentiate Toegepaste Economische Wetenschappen, 1972. *Religion:* Catholic. *Avocational interests:* Reading, gardening, visiting antique markets, cooking, going out for dinner with good friends, playing tennis, traveling, and studying foreign languages.

ADDRESSES: Home—Smetstraat 36, B-3501 Hasselt, Belgium. *Office*—Clavis, Vooruitzichtstraat 42, B-3500 Hasselt, Belgium.

CAREER: Bell-ITT, Antwerp, Belgium, market researcher, 1972-73; Universitaire Faculteiten Sint-Ignatius Te Antwerpen, Belgium, economic researcher, 1973-75; Limburgs Universitair Centrum, Diepenbeek, Belgium, economic researcher, 1975-79; Poespas (children's book store), Hasselt, Belgium, owner and bookseller, 1979—; Clavis (children's book publisher), Hasselt, editor and co-founder, 1984—; conducted a radio talk show about children's books for fourteen years.

MEMBER: Soroptimists of Hasselt.

AWARDS, HONORS: Briljanten Leeuwtje, Province of Limburg (Belgium), for dedication to the promotion of children's books, 1996.

WRITINGS:

IN ENGLISH TRANSLATION

Ducks Like to Swim, illustrations by Anne Westerduin, translation from original Dutch manuscript, *Alle Eendjes Zwemmen in Het Water,* by Dominic Barth, Orchard, 1997.

OTHER

Also author of seventeen other titles for young children that have been published in Dutch and other languages including French, German, and Japanese.

Ducks Like to Swim has also been translated into German and Norwegian.

WORK IN PROGRESS: *A Day at the Playground,* "another picture book for the very young ones, published in Dutch (my native tongue) as *Een Dagje naar de Speeltuin,* 1998."

SIDELIGHTS: Agnes Verboven commented: "As the fifth child out of eight, I started reading at the age of five; my three older brothers and one sister taught me how to read. My real interest in children's books started when my oldest daughter was still very young, and I began reading stories aloud to her. The ultimate pleasure that books gave us made me believe that children's books are indispensable to the education of children.

"While my children were young, my family lived in an area where good children's books were hard to find. That's why my husband and I decided to start a specialized children's bookstore, which we have had now for almost twenty years. Six years after we opened our store, we started our own children's book publishing company, Clavis. Meanwhile, I've done almost everything possible to promote children's books: I've given lectures to children, parents, and teachers, and I had my own little radio show for fourteen years.

"I first started writing stories for picture books because none of our authors at Clavis were coming up with appropriate stories, and I discovered that I really loved writing them. So I started my modest writing career to fill in the gaps in existing children's books. I hope to go on writing story lines for picture books because that's what I like most; it seems easy to do, but it isn't. My oldest daughter is now working with us in the publishing house, and we've found that we share the same love for children's books. It's a nice idea to know that she once inspired all of our publishing success."

Ducks Like to Swim is Verboven's first picture book to have been translated and published in English. The barnyard animals in this story have spoken to children all over the world in four different languages. Mother Duck's conflict defies cultural boundaries: There is simply not enough water in the pond. Rallying behind Mother Duck, the barnyard animals form a chorus and clamor for rain. The "satisfying conclusion" noted by *School Library Journal* reviewer Susan M. Moore, and "the toddler-like antics of the smallest duckling" admired by *Booklist* critic Julie Corsaro will both be likely to please young children. Acknowledging the enthusiastic participatory effect with which the animal choir is apt to infect young readers, a *Kirkus Reviews* critic encouraged adults selecting *Ducks like to Swim* to "plan a noisy story hour."

BIOGRAPHICAL/CRITICAL SOURCES:

PERIODICALS

Booklist, September 1, 1997, p. 136.
Kirkus Reviews, June 15, 1997, p. 958.
School Library Journal, September, 1997, p. 197.*

*   *   *

VIDRINE, Beverly Barras 1938-

PERSONAL: Born September 30, 1938, in New Iberia, LA; daughter of Charles (a building contractor) and Estelle (Rouly) Barras; married Dennis J. Vidrine (an attorney), July 22, 1961; children: Denise Vidrine Torian, William, Kenneth. *Education:* University of Southwestern Louisiana, B.A.; attended Lamar State College of Technology (now Lamar University) and the Institute of Children's Literature. *Religion:* Catholic.

ADDRESSES: *Home*—1000 Kim Dr., Lafayette, LA 70503. *E-mail*—barras@iamerica.net.

CAREER: Elementary school teacher in Lafayette, LA, 1960-61, 1973, 1988-1991, Beaumont, TX, 1961-62, 1964-65, Baton Rouge, LA, 1970-72, and Broussard, LA, 1973-76; law office of Dennis J. Vidrine, Lafayette, office manager, legal secretary, and bookkeeper, 1976-88.

MEMBER: Writers Guild of Acadiana (historian, 1991—), Society of Children's Book Writers and Illustrators.

WRITINGS:

A Mardi Gras Dictionary, illustrated by Patrick Soper, Sunflower (Lafayette, LA), 1994.
A Christmas Dictionary, illustrated by Soper, Pelican (Gretna, LA), 1997.

Contributor of short fiction to magazines, including *U.S. Kids.*

WORK IN PROGRESS: St. Patrick's Day from A to Z and *Easter from A to Z.**

*   *   *

VOSTI, Stephen A.   1955-

PERSONAL: Born February 26, 1955, in California; married; children: three. *Education:* Attended Institute of European Studies, Madrid, Spain, 1975-76; Whitman College, B.A., 1977; University of Pennsylvania, M.Sc., 1981, Ph.D., 1982.

ADDRESSES: Office—Environment and Production Technology Division, International Food Policy Research Institute, 2033 K St. N.W., Washington, DC 20006; fax 202-467-4439. *E-mail*—s.vosti@cgiar .org.

CAREER: Federal University of Minas Gerais, Minas Gerais, Brazil, visiting professor and postdoctoral research fellow in population sciences at Centro de Desenvolvimento e Planejamento Regional, 1985-87; International Food Policy Research Institute, Wash-

ington, DC, research fellow in Environment and Production Technology Division, 1987—.

MEMBER: American Economic Association, American Agricultural Economic Association, Population Association of America, Latin American Studies Association, Associacao Brasileira de Estudos Populacionais, Sociedade Brasileira de Econometria, Sociedade Brasileira de Economia Rural, Phi Beta Kappa.

AWARDS, HONORS: Rockefeller Foundation fellow in Brazil, 1985-87; grants from Empresa Brasileira de Pesquisa Agropecuaria, 1988-92, 1996-98, Rockefeller Foundation, 1990, U.S. Agency for International Development and government of Italy, both 1993, Swiss Development Cooperation, 1996, Overseas Development Administration, 1996, 1997, and Inter-American Development Bank, Global Environmental Fund, International Centre for Research in Agroforestry, and Denmark International Development Agency, all 1996-98.

WRITINGS:

(Editor with T. Reardon, and contributor) *Agricultural Sustainability, Growth, and Poverty Alleviation: A Policy and Agroecological Perspective,* Johns Hopkins University Press (Baltimore, MD), 1997.
(Coauthor of foreword) M. D. Faminow, editor, *Cattle, Deforestation, and Development in the Amazon: An Economic, Agronomic, and Environmental Perspective,* CAB International (Wallingford, England), 1998.

Contributor to professional journals, popular magazines, and newspapers, including *Diversity, Journal of Health Economics, World Development, Coastal Grower, Quarterly Journal of International Agriculture, Washington Economic Reports,* and *Agroforestry Systems.*

W-Z

WALLACE, George C(orley) 1919-1998

OBITUARY NOTICE—See index for *CA* sketch: Born August 25, 1919, in Clio, AL; died of cardiac and respiratory arrest, September 13, 1998, in Montgomery, AL. Attorney, judge, governor, and author. Wallace, a former governor of Alabama, was a career politician best known for his racist policies and inaugural gubernatorial speech in which he vowed, "Segregation now, segregation tomorrow, segregation forever." Wallace grew up a two-time Golden Gloves boxing champion and got a job as a fifteen-year-old page in the Alabama Senate. He worked a variety of jobs while at the University of Alabama, including waiting tables and driving a taxi. He graduated from law school in 1942 and was named assistant attorney general in 1946. From 1947 to 1953 he served as a member of the Barbour County Legislature and followed that with a five-year term as a judge in the third judicial district.

Wallace made his first unsuccessful bid for governor in 1958, with the endorsement of the National Association for the Advancement of Colored People (NAACP), but was defeated by avowed racist John Patterson. After that Wallace strengthened his racial stance and was elected governor in 1962. It was during his first term in office that he found himself at the center of America's civil rights battle. Later that year he had a "stand in the schoolhouse door" to prevent the enrollment of two black students at the University of Alabama. The students were eventually admitted with the help of federal troops, and two years later Wallace again placed himself at the vortex of the civil rights battle when he ordered state troopers to block a march planned by activists between Selma and Montgomery.

As his term neared its end, Wallace unsuccessfully tried to amend the state constitution so he could run again. When the amendment was not approved Wallace talked his cancer-riddled wife Lurleen into running for the post. Lurleen Wallace was elected Alabama's only female governor, but died in office in 1968. It was that year that his first book, *Hear Me Out,* was published. Wallace had run the governor's office during his wife's tenure and he was elected back to the position in the 1970s. Wallace had already made runs for the presidency in 1964 and 1968, and was gearing up for another in 1972 when he was shot during a campaign appearance at a shopping mall in Laurel, Maryland. Wallace's hopes for the Oval Office were effectively ended when one of the five shots lodged a bullet in his spine, paralyzing him from the waist down and confining him to a wheelchair. He was re-elected governor in 1974 and although he started a final presidential campaign in 1976, he was beaten in primaries by Governor Jimmy Carter of Georgia.

Wallace took a brief respite from politics near the end of the decade and authored *Stand up for America* in 1976, but was back in the governor's office in 1983 in an unprecedented fourth term. Wracked with pain and illness related to the shooting, Wallace retired from politics in the late 1980s after attempting a revision of history by saying that he had been wrong about segregation and that his comments never reflected on blacks, apologizing if he was misinterpreted due to lack of clarity about his position.

OBITUARIES AND OTHER SOURCES:

PERIODICALS

Chicago Tribune, September 14, 1998, sec. 4, p.8.

CNN Interactive (electronic), September 14, 1998.
Los Angeles Times, September 14, 1998, p. A1.
New York Times, September 15, 1998, p. B 10.
Times (London), September 15, 1998.
USA Today, September 14, 1998.
Washington Post, September 15, 1998, p. B6.

*   *   *

WATSON, Donald 1946-

PERSONAL: Born March 18, 1946, in Yorkshire, England. *Education:* Cambridge University, M.A., 1974; University of Essex, M.A., 1974.

ADDRESSES: Home and office—54 Woodside House, Woodside, Wimbledon, London SW19 7QN, England; fax +44-181-946-0411. *Agent*—Jeffrey Simmons, 10 Lowndes Sq., London SW1X 9HA, England.

CAREER: Freelance writer, teacher, and trainer of teachers. Lecturer at universities in England and abroad. British Broadcasting Corp., scriptwriter and broadcaster. Healer and teacher of Kabbalah.

MEMBER: National Federation of Spiritual Healers, Society of Authors, Scientific and Medical Network, College of Psychic Studies.

AWARDS, HONORS: Awards from English-speaking Union, 1991 and 1992.

WRITINGS:

A Dictionary of Mind and Spirit, Deutsch (London), 1991.
A Dictionary of Mind and Body, Deutsch, 1995.

WORK IN PROGRESS: A novel.

*   *   *

WATTS, Julia 1969-

PERSONAL: Born November 18, 1969, in Corbin, KY; daughter of Rayford (a professor of English) and June (a sculptor and artist; maiden name, Queener) Watts. *Education:* University of Tennessee, B.A.,

1992; University of Louisville, M.A., 1994. *Religion:* Unitarian Universalist. *Avocational interests:* Movies, reading books, cooking.

ADDRESSES: Home—Knoxville, TN. *E-mail*—Julia W7590@aol.com.

CAREER: Knoxville College, Knoxville, TN, instructor, 1994-97; Knoxville Business College, Knoxville, instructor, 1997—.

AWARDS, HONORS: Grant from Kentucky Foundation for Women, 1995, 1997.

WRITINGS:

Wildwood Flowers (novel), Naiad Press (Tallahassee, FL), 1996.
Phases of the Moon (young adult novel), Naiad Press, 1997.
Piece of My Heart (novel), Naiad Press, 1998.
Wedding Bell Blues (comic novel), Naiad Press, 1999.

WORK IN PROGRESS: Mixed Blessings, a "mainstream adult comic novel."

SIDELIGHTS: Julia Watts commented: "When I was writing *Phases of the Moon,* I was aware that the book could appeal to a younger audience. After all, the novel's protagonist, Glenda Mooney, is under the age of eighteen for most of the novel's duration. But since *Phases* was to be published by Naiad Press, a lesbian/feminist publishing company, I didn't anticipate that the novel would necessarily reach younger readers. I am delighted to hear that younger readers have found the book and have found both meaning and entertainment in its pages.

"Glenda Mooney is my favorite fictional creation to date. Of course, I would be lying if I said I truly created her. Like Athena springing fully formed from the head of Zeus, Glenda sprang from my head as a fully developed character and proceeded to tell me her story. It is a story of growing up in poverty-stricken eastern Kentucky, with the knowledge that she is different from those around her, but still facing life with confidence, humor, and optimism. Like a dutiful copyist, I wrote down her story as she related it to me, and when the story was written and Glenda was gone from my head, I missed her the same way I would miss a close friend who moved away. I hope that Glenda comes alive for readers as much as she came alive for me."*

WEISMAN, Leslie Kanes 1945-

PERSONAL: Born November 8, 1945, in Detroit, MI; daughter of Marvin (a lawyer) and Mollie Kanes. *Education:* Wayne State University, B.F.A. (interior architecture), cum laude, 1967; University of Detroit, M.A. (urban studies), magna cum laude, 1973.

ADDRESSES: Home—99 Bank Street, Apt. 3K, New York, NY 10014. *Office*—School of Architecture, New Jersey Institute of Technology, University Heights, Newark, NJ 07102.

CAREER: Educator and author. University of Detroit, Detroit, assistant professor, 1968-75; New Jersey Institute of Technology, Newark, associate professor of architecture, 1975-97, associate dean, 1984-85, professor of architecture, 1998—; Brooklyn College, visiting professor of women's studies, 1980; Massachusetts Institute of Technology, visiting associate professor of architecture, planning, and women's studies, 1986; University of Illinois at Urbana-Champaign, George A. Miller Endowment Professor, 1995-96. Detroit City Planning Commission and Detroit Historical Society, consultant, both 1969-75; Women's School of Planning and Architecture, co-founder, 1974-81; Networks, Women in Architecture (professional organization), New York City, co-founder, 1977-82; Sheltering Ourselves (international educational forum on housing and economic development for low income women and their families), co-founder, 1987—.

AWARDS, HONORS: Selected as an Outstanding Educator in America, 1971; Excellence in Teaching Award, 1990, Foundation Overseer's Award for Public and Institute Service, 1993, both New Jersey Institute of Technology; *Discrimination by Design: A Feminist Critique of the Man-Made Environment* named "One of the Best Academic Books of 1993," and as "An Outstanding Contribution to Human Rights in the United States," 1994; Association of Collegiate Schools of Architecture, National Creative Achievement Award, 1994; International Book Publishing Award for Excellence in Design Theory, American Institute of Architects, 1997, for *The Sex of Architecture.*

WRITINGS:

Discrimination by Design: A Feminist Critique of the Man-Made Environment, University of Illinois Press (Urbana), 1992.

(Co-editor, with Diane Agrest and Patricia Conway) *The Sex of Architecture,* Abrams (New York City), 1996.

A Chinese language edition of *Discrimination by Design: A Feminist Critique of the Man-Made Environment* was published in 1997.

Contributor of chapters to books, including *Architecture: A Place for Women,* edited by Ellen Perry Berkeley and Matilda McQuaid, Smithsonian Institution Press, 1989; *The Knowledge Explosion: Generations of Feminist Scholarship,* edited by Dale Spender and Cheris Kramarae, Teachers College Press, 1992; *The Encyclopedia of Housing,* edited by Villem van Vliet, Sage Publications, 1998; *The International Encyclopedia of Feminism,* edited by Dale Spender and Cheris Kramarae, Simon & Schuster (New York City), 1999; and *Design and Feminism: Re-Visioning Spaces, Places, and Everyday Things,* edited by Joan Rothschild, Rutgers University Press, 1999.

SIDELIGHTS: Leslie Kanes Weisman, a professor of architecture, looks at the design of the built and planned environment from a feminist perspective. Her 1992 book, *Discrimination by Design: A Feminist Critique of the Man-Made Environment,* traces the social and architectural histories of several kinds of "spatial settings"—from private dwellings to public buildings and spaces. She posits that architecture has often been designed for men's comfort and at the expense of women and children. She notes, for instance, that maternity hospitals were originally designed to maximize male doctors' profits and convenience and that the more women-friendly birthing centers were not designed until women demanded them. Weisman's concerns run from the mundane— the lack of enough toilet facilities for women in many public spaces—to the overarching—the hostility of the urban environment to women who use public transportation in higher numbers than men, and who rent more low-income housing than men. When she turns her attention to the private home, Weisman blames the "family mystique" and patriarchal society for the paucity of housing choices for those who live outside the bounds of the traditional nuclear family unit.

In the *Women's Review of Books* Joni Seagar noted that "space and place matter." Seagar praised *Discrimination by Design* as "a fast-moving, insightful, politically astute and upfront feminist examination of the power struggles in building and controlling space." Moira Kenney, reviewing the work in the *San Francisco Review of Books,* notes that Weisman's book delves into the "symbolic meaning of architecture and the discrimination it engenders" and "details the privatization of public spaces (exemplified by the suburban mall and its high-tech security systems) and the hierarchy of social spaces in gleaming downtown office spires." In *Harvard Design Magazine* Grahame Shane stated that "Weisman convincingly describes, in gruesome detail, how urban space can be repressive and patriarchal, and she demonstrates how public space reveals the social status of women." Shane praised the work's "well-rounded critique."

In an interview in *Designer/Builder* magazine, Weisman noted that "I strongly identify myself as a feminist but my feminist activism and scholarship have always been committed to creating relationships of equity among people, not just equality between genders. As a moral and political concept, equity recognizes that human needs differ and that each person should be able to have what they need in order to live a full, healthy, creative, and productive life, unlike equality, which requires that everyone gets the same." "As a feminist I believe that only when one is able to analyze and evaluate the existing system can one begin to reshape it in ways that create an alternative that speaks to more inclusivity, generosity, and kindness," Weisman added.

Weisman told *CA:* "I wrote my book because I wanted to contribute to furthering our understanding of the complex social processes and power struggles involved in building and controlling space; how the spatial arrangements of our buildings and communities reflect and reinforce the nature of gender, race, and class relations in society; and how we can begin to challenge and change the forms and values encoded in the man-made environment (by which I mean the man-made environment); thereby fostering the transformation of the sexist and racist conditions that delimit and define our daily lives and the cultural assumptions in which they are immersed."

Weisman also elucidated the basic theme of *Discrimination by Design:* "I explain how buildings and communities are designed and used, both symbolically and literally, to keep different groups of people in their respective 'social place.' I maintain that access to built space and control over it is fundamentally related to social status and power. Those who have traditionally held power in our society—mostly white males—have in part done so by confining blacks to the back of the bus and women to the master bedroom, and excluding both from the corporate boardroom. In my book, I trace the social and architectural histories of the skyscraper, maternity hospital, department store, shopping mall, nuclear family suburban dream house, and public housing high rise and I document how each setting, along with cities and suburbs, contributes to the power of some groups over others and the maintenance of human inequality. Further, I propose how we could rebuild and reshape our neighborhoods, workplaces, and dwellings in ways that foster relationships of equality and environmental wholeness."

BIOGRAPHICAL/CRITICAL SOURCES:

PERIODICALS

Choice, October, 1992, p. 290.
Designer/Builder, October, 1998, pp. 5-9.
Harvard Design Magazine, winter/spring, 1997, pp. 74-75.
Journal of American History, September, 1994, p. 834.
San Francisco Review of Books, winter, 1992, p. 18.
Women's Review of Books, January, 1993, pp. 1, 3.

*   *   *

WELLS, G(eorge) A(lbert) 1926-

PERSONAL: Born May 22, 1926, in London, England; married Elisabeth Delhey, 1969. *Ethnicity:* "White." *Education:* University of London, B.A., 1947, M.A., 1950, Ph.D., 1954, B.Sc., 1963. *Politics:* "No affiliation." *Religion:* "None." *Avocational interests:* Walking.

ADDRESSES: Home—35 St. Stephens Ave., St. Albans, Hertfordshire AL3 4AA, England.

CAREER: University of London, London, lecturer, 1949-64, reader in German, 1964-68, professor of German at Birkbeck College, 1968-88, professor emeritus, 1988—. *Wartime service:* Worked as a coal miner, 1944-45.

MEMBER: Academy of Humanism (humanist laureate, 1983).

WRITINGS:

Herder and After, Mouton (The Hague, Netherlands), 1959.
The Plays of Grillparzer, Pergamon (London), 1969.

The Jesus of the Early Christians, Pemberton (London), 1971.

Did Jesus Exist?, Pemberton, 1975, second edition, 1986.

(Editor with D. R. Oppenheimer) F. R. H. Englefield, *Language: Its Origin and Relation to Thought,* Elek/Pemberton (London), 1977.

Goethe and the Development of Science, Sijthoff & Nordhoff (The Netherlands), 1978.

The Historical Evidence for Jesus, Prometheus Books (Buffalo, NY), 1982.

(Editor with Oppenheimer) Englefield, *The Mind at Work and Play,* Prometheus Books, 1985.

The Origin of Language: Aspects of the Discussion from Condillac to Wundt, Open Court (Chicago, IL), 1987.

(Editor) *J. M. Robertson: Liberal, Rationalist, and Scholar,* Pemberton, 1987.

Religious Postures: Essays on Modern Christian Apologists and Religious Problems, Open Court, 1988.

Who Was Jesus? A Critique of the New Testament Record, Open Court, 1989.

(Editor with Oppenheimer) Englefield, *Critique of Pure Verbiage: Essays on Abuses of Language in Literary, Religious, and Philosophical Writings,* Open Court, 1990.

Belief and Make-Believe: Critical Reflections on the Sources of Credulity, Open Court, 1991.

What's in a Name? Reflections on Language, Magic, and Religion, Open Court, 1993.

The Jesus Legend, Open Court, 1996.

(Editor) David Friedrich Strauss, *The Old Faith and the New,* Prometheus Books, 1997.

The Jesus Myth, Open Court, 1998.

Origin of Language (booklet), Rationalist Press Association (London), 1999.

SIDELIGHTS: G. A. Wells told *CA:* "I suppose I have something of the temperament of an investigative scholar. I also enjoy trying to condense a page of my draft into half a page, without loss of substance or clarity."

* * *

WERBACH, Adam 1973-

PERSONAL: Born in 1973, in CA. *Education:* Brown University, B.A. (political science, modern culture, media); Instututo Central America, Guatamala, received advanced degree in Spanish.

ADDRESSES: Office—c/o Sierra Club, 85 Second St., second floor, San Francisco, CA 94105-3441. *Agent*—c/o HarperCollins Publishers, 10 East 53rd St., New York, NY 10022. *E-mail*—adam.werbach@sierraclub.org.

CAREER: Environmental activist. Sierra Student Coalition, founding member and first director, c. early 1990s; Sierra Club, board member, 1994—, president and head of board of directors, 1996—. Vocalist for the music group Brown Derbies; producer and director of films and videos.

MEMBER: Sierra Club.

AWARDS, HONORS: Named "Environmental Hero," Sierra Club Centennial Celebration, 1991; Denny and Ida Wilcher Award; named one of "Ten Most Powerful People in their Twenties," *Swing* Magazine, and "Ten Outstanding Young Americans," U.S. Junior Chamber of Commerce.

WRITINGS:

Act First, Apologize Later: If You Don't Stand up for Something, You'll Fall for Anything, Harper Collins (New York City), 1997.

SIDELIGHTS: When the Sierra Club, founded by famed naturalist John Muir in 1892 to further environmental causes, chose a new president in 1996, the choice caused quite a stir. The uproar was caused by the new president, Adam Werbach, who was only twenty-three years old at the time. The average age of a Sierra Club member is forty-seven, and the executive director who spearheaded the search was old enough to be Werbach's great-grandfather. Many wondered at the time what possessed the board to pick such an unusual candidate—the youngest ever in the Club's history.

Werbach, though tender in years, was an experienced environmental activist. The son of Sierra Club members, Werbach collected two hundred signatures in second grade from fellow elementary students in an effort to get Federal Interior Secretary James Watts to resign. By high school he was ready for a bigger challenge. He founded the student-run Sierra Student Coalition (SSC) and then continued his involvement with the organization while he was an undergraduate at Brown University. The SSC now has thirty thousand members. Reed McManus outlined the Coalition's activities in an article in *Sierra* magazine: "[Werbach] and his SSC colleagues mastered the mundane (such as registering thousands of student voters before the 1992 elections and phone-banking on behalf of the California Desert Protection Act), the dramatic (such as selling black snow cones at fairs and concerts to publicize oil-industry threats to the Arctic National Wildlife Refuge), and the modern (spreading the Club's message on the Internet)." Werbach's activism won him a spot on the Sierra Club's board in 1994 and the presidency two years later.

Werbach has worked on changing the Sierra Club, both in the makeup of its membership and in the way it delivers its message. "We started out as a very exclusive organization," Werbach told Anne W. Wilke of *E* journal. "We don't reach out to the religious community well, and we don't reach out to young people or minorities." To that end Werbach has changed the Sierra Club's focus from the national to the local. He told Wilke, "We have taken 80 percent of the money we spent on direct lobbying two years ago and now spend it on community organizing and community outreach." Werbach has been criticized for "watering down" the Sierra Club's message in the use of such media as the Internet and MTV. Werbach meets this criticism head-on: "Sure you water the message down," he told Wilke, "you just don't water the goals down." More pointedly, Werbach noted, "If Nike can sell me a pair of shoes that I can't afford in five seconds, then I better be able to sell substance in three seconds. The environmental movement right now is content rich but signal poor."

Werbach promoted his message of environmental activism with his first book, *Act First, Apologize Later: If You Don't Stand up for Something, You'll Fall for Anything,* which came out in 1997. In it Werbach relates inspirational tales of grassroots activism—such as the one about a woman poisoned by a hydrogen fluoride leak who organized the Chemical Injury Coalition, and another about a minister who was instrumental in closing down a smelting plant that was polluting his neighborhood. A *Publishers Weekly* review noted that "Werbach's reasoning, though impassioned, is neither subtle nor thorough" but concluded that "his clarion call is bound to recruit a new generation of activists."

BIOGRAPHICAL/CRITICAL SOURCES:

PERIODICALS

E, September/October 1997, pp. 10-13.
Interview, September, 1996, p. 40.

Library Journal, October 15, 1997, p. 89.
New Republic, November 24, 1997, pp. 20-22.
Newsweek, June 17, 1996, p. 71.
People Weekly, September 16, 1996, p. 65.
Publishers Weekly, September 22, 1997, pp. 60-61.
Sierra, September/October 1996, pp. 54-55.
Statesman Journal, September 12, 1997.
Time, June 9, 1997.
U.S. News & World Report, March 31, 1997, p. 33.
Vegetarian Times, April, 1997, p. 128.

OTHER

Adam Werbach Bio, http://werbach.com/adam/bio.ht ml (February 2, 1999).
CNNfn, http://www.cnnfn.com/grapevine/9605/25/ (February 2, 1999).
Infoact, http://www.infoact.com/acts/profile.cfm (February 2, 1999).
The Netizen, http://www.netizen.com/netizen/96/26/ special2a.html (February 2, 1999).
The Planet, http://www.sierraclub.org/planet/199607/ scpresident.html (July/August, 1996).
Readersndex, http://www.readersndex.com/imprint/ 0000018/0000bf9/author.html (February 2, 1999).
Salon Daily Clicks: Newsreal, http://www.salon1999. com/news960528.html (February 2, 1999).
Sierra Student Coalition, http://www.ssc.org/home pg.html (February 2, 1999).
Testimony of Mr. Adam Werbach before the Subcommittees on National Parks and Public Lands and Water and Power Resources of the House of Representatives, http://lakepowell.org/Werbach.htm (February 2, 1999).
Vault Reports Celebrity Profiles, http://www.vault reports.com/career/werbach.html (February 2, 1999).
WhiRrLed, http://werbach.com/whirrled/whirrled.ht ml (February 2, 1999).*

*　　*　　*

WETTSTEIN, Robert M. 1950-

PERSONAL: Born June 4, 1950, in New York, NY; son of Sidney and Bonnie Wettstein; married, wife's name Stacey, 1984. *Ethnicity:* "Caucasian." *Education:* Johns Hopkins University, B.A., 1972; University of California, Los Angeles, M.D., 1976.

ADDRESSES: Office—401 Shady Ave., Suite B103,

Pittsburgh, PA 15206; fax 412-661-0333. *E-mail*—wettsteins@aol.com.

CAREER: University of Pittsburgh, Pittsburgh, PA, faculty psychiatrist and assistant professor of psychiatry, 1984-96; psychiatrist, Pittsburgh, 1996—.

MEMBER: American Academy of Psychiatry and the Law, American Psychiatric Association.

WRITINGS:

(With Barbara Weiner) *Legal Issues in Mental Health Care,* Plenum (New York City), 1993.
(Editor) *Treatment of Offenders with Mental Disorders,* Guilford (New York City), 1998.

Editor, *Behavioral Sciences and the Law,* 1990-96.

*   *   *

WIEDMAN, John Charles 1949-

PERSONAL: Born May 26, 1949, in San Antonio, TX; son of Donald and Donnie S. (a nurse) Wiedman; married Rhonda Chambers, December 16, 1974; children: J. Cary, Bradley Clark, C. Blake. *Ethnicity:* "Caucasian." *Education:* University of Memphis, B.B.A. *Religion:* Methodist.

ADDRESSES: Home and office—Towering Pines Press, Inc., 6442 South Oak Shadows Cir., Memphis, TN 38119; fax 901-681-9269. *E-mail*—weed6442@aol.com.

CAREER: Leader Federal Savings and Loan, Memphis, TN, vice president, 1976-82; Verex, sales representative, 1982-84; Union Planters Investment Banking Group, Memphis, sales representative, 1984-90; Wiedman Mortgage, Inc., Memphis, owner, 1990—.

MEMBER: Memphis University School Parents Association, Mayfair Homeowners Association.

WRITINGS:

Desperately Seeking Snoozin', Towering Pines Press (Memphis, TN), 1998.

SIDELIGHTS: John Charles Wiedman told *CA:* "Inspiration came from a lifelong battle with chronic

insomnia and the desire to share my success in overcoming it with other sufferers. It also came from the many internet readers (of my initial draft) who encouraged me to write this book."

*   *   *

WINTERS, Kay 1936-

PERSONAL: Born October 5, 1936, in Trenton, NJ; daughter of Robert (an aerospace engineer) and Luella (a homemaker; maiden name, Hutchinson) Lanning; married Earl D. Winters (a consultant), August 27, 1960; children: Linda. *Education:* Beaver College, B.S. (elementary education); attended Boston University (graduate work in public relations); Wheelock College, M.S. (education); attended Lehigh University. *Politics:* Democrat. *Religion:* Protestant. *Avocational interests:* Reading, biking, walking, gardening, and traveling.

ADDRESSES: Home and office—Box 339, Richlandtown, PA 18955. *E-mail*—KayWin@aol.com.

CAREER: Children's book author, reviewer, and consultant. Massachusetts Public Schools, Newton, MA, elementary education teacher, 1960-63; Palisades School District, Kintnersville, PA, elementary education teacher and supervisor, 1968-92. American International Schools, education consultant, 1970-80.

MEMBER: International Reading Association, Society of Children's Book Writers and Illustrators.

AWARDS, HONORS: Pick of the List, American Booksellers Association, 1997, for *Wolf Watch.*

WRITINGS:

Did You See What I Saw?: Poems about School, illustrated by Martha Weston, Viking (New York City), 1996.
The Teeny Tiny Ghost, illustrated by Lynn Munsinger, HarperCollins (New York City), 1997.
Wolf Watch, illustrated by Laura Regan, Simon & Schuster (New York City), 1997.
Where Are the Bears?, illustrated by Brian Lies, Bantam (New York City), 1998.
How Will the Easter Bunny Know? ("First Choice Chapter Book"), illustrated by Martha Weston, Yearling, 1999.

Who's Haunting the Teeny Tiny Ghost, illustrated by Lynn Munsinger, HarperCollins, 1999.

OTHER

(With Marta Felber) *The Teachers Copebook: How to End the Year Better Than You Started,* Fearon, 1980.

Winters has also written reading textbooks for Scott Foresman and Houghton Mifflin.

WORK IN PROGRESS: Tiger Trail, a companion book to *Wolf Watch,* illustrated by Laura Regan, for Simon & Schuster, expected publication in 2000; *Abe Lincoln,* illustrated by Nancy Carpenter, for Simon & Schuster, expected publication in 2002.

SIDELIGHTS: Kay Winters commented: "From the time I was seven years old I was a writer. I kept diaries, journals, wrote for the school and camp newspapers, and the college magazine. When I graduated from Beaver College with a bachelor of science degree in elementary education and a minor in English, I took additional writing courses at Boston University. I submitted poems, essays, articles, and stories to educational journals and textbooks. Now and then they were published. But making a living by writing books did not seem like a viable possibility at that time. My husband and I were just out of graduate school, and we had a big educational debt to pay to Massachusetts Institute of Technology (MIT), as well as a new baby.

"For the next twenty-nine years I worked in public schools as a teacher, a reading specialist, an educational consultant, and a college instructor. And I loved it. At every conference I attended I always went to hear the authors instead of the latest theory on the wonder of phonics. I continued to send in manuscripts now and then, but teaching was very consuming. There was little time for writing. In 1980, I coauthored a book for teachers with Marta Felber, *The Teachers Copebook: How to End the Year Better Than You Started.* In order to finish that project, I had to get up every morning at 4 a.m., sneak downstairs to my frosty office, and garbed in a fur robe, woolen gloves, and fleece-lined boots, would type until it was time to teach.

"In 1992, my school board offered early retirement. My resignation was on the superintendent's desk the next day. This was my chance! I was taking it. I started to write full time the day after I retired. I imagined that the Palisades School District was paying me to stay home and write. And write I did. I wrote every day. I went to the New School [for Social Research] in New York and took classes in writing for children with instructors Margaret Gable and Deborah Brodie. I attended conferences and met editors. I went to New York to the Children's Book Council and read all of the picture books from the years 1991 and 1992 that they had on their shelves.

"Gradually, the rejection forms from publishers changed into personal letters. Finally, in 1994, I got a phone call from an editor at HarperCollins. They were interested in *The Teeny Tiny Ghost.* From there, my writing career began to take off. Publishers were soon interested in *Wolf Watch* and *Did You See What I Saw?: Poems about School.* In the meantime, I was also writing reading textbooks. Soon, *Where Are the Bears?* and *How Will the Easter Bunny Know?* were going to press and I was writing *Who's Haunting the Teeny Tiny Ghost,* a sequel to *The Teeny Tiny Ghost,* and *Tiger Trail,* the companion to *Wolf Watch.* I was researching *Abe Lincoln* as well."

Drawing on her twenty-seven years of teaching elementary school, Winters wrote a book of poems devoted to life in the classroom. The day-to-day goings-on in a typical schoolroom are highlighted in *Did You See What I Saw?: Poems about School.* Everything, from the pleasure evoked by a new box of crayons to snow days and passing notes in class, is explored in lighthearted verse. Poems such as "Lots of Spots," about the travails of chicken pox, and "Groundhog Day," paint amusing pictures of school life. "The rhythms and sounds and wordplay . . . are part of the fun," enthused Hazel Rochman in *Booklist.*

In *The Teeny Tiny Ghost,* Winters addresses the importance of mastering one's fears. In this take on a well-known tale, a diminutive specter is afraid of his own boos and howls. On Halloween night, a rap on the door sends shivers through him and his teeny tiny kittens. But summing up all his courage, he swears to protect his feline companions and opens the door to his ghostly pals, who have come to take him trick-or-treating. Janice M. Del Negro, writing in *Bulletin of the Center for Children's Books,* said, "tucked into this humorously written and illustrated tale is the kernel of stout-heartedness that makes young children love the hero." "This tale of banishing fear has just the right blend of wit and supernatural suspense," stated a reviewer for *Publishers Weekly.*

In the award-winning *Wolf Watch* Winters uses poetic quatrains to tell the story of four wolf pups from birth until their first foray out of the den. The habits of a wolf pack are introduced, from howling to hunting and protecting their young. Danger is present in the form of a golden eagle who awaits the chance to prey upon one of the defenseless pups. *School Library Journal* contributor Susan Scheps called *Wolf Watch* "a treasure of a book," and asserted that "there is a lot of information to be gleaned from this sparsely written visual masterpiece." A critic for *Kirkus Reviews* hailed *Wolf Watch* as "a splendid complement to titles with a more fact-based approach to wolf life."

Winters commented: "I write because that's how I know what I think. When I see what I say, ideas that were fuzzy come clear to me. And sometimes I am surprised at what I find out about myself.

"I write because I love to read and I want to give others that pleasure. Some of my happiest moments are when I am curled up by the fire in our old stone farmhouse in Bucks County. My husband and I seldom watch television. On summer evenings we read in the gazebo, which looks out on our ten acres of meadows and woods. The hummingbird stops by for a sip from our feeder. Butterflies light on the cosmos. We have wild turkeys, deer, and pheasants who visit. I hope that children will become more aware of small wonders from my books.

"I write because I love to learn. Writers have the chance to play many parts, hear many voices, and dream many dreams. One of the exciting fringe benefits of being a writer is the ability to pursue what you care about. I am interested in so many things, nature, people, history, humor. Writing gives me a powerful motivation for learning. I loved finding out about wolves, presenting their warm family life, and dispelling the 'big bad wolf' myth in *Wolf Watch*. It's important to examine how to face fears and cope, as I explored in *The Teeny Tiny Ghost,* or how to observe and share experiences and memories, as in *Did You See What I Saw?: Poems about School.* I liked putting myself in the place of a six-year-old, as if I was going to Grandma's house for Easter and had no way of letting the Easter Bunny know of my whereabouts in *How Will the Easter Bunny Know?* Or imagining twin bear cubs, Sassy and Lum, in *Where Are the Bears?,* figuring out which activities they would copy as they met campers for the very first time. As I worked on the book about Abraham Lincoln I lost myself in the wilderness, suffered on his hundred-

mile trek to Indiana and sympathized with Abe as he searched for books and learned to use words to lift himself out of grinding poverty. In *Tiger Trail,* I love putting myself in the place of the mother tigress and feeling her fear, her concern, and her triumph as she taught her cubs survival skills. When I was writing my book on ancient Egypt, the pharaohs seemed to come alive and walk right off the pages in their royal sandals. I hope that as youngsters meet the characters in my stories, they will realize that whatever their own circumstances may be, they can choose—to be brave, to forge ahead, to take positive risks, to be kind, to overcome severe obstacles, to appreciate the moment.

"My work habits are similar to those I used when I was teaching. I work every day. I am always on the watch for a story, even when we are on vacation riding elephants in Thailand or sailing on Lake Nockamixon. I have been very influenced by writers who use poetic prose, such as Karen Hesse, Jane Yolen, and Byrd Baylor. I love poetry by Aileen Fisher. I think Patricia Reilly Giff gets into the heads of her characters in a way I admire. And even though I frequently try to use other genres, poetic prose seems to speak up the most often. I am more interested in character development than plot. The story comes from the characters, and they frequently have a mind of their own. Still, writing the book is only the beginning. I also visit schools, attend book signings, speak at colleges, conferences, and bookstores.

"My advice for aspiring writers is to work, revise, and persist. Treat writing like a job. Make contacts. Go to conferences. Read current children's books. Join a writer's group. I am lucky to have a husband who is an excellent editor. Don't send your manuscript right off when you finish it. Let it breathe. Look at it again. And be grateful that you have chosen a career that makes every day matter. Whatever is going on in your life today will fit somewhere, sometime, in a story."

BIOGRAPHICAL/CRITICAL SOURCES:

PERIODICALS

Booklist, August, 1996, p. 1903; September, 1, 1997, p. 141; November, 1, 1997. p. 485.
Bulletin of the Center for Children's Books, November, 1997, p. 107.
Kirkus Reviews, October 1, 1997, p. 1539.
Publishers Weekly, October 6, 1997, p. 48.

School Library Journal, October, 1996, p. 119; November, 1997, p. 104.*

*   *   *

WOLZIEN, Valerie

PERSONAL: Married; children: a son. *Education:* Attended college in Colorado and Alaska.

ADDRESSES: Home—New Jersey. *Agent*—c/o Fawcett Book Group, 201 East 50th St., New York, NY 10022. *E-mail*—valerie@wolzien.com.

CAREER: Mystery novelist.

WRITINGS:

"SUSAN HENSHAW" SERIES; ALL PUBLISHED BY FAWCETT GOLD MEDAL (NEW YORK CITY), EXCEPT AS INDICATED

Murder at the PTA Luncheon, St. Martin's Press (New York City), 1988.
The Fortieth Birthday Body: A Suburban Mystery, St. Martin's Press (New York City), 1989.
We Wish You a Merry Murder, 1991.
All Hallow's Evil, 1992.
An Old Faithful Murder, 1992.
A Star-Spangled Murder, 1993.
A Good Year for a Corpse, 1994.
"Tis the Season to Be Murdered, 1994.
Remodeled to Death, 1995.
Elected to Die, 1996.
Permit for Murder, 1997.
Weddings Are Murder, 1998.

OTHER

Shore to Die ("Josie Pigeon" series), Fawcett Gold Medal, 1996.

SIDELIGHTS: Valerie Wolzien is the author of several murder mysteries featuring homemaker Susan Henshaw of Hancock, Connecticut, a well-to-do suburban community. Wolzien's eleventh novel, published in 1996, *Shore to Die* shares the same setting but focuses on Josie Pigeon, the owner of an all-female construction company who first appears in the 1995 Henshaw mystery *Remodeled to Death.* In the 1987 novel, *Murder at the PTA Luncheon,* the earliest Henshaw mystery, two prominent members of

Hancock's elementary school PTA succumb to cyanide poisoning. Susan, also a PTA member, is initially a suspect, but eventually Brett and Kathleen, the two good-looking state police officers working on the case, discover the truth with Susan's help. In the *Wilson Library Bulletin,* Kathleen Maio wrote that Brett and Kathleen "are a bit like the Ken and Barbie of detection" but found *Murder at the PTA Luncheon* "a skillful work of light entertainment." *Library Journal*'s Rex E. Klett, however, was scathing. In his view, the novel was spoiled by "inane chitchat, gratuitous details, and flat characters." A critic for *Publishers Weekly* also deemed *Murder at the PTA Luncheon* a disappointment, commenting that the book is crowded with poorly drawn characters and that the "solution to the mystery is labored and murky."

The second Henshaw mystery, *The Fortieth Birthday Body,* appearing in 1989, begins with an expensive fortieth birthday celebration for Susan and the gift of a new Volvo sedan from Jed, her husband. But the car contains an unwanted passenger—Dawn Elliot, shot through the head. Dawn, it turns out, had affairs with many of the men at the party, including Susan's husband, all of whom are suspects. Kathleen of *Murder at the PTA Luncheon,* now retired from the state police, attempts to track down the killer, but it is Susan's ten-year-old son, Chad, who unexpectedly supplies the key piece of information that identifies one of the husbands (not Jed) as the chief perpetrator. A critic writing in *Publishers Weekly* declared that "[a] townful of listless characters and a thin, drawn-out story line stall this pallid mystery." However, *Booklist* reviewer Denise Perry Donavin considered the novel's realistic suburban detail a strength.

Some of the Henshaw mysteries use holidays as a framing device. Halloween, for example, is the occasion for the two murders in the 1992 novel *All Hallows Evil.* One victim is discovered in Hancock's public library by Susan, who sets out to solve the slayings. A contributor in *Publishers Weekly* panned the novel, concluding that it offers little in the way of suspense or believability. The *Publishers Weekly* reviewer also complained that the novel's two potential adulterous romances, one involving Susan and the other, her husband, are ineptly handled.

BIOGRAPHICAL/CRITICAL SOURCES:

BOOKS

Heising, Willetta L., editor, *Detecting Women 2: A Reader's Guide and Checklist for Mystery Series*

Written by Women, Purple Moon Press (Dearborn, MI), 1996.

PERIODICALS

Booklist, June 15, 1989, pp. 1782-1783.
Kirkus Reviews, May 15, 1989, p. 736.
Library Journal, March 1, 1988, p. 80.
New York Times Book Review, May 22, 1988, p. 28.
People Weekly, February 22, 1988, p. 16.
Publishers Weekly, December 18, 1987, p. 58; May 12, 1989, p. 284; April 13, 1992, p. 53; September 14, 1992, p. 116.
Tribune Books (Chicago), February 28, 1988, p. 6.
Wilson Library Bulletin, April, 1988, p. 76.*

* * *

WOO, Wing Thye 1954-

PERSONAL: Born April 13, 1954. *Education:* Swarthmore College, B.Sc. and B.A. (with high honors), 1976; Yale University, M.A., 1978; Harvard University, M.A., Ph.D., 1982.

ADDRESSES: Office—Department of Economics, University of California, Davis, CA 95616; fax 530-758-2625. *E-mail*—wtwoo@ucdavis.edu.

CAREER: University of Maryland at College Park, lecturer in economics, 1982-84; University of California, Davis, professor of economics, and head of Pacific Rim Studies Program at Institute of Governmental Affairs, 1987-95. Brookings Institution, research associate in economic studies, 1982-85; People's University of China, visiting professor, 1989; National Taiwan University, visiting professor, 1990; Institute of Southeast Asian Studies, Singapore, visiting research fellow, 1990; Harvard University, faculty associate of Harvard Institute for International Development, 1998—. U.S. Treasury, special adviser, 1997-98; consultant to governments of China, India, Indonesia, Mongolia, Vietnam, and Ukraine.

AWARDS, HONORS: Grants from Pacific Cultural Foundation and National Science Council (both for Taiwan), 1989-90, Ford Foundation, 1991-94, 1993-95, International Center for Economic Growth, 1993-94, and Asia Foundation, 1994-96.

WRITINGS:

(Contributor) Jeffrey Sachs, editor, *Developing Country Debt and the World Economy,* University of Chicago Press (Chicago), 1989.
(Contributor) Jeffrey Frankel and Miles Kahler, editors, *Regionalism and Rivalry: Japan and the United States in Pacific Asia,* University of Chicago Press, 1993.
(With Bruce Glassburner and Anwar Nasution) *Macroeconomic Crisis and Long-Term Growth: The Case of Indonesia, 1965-1990,* World Bank Press, 1994.
(Contributor) Chung Lee and Helmut Reisen, editors, *From Reform to Growth: China and Other Countries in Transition,* Organization for Economic Cooperation and Development (Paris), 1994.
(With Christopher Heady and Christine Wong) *Economic Reform and Fiscal Management in China,* Oxford University Press, 1995.
(Contributor) Kevin Hoover and Steven Sheffrin, editor, *Monetarism and the Methodology of Economics,* Edward Elgar, 1995.
(Editor with Sachs and Steven Parker, and contributor) *Economies in Transition: Asia and Europe,* MIT Press (Cambridge, MA), 1996.
(Contributor) Konosuke Odaka and Juro Teranishi, editors, *Market and Government: Foes or Friends?,* Maruzen Book (Tokyo, Japan), 1998.

Contributor of articles and reviews to scholarly journals, popular magazines, and newspapers, including *Far Eastern Economic Review, International Economy,* and *Asian Wall Street Journal Weekly.* Assistant editor, *Brookings Papers on Economic Activity,* 1983-85; guest editor, *Journal of Comparative Economics* and *Economic Policy,* both 1994; member of editorial advisory board, *Journal of Asian Business,* 1994—; member of editorial committee, *MOCT-MOST: Economic Policy in Transitional Economies,* 1997—.

WORK IN PROGRESS: Research on international and domestic macroeconomics, economic reforms in socialist countries, and trade and economic development.

* * *

WORSHAM, Lynn 1953-

PERSONAL: Born December 17, 1953, in Tulsa, OK; daughter of William Henry (an electrical engineer) and Arlene (Barlow) Worsham. *Ethnicity:* "Caucasian." *Education:* University of Colorado, B.A., 1976; University of Texas at Arlington, M.A., 1981, Ph.D., 1988. *Avocational interests:* Jazz, gardening.

ADDRESSES: Home—2515 Siena Way, Valrico, FL 33594. *Office*—Department of English, CPR 107, University of South Florida, Tampa, FL 33620; fax 813-974-2270. *E-mail*—lworsham@chuma1.cas.usf. edu.

CAREER: University of Wisconsin—Milwaukee, assistant professor, 1988-94, associate professor of English, 1994-98; University of South Florida, Tampa, professor of English, 1998—.

MEMBER: National Council of Teachers of English, Conference on College Composition and Communication, Modern Language Association of America, Rhetoric Society of America, Phi Beta Kappa.

AWARDS, HONORS: Fellow, Center for Twentieth-Century Studies.

WRITINGS:

Feminism and Composition Studies, Modern Language Association of America (New York City), 1998.
Race, Rhetoric, and the Postcolonial, State University of New York Press (Albany), 1998.

Editor, *JAC: Journal of Composition Theory.*

WORK IN PROGRESS: Terms of Interest: Gayatri Spivak's Rhetorical Theory, publication by State University of New York Press expected in 2000.

SIDELIGHTS: Lynn Worsham told *CA:* "I write to change the hearts and minds of readers. I write to bring greater social justice to the world in which I live."

*   *   *

WRIGHT, Alexandra 1979-

PERSONAL: Born December 13, 1979, in Winchester, MA; daughter of James Allan (a sculptor) and Elena (an editor; maiden name, Dworkin) Wright. *Education:* Attends Drew University, 1997—. *Religion:* Episcopal. *Avocational interests:* Music, architecture, trains, cartography, bicycling, cooking, and studying French, Spanish, history, calculus, physics, piano, violin, and literature.

ADDRESSES: Home—94 Ridge Ave., Newton, MA 02159. *E-mail*—awright@drew.edu.

CAREER: Student, 1997—. Speaker at libraries and public schools.

AWARDS, HONORS: Presidential Scholar, Drew University, 1998.

WRITINGS:

NONFICTION; FOR CHILDREN

Will We Miss Them?: Endangered Species, illustrated by Marshall Peck III, Charlesbridge (Watertown, MA), 1992.
At Home in the Tide Pool, illustrated by Marshall Peck III, Charlesbridge, 1992.
Can We Be Friends?: Nature's Partners, illustrated by Marshall Peck III, Charlesbridge, 1994.

FICTION; FOR CHILDREN

Alice in Pastaland: A Math Adventure, illustrated by Reagan Word, Charlesbridge, 1997.

WORK IN PROGRESS: "The impact of Darwin on science and society"; research on physics and the history of science.

SIDELIGHTS: Alexandra Wright commented: "Writing is an essential part of my day. I find the inspiration to write in everything I do: walking to class, or listening to Mozart; doing the laundry, or pondering a physics problem. People often ask me when I first began to write. I can remember writing books in first grade that had a cover, a picture, and a page of invented spelling that only I could read. The first story I remember writing was based on a family anecdote about baby talk.

"My first published book, *Will We Miss Them?,* began because I was concerned that panda bears were in danger of becoming extinct. When I am interested in something, I like to read about it. I read about endangered animals all through the summer after fifth grade. I was shocked by what was happening to wild animals everywhere. I wrote the book as a way to tell people about it. When I was in sixth grade, the book was published, and I began a series of visits to schools to talk about endangered animals and being a writer. *Will We Miss Them?* was reviewed on the *Reading Rainbow* television show. The book's success made me realize that writing can be powerful.

"I'm interested in practically everything, and one of the ways I explore a new topic is by writing. I write to find out what I think, what questions I have, what bothers me, and how the things I know fit (or don't fit) with what I am learning. Besides writing nonfiction, I enjoy writing humorous and serious poetry, plays, and stories. Besides writing, I enjoy playing violin and piano, and anything to do with trolleys, trains, or maps."

BIOGRAPHICAL/CRITICAL SOURCES:

PERIODICALS

Appraisal: Science Books for Young People, winter, 1992, p. 65.
School Library Journal, March, 1995, p. 22.
Science Books and Films, January, 1992, p. 16; March, 1993, p. 50; January, 1995, p. 22.*

*   *   *

YOKOMITSU RIICHI 1898-1947

PERSONAL: Born in 1898, in Japan; died in 1947; father, a surveying engineer. *Education:* Attended Waseda University, 1916.

CAREER: Writer.

WRITINGS:

NOVELS

Nichirin, published in journal *Shin'-shosetsu,* 1923.
Shanghai, published in journal *Kaizo,* 1928-31.
Shin'en, 1930-32, first half published in newspaper *Osaka mainichi shinbun,* second half published in journal *Bungei shunju.*
Monsho, 1934.
Ryoshu, 1937-46, published in installments in various journals.
Kanashimi no daika, 1955.

SHORT STORIES

Onmi, 1924.
Haru wa basha ni notte, 1927.

Kikai, 1931.
Time, and Others, 1965.
Love and Other Stories of Yokomitsu Riichi, translated and with an introduction by Dennis Keene, University of Tokyo Press (Tokyo), 1974.

Author of "Hae," published in journal *Bungei shunju,* 1923 (translated as "The Fly," published in journal *Japan Quarterly,* 1965); author of "Atama narabi ni hara," published in journal *Bungei jidai,* 1924.

OTHER

The Roof-Garden and Other One-Act Plays, 1934.
Oboegaki (memoirs), 1935.
Young Forever and Five Other Novelettes, 1941.
Yoru no kutsu (diary), 1945.
Yokomitsu Riichi zenshu (complete works), twelve volumes, 1955-56.

SIDELIGHTS: Yokomitsu Riichi's fiction exemplifies the tenets of the Shinkankakuha movement, which existed in Japan from 1924 to 1927. In response to the naturalist school of Japanese literature represented by the Shirakaba writers, who concerned themselves with the realistic presentation of life, Yokomitsu and other members of the Shinkankakuha group held that writing should present readers with an unsubjective record of their characters' sensations. Although Yokomitsu adopted some of the techniques of the "I-novel"—the predominant Japanese prose form of his day, in which authors related actual events of their lives through highly detailed confession yet made use of dialogue, narrative, and other devices of fiction—he sought to avoid the subjectivity of the "I-novel" by objectively describing situations separate from his own experiences. In his *Contemporary Japanese Fiction,* Mitsuo Nakamura asserted: "Probably Yokomitsu wished to say that he had created something fresh and new which had never been seen before. He was aiming at creating style and story, and it was his program to escape from 'I' novel type realism. For him, sense is the synonym of style, but he himself knew very well that it was impossible to construct a novel with it only. The frame which he chose for supporting 'sense' . . . was the paradoxical elucidation of the opposing elements of human psychology. . . . When human beings appear, his attention is always paid to the mental activity for outdoing the other party, and the mutual misunderstanding and complications are observed mainly from the viewpoint of victory and defeat. To him the human deeds are, like words, partial and therefore, an incomplete expression of psychology; hence ethics becomes meaningless."

Yokomitsu endured an unsettled and often lonely youth; his father was a surveying engineer for new railways, which demanded that the family move frequently from one job site to another. Yokomitsu entered Waseda University in 1916 but gradually lost interest in his studies and decided to pursue a career as a writer. In 1923 he began contributing short stories to literary magazines and in the same year published *Nichirin*, his first novel. The devastating Kanto earthquake, which levelled much of Tokyo in September 1923, instilled in Yokomitsu a sense of being at the mercy of uncontrollable natural forces. According to Mitsuo Nakamura, Yokomitsu believed that this experience of powerlessness in the face of nature had a great effect on the thought of the upcoming generation of writers. In October, Yokomitsu founded the Shinkankakuha movement with Kawabata Yasunari. By 1927 the movement was considered to have outlived its usefulness as an experimental forum, and many of its writers had defected to Japan's proletarian school of literature. With other non-Marxist writers Yokomitsu formed a new group that continued the modernist ideal of "art for art's sake" and emphasized the subjective process of psychological experience. He journeyed to China in 1928 to research *Shanhai*, the novel which marked the end of his experimentation with Shinkankakuha techniques. Over the next few years, he established himself as Japan's most popular novelist. His last novel, *Ryoshu*, is based on the clash of Eastern and Western cultures he experienced while traveling in Europe during the 1930s. With the advent of World War II, Yokomitsu virtually ceased writing. The few works he published during and after the war advocated the superiority of traditional Japanese culture to Western culture and reflected his despair over the Japanese defeat by Allied forces. He died in 1947.

In his short stories and novels Yokomitsu strove to reform the predominant conception of the modern Japanese novel, which at the time served as either a vehicle for confession or propaganda. He believed that the "I-novel", which was intended to express the author's state of mind, was incapable of conveying the effects of tragedy on the human psyche. He also maintained that the proletarian novel, basically an "I-novel" concerned with social reform, obscured the psychological motivations of characters due to its political intent. Although Yokomitsu's novels achieved enormous popular success in the 1930s, these works as well as his criticism and literary theories are viewed as simplistic by many modern scholars. Critics reserve their praise instead for several of Yokomitsu's short stories. Early stories such as

"Maketa otto" (1924; "The Defeated Husband") and later stories such as "Kikai" (1930; "The Machine") reflect his shift from an emphasis on his characters' external sensory perception to one emphasizing their internal psychological states. "The Defeated Husband" centers on the developing jealousy of a husband who suspects his wife of infidelity. Written during Yokomitsu's Shinkankakuha period, "The Defeated Husband" relies heavily on characters' actions, details of setting, and dialogue to reveal his protagonist's psychological trauma. In "The Machine," which examines a character who believes his ideas are being appropriated by his rivals at a small factory, Yokomitsu balances sensory details with confessional narrative to expand on the perceptions presented in the main character's confessions. On the basis of these and other stories, Yokomitsu is regarded by Western critics as an innovative writer whose works anticipated the more conspicuous emergence of modernist literary forms which took place in Japan following World War II. Donald Keene, in his *Dawn to the West, Japanese Literature of the Modern Era: Fiction,* declared: "The New Sensationalist school failed. Yokomitsu Riichi, despite some real successes and great popular acclaim, also failed to create a consistent style. . . . But it would be a mistake to infer from his failures that little had been achieved. . . . The failure of Yokomitsu was tragic and more deeply affecting than any of his works of fiction. His career and the Japan he lived in are mirrored in the novels, and even if a time should come when they are no longer read as works of pure literature they will remain a memorable segment of the continuing effort of Japanese writers to join the mainstream of modern world literature."

BIOGRAPHICAL/CRITICAL SOURCES:

BOOKS

Keene, Dennis, editor, *Love, and Other Stories of Yokomitsu Riichi,* University of Tokio Press, 1974.

Keene, Dennis, *Yokomitsu Riichi: Modernist,* Columbia University Press, 1980.

Keene, Donald, *Dawn to the West, Japanese Literature of the Modern Era: Fiction,* Volume 1, Holt, Rinehart, and Winston, 1984.

Lippit, Noriko Mizuta, *Reality and Fiction in Modern Japanese Literature,* M. E. Sharpe, 1980.

Nakamura, Mitsuo, *Contemporary Japanese Fiction: 1926-1968,* edited by John Krummel, translated by Ryoko Suetsugu, Kokusai Bunka Shinkokai, 1969.

PERIODICALS

Times Literary Supplement, April 10, 1981, p. 404.*

*   *   *

YOUNG, Patrick   1937-

PERSONAL: Born October 19, 1937, in Ladysmith, WI; son of Rodney Lee (a lawyer) and Janice (a medical technologist; maiden name, Wolf) Young; married Leah Ruth Figelman (a reporter), October 8, 1966; children: Justine Rebecca. *Education:* University of Colorado, B.A. (cum laude), 1960.

ADDRESSES: Home—7711 Hyacinth Court, Laurel, MD 20810. *Agent*—c/o Chelsea House Publishers, P.O. Box 914, Broomall, PA 19008.

CAREER: United Press International, Washington, DC, reporter, 1961-62; USN, journalist, 1963-64; *National Observer,* Silver Spring, MD, staff writer, 1965-77; freelance writer, 1977-79, 1995—; Newhouse News Service, Washington, DC, chief science and medical writer, 1980-88; *Science News,* Washington, DC, editor, 1988-95.

MEMBER: National Association of Science Writers, National Press Club.

AWARDS, HONORS: Howard W. Blakeslee Award, American Heart Association, 1971; science writing award in physics and astronomy, American Institute of Physics, 1974; James T. Grady Award, American Chemistry Society, 1977.

WRITINGS:

Drifting Continents, Shifting Seas: An Introduction to Plate Tectonics, F. Watts (New York City), 1976.
Asthma and Allergies: An Optimistic Future, U.S. Department of Health and Human Services (Bethesda, MD), 1980.
Drugs and Pregnancy, Chelsea House (New York City), 1987.
Mental Disturbances, Chelsea House (New York City), 1988.
Schizophrenia, with introduction by C. Everett Koop, Chelsea House (New York City), 1988.
(With Alan R. Figelman) *Keeping Young Athletes Healthy,* Simon & Schuster (New York City), 1991.

Also contributor of articles to periodicals, including *Science News.*

SIDELIGHTS: Patrick Young's *Drugs and Pregnancy,* published in 1987, informs readers of the effects of drugs and other substances taken by pregnant women on the development of their fetuses. Young followed with two other volumes the next year: *Mental Disturbances* and *Schizophrenia.* The latter included an introduction by then-U.S. Surgeon General C. Everett Koop.

Drugs and Pregnancy not only discusses the effects of drugs on embryos and fetuses, but lays out the basic biology of pregnancy. In particular, Young emphasizes the role that the placenta plays in the process by allowing drugs to pass through the mother's system and into that of the fetus. Young also warns his audience about fetal alcohol syndrome, which occurs in the fetus of women who drink too much alcohol while pregnant. In addition, he provides information about many over-the-counter medications and how they interact with pregnancy. Other topics covered in *Drugs and Pregnancy* include dangers to nursing infants from substances ingested by their mothers, as well as some of the challenges faced by babies who, because of their mother's drug abuse, are born addicted to dangerous drugs such as heroin and crack cocaine. *Booklist* reviewer Stephanie Zvirin praised the volume as "responsible and informative," while noting that despite the dangers involved, Young's tone is "never shrill" in discussing the risks of drug usage.

Mental Disturbances discusses several mental illnesses, and emphasizes those that most often threaten adolescents, such as manic depression, anorexia nervosa and bulimia, anxiety, and schizophrenia. As a *Booklist* critic reported, when Young provides information about the causes of these afflictions, he often follows the teachings and opinions of pioneering Austrian psychiatrist Sigmund Freud. Young also cites the symptoms for these and other conditions, as well as some of the possible treatments. Though the reviewer expressed a wish for further documentation and footnotes, the *Booklist* critic concluded that *Mental Disturbances* is "a fascinating survey."

Touched on in *Mental Disturbances,* schizophrenia provides the main subject for Young's second 1988 effort. He explains in *Schizophrenia* that many experts believe the affliction is composed of several components rather than standing alone as a single mental illness. He lists the symptoms of schizophrenia—which include disrupted patterns of speech and thought, hallucinations, and delusions—and discusses probable causes both environmental and genetic. He also mentions treatments, including recent medical breakthroughs that have greatly improved the quality of life for schizophrenics. Young considers the trials faced by the families of schizophrenics and includes testimony from those afflicted by it. *Booklist* critic Sally Estes described *Schizophrenia* as "a compassionate look at a puzzling illness."

BIOGRAPHICAL/CRITICAL SOURCES:

PERIODICALS

Booklist, May 1, 1976; August, 1987, p. 1736; July, 1988, p. 1818.
School Library Journal, September, 1976.*

* * *

ZELLMAN, Shelley 1948-

PERSONAL: Born October 24, 1948, in Los Angeles, CA; daughter of Emanuel (a men's clothing retailer) and Harriet (Schireson) Zellman; married Brian Scott Bennett (a composer), June 20, 1992; children: Skye Richard. *Education:* Antioch College, B.A., 1970; attended University of Southern California. *Politics:* Democrat. *Religion:* Jewish. *Avocational interests:* Animals, music, children, film.

ADDRESSES: Home—Studio City, CA. *Agent*—Roger Strull, Preferred Artists, 16633 Ventura, Suite 1421, Encino, CA 91436.

CAREER: Television writer and producer, 1978—. Story editor for episodes of television series, *Barney Miller,* ABC-TV, and *James at Fifteen,* FOX-TV; executive story editor of television episodes for *Three's Company,* ABC-TV; producer of episodes for series *Dear John,* NBC-TV; supervising producer of episodes for series *Newhart,* CBS-TV; co-creator of television series *FM,* CBS-TV.

MEMBER: Writers Guild of America West.

AWARDS, HONORS: Annual Cable Excellence (ACE) Award, outstanding children's television series, 1996, for *Madeline;* Emmy Award nomination, outstanding animated children's program special, American Academy of Television Arts and Sciences, 1997.

WRITINGS:

(With husband, Brian Bennett) *Autobiography of an Angel* (nonfiction), Journey into Light, 1998.

Staff writer for television series *Donny and Marie,* ABC-TV; writer of episodes for television series *Madeline,* ABC-TV, and for *James at Fifteen, Barney Miller, Three's Company, Dear John,* and *Newhart.*

* * *

ZWEIG, Stefan 1881-1942

PERSONAL: Born November 28, 1881, in Vienna, Austria; immigrated to England, 1934, became a naturalized citizen, 1940; committed suicide, February 22, 1942, in Petropolis, Brazil; son of Moritz (a textile manufacturer) and Ida Brettauer Zweig; married Friderike Maria Burger von Winternitz (a writer), in 1919 (divorced); married Elisabeth Charlotte Altmann, in 1939. *Education:* University of Vienna, studied German and Romance literatures, earned doctorate in 1904. *Politics:* Pacifist. *Religion:* Jewish. *Avocational interests:* Collecting literary and musical manuscripts.

CAREER: Novelist, biographer, playwright, poet, and critic. *Wartime service:* Worked in the Austrian War Archives during World War I.

WRITINGS:

Silberne Satien (poetry), Schuster & Loeffler (Berlin and Leipzig), 1901.
Die Liebe der Erika Ewald (novellas), Fleischel (Berlin), 1904.
Verlaine (biography) Schuster and Loeffler (Berlin and Leipzig), 1905, translation by O. F. Theis published as *Paul Verlaine,* Luce (Boston), 1913.
Tersites: Ein Traurspiel (drama), Insel (Leipzig), 1907.
Emile Verhaeren (biography), Insel, 1910, translation by Jethro Bithell, Houghton Mifflin (Boston and New York City), 1914.
Brennendes Geheimnis: Eine Erzahlung (novella), Insel, 1911.
Erstes Erlebnis (short stories and novellas), Insel, 1911.
Das Haus am Meer (play), Insel, 1912.
Der verwandelte Komodant (play), Insel 1913.

Jeremias (play), Insel, 1917, translation by Eden and Cedar Paul published as *Jeremiah,* Seltzer (New York City), 1922.

Legende eines Lebens (play), Insel, 1919.

Angst (novella), Hermann (Berlin), 1920.

Drei Meister: Balzac, Dickens, Dostojewski (biography), Insel, 1920, translation by Eden and Cedar Paul published as *Three Masters: Balzac, Dickens, Dostoeffsky,* Viking (New York City), 1930.

Der Zwang (novella), Insel, 1920.

Romain Rolland (biography), Rutten & Loening (Frankfurt am Main), 1921, translation by Eden and Cedar Paul, Seltzer (New York City), 1921.

Amok (novellas), Insel, 1922.

Die Augen des Ewigen Bruders (novella), Insel, 1922.

Die gesammelten Gedichte (poetry), Insel, 1924.

Passion and Pain (translated short stories and novellas), Chapman & Hall (London), 1924, Richards (New York City), 1925.

Der Kampf mit dem Damon: Holerin, Kleist, Nietzsche (biography), Insel, 1925, translation by Eden and Cedar Paul published as *The Struggle with the Demon,* Viking, 1929.

Volpone (adapted from play by Ben Johnson), Kiepenheuer (Berlin), 1926, translation by Ruth Langner published as *Ben Jonson's Volpone: A Loveless Comedy in Three Acts,* Allen & Unwin (London), 1926, Viking, 1929.

Abschied von Rilke (essay), Wunderlich (Tubingen), 1927, translation by Marion Sonnenfeld published as *Farewell to Rilke,* Friends of the Daniel Reed Library, State University College (Fredonia, NY), 1975.

Die Flucht zu Gott (drama), Floch (Berlin), 1927.

Verwirrung der Gefuhle (novellas), Insel, 1927, translation by Eden and Cedar Paul published as *Conflicts,* Viking, 1927.

Drei Dichter ihres Lebens: Casanova, Stendhal, Tolstoi (biography), Insel, 1928, translation by Eden and Cedar Paul published as *Adepts in Self-Portraiture: Casanova, Stendhal, Tolstoy,* Viking, 1928.

Joseph Fouche (biography), 1929, translation by Eden and Cedar Paul, Viking, 1930.

Die Heilung durch den Geist: Franz Anton Mesmer, Mary Baker Eddy, Sigmund Freud (biography), Insel, 1931, translation by Eden and Cedar Paul published as *Mental Healers,* Viking, 1932.

Marie Antoinette (biography), 1932, translation by Eden and Cedar Paul, Viking, 1933.

Triumph und Tragik des Erasmus von Rotterdam (biography), 1934, translation by Eden and Cedar Paul published as *Erasmus of Rotterdam,* Viking, 1934.

Maria Stuart (biography), Reichner (Vienna, Peipzig and Zurich), 1935, translation by Eden and Cedar Paul published as *Mary, the Queen of Scotland and the Isles,* Viking, 1935.

Die schweigsame Frau (libretto adapted from a drama by Ben Jonson), Furstner (Berlin), 1935.

Der begrabene Leuchter (novella), Reichner, 1936, translation by Eden and Cedar Paul published as *The Buried Candelabrum,* Viking, 1937.

Castellio gegen Calvin; oder, Ein Gewissen gegen die Gewalt (biography), Reichner, 1936, translation by Eden and Cedar Paul published as *The Right to Heresy: Castellio against Calvin,* Viking, 1936.

Kaleidoskop (short stories and novellas), Reichner, 1936, translation published as *Kaleidoscope,* 1934.

Begegnungen mit Menschen, Buchern, Stadten (essays and criticism), Reichner, 1937.

The Old Book Peddlar, and Other Tales for Bibliophiles (short stories), translation by Theodore W. Koch, Northwestern University (Evanston, IL), 1937.

Magellan (biography), Reichner, 1938, translation by Eden and Cedar Paul published as *Conqueror of the Seas,* Viking, 1938.

Ungeduld des Herzens (novel), Bermann-Fischer (Stockholm), 1939, translation by Phyllis and Trevor Blewitt published as *Beware of Pity,* Viking, 1939.

Brazilien: Ein Land der Zukunft (travel), Bermann-Fischer, 1941, translation by Andrew St. James published as *Brazil, Land of the Future,* Viking, 1941.

Schachnovelle (novella), Pigmalion (Buenos Aires), 1942, published as *The Royal Game,* Viking, 1944.

Amerigo (biography), translation by Andrew St. James, Viking, 1942.

The World of Yesterday (autobiography), translation by Benjamin W. Huebsch and Helmut Ripperger, Viking, 1943.

Balzac (biography), Bermann-Fischer, 1946, translation by William and Dorothy Rose, Viking, 1946.

Briefwechsel: Stefan Zweig-Friderike Maria Zweig, 1912-42 (letters), Scherz (Bern), 1951, translation by Henry G. Alsberg and Erna McArthur published as *Stefan Zweig and Friderike Maria Zweig: Their Correspondence,* Hastings House (New York City), 1954.

Stories and Legends (short stories and novellas), translation by Eden and Cedar Paul and Constantine Fitzgibbon, Cassell (London), 1955.

Briefwechsel zwischen Richard Strauss und Stefan Zweig (letters), edited by Willi Schuh, Fischer (Frankfurt am Main), 1957, translation by Max

Knight published as *A Confidential Matter: The Letters of Richard Strauss and Stefan Zweig, 1931-35,* University of California Press (Berkeley), 1977.

Brief an Freunde (letters), Fischer, 1978.

Briefweschsel mit Hermann Bahr, Sigmund Freud, Ranier Maria Rilke und Arthur Schnitzler (letters), Fischer, 1987.

SIDELIGHTS: One of the most widely translated authors of his day, Austrian native Stefan Zweig wrote poetry, novellas, biographies, plays, and criticism. However, his literary legacy has been obscured by certain events and criticism that marked his career. In the politically charged atmosphere of Europe during World Wars I and II, Zweig was sometimes maligned for being a pacifist who would not join in open condemnation of Fascism and a Jew who did not show solidarity with his people. In fact, the events of World War II devastated Zweig, who was passionately dedicated to promoting an intellectually unified Europe. He saw the war as proof that his ideals would never be achieved, and in a dual suicide by poison with his second wife, ended his life in despair. While his varied publications were extremely popular during his lifetime, they fell out of fashion soon after his death. Zweig's works have been treated as modern classics in Germany and continued to be read in South America, but they lost their larger English-reading audience. It was not until the 1980s that a renewed critical interest developed and his body of work began to be reevaluated.

Zweig was born into wealth in Vienna as the son of a successful textile manufacturer. While he hated the authoritarian schools he attended as a child, Zweig learned to love the arts and was a voracious reader. As a young man Zweig published the volume of poetry *Silbern Saiten* (title means "Silver Strings") in 1901, and he became known as one of the literary group Young Vienna. He went on to study German and Romance literatures at the University of Vienna, earning his doctorate in 1904. This work had been interrupted, however, when Zweig met the Belgian poet Emile Verhaeren and embarked on a two-year project translating his poetry into German. Thus, Verhaeren become one of Zweig's greatest literary influences, with his philosophy of humanism and positive outlook. Zweig's other great mentor was French writer Romain Rolland, another humanist, and a pacifist who sought European unity.

Prior to the start of World War I in 1914, Zweig traveled extensively, visiting China, India, Africa, and North America. During this time he also became acquainted with the leading intellectual figures of Europe. When war broke out, he went to work in the Austrian War Archives, but he also found time to write a play. *Jeremias,* an anti-war drama, premiered in neutral Switzerland in 1917.

Zweig moved to Salzburg in 1919, where he and his first wife, writer Friderike Maria Burger von Winternitz, played host to many important cultural figures. The couple numbered Sigmund Freud, Hermann Hesse, and Arturo Toscanini among their friends and associates. It is important to note, however, that Zweig carefully avoided being associated with any group, including pan-European organizations. Zweig also spent time creating an impressive collection of literary and musical manuscripts. In Salzburg, Zweig was productive and happy, developing a multi-faceted career. As scholar Harry Zohn noted in the *Dictionary of Literary Biography,* he had become "a translator in a wider and higher sense, a man who strove to inform, educate, inspire, and arouse appreciation and enthusiasm across literary, cultural, political, and personal boundaries."

Several tragic events marred Zweig's experiences as a playwright and made him wary of the genre. Four deaths hindered productions of his plays, and as a result the prolific Zweig wrote only eight plays. *Jeremias* is Zweig's best-known original drama; the author used the biblical story of Jeremiah, who is selected by God to deliver a message of peace, to show the spiritual superiority of the defeated. The play was well received by critics and when it reached the United States after the end of the war, a *New York Times Book Review* critic asserted the drama's importance was not just due to the current political climate: "The scale and sweep of Zweig's tragedy, its vivid characterization and the fervor and loftiness of its diction, would have attracted attention at any time." Zweig's 1925 adaptation of Ben Jonson's Elizabethan play *Volpone* was also a dramatic success internationally. This was a rare comedic turn for Zweig, who otherwise rarely used humor or irony in his writings.

As a writer of fiction, Zweig mastered the short novella form, but only completed one novel during his lifetime. His novellas most often were careful psychological explorations of individuals who were experiencing violent emotions and were gripped by an obsession. These works comprised several collections, including the translations *Passion and Pain* and *Kaleidoscope.* On the occasion of reviewing this second collection, *New Republic* writer Barthold Fles reflected, "always [Zweig] remains essentially the same, revealing in all . . . mediums his subtlety of style, his profound psychological knowledge and his inherent humaneness." Taken individually, Zweig's notable novelettes include *Letter from an Unknown Woman,* which *New York Times Book Review* writer Harold Strauss saw as having "all the richness and force of a full-bodied novel, and [adding] to that a delicacy entirely its own, a high point in the development of the short narrative form." Zweig's last novelette, *The Royal Game,* is also considered one of his best in its depiction of a released Nazi prisoner who, having kept himself same by playing chess against himself, goes mad when drawn into a real game with a chess master.

The author's best-received works, however, were his psychological biographies. Zweig recreated the lives of historical figures such as Erasmus, Magellan, George Frederick Handel, and Mary Stuart. He did exhaustive historical research, particularly for the highly popular *Marie Antoinette: The Portrait of an Average Woman.* Herbert Gorman's *New York Times Book Review* article on this work noted, "[Zweig] possesses a dogged psychological curiosity, a brutal frankness, a supreme impartiality and had access to hitherto unused documentation. The result of this concentration of talents is a full-bodied and frank exposition." A number of Zweig's biographies were comparative works that focused on multiple figures, such as *Three Masters: Balzac, Dickens, Dostoeffsky, Mental Healers: Franz Anton Mesmer, Mary Baker Eddy, Sigmund Freud,* and *The Right to Heresy: Castellio against Calvin.* Zweig's vivid narration and imaginative presentation of personalities earned him many readers, but his biographical works were also criticized for being melodramatic and politically naive.

The year 1934 was a pivotal period in Zweig's life, for political tensions in Europe began to bear directly on his life. He completed a collaboration with Richard Strauss, writing the libretto for the opera *Die schweigsame Frau.* Because Strauss served as the president of the Reich Music Chamber, the opera came under the scrutiny of the Nazi regime. Having intercepted a warm letter from the composer to his Jewish librettist, officials canceled the opera's production after four performances and Strauss was removed from his position. That same year, Zweig's home was searched by police looking for weapons hidden by a socialist organization. Zweig became restless and uneasy in his beloved home and he soon moved to the safety of England.

Zweig's transplantation, however, did not proceed smoothly. His wife, upon whom he relied in all domestic and practical matters, remained in Salzburg, arranging the disposition of their home and belongings. Meanwhile, Zweig met Elisabeth Charlotte Altmann, who became his secretary. The married couple remained apart for several years and their relationship disintegrated. Zweig married Altmann in England in 1939. Through all of these events, the writer was beset with depression and guilt about leaving his homeland. He remained ill at ease in England and sought escape in travel. In 1940 Zweig traveled to the United States and then to South America, where he applied for a permanent visa in Brazil. He had just become a British citizen, but believed that his possessions in England had been destroyed by the war. He began to write his autobiography, *The World of Yesterday.* This volume rivals all of Zweig's former work in its literary impact. According to Ruth V. Gross in the *Dictionary of Literary Biography,* "the text is so vividly evocative and the sense of loss so palpable that the persona that emerges—an Austrian who has outlived his age—became the Stefan Zweig that people remembered." In fact, *The World of Yesterday* served as a timely post script to Zweig's life, being published a year after his death. He took poison with his wife on February 23, 1942, leaving a suicide note expressing the wish that his friends would see the end of the horrors that had crushed him.

A number of Zweig's other writings were published posthumously, including some unfinished novels. One such novel was *Clarissa,* which its editor Knut Beck deemed a fictional variation on Zweig's autobiography. Reviewed in *World Literature Today,* Harry Zohn called it "absorbing enough, but what we have here is not vintage Zweig; once again one suspects that the novel was not this writer's favorite form." Several volumes of Zweig's correspondence with figures such as Sigmund Freud, Hermann Hesse, Romain Rolland, Martin Buber, and many others have been published, as have his diaries and notebooks in a volume titled *Tagebucher.* Zohn marveled at the diaries in *World Literature Today:* "That so much hitherto unknown material should have surfaced more than four decades after the author's death is one of the minor mysteries of the literary scene."

Among Zweig's works to be reissued during the 1980s were his autobiography and the translated novel *Beware of Pity.* Writing for the *Times Literary Supplement,* Peter Kemp was fascinated by *The World of Yesterday;* he commented on the impersonal narrative technique—Zweig himself compared it to being an "intellectual lecturer"—saying, "the result is as informative as this would suggest—and far more elegant and alluring. As much the history of a generation and a continent as of an individual. . . . Zweig makes his book a triumph of long perspectives and wide horizons." Kemp concluded, "Zweig's story . . . is an unwaveringly civilized account of a civilization's collapse." *Beware of Pity* elicited conflicting reviews. S. S. Prawer, knowing the pitiable circumstances of Zweig's last years, reluctantly remarked that "page after wordy page . . . [made] one realize why Musil was so scornful of his compatriot Zweig and why the anti-novel had to be invented." *Spectator* reviewer P. J. Kavanagh had an entirely different reaction to the novel, and called it "a profound book but easy to read, and enthralling, which is a rare combination."

BIOGRAPHICAL/CRITICAL SOURCES:

BOOKS

Gross, Ruth V., *Dictionary of Literary Biography,* Volume 81: *Austrian Fiction Writers, 1875-1913,* edited by James Hardin and Donald G. Daviau, Gale (Detroit, MI), 1989.

Klein, Leonard S., editor, *Encyclopedia of World Literature in the Twentieth Century,* Continuum, 1993.

Twentieth-Century Literary Criticism, Volume 17, Gale, 1985.

Zohn, Harry, *Dictionary of Literary Biography,* Volume 118: *Twentieth-Century German Dramatists,* edited by Wolfgang D. Elfe and James Hardin, Gale, 1992.

PERIODICALS

New Republic, July 4, 1934, pp. 216-217.

New York Times Book Review, December 24, 1922, p. 17; June 19, 1932, p. 6; April 2, 1933, p 3.

Spectator, November 6, 1982, p. 27.

Times Literary Supplement, November 19, 1982, p. 1268; November 13-19, 1987, p. 1258.

World Literature Today, summer, 1985, p. 424; summer, 1991, p. 480.*